ECONOMICS IN PRACTICE FEATURE

To help pique students' interest in the economic world, the authors have created a new feature entitled *Economics in Practice*. This feature either (1) describes a personal observation or a research idea and provides an analysis using the concepts of the chapter or (2) presents a newspaper excerpt that relates to the concepts of the chapter.

NINTH EDITION

Principles of Economics

Karl E. Case
Wellesley College

Ray C. Fair
Yale University

Sharon M. Oster
Yale University

Prentice Hall
UPPER SADDLE RIVER, NJ 07458

Library of Congress Cataloging-in-Publication Data
Case, Karl E.
Principles of economics / Karl E. Case, Ray C. Fair, Sharon M. Oster. — 9th ed.
p. cm.
Includes index.
ISBN-13: 978-0-13-605548-8 (pbk.)
ISBN-10: 0-13-605548-6 (pbk.)
1. Economics. I. Fair, Ray C. II. Oster, Sharon M. III. Title.
HB171.5.C3123 2008
330—dc22
2008031127

Dedicated To
Professor Richard A. Musgrave
and
Professor Robert M. Solow
and
Professor Richard Caves

VP/Publisher: Natalie E. Anderson
Acquisitions Editor, Print: Jodi Bolognese
Senior Development Editor: Lena Buonanno
Director, Product Development: Pamela Hersperger
Editorial Project Manager: Virginia Guariglia
VP/Director of Development: Steve Deitmer
Editorial Assistant: Terenia McHenry
AVP/Executive Editor, Media: Richard Keaveny
Advanced Media Project Manager: Dana Davis
Editorial Media Project Manager: Alana Coles
Production Media Project Manager: Lorena Cerisano
Director of Marketing: Kate Valentine
AVP/Marketing Manager: Lori DeShazo
Marketing Assistant: Justin Jacob
Senior Managing Editor: Cynthia Zonneveld
Production Project Manager: Lynne Breitfeller
Manager of Rights & Permissions: Charles Morris
Senior Operations Specialist: Nick Sklitsis
Senior Art Director: Jonathan Boylan
AV Project Manager: Rhonda Aversa
Interior Design: John Christiana
Cover Design: Jonathan Boylan
Illustration (Interior): LaserWords
Director, Image Resource Center: Melinda Patelli
Manager, Rights and Permissions: Zina Arabia
Manager, Visual Research: Beth Brenzel
Image Permission Coordinator: Cynthia Vincenti
Photo Researcher: Sheila Norman
Composition: GEX Publishing Services
Full-Service Project Management: GEX Publishing Services
Printer/Binder: Courier
Typeface: 10/12 Minion

Credits and acknowledgments borrowed from other sources and reproduced, with permission, in this textbook appear on appropriate page within text (or on page 779)

Pearson Education Ltd., London
Pearson Education Singapore, Pte. Ltd
Pearson Education, Canada, Inc.
Pearson Education–Japan
Pearson Education North Asia Ltd., Hong Kong
Pearson Educación de Mexico, S.A. de C.V.
Pearson Education Malaysia, Pte. Ltd.
Pearson Education, Upper Saddle River, New Jersey
Pearson Education Australia PTY, Limited

Prentice Hall
is an imprint of

www.pearsonhighered.com

10 9 8 7 6 5 4 3 2 1
ISBN-13: 978-0-13-605548-8
ISBN-10: 0-13-605548-6

About the Authors

Karl E. Case is the Katharine Coman and A. Barton Hepburn Professor of Economics at Wellesley College, where he has taught for over 30 years and served several tours of duty as Department Chair. For two decades, he has been a Visiting Scholar at the Federal Reserve Bank of Boston where he serves as a member of the Bank's Academic Advisory Board.

Before coming to Wellesley, he served as Head Tutor in Economics (director of undergraduate studies) at Harvard, where he won the Allyn Young Teaching Prize. He was Associate Editor of the *Journal of Economic Perspectives* and the *Journal of Economic Education* and was a member of the AEA's Committee on Economic Education. He teaches at least one section of the principles course every year.

Professor Case received his B.A. from Miami University in 1968; spent three years on active duty in the Army, including a year in Vietnam; and received his Ph.D. in Economics from Harvard University in 1976.

Professor Case's research has been in the areas of real estate, housing, and public finance. He is author or coauthor of five books, including *Principles of Economics, Economics and Tax Policy*, and *Property Taxation: The Need for Reform*, and has published numerous articles in professional journals.

He also is a founding partner in the real estate research firm of Fiserv Case Shiller Weiss, Inc., which produces the S&P Case Shiller Indexes of home prices and serves as a member of the Boards of Directors of the Mortgage Guaranty Insurance Corporation (MGIC) and the Depositors Insurance Fund of Massachusetts.

Ray C. Fair is Professor of Economics at Yale University. He is a member of the Cowles Foundation at Yale and a Fellow of the Econometric Society. He received a B.A. in Economics from Fresno State College in 1964 and a Ph.D. in economics from MIT in 1968. He taught at Princeton University from 1968 to 1974 and has been at Yale since 1974.

Professor Fair's research has primarily been in the areas of macroeconomics and econometrics, with particular emphasis on macroeconometric model building. He also has done work in the areas of finance, voting behavior, and aging in sports. His publications include *Specification, Estimation, and Analysis of Macroeconometric Models* (Harvard Press, 1984); *Testing Macroeconometric Models* (Harvard Press, 1994); and *Estimating How the Macroeconomy Works* (Harvard Press, 2004).

Professor Fair has taught introductory and intermediate macroeconomics at Yale. He has also taught graduate courses in macroeconomic theory and macroeconometrics.

Professor Fair's U.S. and multicountry models are available for use on the Internet free of charge. The address is http://fairmodel.econ.yale.edu. Many teachers have found that having students work with the U.S. model on the Internet is a useful complement to an introductory macroeconomics course.

Sharon M. Oster is Professor of Economics at Yale University. She is a new coauthor to this ninth edition. Professor Oster is the Frederic Wolfe Professor of Management and Entrepreneurship at the Yale School of Management. She has a B.A. in Economics from Hofstra University and a Ph.D. in Economics from Harvard University.

Professor Oster's research is in the area of industrial organization. She has worked on problems of diffusion of innovation in a number of different industries, on the effect of regulations on business, and on competitive strategy. She has published a number of articles in these areas and is the author of several books, including *Modern Competitive Analysis* and *The Strategic Management of Nonprofits.*

Prior to joining the School of Management at Yale, Professor Oster taught for a number of years in Yale's Department of Economics. In the department, Professor Oster taught introductory and intermediate microeconomics to undergraduates as well as several graduate courses in industrial organization. Since 1982, Professor Oster has taught primarily in the Management School, where she teaches the core microeconomics class for MBA students and a course in the area of competitive strategy. Professor Oster also consults widely for businesses and nonprofit organizations and has served on the boards of several publicly traded companies and nonprofit organizations.

Brief Contents

Contents

8 Short-Run Costs and Output Decisions 155

9 Long-Run Costs and Output Decisions 177

10 Input Demand: The Labor and Land Markets 203

11 Input Demand: The Capital Market and the Investment Decision 221

Preface

Our goal in the ninth edition, as it was in the first edition, is to instill in students a fascination with both the functioning of the economy and the power and breadth of economics. The first line of every edition of our book has been "The study of economics should begin with a sense of wonder." We hope that readers will come away from our book with a basic understanding of how market economies function, an appreciation for the things they do well, and a sense of the things they do poorly. We hope too that readers will learn that the proper role of government in a market economy is the subject of great debate around the world. That debate serves as the organizing principle behind this book.

For an economics text to be effective, it must address the economic issues of the time. Since the publication of our eighth edition, the economic landscape has changed substantially.

From 2003 through the end of 2007, the U.S. economy added over 8 million payroll jobs to the labor market, bringing the total to over 138 million. From a high of 6.3 percent in 2003, the unemployment rate dropped steadily to 4.4 percent by mid-2007.

The beginning of 2008 brought worries that the United States was in recession. During the first two quarters, the number of payroll jobs fell by nearly half a million and the unemployment rate jumped back up to 5.5 percent. The biggest issue facing the economy was a sharp downturn in the housing market and the resulting partial collapse of the mortgage market.

The housing downturn first hit the economy through a sharp downturn in the demand for housing and a 55 percent drop in new home construction. Prices of homes also fell nationwide for the first time in over 30 years. Falling home prices led to a decline in household wealth and a dramatic increase in mortgage defaults and foreclosures. This was made worse by the significant increase in lending to less creditworthy borrowers in what is called the subprime market.

The collapse of the usually stable mortgage market sent shock waves through the financial system worldwide. Banks, investment houses, and other financial service companies, as well as private investors lost hundreds of billions of dollars as many investors lost faith in the credit markets. To make matters worse, oil prices rose to over $147 per barrel, squeezing corporate profits, causing more layoffs, and pushing gasoline prices up.

The government reacted in several ways. Congress and the president announced a fiscal stimulus package including rebates to taxpayers of over $120 billion. The Federal Reserve dropped interest rates for the seventh consecutive time in early 2008 and took unprecedented action, directly participating in the rescue of Bear Stearns, the fifth-largest U.S. investment bank, from bankruptcy. In July, the Treasury and Federal Reserve jointly announced a plan to prevent the collapse of Fannie Mae and Freddie Mac, publicly held companies originally set up by the government to channel money into the mortgage market. Fannie and Freddie together held over $5 trillion in mortgages, about half of all the mortgages in the United States. This precipitated a national debate on the role of the Federal Reserve, which will not be easily resolved.

Internationally, the rise in oil prices was accompanied by a decline in the value of the dollar, making U.S. imports more expensive. Given this fact and a sharp increase in food and commodity prices, the possibility of serious inflation in the United States increased. The word *stagflation* came back in vogue.

On the positive side, the cheaper dollar led to a dramatic increase in U.S. net exports. Nonresidential construction continued to boom, and consumption remained surprisingly strong despite a huge drop in consumer confidence and the loss in housing wealth. While many were convinced that a recession was under way by the second quarter of 2008, others claimed that it was not yet in the numbers. All of this will influence the election of a new president in November 2008.

To understand these events requires a working knowledge of at least the basic "vocabulary" of economics.

New to this Edition

We have made every effort in this new edition to be responsive to the rapidly changing times, the recommendations of our reviewers, and our own teaching experiences. Here is a summary of the key changes:

1. Added a new chapter on uncertainty and asymmetric information
2. Improved the organization of the market structure chapters by including a full chapter on monopolistic competition and a full chapter on oligopoly
3. Revised the organization of the aggregate demand and aggregate supply presentation
4. Added a new feature, *Economics in Practice*, to help students think critically about economics in the world around them
5. Added modern topics, including behavioral economics
6. Streamlined the stock market chapter and merged the relevant content into Chapter 30, "Policy Timing, Deficit Targeting, and Stock Market Effects"
7. Streamlined the globalization chapter and merged the relevant content into Chapter 34, "International Trade, Comparative Advantage, and Protectionism"

New Chapter: "Uncertainty and Asymmetric Information"

Chapter 17, "Uncertainty and Asymmetric Information," explores how consumers and firms make decisions using incomplete information. The chapter covers attitudes toward risk, adverse selection, moral hazard, market signaling, expected value and expected utility, and incentives in the health care industry. We use familiar examples, such as how people evaluate different salary offers and make decisions about health insurance.

Improved Organization of Market Structure Chapters

In the previous edition, we covered monopolistic competition and oligopoly in one chapter. In this new edition, we devote a full chapter to each market structure. This new organization allows us to expand several key topics and provide more examples. Chapter 14, "Oligopoly," includes expanded coverage of game theory, new real-world examples, and new coverage of the five forces model. Chapter 15, "Monopolistic Competition," includes new coverage of behavioral economics and expanded coverage of product differentiation and advertising. Business students should find some of the new material in these chapters interesting.

New Organization of Aggregate Demand and Aggregate Supply Chapters

The *AD* curve is now derived at the end of Chapter 27, "Aggregate Demand in the Goods and Money Markets" (rather than as before in Chapter 28). Since each point on the *AD* curve is an equilibrium in the goods and money markets and since Chapter 27 combines the goods and money markets, it is natural to derive the *AD* curve at the end of this chapter. Chapter 28, "Aggregate Supply and the Equilibrium Price Level," then presents the *AS* curve, which allows the equilibrium price level to be determined. We are then in a position to use the complete *AS/AD* framework for analysis—all but the labor market, which is discussed in Chapter 29, "The Labor Market in the Macroeconomy."

New Feature: *Economics in Practice*

To help pique students' interest in the economic world, we have created a new feature entitled "Economics in Practice." This feature either (1) describes a personal observation or a research idea and provides an analysis using the concepts of the chapter or (2) presents a newspaper excerpt that relates to the concepts of the chapter. The *Economics in Practice* feature saves instructors time by providing real-world examples and helps keep students engaged in the chapters. Each feature includes a related end-of-chapter problem so that instructors can test students' understanding of the concepts applied in the feature. Additional *Economics in Practice* features appear in the *Instructor's Manuals* so that instructors can present real-world examples in class that do not appear in the main text and in the PowerPoint® to aid in class discussion of the topics. Also, MyEconLab and the Test Item Files include questions related to the *Economics in Practice* feature for instructors who want to assess students' understanding of the examples presented.

Here, to the right, is an example of an *Economics in Practice* feature that appears in Chapter 3, "Demand, Supply, and Market Equilibrium."

For a complete list of the Economics in Practice features in this book, please see the detailed table of contents, which begins on page v.

CHAPTER 3 Demand, Supply, and Market Equilibrium 69

ECONOMICS IN PRACTICE

Why Do the Prices of Newspapers Rise?

In 2006, the average price for a daily edition of a Baltimore newspaper was $0.50. In 2007, the average price had risen to $0.75. Three different analysts have three different explanations for the higher equilibrium price.

Analyst 1: The higher price for Baltimore newspapers is good news because it means the population is better informed about public issues. These data clearly show that the citizens of Baltimore have a new, increased regard for newspapers.

Analyst 2: The higher price for Baltimore newspapers is bad news for the citizens of Baltimore. The higher cost of paper, ink, and distribution reflected in these higher prices will further diminish the population's awareness of public issues.

Analyst 3: The higher price for Baltimore newspapers is an unfortunate result of newspapers trying to make money as many consumers have turned to the Internet to access news coverage for free.

As economists, we are faced with two tasks in looking at these explanations: Do they make sense based on what we know about economic principles? And if they do make sense, can we figure out which explanation applies to the case of rising newspaper prices in Baltmore?

What is Analyst 1 saying? Her observation about consumers' new increased regard for newspapers tells us something about the demand curve. Analyst 1 seems to be arguing that tastes have changed in favor of newspapers, which would mean a shift in the demand curve to the right. With upward-sloping supply, such a shift would produce a price increase. So Analyst 1's story is plausible.

Analyst 2 refers to an increased cost of newsprint. This would cause production costs of newspapers to rise, shifting the supply curve to the left. A downward-sloping demand curve also results in increased prices. So Analyst 2 also has a plausible story.

Since Analyst 1 and Analyst 2 have plausible stories based on economic principles, we can look at evidence to see who is in fact right. If you go back to the graphs in Figure 3.12 on p. 66, you will find a clue. When demand shifts to the right (as in Analyst 1's story) the price rises, but so does the quantity as shown in Figure (a) below. When supply shifts to the left (as in Analyst 2's story) the price rises, but the quantity falls as shown in Figure (b) below. So we would look at what happened to newspaper circulation during this period to see whether the price increase is from the demand side or the supply side. In fact, in most markets, including Baltimore, quantities of newspapers bought have been falling, so Analyst 2 is most likely correct.

But be careful. Both analysts may be correct. If demand shifts to the right and supply shifts to the left by a greater amount, the price will rise and the quantity sold will fall.

What about Analyst 3? Analyst 3 clearly never had an economics course! Free Internet access to news is a substitute for print media. A decrease in the price of this substitute should shift the demand for newspapers to the left. The result should be a lower price, not a price increase. The fact that the newspaper publishers are "trying to make money" faced with this new competition does not change the laws of supply and demand.

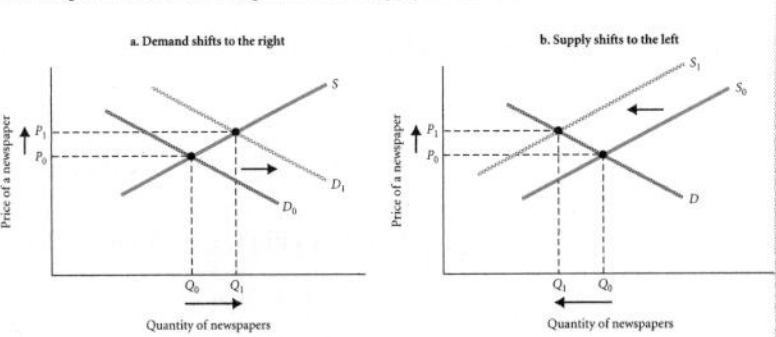

Modern Topics

In Chapter 11, "Input Demand: The Capital Market and the Investment Decision," we have a new section on mortgages and the mortgage market to help students understand the housing crisis that began in 2007. Chapter 13, "Monopoly and Antitrust Policy," includes a new section on network externalities that helps students understand why they benefit from products because many other people also use them and why network externalities may create a barrier to entry for firms. Chapter 14, "Oligopoly," includes new coverage of Michael Porter's five forces framework. As noted earlier, we cover behavioral economics in Chapter 15, "Monopolistic Competition." Examples of behavioral economics also appear in Chapter 18, "Income Distribution and Poverty." Chapter 16, "Externalities, Public Goods, and Social Choice," includes a new section on positive externalities to complement the coverage of negative externalities and provides a more detailed example of tradable permits.

We have added examples and coverage of behavioral economics and experimental economics.

For example, Chapter 23, "Aggregate Expenditure and Equilibrium Output," includes material on anomalies in saving decisions: Do pension savings respond to opt-in versus opt-out requirements?

We have also updated the chapters with current events regarding fiscal policy and monetary policy and the recent housing crisis. Here are some examples of the new coverage:

- Chapter 20, "Introduction to Macroeconomics," covers the economy in 2008 and the way it affected the presidential election outcome.
- Chapter 28, "Aggregate Supply and the Equilibrium Price Level," covers Federal Reserve Board policies through 2008.
- Chapter 30, "Policy Timing, Deficit Targeting, and Stock Market Effects," covers the bursting of the housing bubble and its implications for Federal Reserve policy. The chapter also covers the 2008 fiscal stimulus package.
- Chapter 32, "Long-Run Growth," covers how firms are dealing with high health care costs by increasing the availability of wellness programs for diet, exercise, and smoking cessation, for example. Also included in this chapter is a new section on "Growth and Environmental Issues of Sustainability." This section covers the Millennium Development Goals adopted by the United Nations.

Streamlined and Integrated Stock Market and Globalization Chapters

We moved the relevant material in the old stock market chapter into Chapter 30, "Policy Timing, Deficit Targeting, and Stock Market Effects." We moved the relevant material in the old globalization chapter into Chapter 34, "International Trade, Comparative Advantage, and Protectionism."

In addition to the preceding changes, we also updated all tables and graphs with the latest data.

The Foundation

Despite a new chapter, a new feature, updates, and other revisions, the themes of *Principles of Economics*, Ninth Edition, are the same themes of the first eight editions. The purposes of this book are to introduce the discipline of economics and to provide a basic understanding of how economies function. This requires a blend of economic theory, institutional material, and real-world applications. We have maintained a balance between these ingredients in every chapter. The hallmark features of our book are its:

1. Three-tiered explanations of key concepts (*stories-graphs-equations*).
2. Intuitive and accessible structure.
3. International coverage.

Three-Tiered Explanations: Stories-Graphs-Equations

Professors who teach principles of economics are faced with a classroom of students with different abilities, backgrounds, and learning styles. For some students, analytical material is difficult no matter how it is presented; for others, graphs and equations seem to come naturally. The problem facing instructors and textbook authors is how to convey the core principles of the discipline to as many students as possible without selling the better students short. Our approach to this problem is to present most core concepts in the following three ways:

First, we present each concept in the context of a simple intuitive ***story*** or example in words often followed by a table. Second, we use a ***graph*** in most cases to illustrate the story or example. And finally, in many cases where appropriate, we use an ***equation*** to present the concept with a mathematical formula.

Microeconomic Structure

The organization of the microeconomic chapters continues to reflect our belief that the best way to understand how market economies operate—and the best way to understand basic economic theory—is to work through the perfectly competitive model first, including discussions of output markets (goods and services) and input markets (land, labor, and capital), and the connections between them before turning to noncompetitive market structures such as monopoly and oligopoly. When students understand how a simple, perfectly competitive system works, they can start thinking about how the pieces of the economy "fit together." We think this is a better approach to teaching economics than some of the more traditional approaches, which encourage students to think of economics as a series of disconnected alternative market models.

Learning perfect competition first also enables students to see the power of the market system. It is impossible for students to discuss the efficiency of markets as well as the problems that arise from markets until they have seen how a simple, perfectly competitive market system produces and distributes goods and services. This is our purpose in Chapter 6 through 11.

Chapter 12, "General Equilibrium and the Efficiency of Perfect Competition," is a pivotal chapter that links simple, perfectly competitive markets with a discussion of market imperfections and the role of government. Chapter 13 through 15 cover three noncompetitive market structures—monopoly, monopolistic competition, and oligopoly. Chapter 16 covers externalities, public goods, and social choice. Chapter 17, which is new to this edition, covers uncertainty and asymmetric information. Chapters 18 and 19 cover income distribution as well as taxation and government finance. The visual at the top of the next page (Figure II.2 from page 108), gives you an overview of our structure.

Macroeconomic Structure

We remain committed to the view that it is a mistake simply to throw aggregate demand and aggregate supply curves at students in the first few chapters of a principles book. To understand the *AS* and *AD* curves, students need to know about the functioning of both the goods market and the money market. The logic behind the simple demand curve is wrong when it is applied to the relationship between aggregate demand and the price level. Similarly, the logic behind the simple supply curve is wrong when it is applied to the relationship between aggregate supply and the price level.

Part of teaching economics is teaching economic reasoning. Our discipline is built around deductive logic. Once we teach students a pattern of logic, we want and expect them to apply it

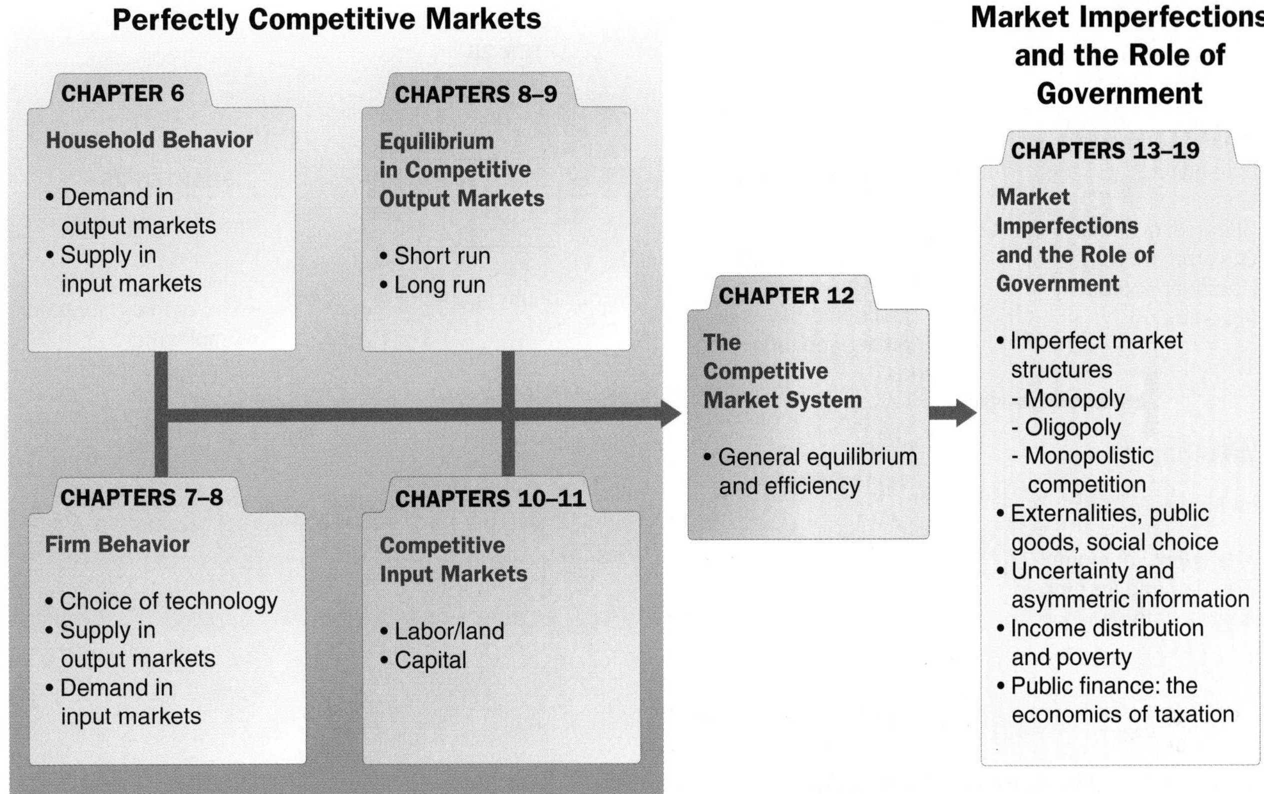

▲ FIGURE II.2 **Understanding the Microeconomy and the Role of Government**

to new circumstances. When they apply the logic of a simple demand curve or a simple supply curve to the aggregate demand or aggregate supply curve, the logic does not fit. We believe that the best way to teach the reasoning embodied in the aggregate demand and aggregate supply curves without creating confusion for students is to build up to those topics carefully.

In Chapter 23, "Aggregate Expenditure and Equilibrium Output," and Chapter 24, "The Government and Fiscal Policy," we examine the market for goods and services. In Chapter 25, "The Money Supply and the Federal Reserve System," and Chapter 26, "Money Demand and the Equilibrium Interest Rate," we examine the money market. We bring the two markets together in Chapter 27, "Aggregate Demand in the Goods and Money Markets," which explains the links between aggregate output (Y) and the interest rate (r) and derives the *AD* curve. In Chapter 28, "Aggregate Supply and the Equilibrium Price Level," we introduce the *AS* curve and determine the equilibrium price level (P). We then explain in Chapter 29, "The Labor Market in the Macroeconomy," how the labor markets fits into this macroeconomic picture. The figure at the top of the next page (Figure V.1 from page 451) gives you an overview of this structure.

One of the big issues in the organization of the macroeconomic material is whether long-run growth issues should be taught before short-run chapters on the determination of national income and countercyclical policy. In the last three editions, we moved a significant discussion of growth to Chapter 22, "Unemployment, Inflation, and Long-Run Growth," and highlighted it. However, while we wrote the major chapter on long-run growth, Chapter 32, "Long-Run Growth," so that it can be taught before or after the short-run chapters, we remain convinced that it is easier for students to understand the growth issue once they have come to grips with the logic and controversies of short-run cycles, inflation, and unemployment.

International Coverage

As in previous editions, we continue to integrate international examples and applications in many chapters. Here are examples of our coverage:

- Chapter 1, "The Scope and Method of Economics," discusses the many countries that contribute to creating the iPod.

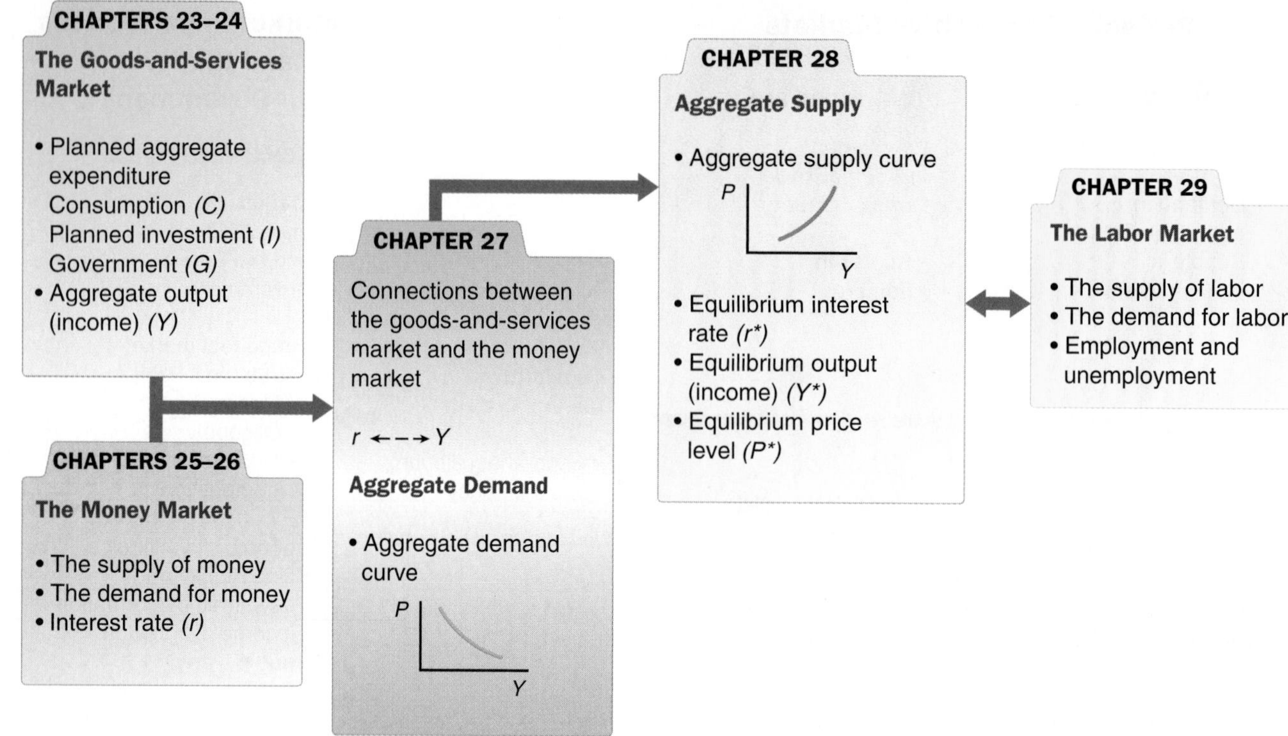

▲ FIGURE V.1 **The Core of Macroeconomic Theory**

- Chapter 7, "The Production Process: The Behavior of Profit-Maximizing Firms," discusses how United Parcel Service is using technology to speed worldwide delivery.
- Chapter 18, "Income Distribution and Poverty," includes a section on the distribution of income in various parts of the world, including sub-Saharan Africa, the Middle East, and Mexico. The chapter also discusses how technology affects income distribution.
- Chapter 26, "Money Demand and the Equilibrium Interest Rate," discusses ATM use in Italy.
- Chapter 32, "Long-Run Growth," compares GDP growth rates in various countries and discusses the role of institutions in attracting capital. The chapter explains how market reforms in China affected its productivity gains in the last 20 years and its recent foreign direct investments in parts of Africa and Asia. Also included in this chapter is a discussion of industrial policy in developing countries such as Taiwan.

We also include two full chapters on the world economy: Chapter 34, "International Trade, Comparative Advantage, and Protectionism," and Chapter 36, "Economic Growth in Developing and Transitional Economies." These chapters cover the increasing economic interdependence among countries and their citizens. We focus on the causes and consequences of increased international trade of goods and services, increased cross-border movements of labor, and the outsourcing of jobs to low-wage labor markets outside the United States.

Tools for Learning

As authors and teachers, we understand the challenges of the principles of economics course. Our pedagogical features are designed to illustrate and reinforce key economic concepts through real-world examples and applications.

Economics in Practice

As described earlier, the *Economics in Practice* feature presents a real-world personal observation, current research work, or a news article that supports the key concept of the chapter and helps students think critically about how economics is a part of their daily lives. The end-of-chapter problem sets include a question specific to each *Economics in Practice* feature. Students can visit www.myeconlab.com for additional updated news articles and related exercises.

Graphs

Reading and interpreting graphs is a key part of understanding economic concepts. The Chapter 1 Appendix, "How to Read and Understand Graphs," shows readers how to interpret the 200-plus graphs featured in this book. We use red curves to illustrate the behavior of firms and blue curves to show the behavior of households. We use a different shade of red and blue to signify a shift in a curve.

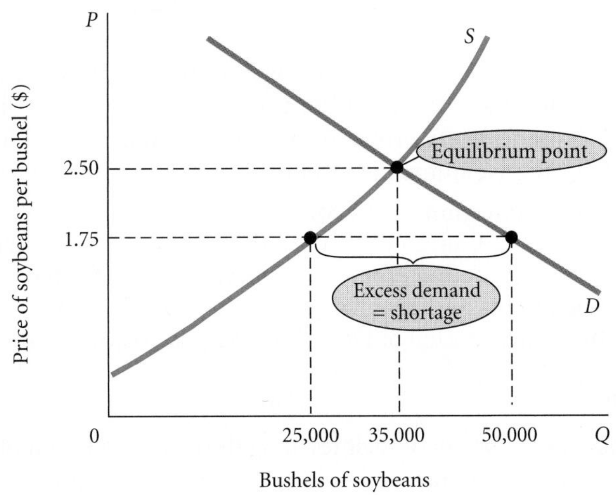

FIGURE 3.9 Excess Demand, or Shortage
At a price of $1.75 per bushel, quantity demanded exceeds quantity supplied. When excess *demand* exists, there is a tendency for price to rise. When quantity demanded equals quantity supplied, excess demand is eliminated and the market is in equilibrium. Here the equilibrium price is $2.50 and the equilibrium quantity is 35,000 bushels.

Problems and Solutions

Each chapter and appendix ends with a problem set that asks students to think about and apply what they've learned in the chapter. These problems are not simple memorization questions. Rather, they ask students to perform graphical analysis or to apply economics to a real-world situation or policy decision. More challenging problems are indicated by an asterisk. Additional questions specific to the *Economics in Practice* feature have been added. Several problems have been updated. The solutions to all of the problems are available in the *Instructor's Manuals*. Instructors can provide the solutions to their students so they can check their understanding and progress.

MyEcon Lab myeconlab

Both the text and supplement package provide ways for instructors and students to assess their knowledge and progress through the course. MyEconLab, the new standard in personalized online learning, is a key part of Case, Fair, and Oster's integrated learning package for the ninth edition.

For the Instructor

MyEconLab is an online course management, testing, and tutorial resource. Instructors can choose how much or how little time to spend setting up and using MyEconLab. Each chapter contains two Sample Tests, Study Plan Exercises, and Tutorial Resources. Student use of these materials requires no initial set-up by their instructor. The online Gradebook records each student's performance and time spent on the Tests and Study Plan and generates reports by student or by chapter. Instructors can assign tests, quizzes, and homework in MyEconLab using four resources:

- Preloaded Sample Test questions
- Problems similar to the end-of-chapter problems
- Test Item File questions
- Self-authored questions using Econ Exercise Builder

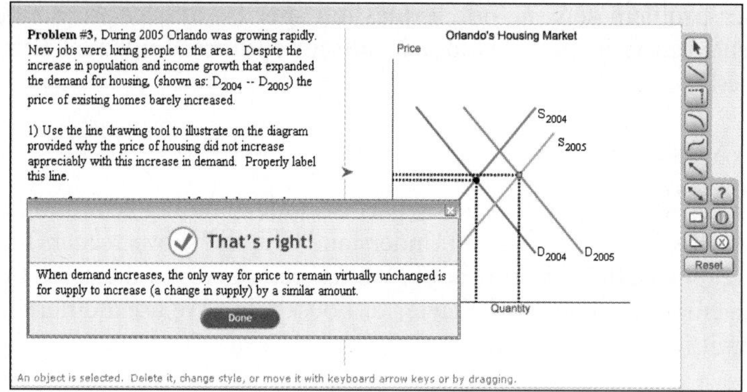

Exercises use multiple-choice, graph drawing, and free-response items, many of which are generated algorithmically so that each time a student works them, a different variation is presented. MyEconLab grades every problem, even those with graphs. When working homework exercises, students receive immediate feedback with links to additional learning tools.

Customization and Communication MyEconLab in CourseCompass™ provides additional optional customization and communication tools. Instructors who teach distance learning courses or very large lecture sections find the CourseCompass format useful because they can upload course documents and assignments, customize the order of chapters, and use communication features such as Digital Drop Box and Discussion Board.

For the Student

MyEconLab puts students in control of their learning through a collection of tests, practice, and study tools tied to the online, interactive version of the textbook, and other media resources. Within MyEconLab's structured environment, students practice what they learn, test their understanding, and pursue a personalized Study Plan generated from their performance on Sample Tests and tests set by their instructors. At the core of MyEconLab are the following features:

- Sample Tests, two per chapter
- Personal Study Plan
- Tutorial Instruction
- Graphing Tool

Sample Tests Two Sample Tests for each chapter are preloaded in MyEconLab, enabling students to practice what they have learned, test their understanding, and identify areas in which they need further work. Students can study on their own, or they can complete assignments created by their instructor.

Personal Study Plan Based on a student's performance on tests, MyEconLab generates a personal Study Plan that shows where the student needs further study. The Study Plan consists of a series of additional practice exercises with detailed feedback and guided solutions and keyed to other tutorial resources.

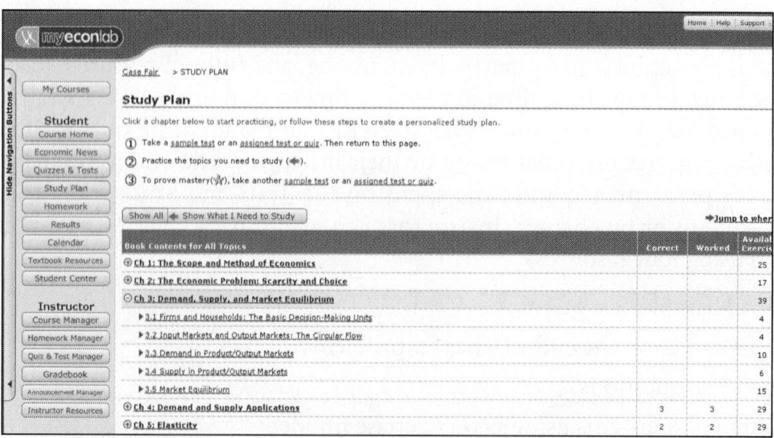

Tutorial Instruction Launched from many of the exercises in the Study Plan, MyEconLab provides tutorial instruction in the form of step-by-step solutions and other media-based explanations.

Graphing Tool A graphing tool is integrated into the Tests and Study Plan exercises to enable students to make and manipulate graphs. This feature helps students understand how concepts, numbers, and graphs connect.

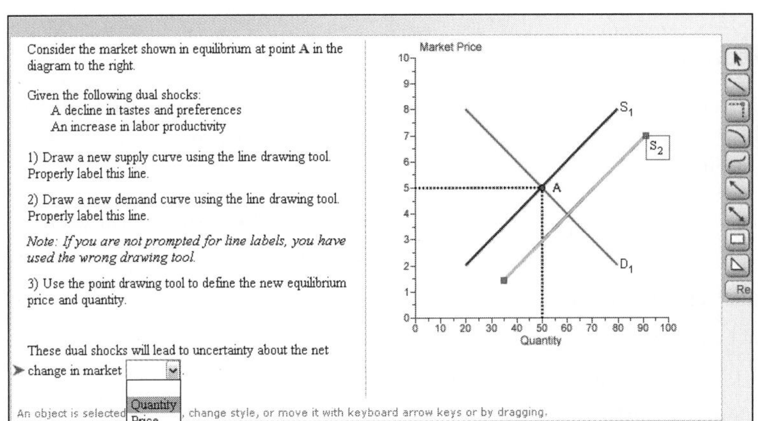

Additional MyEconLab Tools MyEconLab includes the following additional features:

1. **Economics in the News**—This feature provides weekly updates during the school year of news items with links to sources for further reading and discussion questions. Instructors can assign these articles with related, auto-graded questions to assess students' understanding of what they've read.
2. **eText**—While students are working in the Study Plan or completing homework assignments, part of the tutorial resources available is a direct link to the relevant page of the text so that students can review the appropriate material to help them complete the exercise.
3. **Glossary**—This searchable version of the textbook glossary provides additional examples and links to related terms.
4. **Glossary Flashcards**—Every key term is available as a flashcard, allowing students to quiz themselves on vocabulary from one or more chapters at a time.
5. **Ask the Author**—Students can e-mail economics-related questions to the author.
6. **Research Navigator (CourseCompass™ version only)**—This feature offers extensive help on the research process and provides four exclusive databases of credible and reliable source material, including *The New York Times*, the *Financial Times*, and peer-reviewed journals.

   MyEconLab content has been created through the efforts of:

   Charles Baum, Middle Tennessee State University; Sarah Ghosh, University of Scranton; Russell Kellogg, University of Colorado–Denver; Bert G.Wheeler, Cedarville University; and Noel Lotz and Douglas A. Ruby, Pearson Education

Resources for the Instructor

The following supplements are designed to make teaching and testing flexible and easy.

Instructor's Manuals

Two *Instructor's Manuals*, one for *Principles of Microeconomics* and one for *Principles of Macroeconomics*, were prepared by Tony Lima of California State University, Hayward. The *Instructor's Manuals* are designed to provide the utmost teaching support for instructors. They include the following content:

- Detailed *Chapter Outlines* include key terminology, teaching notes, and lecture suggestions.
- *Topics for Class Discussion* provide topics and real-world situations that help ensure that economic concepts resonate with students.
- Unique *Economics in Practice* features that are not in the main text provide extra real-world examples to present and discuss in class.

- *Teaching Tips* provide tips for alternative ways to cover the material and brief reminders on additional help to provide students. These tips include suggestions for exercises and experiments to complete in class.
- *Extended Applications* include exercises, activities, and experiments to help make economics relevant to students.
- *Solutions* are provided for all problems in the book.

Six Test Item Files

We have tailored the Test Item Files to help instructors easily and efficiently assess student understanding of economic concepts and analyses. Test questions are annotated with the following information:

- **Difficulty:** 1 for straight recall, 2 for some analysis, 3 for complex analysis
- **Type:** multiple-choice, true/false, short-answer, essay
- **Topic:** the term or concept the question supports
- **Skill:** fact, definition, analytical, conceptual
- **AACSB** (see description that follows)
- **Special feature in the main book:** *Economics in Practice*

The Test Item Files include questions with tables that students must analyze to solve for numerical answers. The Test Item Files also contain questions based on the graphs that appear in the book. The questions ask students to interpret the information presented in the graph. Many questions require students to sketch a graph on their own and interpret curve movements.

Microeconomics Test Item File 1, by Tisha Emerson of Baylor University: Test Item File 1 (TIF1) includes over 2,200 questions. All questions are machine-gradable and are either multiple-choice or true-false. This Test Item File is for use with the ninth edition of *Principles of Microeconomics* in the first year of publication. TIF1 is available in a computerized format using TestGen EQ test-generating software.

Microeconomics Test Item File 2, by Tisha Emerson of Baylor University: This additional Test Item File contains another 2,200 machine-gradable questions based on the TIF1 but regenerated to provide instructors with fresh questions when using the book the second year. This Test Item File is available in a computerized format using TestGen EQ test-generating software.

Microeconomics Test Item File 3, by Richard Gosselin of Houston Community College: This third Test Item File includes 1,000 conceptual problems, essay questions, and short-answer questions. Application-type problems ask students to draw graphs and analyze tables. The Word files are available on the Instructor's Resource Center. (**www.prenhall.com/casefair**)

Macroeconomics Test Item File 1, by Randy Methenitis of Richland College: Test Item File 1 (TIF1) includes over 2,200 questions. All questions are machine-gradable and are either multiple-choice or true-false. This Test Item File is for use with the ninth edition of *Principles of Macroeconomics* in the first year of publication. This Test Item File is available in a computerized format using TestGen EQ test-generating software.

Macroeconomics Test Item File 2, by Randy Methenitis of Richland College: This additional Test Item File contains another 2,200 machine-gradable questions based on the TIF1 but regenerated to provide instructors with fresh questions when using the book the second year. This Test Item File is available in a computerized format using TestGen EQ test-generating software.

Macroeconomics Test Item File 3, by Richard Gosselin of Houston Community College: This third Test Item File includes 1,000 conceptual problems, essay questions, and short-answer questions. Application-type problems ask students to draw graphs and analyze tables. The Word files are available on the Instructor's Resource Center. (**www.prenhall.com/casefair**)

The Test Item Files were checked for accuracy by the following professors:

Leon J. Battista, Bronx Community College; Margaret Brooks, Bridgewater State College; Mike Cohick, Collin County Community College; Dennis Debrecht, Carroll College; Amrik

Dua, California State Polytechnic University, Pomona; Mitchell Dudley, The College of William & Mary; Ann Eike, University of Kentucky; Connel Fullencamp, Duke University; Craig Gallet, California State University, Sacramento; Michael Goode, Central Piedmont Community College; Steve Hamilton, California State Polytechnic University; James R. Irwin, Central Michigan University; Aaron Jackson, Bentley College; Rus Janis, University of Massachusetts, Amherst; Jonatan Jelen, The City College of New York; Kathy A. Kelly, University of Texas, Arlington; Kate Krause, University of New Mexico; Gary F. Langer, Roosevelt University; Leonard Lardaro, University of Rhode Island; Ross LaRoe, Denison University; Melissa Lind, University of Texas, Arlington; Solina Lindahl, California State Polytechnic University; Pete Mavrokordatos, Tarrant County College; Roberto Mazzoleni, Hofstra University; Kimberly Mencken, Baylor University; Ida Mirzaie, Ohio State University; Shahruz Mohtadi, Suffolk University; Mary Pranzo, California State University, Fresno; Ed Price, Oklahoma State University; Robert Shoffner, Central Piedmont Community College; James Swofford, University of South Alabama; Helen Tauchen, University of North Carolina, Chapel Hill; Eric Taylor, Central Piedmont Community College; Henry Terrell, University of Maryland; John Tommasi, Bentley College; Mukti Upadhyay, Eastern Illinois University; Robert Whaples, Wake Forest University; and Timothy Wunder, University of Texas, Arlington.

The Association to Advance Collegiate Schools of Business (AACSB) The authors of the Test Item File have connected select Test Item File questions to the general knowledge and skill guidelines found in the AACSB assurance of learning standards.

What Is the AACSB? AACSB is a not-for-profit corporation of educational institutions, corporations, and other organizations devoted to the promotion and improvement of higher education in business administration and accounting. A collegiate institution offering degrees in business administration or accounting may volunteer for AACSB accreditation review. The AACSB makes initial accreditation decisions and conducts periodic reviews to promote continuous quality improvement in management education. Pearson Education is a proud member of the AACSB and is pleased to provide advice to help you apply AACSB assurance of learning standards.

What Are AACSB Assurance of Learning Standards? One of the criteria for AACSB accreditation is quality of the curricula. Although no specific courses are required, the AACSB expects a curriculum to include learning experiences in areas such as the following:

- Communication
- Ethical Reasoning
- Analytic Skills
- Use of Information Technology
- Multicultural and Diversity
- Reflective Thinking

Questions that test skills relevant to these guidelines are appropriately tagged. For example, a question testing the moral questions associated with externalities would receive the Ethical Reasoning tag.

How Can Instructors Use the AACSB Tags? Tagged questions help you measure whether students are grasping the course content that aligns with the AACSB guidelines noted. In addition, the tagged questions may help instructors identify potential applications of these skills. This in turn may suggest enrichment activities or other educational experiences to help students achieve these skills.

TestGen

The computerized TestGen package allows instructors to customize, save, and generate classroom tests. The test program permits instructors to edit, add, or delete questions from the Test Item Files; edit existing graphics and create new graphics; analyze test results; and organize a database of tests and student results. This software allows for extensive flexibility and ease of use. It provides many options for organizing and displaying tests, along with search and sort features. The software and the Test Item Files can be downloaded from the Instructor's Resource Center (**www.prenhall.com/casefair**).

PowerPoint® Lecture Presentations

Three sets of PowerPoint® slides, three for *Principles of Microeconomics* and three for *Principles of Macroeconomics*, prepared by Fernando and Yvonn Quijano, are available:

1. A comprehensive set of PowerPoint® slides that can be used by instructors for class presentations or by students for lecture preview or review. The presentation includes all the graphs, tables, and equations in the textbook. Two versions are available—the first is in step-by-step mode so that you can build graphs as you would on a blackboard, and in an automated mode, using a single click per slide.
2. A comprehensive set of PowerPoint® slides with Classroom Response Systems (CRS) questions built in so that instructors can incorporate CRS "clickers" into their classroom lectures. For more information on Prentice Hall's partnership with CRS, see the description below. Instructors may download these PowerPoint presentations from the Instructor's Resource Center (**www.prenhall.com/casefair**).
3. A student version of the PowerPoints is available as .pdf files from the book's companion website at www.prenhall.com/case. This version allows students to print the slides and bring them to class for note taking.

Instructor's Resource CD-ROM

The Instructor's Resource CD-ROM contains all the faculty and student resources that support this text. Instructors have the ability to access and edit the following three supplements:

- Instructor's Manuals
- Test Item Files
- PowerPoint® presentations

By clicking on a chapter or searching for a key word, faculty can access an interactive library of resources. Faculty can pick and choose from the various supplements and export them to their hard drives.

Classroom Response Systems

Classroom Response Systems (CRS) is an exciting new wireless polling technology that makes large and small classrooms even more interactive because it enables instructors to pose questions to their students, record results, and display the results instantly. Students can answer questions easily by using compact remote-control transmitters. Prentice Hall has partnerships with leading providers of classroom response systems and can show you everything you need to know about setting up and using a CRS system. We provide the classroom hardware, text-specific PowerPoint® slides, software, and support; and we show you how your students can benefit. Learn more at www.prenhall.com/crs.

Blackboard® and WebCT® Course Content

Prentice Hall offers fully customizable course content for the Blackboard® and WebCT® Course Management Systems.

Resources for the Student

The following supplements are designed to help students understand and retain the key concepts of each chapter.

MyEconLab

MyEconLab allows students to practice what they learn, test their understanding, and pursue a personalized Study Plan generated from their performance on Sample Tests and tests set by their instructors. Here are MyEconLab's key features. (See page xxi of this preface for more details on MyEconLab.)

- Sample Tests, two per chapter
- Personal Study Plan

- Tutorial Instruction
- Graphing Tool

Study Guides

Two *Study Guides*, one for *Principles of Microeconomics* and one for *Principles of Macroeconomics*, were prepared by Thomas M. Beveridge of Durham Technical Community College. They provide students with additional applications and exercises.

Each chapter of the *Study Guides* contains the following elements:

- **Point-by-Point Chapter Objectives** A list of learning goals for the chapter. Each objective is followed up with a summary of the material, learning tips for each concept, and practice questions with solutions.
- ***Economics in Practice* Questions** A question that requires students to apply concepts of the chapter to the *Economics in Practice* feature. The answer accompanies the question.
- **Practice Tests** Approximately 20 multiple-choice questions and answers and application questions that require students to use graphic or numerical analysis to solve economic problems.
- **Solutions** Worked-out solutions to all questions in the *Study Guide*
- **Comprehensive Part Exams** Multiple-choice and application questions to test students' overall comprehension. Solutions to all questions are also provided.

CourseSmart

CourseSmart is an exciting new *choice* for students looking to save money. As an alternative to purchasing the print textbook, students can purchase an electronic version of the same content and save up to 50 percent off the suggested list price of the print text. With a CourseSmart eTextbook, students can search the text, make notes online, print out reading assignments that incorporate lecture notes, and bookmark important passages for later review. For more information or to purchase access to the CourseSmart eTextbook, visit www.coursesmart.com.

Student Subscriptions

Staying on top of current economic issues is critical to understanding and applying microeconomic theory in and out of class. Keep students engaged by packaging, at a discount, a semester-long subscription to The *Wall Street Journal*, the *Financial Times*, or Economist.com with each student text. Contact your local Prentice Hall representative for more information about benefits of these subscriptions and how to order one for your students.

Acknowledgments

We are grateful to the many people who helped us prepare the ninth edition. We thank Jodi Bolognese, our editor, and Virginia Guariglia, our project manager, for their help and enthusiasm. We are also grateful to Lena Buonanno, Developmental Editor, for overseeing the entire project. The quality of the book owes much to her guidance. Steve Deitmer, Director of Development, brought sound judgment to many decisions required during a revision.

Lori DeShazo, Executive Marketing Manager, carefully crafted the marketing message. Lynne Breitfeller, Production Editor, and Cynthia Zonneveld, our production managing editor, ensured that the production process of the book went smoothly. In addition, we also want to thank Marisa Taylor of GEX Publishing Services, who kept us on schedule, and Sheila Norman, who researched the many photographs that appear in the book.

We want to give special thanks to Patsy Balin, Murielle Dawdy, and Tracy Waldman for their research assistance.

We also owe a debt of gratitude to those who reviewed and accuracy-checked the ninth edition. They provided us with valuable insight as we prepared this edition and its supplement package.

Consultant Board

The guidance and recommendations of the following professors helped us develop our revision plan and select *Economics in Practice* features for each chapter.

Brett Katzman, Kennesaw State University
Margaret D. Ledyard, University of Texas, Austin
Nathan Perry, University of Utah
Joseph A. Petry, University of Illinois
Chris Phillips, Somerset Community College
Jeff Rubin, Rutgers University
William Walsh, University of St. Thomas
Robert Whaples, Wake Forest University

Accuracy Reviewers

A dedicated team of economics professors accuracy-checked the text for the ninth edition:

Fatma Abdel-Raouf, Goldey-Beacom College
Charles Callahan, III, State University of New York, Brockport
Tisha Emerson, Baylor University
Daniel Lawson, Drew University
Randy Methenitis, Richland College
Robert Whaples, Wake Forest University

Reviewers of the Current Edition

The guidance and recommendations of the following professors helped us develop the revision plans for our new edition and shape the content of the new chapters:

Cynthia Abadie, Southwest Tennessee Community College
Shawn Abbott, College of the Siskiyous
Rebecca Abraham, Nova Southeastern University
Basil Adams, Notre Dame de Namur University
Carlos Aguilar, El Paso Community College
Ehsan Ahmed, James Madison University
Ferhat Akbas, Texas A&M University
Terence Alexander, Iowa State University
Hassan Aly, Ohio State University
David Anderson, Centre College
Joan Anderssen, Arapahoe Community College
Bevin Ashenmiller, Occidental College
Birjees Ashraf, Houston Community College Southwest
Musa Ayar, University of Texas, Austin
Asatar Bair, City College of San Francisco
Nick Barcia, Baruch College
Laurie Bates, Bryant University
Diana Bajrami, College of Alameda
Rita Balaban, University of North Carolina, Chapel Hill
Henry Barker, Tiffin University
Robin Bartlett, Denison University
Leon Battista, City University of New York
Amanda Bayer, Swarthmore College
Klaus Becker, Texas Tech University
Clive Belfield, Queens College
Richard Beil, Auburn University
Emil Berendt, Siena Heights University
Kurt Beron, University of Texas, Dallas
Derek Berry, Calhoun Community College
Tibor Besedes, Georgia Institute of Technology
Thomas Beveridge, Durham Technical Community College
Anoop Bhargava, Finger Lakes CC
Eugenie Bietry, Pace University
Kelly Blanchard, Purdue University
Mark Bock, Loyola College in Maryland
Howard Bodenhorn, Lafayette College
Jeff Bookwalter, University of Montana
Antonio Bos, Tusculum College
Barry Brown, Murray State University
Bruce Brown, California State Polytechnic University, Pomona
Jennifer Brown, Eastern Connecticut State University
Don Brunner, Spokane Falls Community College
Jeff Bruns, Bacone College
David Bunting, Eastern Washington University
Barbara Burnell, College of Wooster
Alison Butler, Willamette University
Fred Campano, Fordham University
Douglas Campbell, University of Memphis
Beth Cantrell, Central Baptist College
Kevin Carlson, University of Massachusetts, Boston
Leonard Carlson, Emory University
Arthur Schiller Casimir, Western New England College
Cesar Corredor, Texas A&M University
Suparna Chakraborty, Baruch College of the City University of New York
David Ching, University of Hawaii – Honolulu
Dmitriy Chulkov, Indiana University, Kokomo
Karen Conway, University of New Hampshire
Tyler Cowen, George Mason University
Amy Cramer, Pima Community College, West Campus
Jerry Crawford, Arkansas State University
James Cunningham, Chapman University
Barbara Craig, Oberlin College
James D'Angelo, University of Cincinnati
David Dahl, University of St. Thomas
Sonia Dalmia, Grand Valley State University
Sheryll Dahlke, Lees-McRae College
Joseph Dahms, Hood College
Rosa Lea Danielson, College of DuPage
David Danning, University of Massachusetts, Boston
Amlan Datta, Cisco Junior College
David Davenport, McLennan Community College
Stephen Davis, Southwest Minnesota State University
Dale DeBoer, Colorado University, Colorado Springs
Dennis Debrecht, Carroll College
Juan J. DelaCruz, Fashion Institute of Technology and Lehman College
Greg Delemeester, Marietta College
Amy Diduch, Mary Baldwin College
Yanan Di, State University of New York, Stony Brook
Timothy Diette, Washington and Lee University
Alan Dobrowolksi, Manchester Community College
Eric Dodge, Hanover College
Carol Dole, Jacksonville University
Shahpour Dowlatshahi, Fayetteville Technical Community College
Kevin Duncan, Colorado State University
Ann Eike, University of Kentucky
Eugene Elander, Plymouth State University
Tisha Emerson, Baylor University
Michael Enz, Western New England College
Erwin Erhardt III, University of Cincinnati
William Even, Miami University
Dr. Ali Faegh, Houston Community College, Northwest
Deborah Figart, Richard Stockton College
Fred Foldvary, Santa Clara University
Kevin Foster, The City College of New York
Johanna Francis, Fordham University
Mark Frascatore, Clarkson University
Amanda Freeman, Kansas State University
Morris Frommer, Owens Community College
Brandon Fuller, University of Montana
David Fuller, University of Iowa
Mark Funk, University of Arkansas, Little Rock
Craig Gallet, California State University, Sacramento
Bill Ganley, Buffalo State College
Jeff Gerlach, Sungkyunkwan Graduate School of Business
Lynn G. Gillette, Spalding University

Donna Ginther, University of Kansas
Amy Glass, Texas A&M University
Bill Godair, Landmark College
Joshua Goodman, New York University
Ophelia Goma, DePauw University
John Gonzales, University of San Francisco
David Gordon, Illinois Valley College
Eugene Gotwalt, Sweet Briar College
Osman Gulseven, North Carolina State University
Mike Gumpper, Millersville University
Thomas A. Gresik, University of Notre Dame
Wayne Grove, Le Moyne College
Daryl Gruver, Mount Vernon Nazarene University
Anthony Gyapong, Penn State University, Abington
Bradley Hansen, University of Mary Washington
Mehdi Haririan, Bloomsburg University of Pennsylvania
David Harris, Benedictine College
David Harris, San Diego State University
James Hartley, Mount Holyoke College
Bruce Hartman, California Maritime Academy of California State University
Dewey Heinsma, Mt. San Jacinto College
Sara Helms, University of Alabama, Birmingham
Brian Hill, Salisbury University
Arleen Hoag, Owens Community College
Carol Hogan, University of Michigan, Dearborn
Ward Hooker, Orangeburg-Calhoun Technical College
Daniel Horton, Cleveland State University
Ying Huang, Manhattan College
Creed Hyatt, Lehigh Carbon Community College
Ana Ichim, Louisiana State University
Aaron Iffland, Rocky Mountain College
Aaron Jackson, Bentley College
Brian Jacobsen, Wisconsin Lutheran College
Russell Janis, University of Massachusetts, Amherst
Jonatan Jelen, The City College of New York
Aaron Johnson, Missouri State University
Paul Johnson, University of Alaska Anchorage
Donn Johnson, Quinnipiac University
Dennis Kaufman, University of Wisconsin, Parkside
Pavel Kapinos, Carleton College
Russell Kashian, University of Wisconsin, Whitewater
Amoz Kats, Virginia Technical University
David Kaun, University of California, Santa Cruz
Brett Katzman, Kennesaw State University
Fred Keast, Portland State University
Stephanie Kelton, University of Missouri, Kansas City
Deborah Kelly, Palomar College
Erasmus Kersting, Texas A&M University
Randall Kesselring, Arkansas State University
Alan Kessler, Providence College
Gary Kikuchi, University of Hawaii, Manoa
Keon-Ho Kim, University of Utah
Kil-Joong Kim, Austin Peay State University
Sang W. Kim, Hood College
Janet Koscianski, Shippensburg University
Vani Kotcherlakota, University of Nebraska, Kearney
Stephan Kroll, California State University, Sacramento
Joseph Kubec, Park University
Jacob Kurien, Helzberg School of Management
Barry Kotlove, Edmonds Community College
Kate Krause, University of New Mexico
David Kroeker, Tabor College
Sally Kwak, University of Hawaii- Manoa
David Lang, California State University, Sacramento
Gary Langer, Roosevelt University
Anthony Laramie, Merrimack College
Leonard Lardaro, University of Rhode Island
Ross LaRoe, Denison University
Pareena Lawrence, Unversity of Minnesota, Morris
Mary Rose Leacy, Wagner College
Alan Leonard, Wilson Technical Community College
Ding Li, Northern State University
Zhe Li, Stony Brook University
Benjamin Liebman, Saint Joseph's University
Larry Lichtenstein, Canisius College
Jesse Liebman, Kennesaw State University
Melissa Lind, University of Texas, Arlington
Charles Link, University of Delaware
Samuel Liu, West Valley College
Jeffrey Livingston, Bentley College
Ming Chien Lo, Saint Cloud University
Alina Luca, Drexel University
Adrienne Lucas, Wellesley College
Nancy Lutz, Virginia Technical University, Virginia Tech
Kristina Lybecker, Colorado College
Ann E. Lyon, University of Alaska Anchorage
Bruce Madariaga, Montgomery College
Tim Mason, Eastern Illinois University
Don Mathews, Coastal Georgia Community College
Roberto Mazzoleni, Hofstra University
Patrick McEwan, Wellesley College
Dawn McLaren, Mesa Community College
B. Starr McMullen, Oregon State University
Martin Melkonian, Hofstra University
Alice Melkumian, Western Illinois University
William Mertens, University of Colorado, Boulder
Randy Methenitis, Richland College
Carrie A. Meyer, George Mason University
David Mitchell, Missouri State University
Ida Mirzaie, The Ohio State University
Bijan Moeinian, Osceola Campus
Robert Mohr, University of New Hampshire
Shahruz Mohtadi, Suffolk University
Amyaz Moledina, College of Wooster
Gary Mongiovi, St. John's University
Terry Monson, Michigan Technological University
Barbara A. Moore, University of Central Florida
W. Douglas Morgan, University of California, Santa Barbara
David Murphy, Boston College
Ellen Mutari, Richard Stockton College of New Jersey
Steven C. Myers, University of Akron
Doug Nelson, Spokane Community College
Sung No, Southern University and A&M College
Albert Okunade, University of Memphis
Constantin Ogloblin, Georgia Southern University
David O'Hara, Metropolitan State University
Ronald Olive, University of Massachusetts, Lowell
Martha Olney, University of California, Berkeley
Mete Ozcan, Brooklyn College
Alexandre Padilla, Metropolitan State College of Denver
Aaron Pankratz, Fresno City College
Spiro Patton, Rasmussen College
Andrew Pearlman, Bard College
Richard Peck, University of Illinois at Chicago
Don Peppard, Connecticut College
Elizabeth Perry, Randolph College
Nathan Perry, University of Utah
Chris Phillips, Somerset Community College
Frankie Pircher, University of Missouri, Kansas City
Dennis Placone, Clemson University
Linnea Polgreen, University of Iowa
Bob Potter, University of Central Florida
Ed Price, Oklahoma State University

Ramkishen S. Rajan, George Mason University
James Rakowski, University of Notre Dame
Amy Ramirez-Gay, Eastern Michigan University
Artatrana Ratha, St. Cloud State University
Brian Roberson, Miami University
Michael Robinson, Mount Holyoke College
Juliette Roddy, University of Michigan, Dearborn
Belinda Roman, Palo Alto College
Paul Roscelli, Canada College
Charles Roussel, Louisiana State University
Brian Rosario, University of California, Davis
Greg Rose, Sacramento City College
Howard Ross, Baruch College
Robert Rosenthal, Stonehill College
Jeff Rubin, Rutgers University, Rutgers
Luz A. Saavedra, University of St. Thomas
William Samuelson, Boston University School of Management
Allen Sanderson, University of Chicago
David Saner, Springfield College – Benedictine University
Ahmad Saranjam, Bridgewater State College
Eric Schansberg, Indiana University – Southeast
Robert Schenk, Saint Joseph's College
Adina Schwartz, Lakeland College
Amy Scott, DeSales University
Atindra Sen, Miami University
Chad Settle, University of Tulsa
Ronald Shadbegian, University of Massachusetts, Dartmouth
Paul Shea, University of Oregon
Gerald Shilling, Eastfield College
Dongsoo Shin, Santa Clara University
William Simeone, Providence College
Larry Singell, University of Oregon
Dennis Shannon, Southwestern Illinois College
David Shideler, Murray State University
Elias Shukralla, St. Louis Community College, Meramec
Anne Shugars, Harford Community College
Richard Sicotte, University of Vermont
Priyanka Singh, University of Texas, Dallas
Edward Skelton, Southern Methodist University
Ken Slaysman, York College
John Smith, New York University
Donald Snyder, Utah State University
Marcia Snyder, College of Charleston
John Solow, University of Iowa
Angela Sparkman, Itawamba Community College
Martin Spechler, Indiana University
Arun Srinivasa, Indiana University, Southeast
Sarah Stafford, College of William & Mary
Richard Stahl, Louisiana State University
Mary Stevenson, University of Massachusetts, Boston
Courtenay Stone, Ball State University
Edward Stuart, Northeastern Illinois University
Chuck Stull, Kalamazoo College
Della Sue, Marist College
Abdulhamid Sukar, Cameron University
Christopher Surfield, Saginaw Valley State University
Bernica Tackett, Pulaski Technical College
William Taylor, New Mexico Highlands University
Samia Costa Tavares, Rochester Institute of Technology
Henry Terrell, University of Maryland
Jennifer Thacher, University of New Mexico
Donna Thompson, Brookdale Community College
David Tolman, Boise State University
Susanne Toney, Hampton University
Boone Turchi, University of North Carolina, Chapel Hill
Kristin Van Gaasbeck, California State University, Sacramento
HuiKuan Tseng, University of North Carolina at Charlotte
Amy Vander Laan, Hastings College
William Walsh, University of St. Thomas
Chunbei Wang, University of St. Thomas
Bruce Webb, Gordon College
Ross Weiner, The City College of New York
Elaine Wendt, Milwaukee Area Technical College
Christopher Westley, Jacksonville State University
Robert Whaples, Wake Forest University
Alex Wilson, Rhode Island College
Wayne Winegarden, Marymount University
Jennifer Wissink, Cornell University
Arthur Woolf, University of Vermont
Bill Yang, Georgia Southern University
Jay Zagorsky, Boston University
Alexander Zampieron, Bentley College
Sourushe Zandvakili, University of Cincinnati
Walter J. Zeiler, University of Michigan

Reviewers of Previous Editions

The following individuals were of immense help in reviewing all or part of previous editions of this book and the teaching/learning package in various stages of development:

Lew Abernathy, University of North Texas
Jack Adams, University of Maryland
Douglas K. Adie, Ohio University
Douglas Agbetsiafa, Indiana University, South Bend
Sheri Aggarwal, University of Virginia
Sam Alapati, Rutgers University
John W. Allen, Texas A&M University
Polly Allen, University of Connecticut
Stuart Allen, University of North Carolina at Greensboro
Alex Anas, University at Buffalo, The State University of New York
Jim Angresano, Hampton-Sydney College
Kenneth S. Arakelian, University of Rhode Island
Harvey Arnold, Indian River Community College
Nick Apergis, Fordham University
Richard Ashley, Virginia Technical University
Kidane Asmeron, Pennsylvania State University
James Aylesworth, Lakeland Community College
Moshen Bahmani, University of Wisconsin-Milwaukee
Mohammad Bajwa, Northampton Community College
A. Paul Ballantyne, University of Colorado, Colorado Springs
Richard J. Ballman, Jr., Augustana College
King Banaian, St. Cloud State University
Kari Battaglia, University of North Texas
Leon Battista, Bronx Community College
Willie J. Belton, Jr., Georgia Institute of Technology
Daniel K. Benjamin, Clemson University
Charles A. Bennett, Gannon University
Daniel Berkowitz, University of Pittsburgh
Bruce Bolnick, Northeastern University
Frank Bonello, University of Notre Dame
Jeffrey Bookwalter, University of Montana
Maristella Botticini, Boston University
G. E. Breger, University of South Carolina
Dennis Brennan, William Rainey Harper Junior College
Anne E. Bresnock, California State Polytechnic University, Pomona, and the University of California, Los Angeles

David Brownstone, University of California, Irvine
Charles Callahan, III, State University of New York at Brockport
Lindsay Caulkins, John Carroll University
Atreya Chakraborty, Boston College
Winston W. Chang, University at Buffalo, The State University of New York
Janie Chermak, University of New Mexico
Harold Christensen, Centenary College
Daniel Christiansen, Albion College
Susan Christoffersen, Philadelphia University
Samuel Kim-Liang Chuah, Walla Walla College
David Colander, Middlebury College
Daniel Condon, University of Illinois at Chicago; Moraine Valley Community College
David Cowen, University of Texas, Austin
Peggy Crane, Southwestern College
Minh Quang Dao, Eastern Illinois University
Vernon J. Dixon, Haverford College
Michael Donihue, Colby College
Joanne M. Doyle, James Madison University
Robert Driskill, Ohio State University
James Dulgeroff, San Bernardino Valley College
Yvonne Durham, Western Washington University
Debra Sabatini Dwyer, State University of New York, Stony Brook
Gary Dymski, University of Southern California
David Eaton, Murray State University
Jay Egger, Towson State University
Ronald D. Elkins, Central Washington University
Noel J. J. Farley, Bryn Mawr College
Mosin Farminesh, Temple University
Dan Feaster, Miami University of Ohio
Susan Feiner, Virginia Commonwealth University
Getachew Felleke, Albright College
Lois Fenske, South Puget Sound Community College
William Field, DePauw University
Mary Flannery, Santa Clara University
Bill Foeller, State University of New York, Fredonia
Roger Nils Folsom, San Jose State University
Mathew Forstater, University of Missouri-Kansas City
Richard Fowles, University of Utah
Sean Fraley, College of Mount Saint Joseph
Roger Frantz, San Diego State University
Alejandro Gallegos, Winona State University
N. Galloro, Chabot College
Martin A. Garrett, Jr., College of William and Mary
Tom Gausman, Northern Illinois University
Shirley J. Gedeon, University of Vermont
Lisa Giddings, University of Wisconsin, La Crosse
Gary Gigliotti, Rutgers University
Lynn Gillette, Texas A&M University
Donna Ginther, University of Kansas
James N. Giordano, Villanova University
Sarah L. Glavin, Boston College
Roy Gobin, Loyola University, Chicago
Bill Goffe, University of Mississippi
Devra Golbe, Hunter College
Roger Goldberg, Ohio Northern University
Richard Gosselin, Houston Community College
John W. Graham, Rutgers University
Douglas Greenley, Morehead State University
Thomas A. Gresik, University of Notre Dame
Lisa M. Grobar, California State University, Long Beach
Wayne A. Grove, Syracuse University
Benjamin Gutierrez, Indiana University, Bloomington
A. R. Gutowsky, California State University, Sacramento
David R. Hakes, University of Missouri, St. Louis
Stephen Happel, Arizona State University
Mitchell Harwitz, University at Buffalo, The State University of New York
David Hoaas, Centenary College
Harry Holzer, Michigan State University
Bobbie Horn, University of Tulsa
John Horowitz, Ball State University
Janet Hunt, University of Georgia
E. Bruce Hutchinson, University of Tennessee, Chattanooga
Fred Inaba, Washington State University
Richard Inman, Boston College
Russell A. Janis, University of Massachusetts, Amherst
Eric Jensen, The College of William & Mary
Shirley Johnson, Vassar College
Farhoud Kafi, Babson College
R. Kallen, Roosevelt University
Arthur E. Kartman, San Diego State University
Hirshel Kasper, Oberlin College
Brett Katzman, Kennesaw State University
Bruce Kaufman, Georgia State University
Fred Keast, Portland State University
Stephanie Kelton, University of Missouri-Kansas City
Dominique Khactu, The University of North Dakota
Hwagyun Kim, State University of New York, Buffalo
Phillip King, San Francisco State University
Barbara Kneeshaw, Wayne County Community College
Inderjit Kohli, Santa Clara University
Heather Kohls, Marquette University
Barry Kotlove, Elmira College
David Kraybill, University of Georgia
Rosung Kwak, University of Texas at Austin
Steven Kyle, Cornell University
Anil K. Lal, Pittsburg State University
Melissa Lam, Wellesley College
Micheal Lawlor, Wake Forest University
Jim Lee, Fort Hays State University
Judy Lee, Leeward Community College
Sang H. Lee, Southeastern Louisiana University
Don Leet, California State University, Fresno
Robert J. Lemke, Lake Forest College
Gary Lemon, DePauw University
Alan Leonard, Northern Illinois University
Mary Lesser, Iona College
George Lieu, Tuskegee University
Stephen E. Lile, Western Kentucky University
Jane Lillydahl, University of Colorado at Boulder
Anthony K. Lima, California State University at Hayward
Al Link, University of North Carolina Greensboro
Charles R. Link, University of Delaware
Robert Litro, U.S. Air Force Academy
Ming Chien Lo, St. Cloud State University
Burl F. Long, University of Florida
Gerald Lynch, Purdue University
Karla Lynch, University of North Texas
Michael Magura, University of Toledo
Marvin S. Margolis, Millersville University of Pennsylvania
Don Maxwell, Central State University
Nan Maxwell, California State University at Hayward
Cynthia S. McCarty, Jacksonville State University
J. Harold McClure, Jr., Villanova University
Rick McIntyre, University of Rhode Island
James J. McLain, University of New Orleans
K. Mehtaboin, College of St. Rose
Art Meyer, Lincoln Land Community College
Carrie Meyer, George Mason University
Meghan Millea, Mississippi State University

Jenny Minier, University of Miami
Shahruz Mohtadi, Suffolk University
Terry D. Monson, Michigan Tech University
Barbara A. Moore, University of Central Florida
Joe L. Moore, Arkansas Technical University
Myra Moore, University of Georgia
Robert Moore, Occidental College
Norma C. Morgan, Curry College
W. Douglas Morgan, University of California, Santa Barbara
John Murphy, North Shore Community College, Massachusetts
Veena Nayak, University at Buffalo, The State University of New York
Ron Necoechea, Robert Wesleyan College
Randy Nelson, Colby College
David Nickerson, University of British Columbia
Rachel Nugent, Pacific Lutheran University
Akorlie A. Nyatepe-Coo, University of Wisconsin LaCrosse
Norman P. Obst, Michigan State University
William C. O'Connor, Western Montana College
Martha L. Olney, University of California, Berkeley
Kent Olson, Oklahoma State University
Jaime Ortiz, Florida Atlantic University
Theresa Osborne, Hunter College
Donald J. Oswald, California State University, Bakersfield
Niki Papadopoulou, University of Cyprus
Walter Park, American University
Carl Parker, Fort Hays State University
Spirog Patton, Neumann College
Mary Ann Pevas, Winona State University
Tony Pizelo, Spokane Community College
Mike Pogodzinski, San Jose State University
Elizabeth Porter, University of North Florida
Abe Qastin, Lakeland College
Kevin Quinn, St. Norbert College
Paul Rappoport, Temple University
Michael Rendich, Westchester Community College
Lynn Rittenoure, University of Tulsa
Michael Rolleigh, University of Minnesota
S. Scanlon Romer, Delta College
David C. Rose, University of Missouri-St. Louis
Greg Rose, Sacramento City College
Richard Rosenberg, Pennsylvania State University
Robert Rosenman, Washington State University
Paul Rothstein, Washington University
Jeff Rubin, Rutgers University
Mark Rush, University of Florida
Dereka Rushbrook, Ripon College
Jerard Russo, University of Hawaii
David L. Schaffer, Haverford College
Ramon Schreffler, Houston Community College System (retired)
Jerry Schwartz, Broward Community College
Gary Sellers, University of Akron
Jean Shackleford, Bucknell University
Linda Shaffer, California State University, Fresno
Stephen L Shapiro, University of North Florida
Geoff Shepherd, University of Massachusetts Amherst
Bih-Hay Sheu, University of Texas at Austin
Alden Shiers, California Polytechnic State University
Scott Simkins, North Carolina Agricultural and Technical State University
Sue Skeath, Wellesley College
Paula Smith, Central State University, Oklahoma
David Sobiechowski, Wayne State University
John Solow, University of Iowa
David J. St. Clair, California State University at Hayward
Rebecca Stein, University of Pennsylvania
Susan Stojanovic, Washington University, St. Louis
Ernst W. Stromsdorfer, Washington State University
Chris Stufflebean, Southwestern Oklahoma State University
Rodney B. Swanson, University of California, Los Angeles
James Swofford, University of Alabama
Michael Taussig, Rutgers University
Samia Tavares, Rochester Institute of Technology
Timothy Taylor, Stanford University
Sister Beth Anne Tercek, SND, Notre Dame College of Ohio
Henry Terrell, University of Maryland, College Park
Robert Tokle, Idaho State University
Karen M. Travis, Pacific Lutheran University
Jack Trierweler, Northern State University
Brian M. Trinque, University of Texas at Austin
Ann Velenchik, Wellesley College
Lawrence Waldman, University of New Mexico
Chris Waller, Indiana University, Bloomington
Walter Wessels, North Carolina State University
Joan Whalen-Ayyappan, DeVry Institute of Technology
Robert Whaples, Wake Forest University
Leonard A. White, University of Arkansas
Paula Worthington, Northwestern University
Ben Young, University of Missouri, Kansas City
Darrel Young, University of Texas
Michael Youngblood, Rock Valley College
Abera Zeyege, Ball State University
James Ziliak, Indiana University, Bloomington
Jason Zimmerman, South Dakota State University

We welcome comments about the ninth edition. Please write to us care of Economics Editor, Prentice Hall Higher Education Division, One Lake Street, Upper Saddle River, NJ 07458.

Karl E. Case

Ray C. Fair

Sharon M. Oster

Save a Tree!

Many of the components of the teaching and learning package are available online. Online supplements conserve paper and allow you to select and print only the material you plan to use. For more information, please contact your Prentice Hall sales representative.

The Scope and Method of Economics

1

CHAPTER OUTLINE

The study of economics should begin with a sense of wonder. Pause for a moment and consider a typical day in your life. It might start with a bagel made in a local bakery with flour produced in Minnesota from wheat grown in Kansas and bacon from pigs raised in Ohio packaged in plastic made in New Jersey. You spill coffee from Colombia on your shirt made in Texas from textiles shipped from South Carolina.

After class you drive with a friend on an interstate highway that is part of a system that took 20 years and billions of dollars to build. You stop for gasoline refined in Louisiana from Saudi Arabian crude oil brought to the United States on a supertanker that took 3 years to build at a shipyard in Maine.

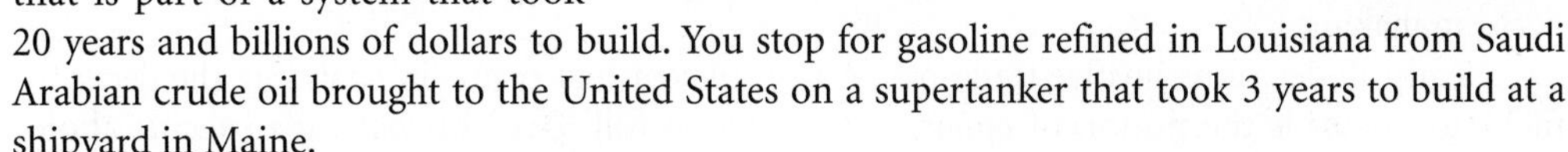

Later you log onto the Web with a laptop computer assembled in Indonesia from parts made in China and send an e-mail to your brother in Mexico City, and you call a buddy on a cell phone made by a company in Finland. Your call is picked up by a microwave dish hidden in a church steeple rented from the church by a cellular company that was just bought by a European conglomerate.

You use or consume tens of thousands of things, both tangible and intangible, every day: buildings, rock music, iPods, telephone services, staples, paper, toothpaste, tweezers, pizza, soap, digital watches, fire protection, banks, electricity, eggs, insurance, football fields, computers, buses, rugs, subways, health services, sidewalks, and so forth. Somebody made all these things. Somebody organized men and women and materials to produce and distribute them. Thousands of decisions went into their completion. Somehow they got to you.

In the United States, over 146 million people—almost half the total population—work at hundreds of thousands of different jobs producing over $14 trillion worth of goods and services every year. Some cannot find work; some choose not to work. Some are rich; others are poor.

The United States imports over $257 billion worth of automobiles and parts and about $229 billion worth of petroleum and petroleum products each year; it exports around $62 billion worth of agricultural products, including food. High-rise office buildings go up in central cities. Condominiums and homes are built in the suburbs. In other places, homes are abandoned and boarded up.

Some countries are wealthy. Others are impoverished. Some are growing. Some are not. Some businesses are doing well. Others are going bankrupt.

At any moment in time, every society faces constraints imposed by nature and by previous generations. Some societies are handsomely endowed by nature with fertile land, water, sunshine, and natural resources. Others have deserts and few mineral resources. Some societies receive much from previous generations—art, music, technical knowledge, beautiful buildings, and productive factories. Others are left with overgrazed, eroded land, cities leveled by war, or polluted natural environments. *All* societies face limits.

economics The study of how individuals and societies choose to use the scarce resources that nature and previous generations have provided.

Economics is the study of how individuals and societies choose to use the scarce resources that nature and previous generations have provided. The key word in this definition is *choose*. Economics is a behavioral, or social, science. In large measure, it is the study of how people make choices. The choices that people make, when added up, translate into societal choices.

The purpose of this chapter and the next is to elaborate on this definition and to introduce the subject matter of economics. What is produced? How is it produced? Who gets it? Why? Is the result good or bad? Can it be improved?

Why Study Economics?

There are four main reasons to study economics: to learn a way of thinking, to understand society, to understand global affairs, and to be an informed citizen.

To Learn a Way of Thinking

Probably the most important reason for studying economics is to learn a way of thinking. Economics has three fundamental concepts that, once absorbed, can change the way you look at everyday choices: opportunity cost, marginalism, and the working of efficient markets.

Opportunity Cost What happens in an economy is the outcome of thousands of individual decisions. People must decide how to divide their incomes among all the goods and services available in the marketplace. They must decide whether to work, whether to go to school, and how much to save. Businesses must decide what to produce, how much to produce, how much to charge, and where to locate. It is not surprising that economic analysis focuses on the process of decision making.

Nearly all decisions involve trade-offs. A key concept that recurs in analyzing the decision-making process is the notion of *opportunity cost*. The full "cost" of making a specific choice includes what we give up by not making the alternative choice. The best alternative that we forgo, or give up, when we make a choice or a decision is called the **opportunity cost** of that decision.

opportunity cost The best alternative that we forgo, or give up, when we make a choice or a decision.

When asked how much a movie costs, most people cite the ticket price. For an economist, this is only part of the answer: to see a movie takes not only a ticket but also time. The opportunity cost of going to a movie is the value of the other things you could have done with the same money and time. If you decide to take time off from work, the opportunity cost of your leisure is the pay that you would have earned had you worked. Part of the cost of a college education is the income you could have earned by working full-time instead of going to school. If a firm purchases a new piece of equipment for $3,000, it does so because it expects that equipment to generate more profit. There is an opportunity cost, however, because that $3,000 could have been deposited in an interest-earning account. To a society, the opportunity cost of using resources to launch astronauts on a space shuttle is the value of the private/civilian or other government goods that could have been produced with the same resources.

scarce Limited.

Opportunity costs arise because resources are scarce. **Scarce** simply means limited. Consider one of our most important resources—time. There are only 24 hours in a day, and we must live our lives under this constraint. A farmer in rural Brazil must decide whether it is better to continue to farm or to go to the city and look for a job. A hockey player at the University of Vermont must decide whether to play on the varsity team or spend more time studying.

marginalism The process of analyzing the additional or incremental costs or benefits arising from a choice or decision.

Marginalism A second key concept used in analyzing choices is the notion of **marginalism**. In weighing the costs and benefits of a decision, it is important to weigh only the costs and benefits that arise from the decision. Suppose, for example, that you live in New Orleans and that you are weighing the costs and benefits of visiting your mother in Iowa. If business required that you travel to Kansas City, the cost of visiting Mom would be only the additional, or *marginal*, time and money cost of getting to Iowa from Kansas City.

Consider the music business. To produce a typical CD, music labels spend approximately $300,000 on recording the music and music video, developing marketing materials, and distributing the album. Once the label has made this investment, physically producing another copy of the CD for sale typically costs about $2. When the music label is deciding whether to sign a new artist and produce a CD, the $300,000 investment is important. Companies such as EMI and Columbia Records spend a great deal of time thinking about whether a new CD by a newly discovered artist will sell enough copies to make a profit. But once an artist is signed and the investment is made and the music label is trying to decide whether to manufacture the 100,001st copy of a new CD, the key cost number is $2. Every new copy costs only $2, and as long as EMI can sell that copy for more than $2, it is better off making the copy. The original investment made to create the music is irrelevant—a **sunk cost**. Sunk costs are costs that cannot be avoided because they have already been incurred.

sunk costs Costs that cannot be avoided because they have already been incurred.

Technically, we call the incremental cost of producing one more unit of a good or service the *marginal cost*. One of the interesting changes in the music business is what has happened to the marginal cost of producing another copy of a CD given the introduction of iTunes as an alternative to the physical CD. While it is not always easy to figure out what the marginal cost is (and we will spend some time in this text honing your skills in this area), understanding the idea of marginalism when thinking about choices is critical.

There are numerous examples in which the concept of marginal cost is useful. For an airplane that is about to take off with empty seats, the marginal cost of an extra passenger is essentially zero; the total cost of the trip is roughly unchanged by the addition of an extra passenger. Thus, setting aside a few seats to be sold at big discounts through www.priceline.com or other Web sites can be profitable even if the fare for those seats is far below the average cost per seat of making the trip. As long as the airline succeeds in filling seats that would otherwise have been empty, doing so is profitable.

Efficient Markets—No Free Lunch Suppose you are ready to check out of a busy grocery store on the day before a storm and seven checkout registers are open with several people in each line. Which line should you choose? Usually, the waiting time is approximately the same no matter which register you choose (assuming you have more than 12 items). If one line is much shorter than the others, people will quickly move into it until the lines are equalized again.

As you will see later, the term *profit* in economics has a very precise meaning. Economists, however, often loosely refer to "good deals" or risk-free ventures as *profit opportunities*. Using the term loosely, a profit opportunity exists at the checkout lines when one line is shorter than the others. In general, such profit opportunities are rare. At any time, many people are searching for them; as a consequence, few exist. Markets like this, where any profit opportunities are eliminated almost instantaneously, are said to be **efficient markets**. (We discuss *markets*, the institutions through which buyers and sellers interact and engage in exchange, in detail in Chapter 2.)

efficient market A market in which profit opportunities are eliminated almost instantaneously.

The common way of expressing the efficient markets concept is "there's no such thing as a free lunch." How should you react when a stockbroker calls with a hot tip on the stock market? With skepticism. Thousands of individuals each day are looking for hot tips in the market. If a particular tip about a stock is valid, there will be an immediate rush to buy the stock, which will quickly drive up its price. This view that very few profit opportunities exist can, of course, be carried too far. There is a story about two people walking along, one an economist and one not. The noneconomist sees a $20 bill on the sidewalk and says, "There's a $20 bill on the sidewalk." The economist replies, "That is not possible. If there were, somebody would already have picked it up."

There are clearly times when profit opportunities exist. Someone has to be first to get the news, and some people have quicker insights than others. Nevertheless, news travels fast and there are thousands of people with quick insights. The general view that large profit opportunities are rare is close to the mark.

The study of economics teaches us a way of thinking and helps us make decisions.

To Understand Society

Another reason for studying economics is to understand society better. Past and present economic decisions have an enormous influence on the character of life in a society. The current state of the physical environment, the level of material well-being, and the nature and number of jobs are all products of the economic system.

To get a sense of the ways in which economic decisions have shaped our environment, imagine looking out a top-floor window of an office tower in any large city. The workday is about to begin. All around you are other tall glass and steel buildings full of workers. In the distance, you see the smoke of factories. Looking down, you see thousands of commuters pouring off trains and buses and cars backed up on freeway exit ramps. You see trucks carrying goods from one place to another. You also see the face of urban poverty: Just beyond the freeway is a large public housing project and, beyond that, burned-out and boarded-up buildings.

What you see before you is the product of millions of economic decisions made over hundreds of years. People at some point decided to spend time and money building those buildings and factories. Somebody cleared the land, laid the tracks, built the roads, and produced the cars and buses.

Economic decisions not only have shaped the physical environment but also have determined the character of society. At no time has the impact of economic change on a society been more evident than in England during the late eighteenth and early nineteenth centuries, a period that we now call the **Industrial Revolution**. Increases in the productivity of agriculture, new manufacturing technologies, and development of more efficient forms of transportation led to a massive movement of the British population from the countryside to the city. At the beginning of the eighteenth century, approximately 2 out of 3 people in Great Britain worked in agriculture. By 1812, only 1 in 3 remained in agriculture; by 1900, the figure was fewer than 1 in 10. People jammed into overcrowded cities and worked long hours in factories. England had changed completely in two centuries—a period that in the run of history was nothing more than the blink of an eye.

Industrial Revolution The period in England during the late eighteenth and early nineteenth centuries in which new manufacturing technologies and improved transportation gave rise to the modern factory system and a massive movement of the population from the countryside to the cities.

It is not surprising that the discipline of economics began to take shape during this period. Social critics and philosophers looked around and knew that their philosophies must expand to accommodate the changes. Adam Smith's *Wealth of Nations* appeared in 1776. It was followed by the writings of David Ricardo, Karl Marx, Thomas Malthus, and others. Each tried to make sense out of what was happening. Who was building the factories? Why? What determined the level of wages paid to workers or the price of food? What would happen in the future, and what *should* happen? The people who asked these questions were the first economists.

Similar changes continue to affect the character of life in more recent times. In fact, many argue that the late 1990s marked the beginning of a new Industrial Revolution. As we turned the corner into the new millennium, the "e" revolution was clearly having an impact on virtually every aspect of our lives: the way we buy and sell products, the way we get news, the way we plan vacations, the way we communicate with each other, the way we teach and take classes, and on and on. These changes have had and will clearly continue to have profound impacts on societies across the globe, from Beijing to Calcutta to New York.

These changes have been driven by economics. Although the government was involved in the early years of the World Wide Web, private firms that exist to make a profit (such as Facebook, YouTube, Yahoo!, Microsoft, Google, Monster.com, Amazon.com, and E-Trade) created almost all the new innovations and products. How does one make sense of all this? What will the effects of these innovations be on the number of jobs, the character of those jobs, the family incomes, the structure of our cities, and the political process both in the United States and in other countries?

During the last days of August 2005, Hurricane Katrina slammed into the coasts of Louisiana and Mississippi, causing widespread devastation, killing thousands, and leaving hundreds of thousands homeless. The economic impact of this catastrophic storm was huge. Thinking about various markets involved helps frame the problem.

For example, the labor market was massively affected. By some estimates, over 400,000 jobs were lost as the storm hit. Hotels, restaurants, small businesses, and oil refineries, to name just a few, were destroyed. All the people who worked in those establishments instantaneously lost their jobs and their incomes. The cleanup and rebuilding process took time to organize, and it eventually created a great deal of employment.

The storm created a major disruption in world oil markets. Loss of refinery capacity sent gasoline prices up immediately, nearly 40 percent to over $4 per gallon in some locations. The price per gallon of crude oil rose to over $70 per barrel. Local governments found their tax bases destroyed, with no resources to pay teachers and local officials. Hundreds of hospitals were destroyed, and colleges and universities were forced to close their doors, causing tens of thousands of students to change their plans.

While the horror of the storm hit all kinds of people, the worst hit were the very poor, who could not get out of the way because they had no cars or other means of escape. The storm raised fundamental issues of fairness, which we will be discussing for years to come.

The study of economics is an essential part of the study of society.

To Understand Global Affairs

A third reason for studying economics is to understand global affairs. News headlines are filled with economic stories. International events often have enormous economic consequences. The destruction of the World Trade Center towers in New York City in 2001 and the subsequent war on terror in Afghanistan and elsewhere led to a huge decline in both tourism and business travel. Several major airlines, including U.S. Airways and Swissair, went bankrupt. Hotel operators worldwide suffered huge losses. The war in Iraq and a strike in Venezuela, a major oil exporter, in 2003 sent oil markets gyrating dramatically, initially increasing the cost of energy across the globe. The rapid spread of HIV and AIDS across Africa will continue to have terrible economic consequences for the continent and ultimately for the world.

Some claim that economic considerations dominate international relations. Certainly, politicians place the economic well-being of their citizens near the top of their priority lists. It would be surprising if that were not so. Thus, the economic consequences of things such as environmental policy, free trade, and immigration play a huge role in international negotiations and policies.

Great Britain and the other countries of the European Union have struggled with the agreement among most members to adopt a common currency, the euro. In 2005, France and the Netherlands rejected a proposed European constitution that would have gone a long way toward a completely open economy in Europe. The nations of the former Soviet Union are wrestling with a growing phenomenon that clouds their efforts to "privatize" formerly state-owned industries: organized crime.

Another important issue in today's world is the widening gap between rich and poor nations. In 2007, world population was over 6.5 billion. Of that number, over 2.4 billion lived in low-income (less than $900 annually per capita) countries and just over 1 billion lived in high-income (over $11,000 per capita per year) countries. The 37 percent of the world's population that lives in the low-income countries receives less than 3.3 percent of the world's income. In dozens of countries, per capita income is only a few hundred dollars a year. The 15 percent of the population in high-income countries earn 75 percent of the world's income.

An understanding of economics is essential to an understanding of global affairs.

To Be an Informed Citizen

A knowledge of economics is essential to being an informed citizen. During the last 35 years, the U.S. economy has been on a roller coaster. In 1973–1974, the Organization of Petroleum Exporting Countries (OPEC) succeeded in raising the price of crude oil by 400 percent. Simultaneously, a sequence of events in the world food market drove food prices up by 25 percent. By mid-1974, prices in the United States were rising across the board at a very rapid rate. Partially as a result of government policy to fight runaway inflation, the economy went into a recession in 1975. (An *inflation* is an increase in the overall price level in the economy; a *recession* is a period of decreasing output and rising unemployment.) The recession succeeded in slowing price increases, but in the process, millions found themselves unemployed.

From 1979 through 1983, it happened all over again. Prices rose rapidly, the government reacted with more policies designed to stop prices from rising, and the United States ended up with an even worse recession in 1982. By the end of that year, 10.8 percent of the work force was unemployed. Then, in mid-1990—after almost 8 years of strong economic performance—the

ECONOMICS IN PRACTICE

iPod and the World

It is impossible to understand the workings of an economy without first understanding the ways in which economies are connected across borders. The United States was importing goods and services at a rate of over $2 trillion per year in 2007 and was exporting at a rate of over $1.5 trillion per year.

For literally hundreds of years, the virtues of free trade have been the subject of heated debate. Opponents have argued that buying foreign-produced goods costs Americans jobs and hurts American producers. Proponents argue that there are gains from trade—that all countries can gain from specializing in the production of the goods and services that they produce best.

But in today's global economy, it is often unclear what is an import and what is an export. Consider the following column in *The New York Times* in 2007:

An iPod Has Global Value. Ask the (Many) Countries That Make It.

The New York Times

Who makes the Apple iPod? Here's a hint: It is not Apple. The company outsources the entire manufacture of the device to a number of Asian enterprises, among them Asustek, Inventec Appliances, and Foxconn.

But this list of companies isn't a satisfactory answer either: They only do final assembly. What about the 451 parts that go into the iPod? Where are they made and by whom?

Three researchers at the University of California, Irvine—Greg Linden, Kenneth L. Kraemer, and Jason Dedrick—applied some investigative cost accounting to this question, using a report from Portelligent Inc. that examined all the parts that went into the iPod.

Their study, sponsored by the Sloan Foundation, offers a fascinating illustration of the complexity of the global economy, and how difficult it is to understand that complexity by using only conventional trade statistics.

The retail value of the 30-gigabyte video iPod that the authors examined was $299. The most expensive component in it was the hard drive, which was manufactured by Toshiba and costs about $73. The next most costly components were the display module (about $20), the video/multimedia processor chip ($8), and the controller chip ($5). They estimated that the final assembly, done in China, cost only about $4 a unit.

The researchers estimated that $163 of the iPod's $299 retail value in the United States was captured by American companies and workers, breaking it down to $75 for distribution and retail costs, $80 to Apple, and $8 to various domestic component makers. Japan contributed about $26 to the value added (mostly via the Toshiba disk drive), while Korea contributed less than $1.

The real value of the iPod doesn't lie in its parts or even in putting those parts together. The bulk of the iPod's value is in the conception and design of the iPod. That is why Apple gets $80 for each of these video iPods it sells, which is by far the largest piece of value added in the entire supply chain.

Those clever folks at Apple figured out how to combine 451 mostly generic parts into a valuable product. They may not make the iPod, but they created it. In the end, that's what really matters.

Source: Hal R. Varian, Published: June 28, 2007, The New York Times, *reprinted with permission.*

U.S. economy went into another recession. During the third and fourth quarters of 1990 and the first quarter of 1991, *gross domestic product (GDP,* a measure of the total output of the U.S. economy) fell and unemployment again increased sharply. The election of Bill Clinton late in 1992 was no doubt in part influenced by the so-called "jobless recovery."

From the second quarter of 1991 through the early part of the new millennium, the U.S. economy experienced the longest expansion in its history. More than 24 million new jobs were created, pushing unemployment below 4 percent by the year 2000. The stock market boomed to historic levels, and the biggest worry facing the American economy was that things were too good!

The presidential election of 2000 was close, to say the least, with the outcome not known until early December. In mid-December, President-elect George W. Bush and his economic advisers began to worry about the possibility of a recession occurring in 2001. The stock market was below its highs for the year, corporate profits were not coming in as well as expected, and there were some signs that demand for goods was slowing.

Indeed, following the election, the economy slipped into a recession and economic conditions were made worse by the September 11, 2001, attacks on the World Trade Center and on the Pentagon. The stock market, which suffered losses as early as 2000, fell for 3 consecutive years, reducing people's wealth by trillions of dollars. Total employment dropped by nearly 2.7 million. But by 2002, the economy began to grow again, slowly, and by 2005, nearly 3.5 million jobs had been created.

The war in Iraq and the threat of international terrorism following the 9/11 attacks increased military expenditures in the United States substantially. At the same time, tax cuts proposed by President Bush and passed by Congress led to large deficits in the federal budget.

The housing market began to boom in 2001. Fueled by lower interest rates that made borrowing less expensive, foreign demand, and a highly competitive mortgage market that made mortgage credit available to virtually any applicant, house prices rose substantially around the country. Housing starts, the number of new housing units begun each period, rose steadily to a record high by 2005 of over 2 million annually. Sales of existing homes at the same time rose above 7 million per year. In addition, as house values rose, home owners had higher wealth and increased their spending. Much spending was driven by borrowing against the house. When you add all the services surrounding house sales, the huge spending on new units, and the purchases at stores such as Home Depot that go with new house sales, the economy was strongly stimulated by the housing market until the middle of 2006, when housing began to slow.

One of the key factors that fueled the housing boom was the expansion of mortgage credit to borrowers who in earlier years would have not have qualified. Some borrowers had bad credit histories, low incomes, or other substantial debts. These mortgages came to be called subprime loans. In addition, mortgage loans that carried low monthly payments for a few years that were later followed by substantially higher payments became prevalent.

In the summer of 2007, the housing market stalled, prices began to fall, and the huge amount of mortgage debt outstanding (over $10 trillion by 2007) experienced rising delinquency and default. Losses were huge and sent financial markets, including the stock market, into a sharp decline. The question at the start of 2008 was whether the sharp slowdown of the housing market combined with the problems of the credit markets would lead the economy as a whole into a recession.

To be an informed citizen requires a basic understanding of economics.

The Scope of Economics

Most students taking economics for the first time are surprised by the breadth of what they study. Some think that economics will teach them about the stock market or what to do with their money. Others think that economics deals exclusively with problems such as inflation and unemployment. In fact, it deals with all those subjects, but they are pieces of a much larger puzzle.

Economics has deep roots in and close ties to social philosophy. An issue of great importance to philosophers, for example, is distributional justice. Why are some people rich and others poor? And whatever the answer, is this fair? A number of nineteenth-century social philosophers wrestled with these questions, and out of their musings, economics as a separate discipline was born.

The easiest way to get a feel for the breadth and depth of what you will be studying is to explore briefly the way economics is organized. First of all, there are two major divisions of economics: microeconomics and macroeconomics.

Microeconomics and Macroeconomics

microeconomics The branch of economics that examines the functioning of individual industries and the behavior of individual decision-making units—that is, firms and households.

Microeconomics deals with the functioning of individual industries and the behavior of individual economic decision-making units: firms and households. Firms' choices about what to produce and how much to charge and households' choices about what and how much to buy help to explain why the economy produces the goods and services it does.

Another big question addressed by microeconomics is who gets the goods and services that are produced. Wealthy households get more than poor households, and the forces that determine this distribution of output are the province of microeconomics. Why does poverty exist? Who is poor? Why do some jobs pay more than others?

Think again about what you consume in a day and then think back to that view over a big city. Somebody decided to build those factories. Somebody decided to construct the roads, build the housing, produce the cars, and smoke the bacon. Why? What is going on in all those buildings? It is easy to see that understanding individual microdecisions is very important to any understanding of society.

macroeconomics The branch of economics that examines the economic behavior of aggregates—income, employment, output, and so on—on a national scale.

Macroeconomics looks at the economy as a whole. Instead of trying to understand what determines the output of a single firm or industry or what the consumption patterns are of a single household or group of households, macroeconomics examines the factors that determine national output, or national product. Microeconomics is concerned with *household* income; macroeconomics deals with *national* income.

Whereas microeconomics focuses on individual product prices and relative prices, macroeconomics looks at the overall price level and how quickly (or slowly) it is rising (or falling). Microeconomics questions how many people will be hired (or fired) this year in a particular industry or in a certain geographic area and focuses on the factors that determine how much labor a firm or an industry will hire. Macroeconomics deals with *aggregate* employment and unemployment: how many jobs exist in the economy as a whole and how many people who are willing to work are not able to find work.

To summarize:

Microeconomics looks at the individual unit—the household, the firm, the industry. It sees and examines the "trees." Macroeconomics looks at the whole, the aggregate. It sees and analyzes the "forest."

Table 1.1 summarizes these divisions of economics and some of the subjects with which they are concerned.

TABLE 1.1 Examples of Microeconomic and Macroeconomic Concerns

Division of Economics	Production	Prices	Income	Employment
Microeconomics	*Production/output in individual industries and businesses* How much steel How much office space How many cars	*Prices of individual goods and services* Price of medical care Price of gasoline Food prices Apartment rents	*Distribution of income and wealth* Wages in the auto industry Minimum wage Executive salaries Poverty	*Employment by individual businesses and industries* Jobs in the steel industry Number of employees in a firm Number of accountants
Macroeconomics	*National production/output* Total industrial output Gross domestic product Growth of output	*Aggregate price level* Consumer prices Producer prices Rate of inflation	*National income* Total wages and salaries Total corporate profits	*Employment and unemployment in the economy* Total number of jobs Unemployment rate

The Diverse Fields of Economics

Individual economists focus their research and study in many diverse areas. Many of these specialized fields are reflected in the advanced courses offered at most colleges and universities. Some are concerned with economic history or the history of economic thought. Others focus on international economics or growth in less developed countries. Still others study the economics of cities (urban economics) or the relationship between economics and law. These fields are summarized in Table 1.2.

Economists also differ in the emphasis they place on theory. Some economists specialize in developing new theories, whereas other economists spend their time testing the theories of others. Some economists hope to expand the frontiers of knowledge, whereas other economists are more interested in applying what is already known to the formulation of public policies.

TABLE 1.2 The Fields of Economics

Comparative economic systems	examines the ways alternative economic systems function. What are the advantages and disadvantages of different systems?
Econometrics	applies statistical techniques and data to economic problems in an effort to test hypotheses and theories. Most schools require economics majors to take at least one course in statistics or econometrics.
Economic development	focuses on the problems of low-income countries. What can be done to promote development in these nations? Important concerns of development economists include population growth and control, provision for basic needs, and strategies for international trade.
Economic history	traces the development of the modern economy. What economic and political events and scientific advances caused the Industrial Revolution? What explains the tremendous growth and progress of post–World War II Japan? What caused the Great Depression of the 1930s?
Economics of race and gender	examines the role of race and gender in economic theory, in economic life, and in policymaking. How has discrimination by race or gender affected the well-being of households and the distribution of income and wealth?
Environmental economics	studies the potential failure of the market system to account fully for the impacts of production and consumption on the environment and on natural resource depletion. Have alternative public policies and new economic institutions been effective in correcting these potential failures?
Finance	examines the ways in which households and firms actually pay for, or finance, their purchases. It involves the study of capital markets (including the stock and bond markets), futures and options, capital budgeting, and asset valuation.
The history of economic thought,	which is grounded in philosophy, studies the development of economic ideas and theories over time, from Adam Smith in the eighteenth century to the works of economists such as Thomas Malthus, Karl Marx, and John Maynard Keynes. Because economic theory is constantly developing and changing, studying the history of ideas helps give meaning to modern theory and puts it in perspective.
Industrial organization	looks carefully at the structure and performance of industries and firms within an economy. How do businesses compete? Who gains and who loses?
International economics	studies trade flows among countries and international financial institutions. What are the advantages and disadvantages for a country that allows its citizens to buy and sell freely in world markets? Why is the dollar strong or weak?
Labor economics	deals with the factors that determine wage rates, employment, and unemployment. How do people decide whether to work, how much to work, and at what kind of job? How have the roles of unions and management changed in recent years?
Law and economics	analyzes the economic function of legal rules and institutions. How does the law change the behavior of individuals and businesses? Do different liability rules make accidents and injuries more or less likely? What are the economic costs of crime?
Public economics	examines the role of government in the economy. What are the economic functions of government, and what should they be? How should the government finance the services that it provides? What kinds of government programs should confront the problems of poverty, unemployment, and pollution? What problems does government involvement create?
Urban and regional economics	studies the spatial arrangement of economic activity. Why do we have cities? Why are manufacturing firms locating farther and farther from the center of urban areas?

As you begin your study of economics, look through your school's course catalog and talk to the faculty about their interests. You will discover that economics encompasses a broad range of inquiry and is linked to many other disciplines.

The Method of Economics

positive economics An approach to economics that seeks to understand behavior and the operation of systems without making judgments. It describes what exists and how it works.

normative economics An approach to economics that analyzes outcomes of economic behavior, evaluates them as good or bad, and may prescribe courses of action. Also called *policy economics*.

Economics asks and attempts to answer two kinds of questions: positive and normative. **Positive economics** attempts to understand behavior and the operation of economic systems *without making judgments* about whether the outcomes are good or bad. It strives to describe what exists and how it works. What determines the wage rate for unskilled workers? What would happen if we abolished the corporate income tax? The answers to such questions are the subject of positive economics.

In contrast, **normative economics** looks at the outcomes of economic behavior and asks whether they are good or bad and whether they can be made better. Normative economics involves judgments and prescriptions for courses of action. Should the government subsidize or regulate the cost of higher education? Should medical benefits to the elderly under Medicare be available only to those with incomes below some threshold? Should the United States allow importers to sell foreign-produced goods that compete with U.S.-produced products? Should we reduce or eliminate inheritance taxes? Normative economics is often called *policy economics*.

Of course, most normative questions involve positive questions. To know whether the government *should* take a particular action, we must know first if it *can* and second what the consequences are likely to be. (For example, if we lower import fees, will there be more competition and lower prices?)

Some claim that positive, value-free economic analysis is impossible. They argue that analysts come to problems with biases that cannot help but influence their work. Furthermore, even in choosing what questions to ask or what problems to analyze, economists are influenced by political, ideological, and moral views.

Although this argument has some merit, it is nevertheless important to distinguish between analyses that attempt to be positive and those that are intentionally and explicitly normative. Economists who ask explicitly normative questions should be forced to specify their grounds for judging one outcome superior to another.

Descriptive Economics and Economic Theory

descriptive economics The compilation of data that describe phenomena and facts.

Positive economics is often divided into descriptive economics and economic theory. **Descriptive economics** is simply the compilation of data that describe phenomena and facts. Examples of such data appear in the *Statistical Abstract of the United States*, a large volume of data published by the Department of Commerce every year that describes many features of the U.S. economy. Massive volumes of data can now be found on the World Wide Web. As an example, look at www.bls.gov (Bureau of Labor Statistics).

Where do all these data come from? The Census Bureau collects an enormous amount of raw data every year, as do the Bureau of Labor Statistics, the Bureau of Economic Analysis, and nongovernment agencies such as the University of Michigan Survey Research Center. One important study now published annually is the *Survey of Consumer Expenditure*, which asks individuals to keep careful records of all their expenditures over a long period of time. Another is the *National Longitudinal Survey of Labor Force Behavior*, conducted over many years by the Center for Human Resource Development at The Ohio State University.

economic theory A statement or set of related statements about cause and effect, action and reaction.

Economic theory attempts to generalize about data and interpret them. An **economic theory** is a statement or set of related statements about cause and effect, action and reaction. One of the first theories you will encounter in this text is the *law of demand*, which was most clearly stated by Alfred Marshall in 1890: When the price of a product rises, people tend to buy less of it; when the price of a product falls, people tend to buy more.

Theories do not always arise out of formal numerical data. All of us have been collecting observations of people's behavior and their responses to economic stimuli for most of our lives. We may have observed our parents' reaction to a sudden increase—or decrease—in income or to the loss of a job or the acquisition of a new one. We all have seen people standing in line waiting for a bargain. Of course, our own actions and reactions are another important source of data.

Theories and Models

In many disciplines, including physics, chemistry, meteorology, political science, and economics, theorists build formal models of behavior. A **model** is a formal statement of a theory. It is usually a mathematical statement of a presumed relationship between two or more variables.

model A formal statement of a theory, usually a mathematical statement of a presumed relationship between two or more variables.

A **variable** is a measure that can change from time to time or from observation to observation. Income is a variable—it has different values for different people and different values for the same person at different times. The rental price of a movie on a DVD is a variable; it has different values at different stores and at different times. There are countless other examples.

variable A measure that can change from time to time or from observation to observation.

Because all models simplify reality by stripping part of it away, they are abstractions. Critics of economics often point to abstraction as a weakness. Most economists, however, see abstraction as a real strength.

The easiest way to see how abstraction can be helpful is to think of a map. A map is a representation of reality that is simplified and abstract. A city or state appears on a piece of paper as a series of lines and colors. The amount of reality that the mapmaker can strip away before the map loses something essential depends on what the map will be used for. If you want to drive from St. Louis to Phoenix, you need to know only the major interstate highways and roads. You lose absolutely nothing and gain clarity by cutting out the local streets and roads. However, if you need to get around Phoenix, you may need to see every street and alley.

Most maps are two-dimensional representations of a three-dimensional world; they show where roads and highways go but do not show hills and valleys along the way. Trail maps for hikers, however, have "contour lines" that represent changes in elevation. When you are in a car, changes in elevation matter very little; they would make a map needlessly complex and more difficult to read. However, if you are on foot carrying a 50-pound pack, a knowledge of elevation is crucial.

Like maps, economic models are abstractions that strip away detail to expose only those aspects of behavior that are important to the question being asked. The principle that irrelevant detail should be cut away is called the principle of **Ockham's razor** after the fourteenth-century philosopher William of Ockham.

Ockham's razor The principle that irrelevant detail should be cut away.

Be careful—although abstraction is a powerful tool for exposing and analyzing specific aspects of behavior, it is possible to oversimplify. Economic models often strip away a good deal of social and political reality to get at underlying concepts. When an economic theory is used to help formulate actual government or institutional policy, political and social reality must often be reintroduced if the policy is to have a chance of working.

The key here is that the appropriate amount of simplification and abstraction depends on the use to which the model will be put. To return to the map example: you do not want to walk around San Francisco with a map made for drivers—there are too many very steep hills.

All Else Equal: *Ceteris Paribus* It is usually true that whatever you want to explain with a model depends on more than one factor. Suppose, for example, that you want to explain the total number of miles driven by automobile owners in the United States. The number of miles driven will change from year to year or month to month; it is a variable. The issue, if we want to understand and explain changes that occur, is what factors cause those changes.

Obviously, many things might affect total miles driven. First, more or fewer people may be driving. This number, in turn, can be affected by changes in the driving age, by population growth, or by changes in state laws. Other factors might include the price of gasoline, the household's income, the number and age of children in the household, the distance from home to work, the location of shopping facilities, and the availability and quality of public transport. When any of these variables change, the members of the household may drive more or less. If changes in any of these variables affect large numbers of households across the country, the total number of miles driven will change.

Very often we need to isolate or separate these effects. For example, suppose we want to know the impact on driving of a higher tax on gasoline. This change would raise the price of gasoline at the pump but would not (at least in the short run) affect income, workplace location, number of children, and so on.

ceteris paribus, *or* **all else equal** A device used to analyze the relationship between two variables while the values of other variables are held unchanged.

To isolate the impact of one single factor, we use the device of ***ceteris paribus,*** or **all else equal.** We ask: What is the impact of a change in gasoline price on driving behavior, *ceteris paribus*, or assuming that nothing else changes? If gasoline prices rise by 10 percent, how much less driving will there be, assuming no simultaneous change in anything else—that is, assuming that income, number of children, population, laws, and so on, all remain constant? Using the device of *ceteris paribus* is one part of the process of abstraction. In formulating economic theory, the concept helps us simplify reality to focus on the relationships that interest us.

Expressing Models in Words, Graphs, and Equations Consider the following statements: Lower airline ticket prices cause people to fly more frequently. Higher interest rates slow the rate of home sales. When firms produce more output, employment increases. Higher gasoline prices cause people to drive less and to buy more fuel-efficient cars.

Each of those statements expresses a relationship between two variables that can be quantified. In each case, there is a stimulus and a response, a cause and an effect. Quantitative relationships can be expressed in a variety of ways. Sometimes words are sufficient to express the essence of a theory, but often it is necessary to be more specific about the nature of a relationship or about the size of a response. The most common method of expressing the quantitative relationship between two variables is *graphing* that relationship on a two-dimensional plane. In fact, we will use graphic analysis extensively in Chapter 2 and beyond. Because it is essential that you be familiar with the basics of graphing, the Appendix to this chapter presents a careful review of graphing techniques.

Quantitative relationships between variables can also be presented through *equations*. For example, suppose we discovered that over time, U.S. households collectively spend, or consume, 90 percent of their income and save 10 percent of their income. We could then write:

$$C = .90\,Y \text{ and } S = .10Y$$

where C is consumption spending, Y is income, and S is saving. Writing explicit algebraic expressions like these helps us understand the nature of the underlying process of decision making. Understanding this process is what economics is all about.

Cautions and Pitfalls In formulating theories and models, it is especially important to avoid two pitfalls: the *post hoc* fallacy and the fallacy of composition.

The* Post Hoc *Fallacy Theories often make statements or sets of statements about cause and effect. It can be quite tempting to look at two events that happen in sequence and assume that the first caused the second to happen. This is not always the case. This common error is called the ***post hoc, ergo propter hoc*** (or "after this, therefore because of this") fallacy.

post hoc, ergo propter hoc Literally, "after this (in time), therefore because of this." A common error made in thinking about causation: If Event A happens before Event B, it is not necessarily true that A caused B.

There are thousands of examples. The Colorado Rockies have won seven games in a row. Last night you went to the game and they lost. You must have jinxed them. They lost *because* you went to the game.

Stock market analysts indulge in what is perhaps the most striking example of the *post hoc* fallacy in action. Every day the stock market goes up or down, and every day some analyst on some national news program singles out one or two of the day's events as *the* cause of some change in the market: "Today the Dow Jones industrial average rose 5 points on heavy trading; analysts say that the increase was due to progress in talks between Israel and Syria." Research has shown that daily changes in stock market averages are very largely random. Although major news events clearly have a direct influence on certain stock prices, most daily changes cannot be linked directly to specific news stories.

Very closely related to the *post hoc* fallacy is the often erroneous link between correlation and causation. Two variables are said to be *correlated* if one variable changes when the other variable changes. However, correlation does not imply causation. Cities that have high crime rates also have many automobiles, so there is a very high degree of correlation between number of cars and crime rates. Can we argue, then, that cars *cause* crime? No. The reason for the correlation may have nothing to do with cause and effect. Big cities have many people, many people have many cars; therefore, big cities have many cars. Big cities also have high crime rates for many reasons—crowding, poverty, anonymity, unequal distribution of wealth, and readily available drugs, to mention only a few. However, the presence of cars is probably not one of them.

This caution must also be viewed in reverse. Sometimes events that seem entirely unconnected actually *are* connected. In 1978, Governor Michael Dukakis of Massachusetts ran for reelection. Still quite popular, Dukakis was nevertheless defeated in the Democratic primary that year by a razor-thin margin. The weekend before, the Boston Red Sox, in the thick of the division championship race, had been badly beaten by the New York Yankees in four straight games. Some very respectable political analysts believe that hundreds of thousands of Boston sports fans vented their anger on the incumbent governor the following Tuesday.

The Fallacy of Composition To conclude that what is true for a part is necessarily true for the whole is to fall into the **fallacy of composition**. Suppose that a large group of cattle ranchers graze their cattle on the same range. To an individual rancher, more cattle and more grazing mean a higher income. However, because its capacity is limited, the land can support only so many cattle. If every cattle rancher increased the number of cattle sent out to graze, the land would become overgrazed and barren; as a result, everyone's income would fall. In short, theories that seem to work well when applied to individuals or households often break down when they are applied to the whole.

fallacy of composition The erroneous belief that what is true for a part is necessarily true for the whole.

Testing Theories and Models: Empirical Economics In science, a theory is rejected when it fails to explain what is observed or when another theory better explains what is observed. Prior to the sixteenth century, almost everyone believed that Earth was the center of the universe and that the sun and stars rotated around it. The astronomer Ptolemy (A.D. 127 to 151) built a model that explained and predicted the movements of the heavenly bodies in a geocentric (Earth-centered) universe. Early in the sixteenth century, however, the Polish astronomer Nicholas Copernicus found himself dissatisfied with the Ptolemaic model and proposed an alternative theory or model, placing the sun at the center of the known universe and relegating Earth to the status of one planet among many. The battle between the competing models was waged, at least in part, with data based on observations—actual measurements of planetary movements. The new model ultimately predicted much better than the old, and in time it came to be accepted.

In the seventeenth century, building on the works of Copernicus and others, Sir Isaac Newton constructed yet another body of theory that seemed to predict planetary motion with still more accuracy. Newtonian physics became the accepted body of theory, relied on for almost 300 years. Then, in the early twentieth century, Albert Einstein's theory of relativity replaced Newtonian physics for particular types of problems because it was able to explain some problems that earlier theories could not.

Economic theories are also confronted with new and often conflicting data from time to time. The collection and use of data to test economic theories is called **empirical economics**.

empirical economics The collection and use of data to test economic theories.

Numerous large data sets are available to facilitate economic research. For example, economists studying the labor market can now test behavioral theories against the actual working experiences of thousands of randomly selected people who have been surveyed continuously since the 1960s by economists at The Ohio State University. Macroeconomists continuously monitoring and studying the behavior of the national economy pass thousands of items of data, collected by both government agencies and private companies, back and forth over the Internet.

Scientific research often seeks to isolate and measure the responsiveness of one variable to a change in another variable, *ceteris paribus*. Physical scientists such as physicists and geologists can often impose the condition of *ceteris paribus* by conducting controlled experiments. They can, for example, measure the effect of one chemical on another while literally holding all else constant in an environment that they control completely. Social scientists, who study people, rarely have this luxury.

Although controlled experiments are difficult in economics and other social sciences, they are not impossible. During recent presidential and congressional elections, many candidates pointed to dramatic declines in crime rates in most American cities. Of course, incumbent candidates took credit, claiming that the decline was due to their policies. In fact, careful analysis shows that the decline in crime was largely due to two factors essentially beyond the control of political leaders: fewer people in the age groups that tend to commit crimes and a very strong economy with low unemployment. How do researchers know this? They look at data over time on crimes committed by people of various ages, they look at crime rates across states with different economic conditions, and they look at the pattern of crime rates nationally over time under different economic conditions. Even though economists cannot generally do controlled experiments, fluctuations in economic conditions and factors such as birthrate patterns in a way set up natural experiments.

Economic Policy

Economic theory helps us understand how the world works, but the formulation of *economic policy* requires a second step. We must have objectives. What do we want to change? Why? What is good and what is bad about the way the system is operating? Can we make it better?

Such questions force us to be specific about the grounds for judging one outcome superior to another. What does it mean to be better? Four criteria are frequently applied in judging economic outcomes:

1. Efficiency
2. Equity
3. Growth
4. Stability

Efficiency In physics, "efficiency" refers to the ratio of useful energy delivered by a system to the energy supplied to it. An efficient automobile engine, for example, is one that uses a small amount of fuel per mile for a given level of power.

efficiency In economics, allocative efficiency. An efficient economy is one that produces what people want at the least possible cost.

In economics, **efficiency** means *allocative efficiency*. An efficient economy is one that produces what people want at the least possible cost. If the system allocates resources to the production of goods and services that nobody wants, it is inefficient. If all members of a particular society were vegetarians and somehow half of all that society's resources were used to produce meat, the result would be inefficient. It is inefficient when steel beams lie in the rain and rust because somebody fouled up a shipping schedule. If a firm could produce its product using 25 percent less labor and energy without sacrificing quality, it too is inefficient.

The clearest example of an efficient change is a voluntary exchange. If you and I each want something that the other has and we agree to exchange, we are both better off and no one loses. When a company reorganizes its production or adopts a new technology that enables it to produce more of its product with fewer resources, without sacrificing quality, it has made an efficient change. At least potentially, the resources saved could be used to produce more of something.

Inefficiencies can arise in numerous ways. Sometimes they are caused by government regulations or tax laws that distort otherwise sound economic decisions. Suppose that land in Ohio is best suited for corn production and that land in Kansas is best suited for wheat production. A law that requires Kansas to produce only corn and Ohio to produce only wheat would be inefficient. If firms that cause environmental damage are not held accountable for their actions, the incentive to minimize those damages is lost and the result is inefficient.

equity Fairness.

Equity While efficiency has a fairly precise definition that can be applied with some degree of rigor, **equity** (fairness) lies in the eye of the beholder. To many, fairness implies a more equal distribution of income and wealth. Fairness may imply alleviating poverty, but the extent to which the poor should receive cash benefits from the government is the subject of enormous disagreement. For thousands of years, philosophers have wrestled with the principles of justice that should guide social decisions. They will probably wrestle with such questions for thousands of years to come.

Despite the impossibility of defining equity or fairness universally, public policy makers judge the fairness of economic outcomes all the time. Rent control laws were passed because some legislators thought that landlords treated low-income tenants unfairly. Certainly, most social welfare programs are created in the name of equity.

Growth As the result of technological change, the building of machinery, and the acquisition of knowledge, societies learn to produce new goods and services and to produce old ones better. In the early days of the U.S. economy, it took nearly half the population to produce the required food supply. Today less than 2.5 percent of the country's population works in agriculture.

When we devise new and better ways of producing the goods and services we use now and when we develop new goods and services, the total amount of production in the economy increases. **Economic growth** is an increase in the total output of an economy. If output grows faster than the population, output per capita rises and standards of living increase. Presumably, when an economy grows, it produces more of what people want. Rural and agrarian societies become modern industrial societies as a result of economic growth and rising per capita output.

economic growth An increase in the total output of an economy.

Some policies discourage economic growth, and others encourage it. Tax laws, for example, can be designed to encourage the development and application of new production techniques. Research and development in some societies are subsidized by the government. Building roads, highways, bridges, and transport systems in developing countries may speed up the process of economic growth. If businesses and wealthy people invest their wealth outside their country rather than in their country's industries, growth in their home country may be slowed.

Stability Economic **stability** refers to the condition in which national output is growing steadily, with low inflation and full employment of resources. During the 1950s and 1960s, the U.S. economy experienced a long period of relatively steady growth, stable prices, and low unemployment. Between 1951 and 1969, consumer prices never rose more than 5 percent in a single year and in only 2 years did the number of unemployed exceed 6 percent of the labor force. From the end of the Gulf War in 1991 to the beginning of 2001, the U.S. economy enjoyed price stability and strong economic growth with rising employment. It was the longest expansion in American history.

stability A condition in which national output is growing steadily, with low inflation and full employment of resources.

The decades of the 1970s and 1980s, however, were not as stable. The United States experienced two periods of rapid price inflation (over 10 percent) and two periods of severe unemployment. In 1982, for example, 12 million people (10.8 percent of the workforce) were looking for work. The beginning of the 1990s was another period of instability, with a recession occurring in 1990–1991. Around the world, economic fluctuations have been severe in recent years. During the late 1990s, many economies in Asia fell into recessions with falling incomes and rising unemployment. The transition economies of Eastern Europe and the former Soviet Union have experienced periods of decline as well as periods of rapidly rising prices since the fall of the Berlin Wall in 1989.

The causes of instability and the ways in which governments have attempted to stabilize the economy are the subject matter of macroeconomics.

An Invitation

This chapter has prepared you for your study of economics. The first part of the chapter invited you into an exciting discipline that deals with important issues and questions. You cannot begin to understand how a society functions without knowing something about its economic history and its economic system.

The second part of the chapter introduced the method of reasoning that economics requires and some of the tools that economics uses. We believe that learning to think in this very powerful way will help you better understand the world.

As you proceed, it is important that you keep track of what you have learned in earlier chapters. This book has a plan; it proceeds step-by-step, each section building on the last. It would be a good idea to read each chapter's table of contents at the start of each chapter and scan each chapter before you read it to make sure you understand where it fits in the big picture.

SUMMARY

1. *Economics* is the study of how individuals and societies choose to use the scarce resources that nature and previous generations have provided.

WHY STUDY ECONOMICS? *p. 2*

2. There are many reasons to study economics, including (a) to learn a way of thinking, (b) to understand society, (c) to understand global affairs, and (d) to be an informed citizen.
3. The best alternative that we forgo when we make a choice or a decision is the *opportunity cost* of that decision.

THE SCOPE OF ECONOMICS *p. 7*

4. *Microeconomics* deals with the functioning of individual markets and industries and with the behavior of individual decision-making units: business firms and households.
5. *Macroeconomics* looks at the economy as a whole. It deals with the economic behavior of aggregates—national output, national income, the overall price level, and the general rate of inflation.
6. Economics is a broad and diverse discipline with many special fields of inquiry. These include economic history, international economics, and urban economics.

THE METHOD OF ECONOMICS *p. 10*

7. Economics asks and attempts to answer two kinds of questions: positive and normative. *Positive economics* attempts to understand behavior and the operation of economies without making judgments about whether the outcomes are good or bad. *Normative economics* looks at the results of economic behavior and asks whether they are good or bad and whether they can be improved.
8. Positive economics is often divided into two parts. *Descriptive economics* involves the compilation of data that accurately describe economic facts and events. *Economic theory* attempts to generalize and explain what is observed. It involves statements of cause and effect—of action and reaction.
9. An economic *model* is a formal statement of an economic theory. Models simplify and abstract from reality.
10. It is often useful to isolate the effects of one variable on another while holding "all else constant." This is the device of *ceteris paribus*.
11. Models and theories can be expressed in many ways. The most common ways are in words, in graphs, and in equations.
12. Because one event happens before another, the second event does not necessarily happen as a result of the first. To assume that "after" implies "because" is to commit the fallacy of *post hoc, ergo propter hoc*. The erroneous belief that what is true for a part is necessarily true for the whole is the *fallacy of composition*.
13. *Empirical economics* involves the collection and use of data to test economic theories. In principle, the best model is the one that yields the most accurate predictions.
14. To make policy, one must be careful to specify criteria for making judgments. Four specific criteria are used most often in economics: *efficiency, equity, growth,* and *stability*.

REVIEW TERMS AND CONCEPTS

ceteris paribus, or all else equal, *p. 12*
descriptive economics, *p. 10*
economic growth, *p. 15*
economic theory, *p. 10*
economics, *p. 2*
efficiency, *p. 14*
efficient market, *p. 3*
empirical economics, *p. 13*
equity, *p. 14*
fallacy of composition, *p. 13*
Industrial Revolution, *p. 4*
macroeconomics, *p. 8*
marginalism, *p. 2*
microeconomics, *p. 8*
model, *p. 11*
normative economics, *p. 10*
Ockham's razor, *p. 11*
opportunity cost, *p. 2*
positive economics, *p. 10*
post hoc, ergo propter hoc, *p. 12*
scarce, *p. 2*
stability, *p. 15*
sunk costs, *p. 3*
variable, *p. 11*

PROBLEMS

Visit **www.myeconlab.com** to complete the problems marked in orange online. You will receive instant feedback on your answers, tutorial help, and access to additional practice problems.

1. One of the scarce resources that constrain our behavior is time. Each of us has only 24 hours in a day. How do you go about allocating your time in a given day among competing alternatives? How do you go about weighing the alternatives? Once you choose a most important use of time, why do you not spend all your time on it? Use the notion of opportunity cost in your answer.

2. In the summer of 2007, the housing market and the mortgage market were both in decline. Housing prices in most U.S. cities began to decline in mid-2006. With prices falling and the inventory of unsold houses rising, the production of new homes fell to around 1.5 million in 2007 from 2.3 million in 2005. With new construction falling dramatically, it was expected that construction *employment* would fall and that this would have the potential of slowing the national economy and increasing the general unemployment rate. Go to www.bls.gov and check out the recent data on total employment and construction employment. Have they gone up or down from their levels in August 2007? What has happened to the unemployment rate? Go to www.ofheo.gov and look at the housing price index. Have home prices risen or fallen since August 2007? Finally, look at the latest GDP release at www.bea.gov. Look at residential and nonresidential investment (Table 1.1.5) during the last 2 years. Do you see a pattern? Does it explain the employment numbers? Explain your answer.

3. Which of the following statements are examples of positive economic analysis? Which are examples of normative analysis?
   a. The inheritance tax should be repealed because it is unfair.
   b. Allowing Chile to join NAFTA would cause wine prices in the United States to drop.
   c. The first priorities of the new regime in the Democratic Republic of Congo (DRC, formerly Zaire) should be to rebuild schools and highways and to provide basic health care.

4. Selwyn signed up with an Internet provider for a fixed fee of $19.95 per month. For this fee, he gets unlimited access to the World Wide Web. During the average month in 2007, he was logged onto the Web for 17 hours. What is the average cost of an hour of Web time to Selwyn? What is the marginal cost of an additional hour?

5. A question facing many U.S. states is whether to allow casino gambling. States with casino gambling have seen a substantial increase in tax revenue flowing to state government. This revenue can be used to finance schools, repair roads, maintain social programs, or reduce other taxes.
   a. Recall that efficiency means producing what people want at the least cost. Can you make an efficiency argument in favor of allowing casinos to operate?
   b. What nonmonetary costs might be associated with gambling? Would these costs have an impact on the efficiency argument you presented in part **a**?
   c. Using the concept of equity, argue for or against the legalization of casino gambling.

6. For each of the following situations, identify the full cost (opportunity cost) involved:
   a. A worker earning an hourly wage of $8.50 decides to cut back to part-time to attend Houston Community College.
   b. Sue decides to drive to Los Angeles from San Francisco to visit her son, who attends UCLA.
   c. Tom decides to go to a wild fraternity party and stays out all night before his physics exam.
   d. Annie spends $200 on a new dress.
   e. The Confab Company spends $1 million to build a new branch plant that will probably be in operation for at least 10 years.
   f. Alex's father owns a small grocery store in town. Alex works 40 hours a week in the store but receives no compensation.

7. **[Related to the *Economics in Practice* on *p. 6*]** Log onto www.census.gov. Click on "Foreign Trade," then on "Statistics," and finally on "State Export Data." There you will find a list of the products produced in your state and exported to countries around the world. In looking over that list, are you surprised by anything? Do you know of any firms that produce these items? Search the Web to find a company that does. Do some research and write a paragraph about your company: what it produces, how many people it employs, and whatever else you can learn about the firm. You might even call the company to obtain the information.

APPENDIX

HOW TO READ AND UNDERSTAND GRAPHS

Economics is the most quantitative of the social sciences. If you flip through the pages of this or any other economics text, you will see countless tables and graphs. These serve a number of purposes. First, they illustrate important economic relationships. Second, they make difficult problems easier to understand and analyze. Finally, they can show patterns and regularities that may not be discernible in simple lists of numbers.

A **graph** is a two-dimensional representation of a set of numbers, or data. There are many ways that numbers can be illustrated by a graph.

TIME SERIES GRAPHS

It is often useful to see how a single measure or variable changes over time. One way to present this information is to plot the values of the variable on a graph, with each value corresponding to a different time period. A graph of this kind is called a **time series graph.** On a time series graph, time is measured along the horizontal scale and the variable being graphed is measured along the vertical scale. Figure 1A.1 is a time series graph that presents the total disposable personal income in the U.S. economy for each year between 1975 and 2006.[1] This graph is based on the data found in Table 1A.1. By displaying these data graphically, we can see that (1) total disposable personal income has increased steadily since 1975 and (2) during certain periods, income has increased at a faster rate than during other periods.

[1] The measure of income presented in Table 1A.1 and in Figure 1A.1 is disposable personal income in billions of dollars. It is the total personal income received by all households in the United States minus the taxes that they pay.

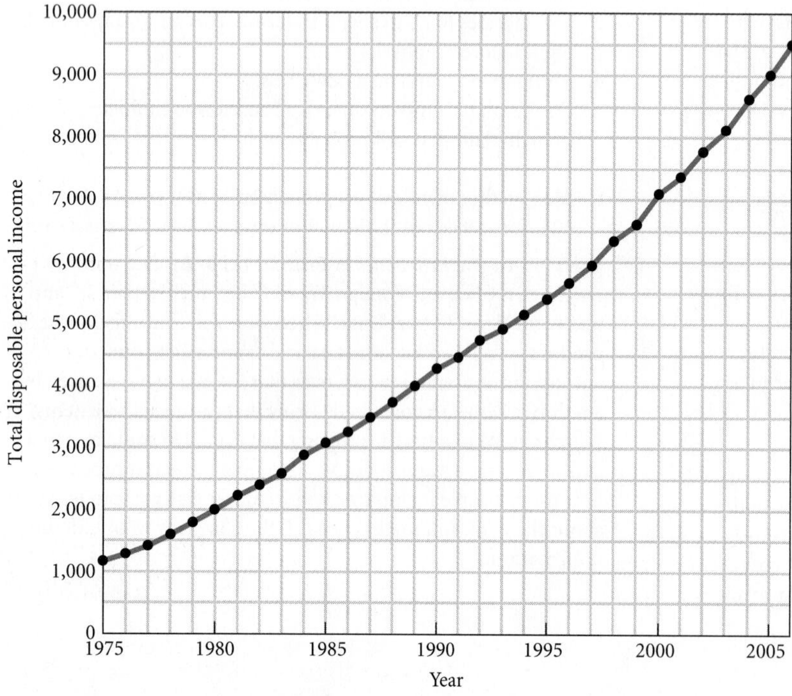

▲ **FIGURE 1A.1 Total Disposable Personal Income in the United States: 1975–2006 (in billions of dollars)**

Source: See Table 1A.1.

TABLE 1A.1 Total Disposable Personal Income in the United States, 1975–2006 (in billions of dollars)

Year	Total Disposable Personal Income	Year	Total Disposable Personal Income
1975	1,181.4	1991	4,474.8
1976	1,299.9	1992	4,754.6
1977	1,436.0	1993	4,935.3
1978	1,614.8	1994	5,165.4
1979	1,808.2	1995	5,422.6
1980	2,019.8	1996	5,677.7
1981	2,247.9	1997	5,968.2
1982	2,406.8	1998	6,355.6
1983	2,586.0	1999	6,627.4
1984	2,887.6	2000	7,120.2
1985	3,086.5	2001	7,393.2
1986	3,262.5	2002	7,827.7
1987	3,459.5	2003	8,159.9
1988	3,752.4	2004	8,646.9
1989	4,016.3	2005	9,019.1
1990	4,293.6	2006	9,501.5

Source: U.S. Department of Commerce, Bureau of Economic Analysis.

GRAPHING TWO VARIABLES ON A CARTESIAN COORDINATE SYSTEM

More important than simple graphs of one variable are graphs that contain information on two variables at the same time. The most common method of graphing two variables is the **Cartesian coordinate system**. This system is constructed by drawing two perpendicular lines: a horizontal line, or ***X*-axis**, and a vertical line, or ***Y*-axis**. The axes contain measurement scales that intersect at 0 (zero). This point is called the **origin**. On the vertical scale, positive numbers lie above the horizontal axis (that is, above the origin) and negative numbers lie below it. On the horizontal scale, positive numbers lie to the right of the vertical axis (to the right of the origin) and negative numbers lie to the left of it. The point at which the graph intersects the *Y*-axis is called the ***Y*-intercept**. The point at which the graph intersects the *X*-axis is called the ***X*-intercept**.

When two variables are plotted on a single graph, each point represents a pair of numbers. The first number is measured on the *X*-axis, and the second number is measured on the *Y*-axis. For example, the following points (X, Y) are plotted on the set of axes drawn in Figure 1A.2: (4, 2), (2, −1), (−3, 4), (−3, −2). Most, but not all, of the graphs in this book are plots of two variables where both values are positive numbers [such as (4, 2) in Figure 1A.2]. On these graphs, only the upper right quadrant of the coordinate system (that is, the quadrant in which all *X* and *Y* values are positive) will be drawn.

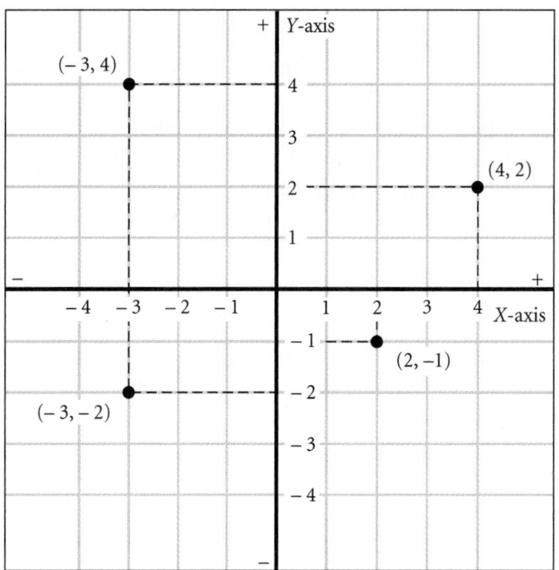

▲ **FIGURE 1A.2 A Cartesian Coordinate System**

A Cartesian coordinate system is constructed by drawing two perpendicular lines: a vertical axis (the *Y*-axis) and a horizontal axis (the *X*-axis). Each axis is a measuring scale.

PLOTTING INCOME AND CONSUMPTION DATA FOR HOUSEHOLDS

Table 1A.2 presents data collected by the Bureau of Labor Statistics (BLS). In a recent survey, 5,000 households were asked to keep track of all their expenditures. This table shows average income and average spending for those households, ranked by income. For example, the average income for the top fifth (20 percent) of the households was $147,737. The average spending for the top 20 percent was $90,469.

Figure 1A.3 presents the numbers from Table 1A.2 graphically using the Cartesian coordinate system. Along the horizontal scale, the *X*-axis, we measure average income. Along the vertical scale, the *Y*-axis, we measure average consumption spending. Each of the five pairs of numbers from the table is represented by a point on the graph. Because all numbers are positive numbers, we need to show only the upper right quadrant of the coordinate system.

To help you read this graph, we have drawn a dotted line connecting all the points where consumption and income would be equal. *This 45° line does not represent any data.* Instead, it represents the line along which all variables on the *X*-axis correspond exactly to the variables on the *Y*-axis, for example, [10,000, 10,000], [20,000, 20,000], and [37,000, 37,000]. The heavy blue line traces the data; the purpose of the dotted line is to help you read the graph.

There are several things to look for when reading a graph. The first thing you should notice is whether the line slopes upward or downward as you move from left to right. The blue line in Figure 1A.3 slopes upward, indicating that there seems to be a **positive relationship** between income and spending: The higher a household's income, the more a household tends to consume. If we had graphed the percentage of each group receiving welfare payments along the *Y*-axis, the line would presumably slope downward, indicating that welfare payments are lower at higher income levels. The income level/welfare payment relationship is thus a **negative relationship**.

TABLE 1A.2 Consumption Expenditures and Income, 2005

	Average Income Before Taxes	Average Consumption Expenditures
Bottom fifth	$ 9,676	$19,120
2nd fifth	25,546	28,921
3rd fifth	42,622	39,098
4th fifth	67,813	54,354
Top fifth	147,737	90,469

Source: Consumer Expenditures in 2005, U.S. Bureau of Labor Statistics; Report 998, Feb. 2007.

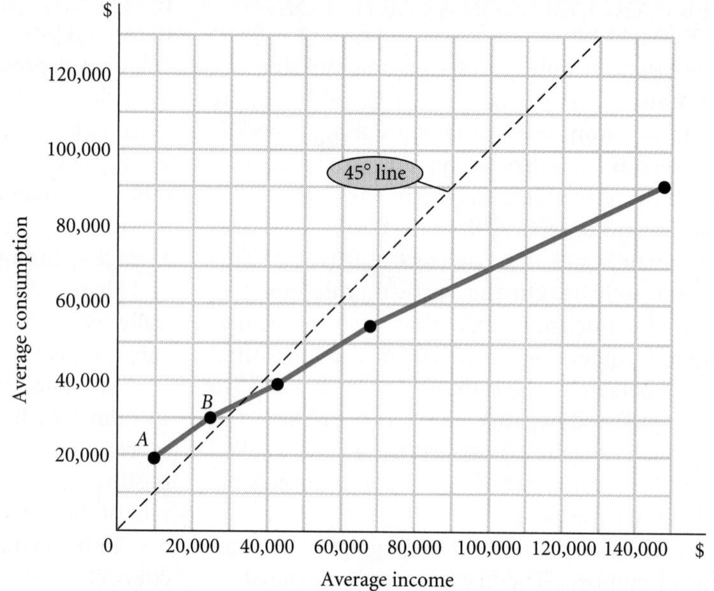

FIGURE 1A.3 Household Consumption and Income

A graph is a simple two-dimensional geometric representation of data. This graph displays the data from Table 1A.2. Along the horizontal scale (X-axis), we measure household income. Along the vertical scale (Y-axis), we measure household consumption. *Note*: At point *A*, consumption equals $19,120 and income equals $9,676. At point *B*, consumption equals $28,921 and income equals $25,546.

Source: See Table 1A.2.

SLOPE

The **slope** of a line or curve is a measure that indicates whether the relationship between the variables is positive or negative and how much of a response there is in *Y* (the variable on the vertical axis) when *X* (the variable on the horizontal axis) changes. The slope of a line between two points is the change in the quantity measured on the *Y*-axis divided by the change in the quantity measured on the *X*-axis. We will normally use Δ (the Greek letter *delta*) to refer to a change in a variable. In Figure 1A.4, the slope of the line between points *A* and *B* is ΔY divided by ΔX. Sometimes it is easy to remember slope as "the rise over the run," indicating the vertical change over the horizontal change.

To be precise, ΔX between two points on a graph is simply X_2 minus X_1, where X_2 is the *X* value for the second point and X_1 is the *X* value for the first point. Similarly, ΔY is defined as Y_2 minus Y_1, where Y_2 is the *Y* value for the second point and Y_1 is the *Y* value for the first point. Slope is equal to

$$\frac{\Delta Y}{\Delta X} = \frac{Y_2 - Y_1}{X_2 - X_1}$$

As we move from *A* to *B* in Figure 1A.4(a), both *X* and *Y* increase; the slope is thus a positive number. However, as we move from *A* to *B* in Figure 1A.4(b), *X* increases $[(X_2 - X_1)$ is a positive number$]$, but *Y* decreases $[(Y_2 - Y_1)$ is a negative number$]$. The slope in Figure 1A.4(b) is thus a negative number, because a negative number divided by a positive number results in a negative quotient.

To calculate the numerical value of the slope between points *A* and *B* in Figure 1A.3, we need to calculate ΔY and ΔX. Because consumption is measured on the *Y*-axis, ΔY is 9,801 $[(Y_2 - Y_1) = (28{,}921 - 19{,}120)]$. Because income is measured along the *X*-axis, ΔX is 15,870 $[(X_2 - X_1) = (25{,}546 - 9{,}676)]$. The slope between *A* and *B* is $\Delta Y/\Delta X = 9{,}801/15{,}870 = +0.62$.

Another interesting thing to note about the data graphed in Figure 1A.3 is that all the points lie roughly along a straight line. (If you look very closely, however, you can see that the slope declines as you move from left to right; the line becomes slightly less steep.) A straight line has a constant slope. That is, if you pick any two points along it and calculate the slope, you will always get the same number. A horizontal line has a zero slope (ΔY is zero); a vertical line has an "infinite" slope because ΔY is too big to be measured.

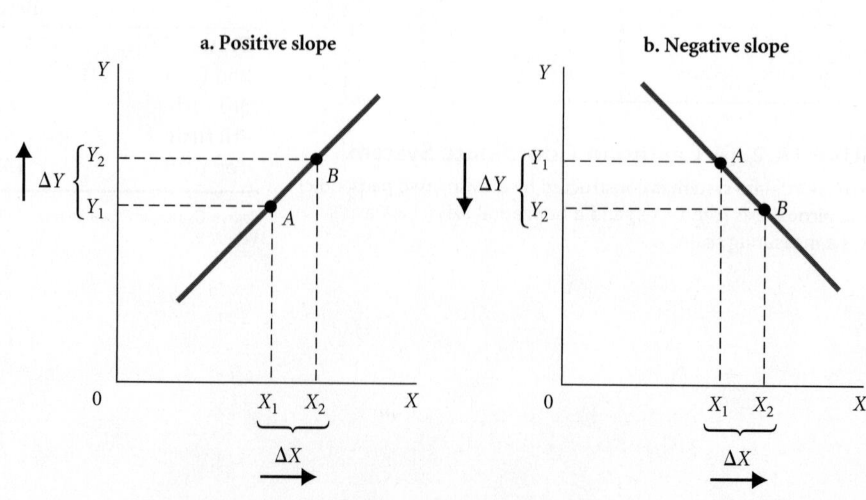

FIGURE 1A.4 A Curve with (a) Positive Slope and (b) Negative Slope

A *positive* slope indicates that increases in *X* are associated with increases in *Y* and that decreases in *X* are associated with decreases in *Y*. A *negative* slope indicates the opposite—when *X* increases, *Y* decreases; and when *X* decreases, *Y* increases.

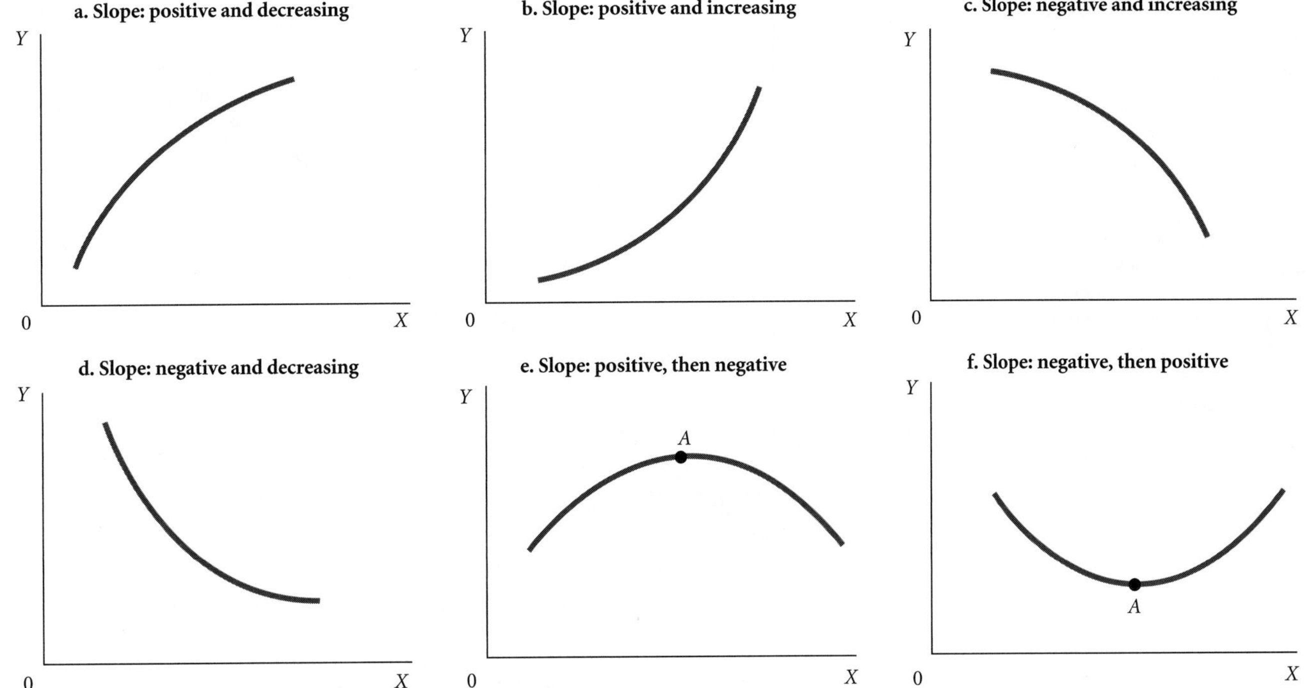

▲ **FIGURE 1A.5 Changing Slopes Along Curves**

Unlike the slope of a straight line, the slope of a *curve* is continually changing. Consider, for example, the curves in Figure 1A.5. Figure 1A.5(a) shows a curve with a positive slope that decreases as you move from left to right. The easiest way to think about the concept of increasing or decreasing slope is to imagine what it is like walking up a hill from left to right. If the hill is steep, as it is in the first part of Figure 1A.5(a), you are moving more in the Y direction for each step you take in the X direction. If the hill is less steep, as it is further along in Figure 1A.5(a), you are moving less in the Y direction for every step you take in the X direction. Thus, when the hill is steep, slope ($\Delta Y/\Delta X$) is a larger number than it is when the hill is flatter. The curve in Figure 1A.5(b) has a positive slope, but its slope *increases* as you move from left to right.

The same analogy holds for curves that have a negative slope. Figure 1A.5(c) shows a curve with a negative slope that increases (in absolute value) as you move from left to right. This time think about skiing down a hill. At first, the descent in Figure 1A.5(c) is gradual (low slope); but as you proceed down the hill (to the right), you descend more quickly (high slope). Figure 1A.5(d) shows a curve with a negative slope that *decreases* (in absolute value) as you move from left to right.

In Figure 1A.5(e), the slope goes from positive to negative as X increases. In Figure 1A.5(f), the slope goes from negative to positive. At point A in both, the slope is zero. [Remember, slope is defined as $\Delta Y/\Delta X$. At point A, Y is not changing ($\Delta Y = 0$). Therefore, slope at point A is zero.]

SOME PRECAUTIONS

When you read a graph, it is important to think carefully about what the points in the space defined by the axes represent. Table 1A.3 and Figure 1A.6 present a graph of consumption and income that is very different from the one in Table 1A.2 and Figure 1A.3. First, each point in Figure 1A.6 represents a different year; in Figure 1A.3, each point represented a different group of households at the *same* point in time (2005). Second, the points in Figure 1A.6 represent *aggregate* consumption and income for the whole nation measured in *billions* of dollars; in Figure 1A.3, the points represented average *household* income and consumption measured in dollars.

It is interesting to compare these two graphs. All points on the aggregate consumption curve in Figure 1A.6 lie below the 45° line, which means that aggregate consumption is always less than aggregate income. However, the graph of average household income and consumption in Figure 1A.3 crosses the 45° line, implying that for some households, consumption is larger than income.

TABLE 1A.3 Aggregate National Income and Consumption for the United States, 1930–2006 (in billions of dollars)

	Aggregate National Income	Aggregate Consumption
1930	75.6	70.2
1940	81.1	71.2
1950	241.0	192.7
1960	427.5	332.3
1970	837.5	648.9
1980	2,243.0	1,762.9
1990	4,642.1	3,831.5
2000	7,984.4	6,683.7
2004	10,306.8	8,195.9
2005	10,887.6	8,707.8
2006	11,655.6	9,224.5

Source: U.S. Department of Commerce, Bureau of Economic Analysis.

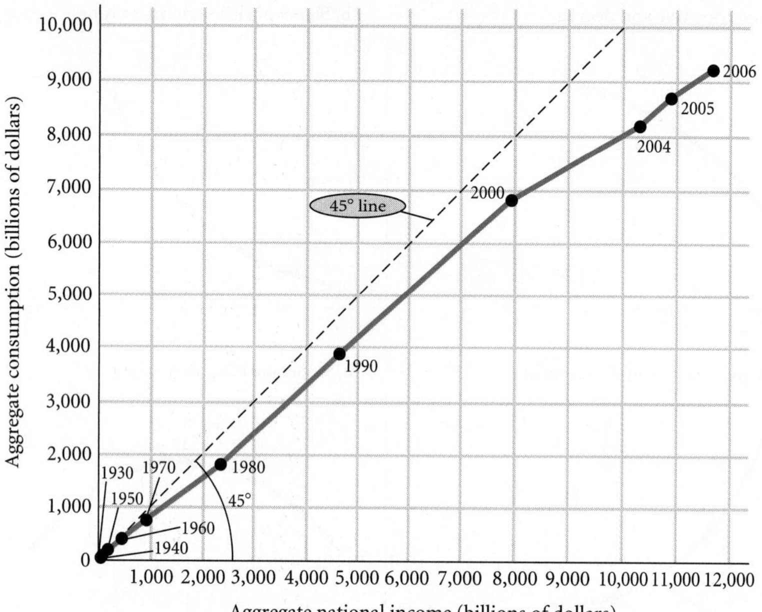

▶ FIGURE 1A.6 National Income and Consumption

It is important to think carefully about what is represented by points in the space defined by the axes of a graph. In this graph, we have graphed income with consumption, as in Figure 1A.3, but here each observation point is national income and aggregate consumption in *different years*, measured in billions of dollars.

Source: See Table 1A.3.

SUMMARY

1. A *graph* is a two-dimensional representation of a set of numbers, or data. A *time series graph* illustrates how a single variable changes over time.
2. The most common method of graphing two variables on one graph is the *Cartesian coordinate system*, which includes an *X* (horizontal)-*axis* and a *Y* (vertical)-*axis*. The points at which the two axes intersect is called the *origin*. The point at which a graph intersects the *Y*-axis is called the *Y-intercept*. The point at which a graph intersects the *X*-axis is called the *X-intercept*.
3. The *slope* of a line or curve indicates whether the relationship between the two variables graphed on a Cartesian coordinate system is positive or negative and how much of a response there is in *Y* (the variable on the vertical axis) when *X* (the variable on the horizontal axis) changes. The slope of a line between two points is the change in the quantity measured on the *Y*-axis divided by the change in the quantity measured on the *X*-axis.

REVIEW TERMS AND CONCEPTS

Cartesian coordinate system A common method of graphing two variables that makes use of two perpendicular lines against which the variables are plotted. *p. 19*

graph A two-dimensional representation of a set of numbers, or data. *p. 18*

negative relationship A relationship between two variables, *X* and *Y*, in which a decrease in *X* is associated with an increase in *Y* and an increase in *X* is associated with a decrease in *Y*. *p. 19*

origin On a Cartesian coordinate system, the point at which the horizontal and vertical axes intersect. *p. 19*

positive relationship A relationship between two variables, *X* and *Y*, in which a decrease in *X* is associated with a decrease in *Y*, and an increase in *X* is associated with an increase in *Y*. *p. 19*

slope A measurement that indicates whether the relationship between variables is positive or negative and how much of a response there is in *Y* (the variable on the vertical axis) when *X* (the variable on the horizontal axis) changes. *p. 20*

time series graph A graph illustrating how a variable changes over time. *p. 18*

***X*-axis** On a Cartesian coordinate system, the horizontal line against which a variable is plotted. *p. 19*

***X*-intercept** The point at which a graph intersects the *X*-axis. *p. 19*

***Y*-axis** On a Cartesian coordinate system, the vertical line against which a variable is plotted. *p. 19*

***Y*-intercept** The point at which a graph intersects the *Y*-axis. *p. 19*

PROBLEMS

1. Graph each of the following sets of numbers. Draw a line through the points and calculate the slope of each line.

1		2		3		4		5		6	
X	*Y*	*X*	*Y*	*X*	*Y*	*X*	*Y*	*X*	*Y*	*X*	*Y*
1	5	1	25	0	0	0	40	0	0	0.1	100
2	10	2	20	10	10	10	30	10	10	0.2	75
3	15	3	15	20	20	20	20	20	20	0.3	50
4	20	4	10	30	30	30	10	30	10	0.4	25
5	25	5	5	40	40	40	0	40	0	0.5	0

2. For each of the graphs in Figure 1, determine whether the curve has a positive or negative slope. Give an intuitive explanation for what is happening with the slope of each curve.

3. For each of the following equations, graph the line and calculate its slope.
   a. $P = 10 - 2q_D$ (Put q_D on the *X*-axis.)
   b. $P = 100 - 4q_D$ (Put q_D on the *X*-axis.)
   c. $P = 50 + 6q_S$ (Put q_S on the *X*-axis.)
   d. $I = 10{,}000 - 500r$ (Put *I* on the *X*-axis.)

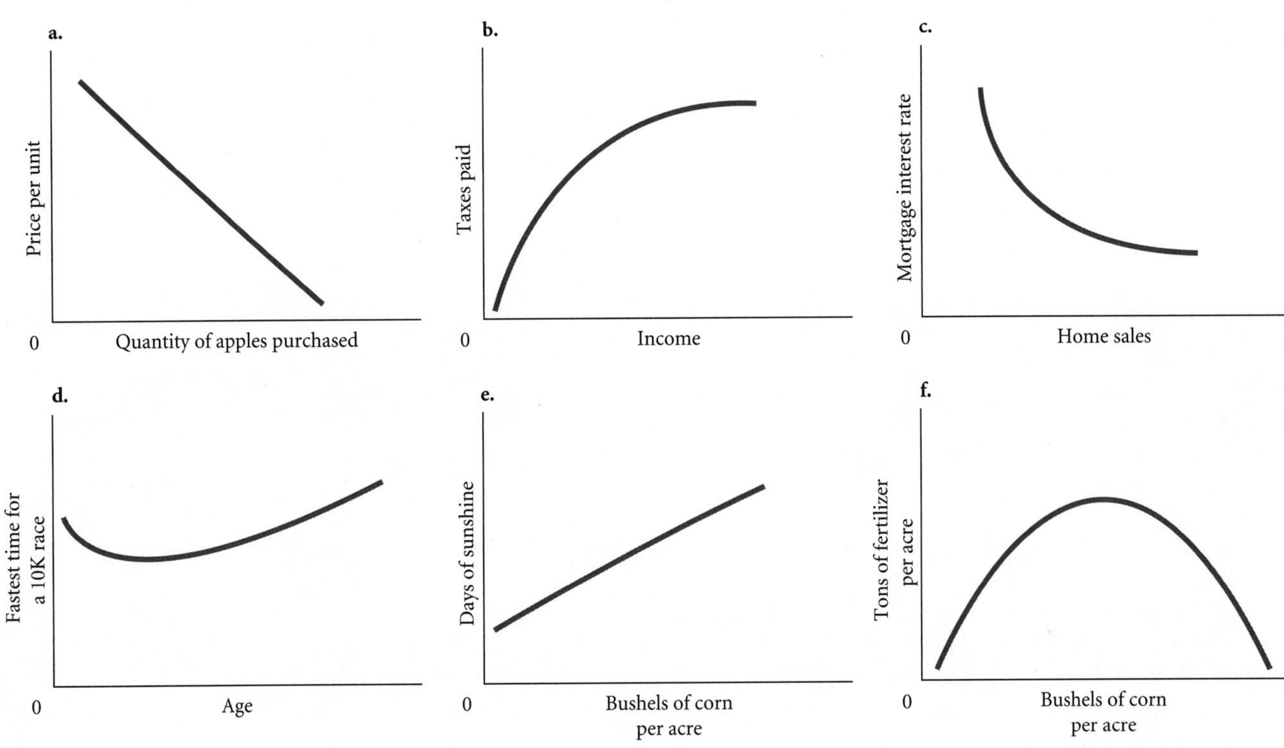

▲ FIGURE 1

The Economic Problem: Scarcity and Choice

2

CHAPTER OUTLINE

Chapter 1 began with a very broad definition of economics. Every society, no matter how small or large, no matter how simple or complex, has a system or process that works to transform the resources that nature and previous generations provide into useful form. Economics is the study of that process and its outcomes.

Figure 2.1 illustrates three basic questions that must be answered to understand the functioning of the economic system:

- What gets produced?
- How is it produced?
- Who gets what is produced?

This chapter explores these questions in detail. In a sense, this entire chapter *is* the definition of economics. It lays out the central problems addressed by the discipline and presents a framework that will guide you through the rest of the book. The starting point is the presumption that *human wants are unlimited but resources are not.* Limited or scarce resources force individuals and societies to choose among competing uses of resources—alternative combinations of produced goods and services—and among alternative final distributions of what is produced among households.

These questions are *positive* or *descriptive*. That is, they ask how the system functions without passing judgment about whether the result is good or bad. They must be answered first before we ask more normative questions such as these:

- Is the outcome good or bad?
- Can it be improved?

The term *resources* is very broad. The sketch on the left side of Figure 2.1 shows several categories of resources. Some resources are the products of nature: land, wildlife, fertile soil, minerals, timber, energy, and even the rain and wind. In addition, the resources available to an economy include things such as buildings and equipment that have been produced in the past but are now being used to produce other things. And perhaps the most important resource of a society is its human workforce with people's talents, skills, and knowledge.

Things that are produced and then used in the production of other goods and services are called capital resources, or simply **capital**. Buildings, equipment, desks, chairs, software, roads, bridges, and highways are a part of the nation's stock of capital.

The basic resources available to a society are often referred to as **factors of production**, or simply **factors**. The three key factors of production are land, labor, and capital. The process that transforms scarce resources into useful goods and services is called **production**. In many societies, most of the production of goods and services is done by private firms. Private airlines in

capital Things that are produced and then used in the production of other goods and services.

factors of production (*or* factors) The inputs into the process of production. Another term for resources.

production The process that transforms scarce resources into useful goods and services.

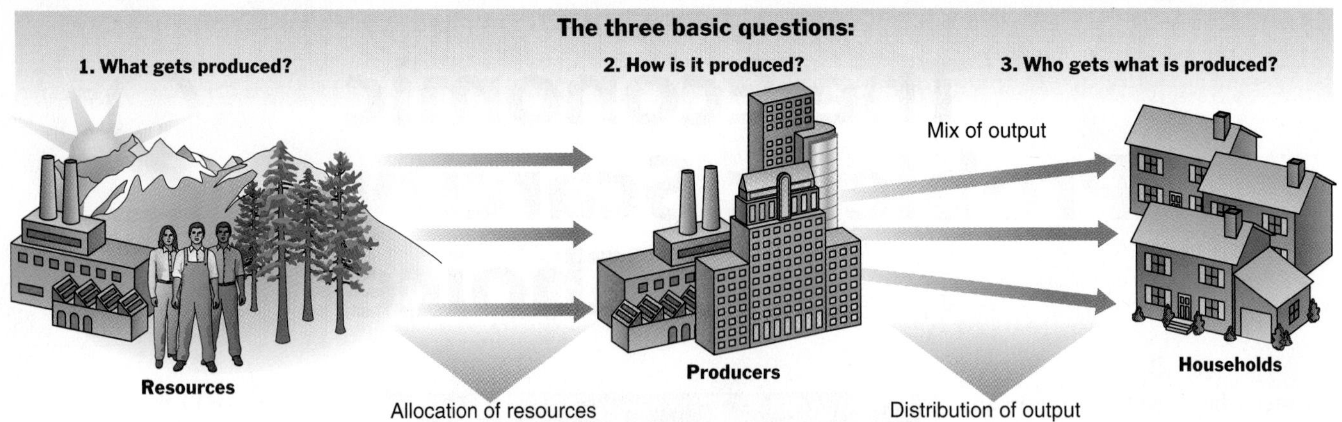

▲ **FIGURE 2.1 The Three Basic Questions**

Every society has some system or process that transforms its scarce resources into useful goods and services. In doing so, it must decide what gets produced, how it is produced, and to whom it is distributed. The primary resources that must be allocated are land, labor, and capital.

the United States use land (runways), labor (pilots and mechanics), and capital (airplanes) to produce transportation services. But in all societies, some production is done by the public sector, or government. Examples of government-produced or government-provided goods and services include national defense, public education, police protection, and fire protection.

inputs *or* resources Anything provided by nature or previous generations that can be used directly or indirectly to satisfy human wants.

outputs Goods and services of value to households.

Resources or factors of production are the **inputs** into the process of production; goods and services of value to households are the **outputs** of the process of production.

Scarcity, Choice, and Opportunity Cost

In the second half of this chapter we discuss the global economic landscape. Before you can understand the different types of economic systems, it is important to master the basic economic concepts of scarcity, choice, and opportunity cost.

Scarcity and Choice in a One-Person Economy

The simplest economy is one in which a single person lives alone on an island. Consider Bill, the survivor of a plane crash, who finds himself cast ashore in such a place. Here individual and society are one; there is no distinction between social and private. *Nonetheless, nearly all the same basic decisions that characterize complex economies must also be made in a simple economy.* That is, although Bill will get whatever he produces, he still must decide how to allocate the island's resources, what to produce, and how and when to produce it.

First, Bill must decide *what* he wants to produce. Notice that the word *needs* does not appear here. Needs are absolute requirements; but beyond just enough water, basic nutrition, and shelter to survive, needs are very difficult to define. What is an "absolute necessity" for one person may not be for another person. In any case, Bill must put his wants in some order of priority and make some choices.

Next, he must look at the *possibilities*. What can he do to satisfy his wants given the limits of the island? In every society, no matter how simple or complex, people are constrained in what they can do. In this society of one, Bill is constrained by time, his physical condition, his knowledge, his skills, and the resources and climate of the island.

Given that resources are limited, Bill must decide *how* to best use them to satisfy his hierarchy of wants. Food would probably come close to the top of his list. Should he spend his time gathering fruits and berries? Should he hunt for game? Should he clear a field and plant seeds? The answers to those questions depend on the character of the island, its climate, its flora and fauna (*are* there any fruits and berries?), the extent of his skills and knowledge (does he know anything about farming?), and his preferences (he may be a vegetarian).

Opportunity Cost The concepts of *constrained choice* and *scarcity* are central to the discipline of economics. They can be applied when discussing the behavior of individuals such as Bill and when analyzing the behavior of large groups of people in complex societies.

Given the scarcity of time and resources, if Bill decides to hunt, he will have less time to gather fruits and berries. He faces a trade-off between meat and fruit. There is a trade-off between food and shelter too. If Bill likes to be comfortable, he may work on building a nice place to live, but that may require giving up the food he might have produced. As we noted in Chapter 1, the best alternative that we give up, or forgo, when we make a choice is the **opportunity cost** of that choice.

opportunity cost The best alternative that we give up, or forgo, when we make a choice or decision.

Bill may occasionally decide to rest, to lie on the beach, and to enjoy the sun. In one sense, that benefit is free—he does not have to buy a ticket to lie on the beach. In reality, however, relaxing does have an opportunity cost. The true cost of that leisure is the value of the other things Bill could have produced, but did not, during the time he spent on the beach.

The Houston Dynamos are a championship soccer team currently playing in an old arena on the University of Houston campus. In the summer of 2007, the Harris County Houston Sports Authority and local politicians were actively debating whether to spend taxpayers money on a new arena for the team. An important part of that debate was the opportunity cost of the taxpayers' dollars: what else could tax dollars be spent on, and how much value would the alternatives bring to the local taxpayers? Perhaps without the new arena, taxes could be lower. Here the opportunity cost would include the value taxpayers receive from goods and services they would consume with the earnings that are no longer taxed. Most discussions of public expenditures at all levels of government include active considerations of opportunity costs.

In making everyday decisions, it is often helpful to think about opportunity costs. Should you go to the dorm party or not? First, it costs $4 to attend. When you pay money for anything, you give up the other things you could have bought with that money. Second, it costs 2 or 3 hours. Time is a valuable commodity for a college student. You have exams next week, and you need to study. You could go to a movie instead of the party. You could go to another party. You could sleep. Just as Bill must weigh the value of sunning on the beach against more food or better housing, so you must weigh the value of the fun you may have at the party against everything else you might otherwise do with the time and money.

Scarcity and Choice in an Economy of Two or More

Now suppose that another survivor of the crash, Colleen, appears on the island. Now that Bill is not alone, things are more complex and some new decisions must be made. Bill's and Colleen's preferences about what things to produce are likely to be different. They will probably not have the same knowledge or skills. Perhaps Colleen is very good at tracking animals and Bill has a knack for building things. How should they split the work that needs to be done? Once things are produced, the two castaways must decide how to divide them. How should their products be distributed?

The mechanism for answering these fundamental questions is clear when Bill is alone on the island. The "central plan" is his; he simply decides what he wants and what to do about it. The minute someone else appears, however, a number of decision-making arrangements immediately become possible. One or the other may take charge, in which case that person will decide for both of them. The two may agree to cooperate, with each having an equal say, and come up with a joint plan; or they may agree to split the planning as well as the production duties. Finally, they may go off to live alone at opposite ends of the island. Even if they live apart, however, they may take advantage of each other's presence by specializing and trading.

Modern industrial societies must answer the same questions that Colleen and Bill must answer, but the mechanics of larger economies are more complex. Instead of two people living together, the United States has over 300 million people. Still, decisions must be made about what to produce, how to produce it, and who gets it.

Specialization, Exchange, and Comparative Advantage The idea that members of society benefit by specializing in what they do best has a long history and is one of the most important and powerful ideas in all of economics. David Ricardo, a major nineteenth-century British economist, formalized the point precisely. According to Ricardo's **theory of comparative advantage**, specialization and free trade will benefit all trading parties, even

theory of comparative advantage Ricardo's theory that specialization and free trade will benefit all trading parties, even those that may be "absolutely" more efficient producers.

ECONOMICS IN PRACTICE

Frozen Foods and Opportunity Costs

In 2007, $27 billion of frozen foods were sold in U.S. grocery stores, one quarter of it in the form of frozen dinners and entrees. In the mid-1950s, sales of frozen foods amounted to only $1 billion, a tiny fraction of the overall grocery store sales. One industry observer attributes this growth to the fact that frozen food tastes much better than it did in the past. Can you think of anything else that might be occurring?

The growth of the frozen dinner entrée market in the last 50 years is a good example of the role of opportunity costs in our lives. One of the most significant social changes in the U.S. economy in this period has been the increased participation of women in the labor force. In 1950, only 24 percent of married women worked; by 2000, that fraction had risen to 61 percent. Producing a meal takes two basic ingredients: food and time. When both husbands and wives work, the opportunity cost of time for housework—including making meals—goes up. This tells us that making a home-cooked meal became more expensive in the last 50 years. A natural result is to shift people toward labor-saving ways to make meals. Frozen foods are an obvious solution to the problem of increased opportunity costs.

Another, somewhat more subtle, opportunity cost story is at work encouraging the consumption of frozen foods. In 1960, the first microwave oven was introduced. The spread of this device into America's kitchens was rapid. The microwave turned out to be a quick way to defrost and cook those frozen entrées. So this technology lowered the opportunity cost of making frozen dinners, reinforcing the advantage these meals had over home-cooked meals. Microwaves made cooking with frozen foods cheaper once opportunity cost was considered while home-cooked meals were becoming more expensive.

The entrepreneurs among you also might recognize that the rise we described in the opportunity cost of the home-cooked meal *contributed* in part to the spread of the microwave, creating a reinforcing cycle. In fact, many entrepreneurs find that the simple tools of economics—like the idea of opportunity costs—help them anticipate what products will be profitable for them to produce in the future. The growth of the two-worker family has stimulated many entrepreneurs to search for labor-saving solutions to family tasks.

The public policy students among you might be interested to know that some researchers attribute part of the growth in obesity in the United States to the lower opportunity costs of making meals associated with the growth of the markets for frozen foods and the microwave. (See David M.Cutler, Edward L. Glaeser, and Jesse M. Shapiro, "Why Have Americans Become More Obese?" *Journal of Economic Perspectives*, Summer 2003, 93–118.)

when some are "absolutely" more efficient producers than others. Ricardo's basic point applies just as much to Colleen and Bill as it does to different nations.

To keep things simple, suppose that Colleen and Bill have only two tasks to accomplish each week: gathering food to eat and cutting logs to burn. If Colleen could cut more logs than Bill in 1 day and Bill could gather more nuts and berries than Colleen could, specialization would clearly lead to more total production. Both would benefit if Colleen only cuts logs and Bill only gathers nuts and berries, as long as they can trade. Suppose that Bill is slow and somewhat clumsy in his nut gathering and that Colleen is better at cutting logs *and* gathering food.

At first, it might seem that since Colleen is better at everything, she should do everything. But that cannot be right. Colleen's time is limited after all, and even though Bill is clumsy and not very clever, he must be able to contribute something.

One of Ricardo's lasting contributions to economics has been his analysis of exactly this situation. His analysis, which is illustrated in Figure 2.2, shows both how Colleen and Bill should divide the work of the island and how much they will gain from specializing and exchanging even if, as in this example, one party is absolutely better at everything than the other party.

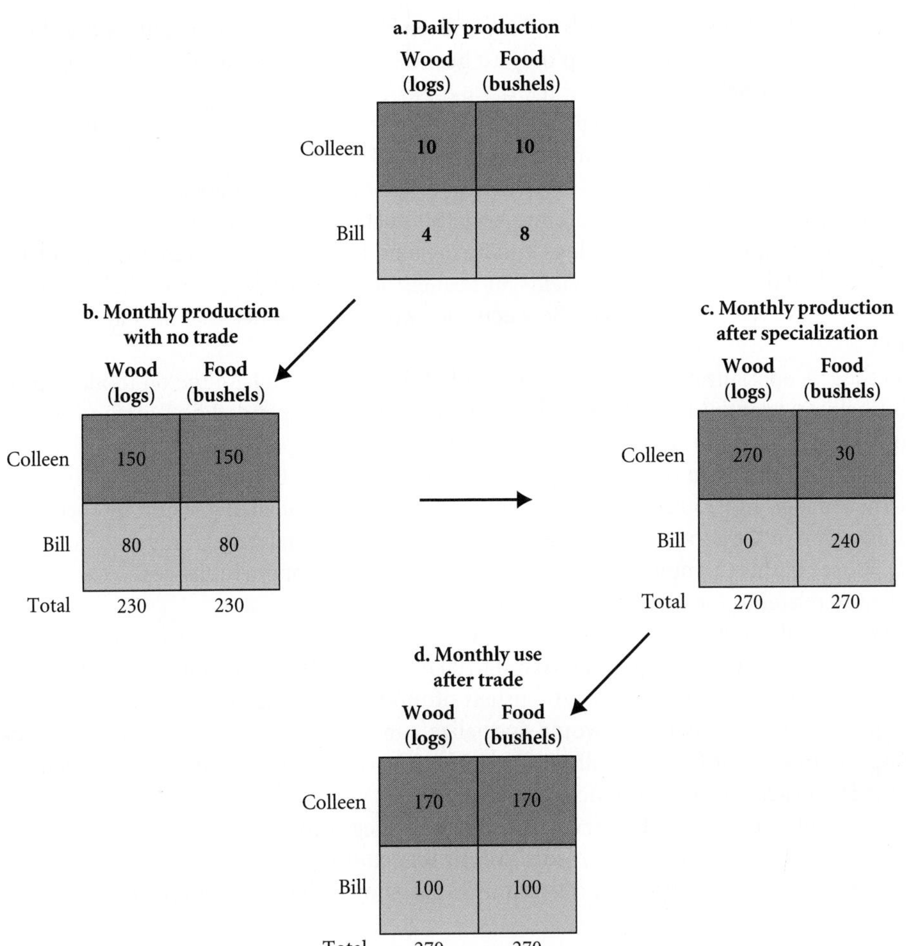

FIGURE 2.2
Comparative Advantage and the Gains from Trade

In this figure, (a) shows the number of logs and bushels of food that Colleen and Bill can produce for every day spent at the task and (b) shows how much output they could produce in a month, assuming they wanted an equal number of logs and bushels. Colleen would split her time 50/50, devoting 15 days to each task and achieving total output of 150 logs and 150 bushels of food. Bill would spend 20 days cutting wood and 10 days gathering food. As shown in (c) and (d), by specializing and trading, both Colleen and Bill will be better off. Going from (c) to (d), Colleen trades 100 logs to Bill in exchange for 140 bushels of food.

Suppose Colleen can cut 10 logs per day and Bill can cut only 4. Also suppose Colleen can gather 10 bushels of food per day and Bill can gather only 8. A producer has an **absolute advantage** over another in the production of a good or service if he or she can produce the good or service using fewer resources, including time. Since Colleen can cut more logs per day than Bill, we say that she has an absolute advantage in the production of logs. Similarly, Colleen has an absolute advantage over Bill in the production of food.

absolute advantage A producer has an absolute advantage over another in the production of a good or service if he or she can produce that product using fewer resources.

Thinking just about productivity and the output of food and logs, you might conclude that it would benefit Colleen to move to the other side of the island and be by herself. Since she is more productive in cutting logs and gathering food, would she not be better off on her own? How could she benefit by hanging out with Bill and sharing what they produce?

To answer that question we must remember that Colleen's time is limited: This limit creates opportunity cost. A producer has a **comparative advantage** over another in the production of a good or service if he or she can produce the good or service at a lower opportunity cost. First, think about Bill. He can produce 8 bushels of food per day, or he can cut 4 logs. To get 8 additional bushels of food, he must give up cutting 4 logs. Thus, *for Bill, the opportunity cost of 8 bushels of food is 4 logs*. Think next about Colleen. She can produce 10 bushels of food per day, or she can cut 10 logs. She thus gives up 1 log for each additional bushel; so *for Colleen, the opportunity cost of 8 bushels of food is 8 logs*. Bill has a comparative advantage over Colleen in the production of food because he gives up only 4 logs for an additional 8 bushels, whereas Colleen gives up 8 logs.

comparative advantage A producer has a comparative advantage over another in the production of a good or service if he or she can produce that product at a lower *opportunity cost*.

Think now about what Colleen must give up in terms of food to get 10 logs. To produce 10 logs she must work a whole day. If she spends a day cutting 10 logs, she gives up a day of gathering 10 bushels of food. Thus, *for Colleen, the opportunity cost of 10 logs is 10 bushels of food*. What must Bill give up to get 10 logs? To produce 4 logs, he must work 1 day. For each day he cuts logs, he gives up 8 bushels of food. He thus gives up 2 bushels of food for each log; so *for Bill, the opportunity cost of 10 logs is 20 bushels of food.* Colleen has a comparative advantage over Bill in the production of logs since she gives up only 10 bushels of food for an additional 10 logs, whereas Bill gives up 20 bushels.

Ricardo then argues that two parties can benefit from specialization and trade even if one party has an absolute advantage in the production of both goods. Suppose Colleen and Bill both want equal numbers of logs and bushels of food. If Colleen goes off on her own, in a 30-day month, she can produce 150 logs and 150 bushels, devoting 15 days to each task. For Bill to produce equal numbers of logs and bushels on his own requires that he spend 10 days on food and 20 days on logs. This yields 80 bushels of food (10 days × 8 bushels per day) and 80 logs (20 days × 4 logs per day). Between the two, they produce 230 logs and 230 bushels of food.

Let's see if specialization and trade can work. If Bill spends all his time on food, he produces 240 bushels in a month (30 days × 8 bushels per day). If Colleen spends 3 days on food and 27 days on logs, she produces 30 bushels of food (3 days × 10 bushels per day) and 270 logs (27 days × 10 logs per day). Between the two, they produce 270 logs and 270 bushels of food, which is more than the 230 logs and 230 bushels they produced when not specializing. Thus, by specializing in the production of the good in which they enjoyed a comparative advantage, there are more of both goods. We see in this example how the fundamental concept of opportunity cost covered earlier in this chapter relates to the theory of comparative advantage.

Even if Colleen were to live at another place on the island, she could specialize, producing 30 bushels of food and 270 logs, then trading 100 of her logs to Bill for 140 bushels of food. This would leave her with 170 logs and 170 bushels of food, which is more than the 150 of each she could produce on her own. Bill would specialize completely in food, producing 240 bushels. Trading 140 bushels of food to Colleen for 100 logs leaves him with 100 of each, which is more than the 80 of each he could produce on his own.

The simple example of Bill and Colleen should begin to give you some insight into why most economists see value in free trade. Even if one country is absolutely better than another country at producing everything, our example has shown that there are gains to specializing and trading.

A Graphical Presentation of Comparative Advantage and Gains from Trade Graphs can also be used to show the benefits from specialization and trade in the example of Colleen and Bill. To construct a graph reflecting Colleen's production choices (Figure 2.3 (a)), we start with the end points. If she were to devote an entire month (30 days) to log production, she could cut 300 logs—10 logs per day × 30 days. Similarly, if she were to devote an entire month to food gathering, she could produce 300 bushels. If she chose to split her time evenly (15 days to logs and 15 days to food), she would have 150 bushels and 150 logs. Her production possibilities are illustrated by the straight line between *A* and *B* and illustrate the trade-off that she faces between logs and food: By reducing her time spent in food gathering, Colleen is able to devote more time to logs; and for every 10 bushels of food that she gives up, she gets 10 logs.

In Figure 2.3(b), we construct a graph of Bill's production possibilities. Recall that Bill can produce 8 bushels of food per day, but he can cut only 4 logs. Again, starting with the end points, if Bill devoted all his time to food production, he could produce 240 bushels—8 bushels of food per day × 30 days. Similarly, if he were to devote the entire 30 days to log cutting, he could cut 120 logs—4 logs per day × 30 days. By splitting his time, with 20 days spent on log cutting and 10 days spent gathering food, Bill could produce 80 logs and 80 bushels of food. His production possibilities are illustrated by the straight line between *D* and *E*. By shifting his resources and time from logs to food, he gets 2 bushels for every log.

Figures 2.3(a) and 2.3(b) illustrate the maximum amounts of food and logs that Bill and Colleen can produce acting independently with no specialization or trade, which is 230 logs and 230 bushels. Now let us have each specialize in producing the good in which he or she has a comparative advantage. Back in Figure 2.2 on p. 29, we showed that if Bill devoted all his time to food production, producing 240 bushels (30 days × 8 bushels per day), and Colleen devoted the vast majority of her time to cutting logs (27 days) and just a few days to gathering food (3 days), their combined total would be 270 logs and 270 bushels of food. Colleen would produce 270 logs and 30 bushels of food to go with Bill's 240 bushels of food.

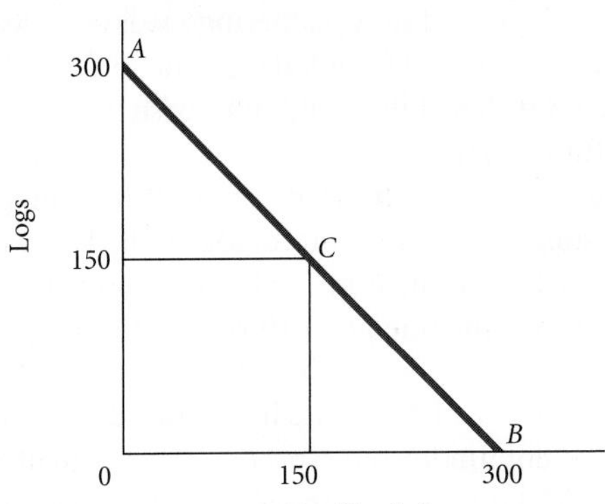

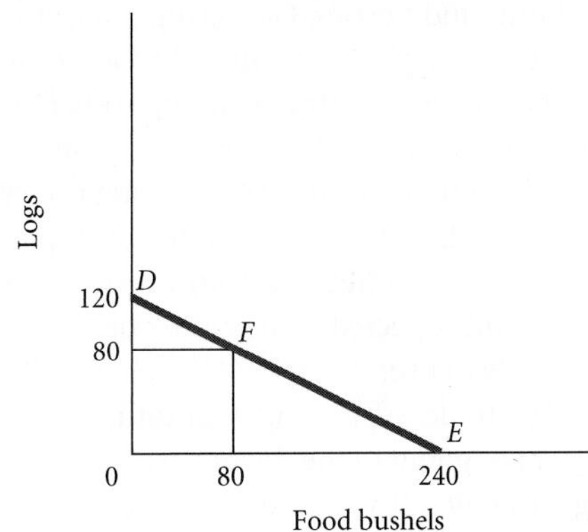

▲ **FIGURE 2.3 Production Possibilities with No Trade**

The figure in (a) shows all of the combinations of logs and bushels of food that Colleen can produce by herself. If she spends all 30 days each month on logs, she produces 300 logs and no food (point *A*). If she spends all 30 days on food, she produces 300 bushels of food and no logs (point *B*). If she spends 15 days on logs and 15 days on food, she produces 150 of each (point *C*).

The figure in (b) shows all of the combinations of logs and bushels of food that Bill can produce by himself. If he spends all 30 days each month on logs, he produces 120 logs and no food (point *D*). If he spends all 30 days on food, he produces 240 bushels of food and no logs (point *E*). If he spends 20 days on logs and 10 days on food, he produces 80 of each (point *F*).

Finally, we arrange a trade, and the result is shown in Figures 2.4(a) and 2.4(b). Bill trades 140 bushels of food to Colleen for 100 logs; and he ends up with 100 logs and 100 bushels of food, 20 more of each than he would have had before the specialization and trade.

Colleen ends up with 170 logs and 170 bushels, again 20 more of each than she would have had before the specialization and trade. Both are better off. Both move beyond their individual production possibilities.

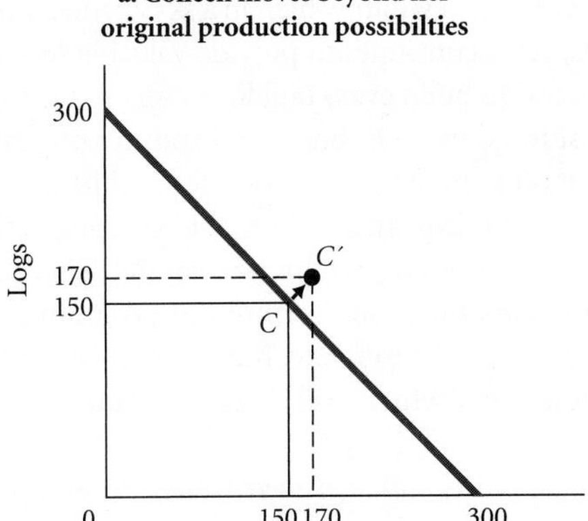

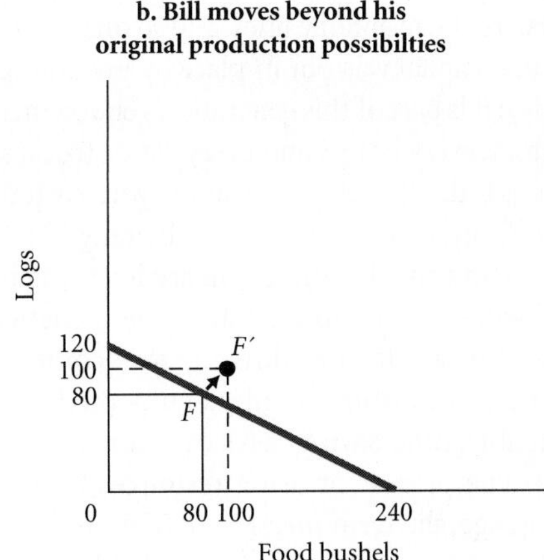

▲ **FIGURE 2.4 Colleen and Bill Gain from Trade**

By specializing and engaging in trade, Colleen and Bill can move beyond their own production possibilities. If Bill spends all his time producing food, he will produce 240 bushels of food and no logs. If he can trade 140 of his bushels of food to Colleen for 100 logs, he will end up with 100 logs and 100 bushels of food. The figure in (b) shows that he can move from point *F* to point *F′*.

If Colleen spends 27 days cutting logs and 3 days producing food, she will produce 270 logs and 30 bushels of food. If she can trade 100 of her logs to Bill for 140 bushels of food, she will end up with 170 logs and 170 bushels of food. The figure in (a) shows that she can move from point *C* to point *C′*.

Weighing Present and Expected Future Costs and Benefits Very often we find ourselves weighing benefits available today against benefits available tomorrow. Here, too, the notion of opportunity cost is helpful.

While alone on the island, Bill had to choose between cultivating a field and just gathering wild nuts and berries. Gathering nuts and berries provides food now; gathering seeds and clearing a field for planting will yield food tomorrow if all goes well. Using today's time to farm may well be worth the effort if doing so will yield more food than Bill would otherwise have in the future. By planting, Bill is trading present value for future value.

The simplest example of trading present for future benefits is the act of saving. When you put income aside today for use in the future, you give up some things that you could have had today in exchange for something tomorrow. Because nothing is certain, some judgment about future events and expected values must be made. What will your income be in 10 years? How long are you likely to live?

We trade off present and future benefits in small ways all the time. If you decide to study instead of going to the dorm party, you are trading present fun for the expected future benefits of higher grades. If you decide to go outside on a very cold day and run 5 miles, you are trading discomfort in the present for being in better shape later.

Capital Goods and Consumer Goods A society trades present for expected future benefits when it devotes a portion of its resources to research and development or to investment in capital. As we said earlier in this chapter, *capital* in its broadest definition is anything that has already been produced that will be used to produce other valuable goods or services over time.

Building capital means trading present benefits for future ones. Bill and Colleen might trade gathering berries or lying in the sun for cutting logs to build a nicer house in the future. In a modern society, resources used to produce capital goods could have been used to produce **consumer goods**—that is, goods for present consumption. Heavy industrial machinery does not directly satisfy the wants of anyone, but producing it requires resources that could instead have gone into producing things that do satisfy wants directly—for example, food, clothing, toys, or golf clubs.

consumer goods Goods produced for present consumption.

Capital is everywhere. A road is capital. Once a road is built, we can drive on it or transport goods and services over it for many years to come. A house is also capital. Before a new manufacturing firm can start up, it must put some capital in place. The buildings, equipment, and inventories that it uses comprise its capital. As it contributes to the production process, this capital yields valuable services over time.

In Chapter 1, we talked about the enormous amount of capital—buildings, factories, housing, cars, trucks, telephone lines, and so on—that you might see from a window high in a skyscraper. Much of that capital was put in place by previous generations, yet it continues to provide valuable services today; it is part of this generation's endowment of resources. To build every building, every road, every factory, every house, and every car or truck, society must forgo using resources to produce consumer goods today. To get an education, you pay tuition and put off joining the workforce for a while.

Capital does not need to be tangible. When you spend time and resources developing skills or getting an education, you are investing in human capital—your own human capital. This capital will continue to exist and yield benefits to you for years to come. A computer program produced by a software company may come on a CD that costs 75¢ to make, but its true intangible value comes from the ideas embodied in the program itself, which will drive computers to do valuable, time-saving tasks over time. It too is capital.

investment The process of using resources to produce new capital.

The process of using resources to produce new capital is called **investment**. (In everyday language, the term *investment* often refers to the act of buying a share of stock or a bond, as in "I invested in some Treasury bonds." In economics, however, investment *always* refers to the creation of capital: the purchase or putting in place of buildings, equipment, roads, houses, and the like.) A wise investment in capital is one that yields future benefits that are more valuable than the present cost. When you spend money for a house, for example, presumably you value its future benefits. That is, you expect to gain more from living in it than you would from the things you could buy today with the same money. Because resources are scarce, the opportunity cost of every investment in capital is forgone present consumption.

The Production Possibility Frontier

production possibility frontier (ppf) A graph that shows all the combinations of goods and services that can be produced if all of society's resources are used efficiently.

A simple graphic device called the **production possibility frontier (ppf)** illustrates the principles of constrained choice, opportunity cost, and scarcity. The ppf is a graph that shows all the combinations of goods and services that can be produced if all of a society's resources are used efficiently. Figure 2.5 shows a ppf for a hypothetical economy.

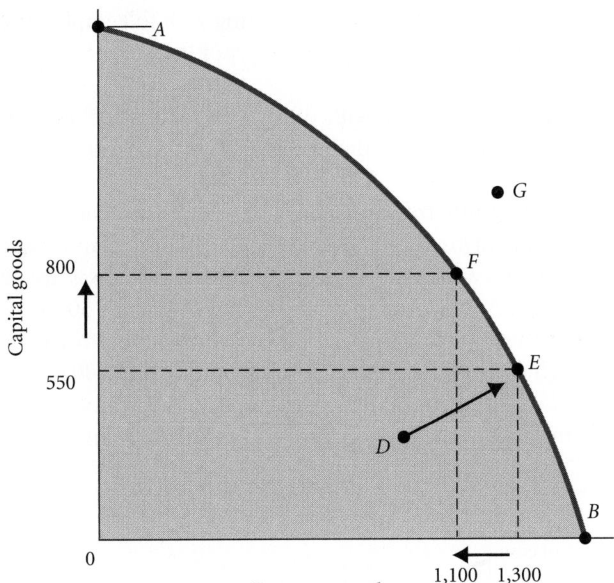

◀ **FIGURE 2.5 Production Possibility Frontier**

The ppf illustrates a number of economic concepts. One of the most important is *opportunity cost*. The opportunity cost of producing more capital goods is fewer consumer goods. Moving from *E* to *F*, the number of capital goods increases from 550 to 800, but the number of consumer goods decreases from 1,300 to 1,100.

On the *Y*-axis, we measure the quantity of capital goods produced. On the *X*-axis, we measure the quantity of consumer goods. All points below and to the left of the curve (the shaded area) represent combinations of capital and consumer goods that are possible for the society given the resources available and existing technology. Points above and to the right of the curve, such as point *G*, represent combinations that cannot be reached. If an economy were to end up at point *A* on the graph, it would be producing no consumer goods at all; all resources would be used for the production of capital. If an economy were to end up at point *B*, it would be devoting all its resources to the production of consumer goods and none of its resources to the formation of capital.

While all economies produce some of each kind of good, different economies emphasize different things. About 17.1 percent of gross output in the United States in 2005 was new capital. In Japan, capital historically accounted for a much higher percent of gross output, while in the Congo, the figure was 7 percent. Japan is closer to point *A* on its ppf, the Congo is closer to *B*, and the United States is somewhere in between.

Points that are actually on the ppf are points of both full resource employment and production efficiency. (Recall from Chapter 1 that an efficient economy is one that produces the things that people want at the least cost. *Production efficiency* is a state in which a given mix of outputs is produced at the least cost.) Resources are not going unused, and there is no waste. Points that lie within the shaded area but that are not on the frontier represent either unemployment of resources or production inefficiency. An economy producing at point *D* in Figure 2.5 can produce more capital goods and more consumer goods, for example, by moving to point *E*. This is possible because resources are not fully employed at point *D* or are not being used efficiently.

Unemployment During the Great Depression of the 1930s, the U.S. economy experienced prolonged unemployment. Millions of workers found themselves without jobs. In 1933, 25 percent of the civilian labor force was unemployed. This figure stayed above 14 percent until 1940, when increased defense spending by the United States created millions of jobs. In June 1975, the unemployment rate went over 9 percent for the first time since the 1930s. In December 1982, when the unemployment rate hit 10.8 percent, nearly 12 million people were looking for work. In 2007, the figure was 7.1 million.

In addition to the hardship that falls on the unemployed, unemployment of labor means unemployment of capital. During economic downturns or recessions, industrial plants run at less than their total capacity. When there is unemployment of labor and capital, we are not producing all that we can.

Periods of unemployment correspond to points inside the ppf, points such as *D* in Figure 2.5. Moving onto the frontier from a point such as *D* means achieving full employment of resources.

Inefficiency Although an economy may be operating with full employment of its land, labor, and capital resources, it may still be operating inside its ppf (at a point such as *D* in Figure 2.5). It could be using those resources *inefficiently*.

Waste and mismanagement are the results of a firm operating below its potential. If you are the owner of a bakery and you forget to order flour, your workers and ovens stand idle while you figure out what to do.

Sometimes inefficiency results from mismanagement of the economy instead of mismanagement of individual private firms. Suppose, for example, that the land and climate in Ohio are best suited for corn production and that the land and climate in Kansas are best suited for wheat production. If Congress passes a law forcing Ohio farmers to plant 50 percent of their acreage with wheat and Kansas farmers to plant 50 percent with corn, neither corn nor wheat production will be up to potential. The economy will be at a point such as *A* in Figure 2.6—inside the ppf. Allowing each state to specialize in producing the crop that it produces best increases the production of both crops and moves the economy to a point such as *B* in Figure 2.6.

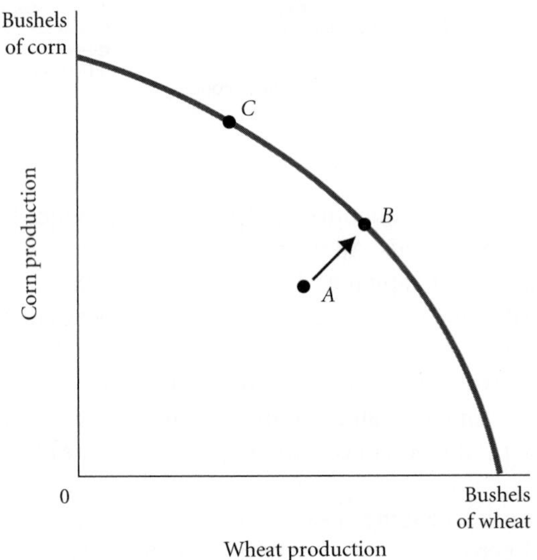

FIGURE 2.6 Inefficiency from Misallocation of Land in Farming

Society can end up inside its ppf at a point such as *A* by using its resources inefficiently. If, for example, Ohio's climate and soil were best suited for corn production and those of Kansas were best suited for wheat production, a law forcing Kansas farmers to produce corn and Ohio farmers to produce wheat would result in less of both. In such a case, society might be at point *A* instead of point *B*.

The Efficient Mix of Output To be efficient, an economy must produce what people want. This means that in addition to operating *on* the ppf, the economy must be operating at the *right point* on the ppf. This is referred to as *output efficiency*, in contrast to production efficiency. Suppose that an economy devotes 100 percent of its resources to beef production and that the beef industry runs efficiently using the most modern techniques. Also suppose that everyone in the society is a vegetarian. The result is a total waste of resources (assuming that the society cannot trade its beef for vegetables produced in another country).

Points *B* and *C* in Figure 2.6 are points of production efficiency and full employment. Whether *B* is more or less efficient than *C*, however, depends on the preferences of members of society and is not shown in the ppf graph.

Negative Slope and Opportunity Cost As we have seen, points that lie on the ppf represent points of full resource employment and production efficiency. Society can choose only one point on the curve. Because a society's choices are constrained by available resources and existing technology, when those resources are fully and efficiently employed, it can produce more capital goods only by reducing production of consumer goods. The opportunity cost of the additional capital is the forgone production of consumer goods.

The fact that scarcity exists is illustrated by the negative slope of the ppf. (If you need a review of slope, see the Appendix to Chapter 1.) In moving from point *E* to point *F* in Figure 2.5, capital production *increases* by 800 − 550 = 250 units (a positive change), but that increase in capital can be achieved only by shifting resources out of the production of consumer goods. Thus, in moving from point *E* to point *F* in Figure 2.5, consumer goods production *decreases* by

1,300 − 1,100 = 200 units (a negative change). The slope of the curve, the ratio of the change in capital goods to the change in consumer goods, is negative.

The value of the slope of a society's ppf is called the **marginal rate of transformation (MRT)**. In Figure 2.5, the MRT between points *E* and *F* is simply the ratio of the change in capital goods (a positive number) to the change in consumer goods (a negative number).

marginal rate of transformation (MRT) The slope of the production possibility frontier (ppf).

The Law of Increasing Opportunity Cost The negative slope of the ppf indicates the trade-off that a society faces between two goods. We can learn something further about the shape of the frontier and the terms of this trade-off. Let's look at the trade-off between corn and wheat production in Ohio and Kansas. In a recent year, Ohio and Kansas together produced 510 million bushels of corn and 380 million bushels of wheat. Table 2.1 presents these two numbers, plus some hypothetical combinations of corn and wheat production that might exist for Ohio and Kansas together. Figure 2.7 graphs the data from Table 2.1.

TABLE 2.1 Production Possibility Schedule for Total Corn and Wheat Production in Ohio and Kansas

Point on ppf	Total Corn Production (Millions of Bushels Per Year)	Total Wheat Production (Millions of Bushels Per Year)
A	700	100
B	650	200
C	510	380
D	400	500
E	300	550

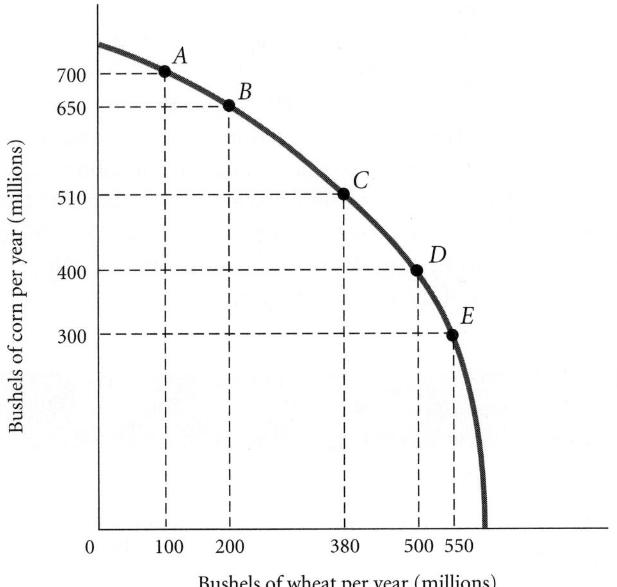

◀ **FIGURE 2.7 Corn and Wheat Production in Ohio and Kansas**
The ppf illustrates that the opportunity cost of corn production increases as we shift resources from wheat production to corn production. Moving from point *E* to *D*, we get an additional 100 million bushels of corn at a cost of 50 million bushels of wheat. Moving from point *B* to *A*, we get only 50 million bushels of corn at a cost of 100 million bushels of wheat. The *cost per bushel* of corn—measured in lost wheat—has increased.

Suppose that society's demand for corn dramatically increases. If this happens, farmers would probably shift some of their acreage from wheat production to corn production. Such a shift is represented by a move from point *C* (where corn = 510 and wheat = 380) up and to the left along the ppf toward points *A* and *B* in Figure 2.7. As this happens, it becomes more difficult to produce additional corn. The best land for corn production was presumably already in corn, and the best land for wheat production was already in wheat. As we try to produce more corn, the land is less well suited to that crop. As we take more land out of wheat production, we are taking increasingly better wheat-producing land. In other words, the opportunity cost of more corn, measured in terms of wheat, increases.

Moving from point *E* to *D*, Table 2.1 shows that we can get 100 million bushels of corn (400 − 300) by sacrificing only 50 million bushels of wheat (550 − 500)—that is, we get

2 bushels of corn for every bushel of wheat. However, when we are already stretching the ability of the land to produce corn, it becomes harder to produce more and the opportunity cost increases. Moving from point *B* to *A*, we can get only 50 million bushels of corn (700 − 650) by sacrificing 100 million bushels of wheat (200 − 100). For every bushel of wheat, we now get only half a bushel of corn. However, if the demand for *wheat* were to increase substantially and we were to move down and to the right along the ppf, it would become increasingly difficult to produce wheat and the opportunity cost of wheat, in terms of corn, would increase. This is the *law of increasing opportunity cost.*

If you think about the example we discussed earlier of Colleen and Bill producing logs and food on an island, you will recognize that the production possibilities described were highly simplified. In that example, we drew a downward slope, *straight line ppf*; to make the problem easier, we assume constant opportunity costs. In a real economy, ppf's would be expected to look like Figure 2.5.

Although it exists only as an abstraction, the ppf illustrates a number of very important concepts that we will use throughout the rest of this book: scarcity, unemployment, inefficiency, opportunity cost, the law of increasing opportunity cost, economic growth, and the gains from trade.

It is important to remember that the ppf represents choices available within the constraints imposed by the current state of agricultural technology. In the long run, technology may improve, and when that happens, we have *growth.*

economic growth An increase in the total output of an economy. It occurs when a society acquires new resources or when it learns to produce more using existing resources.

Economic Growth

Economic growth is characterized by an increase in the total output of an economy. It occurs when a society acquires new resources or learns to produce more with existing resources. New resources may mean a larger labor force or an increased capital stock. The production and use of new machinery and equipment (capital) increase workers' productivity. (Give a man a shovel, and he can dig a bigger hole; give him a steam shovel, and wow!) Improved productivity also comes from technological change and *innovation*, the discovery and application of new, more efficient production techniques.

In the past few decades, the productivity of U.S. agriculture has increased dramatically. Based on data compiled by the Department of Agriculture, Table 2.2 shows that yield per acre in corn production has increased fivefold since the late 1930s, while the labor required to produce it has dropped significantly. Productivity in wheat production has also increased, at only a slightly less remarkable rate: Output per acre has more than tripled, while labor requirements are down nearly 90 percent. These increases are the result of more efficient farming techniques, more and better capital (tractors, combines, and other equipment), and advances in scientific knowledge and technological change (hybrid seeds, fertilizers, and so on). As you can see in Figure 2.8, increases such as these shift the ppf up and to the right.

TABLE 2.2 Increasing Productivity in Corn and Wheat Production in the United States, 1935–2007

	Corn		Wheat	
	Yield Per Acre (Bushels)	Labor Hours Per 100 Bushels	Yield Per Acre (Bushels)	Labor Hours Per 100 Bushels
1935–1939	26.1	108	13.2	67
1945–1949	36.1	53	16.9	34
1955–1959	48.7	20	22.3	17
1965–1969	78.5	7	27.5	11
1975–1979	95.3	4	31.3	9
1981–1985	107.2	3	36.9	7
1985–1990	112.8	NA[a]	38.0	NA[a]
1990–1995	120.6	NA[a]	38.1	NA[a]
1998	134.4	NA[a]	43.2	NA[a]
2001	138.2	NA[a]	43.5	NA[a]
2006	145.6	NA[a]	42.3	NA[a]
2007	152.8	NA[a]	40.6	NA[a]

[a]Data not available.

Source: U.S. Department of Agriculture, Economic Research Service, Agricultural Statistics, Crop Summary. www.ers.usda.gov, *August 2007.*

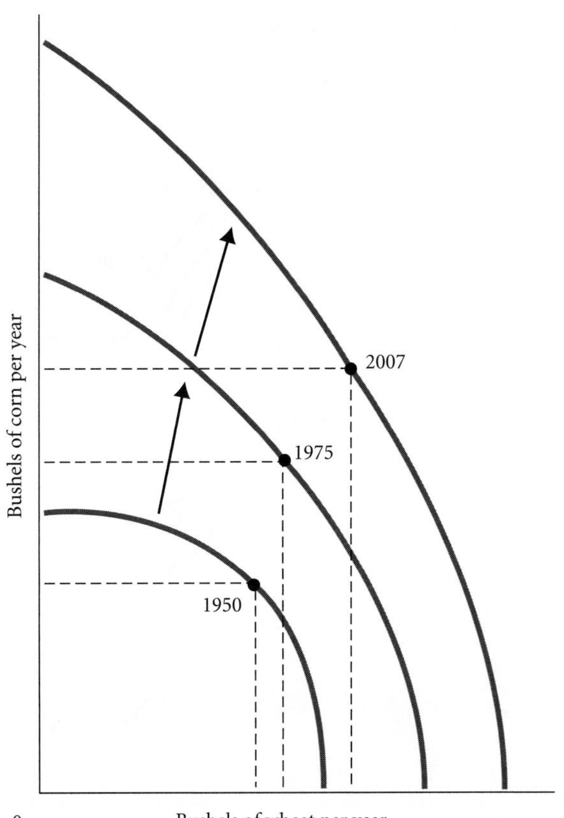

◀ **FIGURE 2.8 Economic Growth Shifts the PPF Up and to the Right**

Productivity increases have enhanced the ability of the United States to produce both corn and wheat. As Table 2.2 shows, productivity increases were more dramatic for corn than for wheat. Thus, the shifts in the ppf were not parallel.

Note: The ppf also shifts if the amount of land or labor in corn and wheat production changes. Although we emphasize productivity increases here, the actual shifts between years were due in part to land and labor changes.

Sources of Growth and the Dilemma of Poor Countries Economic growth arises from many sources, the two most important over the years having been the accumulation of capital and technological advances. For poor countries, capital is essential; they must build the communication networks and transportation systems necessary to develop industries that function efficiently. They also need capital goods to develop their agricultural sectors.

Recall that capital goods are produced only at a sacrifice of consumer goods. The same can be said for technological advances. Technological advances come from research and development that use resources; thus, they too must be paid for. The resources used to produce capital goods—to build a road, a tractor, or a manufacturing plant—*and* to develop new technologies could have been used to produce consumer goods.

When a large part of a country's population is very poor, taking resources out of the production of consumer goods (such as food and clothing) is very difficult. In addition, in some countries, people wealthy enough to invest in domestic industries choose instead to invest abroad because of political turmoil at home. As a result, it often falls to the governments of poor countries to generate revenues for capital production and research out of tax collections.

All these factors have contributed to the growing gap between some poor and rich nations. Figure 2.9 shows the result using ppf's. On the left, the rich country devotes a larger portion of its production to capital while the poor country produces mostly consumer goods. On the right, you see the results: the ppf of the rich country shifts up and out farther and faster.

The importance of capital goods and technological developments to the position of workers in less developed countries is well illustrated by Robert Jensen's study of South India's industry. Conventional telephones require huge investments in wires and towers and, as a result, many less developed areas are without landlines. Mobile phones, on the other hand, require a less expensive investment; thus, in many areas, people upgraded from no phones directly to cell phones. Jensen found that in small fishing villages, the advent of cell phones allowed fishermen to determine on any given day where to take their catch to sell, resulting in a large decrease in fish wasted and an increase in fishing profits. The ability of newer communication technology to aid development is one of the exciting features of our times. (See Robert Jensen, "The Digital Provide: Information Technology, Market Performance, and Welfare in the South Indian Fisheries Sector," *Quarterly Journal of Economics*, August 2007, 879–924.)

▶ **FIGURE 2.9 Capital Goods and Growth in Poor and Rich Countries**

Rich countries find it easier than poor countries to devote resources to the production of capital, and the more resources that flow into capital production, the faster the rate of economic growth. Thus, the gap between poor and rich countries has grown over time.

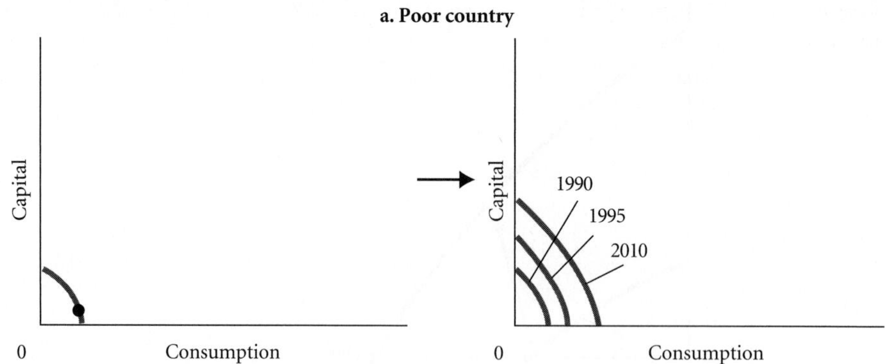

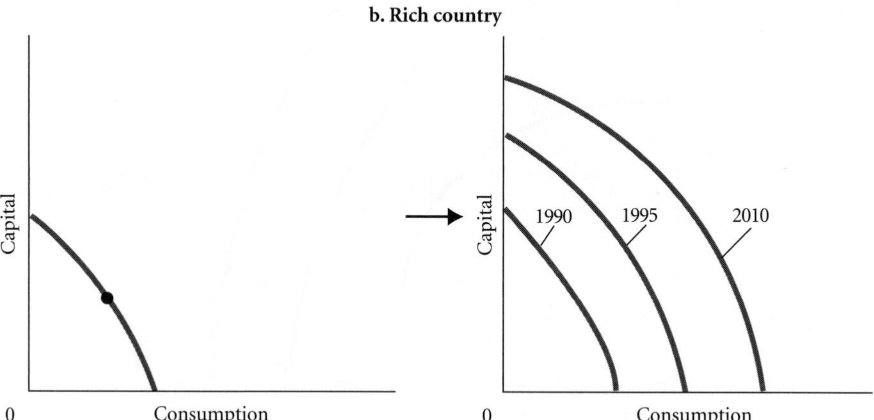

The Economic Problem

Recall the three basic questions facing all economic systems: (1) What gets produced? (2) How is it produced? and (3) Who gets it?

When Bill was alone on the island, the mechanism for answering those questions was simple: He thought about his own wants and preferences, looked at the constraints imposed by the resources of the island and his own skills and time, and made his decisions. As Bill set about his work, he allocated available resources quite simply, more or less by dividing up his available time. Distribution of the output was irrelevant. Because Bill was the society, he got it all.

Introducing even one more person into the economy—in this case, Colleen—changed all that. With Colleen on the island, resource allocation involves deciding not only how each person spends his or her time but also who does what; and now there are two sets of wants and preferences. If Bill and Colleen go off on their own and form two separate self-sufficient economies, there will be lost potential. Two people can do more things together than each person can do alone. They may use their comparative advantages in different skills to specialize. Cooperation and coordination may give rise to gains that would otherwise not be possible.

When a society consists of millions of people, the problem of coordination and cooperation becomes enormous, but so does the potential for gain. In large, complex economies, specialization can go wild, with people working in jobs as different in their detail as an impressionist painting is from a blank page. The range of products available in a modern industrial society is beyond anything that could have been imagined a hundred years ago, and so is the range of jobs.

The amount of coordination and cooperation in a modern industrial society is almost impossible to imagine. Yet something seems to drive economic systems, if sometimes clumsily and inefficiently, toward producing the goods and services that people want. Given scarce resources, how do large, complex societies go about answering the three basic economic questions? This is the economic problem, which is what this text is about.

Economic Systems

Now that you understand the economic problem, we can explore how different economic systems go about answering the three basic questions.

In the long struggle between the United States and the USSR in the post–World War II period, there was a general view that authoritarian political systems went hand in hand with highly centralized and governmentally controlled economic systems. The recent explosive growth in China and the structure of the Chinese economy have created some debate over that connection.

China has become a magnet for private capital and entrepreneurship and has one of the most rapidly growing economies in the world. For the last decade, China has been growing at double-digit rates. Between 2001 and 2004, China's national output went up almost 50 percent. In the single month of June 2005, the Chinese sold $21 billion worth of goods and services to the United States, while the United States sold only $3.4 billion to China. While the Chinese political system is still highly controlled, the economy has many hallmarks of a free market system. Exciting new work is taking place to help better understand the connections between the economic system and the political system.

Command Economies

In a pure **command economy**, the basic economic questions are answered by a central government. Through a combination of government ownership of state enterprises and central planning, the government, either directly or indirectly, sets output targets, incomes, and prices.

command economy An economy in which a central government either directly or indirectly sets output targets, incomes, and prices.

While the extremes of central planning have been rejected, so too has the idea that "markets solve all problems." The real debate is not about whether we have government at all, it is about the extent and the character of a limited government role in the economy. One of the major themes of this book is that government involvement, in theory, may improve the efficiency and fairness of the allocation of a nation's resources. At the same time, a poorly functioning government can destroy incentives, lead to corruption, and result in the waste of a society's resources.

Laissez-Faire Economies: The Free Market

At the opposite end of the spectrum from the command economy is the **laissez-faire economy**. The term *laissez-faire*, which translated literally from French means "allow [them] to do," implies a complete lack of government involvement in the economy. In this type of economy, individuals and firms pursue their own self-interest without any central direction or regulation; the sum total of millions of individual decisions ultimately determines all basic economic outcomes. The central institution through which a laissez-faire system answers the basic questions is the **market**, a term that is used in economics to mean an institution through which buyers and sellers interact and engage in exchange.

laissez-faire economy Literally from the French: "allow [them] to do." An economy in which individual people and firms pursue their own self-interest without any central direction or regulation.

market The institution through which buyers and sellers interact and engage in exchange.

The interactions between buyers and sellers in any market range from simple to complex. Early explorers of the North American Midwest who wanted to exchange with Native Americans did so simply by bringing their goods to a central place and trading them. Today the World Wide Web is revolutionizing exchange. A jewelry maker in upstate Maine can exhibit wares through digital photographs on the Web. Buyers can enter orders or make bids and pay by credit card. Companies such as eBay facilitate the worldwide interaction of tens of thousands of buyers and sellers sitting at their computers.

In short:

> Some markets are simple and others are complex, but they all involve buyers and sellers engaging in exchange. The behavior of buyers and sellers in a laissez-faire economy determines what gets produced, how it is produced, and who gets it.

The following chapters explore market systems in great depth. A quick preview is worthwhile here, however.

Consumer Sovereignty In a free, unregulated market, goods and services are produced and sold only if the supplier can make a profit. In simple terms, making a *profit* means selling goods or services for more than it costs to produce them. You cannot make a profit unless someone wants the product that you are selling. This logic leads to the notion of **consumer sovereignty**: The mix of output found in any free market system is dictated ultimately by the

consumer sovereignty The idea that consumers ultimately dictate what will be produced (or not produced) by choosing what to purchase (and what not to purchase).

tastes and preferences of consumers who "vote" by buying or not buying. Businesses rise and fall in response to consumer demands. No central directive or plan is necessary.

Individual Production Decisions: Free Enterprise Under a free market system, individual producers must also determine how to organize and coordinate the actual production of their products or services. The owner of a small shoe repair shop must alone buy the needed equipment and tools, hang signs, and set prices. In a big corporation, so many people are involved in planning the production process that in many ways, corporate planning resembles the planning in a command economy. In a free market economy, producers may be small or large. One person who hand-paints eggshells may start to sell them as a business; a person good with computers may start a business designing Web sites. On a larger scale, a group of furniture designers may put together a large portfolio of sketches, raise several million dollars, and start a bigger business. At the extreme are huge corporations such as Microsoft, Mitsubishi, and Intel, each of which sells tens of billions of dollars' worth of products every year. Whether the firms are large or small, however, production decisions in a market economy are made by separate private organizations acting in what they perceive to be their own interests.

free enterprise The freedom of individuals to start and operate private businesses in search of profits.

Often the market system is called a free enterprise system. **Free enterprise** means the freedom of individuals to start private businesses in search of profits. Because new businesses require capital investment before they can begin operation, starting a new business involves risk. A well-run business that produces a product for which demand exists is likely to succeed; a poorly run business or one that produces a product for which little demand exists now or in the future is likely to fail. It is through free enterprise that new products and new production techniques find their way into use.

Proponents of free market systems argue that free enterprise leads to more efficient production and better response to diverse and changing consumer preferences. If a producer produces inefficiently, competitors will come along, fight for the business, and eventually take it away. Thus, in a free market economy, competition forces producers to use efficient techniques of production. It is competition, then, that ultimately dictates how output is produced.

Distribution of Output In a free market system, the distribution of output—who gets what—is also determined in a decentralized way. The amount that any one household gets depends on its income and wealth. *Income* is the amount that a household earns each year. It comes in a number of forms: wages, salaries, interest, and the like. *Wealth* is the amount that households have accumulated out of past income through saving or inheritance.

To the extent that income comes from working for a wage, it is at least in part determined by individual choice. You will work for the wages available in the market only if these wages (and the products and services they can buy) are sufficient to compensate you for what you give up by working. Your leisure certainly has a value also. You may discover that you can increase your income by getting more education or training. You *cannot* increase your income, however, if you acquire a skill that no one wants.

Price Theory The basic coordinating mechanism in a free market system is price. A price is the amount that a product sells for per unit, and it reflects what society is willing to pay. Prices of inputs—labor, land, and capital—determine how much it costs to produce a product. Prices of various kinds of labor, or *wage rates*, determine the rewards for working in different jobs and professions. Many of the independent decisions made in a market economy involve the weighing of prices and costs, so it is not surprising that much of economic theory focuses on the factors that influence and determine prices. This is why microeconomic theory is often simply called *price theory*.

In sum:

> In a free market system, the basic economic questions are answered without the help of a central government plan or directives. This is what the "free" in free market means—the system is left to operate on its own with no outside interference. Individuals pursuing their own self-interest will go into business and produce the products and services that people want. Other individuals will decide whether to acquire skills; whether to work; and whether to buy, sell, invest, or save the income that they earn. The basic coordinating mechanism is price.

Mixed Systems, Markets, and Governments

The differences between command economies and laissez-faire economies in their pure forms are enormous. In fact, these pure forms do not exist in the world; all real systems are in some sense "mixed." That is, individual enterprise exists and independent choice is exercised even in economies in which the government plays a major role.

Conversely, no market economies exist without government involvement and government regulation. The United States has basically a free market economy, but government purchases accounted for about 19.4 percent of the country's total production in 2007. Governments in the United States (local, state, and federal) directly employ about 16 percent of all workers, counting the military. They also redistribute income by means of taxation and social welfare expenditures, and they regulate many economic activities.

One of the major themes in this book, and indeed in economics, is the tension between the advantages of free, unregulated markets and the desire for government involvement. Advocates of free markets argue that such markets work best when left to themselves. They produce only what people want; without buyers, sellers go out of business. Competition forces firms to adopt efficient production techniques. Wage differentials lead people to acquire needed skills. Competition also leads to innovation in both production techniques and products. The result is quality and variety, but market systems have problems too. Even staunch defenders of the free enterprise system recognize that market systems are not perfect. First, they do not always produce what people want at the lowest cost—there are inefficiencies. Second, rewards (income) may be unfairly distributed and some groups may be left out. Third, periods of unemployment and inflation recur with some regularity.

Many people point to these problems as reasons for government involvement. Indeed, for some problems, government involvement may be the only solution. However, government decisions are made by people who presumably, like the rest of us, act in their own self-interest. While governments may be called on to improve the functioning of the economy, there is no guarantee that they will do so. Just as markets may fail to produce an allocation of resources that is perfectly efficient and fair, governments may fail to improve matters. We return to this debate many times throughout this text.

Looking Ahead

This chapter described the economic problem in broad terms. We outlined the questions that all economic systems must answer. We also discussed very broadly the two kinds of economic systems. In the next chapter, we analyze the way market systems work.

SUMMARY

1. Every society has some system or process for transforming into useful form what nature and previous generations have provided. Economics is the study of that process and its outcomes.

2. *Producers* are those who take resources and transform them into usable products, or *outputs*. Private firms, households, and governments all produce something.

SCARCITY, CHOICE, AND OPPORTUNITY COST *p. 26*

3. All societies must answer *three basic questions*: What gets produced? How is it produced? Who gets what is produced? These three questions make up the *economic problem*.

4. One person alone on an island must make the same basic decisions that complex societies make. When a society consists of more than one person, questions of distribution, cooperation, and specialization arise.

5. Because resources are scarce relative to human wants in all societies, using resources to produce one good or service implies *not* using them to produce something else. This concept of *opportunity cost* is central to an understanding of economics.

6. Using resources to produce *capital* that will in turn produce benefits in the future implies *not* using those resources to produce consumer goods in the present.

7. Even if one individual or nation is absolutely more efficient at producing goods than another, all parties will gain if they specialize in producing goods in which they have a *comparative advantage*.

8. A *production possibility frontier* (ppf) is a graph that shows all the combinations of goods and services that can be produced if all of society's resources are used efficiently. The ppf illustrates a number of important economic concepts: scarcity, unemployment, inefficiency, increasing opportunity cost, and economic growth.

9. *Economic growth* occurs when society produces more, either by acquiring more resources or by learning to produce more with existing resources. Improved productivity may come from additional capital or from the discovery and application of new, more efficient techniques of production.

ECONOMIC SYSTEMS *p. 38*

10. In some modern societies, government plays a big role in answering the three basic questions. In pure *command economies*, a central authority directly or indirectly sets output targets, incomes, and prices.

11. A *laissez-faire economy* is one in which individuals independently pursue their own self-interest, without any central direction or regulation, and ultimately determine all basic economic outcomes.

12. A *market* is an institution through which buyers and sellers interact and engage in exchange. Some markets involve simple face-to-face exchange; others involve a complex series of transactions, often over great distances or through electronic means.

13. There are no purely planned economies and no pure laissez-faire economies; all economies are mixed. Individual enterprise, independent choice, and relatively free markets exist in centrally planned economies; and there is significant government involvement in market economies such as that of the United States.

14. One of the great debates in economics revolves around the tension between the advantages of free, unregulated markets and the desire for government involvement in the economy. Free markets produce what people want, and competition forces firms to adopt efficient production techniques. The need for government intervention arises because free markets are characterized by inefficiencies and an unequal distribution of income and experience regular periods of inflation and unemployment.

REVIEW TERMS AND CONCEPTS

absolute advantage, *p. 29*
capital, *p. 25*
command economy, *p. 39*
comparative advantage, *p. 29*
consumer goods, *p. 32*
consumer sovereignty, *p. 39*
economic growth, *p. 36*
factors of production (*or* factors), *p. 25*
free enterprise, *p. 40*
inputs *or* resources, *p. 26*
investment, *p. 32*
laissez-faire economy, *p. 39*
marginal rate of transformation (MRT), *p. 35*
market, *p. 39*
opportunity cost, *p. 27*
outputs, *p. 26*
production, *p. 25*
production possibility frontier (ppf), *p. 32*
theory of comparative advantage, *p. 27*

PROBLEMS

Visit **www.myeconlab.com** to complete the problems marked in orange online. You will receive instant feedback on your answers, tutorial help, and access to additional practice problems.

1. For each of the following, describe some of the potential opportunity costs:
   a. Studying for your economics test
   b. Spending 2 hours playing computer games
   c. Buying a new car instead of keeping the old one
   d. A local community voting to raise property taxes to increase school expenditures and to reduce class size
   e. A number of countries working together to build a space station
   f. Going to graduate school

2. "As long as all resources are fully employed and every firm in the economy is producing its output using the best available technology, the result will be efficient." Do you agree or disagree with this statement? Explain your answer.

3. You are an intern to the editor of a small-town newspaper in Mallsburg, Pennsylvania. Your boss, the editor, asks you to write the first draft of an editorial for this week's paper. Your assignment is to describe the costs and the benefits of building a new bridge across the railroad tracks in the center of town. Currently, most people who live in this town must drive 2 miles through thickly congested traffic to the existing bridge to get to the main shopping and employment center. The bridge will cost the citizens of Mallsburg $25 million, which will be paid for with a tax on their incomes over the next 20 years. What are the opportunity costs of building this bridge? What are the benefits that citizens will likely receive if the bridge is built? What other factors might you consider in writing this editorial?

4. Kristen and Anna live in the beach town of Santa Monica. They own a small business in which they make wristbands and pot holders and sell them to people on the beach. As shown in the table on the following page, Kristen can make 15 wristbands per hour but only 3 pot holders. Anna is a bit slower and can make only 12 wristbands or 2 pot holders in an hour.

	OUTPUT PER HOUR	
	WRISTBANDS	POT HOLDERS
Kristen	15	3
Anna	12	2

a. For Kristen and for Anna, what is the opportunity cost of a pot holder? Who has a comparative advantage in the production of pot holders? Explain your answer.
b. Who has a comparative advantage in the production of wristbands? Explain your answer.
c. Assume that Kristen works 20 hours per week in the business. Assuming Kristen is in business on her own, graph the possible combinations of pot holders and wristbands that she could produce in a week. Do the same for Anna.
d. If Kristen devoted half of her time (10 out of 20 hours) to wristbands and half of her time to pot holders, how many of each would she produce in a week? If Anna did the same, how many of each would she produce? How many wristbands and pot holders would be produced in total?
e. Suppose that Anna spent all 20 hours of her time on wristbands and Kristen spent 17 hours on pot holders and 3 hours on wristbands. How many of each item would be produced?
f. Suppose that Kristen and Anna can sell all their wristbands for $1 each and all their pot holders for $5.50 each. If each of them worked 20 hours per week, how should they split their time between wristbands and pot holders? What is their maximum joint revenue?

5. Briefly describe the trade-offs involved in each of the following decisions. Specifically, list some of the opportunity costs associated with each decision, paying particular attention to the trade-offs between present and future consumption.
a. After a stressful senior year in high school, Sherice decides to take the summer off instead of working before going to college.
b. Frank is overweight and decides to work out every day and to go on a diet.
c. Mei is diligent about taking her car in for routine maintenance even though it takes 2 hours of her time and costs $100 four times each year.
d. Jim is in a hurry. He runs a red light on the way to work.

*6. The countries of Figistan and Blah are small island countries in the South Pacific. Both produce fruit and timber. Each island has a labor force of 1,200. The following table gives production per month for each worker in each country.

	BASKETS OF FRUIT	BOARD FEET OF TIMBER
Figistan workers	10	5
Blah workers	30	10

Productivity of one worker for one month

a. Which country has an absolute advantage in the production of fruit? Which country has an absolute advantage in the production of timber?
b. Which country has a comparative advantage in the production of fruit? of timber?
c. Sketch the ppf's for both countries.
d. Assuming no trading between the two, if both countries wanted to have equal numbers of feet of timber and baskets of fruit, how would they allocate workers to the two sectors?
e. Show that specialization and trade can move both countries beyond their ppf's.

7. Suppose that a simple society has an economy with only one resource, labor. Labor can be used to produce only two commodities—X, a necessity good (food), and Y, a luxury good (music and merriment). Suppose that the labor force consists of 100 workers. One laborer can produce either 5 units of necessity per month (by hunting and gathering) or 10 units of luxury per month (by writing songs, playing the guitar, dancing, and so on).
a. On a graph, draw the economy's ppf. Where does the ppf intersect the Y-axis? Where does it intersect the X-axis? What meaning do those points have?
b. Suppose the economy produced at a point *inside* the ppf. Give at least two reasons why this could occur. What could be done to move the economy to a point *on* the ppf?
c. Suppose you succeeded in lifting your economy to a point on its ppf. What point would you choose? How might your small society decide the point at which it wanted to be?
d. Once you have chosen a point on the ppf, you still need to decide how your society's production will be divided. If you were a dictator, how would you decide? What would happen if you left product distribution to the free market?

*8. Match each diagram in Figure 1 on the next page with its description here. Assume that the economy is producing or attempting to produce at point A and that most members of society like meat and not fish. Some descriptions apply to more than one diagram, and some diagrams have more than one description.
a. Inefficient production of meat and fish
b. Productive efficiency
c. An inefficient mix of output
d. Technological advances in the production of meat and fish
e. The law of increasing opportunity cost
f. An impossible combination of meat and fish

9. A nation with fixed quantities of resources is able to produce any of the following combinations of bread and ovens:

LOAVES OF BREAD (MILLIONS)	OVENS (THOUSANDS)
75	0
60	12
45	22
30	30
15	36
0	40

These figures assume that a certain number of previously produced ovens are available in the current period for baking bread.
a. Using the data in the table, graph the ppf (with ovens on the vertical axis).
b. Does the principle of "increasing opportunity cost" hold in this nation? Explain briefly. (*Hint:* What happens to the opportunity cost of bread—measured in number of ovens—as bread production increases?)
c. If this country chooses to produce both ovens and bread, what will happen to the ppf over time? Why?

Now suppose that a new technology is discovered that allows twice as many loaves of bread to be baked in each existing oven.
d. Illustrate (on your original graph) the effect of this new technology on the ppf.
e. Suppose that before the new technology is introduced, the nation produces 22 ovens. After the new technology is

*Note: Problems marked with an asterisk are more challenging.

introduced, the nation produces 30 ovens. What is the effect of the new technology on the production of bread? (Give the number of loaves before and after the change.)

10. **[Related to the *Economics in Practice* on p. 28]** An analysis of a large-scale survey of consumer food purchases by Mark Aguiar and Erik Hurst indicates that retired people spend less *for the same market basket of food* than working people do. Use the concept of opportunity cost to explain this fact.

*11. Dr. Falk is a dentist who performs two basic procedures: filling cavities and whitening teeth. Falk charges $50 per cavity filled, a process that takes him 15 minutes per tooth and requires no help or materials. For tooth whitening, a process requiring 30 minutes, Falk charges $150 net of materials. Again, no help is required. Is anything puzzling about Falk's pricing pattern? Explain your answer.

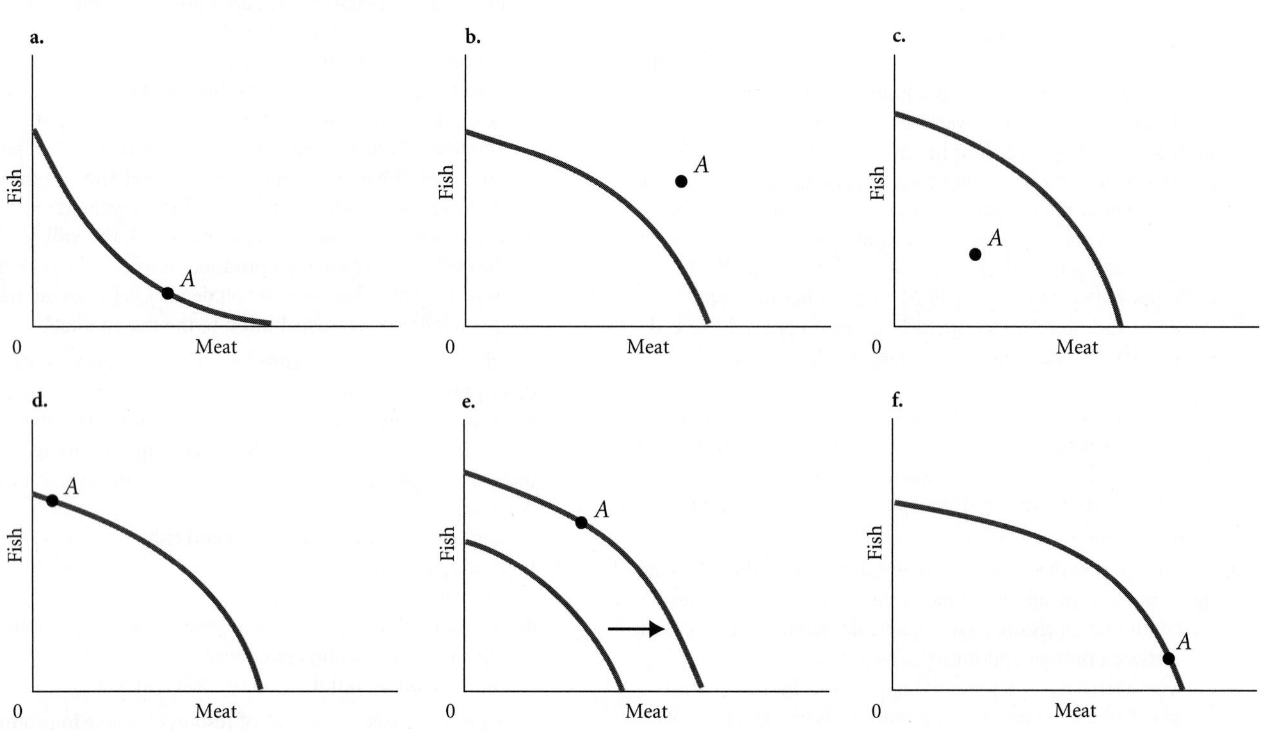

▲ FIGURE 1

Demand, Supply, and Market Equilibrium

3

CHAPTER OUTLINE

Chapters 1 and 2 introduced the discipline, methodology, and subject matter of economics. We now begin the task of analyzing how a market economy actually works. This chapter and the next present an overview of the way individual markets work. They introduce some of the concepts needed to understand both microeconomics and macroeconomics.

As we proceed to define terms and make assumptions, it is important to keep in mind what we are doing. In Chapter 1 we explained what economic theory attempts to do. Theories are abstract representations of reality, like a map that represents a city. We believe that the models presented here will help you understand the workings of the economy just as a map helps you find your way around a city. Just as a map presents one view of the world, so too does any given theory of the economy. Alternatives exist to the theory that we present. We believe, however, that the basic model presented here, while sometimes abstract, is useful in gaining an understanding of how the economy works.

In the simple island society discussed in Chapter 2, Bill and Colleen solved the economic problem directly. They allocated their time and used the island's resources to satisfy their wants. Bill might be a farmer, Colleen a hunter and carpenter. He might be a civil engineer, she a doctor. Exchange occurred, but complex markets were not necessary.

In societies of many people, however, production must satisfy wide-ranging tastes and preferences. Producers therefore specialize. Farmers produce more food than they can eat so that they can sell it to buy manufactured goods. Physicians are paid for specialized services, as are attorneys, construction workers, and editors. When there is specialization, there must be exchange, and *markets* are the institutions through which exchange takes place.

This chapter begins to explore the basic forces at work in market systems. The purpose of our discussion is to explain how the individual decisions of households and firms together, without any central planning or direction, answer the three basic questions: What gets produced? How is it produced? Who gets what is produced? We begin with some definitions.

Firms and Households: The Basic Decision-Making Units

Throughout this book, we discuss and analyze the behavior of two fundamental decision-making units: *firms*—the primary producing units in an economy—and *households*—the consuming units in an economy. Both are made up of people performing different functions and playing different roles. In essence, what we are developing is a theory of human behavior.

firm An organization that transforms resources (inputs) into products (outputs). Firms are the primary producing units in a market economy.

A **firm** exists when a person or a group of people decides to produce a product or products by transforming *inputs*—that is, resources in the broadest sense—into *outputs*, the products that are sold in the market. Some firms produce goods; others produce services. Some are large, many are small, and some are in between. All firms exist to transform resources into goods and services that people want. The Colorado Symphony Orchestra takes labor, land, a building, musically talented people, instruments, and other inputs and combines them to produce concerts. The production process can be extremely complicated. For example, the first flautist in the orchestra uses training, talent, previous performance experience, score, instrument, conductor's interpretation, and personal feelings about the music to produce just one contribution to an overall performance.

Most firms exist to make a profit for their owners, but some do not. Columbia University, for example, fits the description of a firm: It takes inputs in the form of labor, land, skills, books, and buildings and produces a service that we call education. Although the university sells that service for a price, it does not exist to make a profit; instead, it exists to provide education of the highest quality possible.

Still, most firms exist to make a profit. They engage in production because they can sell their product for more than it costs to produce it. The analysis of a firm's behavior that follows rests on the assumption that *firms make decisions in order to maximize profits.*

entrepreneur A person who organizes, manages, and assumes the risks of a firm, taking a new idea or a new product and turning it into a successful business.

An **entrepreneur** is a person who organizes, manages, and assumes the risks of a firm. When a new firm is created, someone must organize the new firm, arrange financing, hire employees, and take risks. That person is an entrepreneur. Sometimes existing firms introduce new products, and sometimes new firms develop or improve on an old idea, but at the root of it all is entrepreneurship, which some see as the core of the free enterprise system.

At the heart of the debate about the potential of free enterprise in formerly socialist Eastern Europe is the question of entrepreneurship. Does an entrepreneurial spirit exist in that part of the world? If not, can it be developed? Without it, the free enterprise system breaks down.

households The consuming units in an economy.

The consuming units in an economy are **households**. A household may consist of any number of people: a single person living alone, a married couple with four children, or 15 unrelated people sharing a house. Household decisions are presumably based on individual tastes and preferences. The household buys what it wants and can afford. In a large, heterogeneous, and open society such as the United States, wildly different tastes find expression in the marketplace. A six-block walk in any direction on any street in Manhattan or a drive from the Chicago Loop south into rural Illinois should be enough to convince someone that it is difficult to generalize about what people do and do not like.

Even though households have wide-ranging preferences, they also have some things in common. All—even the very rich—have ultimately limited incomes, and all must pay in some way for the goods and services that they consume. Although households may have some control over their incomes—they can work more hours or fewer hours—they are also constrained by the availability of jobs, current wages, their own abilities, and their accumulated and inherited wealth (or lack thereof).

Input Markets and Output Markets: The Circular Flow

product *or* output markets The markets in which goods and services are exchanged.

input *or* factor markets The markets in which the resources used to produce goods and services are exchanged.

Households and firms interact in two basic kinds of markets: product (or output) markets and input (or factor) markets. Goods and services that are intended for use by households are exchanged in **product *or* output markets**. In output markets, firms *supply* and households *demand.*

To produce goods and services, firms must buy resources in **input *or* factor markets**. Firms buy inputs from households, which supply these inputs. When a firm decides how much to produce (supply) in output markets, it must simultaneously decide how much of each input it needs to produce the desired level of output. To produce automobiles, Ford Motor Company must use many inputs, including tires, steel, complicated machinery, and many different kinds of labor.

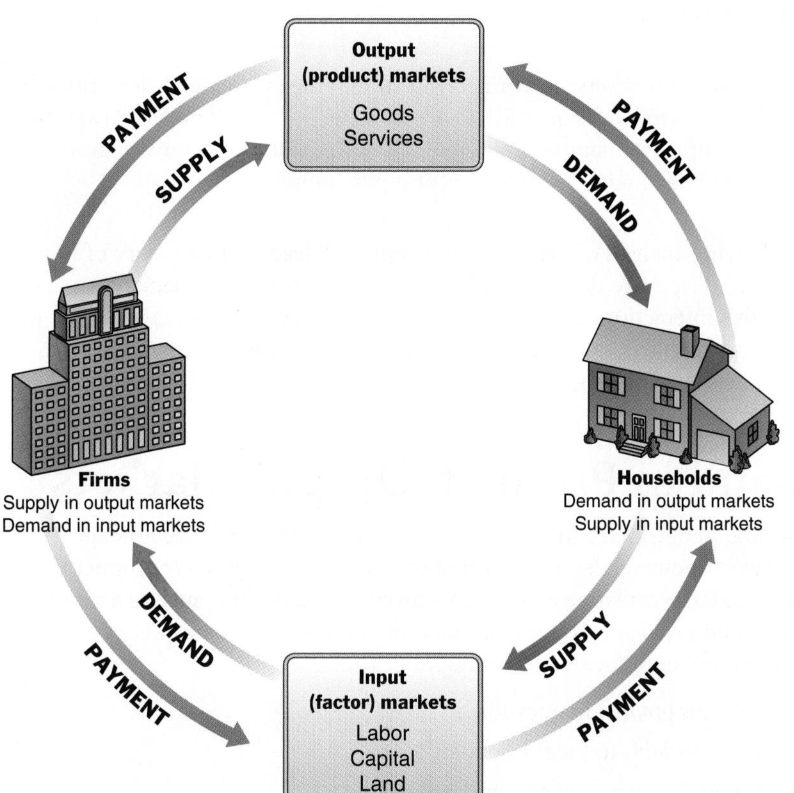

FIGURE 3.1 The Circular Flow of Economic Activity
Diagrams like this one show the circular flow of economic activity, hence the name *circular flow diagram*. Here goods and services flow clockwise: Labor services supplied by households flow to firms, and goods and services produced by firms flow to households. Payment (usually money) flows in the opposite (counterclockwise) direction: Payment for goods and services flows from households to firms, and payment for labor services flows from firms to households.

Note: Color Guide—In Figure 3.1 households are depicted in *blue* and firms are depicted in *red*. From now on all diagrams relating to the behavior of households will be blue or shades of blue and all diagrams relating to the behavior of firms will be red or shades of red.

Figure 3.1 shows the *circular flow* of economic activity through a simple market economy. Note that the flow reflects the direction in which goods and services flow through input and output markets. For example, goods and services flow from firms to households through output markets. Labor services flow from households to firms through input markets. Payment (most often in money form) for goods and services flows in the opposite direction.

In input markets, households *supply* resources. Most households earn their incomes by working—they supply their labor in the **labor market** to firms that demand labor and pay workers for their time and skills. Households may also loan their accumulated or inherited savings to firms for interest or exchange those savings for claims to future profits, as when a household buys shares of stock in a corporation. In the **capital market**, households supply the funds that firms use to buy capital goods. Households may also supply land or other real property in exchange for rent in the **land market.**

labor market The input/factor market in which households supply work for wages to firms that demand labor.

capital market The input/factor market in which households supply their savings, for interest or for claims to future profits, to firms that demand funds to buy capital goods.

land market The input/factor market in which households supply land or other real property in exchange for rent.

Inputs into the production process are also called **factors of production**. Land, labor, and capital are the three key factors of production. Throughout this text, we use the terms *input* and *factor of production* interchangeably. Thus, input markets and factor markets mean the same thing.

factors of production The inputs into the production process. Land, labor, and capital are the three key factors of production.

Early economics texts included entrepreneurship as a type of input, just like land, labor, and capital. Treating entrepreneurship as a separate factor of production has fallen out of favor, however, partially because it is unmeasurable. Most economists today implicitly assume that entrepreneurship is in plentiful supply. That is, if profit opportunities exist, it is likely that entrepreneurs will crop up to take advantage of them. This assumption has turned out to be a good predictor of actual economic behavior and performance.

The supply of inputs and their prices ultimately determine household income. Thus, the amount of income a household earns depends on the decisions it makes concerning what types of inputs it chooses to supply. Whether to stay in school, how much and what kind of training to get, whether to start a business, how many hours to work, whether to work at all, and how to invest savings are all household decisions that affect income.

As you can see:

Input and output markets are connected through the behavior of both firms and households. Firms determine the quantities and character of outputs produced and the types and quantities of inputs demanded. Households determine the types and quantities of products demanded and the quantities and types of inputs supplied.[1]

The following analysis of demand and supply will lead up to a theory of how market prices are determined. Prices are determined by the interaction between demanders and suppliers. To understand this interaction, we first need to know how product prices influence the behavior of demanders and suppliers *separately*. Therefore, we discuss output markets by focusing first on demanders, then on suppliers, and finally on their interaction.

Demand in Product/Output Markets

In real life, households make many decisions at the same time. To see how the forces of demand and supply work, however, let us focus first on the amount of a *single* product that an *individual* household decides to consume within some given period of time, such as a month or a year.

A household's decision about what quantity of a particular output, or product, to demand depends on a number of factors, including:

- The *price of the product* in question.
- The *income available* to the household.
- The household's *amount of accumulated wealth.*
- The *prices of other products* available to the household.
- The household's *tastes and preferences.*
- The household's *expectations* about future income, wealth, and prices.

quantity demanded The amount (number of units) of a product that a household would buy in a given period if it could buy all it wanted at the current market price.

Quantity demanded is the amount (number of units) of a product that a household would buy in a given period *if it could buy all it wanted at the current market price.* Of course, the amount of a product that households finally purchase depends on the amount of product actually available in the market. The expression *if it could buy all it wanted* is critical to the definition of quantity demanded because it allows for the possibility that quantity supplied and quantity demanded are unequal.

Changes in Quantity Demanded versus Changes in Demand

The most important relationship in individual markets is that between market price and quantity demanded. For this reason, we need to begin our discussion by analyzing the likely response of households to changes in price using the device of *ceteris paribus*, or "all else equal." That is, we will attempt to derive a relationship between the quantity demanded of a good per time period and the price of that good, holding income, wealth, other prices, tastes, and expectations constant.

It is very important to distinguish between price changes, which affect the quantity of a good demanded, and changes in other factors (such as income), which change the entire relationship between price and quantity. For example, if a family begins earning a higher income, it might buy more of a good at every possible price. To be sure that we distinguish between changes in price

[1] Our description of markets begins with the behavior of firms and households. Modern orthodox economic theory essentially combines two distinct but closely related theories of behavior. The "theory of household behavior," or "consumer behavior," has its roots in the works of nineteenth century utilitarians such as Jeremy Bentham, William Jevons, Carl Menger, Leon Walras, Vilfredo Parcto, and F. Y. Edgeworth. The "theory of the firm" developed out of the earlier classical political economy of Adam Smith, David Ricardo, and Thomas Malthus. In 1890, Alfred Marshall published the first of many editions of his *Principles of Economics*. That volume pulled together the main themes of both the classical economists and the utilitarians into what is now called *neoclassical economics*. While there have been many changes over the years, the basic structure of the model that we build can be found in Marshall's work.

and other changes that affect demand, throughout the rest of the text, we will be very precise about terminology. Specifically:

> Changes in the price of a product affect the *quantity demanded* per period. Changes in any other factor, such as income or preferences, affect *demand*. Thus, we say that an increase in the price of Coca-Cola is likely to cause a decrease in the *quantity of Coca-Cola demanded.* However, we say that an increase in income is likely to cause an increase in the *demand* for most goods.

Price and Quantity Demanded: The Law of Demand

A **demand schedule** shows the quantities of a product that a household would be willing to buy at different prices. Table 3.1 presents a hypothetical demand schedule for Anna, a student who goes off to college to study economics while her boyfriend goes to art school. If telephone calls were free (a price of zero), Anna would call her boyfriend every day, or 30 times a month. At a price of $0.50 per call, she makes 25 calls a month. When the price hits $3.50, she cuts back to seven calls a month. This same information presented graphically is called a **demand curve**. Anna's demand curve is presented in Figure 3.2.

demand schedule A table showing how much of a given product a household would be willing to buy at different prices.

demand curve A graph illustrating how much of a given product a household would be willing to buy at different prices.

You will note in Figure 3.2 that *quantity* (q) is measured along the horizontal axis and *price* (P) is measured along the vertical axis. This is the convention we follow throughout this book.

TABLE 3.1 Anna's Demand Schedule for Telephone Calls

Price (Per Call)	Quantity Demanded (Calls Per Month)
$ 0.00	30
0.50	25
3.50	7
7.00	3
10.00	1
15.00	0

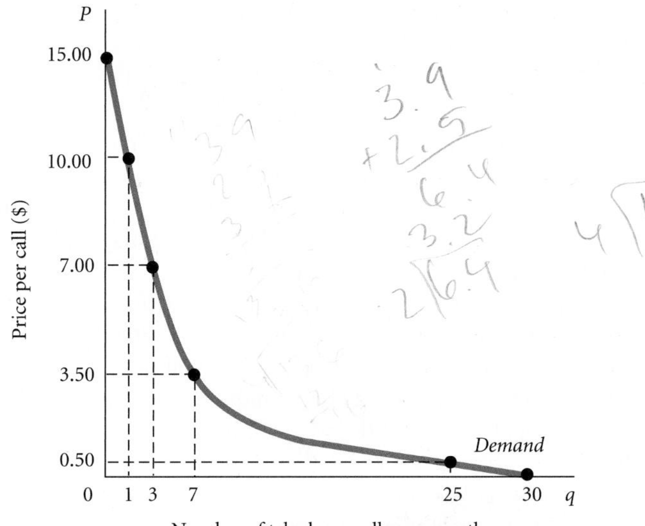

FIGURE 3.2 Anna's Demand Curve
The relationship between price (P) and quantity demanded (q) presented graphically is called a demand curve. Demand curves have a negative slope, indicating that lower prices cause quantity demanded to increase. Note that Anna's demand curve is blue; demand in product markets is determined by household choice.

Demand Curves Slope Downward The data in Table 3.1 show that at lower prices, Anna calls her boyfriend more frequently; at higher prices, she calls less frequently. Thus, there is a *negative, or inverse, relationship between quantity demanded and price.* When price rises, quantity demanded falls, and when price falls, quantity demanded rises. Thus, demand curves always slope downward. This negative relationship between price and quantity demanded is often referred to as the **law of demand**, a term first used by economist Alfred Marshall in his 1890 textbook.

law of demand The negative relationship between price and quantity demanded: As price rises, quantity demanded decreases; as price falls, quantity demanded increases.

Some people are put off by the abstraction of demand curves. Of course, we do not actually draw our own demand curves for products. When we want to make a purchase, we usually face only a single price and how much we would buy at other prices is irrelevant. However, demand curves help analysts understand the kind of behavior that households are *likely* to exhibit if they are actually faced with a higher or lower price. We know, for example, that if the price of a good rises enough, the quantity demanded must ultimately drop to zero. The demand curve is thus a tool that helps us explain economic behavior and predict reactions to possible price changes.

Marshall's definition of a social "law" captures the idea:

> The term "law" means nothing more than a general proposition or statement of tendencies, more or less certain, more or less definite . . . a *social law* is a statement of social tendencies; that is, that a certain course of action may be expected from the members of a social group under certain conditions.[2]

It seems reasonable to expect that consumers will demand more of a product at a lower price and less of it at a higher price. Households must divide their incomes over a wide range of goods and services. If you spend $4.50 for a pound of prime beef, you are sacrificing the other things that you might have bought with that $4.50. If the price of prime beef were to jump to $7 per pound while chicken breasts remained at $1.99 (remember *ceteris paribus*—we are holding all else constant), you would have to give up more chicken and/or other items to buy that pound of beef. So you would probably eat more chicken and less beef. Anna calls her boyfriend three times when phone calls cost $7 each. A fourth call would mean sacrificing $7 worth of other purchases. At a price of $3.50, however, the opportunity cost of each call is lower and she calls more frequently.

Another explanation for the fact that demand curves slope downward rests on the notion of *utility*. Economists use the concept of *utility* to mean happiness or satisfaction. Presumably, we consume goods and services because they give us utility. As we consume more of a product within a given period of time, it is likely that each additional unit consumed will yield successively less satisfaction. The utility you gain from a second ice cream cone is likely to be less than the utility you gained from the first, the third is worth even less, and so on. This *law of diminishing marginal utility* is an important concept in economics. If each successive unit of a good is worth less to you, you are not going to be willing to pay as much for it. Thus, it is reasonable to expect a downward slope in the demand curve for that good.

The idea of diminishing marginal utility also helps to explain Anna's behavior. The demand curve is a way of representing what she is willing to pay per phone call. At a price of $7, she calls her boyfriend three times per month. A fourth call, however, is worth less than the third—that is, the fourth call is worth less than $7 to her—so she stops at three. If the price were only $3.50, however, she would continue calling. Even at $3.50, she would stop at seven calls per month. This behavior reveals that the eighth call has less value to Anna than the seventh.

Thinking about the ways that people are affected by price changes also helps us see what is behind the law of demand. Consider this example: Luis lives and works in Mexico City. His elderly mother lives in Santiago, Chile. Last year the airlines servicing South America got into a price war, and the price of flying between Mexico City and Santiago dropped from 20,000 pesos to 10,000 pesos. How might Luis's behavior change?

First, he is better off. Last year he flew home to Chile three times at a total cost of 60,000 pesos. This year he can fly to Chile the same number of times, buy exactly the same combination of other goods and services that he bought last year, and have 30,000 pesos left over. Because he is better off—his income can buy more—he may fly home more frequently. Second, the opportunity cost of flying home has changed. Before the price war, Luis had to sacrifice 20,000 pesos worth of other goods and services each time he flew to Chile. After the price war, he must sacrifice only 10,000 pesos worth of other goods and services for each trip. The trade-off has changed. Both of these effects are likely to lead to a higher quantity demanded in response to the lower price.

In sum:

> It is reasonable to expect quantity demanded to fall when price rises, *ceteris paribus*, and to expect quantity demanded to rise when price falls, *ceteris paribus*. Demand curves have a negative slope.

[2] Alfred Marshall, *Principles of Economics*, 8th ed. (New York: Macmillan, 1948), p. 33. (The first edition was published in 1890.)

Other Properties of Demand Curves Two additional things are notable about Anna's demand curve. First, it intersects the *Y*-, or price, axis. This means that there is a price above which no calls will be made. In this case, Anna simply stops calling when the price reaches $15 per call. As long as households have limited incomes and wealth, all demand curves will intersect the price axis. For any commodity, there is always a price above which a household will not or cannot pay. Even if the good or service is very important, all households are ultimately constrained, or limited, by income and wealth.

Second, Anna's demand curve intersects the *X*-, or quantity, axis. Even at a zero price, there is a limit to the number of phone calls Anna will make. If telephone calls were free, she would call 30 times a month, but not more. That demand curves intersect the quantity axis is a matter of common sense. Demand in a given period of time is limited, if only by time, even at a zero price.

To summarize what we know about the shape of demand curves:

1. They have a negative slope. An increase in price is likely to lead to a decrease in quantity demanded, and a decrease in price is likely to lead to an increase in quantity demanded.
2. They intersect the quantity (*X*-) axis, a result of time limitations and diminishing marginal utility.
3. They intersect the price (*Y*-) axis, a result of limited income and wealth.

That is all we can say; it is not possible to generalize further. The actual shape of an individual household demand curve—whether it is steep or flat, whether it is bowed in or bowed out—depends on the unique tastes and preferences of the household and other factors. Some households may be very sensitive to price changes; other households may respond little to a change in price. In some cases, plentiful substitutes are available; in other cases, they are not. Thus, to fully understand the shape and position of demand curves, we must turn to the other determinants of household demand.

Other Determinants of Household Demand

Of the many factors likely to influence a household's demand for a specific product, we have considered only the price of the product. Other determining factors include household income and wealth, the prices of other goods and services, tastes and preferences, and expectations.

Income and Wealth Before we proceed, we need to define two terms that are often confused, *income* and *wealth*. A household's **income** is the sum of all the wages, salaries, profits, interest payments, rents, and other forms of earnings received by the household *in a given period of time*. Income is thus a *flow* measure: We must specify a time period for it—income *per month* or *per year*. You can spend or consume more or less than your income in any given period. If you consume less than your income, you save. To consume more than your income in a period, you must either borrow or draw on savings accumulated from previous periods.

income The sum of all a household's wages, salaries, profits, interest payments, rents, and other forms of earnings in a given period of time. It is a flow measure.

Wealth is the total value of what a household owns minus what it owes. Another word for wealth is **net worth**—the amount a household would have left if it sold all of its possessions and paid all of its debts. Wealth is a *stock* measure: It is measured at a given point in time. If, in a given period, you spend less than your income, you save; the amount that you save is added to your wealth. Saving is the flow that affects the stock of wealth. When you spend more than your income, you *dissave*—you reduce your wealth.

wealth *or* net worth The total value of what a household owns minus what it owes. It is a stock measure.

Households with higher incomes and higher accumulated savings or inherited wealth can afford to buy more goods and services. In general, we would expect higher demand at higher levels of income/wealth and lower demand at lower levels of income/wealth. Goods for which demand goes up when income is higher and for which demand goes down when income is lower are called **normal goods**. Movie tickets, restaurant meals, telephone calls, and shirts are all normal goods.

normal goods Goods for which demand goes up when income is higher and for which demand goes down when income is lower.

However, generalization in economics can be hazardous. Sometimes demand for a good falls when household income rises. Consider, for example, the various qualities of meat available. When a household's income rises, it is likely to buy higher-quality meats—its demand for filet mignon is likely to rise—but its demand for lower-quality meats—chuck steak, for example—is likely to fall. Transportation is another example. At higher incomes, people can afford to fly. People who can afford to fly are less likely to take the bus long distances. Thus, higher income may *reduce* the number of times someone takes a bus. Goods for which demand tends to fall when income rises are called **inferior goods**.

inferior goods Goods for which demand tends to fall when income rises.

Prices of Other Goods and Services No consumer decides in isolation on the amount of any one commodity to buy. Instead, each decision is part of a larger set of decisions that are made simultaneously. Households must apportion their incomes over many different goods and services. As a result, the price of any one good can and does affect the demand for other goods.

This is most obviously the case when goods are substitutes for one another. To return to our lonesome first-year student: If the price of a telephone call rises to $10, Anna will call her boyfriend only once a month. (See Table 3.1 on p. 49.) Of course, she can get in touch with him in other ways. Presumably she substitutes some other, less costly form of communication, such as writing more letters or sending more e-mails.

When an *increase* in the price of one good causes demand for another good to *increase* (a positive relationship), we say that the goods are **substitutes.** A *fall* in the price of a good causes a *decline* in demand for its substitutes. Substitutes are goods that can serve as replacements for one another.

substitutes Goods that can serve as replacements for one another; when the price of one increases, demand for the other increases.

perfect substitutes Identical products.

To be substitutes, two products do not need to be identical. Identical products are called **perfect substitutes.** Japanese cars are not identical to American cars. Nonetheless, all have four wheels, are capable of carrying people, and run on gasoline. Thus, significant changes in the price of one country's cars can be expected to influence demand for the other country's cars. Restaurant meals are substitutes for meals eaten at home, and flying from New York to Washington, D.C., is a substitute for taking the train.

Often two products "go together"—that is, they complement each other. Our lonesome letter writer, for example, will find her demand for stamps and stationery rising as she writes more letters and her demand for Internet access rising as she sends more e-mails. Bacon and eggs are **complementary goods**, as are cars and gasoline, and cameras and film. When two goods are **complements**, a *decrease* in the price of one results in an *increase* in demand for the other and vice versa. In mid-2007, Microsoft coordinated the release of its wildly popular game *Halo 3* for the Xbox 360 with the introduction of its new, improved wireless headset because Microsoft understood that the game was a complement to the headset and would thus increase the demand for that product.

complements, complementary goods Goods that "go together"; a decrease in the price of one results in an increase in demand for the other and vice versa.

Because any one good may have many potential substitutes and complements at the same time, a single price change may affect a household's demands for many goods simultaneously; the demand for some of these products may rise while the demand for others may fall. For example, consider the compact disc read-only memory (CD-ROM). Massive amounts of data can be stored digitally on CDs that can be read by personal computers with a CD-ROM drive. When these drives first came on the market, they were quite expensive, selling for several hundred dollars each. Now they are much less expensive, and most new computers have them built in. As a result, the demand for CD-ROM discs (complementary goods) has soared. As more students adopted the CD technology and the price of CDs and CD hardware fell, fewer students bought printed reference books such as encyclopedias and dictionaries (substitute goods).

Tastes and Preferences Income, wealth, and prices of goods available are the three factors that determine the combinations of goods and services that a household is *able* to buy. You know that you cannot afford to rent an apartment at $1,200 per month if your monthly income is only $400, but within these constraints, you are more or less free to choose what to buy. Your final choice depends on your individual tastes and preferences.

Changes in preferences can and do manifest themselves in market behavior. Thirty years ago the major big-city marathons drew only a few hundred runners. Now tens of thousands enter and run. The demand for running shoes, running suits, stopwatches, and other running items has greatly increased. For many years, people drank soda for refreshment. Today convenience stores are filled with a dizzying array of iced teas, fruit juices, natural beverages, and mineral waters.

Within the constraints of prices and incomes, preference shapes the demand curve, but it is difficult to generalize about tastes and preferences. First, they are volatile: Five years ago more people smoked cigarettes and fewer people had computers. Second, tastes are idiosyncratic: Some people like to talk on the telephone, whereas others prefer to use e-mail; some people prefer dogs, whereas others are crazy about cats; some people like chicken wings, whereas others prefer drumsticks. The diversity of individual demands is almost infinite.

One of the interesting questions in economics is why, in some markets, diverse consumer tastes give rise to a variety of styles, while in other markets, despite a seeming diversity in tastes, we find only one or two varieties. All sidewalks in the United States are a similar gray color, yet houses are painted a rainbow of colors. Yet it is not obvious on the face of it that people would not prefer as much variety in their sidewalks as in their houses. To answer this type of question, we need to move beyond the demand curve. We will revisit this question in a later chapter.

Expectations What you decide to buy today certainly depends on today's prices and your current income and wealth. You also have expectations about what your position will be in the future. You may have expectations about future changes in prices too, and these may affect your decisions today.

There are many examples of the ways expectations affect demand. When people buy a house or a car, they often must borrow part of the purchase price and repay it over a number of years. In deciding what kind of house or car to buy, they presumably must think about their income today, as well as what their income is likely to be in the future.

As another example, consider a student in the final year of medical school living on a scholarship of $12,000. Compare that student with another person earning $6 an hour at a full-time job, with no expectation of a significant change in income in the future. The two have virtually identical incomes because there are about 2,000 working hours in a year (40 hours per week × 50 work weeks per year). But even if they have the same tastes, the medical student is likely to demand different goods and services, simply because of the expectation of a major increase in income later on.

Increasingly, economic theory has come to recognize the importance of expectations. We will devote a good deal of time to discussing how expectations affect more than just demand. For the time being, however, it is important to understand that demand depends on more than just *current* incomes, prices, and tastes.

Shift of Demand versus Movement Along a Demand Curve

Recall that a demand curve shows the relationship between quantity demanded and the price of a good. Demand curves are derived while holding income, tastes, and other prices constant. If income, tastes, or other prices change, we would have to derive an entirely new relationship between price and quantity.

Let us return once again to Anna. (See Table 3.1 and Figure 3.2 on p. 49.) Suppose that when we derived the demand schedule in Table 3.1, Anna had a part-time job that paid $300 per month. Now suppose that her parents inherit some money and begin sending her an additional $300 per month. Assuming that she keeps her job, Anna's income is now $600 per month.

With her higher income, Anna would probably call her boyfriend more frequently, regardless of the price of a call. Table 3.2 and Figure 3.3 present Anna's original income schedule (D_0) and increased income demand schedule (D_1). Our models tell us that with a higher income, Anna likely makes more calls at each price level. In Table 3.2, we have drawn an example that illustrates this pattern. At $0.50 per call, the frequency of her calls (the quantity she demands) increases from 25 to 33 calls per month; at $3.50 per call, frequency increases from 7 to 18 calls per month; at $10.00 per call, frequency increases from 1 to 7 calls per month. (Note in Figure 3.3 that even if calls are free, Anna's income matters; at zero price, her demand increases. With a higher income, she may visit her boyfriend more, for example, and more visits might mean more phone calls to organize and plan.)

The fact that demand *increased* when income increased implies that telephone calls are *normal goods* to Anna.

The conditions that were in place at the time we drew the original demand curve have now changed. In other words, a factor that affects Anna's demand for telephone calls (in this case, her income) has changed, and there is now a new relationship between price and quantity demanded. Such a change is referred to as a **shift of a demand curve.**

shift of a demand curve The change that takes place in a demand curve corresponding to a new relationship between quantity demanded of a good and price of that good. The shift is brought about by a change in the original conditions.

It is very important to distinguish between a change in quantity demanded—that is, some movement *along* a demand curve—and a shift of demand. Demand schedules and demand curves show the relationship between the price of a good or service and the quantity demanded per period, *ceteris paribus.* If price changes, quantity demanded will change—this is a

TABLE 3.2 Shift of Anna's Demand Schedule Due to Increase in Income

	Schedule D_0	Schedule D_1
Price (Per Call)	Quantity Demanded (Calls per Month at an Income of $300 per Month)	Quantity Demanded (Calls per Month at an Income of $600 per Month)
$ 0.00	30	35
0.50	25	33
3.50	7	18
7.00	3	12
10.00	1	7
15.00	0	2
20.00	0	0

movement along a demand curve The change in quantity demanded brought about by a change in price.

movement along a demand curve. When any of the *other* factors that influence demand change, however, a new relationship between price and quantity demanded is established—this is a *shift of a demand curve.* The result, then, is a *new* demand curve. Changes in income, preferences, or prices of other goods cause a demand curve to shift:

Change in price of a good or service leads to
→ Change in *quantity demanded* (**movement along a demand curve**).

Change in income, preferences, or prices of other goods or services leads to
→ Change in *demand* (**shift of a demand curve**).

Figure 3.4 illustrates the differences between movement along a demand curve and shifting demand curves. In Figure 3.4(a), an increase in household income causes demand for hamburger (an inferior good) to decline, or shift to the left from D_0 to D_1. (Because quantity is measured on the horizontal axis, a decrease means a *shift to the left.*) In contrast, demand for steak (a normal good) increases, or *shifts to the right,* when income rises.

In Figure 3.4(b), an increase in the price of hamburger from $1.49 to $3.09 a pound causes a household to buy less hamburger each month. In other words, the higher price causes the *quantity demanded* to decline from 10 pounds to 5 pounds per month. This change represents a movement *along* the demand curve for hamburger. In place of hamburger, the household buys more chicken. The household's demand for chicken (a substitute for hamburger) rises—the demand curve shifts to the right. At the same time, the demand for ketchup (a good that complements hamburger) declines—its demand curve shifts to the left.

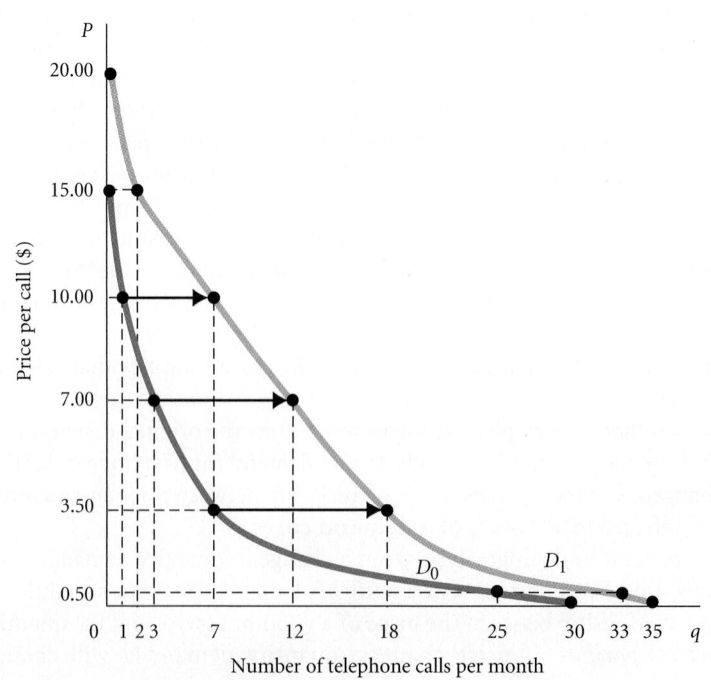

FIGURE 3.3 Shift of a Demand Curve Following a Rise in Income

When the price of a good changes, we move *along* the demand curve for that good. When any other factor that influences demand changes (income, tastes, and so on), the relationship between price and quantity is different; there is a *shift* of the demand curve, in this case from D_0 to D_1. Telephone calls are normal goods.

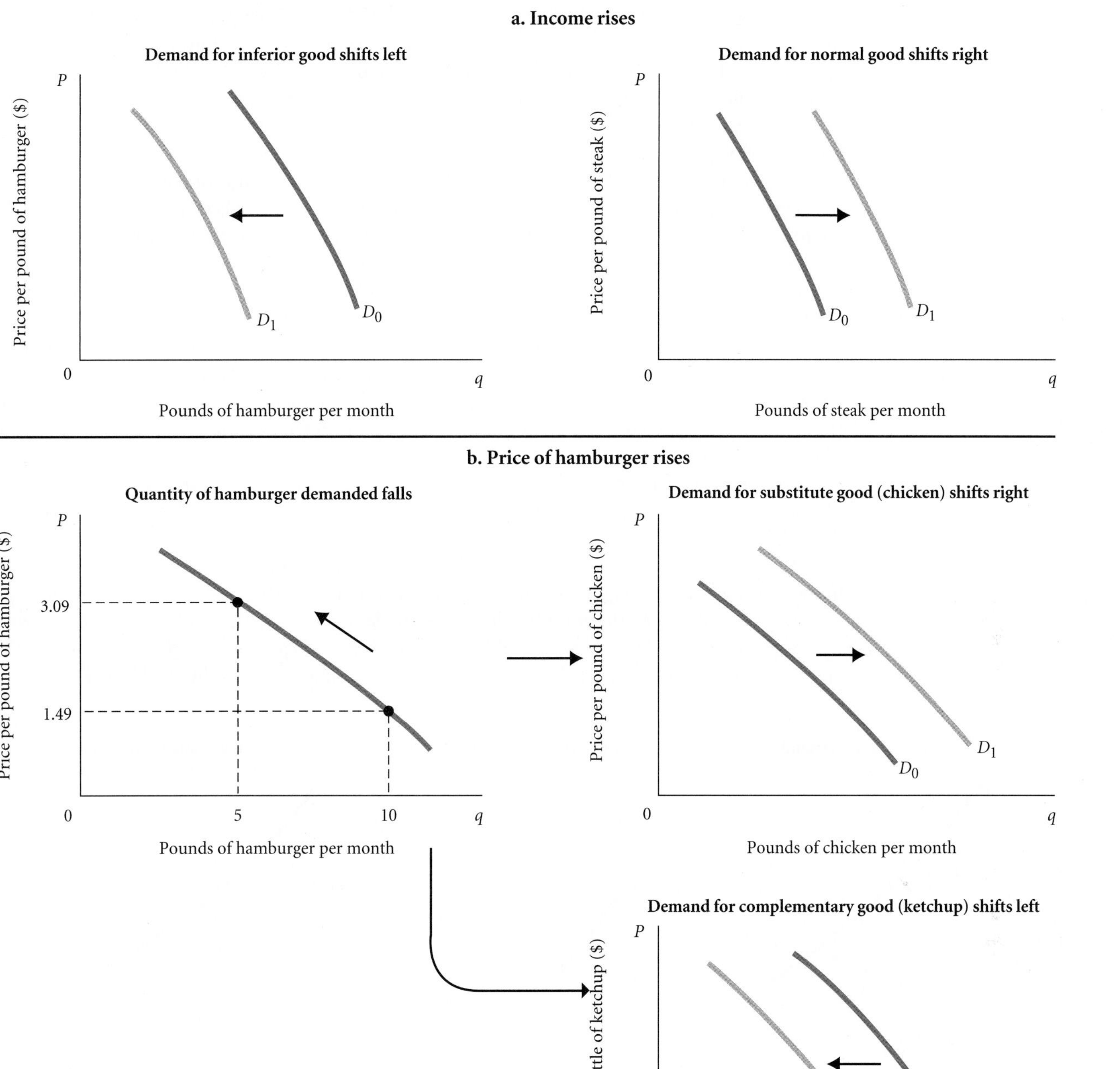

▲ **FIGURE 3.4 Shifts versus Movement Along a Demand Curve**
a. When income increases, the demand for inferior goods *shifts to the left* and the demand for normal goods *shifts to the right*. **b.** If the price of hamburger rises, the quantity of hamburger demanded declines—this is a movement along the demand curve. The same price rise for hamburger would shift the demand for chicken (a substitute for hamburger) to the right and the demand for ketchup (a complement to hamburger) to the left.

From Household Demand to Market Demand

market demand The sum of all the quantities of a good or service demanded per period by all the households buying in the market for that good or service.

Market demand is simply the sum of all the quantities of a good or service demanded per period by all the households buying in the market for that good or service. Figure 3.5 shows the derivation of a market demand curve from three individual demand curves. (Although this market demand curve is derived from the behavior of only three people, most markets have thousands, or even millions of demanders.) As the table in Figure 3.5 shows, when the price of a pound of coffee is $3.50, both household A and household C would purchase 4 pounds per month, while household B would buy none. At that price, presumably, B drinks tea. Market demand at $3.50 would thus be a total of 4 + 4, or 8 pounds. At a price of $1.50 per pound, however, A would purchase 8 pounds per month; B, 3 pounds; and C, 9 pounds. Thus, at $1.50 per pound, market demand would be 8 + 3 + 9, or 20 pounds of coffee per month.

The total quantity demanded in the marketplace at a given price is simply the sum of all the quantities demanded by all the individual households shopping in the market *at that price.* A market demand curve shows the total amount of a product that would be sold at each price if households could buy all they wanted at that price. As Figure 3.5 shows, the market demand curve is the sum of all the individual demand curves—that is, the sum of all the individual quantities demanded at each price. Thus, the market demand curve takes its shape and position from the shapes, positions, and number of individual demand curves. If more people decide to shop in a market, more demand curves must be added and the market demand curve will shift to the right. Market demand curves may also shift as a result of preference changes, income changes, or changes in the number of demanders.

An interesting fact about the market demand curve in Figure 3.5 is that at different prices, not only the number of people demanding the product may change but also the *type* of people demanding the product. When Apple halved the price of its iPhone in fall 2007, it announced that it wanted to make the iPhone available to a broader group of people. When prices fall, people like those in household B in Figure 3.5 move into markets that are otherwise out of their reach.

As a general rule throughout this book, capital letters refer to the entire market and lowercase letters refer to individual households or firms. Thus, in Figure 3.5, Q refers to total quantity demanded in the market, while q refers to the quantity demanded by individual households.

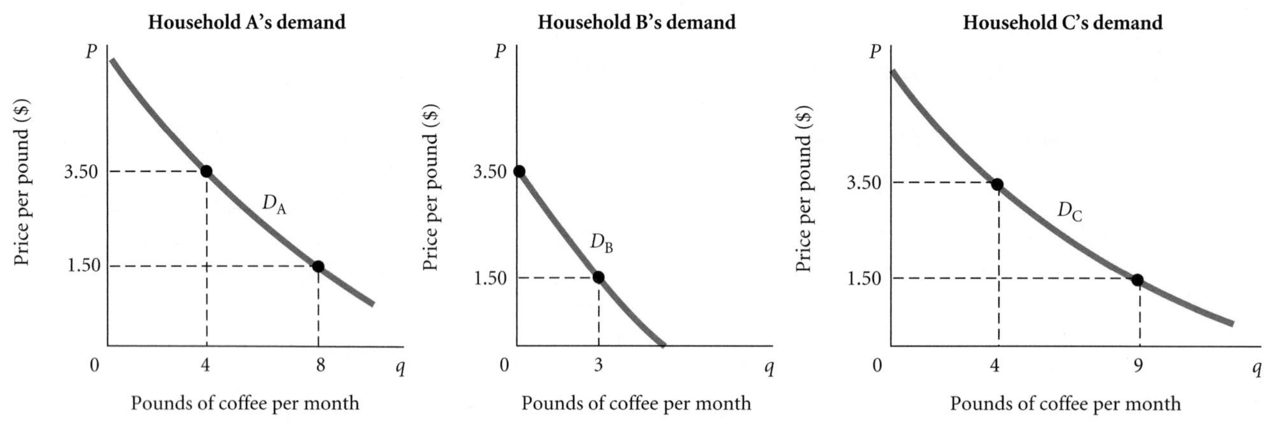

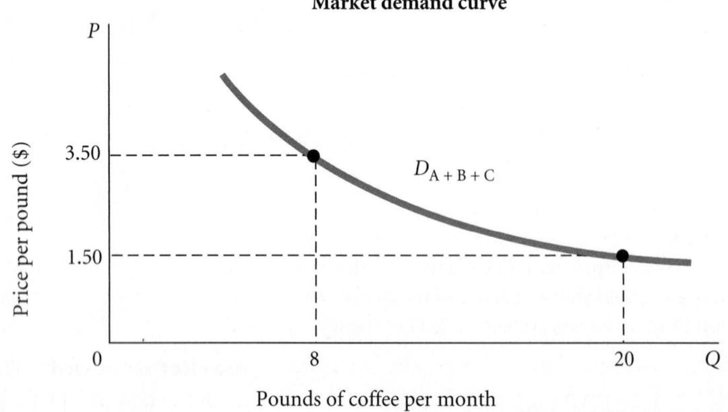

Price	Quantity (q) Demanded by A	B	C	Total Quantity Demanded in the Market (Q)
$3.50	4 +	0 +	4	= 8
1.50	8 +	3 +	9	= 20

▲ **FIGURE 3.5 Deriving Market Demand from Individual Demand Curves**
Total demand in the marketplace is simply the sum of the demands of all the households shopping in a particular market. It is the sum of all the individual demand curves—that is, the sum of all the individual quantities demanded at each price.

Supply in Product/Output Markets

In addition to dealing with household demands for outputs, economic theory deals with the behavior of business firms, which supply in output markets and demand in input markets. (See Figure 3.1 on p. 47 again.) Firms engage in production, and we assume that they do so for profit. Successful firms make profits because they are able to sell their products for more than it costs to produce them.

Thus, supply decisions can be expected to depend on profit potential. Because **profit** is the difference between revenues and costs, supply is likely to react to changes in revenues and changes in production costs. The amount of revenue that a firm earns depends on what the price of its product in the market is and on how much it sells. Costs of production depend on many factors, the most important of which are (1) the kinds of inputs needed to produce the product, (2) the amount of each input required, and (3) the prices of inputs.

profit The difference between revenues and costs.

The supply decision is just one of several decisions that firms make to maximize profit. There are usually a number of ways to produce any given product. A golf course can be built by hundreds of workers with shovels and grass seed or by a few workers with heavy earth-moving equipment and sod blankets. Hamburgers can be fried individually by a short-order cook or grilled by the hundreds on a mechanized moving grill. Firms must choose the production technique most appropriate to their products and projected levels of production. The best method of production is the one that minimizes cost, thus maximizing profit.

Which production technique is best, in turn, depends on the prices of inputs. Where labor is cheap and machinery is expensive and difficult to transport, firms are likely to choose production techniques that use a great deal of labor. Where machines or resources to produce machines are readily available and labor is scarce or expensive, firms are likely to choose more capital-intensive methods. Obviously, the technique ultimately chosen determines input requirements. Thus, by choosing an output supply target and the most appropriate technology, firms determine which inputs to demand.

With the caution that no decision exists in a vacuum, let us begin our examination of firm behavior by focusing on the output supply decision and the relationship between quantity supplied and output price, *ceteris paribus*.

Price and Quantity Supplied: The Law of Supply

Quantity supplied is the amount of a particular product that firms would be willing and able to offer for sale at a particular price during a given time period. A **supply schedule** shows how much of a product firms will sell at alternative prices.

quantity supplied The amount of a particular product that a firm would be willing and able to offer for sale at a particular price during a given time period.

supply schedule A table showing how much of a product firms will sell at alternative prices.

Let us look at an agricultural market as an example. Table 3.3 itemizes the quantities of soybeans that an individual representative farmer such as Clarence Brown might sell at various prices. If the market paid $1.50 or less for a bushel for soybeans, Brown would not supply any soybeans: When Farmer Brown looks at the costs of growing soybeans, including the opportunity cost of his time and land, $1.50 per bushel will not compensate him for those costs. At $1.75 per bushel, however, at least some soybean production takes place on Brown's farm, and a price increase from $1.75 to $2.25 per bushel causes the quantity supplied by Brown to increase from 10,000 to 20,000 bushels per year. The higher price may justify shifting land from wheat to soybean production or putting previously fallow land into soybeans, or it may lead to more intensive farming of land already in soybeans, using expensive fertilizer or equipment that was not cost-justified at the lower price.

Generalizing from Farmer Brown's experience, we can reasonably expect an increase in market price, *ceteris paribus*, to lead to an increase in quantity supplied for Brown and farmers like him. In other words, there is a positive relationship between the quantity of a good supplied and price. This statement sums up the **law of supply**: An increase in market price will lead to an increase in quantity supplied, and a decrease in market price will lead to a decrease in quantity supplied.

law of supply The positive relationship between price and quantity of a good supplied: An increase in market price will lead to an increase in quantity supplied, and a decrease in market price will lead to a decrease in quantity supplied.

The information in a supply schedule may be presented graphically in a **supply curve**. Supply curves slope upward. The upward, or positive, slope of Brown's curve in Figure 3.6 reflects this positive relationship between price and quantity supplied.

supply curve A graph illustrating how much of a product a firm will sell at different prices.

TABLE 3.3 Clarence Brown's Supply Schedule for Soybeans

Price (Per Bushel)	Quantity Supplied (Bushels Per Year)
$1.50	0
1.75	10,000
2.25	20,000
3.00	30,000
4.00	45,000
5.00	45,000

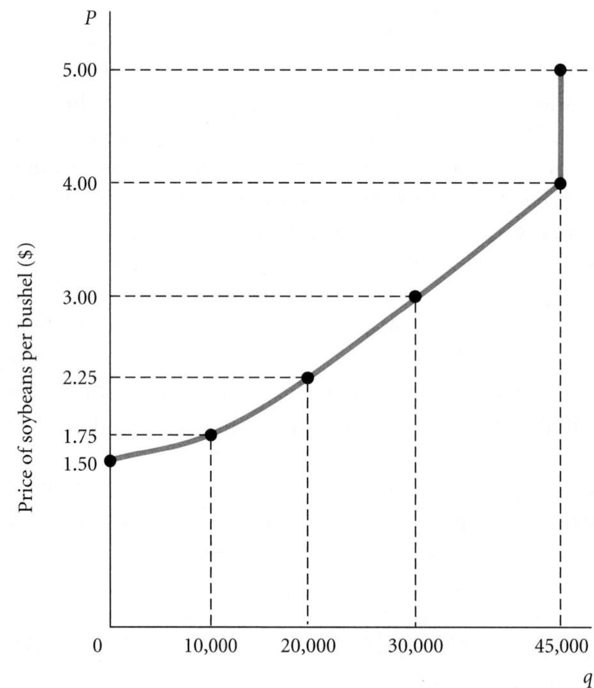

FIGURE 3.6 Clarence Brown's Individual Supply Curve
A producer will supply more when the price of output is higher. The slope of a supply curve is positive. Note that the supply curve is red: Supply is determined by choices made by firms.

Note in Brown's supply schedule, however, that when price rises from $4 to $5, quantity supplied no longer increases. Often an individual firm's ability to respond to an increase in price is constrained by its existing scale of operations, or capacity, in the short run. For example, Brown's ability to produce more soybeans depends on the size of his farm, the fertility of his soil, and the types of equipment he has. The fact that output stays constant at 45,000 bushels per year suggests that he is running up against the limits imposed by the size of his farm, the quality of his soil, and his existing technology.

In the longer run, however, Brown may acquire more land or technology may change, allowing for more soybean production. The terms *short run* and *long run* have very precise meanings in economics; we will discuss them in detail later. Here it is important only to understand that time plays a critical role in supply decisions. When prices change, firms' immediate response may be different from what they are able to do after a month or a year. Short-run and long-run supply curves are often different.

Other Determinants of Supply

Of the factors we have listed that are likely to affect the quantity of output supplied by a given firm, we have thus far discussed only the price of output. Other factors that affect supply include the cost of producing the product and the prices of related products.

The Cost of Production In order for a firm to make a profit, its revenue must exceed its costs. As an individual producer, like Farmer Brown, thinks about how much to supply at a particular price, the producer will be looking at his or her costs. Brown's supply decision is likely to change in response to changes in the cost of production. Cost of production depends on a number of factors, including the available technologies and the prices and quantities of the inputs needed by the firm (labor, land, capital, energy, and so on).

Technological change can have an enormous impact on the cost of production over time. Consider agriculture. The introduction of fertilizers, the development of complex farm machinery, and the use of bioengineering to increase the yield of individual crops have all powerfully affected the cost of producing agricultural products. Farm productivity in the United States has been increasing dramatically for decades. Yield per acre of corn production has increased fivefold since the late 1930s, and the amount of labor required to produce 100 bushels of corn has fallen from 108 hours in the late 1930s to 20 hours in the late 1950s to less than 3 hours today. (See Table 2.2 on p. 36.)

When a technological advance lowers the cost of production, output is likely to increase. When yield per acre increases, individual farmers can and do produce more. The output of the Ford Motor Company increased substantially after the introduction of assembly-line techniques. The production of electronic calculators, and later personal computers, boomed with the development of inexpensive techniques to produce microprocessors.

Cost of production is also directly affected by the price of the factors of production. In the spring of 2008, the world price of oil rose to more than $100 per barrel from below $20 in 2002. As a result, cab drivers faced higher gasoline prices, airlines faced higher fuel costs, and manufacturing firms faced higher heating bills. The result: Cab drivers probably spent less time driving around looking for customers, airlines cut a few low-profit routes, and some manufacturing plants stopped running extra shifts. The moral of this story: Increases in input prices raise costs of production and are likely to reduce supply.

The Prices of Related Products Firms often react to changes in the prices of related products. For example, if land can be used for either corn or soybean production, an increase in soybean prices may cause individual farmers to shift acreage out of corn production into soybeans. Thus, an increase in soybean prices actually affects the amount of corn supplied.

Similarly, if beef prices rise, producers may respond by raising more cattle. However, leather comes from cowhide. Thus, an increase in beef prices may actually increase the supply of leather.

To summarize:

Assuming that its objective is to maximize profits, a firm's decision about what quantity of output, or product, to supply depends on:

1. The price of the good or service.
2. The cost of producing the product, which in turn depends on:
   - The price of required inputs (labor, capital, and land).
   - The technologies that can be used to produce the product.
3. The prices of related products.

Shift of Supply versus Movement Along a Supply Curve

A supply curve shows the relationship between the quantity of a good or service supplied by a firm and the price that good or service brings in the market. Higher prices are likely to lead to an increase in quantity supplied, *ceteris paribus*. Remember: The supply curve is derived holding everything constant except price. When the price of a product changes *ceteris paribus*, a change in the quantity supplied follows—that is, a **movement along a supply curve** takes place. As you have seen, supply decisions are also influenced by factors other than price. New relationships between price and quantity supplied come about when factors other than price change, and the result is a **shift of a supply curve**. When factors other than price cause supply curves to shift, we say that there has been a *change in supply*.

movement along a supply curve The change in quantity supplied brought about by a change in price.

shift of a supply curve The change that takes place in a supply curve corresponding to a new relationship between quantity supplied of a good and the price of that good. The shift is brought about by a change in the original conditions.

Recall that the cost of production depends on the price of inputs and the technologies of production available. Now suppose that a major breakthrough in the production of soybeans has occurred: Genetic engineering has produced a superstrain of disease- and pest-resistant seed. Such a technological change would enable individual farmers to supply more soybeans at *any* market price. Table 3.4 and Figure 3.7 describe this change. At $3 a bushel, farmers would have produced 30,000 bushels from the old seed (schedule S_0 in Table 3.4); with the lower cost of production and higher yield resulting from the new seed, they produce 40,000 bushels (schedule S_1 in Table 3.4). At $1.75 per bushel, they would have produced 10,000 bushels from the old seed; but with the lower costs and higher yields, output rises to 23,000 bushels.

TABLE 3.4 Shift of Supply Schedule for Soybeans Following Development of a New Disease-Resistant Seed Strain

	Schedule S_0	Schedule S_1
Price (per Bushel)	Quantity Supplied (Bushels per Year Using Old Seed)	Quantity Supplied (Bushels per Year Using New Seed)
$1.50	0	5,000
1.75	10,000	23,000
2.25	20,000	33,000
3.00	30,000	40,000
4.00	45,000	54,000
5.00	45,000	54,000

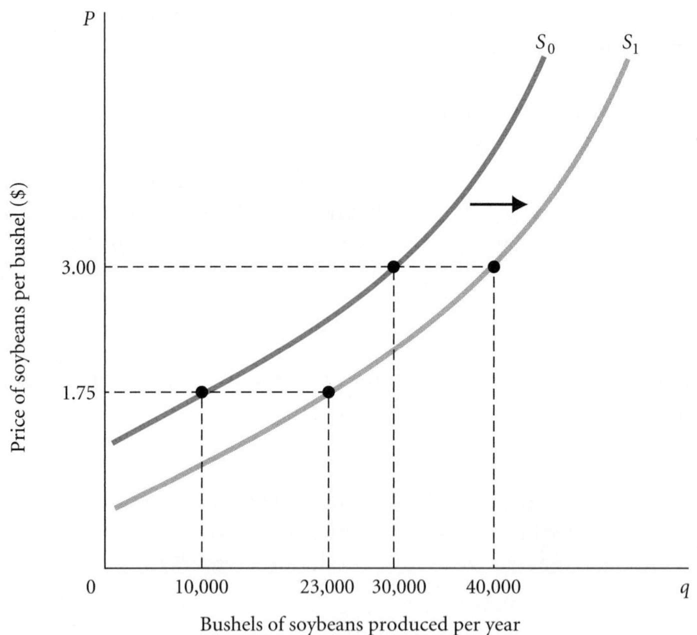

FIGURE 3.7 Shift of the Supply Curve for Soybeans Following Development of a New Seed Strain

When the price of a product changes, we move *along* the supply curve for that product; the quantity supplied rises or falls. When any other factor affecting supply changes, the supply curve *shifts*.

Increases in input prices may also cause supply curves to shift. If Farmer Brown faces higher fuel costs, for example, his supply curve will shift to the left—that is, he will produce less at any given market price. If Brown's soybean supply curve shifted far enough to the left, it would intersect the price axis at a higher point, meaning that it would take a higher market price to induce Brown to produce any soybeans at all.

As with demand, it is very important to distinguish between *movements along* supply curves (changes in quantity supplied) and *shifts in* supply curves (changes in supply):

Change in price of a good or service leads to
→ Change in *quantity supplied* (**movement along a supply curve**).

Change in costs, input prices, technology, or prices of related goods and services leads to
→ Change in *supply* (**shift of a supply curve**).

From Individual Supply to Market Supply

Market supply is determined in the same fashion as market demand. It is simply the sum of all that is supplied each period by all producers of a single product. Figure 3.8 derives a market supply curve from the supply curves of three individual firms. (In a market with more firms, total market supply would be the sum of the amounts produced by each of the firms in that market.) As the table in Figure 3.8 shows, at a price of $3, farm A supplies 30,000 bushels of soybeans, farm B supplies 10,000 bushels, and farm C supplies 25,000 bushels. At this price, the total amount supplied in the market is 30,000 + 10,000 + 25,000, or 65,000 bushels. At a price of $1.75, however, the total amount supplied is only 25,000 bushels (10,000 + 5,000 + 10,000). Thus, the market supply curve is the simple addition of the individual supply curves of all the firms in a particular market—that is, the sum of all the individual quantities supplied at each price.

market supply The sum of all that is supplied each period by all producers of a single product.

The position and shape of the market supply curve depends on the positions and shapes of the individual firms' supply curves from which it is derived. The market supply curve also depends on the number of firms that produce in that market. If firms that produce for a particular market are earning high profits, other firms may be tempted to go into that line of business. When the technology to produce computers for home use became available, literally hundreds of new firms got into the act. The popularity and profitability of professional football has, three times, led to the formation of new leagues. When new firms enter an industry, the supply curve shifts to the right. When firms go out of business, or "exit" the market, the supply curve shifts to the left.

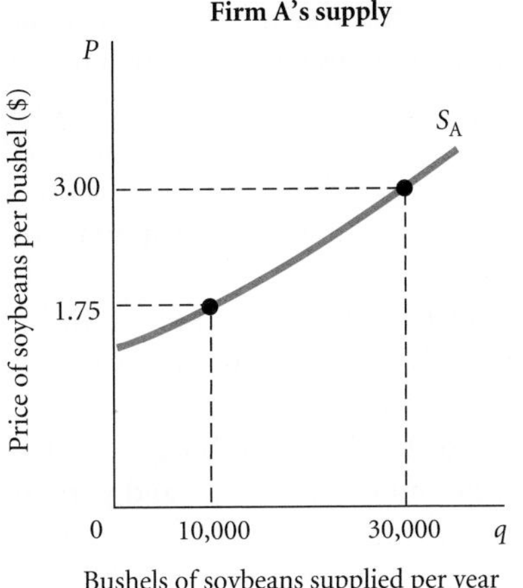

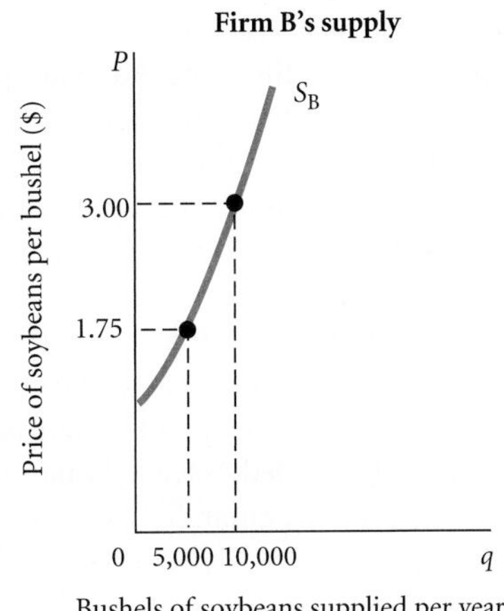

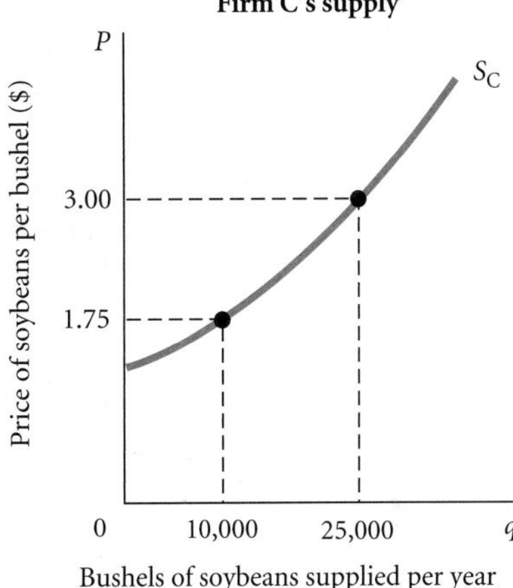

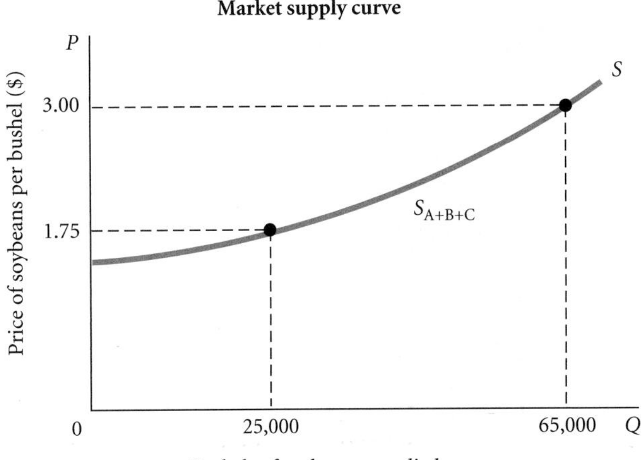

Price	Quantity (q) Supplied by A	B	C		Total Quantity Supplied in the Market (Q)
$3.00	30,000 +	10,000 +	25,000	=	65,000
1.75	10,000 +	5,000 +	10,000	=	25,000

▲ **FIGURE 3.8 Deriving Market Supply from Individual Firm Supply Curves**
Total supply in the marketplace is the sum of all the amounts supplied by all the firms selling in the market. It is the sum of all the individual quantities supplied at each price.

Market Equilibrium

So far, we have identified a number of factors that influence the amount that households demand and the amount that firms supply in product (output) markets. The discussion has emphasized the role of market price as a determinant of both quantity demanded and quantity supplied. We are now ready to see how supply and demand in the market interact to determine the final market price.

We have been very careful in our discussions thus far to separate household decisions about how much to demand from firm decisions about how much to supply. The operation of the market, however, clearly depends on the interaction between suppliers and demanders. At any moment, one of three conditions prevails in every market: (1) The quantity demanded exceeds the quantity supplied at the current price, a situation called *excess demand*; (2) the quantity supplied exceeds the quantity demanded at the current price, a situation called *excess supply*; or (3) the quantity supplied equals the quantity demanded at the current price, a situation called **equilibrium**. At equilibrium, no tendency for price to change exists.

equilibrium The condition that exists when quantity supplied and quantity demanded are equal. At equilibrium, there is no tendency for price to change.

Excess Demand

excess demand *or* **shortage** The condition that exists when quantity demanded exceeds quantity supplied at the current price.

Excess demand, or a **shortage**, exists when quantity demanded is greater than quantity supplied at the current price. Figure 3.9, which plots both a supply curve and a demand curve on the same graph, illustrates such a situation. As you can see, market demand at $1.75 per bushel (50,000 bushels) exceeds the amount that farmers are currently supplying (25,000 bushels).

When excess demand occurs in an unregulated market, there is a tendency for price to rise as demanders compete against each other for the limited supply. The adjustment mechanisms may differ, but the outcome is always the same. For example, consider the mechanism of an auction. In an auction, items are sold directly to the highest bidder. When the auctioneer starts the bidding at a low price, many people bid for the item. At first, there is a shortage: Quantity demanded exceeds quantity supplied. As would-be buyers offer higher and higher prices, bidders drop out until the one who offers the most ends up with the item being auctioned. Price rises until quantity demanded and quantity supplied are equal.

At a price of $1.75 (see Figure 3.9 again), farmers produce soybeans at a rate of 25,000 bushels per year, but at that price, the demand is for 50,000 bushels. Most farm products are sold to local dealers who in turn sell large quantities in major market centers, where bidding would push prices up if quantity demanded exceeded quantity supplied. As price rises above $1.75, two things happen: (1) The quantity demanded falls as buyers drop out of the market and perhaps choose a substitute, and (2) the quantity supplied increases as farmers find themselves receiving a higher price for their product and shift additional acres into soybean production.[3]

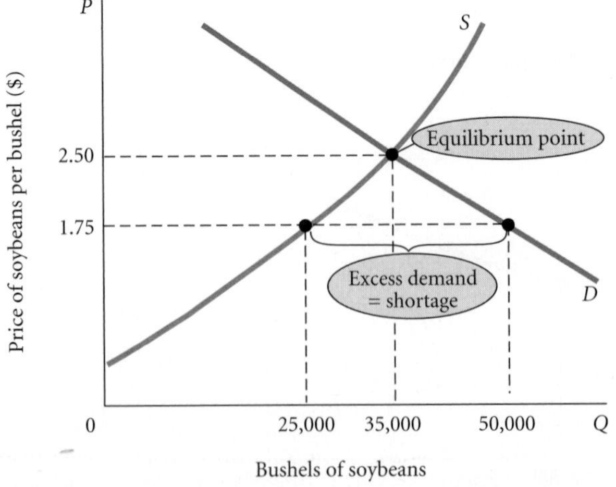

▶ **FIGURE 3.9 Excess Demand, or Shortage**
At a price of $1.75 per bushel, quantity demanded exceeds quantity supplied. When excess *demand* exists, there is a tendency for price to rise. When quantity demanded equals quantity supplied, excess demand is eliminated and the market is in equilibrium. Here the equilibrium price is $2.50 and the equilibrium quantity is 35,000 bushels.

[3] Once farmers have produced in any given season, they cannot change their minds and produce more, of course. When we derived Clarence Brown's supply schedule in Table 3.3, we imagined him reacting to prices that existed at the time he decided how much land to plant in soybeans. In Figure 3.9, the upward slope shows that higher prices justify shifting land from other crops. Final price may not be determined until final production figures are in. For our purposes here, however, we have ignored this timing problem. The best way to think about it is that demand and supply are *flows*, or *rates*, of production—that is, we are talking about the number of bushels produced *per production period*. Adjustments in the rate of production may take place over a number of production periods.

This process continues until the shortage is eliminated. In Figure 3.9, this occurs at $2.50, where quantity demanded has fallen from 50,000 to 35,000 bushels per year and quantity supplied has increased from 25,000 to 35,000 bushels per year. When quantity demanded and quantity supplied are equal and there is no further bidding, the process has achieved an equilibrium, a situation in which *there is no natural tendency for further adjustment*. Graphically, the point of equilibrium is the point at which the supply curve and the demand curve intersect.

Increasingly, items are auctioned over the Internet. Companies such as eBay connect buyers and sellers of everything from automobiles to wine and from computers to airline tickets. Auctions are occurring simultaneously with participants located across the globe. The principles through which prices are determined in these auctions are the same: When excess demand exists, prices rise.

While the principles are the same, the process through which excess demand leads to higher prices is different in different markets. Consider the market for houses in the hypothetical town of Boomville with a population of 25,000 people, most of whom live in single-family homes. Normally, about 75 homes are sold in the Boomville market each year. However, last year a major business opened a plant in town, creating 1,500 new jobs that pay good wages. This attracted new residents to the area, and real estate agents now have more buyers than there are properties for sale. Quantity demanded now exceeds quantity supplied. In other words, there is a shortage.

Auctions are not unheard of in the housing market, but they are rare. This market usually works more subtly, but the outcome is the same. Properties are sold very quickly, and housing prices begin to rise. Boomville sellers soon learn that there are more buyers than usual, and they begin to hold out for higher offers. As prices for Boomville houses rise, quantity demanded eventually drops off and quantity supplied increases. Quantity supplied increases in at least two ways: (1) Encouraged by the high prices, builders begin constructing new houses, and (2) some people, attracted by the higher prices their homes will fetch, put their houses on the market. Discouraged by higher prices, however, some potential buyers (demanders) may begin to look for housing in neighboring towns and settle on commuting. Eventually, equilibrium will be reestablished, with the quantity of houses demanded just equal to the quantity of houses supplied.

Although the mechanics of price adjustment in the housing market differ from the mechanics of an auction, the outcome is the same:

> When quantity demanded exceeds quantity supplied, price tends to rise. When the price in a market rises, quantity demanded falls and quantity supplied rises until an equilibrium is reached at which quantity demanded and quantity supplied are equal.

This process is called *price rationing*. When a shortage exists, some people will be satisfied and some will not. When the market operates without interference, price increases will distribute what is available to those who are willing and able to pay the most. As long as there is a way for buyers and sellers to interact, those who are willing to pay more will make that fact known somehow. (We discuss the nature of the price system as a rationing device in detail in Chapter 4.)

Excess Supply

Excess supply, or a **surplus**, exists when the quantity supplied exceeds the quantity demanded at the current price. As with a shortage, the mechanics of price adjustment in the face of a surplus can differ from market to market. For example, if automobile dealers find themselves with unsold cars in the fall when the new models are coming in, you can expect to see price cuts. Sometimes dealers offer discounts to encourage buyers; sometimes buyers themselves simply offer less than the price initially asked. In any event, products do no one any good sitting in dealers' lots or on warehouse shelves. The auction metaphor introduced earlier can also be applied here: If the initial asking price is too high, no one bids and the auctioneer tries a lower price. It is almost always true, and 2007 was no exception, that certain items do not sell as well as anticipated during the Christmas holidays. After Christmas, most stores have big sales during which they lower the prices of overstocked items. Quantities supplied exceeded quantities demanded at the current prices, so stores cut prices.

excess supply *or* **surplus** The condition that exists when quantity supplied exceeds quantity demanded at the current price.

Across the state from Boomville is Bustville, where last year a drug manufacturer shut down its operations and 1,500 people found themselves out of work. With no other prospects for work, many residents decided to pack up and move. They put their houses up for sale, but there were few buyers. The result was an excess supply, or surplus, of houses: The quantity of houses supplied exceeded the quantity demanded at the current prices.

As houses sit unsold on the market for months, sellers start to cut their asking prices. Potential buyers begin offering considerably less than sellers are asking. As prices fall, two things are likely to happen. First, the low housing prices may attract new buyers. People who might have bought in a neighboring town see that housing bargains are to be had in Bustville, and quantity demanded rises in response to price decline. Second, some of those people who put their houses on the market may be discouraged by the lower prices and decide to stay in Bustville. Developers are certainly not likely to be building new housing in town. Thus, lower prices lead to a decline in quantity supplied as potential sellers pull their houses from the market. This was the situation in New England and California in the early 1990s.

Figure 3.10 illustrates another excess supply/surplus situation. At a price of $3 per bushel, suppose farmers are supplying soybeans at a rate of 40,000 bushels per year, but buyers are demanding only 20,000. With 20,000 (40,000 minus 20,000) bushels of soybeans going unsold, the market price falls. As price falls from $3.00 to $2.50, quantity supplied decreases from 40,000 bushels per year to 35,000. The lower price causes quantity demanded to rise from 20,000 to 35,000. At $2.50, quantity demanded and quantity supplied are equal. For the data shown here, $2.50 and 35,000 bushels are the equilibrium price and quantity, respectively.

Although oil prices rose to record levels in 2008, back in 2001, crude oil production worldwide exceeded the quantity demanded and prices fell significantly as competing producer countries tried to maintain their share of world markets. Although the mechanism by which price is adjusted is different for automobiles, housing, soybeans, and crude oil, the outcome is the same:

> When quantity supplied exceeds quantity demanded at the current price, the price tends to fall. When price falls, quantity supplied is likely to decrease and quantity demanded is likely to increase until an equilibrium price is reached where quantity supplied and quantity demanded are equal.

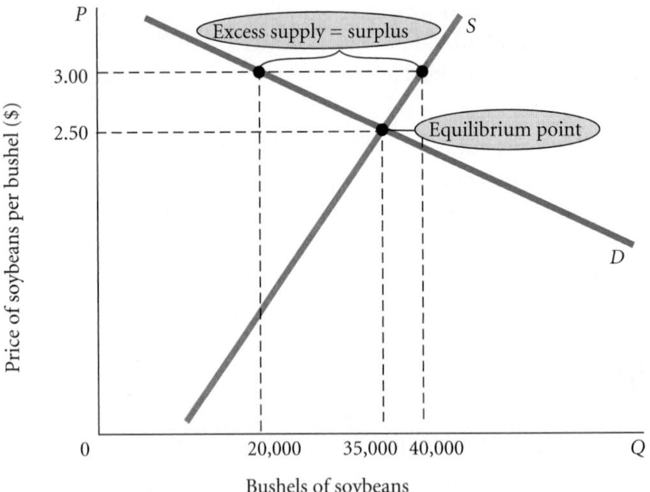

FIGURE 3.10 Excess Supply, or Surplus
At a price of $3.00, quantity supplied exceeds quantity demanded by 20,000 bushels. This excess supply will cause the price to fall.

Changes in Equilibrium

When supply and demand curves shift, the equilibrium price and quantity change. The following example will help to illustrate this point.

South America is a major producer of coffee beans. A cold snap there can reduce the coffee harvest enough to affect the world price of coffee beans. In the mid-1990s, a major freeze hit Brazil and Colombia and drove up the price of coffee on world markets to a record $2.40 per pound. Severe hurricanes in the Caribbean caused a similar shift of supply in 2005.

Figure 3.11 illustrates how the freeze pushed up coffee prices. Initially, the market was in equilibrium at a price of $1.20. At that price, the quantity demanded was equal to quantity supplied (13.2 billion pounds). At a price of $1.20 and a quantity of 13.2 billion pounds, the demand curve (labeled *D*) intersected the initial supply curve (labeled S_0). (Remember that equilibrium exists when quantity demanded equals quantity supplied—the point at which the supply and demand curves intersect.)

The freeze caused a decrease in the supply of coffee beans. That is, the freeze caused the supply curve to shift to the left. In Figure 3.11, the new supply curve (the supply curve that shows the relationship between price and quantity supplied after the freeze) is labeled S_1.

At the initial equilibrium price, $1.20, there is now a shortage of coffee. If the price were to remain at $1.20, quantity demanded would not change; it would remain at 13.2 billion pounds. However, at that price, quantity supplied would drop to 6.6 billion pounds. At a price of $1.20, quantity demanded is greater than quantity supplied.

When excess demand exists in a market, price can be expected to rise, and rise it did. As the figure shows, price rose to a new equilibrium at $2.40. At $2.40, quantity demanded is again equal to quantity supplied, this time at 9.9 billion pounds—the point at which the new supply curve (S_1) intersects the demand curve.

Notice that as the price of coffee rose from $1.20 to $2.40, two things happened. First, the quantity demanded declined (a movement along the demand curve) as people shifted to substitutes such as tea and hot cocoa. Second, the quantity supplied began to rise, but within the limits imposed by the damage from the freeze. (It might also be that some countries or areas with high costs of production, previously unprofitable, came into production and shipped to the world market at the higher price.) That is, the quantity supplied increased in response to the higher price *along* the new supply curve, which lies to the left of the old supply curve. The final result was a higher price ($2.40), a smaller quantity finally exchanged in the market (9.9 billion pounds), and coffee bought only by those willing to pay $2.40 per pound.

Since many market prices are driven by the interaction of millions of buyers and sellers, it is often difficult to predict how they will change. A series of events in the mid-1990s led to the leftward shift in supply, thus driving up the price of coffee, but the opposite occurred more recently. Today coffee beans are exported by over 50 countries, with Brazil being the largest producer with about 30 percent of the market. Large increases in production have kept prices low. In July 2007, the average price per pound was $1.06.

Figure 3.12 summarizes the possible supply and demand shifts that have been discussed and the resulting changes in equilibrium price and quantity. Study the graphs carefully to ensure that you understand them.

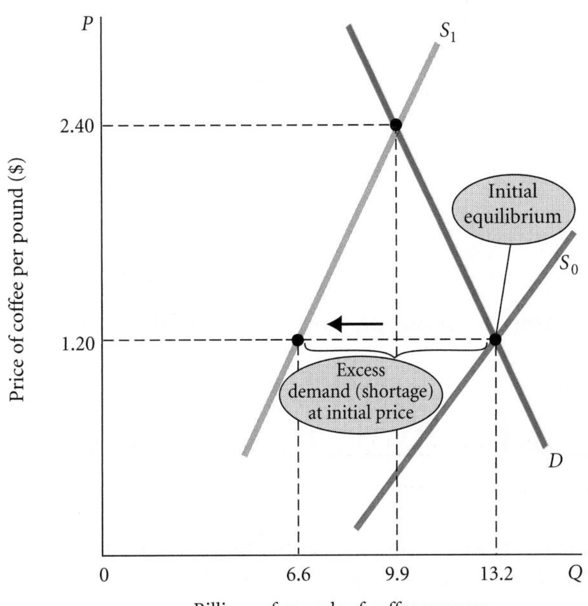

FIGURE 3.11 The Coffee Market: A Shift of Supply and Subsequent Price Adjustment
Before the freeze, the coffee market was in equilibrium at a price of $1.20 per pound. At that price, quantity demanded equaled quantity supplied. The freeze shifted the supply curve to the left (from S_0 to S_1), increasing the equilibrium price to $2.40.

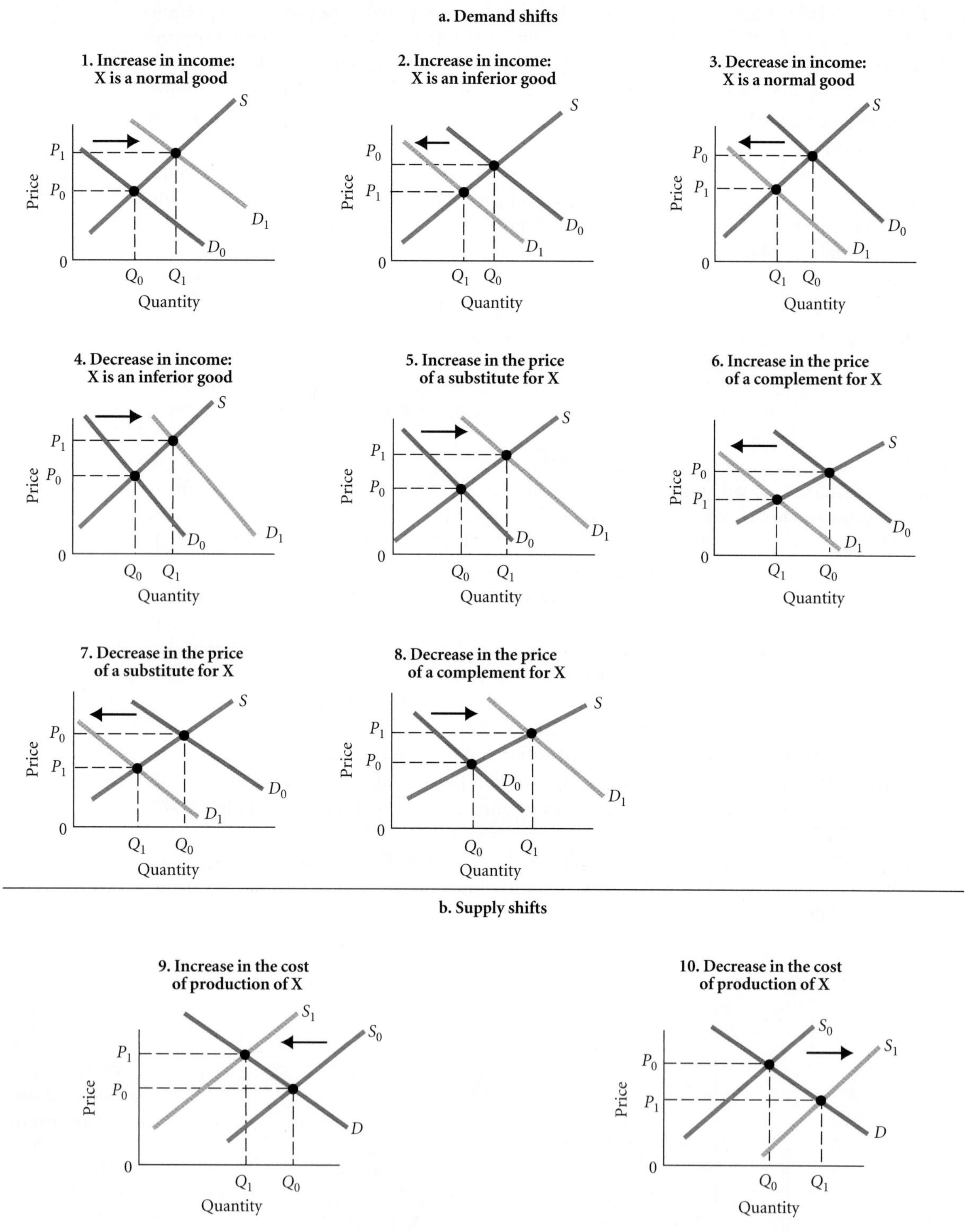

a. Demand shifts
1. Increase in income: X is a normal good
2. Increase in income: X is an inferior good
3. Decrease in income: X is a normal good
4. Decrease in income: X is an inferior good
5. Increase in the price of a substitute for X
6. Increase in the price of a complement for X
7. Decrease in the price of a substitute for X
8. Decrease in the price of a complement for X
b. Supply shifts
9. Increase in the cost of production of X
10. Decrease in the cost of production of X
Price
Quantity
0
P_0
P_1
Q_0
Q_1
D_0
D_1
D
S
S_0
S_1

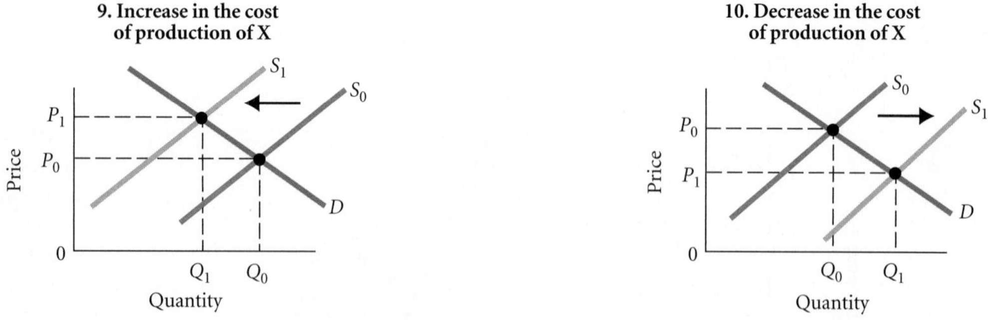

▲ **FIGURE 3.12 Examples of Supply and Demand Shifts for Product X**

Demand and Supply in Product Markets: A Review

As you continue your study of economics, you will discover that it is a discipline full of controversy and debate. There is, however, little disagreement about the basic way that the forces of supply and demand operate in free markets. If you hear that a freeze in Florida has destroyed a good portion of the citrus crop, you can bet that the price of oranges will rise.

ECONOMICS IN PRACTICE

Bad News for Orange Juice Fanatics

This article once again shows the way in which the laws of supply and demand end up affecting our lives. In this article, the bad weather in California caused the supply of oranges—an essential input into orange juice (OJ)—to drop dramatically. This shift in the supply curve to the left raised the price of those oranges for companies such as Tropicana as we see in the graph below. The most likely result is the one described here: an increase in the price of orange juice.

For those of you interested in this topic, you might enjoy Eddie Murphy in the movie *Trading Places*. In the movie, a freeze in Florida and the resulting change in the price of orange juice futures contracts play an important role.

We should also note that while the story told in the article is most likely the case in practice, in theory a freeze has the potential to actually lower frozen orange juice prices. Frozen oranges are useless as fresh fruit, but some fraction can typically be salvaged for frozen juice. Thus while the overall supply of oranges falls with a freeze, we may also see a shift in the remaining oranges from fresh to frozen. In theory this could shift the supply to frozen OJ firms to the right, lowering price. In Florida, most oranges are currently used for frozen orange juice, and so the story told in the article is most likely the case in practice.

Orange Juice Prices Could Skyrocket After Freeze Destroys Most of California Output

City News

It's not a place where they often talk about the cold.

But farmers in California aren't thinking about much else this week, and you may soon be sharing their distress.

The freak cold snap that has left oranges from the Golden State frozen amid icicles on the trees could send the cost of your morning glass of OJ skyrocketing.

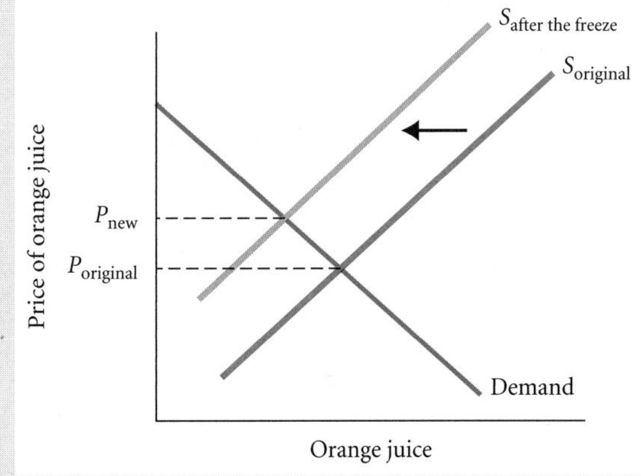

New figures show that three days of below freezing temperatures have destroyed as much as three quarters of the state's $1 billion citrus crop, a devastating blow unseen since a similar spell in December 1998 left growers with a $700 million loss.

It's believed 50–75 percent of all crops were lost to the weather, and while the farmers tried to save what they could before the big blast hit, a labour shortage kept them from getting too much of it.

"When you're already cutting the ice within the oranges, you know those are gone," laments Philip LoBue, who represents a growers' trade organization.

It's believed the loss could total some $960 million.

It's some bad weather in a place 3,000 miles away, so what does it mean to you? A lot if you buy fresh fruit or juice.

Last November, the makers of Tropicana warned they might have to raise prices on their popular orange juice by 12.5 percent in 2007, because of a devastating disease that ravaged much of Florida's citrus crop.

With the California output now also in doubt, it's possible the cost of your next morning glass of fruit juice could soar at local supermarkets in the coming weeks.

Source: CityNews.ca staff, January 16, 2007. Reprinted by permission.

If you read that the weather in the Midwest has been good and a record corn crop is expected, you can bet that corn prices will fall. When fishermen in Massachusetts go on strike and stop bringing in the daily catch, you can bet that the price of fish will go up.

Here are some important points to remember about the mechanics of supply and demand in product markets:

1. A demand curve shows how much of a product a household would buy if it could buy all it wanted at the given price. A supply curve shows how much of a product a firm would supply if it could sell all it wanted at the given price.
2. Quantity demanded and quantity supplied are always per time period—that is, per day, per month, or per year.
3. The demand for a good is determined by price, household income and wealth, prices of other goods and services, tastes and preferences, and expectations.
4. The supply of a good is determined by price, costs of production, and prices of related products. Costs of production are determined by available technologies of production and input prices.
5. Be careful to distinguish between movements along supply and demand curves and shifts of these curves. When the price of a good changes, the quantity of that good demanded or supplied changes—that is, a movement occurs along the curve. When any other factor changes, the curve shifts, or changes position.
6. Market equilibrium exists only when quantity supplied equals quantity demanded at the current price.

Looking Ahead: Markets and the Allocation of Resources

You can already begin to see how markets answer the basic economic questions of what is produced, how it is produced, and who gets what is produced. A firm will produce what is profitable to produce. If the firm can sell a product at a price that is sufficient to ensure a profit after production costs are paid, it will in all likelihood produce that product. Resources will flow in the direction of profit opportunities.

- Demand curves reflect what people are willing and able to pay for products; demand curves are influenced by incomes, wealth, preferences, prices of other goods, and expectations. Because product prices are determined by the interaction of supply and demand, prices reflect what people are willing to pay. If people's preferences or incomes change, resources will be allocated differently. Consider, for example, an increase in demand—a shift in the market demand curve. Beginning at an equilibrium, households simply begin buying more. At the equilibrium price, quantity demanded becomes greater than quantity supplied. When there is excess demand, prices will rise, and higher prices mean higher profits for firms in the industry. Higher profits, in turn, provide existing firms with an incentive to expand and new firms with an incentive to enter the industry. Thus, the decisions of independent private firms responding to prices and profit opportunities determine *what* will be produced. No central direction is necessary.

  Adam Smith saw this self-regulating feature of markets more than 200 years ago:

  > Every individual . . . by pursuing his own interest . . . promotes that of society. He is led . . . by an invisible hand to promote an end which was no part of his intention.[4]

  The term Smith coined, the *invisible hand*, has passed into common parlance and is still used by economists to refer to the self-regulation of markets.

- Firms in business to make a profit have a good reason to choose the best available technology—lower costs mean higher profits. Thus, individual firms determine *how* to produce their products, again with no central direction.

---

[4] Adam Smith, *The Wealth of Nations*, Modern Library Edition (New York: Random House, 1937), p. 456 (1st ed., 1776).

ECONOMICS IN PRACTICE

Why Do the Prices of Newspapers Rise?

In 2006, the average price for a daily edition of a Baltimore newspaper was $0.50. In 2007, the average price had risen to $0.75. Three different analysts have three different explanations for the higher equilibrium price.

Analyst 1: The higher price for Baltimore newspapers is good news because it means the population is better informed about public issues. These data clearly show that the citizens of Baltimore have a new, increased regard for newspapers.

Analyst 2: The higher price for Baltimore newspapers is bad news for the citizens of Baltimore. The higher cost of paper, ink, and distribution reflected in these higher prices will further diminish the population's awareness of public issues.

Analyst 3: The higher price for Baltimore newspapers is an unfortunate result of newspapers trying to make money as many consumers have turned to the Internet to access news coverage for free.

As economists, we are faced with two tasks in looking at these explanations: Do they make sense based on what we know about economic principles? And if they do make sense, can we figure out which explanation applies to the case of rising newspaper prices in Baltmore?

What is Analyst 1 saying? Her observation about consumers' new increased regard for newspapers tells us something about the demand curve. Analyst 1 seems to be arguing that tastes have changed in favor of newspapers, which would mean a shift in the demand curve to the right. With upward-sloping supply, such a shift would produce a price increase. So Analyst 1's story is plausible.

Analyst 2 refers to an increased cost of newsprint. This would cause production costs of newspapers to rise, shifting the supply curve to the left. A downward-sloping demand curve also results in increased prices. So Analyst 2 also has a plausible story.

Since Analyst 1 and Analyst 2 have plausible stories based on economic principles, we can look at evidence to see who is in fact right. If you go back to the graphs in Figure 3.12 on p. 66, you will find a clue. When demand shifts to the right (as in Analyst 1's story) the price rises, but so does the quantity as shown in Figure (a) below. When supply shifts to the left (as in Analyst 2's story) the price rises, but the quantity falls as shown in Figure (b) below. So we would look at what happened to newspaper circulation during this period to see whether the price increase is from the demand side or the supply side. In fact, in most markets, including Baltimore, quantities of newspapers bought have been falling, so Analyst 2 is most likely correct.

But be careful. Both analysts may be correct. If demand shifts to the right and supply shifts to the left by a greater amount, the price will rise and the quantity sold will fall.

What about Analyst 3? Analyst 3 clearly never had an economics course! Free Internet access to news is a substitute for print media. A decrease in the price of this substitute should shift the demand for newspapers to the left. The result should be a lower price, not a price increase. The fact that the newspaper publishers are "trying to make money" faced with this new competition does not change the laws of supply and demand.

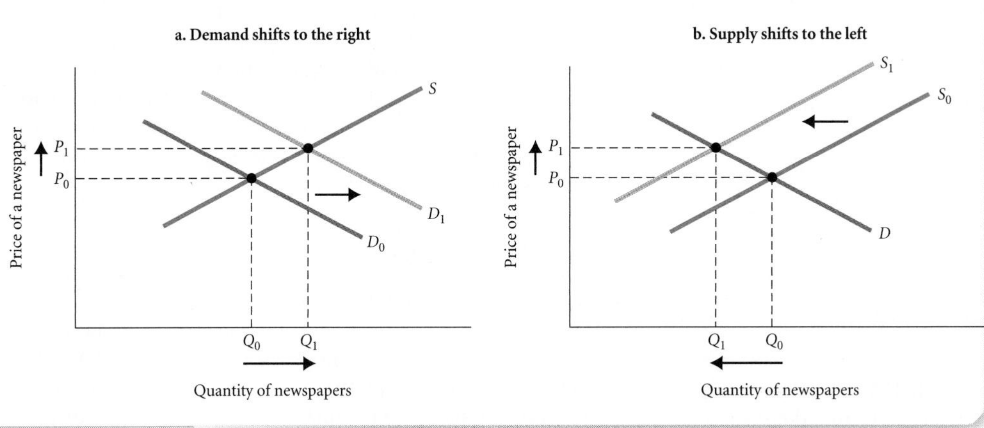

- So far, we have barely touched on the question of distribution—*who* gets what is produced? You can see part of the answer in the simple supply and demand diagrams. When a good is in short supply, price rises. As it does, those who are willing and able to continue buying do so; others stop buying.

The next chapter begins with a more detailed discussion of these topics. How, exactly, is the final allocation of resources (the mix of output and the distribution of output) determined in a market system?

SUMMARY

1. In societies with many people, production must satisfy wide-ranging tastes and preferences, and producers must therefore specialize.

FIRMS AND HOUSEHOLDS: THE BASIC DECISION-MAKING UNITS *p. 45*

2. A *firm* exists when a person or a group of people decides to produce a product or products by transforming resources, or *inputs*, into *outputs*—the products that are sold in the market. Firms are the primary producing units in a market economy. We assume that firms make decisions to try to maximize profits.
3. *Households* are the primary consuming units in an economy. All households' incomes are subject to constraints.

INPUT MARKETS AND OUTPUT MARKETS: THE CIRCULAR FLOW *p. 46*

4. Households and firms interact in two basic kinds of markets: *product* or *output markets* and *input* or *factor markets.* Goods and services intended for use by households are exchanged in output markets. In output markets, competing firms supply and competing households demand. In input markets, competing firms demand and competing households supply.
5. Ultimately, firms choose the quantities and character of outputs produced, the types and quantities of inputs demanded, and the technologies used in production. Households choose the types and quantities of products demanded and the types and quantities of inputs supplied.

DEMAND IN PRODUCT/OUTPUT MARKETS *p. 48*

6. The quantity demanded of an individual product by an individual household depends on (1) price, (2) income, (3) wealth, (4) prices of other products, (5) tastes and preferences, and (6) expectations about the future.
7. *Quantity demanded* is the amount of a product that an individual household would buy in a given period if it could buy all that it wanted at the current price.
8. A *demand schedule* shows the quantities of a product that a household would buy at different prices. The same information can be presented graphically in a *demand curve.*
9. The *law of demand* states that there is a negative relationship between price and quantity demanded: As price rises, quantity demanded decreases and vice versa. Demand curves slope downward.
10. All demand curves eventually intersect the price axis because there is always a price above which a household cannot or will not pay. Also, all demand curves eventually intersect the quantity axis because demand for most goods is limited, if only by time, even at a zero price.
11. When an increase in income causes demand for a good to rise, that good is a *normal good.* When an increase in income causes demand for a good to fall, that good is an *inferior good.*
12. If a rise in the price of good X causes demand for good Y to increase, the goods are *substitutes.* If a rise in the price of X causes demand for Y to fall, the goods are *complements.*
13. *Market demand* is simply the sum of all the quantities of a good or service demanded per period by all the households buying in the market for that good or service. It is the sum of all the individual quantities demanded at each price.

SUPPLY IN PRODUCT/OUTPUT MARKETS *p. 57*

14. *Quantity supplied* by a firm depends on (1) the price of the good or service; (2) the cost of producing the product, which includes the prices of required inputs and the technologies that can be used to produce the product; and (3) the prices of related products.
15. *Market supply* is the sum of all that is supplied in each period by all producers of a single product. It is the sum of all the individual quantities supplied at each price.
16. It is very important to distinguish between *movements* along demand and supply curves and *shifts* of demand and supply curves. The demand curve shows the relationship between price and quantity demanded. The supply curve shows the relationship between price and quantity supplied. A change in price is a movement along the curve. Changes in tastes, income, wealth, expectations, or prices of other goods and services cause demand curves to shift; changes in costs, input prices, technology, or prices of related goods and services cause supply curves to shift.

MARKET EQUILIBRIUM *p. 62*

17. When quantity demanded exceeds quantity supplied at the current price, *excess demand* (or a *shortage*) exists and the price tends to rise. When prices in a market rise, quantity demanded falls and quantity supplied rises until an equilibrium is reached at which quantity supplied and quantity demanded are equal. At *equilibrium*, there is no further tendency for price to change.

18. When quantity supplied exceeds quantity demanded at the current price, *excess supply* (or a *surplus*) exists and the price tends to fall. When price falls, quantity supplied decreases and quantity demanded increases until an equilibrium price is reached where quantity supplied and quantity demanded are equal.

REVIEW TERMS AND CONCEPTS

PROBLEMS

Visit **www.myeconlab.com** to complete the problems marked in orange online. You will receive instant feedback on your answers, tutorial help, and access to additional practice problems.

1. Illustrate the following with supply and demand curves:
   a. With increased access to wireless technology and lighter weight, the demand for laptop computers has increased substantially. Laptops have also become easier and cheaper to produce as new technology has come online. Despite the shift of demand, prices have fallen.
   b. Cranberry production in Massachusetts totaled 1.97 million barrels in 2006, a 39 percent increase from the previous year's production. This year's crop yield averaged 140.9 barrels per acre, an increase of over 40 barrels per acre from the 2005 crop. But demand increased by even more than supply, actually pushing 2006 prices above 2005 prices.
   c. During the high-tech boom in the late 1990s, San Jose office space was in very high demand and rents were very high. With the national recession that began in March 2001, however, the market for office space in San Jose (Silicon Valley) was hit very hard, with rents per square foot falling. In 2005, the employment numbers from San Jose were rising slowly and rents began to rise again. Assume for simplicity that no new office space was built during the period.
   d. Before economic reforms were implemented in the countries of Eastern Europe, regulation held the price of bread substantially below equilibrium. When reforms were implemented, prices were deregulated and the price of bread rose dramatically. As a result, the quantity of bread demanded fell and the quantity of bread supplied rose sharply.
   e. The steel industry has been lobbying for high taxes on imported steel. Russia, Brazil, and Japan have been producing and selling steel on world markets at \$610 per metric ton, well below what equilibrium would be in the United States with no imports. If no imported steel was permitted into the country, the equilibrium price would be \$970 per metric ton. Show supply and demand curves for the United States, assuming no imports; then show what the graph would look like if U.S. buyers could purchase all the steel that they wanted from world markets at \$610 per metric ton; show the quantity of imported steel.
2. On Sunday, August 19, the Detroit Tigers and the New York Yankees played baseball at Yankee Stadium. Both teams were in pursuit of league championships. Tickets to the game were sold out, and many more fans would have attended if additional tickets had been available. On that same day, the Cleveland Indians and the Tampa Bay Devil Rays played each other and sold tickets to only 22,500 people in Tampa.

   The Devil Rays stadium, Tropicana Field, holds 43,772. Yankee Stadium holds 57,478. Assume for simplicity that tickets to all regular-season games are priced at \$40.
   a. Draw supply and demand curves for the tickets to each of the two games. (*Hint:* Supply is fixed. It does not change with price.) Draw one graph for each game.
   b. Is there a pricing policy that would have filled the ballpark for the Tampa game? If the Devil Rays adopted such a strategy, would it bring in more or less revenue?
   c. The price system was not allowed to work to ration the New York tickets when they were initially sold to the public. How do you know? How do you suppose the tickets were rationed?
3. During the last 10 years, Orlando, Florida grew rapidly, with new jobs luring young people into the area. Despite increases in population and income growth that expanded demand for housing, the price of existing houses barely increased. Why? Illustrate your answer with supply and demand curves.

4. Do you agree or disagree with each of the following statements? Briefly explain your answers and illustrate each with supply and demand curves.
   a. The price of a good rises, causing the demand for another good to fall. Therefore, the two goods are substitutes.
   b. A shift in supply causes the price of a good to fall. The shift must have been an increase in supply.
   c. During 2007, incomes rose sharply for most Americans. This change would likely lead to an increase in the prices of both normal and inferior goods.
   d. Two normal goods cannot be substitutes for each other.
   e. If demand increases and supply increases at the same time, price will clearly rise.
   f. The price of good A falls. This causes an increase in the price of good B. Therefore, goods A and B are complements.

5. The U.S. government administers two programs that affect the market for cigarettes. Media campaigns and labeling requirements are aimed at making the public aware of the health dangers of cigarettes. At the same time, the Department of Agriculture maintains price supports for tobacco. Under this program, the supported price is above the market equilibrium price and the government limits the amount of land that can be devoted to tobacco production. Are these two programs at odds with the goal of reducing cigarette consumption? As part of your answer, illustrate graphically the effects of both policies on the market for cigarettes.

6. Housing prices in Boston and Los Angeles have been on a roller-coaster ride. Illustrate each of the following situations with supply and demand curves:
   a. In both cities, an increase in income combined with expectations of a strong market shifted demand and caused prices to rise rapidly during the mid- to late 1980s.
   b. By 1990, the construction industry boomed as more developers started new residential projects. Those new projects expanded the supply of housing just as demand was shifting as a result of falling incomes and expectations during the 1990–1991 recession.

7. The following sets of statements contain common errors. Identify and explain each error:
   a. Demand increases, causing prices to rise. Higher prices cause demand to fall. Therefore, prices fall back to their original levels.
   b. The supply of meat in Russia increases, causing meat prices to fall. Lower prices always mean that Russian households spend more on meat.

8. For each of the following statements, draw a diagram that illustrates the likely effect on the market for eggs. Indicate in each case the impact on equilibrium price and equilibrium quantity.
   a. A surgeon general warns that high-cholesterol foods cause heart attacks.
   b. The price of bacon, a complementary product, decreases.
   c. An increase in the price of chicken feed occurs.
   d. Caesar salads become trendy at dinner parties. (The dressing is made with raw eggs.)
   e. A technological innovation reduces egg breakage during packing.

*9. Suppose the demand and supply curves for eggs in the United States are given by the following equations:

$$Q_d = 100 - 20P$$
$$Q_s = 10 + 40P$$

where Q_d = millions of dozens of eggs Americans would like to buy each year; Q_s = millions of dozens of eggs U.S. farms would like to sell each year; P = price per dozen of eggs.
   a. Fill in the following table:

PRICE (PER DOZEN)	QUANTITY DEMANDED (Q_d)	QUANTITY SUPPLIED (Q_s)
$ .50	_____	_____
$1.00	_____	_____
$1.50	_____	_____
$2.00	_____	_____
$2.50	_____	_____

   b. Use the information in the table to find the equilibrium price and quantity.
   c. Graph the demand and supply curves and identify the equilibrium price and quantity.

*10. Housing policy analysts debate the best way to increase the number of housing units available to low-income households. One strategy—the demand-side strategy—is to provide people with housing vouchers, paid for by the government, that can be used to rent housing supplied by the private market. Another—a supply-side strategy—is to have the government subsidize housing suppliers or to build public housing.
   a. Illustrate supply- and demand-side strategies using supply and demand curves. Which results in higher rents?
   b. Critics of housing vouchers (the demand-side strategy) argue that because the supply of housing to low-income households is limited and does not respond to higher rents, demand vouchers will serve only to drive up rents and make landlords better off. Illustrate their point with supply and demand curves.

*11. Suppose the market demand for pizza is given by $Q_d = 300 - 20P$ and the market supply for pizza is given by $Q_s = 20P - 100$, where P = price (per pizza).
   a. Graph the supply and demand schedules for pizza using $5 through $15 as the value of P.
   b. In equilibrium, how many pizzas would be sold and at what price?
   c. What would happen if suppliers set the price of pizza at $15? Explain the market adjustment process.
   d. Suppose the price of hamburgers, a substitute for pizza, doubles. This leads to a doubling of the demand for pizza. (At each price, consumers demand twice as much pizza as before.) Write the equation for the new market demand for pizza.
   e. Find the new equilibrium price and quantity of pizza.

12. **[Related to the *Economics in Practice* on p. 67]** In the winter, which is the peak season for coats, the price of coats is typically higher than it is in the summer. In the case of strawberries, however, the reverse is true: The price of strawberries is lower in the peak season than it is in the winter season. How do we explain this seeming contradiction?

13. **[Related to the *Economics in Practice* on p. 69]** Analyst 1 suggested that the demand curve for newspapers in Baltimore might have shifted to the right because people were becoming more literate. Think of two other plausible stories that would result in this demand curve shifting to the right.

---

*Note: Problems marked with an asterisk are more challenging.

Demand and Supply Applications

4

CHAPTER OUTLINE

Every society has a system of institutions that determines what is produced, how it is produced, and who gets what is produced. In some societies, these decisions are made centrally, through planning agencies or by government directive. However, in every society, many decisions are made in a *decentralized* way, through the operation of markets.

Markets exist in all societies, and Chapter 3 provided a bare-bones description of how markets operate. In this chapter, we continue our examination of demand, supply, and the price system.

The Price System: Rationing and Allocating Resources

The market system, also called the *price system*, performs two important and closely related functions. First, it provides an automatic mechanism for distributing scarce goods and services. That is, it serves as a **price rationing** device for allocating goods and services to consumers when the quantity demanded exceeds the quantity supplied. Second, the price system ultimately determines both the allocation of resources among producers and the final mix of outputs.

price rationing The process by which the market system allocates goods and services to consumers when quantity demanded exceeds quantity supplied.

Price Rationing

Consider the simple process by which the price system eliminates a shortage. Figure 4.1 shows hypothetical supply and demand curves for lobsters caught off the coast of New England.

Lobsters are considered a delicacy. Maine produces most of the lobster catch in the United States, and anyone who drives up the Maine coast cannot avoid the hundreds of restaurants selling lobster rolls, steamed lobster, and baked stuffed lobster.

As Figure 4.1 shows, the equilibrium price of live New England lobsters was $11.50 per pound in the summer of 2007. At this price, lobster boats brought in lobsters at a rate of 81 million pounds per year—an amount that was just enough to satisfy demand.

Market equilibrium existed at $11.50 per pound because at that price, quantity demanded was equal to quantity supplied. (Remember that equilibrium occurs at the point where the supply and demand curves intersect. In Figure 4.1, this occurs at point *C*.)

Now suppose in 2008 that the waters off a section of the Maine coast become contaminated with a poisonous parasite. As a result, the Department of Agriculture is forced to close 15,000 square miles of the most productive lobstering areas. Even though many of the lobster boats shift their trapping activities to other waters, there is a sharp reduction in the quantity of lobster available for trapping. The supply curve shifts to the left, from S_{2007} to S_{2008}. This shift in

FIGURE 4.1 The Market for Lobsters

Suppose in 2008 that 15,000 square miles of lobstering waters off the coast of Maine are closed. The supply curve shifts to the left. Before the waters are closed, the lobster market is in equilibrium at the price of $11.50 and a quantity of 81 million pounds. The decreased supply of lobster leads to higher prices, and a new equilibrium is reached at $16.10 and 60 million pounds (point *B*).

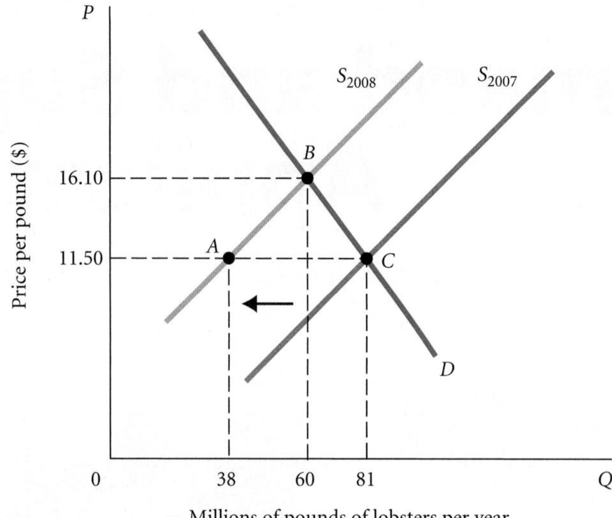

the supply curve creates a situation of excess demand at $11.50. At that price, the quantity demanded is 81 million pounds and the quantity supplied is 38 million pounds. Quantity demanded exceeds quantity supplied by 43 million pounds.

The reduced supply causes the price of lobster to rise sharply. As the price rises, the available supply is "rationed." Those who are willing and able to pay the most get it.

You can see the market's price rationing function clearly in Figure 4.1. As the price rises from $11.50, the quantity demanded declines along the demand curve, moving from point *C* (81 million pounds) toward point *B* (60 million pounds). The higher prices mean that restaurants must charge more for lobster rolls and stuffed lobsters. As a result, many people stop buying lobster or order it less frequently when they dine out. Some restaurants drop lobster from the menu entirely, and some shoppers at the fish counter turn to lobster substitutes such as swordfish and salmon.

As the price rises, lobster trappers (suppliers) also change their behavior. They stay out longer and put out more traps than they did when the price was $11.50 per pound. Quantity supplied increases from 38 million pounds to 60 million pounds. This increase in price brings about a movement along the 2008 supply curve from point *A* to point *B*.

Finally, a new equilibrium is established at a price of $16.10 per pound and a total output of 60 million pounds. The market has determined who gets the lobsters: *The lower total supply is rationed to those who are willing and able to pay the higher price.*

This idea of "willingness to pay" is central to the distribution of available supply, and willingness depends on both desire (preferences) and income/wealth. Willingness to pay does not necessarily mean that only the very rich will continue to buy lobsters when the price increases. For anyone to continue to buy lobster at a higher price, his or her enjoyment comes at a higher cost in terms of other goods and services.

In sum:

> The adjustment of price is the rationing mechanism in free markets. Price rationing means that whenever there is a need to ration a good—that is, when a shortage exists—in a free market, the price of the good will rise until quantity supplied equals quantity demanded—that is, until the market clears.

There is some price that will clear any market you can think of. Consider the market for a famous painting such as Jackson Pollock's *No. 5, 1948*, illustrated in Figure 4.2. At a low price, there would be an enormous excess demand for such an important painting. The price would be bid up until there was only one remaining demander. Presumably, that price would be very high. In fact, the Pollock painting sold for a record $140 million in 2006. If the product is in strictly scarce supply, as a single painting is, its price is said to be *demand-determined.* That is, its price is determined solely and exclusively by the amount that the highest bidder or highest bidders are willing to pay.

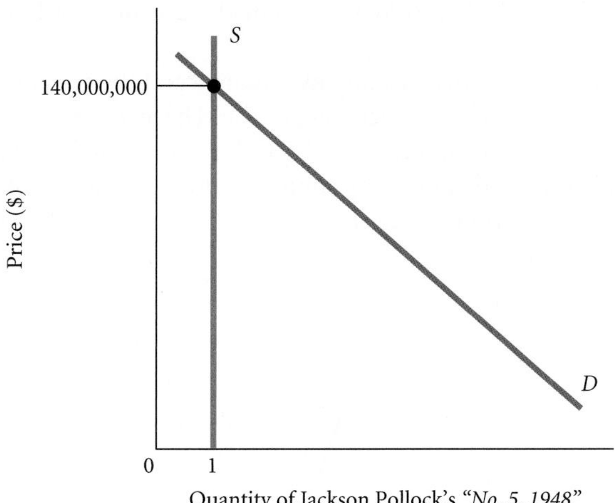

◀ **FIGURE 4.2 Market for a Rare Painting**

There is some price that will clear any market, even if supply is strictly limited. In an auction for a unique painting, the price (bid) will rise to eliminate excess demand until there is only one bidder willing to purchase the single available painting. Some estimate that the *Mona Lisa* would sell for $600 million if auctioned.

One might interpret the statement that "there is some price that will clear any market" to mean "everything has its price," but that is not exactly what it means. Suppose you own a small silver bracelet that has been in your family for generations. It is quite possible that you would not sell it for *any* amount of money. Does this mean that the market is not working, or that quantity supplied and quantity demanded are not equal? Not at all. It simply means that *you* are the highest bidder. By turning down all bids, you must be willing to forgo what anybody offers for it.

Constraints on the Market and Alternative Rationing Mechanisms

On occasion, both governments and private firms decide to use some mechanism other than the market system to ration an item for which there is excess demand at the current price. Policies designed to stop price rationing are commonly justified in a number of ways.

The rationale most often used is fairness. It is not "fair" to let landlords charge high rents, not fair for oil companies to run up the price of gasoline, not fair for insurance companies to charge enormous premiums, and so on. After all, the argument goes, we have no choice but to pay—housing and insurance are necessary, and one needs gasoline to get to work. Although it is not precisely true that price rationing allocates goods and services solely on the basis of income and wealth, income and wealth do constrain our wants. Why should all the gasoline or all the tickets to the World Series go just to the rich?

Various schemes to keep price from rising to equilibrium are based on several perceptions of injustice, among them (1) that price-gouging is bad, (2) that income is unfairly distributed, and (3) that some items are necessities and everyone should be able to buy them at a "reasonable" price. Regardless of the rationale, the following examples will make two things clear:

1. Attempts to bypass price rationing in the market and to use alternative rationing devices are more difficult and more costly than they would seem at first glance.
2. Very often such attempts distribute costs and benefits among households in unintended ways.

Oil, Gasoline, and OPEC In 1973 and 1974, OPEC imposed an embargo on shipments of crude oil to the United States. What followed was a drastic reduction in the quantity of gasoline available at local gas pumps.

Had the market system been allowed to operate, refined gasoline prices would have increased dramatically until quantity supplied was equal to quantity demanded. However, the government decided that rationing gasoline only to those who were willing and able to pay the most was unfair, and Congress imposed a **price ceiling**, or maximum price, of $0.57 per gallon of leaded regular gasoline. That price ceiling was intended to keep gasoline "affordable," but it also perpetuated the shortage. At the restricted price, quantity demanded remained greater than

price ceiling A maximum price that sellers may charge for a good, usually set by government.

quantity supplied and the available gasoline had to be divided up somehow among all potential demanders.

You can see the effects of the price ceiling by looking carefully at Figure 4.3. If the price had been set by the interaction of supply and demand, it would have increased to approximately $1.50 per gallon. Instead, Congress made it illegal to sell gasoline for more than $0.57 per gallon. At that price, quantity demanded exceeded quantity supplied and a shortage existed. Because the price system was not allowed to function, an alternative rationing system had to be found to distribute the available supply of gasoline.

FIGURE 4.3 Excess Demand (Shortage) Created by a Price Ceiling

In 1974, a ceiling price of $0.57 cents per gallon of leaded regular gasoline was imposed. If the price had been set by the interaction of supply and demand instead, it would have increased to approximately $1.50 per gallon. At $0.57 per gallon, the quantity demanded exceeded the quantity supplied. Because the price system was not allowed to function, an alternative rationing system had to be found to distribute the available supply of gasoline.

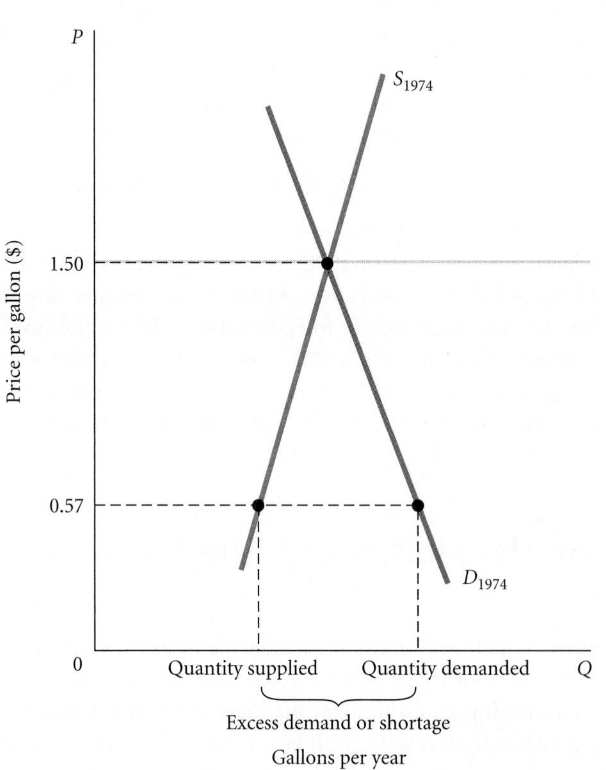

queuing Waiting in line as a means of distributing goods and services: a nonprice rationing mechanism.

favored customers Those who receive special treatment from dealers during situations of excess demand.

ration coupons Tickets or coupons that entitle individuals to purchase a certain amount of a given product per month.

Several devices were tried. The most common of all nonprice rationing systems is **queuing**, a term that means waiting in line. During 1974, very long lines formed daily at gas stations, starting as early as 5 A.M. Under this system, gasoline went to those people who were willing to pay the most, but the sacrifice was measured in hours and aggravation instead of dollars.[1]

A second nonprice rationing device used during the gasoline crisis was that of **favored customers**. Many gas station owners decided not to sell gasoline to the general public, but to reserve their scarce supplies for friends and favored customers. Not surprisingly, many customers tried to become "favored" by offering side payments to gas station owners. Owners also charged high prices for service. By doing so, they increased the real price of gasoline but hid it in service overcharges to get around the ceiling.

Yet another method of dividing up available supply is the use of **ration coupons**. It was suggested in both 1974 and 1979 that families be given ration tickets or coupons that would entitle them to purchase a certain number of gallons of gasoline each month. That way, everyone would get the same amount regardless of income. Such a system had been employed in the United States

[1] You can also show formally that the result is inefficient—that there is a resulting net loss of total value to society. First, there is the cost of waiting in line. Time has a value. With price rationing, no one has to wait in line and the value of that time is saved. Second, there may be additional lost value if the gasoline ends up in the hands of someone who places a lower value on it than someone else who gets no gas. Suppose, for example, that the market price of gasoline if unconstrained would rise to $2 but that the government has it fixed at $1. There will be long lines to get gas. Imagine that to motorist A, 10 gallons of gas is worth $35 but that she fails to get gas because her time is too valuable to wait in line. To motorist B, 10 gallons is worth only $15, but his time is worth much less; so he gets the gas. In the end, A could pay B for the gas and both would be better off. If A pays B $30 for the gas, A is $5 better off and B is $15 better off. In addition, A does not have to wait in line. Thus, the allocation that results from nonprice rationing involves a net loss of value. Such losses are called *deadweight losses*. See p. 84 of this chapter.

during the 1940s when wartime price ceilings on meat, sugar, butter, tires, nylon stockings, and many other items were imposed.

When ration coupons are used with no prohibition against trading them, however, the result is almost identical to a system of price rationing. Those who are willing and able to pay the most buy up the coupons and use them to purchase gasoline, chocolate, fresh eggs, or anything else that is sold at a restricted price.[2] This means that the price of the restricted good will effectively rise to the market-clearing price. For instance, suppose that you decide not to sell your ration coupon. You are then forgoing what you would have received by selling the coupon. Thus, the "real" price of the good you purchase will be higher (if only in opportunity cost) than the restricted price. Even when trading coupons is declared illegal, it is virtually impossible to stop black markets from developing. In a **black market**, illegal trading takes place at market-determined prices.

black market A market in which illegal trading takes place at market-determined prices.

Rationing Mechanisms for Concert and Sports Tickets On September 16, 2007, Justin Timberlake performed at the Staples Center in Los Angeles. The day before the concert, you could buy a front row ticket for $16,000 on the StubHub Web site. Tickets for sporting events such as the World Series, the Super Bowl, and the World Cup command huge prices in the open market. In many cases, the prices are substantially above the original issue price.

The Staples Center seats 20,000 for concerts. Figure 4.4 illustrates the situation. The supply of tickets is fixed. Of course, there are good seats and bad seats; but to keep things simple, let's assume that all the seats are the same and that the promoters originally charged $50 for all tickets. Supply is represented by a vertical line at 20,000. A higher price does not increase the supply of seats. At the original issue price, the quantity demanded is 38,000, which is greater than the quantity supplied.

The first question is why would a profit-maximizing enterprise not charge the highest price it could charge? The answer depends on the event. If the Chicago Cubs got into the World Series,

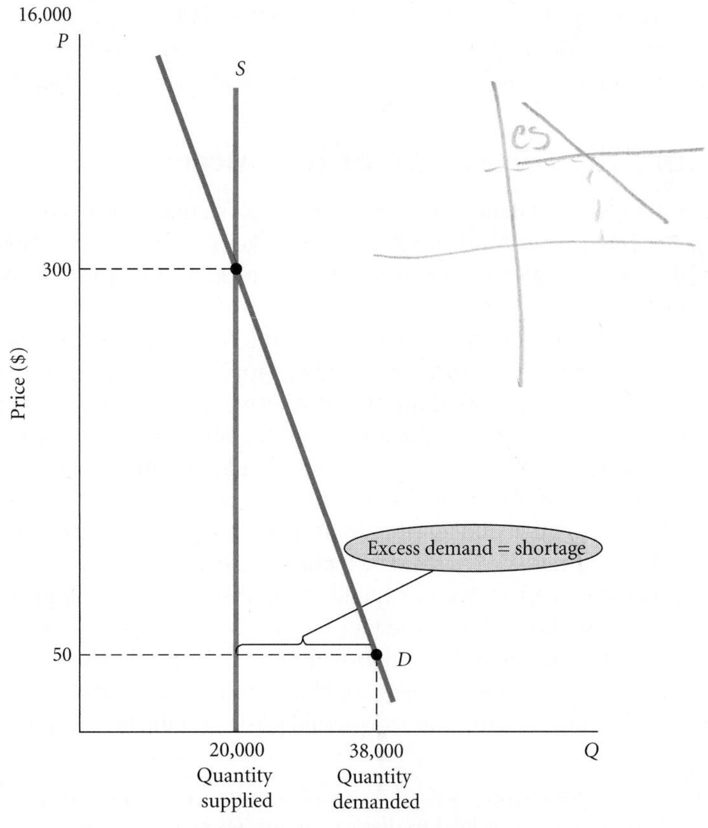

FIGURE 4.4 Supply of and Demand for a Concert in 2007

The face value of a ticket to the Justin Timberlake concert on September 16, 2007, at the Staples Center in Los Angeles was $50. The Staples Center holds 20,000. The supply curve is vertical at 20,000. At $50, the quantity supplied is below the quantity demanded. The diagram shows that the quantity demanded and the quantity supplied would be equal at $300. The Web shows that one ticket could be worth $16,000.

[2] Of course, if you are assigned a number of tickets and you sell them, you are better off than you would be with price rationing. Ration coupons thus serve as a way of redistributing income.

the people of Chicago would buy all the tickets available for thousands of dollars each. But if the Cubs actually *charged* $2,000 a ticket, the hard-working fans would be furious: "Greedy Cubs Gouge Fans" the headlines would scream. Ordinary loyal fans earning reasonable salaries would not be able to afford those prices. Next season, perhaps some of those irate fans would change loyalties, supporting the White Sox over the Cubs. In part to keep from alienating loyal fans, prices for championship games are held down.

Not every concert promoter or sports team behaves that way. In 2000, Barbra Streisand gave a concert in Sydney, Australia. Tickets were issued with a *face value* of $1,530, a record for a concert that still stands today.

If all the Justin Timberlake tickets were sold for $50, the sold-out concert would take in $1 million dollars. But who would get the tickets? As in the case of gasoline, a variety of rationing mechanisms might be used. The most common is queuing, waiting in line. The tickets would go on sale at a particular time, and people would show up and wait. Now ticket sellers have virtual waiting rooms online. Tickets for the World Series go on sale at a particular time in September, and the people who log on to team Web sites at the right moment get into an electronic queue and can buy tickets. Often tickets are sold out in a matter of minutes.

Again there are also favored customers. Those who get tickets without queuing are local politicians, sponsors, and friends of the artist or friends of the players.

But "once the dust settles," the power of technology and the concept of *opportunity cost* take over. Even if you get the Timberlake ticket for the (relatively) low price of $50, that is not the true cost. The true cost is what you give up to sit in the seat. If people on eBay, StubHub, or Ticketmaster are willing to pay $500 for your ticket, that's what you must pay, or sacrifice, to go to the concert. Many people—even strong fans—will choose to sell that ticket. Once again, it is difficult to stop the market from rationing the tickets to those people who are willing and able to pay the most.

No matter how good the intentions of private organizations and governments, it is very difficult to prevent the price system from operating and to stop people's willingness to pay from asserting itself. Every time an alternative is tried, the price system seems to sneak in the back door. With favored customers and black markets, the final distribution may be even more unfair than that which would result from simple price rationing.

Prices and the Allocation of Resources

Thinking of the market system as a mechanism for allocating scarce goods and services among competing demanders is very revealing, but the market determines more than just the distribution of final outputs. It also determines what gets produced and how resources are allocated among competing uses.

Consider a change in consumer preferences that leads to an increase in demand for a specific good or service. During the 1980s, for example, people began going to restaurants more frequently than before. Researchers think that this trend, which continues today, is partially the result of social changes (such as a dramatic rise in the number of two-earner families) and partially the result of rising incomes. The market responded to this change in demand by shifting resources, both capital and labor, into more and better restaurants.

With the increase in demand for restaurant meals, the price of eating out rose and the restaurant business became more profitable. The higher profits attracted new businesses and provided old restaurants with an incentive to expand. As new capital, seeking profits, flowed into the restaurant business, so did labor. New restaurants need chefs. Chefs need training, and the higher wages that came with increased demand provided an incentive for them to get it. In response to the increase in demand for training, new cooking schools opened and existing schools began to offer courses in the culinary arts. This story could go on and on, but the point is clear:

Price changes resulting from shifts of demand in output markets cause profits to rise or fall. Profits attract capital; losses lead to disinvestment. Higher wages attract labor and encourage workers to acquire skills. At the core of the system, supply, demand, and prices in input and output markets determine the allocation of resources and the ultimate combinations of goods and services produced.

ECONOMICS IN PRACTICE

The Price Mechanism at Work for Shakespeare

Every summer, New York City puts on free performances of Shakespeare in the Park. Tickets are distributed on a first-come-first-serve basis at the Delacorte Theatre in the Park beginning at 1 P.M. on the day of the show. People usually begin lining up at 6 A.M. when the park opens; and by 10 A.M. the line has typically reached a length sufficient to give away all available tickets.

When you examine the people standing in line for these tickets, most of them seem to be fairly young. Many carry book bags identifying them as students in one of New York's many colleges. Of course, all college students may be fervent Shakespeare fans, but can you think of another reason for the composition of the line? Further, when you attend one of the plays and look around, the audience appears much older and much sleeker than the people who were standing in line. What is going on?

While the tickets are "free" in terms of financial costs, their true price includes the value of the time spent standing in line. Thus, the tickets are cheaper for people (for example, students) whose time value is lower than they are for high-wage earners, like an investment banker from Goldman Sachs. The true cost of a ticket is $0 plus the opportunity cost of the time spent in line. If the average person spends 4 hours in line, as is done in the Central Park case, for someone with a high wage, the true cost of the ticket might be very high. For example, a lawyer who earns $300 an hour would be giving up $1,200 to wait in line. It should not surprise you to see more people waiting in line for whom the tickets are inexpensive.

What about the people who are at the performance? Think about our discussion of the power of entrepreneurs. In this case, the students who stand in line as consumers of the tickets also can play a role as producers. In fact, the students can produce tickets relatively cheaply by waiting in line. They can then turn around and sell those tickets to the high-wage Shakespeare lovers. These days eBay is a great source of tickets to free events, sold by individuals with low opportunity costs of their time who queued up. Craigslist even provides listings for people who are willing to wait in line for you.

Of course, now and again we do encounter a busy businessperson in one of the Central Park lines. Recently, one of the authors encountered one and asked him why he was waiting in line rather than using eBay, and he replied that it reminded him of when he was young, waiting in line for rock concerts.

Price Floors

As we have seen, price ceilings, often imposed because price rationing is viewed as unfair, result in alternative rationing mechanisms that are inefficient and may be equally unfair. Some of the same arguments can be made for price floors. A **price floor** is a minimum price below which exchange is not permitted. If a price floor is set above the equilibrium price, the result will be excess supply; quantity supplied will be greater than quantity demanded.

price floor A minimum price below which exchange is not permitted.

The most common example of a price floor is the **minimum wage**, which is a floor set for the price of labor. Employers (who demand labor) are not permitted under federal law to pay a wage less than $6.55 per hour (in 2008) to workers (who supply labor). Critics argue that since the minimum wage is above equilibrium, the result will be wasteful unemployment. At the wage of $6.55, the quantity of labor demanded is less than the quantity of labor supplied. Whenever a price floor is set above equilibrium, there will be an excess supply.

minimum wage A price floor set for the price of labor.

Supply and Demand Analysis: An Oil Import Fee

The basic logic of supply and demand is a powerful tool of analysis. As an extended example of the power of this logic, we will consider a recent proposal to impose a tax on imported oil. The idea of taxing imported oil is hotly debated, and the tools we have learned thus far will show us the effects of such a tax.

Consider the facts. Between 1985 and 1989, the United States increased its dependence on oil imports dramatically. In 1989, total U.S. demand for crude oil was 13.6 million barrels per day. Of that amount, only 7.7 million barrels per day (57 percent) were supplied by U.S. producers, with the remaining 5.9 million barrels per day (43 percent) imported. The price of oil on world markets that year averaged about $18. This heavy dependence on foreign oil left the United States vulnerable to the price shock that followed the Iraqi invasion of Kuwait in August 1990. In the months following the invasion, the price of crude oil on world markets shot up to $40 per barrel.

Even before the invasion, many economists and some politicians had recommended a stiff oil import fee (or tax) that would, it was argued, reduce the U.S. dependence on foreign oil by (1) reducing overall consumption and (2) providing an incentive for increased domestic production. An added bonus would be improved air quality from the reduction in driving.

Supply and demand analysis makes the arguments of the import fee proponents easier to understand. Figure 4.5(a) shows the U.S. market for oil. The world price of oil is assumed to be $18, and the United States is assumed to be able to buy *all the oil that it wants* at this price. This

▶ FIGURE 4.5 The U.S. Market for Crude Oil, 1989

At a world price of $18, domestic production is 7.7 million barrels per day and the total quantity of oil demanded in the United States is 13.6 million barrels per day. The difference is total imports (5.9 million barrels per day).

If the government levies a 33 1/3 percent tax on imports, the price of a barrel of oil rises to $24. The quantity demanded falls to 12.2 million barrels per day. At the same time, the quantity supplied by domestic producers increases to 9.0 million barrels per day and the quantity imported falls to 3.2 million barrels per day.

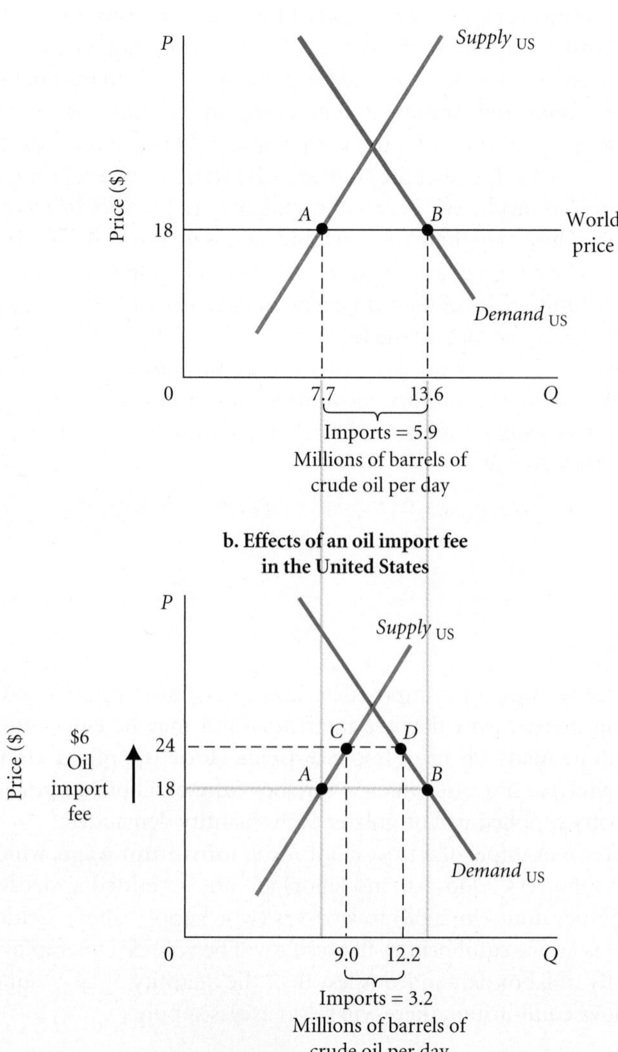

means that domestic producers cannot get away with charging any more than $18 per barrel. The curve labeled $Supply_{US}$ shows the amount that domestic suppliers will produce at each price level. At a price of $18, domestic production is 7.7 million barrels. Stated somewhat differently, U.S. producers will produce at point *A* on the supply curve. The total quantity of oil demanded in the United States in 1989 was 13.6 million barrels per day. At a price of $18, the quantity demanded in the United States is point *B* on the demand curve.

The difference between the total quantity demanded (13.6 million barrels per day) and domestic production (7.7 million barrels per day) is total imports (5.9 million barrels per day).

Now suppose that the government levies a tax of 33 1/3 percent on imported oil. Because the import price is $18, a tax of $6 (or .3333 × $18) per barrel means that importers of oil in the United States will pay a total of $24 per barrel ($18 + $6). This new, higher price means that U.S. producers can also charge up to $24 for a barrel of crude. Note, however, that the tax is paid only on imported oil. Thus, the entire $24 paid for domestic crude goes to domestic producers.

Figure 4.5(b) shows the result of the tax. First, because of a higher price, the quantity demanded drops to 12.2 million barrels per day. This is a movement *along* the demand curve from point *B* to point *D*. At the same time, the quantity supplied by domestic producers increased to 9.0 million barrels per day. This is a movement *along* the supply curve from point *A* to point *C*. With an increase in domestic quantity supplied and a decrease in domestic quantity demanded, imports decrease to 3.2 million barrels per day (12.2 – 9.0).[3]

The tax also generates revenues for the federal government. The total tax revenue collected is equal to the tax per barrel ($6) times the number of imported barrels. When the quantity imported is 3.2 million barrels per day, total revenue is $6 × 3.2 million, or $19.2 million *per day* (about $7 billion per year).

What does all of this mean? In the final analysis, an oil import fee would (1) increase domestic production and (2) reduce overall consumption. To the extent that one believes that Americans are consuming too much oil and polluting the environment, the reduced consumption may be a good thing.

Supply and Demand and Market Efficiency

Clearly, supply and demand curves help explain the way that markets and market prices work to allocate scarce resources. Recall that when we try to understand "how the system works," we are doing "positive economics."

Supply and demand curves can also be used to illustrate the idea of market efficiency, an important aspect of "normative economics." To understand the ideas, you first must understand the concepts of consumer and producer surplus.

Consumer Surplus

The argument, made several times already, that the market forces us to reveal a great deal about our personal preferences is an extremely important one; and it bears repeating at least once more here. If you are free to choose within the constraints imposed by prices and your income and you decide to buy, for example, a hamburger for $2.50, you have "revealed" that a hamburger is worth at least $2.50 to you.

A simple market demand curve such as the one in Figure 4.6(a) illustrates this point quite clearly. At the current market price of $2.50, consumers will purchase 7 million hamburgers per month. There is only one price in the market, and the demand curve tells us how many hamburgers households would buy if they could purchase all they wanted at the posted price of $2.50. Anyone who values a hamburger at $2.50 or more will buy it. Anyone who does not value a hamburger that highly will not buy it.

[3] These figures were not chosen randomly. It is interesting to note that in 1985, the world price of crude oil averaged about $24 a barrel. Domestic production was 9.0 million barrels per day and domestic consumption was 12.2 million barrels per day, with imports of only 3.2 million. The drop in the world price between 1985 and 1989 increased imports to 5.9 million, an 84 percent increase.

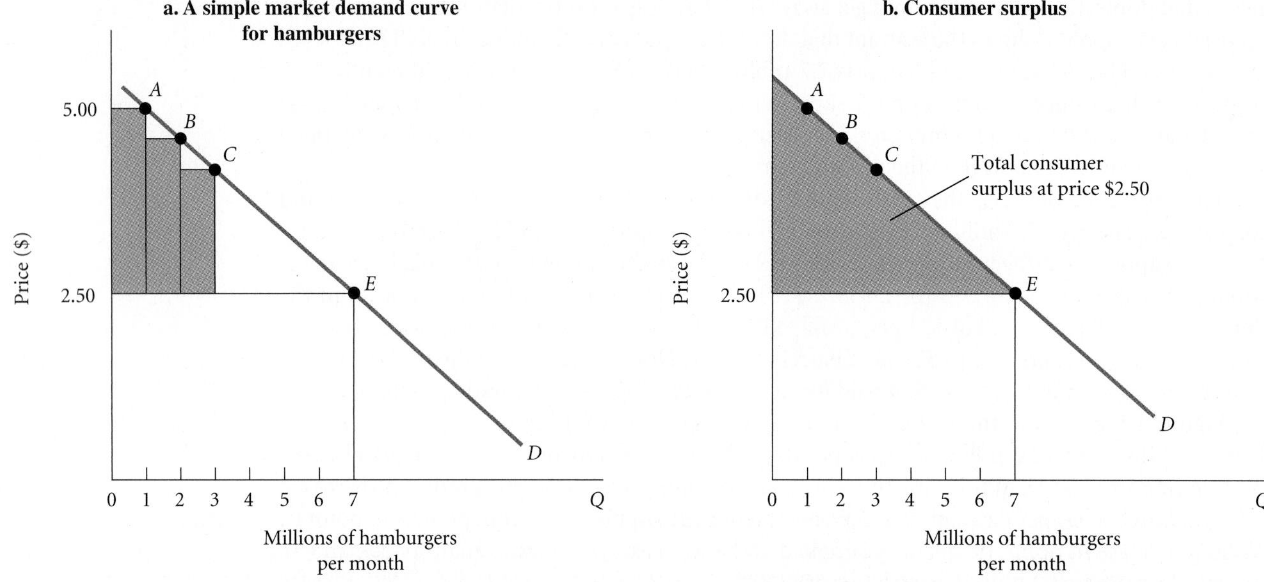

▲ **FIGURE 4.6 Market Demand and Consumer Surplus**
As illustrated in Figure 4.6(a), some consumers (see point *A*) are willing to pay as much as $5.00 each for hamburgers. Since the market price is just $2.50, they receive a consumer surplus of $2.50 for each hamburger that they consume. Others (see point *B*) are willing to pay something less than $5.00 and receive a slightly smaller surplus. Since the market price of hamburgers is just $2.50, the area of the shaded triangle in Figure 4.6(b) is equal to total consumer surplus.

consumer surplus The difference between the maximum amount a person is willing to pay for a good and its current market price.

Some people, however, value hamburgers at more than $2.50. As Figure 4.6(a) shows, even if the price were $5.00, consumers would still buy 1 million hamburgers. If these people were able to buy the good at a price of $2.50, they would earn a **consumer surplus**. Consumer surplus is the difference between the maximum amount a person is willing to pay for a good and its current market price. The consumer surplus earned by the people willing to pay $5.00 for a hamburger is approximately equal to the shaded area between point *A* and the price, $2.50.

The second million hamburgers in Figure 4.6(a) are valued at more than the market price as well, although the consumer surplus gained is slightly less. Point *B* on the market demand curve shows the maximum amount that consumers would be willing to pay for the second million hamburgers. The consumer surplus earned by these people is equal to the shaded area between *B* and the price, $2.50. Similarly, for the third million hamburgers, maximum willingness to pay is given by point *C*; consumer surplus is a bit lower than it is at points *A* and *B*, but it is still significant.

The total value of the consumer surplus suggested by the data in Figure 4.6(a) is roughly equal to the area of the shaded triangle in Figure 4.6(b). To understand why this is so, think about offering hamburgers to consumers at successively lower prices. If the good were actually sold for $2.50, those near point *A* on the demand curve would get a large surplus; those at point *B* would get a smaller surplus. Those at point *E* would get no surplus.

Producer Surplus

Similarly, the supply curve in a market shows the amount that firms willingly produce and supply to the market at various prices. Presumably it is because the price is sufficient to cover the costs or the opportunity costs of production and give producers enough profit to keep them in business. When speaking of cost of production, we include everything that a producer must give up in order to produce a good.

A simple market supply curve like the one in Figure 4.7(a) illustrates this point quite clearly. At the current market price of $2.50, producers will produce and sell 7 million hamburgers. There is only one price in the market, and the supply curve tells us the quantity supplied at each price.

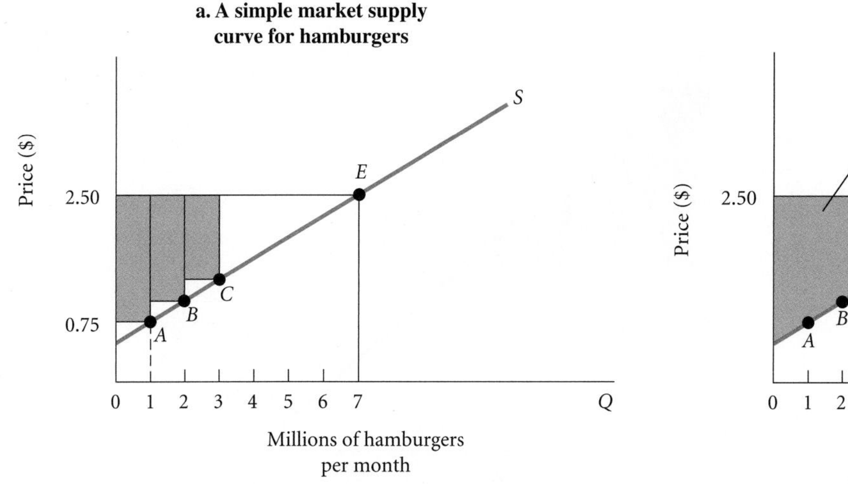

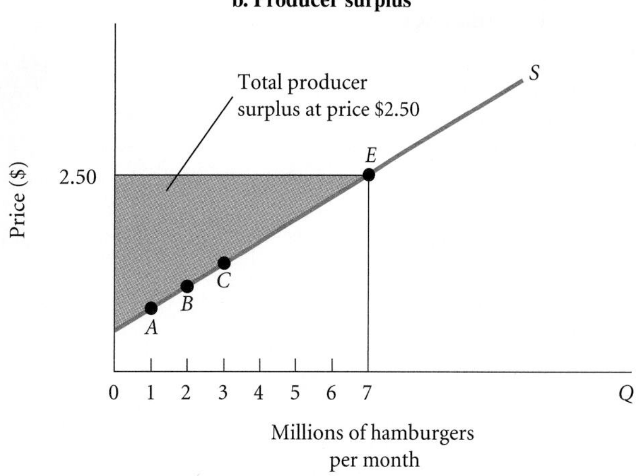

▲ **FIGURE 4.7 Market Supply and Producer Surplus**

As illustrated in Figure 4.7(a), some producers are willing to produce hamburgers for a price of $0.75 each. Since they are paid $2.50, they earn a producer surplus equal to $1.75. Other producers are willing to supply hamburgers at a price of $1.00; they receive a producer surplus equal to $1.50. Since the market price of hamburgers is $2.50, the area of the shaded triangle in Figure 4.7(b) is equal to total producer surplus.

Notice, however, that if the price were just $0.75 (75 cents), although production would be much lower—most producers would be out of business at that price—a few producers would actually be supplying burgers. In fact, producers would supply about 1 million burgers to the market. These firms must have lower costs: They are more efficient or they have access to raw beef at a lower price or perhaps they can hire low-wage labor.

If these efficient, low-cost producers are able to charge $2.50 for each hamburger, they are earning what is called a **producer surplus**. Producer surplus is the difference between the current market price and the full cost of production for the firm. The first 1 million hamburgers would generate a producer surplus of $2.50 minus $0.75, or $1.75 per hamburger: a total of $1.75 million. The second million hamburgers would also generate a producer surplus because the price of $2.50 exceeds the producers' total cost of producing these hamburgers, which is above $0.75 but much less than $2.50.

producer surplus The difference between the current market price and the full cost of production for the firm.

The total value of the producer surplus received by producers of hamburgers at a price of $2.50 per burger is roughly equal to the shaded triangle in Figure 4.7(b). Those producers just able to make a profit producing burgers will be near point *E* on the supply curve and will earn very little in the way of surplus.

Competitive Markets Maximize the Sum of Producer and Consumer Surplus

In the preceding example, the quantity of hamburgers supplied and the quantity of hamburgers demanded are equal at $2.50. Figure 4.8 shows the total net benefits to consumers and producers resulting from the production of 7 million hamburgers. Consumers receive benefits in excess of the price they pay and equal to the blue shaded area between the demand curve and the price line at $2.50; the area is equal to the amount of consumer surplus being earned. Producers receive compensation in excess of costs and equal to the red shaded area between the supply curve and the price line at $2.50; the area is equal to the amount of producer surplus being earned.

Now consider the result to consumers and producers if production were to be reduced to 4 million burgers. Look carefully at Figure 4.9(a). At 4 million burgers, consumers are willing to pay $3.75 for hamburgers and there are firms whose cost makes it worthwhile to supply at a price as low as $1.50, yet something is stopping production at 4 million. The result is a loss of both consumer and producer surplus. You can see in Figure 4.9(a) that if production were expanded from 4 million to 7 million, the market would yield more consumer surplus and more producer surplus.

FIGURE 4.8 Total Producer and Consumer Surplus

Total producer and consumer surplus is greatest where supply and demand curves intersect at equilibrium.

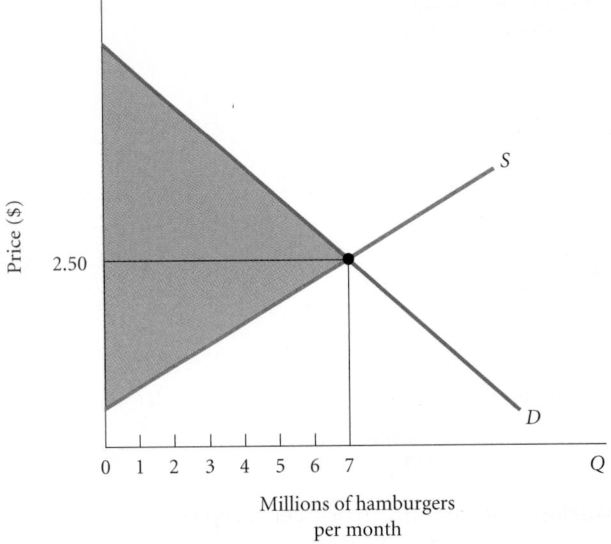

deadweight loss The total loss of producer and consumer surplus from underproduction or overproduction.

The total loss of producer and consumer surplus from *underproduction* and, as we will see shortly, from overproduction is referred to as a **deadweight loss**. In Figure 4.9(a) the deadweight loss is equal to the area of triangle *ABC* shaded in yellow.

Figure 4.9(b) illustrates how a deadweight loss of both producer and consumer surplus can result from *overproduction* as well. For every hamburger produced above 7 million, consumers are willing to pay less than the cost of production. The cost of the resources needed to produce hamburgers above 7 million exceeds the benefits to consumers, resulting in a net loss of producer and consumer surplus equal to the yellow shaded area *ABC*.

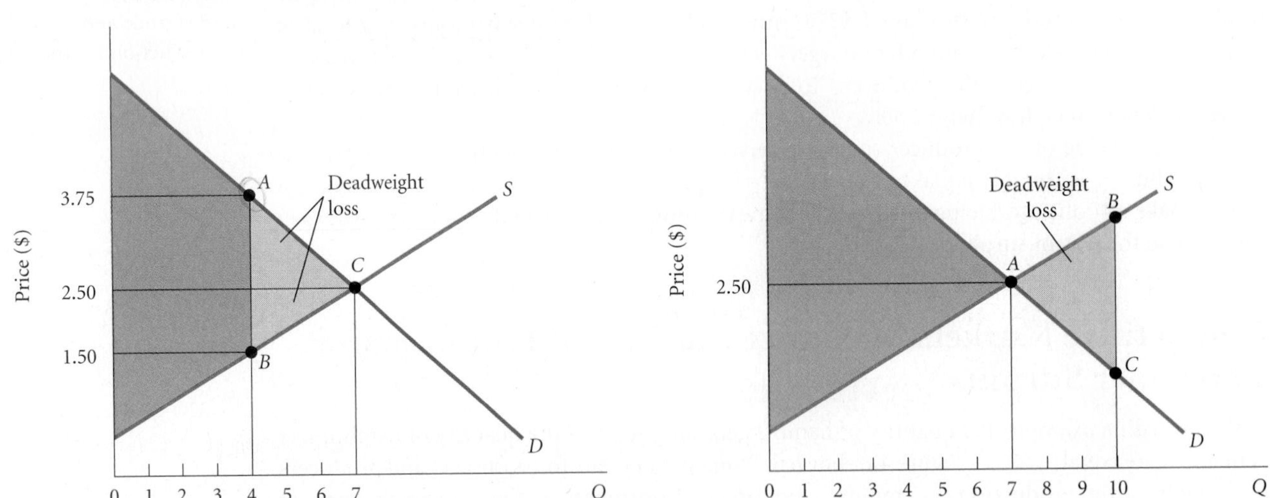

FIGURE 4.9 Deadweight Loss

Figure 4.9(a) shows the consequences of producing 4 million hamburgers per month instead of 7 million hamburgers per month. Total producer and consumer surplus is reduced by the area of triangle *ABC* shaded in yellow. This is called the deadweight loss from underproduction. Figure 4.9(b) shows the consequences of producing 10 million hamburgers per month instead of 7 million hamburgers per month. As production increases from 7 million to 10 million hamburgers, the full cost of production rises above consumers' willingness to pay, resulting in a deadweight loss equal to the area of triangle *ABC*.

Potential Causes of Deadweight Loss From Under- and Overproduction

Most of the next few chapters will discuss perfectly competitive markets in which prices are determined by the free interaction of supply and demand. As you will see, when supply and demand interact freely, competitive markets produce what people want at the least cost, that is, they are efficient. Beginning in Chapter 13, however, we will begin to relax assumptions and will discover a number of naturally occurring sources of market failure. Monopoly power gives firms the incentive to underproduce and overprice, taxes and subsidies may distort consumer choices, external costs such as pollution and congestion may lead to over- or underproduction of some goods, and artificial price floors and price ceilings may have the same effects.

Looking Ahead

We have now examined the basic forces of supply and demand and discussed the market/price system. These fundamental concepts will serve as building blocks for what comes next. Whether you are studying microeconomics or macroeconomics, you will be studying the functions of markets and the behavior of market participants in more detail in the following chapters.

Because the concepts presented in the first four chapters are so important to your understanding of what is to come, this might be a good time for you to review this material.

SUMMARY

THE PRICE SYSTEM: RATIONING AND ALLOCATING RESOURCES *p. 73*

1. In a market economy, the market system (or price system) serves two functions. It determines the allocation of resources among producers and the final mix of outputs. It also distributes goods and services on the basis of willingness and ability to pay. In this sense, it serves as a *price rationing* device.
2. Governments as well as private firms sometimes decide not to use the market system to ration an item for which there is excess demand. Examples of nonprice rationing systems include *queuing*, *favored customers*, and *ration coupons*. The most common rationale for such policies is "fairness."
3. Attempts to bypass the market and use alternative nonprice rationing devices are more difficult and costly than it would seem at first glance. Schemes that open up opportunities for favored customers, black markets, and side payments often end up less "fair" than the free market.

SUPPLY AND DEMAND ANALYSIS: AN OIL IMPORT FEE *p. 80*

1. The basic logic of supply and demand is a powerful tool for analysis. For example, supply and demand analysis shows that an oil import tax will reduce quantity of oil demanded, increase domestic production, and generate revenues for the government.

SUPPLY AND DEMAND AND MARKET EFFICIENCY *p. 81*

1. Supply and demand curves can also be used to illustrate the idea of market efficiency, an important aspect of normative economics.
2. *Consumer surplus* is the difference between the maximum amount a person is willing to pay for a good and the current market price.
3. *Producer surplus* is the difference between the current market price and the full cost of production for the firm.
4. At free market equilibrium with competitive markets, the sum of consumer surplus and producer surplus is maximized.
5. The total loss of producer and consumer surplus from underproduction or overproduction is referred to as a *deadweight loss*.

REVIEW TERMS AND CONCEPTS

black market, *p. 77*
consumer surplus, *p. 82*
deadweight loss, *p. 84*
favored customers, *p. 76*
minimum wage, *p. 79*
price ceiling, *p. 75*
price floor, *p. 79*
price rationing, *p. 73*
producer surplus, *p. 83*
queuing, *p. 76*
ration coupons, *p. 76*

PROBLEMS

Visit **www.myeconlab.com** to complete the problems marked in orange online. You will receive instant feedback on your answers, tutorial help, and access to additional practice problems.

1. Illustrate the following with supply and demand curves:
   a. In the summer of 2006, Viennese artist Gustav Klimt's Portrait of Adele Bloch-Bauer was sold in New York for $135 million.
   b. In 2008, hogs in the United States were selling for $67 each, down from $75 a year before. This was due primarily to the fact that supply had increased during the period to 1.8 million hogs per week.
   c. Early in 2009, a survey of greenhouses indicated that the demand for houseplants was rising sharply. At the same time, large numbers of low-cost producers started growing plants for sale. The overall result was a drop in the average price of houseplants and an increase in the number of plants sold.
2. Every demand curve must eventually hit the quantity axis because with limited incomes, there is always a price so high that there is no demand for the good. Do you agree or disagree? Why?
3. When excess demand exists for tickets to a major sporting event or a concert, profit opportunities exist for scalpers. Explain briefly using supply and demand curves to illustrate. Some argue that scalpers work to the advantage of everyone and are "efficient." Do you agree or disagree? Explain briefly.
4. In an effort to "support" the price of some agricultural goods, the Department of Agriculture pays farmers a subsidy in cash for every acre that they leave *unplanted*. The Agriculture Department argues that the subsidy increases the "cost" of planting and that it will reduce supply and increase the price of competitively produced agricultural goods. Critics argue that because the subsidy is a payment to farmers, it will reduce costs and lead to lower prices. Which argument is correct? Explain.
5. The rent for apartments in New York City has been rising sharply. Demand for apartments in New York City has been rising sharply as well. This is hard to explain because the law of demand says that higher prices should lead to lower demand. Do you agree or disagree? Explain your answer.
6. Illustrate the following with supply and/or demand curves:
   a. The federal government "supports" the price of wheat by paying farmers not to plant wheat on some of their land.
   b. An increase in the price of chicken has an impact on the price of hamburger.
   c. Incomes rise, shifting the demand for gasoline. Crude oil prices rise, shifting the supply of gasoline. At the new equilibrium, the quantity of gasoline sold is less than it was before. (Crude oil is used to produce gasoline.)
7. Illustrate the following with supply and/or demand curves:
   a. A situation of excess labor supply (unemployment) caused by a "minimum wage" law.
   b. The effect of a sharp increase in heating oil prices on the demand for insulation material.
8. Suppose that the world price of oil is $70 per barrel and that the United States can buy all the oil it wants at this price. Suppose also that the demand and supply schedules for oil in the United States are as follows:

PRICE ($ PER BARREL)	U.S. QUANTITY DEMANDED	U.S. QUANTITY SUPPLIED
68	16	4
70	15	6
72	14	8
74	13	10
76	12	12

   a. On graph paper, draw the supply and demand curves for the United States.
   b. With free trade in oil, what price will Americans pay for their oil? What quantity will Americans buy? How much of this will be supplied by American producers? How much will be imported? Illustrate total imports on your graph of the U.S. oil market.
   c. Suppose the United States imposes a tax of $4 per barrel on imported oil. What quantity would Americans buy? How much of this would be supplied by American producers? How much would be imported? How much tax would the government collect?
   d. Briefly summarize the impact of an oil import tax by explaining who is helped and who is hurt among the following groups: domestic oil consumers, domestic oil producers, foreign oil producers, and the U.S. government.
9. Use the data in the preceding problem to answer the following questions. Now suppose that the United States allows no oil imports.
   a. What are the equilibrium price and quantity for oil in the United States?
   b. If the United States imposed a price ceiling of $74 per barrel on the oil market and prohibited imports, would there be an excess supply or an excess demand for oil? If so, how much?
   c. Under the price ceiling, quantity supplied and quantity demanded differ. Which of the two will determine how much oil is purchased? Briefly explain why.

10. Use the following diagram to calculate total consumer surplus at a price of $8 and production of 6 million meals per day. For the same equilibrium, calculate total producer surplus. Assuming price remained at $8 but production was cut to 3 million meals per day, calculate producer surplus and consumer surplus. Calculate the deadweight loss from underproduction.

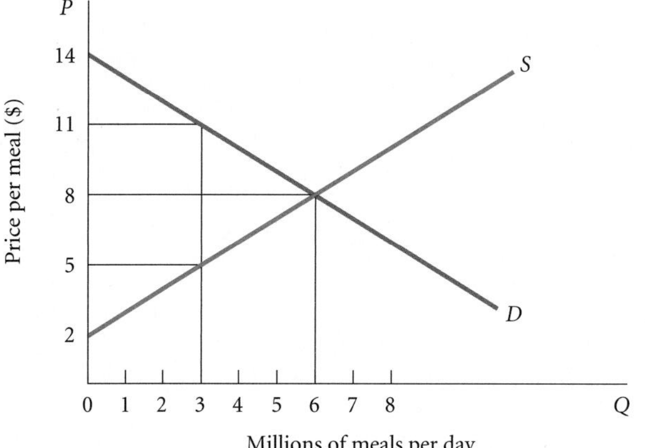

11. In early 2008, many predicted that in a relatively short period of time, unleaded regular gasoline at the pump would be selling for over $4. Do some research on the price of gasoline. Have those dire predictions materialized? What is the price of unleaded regular today in your city or town? If it is below $4 per gallon, what are the reasons? Similarly, if it is higher than $4, what has happened to drive up the price? Illustrate with supply and demand curves.

12. **[Related to the *Economics in Practice* on *p. 79*]** Many cruise lines offer 5-day trips. A disproportionate number of these trips leave port on Thursday and return late Monday. Why might this be true?

13. **[Related to the *Economics in Practice* on *p. 79*]** Lines for free tickets to see Shakespeare in Central Park are often long. A local politician has suggested that it would be a great service if the Park provided music to entertain those who are waiting in line. What do you think of this suggestion?

Elasticity

5

CHAPTER OUTLINE

In economics, simple logic often tells us how a change in one variable, such as the price of a good or an interest rate, is likely to affect behavior. It is a safe bet, for example, that when Apple halved the price of its iPhones in 2007, sales increased. When many universities lowered the price of football tickets to students (many to a price of zero), the schools did so in an attempt to increase the number of student fans in their stadiums. If the government helps to raise the price of cigarettes by increasing cigarette taxes, it is likely that tobacco sales will suffer.

The work we did in earlier chapters tells us the direction of the changes we would expect to see from price changes in markets. But in each of the preceding examples and in most other situations, knowing the direction of a change is not enough. What we really need to know to help us make the right decisions is how big the reactions are. How many more fans would come to a football game if the price were lowered? Is the added team spirit worth the lost ticket revenue? Would the university get more fans by charging students but giving them free hot dogs at the game? For a profit-making firm such as Apple, knowing the number of new phones that would be sold at the lowered price is key. If sales increases following the iPhone price cut are large enough, Apple's revenues may actually rise. With small sales increases, Apple's price-cutting strategy will leave the company with reduced revenues. To answer these questions, we must know more than just direction; we must know something about market responsiveness.

Understanding the responsiveness of consumers and producers in markets to price changes is key to answering a wide range of economic problems. Should McDonald's lower the price of its Big Mac? For McDonald's, the answer depends on whether that price cut increases or decreases its profits. The answer to that, in turn, depends on how its customers are likely to respond to the price cut. How many more Big Macs will be sold, and will the new sales come at the expense of the sandwiches sold at Subway or be a substitution of McDonald's Chicken McNuggets for Big Macs? Can universities change the social behavior of their students by lowering fees on campus sports, theatrical events, and concerts? How many potential new smokers will be deterred from smoking by higher cigarette prices the government has induced? Questions such as these lie at the core of economics. To answer these questions, we need to measure the magnitude of market responses.

The importance of actual measurement cannot be overstated. Without the ability to measure and predict how much people are likely to respond to economic changes, all the economic theory in the world would be of little help to policy makers. In fact, much of the research being done in economics today involves the collection and analysis of quantitative data that measure behavior. The ability to analyze large amounts of data increased enormously with the advent of modern computers.

Economists commonly measure responsiveness using the concept of **elasticity**. Elasticity is a general concept that can be used to quantify the response in one variable when another variable

elasticity A general concept used to quantify the response in one variable when another variable changes.

changes. If some variable A changes in response to changes in another variable B, the elasticity of A with respect to B is equal to the percentage change in A divided by the percentage change in B:

$$\text{elasticity of } A \text{ with respect to } B = \frac{\%\Delta A}{\%\Delta B}$$

In the examples discussed previously, we often consider responsiveness or elasticity by looking at prices: How does demand for a product respond when its price changes? This is known as the price elasticity of demand. How does supply respond when prices change? This is the price elasticity of supply. As in the McDonald's example, sometimes it is important to know how the price of one good—for example, the Big Mac—affects the demand for another good—Chicken McNuggets. This is called the cross-price elasticity of demand.

But the concept of elasticity goes well beyond responsiveness to price changes. As we will see, we can look at elasticities as a way to understand responses to changes in income and almost any other major determinant of supply and demand in a market. We begin with a discussion of price elasticity of demand.

Price Elasticity of Demand

You have already seen the law of demand at work. Recall that, *ceteris paribus*, when prices rise, quantity demanded can be expected to decline. When prices fall, quantity demanded can be expected to rise. The normal negative relationship between price and quantity demanded is reflected in the downward slope of demand curves.

Slope and Elasticity

The slope of a demand curve may in a rough way reveal the responsiveness of the quantity demanded to price changes, but slope can be quite misleading. In fact, it is not a good formal measure of responsiveness.

Consider the two identical demand curves in Figure 5.1. The only difference between the two is that quantity demanded is measured in pounds in the graph on the left and in ounces in the graph on the right. When we calculate the numerical value of each slope, however, we get very different answers. The curve on the left has a slope of $-1/5$, and the curve on the right has a slope of $-1/80$; yet the two curves represent the *exact same behavior*. If we had changed dollars to cents on the Y-axis, the two slopes would be -20 and -1.25, respectively. (Review the Appendix to Chapter 1 if you do not understand how these numbers are calculated.)

▶ FIGURE 5.1 Slope Is Not a Useful Measure of Responsiveness

Changing the unit of measure from pounds to ounces changes the numerical value of the demand slope dramatically, but the behavior of buyers in the two diagrams is identical.

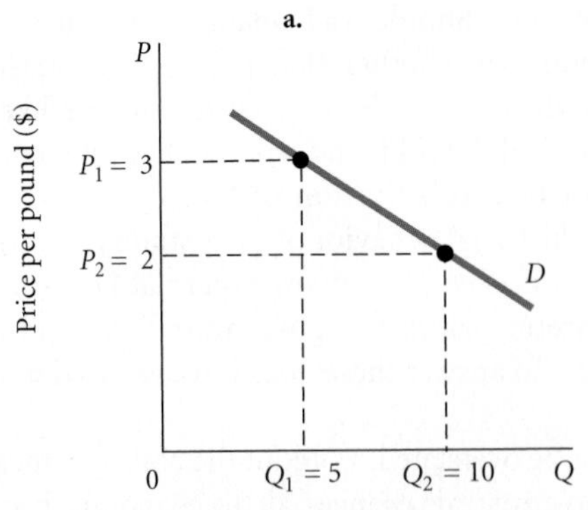

Pounds of steak per month

$$\text{Slope: } \frac{\Delta Y}{\Delta X} = \frac{P_2 - P_1}{Q_2 - Q_1} = \frac{2-3}{10-5} = -\frac{1}{5}$$

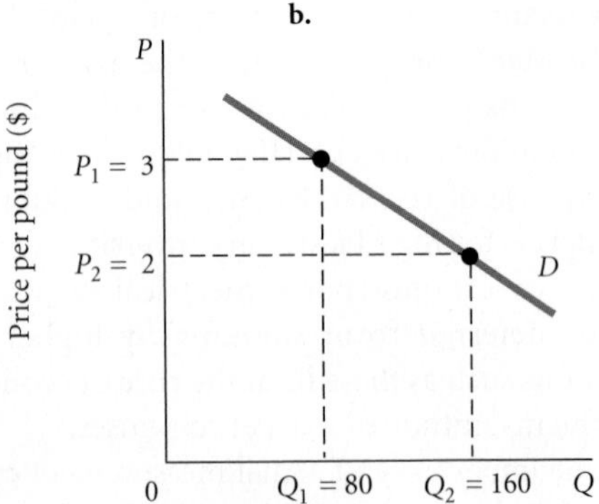

Ounces of steak per month

$$\text{Slope: } \frac{\Delta Y}{\Delta X} = \frac{P_2 - P_1}{Q_2 - Q_1} = \frac{2-3}{160-80} = -\frac{1}{80}$$

The problem is that the numerical value of slope depends on the units used to measure the variables on the axes. To correct this problem, we must convert the changes in price and quantity to *percentages.* By looking at by how much the *percent* quantity demanded changes for a given *percent* price change, we have a measure of responsiveness that does not change with the unit of measurement. The price increase in Figure 5.1 leads to a decline of 5 pounds, or 80 ounces, in the quantity of steak demanded—a decline of 50 percent from the initial 10 pounds, or 160 ounces, whether we measure the steak in pounds or ounces.

We define **price elasticity of demand** simply as the ratio of the percentage of change in quantity demanded to the percentage change in price.

price elasticity of demand The ratio of the percentage of change in quantity demanded to the percentage of change in price; measures the responsiveness of quantity demanded to changes in price.

$$\text{price elasticity of demand} = \frac{\%\ \text{change in quantity demanded}}{\%\ \text{change in price}}$$

Percentage changes should always carry the sign (plus or minus) of the change. Positive changes, or increases, take a (+). Negative changes, or decreases, take a (−). The law of demand implies that price elasticity of demand is nearly always a negative number: Price increases (+) will lead to decreases in quantity demanded (−), and vice versa. Thus, the numerator and denominator should have opposite signs, resulting in a negative ratio.

Types of Elasticity

Table 5.1 gives the hypothetical responses of demanders to a 10 percent price increase in four markets. Insulin is absolutely necessary to an insulin-dependent diabetic, and the quantity demanded is unlikely to respond to an increase in price. When the quantity demanded does not respond at all to a price change, the percentage of change in quantity demanded is zero and the elasticity is zero. In this case, we say that the demand for the product in the region we are measuring is **perfectly inelastic.** Figure 5.2(a) illustrates the perfectly inelastic demand for insulin. Because quantity demanded does not change *at all* when price changes, the demand curve is a vertical line.

perfectly inelastic demand Demand in which quantity demanded does not respond at all to a change in price.

TABLE 5.1 Hypothetical Demand Elasticities for Four Products

Product	% Change in Price ($\% \Delta P$)	% Change in Quantity Demanded ($\% \Delta Q_D$)	Elasticity ($\% \Delta Q_D \div \% \Delta P$)
Insulin	+10%	0%	.0 ⟶ Perfectly inelastic
Basic telephone service	+10%	-1%	-.1 ⟶ Inelastic
Beef	+10%	-10%	-1.0 ⟶ Unitarily elastic
Bananas	+10%	-30%	-3.0 ⟶ Elastic

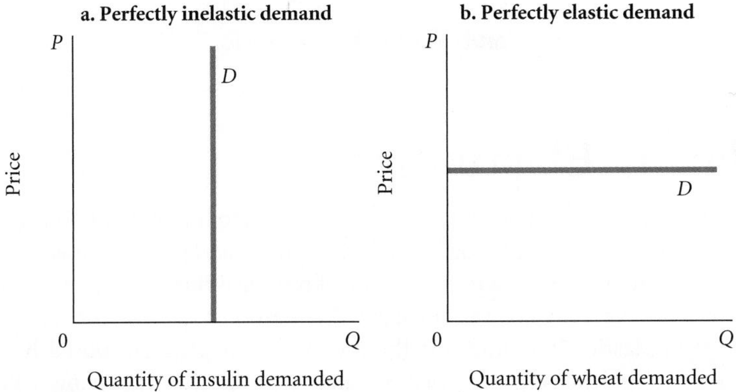

▲ **FIGURE 5.2 Perfectly Inelastic and Perfectly Elastic Demand Curves**

Figure 5.2(a) shows a perfectly inelastic demand curve for insulin. Price elasticity of demand is zero. Quantity demanded is fixed; it does not change at all when price changes. Figure 5.2(b) shows a perfectly elastic demand curve facing a wheat farmer. A tiny price increase drives the quantity demanded to zero. In essence, perfectly elastic demand implies that individual producers can sell all they want at the going market price but cannot charge a higher price.

Unlike insulin, basic telephone service is generally considered a necessity, but not an absolute necessity. If a 10 percent increase in telephone rates results in a 1 percent decline in the quantity of service demanded, demand elasticity is (−1 ÷ 10) = −.1.

inelastic demand Demand that responds somewhat, but not a great deal, to changes in price. Inelastic demand always has a numerical value between zero and −1.

When the percentage change in quantity demanded is smaller in absolute size than the percentage change in price, as is the case with telephone service, elasticity is less than 1 in absolute size.[1] When a product has an elasticity between zero and −1, we say that demand is inelastic. The demand for basic telephone service in our example is **inelastic** at −.1. Stated simply, inelastic demand means that there is some responsiveness of demand, but not a great deal, to a change in price.

A warning: You must be very careful about signs. Because it is generally understood that demand elasticities are negative (demand curves have a negative slope), they are often reported and discussed without the negative sign. For example, a technical paper might report that the demand for housing "appears to be inelastic with respect to price, or less than 1 (.6)." What the writer means is that the estimated elasticity is −.6, which is between zero and −1. Its absolute value is less than 1.

Returning to Table 5.1 on p. 91, we see that a 10 percent increase in beef prices drives down the quantity of beef demanded by 10 percent. Demand elasticity is thus (−10 ÷ 10) = −1 in the region we are measuring. When the percentage change in quantity of product demanded is the same as the percentage change in price in absolute value, we say that the demand for that product has **unitary elasticity**. The elasticity is minus one (−1). As Table 5.1 shows, the demand for beef has unitary elasticity.

unitary elasticity A demand relationship in which the percentage change in quantity of a product demanded is the same as the percentage change in price in absolute value (a demand elasticity of −1).

When the percentage change in quantity demanded is larger than the percentage change in price in absolute value, we say that demand is **elastic**. The demand for bananas, for example, is likely to be quite elastic because there are many substitutes for bananas—other fruits, for instance. If a 10 percent increase in the price of bananas leads to a 30 percent decrease in the quantity of bananas demanded, the price elasticity of demand for bananas is (−30 ÷ 10) = −3. When the absolute value of elasticity exceeds 1, demand is elastic.

elastic demand A demand relationship in which the percentage change in quantity demanded is larger than the percentage change in price in absolute value (a demand elasticity with an absolute value greater than 1).

Finally, if a small increase in the price of a product causes the quantity demanded to drop immediately to zero, demand for that product is said to be **perfectly elastic**. Suppose, for example, that you produce a product that can be sold only at a predetermined fixed price. If you charged even one penny more, no one would buy your product because people would simply buy from another producer who had not raised the price. This is very close to reality for farmers, who cannot charge more than the current market price for their crops.

perfectly elastic demand Demand in which quantity drops to zero at the slightest increase in price.

A perfectly elastic demand curve is illustrated in Figure 5.2(b) on p. 91. Because the quantity demanded drops to zero above a certain price, the demand curve for such a good is a horizontal line. A good way to remember the difference between the two "perfect" elasticities is

Perfectly Elastic
and Perfectly Inelastic

Calculating Elasticities

Elasticities must be calculated cautiously. Return for a moment to the demand curves in Figure 5.1 on p. 90. The fact that these two identical demand curves have dramatically different slopes should be enough to convince you that slope is a poor measure of responsiveness. As we will see shortly, a given straight line, which has the same slope all along it, will show different elasticities at various points.

The concept of elasticity circumvents the measurement problem posed by the graphs in Figure 5.1 by converting the changes in price and quantity to percentage changes. Recall that elasticity of demand is the *percentage* change in quantity demanded divided by the *percentage* change in price.

[1] The term *absolute size* or *absolute value* means ignoring the sign. The absolute value of −4 is 4; the absolute value of −3.8 is greater than the absolute value of 2.

Calculating Percentage Changes

Because we need to know percentage changes to calculate elasticity, let us begin our example by calculating the percentage change in quantity demanded. Figure 5.1(a) shows that the quantity of steak demanded increases from 5 pounds (Q_1) to 10 pounds (Q_2) when price drops from \$3 to \$2 per pound. Thus, the change in quantity demanded is equal to $Q_2 - Q_1$, or 5 pounds.

To convert this change into a percentage change, we must decide on a *base* against which to calculate the percentage. It is often convenient to use the initial value of quantity demanded (Q_1) as the base.

To calculate percentage change in quantity demanded using the initial value as the base, the following formula is used:

$$\begin{aligned}\text{\% change in quantity demanded} &= \frac{\text{change in quantity demanded}}{Q_1} \times 100\% \\ &= \frac{Q_2 - Q_1}{Q_1} \times 100\%\end{aligned}$$

In Figure 5.1, $Q_2 = 10$ and $Q_1 = 5$. Thus,

$$\text{\% change in quantity demanded} = \frac{10 - 5}{5} \times 100\% = \frac{5}{5} \times 100\% = 100\%$$

Expressing this equation verbally, we can say that an increase in quantity demanded from 5 pounds to 10 pounds is a 100 percent increase from 5 pounds. Note that you arrive at exactly the same result if you use the diagram in Figure 5.1(b), in which quantity demanded is measured in ounces. An increase from Q_1 (80 ounces) to Q_2 (160 ounces) is a 100 percent increase.

We can calculate the percentage change in price in a similar way. Once again, let us use the initial value of *P*—that is, P_1—as the base for calculating the percentage. By using P_1 as the base, the formula for calculating the percentage of change in *P* is

$$\begin{aligned}\text{\% change in price} &= \frac{\text{change in price}}{P_1} \times 100\% \\ &= \frac{P_2 - P_1}{P_1} \times 100\%\end{aligned}$$

In Figure 5.1(a), P_2 equals 2 and P_1 equals 3. Thus, the change in *P*, or ΔP, is a negative number: $P_2 - P_1 = 2 - 3 = -1$. This is true because the change is a decrease in price. Plugging the values of P_1 and P_2 into the preceding equation, we get

$$\text{\% change in price} = \frac{2 - 3}{3} \times 100\% = \frac{-1}{3} \times 100\% = -33.3\%$$

In other words, decreasing the price from \$3 to \$2 is a 33.3 percent decline.

Elasticity Is a Ratio of Percentages

Once the changes in quantity demanded and price have been converted to percentages, calculating elasticity is a matter of simple division. Recall the formal definition of elasticity:

$$\text{price elasticity of demand} = \frac{\text{\% change in quantity demanded}}{\text{\% change in price}}$$

If demand is elastic, the ratio of percentage change in quantity demanded to percentage change in price will have an absolute value greater than 1. If demand is inelastic, the ratio will have an absolute value between 0 and 1. If the two percentages are equal, so that a given percentage change in price causes an equal percentage change in quantity demanded, elasticity is equal to −1; this is unitary elasticity.

Substituting the preceding percentages, we see that a 33.3 percent decrease in price leads to a 100 percent increase in quantity demanded; thus,

$$\text{price elasticity of demand} = \frac{+100\%}{-33.3\%} = -3.0$$

According to these calculations, the demand for steak is elastic when we look at the range between \$2 and \$3.

The Midpoint Formula

Although simple, the use of the initial values of P and Q as the bases for calculating percentage changes can be misleading. Let us return to the example of demand for steak in Figure 5.1(a), where we have a change in quantity demanded of 5 pounds. Using the initial value Q_1 as the base, we calculated that this change represents a 100 percent increase over the base. Now suppose that the price of steak rises to \$3 again, causing the quantity demanded to drop back to 5 pounds. How much of a percentage decrease in quantity demanded is this? We now have $Q_1 = 10$ and $Q_2 = 5$. With the same formula we used earlier, we get

$$\begin{aligned} \text{\% change in quantity demanded} &= \frac{\text{change in quantity demanded}}{Q_1} \times 100\% \\ &= \frac{Q_2 - Q_1}{Q_1} \times 100\% \\ &= \frac{5 - 10}{10} \times 100\% = -50\% \end{aligned}$$

Thus, an increase from 5 pounds to 10 pounds is a 100 percent increase (because the initial value used for the base is 5), but a decrease from 10 pounds to 5 pounds is only a 50 percent decrease (because the initial value used for the base is 10). This does not make much sense because in both cases, we are calculating elasticity on the same interval on the demand curve. Changing the "direction" of the calculation should not change the elasticity.

To describe percentage changes more accurately, a simple convention has been adopted. Instead of using the initial values of Q and P as the bases for calculating percentages, we use the *midpoints* of these variables as the bases. That is, we use the value halfway between P_1 and P_2 for the base in calculating the percentage change in price and the value halfway between Q_1 and Q_2 as the base for calculating percentage change in quantity demanded.

midpoint formula A more precise way of calculating percentages using the value halfway between P_1 and P_2 for the base in calculating the percentage change in price and the value halfway between Q_1 and Q_2 as the base for calculating the percentage change in quantity demanded.

Thus, the **midpoint formula** for calculating the percentage change in quantity demanded becomes

$$\begin{aligned} \text{\% change in quantity demanded} &= \frac{\text{change in quantity demanded}}{(Q_1 + Q_2)/2} \times 100\% \\ &= \frac{Q_2 - Q_1}{(Q_1 + Q_2)/2} \times 100\% \end{aligned}$$

Substituting the numbers from the original Figure 5.1(a), we get

$$\text{\% change in quantity demanded} = \frac{10 - 5}{(5 + 10)/2} \times 100\% = \frac{5}{7.5} \times 100\% = 66.7\%$$

Using the point halfway between P_1 and P_2 as the base for calculating the percentage change in price, we get

$$\begin{aligned} \text{\% change in price} &= \frac{\text{change in price}}{(P_1 + P_2)/2} \times 100\% \\ &= \frac{P_2 - P_1}{(P_1 + P_2)/2} \times 100\% \end{aligned}$$

Substituting the numbers from the original Figure 5.1(a) yields

$$\% \text{ change in price} = \frac{2 - 3}{(3 + 2)/2} \times 100\% = \frac{-1}{2.5} \times 100\% = -40.0\%$$

We can thus say that a change from a quantity of 5 to a quantity of 10 is a +66.7 percent change using the midpoint formula and that a change in price from \$3 to \$2 is a −40 percent change using the midpoint formula.

Using these percentages to calculate elasticity yields

$$\text{price elasticity of demand} = \frac{\% \text{ change in quantity demanded}}{\% \text{ change in price}} = \frac{66.7\%}{-40.0\%} = -1.67$$

Using the midpoint formula in this case gives a lower demand elasticity, but the demand remains elastic because the percentage change in quantity demanded is still greater than the percentage change in price in absolute size.

The calculations based on the midpoint approach are summarized in Table 5.2.

TABLE 5.2 Calculating Price Elasticity with the Midpoint Formula

First, Calculate Percentage Change in Quantity Demanded ($\%\Delta Q_D$):

$$\frac{\% \text{ change in}}{\text{quantity demanded}} = \frac{\text{change in quantity demanded}}{(Q_1 + Q_2)/2} \times 100\% = \frac{Q_2 - Q_1}{(Q_1 + Q_2)/2} \times 100\%$$

By substituting the numbers from Figure 5.1(a):

$$\% \text{ change in quantity demanded} = \frac{10 - 5}{(5 + 10)/2} \times 100\% = \frac{5}{7.5} \times 100\% = 66.7\%$$

Next, Calculate Percentage Change in Price ($\%\Delta P$):

$$\% \text{ change in price} = \frac{\text{change in price}}{(P_1 + P_2)/2} \times 100\% = \frac{P_2 - P_1}{(P_1 + P_2)/2} \times 100\%$$

By substituting the numbers from Figure 5.1(a):

$$\% \text{ change in price} = \frac{2 - 3}{(3 + 2)/2} \times 100\% = \frac{-1}{2.5} \times 100\% = -40.0\%$$

Price elasticity compares the percentage change in quantity demanded and the percentage change in price.

$$\frac{\%\Delta Q_D}{\%\Delta P} = \frac{66.7\%}{-40.0\%}$$

= −1.67

= Price elasticity of demand

Demand is elastic

Elasticity Changes Along a Straight-Line Demand Curve

An interesting and important point is that elasticity changes from point to point along a demand curve even when the slope of that demand curve does not change—that is, even along a straight-line demand curve. Indeed, the differences in elasticity along a demand curve can be quite large.

Before we go through the calculations to show how elasticity changes along a demand curve, it is useful to think *why* elasticity might change as we vary price. Consider again McDonald's decision to reduce the price of a Big Mac. Suppose McDonald's found that at the current price of \$3, a small price cut would generate a large number of new customers who wanted burgers. Demand, in short, was relatively elastic. What happens as McDonald's continues to cut its price? As the price moves from \$2.50 to \$2.00, for example, new customers lured in by the price cuts are likely to decrease; in some sense, McDonald's will be running out of customers who are interested in its burgers at any price. It should come as no surprise that as we move down a typical straight-line demand curve, price elasticity falls. Demand becomes less elastic as price is reduced. This lesson has important implications for price-setting strategies of firms.

Consider the demand schedule shown in Table 5.3 and the demand curve in Figure 5.3. Herb works about 22 days per month in a downtown San Francisco office tower. On the top floor of the building is a nice dining room. If lunch in the dining room were \$10, Herb would eat there only twice a month. If the price of lunch fell to \$9, he would eat there 4 times a month. (Herb would bring his lunch to work on other days.) If lunch were only a dollar, he would eat there 20 times a month.

Let us calculate price elasticity of demand between points *A* and *B* on the demand curve in Figure 5.3. Moving from *A* to *B*, the price of a lunch drops from \$10 to \$9 (a decrease of \$1) and

TABLE 5.3 Demand Schedule for Office Dining Room Lunches

Price (per Lunch)	Quantity Demanded (Lunches per Month)
$11	0
10	2
9	4
8	6
7	8
6	10
5	12
4	14
3	16
2	18
1	20
0	22

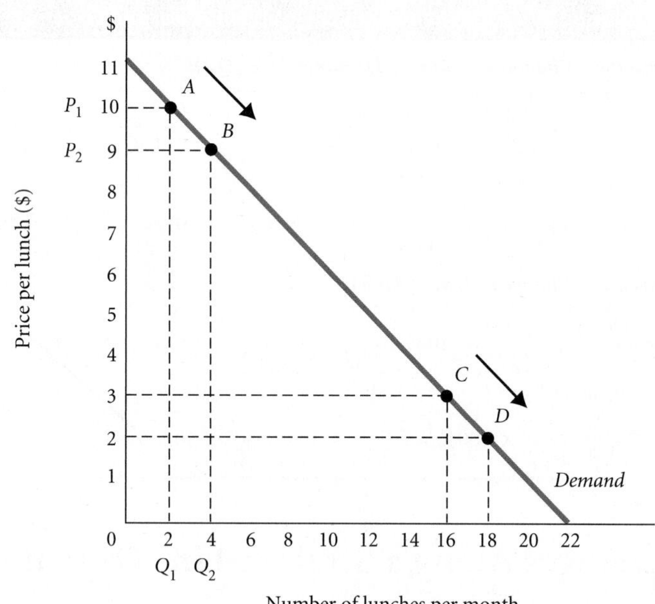

FIGURE 5.3 Demand Curve for Lunch at the Office Dining Room

Between points *A* and *B*, demand is quite elastic at −6.4. Between points *C* and *D*, demand is quite inelastic at −.294.

the number of dining room lunches that Herb eats per month increases from two to four (an increase of two). We will use the midpoint approach.

First, we calculate the percentage change in quantity demanded:

$$\text{\% change in quantity demanded} = \frac{Q_2 - Q_1}{(Q_1 + Q_2)/2} \times 100\%$$

Substituting the numbers from Figure 5.3, we get

$$\text{\% change in quantity demanded} = \frac{4 - 2}{(2 + 4)/2} \times 100\% = \frac{2}{3} \times 100\% = 66.7\%$$

Next, we calculate the percentage change in price:

$$\text{\% change in price} = \frac{P_2 - P_1}{(P_1 + P_2)/2} \times 100\%$$

Substituting the numbers from Figure 5.3, we get

$$\text{\% change in price} = \frac{9 - 10}{(10 + 9)/2} \times 100\% = \frac{-1}{9.5} \times 100\% = -10.5\%$$

Finally, we calculate elasticity by dividing

$$\text{elasticity of demand} = \frac{\%\text{ change in quantity demanded}}{\%\text{ change in price}}$$

$$= \frac{66.7\%}{-10.5\%} = -6.4$$

The percentage change in quantity demanded is 6.4 times larger than the percentage change in price. In other words, Herb's demand between points *A* and *B* is quite responsive; his demand between points *A* and *B* is elastic.

Now consider a different movement along the *same* demand curve in Figure 5.3. Moving from point *C* to point *D*, the graph indicates that at a price of $3, Herb eats in the office dining room 16 times per month. If the price drops to $2, he will eat there 18 times per month. These changes expressed in numerical terms are exactly the same as the price and quantity changes between points *A* and *B* in the figure—price falls $1, and quantity demanded increases by two meals. Expressed in *percentage* terms, however, these changes are very different.

By using the midpoints as the base, the $1 price decline is only a 10.5 percent reduction when price is around $9.50, between points *A* and *B*. The same $1 price decline is a 40 percent reduction when price is around $2.50, between points *C* and *D*. The two-meal increase in quantity demanded is a 66.7 percent increase when Herb averages only 3 meals per month, but it is only an 11.76 percent increase when he averages 17 meals per month. The elasticity of demand between points *C* and *D* is thus 11.76 percent divided by −40 percent, or −.294. (Work these numbers out for yourself by using the midpoint formula.)

The percentage changes between *A* and *B* are very different from those between *C* and *D*, and so are the elasticities. Herb's demand is quite elastic (−6.4) between points *A* and *B*; a 10.5 percent reduction in price caused a 66.7 percent increase in quantity demanded. However, his demand is inelastic (−.294) between points *C* and *D*; a 40 percent decrease in price caused only an 11.76 percent increase in quantity demanded.

Again, it is useful to keep in mind the underlying economics as well as the mathematics. At high prices, there is a great deal of potential demand for the dining room to capture. Hence, quantity is likely to respond well to price cuts. At low prices, everyone who is likely to come to the dining room already has.

Elasticity and Total Revenue

Consider the oil-producing countries, which have had some success keeping oil prices high by controlling supply. To some extent, reducing supply and driving up prices has increased the total oil revenues to the producing countries. As a result, we might expect this strategy to work for everyone. If the organization of banana-exporting countries (OBEC) had done the same thing, however, the strategy would not have worked.

Why? Suppose OBEC decides to cut production by 30 percent to drive up the world price of bananas. At first, when the quantity of bananas supplied declines, the quantity demanded is greater than the quantity supplied and the world price rises. The issue for OBEC, however, is *how much* the world price will rise. That is, how much will people be willing to pay to continue consuming bananas? Unless the percentage *increase* in price is greater than the percentage *decrease* in output, the OBEC countries will lose revenues.

A little research shows us that the prospects are not good for OBEC. There are many reasonable substitutes for bananas. As the price of bananas rises, people simply eat fewer bananas as they switch to eating more pineapples or oranges. Many people are simply not willing to pay a higher price for bananas. The quantity of bananas demanded declines 30 percent—to the new quantity supplied—after only a modest price rise, and OBEC fails in its mission; its revenues decrease instead of increase.

We have seen that oil-producing countries often can increase their revenues by restricting supply and pushing up the market price of crude oil. We also argued that a similar strategy by banana-producing countries would probably fail. Why? The quantity of oil demanded is not as responsive to a change in price as is the quantity of bananas demanded. In other words, the demand for oil is more inelastic than is the demand for bananas. One of the very useful features of elasticity is that knowing the value of price elasticity allows us to quickly see what happens to a firm's revenue as it raises and cuts its prices. When demand is inelastic, raising prices will raise revenues; when (as in the banana case) demand is elastic, price increases reduce revenues.

We can now use the more formal definition of elasticity to make more precise our argument of why oil producers would succeed and banana producers would fail as they raise prices. In any market, $P \times Q$ is total revenue (TR) received by producers:

$$TR = P \times Q$$
$$\text{total revenue} = \text{price} \times \text{quantity}$$

The oil producers' total revenue is the price per barrel of oil (P) times the number of barrels its participant countries sell (Q). To banana producers, total revenue is the price per bunch times the number of bunches sold.

When price increases in a market, quantity demanded declines. As we have seen, when price (P) declines, quantity demanded (Q_D) increases. This is true in all markets. The two factors, P and Q_D, move in opposite directions:

effects of price changes on quantity demanded: $P \uparrow \rightarrow Q_D \downarrow$ and $P \downarrow \rightarrow Q_D \uparrow$

Because total revenue is the product of P and Q, whether TR rises or falls in response to a price increase depends on which is bigger: the percentage increase in price or the percentage decrease in quantity demanded. If the percentage decrease in quantity demanded is smaller than the percentage increase in price, total revenue will rise. This occurs when demand is *inelastic*. In this case, the percentage price rise simply outweighs the percentage quantity decline and $P \times Q = (TR)$ rises:

effect of price increase on a product with inelastic demand: $\uparrow P \times Q_D \downarrow = TR \uparrow$

If, however, the percentage decline in quantity demanded following a price increase is larger than the percentage increase in price, total revenue will fall. This occurs when demand is *elastic*. The percentage price increase is outweighed by the percentage quantity decline:

effect of price increase on a product with elastic demand: $\uparrow P \times Q_D \downarrow = TR \downarrow$

The opposite is true for a price cut. When demand is elastic, a cut in price increases total revenues:

effect of price cut on a product with elastic demand: $\downarrow P \times Q_D \uparrow = TR \uparrow$

When demand is inelastic, a cut in price reduces total revenues:

effect of price cut on a product with inelastic demand: $\downarrow P \times Q_D \uparrow = TR \downarrow$

Review the logic of these equations to make sure you thoroughly understand the reasoning. Having a responsive (or elastic) market is good when we are lowering price because it means that we are dramatically increasing our units sold. But that same responsiveness is unattractive as we contemplate raising prices because now it means that we are losing customers. And, of course, the reverse logic works in the inelastic market. Note that if there is unitary elasticity, total revenue is unchanged if the price changes.

With this knowledge, we can now see why reducing supply by the oil-producing countries was so effective. The demand for oil is inelastic. Restricting the quantity of oil available led to a huge increase in the price of oil—the percentage increase was larger in absolute value than the percentage decrease in the quantity of oil demanded. Hence, oil producers' total revenues went up. In contrast, a banana cartel would not be effective because the demand for bananas is elastic. A small increase in the price of bananas results in a large decrease in the quantity of bananas demanded and thus causes total revenues to fall.

The Determinants of Demand Elasticity

Elasticity of demand is a way of measuring the responsiveness of consumers' demand to changes in price. As a measure of behavior, it can be applied to individual households or to market demand as a whole. You love peaches, and you would hate to give them up. Your demand for peaches is therefore inelastic. However, not everyone is crazy about peaches; in fact, the market demand for peaches is relatively elastic. Because no two people have exactly the same preferences, reactions to price changes will be different for different people, which makes generalizations risky. Nonetheless, a few principles do seem to hold.

Availability of Substitutes

Perhaps the most obvious factor affecting demand elasticity is the availability of substitutes. Consider a number of farm stands lined up along a country road. If every stand sells fresh corn of roughly the same quality, Mom's Green Thumb will find it very difficult to charge a price much higher than the competition charges because a nearly perfect substitute is available just down the road. The demand for Mom's corn is thus likely to be very elastic: An increase in price will lead to a rapid decline in the quantity demanded of Mom's corn.

In the oil versus banana example, the demand for oil is inelastic in large measure due to the lack of substitutes. When the price of crude oil went up in the early 1970s, 130 million motor vehicles, getting an average of 12 miles per gallon and consuming over 100 billion gallons of gasoline each year, were on the road in the United States. Millions of homes were heated with oil, and industry ran on equipment that used petroleum products. When the oil-producing countries (OPEC) cut production, the price of oil rose sharply. Quantity demanded fell somewhat, but price increased over 400 percent. What makes the cases of OPEC and OBEC different is the *magnitude* of the response in the quantity demanded to a change of price.

In Table 5.1, we considered two products that have no readily available substitutes, local telephone service and insulin for diabetics. There are many others. Demand for these products is likely to be quite inelastic.

The Importance of Being Unimportant

When an item represents a relatively small part of our total budget, we tend to pay little attention to its price. For example, if you pick up a pack of mints once in a while, you might not notice an increase in price from 25 cents to 35 cents. Yet this is a 40 percent increase in price (33.3 percent using the midpoint formula). In cases such as these, we are not likely to respond very much to changes in price and demand is likely to be inelastic.

The Time Dimension

When the oil-producing nations first cut output and succeeded in pushing up the price of crude oil, few substitutes were immediately available. Demand was relatively inelastic, and prices rose substantially. During the last 30 years, however, there has been some adjustment to higher oil prices. Automobiles manufactured today get on average more miles per gallon, and some drivers have cut down on their driving. Millions of home owners have insulated their homes, most people have turned down their thermostats, and some people have explored alternative energy sources.

Oil prices again rose dramatically during the weeks following Hurricane Katrina in 2005 because of the disruption to oil refineries and oil rigs. Once again, the response of demand to the

ECONOMICS IN PRACTICE

Who Are the Elastic Smokers?

In the United States, taxes are imposed on cigarettes at the state level. As a result, there are large differences among states. In 2007, New Jersey imposed a tax of $2.57 per pack while South Carolina's tax was only $0.07. The following article describes a proposal to raise taxes by $1.00 per pack in the state of Washington.

We would expect an increase in the tax on cigarettes to increase their price to consumers. An interesting question from the point of view of health and tax revenue is how much a price increase lowers demand. One of the commentators in the article claims that increasing cigarette prices by 10 percent reduces youth smokers by 6–7 percent; this is an implied demand elasticity of –.6 (6%/10%). How do you think this compares to what we would expect from adult smokers? Many people would argue that because more young people are new smokers and because they have less money than adults, their demand for cigarettes would be more elastic. On the other hand, if peer pressure favors smoking, this could lower demand elasticity for youths.

One problem that states face as they increase their cigarette taxes is that people will seek cigarette substitutes from cheaper areas. In Washington, the state pressured Indian tribes to raise the tribal tax rate on cigarettes to the overall state level. By making these substitutes to state-taxed cigarettes more expensive, the loss of customers in response to the state tax increase would be less.

Bill aims to raise tax on cigarettes

Seattle Times

OLYMPIA—If lawmakers pass a House bill raising the state cigarette tax to $2.50 a pack, Washington would be the second most expensive place in the country to buy cigarettes.

The proposed tax would raise the current $1.425 a pack by more than a dollar. The additional revenue would generate an estimated $300 million in two years for the state's health-care fund, according to bill sponsors. Proponents also say the substantial tax would deter people from smoking, saving nearly $1 billion in future health-care costs.

Eric Lindblom, manager for policy research at Campaign for Tobacco-Free Kids, said "raising cigarette prices is one of the quickest, most effective ways to reduce youth smoking."

Every time a state increases cigarette taxes by 10 percent, there is a 6 to 7 percent decrease in youth smokers, he said.

By Christina Siderius, Seattle Times Olympia Bureau, February 25, 2005

resulting higher gasoline prices took place slowly over time. This time many former SUV drivers switched to hybrids.

All of this illustrates a very important point: The elasticity of demand in the short run may be very different from the elasticity of demand in the long run. In the longer run, demand is likely to become more elastic, or responsive, simply because households make adjustments over time and producers develop substitute goods.

ECONOMICS IN PRACTICE

Elasticities at a Delicatessen in the Short Run and Long Run

Frank runs a corner delicatessen and decides one Monday morning to raise the prices of his sandwiches by 10 percent. Since Frank knows a little economics, he expects that this price increase will cause him to lose some business, since demand curves slope down, but he decides to try it anyway. At the end of the day, Frank discovers that his revenue has, in fact, gone up in the sandwich department. Feeling pleased with himself, Frank hires someone to create signs showing the new prices for the sandwich department. At the end of the month, however, he discovers that sandwich revenue is way down. What is going on?

The first thing to notice about this situation is that it poses a puzzle about what happens to revenue following a price increase. Seeing a linkage between price increases (or cuts) and revenue immediately leads an economist to think about *elasticity*. We remember from earlier in the chapter that *when demand is elastic*, (that is, an *absolute value* greater than 1), *price increases reduce revenue* because a small price increase will bring a large quantity decrease, thus depressing revenue. Conversely, when demand is inelastic (that is, an absolute value less than 1), price increases do little to curb demand and revenues rise. In this case, Monday's price increase brings increases in revenue; therefore, this pattern tells us that the demand from Frank's customers appears to be inelastic. In the longer term, however, demand appears to be more elastic (revenue is down after a month). Another way to pose this puzzle is to ask why the monthly demand curve might have a different elasticity than the daily demand.

To answer that question, you need to think about what determines elasticity. The most fundamental determinant of demand elasticity is the availability of substitutes. In this case, the product we are looking at is sandwiches. At first, you might think that the substitutes for Monday's sandwich would be the same as the substitutes for the sandwiches for the rest of the month. But this is not correct. Once you are in Frank's store, planning to buy a sandwich, your demand tends to be relatively inelastic because your ability to substitute by going elsewhere or choosing a different lunch item is relatively limited. You have already come to the part of town where Frank's Delicatessen is located, and you may already have chosen chips and a beverage to go along with your sandwich. Once you know that Frank's sandwiches are expensive, you can make different plans, and this broadening of your substitute choices increases your elasticity. In general, longer-term demand curves tend to be more elastic than shorter-term curves because customers have more choices.

The graph below shows the expected relationship between long-run and short-run demand for Frank's sandwiches. Notice if you raise prices above the current level, the expected quantity change read off the short-run curve is less than that from the long-run curve.

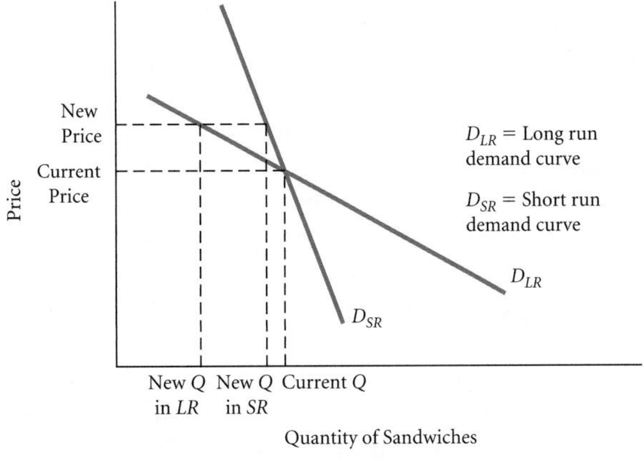

Other Important Elasticities

So far, we have been discussing price elasticity of demand, which measures the responsiveness of quantity demanded to changes in price. However, as we noted earlier, elasticity is a general concept. If *B* causes a change in *A* and we can measure the change in both, we can calculate the elasticity of *A* with respect to *B*. Let us look briefly at three other important types of elasticity.

Income Elasticity of Demand

income elasticity of demand A measure of the responsiveness of demand to changes in income.

Income elasticity of demand, which measures the responsiveness of demand to changes in income, is defined as

$$\text{income elasticity of demand} = \frac{\%\text{ change in quantity demanded}}{\%\text{ change in income}}$$

Measuring income elasticity is important for many reasons. Government policy makers spend a great deal of time and money weighing the relative merits of different policies. During the 1970s, for example, the Department of Housing and Urban Development (HUD) conducted a huge experiment in four cities to estimate the income elasticity of housing demand. In this "housing allowance demand experiment," low-income families received housing vouchers over an extended period of time and researchers watched their housing consumption for several years. Most estimates, including the ones from the HUD study, put the income elasticity of housing demand between .5 and .8. That is, a 10 percent increase in income can be expected to raise the quantity of housing demanded by a household by 5 percent to 8 percent.

Income elasticities can be positive or negative. During periods of rising income, people increase their spending on some goods (positive income elasticity) but reduce their spending on other goods (negative income elasticity). The income elasticity of demand for jewelry is positive, while the income elasticity of demand for low-quality beef is negative. As incomes rise in many low-income countries, the birth rate falls, implying a negative income elasticity of demand for children. Also, as incomes rise in most countries, the demand for education and health care rises, a positive income elasticity.

Cross-Price Elasticity of Demand

cross-price elasticity of demand A measure of the response of the quantity of one good demanded to a change in the price of another good.

Cross-price elasticity of demand, which measures the response of quantity of one good demanded to a change in the price of another good, is defined as

$$\text{cross-price elasticity of demand} = \frac{\%\text{ change in quantity of } Y \text{ demanded}}{\%\text{ change in price of } X}$$

Like income elasticity, cross-price elasticity can be either positive or negative. A *positive* cross-price elasticity indicates that an increase in the price of *X* causes the demand for *Y* to rise. This implies that the goods are substitutes. For McDonald's, Big Macs and Chicken McNuggets are substitutes with a positive cross-price elasticity. In our earlier example, as McDonald's lowered the price of Big Macs, it saw a decline in the quantity of McNuggets sold as consumers substituted between the two meals. If cross-price elasticity turns out to be *negative*, an increase in the price of *X* causes a decrease in the demand for *Y*. This implies that the goods are complements. Hot dogs and football games are complements with a negative cross-price elasticity.

As we have already seen, knowing the cross-price elasticity can be a very important part of a company's business strategy. Sony and Toshiba recently competed in the market for high-definition DVD players: Sony's Blu-ray versus Toshiba's HD DVD. Both firms recognized that an important driver of a customer's choice of a DVD player is movie price and availability. No one wants a new high-definition player if there is nothing to watch on it or if the price of movies is expensive. Inexpensive and available movies are a key complement to new DVD players. The cross-price elasticity of movies and high-definition DVD players is strong and negative. Sony won, and some observers think that Sony's ownership of a movie studio gave it an important advantage.

Elasticity of Supply

So far, we have focused on the consumer part of the market. But elasticity also matters on the producer's side.

Elasticity of supply, which measures the response of quantity of a good supplied to a change in price of that good, is defined as

elasticity of supply A measure of the response of quantity of a good supplied to a change in price of that good. Likely to be positive in output markets.

$$\text{elasticity of supply} = \frac{\text{\% change in quantity supplied}}{\text{\% change in price}}$$

In output markets, the elasticity of supply is likely to be a positive number—that is, a higher price leads to an increase in the quantity supplied, *ceteris paribus*. (Recall our discussion of upward-sloping supply curves in the preceding two chapters.)

The elasticity of supply is a measure of how easily producers can adapt to a price increase and bring increased quantities to market. In some industries, it is relatively easy for firms to increase their output. Ballpoint pens fall into this category, as does most software that has already been developed. For these products, the elasticity of supply is very high. In the oil industry, supply is inelastic, much like demand.

In input markets, however, some interesting problems arise in looking at elasticity. Perhaps the most studied elasticity of all is the **elasticity of labor supply**, which measures the response of labor supplied to a change in the price of labor. Economists have examined household labor supply responses to government programs such as welfare, Social Security, the income tax system, need-based student aid, and unemployment insurance.

elasticity of labor supply A measure of the response of labor supplied to a change in the price of labor.

In simple terms, the elasticity of labor supply is defined as

$$\text{elasticity of labor supply} = \frac{\text{\% change in quantity of labor supplied}}{\text{\% change in the wage rate}}$$

It seems reasonable at first glance to assume that an increase in wages increases the quantity of labor supplied. That would imply an upward-sloping supply curve and a positive labor supply elasticity, but this is not necessarily so. An increase in wages makes workers better off: They can work the same number of hours and have higher incomes. One of the things workers might like to "buy" with that higher income is more leisure time. "Buying" leisure simply means working fewer hours, and the "price" of leisure is the lost wages. Thus, it is quite possible that to some groups, an increase in wages above some level will lead to a reduction in the quantity of labor supplied.

Looking Ahead

The purpose of this chapter was to convince you that measurement is important. If all we can say is that a change in one economic factor causes another to change, we cannot say whether the change is important or whether a particular policy is likely to work. The most commonly used tool of measurement is elasticity, and the term will recur as we explore economics in more depth.

We now return to the study of basic economics by looking in detail at household behavior. Recall that households *demand* goods and services in product markets but *supply* labor and savings in input or factor markets.

SUMMARY

1. *Elasticity* is a general measure of responsiveness that can be used to quantify many different relationships. If one variable A changes in response to changes in another variable B, the elasticity of A with respect to B is equal to the percentage change in A divided by the percentage change in B.

2. The slope of a demand curve is an inadequate measure of responsiveness because its value depends on the units of measurement used. For this reason, elasticities are calculated using percentages.

PRICE ELASTICITY OF DEMAND *p. 90*

3. *Price elasticity of demand* is the ratio of the percentage change in quantity demanded of a good to the percentage change in price of that good.
4. *Perfectly inelastic* demand is demand whose quantity demanded does not respond at all to changes in price; its numerical value is zero.
5. *Inelastic* demand is demand whose quantity demanded responds somewhat, but not a great deal, to changes in price; its numerical value is between zero and −1.
6. *Elastic* demand is demand in which the percentage change in quantity demanded is larger in absolute value than the percentage change in price. Its numerical value is less than −1.
7. *Unitary elasticity* of demand describes a relationship in which the percentage change in the quantity of a product demanded is the same as the percentage change in price; unitary elasticity has a numerical value of −1.
8. *Perfectly elastic* demand describes a relationship in which a small increase in the price of a product causes the quantity demanded for that product to drop to zero.

CALCULATING ELASTICITIES *p. 92*

9. If demand is elastic, a price increase will reduce the quantity demanded by a larger percentage than the percentage increase in price and total revenue ($P \times Q$) will fall. If demand is inelastic, a price increase will increase total revenue.
10. If demand is elastic, a price cut will cause quantity demanded to increase by a greater percentage than the percentage decrease in price and total revenue will rise. If demand is inelastic, a price cut will cause quantity demanded to increase by a smaller percentage than the percentage decrease in price and total revenue will fall.

THE DETERMINANTS OF DEMAND ELASTICITY *p. 99*

11. The elasticity of demand depends on (1) the availability of substitutes, (2) the importance of the item in individual budgets, and (3) the time frame in question.

OTHER IMPORTANT ELASTICITIES *p. 102*

12. There are several important elasticities. *Income elasticity of demand* measures the responsiveness of the quantity demanded with respect to changes in income. *Cross-price elasticity of demand* measures the response of the quantity of one good demanded to a change in the price of another good. *Elasticity of supply* measures the response of the quantity of a good supplied to a change in the price of that good. The *elasticity of labor supply* measures the response of the quantity of labor supplied to a change in the price of labor.

REVIEW TERMS AND CONCEPTS

PROBLEMS

Visit **www.myeconlab.com** to complete the problems marked in orange online. You will receive instant feedback on your answers, tutorial help, and access to additional practice problems.

1. Fill in the missing amounts in the following table:

	% CHANGE IN PRICE	% CHANGE IN QUANTITY	ELASTICITY
Demand for Ben & Jerry's Ice Cream	+10%	−12%	**a.**
Demand for beer at San Francisco 49ers football games	−20%	**b.**	−.5
Demand for Broadway theater tickets in New York	**c.**	−15%	−1.0
Supply of chickens	+10%	**d.**	+1.2
Supply of beef cattle	−15%	−10%	**e.**

2. Use the table in the preceding problem to defend your answers to the following questions:
   a. Would you recommend that Ben & Jerry's move forward with a plan to raise prices if the company's only goal is to increase revenues?
   b. Would you recommend that beer stands cut prices to increase revenues at 49ers football games next year?

3. Using the midpoint formula, calculate elasticity for each of the following changes in demand by a household.

	P_1	P_2	Q_1	Q_2
Demand for:				
a. Long-distance telephone service	$0.25 per min.	$0.15 per min.	300 min. per month	400 min. per month
b. Orange juice	1.49 per qt	1.89 per qt	14 qt per month	12 qt per month
c. Big Macs	2.89	1.00	3 per week	6 per week
d. Cooked shrimp	$9 per lb	$12 per lb	2 lb per month	1.5 lb per month

4. A sporting goods store has estimated the demand curve for a popular brand of running shoes as a function of price. Use the diagram to answer the questions that follow.

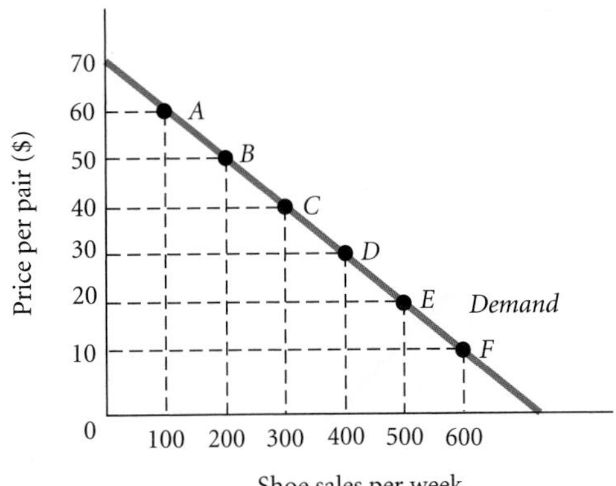

a. Calculate demand elasticity using the midpoint formula between points *A* and *B*, between points *C* and *D*, and between points *E* and *F*.
b. If the store currently charges a price of $50, then increases that price to $60, what happens to total revenue from shoe sales (calculate $P \times Q$ before and after the price change)? Repeat the exercise for initial prices being decreased to $40 and $20, respectively.
c. Explain why the answers to a. can be used to predict the answers to b.

5. For each of the following scenarios, decide whether you agree or disagree and explain your answer.
   a. If the elasticity of demand for cocaine is −.2 and the Drug Enforcement Administration succeeds in reducing supply substantially, causing the street price of the drug to rise by 50%, buyers will spend less on cocaine.
   b. Every year Christmas tree vendors bring tens of thousands of trees from the forests of New England to New York City and Boston. During the last two years, the market has been very competitive; as a result, price has fallen by 10 percent. If the price elasticity of demand was −1.3, vendors would lose revenues altogether as a result of the price decline.
   c. If the demand for a good has unitary elasticity, or elasticity is −1, it is always true that an increase in its price will lead to more revenues for sellers taken as a whole.

6. For the following statements, decide whether you agree or disagree and explain your answer.
   a. The demand curve pictured here is elastic.

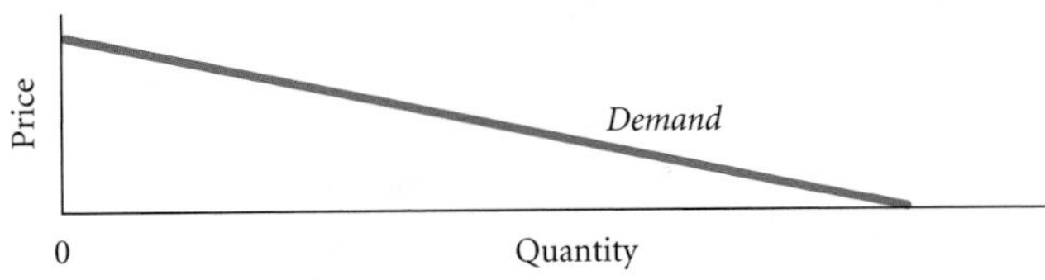

   b. If supply were to increase slightly in the following diagram, prices would fall and firms would earn less revenue.

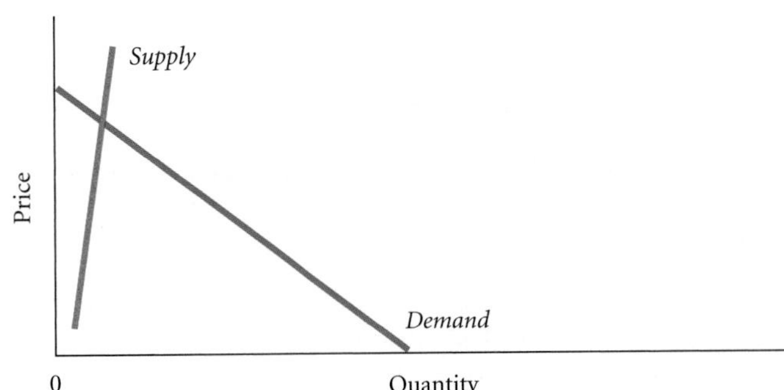

7. Taxicab fares in most cities are regulated. Several years ago taxicab drivers in Boston obtained permission to raise their fares 10 percent, and they anticipated that revenues would increase by about 10 percent as a result. They were disappointed, however. When the commissioner granted the 10 percent increase, revenues increased by only about 5 percent. What can you infer about the elasticity of demand for taxicab rides? What were taxicab drivers assuming about the elasticity of demand?

*8. Studies have fixed the short-run price elasticity of demand for gasoline at the pump at −.20. Suppose that international hostilities lead to a sudden cutoff of crude oil supplies. As a result, U.S. supplies of refined gasoline drop 10 percent.
   a. If gasoline were selling for $2.60 per gallon before the cutoff, how much of a price increase would you expect to see in the coming months?
   b. Suppose that the government imposes a price ceiling on gas at $2.60 per gallon. How would the relationship between consumers and gas station owners change?

9. Prior to 2005, it seemed like house prices always rose and never fell. When the demand for housing increases, prices in the housing market rise but not always by very much. For prices to rise substantially, the supply of housing must be relatively inelastic. That is, if the quantity supplied increases rapidly whenever house prices rise, price increases will remain small. Many have suggested government policies to increase the elasticity of supply. What specific policies might hold prices down when demand increases? Explain.

10. For each of the following statements, state the relevant elasticity and state what its value should be (negative, positive, greater than one, zero, and so on).
   a. The supply of labor is inelastic but slightly backward-bending.
   b. The demand for BMWs in an area increases during times of rising incomes just slightly faster than income rises.
   c. The demand for lobsters falls when lobster prices rise (*ceteris paribus*), but the revenue received by restaurants from the sale of lobsters stays the same.
   d. Demand for many goods rise when the price of substitutes rise.
   e. Land for housing development near Youngstown, Ohio, is in plentiful supply. At the current price, there is essentially an infinite supply.

11. **[Related to the *Economics in Practice* on *p. 100*]** A number of towns in the United States have begun charging their residents for garbage pickup based on the number of garbage cans filled per week. The town of Chase decided to increase its per-can price from 10 cents to 20 cents per week. In the first week, Chase found that the number of cans that were brought to the curb fell from 550 to 525 (although the city workers complained that the cans were heavier). The town economist ran the numbers, informed the mayor that the demand for disposal was inelastic, and recommended that the city raise the price more to maximize town revenue from the program. Six months later, at a price of 30 cents per can, the number of cans has fallen to 125 and town revenues are down. What might have happened?

12. **[Related to the *Economics in Practice* on *p. 100*]** At Frank's Delicatessen, Frank noticed that the elasticity of customers differed in the short and longer term. Frank also noticed that his increase in the price of sandwiches had other effects on his store. In particular, the number of sodas sold declined while the number of yogurts sold went up. How might you explain this pattern?

*Note: Problems marked with an asterisk are more challenging.

APPENDIX

POINT ELASTICITY (OPTIONAL)

Two different elasticities were calculated along the demand curve in Figure 5.3 on p. 96. Between points *A* and *B*, we discovered that Herb's demand for lunches in the fancy dining room was very elastic: A price decline of only 10.5 percent resulted in his eating 66.7 percent more lunches in the dining room (elasticity = −6.4). Between points *C* and *D*, however, on the same demand curve, we discovered that his demand for meals was very inelastic: A price decline of 40 percent resulted in only a modest increase in lunches consumed of 11.76 percent (elasticity = −0.294).

Now consider the straight-line demand curve in Figure 5A.1. We can write an expression for elasticity at point *C* as follows:

$$\text{elasticity} = \frac{\%\Delta Q}{\%\Delta P} = \frac{\frac{\Delta Q}{Q}\cdot 100}{\frac{\Delta P}{P}\cdot 100} = \frac{\frac{\Delta Q}{Q_1}}{\frac{\Delta P}{P_1}} = \boxed{\frac{\Delta Q}{\Delta P}\cdot\frac{P_1}{Q_1}}$$

$\Delta Q/\Delta P$ is the *reciprocal* of the slope of the curve. Slope in the diagram is constant along the curve, and it is negative. To calculate the reciprocal of the slope to plug into the previous elasticity equation, we take Q_1B, or M_1 and divide by *minus* the length of line segment CQ_1. Thus,

$$\frac{\Delta Q}{\Delta P} = \frac{M_1}{CQ_1}$$

Since the length of CQ_1 is equal to P_1, we can write

$$\frac{\Delta Q}{\Delta P} = \frac{M_1}{P_1}$$

By substituting, we get

$$\text{elasticity} = \frac{M_1}{P_1}\cdot\frac{P_1}{Q_1} = \frac{M_1}{P_1}\cdot\frac{P_1}{M_2} = \boxed{\frac{M_1}{M_2}}$$

(The second equal sign uses the fact that Q_1 equals M_2 in Figure 5A.1.)

Elasticity at point *C* is simply the ratio of line segment M_1 to line segment M_2. It is easy to see that if we had chosen a point to the left of Q_1, M_1 would have been larger and M_2 would have been smaller, indicating a higher elasticity. If we had chosen a point to the right of Q_1, M_1 would have been smaller and M_2 would have been larger, indicating a lower elasticity.

In Figure 5A.2, you can see that elasticity is unitary (equal to −1) at the midpoint of the demand curve, Q_3. At points to the right, such as Q_2, segment Q_2C (M_1 from Figure 5A.1) is smaller than segment $0Q_1$ (M_2 from Figure 5A.1). This means that the absolute size of the ratio is *less than 1* and that demand is *inelastic* at point *A*. At points to the left, such as Q_1, segment Q_1C (M_1) is larger than segment $0Q_1$ (M_2). This means that the absolute size of the ratio is *greater than 1* and that demand is elastic at point *B*.

Compare the results here with the results using the midpoint formula for elasticity for Herb.

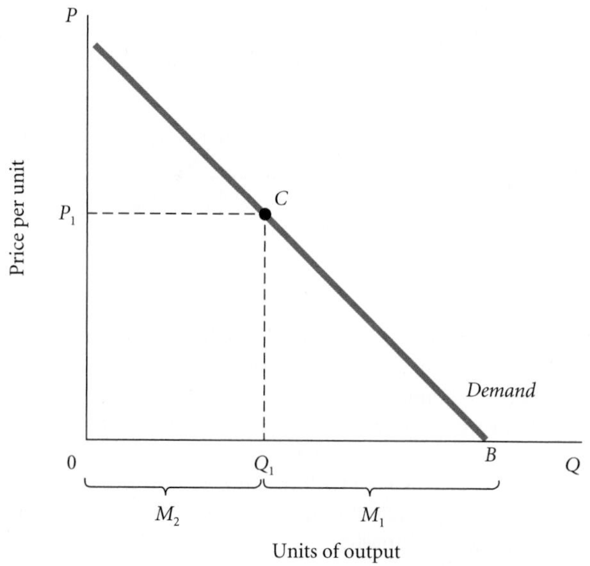

▲ **FIGURE 5A.1 Elasticity at a Point Along a Demand Curve**

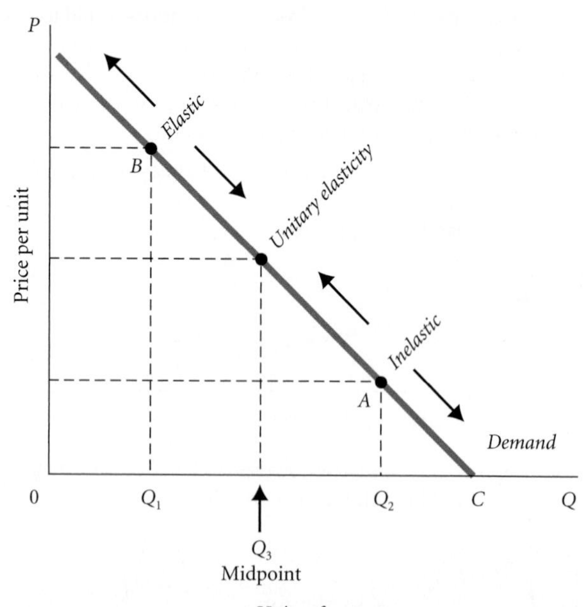

▲ **FIGURE 5A.2 Point Elasticity Changes Along a Demand Curve**

part II
The Market System
Choices Made by Households and Firms

Now that we have discussed the basic forces of supply and demand, we can explore the underlying behavior of the two fundamental decision-making units in the economy: households and firms.

Figure II.1 presents a diagram of a simple competitive economy. The figure is an expanded version of the circular flow diagram first presented in Figure 3.1 on p. 47. It is designed to guide you through Part II (Chapter 6 through Chapter 12) of this book. You will

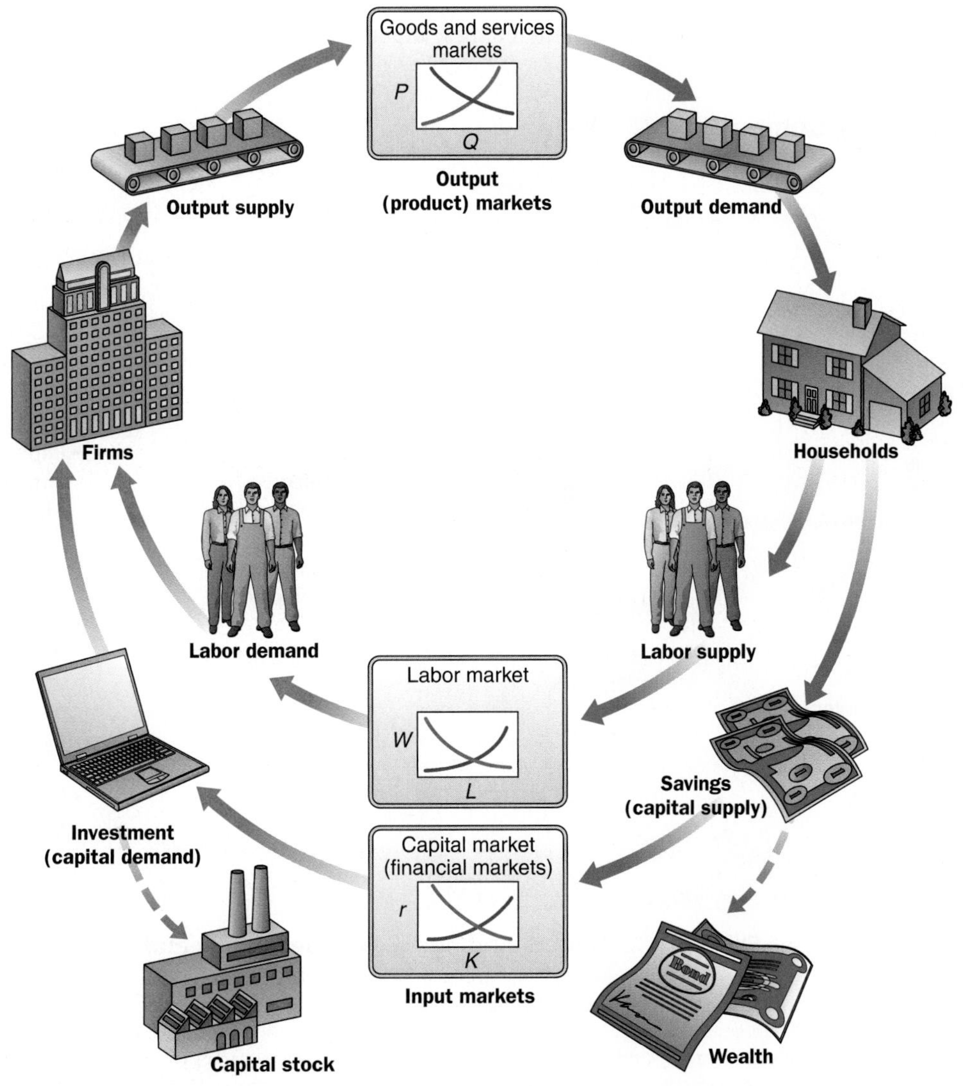

▲ **FIGURE II.1 Firm and Household Decisions**

Households demand in output markets and supply labor and capital in input markets. To simplify our analysis, we have not included the government and international sectors in this circular flow diagram. These topics will be discussed in detail later.

see the big picture more clearly if you follow this diagram closely as you work your way through this part of the book.

Recall that households and firms interact in two kinds of markets: output (product) markets, shown at the top of Figure II.1, and input (factor) markets, shown at the bottom. Households *demand* outputs and *supply* inputs. In contrast, firms *supply* outputs and *demand* inputs. Chapter 6 explores the behavior of households, focusing first on household demand for outputs and then on household supply in labor and capital markets.

The remaining chapters in Part II focus on firms and the interaction between firms and households. Chapter 7 through Chapter 9 analyze the behavior of firms in output markets in both the short run and the long run. Chapter 10 focuses on the behavior of firms in input markets in general, especially the labor and land markets. Chapter 11 discusses the capital market in more detail. Chapter 12 puts all the pieces together and analyzes the functioning of a complete market system. Following Chapter 12, Part III of the book relaxes many assumptions and analyzes market imperfections as well as the potential for and pitfalls of government involvement in the economy. The plan for Chapter 6 through Chapter 19 is outlined in Figure II.2.

Recall that throughout this book, all diagrams that describe the behavior of households are drawn or highlighted in *blue*. All diagrams that describe the behavior of firms are drawn or highlighted in *red*. Look carefully at the supply and demand diagrams in Figure II.1; notice that in both the labor and capital markets, the supply curves are blue. The reason is that labor and capital are supplied by households. The demand curves for labor and capital are red because firms demand these inputs for production.

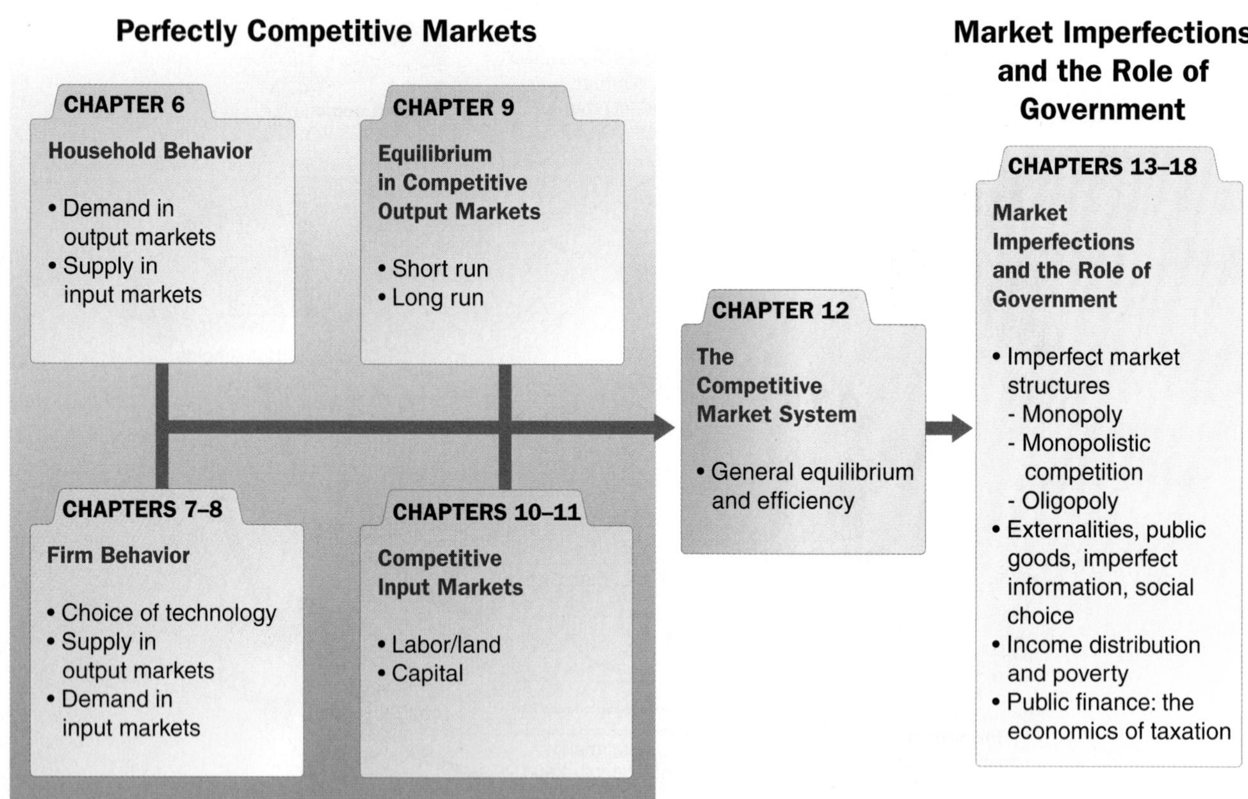

▲ **FIGURE II.2 Understanding the Microeconomy and the Role of Government**

To understand how the economy works, it helps to build from the ground up. We start in Chapters 6–8 with an overview of **household** and **firm** decision making in simple perfectly competitive markets. In Chapters 9–11, we see how firms and households interact in **output markets** (product markets) and **input markets** (labor/land and capital) to determine prices, wages, and profits. Once we have a picture of how a simple perfectly competitive economy works, we begin to relax assumptions. Chapter 12 is a pivotal chapter that links perfectly competitive markets with a discussion of market imperfections and the role of government. In Chapters 13–19, we cover the three noncompetitive market structures (monopoly, oligopoly, and monopolistic competition), externalities, public goods, uncertainty and asymmetric information, and income distribution as well as taxation and government finance.

In Figure II.1, much of the detail of the real world is stripped away just as it is on a highway map. A map is a highly simplified version of reality, but it is a very useful tool when you need to know where you are. Figure II.1 is intended to serve as a map to help you understand basic market forces before we add more complicated market structures and government.

Before we proceed with our discussion of household choice, we need to make a few basic assumptions. These assumptions pertain to all of Chapters 6 through Chapter 12.

We first assume that households and firms possess all the information they need to make market choices. Specifically, we assume that households possess knowledge of the qualities and prices of everything available in the market. Firms know all that there is to know about wage rates, capital costs, and output prices. This assumption is often called the assumption of **perfect knowledge**.

The next assumption is **perfect competition**. Perfect competition is a precisely defined form of industry structure. (The word *perfect* here does not refer to virtue. It simply means "total" or "complete.") In a perfectly competitive industry, no single firm has control over prices. That is, no single firm is large enough to affect the market price of its product or the prices of the inputs that it buys. This follows from two characteristics of competitive industries. First, a competitive industry is composed of many firms, each one small relative to the size of the industry. Second, every firm in a perfectly competitive industry produces exactly the same product; the output of one firm cannot be distinguished from the output of the others. Products in a perfectly competitive industry are said to be **homogeneous**.

These characteristics limit the decisions open to competitive firms and simplify the analysis of competitive behavior. Because all firms in a perfectly competitive industry produce virtually identical products and because each firm is small relative to the market, perfectly competitive firms have no control over the prices at which they sell their output. By taking prices as a given, each firm can decide only how much output to produce and how to produce it.

Consider agriculture, the classic example of a perfectly competitive industry. A wheat farmer in South Dakota has absolutely no control over the price of wheat. Prices are determined not by the individual farmers, but by the interaction of many suppliers and many demanders. The only decisions left to the wheat farmer are how much wheat to plant and when and how to produce the crop.

We finally assume that each household is small relative to the size of the market. Households face a set of product prices that they individually cannot control. Prices again are set by the interaction of many suppliers and many demanders.

By the end of Chapter 10, we will have a complete picture of an economy, but it will be based on this set of fairly restrictive assumptions. At first, this may seem unrealistic to you, but keep the following in mind. Much of the economic analysis in the chapters that follow applies to all forms of market structure. Indeed, much of the power of economic reasoning is that it is quite general. As we continue in microeconomics, in Chapters 13–14, we will define and explore several different kinds of market organization and structure, including monopoly, oligopoly, and monopolistic competition. Because monopolists, oligopolists, monopolistic competitors, and perfect competitors share the objective of maximizing profits, it should not be surprising that their behavior is in many ways similar. We focus here on perfect competition because many of these basic principles are easier to learn using the simplest of cases.

perfect knowledge The assumption that households possess a knowledge of the qualities and prices of everything available in the market and that firms have all available information concerning wage rates, capital costs, and output prices.

perfect competition An industry structure in which there are many firms, each being small relative to the industry and producing virtually identical products, and in which no firm is large enough to have any control over prices.

homogeneous products Undifferentiated outputs; products that are identical to or indistinguishable from one another.

Household Behavior and Consumer Choice

6

CHAPTER OUTLINE

Every day people in a market economy make decisions. Some of those decisions involve the products they plan to buy: Should you buy a Coke for lunch or just drink water? Should you purchase a laptop computer or stick with your old desktop? Some decisions are about the labor market: Should you continue your schooling or go to work instead? If you do start working, how much should you work? Should you work more when you get a raise or just take it easy? Many decisions involve a time element. If you decide to buy a laptop, you may have to use your savings or borrow money. That will leave you with fewer choices about what you can buy in the future. On the other hand, the laptop itself is an investment.

To many people, the decisions listed in the previous paragraph seem very different from one another. As you will see in this chapter, however, from an economics perspective, these decisions have a great deal in common. In this chapter, we will develop a set of principles that can be used to understand decisions in the product market and the labor market—decisions for today and for the future.

As you read this chapter, you might want to think about some of the following questions, questions that you will be able to answer by chapter's end. Baseball, even when it was more popular than it is today, was never played year-round. Indeed, no professional sport has a year-round season. Is this break necessary to give the athletes a rest, or is there something about household choice that helps explain this pattern? When the price of gasoline rises, people drive less, but one study suggests that they also switch from brand name products to generics or store brands.[1] Why might this be? Studying household choice will help you understand many decisions that underpin our market economy.

Household Choice in Output Markets

Every household must make three basic decisions:

1. How much of each product, or output, to demand
2. How much labor to supply
3. How much to spend today and how much to save for the future

As we begin our look at demand in output markets, you must keep in mind that the choices underlying the demand curve are only part of the larger household choice problem. Closely related decisions about how much to work and how much to save are equally important and must be made simultaneously with output–demand decisions.

[1] Dora Gicheva, Justine Hastings, and Sofia Villas-Boas, "Revisiting the Income Effect: Gasoline Prices and Grocery Purchases," NBER Working Paper No. 13614, October 2007.

The Determinants of Household Demand

As we saw in Chapter 3, several factors influence the quantity of a given good or service demanded by a single household:

- The price of the product
- The income available to the household
- The household's amount of accumulated wealth
- The prices of other products available to the household
- The household's tastes and preferences
- The household's expectations about future income, wealth, and prices

Recall that demand schedules and demand curves express the relationship between quantity demanded and price, *ceteris paribus*. A change in price leads to a movement along a demand curve. Changes in income, in other prices, or in preferences shift demand curves to the left or right. We refer to these shifts as "changes in demand." However, the interrelationship among these variables is more complex than the simple exposition in Chapter 3 might lead you to believe.

The Budget Constraint

Before we examine the household choice process, we need to discuss what choices are open and not open to households. If you look carefully at the list of items that influence household demand, you will see that the first four actually define the set of options available. Information on household income and wealth, together with information on product prices, makes it possible to distinguish those combinations of goods and services that are affordable from those that are not.[2]

budget constraint The limits imposed on household choices by income, wealth, and product prices.

Income, wealth, and prices thus define what we call household **budget constraint**. The budget constraint facing any household results primarily from limits imposed externally by one or more markets. In competitive markets, for example, households cannot control prices; they must buy goods and services at market-determined prices. A household has some control over its income: Its members can choose whether to work, and they can sometimes decide how many hours to work and how many jobs to hold. However, constraints exist in the labor market too. The amount that household members are paid is limited by current market wage rates. Whether they can get a job is determined by the availability of jobs.

Although income does depend, at least in part, on the choices that households make, we will treat it as a given for now. Later in this chapter, we will relax this assumption and explore labor supply choices in more detail.

The income, wealth, and price constraints that surround choice are best illustrated with an example. Consider Barbara, a recent graduate of a midwestern university who takes a job as an account manager at a public relations firm. Let us assume that she receives a salary of $1,000 per month (after taxes) and that she has no wealth and no credit. Barbara's monthly expenditures are limited to her flow of income. Table 6.1 summarizes some of the choices open to her.

TABLE 6.1 Possible Budget Choices of a Person Earning $1,000 per Month After Taxes

Option	Monthly Rent	Food	Other Expenses	Total	Available?
A	$ 400	$250	$350	$1,000	Yes
B	600	200	200	1,000	Yes
C	700	150	150	1,000	Yes
D	1,000	100	100	1,200	No

A careful search of the housing market reveals four vacant apartments. The least expensive is a one-room studio with a small kitchenette that rents for $400 per month, including utilities (option A). If she lived there, Barbara could afford to spend $250 per month on food and still have $350 left over for other things.

[2] Remember that we drew the distinction between income and wealth in Chapter 3. *Income* is the sum of household earnings within a given period; it is a flow variable. In contrast, *wealth* is a stock variable; it is what a household owns minus what it owes at a given point in time.

About four blocks away is a one-bedroom apartment with wall-to-wall carpeting and a larger kitchen. It has more space, but the rent is $600, including utilities. If Barbara took this apartment, she might cut her food expenditures by $50 per month and have only $200 per month left for everything else.

In the same building as the one-bedroom apartment is an identical unit on the top floor of the building with a balcony facing west toward the sunset. The balcony and view add $100 to the monthly rent. To live there, Barbara would be left with only $300 to split between food and other expenses.

Just because she was curious, Barbara looked at a townhouse in the suburbs that was renting for $1,000 per month. Obviously, unless she could get along without eating or doing anything else that cost money, she could not afford it. The combination of the townhouse and any amount of food is outside her budget constraint.

Notice that we have used the information that we have on income and prices to identify different combinations of housing, food, and other items that are available to a single-person household with an income of $1,000 per month. We have said nothing about the process of choosing. Instead, we have carved out what is called a **choice set** or **opportunity set**, the set of options that is defined and limited by Barbara's budget constraint.

choice set *or* opportunity set The set of options that is defined and limited by a budget constraint.

Preferences, Tastes, Trade-Offs, and Opportunity Cost So far, we have identified only the combinations of goods and services that are and are not available to Barbara. Within the constraints imposed by limited incomes and fixed prices, however, households are free to choose what they will and will not buy. Their ultimate choices are governed by their individual preferences and tastes.

It will help you to think of the household choice process as a process of allocating income over a large number of available goods and services. Final demand of a household for any single product is just one of many outcomes that result from the decision-making process. Think, for example, of a demand curve that shows a household's reaction to a drop in the price of air travel. During certain periods when people travel less frequently, special fares flood the market and many people decide to take trips that they otherwise would not have taken. However, if you live in Florida and decide to spend $400 to visit your mother in Nashville, you cannot spend that $400 on new clothes, dinners at restaurants, or a new set of tires.

A change in the price of a single good changes the constraints within which households choose, and this may change the entire allocation of income. Demand for some goods and services may rise while demand for others falls. A complicated set of trade-offs lies behind the shape and position of a household demand curve for a single good. Whenever a household makes a choice, it is weighing the good or service that it chooses against all the other things that the same money could buy.

Consider again our young account manager and her options listed in Table 6.1. If she hates to cook, likes to eat at restaurants, and goes out three nights a week, she will probably trade off some housing for dinners out and money to spend on clothes and other things. She will probably rent the studio for $400. She may, however, love to spend long evenings at home reading, listening to classical music, and sipping tea while watching the sunset. In that case, she will probably trade off some restaurant meals, evenings out, and travel expenses for the added comfort of the larger apartment with the balcony and the view. As long as a household faces a limited budget—and all households ultimately do—the real cost of any good or service is the value of the other goods and services that could have been purchased with the same amount of money. The real cost of a good or service is its opportunity cost, and opportunity cost is determined by relative prices.

The Budget Constraint More Formally Ann and Tom are struggling graduate students in economics at the University of Virginia. Their tuition is paid by graduate fellowships. They live as resident advisers in a first-year dormitory, in return for which they receive an apartment and meals. Their fellowships also give them $200 each month to cover all their other expenses. To simplify things, let us assume that Ann and Tom spend their money on only two things: meals at a local Thai restaurant and nights at a local jazz club, The Hungry Ear. Thai meals go for a fixed price of $20 per couple. Two tickets to the jazz club, including espresso, are $10.

As Figure 6.1 shows, we can graphically depict the choices that are available to our dynamic duo. The axes measure the *quantities* of the two goods that Ann and Tom buy. The horizontal axis measures the number of Thai meals consumed per month, and the vertical axis measures the number of trips to The Hungry Ear. (Note that price is not on the vertical axis here.) Every point in the space between the axes represents some combination of Thai meals and nights at the jazz club. The question is this: Which of these points can Ann and Tom purchase with a fixed budget of $200 per month? That is, which points are in the opportunity set and which are not?

One possibility is that the students in the dorm are driving Ann and Tom crazy. The two grad students want to avoid the dining hall at all costs. Thus, they might decide to spend all their money on Thai food and none of it on jazz. This decision would be represented by a point *on* the horizontal axis because all the points on that axis are points at which Ann and Tom make no jazz club visits. How many meals can Ann and Tom afford? The answer is simple: When income is $200 and the price of Thai meals is $20, they can afford $200 ÷ $20 = 10 meals. This point is labeled *A* on the budget constraint in Figure 6.1.

FIGURE 6.1 Budget Constraint and Opportunity Set for Ann and Tom

A budget constraint separates those combinations of goods and services that are available, given limited income, from those that are not. The available combinations make up the opportunity set.

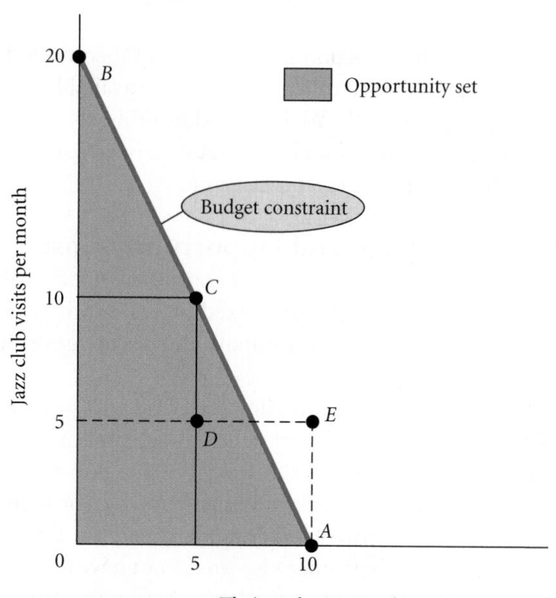

Another possibility is that general exams are coming up and Ann and Tom decide to relax at The Hungry Ear to relieve stress. Suppose they choose to spend all their money on jazz and none of it on Thai food. This decision would be represented by a point *on* the vertical axis because all the points on this axis are points at which Ann and Tom eat no Thai meals. How many jazz club visits can they afford? Again, the answer is simple: With an income of $200 and with the price of jazz/espresso at $10, they can go to The Hungry Ear $200 ÷ $10 = 20 times. This is the point labeled *B* in Figure 6.1. The line connecting points *A* and *B* is Ann and Tom's budget constraint.

What about all the points between *A* and *B* on the budget constraint? Starting from point *B*, suppose Ann and Tom give up trips to the jazz club to buy more Thai meals. Each additional Thai meal "costs" two trips to The Hungry Ear. The opportunity cost of a Thai meal is two jazz club trips.

Point *C* on the budget constraint represents a compromise. Here Ann and Tom go to the club 10 times and eat at the Thai restaurant 5 times. To verify that point *C* is on the budget constraint, price it out: 10 jazz club trips cost a total of $10 × 10 = $100, and 5 Thai meals cost a total of $20 × 5 = $100. The total is $100 + $100 = $200.

The budget constraint divides all the points between the axes into two groups: those that can be purchased for $200 or less (the opportunity set) and those that are unavailable. Point *D* on the diagram costs less than $200; point *E* costs more than $200. (Verify that this is true.) The opportunity set is the shaded area in Figure 6.1.

real income The set of opportunities to purchase real goods and services available to a household as determined by prices and money income.

Clearly, both prices and incomes affect the size of a household's opportunity set. If a price or a set of prices falls but income stays the same, the opportunity set gets bigger and the household is better off. If we define **real income** as the set of opportunities to purchase real goods and services, "real income" will have gone up in this case even if the household's money income has not. A consumer's opportunity set expands as the result of a price decrease. On the other hand, when money income increases and prices go up even more, we say that the household's "real income" has fallen.

The concept of real income is very important in macroeconomics, which is concerned with measuring real output and the price level.

The Equation of the Budget Constraint

Yet another way to look at the budget constraint is to write the consumer's problem as an equation. In the previous example, the constraint is that total expenditure on Thai meals plus total expenditure on jazz club visits must be less than or equal to Ann and Tom's income. Total expenditure on Thai meals is equal to the *price* of Thai meals times the number, or *quantity*, of meals consumed. Total expenditure on jazz club visits is equal to the *price* of a visit times the number, or *quantity*, of visits. That is,

$$\$20 \times \text{Thai meals} + \$10 \times \text{jazz visits} \leq \$200$$

If we let X represent the number of Thai meals and we let Y represent the number of jazz club visits and we assume that Ann and Tom spend their entire income on either X or Y, this can be written as follows:

$$20X + 10Y = \$200$$

This is the equation of the budget constraint—the line connecting points A and B in Figure 6.1. Notice that when Ann and Tom spend nothing at the jazz club, $Y = 0$. When you plug $Y = 0$ into the equation of the budget constraint, $20X = 200$ and $X = 10$. Since X is the number of Thai meals, Ann and Tom eat Thai food 10 times. Similarly, when $X = 0$, you can solve for Y, which equals 20. When Ann and Tom eat no Thai food, they can go to the jazz club 20 times.

In general, the budget constraint can be written

$$P_X X + P_Y Y = I,$$

where P_X = the price of X, X = the quantity of X consumed, P_Y = the price of Y, Y = the quantity of Y consumed, and I = household income.[3]

Budget Constraints Change When Prices Rise or Fall Now suppose the Thai restaurant is offering two-for-one certificates good during the month of November. In effect, this means that the price of Thai meals drops to \$10 for Ann and Tom. How would the budget constraint in Figure 6.1 change?

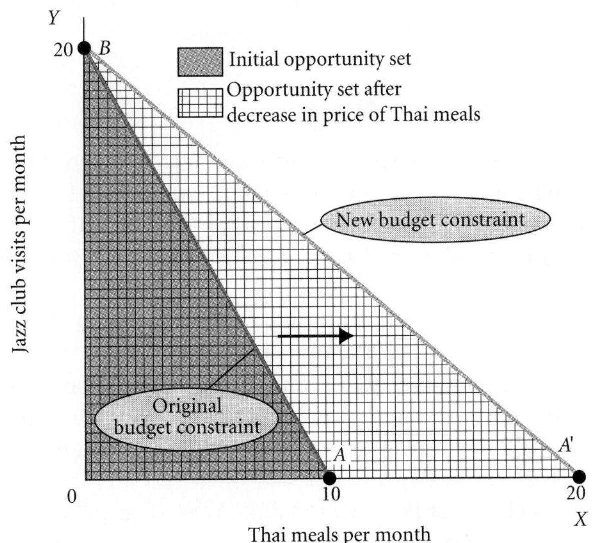

FIGURE 6.2 The Effect of a Decrease in Price on Ann and Tom's Budget Constraint

When the price of a good decreases, the budget constraint swivels to the right, increasing the opportunities available and expanding choice.

First, point B would not change. If Ann and Tom spend all their money on jazz, the price of Thai meals is irrelevant. Ann and Tom can still afford only 20 trips to the jazz club. What has changed is point A, which moves to point A' in Figure 6.2. At the new lower price of \$10, if Ann and Tom spent all their money on Thai meals, they could buy twice as many, $\$200 \div \$10 = 20$. The budget constraint *swivels*, as shown in Figure 6.2.

[3] You can calculate the slope of the budget constraint as $-P_X/P_Y$, the ratio of the price of X to the price of Y. This gives the trade-off that consumers face. In the example, $-P_X/P_Y = -2$, meaning to get another Thai meal, Ann and Tom must give up two trips to the jazz club.

The new, flatter budget constraint reflects the new trade-off between Thai meals and Hungry Ear visits. Now after the price of Thai meals drops to $10, the opportunity cost of a Thai meal is only one jazz club visit. The opportunity set has expanded because at the lower price more combinations of Thai meals and jazz are available.

Figure 6.2 thus illustrates a very important point. When the price of a single good changes, more than just the quantity demanded of that good may be affected. The household now faces an entirely different problem with regard to choice—the opportunity set has expanded. At the same income of $200, the new lower price means that Ann and Tom might choose more Thai meals, more jazz club visits, or more of both. They are clearly better off. The budget constraint is defined by income, wealth, and prices. Within those limits, households are free to choose, and the household's ultimate choice depends on its own likes and dislikes.

Notice that when the price of meals falls to $10, the equation of the budget constraint changes to $10X + 10Y = 200$, which is the equation of the line connecting points A' and B in Figure 6.2.

The range of goods and services available in a modern society is as vast as consumer tastes are variable, and this makes any generalization about the household choice process risky. Nonetheless, the theory of household behavior that follows is an attempt to derive some logical propositions about the way households make choices.

The Basis of Choice: Utility

Somehow, from the millions of things that are available, each of us manages to sort out a set of goods and services to buy. When we make our choices, we make specific judgments about the relative worth of things that are very different.

utility The satisfaction a product yields.

During the nineteenth century, the weighing of values was formalized into a concept called utility. Whether one item is preferable to another depends on how much **utility**, or satisfaction, it yields relative to its alternatives. How do we decide on the relative worth of a new puppy or a stereo? A trip to the mountains or a weekend in New York City? Working or not working? As we make our choices, we are effectively weighing the utilities we would receive from all the possible available goods.

Certain problems are implicit in the concept of utility. First, it is impossible to measure utility. Second, it is impossible to compare the utilities of different people—that is, we cannot say whether person A or person B has a higher level of utility. Despite these problems, however, the idea of utility helps us better understand the process of choice.

Diminishing Marginal Utility

In making their choices, most people spread their incomes over many different kinds of goods. One reason people prefer variety is that consuming more and more of any one good reduces the marginal, or extra, satisfaction they get from further consumption of the same good. Formally, **marginal utility (*MU*)** is the additional satisfaction gained by the consumption or use of *one more* unit of a good or service.

marginal utility (*MU*) The additional satisfaction gained by the consumption or use of *one more* unit of a good or service.

total utility The total amount of satisfaction obtained from consumption of a good or service.

It is important to distinguish marginal utility from total utility. **Total utility** is the total amount of satisfaction obtained from consumption of a good or service. Marginal utility comes only from the *last unit* consumed; total utility comes from *all* units consumed.

Suppose you live next to a store that sells homemade ice cream that you are crazy about. Even though you get a great deal of pleasure from eating ice cream, you do not spend your entire income on it. The first cone of the day tastes heavenly. The second is merely delicious. The third is still very good, but it is clear that the glow is fading. Why? The answer is because the more of any one good we consume in a given period, the less satisfaction, or utility, we get from each additional, or marginal, unit. In 1890, Alfred Marshall called this "familiar and fundamental tendency of human nature" the **law of diminishing marginal utility**.

law of diminishing marginal utility The more of any one good consumed in a given period, the less satisfaction (utility) generated by consuming each additional (marginal) unit of the same good.

Consider this simple example. Frank loves country music, and a country band is playing seven nights a week at a club near his house. Table 6.2 shows how the utility he derives from the band might change as he goes to the club more frequently. The first visit generates 12 "utils," or units of utility. When Frank goes back another night, he enjoys it, but not quite as much as the first night. The second night by itself yields 10 additional utils. *Marginal utility* is 10, while the *total utility* derived from two nights at the club is 22. Three nights per week at the club provide 28 total utils; the marginal utility of the third night is 6 because total utility rose from 22 to 28. Figure 6.3 graphs total and marginal utility using the data in Table 6.2. Total utility increases up

TABLE 6.2 Total Utility and Marginal Utility of Trips to the Club Per Week

Trips to Club	Total Utility	Marginal Utility
1	12	12
2	22	10
3	28	6
4	32	4
5	34	2
6	34	0

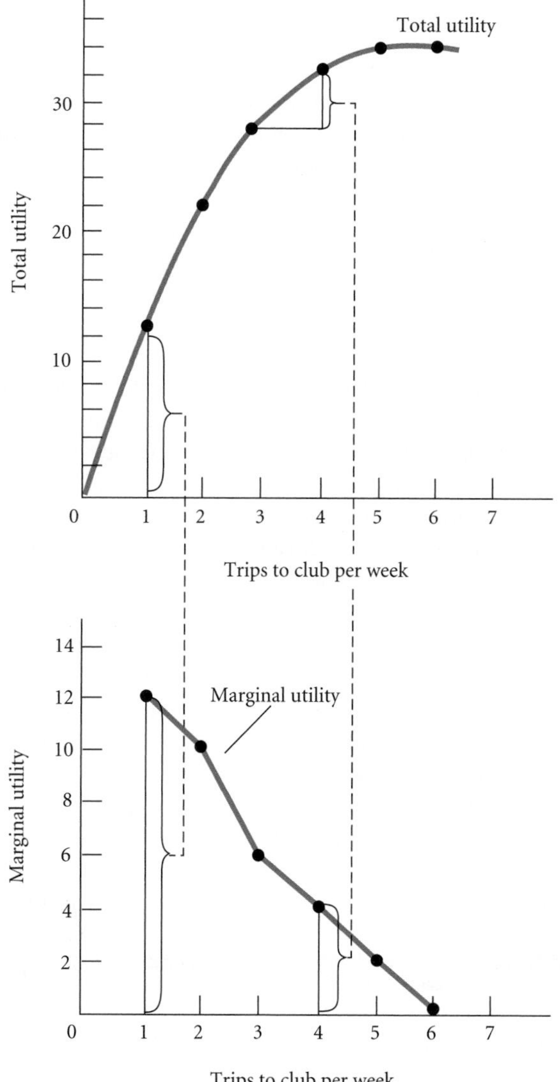

◀ FIGURE 6.3 Graphs of Frank's Total and Marginal Utility

Marginal utility is the additional utility gained by consuming one additional unit of a commodity—in this case, trips to the club. When marginal utility is zero, total utility stops rising.

through Frank's fifth trip to the club but levels off on the sixth night. Marginal utility, which has declined from the beginning, is now at zero.

Diminishing marginal utility helps explain the reason most sports have limited seasons. Even rabid fans have had enough baseball by late October. Given this fact, it would be hard to sell out ball games for a year-round season. While diminishing marginal utility is a simple and intuitive idea, it has great power in helping us understand the economic world.

Allocating Income to Maximize Utility

How many times in one week would Frank go to the club to hear his favorite band? The answer depends on three things: Frank's income, the price of admission to the club, and the alternatives available. If the price of admission was zero and no alternatives existed, he would probably go to the club five nights a week. (Remember, the sixth night does not increase his utility, so why should he bother to go?) However, Frank is also a basketball fan. His city has many good high school and college teams, and he can go to games six nights a week if he so chooses.

Let us say for now that admission to both the country music club and the basketball games is free—that is, there is no price/income constraint. There is a time constraint, however, because there are only seven nights in a week. Table 6.3 lists Frank's total and marginal utilities from attending basketball games and going to country music clubs. From column 3 of the table, we can conclude that on the first night, Frank will go to a basketball game. The game is worth far more to him (21 utils) than a trip to the club (12 utils).

On the second night, Frank's decision is not so easy. Because he has been to one basketball game this week, the second game is worth less (12 utils as compared to 21 for the first basketball game). In fact, because it is worth the same as a first trip to the club, he is indifferent as to whether he goes to the game or the club. So he splits the next two nights: One night he sees ball game number two (12 utils); the other night he spends at the club (12 utils). At this point, Frank has been to two ball games and has spent one night at the club. Where will Frank go on evening four? He will go to the club again because the marginal utility from a second trip to the club (10 utils) is greater than the marginal utility from attending a third basketball game (9 utils).

Frank is splitting his time between the two activities to maximize total utility. At each successive step, he chooses the activity that yields the most marginal utility. Continuing with this logic, you can see that spending three nights at the club and four nights watching basketball produces total utility of 76 utils each week (28 plus 48). No other combination of games and club trips can produce as much utility.

So far, the only cost of a night of listening to country music is a forgone basketball game and the only cost of a basketball game is a forgone night of country music. Now let us suppose that it costs $3 to get into the club and $6 to go to a basketball game. Suppose further that after paying rent and taking care of other expenses, Frank has only $21 left to spend on entertainment. Typically, consumers allocate limited incomes, or budgets, over a large set of goods and services. Here we have a limited income ($21) being allocated between only two goods, but the principle is the same. Income ($21) and prices ($3 and $6) define Franks budget constraint. Within that constraint, Frank chooses to maximize utility.

Because the two activities now cost different amounts, we need to find the *marginal utility per dollar* spent on each activity. If Frank is to spend his money on the combination of activities lying within his budget constraint that gives him the most total utility, each night he must choose the activity that gives him the *most utility per dollar spent.* As you can see from column 5 in Table 6.3, Frank gets 4 utils per dollar on the first night he goes to the club (12 utils ÷ $3 = 4 utils per dollar). On night two, he goes to a game and gets 3.5 utils per dollar (21 utils ÷ $6 = 3.5 utils per dollar). On night three, it is back to the club. Then what happens? When all is said and done—work this out for yourself—Frank ends up going to two games and spending three nights at the club. No other combination of activities that $21 will buy yields more utility.

TABLE 6.3 Allocation of Fixed Expenditure per Week Between Two Alternatives

(1) Trips to Club per Week	(2) Total Utility	(3) Marginal Utility (*MU*)	(4) Price (*P*)	(5) Marginal Utility per Dollar (*MU/P*)
1	12	12	$3.00	4.0
2	22	10	3.00	3.3
3	28	6	3.00	2.0
4	32	4	3.00	1.3
5	34	2	3.00	.7
6	34	0	3.00	0
(1) Basketball Games per Week	**(2) Total Utility**	**(3) Marginal Utility (*MU*)**	**(4) Price (*P*)**	**(5) Marginal Utility per Dollar (*MU/P*)**
1	21	21	$6.00	3.5
2	33	12	6.00	2.0
3	42	9	6.00	1.5
4	48	6	6.00	1.0
5	51	3	6.00	.5
6	51	0	6.00	0

The Utility-Maximizing Rule

In general, utility-maximizing consumers spread out their expenditures until the following condition holds:

$$\text{utility-maximizing rule:} \quad \frac{MU_X}{P_X} = \frac{MU_Y}{P_Y} \text{ for all goods}$$

where MU_X is the marginal utility derived from the last unit of X consumed, MU_Y is the marginal utility derived from the last unit of Y consumed, P_X is the price per unit of X, and P_Y is the price per unit of Y.

To see why this **utility-maximizing rule** is true, think for a moment about what would happen if it were *not* true. For example, suppose MU_X/P_X was greater than MU_Y/P_Y; that is, suppose a consumer purchased a bundle of goods so that the marginal utility from the last dollar spent on X was greater than the marginal utility from the last dollar spent on Y. This would mean that the consumer could increase his or her utility by spending a dollar less on Y and a dollar more on X. As the consumer shifts to buying more X and less Y, he or she runs into diminishing marginal utility. Buying more units of X *decreases* the marginal utility derived from consuming additional units of X. As a result, the marginal utility of another dollar spent on X falls. Now *less* is being spent on Y, and that means its marginal utility *increases*. This process continues until $MU_X/P_X = MU_Y/P_Y$. When this condition holds, there is no way for the consumer to increase his or her utility by changing the bundle of goods purchased.

utility-maximizing rule Equating the ratio of the marginal utility of a good to its price for all goods.

You can see how the utility-maximizing rule works in Frank's choice between country music and basketball. At each stage, Frank chooses the activity that gives him the most utility per dollar. If he goes to a game, the utility he will derive from the next game—marginal utility—falls. If he goes to the club, the utility he will derive from his next visit falls, and so on.

The principles we have been describing help us understand an old puzzle dating from the time of Plato and familiar to economists beginning with Adam Smith. Adam Smith wrote about it in 1776:

> The things which have the greatest value in use have frequently little or no value in exchange; and on the contrary, those which have the greatest value in exchange have frequently little or no value in use. Nothing is more useful than water: but it will purchase scarce any thing; scarce anything can be had in exchange for it. A diamond, on the contrary, has scarce any value in use; but a very great quantity of other goods may frequently be had in exchange for it.[4]

Although diamonds have arguably more than "scarce any value in use" today (for example, they are used to cut glass), Smith's **diamond/water paradox** is still instructive, at least where water is concerned.

diamond/water paradox A paradox stating that (1) the things with the greatest value in use frequently have little or no value in exchange and (2) the things with the greatest value in exchange frequently have little or no value in use.

The low price of water owes much to the fact that it is in plentiful supply. Even at a price of zero, we do not consume an infinite amount of water. We consume up to the point where *marginal* utility drops to zero. The *marginal* value of water is zero. Each of us enjoys an enormous consumer surplus when we consume nearly free water. At a price of zero, consumer surplus is the entire area under the demand curve. We tend to take water for granted, but imagine what would happen to its price if there were not enough for everyone. It would command a high price indeed.

Diminishing Marginal Utility and Downward-Sloping Demand

The concept of diminishing marginal utility offers one reason why people spread their incomes over a variety of goods and services instead of spending all income on one or two items. It also leads us to conclude that demand curves slope downward.

To see why this is so, let us return to our friends Ann and Tom, the struggling graduate students. Recall that they chose between meals at a Thai restaurant and trips to a jazz club. Now

[4] Adam Smith, *The Wealth of Nations*, Modern Library Edition (New York: Random House, 1937), p. 28 (1st ed. 1776). The cheapness of water is referred to by Plato in *Euthydem.*, 304B.

think about their demand curve for Thai meals, shown in Figure 6.4. When the price of a meal is $40, they decide not to buy any Thai meals. What they are really deciding is that the utility gained from even that first scrumptious meal each month is not worth the utility that would come from the other things that $40 can buy.

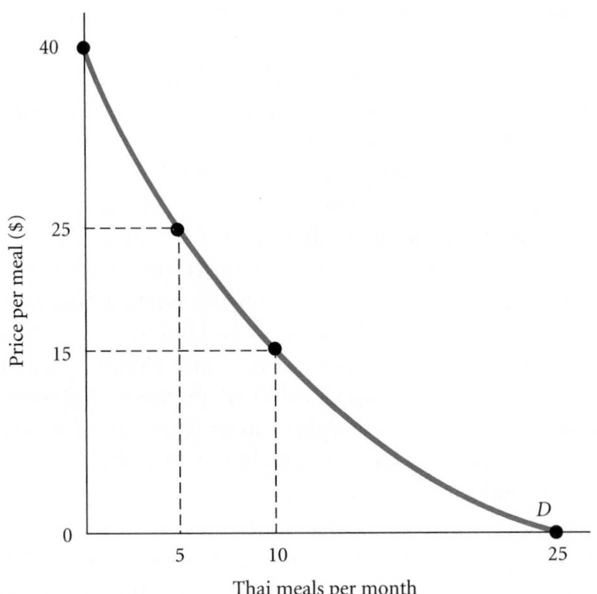

FIGURE 6.4 Diminishing Marginal Utility and Downward-Sloping Demand

At a price of $40, the utility gained from even the first Thai meal is not worth the price. However, a lower price of $25 lures Ann and Tom into the Thai restaurant 5 times a month. (The utility from the sixth meal is not worth $25.) If the price is $15, Ann and Tom will eat Thai meals 10 times a month—until the marginal utility of a Thai meal drops below the utility they could gain from spending $15 on other goods. At 25 meals a month, they cannot tolerate the thought of another Thai meal even if it is free.

Now consider a price of $25. At this price, Ann and Tom buy five Thai meals. The first, second, third, fourth, and fifth meals each generate enough utility to justify the price. Tom and Ann "reveal" this by buying five meals. After the fifth meal, the utility gained from the next meal is not worth $25.

Ultimately, every demand curve hits the quantity (horizontal) axis as a result of diminishing marginal utility—in other words, demand curves slope downward. How many times will Ann and Tom go to the Thai restaurant if meals are free? Twenty-five times is the answer; and after 25 times a month, they are so sick of Thai food that they will not eat any more even if it is free. That is, marginal utility—the utility gained from the last meal—has dropped to zero. If you think this is unrealistic, ask yourself how much water you drank today.

Income and Substitution Effects

Although the idea of utility is a helpful way of thinking about the choice process, there is an explanation for downward-sloping demand curves that does not rely on the concept of utility or the assumption of diminishing marginal utility. This explanation centers on income and substitution effects.

Keeping in mind that consumers face constrained choices, consider the probable response of a household to a decline in the price of some heavily used product, *ceteris paribus*. How might a household currently consuming many goods be likely to respond to a fall in the price of one of those goods if the household's income, its preferences, and all other prices remained unchanged? The household would face a new budget constraint, and its final choice of all goods and services might change. A decline in the price of gasoline, for example, may affect not only how much gasoline you purchase but also what kind of car you buy, when and how much you travel, where you go, and (not so directly) how many movies you see this month and how many projects around the house you get done.

The Income Effect

Price changes affect households in two ways. First, if we assume that households confine their choices to products that improve their well-being, then a decline in the price of any product, *ceteris paribus*, will make the household unequivocally better off. In other words, if a household continues to buy the same amount of every good and service after the price decrease, it will have income left over. That extra income may be spent on the product whose price has declined, hereafter called good X, or on other products. The change in consumption of X due to this improvement in well-being is called the *income effect of a price change.*

Suppose you live in Florida and four times a year you fly to Nashville to visit your mother. Suppose further that last year a round-trip ticket to Nashville cost $400. Thus, you spend a total of $1,600 per year on trips to visit Mom. This year, however, increased competition among the airlines has led one airline to offer round-trip tickets to Nashville for $200. Assuming the price remains $200 all year, you can now fly home the same number of times and you will have spent $800 less for airline tickets than you did last year. Now that you are better off, you have additional opportunities. You can fly home a fifth time this year, leaving $600 ($800 − $200) to spend on other things, or you can fly home the same number of times (four) and spend the extra $800 on other things. When the price of something we buy falls, we are *better off.* When the price of something we buy rises, we are *worse off.*

Look back at Figure 6.2 on p. 115. When the price of Thai meals fell, the opportunity set facing Tom and Ann expanded—they were able to afford more Thai meals, more jazz club trips, or more of both. They were unequivocally better off because of the price decline. In a sense, their "real" income was higher.

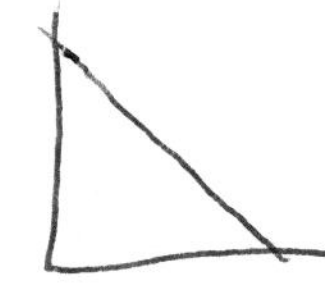

Now recall from Chapter 3 the definition of a *normal good.* When income rises, demand for normal goods increases. Most goods are normal goods. Because of the price decline, Tom and Ann can afford to buy more. If Thai food is a normal good, a decline in the price of Thai food should lead to an increase in the quantity demanded of Thai food.

The Substitution Effect

The fact that a price decline leaves households better off is only part of the story. When the price of a product falls, that product also becomes *relatively* cheaper. That is, it becomes more attractive relative to potential substitutes. A fall in the price of product X might cause a household to shift its purchasing pattern away from substitutes toward X. This shift is called the *substitution effect of a price change.*

Earlier we made the point that the "real" cost or price of a good is what one must sacrifice to consume it. This opportunity cost is determined by relative prices. To see why this is so, consider again the choice that you face when a round-trip ticket to Nashville costs $400. Each trip that you take requires a sacrifice of $400 worth of other goods and services. When the price drops to $200, the opportunity cost of a ticket has dropped by $200. In other words, after the price decline, you have to sacrifice only $200 (instead of $400) worth of other goods and services to visit Mom.

To clarify the distinction between the income and substitution, imagine how you would be affected if two things happened to you at the same time. First, the price of round-trip air travel between Florida and Nashville drops from $400 to $200. Second, your income is reduced by $800. You are now faced with new relative prices, but—assuming you flew home four times last year—you are no better off now than you were before the price of a ticket declined. The decrease in the price of air travel has offset your decrease in income.

You are still likely to take more trips home. Why? The opportunity cost of a trip home is now lower, *ceteris paribus*—that is, assuming no change in the prices of other goods and services. A trip to Nashville now requires a sacrifice of only $200 worth of other goods and services, not the $400 worth that it did before. Thus, you will substitute away from other goods toward trips to see your mother.

Everything works in the opposite direction when a price rises, *ceteris paribus.* A price increase makes households worse off. If income and other prices do not change, spending the same amount of money buys less and households will be forced to buy less. This is the income effect. In addition, when the price of a product rises, that item becomes more expensive relative to potential substitutes and the household is likely to substitute other goods for it. This is the substitution effect.

What do the income and substitution effects tell us about the demand curve? Both the income and the substitution effects imply a negative relationship between price and quantity demanded—in other words, downward-sloping demand. When the price of something falls, *ceteris paribus*, we are better off and we are likely to buy more of that good and other goods (income effect). Because lower price also means "less expensive relative to substitutes," we are likely to buy more of the good (substitution effect). When the price of something rises, we are worse off and we will buy less of it (income effect). Higher price also means "more expensive relative to substitutes," and we are likely to buy less of it and more of other goods (substitution effect).[5]

Figure 6.5 summarizes the income and substitution effects of a price change of gasoline prices.

If you recall the example of gasoline prices from early in the chapter, income and substitution effects help us answer questions. When gas prices rise, the income effects can cause a fall in the demand for other goods. Since gas is a big part of many budgets, these income effects can be very large. It is the income effect from gasoline price increases that some argue causes consumers to switch away from high-priced brand name products.

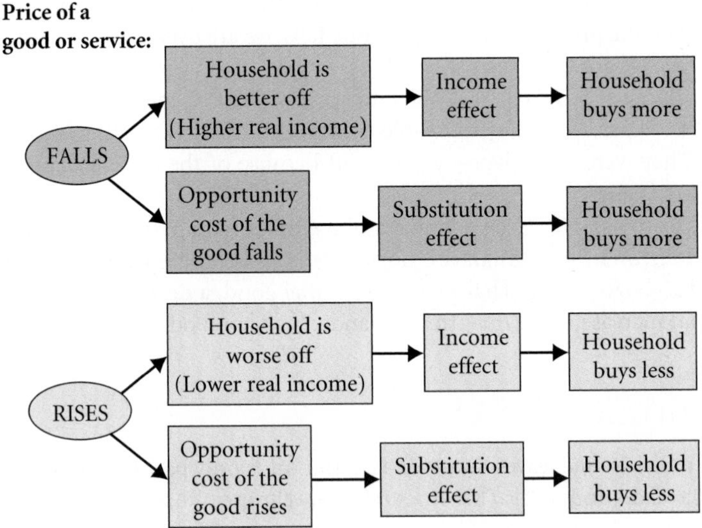

FIGURE 6.5 Income and Substitution Effects of a Price Change
For normal goods, the income and substitution effects work in the same direction. Higher prices lead to a lower quantity demanded, and lower prices lead to a higher quantity demanded.

Household Choice in Input Markets

So far, we have focused on the decision-making process that lies behind output demand curves. Households with limited incomes allocate those incomes across various combinations of goods and services that are available and affordable. In looking at the factors affecting choices in the output market, we assumed that income was fixed, or given. We noted at the outset, however, that income is in fact partially determined by choices that households make in input markets. (Look back at Figure II.1 on p. 107) We now turn to a brief discussion of the two decisions that households make in input markets: the labor supply decision and the saving decision.

The Labor Supply Decision

Most income in the United States is wage and salary income paid as compensation for labor. Household members supply labor in exchange for wages or salaries. As in output markets, households face constrained choices in input markets. They must decide

1. Whether to work
2. How much to work
3. What kind of a job to work at

[5] For some goods, the income and substitution effects work in opposite directions. When our income rises, we may buy less of some goods. In Chapter 3, we called such goods *inferior goods*. When the price of an inferior good rises, it is, like any other good, more expensive relative to substitutes and we are likely to replace it with lower-priced substitutes. However, when we are worse off, we increase our demand for inferior goods. Thus, the income effect could lead us to buy more of the good, partially offsetting the substitution effect.

Even if a good is "very inferior," demand curves will slope downward as long as the substitution effect is larger than the income effect. It is possible, at least in theory, for the income effect to be larger. In such a case, a price increase would actually lead to an increase in quantity demanded. This possibility was pointed out by Alfred Marshall in *Principles of Economics*. Marshall attributes the notion of an upward-sloping demand curve to Sir Robert Giffen; and for this reason, the notion is often referred to as *Giffen's paradox*. Fortunately or unfortunately, no one has ever demonstrated that a Giffen good has existed.

ECONOMICS IN PRACTICE

Substitution and Market Baskets

In driving to work one day, one of the authors of this text heard the following advertisement for a local grocery store, which we will call Cheap Foods:

"Cheap Foods has the best prices in town, and we can prove it! Yesterday we chose Ms. Smith out of our checkout line for a comparison test. Ms. Smith is an average consumer, much like you and me. In doing her weekly grocery shopping yesterday at Cheap Foods, she spent $125. We then sent Ms. Smith to the neighboring competitor with instructions to buy the same market basket of food. When she returned with her food, she saw that her grocery total was $134. You too will see that Cheap Foods can save you money!"

Advertisements like this one are commonplace. As you evaluate the claims in the ad, several things may come to mind. Perhaps Ms. Smith is not representative of consumers or is not much like you. That might make Cheap Foods a good deal for her but not for you. (So your demand curve looks different from Ms. Smith's.) Or perhaps yesterday was a sale day, meaning yesterday was not typical of Cheap Foods' prices. But there is something more fundamentally wrong with the claims in this ad even if you are just like Ms. Smith and Cheap Foods offers the same prices every day. The fundamental error in this ad is revealed by the work you have done in this chapter.

When Ms. Smith shopped, she presumably looked at the prices of the various food choices offered at the market and tried to do the best she could for her family given those prices and her family's tastes. If we go back to the utility-maximizing rule that you learned in this chapter, we see that Ms. Smith was comparing the marginal utility of each product she consumes relative to its price in deciding what bundle to buy. In pragmatic terms, if Ms. Smith likes apples and pears about the same, while she was shopping in Cheap Foods, she would have bought the cheaper of the two. When she was sent to the neighboring store, however, she was constrained to buy the same goods that she bought at Cheap Foods. (So she was forced to buy pears even if they were more expensive just to duplicate the bundle.) When we artificially restrict Ms. Smith's ability to substitute goods, we almost inevitably give her a more expensive bundle. The real question is this: Would Ms. Smith have been more happy or less happy with her market basket after spending $125 at Cheap Foods or at its rival? Without knowing more about the shape of Ms. Smith's utility curve and the prices she faces we cannot answer that question. The dollar comparison in the ad doesn't tell the whole story!

In essence, household members must decide how much labor to supply. The choices they make are affected by

1. Availability of jobs
2. Market wage rates
3. Skills they possess

As with decisions in output markets, the labor supply decision involves a set of trade-offs. There are basically two alternatives to working for a wage: (1) not working and (2) doing unpaid work. If you do not work, you sacrifice income for the benefits of staying home and reading, watching TV, swimming, or sleeping. Another option is to work, but not for a money wage. In this case, you sacrifice money income for the benefits of growing your own food, raising your children, or taking care of your house.

As with the trade-offs in output markets, your final choice depends on how you value the alternatives available. If you work, you earn a wage that you can use to buy things. Thus, the trade-off is between the value of the goods and services you can buy with the wages you earn versus the value of things you can produce at home—home-grown food, manageable children, clean clothes, and so on—or the value you place on leisure. This choice is illustrated in Figure 6.6. In general, the wage rate can be thought of as the price—or the opportunity cost—of the benefits of either unpaid work or leisure. Just as you choose among different goods by comparing the marginal utility of each relative to its price, you also choose between leisure and other goods by comparing the marginal utility of leisure relative to its price (the wage rate) with the marginal utility of other goods relative to their prices.

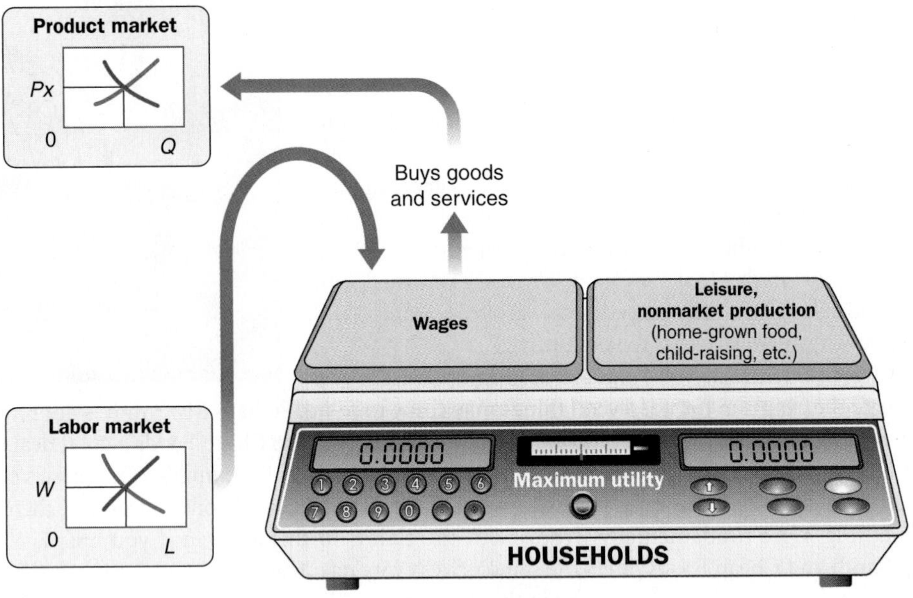

FIGURE 6.6 The Trade-Off Facing Households

The decision to enter the workforce involves a trade-off between wages (and the goods and services that wages will buy) on the one hand and leisure and the value of nonmarket production on the other hand.

The Price of Leisure

In our analysis in the early part of this chapter, households had to allocate a limited budget across a set of goods and services. Now they must choose among goods, services, and *leisure*.

When we add leisure to the picture, we do so with one important distinction. Trading one good for another involves buying less of one and more of another, so households simply reallocate *money* from one good to the other. "Buying" more leisure, however, means reallocating time between work and nonwork activities. For each hour of leisure that you decide to consume, you give up one hour's wages. Thus, the wage rate is the *price of leisure*.

Conditions in the labor market determine the budget constraints and final opportunity sets that households face. The availability of jobs and these job wage rates determine the final combinations of goods and services that a household can afford. The final choice within these constraints depends on the unique tastes and preferences of each household. Different people place more or less value on leisure—but everyone needs to put food on the table.

Income and Substitution Effects of a Wage Change

labor supply curve A curve that shows the quantity of labor supplied at different wage rates. Its shape depends on how households react to changes in the wage rate.

A **labor supply curve** shows the quantity of labor supplied at different wage rates. The shape of the labor supply curve depends on how households react to changes in the wage rate.

Consider an increase in wages. First, an increase in wages makes households better off. If they work the same number of hours—that is, if they supply the same amount of labor—they will earn higher incomes and be able to buy more goods and services. They can also buy more leisure. If leisure is a normal good—that is, a good for which demand increases as income increases—an increase in income will lead to a higher demand for leisure and a lower labor supply. This is the *income effect of a wage increase*.

However, there is also a potential *substitution effect of a wage increase*. A higher wage rate means that leisure is more expensive. If you think of the wage rate as the price of leisure, each individual hour of leisure consumed at a higher wage costs more in forgone wages. As a result, we would expect households to substitute other goods for leisure. This means working more, or a lower quantity demanded of leisure and a higher quantity supplied of labor.

Note that in the labor market, the income and substitution effects work in *opposite* directions when leisure is a normal good. The income effect of a wage increase implies buying more leisure and working less; the substitution effect implies buying less leisure and working more. Whether households will supply more labor overall or less labor overall when wages rise depends on the relative strength of both the income and the substitution effects.

If the substitution effect is greater than the income effect, the wage increase will increase labor supply. This suggests that the labor supply curve slopes upward, or has a positive slope, like the one in Figure 6.7(a). If the income effect outweighs the substitution effect, however, a higher wage will lead to added consumption of leisure and labor supply will decrease. This implies that the labor supply curve "bends back," as the one in Figure 6.7(b) does.

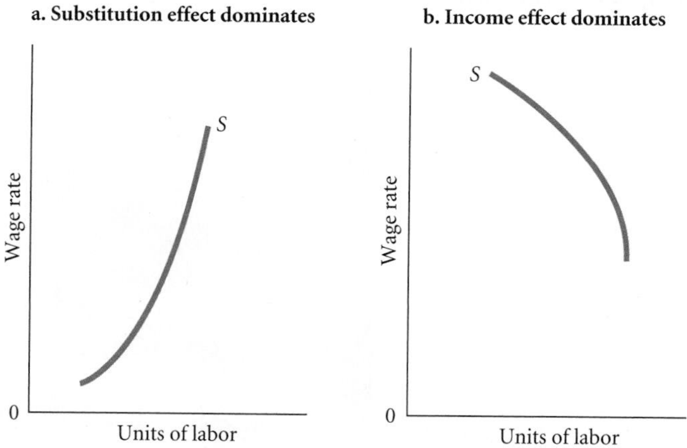

FIGURE 6.7 Two Labor Supply Curves

When the substitution effect outweighs the income effect, the labor supply curve slopes upward (a). When the income effect outweighs the substitution effect, the result is a "backward-bending" labor supply curve: The labor supply curve slopes downward (b).

During the early years of the Industrial Revolution in late eighteenth century Great Britain, the textile industry operated under what was called the "putting-out" system. Spinning and weaving were done in small cottages to supplement the family farm income—hence the term *cottage industry*. During that period, wages and household incomes rose considerably. Some economic historians claim that this higher income actually led many households to take more leisure and work fewer hours; the empirical evidence suggests a backward-bending labor supply curve.

Just as income and substitution effects helped us understand household choices in output markets, they now help us understand household choices in input markets. The point here is simple: When leisure is added to the choice set, the line between input and output market decisions becomes blurred. In fact, households decide simultaneously how much of each good to consume and how much leisure to consume.

Saving and Borrowing: Present versus Future Consumption

We began this chapter by examining the way households allocate a fixed income over a large number of goods and services. We then pointed out that, at least in part, choices made by households determine income levels. Within the constraints imposed by the market, households decide whether to work and how much to work.

So far, however, we have talked about only the current period—the allocation of current income among alternative uses and the work/leisure choice *today*. Households can also (1) use present income to finance future spending—they can *save*—or (2) use future income to finance present spending—they can *borrow*.

When a household decides to save, it is using current income to finance future consumption. That future consumption may come in 3 years, when you use your savings to buy a car; in 10 years, when you sell stock to put a deposit on a house; or in 45 years, when you retire and begin to receive money from your pension plan. Most people cannot finance large purchases—a house or condominium, for example—out of current income and savings. They almost always borrow money and sign a mortgage. When a household borrows, it is in essence financing a current purchase with future income. It pays back the loan out of future income.

Even in simple economies such as the two-person desert-island economy of Colleen and Bill (see Chapter 2), people must make decisions about *present versus future consumption*. Colleen and Bill could (1) produce goods for today's consumption by hunting and gathering, (2) consume leisure by sleeping on the beach, or (3) work on projects to enhance future consumption opportunities. Building a house or a boat over a 5-year period is trading present consumption for

ECONOMICS IN PRACTICE

Google: Is It Work or Is It Leisure?

A recent article on work life at Google included the following descriptions of the workplace:

Google is No. 1: Search and Enjoy!

CNNMoney.com

At Google it always comes back to the food. For human resources director Stacy Sullivan, it's the Irish oatmeal with fresh berries at the Plymouth Rock Café, located in building 1550 near the "people operations" group. "I sometimes dream about it," she says. "Seriously." As a seven-year veteran of the company, engineer Jen Fitzpatrick has developed a more sophisticated palate, preferring the raw bar at the Basque-themed Café Pintxo, a tapas joint in building 47. Her mother is thrilled she's eating well at work: "She came in for lunch once and thanked the chef," says Fitzpatrick. Joshua Bloch, an expert on the Java software language, swears by the roast quail at haute eatery Café Seven, professing it to be the best meal on campus. "It's uniformly excellent," he raves.

Of course, when it comes to America's new Best Company to Work For, the food is, well, just the appetizer. At Google you can do your laundry; drop off your dry cleaning; get an oil change, then have your car washed; work out in the gym; attend subsidized exercise classes; get a massage; study Mandarin, Japanese, Spanish, and French; and ask a personal concierge to arrange dinner reservations. Naturally you can get haircuts onsite. Want to buy a hybrid car? The company will give you $5,000 toward that environmentally friendly end. Care to refer a friend to work at Google? Google would like that too, and it'll give you a $2,000 reward. Just have a new baby? Congratulations! Your employer will reimburse you up to $500 in takeout food to ease your first four weeks at home. Looking to make new friends? Attend a weekly TGIF party, where there's usually a band playing. Five onsite doctors are available to give you a checkup, free of charge.

Google is well known for bringing the spirit of college life to the workplace. But the broad range and high quality of services that Google offers its employees on-site has an economic explanation as well. In our discussion in this chapter on the work/leisure choice, we indicated that people were looking at the marginal utility of leisure relative to the wage in deciding how much to work. While people use some of their leisure time for recreation, some part of the reason people value leisure is that they need the time to do a range of household chores—drop off the dry cleaning, cook, take care of the children, and so on. By providing many of these services at the workplace, Google has potentially affected the trade-off people make between work and leisure. In the end, without increasing wages, Google may have reduced the marginal utility of leisure and made people more willing to work longer hours. In fact, later in the same article, one Google employee comments:

"Hardcore geeks are here because there's no place they'd rather be," says Dennis Hwang, a Google Webmaster who doubles as the artist who draws all the fancifully dressed-up versions of Google's home-page logo, called Doodles.

Source: CNNMoney.com, Fortune, *"Google Is No. 1: Search and Enjoy," January 10, 2007. Excerpted with permission.*

future consumption. As with all of the other choices we have examined in this chapter, the broad principle will be to look at marginal utilities and prices. How much do Colleen and Bill value having something now versus waiting for the future? How much do they gain by waiting?

When a household saves, it usually puts the money into something that will generate income. There is no sense in putting money under your mattress when you can make it work in so many ways: savings accounts, money market funds, stocks, corporate bonds, and so on—many of which are virtually risk-free. When you put your money in any of these places, you are actually lending it out and the borrower pays you a fee for its use. This fee usually takes the form of *interest*. The interest paid is the possible benefit Colleen and Bill get from forgoing current consumption.

Just as changes in wage rates affect household behavior in the labor market, changes in interest rates affect household behavior in capital markets. Higher interest rates mean that borrowing is more expensive—required monthly payments on a newly purchased house or car will be higher. Higher interest rates also mean that saving will earn a higher return: $1,000 invested in a 5 percent savings account or bond yields $50 per year. If rates rise to 10 percent, the annual interest will rise to $100.

What impact do interest rates have on saving behavior? As with the effect of wage changes on labor supply, the effect of changes in interest rates on saving can best be understood in terms of income and substitution effects. Suppose, for example, that I have been saving for a number of years for retirement. Will an increase in interest rates lead to an increase or a decrease in my saving? The answer is not obvious. First, because each dollar saved will earn a higher rate of return, the "price" of spending today in terms of forgone future spending is higher. That is, each dollar that I spend today (instead of saving) costs me more in terms of future consumption because my saving will now earn a higher return. On this score, I will be led to save *more*, which is the substitution effect at work.

However, higher interest rates mean more than that. Higher interest rates mean that it will take less saving today to reach a specific target amount of savings tomorrow. I will not need to save as much for retirement or future consumption as I did before. One hundred dollars put into a savings account with 5 percent compound interest will double in 14 years. If interest was paid at a rate of 10 percent, I would have my $200 in just 7 years. Consequently, I may be led to save less, which is the income effect at work. Higher interest rates mean savers are better off; so higher interest rates may lead to less saving. The final impact of a change in interest rates on saving depends on the relative size of the income and substitution effects. Most empirical evidence indicates that saving tends to increase as the interest rate rises. In other words, the substitution effect is larger than the income effect.

Saving and investment decisions involve a huge and complex set of institutions, the **financial capital market**, in which the suppliers of capital (households that save) and the demand for capital (firms that want to invest) interact. The amount of capital investment in an economy is constrained in the long run by that economy's saving rate. You can think of household *saving* as the economy's supply of capital. When a firm borrows to finance a capital acquisition, it is almost as if households have supplied the capital for the fee we call interest. We treat capital markets in detail in Chapter 11.[6]

financial capital market The complex set of institutions in which suppliers of capital (households that save) and the demand for capital (firms wanting to invest) interact.

A Review: Households in Output and Input Markets

In probing the behavior of households in both input and output markets and examining the nature of constrained choice, we went behind the household demand curve using the simplifying assumption that income was fixed and given. Income, wealth, and prices set the limits, or *constraints*, within which households make their choices in output markets. Within those limits, households make their choices on the basis of personal tastes and preferences.

The notion of *utility* helps explain the process of choice. The law of *diminishing marginal utility* partly explains why people seem to spread their incomes over many different goods and services and why demand curves have a negative slope. Another important explanation behind the negative relationship between price and quantity demanded lies in *income effects* and *substitution effects*.

---

[6] Here in Chapter 6 we are looking at a country as if it were isolated from the rest of the world. Very often, however, capital investment is financed by funds loaned or provided by foreign citizens or governments. For example, in recent years, a substantial amount of foreign savings has found its way into the United States for the purchase of stocks, bonds, and other financial instruments. In part, these flows finance capital investment. Also, the United States and other countries that contribute funds to the World Bank and the International Monetary Fund have provided billions in outright grants and loans to help developing countries produce capital. For more information on these institutions, see Chapter 21.

As we turned to input markets, we relaxed the assumption that income was fixed and given. In the labor market, households are forced to weigh the value of leisure against the value of goods and services that can be bought with wage income. Once again, we found household preferences for goods and leisure operating within a set of constraints imposed by the market. Households also face the problem of allocating income and consumption over more than one period of time. They can finance spending in the future with today's income by saving and earning interest, or they can spend tomorrow's income today by borrowing.

We now have a rough sketch of the factors that determine output demand and input supply. (You can review these in Figure II.1 on p. 107.) In the next three chapters, we turn to firm behavior and explore in detail the factors that affect output supply and input demand.

SUMMARY

HOUSEHOLD CHOICE IN OUTPUT MARKETS *p. 111*

1. Every household must make three basic decisions: (1) how much of each product, or output, to demand; (2) how much labor to supply; and (3) how much to spend today and how much to save for the future.
2. Income, wealth, and prices define household *budget constraint*. The budget constraint separates those combinations of goods and services that are available from those that are not. All the points below and to the left of a graph of a household budget constraint make up the *choice set*, or *opportunity set*.
3. It is best to think of the household choice problem as one of allocating income over a large number of goods and services. A change in the price of one good may change the entire allocation. Demand for some goods may rise, while demand for others may fall.
4. As long as a household faces a limited income, the real cost of any single good or service is the value of the next preferred *other* goods and services that could have been purchased with the same amount of money.
5. Within the constraints of prices, income, and wealth, household decisions ultimately depend on preferences—likes, dislikes, and tastes.

THE BASIS OF CHOICE: UTILITY *p. 116*

6. Whether one item is preferable to another depends on how much *utility*, or satisfaction, it yields relative to its alternatives.
7. The *law of diminishing marginal utility* says that the more of any good we consume in a given period of time, the less satisfaction, or utility, we get out of each additional (or marginal) unit of that good.
8. Households allocate income among goods and services to maximize utility. This implies choosing activities that yield the highest marginal utility per dollar. In a two-good world, households will choose to equate the marginal utility per dollar spent on X with the marginal utility per dollar spent on Y. This is the *utility-maximizing rule*.

INCOME AND SUBSTITUTION EFFECTS *p. 120*

9. The fact that demand curves have a negative slope can be explained in two ways: (1) Marginal utility for all goods diminishes. (2) For most normal goods, both the *income and the substitution effects* of a price decline lead to more consumption of the good.

HOUSEHOLD CHOICE IN INPUT MARKETS *p. 122*

10. In the labor market, a trade-off exists between the value of the goods and services that can be bought in the market or produced at home and the value that one places on leisure. The opportunity cost of paid work is leisure and unpaid work. The wage rate is the price, or opportunity cost, of the benefits of unpaid work or leisure.
11. The income and substitution effects of a change in the wage rate work in opposite directions. Higher wages mean that (1) leisure is more expensive (likely response: people work *more*—substitution effect) and (2) more income is earned in a given number of hours, so some time may be spent on leisure (likely response: people work *less*—income effect).
12. In addition to deciding how to allocate its present income among goods and services, a household may also decide to save or borrow. When a household decides to save part of its current income, it is using current income to finance future spending. When a household borrows, it finances current purchases with future income.
13. An increase in interest rates has a positive effect on saving if the substitution effect dominates the income effect and a negative effect if the income effect dominates the substitution effect. Most empirical evidence shows that the substitution effect dominates here.

REVIEW TERMS AND CONCEPTS

budget constraint, *p. 112*
choice set *or* opportunity set, *p. 113*
diamond/water paradox, *p. 119*
financial capital market, *p. 127*
homogeneous products, *p. 109*
labor supply curve, *p. 124*
law of diminishing marginal utility, *p. 116*
marginal utility (*MU*), *p. 116*
perfect competition, *p. 109*
perfect knowledge, *p. 109*
real income, *p. 114*
total utility, *p. 116*
utility, *p. 116*
utility-maximizing rule, *p. 119*

PROBLEMS

Visit www.myeconlab.com to complete the problems marked in orange online. You will receive instant feedback on your answers, tutorial help, and access to additional practice problems.

1. For each of the following events, consider how you might react. What things might you consume more or less of? Would you work more or less? Would you increase or decrease your saving? Are your responses consistent with the discussion of household behavior in this chapter?
   a. You have a very close friend who lives in another city, a 3-hour bus ride away. The price of a round-trip ticket rises from $20 to $45.
   b. Tuition at your college is cut 25 percent.
   c. You receive an award that pays you $300 per month for the next 5 years.
   d. Interest rates rise dramatically, and savings accounts are now paying 10% interest annually.
   e. The price of food doubles. (If you are on a meal plan, assume that your board charges double.)
   f. A new business opens up nearby offering part-time jobs at $20 per hour.

2. The following table gives a hypothetical total utility schedule for the Cookie Monster (CM):

NUMBER OF COOKIES	TOTAL UTILITY
0	0
1	100
2	200
3	275
4	325
5	350
6	360
7	360

   Calculate the CM's marginal utility schedule. Draw a graph of total and marginal utility. If cookies cost the CM 5 cents each and CM had a good income, what is the maximum number of cookies he would most likely eat?

3. Kamika lives in Chicago but goes to school in Tucson, Arizona. For the last 2 years, she has made four trips home each year. During 2008, the price of a round-trip ticket from Chicago to Tucson increased from $350 to $600. As a result, Kamika decided not to buy a new outfit that year and decided not to drive to Phoenix with friends for an expensive rock concert.
   a. Explain how Kamika's demand for clothing and concert tickets can be affected by an increase in air travel prices.
   b. By using this example, explain why both income and substitution effects might be expected to reduce Kamika's number of trips home.

4. Sketch the following budget constraints:

	P_X	P_Y	INCOME
a.	$20	$50	$1,000
b.	40	50	1,000
c.	20	100	1,000
d.	20	50	2,000
e.	0.25	0.25	7.00
f.	0.25	0.50	7.00
g.	0.50	0.25	7.00

5. On January 1, Professor Smith made a resolution to lose some weight and save some money. He decided that he would strictly budget $100 for lunches each month. For lunch, he has only two choices: the faculty club, where the price of a lunch is $5, and Alice's Restaurant, where the price of a lunch is $10. Every day that he does not eat lunch, he runs 5 miles.
   a. Assuming that Professor Smith spends the $100 each month at either Alice's or the club, sketch his budget constraint. Show actual numbers on the axes.
   b. Last month Professor Smith chose to eat at the club 10 times and at Alice's 5 times. Does this choice fit within his budget constraint? Explain your answer.
   c. Last month Alice ran a half-price lunch special all month. All lunches were reduced to $5. Show the effect on Professor Smith's budget constraint.

6. During 2007, Congress debated the advisability of retaining several temporary tax cut proposals that had been put forward by President Bush. By reducing tax rates across the board, take-home pay for all taxpaying workers would increase. The purpose, in part, was to encourage work and increase the supply of labor. Households would respond the way the president hoped, but only if income effects were stronger than substitution effects. Do you agree or disagree? Explain your answer.

7. Assume that Mei has $100 per month to divide between dinners at a Chinese restaurant and evenings at Zanzibar, a local pub. Assume that going to Zanzibar costs $20 and eating at the Chinese restaurant costs $10. Suppose Mei spends two evenings at Zanzibar and eats six times at the Chinese restaurant.
   a. Draw Mei's budget constraint and show that she can afford six dinners and two evenings at Zanzibar.
   b. Assume that Mei comes into some money and can now spend $200 per month. Draw her new budget constraint.
   c. As a result of the increase in income, Mei decides to spend eight evenings at Zanzibar and eat at the Chinese restaurant four times. What kind of a good is Chinese food? What kind of a good is a night at Zanzibar?
   d. What part of the increase in Zanzibar trips is due to the income effect, and what part is due to the substitution effect? Explain your answer.

8. Decide whether you agree or disagree with each of the following statements and explain your reason:
   a. If the income effect of a wage change dominates the substitution effect for a given household and the household works longer hours following a wage change, wages must have risen.
   b. In product markets, when a price falls, the substitution effect leads to more consumption; but for normal goods, the income effect leads to less consumption.

9. Suppose the price of *X* is $5 and the price of *Y* is $10 and a hypothetical household has $500 to spend per month on goods *X* and *Y*.
   a. Sketch the household budget constraint.
   b. Assume that the household splits its income equally between *X* and *Y*. Show where the household ends up on the budget constraint.

c. Suppose the household income doubles to $1,000. Sketch the new budget constraint facing the household.
d. Suppose after the change the household spends $200 on *Y* and $800 on *X*. Does this imply that *X* is a normal or an inferior good? What about *Y*?

10. For this problem, assume that Joe has $80 to spend on books and movies each month and that both goods must be purchased whole (no fractional units). Movies cost $8 each, and books cost $20 each. Joe's preferences for movies and books are summarized by the following information:

MOVIES				BOOKS			
NO. PER MONTH	*TU*	*MU*	*MU*/$	NO. PER MONTH	*TU*	*MU*	*MU*/$
1	50	—	—	1	22	—	—
2	80	—	—	2	42	—	—
3	100	—	—	3	52	—	—
4	110	—	—	4	57	—	—
5	116	—	—	5	60	—	—
6	121	—	—	6	62	—	—
7	123	—	—	7	63	—	—

a. Fill in the figures for marginal utility and marginal utility per dollar for both movies and books.
b. Are these preferences consistent with the law of diminishing marginal utility? Explain briefly.
c. Given the budget of $80, what quantity of books and what quantity of movies will maximize Joe's level of satisfaction? Explain briefly.
d. Draw the budget constraint (with books on the horizontal axis) and identify the optimal combination of books and movies as point *A*.
e. Now suppose the price of books falls to $10. Which of the columns in the table must be recalculated? Do the required recalculations.
f. After the price change, how many movies and how many books will Joe purchase?
g. Draw the new budget constraint and identify the new optimal combination of books and movies as point *B*.
h. If you calculated correctly, you found that a decrease in the price of books caused Joe to buy more movies as well as more books. How can this be?

11. **[Related to the *Economics in Practice* on *p. 123*]** John's New York–based firm has sent him to work in its Paris office. Recognizing that the cost of living differs between Paris and New York, the company wants to adjust John's salary so that John is as well off (or happy) in Paris as he was in New York. John suggests that he submit a list of the things he bought in New York in a typical month. The firm can use the list to determine John's salary by figuring out how much the same items cost in Paris. Is this a good idea? Explain your answer.

12. **[Related to the *Economics in Practice* on *p. 126*]** Using graphs, show what you would expect to see happen to the labor supply curve facing Google as it increases the number of services it provides to potential workers.

APPENDIX

INDIFFERENCE CURVES

Early in this chapter, we saw how a consumer choosing between two goods is constrained by the prices of those goods and by his or her income. This Appendix returns to that example and analyzes the process of choice more formally. (Before we proceed, carefully review the text under the heading "The Budget Constraint More Formally.")

ASSUMPTIONS

We base the following analysis on four assumptions:

1. We assume that this analysis is restricted to goods that yield positive marginal utility, or, more simply, that "more is better." One way to justify this assumption is to say that when more of something makes you worse off, you can simply throw it away at no cost. This is the assumption of free disposal.
2. The **marginal rate of substitution** is defined as MU_X/MU_Y, or the ratio at which a household is willing to substitute *X* for *Y*. When MU_X/MU_Y is equal to 4, for example, I would be willing to trade 4 units of *Y* for 1 additional unit of *X*.

   We assume a diminishing marginal rate of substitution. That is, as more of *X* and less of *Y* are consumed, MU_X/MU_Y declines. As you consume more of *X* and less of *Y*, *X* becomes less valuable in terms of units of *Y*, or *Y* becomes more valuable in terms of *X*. This is almost but not precisely equivalent to assuming diminishing marginal utility.
3. We assume that consumers have the ability to choose among the combinations of goods and services available. Confronted with the choice between two alternative combinations of goods and services, *A* and *B*, a consumer responds in one of three ways: (1) She prefers *A* over *B*, (2) she prefers *B* over *A*, or (3) she is indifferent between *A* and *B*—that is, she likes *A* and *B* equally.
4. We assume that consumer choices are consistent with a simple assumption of rationality. If a consumer shows that he prefers *A* to *B* and subsequently shows that he prefers *B* to a third alternative, *C*, he should prefer *A* to *C* when confronted with a choice between the two.

DERIVING INDIFFERENCE CURVES

If we accept these four assumptions, we can construct a "map" of a consumer's preferences. These preference maps are made up of indifference curves. An **indifference curve** is a set of points, each point representing a combination of goods *X* and *Y*, all of which yield the same total utility.

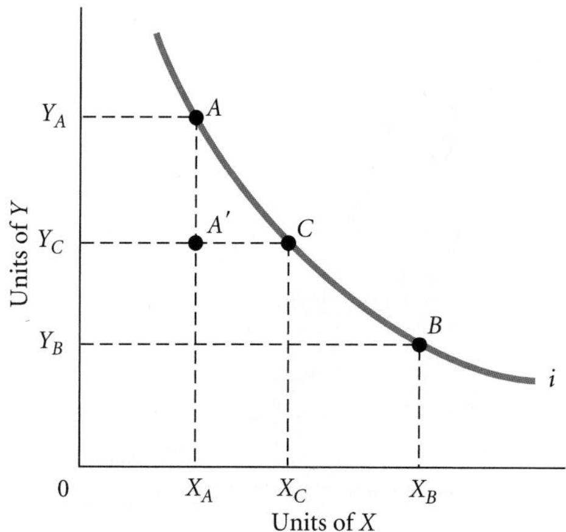

▲ **FIGURE 6A.1 An Indifference Curve**

An indifference curve is a set of points, each representing a combination of some amount of good *X* and some amount of good *Y*, that all yield the same amount of total utility. The consumer depicted here is indifferent between bundles *A* and *B*, *B* and *C*, and *A* and *C*.

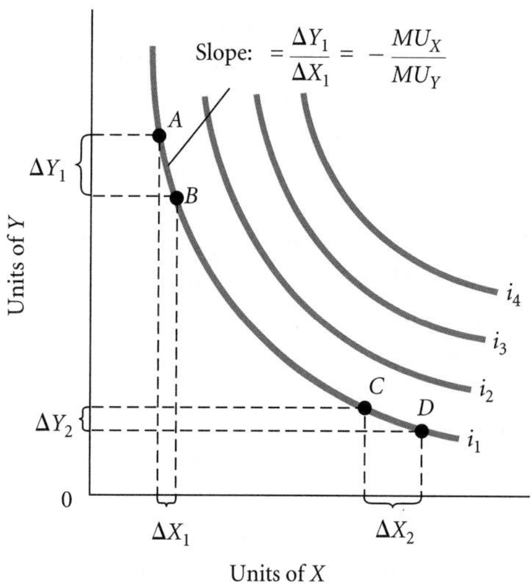

▲ **FIGURE 6A.2 A Preference Map: A Family of Indifference Curves**

Each consumer has a unique family of indifference curves called a preference map. Higher indifference curves represent higher levels of total utility.

Figure 6A.1 shows how we might go about deriving an indifference curve for a hypothetical consumer. Each point in the diagram represents some amount of *X* and some amount of *Y*. Point *A* in the diagram, for example, represents X_A units of *X* and Y_A units of *Y*. Now suppose we take some amount of *Y* away from our hypothetical consumer, moving the individual to *A′*. At *A′*, the consumer has the same amount of *X*—that is, X_A units—but less *Y* and now has only Y_C units of *Y*. Because "more is better," our consumer is unequivocally worse off at *A′* than at *A*.

To compensate for the loss of *Y*, we begin giving our consumer some more *X*. If we give the individual just a little, our consumer will still be worse off than at *A*. If we give this individual a great deal of *X*, our consumer will be better off. There must be some quantity of *X* that will just compensate for the loss of *Y*. By giving the consumer that amount, we will have put together a bundle, Y_C and X_C, that yields the same total utility as bundle *A*. This is bundle *C* in Figure 6A.1. If confronted with a choice between bundles *A* and *C*, our consumer will say, "Either one; I do not care." In other words, the consumer is *indifferent* between *A* and *C*. When confronted with a choice between bundles *C* and *B* (which represent X_B and Y_B units of *X* and *Y*), this person is also indifferent. The points along the curve labeled *i* in Figure 6A.1 represent all the combinations of *X* and *Y* that yield the same total utility to our consumer. That curve is thus an indifference curve.

Each consumer has a whole set of indifference curves. Return for a moment to Figure 6A.1. Starting at point *A* again, imagine that we give the consumer a tiny bit more *X and* a tiny bit more *Y*. Because more is better, we know that the new bundle will yield a higher level of total utility and the consumer will be better off. Now just as we constructed the first indifference curve, we can construct a second one. What we get is an indifference curve that is *higher* and to the *right* of the first curve. Because utility along an indifference curve is constant at all points, every point along the new curve represents a higher level of total utility than every point along the first.

Figure 6A.2 shows a set of four indifference curves. The curve labeled i_4 represents the combinations of *X* and *Y* that yield the highest level of total utility among the four. Many other indifference curves exist between those shown on the diagram; in fact, their number is infinite. Notice that as you move up and to the right, utility increases.

The shapes of the indifference curves depend on the preferences of the consumer, and the whole set of indifference curves is called a **preference map**. Each consumer has a unique preference map.

PROPERTIES OF INDIFFERENCE CURVES

The indifference curves shown in Figure 6A.2 are drawn bowing in toward the origin, or zero point, on the axes. In other words, the absolute value of the slope of the indifference curves decreases, or the curves get flatter, as we move to the right. Thus, we say that indifference curves are convex toward the origin. This shape follows directly from the assumption of diminishing marginal rate of substitution and makes sense if you remember the law of diminishing marginal utility.

To understand the convex shape, compare the segment of curve i_1 between *A* and *B* with the segment of the same curve between *C* and *D*. Moving from *A* to *B*, the consumer is willing to give up a substantial amount of *Y* to get a small amount of *X*. (Remember that total utility is constant along an indifference curve; the consumer is therefore indifferent between *A* and *B*.) Moving from *C* and *D*, however, the consumer is willing to give up only a small amount of *Y* to get more *X*.

This changing trade-off makes complete sense when you remember the law of diminishing marginal utility. Notice that between *A* and *B*, a great deal of *Y* is consumed and the marginal utility derived from a unit of *Y* is likely to be small. At the same time, though, only a little of *X* is being consumed; so the marginal utility derived from consuming a unit of *X* is likely to be high.

Suppose, for example, that *X* is pizza and *Y* is soda. Near *A* and *B*, a thirsty, hungry football player who has 10 sodas in front of him but only one slice of pizza will trade several sodas for another slice. Down around C and D, however, he has 20 slices of pizza and a single soda. Now he will trade several slices of pizza to get an additional soda.

We can show how the trade-off changes more formally by deriving an expression for the slope of an indifference curve. Let us look at the arc (that is, the section of the curve) between A and B. We know that in moving from A to B, total utility remains constant. That means that the utility lost as a result of consuming less Y must be matched by the utility gained from consuming more X. We can approximate the loss of utility by multiplying the marginal utility of Y (MU_Y) by the number of units by which consumption of Y is curtailed (ΔY). Similarly, we can approximate the utility gained from consuming more X by multiplying the marginal utility of X (MU_X) by the number of additional units of X consumed (ΔX). Remember: Because the consumer is indifferent between points A and B, total utility is the same at both points. Thus, these two must be equal in magnitude—that is, the gain in utility from consuming more X must equal the loss in utility from consuming less Y. Because ΔY is a negative number (because consumption of Y decreases from A to B), it follows that

$$MU_X \cdot \Delta X = -(MU_Y \cdot \Delta Y)$$

When we divide both sides by MU_Y and by ΔX, we obtain

$$\frac{\Delta Y}{\Delta X} = -\text{¢}\frac{MU_X}{MU_Y}\text{†}$$

Recall that the slope of any line is calculated by dividing the change in Y—that is, ΔY—by the change in X—that is, ΔX. Thus, the slope of an indifference curve is the ratio of the marginal utility of X to the marginal utility of Y, and it is negative.

Now let us return to our pizza (X) and soda (Y) example. As we move down from the A:B area to the C:D area, our football player is consuming less soda and more pizza. The marginal utility of pizza (MU_X) is falling, and the marginal utility of soda (MU_Y) is rising. That means that MU_X/MU_Y (the marginal rate of substitution) is falling and the absolute value of the slope of the indifference curve is declining. Indeed, it does get flatter.

CONSUMER CHOICE

As you recall, demand depends on income, the prices of goods and services, and preferences or tastes. We are now ready to see how preferences as embodied in indifference curves interact with budget constraints to determine how the final quantities of X and Y will be chosen.

In Figure 6A.3 a set of indifference curves is superimposed on a consumers budget constraint. Recall that the budget constraint separates those combinations of X and Y that are available from those that are not. The constraint simply shows those combinations that can be purchased with an income of I at prices P_X and P_Y. The budget constraint crosses the X-axis at I/P_X, or the number of units of X that can be purchased with I if nothing is spent on Y. Similarly, the budget constraint crosses the Y-axis at I/P_Y, or the number of units of Y that can be purchased with an income of I if nothing is spent on X. The shaded area is the consumers opportunity set. The slope of a budget constraint is $-P_X/P_Y$.

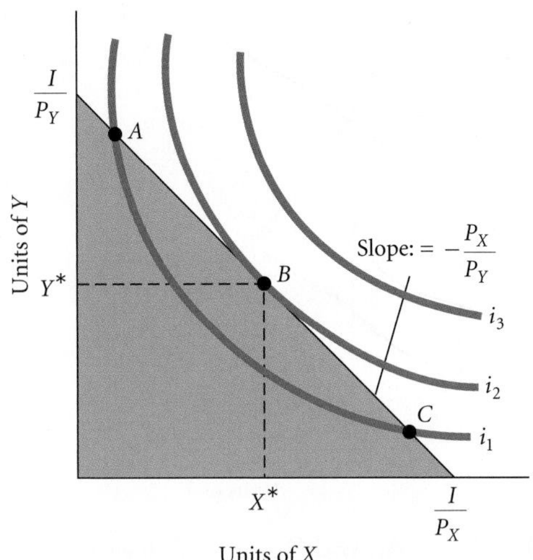

▲ **FIGURE 6A.3 Consumer Utility-Maximizing Equilibrium**

Consumers will choose the combination of X and Y that maximizes total utility. Graphically, the consumer will move along the budget constraint until the highest possible indifference curve is reached. At that point, the budget constraint and the indifference curve are tangent. This point of tangency occurs at X^* and Y^* (point B).

Consumers will choose from among available combinations of X and Y the one that maximizes utility. In graphic terms, a consumer will move along the budget constraint until he or she is on the highest possible indifference curve. Utility rises by moving from points such as A or C (which lie on i_1) toward B (which lies on i_2). Any movement away from point B moves the consumer to a lower indifference curve—a lower level of utility. In this case, utility is maximized when our consumer buys X^* units of X and Y^* units of Y. At point B, the budget constraint is just tangent to—that is, just touches—indifference curve i_2. As long as indifference curves are convex to the origin, utility maximization will take place at that point at which the indifference curve is just tangent to the budget constraint.

The tangency condition has important implications. Where two curves are tangent, they have the same slope, which implies that the slope of the indifference curve is equal to the slope of the budget constraint at the point of tangency:

$$\underbrace{-\frac{MU_X}{MU_Y}}_{} = \underbrace{-\frac{P_X}{P_Y}}_{}$$

slope of indifference curve = slope of budget constraint

By multiplying both sides of this equation by MU_Y and dividing both sides by P_X, we can rewrite this utility-maximizing rule as

$$\frac{MU_X}{P_X} = \frac{MU_Y}{P_Y}$$

This is the same rule derived in our earlier discussion without using indifference curves. We can describe this rule intuitively by saying that consumers maximize their total utility by equating the marginal utility per dollar spent on X with the marginal utility per dollar spent on Y. If this rule did not hold, utility could be increased by shifting money from one good to the other.

DERIVING A DEMAND CURVE FROM INDIFFERENCE CURVES AND BUDGET CONSTRAINTS

We now turn to the task of deriving a simple demand curve from indifference curves and budget constraints. A demand curve shows the quantity of a single good, X in this case, that a consumer will demand at various prices. To derive the demand curve, we need to confront our consumer with several alternative prices for X while keeping other prices, income, and preferences constant.

Figure 6A.4 shows the derivation. We begin with price P_X^1. At that price, the utility-maximizing point is A, where the consumer demands X_1 units of X. Therefore, in the right-hand diagram, we plot P_X^1 against X_1. This is the first point on our demand curve.

Now we lower the price of X to P_X^2. Lowering the price expands the opportunity set, and the budget constraint swivels to the right. Because the price of X has fallen, when our consumer spends all of the income on X, the individual can buy more of it. Our consumer is also better off because of being able to move to a higher indifference curve. The new utility-maximizing point is B, where the consumer demands X_2 units of X. Because the consumer demands X_2 units of X at a price of P_X^2, we plot P_X^2 against X_2 in the right-hand diagram. A second price cut to P_X^3 moves our consumer to point C, with a demand of X_3 units of X, and so on. Thus, we see how the demand curve can be derived from a consumers preference map and budget constraint.

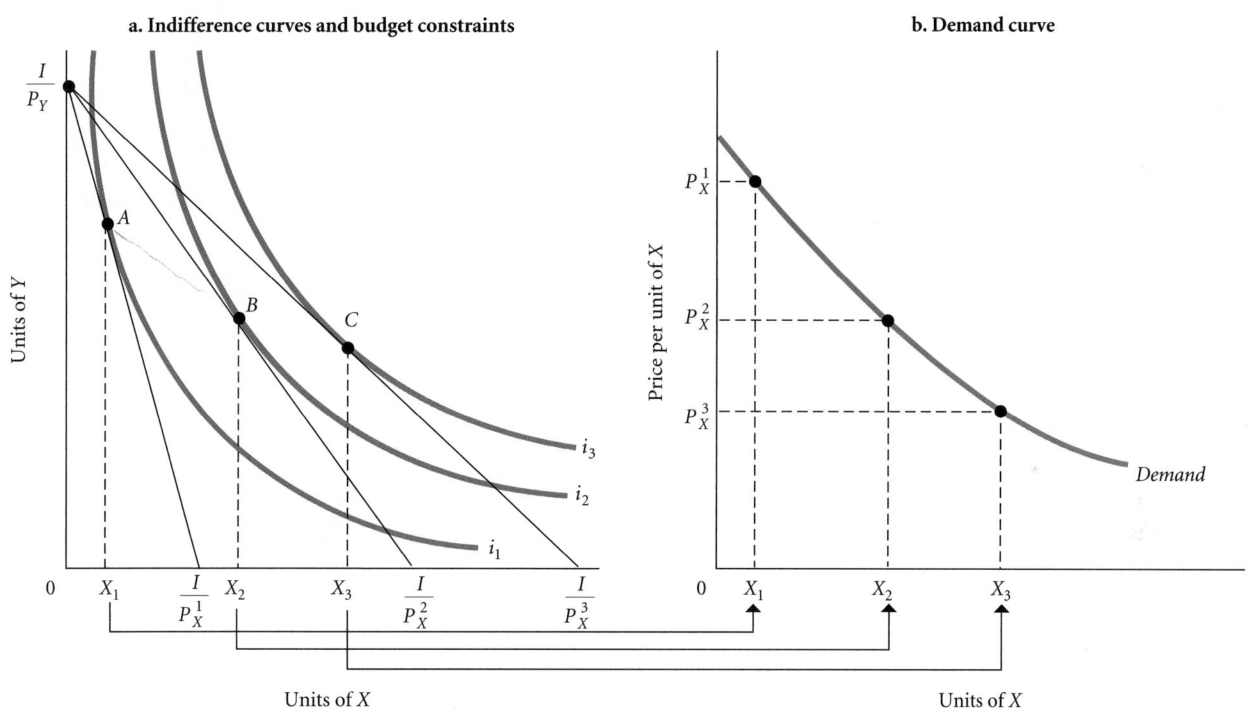

▲ FIGURE 6A.4 Deriving a Demand Curve from Indifference Curves and Budget Constraint

Indifference curves are labeled i_1, i_2, and i_3; budget constraints are shown by the three diagonal lines from I/P_Y to I/P_X^1, I/P_X^2, and I/P_X^3. Lowering the price of X from P_X^1 to P_X^2 and then to P_X^3 swivels the budget constraint to the right. At each price, there is a different utility-maximizing combination of X and Y. Utility is maximized at point A on i_1, point B on i_2, and point C on i_3. Plotting the three prices against the quantities of X chosen results in a standard downward-sloping demand curve.

SUMMARY

1. An *indifference curve* is a set of points, each point representing a combination of goods X and Y, all of which yield the same total utility. A particular consumer's set of indifference curves is called a *preference map*.
2. The slope of an indifference curve is the ratio of the marginal utility of X to the marginal utility of Y, and it is negative.
3. As long as indifference curves are convex to the origin, utility maximization will take place at that point at which the indifference curve is just tangent to—that is, just touches—the budget constraint. The utility-maximizing rule can also be written as $MU_X/P_X = MU_Y/P_Y$.

REVIEW TERMS AND CONCEPTS

Indifference curve A set of points, each point representing a combination of goods *X* and *Y*, all of which yield the same total utility. *p. 130*

Marginal rate of substitution MU_X/MU_Y; the ratio at which a household is willing to substitute good *Y* for good *X*. *p. 130*

Preference map A consumer's set of indifference curves. *p. 131*

PROBLEMS

1. Which of the four assumptions that were made at the beginning of the Appendix are violated by the indifference curves in Figure 1? Explain.
2. Assume that a household receives a weekly income of $100. If Figure 2 represents the choices of that household as the price of *X* changes, plot three points on the household demand curve.
3. If Ann's marginal rate of substitution of *X* for *Y* is 5—that is, $MU_X/MU_Y = 5$—the price of *X* is $9, and the price of *Y* is $2, she is spending too much of her income on *Y*. Do you agree or disagree? Explain your answer using a graph.

*4. Assume that Jim is a rational consumer who consumes only two goods, apples (*A*) and nuts (*N*). Assume that his marginal rate of substitution of apples for nuts is given by the following formula:

$$MRS = MU_N/MU_A = A/N$$

That is, Jim's *MRS* is equal to the ratio of the number of apples consumed to the number of nuts consumed.

a. Assume that Jim's income is $100, the price of nuts is $5, and the price of apples is $10. What quantities of apples and nuts will he consume?

b. Find two additional points on his demand curve for nuts ($P_N = \$10$ and $P_N = \$2$).

c. Sketch one of the equilibrium points on an indifference curve graph.

*Note: Problems marked with an asterisk are more challenging.

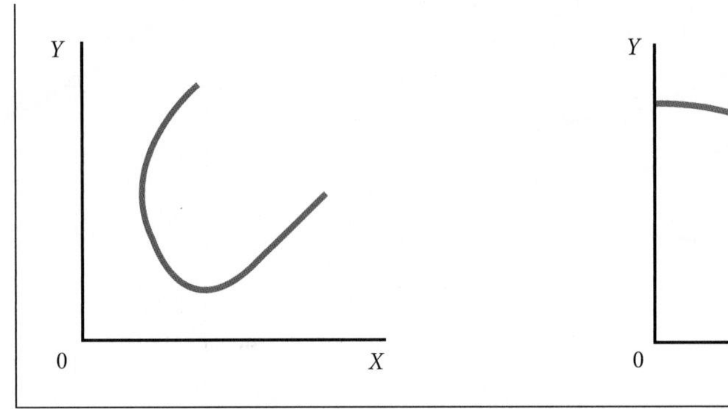

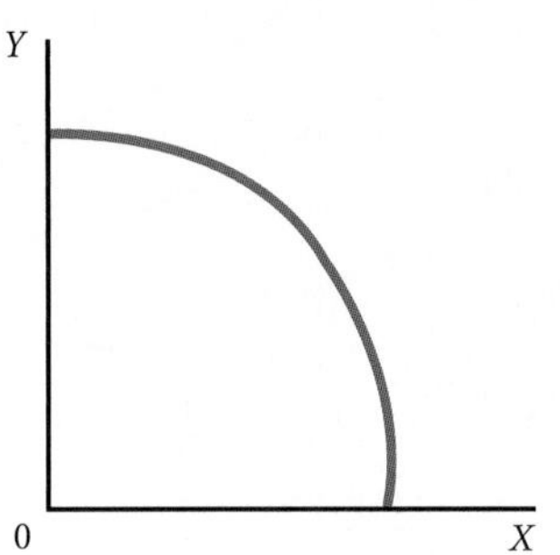

▲ FIGURE 1

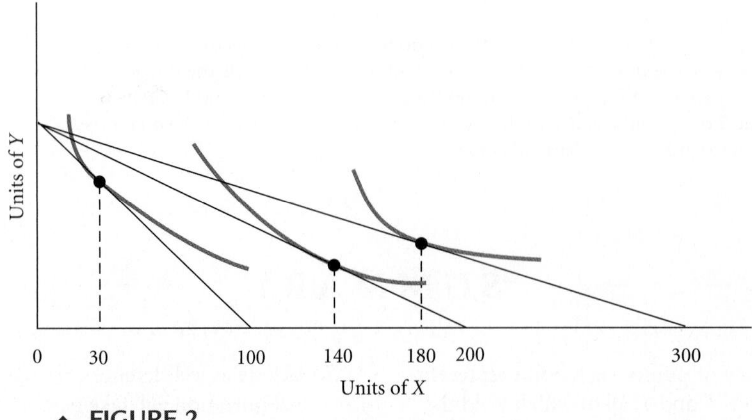

▲ FIGURE 2

The Production Process: The Behavior of Profit-Maximizing Firms

7

CHAPTER OUTLINE

In Chapter 6, we took a brief look at the household decisions that lie behind supply and demand curves. We spent some time discussing household choices: how much to work and how to choose among the wide range of goods and services available within the constraints of prices and income. We also identified some of the influences on household demand in output markets, as well as some of the influences on household supply behavior in input markets.

We now turn to the other side of the system and examine the behavior of firms. Firms purchase inputs to produce and sell outputs that range from computers to string quartet performances. In other words, they *demand* factors of production in input markets and *supply* goods and services in output markets. In this chapter, we look inside the firm at the production process that transforms inputs into outputs. Although Chapters 7 through 12 describe the behavior of perfectly competitive firms, much of what we say in these chapters also applies to firms that are not perfectly competitive. For example, when we turn to monopoly in Chapter 13, we will be describing firms that are similar to competitive firms in many ways. All firms, whether competitive or not, demand inputs, engage in production, and produce outputs. All firms have an incentive to maximize profits and thus to minimize costs.

Central to our analysis is **production**, the process by which inputs are combined, transformed, and turned into outputs. Firms vary in size and internal organization, but they all take inputs and transform them into goods and services for which there is some demand. For example, an independent accountant combines labor, paper, telephone and e-mail service, time, learning, and a Web site to provide help to confused taxpayers. An automobile plant uses steel, labor, plastic, electricity, machines, and countless other inputs to produce cars. If we want to understand a firm's costs, we first need to understand how it efficiently combines inputs to produce goods and services. Before we begin our discussion of the production process, however, we need to clarify some of the assumptions on which our analysis is based.

production The process by which inputs are combined, transformed, and turned into outputs.

Production Is Not Limited to Firms Although our discussions in the next several chapters focus on profit-making business firms, it is important to understand that production and productive activity are not confined to private business firms. Households also engage in transforming factors of production (labor, capital, energy, natural resources, and so on) into useful things. When you work in your garden, you are combining land, labor, fertilizer, seeds, and tools (capital) into the vegetables you eat and the flowers you enjoy. The government also combines land, labor, and capital to produce public services for which demand exists: national defense, homeland security, police and fire protection, and education, to name a few.

firm An organization that comes into being when a person or a group of people decides to produce a good or service to meet a perceived demand.

Private business firms are set apart from other producers, such as households and government, by their purpose. A **firm** exists when a person or a group of people decides to produce a good or service to meet a perceived demand. Firms engage in production—that is, they transform inputs into outputs—because they can sell their products for more than it costs to produce them.

The Behavior of Profit-Maximizing Firms

All firms must make several basic decisions to achieve what we assume to be their primary objective—maximum profits.

As Figure 7.1 states, the three decisions that all firms must make include:

1. How much output to supply (quantity of product)
2. How to produce that output (which production technique/technology to use)
3. How much of each input to demand

FIGURE 7.1 The Three Decisions That All Firms Must Make

1. How much output to supply	2. Which production technology to use	3. How much of each input to demand

The first and last choices are linked by the second choice. Once a firm has decided how much to produce, the choice of a production method determines the firm's input requirements. If a sweater company decides to produce 5,000 sweaters this month, it knows how many production workers it will need, how much electricity it will use, how much raw yarn to purchase, and how many sewing machines to run.

Similarly, given a technique of production, any set of input quantities determines the amount of output that can be produced. Certainly, the number of machines and workers employed in a sweater mill determines how many sweaters can be produced.

Changing the *technology* of production will change the relationship between input and output quantities. An apple orchard that uses expensive equipment to raise pickers up into the trees will harvest more fruit with fewer workers in a given period of time than an orchard in which pickers use simple ladders. It is also possible that two different technologies can produce the same quantity of output. For example, a fully computerized textile mill with only a few workers running the machines may produce the same number of sweaters as a mill with no sophisticated machines but many workers. A profit-maximizing firm chooses the technology that minimizes its costs for a given level of output.

In this chapter, all firms in a given industry produce the same exact product and we are concerned solely with production. In later chapters, these three basic decisions will be expanded to include the setting of prices and the determination of product quality.

Profits and Economic Costs

profit (economic profit) The difference between total revenue and total cost.

total revenue The amount received from the sale of the product ($q \times P$).

total cost (total economic cost) The total of (1) out-of-pocket costs and (2) opportunity cost of all factors of production.

We assume that firms are in business to make a profit and that a firm's behavior is guided by the goal of maximizing profits. What is profit? **Profit** is the difference between total revenue and total cost:

$$\text{profit} = \text{total revenue} - \text{total cost}$$

Total revenue is the amount received from the sale of the product; it is equal to the number of units sold (q) times the price received per unit (P). **Total cost** is less straightforward to define. We define total cost here to include (1) out-of-pocket costs and (2) opportunity cost of all inputs or factors of production. *Out-of-pocket costs* are sometimes referred to as *explicit costs* or *accounting costs*. These refer to costs as an accountant would calculate them. *Economic costs* include the opportunity cost of every input. These opportunity costs are often referred to as *implicit costs*. The term *profit* will from here on refer to *economic profit*. So whenever we say profit = total revenue − total cost, what we really mean is

economic profit = total revenue − total economic cost

The reason we take opportunity costs into account is that we are interested in analyzing the behavior of firms from the standpoint of a potential investor or a potential new competitor. If I am thinking about buying a firm or shares in a firm or entering an industry as a new firm, I need to consider the *full* costs of production. For example, if a family business employs three family members but pays them no wage, there is still a cost: the opportunity cost of their labor. In evaluating the business from the outside, these costs must be added if we want to figure out whether the business is successful.

The most important opportunity cost that is included in economic cost is the opportunity cost of capital. The way we treat the opportunity cost of capital is to add a *normal rate of return* to capital as part of economic cost.

Normal Rate of Return When someone decides to start a firm, that person must commit resources. To operate a manufacturing firm, you need a plant and some equipment. To start a restaurant, you need to buy grills, ovens, tables, chairs, and so on. In other words, you must invest in capital. To start an e-business, you need a host site, some computer equipment, some software, and a Web-site design. Such investment requires resources that stay tied up in the firm as long as it operates. Even firms that have been around a long time must continue to invest. Plant and equipment wear out and must be replaced. Firms that decide to expand must put new capital in place. This is as true of proprietorships, where the resources come directly from the proprietor, as it is of corporations, where the resources needed to make investments come from shareholders.

Whenever resources are used to invest in a business, there is an opportunity cost. Instead of opening a candy store, you could put your funds into an alternative use such as a certificate of deposit or a government bond, both of which earn interest. Instead of using its retained earnings to build a new plant, a firm could earn interest on those funds or pay them out to shareholders.

Rate of return is the annual flow of net income generated by an investment expressed as a percentage of the total investment. For example, if someone makes a $100,000 investment in capital to start a small restaurant and the restaurant produces a flow of profit of $15,000 every year, we say the project has a "rate of return" of 15 percent. Sometimes we refer to the rate of return as the *yield* of the investment.

A **normal rate of return** is the rate that is just sufficient to keep owners and investors satisfied. If the rate of return were to fall below normal, it would be difficult or impossible for managers to raise resources needed to purchase new capital. Owners of the firm would be receiving a rate of return that was lower than what they could receive elsewhere in the economy, and they would have no incentive to invest in the firm.

normal rate of return A rate of return on capital that is just sufficient to keep owners and investors satisfied. For relatively risk-free firms, it should be nearly the same as the interest rate on risk-free government bonds.

If the firm has fairly steady revenues and the future looks secure, the normal rate of return should be very close to the interest rate on risk-free government bonds. A firm certainly will not keep investors interested in it if it does not pay them a rate of return at least as high as they can get from a risk-free government or corporate bond. If a firm is rock solid and the economy is steady, it may not have to pay a much higher rate. However, if a firm is in a very speculative industry and the future of the economy is shaky, it may have to pay substantially more to keep its shareholders happy. In exchange for taking such a risk, the shareholders will expect a higher return.

A normal rate of return is considered a part of the total cost of a business. Adding a normal rate of return to total cost has an important implication: When a firm earns a normal rate of return, it is earning a zero profit as we have defined profit. If the level of profit is positive, the firm is earning an above-normal rate of return on capital.

A simple example will illustrate the concepts of a normal rate of return being part of total cost. Suppose that Sue and Ann decide to start a small business selling turquoise belts in the Denver airport. To get into the business, they need to invest in a fancy pushcart. The price of the pushcart is $20,000 with all the displays and attachments included. Suppose that Sue and Ann estimate that they will sell 3,000 belts each year for $10 each. Further assume that each belt costs

$5 from the supplier. Finally, the cart must be staffed by one clerk, who works for an annual wage of $14,000. Is this business going to make a profit?

To answer this question, we must determine total revenue and total cost. First, annual revenue is $30,000 (3,000 belts × $10). Total cost includes the cost of the belts—$15,000 (3,000 belts × $5)—plus the labor cost of $14,000, for a total of $29,000. Thus, on the basis of the annual revenue and cost flows, the firm *seems* to be making a profit of $1,000 ($30,000 − $29,000).

What about the $20,000 initial investment in the pushcart? This investment is *not* a direct part of the cost of Sue and Ann's firm. If we assume that the cart maintains its value over time, *the only thing that Sue and Ann are giving up is the interest they might have earned had they not tied up their funds in the pushcart.* That is, the only real cost is the opportunity cost of the investment, which is the forgone interest on the $20,000.

Now suppose that Sue and Ann want a minimum return equal to 10 percent—which is, say, the rate of interest that they could have gotten by purchasing corporate bonds. This implies a normal return of 10 percent, or $2,000 annually (= $20,000 × 0.10) on the $20,000 investment. As we determined earlier, Sue and Ann will earn only $1,000 annually. This is only a 5 percent return on their investment. Thus, they are really earning a below-normal return. Recall that the opportunity cost of capital must be added to total cost in calculating profit. Thus, the total cost in this case is $31,000 ($29,000 + $2,000 in forgone interest on the investment). The level of profit is negative: $30,000 minus $31,000 equals −$1,000. These calculations are summarized in Table 7.1. Because the level of profit is negative, Sue and Ann are actually suffering a *loss* on their belt business.

TABLE 7.1 Calculating Total Revenue, Total Cost, and Profit

Initial Investment:	$20,000
Market Interest Rate Available:	0.10, or 10%
Total revenue (3,000 belts × $10 each)	**$30,000**
Costs	
Belts from supplier	$15,000
Labor cost	14,000
Normal return/opportunity cost of capital ($20,000 × 0.10)	2,000
Total Cost	**$31,000**
Profit = total revenue − total cost	**−$1,000**[a]

[a]There is a loss of $1,000.

When a firm earns a *positive* level of profit, it is earning more than is sufficient to retain the interest of investors. In fact, positive profits are likely to attract new firms into an industry and cause existing firms to expand.

When a firm suffers a *negative* level of profit—that is, when it incurs a loss—it is earning at a rate below that required to keep investors happy. Such a loss may or may not be a loss as an accountant would measure it. Even if a firm is earning a rate of return of 10 percent it is earning a below-normal rate of return, or a loss, if a normal return for its industry is 15 percent. Losses may cause some firms to exit the industry; others will contract in size. Certainly, new investment will not flow into such an industry.

Short-Run Versus Long-Run Decisions

The decisions made by a firm—how much to produce, how to produce it, and what inputs to demand—all take time into account. If a firm decides that it wants to double or triple its output, it may need time to arrange financing, hire architects and contractors, and build a new plant. Planning for a major expansion can take years. In the meantime, the firm must decide how much to produce within the constraint of its existing plant. If a firm decides to get out of a particular business, it may take time to arrange an orderly exit. There may be contract obligations to fulfill, equipment to sell, and so on. Once again, the firm must decide what to do in the meantime.

A firm's immediate response to a change in the economic environment may differ from its response over time. Consider, for example, a small restaurant with 20 tables that becomes very popular. The immediate problem for the owners is getting the most profit within the constraint of the existing restaurant. The owner might consider adding a few tables or speeding up service to squeeze in a few more customers. Some popular restaurants do not take reservations, forcing people to wait at the bar. This practice increases drink revenues and keeps tables full at all times. At the same time, the owner may be thinking of expanding the current facility, moving to a larger facility, or opening a second restaurant. In the future, the owner might buy the store next door and double the capacity. Such decisions might require negotiating a lease, buying new equipment, and hiring more staff. It takes time to make and implement these decisions.

Because the character of immediate response differs from long-run adjustment, it is useful to define two time periods: the short run and the long run. Two assumptions define the **short run**: (1) a fixed scale (or a fixed factor of production) and (2) no entry into or exit from the industry. First, the short run is defined as that period during which existing firms have some *fixed factor of production*—that is, during which time some factor locks them into their current scale of operations. Second, new firms cannot enter and existing firms cannot exit an industry in the short run. Firms may curtail operations, but they are still locked into some costs even though they may be in the process of going out of business.

short run The period of time for which two conditions hold: The firm is operating under a fixed scale (fixed factor) of production, and firms can neither enter nor exit an industry.

Which factor or factors of production are fixed in the short run differs from industry to industry. For a manufacturing firm, the size of the physical plant is often the greatest limitation. A factory is built with a given production rate in mind. Although that rate can be increased, output cannot increase beyond a certain limit in the short run. For a private physician, the limit may be the capacity to see patients; the day has only so many hours. In the long run, the doctor may invite others to join the practice and expand; but for now, in the short run, this sole physician *is* the firm, with a capacity that is the firm's only capacity. For a farmer, the fixed factor may be land. The capacity of a small farm is limited by the number of acres being cultivated.

In the **long run**, there are no fixed factors of production. Firms can plan for any output level they find desirable. They can double or triple output, for example. In addition, new firms can start up operations (enter the industry), and existing firms can go out of business (exit the industry).

long run That period of time for which there are no fixed factors of production: Firms can increase or decrease the scale of operation, and new firms can enter and existing firms can exit the industry.

No hard-and-fast rule specifies how long the short run is. The point is that firms make two basic kinds of decisions: those that govern the day-to-day operations of the firm and those that involve longer-term strategic planning. Sometimes major decisions can be implemented in weeks. Often, however, the process takes years.

The Bases of Decisions: Market Price of Outputs, Available Technology, and Input Prices

As we said earlier, a firm's three fundamental decisions are made with the objective of maximizing profits. Because profits equal total revenues minus total costs, each firm needs to know how much it costs to produce its product and how much its product can be sold for.

To know how much it costs to produce a good or service, a firm needs to know something about the production techniques that are available and about the prices of the inputs required. To estimate how much it will cost to operate a gas station, for instance, a firm needs to know what equipment is needed, how many workers, what kind of a building, and so on. The firm also needs to know the going wage rates for mechanics and unskilled laborers, the cost of gas pumps, interest rates, the rents per square foot of land on high-traffic corners, and the wholesale price of gasoline. Of course, the firm also needs to know how much it can sell gasoline and repair services for.

In the language of economics, a firm needs to know three things:

1. The market price of output
2. The techniques of production that are available
3. The prices of inputs

Output price determines potential revenues. The techniques available tell me how much of each input I need, and input prices tell me how much they will cost. Together the available production techniques and the prices of inputs determine costs.

The rest of this chapter and the next chapter focus on costs of production. We begin at the heart of the firm, with the production process. Faced with a set of input prices, firms must decide on the best, or optimal, method of production (Figure 7.2). The **optimal method of production** is the one that minimizes cost. With cost determined and the market price of output known, a firm will make a final judgment about the quantity of product to produce and the quantity of each input to demand.

optimal method of production The production method that minimizes cost.

▶ **FIGURE 7.2 Determining the Optimal Method of Production**

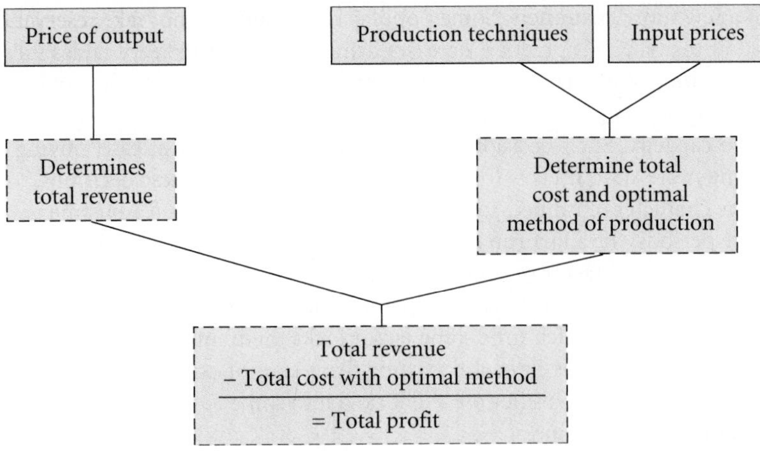

The Production Process

production technology The quantitative relationship between inputs and outputs.

Production is the process through which inputs are combined and transformed into outputs. **Production technology** relates inputs to outputs. Specific quantities of inputs are needed to produce any given service or good. A loaf of bread requires certain amounts of water, flour, and yeast; some kneading and patting; and an oven and gas or electricity. A trip from downtown New York to Newark, New Jersey, can be produced with a taxicab, 45 minutes of a driver's labor, some gasoline, and so on.

labor-intensive technology Technology that relies heavily on human labor instead of capital.

capital-intensive technology Technology that relies heavily on capital instead of human labor.

Most outputs can be produced by a number of different techniques. You can tear down an old building and clear a lot to create a park in several ways, for example. Five hundred men and women could descend on the park with sledgehammers and carry the pieces away by hand; this would be a **labor-intensive technology**. The same park could be produced by two people with a wrecking crane, a steam shovel, a backhoe, and a dump truck; this would be a **capital-intensive technology**. Similarly, different inputs can be combined to transport people from Oakland to San Francisco. The Bay Area Rapid Transit carries thousands of people simultaneously under San Francisco Bay and uses a massive amount of capital relative to labor. Cab rides to San Francisco require more labor relative to capital; a driver is needed for every few passengers.

In choosing the most appropriate technology, firms choose the one that minimizes the cost of production. For a firm in an economy with a plentiful supply of inexpensive labor but not much capital, the optimal method of production will involve labor-intensive techniques. For example, assembly of items such as running shoes is done most efficiently by hand. That is why Nike produces virtually all its shoes in developing countries where labor costs are very low. In contrast, firms in an economy with high wages and high labor costs have an incentive to substitute away from labor and to use more capital-intensive, or labor-saving, techniques. Suburban office parks use more land and have more open space in part because land in the suburbs is more plentiful and less expensive than land in the middle of a big city.

Production Functions: Total Product, Marginal Product, and Average Product

production function *or* **total product function** A numerical or mathematical expression of a relationship between inputs and outputs. It shows units of total product as a function of units of inputs.

The relationship between inputs and outputs—that is, the production technology—expressed numerically or mathematically is called a **production function** (or **total product function**). A production function shows units of total product as a function of units of inputs.

Imagine, for example, a small sandwich shop. All the sandwiches made in the shop are grilled; and the shop owns only one grill, which can accommodate only two workers comfortably. As columns 1 and 2 of the production function in Table 7.2 show, one person working alone can produce only 10 sandwiches per hour in addition to answering the phone, waiting on customers, keeping the tables clean, and so on. The second worker can stay at the grill full-time and not worry about anything except making sandwiches. Because the two workers together can produce 25 sandwiches, the second worker can produce 25 – 10 = 15 sandwiches per hour. A third person trying to use the grill produces crowding; but with careful use of space, more sandwiches can be

TABLE 7.2 Production Function

(1) Labor Units (Employees)	(2) Total Product (Sandwiches per Hour)	(3) Marginal Product of Labor	(4) Average Product of Labor (Total Product ÷ Labor Units)
0	0	–	–
1	10	10	10.0
2	25	15	12.5
3	35	10	11.7
4	40	5	10.0
5	42	2	8.4
6	42	0	7.0

produced. The third worker adds 10 sandwiches per hour. Note that the added output from hiring a third worker is less because of the capital constraint, *not* because the third worker is somehow less efficient or hardworking. We assume that all workers are equally capable.

The fourth and fifth workers can work at the grill only while the first three are putting the pickles, onions, and wrapping on the sandwiches they have made. Then the first three must wait to get back to the grill. Worker four adds five sandwiches per hour to the total, and worker five adds just two. Adding a sixth worker adds no output at all: The current maximum capacity of the shop is 42 sandwiches per hour.

Figure 7.3(a) graphs the total product data from Table 7.2. As you look at Table 7.2 and think about marginal product, you should begin to see how important the nature of the production function is to a firm. We see that the sandwich firm that hires a fourth worker will be expanding its sandwich production by five. Is it worth it? That will in turn depend on how much the worker costs and for how much the shop can sell the sandwich. As we proceed to analyze the firm's decision in the next few chapters, we will explore this further.

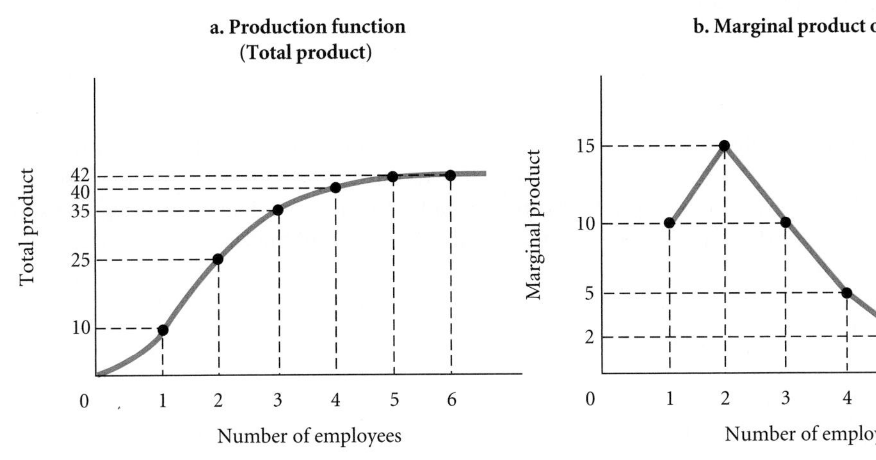

FIGURE 7.3 Production Function for Sandwiches

A *production function* is a numerical representation of the relationship between inputs and outputs. In Figure 7.3(a), total product (sandwiches) is graphed as a function of labor inputs. The *marginal product* of labor is the additional output that one additional unit of labor produces. Figure 7.3(b) shows that the marginal product of the second unit of labor at the sandwich shop is 15 units of output; the marginal product of the fourth unit of labor is 5 units of output.

Marginal Product and the Law of Diminishing Returns

Marginal product is the additional output that can be produced by hiring one more unit of a specific input, holding all other inputs constant. As column 3 of Table 7.2 shows, the marginal product of the first unit of labor in the sandwich shop is 10 sandwiches; the marginal product of the second is 15; the third, 10; and so on. The marginal product of the sixth worker is zero. Figure 7.3(b) graphs the marginal product of labor curve from the data in Table 7.2.

marginal product The additional output that can be produced by adding one more unit of a specific input, *ceteris paribus*.

The **law of diminishing returns** states that *after a certain point, when additional units of a variable input are added to fixed inputs* (in this case, the building and grill), *the marginal product of the variable input* (in this case, labor) *declines*. The British economist David Ricardo first formulated the law of diminishing returns on the basis of his observations of agriculture in nineteenth-century England. Within a given area of land, he noted, successive "doses" of labor and capital yielded smaller and smaller increases in crop output. The law of diminishing returns is true in agriculture because only so much more can be produced by farming the same land more intensely.

law of diminishing returns When additional units of a variable input are added to fixed inputs after a certain point, the marginal product of the variable input declines.

In manufacturing, diminishing returns set in when a firm begins to strain the capacity of its existing plant.

At our sandwich shop, diminishing returns set in when the third worker is added. The marginal product of the second worker is actually higher than the first [Figure 7.3(b)]. The first worker takes care of the phone and the tables, thus freeing the second worker to concentrate exclusively on sandwich making. From that point on, the grill gets crowded.

Diminishing returns characterize many productive activities. Consider, for example, an independent accountant who works primarily for private citizens preparing their tax returns. As more and more clients are added, the accountant must work later and later into the evening. An hour spent working at 1 A.M. after a long day is likely to be less productive than an hour spent working at 10 A.M. Here the fixed factor of production is the accountant, whose mind and body capacity ultimately limits production, much as the size of a plant limits production in a factory.

Diminishing returns, or *diminishing marginal product*, begin to show up when more and more units of a variable input are added to a fixed input, such as the scale of the plant. Recall that we defined the short run as that period in which some fixed factor of production constrains the firm. It then follows that diminishing returns always apply in the short run and that in the short run, every firm will face diminishing returns. This means that every firm finds it progressively more difficult to increase its output as it approaches capacity production.

average product The average amount produced by each unit of a variable factor of production.

Marginal Product Versus Average Product

Average product is the average amount produced by each unit of a variable factor of production. At our sandwich shop with one grill, that variable factor is labor. In Table 7.2, you saw that the first two workers together produce 25 sandwiches per hour. Their average product is therefore 12.5 (25 ÷ 2). The third worker adds only 10 sandwiches per hour to the total. These 10 sandwiches are the *marginal* product of labor. The *average product* of the first three units of labor, however, is 11.7 (the average of 10, 15, and 10). Stated in equation form, the average product of labor is the *total* product divided by total units of labor:

$$\text{average product of labor} = \frac{\text{total product}}{\text{total units of labor}}$$

Average product "follows" marginal product, but it does not change as quickly. If marginal product is above average product, the average rises; if marginal product is below average product, the average falls. Suppose, for example, that you have had six exams and that your average is 86. If you score 75 on the next exam, your average score will fall, but not all the way to 75. In fact, it will fall only to 84.4. If you score a 95 instead, your average will rise to 87.3. As columns 3 and 4 of Table 7.2 show, marginal product at the sandwich shop declines continuously after the third worker is hired. Average product also decreases, but more slowly.

Figure 7.4 shows a typical production function and the marginal and average product curves derived from it. The marginal product curve is a graph of the slope of the total product curve—that is, of the production function. Average product and marginal product start out equal, as they do in Table 7.2. As marginal product climbs, the graph of average product follows it, but more slowly, up to L_1 (point *A*).

Notice that marginal product starts out increasing. (It did so in the sandwich shop as well.) Most production processes are designed to be run well by more than one worker. Take an assembly line, for example. To work efficiently, an assembly line needs a worker at every station; it's a cooperative process. The marginal product of the first workers is low or zero. As workers are added, the process starts to run and marginal product rises.

At point *A* (L_1 units of labor), marginal product begins to fall. Because every plant has a finite capacity, efforts to increase production will always run into the limits of that capacity. At point *B* (L_2 units of labor), marginal product has fallen to equal the average product, which has been increasing. Between point *B* and point *C* (between L_2 and L_3 units of labor), marginal product falls below average product and average product begins to follow it *down*. Average product is at its maximum at point *B*, where it is equal to marginal product. At L_3, more labor yields no more output and marginal product is zero—the assembly line has no more positions, the grill is jammed, and the accountant is too tired to see another client.

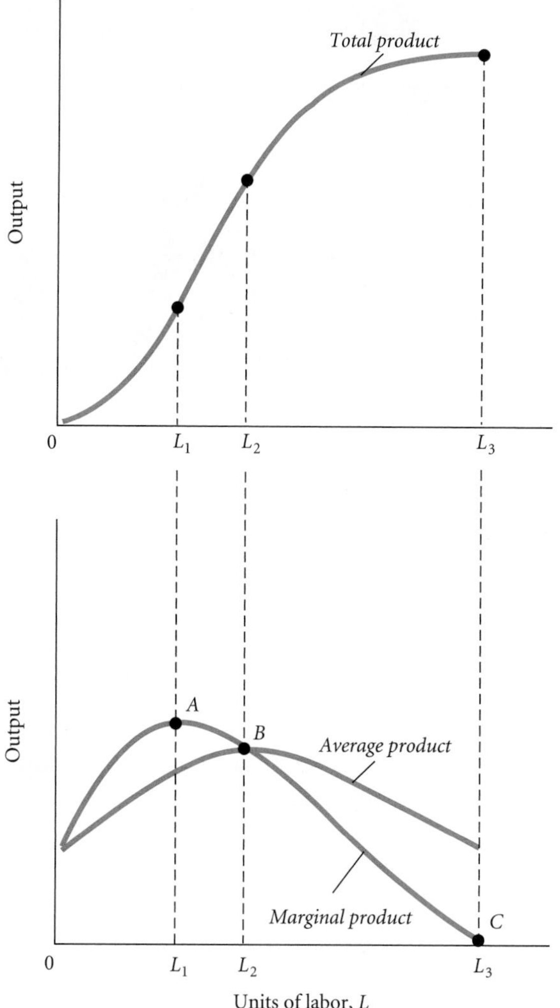

FIGURE 7.4 Total Average and Marginal Product

Marginal and average product curves can be derived from total product curves. Average product is at its maximum at the point of intersection with marginal product.

Production Functions with Two Variable Factors of Production

So far, we have considered production functions with only one variable factor of production. However, inputs work together in production. In general, additional capital increases the productivity of labor. Because capital—buildings, machines, and so on—is of no use without people to operate it, we say that capital and labor are *complementary inputs*.

A simple example will clarify this point. Consider again the sandwich shop. If the demand for sandwiches began to exceed the capacity of the shop to produce them, the shop's owner might decide to expand capacity. This would mean purchasing more capital in the form of a new grill.

A second grill would essentially double the shop's productive capacity. The new higher capacity would mean that the sandwich shop would not run into diminishing returns as quickly. With only one grill, the third and fourth workers are less productive because the single grill gets crowded. With two grills, however, the third and fourth workers could produce 15 sandwiches per hour using the second grill. In essence, the added capital raises the *productivity* of labor—that is, the amount of output produced per worker per hour.

Just as the new grill enhances the productivity of workers in the sandwich shop, new businesses and the capital they put in place raise the productivity of workers in countries such as Malaysia, India, and Kenya.

This simple relationship lies at the heart of worries about productivity at the national and international levels. Building new, modern plants and equipment enhances a nation's productivity. In the last decade, China has accumulated capital (that is, built plant and equipment) at a very high rate. The result is growth in the average quantity of output per worker in China.

ECONOMICS IN PRACTICE

UPS Technology Speeds Global Shipping

In this chapter we have described the way that firms combine labor and capital in producing output of various types. The article below describes that process at UPS. There, the capital consists of a huge fleet of trucks and planes as well as advanced, highly automated package sorting facilities.

As you read about production, you might have wondered where production functions come from. Here we see UPS's search for new production techniques, ones that will allow their labor force and trucks to deliver an increasing number of packages per day. A major focus of research at many firms, including UPS, is looking for better ways to combine labor and capital in the production process.

New UPS Technologies Aim to Speed Worldwide Package Delivery

Information Week

Somewhere behind UPS's 600-aircraft fleet, the hundreds of thousands of packages UPS processes per hour, and the 550,000 customers using its software is the package-delivery company's technology. That technology was formally enhanced this week as UPS unveiled software that uses the Internet to streamline its booming global shipping services.

UPS's technology can track and link together global shipments across oceans and continents, Kurt Kuehn, UPS senior VP of worldwide sales and marketing, said Tuesday. By leveraging technology, UPS is a catalyst for promoting free trade, he said.

Customers had a great deal of input in the development of the new enhancements, noted Jordan Colletta, VP of UPS's customer technology marketing.

A former UPS driver himself, Colletta knows just how important feedback from the field and customers can be as the company enhances its technology and develops new services. The enhancements UPS unveiled this week beef up the company's main technology offerings, which include WorldShip 9.0, Quantum View Manage, and UPS Billing Solutions.

Taken together, the offerings give users applications that range far and wide from traditional shipping functions and emphasize making international shipping easier. With WorldShip, which typically resides on a PC and requires just 128 Mbytes of RAM, users can import shipping information using XML schema. Now available in 14 languages, WorldShip simplifies international shipments, giving users the opportunity to choose from three time-of-day shipping options.

With new features in Quantum View Manage, users can search, sort, filter, e-mail, and download shipment data functions. Customer package and freight shipment status is easily displayed, and no tracking number is required. Customers can view scanned images of various documents, including the bill of lading, corrected bill of lading, and delivery receipts.

The heart of UPS technology is centered at its Worldport technology center in Louisville, Kentucky, where UPS maintains 122 miles of high-speed conveyors and a database capable of processing some 60 million transactions an hour. The company also maintains databases elsewhere....

"Our customers told us WorldShip was great," Colletta said. "But they wanted to ship from their desktops, too. It's been a great success, and it's an idea of how we are 'customer-centric.'"

By W. David Gardner, InformationWeek, March 20, 2007. URL: http://www.informationweek.com/story/showArticle.jhtml?articleID=198100187

Choice of Technology

As our sandwich shop example shows, inputs (factors of production) are complementary. Capital enhances the productivity of labor. Workers in the sandwich shop are more productive when they are not crowded at a single grill. Similarly, labor enhances the productivity of capital. When more workers are hired at a plant that is operating at 50 percent of capacity, previously idle machines suddenly become productive.

However, inputs can also be substituted for one another. If labor becomes expensive, firms can adopt labor-saving technologies; that is, they can substitute capital for labor. Assembly lines can be automated by replacing human beings with machines, and capital can be substituted for land when land is scarce. If capital becomes relatively expensive, firms can substitute labor for capital. In short, most goods and services can be produced in a number of ways, through the use of alternative technologies. One of the key decisions that all firms must make is which technology to use.

Consider the choices available to the diaper manufacturer in Table 7.3. Five different techniques of producing 100 diapers are available. Technology *A* is the most labor-intensive, requiring 10 hours of labor and 2 units of capital to produce 100 diapers. (You can think of units of capital as machine hours.) Technology *E* is the most capital-intensive, requiring only 2 hours of labor but 10 hours of machine time.

TABLE 7.3 Inputs Required to Produce 100 Diapers Using Alternative Technologies

Technology	Units of Capital (*K*)	Units of Labor (*L*)
A	2	10
B	3	6
C	4	4
D	6	3
E	10	2

To choose a production technique, the firm must look to input markets to learn the current market prices of labor and capital. What is the wage rate (P_L), and what is the cost per hour of capital (P_K)? The right choice among inputs depends on how productive an input is and what its price is.

Suppose that labor and capital are both available at a price of $1 per unit. Column 4 of Table 7.4 presents the calculations required to determine which technology is best. The winner is technology *C*. Assuming that the firm's objective is to maximize profits, it will choose the least-cost technology. Using technology *C*, the firm can produce 100 diapers for $8. All four of the other technologies produce 100 diapers at a higher cost.

Now suppose that the wage rate (P_L) were to rise sharply, from $1 to $5. You might guess that this increase would lead the firm to substitute labor-saving capital for workers, and you would be right. As column 5 of Table 7.4 shows, the increase in the wage rate means that technology *E* is now the cost-minimizing choice for the firm. Using 10 units of capital and only 2 units of labor, the firm can produce 100 diapers for $20. All other technologies are now more costly. Notice too from the table that the firm's ability to shift its technique of production softened the impact of the wage increase on its costs. The flexibility of a firm's techniques of production is an important determinant of its costs. Two things determine the cost of production: (1) technologies that are available and (2) input prices. Profit-maximizing firms will choose the technology that minimizes the cost of production given current market input prices.

TABLE 7.4 Cost-Minimizing Choice Among Alternative Technologies (100 Diapers)

			(4)	(5)
			Cost = $(L \times P_L) + (K \times P_K)$	
(1) Technology	(2) Units of Capital (K)	(3) Units of Labor (L)	$P_L = \$1$, $P_K = \$1$	$P_L = \$5$, $P_K = \$1$
A	2	10	$12	52
B	3	6	9	33
C	4	4	8	24
D	6	3	9	21
E	10	2	12	20

ECONOMICS IN PRACTICE

How Fast Should a Truck Driver Go?

The trucking business gives us an opportunity to think about choice among technologies in a concrete way.

Suppose you own a truck and use it to haul merchandise for retailers such as Target and Sears. Your typical run is 200 miles, and you hire one person to drive the truck at a cost of $20 per hour. How fast should you instruct him to drive the truck? Consider the cost per trip.

Notice that even with fixed inputs of one truck and one driver, you still have some choices to make. In the language of this chapter, you can think of the choice as one of slow-drive technology (let's say 50 mph) versus fast-drive technology (say, 60 mph).

If the driver's time were the only input, the problem would be simple: Labor costs are minimized if you tell him to drive fast. At 60 mph, a trip takes the driver only 3.33 hours (200 miles divided by 60 mph) and costs you $66.67 given his $20 wage rate. However, at a speed of 50 mph, it takes four hours and costs you $80. With one variable input, the best technology is the one that uses that input most efficiently. In fact, with only one variable input, you would tell the driver to speed regardless of his wage rate.

But, of course, trucks require not only drivers but also fuel, which is where the question gets more interesting. As it turns out, the fuel mileage that a truck gets diminishes with speed beyond about 50 mph. Let's say in this case that the truck gets 15 miles per gallon at 50 mph but only 12 miles per gallon at 60 mph. Now we have a trade-off. When you tell the driver to go fast, your labor costs are lower but your fuel costs are higher.

So what instructions do you give? It should be clear that your instructions depend on the price of fuel. First suppose that fuel costs $3.50 per gallon. If the trucker drives fast, he will get 12 miles per gallon. Since the trucker has to drive 200 miles per trip, he burns 16.66 gallons (200 divided by 12); and total fuel cost is $58.31. Driving fast, the trucker goes 60 miles per hour. You have to pay him for 3.33 hours (200 divided by 60), which at $20 per hour, is a total of $66.67. The total for the trip is $124.97.

On the other hand, if your trucker drives slowly, he will get 15 miles per gallon, which means you need only 13.33 gallons, which costs $46.67. But now it takes more time. He takes four hours, and you must pay him 4 × $20, or $80 per trip. Total cost is now $126.66. Thus, the cost-minimizing solution is to have him drive fast.

Now try a price of $4.50 per gallon. Doing the same calculations, you should be able to show that when driving slowly, the total cost is $139.99; when driving fast, the cost is $141.63. Thus, the higher fuel price means that you tell the driver to slow down.

Going one step further, you should be able to show that at a fuel price of $4, the trip costs the same whether your trucker drives fast or slowly.

In fact, you should be able to see that at fuel prices in excess of $4 per gallon, you tell your driver to slow down, while at cheaper prices, you tell him to speed up. With more than one input, the choice of technologies often depends on the unit cost of those inputs.

The observation that the optimal "technology" to use in trucking depends on fuel prices is one reason we might expect accident rates to fall with rises in fuel prices (in addition to the fact that everyone drives less when fuel is expensive). Modern technology, in the form of on-board computers, allows a modern trucking firm to monitor driving speed and instruct drivers.

Here is a summary of the cost per trip.

Fuel Price	$3.50	$4.00	$4.50
Drive Fast	$124.97	$133.33	$141.63
Drive Slowly	$126.66	$133.33	$139.99

Looking Ahead: Cost and Supply

So far, we have looked only at a *single* level of output. That is, we have determined how much it will cost to produce 100 diapers using the best available technology when $P_K = \$1$ and $P_L = \$1$ or \$5. The best technique for producing 1,000 diapers or 10,000 diapers may be entirely different. The next chapter explores the relationship between cost and the level of output in some detail. One of our main objectives in that chapter is to determine the amount that a competitive firm will choose to *supply* during a given time period.

SUMMARY

1. Firms vary in size and internal organization, but they all take inputs and transform them into outputs through a process called *production*.
2. In perfect competition, no single firm has any control over prices. This follows from two assumptions: (1) Perfectly competitive industries are composed of many firms, each small relative to the size of the industry; and (2) each firm in a perfectly competitive industry produces *homogeneous products*.
3. The demand curve facing a competitive firm is perfectly elastic. If a single firm raises its price above the market price, it will sell nothing. Because it can sell all it produces at the market price, a firm has no incentive to reduce price.

THE BEHAVIOR OF PROFIT-MAXIMIZING FIRMS *p. 136*

4. Profit-maximizing firms in all industries must make three choices: (1) how much output to supply, (2) how to produce that output, and (3) how much of each input to demand.
5. *Profit* equals total revenue minus total cost. Total cost (economic cost) includes (1) out-of-pocket costs and (2) the opportunity cost of each factor of production, including a normal rate of return on capital.
6. A *normal rate of return* on capital is included in total cost because tying up resources in a firm's capital stock has an opportunity cost. If you start a business or buy a share of stock in a corporation, you do so because you expect to make a normal rate of return. Investors will not invest their money in a business unless they expect to make a normal rate of return.
7. A positive profit level occurs when a firm is earning an above-normal rate of return on capital.
8. Two assumptions define the *short run*: (1) a fixed scale or fixed factor of production and (2) no entry to or exit from the industry. In the *long run*, firms can choose any scale of operations they want and new firms can enter and leave the industry.
9. To make decisions, firms need to know three things: (1) the market price of their output, (2) the production techniques that are available, and (3) the prices of inputs.

THE PRODUCTION PROCESS *p. 140*

10. The relationship between inputs and outputs (the *production technology*) expressed numerically or mathematically is called a *production function* or *total product function*.
11. The *marginal product* of a variable input is the additional output that an added unit of that input will produce if all other inputs are held constant. According to the *law of diminishing returns*, when additional units of a variable input are added to fixed inputs, after a certain point the marginal product of the variable input will decline.
12. *Average product* is the average amount of product produced by each unit of a variable factor of production. If marginal product is above average product, the average product rises; if marginal product is below average product, the average product falls.
13. Capital and labor are at the same time complementary and substitutable inputs. Capital enhances the productivity of labor, but it can also be substituted for labor.

CHOICE OF TECHNOLOGY *p. 145*

14. One of the key decisions that all firms must make is which technology to use. Profit-maximizing firms will choose that combination of inputs that minimizes costs and therefore maximizes profits.

REVIEW TERMS AND CONCEPTS

average product, *p. 142*
capital-intensive technology, *p. 140*
firm, *p. 136*
labor-intensive technology, *p. 140*
law of diminishing returns, *p. 141*
long run, *p. 139*
marginal product, *p. 141*
normal rate of return, *p. 137*
optimal method of production, *p. 139*
production, *p. 135*
production function *or* total product function, *p. 140*
production technology, *p. 140*
profit (economic profit), *p. 136*
short run, *p. 139*
total cost (total economic cost), *p. 136*
total revenue, *p. 136*

Profit = *total revenue* − *total cost*

$$\text{Average product of labor} = \frac{\text{total product}}{\text{total units of labor}}$$

PROBLEMS

Visit www.myeconlab.com to complete the problems marked in orange online. You will receive instant feedback on your answers, tutorial help, and access to additional practice problems.

1. Consider a firm that uses capital and labor as inputs and sells 5,000 units of output per year at the going market price of $10. Also assume that total labor costs to the firm are $45,000 annually. Assume further that the total capital stock of the firm is currently worth $100,000, that the return available to investors with comparable risks is 10 percent annually, and that there is no depreciation. Is this a profitable firm? Explain your answer.

2. Two former Northwestern University students worked in an investment bank at a salary of $60,000 each for 2 years after they graduated. Together they saved $50,000. After 2 years, they decided to quit their jobs and start a business designing Web sites. They used the $50,000 to buy computer equipment, desks, and chairs. For the next 2 years, they took in $40,000 in revenue each year, paid themselves $10,000 annually each, and rented an office for $18,000 per year. Prior to the investment, their $50,000 was in bonds earning interest at a rate of 10 percent. Are they now earning economic profits? Explain your answer.

3. Suppose that in 2008, you became president of a small non-profit theater company. Your playhouse has 120 seats and a small stage. The actors have national reputations, and demand for tickets is enormous relative to the number of seats available; every performance is sold out months in advance. You are elected because you have demonstrated an ability to raise funds successfully. Describe some of the decisions that you must make in the short run. What might you consider to be your "fixed factor"? What alternative decisions might you be able to make in the long run? Explain.

4. The following table gives total output or total product as a function of labor units used.

LABOR	TOTAL OUTPUT
0	0
1	5
2	9
3	12
4	14
5	15

a. Define diminishing returns.
b. Does the table indicate a situation of diminishing returns? Explain your answer.

5. Suppose that widgets can be produced using two different production techniques, *A* and *B*. The following table provides the total input requirements for each of five different total output levels.

	Q = 1		Q = 2		Q = 3		Q = 4		Q = 5	
Tech.	*K*	*L*	*K*	*L*	*K*	*L*	*K*	*L*	*K*	*L*
A	2	5	1	10	5	14	6	18	8	20
B	5	2	8	3	11	4	14	5	16	6

a. Assuming that the price of labor (P_L) is $1 and the price of capital (P_K) is $2, calculate the total cost of production for each of the five levels of output using the optimal (least-cost) technology at each level.
b. How many labor hours (units of labor) would be employed at each level of output? How many machine hours (units of capital)?
c. Graph total cost of production as a function of output. (Put cost on the *Y*-axis and output, *q*, on the *X*-axis.) Again assume that the optimal technology is used.
d. Repeat a. through c. under the assumption that the price of labor (P_L) rises from $1 to $3 while the price of capital (P_K) remains at $2.

6. A female student who lives on the fourth floor of Bates Hall is assigned to a new room on the seventh floor during her junior year. She has 11 heavy boxes of books and "stuff" to move. Discuss the alternative combinations of capital and labor that might be used to make the move. How would your answer differ if the move were to a new dorm 3 miles across campus and to a new college 400 miles away?

7. The following is a production function.

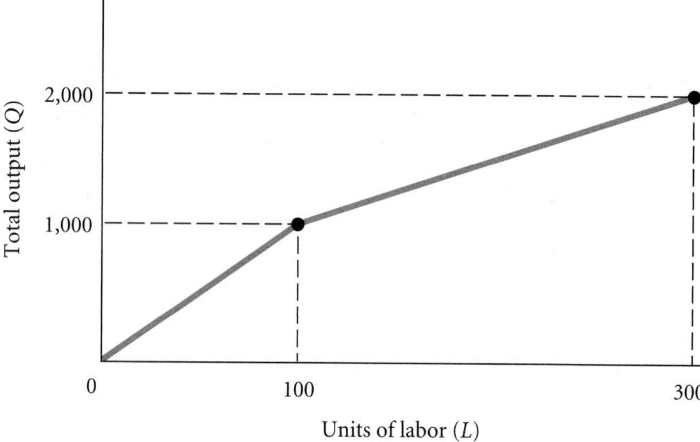

a. Draw a graph of marginal product as a function of output. (*Hint:* Marginal product is the additional number of units of output per unit of labor at each level of output.)
b. Does this graph exhibit diminishing returns? Explain your answer.

8. **[Related to the *Economics in Practice* on p. 144]** Identical sweaters can be made in one of two ways. With a machine that can be rented for $50 per hour and a person to run the machine who can be hired at $25 per hour, five sweaters can be produced in an hour using $10 worth of wool. Alternatively, I can run the machine with a less skilled worker, producing only four sweaters in an hour with the same $10 worth of wool. (The less skilled worker is slower and wastes material.) At what wage rate would I choose the less skilled worker?

9. [Related to the *Economics in Practice* on p. 146] When the price of fuel rises, we typically observe fewer accidents. Can you offer two reasons that this might be true.

10. A firm earning zero economic profits is probably suffering losses from the standpoint of general accounting principles. Do you agree or disagree with this argument? Explain why.

11. During the early phases of industrialization, the number of people engaged in agriculture usually drops sharply, even as agricultural output is growing. Given what you know about production technology and production functions, explain this seeming inconsistency.

12. The number of repairs produced by a computer repair shop depends on the number of workers as follows:

NUMBER OF WORKERS	NUMBER OF REPAIRS (PER WEEK)
0	0
1	8
2	20
3	35
4	45
5	52
6	57
7	60

Assume that all inputs (office space, telephone, and utilities) other than labor are fixed in the short run.

a. Add two additional columns to the table and enter the marginal product and average product for each number of workers.

b. Over what range of labor input are there increasing returns to labor? diminishing returns to labor? negative returns to labor?

c. Over what range of labor input is marginal product greater than average product? What is happening to average product as employment increases over this range?

d. Over what range of labor input is marginal product smaller than average product? What is happening to average product as employment increases over this range?

13. Since the end of World War II, manufacturing firms in the United States and in Europe have been moving farther and farther outside of central cities. At the same time, firms in finance, insurance, and other parts of the service sector have been locating near downtown areas in tall buildings. One major reason seems to be that manufacturing firms find it difficult to substitute capital for land, while service-sector firms that use office space do not.

a. What kinds of buildings represent substitution of capital for land?

b. Why do you think that manufacturing firms might find it difficult to substitute capital for land?

c. Why is it relatively easier for a law firm or an insurance company to substitute capital for land?

d. Why is the demand for land likely to be very high near the center of a city?

*e. One of the reasons for substituting capital for land near the center of a city is that land is more expensive near the center. What is true about the relative supply of land near the center of a city? (*Hint:* What is the formula for the area of a circle?)

14. Ted Baxter runs a small, very stable newspaper company in southern Oregon. The paper has been in business for 25 years. The total value of the firm's capital stock is $1 million, which Ted owns outright. This year the firm earned a total of $250,000 after out-of-pocket expenses. Without taking the opportunity cost of capital into account, this means that Ted is earning a 25 percent return on his capital. Suppose that risk-free bonds are currently paying a rate of 10 percent to those who buy them.

a. What is meant by the "opportunity cost of capital"?

b. Explain why opportunity costs are "real" costs even though they do not necessarily involve out-of-pocket expenses.

c. What is the opportunity cost of Ted's capital?

d. How much excess profit is Ted earning?

15. A firm can use three different production technologies, with capital and labor requirements at each level of output as follows:

	TECHNOLOGY 1		TECHNOLOGY 2		TECHNOLOGY 3	
Daily Output	K	L	K	L	K	L
100	3	7	4	5	5	4
150	3	10	4	7	5	5
200	4	11	5	8	6	6
250	5	13	6	10	7	8

a. Suppose the firm is operating in a high-wage country, where capital cost is $100 per unit per day and labor cost is $80 per worker per day. For each level of output, which technology is cheapest?

b. Now suppose the firm is operating in a low-wage country, where capital cost is $100 per unit per day but labor cost is only $40 per unit per day. For each level of output, which technology is cheapest?

c. Suppose the firm moves from a high-wage to a low-wage country but its level of output remains constant at 200 units per day. How will its total employment change?

*Note: Problems marked with an asterisk are more challenging.

APPENDIX

ISOQUANTS AND ISOCOSTS

This chapter has shown that the cost structure facing a firm depends on two key pieces of information: (1) input (factor) prices and (2) technology. This Appendix presents a more formal analysis of technology and factor prices and their relationship to cost.

NEW LOOK AT TECHNOLOGY: ISOQUANTS

Table 7A.1 is expanded from Table 7.3 to show the various combinations of capital (*K*) and labor (*L*) that can be used to produce three different levels of output (*q*). For example, 100 units of *X* can be produced with 2 units of capital and 10 units of labor, with 3 units of *K* and 6 units of *L*, or with 4 units of *K* and 4 units of *L*, and so on. Similarly, 150 units of *X* can be produced with 3 units of *K* and 10 units of *L*, with 4 units of *K* and 7 units of *L*, and so on.

TABLE 7A.1 Alternative Combinations of Capital (*K*) and Labor (*L*) Required to Produce 50, 100, and 150 Units of Output

	$Q_X = 50$		$Q_X = 100$		$Q_X = 150$	
	K	*L*	*K*	*L*	*K*	*L*
A	1	8	2	10	3	10
B	2	5	3	6	4	7
C	3	3	4	4	5	5
D	5	2	6	3	7	4
E	8	1	10	2	10	3

A graph that shows all the combinations of capital and labor that can be used to produce a given amount of output is called an **isoquant**. Figure 7A.1 graphs three isoquants, one each for $q_X = 50$, $q_X = 100$, and $q_X = 150$ based on the data in Table 7A.1. Notice that all the points on the graph have been connected, indicating that there are an infinite number of combinations of labor and capital that can produce each level of output. For example, 100 units of output can also be produced with 3.50 units of labor and 4.75 units of capital. (Verify that this point is on the isoquant labeled $q_X = 100$.)

Figure 7A.1 shows only three isoquants, but many more are not shown. For example, there are separate isoquants for $q_X = 101$, $q_X = 102$, and so on. If we assume that producing fractions of a unit of output is possible, there must be an isoquant for $q_X = 134.57$, for $q_X = 124.82$, and so on. One could imagine an infinite number of isoquants in Figure 7A.1. The higher the level of output, the farther up and to the right the isoquant will lie.

Figure 7A.2 derives the slope of an isoquant. Because points *F* and *G* are both on the $q_X = 100$ isoquant, the two points represent two different combinations of *K* and *L* that can be used to produce 100 units of output. In moving from point *F* to point *G* along the curve, less capital is employed but more labor is used. An approximation of the amount of output lost by using less capital is ΔK times the marginal product of capital (MP_K). The *marginal product of capital* is the number of units of output produced by a single marginal unit of capital. Thus, $\Delta K \cdot MP_K$ is the total output lost by using less capital.

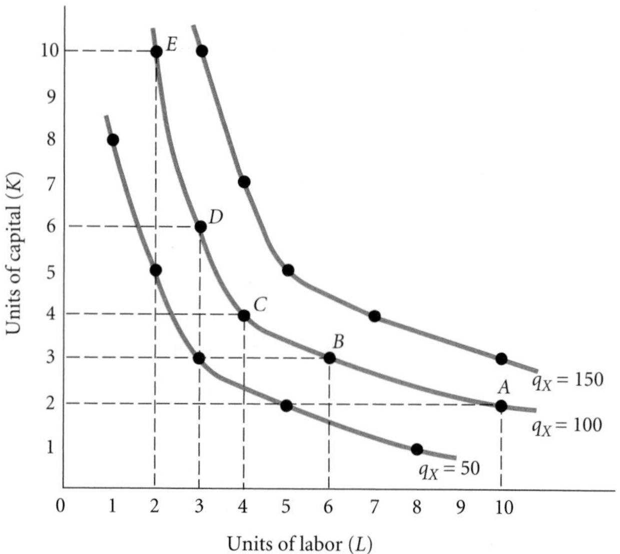

▲ **FIGURE 7A.1 Isoquants Showing All Combinations of Capital and Labor That Can Be Used to Produce 50, 100, and 150 Units of Output**

For output to remain constant (as it must because *F* and *G* are on the same isoquant), the loss of output from using less capital must be matched by the added output produced by using more labor. This amount can be approximated by ΔL times the marginal product of labor (MP_L). Because the two must be equal, it follows that

$$\Delta K \cdot MP_K = -\Delta L \cdot MP_L$$ [1]

If we then divide both sides of this equation by ΔL and then by MP_K, we arrive at the following expression for the slope of the isoquant:

$$\text{slope of isoquant: } \frac{\Delta K}{\Delta L} = -\frac{MP_L}{MP_K}$$

The ratio of MP_L to MP_K is called the **marginal rate of technical substitution**. It is the rate at which a firm can substitute capital for labor and hold output constant.

[1] We need to add the negative sign to ΔL because in moving from point *F* to point *G*, ΔK is a negative number and ΔL is a positive number. The minus sign is needed to balance the equation.

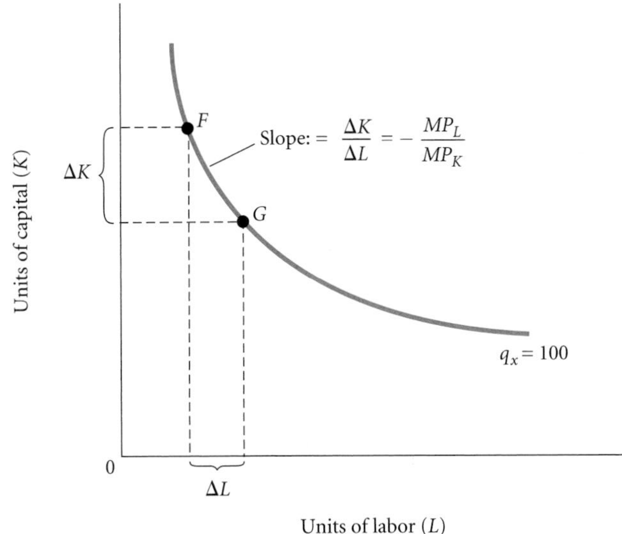

▲ **FIGURE 7A.2 The Slope of an Isoquant Is Equal to the Ratio of MP_L to MP_K**

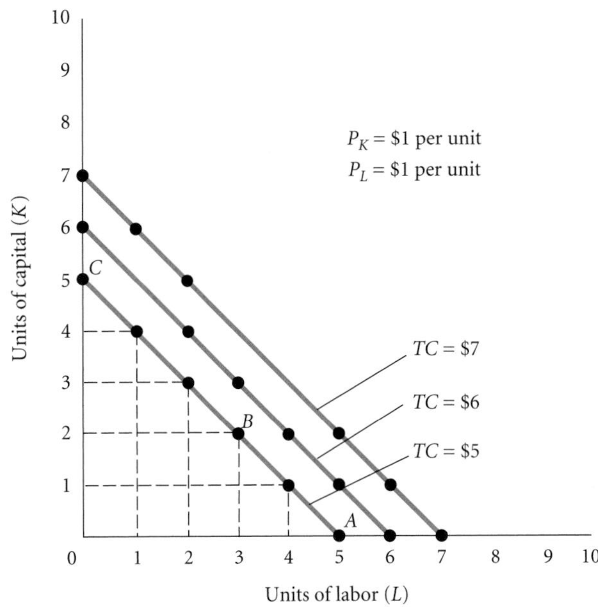

▲ **FIGURE 7A.3 Isocost Lines Showing the Combinations of Capital and Labor Available for \$5, \$6, and \$7**

An isocost line shows all the combinations of capital and labor that are available for a given total cost.

FACTOR PRICES AND INPUT COMBINATIONS: ISOCOSTS

A graph that shows all the combinations of capital and labor that are available for a given total cost is called an **isocost line.** (Recall that total cost includes opportunity costs and normal rate of return.) Just as there are an infinite number of isoquants (one for every possible level of output), there are an infinite number of isocost lines, one for every possible level of total cost.

Figure 7A.3 shows three simple isocost lines assuming that the price of labor (P_L) is \$1 per unit and the price of capital (P_K) is \$1 per unit. The lowest isocost line shows all the combinations of *K* and *L* that can be purchased for \$5. For example, \$5 will buy 5 units of labor and no capital (point *A*), 3 units of labor and 2 units of capital (point *B*), or no units of labor and 5 units of capital (point *C*). All these points lie along a straight line. The equation of that straight line is

$$(P_K \cdot K) + (P_L \cdot L) = TC$$

Substituting our data for the lowest isocost line into this general equation, we get

$$(\$1 \cdot K) + (\$1 \cdot L) = \$5, \text{ or } K + L = 5$$

Remember that the *X*- and *Y*-scales are units of labor and units of capital, not dollars.

On the same graph are two additional isocosts showing the various combinations of *K* and *L* available for a total cost of \$6 and \$7. These are only three of an infinite number of isocosts. At any total cost, there is an isocost that shows all the combinations of *K* and *L* available for that amount.

Figure 7A.4 shows another isocost line. This isocost assumes a different set of factor prices, P_L = \$5 and P_K = \$1. The diagram shows all the combinations of *K* and *L* that can be bought for \$25. One way to draw the line is to determine the endpoints. For example, if the entire \$25 were spent on labor, how much labor could be purchased? The answer is, of course, 5 units (\$25 divided by \$5 per unit). Thus, point *A*, which represents 5 units of labor and no capital, is on the isocost line. Similarly, if all of the \$25 were spent on capital, how much capital could be purchased? The answer is 25 units (\$25 divided by \$1 per unit). Thus, point *B*, which represents 25 units of capital and no labor, is also on the isocost line. Another point on this particular isocost is 3 units of labor and 10 units of capital, point *C*.

The slope of an isocost line can be calculated easily if you first find the endpoints of the line. In Figure 7A.4, we can calculate the slope of the isocost line by taking $\Delta K/\Delta L$ between points *B* and A. Thus,

$$\text{slope of isocost line: } \frac{\Delta K}{\Delta L} = -\frac{TC/P_K}{TC/P_L} = -\frac{P_L}{P_K}$$

Plugging in the endpoints from our example, we get

$$\text{slope of line } AB = -\frac{\$5}{\$1} = -5$$

FINDING THE LEAST-COST TECHNOLOGY WITH ISOQUANTS AND ISOCOSTS

Figure 7A.5 superimposes the isoquant for $q_X = 50$ on the isocost lines in Figure 7A.3, which assume that P_K = \$1 and P_L = \$1. The question now becomes one of choosing among the combinations of *K* and *L* that can be used to produce 50 units of output. Recall that each point on the isoquant (labeled q_X = 50 in Figure 7A.5) represents a different technology—a different combination of *K* and *L*.

We assume that our firm is a perfectly competitive, profit-maximizing firm that will choose the combination that minimizes

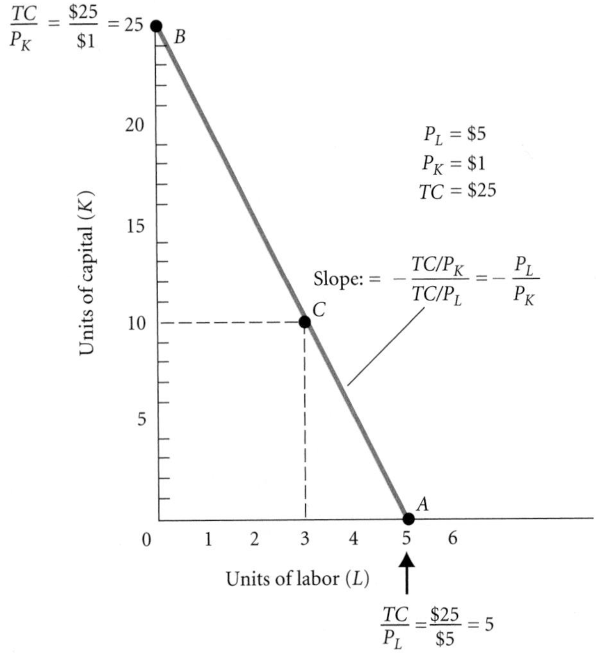

▲ **FIGURE 7A.4 Isocost Line Showing All Combinations of Capital and Labor Available for $25**

One way to draw an isocost line is to determine the endpoints of that line and draw a line connecting them.

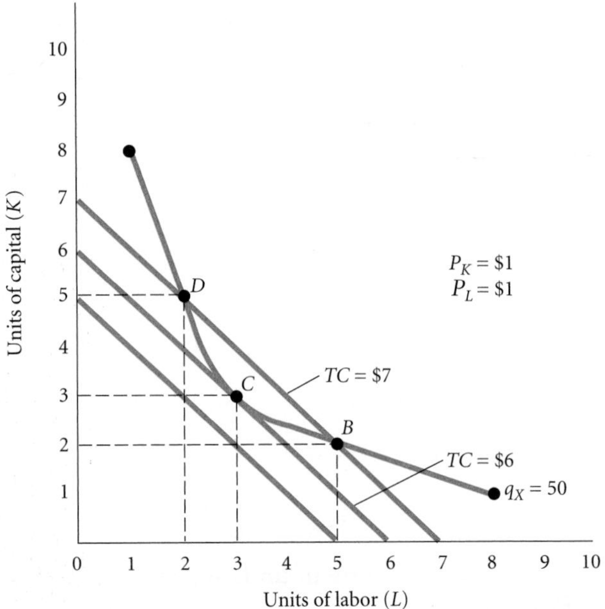

▲ **FIGURE 7A.5 Finding the Least-Cost Combination of Capital and Labor to Produce 50 Units of Output**

Profit-maximizing firms will minimize costs by producing their chosen level of output with the technology represented by the point at which the isoquant is tangent to an isocost line. Here the cost-minimizing technology—3 units of capital and 3 units of labor—is represented by point C.

cost. Because every point on the isoquant lies on some particular isocost line, we can determine the total cost for each combination along the isoquant. For example, point D (5 units of capital and 2 units of labor) lies along the isocost for a total cost of $7. Notice that 5 units of capital and 2 units of labor cost a total of $7. (Remember, $P_K = \$1$ and $P_L = \$1$.) The same amount of output (50 units) can be produced at lower cost. Specifically, by using 3 units of labor and 3 units of capital (point C), total cost is reduced to $6. *No other combination of K and L along isoquant* $q_X = 50$ *is on a lower isocost line.* In seeking to maximize profits, the firm will choose the combination of inputs that is least costly. The least costly way to produce any given level of output is indicated by the point of tangency between an isocost line and the isoquant corresponding to that level of output.[2]

In Figure 7A.5, the least-cost technology of producing 50 units of output is represented by point C, the point at which the $q_X = 50$ isoquant is just tangent to—that is, just touches—the isocost line.

Figure 7A.6 adds the other two isoquants from Figure 7A.1 to Figure 7A.5. Assuming that $P_K = \$1$ and $P_L = \$1$, the firm will move along each of the three isoquants until it finds the least-cost combination of K and L that can be used to produce that particular level of output. The result is plotted in Figure 7A.7. The minimum cost of producing 50 units of X is $6, the minimum cost of producing 100 units of X is $8, and the minimum cost of producing 150 units of X is $10.

THE COST-MINIMIZING EQUILIBRIUM CONDITION

At the point where a line is just tangent to a curve, the two have the same slope. (We have already derived expressions for the slope of an isocost and the slope of an isoquant.) At each point of tangency (such as at points A, B, and C in Figure 7A.6), the following must be true:

$$\text{slope of isoquant} = -\frac{MP_L}{MP_K} = \text{slope of isocost} = -\frac{P_L}{P_K}$$

Thus,

$$\frac{MP_L}{MP_K} = \frac{P_L}{P_K}$$

Dividing both sides by P_L and multiplying both sides by MP_K, we get

$$\frac{MP_L}{P_L} = \frac{MP_K}{P_K}$$

This is the firm's cost-minimizing equilibrium condition.

This expression makes sense if you think about what it says. The left side of the equation is the marginal product of labor divided by the price of a unit of labor. Thus, it is the product

[2] This assumes that the isoquants are continuous and convex (bowed) toward the origin.

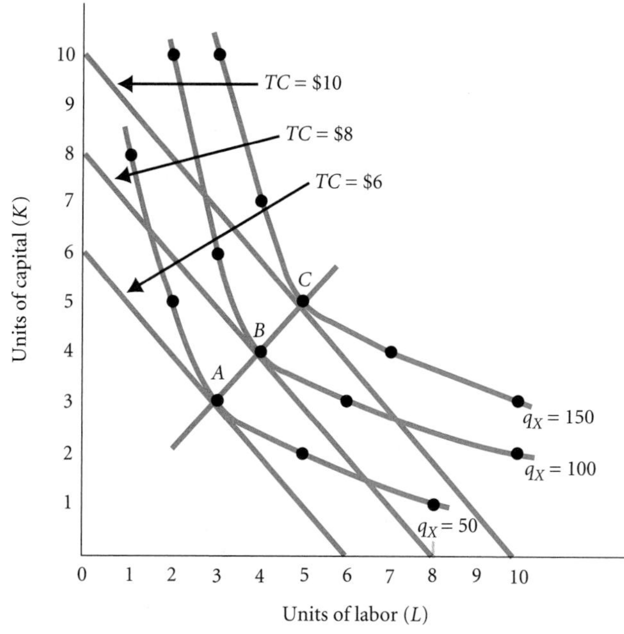

▲ **FIGURE 7A.6 Minimizing Cost of Production for $q_X = 50$, $q_X = 100$, and $q_X = 150$**

Plotting a series of cost-minimizing combinations of inputs—shown in this graph as points *A*, *B*, and *C*—on a separate graph results in a *cost curve* like the one shown in Figure 7A.7.

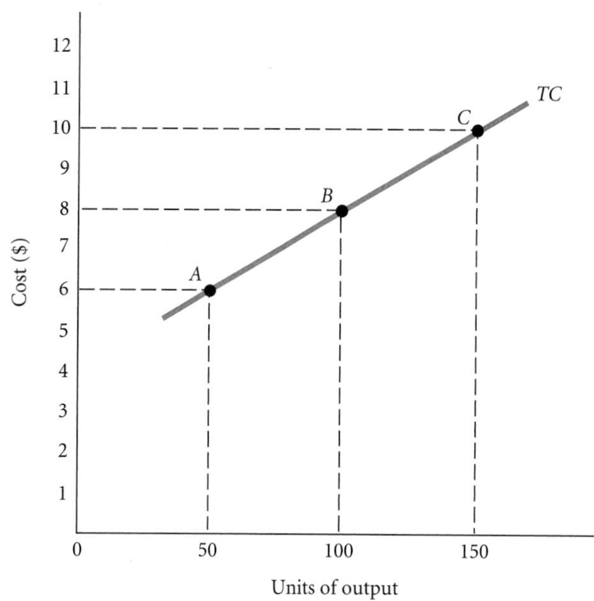

▲ **FIGURE 7A.7 A Cost Curve Shows the *Minimum* Cost of Producing Each Level of Output**

derived from the last dollar spent on labor. The right-hand side of the equation is the product derived from the last dollar spent on capital. If the product derived from the last dollar spent on labor was not equal to the product derived from the last dollar spent on capital, the firm could decrease costs by using more labor and less capital or by using more capital and less labor.

Look back to Chapter 6 and see if you can find a similar expression and some similar logic in our discussion of household behavior. In fact, there is great symmetry between the theory of the firm and the theory of household behavior.

SUMMARY

1. An *isoquant* is a graph that shows all the combinations of capital and labor that can be used to produce a given amount of output. The slope of an isoquant is equal to $-MP_L/MP_K$. The ratio of MP_L to MP_K is the *marginal rate of technical substitution*. It is the rate at which a firm can substitute capital for labor and hold output constant.
2. An *isocost line* is a graph that shows all the combinations of capital and labor that are available for a given total cost. The slope of an isocost line is equal to $-P_L/P_K$.
3. The least-cost method of producing a given amount of output is found graphically at the point at which an isocost line is just tangent to—that is, just touches—the isoquant corresponding to that level of production. The firm's cost-minimizing equilibrium condition is $MP_L/P_L = MP_K/P_K$.

REVIEW TERMS AND CONCEPTS

isocost line A graph that shows all the combinations of capital and labor available for a given total cost. *p. 151*

isoquant A graph that shows all the combinations of capital and labor that can be used to produce a given amount of output. *p. 150*

marginal rate of technical substitution The rate at which a firm can substitute capital for labor and hold output constant. *p. 150*

1. Slope of isoquant:

$$\frac{\Delta K}{\Delta L} = -\frac{MP_L}{MP_K}$$

2. Slope of isocost line:

$$\frac{\Delta K}{\Delta L} = -\frac{TC/P_K}{TC/P_L} = -\frac{P_L}{P_K}$$

PROBLEMS

1. Assume that $MP_L = 5$ and $MP_K = 10$. Assume also that $P_L = \$2$ and $P_K = \$5$. This implies that the firm should substitute labor for capital. Explain why.

2. In the isoquant/isocost diagram (Figure 1) suppose the firm is producing 1,000 units of output at point *A* using 100 units of labor and 200 units of capital. As an outside consultant, what actions would you suggest to management to improve profits? What would you recommend if the firm were operating at point *B*, using 100 units of capital and 200 units of labor?

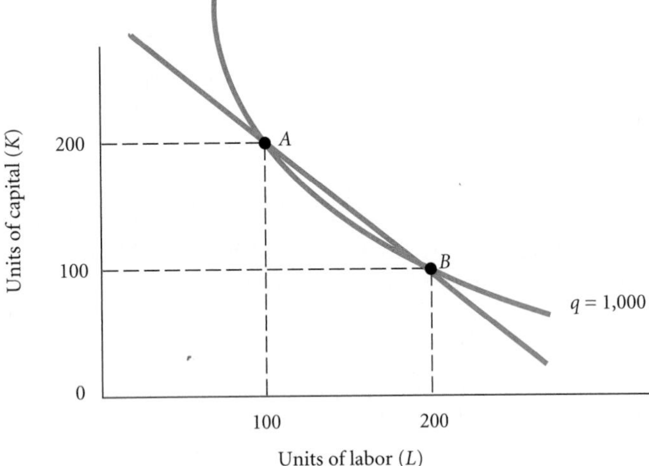

▲ FIGURE 1

3. Using the information from the isoquant/isocost diagram (Figure 2) and assuming that $P_L = P_K = \$2$, complete Table 1.

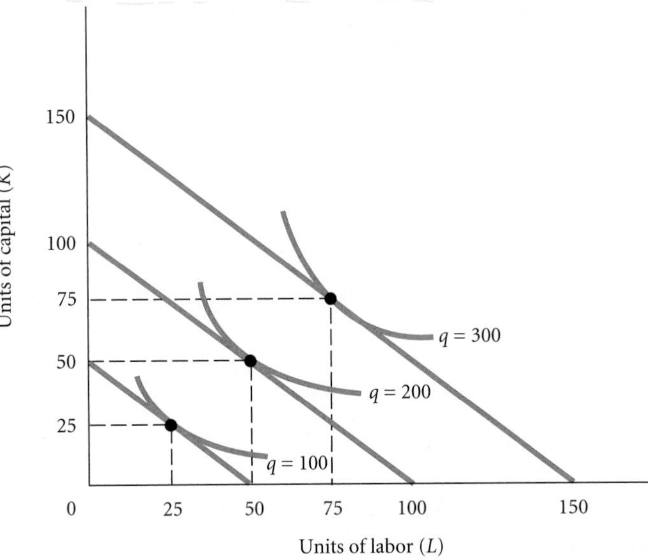

▲ FIGURE 2

TABLE 1

OUTPUT UNITS	TOTAL COST OF OUTPUT	UNITS OF LABOR DEMANDED	UNITS OF CAPITAL DEMANDED
100	______	______	______
200	______	______	______
300	______	______	______

Short-Run Costs and Output Decisions

8

CHAPTER OUTLINE

This chapter continues our examination of the decisions that firms make in their quest for profits. You have seen that firms make three specific decisions (Figure 8.1) involving their production. These decisions are:

1. How much output to supply
2. How to produce that output—that is, which production technique/technology to use
3. What quantity of each input to demand

We have assumed so far that firms are in business to earn profits and that they make choices to maximize those profits. (Remember that *profit* refers to economic profit, the difference between revenues and costs—full economic costs.)

In the last chapter, we focused on the production process. This chapter focuses on the *costs* of production. To calculate costs, a firm must know two things: what quantity and combination of inputs it needs to produce its product and how much those inputs cost. (Do not forget that economic costs include a normal return to capital—the opportunity cost of capital.)

Take a moment and look back at the circular flow diagram, Figure II.1 on p. 107. There you can see where we are in our study of the competitive market system. The goal of this chapter is to look behind the supply curve in output markets. It is important to understand, however, that producing output implies demanding inputs at the same time. You can also see in Figure II.1 two of the information sources that firms use in their output supply and input demand decisions: firms look to *output markets* for the price of output and to *input markets* for the prices of capital and labor.

DECISIONS	**are based on**	INFORMATION
1. The quantity of output to *supply*		1. The price of output
2. How to produce that output (which technique to use)		2. Techniques of production available*
3. The quantity of each input to *demand*		3. The price of inputs*
		*Determines production costs

◀ **FIGURE 8.1 Decisions Facing Firms**

Costs in the Short Run

Our emphasis in this chapter is on costs *in the short run only*. Recall that the short run is that period during which two conditions hold: (1) existing firms face limits imposed by some fixed factor of production, and (2) new firms cannot enter and existing firms cannot exit an industry.

In the short run, all firms (competitive and noncompetitive) have costs that they must bear regardless of their output. In fact, some costs must be paid even if the firm stops producing—that is, even if output is zero. These kinds of costs are called **fixed costs**, and firms can do nothing in the short run to avoid them or to change them. In the long run, a firm has no fixed costs because it can expand, contract, or exit the industry.

fixed cost Any cost that does not depend on the firms' level of output. These costs are incurred even if the firm is producing nothing. There are no fixed costs in the long run.

Firms do have certain costs in the short run that depend on the level of output they have chosen. These kinds of costs are called **variable costs**. Total fixed costs and total variable costs together make up **total costs**:

variable cost A cost that depends on the level of production chosen.

total cost (*TC*) Total fixed costs plus total variable costs.

$$TC = TFC + TVC$$

where *TC* denotes total costs, *TFC* denotes total fixed costs, and *TVC* denotes total variable costs. We will return to this equation after discussing fixed costs and variable costs in detail.

Fixed Costs

In discussing fixed costs, we must distinguish between total fixed costs and average fixed costs.

Total Fixed Cost (*TFC*) Total fixed cost is sometimes called *overhead*. If you operate a factory, you must heat the building to keep the pipes from freezing in the winter. Even if no production is taking place, you may have to keep the roof from leaking, pay a guard to protect the building from vandals, and make payments on a long-term lease. There may also be insurance premiums, taxes, and city fees to pay, as well as contract obligations to workers.

Fixed costs represent a larger portion of total costs for some firms than for others. Electric companies, for instance, maintain generating plants, thousands of miles of distribution wires, poles, transformers, and so on. Usually, such plants are financed by issuing bonds to the public—that is, by borrowing. The interest that must be paid on these bonds represents a substantial part of the utilities' operating cost and is a fixed cost in the short run, no matter how much (if any) electricity they are producing.

For the purposes of our discussion in this chapter, we will assume that firms use only two inputs: labor and capital. Although this may seem unrealistic, virtually everything that we will say about firms using these two factors can easily be generalized to firms that use many factors of production. Recall that capital yields services over time in the production of other goods and services. It is the plant and equipment of a manufacturing firm and the computers, desks, chairs, doors, and walls of a law office; it is the software of a Web-based firm and the boat that Bill and Colleen built on their desert island. It is sometimes assumed that capital is a fixed input in the short run and that labor is the only variable input. To be more realistic, however, we will assume that capital has both a fixed *and* a variable component. After all, some capital can be purchased in the short run.

Consider a small consulting firm that employs several economists, research assistants, and secretaries. It rents space in an office building and has a 5-year lease. The rent on the office space can be thought of as a fixed cost in the short run. The monthly electric and heating bills are also essentially fixed (although the amounts may vary slightly from month to month). So are the salaries of the basic administrative staff. Payments on some capital equipment—a large copying machine and the main word-processing system, for instance—can also be thought of as fixed.

The same firm also has costs that vary with output. When there is a great deal of work, the firm hires more employees at both the professional and research assistant levels. The capital used by the consulting firm may also vary, even in the short run. Payments on the computer system do not change, but the firm may rent additional computer time when necessary. The firm can buy additional personal computers, network terminals, or databases quickly if needed. It must pay for the copy machine, but the machine costs more when it is running than when it is not.

total fixed costs (*TFC*) *or* overhead The total of all costs that do not change with output even if output is zero.

Total fixed costs (*TFC*) *or* overhead are those costs that do not change with output even if output is zero. Column 2 of Table 8.1 presents data on the fixed costs of a hypothetical firm. Fixed costs are $1,000 at all levels of output (q). Figure 8.2(a) shows total fixed costs as a function of output. Because *TFC* does not change with output, the graph is simply a straight horizontal line at $1,000. The important thing to remember here is that firms have no control over fixed costs in the short run.

TABLE 8.1 Short-Run Fixed Cost (Total and Average) of a Hypothetical Firm

(1) *q*	(2) *TFC*	(3) *AFC* (*TFC/q*)
0	$1,000	$ –
1	1,000	1,000
2	1,000	500
3	1,000	333
4	1,000	250
5	1,000	200

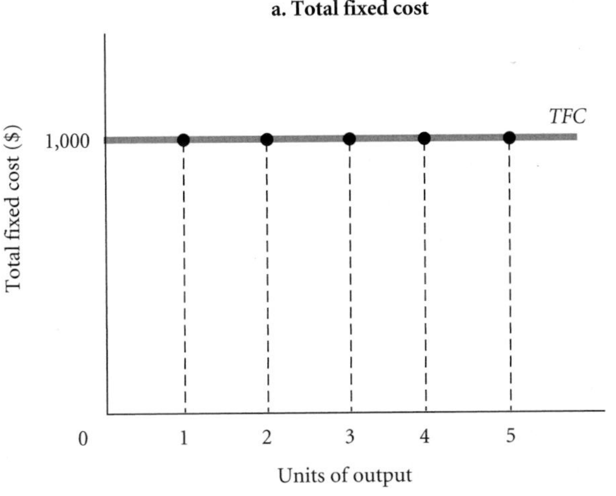

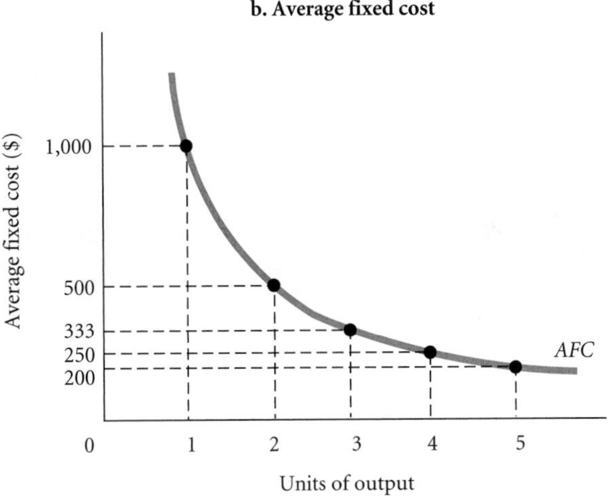

▲ **FIGURE 8.2 Short-Run Fixed Cost (Total and Average) of a Hypothetical Firm**
Average fixed cost is simply total fixed cost divided by the quantity of output. As output increases, average fixed cost declines because we are dividing a fixed number ($1,000) by a larger and larger quantity.

Average Fixed Cost (*AFC*) **Average fixed cost (*AFC*)** is total fixed cost (*TFC*) divided by the number of units of output (*q*):

average fixed cost (*AFC*) Total fixed cost divided by the number of units of output; a per-unit measure of fixed costs.

$$AFC = \frac{TFC}{q}$$

For example, if the firm in Figure 8.2 produced 3 units of output, average fixed costs would be $333 ($1,000 ÷ 3). If the same firm produced 5 units of output, average fixed cost would be $200 ($1,000 ÷ 5). *Average fixed cost falls as output rises* because the same total is being spread over, or divided by, a larger number of units (see column 3 of Table 8.1). This phenomenon is sometimes called **spreading overhead.**

spreading overhead The process of dividing total fixed costs by more units of output. Average fixed cost declines as quantity rises.

Graphs of average fixed cost, like that in Figure 8.2(b) (which presents the average fixed cost data from Table 8.1), are downward-sloping curves. Notice that *AFC* approaches zero as the quantity of output increases. If output were 100,000 units, average fixed cost would equal only 1 cent per unit in our example ($1,000 ÷ 100,000 = $0.01). *AFC* never actually reaches zero.

Variable Costs

Total Variable Cost (*TVC*) **Total variable cost (*TVC*)** is the sum of those costs that vary with the level of output in the short run. To produce more output, a firm uses more inputs. The cost of additional output depends directly on what additional inputs are required and how much they cost.

total variable cost (*TVC*) The total of all costs that vary with output in the short run.

As you saw in Chapter 7, input requirements are determined by technology. Firms generally have a number of production techniques available to them, and the option they choose is assumed to be the one that produces the desired level of output at the least cost. To find out which technology involves the least cost, a firm must compare the total variable costs of producing that level of output using different production techniques.

This is as true of small businesses as it is of large manufacturing firms. Suppose, for example, that you own a small farm. A certain amount of work has to be done to plant and harvest your 120 acres. You might hire four farmhands and divide up the tasks, or you might buy several pieces of complex farm machinery (capital) and do the work single-handedly. Your final choice depends on a number of things. What machinery is available? What does it do? Will it work on small fields such as yours? How much will it cost to buy each piece of equipment? What wage will you have to pay farmhands? How many will you need to hire to get the job done? If machinery is expensive and labor is cheap, you will probably choose the labor-intensive technology. If farm labor is expensive and the local farm equipment dealer is going out of business, you might get a good deal on some machinery and choose the capital-intensive method.

Having compared the costs of alternative production techniques, the firm may be influenced in its choice by the current scale of its operation. Remember, in the short run, a firm is locked into a *fixed* scale of operations. A firm currently producing on a small scale may find that a labor-intensive technique is least costly whether or not labor is comparatively expensive. The same firm producing on a larger scale might find a capital-intensive technique to be less costly.

total variable cost curve
A graph that shows the relationship between total variable cost and the level of a firm's output.

The **total variable cost curve** is a graph that shows the relationship between total variable cost and the level of a firm's output (q). At any given level of output, total variable cost depends on (1) the techniques of production that are available and (2) the prices of the inputs required by each technology. To examine this relationship in more detail, let us look at some hypothetical production figures.

Table 8.2 presents an analysis that might lie behind three points on a typical firm's total variable cost curve. In this case, there are two production techniques available, *A* and *B*, one somewhat more capital intensive than the other. We will assume that the price of labor is $1 per unit and the price of capital is $2 per unit. For the purposes of this example, we focus on *variable capital*—that is, on capital that can be changed in the short run. In practice, some capital (such as buildings and large, specialized machines) is fixed in the short run. In our example, we will use *K* to denote variable capital. Remember, however, that the firm has other capital, capital that is fixed in the short run.

TABLE 8.2 Derivation of Total Variable Cost Schedule from Technology and Factor Prices

Produce	Using Technique	Units of Input Required (Production Function) K	L	Total Variable Cost Assuming $P_K = \$2, P_L = \$1$ $TVC = (K \times P_K) + (L \times P_L)$
1 unit of output	*A*	4	4	$(4 \times \$2) + (4 \times \$1) = \$12$
	B	2	6	$(2 \times \$2) + (6 \times \$1) = \boxed{\$10}$
2 units of output	*A*	7	6	$(7 \times \$2) + (6 \times \$1) = \$20$
	B	4	10	$(4 \times \$2) + (10 \times \$1) = \boxed{\$18}$
3 units of output	*A*	9	6	$(9 \times \$2) + (6 \times \$1) = \boxed{\$24}$
	B	6	14	$(6 \times \$2) + (14 \times \$1) = \$26$

Analysis reveals that to produce 1 unit of output, the labor-intensive technique is least costly. Technique *A* requires 4 units of both capital and labor, which would cost a total of $12. Technique *B* requires 6 units of labor but only 2 units of capital for a total cost of only $10. To maximize profits, the firm would use technique *B* to produce 1 unit. The total variable cost of producing 1 unit of output would thus be $10.

The relatively labor-intensive technique *B* is also the best method of production for 2 units of output. By using *B*, the firm can produce 2 units for $18. If the firm decides to produce 3 units of output, however, technique *A* is cheaper. By using the least-cost technology (*A*), the total variable cost of production is $24. The firm will use 9 units of capital at $2 each and 6 units of labor at $1 each.

Figure 8.3 graphs the relationship between total variable cost and output based on the data in Table 8.2, assuming the firm chooses, for each output, the least-cost technology. The total variable cost curve embodies information about both factor, or input, prices and technology. It shows the cost of production using the best available technique at each output level given current factor prices.

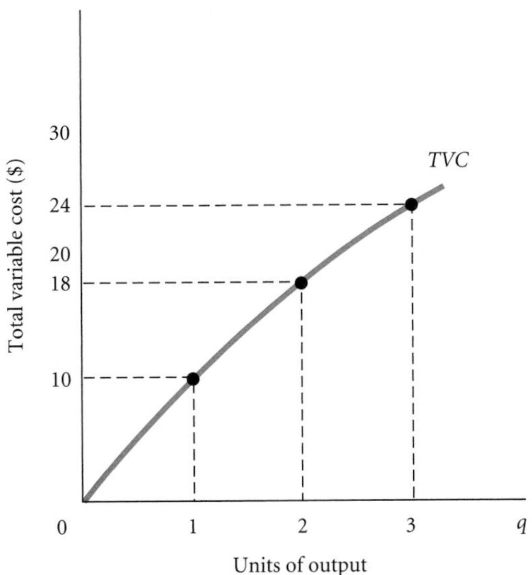

FIGURE 8.3 Total Variable Cost Curve

In Table 8.2, total variable cost is derived from production requirements and input prices. A total variable cost curve expresses the relationship between *TVC* and total output.

Marginal Cost (*MC*) The most important of all cost concepts is that of **marginal cost (*MC*)**, the increase in total cost that results from the production of 1 more unit of output. Let us say, for example, that a firm is producing 1,000 units of output per period and decides to raise its rate of output to 1,001. Producing the extra unit raises costs, and the increase—that is, the cost of producing the 1,001st unit—is the marginal cost. Focusing on the "margin" is one way of looking at variable costs: marginal costs reflect changes in variable costs because they vary when output changes. Fixed costs do not change when output changes.

marginal cost (*MC*) The increase in total cost that results from producing 1 more unit of output. Marginal costs reflect changes in variable costs.

Table 8.3 shows how marginal cost is derived from total variable cost by simple subtraction. The total variable cost of producing the first unit of output is $10. Raising production from 1 unit to 2 units increases total variable cost from $10 to $18; the difference is the marginal cost of the second unit, or $8. Raising output from 2 to 3 units increases total variable cost from $18 to $24. The marginal cost of the third unit, therefore, is $6.

TABLE 8.3 Derivation of Marginal Cost from Total Variable Cost

Units of Output	Total Variable Costs ($)	Marginal Costs ($)
0	0	
1	10	10
2	18	8
3	24	6

It is important to think for a moment about the nature of marginal cost. Specifically, marginal cost is the cost of the added inputs, or resources, needed to produce 1 additional unit of output. Look back at Table 8.2 and think about the additional capital and labor needed to go from 1 unit to 2 units. Producing 1 unit of output with technique *B* requires 2 units of capital and 6 units of labor; producing 2 units of output using the same technique requires 4 units of capital and 10 units of labor. Thus, the second unit requires 2 *additional* units of capital and 4 *additional* units of labor. What, then, is the added, or marginal, cost of the second unit? Two units of capital cost $2 each ($4 total) and 4 units of labor cost $1 each (another $4), for a total marginal cost of $8, which is the number we derived in Table 8.3. Although the easiest way to derive marginal cost is to look at total variable cost and subtract, do not lose sight of the fact that when a firm increases its output level, it hires or demands more inputs. *Marginal cost* measures the *additional* cost of inputs required to produce each successive unit of output.

The Shape of the Marginal Cost Curve in the Short Run The assumption of a fixed factor of production in the short run means that a firm is stuck at its current scale of operation (in our example, the size of the plant). As a firm tries to increase its output, it will eventually find itself trapped by that scale. Thus, our definition of the short run also implies that *marginal cost eventually rises with output.* The firm can hire more labor and use more materials—that is, it can add variable inputs—but diminishing returns eventually set in.

Recall the sandwich shop, with one grill and too many workers trying to prepare sandwiches on it, from Chapter 7. With a fixed grill capacity, more laborers could make more sandwiches; but the marginal product of each successive cook declined as more people tried to use the grill. If each additional unit of labor adds less and less to total output, *it follows that more labor is needed to produce each additional unit of output.* Thus, each additional unit of output costs more to produce. In other words, *diminishing returns, or decreasing marginal product, imply increasing marginal cost* as illustrated in Figure 8.4.

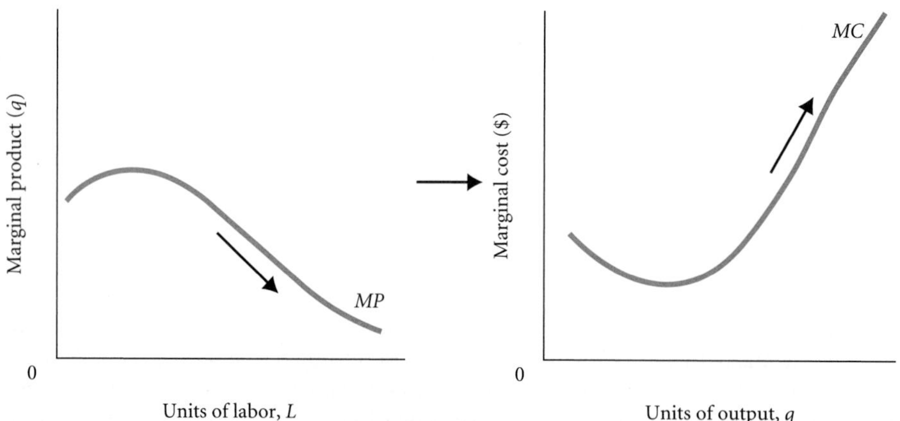

FIGURE 8.4 Declining Marginal Product Implies That Marginal Cost Will Eventually Rise with Output

In the short run, every firm is constrained by some fixed factor of production. A fixed factor implies diminishing returns (declining marginal product) and a limited capacity to produce. As that limit is approached, marginal costs rise.

Recall too the accountant who helps people file their tax returns. He has an office in his home and works alone. His fixed factor of production is that there are only 24 hours in a day and he has only so much stamina. In the long run, he may decide to hire and train an associate. But in the meantime (the short run), he has to decide how much to produce; and that decision is constrained by his current scale of operations. The biggest component of the accountant's cost is time. When he works, he gives up leisure and other things that he could do with his time. With more and more clients, he works later and later into the night. As he does so, he becomes less and less productive, and his hours become more and more valuable for sleep and relaxation. In other words, the marginal cost of doing each successive tax return rises.

To reiterate:

> In the short run, every firm is constrained by some fixed input that (1) leads to diminishing returns to variable inputs and (2) limits its capacity to produce. As a firm approaches that capacity, it becomes increasingly costly to produce successively higher levels of output. Marginal costs ultimately increase with output in the short run.

Graphing Total Variable Costs and Marginal Costs Figure 8.5 shows the total variable cost curve and the marginal cost curve of a typical firm. Notice first that the shape of the marginal cost curve is consistent with short-run diminishing returns. At first, *MC* declines, but eventually the fixed factor of production begins to constrain the firm, and marginal cost rises. Up to 100 units of output, producing each successive unit of output costs slightly less than producing the one before. Beyond 100 units, however, the cost of each successive unit is greater than the one before. (Remember the sandwich shop.)

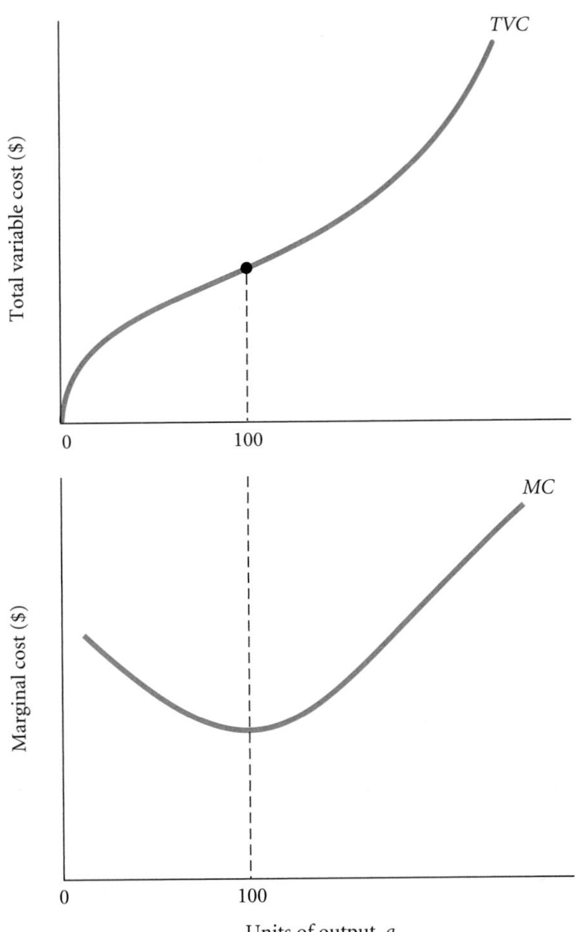

FIGURE 8.5 Total Variable Cost and Marginal Cost for a Typical Firm

Total variable costs always increase with output. Marginal cost is the cost of producing each additional unit. Thus, the marginal cost curve shows how total variable cost changes with single-unit increases in total output.

More output costs more than less output. Total variable costs (*TVC*), therefore, *always increase* when output increases. Even though the cost of each additional unit changes, *total* variable cost rises when output rises. Thus, the *total* variable cost curve always has a positive slope.

You might think of the total variable cost curve as a staircase. Each step takes you out along the quantity axis by a single unit, and the height of each step is the increase in total variable cost. As you climb the stairs, you are always going up; but the steps have different heights. At first, the stairway is steep; but as you climb, the steps get smaller (marginal cost declines). The 100th stair is the smallest. As you continue to walk out beyond 100 units, the steps begin to get larger; the staircase gets steeper (marginal cost increases).

Remember that the slope of a line is equal to the change in the units measured on the *Y*-axis divided by the change in the units measured on the *X*-axis. The slope of a total variable cost curve is thus the change in total variable cost divided by the change in output ($\Delta TVC/\Delta q$). Because marginal cost is by definition the change in total variable cost resulting from an increase in output of one unit ($\Delta q = 1$), *marginal cost actually is the slope of the total variable cost curve*:

$$\text{slope of } TVC = \frac{\Delta\, TVC}{\Delta q} = \frac{\Delta\, TVC}{1} = \Delta\, TVC = MC$$

Notice that up to 100 units, marginal cost decreases and the variable cost curve becomes flatter. The slope of the total variable cost curve is declining—that is, total variable cost increases, but at a *decreasing rate*. Beyond 100 units of output, marginal cost increases and the total variable cost curve gets steeper—total variable costs continue to increase, but at an *increasing rate*.

A more complete picture of the costs of a hypothetical firm appears in Table 8.4. Column 2 shows total variable costs derived from information on input prices and technology. Column 3 derives marginal cost by simple subtraction. For example, raising output from 3 units to 4 units increases variable costs from \$24 to \$32, making the marginal cost of the fourth unit \$8 (\$32 – \$24). The marginal cost of the fifth unit is \$10, the difference between \$32 (*TVC*) for 4 units and \$42 (*TVC*) for 5 units.

average variable cost (*AVC*) Total variable cost divided by the number of units of output.

Average Variable Cost (*AVC*) **Average variable cost (*AVC*)** is total variable cost divided by the number of units of output (q):

$$AVC = \frac{TVC}{q}$$

In Table 8.4, we calculate *AVC* in column 4 by dividing the numbers in column 2 (*TVC*) by the numbers in column 1 (q). For example, if the total variable cost of producing 5 units of output is \$42, then the average variable cost is \$42 ÷ 5, or \$8.40. Marginal cost is the cost of 1 *additional unit*. Average variable cost is the total variable cost divided by the total number of units produced.

TABLE 8.4 Short-Run Costs of a Hypothetical Firm

(1) q	(2) *TVC*	(3) *MC* (Δ*TVC*)	(4) *AVC* (*TVC*/q)	(5) *TFC*	(6) *TC* (*TVC* + *TFC*)	(7) *AFC* (*TFC*/q)	(8) *ATC* (*TC*/q or *AFC* + *AVC*)
0	$ 0	$ –	$ –	$1,000	$1,000	$ –	$ –
1	10	10	10	1,000	1,010	1,000	1,010
2	18	8	9	1,000	1,018	500	509
3	24	6	8	1,000	1,024	333	341
4	32	8	8	1,000	1,032	250	258
5	42	10	8.4	1,000	1,042	200	208.4
–	–	–	–	–	–	–	–
–	–	–	–	–	–	–	–
–	–	–	–	–	–	–	–
500	8,000	20	16	1,000	9,000	2	18

Graphing Average Variable Costs and Marginal Costs The relationship between average variable cost and marginal cost can be illustrated graphically. When marginal cost is *below* average variable cost, average variable cost declines toward it. When marginal cost is *above* average variable cost, average variable cost increases toward it.

Figure 8.6 duplicates the bottom graph for a typical firm in Figure 8.5 but adds average variable cost. As the graph shows, average variable cost *follows* marginal cost but lags behind. As we move from left to right, we are looking at higher and higher levels of output per period. As we increase production, marginal cost—which at low levels of production is above \$3.50 per unit—falls as coordination and cooperation begin to play a role. At 100 units of output, marginal cost has fallen to \$2.50. Notice that average variable cost falls as well, but not as rapidly as marginal cost.

After 100 units of output, we begin to see diminishing returns. Marginal cost begins to increase as higher and higher levels of output are produced. However, notice that average cost is still falling until 200 units because marginal cost remains below it. At 100 units of output, marginal cost is \$2.50 per unit but the *average* variable cost of production is \$3.50. Thus, even though marginal cost is rising after 100 units, it is still pulling the average of \$3.50 downward.

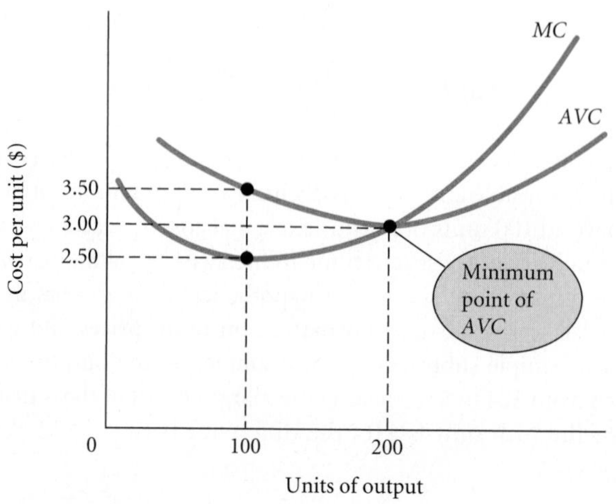

FIGURE 8.6 More Short-Run Costs

When marginal cost is *below* average cost, average cost is declining. When marginal cost is *above* average cost, average cost is increasing. Rising marginal cost intersects average variable cost at the minimum point of *AVC*.

At 200 units, however, marginal cost has risen to \$3 and average cost has fallen to \$3; marginal and average costs are equal. At this point, marginal cost continues to rise with higher output. From 200 units upward, *MC* is *above AVC* and thus exerts an upward pull on the average variable cost curve. At levels of output below 200 units, marginal cost is below average variable cost and average variable cost decreases as output increases. At levels of output above 200 units, *MC* is above *AVC* and *AVC* increases as output increases. If you follow this logic, you will see that marginal cost intersects average variable cost at the lowest, or minimum, point of *AVC*.

An example using test scores should help you understand the relationship between *MC* and *AVC*. Consider the following sequence of test scores: 95, 85, 92, 88. The average of these four scores is 90. Suppose you get an 80 on your fifth test. This score will drag down your average to 88. Now suppose you get an 85 on your sixth test. This score is higher than 80, but its still *below* your 88 average. As a result, your average continues to fall (from 88 to 87.5) even though your marginal test score rose. If instead of an 85 you get an 89—just one point over your average—you have turned your average around; it is now rising.

Total Costs

We are now ready to complete the cost picture by adding total fixed costs to total variable costs. Recall that

$$TC = TFC + TVC$$

Total cost is graphed in Figure 8.7, where the same vertical distance (equal to *TFC*, which is constant) is simply added to *TVC* at every level of output. In Table 8.4, column 6 adds the total fixed cost of \$1,000 to total variable cost to arrive at total cost.

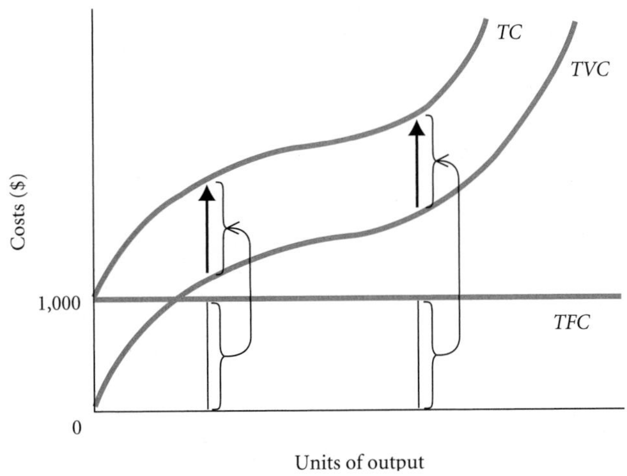

FIGURE 8.7 Total Cost = Total Fixed Cost + Total Variable Cost

Adding *TFC* to *TVC* means adding the same amount of total fixed cost to every level of total variable cost. Thus, the total cost curve has the same shape as the total variable cost curve; it is simply higher by an amount equal to *TFC*.

Average Total Cost (*ATC*)

Average total cost (*ATC*) is total cost divided by the number of units of output (q):

average total cost (*ATC*) Total cost divided by the number of units of output.

$$ATC = \frac{TC}{q}$$

Column 8 in Table 8.4 shows the result of dividing the costs in column 6 by the quantities in column 1. For example, at 5 units of output, *total* cost is \$1,042; *average* total cost is \$1,042 ÷ 5, or \$208.40. The average total cost of producing 500 units of output is only \$18—that is, \$9,000 ÷ 500.

Another, more revealing, way of deriving average total cost is to add average fixed cost and average variable cost together:

$$ATC = AFC + AVC$$

For example, column 8 in Table 8.4 is the sum of column 4 (*AVC*) and column 7 (*AFC*).

Figure 8.8 derives average total cost graphically for a typical firm. The bottom part of the figure graphs average fixed cost. At 100 units of output, average fixed cost is TFC/q = $1,000 ÷ 100 = $10. At 400 units of output, AFC = $1,000 ÷ 400 = $2.50. The top part of Figure 8.8 shows the declining AFC added to AVC at each level of output. Because AFC gets smaller and smaller, ATC gets closer and closer to AVC as output increases, but the two lines never meet.

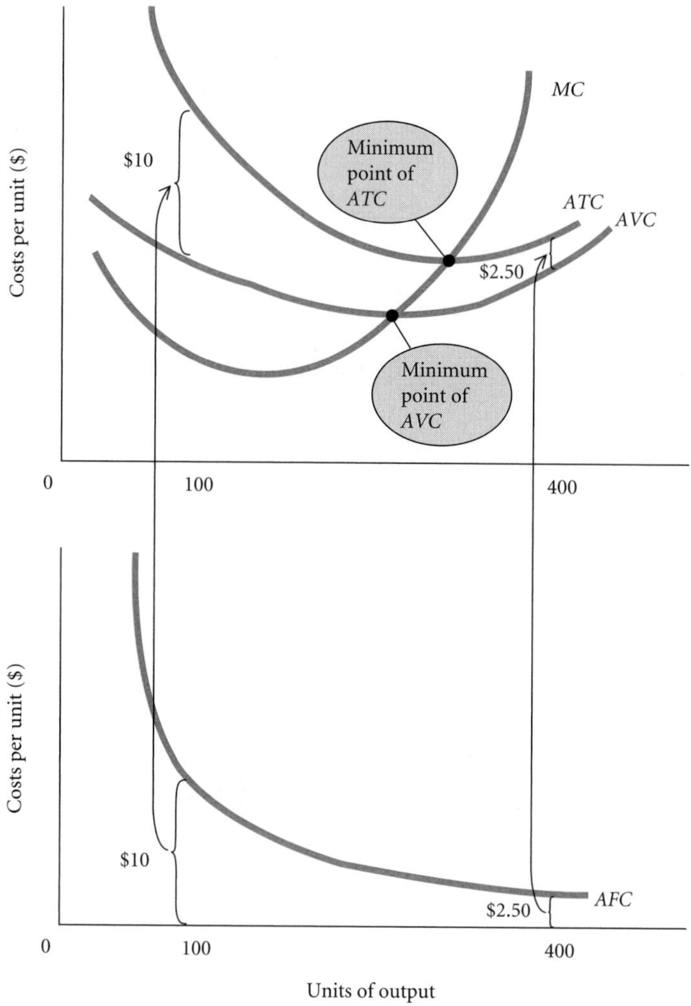

▶ FIGURE 8.8 Average Total Cost = Average Variable Cost + Average Fixed Cost

To get average total cost, we add average fixed and average variable costs at all levels of output. Because average fixed cost falls with output, an ever-declining amount is added to *AVC*. Thus, *AVC* and *ATC* get closer together as output increases, but the two lines never meet.

The Relationship Between Average Total Cost and Marginal Cost The relationship between average *total* cost and marginal cost is exactly the same as the relationship between average *variable* cost and marginal cost. The average total cost curve follows the marginal cost curve but lags behind because it is an average over all units of output. The average total cost curve lags behind the marginal cost curve even more than the average variable cost curve does because the cost of each added unit of production is now averaged not only with the variable cost of all previous units produced but also with fixed costs.

Fixed costs equal $1,000 and are incurred even when the output level is zero. Thus, the first unit of output in the example in Table 8.4 costs $10 in variable cost to produce. The second unit costs only $8 in variable cost to produce. The total cost of 2 units is $1,018; average total cost of the two is ($1,010 + $8)/2, or $509. The marginal cost of the third unit is only $6. The total cost of 3 units is thus $1,024, or $1,018 + $6; and the average total cost of 3 units is ($1,010 + $8 + $6)/3, or $341.

As you saw with the test scores example, marginal cost is what drives changes in average total cost. If marginal cost is *below* average total cost, average total cost will *decline* toward marginal cost. If marginal cost is *above* average total cost, average total cost will *increase*. As a result, marginal cost intersects average *total* cost at *ATC*'s minimum point for the same reason that it intersects the average *variable* cost curve at its minimum point.

Short-Run Costs: A Review

Let us now pause to review what we have learned about the behavior of firms. We know that firms make three basic choices: how much product or output to produce or supply, how to produce that output, and how much of each input to demand to produce what they intend to supply. We assume that these choices are made to maximize profits. Profits are equal to the difference between a firm's revenue from the sale of its product and the costs of producing that product: profit = total revenue – total cost.

So far, we have looked only at costs; but costs are just one part of the profit equation. To complete the picture, we must turn to the output market and see how these costs compare with the price that a product commands in the market. Before we do so, however, it is important to consolidate what we have said about costs.

Before a firm does anything else, it needs to know the different methods that it can use to produce its product. The technologies available determine the combinations of inputs that are needed to produce each level of output. Firms choose the technique that produces the desired level of output at the least cost. The cost curves that result from the analysis of all this information show the cost of producing each level of output using the best available technology.

Remember that so far, we have talked only about short-run costs. The curves we have drawn are therefore *short-run cost curves*. The shape of these curves is determined in large measure by the assumptions that we make about the short run, especially the assumption that some fixed factor of production leads to diminishing returns. Given this assumption, marginal costs eventually rise and average cost curves are likely to be U-shaped. Table 8.5 summarizes the cost concepts that we have discussed.

After gaining a complete knowledge of how to produce a product and how much it will cost to produce it at each level of output, the firm turns to the market to find out what it can sell its product for. We now turn our attention to the output market.

TABLE 8.5 A Summary of Cost Concepts

Term	Definition	Equation
Accounting costs	Out-of-pocket costs or costs as an accountant would define them. Sometimes referred to as *explicit costs*.	–
Economic costs	Costs that include the full opportunity costs of all inputs. These include what are often called *implicit costs*.	–
Total fixed costs (TFC)	Costs that do not depend on the quantity of output produced. These must be paid even if output is zero.	–
Total variable costs (TVC)	Costs that vary with the level of output.	–
Total cost (TC)	The total economic cost of all the inputs used by a firm in production.	$TC = TFC + TVC$
Average fixed costs (AFC)	Fixed costs per unit of output.	$AFC = TFC/q$
Average variable costs (AVC)	Variable costs per unit of output.	$AVC = TVC/q$
Average total costs (ATC)	Total costs per unit of output.	$ATC = TC/q$ $ATC = AFC + AVC$
Marginal costs (MC)	The increase in total cost that results from producing 1 additional unit of output.	$MC = TC/\Delta q$

ECONOMICS IN PRACTICE

Average and Marginal Costs at a College

Pomona College in California has an annual operating budget of $120 million. With this budget, the college educates and houses 1,500 students. So the average total cost of educating a Pomona student is $80,000 per year, some of which comes from the college endowment and gifts. Suppose college administrators are considering a small increase in the number of students it accepts and believe they could do so without sacrificing quality of teaching and research. Given that the level of tuition and room and board is considerably less than $80,000, can the administrators make a financial case to support such a move?

The key issue here is to recognize that for a college like Pomona—and indeed for most colleges—the average total cost of educating a student is higher than the marginal cost. For a very small increase in the number of students, the course-related expenses probably would not go up at all. These students could likely be absorbed into existing courses with no added expense for faculty, buildings, or administrators. Housing might be more of a constraint, but even in that regard administrators might find some flexibility. Thus, from a financial perspective, the key question about expansion is not how the average total cost of education compares to the tuition, but how tuition compares to the marginal cost. For this reason, many colleges would, in fact, find it financially advantageous to expand student populations if they could do so without changing the quality and environment of the school.

Suppose that of Pomona's $120 million budget, $60 million was fixed costs: maintenance of the physical campus, basic salaries, and other fixed operating costs. Suppose further that the full marginal cost of providing the education was $40,000 per student and constant. Using these figures, one can easily create the following table and draw the cost curves.

	Costs in Dollars			
Students	Total Fixed Cost	Total Variable Cost	Total Cost	Average Total Cost
500	$60 million	$ 20 million	$ 80 million	$160,000
1,000	60 million	40 million	100 million	100,000
1,500	60 million	60 million	120 million	80,000
2,000	60 million	80 million	140 million	70,000
2,500	60 million	100 million	160 million	64,000

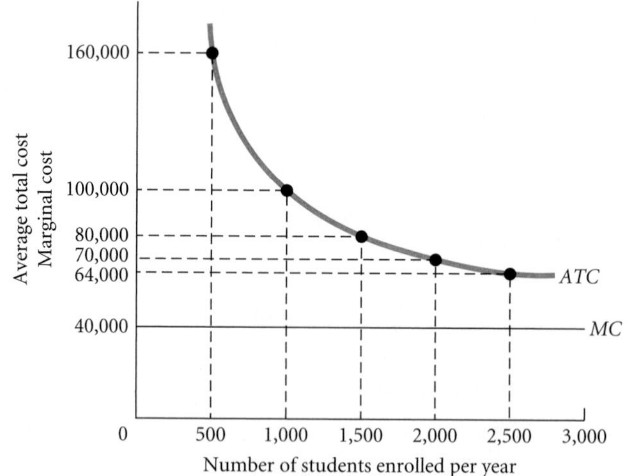

The cost curves also help us understand the downward spiral that can affect colleges as their populations fall. In 2005, Antioch College in Ohio announced that it would be phasing out its undergraduate program. The culprit? Declining attendance caused the average total cost of educating the remaining few students to skyrocket, despite attempts to control costs. Given the inevitability of some fixed costs of education (to educate even a modest student body requires facilities and a college president, for example), as the number of students falls, the average total cost—which is total cost divided by the number of students—rises. For organizations such as colleges and museums, the numbers game is very important to their survival.

Output Decisions: Revenues, Costs, and Profit Maximization

To calculate potential profits, firms must combine their cost analyses with information on potential revenues from sales. After all, if a firm cannot sell its product for more than the cost of production, it will not be in business long. In contrast, if the market gives the firm a price that is significantly greater than the cost it incurs to produce a unit of its product, the firm may have an incentive to expand output. Large profits might also attract new competitors to the market.

Let us now examine in detail how a firm goes about determining how much output to produce. We will begin by examining the decisions of a perfectly competitive firm.

Perfect Competition **Perfect competition** exists in an industry that contains many relatively small firms producing identical products. In a perfectly competitive industry, no single firm has any control over prices. In other words, an individual firm cannot affect the market price of its product or the prices of the inputs that it buys. This important characteristic follows from two assumptions. First, a competitive industry is composed of many firms, each small relative to the size of the industry. Second, every firm in a perfectly competitive industry produces **homogeneous products**, which means that one firm's output cannot be distinguished from the output of the others.

perfect competition An industry structure in which there are many firms, each small relative to the industry, producing identical products and in which no firm is large enough to have any control over prices. In perfectly competitive industries, new competitors can freely enter and exit the market.

homogenous products Undifferentiated products; products that are identical to, or indistinguishable from, one another.

These assumptions limit the decisions open to competitive firms and simplify the analysis of competitive behavior. Firms in perfectly competitive industries do not differentiate their products and do not make decisions about price. Instead, each firm takes prices as given—that is, as determined in the market by the laws of supply and demand—and decides only how much to produce and how to produce it.

The idea that competitive firms are "price-takers" is central to our discussion. Of course, we do not mean that firms cannot affix price tags to their merchandise; all firms have this ability. We mean that given the availability of perfect substitutes, any product priced over the market price will not be sold.

These assumptions also imply that the demand for the product of a competitive firm is perfectly elastic (Chapter 5). For example, consider the Ohio corn farmer whose situation is shown in Figure 8.9. The left side of the diagram represents the current conditions in the market. Corn is currently selling for $6.00 per bushel.[1] The right side of the diagram shows the demand for corn as the farmer sees it. If she were to raise her price, she would sell no corn at all; because there are perfect substitutes available, the quantity demanded of her corn would drop to zero. To lower her price would be silly because she can sell all she wants at the current price. (Remember, each farmer's production is very small relative to the entire corn market.)

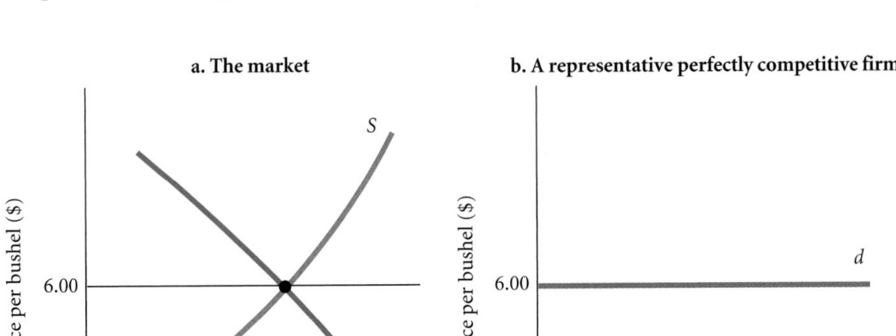

FIGURE 8.9 Demand Facing a Single Firm In a Perfectly Competitive Market

If a representative firm in a perfectly competitive market raises the price of its output above $6.00, the quantity demanded of *that firm's* output will drop to zero. Each firm faces a perfectly elastic demand curve, *d*.

[1] Capital letters refer to the entire market, and lowercase letters refer to representative firms. For example, in Figure 8.9, the market demand curve is labeled *D* and the demand curve facing the firm is labeled *d*.

In perfect competition, we also assume easy entry—that firms can easily enter and exit the industry. If firms in an industry are earning high profits, new firms are likely to spring up. There are no barriers that prevent a new firm from competing. Fast-food restaurants are quick to spring up when a new shopping center opens, and new gas stations appear when a housing development or a new highway is built. When it became clear a number of years ago that many people would be buying products online, thousands of e-commerce start-ups flooded the Web with new online "shops."

We also assume *easy exit.* When a firm finds itself suffering losses or earning low profits, one option is to go out of business, or exit the industry. Everyone knows a favorite restaurant that went out of business. Changes in cost of production, falling prices from international or regional competition, and changing technology may turn business profits into losses and failure.

The best examples of perfect competition are probably found in agriculture. In that industry, products are absolutely homogeneous—it is impossible to distinguish one farmer's wheat from another's—and prices are set by the forces of supply and demand in a huge national market.

Total Revenue and Marginal Revenue

total revenue (*TR*) The total amount that a firm takes in from the sale of its product: the price per unit times the quantity of output the firm decides to produce ($P \times q$).

Profit is the difference between total revenue and total cost. **Total revenue *(TR)*** is the total amount that a firm takes in from the sale of its product. A perfectly competitive firm sells each unit of product for the same price, regardless of the output level it has chosen. Therefore, total revenue is simply the price per unit times the quantity of output that the firm decides to produce:

$$\text{total revenue} = \text{price} \times \text{quantity}$$

$$TR = P \times q$$

marginal revenue (*MR*) The additional revenue that a firm takes in when it increases output by one additional unit. In perfect competition, $P = MR$.

Marginal revenue (*MR*) is the added revenue that a firm takes in when it increases output by 1 additional unit. If a firm producing 10,521 units of output per month increases that output to 10,522 units per month, it will take in an additional amount of revenue each month. The revenue associated with the 10,522nd unit is the amount for which the firm sells that 1 unit. Thus, for a competitive firm, marginal revenue is equal to the current market price of each additional unit sold. In Figure 8.9, for example, the market price is $6.00. Thus, if the representative firm raises its output from 10,521 units to 10,522 units, its revenue will increase by $6.00.

A firm's *marginal revenue curve* shows how much revenue the firm will gain by raising output by 1 unit at every level of output. The *marginal revenue curve and the demand curve facing a competitive firm are identical.* The horizontal line in Figure 8.9(b) can be thought of as both the demand curve facing the firm and its marginal revenue curve:

$$P^* = d = MR$$

Comparing Costs and Revenues to Maximize Profit

The discussion in the next few paragraphs conveys one of the most important concepts in all of microeconomics. As we pursue our analysis, remember that we are working under two assumptions: (1) that the industry we are examining is perfectly competitive and (2) that firms choose the level of output that yields the maximum total profit.

The Profit-Maximizing Level of Output Look carefully at the graphs in Figure 8.10. Once again, we have the whole market, or industry, on the left and a single, typical small firm on the right. And again the current market price is P^*.

First, the firm observes the market price [Figure 8.10(a)] and knows that it can sell all that it wants for $P^* = \$5$ per unit. Next, the firm must decide how much to produce. It might seem reasonable for the firm to pick the output level where marginal cost is at its minimum point—in this case, at an output of 100 units. Here the difference between marginal revenue, $5.00, and marginal cost, $2.50, is the greatest.

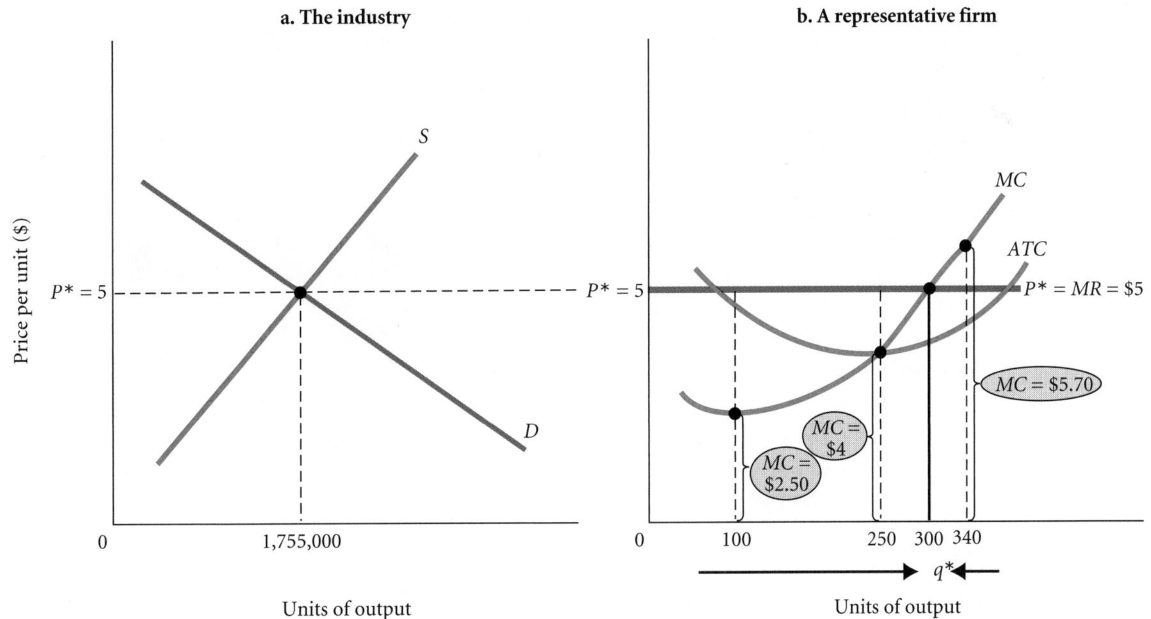

▲ **FIGURE 8.10 The Profit-Maximizing Level of Output for a Perfectly Competitive Firm**

If price is above marginal cost, as it is at 100 and 250 units of output, profits can be increased by raising output; each additional unit increases revenues by more than it costs to produce the additional output. Beyond q^* = 300, however, added output will reduce profits. At 340 units of output, an additional unit of output costs more to produce than it will bring in revenue when sold on the market. Profit-maximizing output is thus q^*, the point at which $P^* = MC$.

Remember that a firm wants to maximize the difference between *total* revenue and *total* cost, not the difference between *marginal* revenue and *marginal* cost. The fact that marginal revenue is greater than marginal cost indicates that profit is *not* being maximized. Think about the 101st unit. Adding that single unit to production each period adds $5.00 to revenues but adds only about $2.50 to cost. Profits each period would be higher by about $2.50. Thus, the optimal (profit-maximizing) level of output is clearly higher than 100 units.

Now look at an output level of 250 units. Here, once again, raising output increases profit. The revenue gained from producing the 251st unit (marginal revenue) is still $5, and the cost of the 251st unit (marginal cost) is only about $4. As long as marginal revenue is greater than marginal cost, even though the difference between the two is getting smaller, added output means added profit. Whenever marginal revenue exceeds marginal cost, the revenue gained by increasing output by 1 unit per period exceeds the cost incurred by doing so. This logic leads us to 300 units of output. At 300 units, marginal cost has risen to $5. At 300 units of output, $P^* = MR = MC = \$5$.

Notice that if the firm were to produce *more* than 300 units, marginal cost would rise above marginal revenue. At 340 units of output, for example, the cost of the 341st unit is about $5.70 while that added unit of output still brings in only $5 in revenue, thus reducing profit. It simply does not pay to increase output above the point where marginal cost rises above marginal revenue because such increases will *reduce* profit. The profit-maximizing perfectly competitive firm will produce up to the point where the price of its output is just equal to short-run marginal cost—the level of output at which $P^* = MC$. Thus, in Figure 8.10, the profit-maximizing level of output, q^*, is 300 units.

Keep in mind, though, that all types of firms (not just those in perfectly competitive industries) are profit maximizers. The profit-maximizing output level for *all* firms is the output level where $MR = MC$. In perfect competition, however, $MR = P$, as shown earlier. Hence, for perfectly competitive firms, we can rewrite our profit-maximizing condition as $P = MC$.

Important note: The key idea here is that firms will produce as long as marginal revenue exceeds marginal cost. When marginal cost rises smoothly, as it does in Figure 8.10, the profit-maximizing condition is that *MR* (or *P*) *exactly equals MC*. If marginal cost moves up in increments—as it does in the following numerical example—marginal revenue or price may never exactly equal marginal cost. The key idea still holds.

ECONOMICS IN PRACTICE

Case Study in Marginal Analysis: An Ice Cream Parlor

The following is a description of the decisions made in 2000 by the owner of a small ice cream parlor in Ohio. After being in business for 1 year, this entrepreneur had to ask herself whether she should stay in business.

The cost figures on which she based her decisions are presented next. These numbers are real, but they do not include one important item: the managerial labor provided by the owner. In her calculations, the entrepreneur did not include a wage for herself; but we will assume an opportunity cost of $30,000 per year ($2,500 per month).

FIXED COSTS

The fixed components of the store's monthly costs include the following:

Rent (1,150 square feet)	$2,012.50
Electricity	325.00
Interest on loan	737.50
Maintenance	295.00
Telephone	65.00
Total	$3,435.00

Not all the items on this list are strictly fixed, however. Electricity costs, for example, would be slightly higher if the store produced more ice cream and stayed open longer, but the added cost would be minimal.

VARIABLE COSTS

The ice cream store's variable costs include two components: (1) behind-the-counter labor costs and (2) cost of making ice cream. The store hires employees at a wage of $5.15 per hour. Including the employer's share of the Social Security tax, the gross cost of labor is $5.54 per hour. Two employees work in the store at all times. The full cost of producing ice cream is $3.27 per gallon. Each gallon contains approximately 12 servings. Customers can add toppings free of charge, and the average cost of the toppings taken by a customer is about $.05:

Gross labor costs	$5.54/hour
Costs of producing one gallon of ice cream (12 servings per gallon)	$3.27
Average cost of added toppings per serving	$.05

REVENUES

The store sells ice cream cones, sundaes, and floats. The average price of a purchase at the store is $1.45. The store is open 8 hours per day, 26 days a month, and serves an average of 240 customers per day:

Average purchase	$1.45
Days open per month	26
Average number of customers per day	240

From the preceding information, it is possible to calculate the store's average monthly profit. Total revenue is equal to 240 customers × $1.45 per customer × 26 days open in an average month: TR = $9,048 per month.

PROFITS

The store sells 240 servings per day. Because there are 12 servings of ice cream per gallon, the store uses exactly 20 gallons per day (240 servings divided by 12). Total costs are $3.27 × 20, or $65.40, per day for ice cream and $12 per day for toppings (240 × $.05). The cost of variable labor is $5.54 × 8 hours × 2 workers, or $88.64 per day. Total variable costs are therefore $166.04 ($65.40 + $12.00 + $88.64) per day. The store is open 26 days a month, so the total variable cost per month is $4,317.04.

Adding fixed costs of $3,435.00 to variable costs of $4,317.04, we get a total cost of operation of $7,752.04 per month. Thus, the firm is averaging a profit of $1,295.96 per month ($9,048.00 – $7,752.04). *This is not an "economic profit" because we have not accounted for the opportunity cost of the owner's time and efforts.* In fact, when we factor in an implicit wage of $2,500 per month for the owner, we see that the store is suffering *losses* of $1,204.04 per month ($1,295.96 – $2,500.00).

Total revenue (*TR*)	$9,048.00
Total fixed cost (*TFC*)	3,435.00
+ Total variable cost (*TVC*)	4,317.04
Total costs (*TC*)	7,752.04
Total profit (*TR* – *TC*)	1,295.96
Adjustment for implicit wage	2,500.00
Economic profit	–1,204.04

Should the entrepreneur stay in business? If she wants to make $2,500 per month and she thinks that nothing about her business will change, she must shut down in the long run. However, two things keep her going: (1) a decision to stay open longer and (2) the hope for more customers in the future.

OPENING LONGER HOURS: MARGINAL COSTS AND MARGINAL REVENUES

The store's normal hours of operation are noon until 8 P.M. On an experimental basis, the owner extends its hours until 11 P.M. for 1 month. The following table shows the average number of additional customers for each of the added hours:

Hours (P.M.)	Customers
8–9	41
9–10	20
10–11	8

Assuming that the late customers spend an average of $1.45, we can calculate the marginal revenue and the marginal cost of staying open longer. The marginal cost of one serving of ice cream is $3.27 divided by 12 = $0.27 + .05 (for topping) = $0.32. (See the table that follows.)

Marginal analysis tells us that the store should stay open for 2 additional hours. Each day that the store stays open from 8 P.M. to 9 P.M. it will make an added profit of $59.45 – $24.20, or $35.25. Staying open from 9 P.M. to 10 P.M. adds $29.00 – $17.48, or $11.52, to profit. Staying open the third hour, however, *decreases* profits because the marginal revenue generated by staying open from 10 P.M. to 11 P.M. is less than the marginal cost. The entrepreneur decides to stay open for 2 additional hours per day. This adds $46.77 ($35.25 + 11.52) to profits each day, a total of $1,216.02 per month.

By adding the 2 hours, the store turns an economic loss of $1,204.04 per month into a small ($11.98) profit after accounting for the owner's implicit wage of $2,500 per month.

The owner decided to stay in business. She now serves over 350 customers per day, and the price of a dish of ice cream has risen to $2.50 while costs have not changed very much. In 2001, she cleared a profit of nearly $10,000 per month.

Hour (P.M.)	Marginal Revenue (*MR*)	Marginal Cost (*MC*)	Added Profit per Hour (*MR* – *MC*)
8–9	$1.45 × 41 = $59.45	Ice cream: $0.32 × 41 = $13.12	$35.25
		Labor: 2 × $5.54 = 11.08	
		Total $24.20	
9–10	1.45 × 20 = $29.00	Ice cream: $0.32 × 20 = $6.40	$11.52
		Labor: 2 × $5.54 = 11.08	
		Total $17.48	
10–11	1.45 × 8 = $11.60	Ice cream: $0.32 × 8 = $2.56	-$2.04
		Labor: 2 × $5.54 = 11.08	
		Total $13.64	

A Numerical Example Table 8.6 presents some data for another hypothetical firm. Let us assume that the market has set a $15 unit price for the firm's product. Total revenue in column 6 is the simple product of $P \times q$ (the numbers in column 1 times $15). The table derives total, marginal, and average costs exactly as Table 8.4 did. Here, however, we have included revenues; and we can calculate the profit, which is shown in column 8.

TABLE 8.6 Profit Analysis for a Simple Firm

(1)	(2)	(3)	(4)	(5)	(6)	(7)	(8)
					TR	*TC*	*PROFIT*
q	*TFC*	*TVC*	*MC*	*P = MR*	(*P* × *q*)	(*TFC* + *TVC*)	(*TR* – *TC*)
0	$10	$ 0	$–	$15	$ 0	$10	$–10
1	10	10	10	15	15	20	–5
2	10	15	5	15	30	25	5
3	10	20	5	15	45	30	15
4	10	30	10	15	60	40	20
5	10	50	20	15	75	60	15
6	10	80	30	15	90	90	0

Column 8 shows that a profit-maximizing firm would choose to produce 4 units of output. At this level, profits are $20. At all other output levels, they are lower. Now let us see if "marginal" reasoning leads us to the same conclusion.

First, should the firm produce at all? If it produces nothing, it suffers losses equal to $10. If it increases output to 1 unit, marginal revenue is $15 (remember that it sells each unit for $15) and marginal cost is $10. Thus, it gains $5, reducing its loss from $10 each period to $5.

Should the firm increase output to 2 units? The marginal revenue from the second unit is again $15, but the marginal cost is only $5. Thus, by producing the second unit, the firm gains $10 ($15 – $5) and turns a $5 loss into a $5 profit. The third unit adds $10 to profits. Again, marginal revenue is $15 and marginal cost is $5, an increase in profit of $10, for a total profit of $15.

The fourth unit offers still more profit. Price is still above marginal cost, which means that producing that fourth unit will increase profits. Price, or marginal revenue, is $15; and marginal cost is just $10. Thus, the fourth unit adds $5 to profit. At unit number five, however, diminishing returns push marginal cost above price. The marginal revenue from producing the fifth unit is $15, while marginal cost is now $20. As a result, profit per period drops by $5, to $15 per period. Clearly, the firm will not produce the fifth unit.

The profit-maximizing level of output is thus 4 units. The firm produces as long as price (marginal revenue) is greater than marginal cost. For an in-depth example of profit maximization, see "Case Study in Marginal Analysis: An Ice Cream Parlor" on p. 170.

The Short-Run Supply Curve

Consider how the typical firm shown in Figure 8.10 on p. 169 would behave in response to an increase in price. In Figure 8.11(a), assume that something causes demand to increase (shift to the right), driving price from $5 to $6 and finally to $7. When price is $5, a profit-maximizing firm will choose an output level of 300 in Figure 8.11(b). To produce any less, or to raise output above that level, would lead to a lower level of profit. At $6, the same firm would increase output to 350; but it would stop there. Similarly, at $7, the firm would raise output to 400 units of output.

The *MC* curve in Figure 8.11(b) relates price and quantity supplied. At any market price, the marginal cost curve shows the output level that maximizes profit. A curve that shows how much output a profit-maximizing firm will produce at every price also fits the definition of a supply curve. (Review Chapter 3 if this point is not clear to you.) Thus, the marginal cost curve of a competitive firm is the firm's short-run supply curve.

As you will see, one very important exception exists to this general rule: There is some price level below which the firm will shut down its operations and simply bear losses equal to fixed costs even if price is above marginal cost. This important point is discussed in Chapter 9.

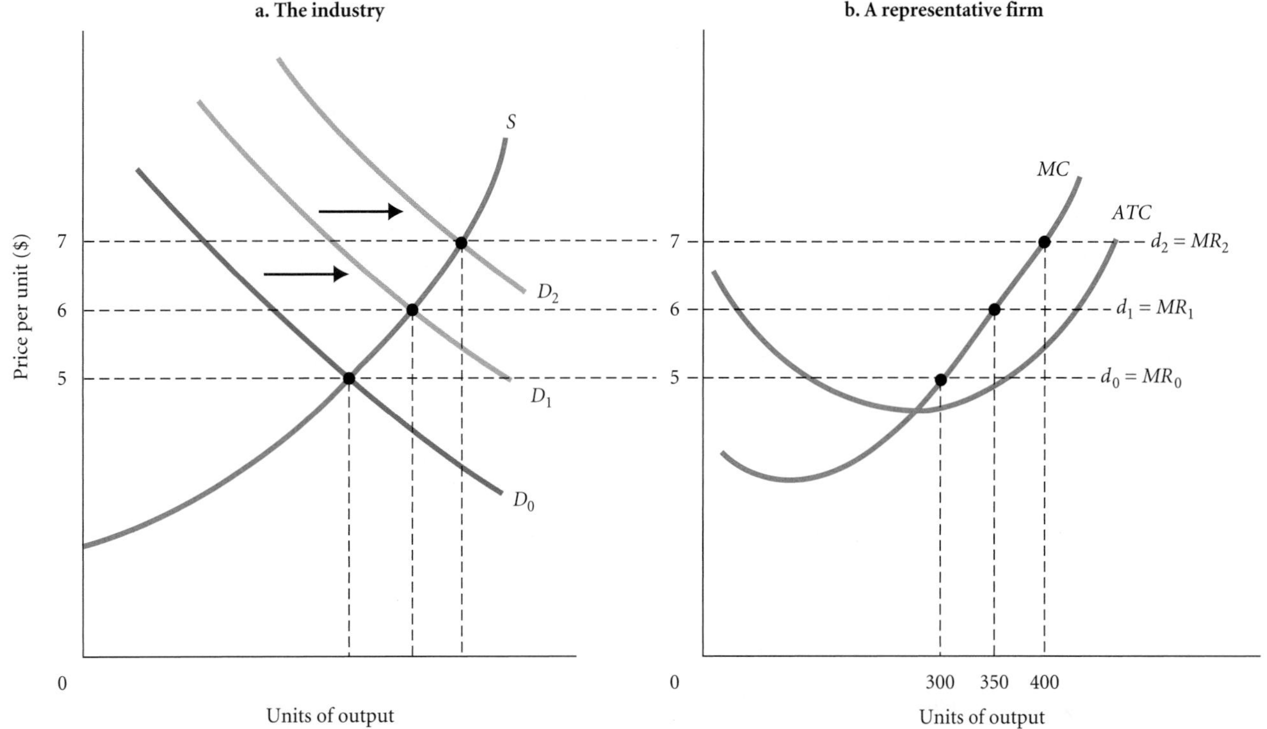

▲ **FIGURE 8.11 Marginal Cost Is the Supply Curve of a Perfectly Competitive Firm**

At any market price,[a] the marginal cost curve shows the output level that maximizes profit. Thus, the marginal cost curve of a perfectly competitive profit-maximizing firm is the firm's short-run supply curve.

[a] This is true except when price is so low that it pays a firm to shut down—a point that will be discussed in Chapter 9.

Looking Ahead

At the beginning of this chapter, we set out to combine information on technology, factor prices, and output prices to understand the supply curve of a competitive firm. We have now accomplished that goal.

Because marginal cost is such an important concept in microeconomics, you should carefully review any sections of this chapter that were unclear to you. Above all, keep in mind that the *marginal cost curve* carries information about both *input prices* and *technology*. The firm looks to output markets for information on potential revenues, and the current market price defines the firm's marginal revenue curve. The point where price (which is equal to marginal revenue in perfect competition) is just equal to marginal cost is the perfectly competitive firm's profit-maximizing level of output. Thus, with one important exception, the marginal cost curve *is* the perfectly competitive firm's supply curve in the short run.

In the next chapter, we turn to the long run. What happens when firms are free to choose their scale of operations without being limited by a fixed factor of production? Without diminishing returns that set in as a result of a fixed scale of production, what determines the shape of cost curves? What happens when new firms can enter industries in which profits are being earned? How do industries adjust when losses are being incurred? How does the structure of an industry evolve over time?

SUMMARY

1. Profit-maximizing firms make decisions to maximize profit (total revenue minus total cost).

2. To calculate production costs, firms must know two things: (1) the quantity and combination of inputs they need to produce their product and (2) the cost of those inputs.

COSTS IN THE SHORT RUN *p. 156*

3. *Fixed costs* are costs that do not change with a firm's output. In the short run, firms cannot avoid fixed costs or change them even if production is zero.
4. *Variable costs* are those costs that depend on the level of output chosen. Fixed costs plus variable costs equal *total costs* ($TC = TFC + TVC$).
5. *Average fixed cost* (AFC) is total fixed cost divided by the quantity of output. As output rises, average fixed cost declines steadily because the same total is being spread over a larger and larger quantity of output. This phenomenon is called *spreading overhead.*
6. Numerous combinations of inputs can be used to produce a given level of output. *Total variable cost* (TVC) is the sum of all costs that vary with output in the short run.
7. *Marginal cost* (MC) is the increase in total cost that results from the production of 1 more unit of output. If a firm is producing 1,000 units, the additional cost of increasing output to 1,001 units is marginal cost. Marginal cost measures the cost of the additional inputs required to produce each successive unit of output. Because fixed costs do not change when output changes, marginal costs reflect changes in variable costs.
8. In the short run, a firm is limited by a fixed factor of production or a fixed scale of a plant. As a firm increases output, it will eventually find itself trapped by that scale. Because of the fixed scale, marginal cost eventually rises with output.
9. Marginal cost is the slope of the total variable cost curve. The total variable cost curve always has a positive slope because total costs always rise with output. However, increasing marginal cost means that total costs ultimately rise at an increasing rate.
10. *Average variable cost* (AVC) is equal to total variable cost divided by the quantity of output.
11. When marginal cost is above average variable cost, average variable cost is *increasing*. When marginal cost is below average variable cost, average variable cost is *declining*. Marginal cost intersects average variable cost at AVC's minimum point.
12. *Average total cost* (ATC) is equal to total cost divided by the quantity of output. It is also equal to the sum of average fixed cost and average variable cost.
13. When marginal cost is below average total cost, average total cost is declining toward marginal cost. When marginal cost is above average total cost, average total cost is increasing. Marginal cost intersects average total cost at ATC's minimum point.

OUTPUT DECISIONS: REVENUES, COSTS, AND PROFIT MAXIMIZATION *p. 167*

14. A perfectly competitive firm faces a demand curve that is a horizontal line (in other words, perfectly elastic demand).
15. *Total revenue* (TR) is simply price times the quantity of output that a firm decides to produce and sell. *Marginal revenue* (MR) is the additional revenue that a firm takes in when it increases output by 1 unit.
16. For a perfectly competitive firm, marginal revenue is equal to the current market price of its product.
17. A profit-maximizing firm in a perfectly competitive industry will produce up to the point at which the price of its output is just equal to short-run marginal cost: $P = MC$. The more general profit-maximizing formula is $MR = MC$ ($P = MR$ in perfect competition). The marginal cost curve of a perfectly competitive firm is the firm's short-run supply curve, with one exception (discussed in Chapter 9).

REVIEW TERMS AND CONCEPTS

average fixed cost (AFC), *p. 157*
average total cost (ATC), *p. 163*
average variable cost (AVC), *p. 162*
fixed cost, *p. 156*
homogeneous product, *p. 167*
marginal cost (MC), *p. 159*
marginal revenue (MR), *p. 168*
perfect competition, *p. 167*
spreading overhead, *p. 157*
total cost (TC), *p. 156*
total fixed costs (TFC) *or* overhead, *p. 156*
total revenue (TR), *p. 168*
total variable cost (TVC), *p. 157*
total variable cost curve, *p. 158*
variable cost, *p. 156*

1. $TC = TFC + TVC$
2. $AFC = TFC/q$
3. Slope of $TVC = MC$
4. $AVC = TVC/q$
5. $ATC = TC/q = AFC + AVC$
6. $TR = P \times q$
7. Profit-maximizing level of output for all firms: $MR = M$
8. Profit-maximizing level of output for perfectly competitive firms: $P = MC$

PROBLEMS

Visit **www.myeconlab.com** to complete the problems marked in orange online. You will receive instant feedback on your answers, tutorial help, and access to additional practice problems.

1. Consider the following costs of owning and operating a car. A \$25,000 Ford Taurus financed over 60 months at 7 percent interest means a monthly payment of \$495.03. Insurance costs \$100 a month regardless of how much you drive. The car gets 20 miles per gallon and uses unleaded regular gasoline that costs \$3.50 per gallon. Finally, suppose that wear and tear on the car costs about 15 cents a mile. Which costs are fixed, and which are variable? What is the marginal cost of a mile driven? In deciding whether to drive from New York to Pittsburgh (about 1,000 miles round-trip) to visit a friend, which costs would you consider? Why?

2. July 23, 2007 LONDON (Reuters)—The final volume of the Harry Potter saga sold more than 11 million copies in the first 24 hours it went on sale in the United States and Britain to become the fastest-selling book in history, publishers said. In book publishing, fixed costs are very high and marginal costs are very low and fairly constant. Suppose that the fixed cost of producing the new Harry Potter volume is $30 million. What is the *average fixed cost* if the publisher produces 5 million copies? 10 million copies? 20 million copies?

Now suppose that the marginal cost of a Harry Potter book is $1.50 per book and is the same for each book up to 40 million copies. Assume that this includes all variable costs. Explain why in this case marginal cost is a horizontal line, as is average variable cost. What is the *average total cost* of the book if the publisher produces 5 million copies? 10 million copies? 20 million copies?

Sketch the average fixed cost curve and the average total cost curve facing the publisher.

3. Do you agree or disagree with this statement? Firms minimize costs; thus, a firm earning short-run economic profits will choose to produce at the minimum point on its average total cost function.

4. You are given the following cost data:

Total fixed costs are 100.

q	*TVC*
0	0
1	5
2	10
3	20
4	40
5	65
6	95

If the price of output is $15, how many units of output will this firm produce? What is total revenue? What is total cost? Briefly explain using the concept of marginal cost. What do you think the firm is likely to do in the short run? In the long run?

5. **[Related to the *Economics in Practice* on p. 166]** While charging admission most days of the week, the Museum of Contemporary Art in Los Angeles offers free admission on Thursday evenings. Why do museums often price this way? Why do they choose Thursday rather than Saturday?

6. The following table gives capital and labor requirements for 10 different levels of production.

q	*K*	*L*
0	0	0
1	2	5
2	4	9
3	6	12
4	8	15
5	10	19
6	12	24
7	14	30
8	16	37
9	18	45
10	20	54

a. Assuming that the price of labor (P_L) is $5 per unit and the price of capital (P_K) is $10 per unit, compute and graph total cost, marginal cost, and average variable cost for the firm.

b. Do the graphs have the shapes that you might expect? Explain.

c. Using the numbers here, explain the relationship between marginal cost and average variable cost.

d. Using the numbers here, explain the meaning of "marginal cost" in terms of additional inputs needed to produce a marginal unit of output.

e. If the output price was $57, how many units of output would the firm produce? Explain.

7. Do you agree or disagree with each of the following statements? Explain your reasons.

a. For a competitive firm facing a market price above average total cost, the existence of economic profits means that the firm should increase output in the short run even if price is below marginal cost.

b. If marginal cost is rising with increasing output, average cost must also be rising.

c. Fixed cost is constant at every level of output except zero. When a firm produces no output, fixed costs are zero in the short run.

8. A firm's cost curves are given in the following table.

q	*TC*	*TFC*	*TVC*	*AVC*	*ATC*	*MC*
0	$100	$100	–	–	–	–
1	130	100	–	–	–	–
2	150	100	–	–	–	–
3	160	100	–	–	–	–
4	172	100	–	–	–	–
5	185	100	–	–	–	–
6	210	100	–	–	–	–
7	240	100	–	–	–	–
8	280	100	–	–	–	–
9	330	100	–	–	–	–
10	390	100	–	–	–	–

a. Complete the table.

b. Graph *AVC*, *ATC*, and *MC* on the same graph. What is the relationship between the *MC* curve and the *ATC* and between *MC* and *AVC*?

c. Suppose market price is $30. How much will the firm produce in the short run? How much are total profits?

d. Suppose market price is $50. How much will the firm produce in the short run? What are total profits?

9. A 2008 Georgia Tech graduate inherited her mother's printing company. The capital stock of the firm consists of three machines of various vintages, all in excellent condition. All machines can be running at the same time.

	COST OF PRINTING AND BINDING PER BOOK	MAXIMUM TOTAL CAPACITY (BOOKS) PER MONTH
Machine 1	$1.00	100
Machine 2	2.00	200
Machine 3	3.00	500

a. Assume that "cost of printing and binding per book" includes *all* labor and materials, including the owner's wages. Assume further that Mom signed a long-term contract (50 years) with a service company to keep the machines in good repair for a fixed fee of $100 per month.

(1) Derive the firm's marginal cost curve.

(2) Derive the firm's total cost curve.

b. At a price of $2.50, how many books would the company produce? What would total revenues, total costs, and total profits be?

10. The following is a total cost curve. Sketch the corresponding marginal cost curve. If the price of output is $3 and there are no fixed costs, what is the profit-maximizing level of output?

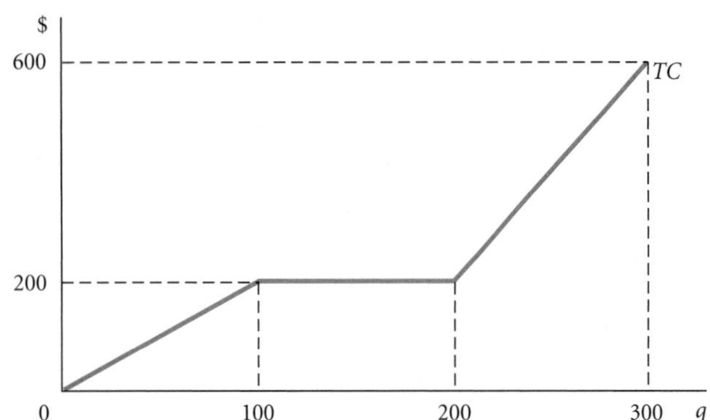

11. The following curve is a production function for a firm that uses just one variable factor of production, labor. It shows total output, or product, for every level of input.
   a. Derive and graph the marginal product curve.
   b. Suppose the wage rate is $4. Derive and graph the firm's marginal cost curve.
   c. If output sells for $6, what is the profit-maximizing level of output? How much labor will the firm hire?

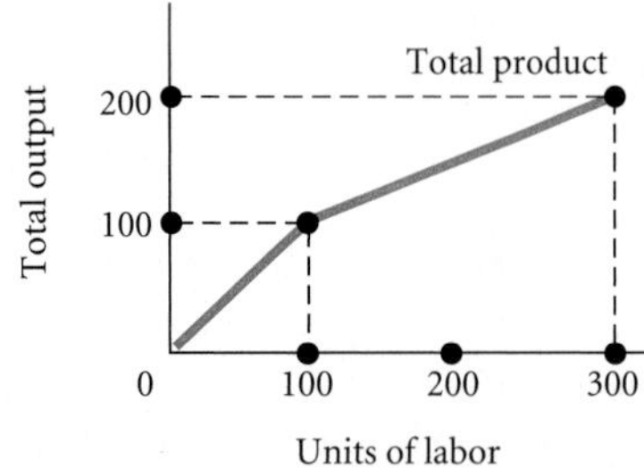

12. **[Related to the *Economics in Practice* on *p. 170*]** Elena and Emmanuel live on the Black Sea in Bulgaria and own a small fishing boat. A crew of four is required to take the boat out fishing. The current wage paid to the four crew members is a total of 5,000 levs per day. (A lev is the Bulgarian unit of currency.) Assume that the cost of operating and maintaining the boat is 1,000 levs per day when fishing and zero otherwise. The following schedule gives the appropriate catch for each period during the year.

PERIOD	CATCH PER DAY (KILOGRAMS)
Prime fishing: 180 days	100
Month 7: 30 days	80
Month 8: 30 days	60
Rest of the year	40

The price of fish in Bulgaria is no longer regulated by the government and is now determined in competitive markets. Suppose the price has been stable all year at 80 levs per kilogram.
   a. What is the marginal product of a day's worth of fishing during prime fishing season? during month 7? during month 8?
   b. What is the marginal cost of a kilogram of fish during prime fishing season? during month 7, during month 8, and during the rest of the year?
   c. If you were Elena and Emmanuel, how many months per year would you hire the crew and go out fishing? Explain your answer using marginal logic.

13. For each of the following businesses, what is the likely fixed factor of production that defines the short run?
   a. Potato farm of 160 acres
   b. Chinese restaurant
   c. Dentist in private practice
   d. Car dealership
   e. Bank

Long-Run Costs and Output Decisions

9

CHAPTER OUTLINE

The last two chapters discussed the behavior of profit-maximizing competitive firms in the short run. Recall that all firms must make three fundamental decisions: (1) how much output to produce or supply, (2) how to produce that output, and (3) how much of each input to demand.

Firms use information on input prices, output prices, and technology to make the decisions that will lead to the most profit. Because profits equal revenues minus costs, firms must know how much their products will sell for and how much production will cost, using the most efficient technology.

In Chapter 8, we saw how cost curves can be derived from production functions and input prices. Once a firm has a clear picture of its short-run costs, the price at which it sells its output determines the quantity of output that will maximize profit. Specifically, a profit-maximizing perfectly competitive firm will supply output up to the point that price (marginal revenue) equals marginal cost. The marginal cost curve of such a firm is thus the same as its supply curve.

In this chapter, we turn from the short run to the long run. The condition in which firms find themselves in the short run (Are they making profits? Are they incurring losses?) determines what is likely to happen in the long run. Remember that output (supply) decisions in the long run are less constrained than in the short run, for two reasons. First, in the long run, the firm can increase any or all of its inputs and thus has no fixed factor of production that confines its production to a given scale. Second, firms are free to enter industries to seek profits and to leave industries to avoid losses.

In thinking about the relationship between the short run and long run, it is useful to put yourself in the position of a manager of a firm. At times, you will be making what we term *short-run* decisions: You are stuck with a particular factory and set of machines, and your decisions involve asking how best to use those assets to produce output. At the same time, you or another manager at the firm will be doing more strategic *long-run* thinking: Should you be in this business at all, or should you close up shop? In better times, you might consider expanding the operation. In thinking about the long run, you will also have to reckon with other firms entering and exiting the industry. Managers simultaneously make short- and long-run decisions, making the best of the current constraints while planning for the future.

In making decisions or understanding industry structure, the shape of the long-run cost curve is important. As we saw in the short run, a fixed factor of production eventually causes marginal cost to increase along with output. In the long run, all factors can be varied. In the earlier sandwich shop example, in the long run, we can add floor space and grills along with more people to make the sandwiches. Under these circumstances, it is no longer inevitable that increased volume comes with higher costs. In fact, as we will see, long-run cost curves need not slope up at all. You might have wondered why there are only a few automobile and steel companies in the United States but dozens of firms producing books and furniture. Differences in the shapes of the long-run cost curves in those industries do a good job of explaining these differences in the industry structures.

We begin our discussion of the long run by looking at firms in three short-run circumstances: (1) firms that earn economic profits, (2) firms that suffer economic losses but continue to operate to reduce or minimize those losses, and (3) firms that decide to shut down and bear losses just equal to fixed costs. We then examine how these firms make their decisions in response to these short-run conditions.

Although we continue to focus on perfectly competitive firms, *all* firms are subject to the spectrum of short-run profit or loss situations regardless of *market structure*. Assuming perfect competition allows us to simplify our analysis and provides us with a strong background for understanding the discussions of imperfectly competitive behavior in later chapters.

Short-Run Conditions and Long-Run Directions

Before beginning our examination of firm behavior, let us review the concept of profit. Recall that a normal rate of return is included in the definition of total cost (Chapter 7). A *normal rate of return* is a rate that is just sufficient to keep current investors interested in the industry. Because we define *profit* as total revenue minus total cost and because total cost includes a normal rate of return, our concept of profit takes into account the opportunity cost of capital. When a firm is earning an above-normal rate of return, it has a positive profit level; otherwise, it does not. When there are positive profits in an industry, new investors are likely to be attracted to the industry.

When we say that a firm is suffering a *loss*, we mean that it is earning a rate of return that is below normal. Such a firm may be suffering a loss as an accountant would measure it; or it may be earning at a very low—that is, below normal—rate. Investors are not going to be attracted to an industry in which there are losses. A firm that is **breaking even**, or earning a zero level of profit, is one that is earning exactly a normal rate of return. New investors are not attracted, but current ones are not running away either.

breaking even The situation in which a firm is earning exactly a normal rate of return.

With these distinctions in mind, we can say that for any firm, one of three conditions holds at any given moment: (1) The firm is making positive profits, (2) the firm is suffering losses, or (3) the firm is just breaking even. Profitable firms will want to maximize their profits in the short run, while firms suffering losses will want to minimize those losses in the short run.

Maximizing Profits

The best way to understand the behavior of a firm that is currently earning profits is by way of example.

Example: The Blue Velvet Car Wash When a firm earns revenues in excess of costs (including a normal rate of return), it is earning positive profits. Let us consider as an example the Blue Velvet Car Wash. Suppose investors have put up $500,000 to construct a building and purchase all equipment required to wash cars. Let us also suppose that investors expect to earn a minimum return of 10 percent on their investment. If the money to set up the business had been borrowed from the bank instead, the car wash owners would have paid a 10 percent interest rate. In either case, total cost must include $50,000 per year (10 percent of $500,000).

The car wash is open 50 weeks per year and washes 800 cars per week. Whether or not it is open and operating, the car wash has fixed costs. Those costs include $1,000 per week to investors—that is, the $50,000 per year normal return to investors—and $1,000 per week in other fixed costs—a basic maintenance contract on the equipment, insurance, and so on.

When the car wash is operating, there are also variable costs. Workers must be paid, and materials such as soap and wax must be purchased. For 800 weekly washes, the wage bill is $1,000 per week. Materials, electricity, and so on run $600 at this capacity. If the car wash is not in operation, there are no variable costs. Table 9.1 summarizes the costs of the Blue Velvet Car Wash.

TABLE 9.1 Blue Velvet Car Wash Weekly Costs

TFC Total Fixed Cost		*TVC* Total Variable Cost (800 Washes)		*TC* Total Cost	*TR* Total Revenue ($P = \$5$)
1. Normal return to investors	\$1,000	1. Labor	\$1,000	$TC = TFC + TVC$	$TR = \$5 \times 800$
		2. Materials	600	$= \$2,000 + \$1,600$	$= \mathbf{\$4,000}$
				$= \mathbf{\$3,600}$	
2. Other fixed costs (maintenance contract, insurance, etc.)	1,000		**\$1,600**		$Profit = TR - TC$
	\$2,000				$= \mathbf{\$400}$

This car wash business is quite competitive. There are many car washes of equal quality in the area, and they offer their service at \$5. If Blue Velvet wants customers, it cannot charge a price above \$5. (Recall the perfectly elastic demand curve facing perfectly competitive firms; review Chapter 8 if necessary.) If we assume that Blue Velvet washes 800 cars each week, it takes in revenue of \$4,000 from operating (800 cars × \$5). Is this total revenue enough to make a positive profit? The answer is yes. Total revenues of \$4,000 is sufficient to cover total fixed cost of \$2,000 and total variable cost of \$1,600, leaving a positive profit of \$400 per week.

Graphic Presentation of the General Case Figure 9.1 graphs the performance of a firm (not the Blue Velvet Car Wash) that is earning a positive profit in the short run. Figure 9.1a illustrates the industry, or the market; and Figure 9.1b illustrates a representative firm. At present, the market is clearing at a price of \$5. Thus, we assume that the individual firm can sell all it wants at a price of $P^* = \$5$, but that it is constrained by its capacity. Its marginal cost curve rises in the short run because of a fixed factor. You already know that a perfectly competitive profit-maximizing firm produces up to the point where price equals marginal cost. As long as price (marginal revenue) exceeds marginal cost, firms can push up profits by increasing short-run output. The firm in the diagram, then, will supply $q^* = 300$ units of output (point A, where $P = MC$).

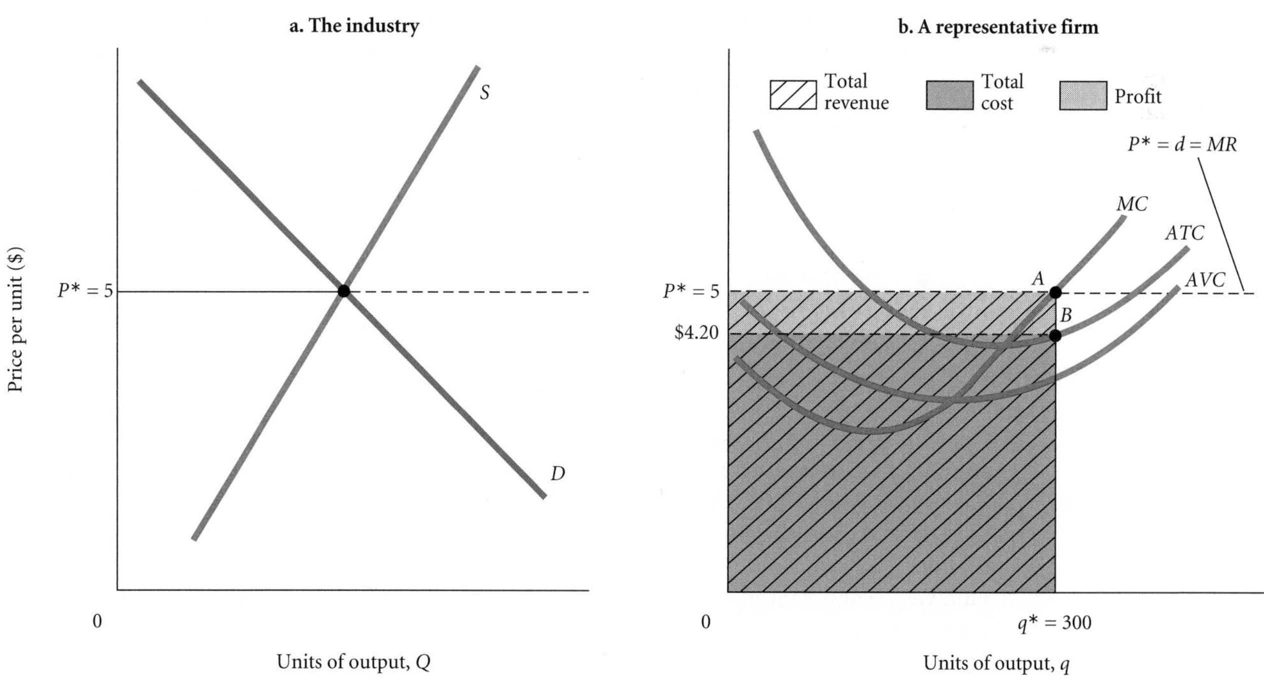

▲ **FIGURE 9.1**

Firm Earning a Positive Profit in the Short Run

A profit-maximizing perfectly competitive firm will produce up to the point where $P^* = MC$. Profit is the difference between total revenue and total cost. At $q^* = 300$, total revenue is $\$5 \times 300 = \$1,500$, total cost is $\$4.20 \times 300 = \$1,260$, and profit $= \$1,500 - \$1,260 = \$240$.

Both revenues and costs are shown graphically. *Total revenue* (TR) is simply the product of price and quantity: $P^* \times q^* = \$5 \times 300 = \$1{,}500$. On the diagram, total revenue is equal to the area of the rectangle P^*Aq^*0. (The area of a rectangle is equal to its length times its width.) At output q^*, average total cost is $4.20 (point B). Numerically, it is equal to the length of line segment q^*B. Because average total cost is derived by dividing total cost by q, we can get back to total cost by *multiplying* average total cost by q. That is,

$$ATC = \frac{TC}{q}$$

and

$$TC = ATC \times q$$

Total cost (TC), then, is $\$4.20 \times 300 = \$1{,}260$, the area shaded blue in the diagram. *Profit* is simply the difference between total revenue (TR) and total cost (TC), or $240. This is the area that is shaded gray in the diagram. This firm is earning positive profits.

A firm that is earning a positive profit in the short run and expects to continue doing so has an incentive to expand its scale of operation in the long run. Managers in these firms will likely be planning to expand even as they concentrate on efficiently producing the 300 units they are capable of in the short run. Those profits also give new firms an incentive to enter and compete in the market.

Minimizing Losses

A firm that is not earning a positive profit or breaking even is suffering a loss. Firms suffering losses fall into two categories: (1) those that find it advantageous to shut down operations immediately and bear losses equal to total fixed costs and (2) those that continue to operate in the short run to minimize their losses. The most important thing to remember here is that firms cannot exit the industry in the short run. The firm can shut down, but it cannot get rid of its fixed costs by going out of business. Fixed costs must be paid in the short run no matter what the firm does.

Whether a firm suffering losses decides to produce or not to produce in the short run depends on the advantages and disadvantages of continuing production. If a firm shuts down, it earns no revenue and has no variable costs to bear. If it continues to produce, it both earns revenue and incurs variable costs. Because a firm must bear fixed costs *whether or not* it shuts down, its decision depends *solely on whether total revenue from operating is sufficient to cover total variable cost.*

- If total revenue exceeds total variable cost, the excess revenue can be used to offset fixed costs and reduce losses, and it will pay the firm to keep operating.
- If total revenue is smaller than total variable cost, the firm that operates will suffer losses in excess of fixed costs. In this case, the firm can minimize its losses by shutting down.

Producing at a Loss to Offset Fixed Costs: The Blue Velvet Revisited

Suppose that competitive pressure pushes the price per wash down to $3. Total revenue for Blue Velvet would fall to $2,400 per week (800 cars × $3). If total variable cost remained at $1,600, total cost would be $3,600 ($1,600 + $2,000 total fixed cost), a figure higher than total revenue. The firm would then be suffering losses of $\$3{,}600 - \$2{,}400 = \$1{,}200$. In the long run, Blue Velvet may want to go out of business, but in the short run it is stuck, and it must decide what to do.

The car wash has two options: operate or shut down. If it shuts down, it has no variable costs but it also earns no revenue, and its losses will be equal to its total fixed cost of $2,000 (Table 9.2, Case 1). If it decides to stay open (Table 9.2, Case 2), revenue will be $2,400, which is more than sufficient to cover total variable cost of $1,600. By operating, the firm gains $800 per week that it can use to offset its fixed costs. By operating, the firm reduces its losses from $2,000 to $1,200.

TABLE 9.2 The Blue Velvet Car Wash Will Operate If Total Revenue Covers Total Variable Cost

Case 1: Shut Down		Case 2: Operate at Price = \$3	
Total revenue ($q = 0$)	\$ 0	Total revenue (\$3 × 800)	\$2,400
Total fixed cost	\$2,000	Total fixed cost	\$2,000
Total variable cost	+ 0	Total variable cost	+ 1,600
Total cost	\$2,000	Total cost	\$3,600
		Total revenue − total variable cost	\$ 800
Profit/loss (total revenue − total cost)	−\$2,000	Profit/loss (total revenue − total cost)	−\$1,200

Graphic Presentation of the General Case Figure 9.2 graphs a firm (not the Blue Velvet Car Wash) suffering losses. The market price, set by the forces of supply and demand, is $P^* = \$3.50$. If the firm decides to operate, it will do best by producing up to the point where price (marginal revenue) is equal to marginal cost—in this case, at an output of $q^* = 225$ units.

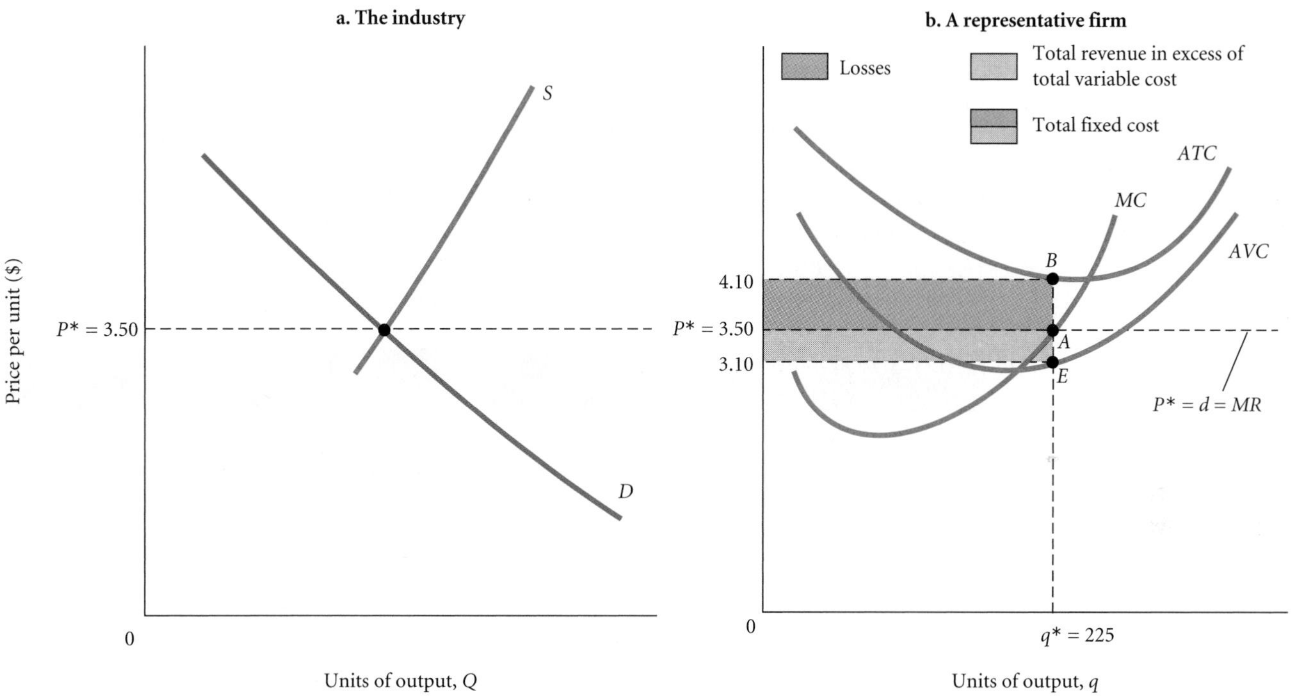

▲ **FIGURE 9.2 A Firm Suffering Losses but Showing Total Revenue in Excess of Total Variable Cost in the Short Run**

When price is sufficient to cover average variable cost, a firm suffering short-run losses will continue operating instead of shutting down. Total revenue ($P^* \times q^*$) covers total variable cost, leaving \$90 to cover part of fixed costs and reduce losses to \$135.

Once again, total revenue (*TR*) is simply the product of price and quantity ($P^* \times q^*$) = \$3.50 × 225 = \$787.50, or the area of rectangle $P^* Aq^*0$. Average total cost at $q^* = 225$ is \$4.10, and it is equal to the length of q^*B. Total cost is the product of average total cost and q^* ($ATC \times q^*$), or \$4.10 × 225 = \$922.50. Because total cost is greater than total revenue, the firm is suffering losses of \$135, shown on the graph by the pink-shaded rectangle.

The difference between total revenue and total *variable* cost can also be identified. On the graph, total revenue (as we said) is \$787.50. *Average* variable cost at q^* is the length of q^*E. Total variable cost is the product of average variable cost and q^* and is therefore equal to \$3.10 × 225 = \$697.50. The excess of total revenue over total variable cost is thus \$787.50 − \$697.50 = \$90, the area of the gray-shaded rectangle.

Remember that average total cost is equal to average fixed cost plus average variable cost. This means that at every level of output, average fixed cost is the difference between average total and average variable cost:

$$ATC = AFC + AVC$$

or

$$AFC = ATC - AVC = \$4.10 - \$3.10 = \$1.00$$

In Figure 9.2, therefore, average fixed cost is equal to the length of *BE* (the difference between *ATC* and *AVC* at q^*, or \$1). Because total fixed cost is average fixed cost of \$1 times $q^* = \$225$, total fixed cost is equal to \$225, the entire red- and gray-shaded rectangle. Thus, if the firm had shut down, its losses would be equal to \$225. By operating, the firm earns an amount equal to the gray-shaded area (\$90) covering some fixed costs and reducing losses to the red-shaded area (\$135).

If we think only in averages, it seems logical that a firm in this position will continue to operate. As long as price (which is equal to average revenue per unit) is sufficient to cover average variable cost, the firm stands to gain by operating instead of shutting down.

Shutting Down to Minimize Loss When total revenue is insufficient to cover total variable cost, a firm suffering losses finds it advantageous to shut down, even in the short run.

Suppose, for example, that competition and the availability of sophisticated new machinery pushed the price of a car wash all the way down to \$1.50. Washing 800 cars per week would yield revenue of only \$1,200 (Table 9.3). With total variable cost at \$1,600, operating would mean losing an additional \$400 *over and above* total fixed cost of \$2,000. This means that losses would amount to \$2,400. A profit-maximizing/loss-minimizing car wash would reduce its losses from \$2,400 to \$2,000 by shutting down, even in the short run.

TABLE 9.3 The Blue Velvet Car Wash Will Shut Down If Total Revenue Is Less Than Total Variable Cost

Case 1: Shut Down		Case 2: Operate at Price = \$1.50	
Total revenue ($q = 0$)	\$ 0	Total revenue (\$1.50 × 800)	\$ 1,200
Total fixed cost	\$2,000		
Total variable cost	+ 0	Total fixed cost	\$ 2,000
Total cost	\$2,000	Total variable cost	+ 1,600
		Total cost	\$ 3,600
		Total revenue − total variable cost	−\$ 400
Profit/loss (total revenue − total cost):	−\$2,000	Profit/loss (total revenue − total cost)	−\$ 2,400

Any time that price (average revenue) is below the minimum point on the average variable cost curve, total revenue will be less than total variable cost and there will be a loss on operation. In other words, when price is below all points on the average variable cost curve, the firm will suffer losses at any possible output level the firm could choose. When this is the case, the firm will stop producing and bear losses equal to total fixed cost. This is why the bottom of the average variable cost curve is called the **shut-down point**. At all prices above this point, the marginal cost curve shows the profit-maximizing level of output. At all prices below this point, optimal short-run output is zero.

shut-down point The lowest point on the average variable cost curve. When price falls below the minimum point on *AVC*, total revenue is insufficient to cover variable costs and the firm will shut down and bear losses equal to fixed costs.

We can now refine our earlier statement that a perfectly competitive firm's marginal cost curve is actually its short-run supply curve. Recall that a profit-maximizing perfectly competitive firm will produce up to the point at which $P = MC$. As we have just seen, though, a firm will shut down when *P* is less than the minimum point on the *AVC* curve. Also recall that the marginal cost curve intersects the *AVC* curve at *AVC*'s lowest point. It therefore follows that the short-run supply curve of a competitive firm is that portion of its marginal cost curve that lies above its average variable cost curve as illustrated in Figure 9.3.

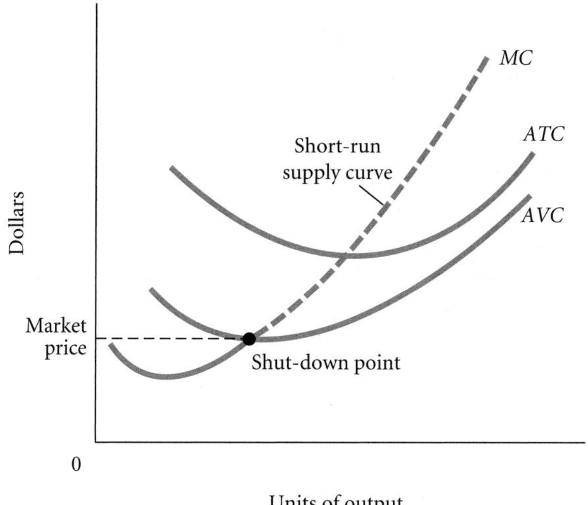

◀ FIGURE 9.3 Short-Run Supply Curve of a Perfectly Competitive Firm

At prices below average variable cost, it pays a firm to shut down rather than continue operating. Thus, the short-run supply curve of a competitive firm is the part of its marginal cost curve that lies *above* its average variable cost curve.

The Short-Run Industry Supply Curve

Supply in a competitive industry is the sum of the quantity supplied by the individual firms in the industry at each price level. The **short-run industry supply curve** is the sum of the individual firm supply curves—that is, the marginal cost curves (above *AVC*) of all the firms in the industry. Because quantities are being added—that is, because we are finding the total quantity supplied in the industry at each price level—the curves are added horizontally.

short-run industry supply curve The sum of the marginal cost curves (above *AVC*) of all the firms in an industry.

Figure 9.4 shows the supply curve for an industry with three identical firms.[1] At a price of $6, each firm produces 150 units, which is the output where $P = MC$. The total amount supplied on the market at a price of $6 is thus 450. At a price of $5, each firm produces 120 units, for an industry supply of 360.

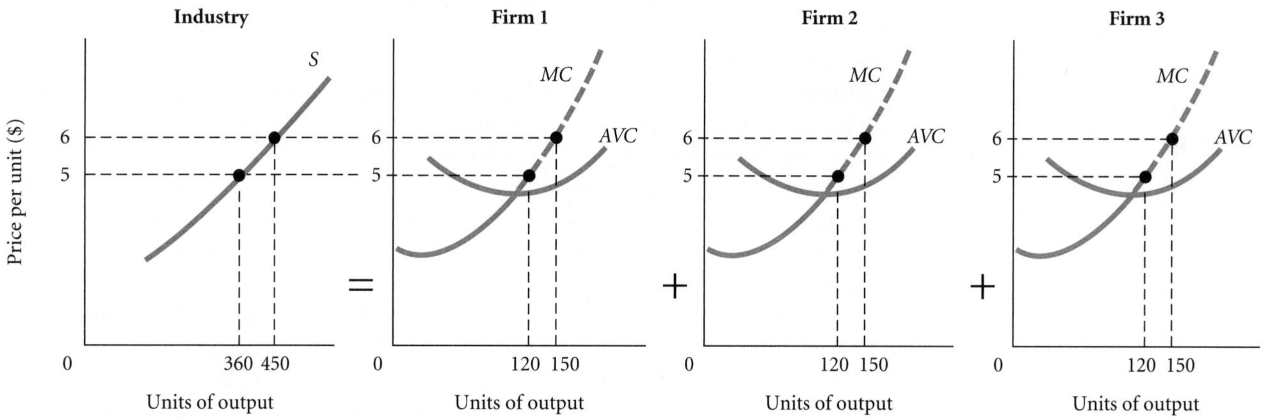

▲ FIGURE 9.4 The Industry Supply Curve in the Short Run Is the Horizontal Sum of the Marginal Cost Curves (above *AVC*) of All the Firms in an Industry

If there are only three firms in the industry, the industry supply curve is simply the sum of all the products supplied by the three firms at each price. For example, at $6 each firm supplies 150 units, for a total industry supply of 450.

Two things can cause the industry supply curve to shift. In the short run, the industry supply curve shifts if something—a decrease in the price of some input, for instance—shifts the marginal cost curves of all the individual firms simultaneously. For example, when the cost of producing

[1] Perfectly competitive industries are assumed to have many firms. Many is, of course, more than three. We use three firms here simply for purposes of illustration. The assumption that all firms are identical is often made when discussing a perfectly competitive industry.

components of home computers decreased, the marginal cost curves of all computer manufacturers shifted downward. Such a shift amounted to the same thing as an outward shift in their supply curves. Each firm was willing to supply more computers at each price level because computers were now cheaper to produce.

In the long run, an increase or decrease in the number of firms—and, therefore, in the number of individual firm supply curves—shifts the total industry supply curve. If new firms enter the industry, the industry supply curve moves to the right; if firms exit the industry, the industry supply curve moves to the left.

We return to shifts in industry supply curves and discuss them further when we take up long-run adjustments later in this chapter.

Long-Run Directions: A Review

Table 9.4 summarizes the different circumstances that perfectly competitive firms may face as they plan for the long run. Profit-making firms will produce up to the point where price and marginal cost are equal in the short run. If there are positive profits, in the long run, there is an incentive for firms to expand their scales of plant and for new firms to enter the industry.

TABLE 9.4 Profits, Losses, and Perfectly Competitive Firm Decisions in the Long and Short Run

	Short-Run Condition	Short-Run Decision	Long-Run Decision
Profits	$TR > TC$	$P = MC$: operate	Expand: new firms enter
Losses	1. $TR \geq TVC$	$P = MC$: operate (loss < total fixed cost)	Contract: firms exit
	2. $TR < TVC$	Shut down: loss = total fixed cost	Contract: firms exit

A firm suffering losses will produce if and only if revenue is sufficient to cover total variable cost. Such firms, like profitable firms, will also produce up to the point where $P = MC$. If a firm suffering losses cannot cover total variable cost by operating, it will shut down and bear losses equal to total fixed cost. Whether a firm that is suffering losses decides to shut down in the short run, it has an incentive to contract in the long run. The simple fact is that when firms are suffering losses, they generally exit the industry in the long run.

In the short run, a firm's decision about how much to produce depends on the market price of its product and the shapes of its cost curves. Remember that the short-run cost curves show costs that are determined by the *current* scale of plant. In the long run, however, firms have to choose among many *potential* scales of plant.

The long-run decisions of individual firms depend on what their costs are likely to be at different scales of operation. Just as firms have to analyze different technologies to arrive at a cost structure in the short run, they must also compare their costs at different scales of plant to arrive at long-run costs. Perhaps a larger scale of operations will reduce average production costs and provide an even greater incentive for a profit-making firm to expand, or perhaps large firms will run into problems that constrain growth. The analysis of long-run possibilities is even more complex than the short-run analysis because more things are variable—scale of plant is not fixed, for example, and there are no fixed costs because firms can exit their industry in the long run. In theory, firms may choose *any* scale of operation; so they must analyze many possible options.

Now let us turn to an analysis of cost curves in the long run.

Long-Run Costs: Economies and Diseconomies of Scale

The shapes of short-run cost curves follow directly from the assumption of a fixed factor of production. As output increases beyond a certain point, the fixed factor (which we usually think of as fixed scale of plant) causes diminishing returns to other factors and thus increasing marginal costs. In the long run, however, there is no fixed factor of production. Firms can choose any scale of production. They can double or triple output or go out of business completely.

The shape of a firm's *long-run* average cost curve depends on how costs vary with scale of operations. In some firms, production technology is such that increased scale, or size, reduces costs. For others, increased scale leads to higher per-unit costs. When an increase in a firm's scale of production leads to lower average costs, we say that there are **increasing returns to scale**, or **economies of scale.** When average costs do not change with the scale of production, we say that there are **constant returns to scale.** Finally, when an increase in a firm's scale of production leads to higher average costs, we say that there are **decreasing returns to scale,** or **diseconomies of scale** . Because these economies of scale are a property of production characteristics of the individual firm, they are considered *internal* economies of scale. In the Appendix to this chapter, we talk about *external* economies of scale, which describe economies or diseconomies of scale on an industry-wide basis.

increasing returns to scale, *or* economies of scale An increase in a firm's scale of production leads to lower costs per unit produced.

constant returns to scale An increase in a firm's scale of production has no effect on costs per unit produced.

decreasing returns to scale, *or* diseconomies of scale An increase in a firm's scale of production leads to higher costs per unit produced.

Increasing Returns to Scale

Technically, the phrase *increasing returns to scale* refers to the relationship between inputs and outputs. When we say that a production function exhibits increasing returns, we mean that a given percentage of increase in inputs leads to a *larger* percentage of increase in the production of output. For example, if a firm doubled or tripled inputs, it would more than double or triple output.

When firms can count on fixed input prices—that is, when the prices of inputs do not change with output levels—increasing returns to scale also means that as output rises, average cost of production falls. The term *economies of scale* refers directly to this reduction in cost per unit of output that follows from larger-scale production.

The Sources of Economies of Scale Most of the economies of scale that immediately come to mind are technological in nature. Automobile production, for example, would be more costly per unit if a firm were to produce 100 cars per year by hand. In the early 1900s, Henry Ford introduced standardized production techniques that increased output volume, reduced costs per car, and made the automobile available to almost everyone. The new technology is not very cost-effective at small volumes of cars, but at larger volumes costs are greatly reduced. Ford's innovation provided a source of scale economics at the plant level of the auto firm.

Some economies of scale result not from technology but from firm-level efficiencies and bargaining power that can come with size. Very large companies, for instance, can buy inputs in volume at discounted prices. Large firms may also produce some of their own inputs at considerable savings, and they can certainly save in transport costs when they ship items in bulk. Wal-Mart has become the largest retailer in the United States in part because of scale economies of this type. Economics of scale have come from advantages of larger *firm* size rather than gains from plant size.

Economies of scale can be seen all around us. A bus that carries 50 people between Vancouver and Seattle uses less labor, capital, and gasoline than 50 people driving 50 different automobiles. The cost per passenger (average cost) is lower on the bus. Roommates who share an apartment are taking advantage of economies of scale. Costs per person for heat, electricity, and space are lower when an apartment is shared than if each person rents a separate apartment.

Example: Economies of Scale in Egg Production Nowhere are economies of scale more visible than in agriculture. Consider the following example. A few years ago a major agribusiness moved to a small Ohio town and set up a huge egg-producing operation. The new firm, Chicken Little Egg Farms Inc., is completely mechanized. Complex machines feed the chickens and collect and box the eggs. Large refrigerated trucks transport the eggs all over the state daily. In the same town, some small farmers still own fewer than 200 chickens. These farmers collect the eggs, feed the chickens, clean the coops by hand, and deliver the eggs to county markets.

Table 9.5 presents some hypothetical cost data for Homer Jones's small operation and for Chicken Little Inc. Jones has his operation working well. He has several hundred chickens and spends about 15 hours per week feeding, collecting, delivering, and so on. During the rest of his time, he raises soybeans. We can value Jones's time at $8 per hour because that is the wage he could earn working at a local manufacturing plant. When we add up all Jones's costs, including a rough estimate of the land and capital costs attributable to egg production, we arrive at $177 per week. Total production on the Jones farm runs about 200 dozen, or 2,400, eggs per week, which means that Jones's average cost comes out to $0.074 per egg.

TABLE 9.5 Weekly Costs Showing Economies of Scale in Egg Production

Jones Farm	Total Weekly Costs
15 hours of labor (implicit value $8 per hour)	$120
Feed, other variable costs	25
Transport costs	15
Land and capital costs attributable to egg production	17
	$177
Total output	2,400 eggs
Average cost	$0.074 per egg
Chicken Little Egg Farms Inc.	**Total Weekly Costs**
Labor	$ 5,128
Feed, other variable costs	4,115
Transport costs	2,431
Land and capital costs	19,230
	$30,904
Total output	1,600,000 eggs
Average cost	$0.019 per egg

The costs of Chicken Little Inc. are much higher in total; weekly costs run over $30,000. A much higher percentage of costs are capital costs—the firm uses a great many pieces of sophisticated machinery that cost millions to put in place. Total output is 1.6 million eggs per week, and the product is shipped all over the Midwest. The comparatively huge scale of plant has driven average production costs all the way down to $0.019 per egg.

Although these numbers are hypothetical, you can see why small farmers in the United States are finding it difficult to compete with large-scale agribusiness concerns that can realize significant economies of scale.

Many large firms have multiple plants or sites where they produce their goods and services. In our discussion in this chapter, we will distinguish between cost changes that come about because a firm decides to build a large versus a small plant and cost changes that result from firms adding volume to their production by building more plants. Coors originally produced its beer in Colorado in what was, at the time, one of the largest U.S. brewing plants; the firm believed that large size at the plant level brought cost savings. Most electronics companies, on the other hand, produce their output in multiple moderate-sized plants and hope to achieve cost savings through firm size. We will be looking at both sources of scale economies.

long-run average cost curve (*LRAC*) The 'envelope' of a series of short-run cost curves.

Graphic Presentation A firm's **long-run average cost curve (*LRAC*)** shows the different scales on which it can choose to operate in the long run. When the firm experiences economies of scale, its *LRAC* will decline with output. A given point on the *LRAC* tells us the average cost of producing the associated level of output. At that point, the existing scale of plant determines the position and shape of the firm's short-run cost curves. The long-run average cost curve shows the positions of the different sets of short-run curves among which the firm must choose. In making the long-run strategic choice of plant scale, the firm then confronts an associated set of short-run cost curves. The long-run average cost curve is the "envelope" of a series of short-run curves; it "wraps around" the set of all possible short-run curves like an envelope.

minimum efficient scale (MES) The smallest size at which the long-run average cost curve is at its minimum.

Figure 9.5 shows short-run and long-run average cost curves for a firm that realizes economies of scale up to about 100,000 units of production and roughly constant returns to scale after that. The 100,000 unit output level in Figure 9.5 is sometimes called the **minimum efficient scale (MES)** of the firm. The MES is the smallest size at which the long-run average

ECONOMICS IN PRACTICE

Economies of Scale in Blood Banks

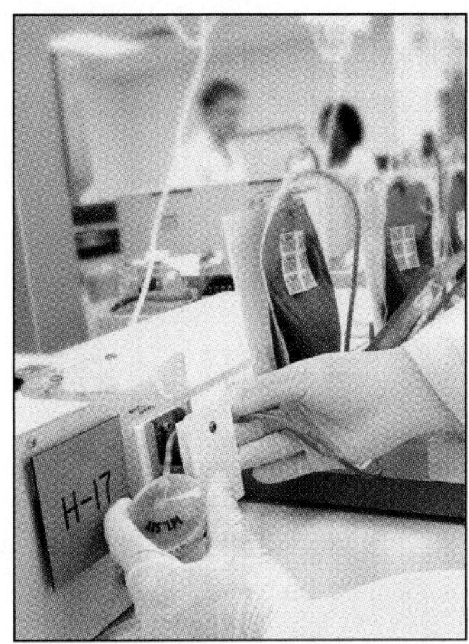

In the text we have described the way in which firms may exhibit economies of scale, so that their average total costs decline with size. Scale economies occur across a wide range of types of organizations. The article below describes a recent merger between two blood banks in Florida and argues that the merger was motivated by a push for scale economies. It is interesting to note that the source of new scale economics in blood banks is the increased government regulations requiring more testing of blood. As regulations grow more complex and testing is done with more capital, size might well be important to cost reductions.

You might also note that in this market, analysts expect the benefits of lower costs to be passed on to hospitals in the form of lower prices.

Blood bank merger 'good' for Manatee

BradentonHerald.com

Two of the Florida's oldest blood banks merged Tuesday, creating a regional network that could help Manatee County in times of emergency, according to a Florida Blood Services spokesman.

Manatee County is served by St. Petersburg-based Florida Blood Services, which has merged with Northwest Florida Blood Center, which has centers in Fort Walton, Panama City and Pensacola.

"Northwest needed to be aligned with a larger organization to achieve economy of scale," said J.B. Gaskins, Florida Blood Services vice president. "That economy of scale is good for the whole network, including Manatee County."

Roy Bertke, chairman of the Florida Blood Services board of directors, said the merger will bring depth to the organization. "The growth of the market, coupled with the more complex testing and regulations from the government, has required all blood banks to operate on a much more sophisticated level with very thin margins," he said.

Those economies of scale will result in more competitive pricing to health care providers, Bertke said.

By DONNA WRIGHT, dwright@bradenton.com

cost curve is at its minimum. Essentially, it is the answer to the question, how large does a firm have to be to have the best per-unit cost position possible? Consider a firm operating in an industry in which all of the firms in that industry face the long-run average cost curve shown in Figure 9.5. If you want your firm to be cost-competitive in that market, you need to produce at least 100,000 units. At smaller volumes, you will have higher costs than other firms in the industry, which makes it hard for you to stay in the industry. Policy makers are often interested in learning how large MES is relative to the total market for a product, since when MES is large relative to the total market size, we typically expect fewer firms to be in the industry. We will discuss this at more length later.

Figure 9.5 shows three potential scales of operation, each with its own set of short-run cost curves. Each point on the *LRAC* curve represents the minimum cost at which the associated output level can be produced. Once the firm chooses a scale on which to produce, it becomes locked into one set of cost curves in the short run. If the firm were to settle on scale 1, it would not realize the major cost advantages of producing on a larger scale. By roughly doubling its scale of operations from 50,000 to 100,000 units (scale 2), the firm reduces average costs per unit significantly.

Figure 9.5 shows that at every moment, firms face two different cost constraints. In the long run, firms can change their scale of operation; and costs may be different as a result. However, at any *given* moment, a particular scale of operation exists, constraining the firm's capacity to produce in the short run. That is why we see both short- and long-run curves in the same diagram.

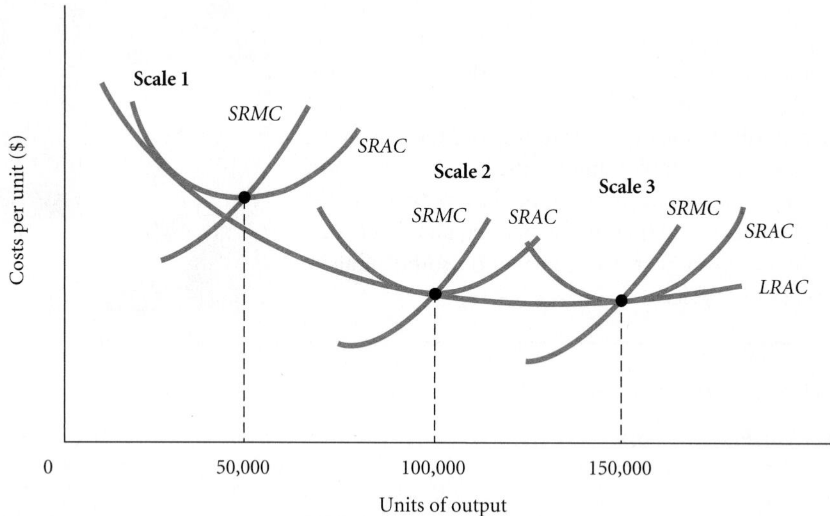

FIGURE 9.5
A Firm Exhibiting Economies of Scale
The long-run average cost curve of a firm shows the different scales on which the firm can choose to operate in the long run. Each scale of operation defines a different short run. Here we see a firm exhibiting economies of scale; moving from scale 1 to scale 3 reduces average cost.

Constant Returns to Scale

Technically, the term *constant returns* means that the quantitative relationship between input and output stays constant, or the same, when output is increased. If a firm doubles inputs, it doubles output; if it triples inputs, it triples output; and so on. Furthermore, if input prices are fixed, constant returns imply that average cost of production does not change with scale. In other words, constant returns to scale mean that the firm's long-run average cost curve remains flat.

The firm in Figure 9.5 exhibits roughly constant returns to scale between scale 2 and scale 3. The average cost of production is about the same in each. If the firm exhibited constant returns at levels above 150,000 units of output, the *LRAC* would continue as a flat, straight line.

Economists have studied cost data extensively over the years to estimate the extent to which economies of scale exist. Evidence suggests that in most industries, firms do not have to be gigantic to realize cost savings from scale economies. In other words, the mes is moderate relative to market size. Perhaps the best example of efficient production on a small scale is the manufacturing sector in Taiwan. Taiwan has enjoyed very rapid growth based on manufacturing firms that employ fewer than 100 workers.

One simple argument supports the empirical result that most industries seem to exhibit constant returns to scale (a flat *LRAC*) after some level of output at least at the level of the plant. Competition always pushes firms to adopt the least-cost technology and scale. If cost advantages result with larger-scale operations, the firms that shift to that scale will drive the smaller, less efficient firms out of business. A firm that wants to grow when it has reached its "optimal" size can do so by building another identical plant. It thus seems logical to conclude that most firms face constant returns to scale at the plant level *as long as* they can replicate their existing plants.

Decreasing Returns to Scale

When average cost increases with scale of production, a firm faces *decreasing returns to scale*, or *diseconomies of scale*. The most often cited example of a diseconomy of scale is bureaucratic inefficiency. As size increases beyond a certain point, operations tend to become more difficult to manage. Large size often entails increased bureaucracy, affecting both managerial incentives and control. The coordination function is more complex for larger firms than for smaller ones, and the chances that it will break down are greater. You can see that this diseconomy of scale is firm-level in type.

A large firm is also more likely than a small firm to find itself facing problems with organized labor. Unions can demand higher wages and more benefits, go on strike, force firms to incur legal expenses, and take other actions that increase production costs. (This does not mean that unions are "bad," but instead that their activities often increase costs.)

Figure 9.6 describes a firm that exhibits both economies of scale and diseconomies of scale. Average costs decrease with scale of plant up to q^* and increase with scale after that. This long-run average cost curve looks very much like the short-run average cost curves we have examined in the last two chapters, but do not confuse the two.

All short-run average cost curves are U-shaped because we assume a fixed scale of plant that constrains production and drives marginal cost upward as a result of diminishing returns. In the long run, we make no such assumption; instead, we assume that scale of plant can be changed.

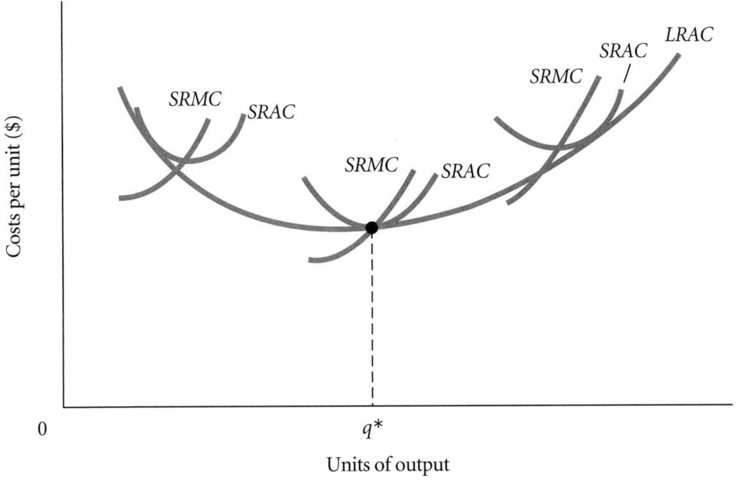

FIGURE 9.6

A Firm Exhibiting Economies and Diseconomies of Scale

Economies of scale push this firm's average costs down to q^*. Beyond q^*, the firm experiences diseconomies of scale; q^* is the level of production at lowest average cost, using optimal scale.

Thus, the same firm can face diminishing returns—a short-run concept—and still have a long-run cost curve that exhibits economies of scale.

The shape of a firm's long-run average cost curve depends on how costs react to changes in scale. Some firms do see economies of scale, and their long-run average cost curves slope downward. Most firms seem to have flat long-run average cost curves. Still others encounter diseconomies, and their long-run average cost curves slope upward.

It is important to note that economic efficiency requires taking advantage of economies of scale (if they exist) and avoiding diseconomies of scale. The **optimal scale of plant** is the scale of plant that minimizes average cost. In fact, as we will see next, competition forces firms to use the optimal scale.

optimal scale of plant The scale of plant that minimizes average cost.

Long-Run Adjustments to Short-Run Conditions

We began this chapter by discussing the different short-run positions in which firms may find themselves. Firms can be operating at a profit or suffering economic losses; they can be shut down or producing. The industry is not in long-run equilibrium if firms have an incentive to enter or exit in the long run. Thus, when firms are earning economic profits (profits above normal, or positive) or are suffering economic losses (profits below normal, or negative), the industry is not at an equilibrium and firms will change their behavior. What firms are likely to do depends in part on costs in the long run. This is why we have spent a good deal of time discussing economies and diseconomies of scale.

ECONOMICS IN PRACTICE

The Long-Run Average Cost Curve: Flat or U-Shaped?

The long-run average cost curve has been a source of controversy in economics for many years. A long-run average cost curve was first drawn as the "envelope" of a series of short-run curves in a classic article written by Jacob Viner in 1931.[a] In preparing that article, Viner gave his draftsman the task of drawing the long-run curve through the minimum points of all the short-run average cost curves.

In a supplementary note written in 1950, Viner commented:

> ... the error in Chart IV is left uncorrected so that future teachers and students may share the pleasure of many of their predecessors of pointing out that if I had known what an envelope was, I would not have given my excellent draftsman the technically impossible and economically inappropriate task of drawing an *AC* curve which would pass through the lowest cost points of all the *AC* curves yet not rise above any *AC* curve at any point....[b]

While this story is an interesting part of the lore of economics, a more recent debate concentrates on the economic content of this controversy. In 1986, Professor Herbert Simon of Carnegie-Mellon University stated bluntly in an interview for *Challenge* magazine that most textbooks are wrong to use the U-shaped long-run cost curve to predict the size of firms. Simon explained that studies show the firm's cost curves are not U-shaped but instead slope down to the right and then level off.[c]

Professor Simon makes an important point. Suppose that we were to redraw Figure 9.7(b) with a flat long-run average cost curve. Figure 1 shows a firm earning short-run profits using scale 1, but there are no economies of scale to be realized.

Despite the lack of economies of scale, expansion of such an industry would likely take place in much the same way as we have described. First, existing firms have an incentive to expand because they are making profits. At current prices, a firm that doubles its scale would earn twice the profits even if average cost did not fall with expansion. Of course, as long as profits persist, new firms have an incentive to enter the industry. Both events will shift the short-run industry supply curve to the right, from S_0 to S_1 and price will fall, from P_0 to P_1. Expansion and entry will stop only when price has fallen to *LRAC*. Only then will profits be eliminated. At equilibrium:

$$P = SRMC = SRAC = LRAC$$

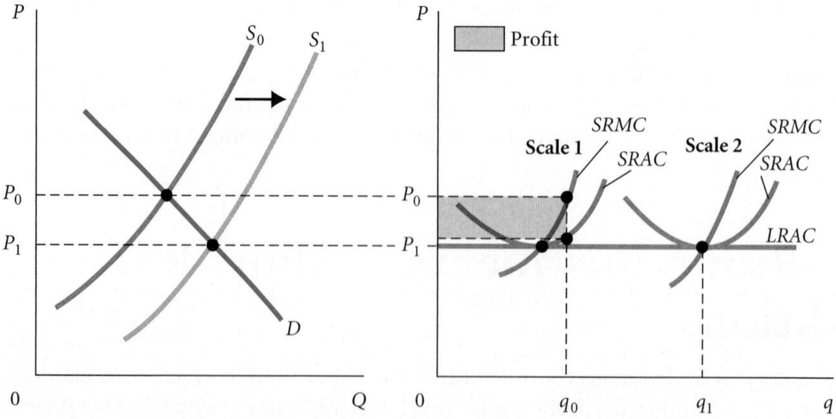

▲ **Long-Run Expansion in an Industry with Constant Returns to Scale**

This model does not predict the final firm size or the structure of the industry. When the long-run *AC* curve is U-shaped, firms stop expanding at the minimum point on *LRAC* because further expansion means higher costs. Thus, optimal firm size is determined technologically. If the *LRAC* curve is flat, however, small firms and large firms have identical average costs.

If this is true, and it seems to be in many industries, the structure of the industry in the long run will depend on whether existing firms expand faster than new firms enter. If new firms enter quickly in response to profit opportunities, the industry will end up with large numbers of small firms, but if existing firms expand more rapidly than new firms enter, the industry may end up with only a few very large firms. There is thus an element of randomness in the way industries expand. In fact, most industries contain some large firms and some small firms, which is exactly what Simon's flat *LRAC* model predicts.

Sources: [a]*Jacob Viner, "Cost Curves and Supply Curves,"* Zeitschrift fur Nationalokonomie, *Vol. 3 (1–1931), 23–46;* [b]*George J. Stigler and Kenneth E. Boulding, eds.,* AEA Readings in Price Theory, *Vol. 6 (Chicago: Richard D. Irwin, 1952), p. 227;* [c]*Based on interview with Herbert A. Simon, "The Failure of Armchair Economics,"* Challenge, *November–December, 1986, 23–24.*

We can now put these two ideas together and discuss the actual long-run adjustments that are likely to take place in response to short-run profits and losses.

Short-Run Profits: Expansion to Equilibrium

We begin our analysis of long-run adjustments with a perfectly competitive industry in which firms are earning positive profits. We assume that all firms in the industry are producing with the same technology of production and that each firm has a long-run average cost curve that is U-shaped. A U-shaped long-run average cost curve implies that there are some economies of scale to be realized in the industry and that all firms ultimately begin to run into diseconomies at some scale of operation.

Figure 9.7 shows a representative perfectly competitive firm initially producing at scale 1. Market price is $P_0 = \$12$, and individual firms are enjoying economic profits. Total revenue at our representative firm, which is producing 1,000 units of output per period, exceeds total cost. Our firm's profit per period is equal to the gray-shaded rectangle. (Make sure you understand why the gray rectangle represents profits. Remember that perfectly competitive firms maximize profit by producing at $P = MC$—in Figure 9.7, at point *A*.)

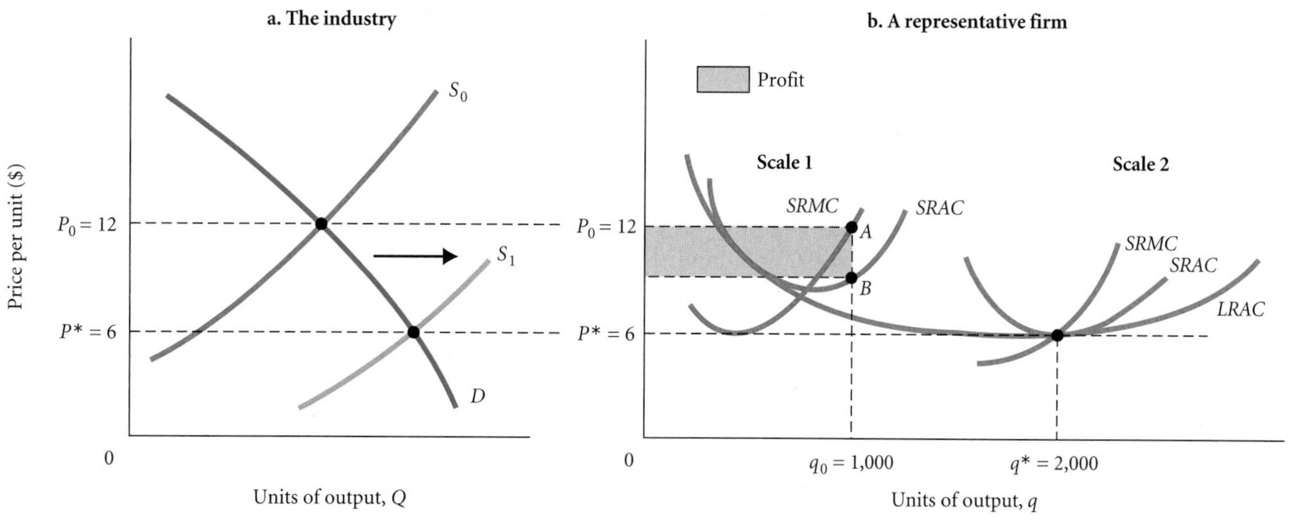

▲ FIGURE 9.7

Firms Expand in the Long Run When Increasing Returns to Scale Are Available

When economies of scale can be realized, firms have an incentive to expand. Thus, firms will be pushed by competition to produce at their optimal scales. Price will be driven to the minimum point on the *LRAC* curve.

At this point, our representative firm has not realized all the economies of scale available to it. By expanding to scale 2, it will reduce average costs significantly and it will increase profits unless price drops. As long as firms are enjoying profits and economies of scale exist, firms will expand as they seek to lower their long-run costs and increase their profits. Thus, the firm in Figure 9.7 shifts to scale 2.

At the same time, the existence of positive profits will attract new entrants to the industry. Both the entrance of new firms and the expansion of existing firms have the same effect on the short-run industry supply curve (Figure 9.7a). Both cause the short-run supply curve to shift to the right, from S_0 to S_1. Because the short-run industry supply curve is the sum of all the marginal cost curves (above the minimum point of *AVC*) of all the firms in the industry, it will shift to the right for two reasons. First, because all firms in the industry are expanding to a larger scale, their individual short-run marginal cost curves shift to the right. Second, with new firms entering the industry, there are more firms and thus more marginal cost curves to add up.

As capital flows into the industry, the supply curve in Figure 9.7a shifts to the right and price falls. The question is where the process will stop. In general, firms will continue to expand as long as there are economies of scale to be realized and new firms will continue to enter as long as positive profits are being earned.

In Figure 9.7a, final equilibrium is achieved only when price falls to $P^* = \$6$ and firms have exhausted all the economies of scale available in the industry. At $P^* = \$6$, no economic profits are being earned and none can be earned by changing the level of output.

Look carefully at the final equilibrium in Figure 9.7. Each firm will choose the scale of plant that produces its product at minimum long-run average cost. Competition drives firms to adopt not just the most efficient technology in the *short* run but also the most efficient scale of operation in the *long* run. In the long run, equilibrium price (P^*) is equal to long-run average cost, short-run marginal cost, and short-run average cost. Profits are driven to zero:

$$P^* = SRMC = SRAC = LRAC$$

where *SRMC* denotes short-run marginal cost, *SRAC* denotes short-run average cost, and *LRAC* denotes long-run average cost. No other price is an equilibrium price. Any price above P^* means that there are profits to be made in the industry and new firms will continue to enter. Any price below P^* means that firms are suffering losses and firms will exit the industry. Only at P^* will economic profits be just equal to zero, and only at P^* will the industry be in equilibrium.

Short-Run Losses: Contraction to Equilibrium

Firms that suffer short-run losses have an incentive to leave the industry in the long run but cannot do so in the short run. As we have seen, some firms incurring losses will choose to shut down and bear losses equal to fixed costs. Others will continue to produce in the short run in an effort to minimize their losses.

Figure 9.8 depicts a firm that will continue to produce $q_0 = 1{,}000$ units of output in the short run, despite its losses. (We are assuming here that the firm has losses that are smaller than the firm's total fixed cost.) With losses, the long-run picture will change. Firms have an incentive to get out of the industry. As they exit, the industry's short-run supply curve shifts to the left. As it shifts, the equilibrium price rises from \$5 to \$6.

Once again the question is how long this adjustment process will continue. In general, as long as losses are being sustained in an industry, firms will shut down and leave the industry, thus reducing supply—shifting the supply curve to the left. As this happens, price rises. This gradual price rise reduces losses for firms remaining in the industry until those losses are ultimately eliminated.

In Figure 9.8, equilibrium occurs when price rises to $P^* = \$9$. At that point, remaining firms will maximize profits by producing $q^* = 1{,}160$ units of output. Price is just sufficient to cover average costs, and economic profits and losses are zero.

Whether we begin with an industry in which firms are earning profits or suffering losses, the final long-run competitive equilibrium condition is the same:

$$P^* = SRMC = SRAC = LRAC$$

and profits are zero. At this point, individual firms are operating at the most efficient scale of plant—that is, at the minimum point on their *LRAC* curve.

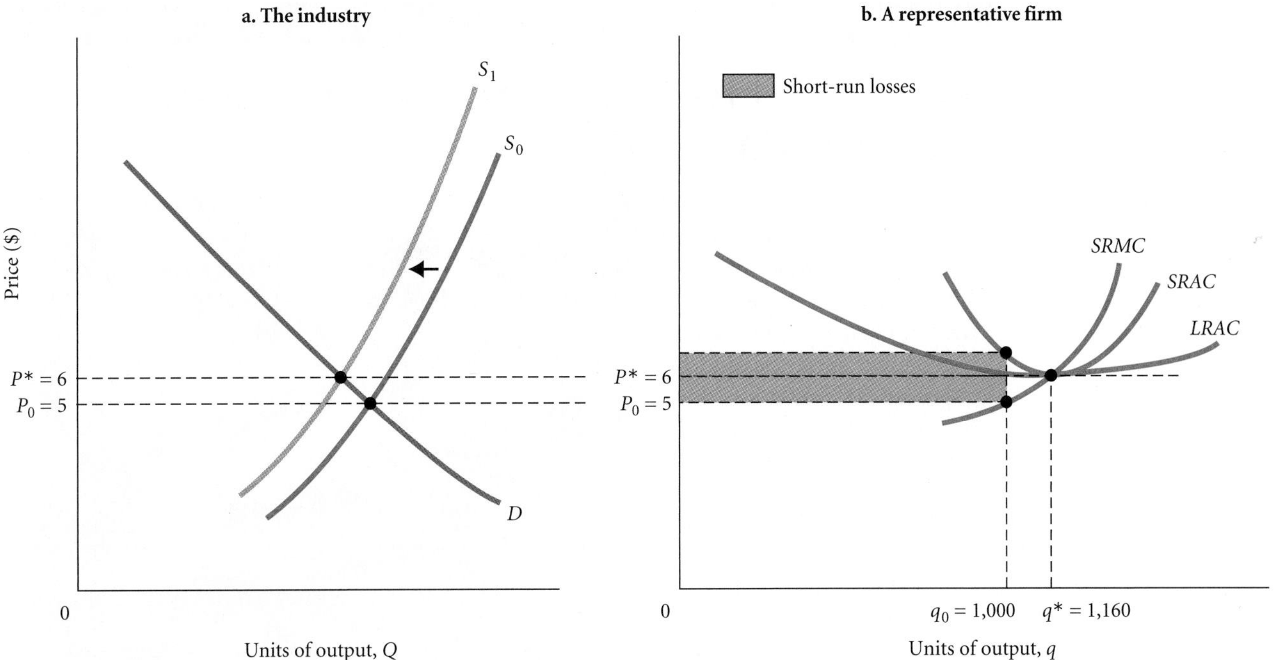

▲ FIGURE 9.8

Long-Run Contraction and Exit in an Industry Suffering Short-Run Losses

When firms in an industry suffer losses, there is an incentive for them to exit. As firms exit, the supply curve shifts from S_0 to S_1, driving price up to P^*. As price rises, losses are eliminated gradually.

The Long-Run Adjustment Mechanism: Investment Flows Toward Profit Opportunities

The central idea in our discussion of entry, exit, expansion, and contraction is this: In efficient markets, investment capital flows toward profit opportunities. The actual process is complex and varies from industry to industry.

We talked about efficient markets in Chapter 1. In efficient markets, profit opportunities are quickly eliminated as they develop. To illustrate this point, we described driving up to a toll booth and suggested that shorter-than-average lines are quickly eliminated as cars shift into those lines. Profits in competitive industries also are eliminated as new competing firms move into open slots, or perceived opportunities, in the industry.

In practice, the entry and exit of firms in response to profit opportunities usually involve the financial capital market. In capital markets, people are constantly looking for profits. When firms in an industry do well, capital is likely to flow into that industry in a variety of forms. Entrepreneurs start new firms, and firms producing entirely different products may join the competition to break into new markets. It happens all around us. The tremendous success of premium ice cream makers Ben and Jerry's and Häagen-Dazs spawned dozens of competitors. In one Massachusetts town of 35,000, a small ice cream store opened to rave reviews, long lines, and high prices and positive profits. Within a year, there were four new ice cream/frozen yogurt stores, no lines, and lower prices. Magic? No, just the natural functioning of competition.

A powerful example of an industry expanding with higher prices and higher economic profits is the housing sector prior to 2007. From the late 1990s until early 2006, the housing market was booming nationally. Demand was shifting to the right for a number of reasons. As it did, housing prices rose substantially and with them the profits being made by builders. As builders responded with higher output, the number of new units started (housing starts) increased to a near record level of over 2.2 million per year in 2005. Construction employment grew to over 7.5 million.

Starting in 2006, housing demand shifted to the left. The inventory of unsold property began to build, and prices started to fall. That turned profits into losses. Home builders cut their production, and many went out of business. These moves had major ramifications for the performance

ECONOMICS IN PRACTICE

Why Are Hot Dogs So Expensive in Central Park?

Recently, one of the authors of this textbook was walking in Central Park in New York City. Since it was lunchtime and she was hungry, she decided to indulge her secret passion for good old-fashioned hot dogs. Because she did this frequently, she was well aware that the standard price for a hot dog in New York City was \$1.50. So she was surprised when she handed the vendor \$2 that she received no change back. As it turned out, the price of a hot dog inside the park was \$2.00, not the \$1.50 vendors charged elsewhere in the city. Since she was trained as an economist, she wanted to know what caused the difference in price.

First, she looked to the demand side of the market. If hot dogs are selling for \$2.00 in the park but only \$1.50 outside the park, people must be willing and able to pay more for them in the park. Why? Perhaps hot dogs are more enjoyable to people when eaten while walking through Central Park. Hot dogs and "walking through the park" may be complementary goods. Or maybe people who walk in the park at noon are richer.

You might ask, if hot dogs are available outside the park for \$1.50, why don't people buy them there and bring them to the park? The fact is that hot dogs are good only when they are hot, and they get cold very quickly. A hot dog purchased 5 minutes away from Central Park will be stone cold by the time someone reaches the park.

But looking at the demand side is not enough to understand a market. We also have to explain the behavior of the hot dog vendors who comprise the supply side of the market. On the supply side, the author knew that the market for hot dogs was virtually perfectly competitive outside the park. First, the product is homogeneous. Essentially all vendors supply the same product: a standard quality-certified hot dog and two varieties of mustard. Second, there is free entry. Since most vendors have wheels on their carts, if the price of hot dogs rises above \$1.50 in one part of town, we would expect vendors to move there. The added supply would then push prices back to Price (*P*) = short-run marginal cost (*SRAC*) = long-run average cost (*LRAC*). At *P* = \$1.50, individual vendors around the city must be earning enough to cover average costs including a normal rate of return (see the discussion in the text on p. 178). If the market price produces excess profits, new vendors will show up to compete those excess profits away.

All of this would suggest that the price of hot dogs should be the same everywhere in New York City. If a vendor is able to charge \$2 in the park and has the same costs as a vendor outside the park, he must be earning above-normal profits. After all, the vendor makes \$.50 more on each hot dog. Something must be preventing the outside vendors from rolling their carts into the park, which would increase the supply of hot dogs and drive the price back to \$1.50.

That something is a more expensive license. In New York, you need a license to operate a hot dog cart, and a license to operate in the park costs more. Since hot dogs are \$0.50 more in the park, the added cost of a license each year must be roughly \$0.50 per hot dog sold. In fact, in New York City, licenses to sell hot dogs in the park are auctioned off for many thousands of dollars, while licenses to operate in more remote parts of the city cost only about \$1,000.

of the whole economy. Go back and look at Figure 9.7 and Figure 9.8. Make sure you understand how these diagrams explain both the expansion and contraction of the housing sector since 2000.

Many believe that part of the explosion of technology-based dot-com companies is due to the very low barriers to entry. All it takes to start a company is an idea, a terminal, and Web access. The number of new firms entering the industry is so large that statistical agencies cannot keep pace.

When there is promise of positive profits, investments are made and output expands. When firms end up suffering losses, firms contract and some go out of business. It can take quite a while, however, for an industry to achieve **long-run competitive equilibrium**, the point at which $P = SRMC = SRAC = LRAC$ and profits are zero. In fact, because costs and tastes are in a constant state of flux, very few industries ever really get there. The economy is always changing. There are always some firms making profits and some firms suffering losses.

long-run competitive equilibrium When $P = SRMC = SRAC = LRAC$ and profits are zero.

This, then, is a story about tendencies:

Investment—in the form of new firms and expanding old firms—will over time tend to favor those industries in which profits are being made; and over time, industries in which firms are suffering losses will gradually contract from disinvestment.

Output Markets: A Final Word

In the last four chapters, we have been building a model of a simple market system under the assumption of perfect competition. Let us provide just one more example to review the actual response of a competitive system to a change in consumer preferences.

Over the past two decades, Americans have developed a taste for wine in general and for California wines in particular. We know that household demand is constrained by income, wealth, and prices and that income is (at least in part) determined by the choices that households make. Within these constraints, households increasingly choose—or demand—wine. The demand curve for wine has shifted to the right, causing excess demand followed by an increase in price.

With higher prices, wine producers find themselves earning positive profits. *This increase in price and consequent rise in profits is the basic signal that leads to a reallocation of society's resources.* In the short run, wine producers are constrained by their current scales of operation. California has only a limited number of vineyards and only a limited amount of vat capacity, for example.

In the long run, however, we would expect to see resources flow in to compete for these profits; and this is exactly what happens. New firms enter the wine-producing business. New vines are planted, and new vats and production equipment are purchased and put in place. Vineyard owners move into new states—Rhode Island, Texas, and Maryland—and established growers increase production. Overall, more wine is produced to meet the new consumer demand. At the same time, competition is forcing firms to operate using the most efficient technology available.

What starts as a shift in preferences thus ends up as a shift in resources. Land is reallocated, and labor moves into wine production. All this is accomplished without any central planning or direction.

You have now seen what lies behind the demand curves and supply curves in competitive output markets. The next two chapters take up competitive *input* markets and complete the picture.

SUMMARY

1. For any firm, one of three conditions holds at any given moment: (1) The firm is earning positive profits, (2) the firm is suffering losses, or (3) the firm is just breaking even—that is, earning a normal rate of return and thus zero profits.

SHORT-RUN CONDITIONS AND LONG-RUN DIRECTIONS p. 178

2. A firm that is earning positive profits in the short run and expects to continue doing so has an incentive to expand in the long run. Profits also provide an incentive for new firms to enter the industry.

3. In the short run, firms suffering losses are stuck in the industry. They can shut down operations ($q = 0$), but they must still bear fixed costs. In the long run, firms suffering losses can exit the industry.
4. A firm's decision about whether to shut down in the short run depends solely on whether its total revenue from operating is sufficient to cover its total variable cost. If total revenue exceeds total variable cost, the excess can be used to pay some fixed costs and thus reduce losses.
5. Anytime that price is below the minimum point on the average variable cost curve, total revenue will be less than total variable cost, and the firm will shut down. The minimum point on the average variable cost curve (which is also the point where marginal cost and average variable cost intersect) is called the *shut-down point*. At all prices above the shut-down point, the *MC* curve shows the profit-maximizing level of output. At all prices below it, optimal short-run output is zero.
6. The *short-run supply curve* of a firm in a perfectly competitive industry is the portion of its marginal cost curve that lies above its average variable cost curve.
7. Two things can cause the industry supply curve to shift: (1) in the short run, anything that causes marginal costs to change across the industry, such as an increase in the price of a particular input and (2) in the long run, entry or exit of firms.

LONG-RUN COSTS: ECONOMIES AND DISECONOMIES OF SCALE *p. 184*

8. When an increase in a firm's scale of production leads to lower average costs, the firm exhibits *increasing returns to scale*, or *economies of scale*. When average costs do not change with the scale of production, the firm exhibits *constant returns to scale*. When an increase in a firm's scale of production leads to higher average costs, the firm exhibits *decreasing returns to scale*, or *diseconomies of scale*.
9. A firm's *long-run average cost curve* (*LRAC*) shows the costs associated with different scales on which it can choose to operate in the long run.

LONG-RUN ADJUSTMENTS TO SHORT-RUN CONDITIONS *p. 189*

10. When short-run profits exist in an industry, firms enter and existing firms expand. These events shift the industry supply curve to the right. When this happens, price falls and ultimately profits are eliminated.
11. When short-run losses are suffered in an industry, some firms exit and some firms reduce scale. These events shift the industry supply curve to the left, raising price and eliminating losses.
12. *Long-run competitive equilibrium* is reached when $P = SRMC = SRAC = LRAC$ and profits are zero.
13. In efficient markets, investment capital flows toward profit opportunities.

REVIEW TERMS AND CONCEPTS

breaking even, *p. 178*
constant returns to scale, *p. 185*
decreasing returns to scale *or* diseconomies of scale, *p. 185*
increasing returns to scale *or* economies of scale, *p. 185*
long-run average cost curve (*LRAC*), *p. 186*
long-run competitive equilibrium, *p. 195*
minimum efficient scale (mes), *p. 186*
optimal scale of plant, *p. 189*
short-run industry supply curve, *p. 183*
shut-down point, *p. 182*
long-run competitive equilibrium, $P = SRMC = SRAC = LRAC$

PROBLEMS

Visit www.myeconlab.com to complete the problems marked in orange online. You will receive instant feedback on your answers, tutorial help, and access to additional practice problems.

1. For each of the following, decide whether you agree or disagree and explain your answer:
   a. Firms that exhibit constant returns to scale have U-shaped long-run average cost curves.
   b. A firm suffering losses in the short run will continue to operate as long as total revenue at least covers fixed cost.
2. Ajax is a competitive firm operating under the following conditions: Price of output is \$5, the profit-maximizing level of output is 20,000 units of output, and the total cost (full economic cost) of producing 20,000 units is \$120,000. The firm's *only* fixed factor of production is a \$300,000 stock of capital (a building). If the interest rate available on comparable risks is 10 percent, should this firm shut down immediately in the short run? Explain your answer.
3. Explain why it is possible that a firm with a production function that exhibits increasing returns to scale can run into diminishing returns at the same time.
4. Which of the following industries do you think are likely to exhibit large economies of scale? Explain why in each case.
   a. Home building
   b. Electric power generation
   c. Vegetable farming
   d. Software development
   e. Aircraft manufacturing

5. For cases *A* through *F* in the following table, would you (1) operate or shut down in the short run and (2) expand your plant or exit the industry in the long run?

	A	B	C	D	E	F
Total revenue	1,500	2,000	2,000	5,000	5,000	5,000
Total cost	1,500	1,500	2,500	6,000	7,000	4,000
Total fixed cost	500	500	200	1,500	1,500	1,500

6. **[Related to the *Economics in Practice* on p. 190]** Do you agree or disagree with the following statements? Explain in a sentence or two.
   a. A firm will never sell its product for less than it costs to produce it.
   b. If the short-run marginal cost curve is U-shaped, the long-run average cost curve is likely to be U-shaped as well.

7. The Smythe chicken farm outside Little Rock, Arkansas, produces 25,000 chickens per month. Total cost of production at Smythe Farm is $28,000. Down the road are two other farms. Faubus Farm produces 55,000 chickens a month, and total cost is $50,050. Mega Farm produces 100,000 chickens per month, at a total cost of $91,000. These data suggest that there are significant economies of scale in chicken production. Do you agree or disagree with this statement? Explain your answer.

8. Indicate whether you agree or disagree with the following statements. Briefly explain your answers.
   a. Increasing returns to scale refers to a situation where an increase in a firm's scale of production leads to higher costs per unit produced.
   b. Constant returns to scale refers to a situation where an increase in a firm's scale of production has no effect on costs per unit produced.
   c. Decreasing returns to scale refers to a situation where an increase in a firm's scale of production leads to lower costs per unit produced.

9. You are given the following cost data:

q	*TFC*	*TVC*
0	12	0
1	12	5
2	12	9
3	12	14
4	12	20
5	12	28
6	12	38

If the price of output is $7, how many units of output will this firm produce? What is the total revenue? What is the total cost? Will the firm operate or shut down in the short run? in the long run? Briefly explain your answers.

10. The concept of economies of scale refers to lower per-unit production costs at higher levels of output. The easiest way to understand this is to look at whether long-run average cost decreases with output (economies of scale) or whether long-run average cost increases with output (diseconomies of scale). If average cost is constant as output rises, there is constant returns to scale. But the concept of falling unit costs is all around us. Explain how the concept of economies of scale helps shed light on each of the following:
   a. car pooling
   b. doubling up to reduce rent
   c. farming
   d. a single-family car versus public transit
   e. a huge refinery

11. According to its Web site, Netflix is the world's largest online entertainment subscription service. It owns 90,000 DVD titles that it rents out to its more than 9 million subscribers. On its Web site, Netflix indicates that its growth strategy is to "focus on subscription growth in order to realize economies of scale." In this business, where do you think scale economies come from?

12. From 2000 to 2005, the home building sector was expanding and new housing construction as measured by housing starts was approaching an all-time high. (At www.census.gov, click "Housing," then click "Construction data.") Big builders such as Lennar Corporation were making exceptional profits. The industry was expanding. Existing home building firms invested in more capacity and raised output. New home building firms entered the industry. During 2006 and 2007, demand for new and existing homes dropped. The inventory of unsold homes grew sharply. Home prices began to fall. Home builders suffered losses, and the industry contracted. Many firms went out of business, and many workers in the construction industry went bankrupt. Use the Web to verify that all of these events happened. Access www.bls.gov for employment data and www.bea.gov for information on residential construction as part of gross domestic product. What has happened since the beginning of 2008? Has the housing market recovered? Have housing starts stopped falling? If so, at what level? Write a short essay about whether the housing sector is about to expand or contract.

13. **[Related to the *Economics in Practice* on p. 194]** St. Mark's Square is a beautiful plaza in Venice that is often frequented by both tourists and pigeons. Ringing the piazza are many small, privately owned cafes. In these cafes, a cappuccino costs 7 euros despite the fact that an equally good cappuccino costs only 3 euros a block a way. What is going on here?

14. The following problem traces the relationship between firm decisions, market supply, and market equilibrium in a perfectly competitive market.
   a. Complete the following table for a single firm in the short run.

OUTPUT	*TFC*	*TVC*	*TC*	*AVC*	*ATC*	*MC*
0	$300	$ 0	—	—	—	—
1	—	100	—	—	—	—
2	—	150	—	—	—	—
3	—	210	—	—	—	—
4	—	290	—	—	—	—
5	—	400	—	—	—	—
6	—	540	—	—	—	—
7	—	720	—	—	—	—
8	—	950	—	—	—	—
9	—	1,240	—	—	—	—
10	—	1,600	—	—	—	—

   b. Using the information in the table, fill in the following supply schedule for this individual firm under perfect competition and indicate profit (positive or negative) at each output level. (*Hint:* At each hypothetical price, what is the *MR* of producing 1 more unit of output? Combine this with the *MC* of another unit to figure out the quantity supplied.)

PRICE	QUANTITY SUPPLIED	PROFIT
$ 50	—	___
70	—	___
100	—	___
130	—	___
170	—	___
220	—	___
280	—	___
350	—	___

c. Now suppose there are 100 firms in this industry, all with identical cost schedules. Fill in the market quantity supplied at each price in this market.

PRICE	MARKET QUANTITY SUPPLIED	MARKET QUANTITY DEMANDED
$ 50	—	1,000
70	—	900
100	—	800
130	—	700
170	—	600
220	—	500
280	—	400
350	—	300

d. Fill in the blanks: From the market supply and demand schedules in c., the equilibrium market price for this good is ____ and the equilibrium market quantity is ____. Each firm will produce a quantity of ____ and earn a ____ (profit/loss) equal to ____.

e. In d., your answers characterize the short-run equilibrium in this market. Do they characterize the long-run equilibrium as well? If so, explain why. If not, explain why not (that is, what would happen in the long run to change the equilibrium and why?).

*15. Assume that you are hired as an analyst at a major New York consulting firm. Your first assignment is to do an industry analysis of the tribble industry. After extensive research and two all-nighters, you have obtained the following information:

- *Long-run costs:*
  Capital costs: $5 per unit of output
  Labor costs: $2 per unit of output
- No economies or diseconomies of scale
- Industry currently earning a normal return to capital (profit of zero)
- Industry perfectly competitive, with each of 100 firms producing the same amount of output
- *Total industry output:* 1.2 million tribbles
  Demand for tribbles is expected to grow rapidly over the next few years to a level twice as high as it is now, but (due to short-run diminishing returns) each of the 100 existing firms is likely to be producing only 50 percent more.

a. Sketch the long-run cost curve of a representative firm.
b. Show the current conditions by drawing two diagrams, one showing the industry and one showing a representative firm.
c. Sketch the increase in demand and show how the industry is likely to respond in the short run and in the long run.

*Note: Problems marked with an asterisk are more challenging.

APPENDIX

EXTERNAL ECONOMIES AND DISECONOMIES AND THE LONG-RUN INDUSTRY SUPPLY CURVE

Sometimes average costs increase or decrease with the size of the industry, in addition to responding to changes in the size of the firm itself. When long-run average costs decrease as a result of industry growth, we say that there are **external economies.** When average costs increase as a result of industry growth, we say that there are **external diseconomies.** (Remember the distinction between internal and external economies: *Internal* economies of scale are found within firms, whereas *external* economies occur on an industry-wide basis.)

The expansion of the home building sector of the economy between 2000 and 2005 illustrates how external diseconomies of scale arise and how they imply a rising long-run average cost curve.

Beginning in 2000, the overall economy suffered a slowdown as the dot-com exuberance turned to a bursting stock market bubble, and the events of 9/11 raised the specter of international terrorism.

One sector, however, came alive between 2000 and 2005: housing. Very low interest rates lowered the monthly cost of home ownership, immigration increased the number of households, millions of baby boomers traded up and bought second homes, and investors who had been burned by the stock market bust turned to housing as a "real" asset.

All of this increased the demand for single-family homes and condominiums around the country. Table 9A.1 shows what happened to house prices, output, and the costs of inputs during the first 5 years of the decade.

First, house prices began to rise faster than other prices while the cost of construction materials stayed flat. Profitability in the home building sector took off. Next, as existing builders expanded their operations, new firms started up. The number of new housing units "started" stood at just over 1.5 million annually in 2000 and then rose to over 2 million by 2005. All of this put pressure on the prices of construction materials such as lumber and wallboard. The table shows that construction materials costs rose more than 8 percent in 2004. These input prices increased the costs of home building. The expanding *industry* caused external diseconomies of scale.

THE LONG-RUN INDUSTRY SUPPLY CURVE

Recall that long-run competitive equilibrium is achieved when entering firms responding to profits or exiting firms fleeing from losses drive price to a level that just covers long-run average

TABLE 9A.1 Construction of New Housing and Construction Materials Costs, 2000–2005

Year	House Prices % Over the Previous Year	Housing Starts (Thousands)	Housing Starts % Change Over the Previous Year	Construction Materials Prices % Change Over the Previous Year	Consumer Prices % Change Over the Previous Year
2000	—	1,573	—	—	—
2001	7.5	1,661	56%	0%	2.8%
2002	7.5	1,710	2.9%	1.5%	1.5%
2003	7.9	1,853	8.4%	1.6%	2.3%
2004	12.0	1,949	5.2%	8.3%	2.7%
2005	13.0	2,053	5.3%	5.4%	2.5%

Source: Economy.com and the Office of Federal Housing Enterprise Oversight (OFHEO).

costs. Profits are zero, and $P = LRAC = SRAC = SRMC$. At this point, individual firms are operating at the most efficient scale of plant—that is, at the minimum point on their *LRAC* curve.

As we saw in the text, long-run equilibrium is not easily achieved. Even if a firm or an industry does achieve long-run equilibrium, it will not remain at that point indefinitely. Economies are dynamic. As population and the stock of capital grow and as preferences and technology change, some sectors will expand and some will contract. How do industries adjust to long-term changes? The answer depends on both internal and external factors.

The extent of *internal* economies (or diseconomies) determines the shape of a firm's long-run average cost curve (*LRAC*). If a firm changes its scale and either expands or contracts, its average costs will increase, decrease, or stay the same *along* the *LRAC* curve. Recall that the *LRAC* curve shows the relationship between a firm's output (q) and average total cost (*ATC*). A firm enjoying internal economies will see costs decreasing as it expands its scale; a firm facing internal diseconomies will see costs increasing as it expands its scale.

However, external economies and diseconomies have nothing to do with the size of *individual* firms in a competitive market. Because individual firms in perfectly competitive industries are very small relative to the market, other firms are affected only minimally when an individual firm changes its output or scale of operation. *External* economies and diseconomies arise from industry expansions; that is, they arise when many firms increase their output simultaneously or when new firms enter an industry. If industry expansion causes costs to increase (external diseconomies), the *LRAC* curves facing individual firms shift upward; costs increase regardless of the level of output finally chosen by the firm. Similarly, if industry expansion causes costs to decrease (external economies), the *LRAC* curves facing individual firms shift downward; costs decrease at all potential levels of output.

An example of an expanding industry facing external economies is illustrated in Figure 9A.1. Initially, the industry and the representative firm are in long-run competitive equilibrium at the price P_0 determined by the intersection of the initial demand curve D_0 and the initial supply curve S_0. P_0 is

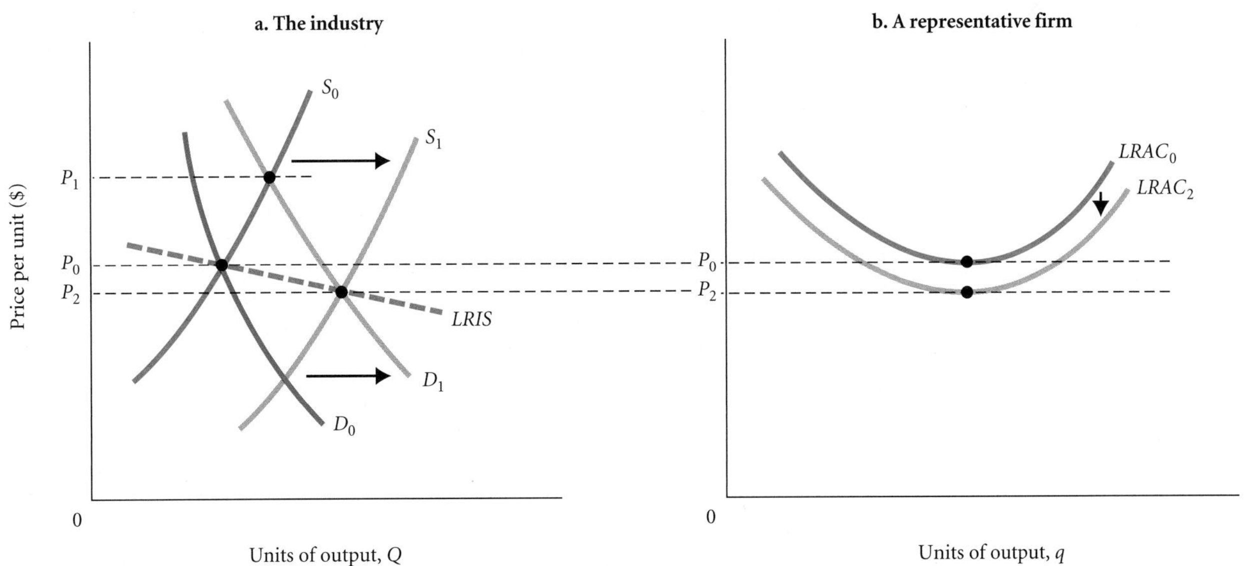

▲ **FIGURE 9A.1 A Decreasing-Cost Industry: External Economies**

In a decreasing-cost industry, average cost declines as the industry expands. As demand expands from D_0 to D_1, price rises from P_0 to P_1. As new firms enter and existing firms expand, supply shifts from S_0 to S_1, driving price down. If costs decline as a result of the expansion to $LRAC_2$, the final price will be below P_0 at P_2. The long-run industry supply curve (*LRIS*) slopes downward in a decreasing-cost industry.

the long-run equilibrium price; it intersects the initial long-run average cost curve ($LRAC_0$) at its minimum point. At this point, economic profits are zero.

Let us assume that as time passes, demand increases—that is, the demand curve shifts to the right from D_0 to D_1. This increase in demand will push price all the way to P_1. Without drawing the short-run cost curves, we know that economic profits now exist and that firms are likely to enter the industry to compete for them. In the absence of external economies or diseconomies, firms would enter the industry, shifting the supply curve to the right and driving price back to the bottom of the long-run average cost curve, where profits are zero. Nevertheless, the industry in Figure 9A.1 enjoys external economies. As firms enter and the industry expands, costs decrease; and as the supply curve shifts to the right from S_0 toward S_1, the long-run average cost curve shifts downward to $LRAC_2$. Thus, to reach the new long-run equilibrium level of price and output, the supply curve must shift all the way to S_1. Only when the supply curve reaches S_1 is price driven down to the new equilibrium price of P_2, the minimum point on the *new* long-run average cost curve.

Presumably, further expansion would lead to even greater savings because the industry encounters external economies. The dashed line in Figure 9A.1(a) that traces out price and total output over time as the industry expands is called the **long-run industry supply curve (*LRIS*)**. When an industry enjoys external economies, its long-run supply curve slopes down. Such an industry is called a **decreasing-cost industry**.

Figure 9A.2 shows the long-run industry supply curve for an industry that faces external *diseconomies*. (These were suffered in the construction industry, you will recall, when increased house building activity drove up lumber prices.) As demand expands from D_0 to D_1, price is driven up from P_0 to P_1. In response to the resulting higher profits, firms enter, shifting the short-run supply schedule to the right and driving price down. However, this time, as the industry expands, the long-run average cost curve shifts up to $LRAC_2$ as a result of external diseconomies. Now, price has to fall back only to P_2 (the minimum point on $LRAC_2$), not all the way to P_0, to eliminate economic profits. This type of industry, whose long-run industry supply curve slopes up to the right, is called an **increasing-cost industry**.

It should not surprise you to know that industries in which there are no external economies or diseconomies of scale have flat, or horizontal, long-run industry supply curves. These industries are called **constant-cost industries**.

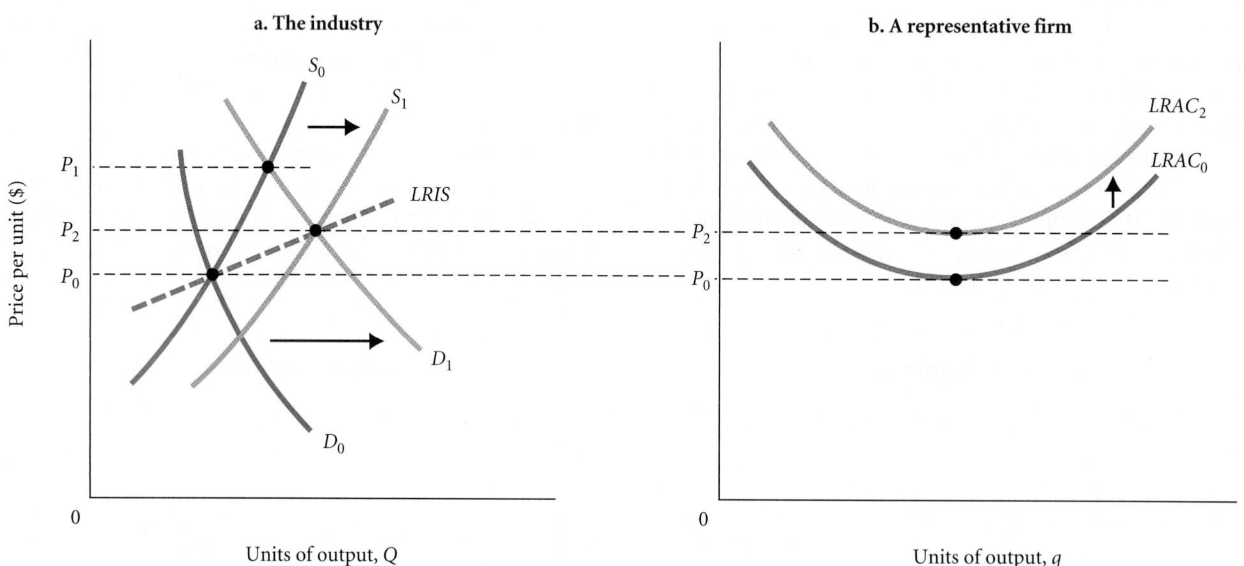

▲ **FIGURE 9A.2 An Increasing-Cost Industry: External Diseconomies**

In an increasing-cost industry, average cost increases as the industry expands. As demand shifts from D_0 to D_1, price rises from P_0 to P_1. As new firms enter and existing firms expand output, supply shifts from S_0 to S_1, driving price down. If long-run average costs rise, as a result, to $LRAC_2$, the final price will be P_2. The long-run industry supply curve (*LRIS*) slopes up in an increasing-cost industry.

SUMMARY

EXTERNAL ECONOMIES AND DISECONOMIES *p. 198*

1. When long-run average costs decrease as a result of industry growth, we say that the industry exhibits *external economies.* When long-run average costs increase as a result of industry growth, we say that the industry exhibits *external diseconomies.*

THE LONG-RUN INDUSTRY SUPPLY CURVE *p. 198*

2. The *long-run industry supply curve* (*LRIS*) is a graph that traces out price and total output over time as an industry expands. A *decreasing-cost industry* is an industry in which average costs fall as the industry expands. It exhibits external economies, and its long-run industry supply curve slopes downward. An *increasing-cost industry* is an industry in which average costs rise as the industry expands. It exhibits external diseconomies, and its long-run industry supply curve slopes upward. A *constant-cost industry* is an industry that shows no external economies or diseconomies as the industry grows. Its long-run industry supply curve is horizontal, or flat.

REVIEW TERMS AND CONCEPTS

constant-cost industry An industry that shows no economies or diseconomies of scale as the industry grows. Such industries have flat, or horizontal, long-run supply curves. *p. 200*

decreasing-cost industry An industry that realizes external economies—that is, average costs decrease as the industry grows. The long-run supply curve for such an industry has a negative slope. *p. 200*

external economies and diseconomies When industry growth results in a decrease of long-run average costs, there are *external economies*; when industry growth results in an increase of long-run average costs, there are *external diseconomies. p. 198*

increasing-cost industry An industry that encounters external diseconomies—that is, average costs increase as the industry grows. The long-run supply curve for such an industry has a positive slope. *p. 200*

long-run industry supply curve (*LRIS*) A graph that traces out price and total output over time as an industry expands. *p. 200*

PROBLEMS

1. In deriving the short-run industry supply curve (the sum of firms' marginal cost curves), we assumed that input prices are constant because competitive firms are price-takers. This same assumption holds in the derivation of the long-run industry supply curve. Do you agree or disagree? Explain.
2. Consider an industry that exhibits external diseconomies of scale. Suppose that over the next 10 years, demand for that industry's product increases rapidly. Describe in detail the adjustments likely to follow. Use diagrams in your answer.
3. A representative firm producing cloth is earning a normal profit at a price of $10 per yard. Draw a supply and demand diagram showing equilibrium at this price. Assuming that the industry is a constant-cost industry, use the diagram to show the long-term adjustment of the industry as demand grows over time. Explain the adjustment mechanism.

Input Demand: The Labor and Land Markets

10

As we have seen, all firms must make three decisions: (1) how much to produce and supply in output markets; (2) how to produce that output—that is, which technology to use; and (3) how much of each input to demand. So far, our discussion of firm behavior has focused on the first two questions. In Chapter 7 through Chapter 9, we explained how profit-maximizing firms choose among alternative technologies and decide how much to supply in output markets.

We now turn to the behavior of firms in perfectly competitive *input* markets, going behind input demand curves in much the same way that we went behind output supply curves in the previous two chapters. When we look behind input demand curves, we discover the exact same set of decisions that we saw when we analyzed output supply curves. In a sense, we have already talked about everything covered in this chapter. It is the *perspective* that is new.

The three main inputs are labor, land, and capital. Transactions in the labor and land markets are fairly straightforward. Households supply their labor to firms that demand it in exchange for a salary or a wage. Landowners sell or rent land to others. Capital markets are a bit more complex but are conceptually very similar. Households supply the resources used for the production of capital by saving and giving up present consumption. Savings flow through financial markets to firms that use these savings to procure capital to be used in production. Households receive interest, dividends, or profits in exchange. This chapter discusses input markets in general, and the next chapter focuses on the capital market in detail. Before reading further, it may be helpful to refer back to Figure II.1 on p. 107, which outlines the interactions of households and firms in the labor and capital markets.

Input Markets: Basic Concepts

Before we begin our discussion of input markets, it will be helpful to establish some basic concepts: derived demand, complementary and substitutable inputs, diminishing returns, and marginal revenue product.

Demand for Inputs: A *Derived* Demand

A firm cannot make a profit unless there is a demand for its product. Households must be willing to pay for the firm's output. The quantity of output that a firm produces (in both the long run and the short run) thus depends on the value the market places on the firm's product. This means that demand for inputs depends on the demand for outputs. In other words, input demand is **derived** from output demand.

derived demand The demand for resources (inputs) that is dependent on the demand for the outputs those resources can be used to produce.

The **productivity of an input** is the amount of output produced per unit of that input. When a large amount of output is produced per unit of an input, the input is said to exhibit *high productivity*. When only a small amount of output is produced per unit of the input, the input is said to exhibit *low productivity*.

productivity of an input The amount of output produced per unit of that input.

> Inputs are demanded by a firm if and only if households demand the good or service produced by that firm.

Prices in competitive input markets depend on firms' demand for inputs, households' supply of inputs, and interaction between the two. In the labor market, for example, households must decide whether to work and how much to work. In Chapter 6, we saw that the opportunity cost of working for a wage is leisure or the value derived from unpaid labor—working in the garden, for instance, or raising children. In general, firms will demand workers as long as the value of what those workers produce exceeds what they must be paid. Households will supply labor as long as the wage they receive exceeds the value of leisure or the value they derive from nonpaid work.

Inputs: Complementary and Substitutable

Inputs can be *complementary* or *substitutable*. Two inputs used together may enhance, or complement, each other. For example, a new machine is often useless without someone to run it. Machines can also be substituted for labor, or—less often—labor can be substituted for machines.

All this means that a firm's input demands are tightly linked to one another. An increase or decrease in wages naturally causes the demand for labor to change, but it may also have an effect on the demand for capital or land. If we are to understand the demand for inputs, therefore, we must understand the connections among labor, capital, and land.

Diminishing Returns

Recall that the short run is the period during which some fixed factor of production limits a firm's capacity to expand. Under these conditions, the firm that decides to increase output will eventually encounter diminishing returns. Stated more formally, a fixed scale of plant means that the marginal product of variable inputs eventually declines.

Recall also that **marginal product of labor (MP_L)** is the additional output produced if a firm hires 1 additional unit of labor. For example, if a firm pays for 400 hours of labor per week—10 workers working 40 hours each—and asks one worker to stay an extra hour, the product of the 401st hour is the marginal product of labor for that firm.

marginal product of labor (MP_L) The additional output produced by 1 additional unit of labor.

In Chapter 7, we talked at some length about declining marginal product at a sandwich shop. The first two columns of Table 10.1 reproduce some of the production data from that shop. You may remember that the shop has only one grill, at which only two or three people can work comfortably. In this example, the grill is the fixed factor of production in the short run. Labor is the variable factor. The first worker can produce 10 sandwiches per hour, and the second worker can produce 15 (column 3 of Table 10.1). The second worker can produce more because the first worker is busy answering the phone and taking care of customers, as well as making sandwiches. After the second worker, however, marginal product declines. The third worker adds only 10 sandwiches per hour because the grill gets crowded. The fourth worker can squeeze in quickly while the others are serving or wrapping, but he or she adds only five additional sandwiches each hour, and so on.

In this case, the grill's capacity ultimately limits output. To see how the firm might make a rational choice about how many workers to hire, we need to know more about the value of the firm's product and the cost of labor.

TABLE 10.1 Marginal Revenue Product per Hour of Labor in Sandwich Production (One Grill)

(1) Total Labor Units (Employees)	(2) Total Product (Sandwiches per Hour)	(3) Marginal Product of Labor (MP_L) (Sandwiches per Hour)	(4) Price (P_X) (Value Added per Sandwich)[a]	(5) Marginal Revenue Product ($MP_L \times P_X$) (per Hour)
0	0	—	—	—
1	10	10	\$0.50	\$5.00
2	25	15	0.50	7.50
3	35	10	0.50	5.00
4	40	5	0.50	2.50
5	42	2	0.50	1.00
6	42	0	0.50	0.00

[a]The "price" is essentially profit per sandwich; see discussion in text.

Marginal Revenue Product

marginal revenue product (*MRP*) The additional revenue a firm earns by employing 1 additional unit of input, *ceteris paribus*.

The **marginal revenue product (*MRP*)** of a variable input is the additional revenue a firm earns by employing 1 additional unit of that input, *ceteris paribus*. If labor is the variable factor, for example, hiring an additional unit will lead to added output (the *marginal product* of labor). The sale of that added output will yield revenue. *Marginal revenue product* is the revenue produced by selling the good or service that is produced by the marginal unit of labor. In a competitive firm, marginal revenue product is the value of a factor's marginal product.

By using labor as our variable factor, we can state this proposition more formally by saying that if MP_L is the marginal product of labor and P_X is the price of output, then the marginal revenue product of labor is

$$MRP_L = MP_L \times P_X$$

When calculating marginal revenue product, we need to be precise about what is being produced. A sandwich shop sells sandwiches, but it does not produce the bread, meat, cheese, mustard, and mayonnaise that go into the sandwiches. What the shop is producing is "sandwich cooking and assembly services." The shop is "adding value" to the meat, bread, and other ingredients by preparing and putting them all together in ready-to-eat form. With this in mind, let us assume that each finished sandwich in our shop sells for \$0.50 over and above the costs of its ingredients. Thus, the *price of the service* the shop is selling is \$0.50 per sandwich, and the only variable cost of providing that service is that of the labor used to put the sandwiches together. Thus, if X is the product of our shop, $P_X = \$0.50$.

Table 10.1, column 5, calculates the marginal revenue product of each worker if the shop charges \$0.50 per sandwich over and above the costs of its ingredients. The first worker produces 10 sandwiches per hour, which at \$0.50 each, generates revenues of \$5.00 per hour. The addition of a second worker yields \$7.50 an hour in revenues. After the second worker, diminishing returns drive MRP_L down. The marginal revenue product of the third worker is \$5.00 per hour, of the fourth worker is only \$2.50, and so on.

Figure 10.1 graphs the data from Table 10.1. Notice that the marginal revenue product curve has the same downward slope as the marginal product curve but that *MRP* is measured in dollars, not units of output. The *MRP* curve shows the dollar value of labor's marginal product.

FIGURE 10.1

Deriving a Marginal Revenue Product Curve from Marginal Product

The marginal revenue product of labor is the price of output, P_X, times the marginal product of labor, MP_L.

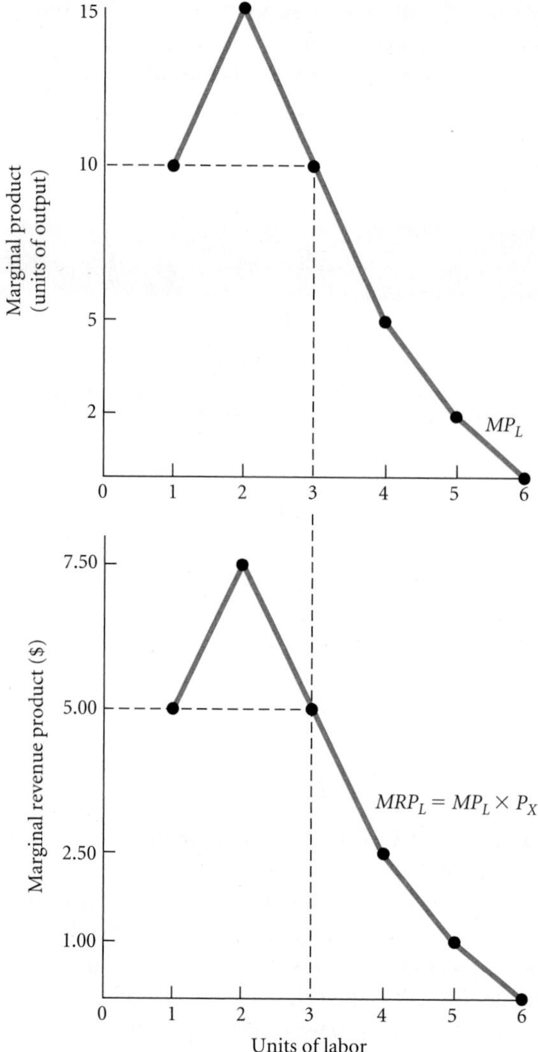

Labor Markets

Let us begin our discussion of input markets by discussing a firm that uses only one variable factor of production.

A Firm Using Only One Variable Factor of Production: Labor

Demand for an input depends on that input's marginal revenue product and its unit cost, or price. The price of labor, for example, is the wage determined in the labor market. (At this point, we are continuing to assume that the sandwich shop uses only one variable factor of production—labor. Remember that competitive firms are price-takers in both output and input markets. Such firms can hire all the labor they want to hire as long as they pay the market wage.) We can think of the hourly wage at the sandwich shop as the marginal cost of a unit of labor. A profit-maximizing firm will add inputs—in the case of labor, it will hire workers—as long as the marginal revenue product of that input exceeds the market price of that input—in the case of labor, the wage.

Look again at the figures for the sandwich shop in Table 10.1, column 5. Now suppose the going wage for sandwich makers is $4 per hour. A profit-maximizing firm would hire three workers. The first worker would yield $5 per hour in revenue, and the second would yield $7.50; but they each would cost only $4 per hour. The third worker would bring in $5 per hour, but still cost only $4 in marginal wages. The marginal product of the fourth worker, however, would not bring in enough revenue ($2.50) to pay this worker's salary. Total profit is thus maximized by hiring three workers.

Figure 10.2 presents this same concept graphically. The labor market appears in Figure 10.2(a); Figure 10.2(b) shows a single firm that employs workers. This firm, incidentally, does not represent just the firms in a single industry. Because firms in many different industries demand labor, the representative firm in Figure 10.2(b) represents any firm in any industry that uses labor.

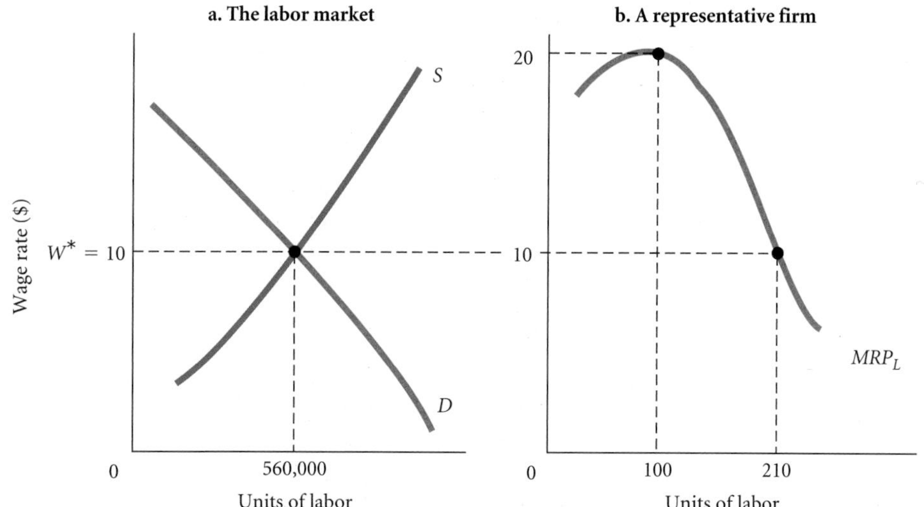

FIGURE 10.2 Marginal Revenue Product and Factor Demand for a Firm Using One Variable Input (Labor)

A competitive firm using only one variable factor of production will use that factor as long as its marginal revenue product exceeds its unit cost. A perfectly competitive firm will hire labor as long as MRP_L is greater than the going wage, W^*. The hypothetical firm will demand 210 units of labor.

The firm faces a market wage rate of \$10. We can think of this as the marginal cost of a unit of labor. (Note that we are now discussing the margin in units of *labor*; in previous chapters, we talked about marginal units of *output*.) Given a wage of \$10, how much labor would the firm demand?

You might think that the firm would hire 100 units, the point at which the difference between marginal revenue product and wage rate is greatest. However, the firm is interested in maximizing *total* profit, not *marginal* profit. Hiring the 101st unit of labor generates \$20 in revenue at a cost of only \$10. Because MRP_L is greater than the cost of the input required to produce it, hiring 1 more unit of labor adds to profit. This will continue to be true as long as MRP_L remains above \$10, which is all the way to 210 units. At that point, the wage rate is equal to the marginal revenue product of labor, or $W^* = MRP_L = 10$. The firm will not demand labor beyond 210 units because the cost of hiring the 211th unit of labor would be greater than the value of what that unit produces. (Recall that the fourth sandwich maker, requiring a wage of \$4 per hour, can produce only an extra \$2.50 an hour in sandwiches.)

Thus, the curve in Figure 10.2(b) tells us how much labor a firm that uses only one variable factor of production will hire at each potential market wage rate. If the market wage falls, the quantity of labor demanded will rise. If the market wage rises, the quantity of labor demanded will fall. This description should sound familiar to you—it is, in fact, the description of a demand curve. Therefore we can now say that when a firm uses only one variable factor of production, that factor's marginal revenue product curve is the firm's demand curve for that factor in the short run.

Comparing Marginal Revenue and Marginal Cost to Maximize Profits In Chapter 8, we saw that a competitive firm's marginal cost curve is the same as its supply curve. That is, at any output price, the marginal cost curve determines how much output a profit-maximizing firm will produce. We came to this conclusion by comparing the marginal revenue that a firm would earn by producing one more unit of output with the marginal cost of producing that unit of output.

There is no difference between the reasoning in Chapter 8 and the reasoning in this chapter. The only difference is that what is being measured at the margin has changed. In Chapter 8, the firm was comparing the marginal revenues and costs of producing *another unit of output*. Here the firm is comparing the marginal revenues and costs of employing *another unit of input*. To see this similarity, look at Figure 10.3. When the only variable factor of production is labor, the condition $W = MRP_L$ is the same condition as $P = MC$. The two statements say exactly the same thing.

▶ FIGURE 10.3
The Two Profit-Maximizing Conditions Are Simply Two Views of the Same Choice Process

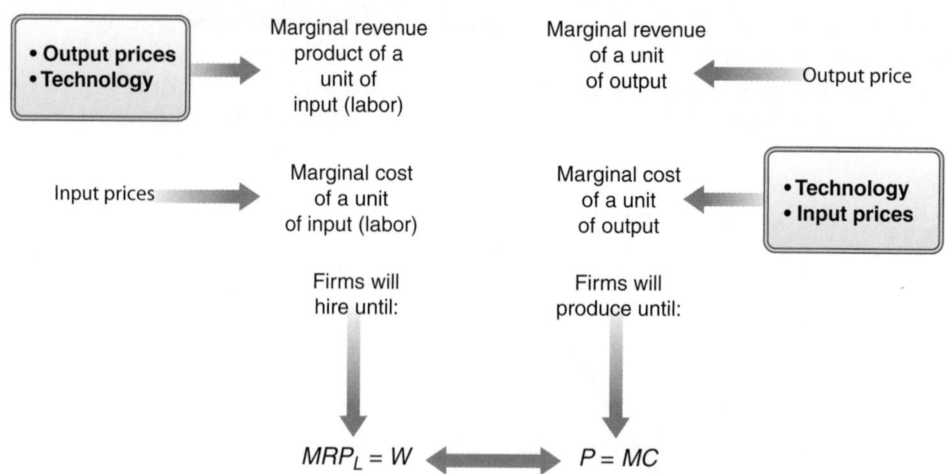

In both cases, the firm is comparing the cost of production with potential revenues from the sale of product *at the margin*. In Chapter 8, the firm compared the price of output (*P*, which is equal to *MR* in perfect competition) directly with cost of production (*MC*), where cost was derived from information on factor prices and technology. (Review the derivation of cost curves in Chapter 8 if this is unclear.) Here information on output price and technology is contained in the marginal revenue product curve, which the firm compares with information on input price to determine the optimal level of input to demand.

The assumption of one variable factor of production makes the trade-off facing firms easy to see. Figure 10.4 shows that, in essence, firms weigh the value of labor as reflected in the market wage against the value of the product of labor as reflected in the price of output. Assuming that labor is the only variable input, if society values a good more than it costs firms to hire the workers to produce that good, the good will be produced. In general, the same logic also holds for more than one input. Firms weigh the value of outputs as reflected in output price against the value of inputs as reflected in marginal costs.

▶ FIGURE 10.4
The Trade-Off Facing Firms

Firms weigh the cost of labor as reflected in wage rates against the value of labor's marginal product. Assume that labor is the only variable factor of production. Then, if society values a good more than it costs firms to hire the workers to produce that good, the good will be produced.

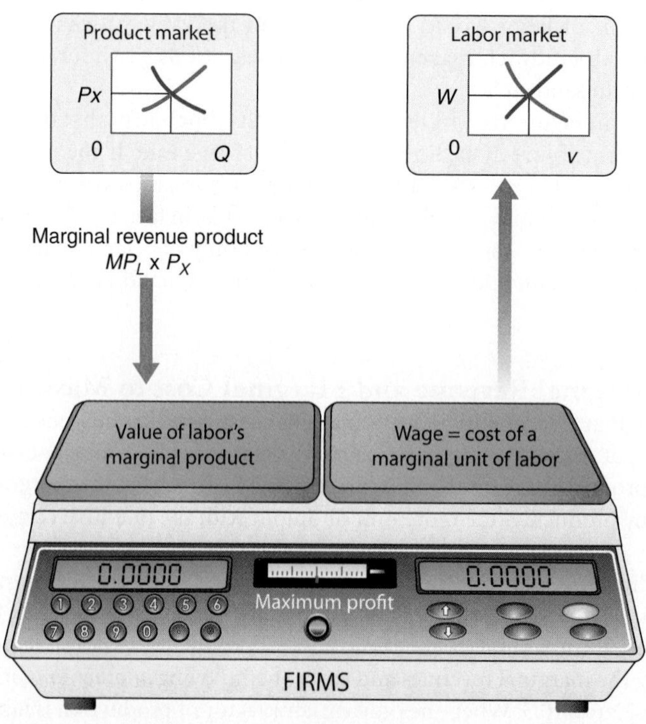

Deriving Input Demands For the small sandwich shop, calculating the marginal product of a variable input (labor) and marginal revenue product was easy. Although it may be more complex, the decision process is essentially the same for both big corporations and small proprietorships.

When an airline hires more flight attendants, for example, it increases the quality of its service to attract more passengers and thus to sell more of its product. In deciding how many flight attendants to hire, the airline must figure out how much new revenue the added attendants are likely to generate relative to their wages.

At the sandwich shop, diminishing returns set in at a certain point. The same holds true for an airplane. Once a sufficient number of attendants are on a plane, additional attendants add little to the quality of service; and beyond a certain level, they might even give rise to negative marginal product. The presence of too many attendants could bother the passengers and make it difficult to get to the restrooms.

In making your own decisions, you also compare marginal gains with input costs in the presence of diminishing returns. Suppose you grow vegetables in your yard. First, you save money at the supermarket. Second, you can plant what you like, and the vegetables taste better fresh from the garden. Third, you simply like to work in the garden.

Like the sandwich shop and the airline, you also face diminishing returns. You have only 625 square feet of garden to work with; and with land as a fixed factor in the short run, your marginal product will certainly decline. You can work all day every day, but your limited space will produce only so many string beans. The first few hours you spend each week watering, fertilizing, and dealing with major weed and bug infestations probably have a high marginal product. However, after 5 or 6 hours, there is little else you can do to increase yield. Diminishing returns also apply to your sense of satisfaction. The farmers' markets are now full of inexpensive fresh produce that tastes nearly as good as yours. Once you have been out in the garden for a few hours, the hot sun and hard work start to lose their charm. Although your gardening does not involve a salary (unlike the sandwich shop and the airline, which pay out wages), the labor you supply has a value that must be weighed. You must weigh the value of additional gardening time against leisure and the other options available to you.

Less labor is likely to be employed as the cost of labor rises. If the competitive labor market pushed the daily wage to $6 per hour, the sandwich shop would hire only two workers instead of three (Table 10.1). If you suddenly became very busy at school, the opportunity cost of your time would rise and you would probably devote fewer hours to gardening.

There is recently in the economy an example of what may seem to be an exception to the rule that workers will be hired only if the revenues they generate are equal to or greater than their wages. Many start-up companies pay salaries to workers before the companies begin to take in revenue. This has been particularly true for Internet start-ups in recent years. How does a company pay workers if it is not earning any revenue? The answer is that the entrepreneur (or the venture capital fund supporting the entrepreneur) is betting that the firm will earn substantial revenue in the future. Workers are hired because the entrepreneur expects that their current efforts will produce future revenue greater than their wage costs.

A Firm Employing Two Variable Factors of Production in the Short and Long Run

When a firm employs more than one variable factor of production, the analysis of input demand becomes more complicated, but the principles stay the same. We shall now consider a firm that employs variable capital (K) and labor (L) inputs and thus faces factor prices P_K and P_L.[1] (Recall that *capital* refers to plant, equipment, and inventory used in production. We assume that some portion of the firm's capital stock is fixed in the short run, but that some of it is variable—for example, some machinery and equipment can be installed quickly.) Our analysis can be applied to any two factors of production and can easily be generalized to three or more. It can also be applied to the long run, when all factors of production are variable.

---

[1] The price of labor, P_L, is the same as the wage rate, W. We will often use the term P_L instead of W to emphasize the symmetry between labor and capital.

You have seen that inputs can be complementary or substitutable. Land, labor, and capital are used *together* to produce outputs. The worker who uses a shovel digs a bigger hole than another worker with no shovel. Add a steam shovel and that worker becomes even more productive. When an expanding firm adds to its stock of capital, it raises the productivity of its labor, and vice versa. Thus, each factor complements the other. At the same time, though, land, labor, and capital can also be *substituted* for one another. If labor becomes expensive, some labor-saving technology—robotics, for example—may take its place.

In firms employing just one variable factor of production, a change in the price of that factor affects only the demand for the factor itself. When more than one factor can vary, however, we must consider the impact of a change in one factor price on the demand for other factors as well.

Substitution and Output Effects of a Change in Factor Price Table 10.2 presents data on a hypothetical firm that employs variable capital and labor. Suppose that the firm faces a choice between two available technologies of production—technique *A*, which is capital intensive, and technique *B*, which is labor intensive. When the market price of labor is $1 per unit and the market price of capital is $1 per unit, the labor-intensive method of producing output is less costly. Each unit costs only $13 to produce using technique *B*, while the unit cost of production using technique *A* is $15. If the price of labor rises to $2, however, technique *B* is no longer less costly. Labor has become more expensive relative to capital. The unit cost rises to $23 for labor-intensive technique *B*, but to only $20 for capital-intensive technique *A*.

TABLE 10.2 Response of a Firm to an Increasing Wage Rate

Technology	Input Requirements per Unit of Output K	L	Unit Cost if $P_L = \$1$ $P_K = \$1$ $(P_L \times L) + (P_K \times K)$	Unit Cost if $P_L = \$2$ $P_K = \$1$ $(P_L \times L) + (P_K \times K)$
A (capital intensive)	10	5	$15	$20
B (labor intensive)	3	10	$13	$23

Table 10.3 shows the impact of such an increase in the price of labor on both capital and labor demand when a firm produces 100 units of output. When the price of labor is $1 and the price of capital is $1, the firm chooses technique *B* and demands 300 units of capital and 1,000 units of labor. Total variable cost is $1,300. An increase in the price of labor to $2 causes the firm to switch from technique *B* to technique *A*. In doing so, the firm *substitutes* capital for labor. The amount of labor demanded drops from 1,000 to 500 units. The amount of capital demanded increases from 300 to 1,000 units, while total variable cost increases to $2,000.

factor substitution effect The tendency of firms to substitute away from a factor whose price has risen and toward a factor whose price has fallen.

The tendency of firms to substitute away from a factor whose relative price has risen and toward a factor whose relative price has fallen is called the **factor substitution effect**. The factor substitution effect is part of the reason that *input demand curves slope downward*. When an input, or factor of production, becomes less expensive, firms tend to substitute it for other factors and thus buy *more* of it. When a particular input becomes more expensive, firms tend to substitute other factors and buy *less* of it.

TABLE 10.3 The Substitution Effect of an Increase in Wages on a Firm Producing 100 Units of Output

	To Produce 100 Units of Output: Total Capital Demanded	Total Labor Demanded	Total Variable Cost
When $P_L = \$1, P_K = \$1$, firm uses technology *B*	300	1,000	$1,300
When $P_L = \$2, P_K = \$1$, firm uses technology *A*	1,000	500	$2,000

ECONOMICS IN PRACTICE

Julia Roberts: Theater or the Movies?

In 2006, Julia Roberts starred in a live performance of *Three days of Rain* in a New York theater. Her pay per week was reported to be \$35,000, and the play ran for 12 weeks—hardly a small sum and well above the average pay earned by Broadway actors, but far below her pay for movies. In 1999, Roberts earned \$15 million for her performance in *Notting Hill*. How do we understand these differences?

In the example in the text, we described the way in which marginal revenue product could be calculated in a sandwich shop. There we could look at the number of sandwiches that were made in an hour and find the profits from those sandwiches. How do we think about the *MRP* of Julia Roberts in film and theater?

A good place to begin is to think about the source of revenues in films versus live theater. For theater, revenues come from the number of patrons in the seats multiplied by the average price for the ticket. Roberts is paid a great deal relative to an unknown actress because the producer believes that Roberts will draw more patrons to the theater. For theaters, once a show is launched, virtually all costs are fixed. No matter how many or how few people are in the seats for a given performance, the producers have to pay the facility costs and the costs of the actors. So an approximate value for Roberts' *MRP* is the average ticket price multiplied by the added tickets the producer thinks he will sell because of Roberts' performance. Roberts' \$35,000 weekly salary is about \$34,000 more than that of a lesser known actor. Given an average New York City ticket price of \$100, producers must think Roberts can bring in 340 more patrons in a given week than they would otherwise draw (340 × \$100). On average, a moderately successful play sells 5,000 tickets in a given week, spread over eight performances, and has some empty seats. So expecting 340 more in incremental sales seems quite reasonable. Indeed, one review of the play was titled "Enough Said about Three Days of Rain! Let's Talk Julia Roberts" (*New York Times*, April 20, 2006).

What about the \$15 million for the movie? Movies take approximately three months to shoot. So the \$15 million works out to over \$1 million per week. Why is Roberts worth \$1 million-plus per week to a movie producer but only \$35,000 per week to the theater? The answer is in the much larger revenue potential for the movie. Looking first at the movie sales, how much is Roberts worth? The average price of a movie ticket is \$10. An ingenue in a big film might earn \$500,000. Is it likely that Roberts will bring 1.45 million [(\$15,000,000 − \$500,000)/\$10] more patrons to the movie over the lifetime of the movie than a lesser star would? In fact, over 30 million people saw *Notting Hill*, with revenues of \$363 million. So expecting 1.45 million more people as a result of Roberts' role does not seem unreasonable. If we count DVD sales, Roberts' potential *MRP* goes up further.

We see in this example that Roberts' *MRP* depends not only on her talent but also on the way that talent is used by employers—in the same way the *MRP* of the sandwich shop employee depended on conditions at the shop (p. 209).

The firm described in Table 10.2 and Table 10.3 continued to produce 100 units of output after the wage rate doubled. An *increase* in the price of a production factor, however, also means an increase in the costs of production. Notice that total variable cost increased from \$1,300 to \$2,000. When a firm faces higher costs, it is likely to produce less in the short run. When a firm decides to decrease output, its demand for all factors declines—including, of

output effect of a factor price increase (decrease) When a firm decreases (increases) its output in response to a factor price increase (decrease), this decreases (increases) its demand for all factors.

course, the factor whose price increased in the first place. This is called the **output effect of a factor price increase.**

A *decrease* in the price of a factor of production, in contrast, means lower costs of production. If their output price remains unchanged, firms will increase output. This, in turn, means that demand for all factors of production will increase. This is the **output effect of a factor price decrease.**

The output effect helps explain why input demand curves slope downward. Output effects and factor substitution effects work in the same direction. Consider, for example, a decline in the wage rate. Lower wages mean that a firm will substitute labor for capital and other inputs. Stated somewhat differently, the factor substitution effect leads to an increase in the quantity of labor demanded. Lower wages mean lower costs, and lower costs lead to more output. This increase in output means that the firm will hire more of all factors of production, including labor. This is the output effect of a factor price decrease. Notice that both effects lead to an increase in the quantity demanded for labor when the wage rate falls.

Many Labor Markets

Although Figure 10.1 depicts "*the* labor market," many labor markets exist. There is a market for baseball players, for carpenters, for chemists, for college professors, and for unskilled workers. Still other markets exist for taxi drivers, assembly-line workers, secretaries, and corporate executives. Each market has a set of skills associated with it and a supply of people with the requisite skills. If labor markets are competitive, the wages in those markets are determined by the interaction of supply and demand. As we have seen, firms will hire additional workers only as long as the value of their product exceeds the relevant market wage. This is true in all competitive labor markets.

Land Markets

Unlike labor and capital, land has a special feature that we have not yet considered: It is in strictly fixed (perfectly inelastic) supply in total. The only real questions about land thus center around how much it is worth and how it will be used.

demand-determined price The price of a good that is in fixed supply; it is determined exclusively by what households and firms are willing to pay for the good.

pure rent The return to any factor of production that is in fixed supply.

Because land is fixed in supply, we say that its price is **demand determined.** In other words, the price of land is determined exclusively by what households and firms are willing to pay for it. The return to any factor of production in fixed supply is called a **pure rent.**

Thinking of the price of land as demand determined can be confusing because all land is not the same. Some land is clearly more valuable than other land. What lies behind these differences? As with any other factor of production, land will presumably be sold or rented to the user who is willing to pay the most for it. The value of land to a potential user may depend on the characteristics of the land or on its location. For example, more fertile land should produce more farm products per acre and thus command a higher price than less fertile land. A piece of property located at the intersection of two highways may be of great value as a site for a gas station because of the volume of traffic that passes the intersection daily.

A numerical example may help to clarify our discussion. Consider the potential uses of a corner lot in a suburb of Kansas City. Alan wants to build a clothing store on the lot. He anticipates that he can earn economic profits of $10,000 per year because of the land's excellent location. Bella, another person interested in buying the corner lot, believes that she can earn $35,000 per year in economic profit if she builds a pharmacy there. Because of the higher profit that she expects to earn, Bella will be able to outbid Alan; and the landowner will sell (or rent) to the highest bidder.

Because location is often the key to profits, landowners are frequently able to "squeeze" their renters. One of the most popular locations in the Boston area, for example, is Harvard Square. There are dozens of restaurants in and around the square, and most of them are full a good deal of the time. Despite this seeming success, most Harvard Square restaurant owners are not getting rich. Why? Because they must pay very high rents on the location of their restaurants. A substantial portion of each restaurant's revenues goes to rent the land that (by virtue of its scarcity) is the key to unlocking those same revenues.

Although Figure 10.5 shows that the supply of land is perfectly inelastic (a vertical line), the supply of land in a *given use* may not be perfectly inelastic or fixed. Think, for example, about farmland available for housing developments. As a city's population grows, housing developers find themselves willing to pay more for land. As land becomes more valuable for development, some farmers sell out; and the supply of land available for development increases. This analysis would lead us to draw an upward-sloping supply curve (not a perfectly inelastic supply curve) for land in the land-for-development category.

Nonetheless, our major point—that land earns a pure rent—is still valid. The supply of land of a *given quality* at a *given location* is truly fixed in supply. Its value is determined exclusively by the amount that the highest bidder is willing to pay for it. Because land cannot be reproduced, supply is perfectly inelastic.

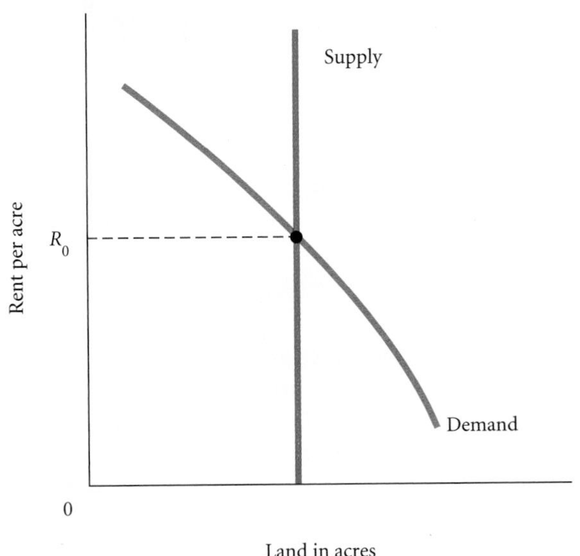

FIGURE 10.5

The Rent on Land Is Demand Determined

Because land in general (and each parcel in particular) is in fixed supply, its price is demand determined. Graphically, a fixed supply is represented by a vertical, perfectly inelastic supply curve. Rent, R_0, depends exclusively on demand—what people are willing to pay.

Rent and the Value of Output Produced on Land

Because the price of land is demand determined, rent depends on what the potential users of the land are willing to pay for it. As we have seen, land will end up being used by whoever is willing to pay the most for it. What determines this willingness to pay? Let us now connect our discussion of land markets with our earlier discussions of factor markets in general.

As our example of two potential users bidding for a plot of land shows, the bids depend on the land's potential for profit. Alan's plan would generate \$10,000 a year; Bella's would generate \$35,000 a year. Nevertheless, these profits do not just materialize. Instead, they come from producing and selling an output that is valuable to households. Land in a popular downtown location is expensive because of what can be produced on it. Note that land is needed as an input into the production of nearly all goods and services. A restaurant located next to a popular theater can charge a premium price because it has a relatively captive clientele. The restaurant must produce a quality product to stay in business, but the location alone provides a substantial profit opportunity.

It should come as no surprise that the demand for land follows the same rules as the demand for inputs in general. A profit-maximizing firm will employ an additional factor of production as long as its marginal revenue product exceeds its market price. For example, a profit-maximizing firm will hire labor as long as the revenue earned from selling labor's product is sufficient to cover the cost of hiring additional labor—which for perfectly competitive firms, equals the wage rate. The same thing is true for land. A firm will pay for and use land as long as the revenue earned from selling the product produced on that land is sufficient to cover the price of the land. Stated in equation form, the firm will use land up to the point at which $MRP_A = P_A$, where A is land (acres).

ECONOMICS IN PRACTICE

Time Is Money: European High-Speed Trains

In the past few years, many parts of Europe have invested in high-speed trains. In the article that follows, we see the way in which these trains increase land value. The rise in land value following the introduction of high-speed trains is another example of the importance of the opportunity cost of time. As train speeds increase, the time cost of living far from one's workplace decreases; the natural result is an increased willingness to live far from one's workplace and thus an increase in outlying land values.

High-Speed Rail Give Short-Haul Air a Run for the Money in Europe, With More Flexible Travel, Greater Comfort, Lower Environmental Impact

Travel Industry News

While air travelers put up with longer delays, cancelled flights and tedious security procedures, and drivers face rising gas prices and ever-increasing congestion, life keeps getting easier for passengers on Europe's expanding network of high-speed trains. The latest developments and the far-reaching benefits of high-speed European train travel were the topics of a press conference, "High-speed trains: Changing the European Experience" held in New York today. Speakers included: CEO of the French National Railroads (SNCF), Guillaume Pepy; Commercial Director of the Eurostar train, Nicholas Mercer; and High-Speed Director of the Paris-based International Railway Association (UIC), Inaki Barron. Rail Europe—North America's leading seller of European rail travel—was the host of the conference.

Traveling at speed of 150 mph or higher (compared to regular trains going 100 mph or less), high-speed trains currently run on 3,034 miles of track in 10 European countries. By 2010, another 1,711 miles are scheduled to be in operation, and there are plans beyond that to add on average 346 miles each year through 2020, according to the UIC's Barron.

High-speed trains not only benefit travelers and the environment, they also boost the economies of communities served. In France, they call it the "TGV effect"—increases in property values, rents/real estate prices and number of jobs/businesses in towns in or near high-speed rail lines.

Real estate prices in Avignon rose more than 30% in the first three years following the launch of TGV Mediterranean. In Vendome, near the TGV Atlantique line (Paris-Tours in the Loire region) real estate prices went up 50% in five years.

Source: Travel Industry Wire, March 24, 2008.

Just as the demand curve for labor reflects the value of labor's product as determined in output markets, so the demand for land depends on the value of land's product in output markets. The profitability of the restaurant located next to the theater results from the fact that the meals produced there command a price in the marketplace.

The allocation of a given plot of land among competing uses thus depends on the trade-off between competing products that can be produced there. Agricultural land becomes developed when its value in producing housing or manufactured goods (or providing space for a minimall) exceeds its value in producing crops. A corner lot in Kansas City becomes the site of a pharmacy instead of a clothing store because the people in that neighborhood have a greater need for a pharmacy.

One final word about land: Because land cannot be moved physically, the value of any one parcel depends to a large extent on the uses to which adjoining parcels are put. A factory belching acrid smoke will probably reduce the value of adjoining land, while a new highway that increases accessibility may enhance it.

The Firm's Profit-Maximizing Condition in Input Markets

Thus far, we have discussed the labor and land markets in some detail. Although we will put off a detailed discussion of capital until the next chapter, it is now possible to generalize about competitive demand for factors of production. Every firm has an incentive to use variable inputs as long as the revenue generated by those inputs covers the costs of those inputs at the margin. More formally, firms will employ each input up to the point that its price equals its marginal revenue product. This condition holds for all factors at all levels of output.

The profit-maximizing condition for the perfectly competitive firm is

$$P_L = MRP_L = (MP_L \times P_X)$$

$$P_K = MRP_K = (MP_K \times P_X)$$

$$P_A = MRP_A = (MP_A \times P_X)$$

where L is labor, K is capital, A is land (acres), X is output, and P_X is the price of that output.

When all these conditions are met, the firm will be using the optimal, or least costly, combination of inputs. If all the conditions hold at the same time, it is possible to rewrite them another way:

$$\frac{MP_L}{P_L} = \frac{MP_K}{P_K} = \frac{MP_A}{P_A} = \frac{1}{P_X}$$

Your intuition tells you much the same thing that these equations do: The marginal product of the last dollar spent on labor must be equal to the marginal product of the last dollar spent on capital, which must be equal to the marginal product of the last dollar spent on land, and so on. If this was not the case, the firm could produce more with less and reduce cost. Suppose, for example, that $MP_L/P_L > MP_K/P_K$. In this situation, the firm can produce more output by shifting dollars out of capital and into labor. Hiring more labor drives down the marginal product of labor, and using less capital increases the marginal product of capital. This means that the ratios come back to equality as the firm shifts out of capital and into labor.

So far, we have used very general terms to discuss the nature of input demand by firms in competitive markets, where input prices and output prices are taken as given. The most important point is that demand for a factor depends on the value that the market places on its marginal product.[2] The rest of this chapter explores the forces that determine the shapes and positions of input demand curves.

Input Demand Curves

In Chapter 5, we considered the factors that influence the responsiveness, or elasticity, of output demand curves. We have not yet talked about *input* demand curves in any detail, however, so we now need to say more about what lies behind them.

Shifts in Factor Demand Curves

Factor (input) demand curves are derived from information on technology—that is, production functions—and output price (see Figure 10.4 on p. 208). A change in the demand for outputs, a change in the quantity of complementary or substitutable inputs, changes in the prices of other

---

[2] If you worked through the Appendix to Chapter 7, you saw this same condition derived graphically from an isocost/isoquant diagram. *Note:* $MP_L/P_L = MP_K/P_K \rightarrow MP_L/MP_K = P_L/P_K$.

inputs, and technological change all can cause factor demand curves to shift. These shifts in demand are important because they directly affect the allocation of resources among alternative uses as well as the level and distribution of income.

The Demand for Outputs A firm will demand an input as long as its marginal revenue product exceeds its market price. Marginal revenue product, which in perfect competition is equal to a factor's marginal product times the price of output, is the value of the factor's marginal product:

$$MRP_L = MP_L \times P_X$$

The amount that a firm is willing to pay for a factor of production depends directly on the value of the things the firm produces. It follows that if product demand increases, product price will rise and marginal revenue product (factor demand) will increase—the *MRP* curve will shift to the right. If product demand declines, product price will fall and marginal revenue product (factor demand) will decrease—the *MRP* curve will shift to the left.

Go back and raise the price of sandwiches from $0.50 to $1.00 in the sandwich shop example examined in Table 10.1 on p. 205 to see that this is so.

To the extent that any input is used intensively in the production of some product, changes in the demand for that product cause factor demand curves to shift and the prices of those inputs to change. Land prices are a good example. Forty years ago, the area in Manhattan along the west side of Central Park from about 80th Street north was a run-down neighborhood full of abandoned houses. The value of land there was virtually zero. During the mid-1980s, increased demand for housing caused rents to hit record levels. Some single-room apartments, for example, rented for as much as $1,400 per month. With the higher price of output (rent), input prices increased substantially. By 2008, small one bedroom apartments on 80th Street and Central Park West sold for well over $500,000, and the value of the land figures very importantly in these prices. In essence, a shift in demand for an output (housing in the area) pushed up the marginal revenue product of land from zero to very high levels.

The Quantity of Complementary and Substitutable Inputs In our discussion thus far, we have kept coming back to the fact that factors of production complement one another. The productivity of, and thus the demand for, any one factor of production depends on the quality and quantity of the other factors with which it works.

The effect of capital accumulation on wages is one of the most important themes in all of economics. In general, the production and use of capital enhances the productivity of labor and normally increases the demand for labor and drives up wages. Consider as an example transportation. In a poor country such as Bangladesh, one person with an ox cart can move a small load over bad roads very slowly. By contrast, the stock of capital used by workers in the transportation industry in the United States is enormous. A truck driver in the United States works with a substantial amount of capital. The typical 18-wheel tractor trailer, for example, is a piece of capital worth over $100,000. The roads themselves are capital that was put in place by the government. The amount of material that a single driver can move between distant points in a short time is staggering relative to what it was just 50 years ago.

The Prices of Other Inputs When a firm has a choice among alternative technologies, the choice it makes depends to some extent on relative input prices. You saw in Table 10.2 and Table 10.3 on p. 210 that an increase in the price of labor substantially increased the demand for capital as the firm switched to a more capital-intensive production technique.

During the 1970s, the large increase in energy prices relative to prices of other factors of production had a number of effects on the demand for those other inputs. Insulation of new buildings, installation of more efficient heating plants, and similar efforts substantially raised the demand for capital as capital was substituted for energy in production. It has also been argued that the energy crisis led to an increase in demand for labor. If capital and energy are complementary inputs—that is, if technologies that are capital-intensive are also energy-intensive—the argument goes, the higher energy prices tended to push firms away from capital-intensive techniques toward more labor-intensive techniques. A new highly automated technique, for example, might need fewer workers, but it would also require a vast amount of electricity to operate. High electricity prices could lead a firm to reject the new techniques and stick with an old, more labor-intensive method of production.

Technological Change Closely related to the impact of capital accumulation on factor demand is the potential impact of **technological change**—that is, the introduction of new methods of production or new products. New technologies usually introduce ways to produce outputs with fewer inputs by increasing the productivity of existing inputs or by raising marginal products. Because marginal revenue product reflects productivity, increases in productivity directly shift input demand curves. If the marginal product of labor rises, for example, the demand for labor shifts to the right (increases). Technological change can and does have a powerful influence on factor demands. As new products and new techniques of production are born, so are demands for new inputs and new skills. As old products become obsolete, so do the labor skills and other inputs needed to produce them.

technological change The introduction of new methods of production or new products intended to increase the productivity of existing inputs or to raise marginal products.

Resource Allocation and the Mix of Output in Competitive Markets

We now have a complete, but simplified picture of household and firm decision making. We have also examined some of the basic forces that determine the allocation of resources and the mix of output in perfectly competitive markets.

In this competitive environment, profit-maximizing firms make three fundamental decisions: (1) how much to produce and supply in output markets, (2) how to produce (which technology to use), and (3) how much of each input to demand. Chapters 7 through 9 looked at these three decisions from the perspective of the output market. We derived the supply curve of a competitive firm in the short run and discussed output market adjustment in the long run. Deriving cost curves, we learned, involves evaluating and choosing among alternative technologies. Finally, we saw how a firm's decision about how much product to supply in output markets implicitly determines input demands. Input demands, we argued, are also derived demands. That is, they are ultimately linked to the demand for output.

To show the connection between output and input markets, this chapter took these same three decisions and examined them from the perspective of input markets. Firms hire up to the point at which each input's marginal revenue product is equal to its price.

The Distribution of Income

In the last few chapters, we have been focusing primarily on the firm. Throughout our study of microeconomics, we have also been building a theory that explains the distribution of income among households. We can now put the pieces of this puzzle together.

As we saw in this chapter, income is earned by households as payment for the factors of production that household members supply in input markets. Workers receive wages in exchange for their labor, owners of capital receive profits and interest in exchange for supplying capital (saving), and landowners receive rents in exchange for the use of their land. The incomes of workers depend on the wage rates determined in the market. The incomes of capital owners depend on the market price of capital (the amount households are paid for the use of their savings). The incomes of landowners depend on the rental values of their land.

If markets are competitive, the equilibrium price of each input is equal to its marginal revenue product ($W^* = MRP_L$, and so on). In other words, at equilibrium, each factor ends up receiving rewards determined by its productivity as measured by marginal revenue product. This is referred to as the **marginal productivity theory of income distribution**. We will turn to a more complete analysis of income distribution in Chapter 18.

marginal productivity theory of income distribution At equilibrium, all factors of production end up receiving rewards determined by their productivity as measured by marginal revenue product.

Looking Ahead

We have now completed our discussion of competitive labor and land markets. The next chapter takes up the complexity of what we have been loosely calling the "capital market." There we discuss the relationship between the market for physical capital and financial capital markets and look at some of the ways that firms make investment decisions. Once we examine the nature of overall competitive equilibrium in Chapter 12, we can finally begin relaxing some of the assumptions that have restricted the scope of our inquiry—most importantly, the assumption of perfect competition in input and output markets.

SUMMARY

1. The same set of decisions that lies behind output supply curves also lies behind input demand curves. Only the perspective is different.

INPUT MARKETS: BASIC CONCEPTS *p. 203*

2. Demand for inputs depends on demand for the outputs that they produce; input demand is thus a *derived demand. Productivity* is a measure of the amount of output produced per unit of input.
3. In general, firms will demand workers as long as the value of what those workers produce exceeds what they must be paid. Households will supply labor as long as the wage exceeds the value of leisure or the value that they derive from nonpaid work.
4. Inputs are at the same time *complementary* and *substitutable.*
5. In the short run, some factor of production is fixed. This means that all firms encounter diminishing returns in the short run. Stated somewhat differently, diminishing returns means that all firms encounter declining marginal product in the short run.
6. The *marginal revenue product* (*MRP*) of a variable input is the additional revenue a firm earns by employing one additional unit of the input, *ceteris paribus. MRP* is equal to the input's marginal product times the price of output.

LABOR MARKETS *p. 206*

7. Demand for an input depends on that input's marginal revenue product. Profit-maximizing perfectly competitive firms will buy an input (for example, hire labor) up to the point where the input's marginal revenue product equals its price. For a firm employing only one variable factor of production, the *MRP* curve is the firm's demand curve for that factor in the short run.
8. For a perfectly competitive firm employing one variable factor of production, labor, the condition $W = MRP_L$ is exactly the same as the condition $P = MC$. Firms weigh the value of outputs as reflected in output price against the value of inputs as reflected in marginal costs.
9. When a firm employs two variable factors of production, a change in factor price has both a *factor substitution effect* and an *output effect.*
10. A wage increase may lead a firm to substitute capital for labor and thus cause the quantity demanded of labor to decline. This is the *factor substitution effect of the wage increase.*
11. A wage increase increases cost, and higher cost may lead to lower output and less demand for all inputs, including labor. This is the *output effect of the wage increase.* The effect is the opposite for a wage decrease.

LAND MARKETS *p. 212*

12. Because land is in strictly fixed supply, its price is *demand determined*—that is, its price is determined exclusively by what households and firms are willing to pay for it. The return to any factor of production in fixed supply is called a *pure rent.* A firm will pay for and use land as long as the revenue earned from selling the product produced on that land is sufficient to cover the price of the land. The firm will use land up to the point at which $MRP_A = P_A$, where A is land (acres).

THE FIRM'S PROFIT-MAXIMIZING CONDITION IN INPUT MARKETS *p. 215*

13. Every firm has an incentive to use variable inputs as long as the revenue generated by those inputs covers the costs of those inputs at the margin. Therefore, firms will employ each input up to the point that its price equals its marginal revenue product. This profit-maximizing condition holds for all factors at all levels of output.

INPUT DEMAND CURVES *p. 215*

14. A shift in a firm's demand curve for a factor of production can be influenced by the demand for the firm's product, the quantity of complementary and substitutable inputs, the prices of other inputs, and changes in technology.

RESOURCE ALLOCATION AND THE MIX OF OUTPUT IN COMPETITIVE MARKETS *p. 217*

15. Because the price of a factor at equilibrium in competitive markets is equal to its marginal revenue product, the distribution of income among households depends in part on the relative productivity of factors. This is the *marginal productivity theory of income distribution.*

REVIEW TERMS AND CONCEPTS

demand-determined price, *p. 212*
derived demand, *p. 204*
factor substitution effect, *p. 210*
marginal product of labor (MP_L), *p. 204*
marginal productivity theory of income distribution, *p. 217*
marginal revenue product (MRP), *p. 205*
output effect of a factor price increase (decrease), *p. 212*
productivity of an input, *p. 204*
pure rent, *p. 212*
technological change, *p. 217*
Equations:
$MRP_L = MP_L \times P_X$

PROBLEMS

Visit **www.myeconlab.com** to complete the problems marked in orange online. You will receive instant feedback on your answers, tutorial help, and access to additional practice problems.

1. In September 2007, average weekly earnings of production workers were \$603. A decade earlier they were \$437. All else equal, such an increase in wages would be expected to reduce the demand for labor and employment should fall. Instead, the quantity demanded for labor has increased dramatically with more than 14.8 million jobs being created between 1997 and 2007. How can you explain this seeming discrepancy?

2. Assume that a firm that manufactures widgets can produce them with one of three processes used alone or in combination. The following table indicates the amounts of capital and labor required by each of the three processes to produce one widget.

	UNITS OF LABOR	UNITS OF CAPITAL
Process 1	4	1
Process 2	2	2
Process 3	1	3

   a. Assuming capital costs \$3 per unit and labor costs \$1 per unit, which process will be employed?
   b. Plot the three points on the firm's *TVC* curve corresponding to $q = 10$, $q = 30$, and $q = 50$.
   c. At each of the three output levels, how much *K* and *L* will be demanded?
   d. Repeat parts a. through c. assuming the price of capital is \$3 per unit and the price of labor has risen to \$4 per unit.

3. During the two decades leading up to the new millennium, wage inequality in the United States increased substantially. That is, high-income workers saw their salaries increase substantially while wages of lower-income workers stagnated or even fell. Using the logic of marginal revenue product, give an explanation for this change in the distribution of income. In your explanation, you may want to consider the rise of the high-technology, high-skill sector and the decline of industries requiring low-skill labor.

4. The following schedule shows the technology of production at the Delicious Apple Orchard for 2006:

WORKERS	TOTAL BUSHELS OF APPLES PER DAY
0	0
1	40
2	70
3	90
4	100
5	105
6	102

If apples sell for \$2 per bushel and workers can be hired in a competitive labor market for \$30 per day, how many workers should be hired? What if workers unionized and the wage rose to \$50? (*Hint:* Create marginal product and marginal revenue product columns for the table.) Explain your answers clearly.

5. The following graph is the production function for a firm using only one variable factor of production, labor.
   a. Graph the marginal product of labor for the firm as a function of the number of labor units hired.
   b. Assuming the price of output, P_X, is equal to \$6, graph the firm's marginal revenue product schedule as a function of the number of labor units hired.
   c. If the current equilibrium wage rate is \$4 per hour, how many hours of labor will you hire? How much output will you produce?

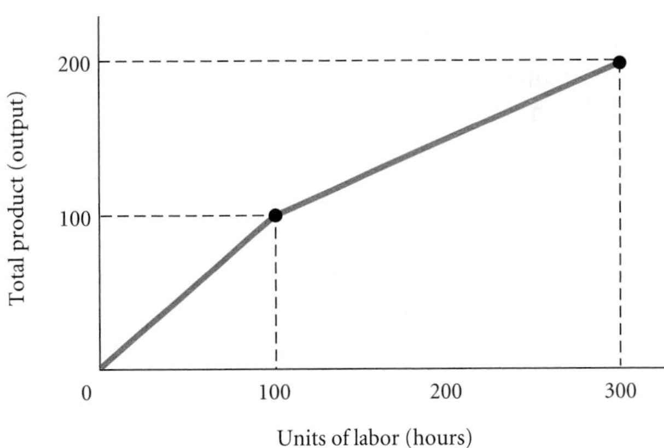

6. Describe how each of the following events would affect (1) demand for construction workers and (2) construction wages in Portland, Oregon. Illustrate with supply and demand curves.
   a. A sharp increase in interest rates on new-home mortgages reduces the demand for new houses substantially.
   b. The economy of the area booms. Office rents rise, creating demand for new office space.
   c. A change in the tax laws in 2008 made real estate developments more profitable. As a result, three major developers start planning to build major shopping centers.

7. The demand for land is a derived demand. Think of a popular location near your school. What determines the demand for land in that area? What outputs are sold by businesses located

there? Discuss the relationship between land prices and the prices of those products.

8. Many states provide firms with an "investment tax credit" that effectively reduces the price of capital. In theory, these credits are designed to stimulate new investment and thus create jobs. Critics have argued that if there are strong factor substitution effects, these subsidies could *reduce* employment in the state. Explain their arguments.

9. Doug's farm in Idaho has four major fields that he uses to grow potatoes. The productivity of each field follows:

	ANNUAL YIELD, HUNDREDS OF POUNDS
Field 1	10,000
Field 2	8,000
Field 3	5,000
Field 4	3,000

Assume that each field is the same size and that the variable costs of farming are $25,000 per year per field. The variable costs cover labor and machinery time, which is rented. Doug must decide each year how many fields to plant. In 2006, potato farmers received $6.35 per 100 pounds. How many fields did Doug plant? Explain. By 2008, the price of potatoes had fallen to $4.50 per 100 pounds. How will this price decrease change Doug's decision? How will it affect his demand for labor? How will it affect the value of Doug's land?

10. Assume that you are living in a house with two other people and that the house has a big lawn that must be mowed. One of your roommates, who dislikes working outdoors, suggests hiring a neighbor's daughter to mow the grass for $40 per week instead of sharing the work and doing it yourselves. How would you go about deciding who will mow the lawn? What factors would you raise in deciding? What are the trade-offs here?

11. Consider the following information for a T-shirt manufacturing firm that can sell as many T-shirts as it wants for $3 per shirt.

NUMBER OF WORKERS	NUMBER OF SHIRTS PRODUCED PER DAY	MP_L	TR	MRP_L
0	0	—	—	—
1	30	—	—	—
2	80	—	—	—
3	110	—	—	—
4	135	—	—	—
5	—	20	—	—
6	170	—	—	—
7	—	—	—	30
8	—	—	—	15

a. Fill in all the blanks in the table.
b. Verify that MRP_L for this firm can be calculated in two ways: (1) change in TR from adding another worker and (2) MP_L times the price of output.
c. If this firm must pay a wage rate of $40 per worker per day, how many workers should it hire? Briefly explain why.
d. Suppose the wage rate rises to $50 per worker. How many workers should be hired now? Why?
e. Suppose the firm adopts a new technology that doubles output at each level of employment and the price of shirts remains at $3. What is the effect of this new technology on MP_L and on MRP_L? At a wage of $50, how many workers should the firm hire now?

12. **[Related to *Economics in Practice* on p. 211]** At some colleges, the highest paid member of the faculty is the football coach. How would you explain this?

13. **[Related to *Economics in Practice* on p. 214]** In Orlando, Florida, the land value went up dramatically when Disney built its theme park there. How do you explain this land price increase?

*14. For a given firm, $MRP_L = \$50$ and $MRP_K = \$100$ while $P_L = \$10$ and $P_K = \$20$.
a. Is the firm maximizing profits? Why or why not?
b. Identify a specific action that would increase this firm's profits.

---

*Note: Problems marked with an asterisk are more challenging.

Input Demand: The Capital Market and the Investment Decision

11

CHAPTER OUTLINE

We saw in Chapter 10 that perfectly competitive firms hire factors of production (inputs) up to the point at which each factor's marginal revenue product is equal to that factor's price. The three main factors of production are land, labor, and capital. We also saw that factor prices are determined by the interaction of supply and demand in the factor markets. The wage rate is determined in the labor market, the price of land is determined in the land market, and the price of capital is determined in the capital market.

In Chapter 10, we explored the labor and land markets in some detail. In this chapter, we consider the capital market more fully. Transactions between households and firms in the labor and land markets are direct. In the labor market, households offer their labor directly to firms in exchange for wages. In the land market, landowners rent or sell their land directly to firms in exchange for rent or an agreed-to price. In the capital market, though, households often *indirectly* supply the financial resources necessary for firms to purchase capital. When households save and add funds to their bank accounts, for example, firms can borrow those funds from the bank to finance their capital purchases.

In Chapter 9 we discussed the incentives new firms have to enter industries in which profit opportunities exist and the incentives that existing firms have to leave industries in which they are suffering losses. We also described the conditions under which existing firms have an incentive either to expand or to reduce their scales of operation. That chapter was in a preliminary way describing the process of capital allocation. When new firms enter an industry or an existing firm expands, someone pays to put capital (plant, equipment, and inventory) in place. Because the future is uncertain, capital investment decisions always involve risk. In market capitalist systems, the decision to put capital to use in a particular enterprise is made by private citizens putting their savings at risk in search of private gain. This chapter describes the set of institutions through which such transactions take place.

Capital, Investment, and Depreciation

Before we proceed with our analysis of the capital market, we need to review some basic economic principles and introduce some related concepts.

Capital

One of the most important concepts in all of economics is the concept of **capital**. Capital goods are those goods produced by the economic system that are used as inputs to produce other goods and services in the future. Capital goods thus yield valuable productive services over time.

capital Those goods produced by the economic system that are used as inputs to produce other goods and services in the future.

physical, *or* tangible, capital Material things used as inputs in the production of future goods and services. The major categories of physical capital are nonresidential structures, durable equipment, residential structures, and inventories.

Tangible Capital When we think of capital, we generally think of the physical, material capital employed by firms. The major categories of **physical,** or **tangible, capital** are (1) nonresidential structures (for example, office buildings, power plants, factories, shopping centers, warehouses, and docks) (2) durable equipment (for example, machines, trucks, sandwich grills, and automobiles), (3) residential structures, and (4) inventories of inputs and outputs that firms have in stock.

Most firms need tangible capital, along with labor and land, to produce their products. A restaurant's capital requirements include a kitchen, ovens and grills, tables and chairs, silverware, dishes, and light fixtures. These items must be purchased up front and maintained if the restaurant is to function properly. A manufacturing firm must have a plant, specialized machinery, trucks, and inventories of parts. A winery needs casks, vats, piping, temperature-control equipment, and cooking and bottling machinery.

The capital stock of a retail pharmacy is made up mostly of inventories. Pharmacies do not produce the aspirin, vitamins, and toothbrushes that they sell. Instead, they buy those items from manufacturers and put them on display. The product actually produced and sold by a pharmacy is convenience. Like any other product, convenience is produced with labor and capital in the form of a store with many products, or inventory, displayed on the sales floor and kept in storerooms. The inventories of inputs and outputs that manufacturing firms maintain are also capital. To function smoothly and meet the demands of buyers, for example, the Ford Motor Company maintains inventories of both auto parts (tires, windshields, and so on) and completed cars.

An apartment building is also capital. Produced by the economic system, it yields valuable services over time and it is used as an input to produce housing services, which are rented.

social capital, *or* infrastructure Capital that provides services to the public. Most social capital takes the form of public works (roads and bridges) and public services (police and fire protection).

Social Capital: Infrastructure Some physical or tangible capital is owned by the public instead of by private firms. **Social capital,** sometimes called **infrastructure**, is capital that provides services to the public. Most social capital takes the form of public works such as highways, roads, bridges, mass transit systems, and sewer and water systems. Police stations, fire stations, city halls, courthouses, and police cars are all forms of social capital that are used as inputs to produce the services that government provides.

All firms use some forms of social capital in producing their outputs. Recent economic research has shown that a country's infrastructure plays a very important role in helping private firms produce their products efficiently. When public capital is not properly cared for—for example, when roads deteriorate or when airports are not modernized to accommodate increasing traffic—private firms that depend on efficient transportation networks suffer.

intangible capital Nonmaterial things that contribute to the output of future goods and services.

human capital A form of intangible capital that includes the skills and other knowledge that workers have or acquire through education and training and that yields valuable services to a firm over time.

Intangible Capital Not all capital is physical. Some things that are intangible (nonmaterial) satisfy every part of our definition of capital. When a firm invests in advertising to establish a brand name, it is producing a form of **intangible capital** called goodwill. This goodwill yields valuable services to the firm over time.

When a firm establishes a training program for employees, it is investing in its workers' skills. We can think of such an investment as the production of an intangible form of capital called **human capital.** It is produced with labor (instructors) and capital (classrooms, computers, projectors, and books). Human capital in the form of new or augmented skills is an input—it will yield valuable productive services for the firm in the future.

When research produces valuable results, such as a new production process that reduces costs or a new formula that creates a new product, the new technology can be considered capital. Furthermore, even ideas can be patented and the rights to them can be sold.

A large number of "new economy" start-up technology companies have responded to the growth of the Internet. These dot-com and e-commerce companies generally start with limited capital, and most of that capital is in the skills and knowledge of their employees: human capital.

The Time Dimension The most important dimension of capital is the fact that it exists through time. Labor services are used at the time they are provided. Households consume services and nondurable goods[1] almost immediately after purchase. However, capital exists now and into the future. The value of capital is only as great as the value of the services it will render over time.[2]

---

[1] Consumer goods are generally divided into two categories: durables and nondurables. Technically, *durable goods* are goods expected to last for more than 1 year. *Nondurable goods* are goods expected to last less than 1 year.

[2] Conceptually, consumer durable goods such as automobiles, washing machines, and the like are capital. They are produced, they yield services over time, and households use them as inputs to produce services such as transportation and clean laundry.

Measuring Capital Labor is measured in hours, and land is measured in square feet or acres. Because capital comes in so many forms, it is virtually impossible to measure it directly in physical terms. The indirect measure generally used is *current market value*. The measure of a firm's **capital stock** is the current market value of its plant, equipment, inventories, and intangible assets. By using value as a measuring stick, business managers, accountants, and economists can, in a sense, add buildings, barges, and bulldozers into a measure of total capital.

Capital is measured as a *stock* value. That is, it is measured at a point in time. The capital stock of the XYZ Corporation on July 31, 2007, is $3,453,231. According to Department of Commerce estimates, the capital stock of the U.S. economy in 2006 was about $40.6 trillion. Of that amount, $17.1 trillion was residential structures, $8.7 trillion was owned by the government (for example, aircraft carriers), and $5.0 trillion was equipment and software.[3]

Although it is measured in terms of money, or value, it is very important to think of the actual capital stock. When we speak of capital, we refer not to money or to financial assets such as bonds and stocks, but instead to the firm's physical plant, equipment, inventory, and intangible assets.

capital stock For a single firm, the current market value of the firm's plant, equipment, inventories, and intangible assets.

Investment and Depreciation

Recall the difference between stock and flow measures discussed in earlier chapters. *Stock measures* are valued at a particular point in time, whereas *flow measures* are valued over a period of time. The easiest way to think of the difference between a stock and a flow is to think about a tub of water. The volume of water in the tub is measured at a point in time and is a stock. The amount of water that flows into the tub *per hour* and the amount of water that evaporates out of the tub *per day* are flow measures. Flow measures have meaning only when the time dimension is added. Water flowing into the tub at a rate of 5 gallons per hour is very different from water flowing at a rate of 5 gallons per year.

Capital stocks are affected over time by two flows: investment and depreciation. When a firm produces or puts in place new capital—a new piece of equipment, for example—it has invested. **Investment** is a flow that increases the stock of capital. Because it has a time dimension, we speak of investment per period (by the month, quarter, or year).

investment New capital additions to a firm's capital stock. Although capital is measured at a given point in time (a stock), investment is measured over a period of time (a flow). The flow of investment increases the capital stock.

As you proceed, keep in mind that the term *investing* is *not* used in economics to describe the act of buying a share of stock or a bond. Although people commonly use the term this way ("I invested in some Union Carbide stock" or "he invested in Treasury bonds"), the term *investment* when used correctly refers *only to an increase in capital.*

Table 11.1 presents data on private investment in the U. S. economy in 2007. About half of the total was equipment and software. Almost all the rest was investment in structures, both residential (apartment buildings, condominiums, houses, and so on) and nonresidential (factories, shopping malls, and so on). Inventory investment was small. Column 3 looks at private investment as a percent of gross domestic product (GDP), a measure of the total output of the economy.

TABLE 11.1 Private Investment in the U.S. Economy, 2007

GDP = $13,841.3 billion

	Billions of Current Dollars	As a Percentage of Total Gross Investment	As a Percentage of GDP
Nonresidential structures	472.1	22.2	3.4
Equipment and software	1,009.7	47.5	7.3
Change in private inventories	2.9	0.1	0.0
Residential structures	640.7	30.2	4.6
Total gross private investment	2,125.4	100.0	15.3
– depreciation	–1,398.7	–65.8	–10.1
Net investment = gross investment – depreciation	726.7	34.2	5.2

Source: U.S. Department of Commerce, Bureau of Economic Analysis.

[3] U.S. Department of Commerce, Bureau of Economic Analysis, *Survey of Current Business*, September 2007.

depreciation The decline in an asset's economic value over time.

Depreciation is the decline in an asset's (resource's) economic value over time. If you have ever owned a car, you are aware that its resale value falls with age. Suppose you bought a new Toyota Prius for $30,500 and you decide to sell it 2 years and 25,000 miles later. Checking the newspaper and talking to several dealers, you find out that, given its condition and mileage, you can expect to get $22,000 for it. It has depreciated $8,500 ($30,500 − $22,000). Table 11.1 shows that in 2007, private depreciation in the U.S. economy was $1,398.7 billion.

A capital asset can depreciate because it wears out physically or because it becomes obsolete. Take, for example, a computer control system in a factory. If a new, technologically superior system does the same job for half the price, the old system may be replaced even if it still functions well. The Prius depreciated because of wear and tear *and* because new models had become available.

The Capital Market

capital market The market in which households supply their savings to firms that demand funds to buy capital goods.

Where does capital come from? How and why is it produced? How much and what kinds of capital are produced? Who pays for it? These questions are answered in the complex set of institutions in which households supply their savings to firms that demand funds to buy capital goods. Collectively, these institutions are called the **capital market**.

Although governments and households make some capital investment decisions, most decisions to produce new capital goods—that is, to invest—are made by firms. However, a firm cannot invest unless it has the funds to do so. Although firms can invest in many ways, it is always the case that the funds that firms use to buy capital goods come, directly or indirectly, from households. When a household decides not to consume a portion of its income, it saves. Investment by firms is the *demand for capital*. Saving by households is the *supply of capital*. Various financial institutions facilitate the transfer of households' savings to firms that use them for capital investment.

Let us use a simple example to see how the system works. Suppose some firm wants to purchase a machine that costs $1,000 and some household decides at the same time to save $1,000 from its income. Figure 11.1 shows one way that the household's decision to save might connect with the firm's decision to invest.

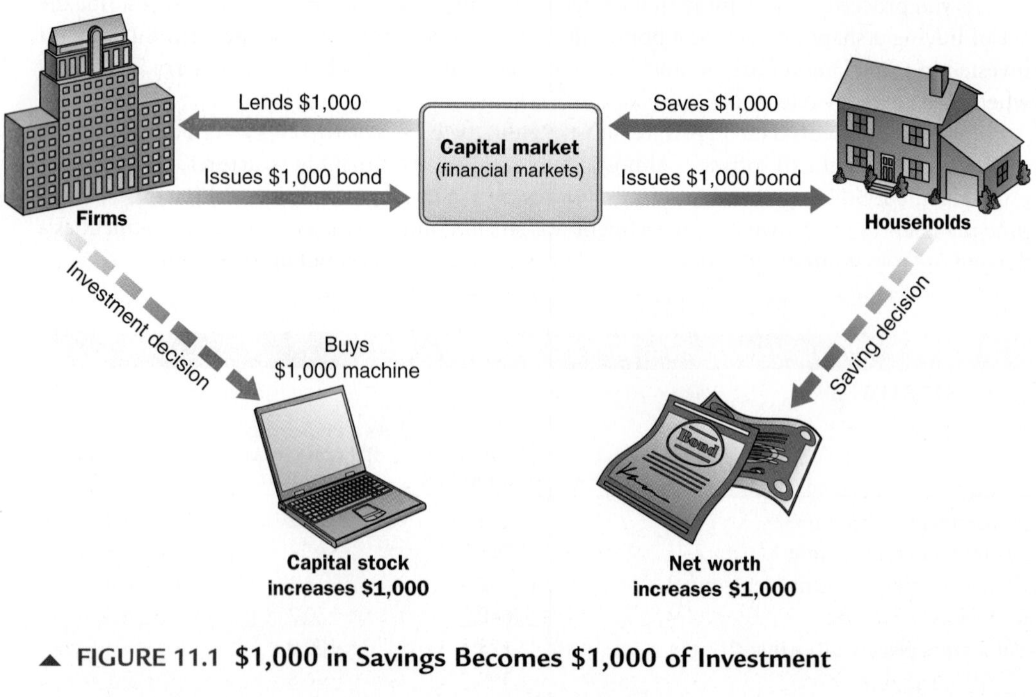

▲ FIGURE 11.1 **$1,000 in Savings Becomes $1,000 of Investment**

Either directly or through a financial intermediary (such as a bank), the household agrees to loan its savings to the firm. In exchange, the firm contracts to pay the household interest at some agreed-to rate each period. Interest is the fee paid by a borrower to a lender or by a bank to a depositor for the use of funds. The interest rate is that fee paid annually, and it is expressed as a percentage of the loan or deposit. If the household lends directly to the firm, the firm gives the household a **bond**, which is nothing more than a contract promising to repay the loan at some specific time in the future. The bond also specifies the flow of interest to be paid in the meantime.

bond A contract between a borrower and a lender, in which the borrower agrees to pay the loan at some time in the future, along with interest payments along the way.

The new saving adds to the household's stock of wealth. The household's *net worth* has increased by the $1,000, which it holds in the form of a bond.[4] The bond represents the firm's promise to repay the $1,000 at some future date with interest. The firm uses the $1,000 to buy a new $1,000 machine, which it adds to its capital stock. In essence, the household has supplied the capital demanded by the firm. It is almost as if the household bought the machine and rented it to the firm for an annual fee. Presumably, this investment will generate added revenues that will facilitate the payment of interest to the household. In general, projects are undertaken as long as the revenues likely to be realized from the investment are sufficient to cover the interest payments to the household.

Sometimes the transfer of household savings through the capital market into investment occurs without a financial intermediary. An *entrepreneur* is one who organizes, manages, and assumes the risk of a new firm. When entrepreneurs start a new business by buying capital with their own savings, they are both demanding capital and supplying the resources (that is, their savings) needed to purchase that capital. No third party is involved in the transaction. Most investment, however, is accomplished with the help of financial intermediaries (third parties such as banks, insurance companies, and pension funds) that stand between the supplier (saver) and the demander (investing firm). The part of the capital market in which savers and investors interact through intermediaries is often called the **financial capital market**.

financial capital market The part of the capital market in which savers and investors interact through intermediaries.

Capital Income: Interest and Profits

It should now be clear to you how capital markets fit into the circular flow: They facilitate the movement of household savings into the most productive investment projects. When households allow their savings to be used to purchase capital, they receive payments; and these payments (along with wages and salaries) are part of household incomes. Income that is earned on savings that have been put to use through financial capital markets is called **capital income**. Capital income is received by households in many forms, the two most important of which are *interest* and *profits*.

capital income Income earned on savings that have been put to use through financial capital markets.

Interest The most common form of capital income received by households is interest. In simplest terms, **interest** is the payment made for the use of money. Banks pay interest to depositors, whose deposits are loaned out to businesses or individuals who want to make investments.[5] Banks also *charge* interest to those who borrow money. Corporations pay interest to households that buy their bonds. The government borrows money by issuing bonds, and the buyers of those bonds receive interest payments.

interest The payments made for the use of money.

The **interest rate** is almost always expressed as an annual rate. It is the annual interest payment expressed as a percentage of the loan or deposit. For example, a $1,000 bond (representing a $1,000 loan from a household to a firm) that carries a fixed 10 percent interest rate will pay the household $100 per year ($1,000 × .10) in interest. A savings account that carries a 5 percent annual interest rate will pay $50 annually on a balance of $1,000.

interest rate Interest payments expressed as a percentage of the loan.

The interest rate is usually agreed to at the time a loan or deposit is made. Sometimes borrowers and lenders agree to periodically adjust the level of interest payments depending on market conditions. These types of loans are called *adjustable* or *floating-rate loans*. (*Fixed rate loans* are loans in which the interest rate never varies.) In recent years, there have even been adjustable rates of interest on savings accounts and certificates of deposit.

A loan's interest rate depends on a number of factors. A loan that involves more risk will generally pay a higher interest rate than a loan with less risk. Similarly, firms that are considered bad

---

[4] Note that the *act of saving* increases the household's wealth, not the act of buying the bond. Buying the bond simply transforms one financial asset (money) into another (a bond). The household could simply have held on to the money.

[5] Although we are focusing on investment by businesses, households can and do make investments also. The most important form of household investment is the construction of a new house, usually financed by borrowing in the form of a mortgage. A household may also borrow to finance the purchase of an existing house; but when it does so, no new investment is taking place.

credit risks will pay higher interest rates than firms with good credit ratings. You have probably heard radio or TV advertisements by finance companies offering to loan money to borrowers "regardless of credit history." This means that they will loan to people or businesses that pose a relatively high risk of *defaulting*, or not paying off the loan. What they do not tell you is that the interest rate will be quite high.

It is generally agreed that the safest borrower is the U.S. government. With the "full faith and credit" of the U.S. government pledged to buyers of U.S. Treasury bonds and bills, most people believe that there is little risk that the government will not repay its loans. For this reason, the U.S. government can borrow money at a lower interest rate than any other borrower.

Profits *Profits* is another word for the net income of a firm: revenue minus costs of production. Some firms are owned by individuals or partners who sell their products for more than it costs to produce them. The profits of proprietors or partnerships generally go directly to the owner or owners who run the firm. Corporations are firms owned by shareholders who usually are not otherwise connected with the firms. Corporations are organized and chartered under state laws that grant limited liability status to their owners or shareholders. Essentially, that means that shareholders cannot lose more than they have invested if the company incurs liabilities it cannot pay.

stock A share of stock is an ownership claim on a firm, entitling its owner to a profit share.

A share of common **stock** is a certificate that represents the ownership of a share of a business, almost always a corporation. For example, Lincoln Electric is a Cleveland-based company that makes welding and cutting equipment. The company has 41 million shares of common stock that are owned by tens of thousands of shareholders, some of whom are private individuals, some of whom are institutions such as Carlton College, and some of whom may be employees of the firm. Shareholders are entitled to a share of the company's profit. When profits are paid directly to shareholders, the payment is called a dividend. Lincoln Electric made a profit of $54 million in a recent year, which was $1.31 per share, of which $0.43 was paid out to shareholders as dividends and the rest retained for investment.[6]

In discussing profit, it is important to distinguish between profit as defined by generally accepting *accounting* practices and *economic* profits as we defined them in Chapter 7. Recall that our definition of profit is total revenue minus total cost, where total cost includes the normal rate of return on capital. We defined profit this way because true economic cost includes the opportunity cost of capital.

Suppose, for example, that I decide to open a candy store that requires an initial investment of $100,000. If I borrow the $100,000 from a bank, I am not making a profit until I cover the interest payments on my loan. Even if I use my own savings or raise the funds I need by selling shares in my business, I am not making a profit until I cover the opportunity cost of using those funds to start my business. Because I always have the option of lending my funds at the current market interest rate, I earn a profit only when my total revenue is large enough to cover my total cost, including the forgone interest revenue I could make from lending my funds at the current market interest rate.

As another example, suppose the Kauai Lamp Company was started in 2006 and 100 percent of the $1 million needed to start up the company (to buy the plant and equipment) was raised by selling shares of stock. Now suppose the company earns $200,000 per year, all of which is paid out to shareholders. Because $200,000 is 20 percent of the company's total capital stock, the shareholders are earning a rate of return of 20 percent; but only part of the $200,000 is profit. If the market interest rate is 11 percent, 11 percent of $1 million ($110,000) will be part of the cost of capital. The shareholders are earning a profit of only $90,000 given our definition of profit.

Functions of Interest and Profit Capital income serves several functions. First, interest may function as an incentive to postpone gratification. When you save, you pass up the chance to buy things that you want right now. One view of interest holds that it is the reward for postponing consumption.

[6] Shares of common stock are traded openly on private stock exchanges or markets. Most of the billions of shares traded every day are one shareholder selling shares to another. When shares are first issued, the proceeds are used to buy capital or to "buy out" the entrepreneurs who started the firm.

Second, profit serves as a reward for innovation and risk taking. Every year *Forbes* magazine publishes the names of the richest people in the United States, and virtually every major fortune listed there is traceable to the founding of some business enterprise that "made it big." In recent years, big winners have included retail stores (the Walton family of Wal-Mart), high-tech companies (Bill Gates of Microsoft and Michael Dell of Dell), and a real estate empire (the Pritzker family).

Many argue that rewards for innovation and risk taking are the essence of the U.S. free enterprise system. Innovation is at the core of economic growth and progress. More efficient production techniques mean that the resources saved can be used to produce new things. There is another side to this story, however: Critics of the free enterprise system claim that such large rewards are not justified and that accumulations of great wealth and power are not in society's best interests.

Financial Markets in Action

When a firm issues a fixed-interest-rate bond, it borrows funds and pays interest at an agreed-to rate to the person or institution that buys the bond. Many other mechanisms, four of which are illustrated in Figure 11.2, also channel household savings into investment projects.

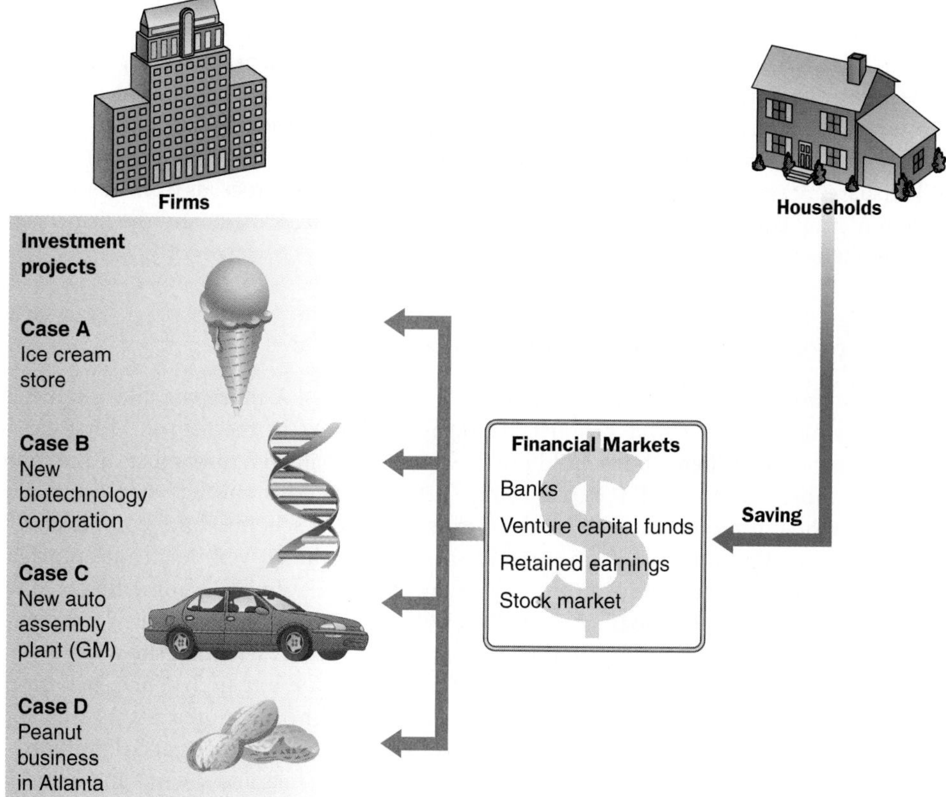

◀ FIGURE 11.2
Financial Markets Link Household Saving and Investment by Firms

Case A: Business Loans As I look around my hometown, I see several ice cream stores doing very well; but I think that I can make better ice cream than they do. To go into the business, I need capital: ice cream-making equipment, tables, chairs, freezers, signs, and a store. Because I put up my house as collateral, I am not a big risk; so the bank grants me a loan at a fairly reasonable interest rate. Banks have these funds to lend only because households deposit their savings there.

Case B: Venture Capital A scientist at a leading university develops an inexpensive method of producing a very important family of virus-fighting drugs, using microorganisms created through gene splicing. The business could very well fail within 12 months; but if it succeeds, the potential for profit is huge.

Our scientist goes to a *venture capital fund* for financing. Such funds take household savings and put them into high-risk ventures in exchange for a share of the profits if the new businesses succeed. By investing in many different projects, the funds reduce the risk of going broke. Once again, household funds make it possible for firms to undertake investments. If a venture succeeds, those owning shares in the venture capital fund receive substantial profits.

Case C: Retained Earnings General Motors Corporation (GM) decides that it wants to build a new assembly plant in Tennessee, and it discovers that it has enough funds to pay for the new facility. The new investment is thus paid for through internal funds, or *retained earnings*.

The result is the same as if the firm had gone to households via some financial intermediary and borrowed the funds. If GM uses its profits to buy new capital, it does so only with the shareholders' implicit consent. When a firm takes its own profit and uses it to buy capital assets instead of paying it out to its shareholders, the total value of the firm goes up, as does the value of the shares held by stockholders. As in our other examples, GM capital stock increases and so does the net worth of households.

When a household owns a share of stock that *appreciates*, or increases in value, the appreciation is part of the household's income. Unless the household sells the stock and consumes the gain, that gain is part of saving. In essence, when a firm retains earnings for investment purposes, it is actually saving on behalf of its shareholders.

Case D: The Stock Market A former high-ranking government official decides to start a new peanut-processing business in Atlanta; he also decides to raise the funds needed by issuing shares of stock. Households buy the shares with income that they decide not to spend. In exchange, they are entitled to a share of the peanut firm's profits.

The shares of stock become part of households' net worth. The proceeds from stock sales are used to buy plant equipment and inventory. Savings flow into investment, and the firm's capital stock goes up by the same amount as household net worth.

Mortgages and the Mortgage Market

Most real estate in the United States is financed by mortgages. A mortgage, like a bond, is a contract in which the borrower promises to repay the lender in the future. Mortgages are backed by real estate. When a household buys a home, it usually borrows most of the money by signing a mortgage in which it agrees to repay the money with interest often over as long as 30 years. While in recent years all kinds of exotic payment schemes have complicated the mortgage market, the most common form of mortgage is the 30-year fixed rate mortgage. Almost all mortgage loans require a monthly payment. As an example, a home financed with a 30-year fixed rate mortgage loan of $250,000 at 6.4 percent will face a monthly payment of $1,563.76. If the borrower pays that amount each month for 30 years, he or she will have paid off the loan while paying interest at a rate of 6.4 percent on the unpaid balance each month. The total value of the homes owned by owner-occupants in the United States was about $21 trillion in 2007. The total mortgage debt owed by households was about $10 trillion.

Until the last decade, most mortgage loans were made by banks and savings and loans. The lenders used depositors' money to make the loans, and the signed promissory notes were kept by the lenders who collected the payment every month.

Recently, the mortgage market changed dramatically and became more complicated. Most mortgages are now written by mortgage brokers or mortgage bankers who immediately sell the mortgages to a secondary market. The secondary market is run by quasi-governmental agencies such as Fannie Mae and Freddie Mac and large investment banks. Loans in this market are "securitized," which means that the mortgage documents are pooled and then mortgage-backed securities are sold to investors who want to take different degrees of risk.

The risk of owning mortgages is primarily the risk that the borrower will default on the obligation. When default occurs, the house may be taken through foreclosure, a procedure in which the lender takes possession of the borrower's house and sells it to get back at least some of the amount that the lender is owed.

In 2007, the mortgage market was hit by a dramatic increase in the number of defaults and foreclosures. Lenders lost billions of dollars, and hundreds of thousands of homes went into foreclosure. The reasons were that home prices began falling for the first time in many years and that a large number of loans were made to buyers who could not make the required payments.

Capital Accumulation and Allocation

You can see from the preceding examples that various, and sometimes complex, connections between households and firms facilitate the movement of savings into productive investment. The methods may differ, but the results are the same.

Think again about Colleen and Bill, whom we discussed in Chapter 2. They found themselves alone on a deserted island. They had to make choices about how to allocate available resources, including their time. By spending long hours working on a house or a boat, Colleen and Bill are saving and investing. First, they are using resources that could be used to produce more immediate rewards—they could gather more food or simply lie in the sun and relax. Second, they are applying those resources to the production of capital and capital accumulation.

Industrialized or agrarian, small or large, simple or complex, all societies exist through time and must allocate resources over time. In simple societies, investment and saving decisions are made by the same people. However:

> In modern industrial societies, investment decisions (capital production decisions) are made primarily by firms. Households decide how much to save; and in the long run, savings limit or constrain the amount of investment that firms can undertake. The capital market exists to direct savings into profitable investment projects.

The Demand for New Capital and the Investment Decision

We saw in Chapter 9 that firms have an incentive to expand in industries that earn positive profits—that is, a rate of return above normal—and in industries in which economies of scale lead to lower average costs at higher levels of output. We also saw that positive profits in an industry stimulate the entry of new firms. The expansion of existing firms and the creation of new firms both involve investment in new capital.

Even when there are no profits in an industry, firms must still do some investing. First, equipment wears out and must be replaced if the firm is to stay in business. Second, firms are constantly changing. A new technology may become available, sales patterns may shift, or the firm may expand or contract its product line.

With these points in mind, we now turn to a discussion of the investment decision process within the individual firm. In the end, we will see (just as we did in Chapter 10) that a perfectly competitive firm invests in capital up to the point at which the marginal revenue product of capital is equal to the price of capital. (Because we based much of our discussion in Chapter 10 on the assumption of perfect competition, it makes sense to continue doing so here. Keep in mind, though, that much of what we say also applies to firms that are not perfectly competitive.)

Forming Expectations

We have already said that the most important dimension of capital is time. Capital produces useful services over *some period of time*. In building an office tower, a developer makes an investment that will be around for decades. In deciding where to build a branch plant, a manufacturing firm commits a large amount of resources to purchase capital that will be in place for a long time.

It is important to remember, though, that capital goods do not begin to yield benefits until they are *used*. Often the decision to build a building or purchase a piece of equipment must be made years before the actual project is completed. Although the acquisition of a small business computer may take only days, the planning process for downtown development projects in big U.S. cities has been known to take decades.

The Expected Benefits of Investments Decision makers must have expectations about what is going to happen in the future. A new plant will be very valuable—that is, it will produce much profit—if the market for a firm's product grows and the price of that product remains high. The same plant will be worth little if the economy goes into a slump or consumers grow tired of the firm's product. An office tower may turn out to be an excellent investment, but not if many new office buildings go up at the same time, flooding the office space market, pushing up the vacancy rate, and driving down rents. The investment process requires that the potential investor evaluate the expected flow of future productive services that an investment project will yield.

Remember that households, firms, and governments all undertake investments. A household must evaluate the future services that a new roof will yield. A firm must evaluate the flow of future revenues that a new plant will generate. Governments must estimate how much benefit society will derive from a new bridge or a war memorial.

An official of the General Electric Corporation (GE) once described the difficulty involved in making such predictions. GE subscribes to a number of different economic forecasting services. In the early 1980s, those services provided the firm with 10-year predictions of new housing construction that ranged from a low of 400,000 new units per year to a high of 4 million new units per year. Because GE sells millions of household appliances to contractors building new houses, condominiums, and apartments, the forecast was critical. If GE decided that the high number was more accurate, it would need to spend billions of dollars on new plant and equipment to prepare for the extra demand. If GE decided that the low number was more accurate, it would need to begin closing several of its larger plants and disinvesting. In fact, GE took the middle road. It assumed that housing production would be between 1.5 and 2 million units—which, in fact, it was.

GE is not an exception. All firms must rely on forecasts to make sensible investment and production decisions, but forecasting is an inexact science because so much depends on events that cannot be foreseen.

Many believe that the Internet and the rise of e-commerce have brought revolutionary change to the world economy and created "a new economy." There is a great deal of uncertainty about where the information age is headed, and this makes expectations all the more important and volatile. A great deal of capital was allocated to thousands and thousands of new technology companies in the 1990s. Many of those firms failed during the dot.com crash of 2000–2003. Only time will tell which technology companies will finally bear fruit for investors.

The Expected Costs of Investments The benefits of any investment project take the form of future profits. These profits must be forecast, but costs must also be evaluated. Like households, firms have access to financial markets, both as borrowers and as lenders. If a firm borrows, it must *pay* interest over time. If it lends, it will *earn* interest. If the firm borrows to finance a project, the interest on the loan is part of the cost of the project.

Even if a project is financed with the firm's own fund instead of through borrowing, an opportunity cost is involved. A thousand dollars put into a capital investment project will generate an expected flow of future profit; the same $1,000 put into the financial market (in essence, loaned to another firm) will yield a flow of interest payments. The project will not be undertaken unless it is expected to yield more than the market interest rate. The cost of an investment project may thus be direct or indirect because the ability to lend at the market rate of interest means that there is an *opportunity cost* associated with every investment project. The evaluation process thus involves not only estimating future benefits but also comparing them with the possible alternative uses of the funds required to undertake the project. At a minimum, those funds could earn interest in financial markets.

ECONOMICS IN PRACTICE

What Makes Venture Capital Green?

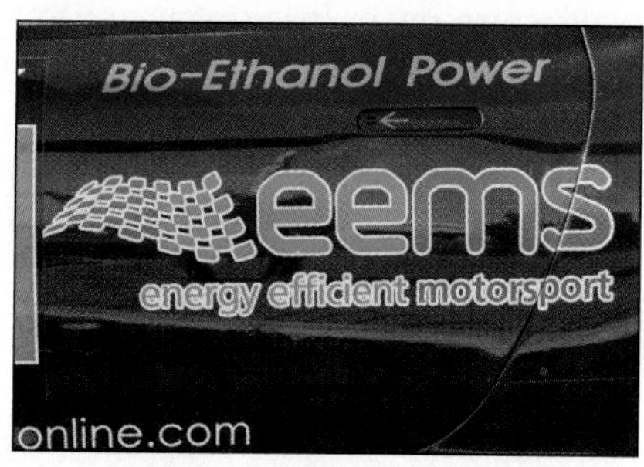

For new and risky firms, the capital needed to grow is something provided by venture capitalists rather than either banks or the stock market. Venture capitalists typically are willing to take more risks than a bank, but expect higher returns when things go well. The article below describes the new excitement that some venture capitalists have evidenced for "green" business, environmentally sustainable, and clean energy firms. What has fueled this enthusiasm? As with any other investment, venture capitalists look to profit potential. Here, some predict that rising fuel prices on the one hand and growing government subsidies for green products on the other hand will produce high profits for this sector.

Venture Capital Goes Big for Green

The Kiplinger Letter

For choosy investors, there's still time to hop on the "green" bandwagon.

For venture capitalists nowadays it's all about green—green companies, that is. Seed money for environmental and clean energy firms is on course to double this year to $3 billion after more than doubling in 2006. Green investments will account for over $1 out of every $10 in venture capital investments, while green initial public offerings will surpass last year's $1.2 billion, which was more than triple the $370 million raised in IPOs in 2005.

The torrid pace brings back memories of the dot-com boom, when investors threw cash at anything even remotely related to the Internet, whether it was making money or not. The numbers tell the story: In 1997, investors put $2.5 billion into Internet start-ups. In 2000, investments ballooned to $43.7 billion.

But there's really no comparison. This time, investors are focused on firms with proven profit potential. In addition, green companies will draw sustained support from long-term trends: rising fuel prices, declines in renewable resources such as oil and natural gas and the need to reduce global warming and worldwide pollution. Government subsidies for environmentally friendly firms are also likely to increase, giving a boost to the bottom lines of green companies for the near future.

Of course, not all green companies will be winners. Some may be betting too heavily on companies that are already expensive, especially these based on solar and biofuel energy technologies. Out of 1500 green-related start-ups last year, 930 were in the energy sector. Several energy-related firms have flopped since their market debuts, prompting others in this category to delay their planned IPOs this year.

Less chancy options include air, water and waste management technologies. Some companies pushing devices that purify and monitor impurities in air and water, as well as ones that desalinate or convert waste to usable fuels, have been overlooked. The waste segment now receives just 4% of venture capital dollars.

Source: By Matthew Mogul, Associate Editor, The Kiplinger Letter, *June 7, 2007.*

Comparing Costs and Expected Return

Once expectations have been formed, firms must quantify them—that is, they must assign some dollars-and-cents value to them. One way to quantify expectations is to calculate an **expected rate of return** on the investment project. For example, if a new computer network that costs

expected rate of return The annual rate of return that a firm expects to obtain through a capital investment.

$400,000 is likely to save $100,000 per year in data processing costs forever after, the expected rate of return on that investment is 25 percent per year. Each year the firm will save $100,000 as a result of the $400,000 investment. The expected rate of return will be less than 25 percent if the computer network wears out or becomes obsolete after a while and the cost saving ceases. The expected rate of return on an investment project depends on the price of the investment, the expected length of time the project provides additional cost savings or revenue, and the expected amount of revenue attributable each year to the project.

Table 11.2 presents a menu of investment choices and expected rates of return that a hypothetical firm faces. Because expected rates of return are based on forecasts of future profits attributable to the investments, any change in expectations would change all the numbers in column 2.

TABLE 11.2 Potential Investment Projects and Expected Rates of Return for a Hypothetical Firm, Based on Forecasts of Future Profits Attributable to the Investment

Project	(1) Total Investment (Dollars)	(2) Expected Rate of Return (Percent)
A. New computer network	400,000	25
B. New branch plant	2,600,000	20
C. Sales office in another state	1,500,000	15
D. New automated billing system	100,000	12
E. Ten new delivery trucks	400,000	10
F. Advertising campaign	1,000,000	7
G. Employee cafeteria	100,000	5

Figure 11.3 graphs the total amount of investment in millions of dollars that the firm would undertake at various interest rates. If the interest rate were 24 percent, the firm would fund only project A, the new computer network. It can borrow at 24 percent and invest in a computer that is expected to yield 25 percent. At 24 percent, the firm's total investment is $400,000. The first vertical red line in Figure 11.3 shows that at any interest rate above 20 percent and below 25 percent, only $400,000 worth of investment (that is, project A) will be undertaken.

▶ **FIGURE 11.3**

Total Investment as a Function of the Market Interest Rate

The demand for new capital depends on the interest rate. When the interest rate is low, firms are more likely to invest in new plant and equipment than when the interest rate is high. This is so because the interest rate determines the direct cost (interest on a loan) or the opportunity cost (alternative investment) of each project.

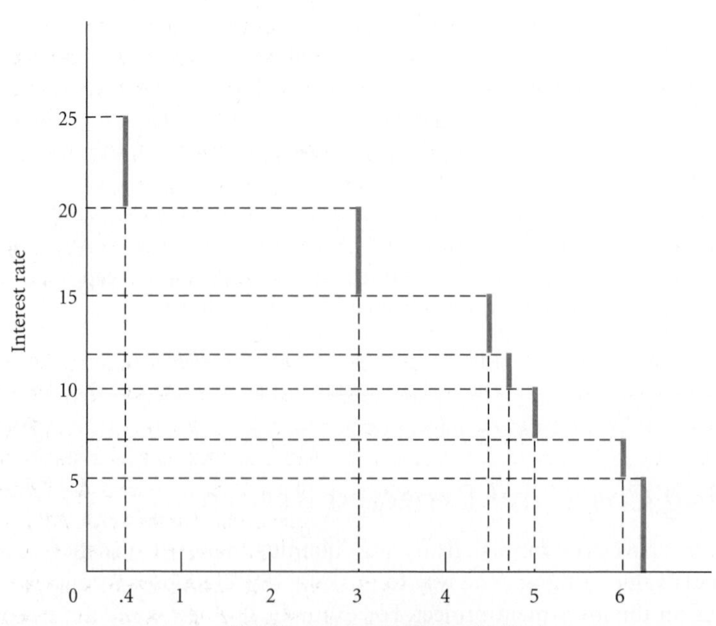

If the interest rate were 18 percent, the firm would fund projects A and B; and its total investment would rise to \$3 million (\$400,000 + \$2,600,000). If the firm could borrow at 18 percent, the flow of additional profits generated by the new computer and the new plant would more than cover the costs of borrowing; but none of the other projects would be justified. The rates of return on projects A and B (25 percent and 20 percent, respectively) both exceed the 18 percent interest rate. Only if the interest rate fell below 5 percent would the firm fund all seven investment projects.

The investment schedule in Table 11.2 and its graphic depiction in Figure 11.3 describe the firm's demand for new capital, expressed as a function of the market interest rate. If we add the total investment undertaken by *all* firms at every interest rate, we arrive at the demand for new capital in the economy as a whole. In other words, the market demand curve for new capital is the sum of all the individual demand curves for new capital in the economy (Figure 11.4). In a sense, the investment demand schedule is a ranking of all the investment opportunities in the economy in order of expected yield. Only those investment projects in the economy that are expected to yield a rate of return higher than the market interest rate will be funded. At lower market interest rates, more investment projects are undertaken.

The most important thing to remember about the investment demand curve is that its shape and position depend critically on the *expectations* of those making the investment decisions. Because many influences affect these expectations, they are usually volatile and subject to frequent change. Thus, although lower interest rates tend to stimulate investment and higher interest rates tend to slow it, many other hard-to-measure and hard-to-predict factors also affect the level of investment spending. These might include government policy changes, election results, global affairs, inflation, and changes in currency exchange rates.

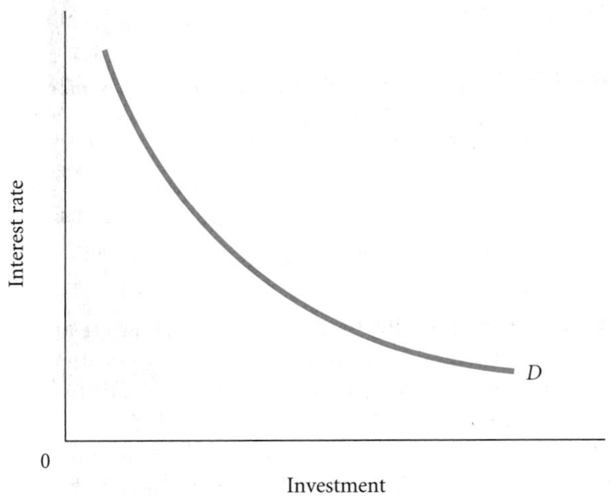

FIGURE 11.4
Investment Demand
Lower interest rates are likely to stimulate investment in the economy as a whole, whereas higher interest rates are likely to slow investment.

The Expected Rate of Return and the Marginal Revenue Product of Capital The concept of the expected rate of return on investment projects is analogous to the concept of the marginal revenue product of capital (MRP_K). Recall that we defined an input's marginal revenue product as the additional revenue a firm earns by employing one additional unit of that input, *ceteris paribus*. Also recall our earlier discussion in Chapter 7 of labor demand in a sandwich shop. If an additional worker can produce 15 sandwiches in 1 hour (the marginal product of labor: $MP_L = 15$) and each sandwich brings in \$0.50 (the price of the service produced by the sandwich shop: $P_X = \$0.50$), the marginal revenue product of labor is equal to \$7.50 ($MRP_L = MP_L \times P_X = 15 \times \$0.50 = \$7.50$).

Now think carefully about the return to an additional unit of new capital (the marginal revenue product of capital). Suppose that the rate of return on an investment in a new machine is 15 percent. This means that the investment project yields the same return as a bond yielding 15 percent. If the current interest rate is less than 15 percent, the investment project will be undertaken because a perfectly competitive profit-maximizing firm will keep investing in new capital up to the point at which the expected rate of return is equal to the interest rate. This is analogous to saying that the firm will continue investing up to the point at which the marginal revenue product of capital is equal to the price of capital, or $MRP_K = P_K$, which is what we learned in Chapter 10.

A Final Word on Capital

The concept of capital is one of the central ideas in economics. Capital is produced by the economic system itself. Capital generates services over time, and it is used as an input in the production of goods and services.

The enormous productivity of modern industrial societies is due in part to the tremendous amount of capital that they have accumulated over the years. It may surprise you to know that the average worker in the United States works with about $170,000 worth of capital. Recall that in the United States, total investment (new capital) was 16.4 percent of GDP in 2007 (Table 11.1). High rates of investment have had enormous impacts in countries such as China and Malaysia. According to recent World Bank figures, capital goods represent 40 percent of China's total output of goods and services; and in Malaysia, the figure is 32 percent. In 2005, China had a growth rate of output of over 9 percent and Malaysia had over 7 percent.

Most of this chapter described the institutions and processes that determine the amount and types of capital produced in a market economy. Existing firms in search of increased profits, potential new entrants to the markets, and entrepreneurs with new ideas are continuously evaluating potential investment projects. At the same time, households are saving. Each year households save some portion of their after-tax incomes. These new savings become part of their net worth, and they want to earn a return on those savings. Each year a good portion of the savings finds its way into the hands of firms that use it to buy new capital goods.

Between households and firms is the financial capital market. Millions of people participate in financial markets every day. There are literally thousands of financial managers, pension funds, mutual funds, brokerage houses, options traders, and banks whose sole purpose is to earn the highest possible rate of return on people's savings.

Brokers, bankers, and financial managers are continuously scanning the financial horizons for profitable investments. What businesses are doing well? What businesses are doing poorly? Should we lend to an expanding firm? All the analysis done by financial managers seeking to earn a high yield for clients, by managers of firms seeking to earn high profits for their stockholders, and by entrepreneurs seeking profits from innovation serves to channel capital into its most productive uses. Within firms, the evaluation of individual investment projects involves forecasting costs and benefits and valuing streams of potential income that will be earned only in future years.

We have now completed our discussion of competitive input and output markets. We have looked at household and firm choices in output markets, labor markets, land markets, and capital markets.

We now turn to a discussion of the allocative process that we have described. How do all the parts of the economy fit together? Is the result good or bad? Can we improve on it? All of this is the subject of Chapter 12.

SUMMARY

CAPITAL, INVESTMENT, AND DEPRECIATION *p. 221*

1. In market capitalist systems, the decision to put capital to use in a particular enterprise is made by private citizens putting their savings at risk in search of private gain. The set of institutions through which such transactions occur is called the *capital market.*

2. *Capital goods* are those goods produced by the economic system that are used as inputs to produce other goods and services in the future. Capital goods thus yield valuable productive services over time.

3. The major categories of *physical,* or *tangible, capital* are nonresidential structures, durable equipment, residential structures, and inventories. *Social capital* (or *infrastructure*) is capital that provides services to the public. *Intangible (nonmaterial) capital* includes *human capital* and goodwill.

4. The most important dimension of capital is that it exists through time. Therefore, its value is only as great as the value of the services it will render over time.

5. The most common measure of a firm's *capital stock* is the current market value of its plant, equipment, inventories, and intangible assets. However, in thinking about capital, it is important to focus on the actual capital stock instead of its simple monetary value.

6. In economics, the term *investment* refers to the creation of new capital, not to the purchase of a share of stock or a bond. Investment is a flow that increases the capital stock.

7. *Depreciation* is the decline in an asset's economic value over time. A capital asset can depreciate because it wears out physically or because it becomes obsolete.

THE CAPITAL MARKET *p. 224*

8. Income that is earned on savings that have been put to use through *financial capital markets* is called *capital income*. The two most important forms of capital income are *interest* and *profits*. Interest is the fee paid by a borrower to a lender. Interest rewards households for postponing gratification, and profit rewards entrepreneurs for innovation and risk taking.

9. In modern industrial societies, investment decisions (capital production decisions) are made primarily by firms. Households decide how much to save; and in the long run, saving limits the amount of investment that firms can undertake. The capital market exists to direct savings into profitable investment projects.

THE DEMAND FOR NEW CAPITAL AND THE INVESTMENT DECISION *p. 229*

10. Before investing, investors must evaluate the expected flow of future productive services that an investment project will yield.

11. The availability of interest to lenders means that there is an opportunity cost associated with every investment project. This cost must be weighed against the stream of earnings that a project is expected to yield.

12. A firm will decide whether to undertake an investment project by comparing costs with expected returns. The *expected rate of return* on an investment project depends on the price of the investment, the expected length of time the project provides additional cost savings or revenue, and the expected amount of revenue attributable each year to the project.

13. The investment demand curve shows the demand for capital in the economy as a function of the market interest rate. Only those investment projects that are expected to yield a rate of return higher than the market interest rate will be funded. Lower interest rates should stimulate investment.

14. A perfectly competitive profit-maximizing firm will keep investing in new capital up to the point at which the expected rate of return is equal to the interest rate. This is equivalent to saying that the firm will continue investing up to the point at which the marginal revenue product of capital is equal to the price of capital, or $MRP_K = P_K$.

REVIEW TERMS AND CONCEPTS

bond, *p. 225*
capital, *p. 221*
capital income, *p. 225*
capital market, *p. 224*
capital stock, *p. 223*
depreciation, *p. 224*
expected rate of return, *p. 231*
financial capital market, *p. 225*
human capital, *p. 222*
intangible capital, *p. 222*
interest, *p. 225*
interest rate, *p. 225*
investment, *p. 223*
physical, *or* tangible, capital, *p. 222*
social capital, *or* infrastructure, *p. 222*
stock, *p. 226*

PROBLEMS

Visit **www.myeconlab.com** to complete the problems marked in orange online. You will receive instant feedback on your answers, tutorial help, and access to additional practice problems.

1. Which of the following are capital, and which are not? Explain your answers.
   a. A video poker game machine at a local bar that takes quarters
   b. A $10 bill
   c. A college education
   d. The Golden Gate Bridge
   e. The shirts on the rack at Sears
   f. A government bond
   g. The Empire State Building
   h. A savings account
   i. The Washington Monument
   j. A Honda plant in Marysville, Ohio

2. For each of the following, decide whether you agree or disagree and explain your answer:
   a. *Savings* and *investment* are just two words for the same thing.
   b. When I buy a share of Microsoft stock, I have invested; when I buy a government bond, I have not.
   c. Higher interest rates lead to more investment because those investments pay a higher return.

3. You and 99 other partners are offered the chance to buy a gas station. Each partner would put up $10,000. The revenues from the operation of the station have been steady at $420,000 per year for several years and are projected to remain steady into the

future. The costs (not including opportunity costs) of operating the station (including maintenance and repair, depreciation, and salaries) have also been steady at $360,000 per year. Currently, 5-year Treasury bills are yielding 7.5 percent interest. Would you go in on the deal? Explain your answer.

4. The board of directors of the Quando Company in Singapore was presented with the following list of investment projects for implementation in 2008:

PROJECT	TOTAL COST SINGAPORE DOLLARS	ESTIMATED RATE OF RETURN
Factory in Kuala Lumpur	17,356,400	13%
Factory in Bangkok	15,964,200	15
A new company aircraft	10,000,000	12
A factory outlet store	3,500,000	18
A new computer network	2,000,000	20
A cafeteria for workers	1,534,000	7

Sketch total investment as a function of the interest rate (with the interest rate on the *Y*-axis). Currently, the interest rate in Singapore is 8 percent. How much investment would you recommend to Quando's board?

5. The Federal Reserve Board of Governors has the power to raise or lower short-term interest rates. Between 2005 and 2006, the Fed aggressively increased the benchmark federal funds interest rate from 2.5 percent in February 2005 to 5.25 percent in June 2006. Assuming that other interest rates also increased, what effects do you think that move had on investment spending in the economy? Explain your answer. What do you think the Fed's objective was?

6. Give at least three examples of how savings can be channeled into productive investment. Why is investment so important for an economy? What do you sacrifice when you save today?

7. From a newspaper such as the *Wall Street Journal*, from the business section of your local daily, or from the Internet, look up the prime interest rate, the corporate bond rate, and the interest rate on 10-year U.S. government bonds today. List some of the reasons these three rates are different.

8. Explain what we mean when we say that "households supply capital and firms demand capital."

9. **[Related to *Economics in Practice* on** *p. 231***].** Venture capital funds have been very active in rapidly developing countries such as China and India. Explain why this is so.

10. Suppose I decide to start a small business. To raise start-up funds, I sell 1,000 shares of stock for $100 each. For the next 5 years, I take in annual revenues of $50,000. My total annual costs of operating the business are $20,000. If all of my earnings are paid out as dividends to shareholders, how much of my total annual earnings can be considered profit? Assume that the current interest rate is 10 percent.

11. Describe the capital stock of your college or university. How would you go about measuring its value? Has your school made any major investments in recent years? If so, describe them. What does your school hope to gain from these investments?

12. In March of 2008, the General Motors building, a skyscraper in Manhattan, was up for bid. At the time, the skyscraper was expected to fetch more than $3 billion, a record for a single building. If you were a real estate investment company considering bidding on this building, what would you want to know first? What specific factors would you need to form expectations about? What information would you need to form those expectations?

13. On October 29, 2007, the Red Sox won the World Series. That same day the stock market rose. The S&P 500 index (an index of the stock prices of the 500 largest corporations in the United States) closed up at 1540.98. Ten-year Treasury notes were paying 4.38% on 10-year obligations of the government. The Fed was poised to announce a cut in the fed funds rate of a quarter of a percent to 4.75 percent.

    Look up today's S&P index, the 10-year treasury interest rate, and the fed funds rate. You can find them at http://money.cnn.com. Provide an explanation for what has happened to those three numbers since 2007.

APPENDIX

CALCULATING PRESENT VALUE

We have seen in this chapter that a firm's major goal in making investment decisions is to evaluate revenue streams that will not materialize until the future. One way for the firm to decide whether to undertake an investment project is to compare the expected rate of return from the investment with the current interest rate available (assuming comparable risk) in the financial market. We discussed this procedure in the text. The purpose of this Appendix is to present a more complete method of evaluating future revenue streams through present-value analysis.

PRESENT VALUE

Consider the investment project described in Table 11A.1. We use the word *project* in this example to refer to buying a machine or a piece of capital for $1,200 and receiving the cash flow given in the right-hand column of the table. Would you do the project? At first glance, you might answer yes. After all, the total flow of cash that you will receive is $1,600, which is $400 greater than the amount that you have to pay. But be careful: The $1,600 comes to you over a 5-year period, and your $1,200 must be paid right now. You must consider the alternative uses and opportunity costs of the $1,200. At the same time, you must consider the risks that you are taking.

TABLE 11A.1 Expected Profits from a $1,200 Investment Project

Year 1	$100
Year 2	100
Year 3	400
Year 4	500
Year 5	500
All later years	0
Total	1,600

What are these alternatives? At a bare minimum, the same $1,200 could be put in a bank account, where it would earn interest. In addition, there are other things that you could do with the same money. You could buy Treasury bonds from the federal government that guarantee you interest of 4 percent for 5 years. Or you might find other projects with a similar degree of risk that produce more than $1,600.

Recall that the *interest rate* is the amount of money that a borrower agrees to pay a lender or a bank agrees to pay a depositor each year, expressed as a percentage of the deposit or the loan. For example, if I deposited $1,000 in an account paying 10 percent interest, I would receive $100 per year for the term of the deposit. Sometimes we use the term *rate of return* to refer to the amount of money that the lender receives from its investment each year, expressed as a percentage of the investment.

The idea is that in deciding to do any project, you must consider the opportunity costs: What are you giving up? If you did not do this project but put the money to use elsewhere, would you do better?

Almost all investments that you might consider involve risks: The project might not work out the way you anticipate, the economy may change, or market interest rates could go up or down. To assess the opportunity costs and to decide whether this project is worth it, you first have to think about those risks and decide on the rate of return that you require to compensate yourself for taking the risks involved.

If there were no risk, the opportunity cost of investing in a project would be the government-guaranteed or bank-guaranteed interest rate. But in considering a project that involves risk, you would want more profit in return for bearing that risk. For example, you might invest in a sure deal if you received a 3 percent annual return comparable to what you might earn with a bank account or certificate of deposit, whereas you might demand 15 percent or even 20 percent on a very risky investment.

Evaluating the opportunity costs of any investment project requires taking the following steps:

Step 1: The first step in evaluating the opportunity costs of an investment project is to look at the market. What are interest rates today? What rates of interest are people earning by putting their money in bank accounts? If there is risk that something could go wrong, what interest rate is the market paying to those who accept that risk? The *discount rate* used to evaluate an investment project is the interest rate that you could earn by investing a similar amount of money in an alternative investment *of comparable risk*.

Let's suppose that the investment project described in Table 11A.1 involved some risk. While you are quite certain that the expected flow of profits in years 1–5 ($100, $100, $400, and so on) is a very good estimate, the future is always uncertain. Let's further suppose that alternative investments of comparable risks are paying a 10 percent rate of interest (rate of return). So you will not do this project unless it earns at least 10 percent. We will thus use a 10 percent discount rate in evaluating the project.

Step 2: Now comes the trick. Is your investment worth it? By doing the project, you must consider the opportunity cost of the money. To do this, imagine a bank that will pay 10 percent on deposits. The question that you must answer is, how much would you have to put in a bank paying 10 percent interest on deposits in order to get the same flow of profits that you would get if you did the project?

If it turns out that you can replicate the flow of profits for *less* money up front than the project costs—$1,200—you will *not* do the project. The project would be paying you less than a 10 percent rate of return. On the other hand, if it turns out that you would have to put *more* than $1,200 in the bank to replicate the flow of profits from the project, the project would be earning more than 10 percent; and you would do it.

The amount of money that you would have to put in the imaginary bank to replicate the flow of profits from an investment project is called the **present discounted value (PDV)** or simply the **present value (PV)** of the expected flow of profits from the project. To determine that flow, we have to look at the flow *1 year at a time.*

At the end of a year, you will receive $100 if you do the project. To receive $100 a year from now from your hypothetical bank, how much would you have to deposit now? The answer is clearly less than $100 because you will earn interest. Let's call the interest rate r. In the example, $r = .10$ (10 percent). To get back $100 next year, you need to deposit X, where X plus a year's interest on X is equal to $100. That is,

$$X + rX = \$100 \text{ or } X(1 + r) = \$100$$

And if we solve for X, we get

$$X = \frac{\$100}{(1 + r)}$$

and that means if $r = .10$,

$$X = \frac{\$100}{1.1}$$

or

$$X = \$90.91$$

To convince yourself that this is right, think of putting $90.91 into your hypothetical bank and coming back in a year. You get back your $90.91 plus interest of 10 percent, which is $9.09. When you add the interest to the initial deposit, you get $90.91 + 9.09, or exactly $100. *We say that the present value of $100 a year from now at a discount rate of 10 percent* ($r = .10$) *is $90.91.*

Notice that if you paid more than $90.91 for the $100 that you will receive from the project after a year, you would be receiving *less than a 10 percent return.* For example, suppose that you paid $95. If you put $95 in an account and came back after a year and found exactly $100, you would have received $5 in interest. Since $5 is just about .0526 (or 5.26 percent) of $95, the interest rate that the bank paid you is only 5.26 percent, not 10 percent.

What about the next year and the years after that? At the end of year 2, you get another $100. How much would you have to put in the bank today to be able to come back in *2* years and take away $100? Assume that you put amount X in the bank today. Then at the end of year 1, you have $X + rX$, which you keep in the account. At the end of year 2, you have $X + rX$ *plus* interest on $X + rX$; so at the end of year 2 you have

$$(X + rX) + r(X + rX)$$

which can be written

$$X(1 + r) + rX(1 + r) \text{ or } X(1 + r)(1 + r) \text{ or } X(1 + r)^2$$

Therefore,

$$X = \frac{\$100}{(1 + r)^2}$$

is the amount you must deposit today to get back $100 in 2 years.

If $r = .10$, then

$$X = \frac{\$100}{(1.1)^2} \quad \text{or} \quad X = \$82.65$$

To convince yourself that this calculation is right, if you put $82.65 in your hypothetical bank today and came back to check the balance after a year, you would have $82.65 plus interest of 10 percent, or $8.26, which is $90.91. But this time you leave it in the bank and receive 10 percent on the entire balance during the second year, which is $9.09. Adding the additional 10 percent, you get back to $100. Thus, if you deposit $82.65 in an account and come back in 2 years, you will have $100. The present value of $100 2 years from now is $82.65.

Now on to year 3. This time you receive a check for $400, but you don't get it until 3 years have passed. Again, how much would you have to put in your hypothetical bank to end up with $400? Without doing all the math, you can show that X, the amount that you must deposit to get back $400 in 3 years, is

$$X = \frac{\$400}{(1 + r)^3}$$

and if $r = .10$,

$$X = \frac{\$400}{(1.1)^3} \quad \text{or} \quad X = \$300.53$$

In general, the present value (PV), or present discounted value, of R dollars to be received in t years is

$$PV = \frac{R}{(1 + r)^t}$$

Step 3: Once you have looked at the project 1 year at a time, you must add up the total present value to see what the whole project is worth. In Table 11A.2, the right-hand column shows the present value of each year's return. If you add up the total, you have arrived at the amount that you would have to put in your hypothetical bank (that pays interest on deposits at 10 percent) today to receive the exact flow that is expected to come from the project. That total is $1,126.06.

So if you go to the bank today and put in $1,126.06, then come back in a year and withdraw $100, then come back after 2 years and withdraw another $100, then come back in 3 years and withdraw $400, and so on, until 5 years have passed, when you show up to close the account at the end of the fifth year, there will be exactly $500 left to withdraw. Lo and behold, you have figured out that you can receive the exact flow of profit that the project is expected to yield for $1,126.06. If you were looking for a 10 percent yield, you would *not* spend $1,200 for it. You would not do the project.

TABLE 11A.2 Calculation of Total Present Value of a Hypothetical Investment Project (Assuming r = 10 Percent)

END OF...	$(r)	DIVIDED BY $(1 + r)^t$	=	PRESENT VALUE ($)
Year 1	100	(1.1)		90.91
Year 2	100	$(1.1)^2$		82.65
Year 3	400	$(1.1)^3$		300.53
Year 4	500	$(1.1)^4$		341.51
Year 5	500	$(1.1)^5$		310.46
Total present value				1,126,06

What you have done is to convert an expected *flow* of dollars from an investment project that comes to you over some extended period of time to a *single number*: the present value of the flow.

We can restate the point this way: If the present value of the income stream associated with an investment is less than the full cost of the investment project, the investment should not be undertaken. This is illustrated in Figure 11A.1.

It is important to remember that we are discussing the *demand for new capital*. Business firms must evaluate potential investments to decide whether they are worth undertaking. This involves predicting the flow of potential future profits arising from each project and comparing those future profits with the return available in the financial market at the current interest rate. The present-value method allows firms to calculate how much it would *cost today* to purchase a contract for the same flow of earnings in the financial market.

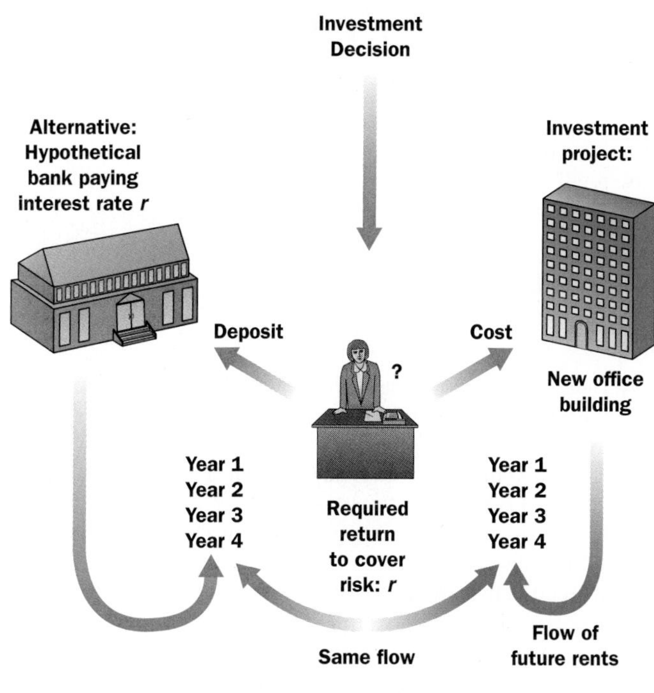

▲ **FIGURE 11A.1 Investment Project: Go or No? A Thinking Map**

LOWER INTEREST RATES, HIGHER PRESENT VALUES

Now consider what would happen if you used a lower interest rate in calculating the present value of a flow of earnings. You might use a lower rate in the analysis because interest rates in general have gone down in financial markets, making the opportunity cost of investment lower in general. You might also find out that the project is less risky than you believed earlier. For whatever reason, let's say that you would now do the project if it produced a return of 5 percent.

In evaluating the present value, the firm now looks at each year's flow of profit and asks how much it would cost to earn that amount if it were able to earn exactly 5 percent on its money in a hypothetical bank. With a lower interest rate, the firm will have to *pay more* now to purchase the same number of future dollars. Consider, for example, the present value of $100 in 2 years. We saw that if the firm puts aside $82.65 at 10 percent interest, it will have $100 in two years—at a 10 percent interest rate, the present discounted value (or current market price) of $100 in 2 years is $82.65. However, $82.65 put aside at a 5 percent interest rate would generate only $4.13 in interest in the first year and $4.34 in the second year, for a total balance of $91.11 after 2 years. To get $100 in 2 years, the firm needs to put aside more than $82.65 now. Solving for X as we did before,

$$X = \frac{\$100}{(1+r)^2} = \frac{\$100}{(1.05)^2} = \$90.70$$

When the interest rate falls from 10 percent to 5 percent, the present value of $100 in 2 years rises by $8.05 ($90.70 − $82.65).

Table 11A.3 recalculates the present value of the full stream at the lower interest rate; it shows that a decrease in the interest rate from 10 percent to 5 percent causes the total present value to rise to $1,334.59. Because the investment project costs less than this (only $1,200), it should be undertaken. It is now a better deal than can be obtained in the financial market. Under these conditions, a profit-maximizing firm will make the investment. As discussed in the chapter, a lower interest rate leads to more investment.

TABLE 11A.3 Calculation of Total Present Value of a Hypothetical Investment Project (Assuming r = 5 Percent)

END OF...	$	DIVIDED BY $(1+r)^t$	=	PRESENT VALUE ($)
Year 1	100	(1.05)		95.24
Year 2	100	$(1.05)^2$		90.70
Year 3	400	$(1.05)^3$		345.54
Year 4	500	$(1.05)^4$		411.35
Year 5	500	$(1.05)^5$		391.76
Total present value				1,334.59

The basic rule is as follows:

If the present value of an expected stream of earnings from an investment exceeds the cost of the investment necessary to undertake it, the investment should be undertaken. However, if the present value of an expected stream of earnings falls short of the cost of the investment, the financial market can generate the same stream of income for a smaller initial investment and the investment should not be undertaken.

SUMMARY

1. The present value (PV) of R dollars to be paid t years in the future is the amount you need to pay today, at current interest rates, to ensure that you end up with R dollars t years from now. It is the current market value of receiving R dollars in t years.
2. If the present value of the income stream associated with an investment is less than the full cost of the investment project, the investment project should not be undertaken. If the present value of an expected stream of income exceeds the cost of the investment necessary to undertake it, the investment should be undertaken.

REVIEW TERMS AND CONCEPTS

present discounted value (PDV) *or* **present value (PV)** The present discounted value of R dollars to be paid t years in the future is the amount you need to pay today, at current interest rates, to ensure that you end up with R dollars t years from now. It is the current market value of receiving R dollars in t years. *p. 237*

$$PV = \frac{R}{(1 + r)^t}$$

PROBLEMS

1. Suppose you were offered \$2,000 to be delivered in 1 year. Further suppose you had the alternative of putting money into a safe certificate of deposit paying annual interest at 10 percent. Would you pay \$1,900 in exchange for the \$2,000 after 1 year? What is the *maximum* amount you would pay for the offer of \$2,000? Suppose the offer was \$2,000, but delivery was to be in 2 years instead of 1 year. What is the maximum amount you would be willing to pay?
2. Your Uncle Joe just died and left \$10,000 payable to you when you turn 30 years old. You are now 20. Currently, the annual rate of interest that can be obtained by buying 10-year bonds is 6.5 percent. Your brother offers you \$6,000 cash right now to sign over your inheritance. Should you do it? Explain your answer.
3. A special task force has determined that the present discounted value of the benefits from a bridge project comes to \$23,786,000. The total construction cost of the bridge is \$25 million. This implies that the bridge should be built. Do you agree with this conclusion? Explain your answer. What impact could a substantial decline in interest rates have on your answer?
4. Calculate the present value of the income streams A to E in Table 1 at an 8 percent interest rate and again at a 10 percent rate.

   Suppose the investment behind the flow of income in E is a machine that cost \$1,235 at the beginning of year 1. Would you buy the machine if the interest rate were 8 percent? if the interest rate were 10 percent?

TABLE 1

END OF YEAR	A	B	C	D	E
1	\$ 80	\$ 80	\$ 100	\$ 100	\$500
2	80	80	100	100	300
3	80	80	1,100	100	400
4	80	80	0	100	300
5	1,080	80	0	100	0
6	0	80	0	1,100	0
7	0	1,080	0	0	0

5. Determine what someone should be willing to pay for each of the following bonds when the market interest rate for borrowing and lending is 5 percent.
   a. A bond that promises to pay \$3,000 in a lump-sum payment after 1 year.
   b. A bond that promises to pay \$3,000 in a lump-sum payment after 2 years.
   c. A bond that promises to pay \$1,000 per year for 3 years.
6. What should someone be willing to pay for each of the bonds in question 5 if the interest rate is 10 percent?
7. Based on your answers to questions 5 and 6, state whether each of the following is true or false:
   a. *Ceteris paribus*, the price of a bond increases when the interest rate increases.
   b. *Ceteris paribus*, the price of a bond increases when any given amount of money is received sooner rather than later.
8. Assume that the present discounted value of an investment project (commercial development) at a discount rate of 7 percent is \$234,756,000. Assume that the building just sold for \$254 million. Will the buyer earn a rate of return of more than 7 percent, exactly 7 percent, or less than 7 percent? Briefly explain.
9. Assume that I promise to pay you \$100 at the end of each of the next 3 years. Using the following formula,

   $$X = 100/(1 + r) + 100/(1 + r)^2 + 100/(1 + r)^3$$

   if $r = 0.075$, then $X = \$260.06$.

   Assuming that somebody of roughly comparable reliability offers to pay out 7.5 percent on anything you let him or her borrow from you, would you be willing to pay me \$270 for my promise? Explain your answer.

General Equilibrium and the Efficiency of Perfect Competition

12

CHAPTER OUTLINE

In the last nine chapters, we have built a model of a simple, perfectly competitive economy. Our discussion has revolved around the two fundamental decision-making units, *households* and *firms*, which interact in two basic market arenas, *input markets* and *output markets*. (Look again at the circular flow diagram, shown in Figure II.1 on p. 107.) By limiting our discussion to perfectly competitive firms, we have been able to examine how the basic decision-making units interact in the two basic market arenas.

Households make constrained choices in both input and output markets. In Chapters 3 and 4, we discussed an individual household demand curve for a single good or service. Then in Chapter 6, we went behind the demand curve and saw how income, wealth, and prices define the budget constraints within which households exercise their tastes and preferences. We soon discovered, however, that we cannot look at household decisions in output markets without thinking about the decisions made simultaneously in input markets. Household income, for example, depends on choices made in input markets: whether to work, how much to work, what skills to acquire, and so on. Input market choices are constrained by such factors as current wage rates, availability of jobs, and interest rates.

Firms are the primary producing units in a market economy. Profit-maximizing firms, to which we have limited our discussion, earn their profits by selling products and services for more than it costs to produce them. With firms, as with households, output markets and input markets cannot be analyzed separately. All firms make three specific decisions simultaneously: (1) how much output to supply, (2) how to produce that output—that is, which technology to use, and (3) how much of each input to demand.

In Chapters 7 through 9, we explored these three decisions from the viewpoint of output markets. We saw that the portion of the marginal cost curve that lies above a firm's average variable cost curve is the supply curve of a perfectly competitive firm in the short run. Implicit in the marginal cost curve is a choice of technology and a set of input demands. In Chapters 10 and 11, we looked at the perfectly competitive firm's three basic decisions from the viewpoint of input markets.

Output and input markets are connected because firms and households make simultaneous choices in both arenas, but there are other connections among markets as well. Firms buy in both capital and labor markets, for example, and they can substitute capital for labor and vice versa. A change in the price of one factor can easily change the demand for other factors. Buying more *capital*, for instance, usually changes the marginal revenue product of *labor* and shifts the labor demand curve. Similarly, a change in the price of a single good or service usually affects household demand for other goods and services, as when a price decrease makes one good more attractive than other close substitutes. The same change also makes households better off when they find that the same amount of income will buy more. Such additional "real income" can be spent on any of the other goods and services that the household buys.

The point here is simple:

Input and output markets cannot be considered as if they were separate entities or as if they operated independently. Although it is important to understand the decisions of individual firms and households and the functioning of individual markets, we now need to add it all up so we can look at the operation of the system as a whole.

You have seen the concept of equilibrium applied both to markets and to individual decision-making units. In individual markets, supply and demand determine an equilibrium price. Perfectly competitive firms are in short-run equilibrium when price and marginal cost are equal ($P = MC$). In the long run, however, equilibrium in a competitive market is achieved only when economic profits are eliminated. Households are in equilibrium when they have equated the marginal utility per dollar spent on each good to the marginal utility per dollar spent on all other goods. This process of examining the equilibrium conditions in individual markets and for individual households and firms separately is called **partial equilibrium analysis**.

partial equilibrium analysis The process of examining the equilibrium conditions in individual markets and for households and firms separately.

general equilibrium The condition that exists when all markets in an economy are in simultaneous equilibrium.

A **general equilibrium** exists when all markets in an economy are in simultaneous equilibrium. An event that disturbs the equilibrium in one market may disturb the equilibrium in many other markets as well. The ultimate impact of the event depends on the way *all* markets adjust to it. Thus, partial equilibrium analysis, which looks at adjustments in one isolated market, may be misleading.

Thinking in terms of a general equilibrium leads to some important questions. Is it possible for all households and firms and all markets to be in equilibrium simultaneously? Are the equilibrium conditions that we have discussed separately compatible with one another? Why is an event that disturbs an equilibrium in one market likely to disturb many other equilibriums simultaneously?

In talking about general equilibrium (the first concept we explore in this chapter), we continue our exercise in *positive economics*—that is, we seek to understand how systems operate without making value judgments about outcomes. Later in the chapter, we turn from positive economics to *normative economics* as we begin to judge the economic system. Are its results good or bad? Can we make them better?

In judging the performance of any economic system, you will recall, it is essential first to establish specific criteria by which to judge. In this chapter, we use two such criteria: *efficiency* and *equity* (fairness). First, we demonstrate the **efficiency** of the allocation of resources—that is, the system produces what people want and does so at the least possible cost—if all the assumptions that we have made thus far hold. When we begin to relax some of our assumptions, however, it will become apparent that free markets may *not* be efficient. Several sources of inefficiency naturally occur within an unregulated market system. In the final part of this chapter, we introduce the potential role of government in correcting market inefficiencies and achieving fairness.

efficiency The condition in which the economy is producing what people want at least possible cost.

General Equilibrium Analysis

Two examples will help illustrate some of the insights that we can gain when we move from partial to general equilibrium analysis. In this section, we will consider the impact on the economy of (1) a major technological advance and (2) a shift in consumer preferences. As you read, remember that we are looking for the connections between markets, particularly between input and output markets.

An Early Technological Advance: The Electronic Calculator

Students working in quantitative fields of study in the late 1960s, and even as late as the early 1970s, recall classrooms filled with noisy mechanical calculators. At that time, a calculator weighed about 40 pounds and was only able to add, subtract, multiply, and divide. The machines had no memories, and they took 20 to 25 seconds to do one multiplication problem.

Major corporations had rooms full of accountants with such calculators on their desks, and the sound when 30 or 40 of them were running was deafening. During the 1950s and 1960s, most firms had these machines, but few people had a calculator in their homes because the cost of a single machine was several hundred dollars. Some high schools had calculators for accounting classes, but most schoolchildren in the United States had never seen one.

In the 1960s, Wang Laboratories developed an electronic calculator. Bigger than a modern personal computer, it had several keyboards attached to a single main processor. It could add, subtract, multiply, and divide, but it also had a memory. Its main virtues were speed and quietness. It did calculations instantaneously without making any noise. The Wang machine sold for around $1,500.

The beginning of the 1970s saw the industry develop rapidly. First, calculators shrank in size. The Bomar Corporation made one of the earliest hand calculators, the Bomar Brain. These early versions could do nothing more than add, subtract, multiply, and divide; they had no memory; and they still sold for several hundred dollars. Then, in the early 1970s, a number of technological breakthroughs made it possible to mass-produce very small electronic circuits (silicon chips). These circuits, in turn, made calculators very inexpensive to produce; and this is the beginning of our general equilibrium story. Costs in the calculator industry shifted downward dramatically, as shown in Figure 12.1(b). As costs fell, profits increased. Attracted by economic profits, new firms rapidly entered the market. Instead of one or two firms producing state-of-the-art machines, dozens of firms began cranking them out by the thousands. As a result, the industry supply curve shifted out to the right, driving down prices toward the new lower costs, as shown in Figure 12.1(a).

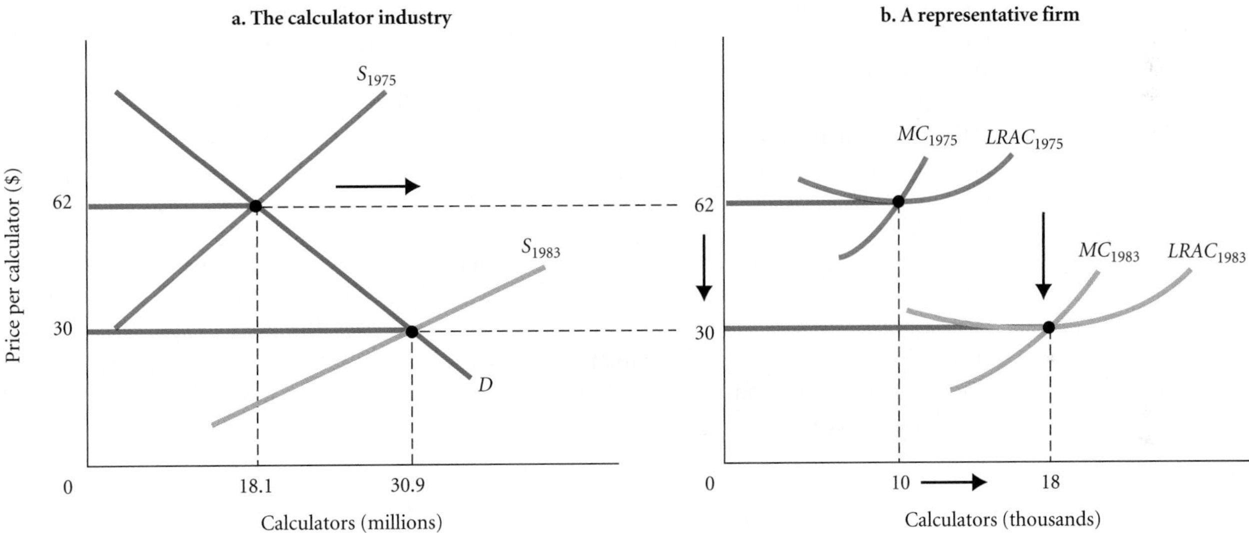

▲ FIGURE 12.1

Cost Saving Technological Change in the Calculator Industry

In the 1970s and 1980s, major technological changes occurred in the calculator industry. In 1975, 18.1 million calculators were sold at an average price of $62. As technology made it possible to produce at lower costs, cost curves shifted downward. As new firms entered the industry and existing firms expanded, output rose and market price dropped. In 1983, 30.9 million calculators were produced and sold at an average price of under $30.

As the price of electronic calculators fell, the market for the old mechanical calculators died a quiet death. With no more demand for their product, producers found themselves suffering losses and got out of the business. As the price of electronic calculators kept falling, thousands of people who had never had a calculator began to buy them. By 1973, calculators were available at discount appliance stores for $60 to $70. By 1975, 18.1 million calculators were produced annually and sold at an average price of $62. The average price fell to under $30 and sales hit 30.9 million by 1983. You can now buy a basic calculator for less than $5—or get one free with a magazine subscription. In 1987, 33.8 million calculators were produced. In 1990, the Commerce Department stopped counting.

The rapid decline in the cost of producing calculators led to a rapid expansion of supply and a decline in price, as shown in Figure 12.1(a). The lower prices increased the quantity demanded to such an extent that most U.S. homes now have at least one calculator. Nowadays most cell phones even have a calculator feature.

This is only a partial equilibrium story, however. The events we have described also had effects on many other markets. In other words, these events disturbed the general equilibrium. When mechanical calculators became obsolete, many people who had over the years developed the skills required to produce and repair those complex machines found themselves unemployed. At the same time, demand boomed for workers in the production, distribution, and sales of the new electronic calculators. The new technology thus caused a reallocation of labor across the labor market.

Capital was also reallocated. New firms invested in the plant and equipment needed to produce electronic calculators. Old capital owned by the firms that previously made mechanical calculators became obsolete and depreciated, and it ended up on the scrap heap. The mechanical calculators, once an integral part of the capital stocks of accounting firms, banks, and so on, were scrapped and replaced by the cheaper, more efficient calculators.

When a large new industry suddenly appears, it earns revenues that might have been spent on other things. Even though the effects of this success on any one other industry are probably small, general equilibrium analysis tells us that in the absence of the new industry and the demand for its product, households will demand other goods and services and other industries will produce more. In this case, society has benefited a great deal. Everyone can now buy a very useful product at a low price. The new calculators raised the productivity of certain kinds of labor and reduced costs in many industries.

Of course, the electronic calculator was just the beginning of a process of product evolution that has led to a complete change in the way we live. Thirty years ago Kenneth Olsen, the president of Digital Equipment Corporation, is widely quoted to have asked, "Why would anyone need their own computer?" Today we do everything from watching movies to paying bills, shopping, dating, and blogging on small but powerful laptops with huge hard drives. A hotel without Wi-Fi (wireless access) is considered a second-class hotel.

Apple sold a staggering 6 million iPods for over a billion dollars during the first 3 months of 2005. The immense popularity of the iPod has fueled the market for music downloads, which are fast becoming the technology of choice for storing and playing music for millions of people worldwide. The bet is that CDs and CD players will soon be obsolete and will fade out as the new technology pushes aside yet another frontier.

All of this change has happened through the market. Declining costs of production and fierce competition have continuously pushed prices down and provided us with a never-ending stream of new and more powerful consumer electronics. A significant—if not sweeping—technological change in a single industry affects many markets. Households face a different structure of prices and must adjust their consumption of many products. Labor reacts to new skill requirements and is reallocated across markets. Capital is also reallocated.

Market Adjustment to Changes in Demand

One thing we know about the U.S. economy and the world economy is that they are dynamic: Change occurs all the time. Markets experience shifts of demand, both up and down; costs and technology change; and prices and outputs change. To show how a change in one market affects other markets and the general equilibrium, we will describe a simple economy with two sectors, *X* and *Y*. The story will be of an increase in demand in one sector and a decline in demand in the other.

As you go through the following diagrams and discussion, you can think of any major sector that might be experiencing an increase in demand. For example, beginning around 2000, the housing market entered a dramatic boom period. Low interest rates and rising incomes led the demand for housing to shift to the right. This rising demand led to higher home prices and new entry by building firms seeking economic profits.

The housing market had even bigger general equilibrium effects on the way down. Beginning in early 2006, the market for single-family homes dropped sharply. It was as if someone blew a whistle and buyers disappeared. People who had their homes on the market did not lower their prices in most cases; and in some instances, people ended up carrying two houses for a substantial monthly cost. The number of existing home sales over the next few months dropped by more than a million. Housing starts, the number of new homes to begin construction, dropped from an annual rate of 2.26 million to 1.19 million, a drop of over a million homes that would not be built. The profits of home builders such as Ryan Homes, Lennar, and Toll Brothers dropped sharply as market prices began to fall.

The decline in housing starts, or housing production, leads to significantly less building. Since the average new house (excluding land) costs about $200,000 to build, when housing starts fell by about a million aggregate spending on new homes fell by about $200 billion. This had a dramatic effect on the labor market, as over a million construction workers lost their jobs. Timber prices fell, and many home builders shut down and exited the industry.

You could also think of the airline industry. New airlines such as JetBlue and AirTran entered the airline industry in response to rising demand as the industry recovered from a dramatic decline following the World Trade Center terrorist attack of 2001. By 2008, several of the new airlines were in bankruptcy as fuel prices increased.

Finally, you might think of the huge automobile industry. In July 2005, 1.8 million cars and light trucks were sold in the United States, with 82 percent being sold by domestic producers. Auto workers accounted for over 1 million workers out of just over 14 million workers in manufacturing in 2005. The auto sector moves cyclically, and periodically demand increases.

Figure 12.2 shows the initial equilibrium in two sectors, called X and Y. We assume that both sectors are initially in long-run competitive equilibrium. Total output in sector X is Q_X^0, the product is selling for a price of P_X^0, and each firm in the industry produces up to where P_X^0 is equal to marginal cost—q_X^0. At that point, price is just equal to average cost and economic profits are zero. The same condition holds initially in sector Y. The market is in zero profit equilibrium at a price of P_Y^0.

Now assume that a change in consumer preferences (or in the age distribution of the population or in something else) shifts the demand for X out to the right from D_X^0 to D_X^1. That shift drives the price up to P_X^1. If households decide to buy more X, without an increase in income, they must buy *less* of something else. Because everything else is represented by Y in this example, the demand for Y must decline and the demand curve for Y shifts to the left, from D_Y^0 to D_Y^1.

With the shift in demand for X, price rises to P_X^1 and profit-maximizing firms immediately increase output to q_X^1 (the point where $P_X^1 = MC_X$). However, now there are positive profits in X. With the downward shift of demand in Y, price falls to P_Y^1. Firms in sector Y cut back to q_Y^1 (the point where $P_Y^1 = MC_Y$), and the lower price causes firms producing Y to suffer losses.

In the short run, adjustment is simple. Firms in both industries are constrained by their current scales of plant. Firms can neither enter nor exit their respective industries. Each firm in industry X raises output somewhat, from q_X^0 to q_X^1. Firms in industry Y cut back from q_Y^0 to q_Y^1.

In response to the existence of profit in sector X, the capital market begins to take notice. In Chapter 9, we saw that new firms are likely to enter an industry in which there are profits to be earned. Financial analysts see the profits as a signal of future healthy growth, and entrepreneurs may become interested in moving into the industry.

Adding all of this together, we would expect to see investment begin to favor sector X. This is indeed the case: Capital begins to flow into sector X. As new firms enter, the short-run supply curve in the industry shifts to the right and continues to do so until all profits are eliminated. In the top-left diagram in Figure 12.2, the supply curve shifts out from S_X^0 to S_X^1, a shift that drives the price back down to P_X^0.

We would also expect to see a movement out of sector Y because of losses. Some firms will exit the industry. In the bottom-left diagram in Figure 12.2, the supply curve shifts back from S_Y^0 to S_Y^1, a shift that drives the price back up to P_Y^0. At this point, all losses are eliminated.

Note that a new general equilibrium is not reached until equilibrium is reestablished in all markets. If costs of production remain unchanged, as they do in Figure 12.2, this equilibrium occurs at the initial product prices, but with more resources and production in X and fewer in Y. In contrast, if an expansion in X drives up the prices of resources used specifically in X, the cost curves in X will shift upward and the final postexpansion zero-profit equilibrium will occur at a higher price. Such an industry is called an *increasing-cost industry.*

Formal Proof of a General Competitive Equilibrium

Economic theorists have struggled with the question of whether a set of prices that equates supply and demand in all markets simultaneously can exist when there are thousands of markets. If all markets are interconnected, how do movements to an equilibrium in one market affect the outcomes in other markets? If a set of prices leading to equilibrium in all markets were not possible, the result could be continuous cycles of expansion, contraction, and instability.

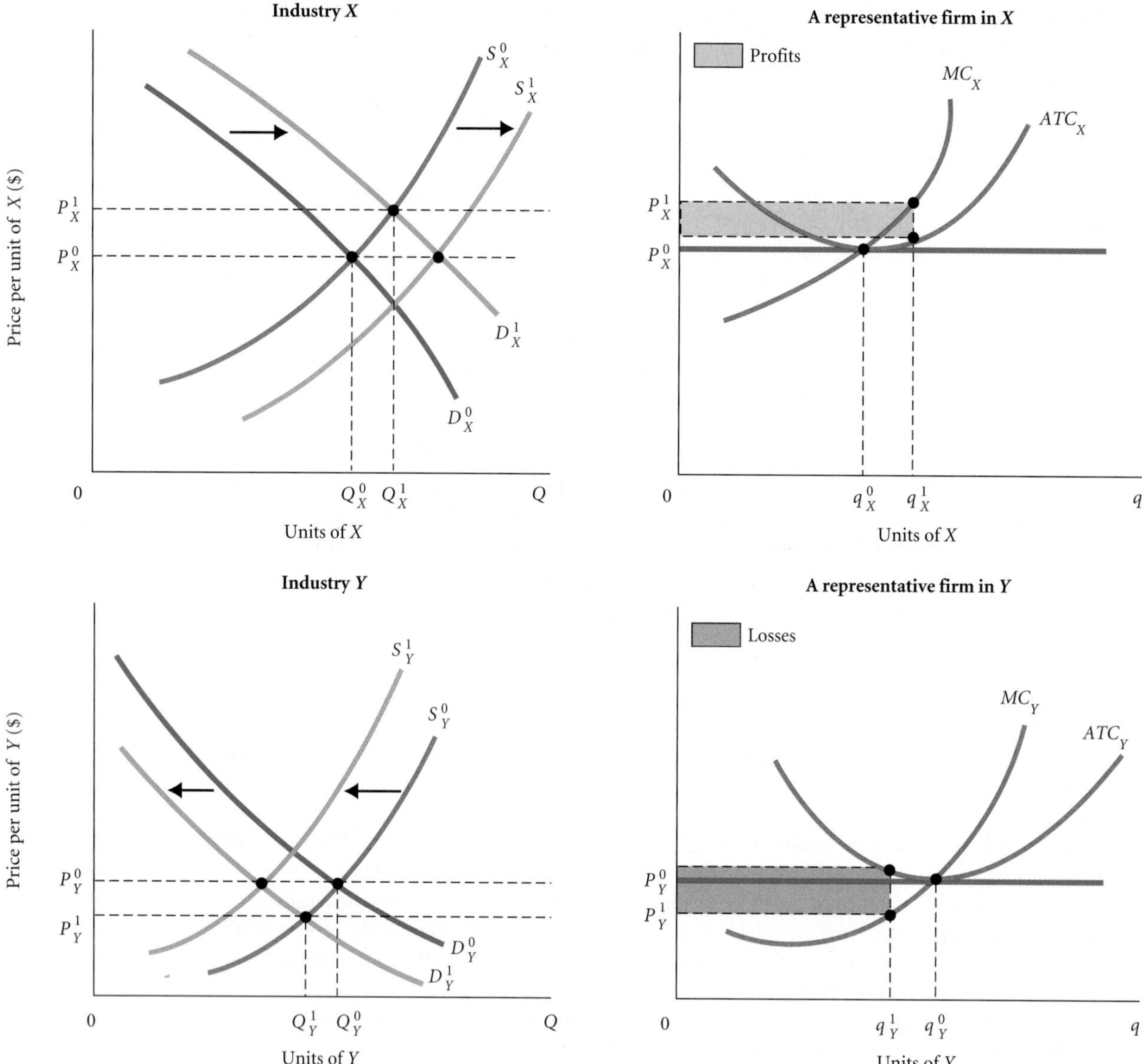

▲ FIGURE 12.2

Adjustment in an Economy with Two Sectors

Initially, demand for X shifts from D_X^0 to D_X^1. This shift pushes the price of X up to P_X^1, creating profits. Demand for Y shifts down from D_Y^0 to D_Y^1, pushing the price of Y down to P_Y^1 and creating losses. Firms have an incentive to leave sector Y and an incentive to enter sector X. Exiting sector Y shifts supply in that industry to S_Y^1, raising price and eliminating losses. Entry shifts supply in X to S_X^1, thus reducing and eliminating profits.

The nineteenth-century French economist Leon Walras struggled with the problem, but he could never provide a formal proof. By using advanced mathematical tools, economists Kenneth Arrow and Gerard Debreu and mathematicians John von Neumann and Abraham Wald showed the existence of at least one set of prices that *will* clear all markets in a large system simultaneously.

Allocative Efficiency and Competitive Equilibrium

Chapters 3 through 11 built a complete model of a simple, perfectly competitive economic system. However, recall that in Chapters 3 and 4 we made a number of important assumptions. We assumed that both output markets and input markets are perfectly competitive—that is, that no individual household or firm is large enough relative to the market to have any control over price. In other words, we assumed that firms and households are *price-takers*.

ECONOMICS IN PRACTICE

Ethanol and Land Prices

The U.S. government provides large subsidies for ethanol, a fuel produced from corn. Proponents of the ethanol subsidies suggest that it is one piece of a policy that can help the United States reduce its dependence on foreign oil. In part, as a result of these subsidies, the midwestern United States has seen a large increase in corn production relative to other grains. The following article traces another of the general equilibrium consequences of the ethanol subsidies: an increase in the price of agricultural land.

Nebraska ethanol boom causing land prices to soar

TheIndependent.com

Ethanol is not only pumping up the price of corn in Nebraska, but also farm real estate market values and cash rent rates values have seen a 14-percent increase, according to the preliminary results of the University of Nebraska-Lincoln's annual Farm Real Estate Market Development Survey.

According to the survey, Nebraska farmland's average value for the year ending Feb. 1 was $1,155 per acre, compared to $1,013 per acre at this time last year, said Bruce Johnson, the UNL agricultural economist who conducts this annual survey.

He said preliminary findings show this was the largest all-land value increase in the past 19 years. It is also the fourth straight year of what Johnson called "solid advances" in land values. He said the state's current all-land average value is more than 50 percent higher than the 2003 level.

Higher prices for corn because of ethanol demand are driving the sharp rise in land prices. By early 2008, Nebraska should have about 25 ethanol plants online, producing 1.2 billion gallons of ethanol and using more than 425 million bushels of corn.

"The demand from rapidly growing ethanol production has triggered the commodity market advances, and, in turn, worked into the agricultural land market dynamic, particularly in the major corn-producing areas of the state," Johnson said.

Source: Robert Pore, robert.pore@theindependent.com.

As we see in the article, a number of markets are affected by the ethanol subsidies. The increase in the demand for ethanol drives up the demand for corn, which in turn increases the demand for land. Since the supply of land is finite, the price of land used to produce corn rises. But what about the rest of the agricultural economy? Increasing land prices increases the cost of other grains, such as wheat. As you learned in Chapter 2, land is a key factor of production. The increase in wheat costs shifts the supply curve to the left, as in the figure below. Wheat prices thus also rise.

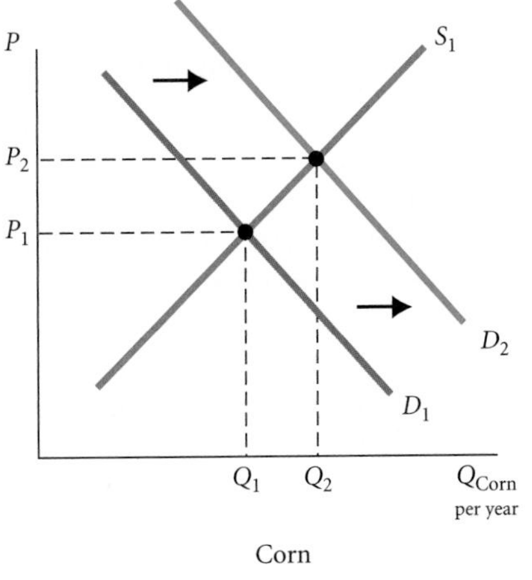

Corn

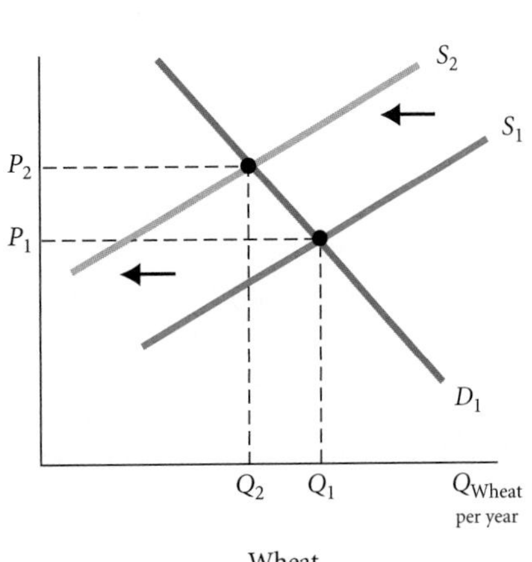

Wheat

We also assumed that households have perfect information on product quality and on all prices available and that firms have perfect knowledge of technologies and input prices. Finally, we said that decision makers in a competitive system always consider all the costs and benefits of their decisions—that there are no "external" costs.

If all these assumptions hold, the economy will produce an efficient allocation of resources. As we relax these assumptions one by one, however, you will discover that the allocation of resources is no longer efficient and that a number of sources of inefficiency occur naturally.

Pareto Efficiency

In Chapter 1, we introduced several specific criteria used by economists to judge the performance of economic systems and to evaluate alternative economic policies. These criteria are (1) efficiency, (2) equity, (3) growth, and (4) stability. In Chapter 1, you also learned that an *efficient* economy is one that produces the things that people want at the least cost. The idea behind the efficiency criterion is that the economic system exists to serve the wants and needs of people. If resources somehow can be reallocated to make people "better off," then they should be. We want to use the resources at our disposal to produce maximum well-being. The trick is defining *maximum well-being*.

For many years, social philosophers wrestled with the problem of "aggregation," or "adding up." When we say "maximum well-being," we mean maximum *for society*. Societies are made up of many people, and the problem has always been how to maximize satisfaction, or well-being, for all members of society. What has emerged is the now widely accepted concept of *allocative efficiency*, first developed by the Italian economist Vilfredo Pareto in the nineteenth century. Pareto's very precise definition of efficiency is often referred to as **Pareto efficiency** or **Pareto optimality**.

Pareto efficiency *or* **Pareto optimality** A condition in which no change is possible that will make some members of society better off without making some other members of society worse off.

Specifically, a change is said to be efficient when it makes some members of society better off without making other members of society worse off. An efficient, or *Pareto optimal*, system is one in which no such changes are possible. An example of a change that makes some people better off and nobody worse off is a simple voluntary exchange. I have apples and you have nuts. I like nuts and you like apples. We trade. We both gain, and no one loses.

For such a definition to have any real meaning, we must answer two questions: (1) What do we mean by "better off"? and (2) How do we account for changes that make some people better off and others worse off?

The answer to the first question is simple. People decide what "better off" and "worse off" mean. I am the only one who knows whether I am better off after a change. If you and I exchange one item for another because I like what you have and you like what I have, we both "reveal" that we are better off after the exchange because we agreed to it voluntarily. If everyone in the neighborhood wants a park and the residents all contribute to a fund to build one, they have consciously changed the allocation of resources and they all are better off for it.

The answer to the second question is more complex. Nearly every change that one can imagine leaves some people better off and some people worse off. If some gain and some lose as the result of a change, and it can be demonstrated that the value of the gains exceeds the value of the losses, then the change is said to be *potentially efficient*. In practice, however, the distinction between a *potentially* and an *actually* efficient change is often ignored and all such changes are simply called *efficient*.

Example: Budget Cuts in Massachusetts Several years ago, in an effort to reduce state spending, the budget of the Massachusetts Registry of Motor Vehicles was cut substantially. Among other things, the state sharply reduced the number of clerks in each office. Almost immediately Massachusetts residents found themselves waiting in line for hours when they had to register their automobiles or get their driver's licenses.

Drivers and car owners began paying a price: standing in line, which used time and energy that could otherwise have been used more productively. However, before we can make sensible efficiency judgments, we must be able to measure, or at least approximate, the value of both the gains and the losses produced by the budget cut. To approximate the losses to car owners and drivers, we might ask how much people would be willing to pay to avoid standing in those long lines.

One office estimated that 500 people stood in line every day for about 1 hour each. If each person were willing to pay just \$2 to avoid standing in line, the damage incurred would be \$1,000 (500 × \$2) per day. If the registry were open 250 days per year, the reduction in labor force at that office alone would create a cost to car owners, conservatively estimated, of \$250,000 (250 × \$1,000) per year.

Estimates also showed that taxpayers in Massachusetts saved about \$80,000 per year by having fewer clerks at that office. If the clerks were reinstated, there would be some gains and some losses. Car owners and drivers would gain, and taxpayers would lose. However, because we can show that the value of the gains would substantially exceed the value of the losses, it can be argued that reinstating the clerks would be an efficient change. Note that the only *net* losers would be those taxpayers who do not own a car and do not hold driver's licenses.[1]

The Efficiency of Perfect Competition

In Chapter 2, we discussed the "economic problem" of dividing up scarce resources among alternative uses. We also discussed the three basic questions that all societies must answer, and we set out to explain how those questions are answered in a competitive economy.

The three basic questions included:

1. *What gets produced?* What determines the final mix of output?
2. *How is it produced?* How do capital, labor, and land get divided up among firms? In other words, what is the allocation of resources among producers?
3. *Who gets what is produced?* What determines which households get how much? What is the distribution of output among consuming households?

The following discussion of efficiency uses these three questions and their answers to prove informally that perfect competition is efficient. To demonstrate that the perfectly competitive system leads to an efficient, or Pareto optimal, allocation of resources, we need to show that no changes are possible that will make some people better off without making others worse off. Specifically, we will show that under perfect competition, (1) resources are allocated among firms efficiently, (2) final products are distributed among households efficiently, and (3) the system produces the things that people want.

Efficient Allocation of Resources Among Firms The simple definition of efficiency holds that firms must produce their products using the best available—that is, lowest-cost—technology. If more output could be produced with the same amount of inputs, it would be possible to make some people better off without making others worse off.

The perfectly competitive model we have been using rests on several assumptions that assure us that resources in such a system would indeed be efficiently allocated among firms. Most important of these is the assumption that individual firms maximize profits. To maximize profit, a firm must minimize the cost of producing its chosen level of output. With a full knowledge of existing technologies, firms will choose the technology that produces the output they want at the least cost.

There is more to this story than meets the eye, however. Inputs must be allocated *across* firms in the best possible way. If we find that it is possible, for example, to take capital from firm A and swap it for labor from firm B and produce more product in both firms, then the original allocation

[1] You might wonder whether there are other gainers and losers. What about the clerks? In analysis like this, it is usually assumed that the citizens who pay lower taxes spend their added income on other things. The producers of those other things need to expand to meet the new demand, and they hire more labor. Thus, a contraction of 100 jobs in the public sector will open up 100 jobs in the private sector. If the economy is fully employed, the transfer of labor to the private sector is assumed to create no net gains or losses to the workers.

was inefficient. Recall our example from Chapter 2. Farmers in Ohio and Kansas both produce wheat and corn. The climate and soil in most of Kansas are best suited to wheat production, and the climate and soil in Ohio are best suited to corn production. Kansas should produce most of the wheat and Ohio should produce most of the corn. A law that forces Kansas land into corn production and Ohio land into wheat production would result in less of both—an inefficient allocation of resources. However, if markets are free and open, Kansas farmers will naturally find a higher return by planting wheat and Ohio farmers will find a higher return in corn. The free market, then, should lead to an efficient allocation of resources among firms. As you think back on Chapter 2, you should now see that societies operating on the production possibility frontier are efficiently using their inputs.

The same argument can be made more general. Misallocation of resources among firms is unlikely as long as every single firm faces the same set of prices and trade-offs in input markets. Recall from Chapter 10 that perfectly competitive firms will hire additional factors of production as long as their marginal revenue product exceeds their market price. As long as all firms have access to the *same* factor markets and the *same* factor prices, the last unit of a factor hired will produce the same value in each firm. Certainly, firms will use different technologies and factor combinations, but at the margin, no single profit-maximizing firm can get more value out of a factor than that factor's current market price. For example, if workers can be hired in the labor market at a wage of $6.50, *all* firms will hire workers as long as the marginal revenue product (MRP_L) produced by the marginal worker (labor's MRP_L) remains above $6.50. *No* firms will hire labor beyond the point at which MRP_L falls below $6.50. Thus, at equilibrium, additional workers are not worth more than $6.50 to any firm, and switching labor from one firm to another will not produce output of any greater value to society. Each firm has hired the profit-maximizing amount of labor. In short:

The assumptions that factor markets are competitive and open, that all firms pay the same prices for inputs, and that all firms maximize profits lead to the conclusion that the allocation of resources among firms is efficient.

You should now have a greater appreciation for the power of the price mechanism in a market economy. Each individual firm needs only to make decisions about which inputs to use by looking at its own labor, capital, and land productivity relative to their prices. But because all firms face identical input prices, the market economy achieves efficient input use among firms. Prices are the instrument of Adam Smith's "invisible hand," allowing for efficiency without explicit coordination or planning.

Efficient Distribution of Outputs Among Households Even if the system is producing the right things and is doing so efficiently, these things still have to get to the right people. Just as open, competitive factor markets ensure that firms do not end up with the wrong inputs, open, competitive output markets ensure that households do not end up with the wrong goods and services.

Within the constraints imposed by income and wealth, households are free to choose among all the goods and services available in output markets. A household will buy a good as long as that good generates utility, or subjective value, greater than its market price. Utility value is revealed in market behavior. You do not go out and buy something unless you are willing to pay *at least* the market price.

Remember that the value you place on any one good depends on what you must give up to have that good. The trade-offs available to you depend on your budget constraint. The trade-offs that are desirable depend on your preferences. If you buy a $300 MP3 player, you may be giving up a trip home. If I buy it, I may be giving up four new tires for my car. We have both revealed that the MP3 player is worth at least as much to us as all the other things that $300 can buy. As long as we are free to choose among all the things that $300 can buy, we will not end up with the wrong things; it is not possible to find a trade that will make us both better off. Again, the price mechanism plays an important role. Each of us faces the same price for the goods that we choose, and that in turn leads us to make choices that ensure that goods are allocated efficiently among consumers.

We all know that people have different tastes and preferences and that they will buy very different things in very different combinations. As long as everyone shops freely in the same markets, no redistribution of final outputs among people will make them better off. If you and I buy in the same markets and pay the same prices and I buy what I want and you buy what you want, we cannot possibly end up with the wrong combination of things. Free and open markets are essential to this result.

Producing What People Want: The Efficient Mix of Output It does no good to produce things efficiently or to distribute them efficiently if the system produces the wrong things. Will competitive markets produce the things that people want?

If the system is producing the wrong mix of output, we should be able to show that producing more of one good and less of another will make people better off. To show that perfectly competitive markets are efficient, we must demonstrate that no such changes in the final mix of output are possible.

The condition that ensures that the right things are produced is $P = MC$. That is, in both the long run and the short run, a perfectly competitive firm will produce at the point where the price of its output is equal to the marginal cost of production. The logic is this: When a firm weighs price and marginal cost, it weighs the value of its product to society *at the margin* against the value of the things that could otherwise be produced with the same resources. Figure 12.3 summarizes this logic.

If $P_X > MC_X$, society gains value by producing *more X*.
If $P_X < MC_X$, society gains value by producing *less X*.

The value placed on good *X* by society through the market, or the social value of a marginal unit of *X*.

Market-determined value of resources needed to produce a marginal unit of *X*. MC_X is equal to the opportunity cost of those resources: lost production of other goods or the value of the resources left unemployed (leisure, vacant land, and so on).

▲ **FIGURE 12.3 The Key Efficiency Condition: Price Equals Marginal Cost**

The argument is quite straightforward. *First, price reflects households' willingness to pay*. By purchasing a good, individual households reveal that it is worth at least as much as the other goods that the same money could buy. Thus, current price reflects the value that households place on a good.

Second, marginal cost reflects the opportunity cost of the resources needed to produce a good. If a firm producing *X* hires a worker, it must pay the market wage. That wage must be sufficient to attract that worker out of leisure or away from firms producing other goods. The same argument holds for capital and land.

Thus, if the price of a good ends up greater than marginal cost, producing more of it will generate benefits to households in excess of opportunity costs, and society gains. Similarly, if the price of a good ends up below marginal cost, resources are being used to produce something that households value less than opportunity costs. Producing less of it creates gains to society.[2]

Society will produce the efficient mix of output if all firms equate price and marginal cost.

---

[2] It is important to understand that firms do not act *consciously* to balance social costs and benefits. In fact, the usual assumption is that firms are self-interested private profit maximizers. It just works out that in perfectly competitive markets, when firms are weighing private benefits against private costs, they are actually (perhaps without knowing it) weighing the benefits and costs to society as well.

ECONOMICS IN PRACTICE

Ticket Scalping in the Electronic Age

A voluntary trade with two willing parties improves the well-being of both, and as long as no one else is harmed it is clearly efficient in the language of economics. But is it always fair? The following essay in the *Boston Globe* explores the issue.

The value of scalping

Boston Globe

SECTION 10, Row M, seats 1 and 2—obstructed view. Lakers and Celtics at the Garden, seventh game of the 1984 NBA championship series. I spent two nights on Causeway Street to get "strips" to the playoffs that year. Nine dollars each!

In those days there was no StubHub or eBay. We did have telephones, and people do talk to each other, so "they" found me—the deep-pocket guys, the people who have willingness and ability to pay.

My 8-year-old daughter called to me in the shower the day before the final game. "Hey, Dad, there's a woman on the phone who wants to buy your tickets to the game tomorrow. Want to sell?"

"Tell her to jump in the Muddy River," I screamed. She yelled back, "Maybe you should talk to her, Dad." The woman was offering $500 each.

A few weeks ago, single-game spring training tickets went on sale on the Red Sox Web site. I will be in Fort Myers when the Red Sox play the Yankees March 12, so I gave it a try. Finding myself in their "virtual waiting room," I sat at my desk for about half an hour hoping to get a couple of reserved seats at the face value of $21. By the time I got out of the virtual queue, the game was sold out. I immediately logged onto StubHub, where dozens of tickets were offered at prices ranging up to $300. Today section 119 is selling for $400 a ticket. Scalpers today are much quicker and more organized than when I got that call 23 years ago.

But the logic is still the same. Ticket scalping is nothing more than the age-old law of supply and demand at work, and it illustrates the eternal tension between the entirely valid case for free markets and the cry that the market system can lead to unfair outcomes.

The argument for unfettered scalping: You have something that I want (tickets), and I have something that you want (money). So we trade. Voluntary free exchange is evidence that the trade makes both parties better off, and the agent gets a commission for bringing them together. Everyone is better off than they would have been had the trade not occurred. The scalper has made a commission for providing a service, and no one is worse off. Stopping scalping clearly makes people less well off, and the state has no business getting involved.

Admittedly, that leaves out a big part of the story. Why are the "cheap" tickets put out there in the first place? And who "should" get them? The Red Sox can't sell tickets for what the market would bear; if they did, people would burn down Fenway Park. It is in the team's long-term interest to have a broad, loyal, culturally and economically diverse fan base to support them no mater what. Besides, doesn't the team really belong to the city? Having seats available at prices that the bulk of the population can afford seems only right.

If you accept this argument, you probably would like to see scalping stopped. But can it be? Probably not. The problem is that the bulk of the population won't fit in Fenway. And once the tickets hit the street, watch out for the market. History is littered with failed efforts to avoid allocating things by consumers' willingness and ability to pay. State stores in the former Soviet Union that sold bread and meat at "fair prices" had shortages and long lines—and were undermined by a powerful black market.

If the system allocates a good (tickets or bread, say) to one group when there are others who are willing and able to pay more, potential buyers will be in touch. With today's technology, there is virtually no way to prevent them from communicating with potential sellers. There will always be scalpers.

On June 12, 1984, the Celtics beat the Lakers 111–102 on the parquet floor for the NBA championship. I was there in section 10. I was also there for the triple overtime against Phoenix in '76 and the double overtime against Milwaukee in '74. And I was there when Roberts stole second. I don't know whether it was good or bad for society that I was in those seats, but I will never forget those games.

I didn't have to discuss where I got tickets with a government official. Nor should I have to.

Source: By Karl E. Case | January 21, 2007. Karl E. Case is a professor of economics at Wellesley College. © Copyright 2007 Globe Newspaper Company.

Figure 12.4 shows how a simple competitive market system leads individual households and firms to make efficient choices in input and output markets. For simplicity, the figure assumes only one factor of production, labor. Households weigh the market wage against the value of leisure and time spent in unpaid household production. However, the wage is a measure of labor's potential product because firms weigh labor cost (wages) against the value of the product produced and hire up to the point at which $W = MRP_L$. Households use wages to buy market-produced goods. Thus, households implicitly weigh the value of market-produced goods against the value of leisure and household production.

When a firm's scale is balanced, it is earning maximum profit; when a household's scale is balanced, it is maximizing utility. Under these conditions, no changes can improve social welfare.

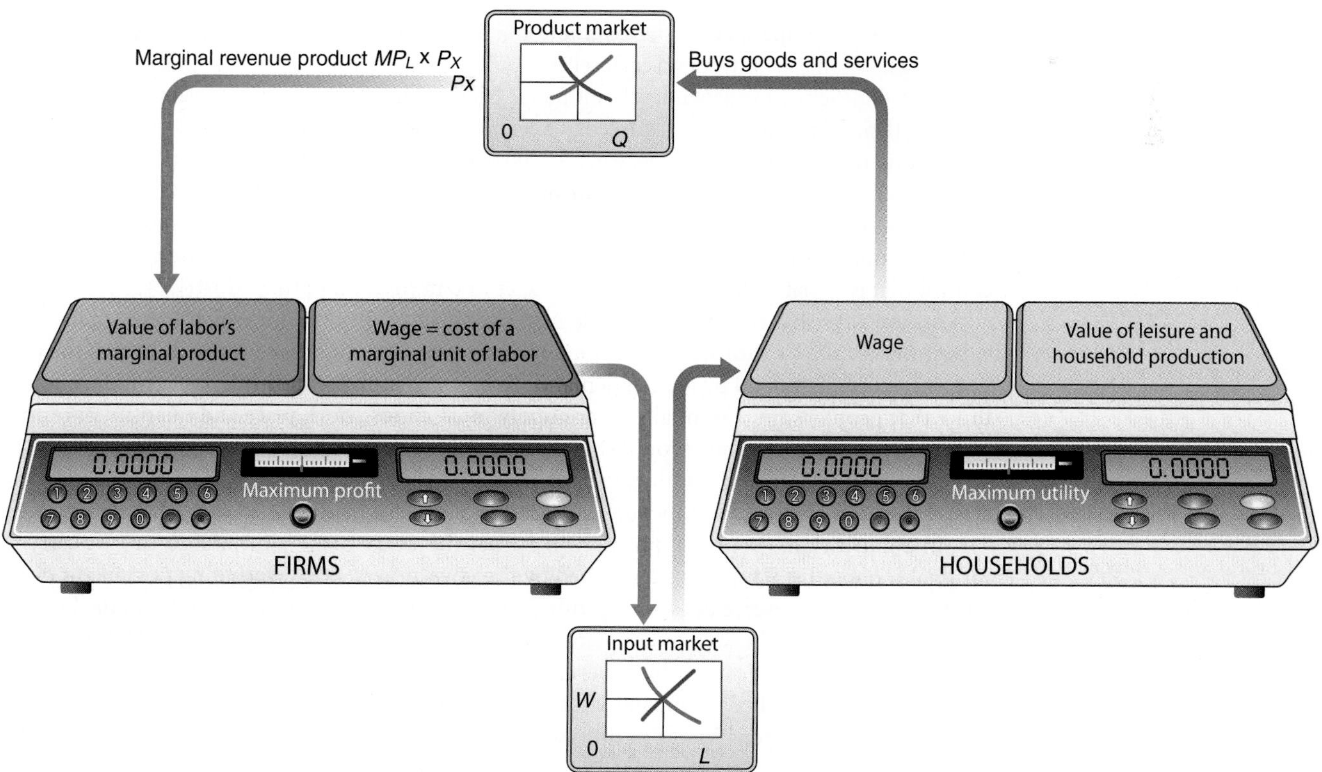

▲ **FIGURE 12.4 Efficiency in Perfect Competition Follows from a Weighing of Values by Both Households and Firms**

Perfect Competition versus Real Markets

So far, we have built a model of a perfectly competitive market system that produces an efficient allocation of resources, an efficient mix of output, and an efficient distribution of output. The perfectly competitive model is built on a set of assumptions, all of which must hold for our conclusions to be fully valid. We have assumed that all firms and households are price-takers in input and output markets, that firms and households have perfect information, and that all firms maximize profits.

These assumptions do not always hold in real-world markets. When this is the case, the conclusion breaks down that free, unregulated markets will produce an efficient outcome. The remainder of this chapter discusses some inefficiencies that occur naturally in markets and some of the strengths, as well as the weaknesses, of the market mechanism. We also discuss the usefulness of the competitive model for understanding the real economy.

The Sources of Market Failure

In suggesting some of the problems encountered in real markets and some of the possible solutions to these problems, the rest of this chapter previews the next part of this book, which focuses on the economics of market failure and the potential role of government in the economy.

market failure Occurs when resources are misallocated, or allocated inefficiently. The result is waste or lost value.

Market failure occurs when resources are misallocated, or allocated inefficiently. The result is waste or lost value. In this section, we briefly describe four important sources of market failure: (1) *imperfect market structure*, or noncompetitive behavior; (2) the existence of *public goods*; (3) the presence of *external costs and benefits*; and (4) *imperfect information*. Each condition results from the failure of one of the assumptions basic to the perfectly competitive model, and each is discussed in more detail in later chapters. Each also points to a potential role for government in the economy. The desirability and the extent of actual government involvement in the economy are hotly debated subjects.

Imperfect Markets

Until now, we have operated on the assumption that the number of buyers and sellers in each market is large. When each buyer and each seller is only one of a great many in the market, no individual buyer or seller can independently influence price. Thus, all economic decision makers are by virtue of their relatively small size forced to take input prices and output prices as given. When this assumption does not hold—that is, when single firms have some control over price and potential competition—the result is **imperfect competition** and an inefficient allocation of resources.

imperfect competition An industry in which single firms have some control over price and competition. Imperfectly competitive industries give rise to an inefficient allocation of resources.

monopoly An industry composed of only one firm that produces a product for which there are no close substitutes and in which significant barriers exist to prevent new firms from entering the industry.

A Kansas wheat farmer is probably a "price-taker," but Microsoft and Mitsubishi most certainly are not. Many firms in many industries do have some control over price. The degree of control that is possible depends on the character of competition in the industry.

An industry that comprises just one firm producing a product for which there are no close substitutes is called a **monopoly**. Although a monopoly has no other firms with which to compete, it is still constrained by market demand. To be successful, the firm still has to produce something that people want. Essentially, a monopoly must choose both price and quantity of output simultaneously because the amount that it will be able to sell depends on the price it sets. If the price is too high, it will sell nothing. Presumably, a monopolist sets price to maximize profit. That price is generally significantly above average costs, and such a firm usually earns economic profits.

In competition, economic profits will attract the entry of new firms into the industry. A rational monopolist who is not restrained by the government does everything possible to block any such entry to preserve economic profits in the long run. As a result, society loses the benefits of more products and lower prices. A number of barriers to entry can be raised. Sometimes a monopoly is actually licensed by government, and entry into its market is prohibited by law. Taiwan has only one beer company; many areas in the United States have only one local telephone company. Ownership of a natural resource can also be the source of monopoly power. If I buy up all the coal mines in the United States and I persuade Congress to restrict coal imports, no one can enter the coal industry and compete with me.

Between monopoly and perfect competition are a number of other imperfectly competitive market structures. *Oligopolistic industries* are made up of a small number of firms, each with a degree of price-setting power. *Monopolistically competitive industries* are made up of a large number of firms that acquire price-setting power by differentiating their products or by establishing a brand name. Only General Mills can produce Wheaties, for example, and only Bayer AG can produce Alka-Seltzer. In all imperfectly competitive industries, output is lower—the product is underproduced—and price is higher than it would be under perfect competition. The equilibrium condition $P = MC$ does not hold, and the system does not produce the most efficient product mix.

In Chapter 13, we will demonstrate that firms with market power underproduce, the result is a deadweight loss of producer and consumer surplus. (See the discussion of deadweight loss in Chapter 4.)

In the United States, many forms of noncompetitive behavior are illegal. A firm that attempts to monopolize an industry or that conspires with other firms to reduce competition risks serious penalties. The most famous recent antitrust case was brought by the Justice Department against Microsoft in the late 1990s. Microsoft was accused of attempting to monopolize the Internet browser market and other anticompetitive practices. In June 2000, the court agreed that Microsoft violated U.S. antitrust laws and ordered that Microsoft be broken up into two separate companies. Although the Microsoft breakup was stopped on appeal, Microsoft was convicted of violating the antitrust laws and is still involved in litigation. In 2007, Microsoft settled numerous cases in the courts of the European Union.

Recently, three industries once thought to be "natural monopolies" are shifting away from government regulation toward becoming fully competitive industries: local telephone service, electricity, and natural gas. (All this is discussed in more detail in Chapters 13 and 14.)

Public Goods

A second major source of inefficiency lies in the fact that private producers do not find it in their best interest to produce everything that members of society want because for one reason or another they are unable to charge prices to reflect values people place on those goods. More specifically, there is a whole class of goods and services called **public goods** or **social goods**, that will be underproduced or not produced at all in a completely unregulated market economy.[3]

public goods, *or* **social goods** Goods and services that bestow collective benefits on members of society. Generally, no one can be excluded from enjoying their benefits. The classic example is national defense.

Public goods are goods and services that bestow collective benefits on society; they are, in a sense, collectively consumed. The classic example is national defense; but there are countless others—police protection, homeland security, preservation of wilderness lands, and public health, to name a few. These things are "produced" using land, labor, and capital just like any other good. Some public goods, such as national defense, benefit the whole nation. Others, such as clean air, may be limited to smaller areas—the air may be clean in a Kansas town but dirty in a southern California city.

Public goods are consumed by everyone, not just by those who pay for them. Once the good is produced, no one can be excluded from enjoying its benefits. Producers of **private goods**, such as hamburgers, can make a profit because they do not hand over the product to you until you pay for it. The inability to exclude nonpayers from consumption of a public good makes it, not surprisingly, hard to charge people a price for the good. Chapters 3 through 11 centered on the production of private goods.

private goods Goods and services produced by firms for sale to individual households.

If the provision of public goods were left to private profit-seeking producers with no power to force payment, a serious problem would arise. Suppose, for example, you value some public good, *X*. If there were a functioning market for *X*, you would be willing to pay for *X*. Suppose you are asked to contribute voluntarily to the production of *X*. Should you contribute? Perhaps you should on moral grounds, but not on the basis of pure self-interest.

At least two problems can get in the way. First, because you cannot be excluded from using *X* for not paying, you get the good whether you pay or not. Why should you pay if you do not have to? Second, because public goods that provide collective benefits to large numbers of people are expensive to produce, any one person's contribution is not likely to make much difference to the amount of the good ultimately produced. Would the national defense suffer, for example, if you did not pay your share of the bill? Probably not. Thus, nothing happens if you do not pay. The output of the good does not change much, and you get it whether you pay or not. Private provision of public goods fails. A completely laissez-faire market system will not produce everything that all members of a society might want. Citizens must band together to ensure that desired public goods are produced, and this is generally accomplished through government spending financed by taxes. Public goods are the subject of Chapter 16.

[3] Although they are normally referred to as public *goods*, many of the things we are talking about are *services*.

Externalities

externality A cost or benefit imposed or bestowed on an individual or a group that is outside, or external to, the transaction.

A third major source of inefficiency is the existence of external costs and benefits. An **externality** is a cost or benefit imposed or bestowed on an individual or a group that is outside, or external to, the transaction—in other words, something that affects a third party. In a city, external costs are pervasive. The classic example is air or water pollution, but there are thousands of others, such as noise, congestion, and your house painted a color that the neighbors think is ugly. Global warming is an externality at the level of the world.

Not all externalities are negative, however. For example, housing investment may yield benefits for neighbors. A farm located near a city provides residents in the area with nice views and a less congested environment.

Externalities are a problem only if decision makers do not take them into account. The logic of efficiency presented earlier in this chapter required that firms weigh social benefits against social costs. If a firm in a competitive environment produces a good, it is because the value of that good to society exceeds the social cost of producing it—this is the logic of $P = MC$. If social costs or benefits are overlooked or left out of the calculations, inefficient decisions result. In essence, if the calculation of either MC or P in the equation is "wrong," equating the two will clearly not lead to an optimal result.

The market itself has no automatic mechanism that provides decision makers an incentive to consider external effects. Through government, however, society has established over the years a number of different institutions for dealing with externalities. Tort law, for example, is a body of legal rules that deal with third-party effects. Under certain circumstances, those who impose costs are held strictly liable for them. In other circumstances, liability is assessed only if the cost results from "negligent" behavior. Tort law deals with small problems as well as larger ones. If your neighbors spray their lawn with a powerful chemical and kill your prize shrub, you can take them to court and force them to pay for it.

The effects of externalities can be enormous. For years, companies piled chemical wastes indiscriminately into dump sites near water supplies and residential areas. In some locations, those wastes seeped into the ground and contaminated the drinking water. In response to the evidence that smoking damages not only the smoker but also others, governments have increased prohibitions against smoking on airplanes and in public places. In 1997, attorneys general for a majority of states approved a tentative agreement with the tobacco industry to pay billions of dollars in damage claims to avoid pending lawsuits filed on behalf of citizens damaged by smoking or breathing secondhand smoke. In July 2005, the Justice Department asked the Supreme Court for the legal authority to seek $280 billion in damages from the tobacco industry. In 2007, scientists working under the auspices of the United Nations released a report suggesting that the worldwide externalities from a range of production and consumption choices were likely to be enormous.

For years, economists have suggested that a carefully designed set of taxes and subsidies could help to "internalize" external effects. For example, if a paper mill that pollutes the air and waterways is taxed in proportion to the damage caused by that pollution, the mill will consider those costs in its production decisions.

Sometimes interaction among and between parties can lead to the proper consideration of externality without government involvement. If someone plays a radio loudly on the fourth floor of your dormitory, that person imposes an externality on the other residents of the building. The residents, however, can get together and negotiate a set of mutually acceptable rules to govern radio playing. The market does not always force consideration of all the costs and benefits of decisions. Yet for an economy to achieve an efficient allocation of resources, all costs and benefits must be weighed. We discuss externalities in detail in Chapter 16.

Imperfect Information

imperfect information The absence of full knowledge concerning product characteristics, available prices, and so on.

The fourth major source of inefficiency is **imperfect information** on the part of buyers and sellers. The conclusion that markets work efficiently rests heavily on the assumption that consumers and producers have full knowledge of product characteristics, available prices, and so on. The absence of full information can lead to transactions that are ultimately disadvantageous.

Some products are so complex that consumers find it difficult to judge the potential benefits and costs of purchase. Buyers of life insurance have a very difficult time sorting out the terms of the more complex policies and determining the true "price" of the product. Consumers of almost any service that requires expertise, such as plumbing and medical care, have a hard time evaluating what is needed, much less how well it is done. It is difficult for a used-car buyer to find out the true "quality" of the cars in Big Jim's Car Emporium.

Some forms of misinformation can be corrected with simple rules such as truth-in-advertising regulations. In some cases, the government provides information to citizens; job banks and consumer information services exist for this purpose. In certain industries, such as medical care, there is no clear-cut solution to the problem of noninformation or misinformation. We discuss all these topics in detail in Chapter 16.

Evaluating the Market Mechanism

Is the market system good or bad? Should the government be involved in the economy, or should it leave the allocation of resources to the free market? So far, our information is mixed and incomplete. To the extent that the perfectly competitive model reflects the way markets really operate, there seem to be some clear advantages to the market system. When we relax the assumptions and expand our discussion to include noncompetitive behavior, public goods, externalities, and the possibility of imperfect information, we see at least a potential role for government.

The market system does seem to provide most participants with the incentive to weigh costs and benefits and to operate efficiently. Firms can make profits only when a demand for their products exists. If there are no externalities or if such costs or benefits are properly internalized, firms *will* weigh social benefits and costs in their production decisions. Under these circumstances, the profit motive should provide competitive firms with an incentive to minimize cost and to produce their products using the most efficient technologies. Likewise, competitive input markets should provide households with the incentive to weigh the value of their time against the social value of what they can produce in the labor force.

However, markets are far from perfect. Freely functioning markets in the real world do not always produce an efficient allocation of resources, and this result provides a potential role for government in the economy. Many have called for government involvement in the economy to correct for market failure—that is, to help markets function more efficiently. As you will see, however, many believe that government involvement in the economy creates more inefficiency than it cures.

An example of inefficiency brought about by government regulation was discussed in Chapter 4. If market-determined prices bring supply and demand into equilibrium, the total value of consumer surplus plus producer surplus will be maximized. Often the government imposes price ceilings and price floors in the name of fairness or equity. An example of a price ceiling is rent control. By holding price below equilibrium, the quantity supplied is reduced and the quantity demanded is increased. The result is a deadweight loss. An example of a price floor is the minimum wage that holds the wage rate above equilibrium in the labor market.

In addition, we have thus far discussed only the criterion of efficiency; but economic systems and economic policies must be judged by many other criteria, not the least of which is *equity*, or fairness. Indeed, some contend that the outcome of any free market is ultimately unfair because some become rich while others remain poor.

Part III, which follows, explores in greater depth the issue of market imperfections and government involvement in the economy.

SUMMARY

GENERAL EQUILIBRIUM ANALYSIS *p. 242*

1. Both firms and households make simultaneous choices in input and output markets. For example, input prices determine output costs and affect firms' output supply decisions. Wages in the labor market affect labor supply decisions, income, and ultimately the amount of output households can and do purchase.

2. A *general equilibrium* exists when all markets in an economy are in simultaneous equilibrium. An event that disturbs the equilibrium in one market may disturb the equilibrium in many other markets as well. *Partial equilibrium* analysis can be misleading because it looks only at adjustments in one isolated market.

ALLOCATIVE EFFICIENCY AND COMPETITIVE EQUILIBRIUM *p. 246*

3. An *efficient* economy is one that produces the goods and services that people want at the least possible cost. A change is said to be efficient if it makes some members of society better off without making others worse off. An efficient, or *Pareto optimal*, system is one in which no such changes are possible.
4. If a change makes some people better off and some people worse off but it can be shown that the value of the gains exceeds the value of the losses, the change is said to be *potentially efficient* or simply *efficient.*
5. If all the assumptions of perfect competition hold, the result is an efficient, or Pareto optimal, allocation of resources. To prove this statement, it is necessary to show that resources are allocated efficiently among firms, that final products are distributed efficiently among households, and that the system produces what people want.
6. The assumptions that factor markets are competitive and open, that all firms pay the same prices for inputs, and that all firms maximize profits lead to the conclusion that the allocation of resources among firms is efficient.
7. People have different tastes and preferences, and they buy very different things in very different combinations. As long as everyone shops freely in the same markets, no redistribution of outputs among people will make them better off. This leads to the conclusion that final products are distributed efficiently among households.
8. Because perfectly competitive firms will produce as long as the price of their product is greater than the marginal cost of production, they will continue to produce as long as a gain for society is possible. The market thus guarantees that the right things are produced. In other words, the perfectly competitive system produces what people want.

THE SOURCES OF MARKET FAILURE *p. 254*

9. When the assumptions of perfect competition do not hold, the conclusion breaks down that free, unregulated markets will produce an efficient allocation of resources.
10. An imperfectly competitive industry is one in which single firms have some control over price and competition. Forms of *imperfect competition* include monopoly, monopolistic competition, and oligopoly. In all imperfectly competitive industries, output is lower and price is higher than they would be in perfect competition. Imperfect competition is a major source of market inefficiency.
11. *Public*, or *social, goods* bestow collective benefits on members of society. Because the benefits of social goods are collective, people cannot, in most cases, be excluded from enjoying them. Thus, private firms usually do not find it profitable to produce public goods. The need for public goods is thus another source of inefficiency.
12. An *externality* is a cost or benefit that is imposed or bestowed on an individual or a group that is outside, or external to, the transaction. If such social costs or benefits are overlooked, the decisions of households or firms are likely to be wrong or inefficient.
13. Market efficiency depends on the assumption that buyers have perfect information on product quality and price and that firms have perfect information on input quality and price. *Imperfect information* can lead to wrong choices and inefficiency.

EVALUATING THE MARKET MECHANISM *p. 257*

14. Sources of market failure—such as imperfect markets, public goods, externalities, and imperfect information—are considered by many to justify the existence of government and governmental policies that seek to redistribute costs and income on the basis of efficiency, equity, or both.

REVIEW TERMS AND CONCEPTS

efficiency, *p. 242*
externality, *p. 256*
general equilibrium, *p. 242*
imperfect competition, *p. 254*
imperfect information, *p. 256*
market failure, *p. 254*
monopoly, *p. 254*
Pareto efficiency *or* Pareto optimality, *p. 248*
partial equilibrium analysis, *p. 242*
private goods, *p. 255*
public goods *or* social goods, *p. 255*
Key efficiency condition in perfect competition: $P_X = MC_X$

PROBLEMS

Visit **www.myeconlab.com** to complete the problems marked in orange online. You will receive instant feedback on your answers, tutorial help, and access to additional practice problems.

1. Cell phones have become very popular. At the same time, new technology has made them less expensive to produce. Assuming that the technological advance caused cost curves to shift downward at the same time that demand was shifting to the right, draw a graph or graphs to show what will happen in the short run and in the long run.
2. Numerous times in history, the courts have issued consent decrees requiring large companies to break up into smaller competing companies for violating the antitrust laws. The two best-known examples are American Telephone and Telegraph (AT&T) in the 1980s and Microsoft 20 years later. (AT&T was broken up into the "Baby Bells"; but the Microsoft breakup was successfully appealed, and the breakup never occurred.)

Many argue that breaking up a monopoly is a Pareto-efficient change. This interpretation cannot be so because breaking up a monopoly makes its owners (or shareholders) worse off. Do you agree or disagree? Explain your answer.

3. **[Related to the *Economics in Practice* on p. 247]** The first *Economics in Practice* in this chapter describes the adjustment of the corn and wheat markets to the massive U.S. subsidy given to ethanol production. The subsidy drives up the prices of other agricultural goods such as wheat and substantially raises the value of farmland. How would this story change if oil prices were to rise extensively at the same time? if oil prices were to fall? Trace these changes on the economy using supply and demand curves.

4. For each of the following, tell a story about what is likely to happen in labor and capital markets using the model of the whole economy that we developed over the first 11 chapters.
   a. A sharp drop in demand for automobiles raises the unemployment rate in Flint, Michigan, and cuts into the profits of local gas stations where my nephew lost his job.
   b. As the baby boomers age, many of them are moving back to the city. They are also buying smaller units. This will have a big effect on owners of suburban homes who find their home values falling.
   c. In 2007–2008, the mortgage markets crashed. This led to a serious decline in the availability of credit to buyers who, a couple of years ago, were able to borrow far more than they needed.

5. A medium-sized bakery has just opened in Slovakia. A loaf of bread is currently selling for 14 koruna (the Slovakian currency) over and above the cost of intermediate goods (flour, yeast, and so on). Assuming that labor is the only variable factor of production, the following table gives the production function for the bread.

WORKERS	LOAVES OF BREAD
0	0
1	15
2	30
3	42
4	52
5	60
6	66
7	70

   a. Suppose the current wage rate in Slovakia is 119 koruna per hour. How many workers will the bakery employ?
   b. Suppose the economy of Slovakia begins to grow, incomes rise, and the price of a loaf of bread is pushed up to 20 koruna. Assuming no increase in the price of labor, how many workers will the bakery hire?
   c. An increase in the demand for labor pushes up wages to 125 koruna per hour. What impact will this increase in cost have on employment and output in the bakery at the 20-koruna price of bread?
   d. If all firms behaved like our bakery, would the allocation of resources in Slovakia be efficient? Explain your answer.

6. Country A has soil that is suited to corn production and yields 135 bushels per acre. Country B has soil that is not suited for corn and yields only 45 bushels per acre. Country A has soil that is not suited for soybean production and yields 15 bushels per acre. Country B has soil that is suited for soybeans and yields 35 bushels per acre. In 2004, there was no trade between A and B because of high taxes and both countries together produced huge quantities of corn and soybeans. In 2005, taxes were eliminated because of a new trade agreement. What is likely to happen? Can you justify the trade agreement on the basis of Pareto efficiency? Why or why not?

7. Do you agree or disagree with each of the following statements? Explain your answer.
   a. Housing is a public good and should be produced by the public sector because private markets will fail to produce it efficiently.
   b. Monopoly power is inefficient because large firms will produce too much product, dumping it on the market at artificially low prices.
   c. Medical care is an example of a potentially inefficient market because consumers do not have perfect information about the product.

8. **[Related to the *Economics in Practice* on p. 252]** The *Economics in Practice* on ticket scalping argues that it is "efficient" for tickets to sporting events to find their way into the hands of those willing and able to pay the most. After all, if you and I make a trade freely, we are both better off after the trade. The result is a "Pareto improvement." It also was argued earlier in the chapter that opportunities for such trades are rare in market economies. If we all shop in the same stores and face the same prices, we end up with those goods and services that we want the most. But when goods sell for different prices to different people, trading becomes common. In 1989, the Berlin Wall separating East Germany and West Germany was dismantled, allowing people to move freely across the border. On the east side, many goods, including bread and meat, were sold at state stores at very low prices on grounds of fairness. In fact, on that side of the wall, prices of goods did not reflect the costs of production. Think of some changes that were likely to have occurred soon after the wall came down. What opportunities existed for Pareto improvements? Also consider the reallocation of inputs (capital, labor, and land). Reread the section "Efficient Allocation of Resources Among Firms" to help you answer this question.

9. Which of the following are examples of Pareto-efficient changes? Explain your answers.
   a. Cindy trades her laptop computer to Bob for his old car.
   b. Competition is introduced into the electric industry, and electricity rates drop. A study shows that benefits to consumers are larger than the lost monopoly profits.
   c. A high tax on wool sweaters deters buyers. The tax is repealed.
   d. A federal government agency is reformed, and costs are cut 23 percent with no loss of service quality.

10. A major source of chicken feed in the United States is anchovies, small fish that can be scooped out of the ocean at low cost. Every 7 years, when the anchovies disappear to spawn, producers must turn to grain, which is more expensive, to feed their chickens. What is likely to happen to the cost of chicken when the anchovies disappear? What are substitutes for chicken? How are the markets for these substitutes affected? Name some complements to chicken. How are the markets for these complements affected? How might the allocation of farmland be changed as a result of the disappearance of anchovies?

11. Suppose two passengers end up with a reservation for the last seat on a train from San Francisco to Los Angeles. Two alternatives are proposed:
    a. Toss a coin
    b. Sell the ticket to the highest bidder

    Compare the two options from the standpoint of efficiency and equity.

12. Assume that there are two sectors in an economy: goods (G) and services (S). Both sectors are perfectly competitive, with large numbers of firms and constant returns to scale. As income rises, households spend a larger portion of their income on S and a smaller portion on G. Using supply and demand curves for both sectors and a diagram showing a representative firm in each sector, explain what would happen to output and prices in the short run and the long run in response to an increase in income. (Assume that the increase in income causes demand for G to shift left and demand for S to shift right.) In the long run, what would happen to employment in the goods sector? in the service sector?(*Hint:* See Figure 12.2 on p. 246.)

13. Which of the following are actual Pareto-efficient changes? Explain briefly.
    a. You buy three oranges for $1 from a street vendor.
    b. You are near death from thirst in the desert and must pay a passing vagabond $10,000 for a glass of water.
    c. A mugger steals your wallet.
    d. You take a taxi ride in downtown Manhattan during rush hour.

14. Each instance that follows is an example of one of the four types of market failure discussed in this chapter. In each case, identify the type of market failure and defend your choice briefly.
    a. An auto repair shop convinces you that you need a $2,000 valve job when all you really need is an oil change.
    b. Everyone in a neighborhood would benefit if an empty lot were turned into a park, but no entrepreneur will come forward to finance the transformation.
    c. Someone who lives in an apartment building buys a Gretchen Wilson CD and then blasts it at full volume at 3 A.M.
    d. The only two airlines flying direct between St. Louis and Atlanta make an agreement to raise their prices.

15. Two factories in the same town hire workers with the same skills. Union agreements require factory A to pay its workers $10 per hour, while factory B must pay $6 per hour. Each factory hires the profit-maximizing number of workers. Is the allocation of labor between these two factories efficient? Explain why or why not.

Monopoly and Antitrust Policy

13

CHAPTER OUTLINE

You may own an iPod by Apple and a computer that runs Windows software by Microsoft. Each of these firms has faced lawsuits accusing it of exercising monopoly power. On New Year's Day 2008, a lawsuit filed against Apple charged the firm with "maintaining an illegal monopoly on the digital music market." By 1992, Microsoft had captured 90 percent of the market for PC operating systems. After years of scrutiny, the government concluded in 1999 that Microsoft was "exercising illegal monopoly power" and ordered the company split in two. A judge overturned the order, and Microsoft eventually agreed to behave more competitively. What is a monopoly, and why are there laws that make it illegal?

In earlier chapters, we described in some detail the workings and benefits of perfect competition. The fact of market competition and undifferentiated or homogeneous products limited the choice of firms in those markets. Firms decided how much to produce and how to produce; but in setting prices, they looked to the market. Moreover, because of entry and competition, firms could do no better than earn the opportunity cost of capital in the long run; there were no excess profits. For firms such as Apple and Microsoft, economic decision making is richer and so is the potential for profit making.

In the next three chapters, we explore markets in which competition is limited, either by the fewness of firms or by product differentiation. After a brief discussion of market structure in general, this chapter will focus on monopoly markets. Chapter 14 will cover oligopolies, while Chapter 15 will deal with monopolistic competition.

Imperfect Competition and Market Power: Core Concepts

A market or industry in which individual firms have some control over the price of their output is **imperfectly competitive**. All firms in an imperfectly competitive market have one thing in common: They exercise **market power**, the ability to raise price without losing all of the quantity demanded for their product. Imperfect competition and market power are major sources of inefficiency. Imperfect competition does not mean that *no* competition exists in the market. In some imperfectly competitive markets, competition occurs in *more* arenas than in perfectly competitive markets. Firms can differentiate their products, advertise, improve quality, market aggressively, cut prices, and so on. But in this competition, we see evidence of some market power.

imperfectly competitive industry An industry in which individual firms have some control over the price of their output.

market power An imperfectly competitive firm's ability to raise price without losing all of the quantity demanded for its product.

What do we mean when we say that a firm has control over its prices? All firms have the *ability* to put a sticker price on their products that is higher than what is charged by the rest of the market. But if the firm is selling a T-shirt identical to those produced by hundreds of other firms, setting a higher price will generate no sales. All the potential customers will go elsewhere.

In the marketplace, we often see T-shirts being sold at different prices and still attracting customers. Shirts with a sports logo generally sell for more that those without; well-known designers can sell their T-shirts for even higher prices. Some customers see these T-shirts as being different from one another. Firms that convince customers that their goods are better and that keep other firms from imitating them have a chance of preserving economic profits. These firms have market power; they do not lose all their customers when they raise prices.

Forms of Imperfect Competition and Market Boundaries

Once we move away from perfectly competitive markets, with its assumption of many firms and undifferentiated products, there is a range of other possible market structures. At one extreme from the perfectly competitive firm lies the monopoly. A *monopoly* is an industry with a single firm in which the entry of new firms is blocked. An *oligopoly* is an industry in which there is a small number of firms, each large enough to have an impact on the market price of its outputs. Firms that differentiate their products in industries with many producers and free entry are called *monopolistic competitors*. We begin our discussion in this chapter with monopoly.

What do we mean when we say that a monopoly firm is the only firm in the industry? In practice, given the prevalence of branding, many firms, especially in the consumer products markets, are alone in producing a specific product. Proctor & Gamble (P&G), for example, is the only producer of Ivory soap. Coca-Cola is the only producer of Coke Classic. And yet we would call neither firm monopolistic because for both, many other firms produce products that are *close substitutes*. Instead of drinking Coke, we could drink Pepsi; instead of washing with Ivory, we could wash with Dove. To be meaningful, therefore, our definition of a monopolistic industry must be more precise. We define a **pure monopoly** as an industry (1) with a single firm that produces a product for which there are *no close substitutes* and (2) in which significant barriers to entry prevent other firms from entering the industry to compete for profits.

pure monopoly An industry with a single firm that produces a product for which there are no close substitutes and in which significant barriers to entry prevent other firms from entering the industry to compete for profits.

As we think about the issue of product substitutes and market power, it is useful to recall the structure of the competitive market. Consider a firm producing an undifferentiated brand of burger meat, Brand X burger. As we show in Figure 13.1 the demand this firm faces is horizontal, perfectly elastic. The demand for hamburgers as a whole, however, likely slopes down. While there are substitutes for hamburgers, they are not perfect and some people will continue to consume hamburgers even with a price increase. As we broaden the category we are considering, the substitution possibilities *outside* the category fall, and demand becomes quite inelastic, as for example for food in general.

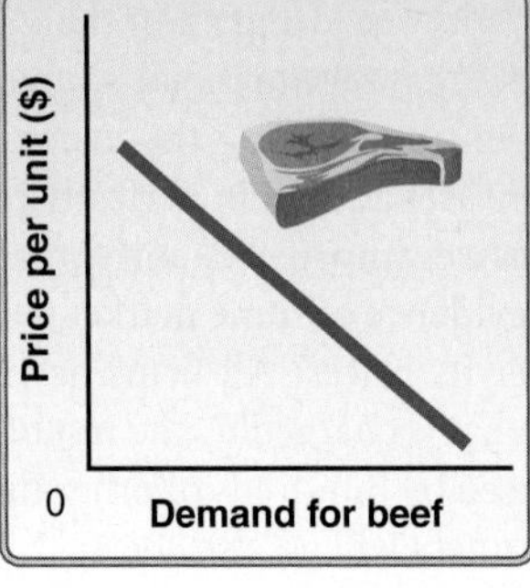

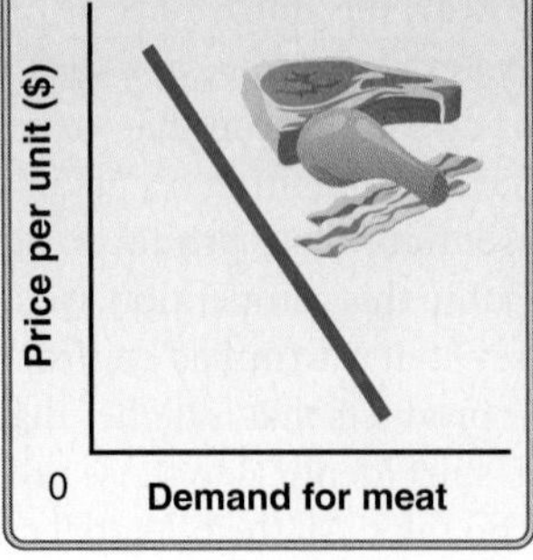

▸ **FIGURE 13.1 The Boundary of a Market and Elasticity**

We can define an industry as broadly or as narrowly as we like. The more broadly we define the industry, the fewer substitutes there are; thus, the less elastic the demand for that industry's product is likely to be. A monopoly is an industry with one firm that produces a product for which there are *no close substitutes*. The producer of brand X hamburger cannot properly be called a monopolist because this producer has no control over market price and there are many substitutes for brand X hamburger.

In practice, figuring out which products are close substitutes for one another to determine monopoly power can be difficult. Are hamburgers and hot dogs close substitutes so that a hamburger monopoly would have little power to raise prices? Are debit cards and checks close substitutes for credit cards so that credit card firms have little market power? The courts in a recent antitrust case said no. How much does the availability of peanut butter affect the ability of major canned tuna producers to raise their prices? Is Microsoft a monopoly, or does it compete with Linux and Apple for software users? These are questions that occupy considerable time for economists, lawyers, and the antitrust courts. In the *Economics in Practice* on p. 279, we explore the issue of product definition in the context of natural foods.

Price and Output Decisions in Pure Monopoly Markets

Consider a market in which we have a single firm producing a good for which there are few substitutes. How does this profit-maximizing monopolist choose its output levels? How does the monopolist take into account the fact that when it raises its prices it will lose at least some customers?

Assume initially that our pure monopolist buys in competitive input markets. Even though the firm is the only one producing for its product market, it is only one among many firms buying factors of production in input markets. The local telephone company must hire labor like any other firm. To attract workers, the company must pay the market wage; to buy fiber-optic cable, it must pay the going price. In these input markets, the monopolistic firm is a price-taker.

On the cost side of the profit equation, a pure monopolist does not differ from a perfect competitor. Both choose the technology that minimizes the cost of production. The cost curve of each represents the minimum cost of producing each level of output. The difference arises on the revenue, or demand, side of the equation, where we begin our analysis.

Demand in Monopoly Markets

A perfectly competitive firm, you will recall, faces a fixed, market-determined price, and we assume that it can sell all it wants to sell at that price. The firm is constrained only by its current capacity in the short run. The demand curve facing such a firm is thus a horizontal line, as shown in Figure 13.2. Raising the price of its product means losing all demand because perfect substitutes are available. The perfectly competitive firm has no incentive to charge a lower price either since it can sell all it wants at the market price.

Because a perfectly competitive firm can charge only one price, regardless of the output level chosen, its *marginal revenue*—the additional revenue that it earns by raising output by 1 unit—is simply the price of the output, or $P^* = \$5$ in Figure 13.2. Remember that marginal revenue is important because a profit-maximizing firm will increase output as long as marginal revenue exceeds marginal cost.

The most important difference between perfect competition and monopoly is that with one firm in a monopoly market, there is no distinction between the firm and the industry. In a monopoly, the firm is the industry. The market demand curve is the demand curve facing the firm, and the total quantity supplied in the market is what the firm decides to produce.

To proceed, we need a few more assumptions. First, we assume that a monopolistic firm cannot price discriminate. It sells its product to all demanders at the same price. (*Price discrimination* means selling to different consumers or groups of consumers at different prices and will be discussed later in this chapter.)

We also assume that the monopoly faces a known demand curve. That is, we assume that the firm has enough information to predict how households will react to different prices. (Many firms use statistical methods to estimate the elasticity of demand for their products. Other firms may use less formal methods, including trial and error, sometimes called "price searching." All firms with market power must have some sense of how consumers are likely to react to various prices.) By knowing the demand curve it faces, the monopolist understands that when it chooses an output level, Q, that choice will affect the price it can obtain. In contrast, the competitive firm reacts to a fixed market price that its output level does not influence. Stated somewhat differently, the monopolist chooses the point on the market demand curve where it wants to be.

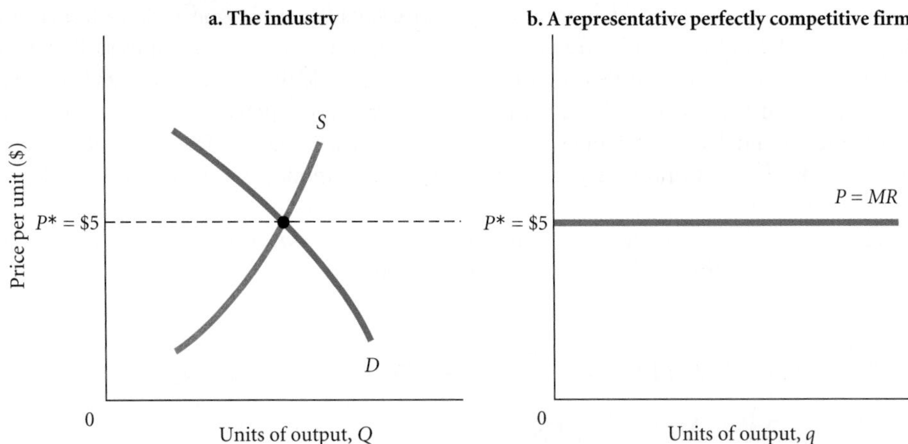

▲ **FIGURE 13.2 The Demand Curve Facing a Perfectly Competitive Firm Is Perfectly Elastic**

Perfectly competitive firms are price-takers; they are small relative to the size of the market and thus cannot influence market price. The implication is that the demand curve facing a perfectly competitive firm is perfectly elastic. If the firm raises its price, it sells nothing and there is no reason for the firm to lower its price if it can sell all it wants at $P^* = \$5$.

Marginal Revenue and Market Demand Just like a competitive firm, a profit-maximizing monopolist will continue to produce output as long as marginal revenue exceeds marginal cost. Because the market demand curve is the demand curve for a monopoly and the monopolist's output choices influence the price it can get, a monopolistic firm faces a downward-sloping demand curve. The downward slope of the demand curve creates a wedge between price and marginal revenue. We explain below.

Consider the hypothetical demand schedule in Table 13.1. Column 3 lists the total revenue that the monopoly would take in at different levels of output. If it were to produce 1 unit, that unit would sell for $10, and total revenue would be $10. Two units would sell for $9 each, in which case total revenue would be $18. As column 4 shows, marginal revenue from the second unit would be $8 ($18 minus $10). Notice that the marginal revenue from increasing output from 1 unit to 2 units ($8) is *less* than the price of the second unit ($9).

Now consider what happens when the firm considers setting production at 4 units instead of 3. The fourth unit would sell for $7, but because the firm cannot price discriminate, it must sell *all 4* units for $7 each. Had the firm chosen to produce only 3 units, it could have sold those 3 units for $8 each. Thus, offsetting the revenue gain of $7 is a revenue loss of $3—that is, $1 for each of the 3 units that would have sold at the higher price. The marginal revenue of the fourth unit is $7 minus $3, or $4, which is considerably below the price of $7. (Remember, unlike a monopoly, a perfectly competitive firm does not have to charge a lower price to sell more. Thus, $P = MR$ in competition.) For a monopolist, an increase in output involves not just producing more and selling it, but also reducing the price of its output to sell it.

Marginal revenue can also be derived by looking at the change in total revenue as output changes by 1 unit. At 3 units of output, total revenue is $24. At 4 units of output, total revenue is $28. Marginal revenue is the difference, or $4.

Moving from 6 to 7 units of output actually reduces total revenue for the firm. At 7 units, marginal revenue is negative. Although it is true that the seventh unit will sell for a positive price ($4), the firm must sell all 7 units for $4 each (for a total revenue of $28). If output had been restricted to 6 units, each would have sold for $5. Thus, offsetting the revenue gain of $4 is a revenue loss of $6—that is, $1 for each of the 6 units that the firm would have sold at the higher price. Increasing output from 6 to 7 units actually decreases revenue by $2. Figure 13.3 graphs the marginal revenue schedule derived in Table 13.1. Notice that at every level of output except 1 unit, marginal revenue is *below* price. Marginal revenue turns from positive to negative after 6 units of output. When the demand curve is a straight line, the marginal revenue curve bisects the quantity axis between the origin and the point where the demand curve hits the quantity axis, as in Figure 13.4.

TABLE 13.1 Marginal Revenue Facing a Monopolist

(1) Quantity	(2) Price	(3) Total Revenue	(4) Marginal Revenue
0	$11	0	—
1	10	$10	$10
2	9	18	8
3	8	24	6
4	7	28	4
5	6	30	2
6	5	30	0
7	4	28	−2
8	3	24	−4
9	2	18	−6
10	1	10	−8

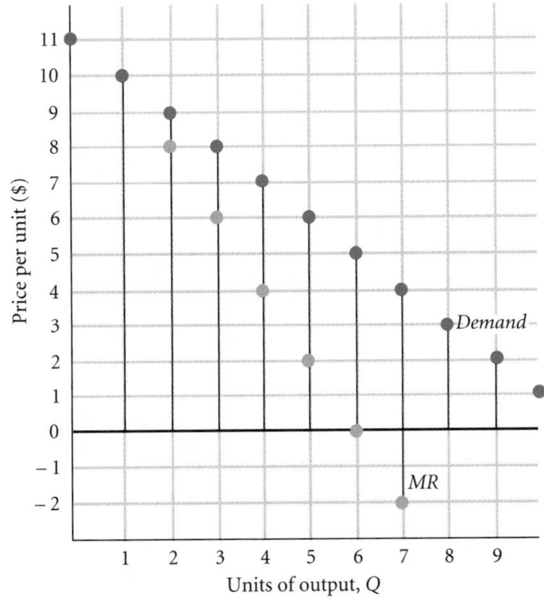

FIGURE 13.3 Marginal Revenue Curve Facing a Monopolist

At every level of output except 1 unit, a monopolist's marginal revenue (*MR*) is below price. This is so because (1) we assume that the monopolist must sell all its product at a single price (no price discrimination) and (2) to raise output and sell it, the firm must lower the price it charges. Selling the additional output will raise revenue, but this increase is offset somewhat by the lower price charged for all units sold. Therefore, the increase in revenue from increasing output by 1 (the marginal revenue) is less than the price.

Look carefully at Figure 13.4. What you can see in the diagram is that a monopoly's marginal revenue curve shows the change in total revenue that results as a firm moves along the segment of the demand curve that lies directly above it. Consider starting at an output of 0 units per period in the top panel of Figure 13.4. At 0 units, of course, total revenue (shown in the bottom panel) is zero because nothing is sold. To begin selling, the firm must lower the product price. Marginal revenue is positive, and total revenue begins to increase. To sell increasing quantities of the good, the firm must lower its price more and more. As output increases between zero and Q^* and the firm moves down its demand curve from point *A* to point *B*, marginal revenue remains positive and total revenue continues to increase. The quantity of output (*Q*) is rising, which tends to push total revenue ($P \times Q$) *up*. At the same time, the price of output (*P*) is falling, which tends to push total revenue ($P \times Q$) *down*. Up to point *B*, the effect of increasing *Q* dominates the effect of falling *P* and total revenue rises: Marginal revenue is positive (above the quantity axis).[1]

What happens as we look at output levels greater than Q^*—that is, farther down the demand curve from point *B* toward point *C*? We are still lowering *P* to sell more output; but at levels greater than Q^*, marginal revenue is negative, and total revenue in the bottom panel starts to fall. Beyond Q^*, the effect of cutting price on total revenue is larger than the effect of

[1] Recall from Chapter 4 that if the percentage change in *Q* is greater than the percentage change in *P* as you move along a demand curve, the absolute value of elasticity of demand is greater than 1. Thus, as we move along the demand curve in Figure 13.4 between point *A* and point *B*, demand is *elastic*.

FIGURE 13.4
Marginal Revenue and Total Revenue

A monopoly's marginal revenue curve bisects the quantity axis between the origin and the point where the demand curve hits the quantity axis. A monopoly's *MR* curve shows the change in total revenue that results as a firm moves along the segment of the demand curve that lies exactly above it.

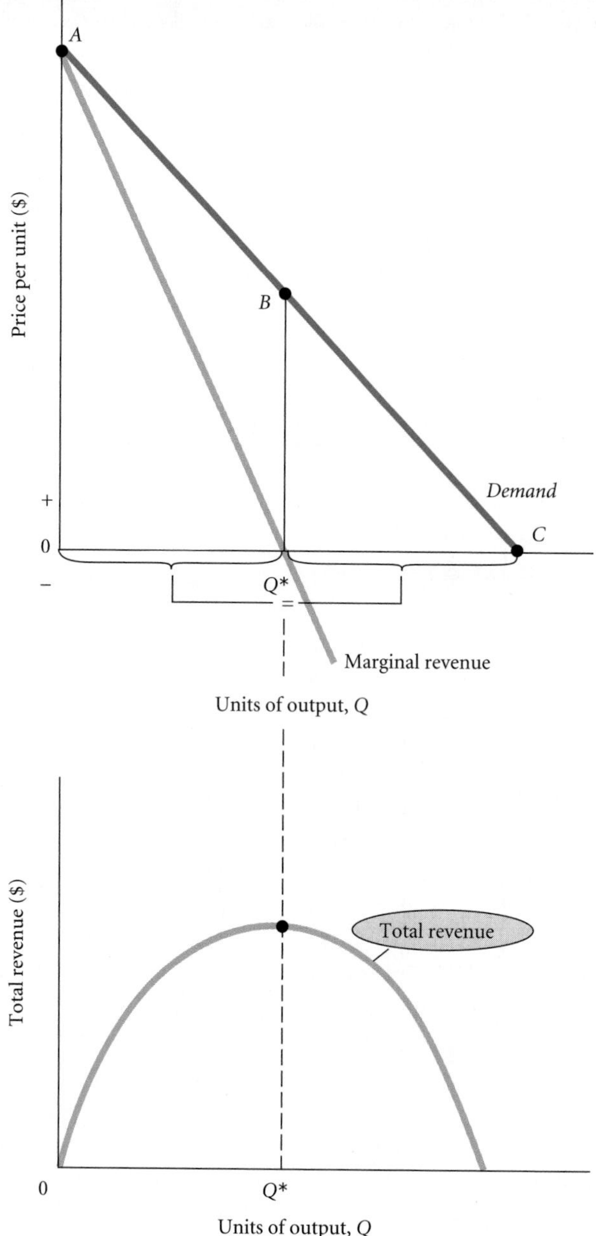

increasing quantity. As a result, total revenue ($P \times Q$) falls. At point *C*, revenue once again is at zero, this time because price has dropped to zero.[2]

The Monopolist's Profit-Maximizing Price and Output We have spent much time defining and explaining marginal revenue because it is an important factor in the monopolist's choice of profit-maximizing price and output. Figure 13.5 superimposes a demand curve and the marginal revenue curve derived from it over a set of cost curves. In determining price and output, a monopolistic firm must go through the same basic decision process that a competitive firm goes through. Any profit-maximizing firm will raise its production as long as the added revenue from the increase outweighs the added cost. In more specific terms, we can say that all firms, including monopolies, raise output as long as marginal revenue is greater than marginal cost. Any positive difference between marginal revenue and marginal cost can be thought of as marginal profit.

[2] Beyond Q^*, between points *B* and *C* on the demand curve in Figure 13.4, the decline in price must be bigger in percentage terms than the increase in quantity. Thus, the absolute value of elasticity beyond point *B* is less than 1: Demand is inelastic. At point *B*, marginal revenue is zero; the decrease in *P* exactly offsets the increase in *Q*, and elasticity is unitary or equal to −1.

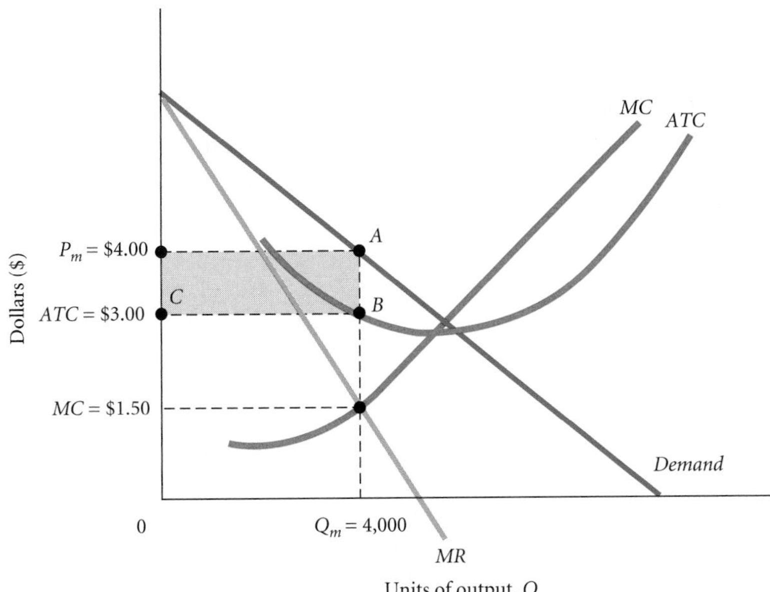

FIGURE 13.5 Price and Output Choice for a Profit-Maximizing Monopolist

A profit-maximizing monopolist will raise output as long as marginal revenue exceeds marginal cost. Maximum profit is at an output of 4,000 units per period and a price of \$4. Above 4,000 units of output, marginal cost is greater than marginal revenue; increasing output beyond 4,000 units would reduce profit. At 4,000 units, $TR = P_mAQ_m0$, $TC = CBQ_m0$, and profit $= P_mABC$.

The optimal price/output combination for the monopolist in Figure 13.5 is P_m = \$4 and Q_m = 4,000 units, the quantity at which the marginal revenue curve and the marginal cost curve intersect. At any output below 4,000, marginal revenue is greater than marginal cost. At any output above 4,000, increasing output would reduce profits because marginal cost exceeds marginal revenue. This leads us to conclude that the profit-maximizing level of output for a monopolist is the one at which marginal revenue equals marginal cost: $MR = MC$.

Because marginal revenue for a monopoly lies below the demand curve, the final price chosen by the monopolist will be above marginal cost. (P_m = \$4.00 is greater than MC = \$1.50.) At 4,000 units of output, price will be fixed at \$4 (point *A* on the demand curve), which is as much as the market will bear, and total revenue will be $P_m \times Q_m$ = \$4 × 4,000 = \$16,000 (area P_mAQ_m0). Total cost is the product of average total cost and units of output, \$3 × 4,000 = \$12,000 (area CBQ_m0). Total profit is the difference between total revenue and total cost, \$16,000 − \$12,000 = \$4,000. In Figure 13.5, total profit is the area of the gray rectangle P_mABC.

Our discussion about the optimal output level for a monopolist points to a common misconception. Even monopolists face constraints on the prices they can charge. Suppose a single firm controlled the production of bicycles. That firm would be able to charge more than could be charged in a competitive marketplace, but the power to raise prices has limits. In this example, as the bike price rises, we will see more people buying inline skates or walking. A particularly interesting case comes from monopolists who sell durable goods, goods that last for some period of time. Microsoft is the only producer for Windows, the operating system that dominates the personal computer (PC) market. But when Microsoft tries to sell a new version of that operating system (for example, Vista, which it introduced in 2007), its price is constrained by the fact that many of the potential consumers it seeks already have an old operating system. If the Vista price is too high, consumers will stay with the older version. Some monopolists may face quite elastic demand curves as a result of the characteristics of the product they sell.

The Absence of a Supply Curve in Monopoly In perfect competition, the supply curve of a firm in the short run is the same as the portion of the firm's marginal cost curve that lies above the average variable cost curve. As the price of the good produced by the firm changes, the perfectly competitive firm simply moves up or down its marginal cost curve in choosing how much output to produce.

As you can see, however, Figure 13.5 contains nothing that we can point to and call a supply curve. The amount of output that a monopolist produces depends on its marginal cost curve *and* on the shape of the demand curve that it faces. In other words, the amount of output that a monopolist supplies is not independent of the shape of the demand curve. A monopoly firm has no supply curve that is independent of the demand curve for its product.

To see why, consider what a firm's supply curve means. A supply curve shows the quantity of output the firm is willing to supply at each price. If we ask a monopolist how much output she is willing to supply at a given price, the monopolist will say that her supply behavior depends not only on marginal cost but also on the marginal revenue associated with that price. To know what that marginal revenue would be, the monopolist must know what her demand curve looks like.

In sum, in perfect competition, we can draw a firm's supply curve without knowing anything more than the firm's marginal cost curve. The situation for a monopolist is more complicated: A monopolist sets both price and quantity, and the amount of output that it supplies depends on its marginal cost curve and the demand curve that it faces.

Perfect Competition and Monopoly Compared

One way to understand monopoly is to compare equilibrium output and price in a perfectly competitive industry with the output and price that would be chosen if the same industry were organized as a monopoly. To make this comparison meaningful, let us exclude from consideration any technological advantage that a single large firm might enjoy.

We begin our comparison with a perfectly competitive industry made up of a large number of firms operating with a production technology that exhibits constant returns to scale in the long run. (Recall that *constant returns to scale* means that average cost is the same whether the firm operates one large plant or many small plants.) Figure 13.6 shows a perfectly competitive industry at long-run equilibrium, a condition in which price is equal to long-run average costs and in which there are no profits.

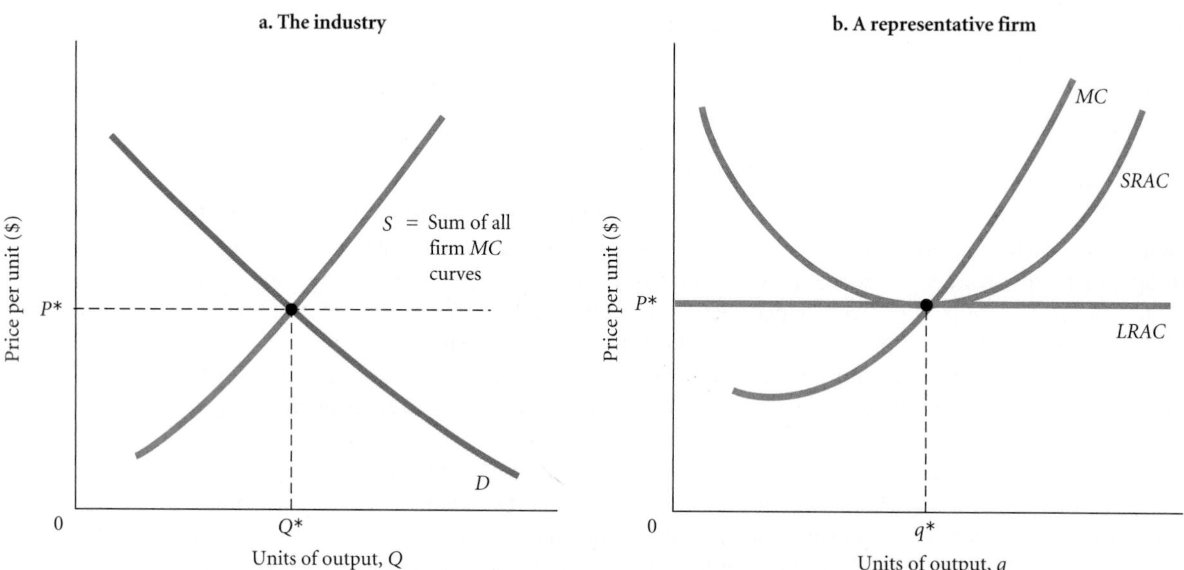

▲ **FIGURE 13.6 A Perfectly Competitive Industry in Long-Run Equilibrium**
In a perfectly competitive industry in the long run, price will be equal to long-run average cost. The market supply curve is the sum of all the short-run marginal cost curves of the firms in the industry. Here we assume that firms are using a technology that exhibits constant returns to scale: *LRAC* is flat. Big firms enjoy no cost advantage.

Suppose the industry were to fall under the control of a single price monopolist. The monopolist now owns one firm with many plants. However, technology has not changed; only the location of decision-making power has. To analyze the monopolist's decisions, we must derive the consolidated cost curves now facing the monopoly.

The marginal cost curve of the new monopoly will be the horizontal sum of the marginal cost curves of the smaller firms, which are now branches of the larger firm. That is, to get the large firm's *MC* curve, at each level of *MC*, we add together the output quantities from each separate plant. To understand why, consider this simple example. Suppose there is perfect competition and the industry is made up of just two small firms, A and B, each with upward-sloping marginal cost curves. Suppose for firm A, *MC* = $5 at an output of 10,000 units and for firm B, *MC* = $5 at an output of 20,000 units. If these firms were merged, what would be the marginal cost of the 30,000th unit of output per period? The answer is \$5 because the new larger firm would produce 10,000 units in plant A and 20,000 in plant B. This means that the marginal cost curve of the new firm is *exactly the same curve* as the supply curve in the industry when it was competitively organized. (Recall from Chapter 9 that the industry supply curve in a perfectly competitive industry is the sum of the marginal cost curves [above average variable cost] of all the individual firms in that industry.)[3]

Figure 13.7 illustrates the cost curves, marginal revenue curve, and demand curve of the consolidated monopoly industry. If the industry were competitively organized, total industry output would have been Q_c = 4,000 and price would have been P_c = \$3. These price and output decisions are determined by the intersection of the competitive supply curve, S_c, and the market demand curve.

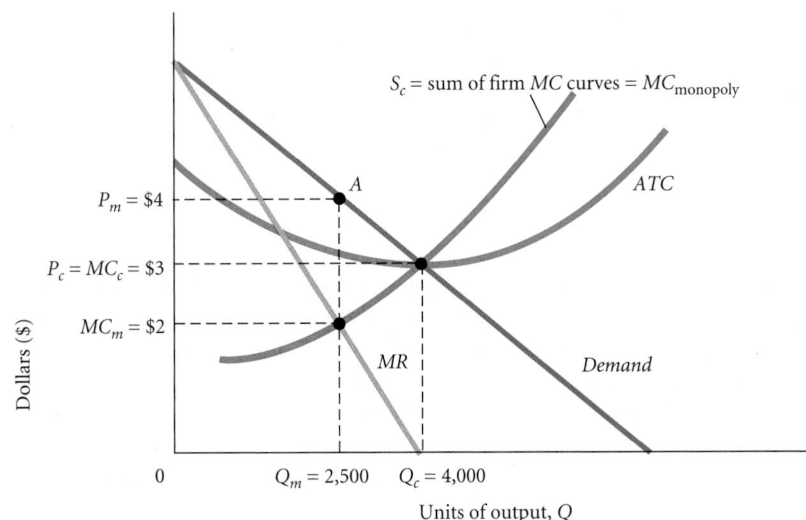

▲ **FIGURE 13.7 Comparison of Monopoly and Perfectly Competitive Outcomes for a Firm with Constant Returns to Scale**

In the newly organized monopoly, the marginal cost curve is the same as the supply curve that represented the behavior of all the independent firms when the industry was organized competitively. Quantity produced by the monopoly will be less than the perfectly competitive level of output, and the monopoly price will be higher than the price under perfect competition. Under monopoly, $P = P_m$ = \$4 and $Q = Q_m$ = 2,500. Under perfect competition, $P = P_c$ = \$3 and $Q = Q_c$ = 4,000.

No longer faced with a price that it cannot influence, however, the monopolist can choose any price/quantity combination along the demand curve. The output level that maximizes profits to the monopolist is Q_m = 2,500—the point at which marginal revenue intersects marginal cost. Output will be priced at P_m = \$4. To increase output beyond 2,500 units or to charge a price below \$4 (which represents the amount consumers are willing to pay) would reduce profit. Relative to a perfectly competitive industry, a monopolist restricts output, charges higher prices, and earns positive profits.

Also remember that all we did was transfer decision-making power from the individual small firms to a consolidated owner. The new firm gains nothing technologically by being big.

Monopoly in the Long Run: Barriers to Entry

What will happen to a monopoly in the long run? Of course, it is possible for a monopolist to suffer losses. Just because a firm is the only producer in a market does not guarantee that anyone will buy its product. Monopolists can end up going out of business just like competitive firms. If, on the contrary, the monopolist is earning positive profits (a rate of return above the normal return to capital), as in Figure 13.5, we would expect other firms to enter as they do in competitive markets. In fact,

[3] The same logic will show that the average cost curve of the consolidated firm is the sum of the average cost curves of the individual plants.

many markets that end up competitive begin with an entrepreneurial idea and a short-lived monopoly position. In the mid-1970s, a California entrepreneur named Gary Dahl "invented" and marketed the Pet Rock. Dahl had the market to himself for about 6 months, during which time he earned millions before scores of competitors entered, driving down the price and profits. (In the end, this product, perhaps not surprisingly, disappeared). *For a monopoly to persist, some factor or factors must prevent entry.* We turn now to a discussion of those factors, commonly termed **barriers to entry**.

barriers to entry Factors that prevent new firms from entering and competing in imperfectly competitive industries.

Return for a moment to Figure 13.5 on p. 267. In that graph, we see that the monopolist is earning a positive economic profit. Such profits can persist only if other firms cannot enter this industry and compete them away. The term *barriers to entry* is used to describe the set of factors that prevent new firms from entering a market with excess profits. Monopoly can persist only in the presence of entry barriers.

Economies of Scale In Chapter 8, we described production technologies in which average costs fall with output increases. In situations in which those scale economies are very large relative to the overall market, the cost advantages associated with size can give rise to monopoly power.

Scale economies come in a number of different forms. Providing cable service requires laying expensive cable; conventional telephones require the installation of poles and wires. For these cases, there are clear cost advantages in having only one set of physical apparatuses. Once a firm has laid the wire, providing service to one more customer is very inexpensive. The semiconductor industry is another case in which production favors the large firms. In 2007, Intel, the world leader in production of semiconductors for the PC, estimated that it would spend $6.2 billion for new production facilities and another $6 billion to support its research efforts to improve the speed of its chips. For Intel, physical production and the importance of research favor the large firm.

In some cases, scale economies come from marketing and advertising. Breakfast cereal can be produced efficiently on a small scale, for example; large-scale production does not reduce costs. However, to compete, a new firm would need an advertising campaign costing millions of dollars. The large front-end investment requirement in advertising is risky and likely to deter would-be entrants to the cereal market.

When scale economies are so large relative to the size of the market that costs are minimized with only one firm in the industry, we have a **natural monopoly**.

natural monopoly An industry that realizes such large economies of scale in producing its product that single-firm production of that good or service is most efficient.

Although Figure 13.8 presents an exaggerated picture, it does serve to illustrate our point. One large-scale plant (Scale 2) can produce 500,000 units of output at an average unit cost of $1. If the industry were restructured into five firms, each producing on a smaller scale (Scale 1), the industry could produce the same amount, but average unit cost would be five times as high ($5). Consumers potentially see a considerable gain when economies of scale are realized. The critical point here is that for a natural monopoly to exist, economies of scale must be realized at a scale that is close to total demand in the market.

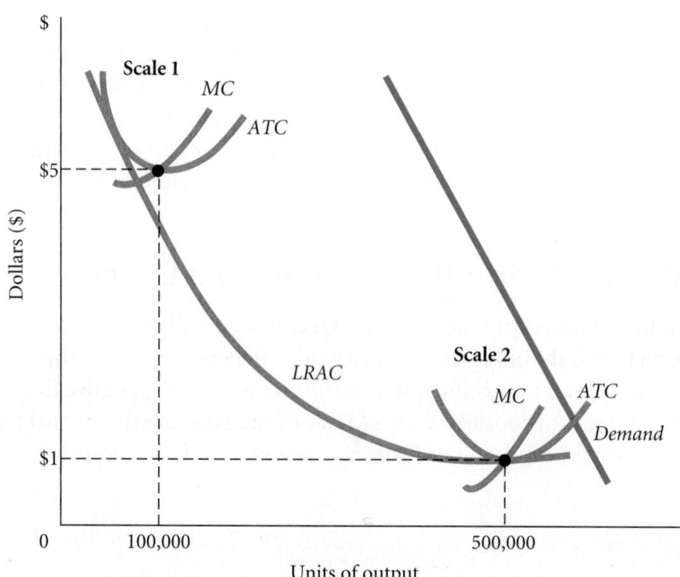

▶ **FIGURE 13.8**

A Natural Monopoly

A natural monopoly is a firm in which the most efficient scale is very large. Here, average total cost declines until a single firm is producing nearly the entire amount demanded in the market. With one firm producing 500,000 units, average total cost is $1 per unit. With five firms each producing 100,000 units, average total cost is $5 per unit.

Notice in Figure 13.8 that the long-run average cost curve continues to decline until it almost hits the market demand curve. If at a price of $1 market demand is 5 *million* units of output, there would be no reason to have only one firm in the industry. Ten firms could each produce 500,000 units, and each could reap the full benefits of the available economies of scale.

Historically, natural monopolies in the United States have been regulated by the state. Public utility commissions in each state monitor electric companies and locally operating telephone companies, regulating prices so that the benefits of scale economies are realized without the inefficiencies of monopoly power. The *Economics in Practice* on page 272 describes the current debate over the regulation of cable television.

Patents **Patents** are legal barriers that prevent entry into an industry by granting exclusive use of the patented product or process to the inventor. Patents are issued in the United States under the authority of Article I, Section 8, of the Constitution, which gives Congress the power to "promote the progress of science and the useful arts, by securing for limited times to authors and inventors the exclusive right to their respective writings and discoveries." Patent protection in the United States is currently granted for a period of 20 years.

patent A barrier to entry that grants exclusive use of the patented product or process to the inventor.

Patents provide an incentive for invention and innovation. New products and new processes are developed through research undertaken by individual inventors and by firms. Research requires resources and time, which have opportunity costs. Without the protection that a patent provides, the results of research would become available to the general public quickly. If research did not lead to expanded profits, little research would be done. On the negative side though, patents do serve as a barrier to competition and they slow down the benefits of research flowing through the market to consumers.

The expiration of patents after a given number of years represents an attempt to balance the benefits of firms and the benefits of households: On the one hand, it is important to stimulate invention and innovation; on the other hand, invention and innovation do society less good when their benefits to the public are constrained.[4]

In recent years, public attention has been focused on the high costs of health care. One factor contributing to these costs is the high price of many prescription drugs. Equipped with newly developed tools of bioengineering, the pharmaceutical industry has been granted thousands of patents for new drugs. When a new drug for treating a disease is developed, the patent holder can charge a high price for the drug. The drug companies argue that these rewards are justified by high research and development costs; others say that these profits are the result of a monopoly protected by the patent system.

Government Rules Patents provide one example of a government-enforced regulation that creates monopoly. For patents, the justification for such intervention is to promote innovation. In some cases, governments impose entry restrictions on firms as a way of controlling activity. In most parts of the United States, governments restrict the sale of alcohol. In fact, in some states (Iowa, Maine, New Hampshire, and Ohio), liquor can be sold only through state-controlled and managed stores. Most states operate lotteries as monopolists. However, when large economies of scale do not exist in an industry or when equity is not a concern, the arguments in favor of government-run monopolies are much weaker. One argument is that the state wants to prevent private parties from encouraging and profiting from "sin," particularly in cases in which society at large can be harmed. Another argument is that government monopolies are a convenient source of revenues.

Ownership of a Scarce Factor of Production You cannot enter the diamond-producing business unless you own a diamond mine. There are not many diamond mines in the world, and most are already owned by a single firm, the DeBeers Company of South Africa. At one time, the Aluminum Company of America (now Alcoa) owned or controlled virtually 100 percent of the known bauxite deposits in the world and until the 1940s monopolized the production and distribution of aluminum. Obviously, if production requires a particular input and one firm owns the entire supply of that input, that firm will control the industry. Ownership alone is a barrier to entry.

---

[4] Another alternative is *licensing*. With licensing, the new technology is used by all producers and the inventor splits the benefits with consumers. Because forcing the non-patent-holding producers to use an inefficient technology results in waste, some analysts have proposed adding mandatory licensing to the current patent system. A key question here involves determining the right licensing fee.

ECONOMICS IN PRACTICE

Managing the Cable Monopoly

Many people subscribe to cable television. Cable systems bundle a collection of network and cable stations and offer them to viewers as packages, ranging from a basic service with only a modest number of offerings to much-expanded premium services. In the last 20 years, the cable system has grown to a multi-billion dollar industry covering most of the country.

What you might not realize about the cable system is that it consists of a network of local monopolies. In any given area, typically just one cable company is in operation. Historically, this monopoly was justified as a natural monopoly, reflecting the expensive cable that needed to be laid to serve the population and the fact that once the cable was laid, the costs of providing service to a new consumer was modest.

What you also may not realize is that when you pay your cable bill, part of your payment goes to your home city. In fact, cities negotiate with the various cable companies to give one of them the right to be the monopoly supplier of cable service in return for a fee that is typically on the order of 5 percent of the cable revenues. Once a firm has bought the right to be a local cable company, it must follow a set of rules, particularly with regard to the availability and price of the basic cable.

One of the hot debates in 2008 was in the cable industry. Cable companies offer programs bundled rather than à la carte programs. Keith Martin, the commissioner of the Federal Communications Commission, which oversees cable, pushed to have cable unbundled, largely in response to parents who were concerned about inappropriate television shows coming into their homes as part of a bundle. What economic logic would justify bundling programs in this way?

Here it is helpful to think about costs again. Once a television show is produced, distributing it to another customer has a zero marginal cost up to the capacity level of the cable. Thus, from a cable company's point of view, having a large customer base for the various shows is typically a profitable strategy. Suppose 100 viewers valued doctor shows at \$2 a week each and lawyer shows at \$1.50 each, while another 100 viewers had the opposite preference. To maximize revenue with à la carte pricing, the cable company would charge \$1.50 for each show, giving it 200 viewers per show for a revenue of \$600 (200 viewers $\times$ 2 shows each $\times$ \$1.50). If the cable company sells the bundle for \$3.50, all viewers buy and it earns \$700. If the cable company sells the bundle for \$3, its revenue is still the original \$600 but now all of its customers are better off and can watch two programs instead of one. When the cost of distributing a good with high fixed costs is zero, bundling is often a way to make both producers and consumers better off.

Network Effects How much value do you get from a telephone or a fax machine? It will depend on how many other people own a machine that can communicate with yours. Products such as these, in which benefits of ownership are a function of how many other people are part of the network, are subject to **network externalities**. For phones and faxes, the network effects are direct. For products such as the Windows operating system and the Xbox, network effects may be indirect. Having a large consumer base increases consumer valuation by encouraging the development of complementary goods. When many people own an Xbox, game developers have an incentive to create games for the system. Good games increase the value of the system.

network externalities The value of a product to a consumer increases with the number of that product being sold or used in the market.

How does the existence of network effects create a barrier to entry? In this situation, a firm that starts early and builds a large product base will have an advantage over a newcomer. Microsoft's dominant position in the operating system market reflects network effects in this business. The high concentration in the game console market (Microsoft, Nintendo, and Sony control this market) also comes from network effects.

The Social Costs of Monopoly

So far, we have seen that a monopoly produces less output and charges a higher price than a competitively organized industry if no large economies of scale exist for the monopoly. We have also seen the way in which barriers to entry can allow monopolists to persist over time. You are probably thinking at this point that producing less and charging more to earn positive profits is not likely to be in the best interests of consumers, and you are right.

Inefficiency and Consumer Loss

In Chapter 12, we argued that price must equal marginal cost ($P = MC$) for markets to produce what people want. This argument rests on two propositions: (1) that price provides a good approximation of the social value of a unit of output and (2) that marginal cost, in the absence of externalities (costs or benefits to external parties not weighed by firms), provides a good approximation of the product's social opportunity cost. In a pure monopoly, price is above the product marginal cost. When this happens, the firm is underproducing from society's point of view. Society would be better off if the firm produced more and charged a lower price. Monopoly leads to an inefficient mix of output.

A slightly simplified version of the monopoly diagram appears in Figure 13.9, which shows how we might make a rough estimate of the size of the loss to social welfare that arises from monopoly. (For clarity, we will ignore the short-run cost curves and assume constant returns to scale in the long run.) Under competitive conditions, firms would produce output up to Q_c = 4,000 units and price would ultimately settle at P_c = $2, equal to long-run average cost. Any price above $2 will mean positive profits, which would be eliminated by the entry of new competing firms in the long run. (You should remember all this from Chapter 9.)

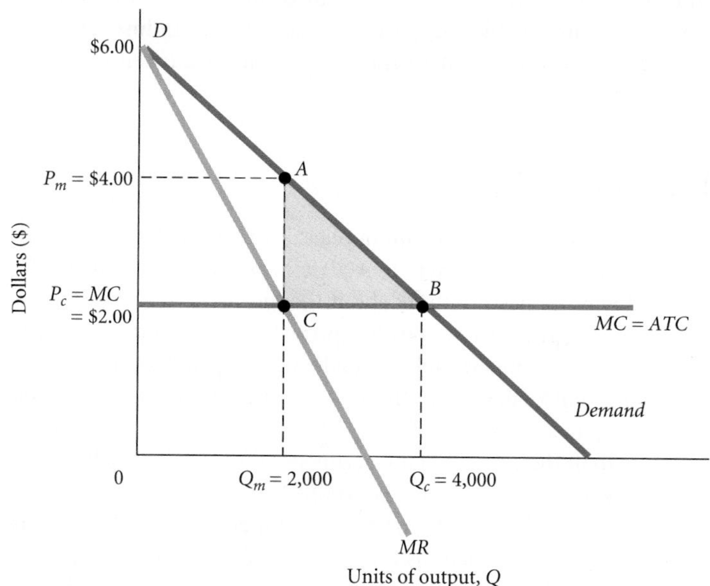

FIGURE 13.9
Welfare Loss from Monopoly
A demand curve shows the amounts that people are willing to pay at each potential level of output. Thus, the demand curve can be used to approximate the benefits to the consumer of raising output above 2,000 units. *MC* reflects the marginal cost of the resources needed. The triangle *ABC* roughly measures the net social gain of moving from 2,000 units to 4,000 units (or the loss that results when monopoly decreases output from 4,000 units to 2,000 units).

A monopoly firm in the same industry, however, would produce only Q_m = 2,000 units per period and charge a price of P_m = $4 because $MR = MC$ at Q_m = 2,000 units. The monopoly would make a profit equal to total revenue minus total cost, or $P_m \times Q_m$ minus $ATC \times Q_m$. Profit to the monopoly is thus equal to the area P_mACP_c, or \$4,000. [(\$4 × 2,000) – (\$2 × 2,000) = \$8,000 – \$4,000 = \$4,000. Remember that $P_c = ATC$ in this example.]

Now consider the gains and losses associated with increasing price from \$2 to \$4 and cutting output from 4,000 units to 2,000 units. As you might guess, the winner will be the monopolist and the loser will be the consumer; but let us see how it works out.

At P_c = \$2, the price under perfect competition, there are no profits. Consumers are paying a price of \$2, but the demand curve shows that many are willing to pay more than that. For example, a substantial number of people would pay \$4 or more. Those people willing to pay more than \$2 are receiving what we earlier called a *consumer surplus*. Consumer surplus is the difference between what households are willing to pay for a product and the current market price. The demand curve shows approximately how much households are willing to pay at each level of output. Thus, the area of triangle DBP_c gives us a rough measure of the "consumer surplus" being enjoyed by households when the price is \$2. Consumers willing to pay exactly \$4 get a surplus equal to \$2. Those who place the highest value on this good—that is, those who are willing to pay the most (\$6)—get a surplus equal to DP_c, or \$4.

Now the industry is reorganized as a monopoly that cuts output to 2,000 units and raises price to \$4. The big winner is the monopolist, who ends up earning profits equal to \$4,000. The big losers are the consumers. Their "surplus" now shrinks from the area of triangle DBP_c to the area of triangle DAP_m. Part of that loss (which is equal to $DBP_c - DAP_m$, or the area P_mABP_c) is covered by the monopolist's gain of P_mACP_c, but not all of it. The loss to consumers exceeds the gain to the monopoly by the area of triangle ABC ($P_mABP_c - P_mACP_c$), which roughly measures the net loss in social welfare associated with monopoly power in this industry. Because the area of a triangle is half its base times its height, the welfare loss is 1/2 × 2,000 × \$2 = \$2,000. If we could push price back down to the competitive level and increase output to 4,000 units, consumers would gain more than the monopolist would lose and the gain in social welfare would approximate the area of *ABC*, or \$2,000.

In this example, the presence of a monopoly also causes an important change in the distribution of real income. In Figure 13.9, area P_mACP_c is a profit of \$4,000 flowing every period to the monopolist. If price were pushed down to \$2 by competition or regulation, those profits would pass to consumers in the form of lower prices. Society may value this resource transfer on equity grounds in addition to efficiency grounds.

Of course, monopolies may have social costs that do not show up on these graphs. Monopolies, which are protected from competition by barriers to entry, may not face the same pressures to cut costs and innovate as competitive firms do. A competitive firm that does not use the most efficient technology will be driven out of business by firms that do. One of the significant arguments against tariffs and quotas to protect such industries as automobiles and steel from foreign competition is that protection lessens the incentive to be efficient and competitive.

Rent-Seeking Behavior

Economists have another concern about monopolies. Triangle *ABC* in Figure 13.9 represents a real net loss to society, but part of rectangle P_mACP_c (the \$4,000 monopoly profit) may also end up lost. To understand why, we need to think about the incentives facing potential monopolists.

The area of rectangle P_mACP_c shows positive profits. If entry into the market were easy and competition were open, these profits would eventually be competed to zero. Owners of businesses earning profits have an incentive to prevent this development. In fact, the graph shows how much they would be willing to pay to prevent it. A rational owner of a monopoly firm would be willing to pay any amount less than the entire rectangle. Any portion of profits left over after expenses is better than zero, which would be the case if free competition eliminated all profits.

Potential monopolists can do many things to protect their profits. One obvious approach is to push the government to impose restrictions on competition. A classic example is the behavior of taxicab driver organizations in New York and other large cities. To operate a cab legally in New York City, you need a license. The city tightly controls the number of licenses available. If entry into the taxi business were open, competition would hold down cab fares to the cost of operating cabs. However, cab drivers have become a powerful lobbying force and have muscled the city into restricting the number of licenses issued. This restriction keeps fares high and preserves monopoly profits.

There are countless other examples. The steel industry and the automobile industry spend large sums lobbying Congress for tariff protection.[5] Some experts claim that establishment of the now-defunct Civil Aeronautics Board in 1937 to control competition in the airline industry and extensive regulation of trucking by the I.C.C. prior to deregulation in the 1970s came about partly through industry efforts to restrict competition and preserve profits.

This kind of behavior, in which households or firms take action to preserve positive profits, is called **rent-seeking behavior**. Recall from Chapter 10 that rent is the return to a factor of production in strictly limited supply. Rent-seeking behavior has two important implications.

rent-seeking behavior Actions taken by households or firms to preserve positive profits.

First, this behavior consumes resources. Lobbying and building barriers to entry are not costless activities. Lobbyists' wages, expenses of the regulatory bureaucracy, and the like must be paid. Periodically faced with the prospect that the city of New York will issue new taxi licenses, cab owners and drivers have become so well organized that they can bring the city to a standstill with a strike or even a limited job action. Indeed, positive profits may be completely consumed through rent-seeking behavior that produces nothing of social value; all it does is help to preserve the current distribution of income.

Second, the frequency of rent-seeking behavior leads us to another view of government. So far, we have considered only the role that government might play in helping to achieve an efficient allocation of resources in the face of market failure—in this case, failures that arise from imperfect market structure. Later in this chapter we survey the measures government might take to ensure that resources are efficiently allocated when monopoly power arises. However, the idea of rent-seeking behavior introduces the notion of **government failure**, in which the government becomes the tool of the rent seeker and the allocation of resources is made even less efficient than before.

government failure Occurs when the government becomes the tool of the rent seeker and the allocation of resources is made even less efficient by the intervention of government.

This idea of government failure is at the center of **public choice theory**, which holds that governments are made up of people, just as business firms are. These people—politicians and bureaucrats—can be expected to act in their own self-interest, just as owners of firms do. We turn to the economics of public choice in Chapter 16.

public choice theory An economic theory that the public officials who set economic policies and regulate the players act in their own self-interest, just as firms do.

Price Discrimination

So far in our discussion of monopoly, we have assumed that the firm faces a known downward-sloping demand curve and must choose a *single price* and a single quantity of output. Indeed, the reason that price and marginal revenue are different for a monopoly and the same for a perfectly competitive firm is that if a monopoly decides to sell more output, it must lower price in order to do so.

In the world, however, there are many examples of firms that charge different prices to different groups of buyers. Charging different prices to different buyers is called **price discrimination**. The motivation for price discrimination is fairly obvious: If a firm can identify those who are willing to pay a higher price for a good, it can earn more profit from them by charging a higher price. The idea is best illustrated using the extreme case where a firm knows what each buyer is willing to pay. A firm that charges the maximum amount that buyers are willing to pay for each unit is practicing **perfect price discrimination.**

price discrimination Charging different prices to different buyers.

perfect price discrimination Occurs when a firm charges the maximum amount that buyers are willing to pay for each unit.

Figure 13.10 is similar to Figure 13.9. For simplicity, assume a firm with a constant marginal cost equal to \$2 per unit. A non-price-discriminating monopolist would have to set one and only one price. That firm would face the marginal revenue curve shown in the diagram and would produce as long as *MR* is above *MC*: Output would be Q_m, and price would be set at \$4 per unit. The firm would earn an economic profit of \$2 per unit for every unit up to Q_m. Consumers would enjoy a consumer surplus equal to the shaded area. Consumer A, for example, is willing to pay \$5.75 but has to pay only \$4.00.

Now consider what would happen if the firm could charge each consumer the maximum amount that that consumer was willing to pay. In Figure 13.10(a), if the firm could charge consumer A a price of \$5.75, the firm would earn \$3.75 in profit on that unit and the consumer would get no consumer surplus. Going on to consumer B, if the firm could determine B's

[5] A tariff is a tax on imports designed to give a price advantage to domestic producers.

maximum willingness to pay and charge \$5.50, profit would be \$3.50 and consumer surplus for B would again be zero. This would continue all the way to point *C* on the demand curve, where total profit would be equal to the entire area under the demand curve and above the *MC* = *ATC* line, as shown in Figure 13.10(b).

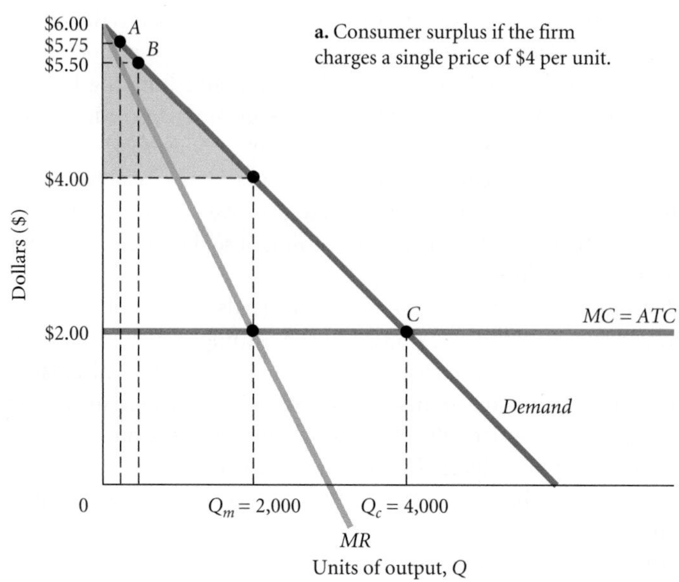

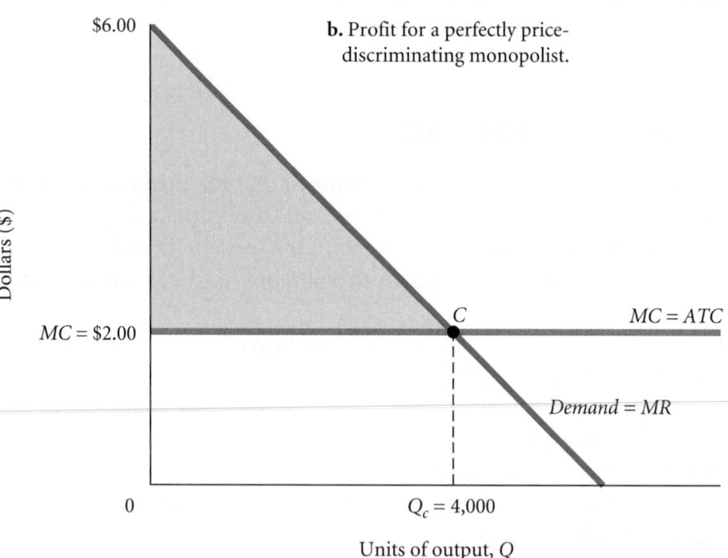

FIGURE 13.10 Price Discrimination

In Figure 13.10(a), consumer A is willing to pay \$5.75. If the price-discriminating firm can charge \$5.75 to A, profit is \$3.75. A monopolist who cannot price discriminate would maximize profit by charging \$4. At a price of \$4.00, the firm makes \$2.00 in profit and consumer A enjoys a consumer surplus of \$1.75. In Figure 13.10(b), for a perfectly price-discriminating monopolist, the demand curve is the same as marginal revenue. The firm will produce as long as *MR* > *MC*, up to Q_c. At Q_c, profit is the entire shaded area and consumer surplus is zero.

Another way to look at the diagram in Figure 13.10(b) is to notice that the demand curve actually becomes the same as the marginal revenue curve. When a firm can charge the maximum that anyone is willing to pay *for each unit*, that price *is* marginal revenue. There is no need to draw a separate *MR* curve as there was when the firm could charge only one price to all consumers. Once again, profit is the entire shaded area and consumer surplus is zero.

It is interesting to note that a perfectly price-discriminating monopolist will actually produce the *efficient* quantity of output—Q_c in Figure 13.10(b), which is the same as the amount that would be produced had the industry been perfectly competitive. The firm will continue to produce as long as benefits to consumers exceed marginal cost; it does not stop at Q_m in Figure 13.10(a). But when a monopolist can perfectly price discriminate, it reaps all the net benefits from higher production. There is no deadweight loss, but there is no consumer surplus either.

Examples of Price Discrimination

Examples of price discrimination are all around us. It used to be that airlines routinely charged those who stayed over Saturday nights a much lower fare than those who did not. Business travelers generally travel during the week, often are unwilling to stay over Saturdays, and generally are willing to pay more for tickets.

Airlines, movie theaters, hotels, and many other industries routinely charge a lower price for children and the elderly. The reason is that children and the elderly generally have a lower willingness to pay. Telephone companies have so many ways of targeting different groups that it is difficult to know what they are really charging.

In each case, the objective of the firm is to segment the market into different identifiable groups, with each group having a different elasticity of demand. Doing so requires firms to ensure that different customers are kept separated, so that they cannot trade with one another. It can be shown, although we will not present the analysis here, that the optimal strategy for a firm that can sell in more than one market is to charge higher prices in markets with low demand elasticities.

Remedies for Monopoly: Antitrust Policy

As we have just seen, the exercise of monopoly power can bring with it considerable social costs. On the other hand, as our discussion of entry barriers suggested, at times, monopolies may bring with them benefits associated with scale economies or innovation gains. Sometimes monopolies result from the natural interplay of market and technological forces, while at other times firms actively and aggressively pursue monopoly power, doing their best to eliminate the competition. In the United States, the rules set out in terms of what firms can and cannot do in their markets are contained in two pieces of antitrust legislation: the Sherman Act passed in 1890 and the Clayton Act passed in 1914.

Major Antitrust Legislation

The following are some of the major antitrust legislation that have been passed in the United States.

The Sherman Act of 1890 The substance of the Sherman Act is contained in two short sections:

> *Section 1.* Every contract, combination in the form of trust or otherwise, or conspiracy, in restraint of trade or commerce among the several States, or with foreign nations, is hereby declared to be illegal....
> *Section 2.* Every person who shall monopolize, or attempt to monopolize, or combine or conspire with any other person or persons, to monopolize any part of the trade or commerce among the several States, or with foreign nations, shall be deemed guilty of a misdemeanor, and, on conviction thereof, shall be punished by fine not exceeding five thousand dollars, or by imprisonment not exceeding one year, or by both said punishments, in the discretion of the court.

For our treatment of monopoly, the relevant part of the Sherman Act is Section 2, the rule against monopolization or attempted monopolization. The language of the act is quite broad, so it is the responsibility of the courts to judge conduct that is legal and conduct that is illegal. As a firm competes in the hopes of winning business, what kind of behavior is acceptable hard competition and what is not? Two different administrative bodies have the responsibility for initiating actions on behalf of the U.S. government against individuals or companies thought to be in violation of the antitrust laws. These agencies are the Antitrust Division of the Justice Department and the Federal Trade Commission (FTC). In addition, private citizens can initiate antitrust actions.

In 1911, two major antitrust cases were decided by the Supreme Court. The two companies involved, Standard Oil and American Tobacco, seemed to epitomize the textbook definition of monopoly, and both appeared to exhibit the structure and the conduct outlawed by the Sherman Act. Standard Oil controlled about 91 percent of the refining industry; and although the exact figure is still disputed, the American Tobacco Trust probably controlled between 75 percent and 90 percent of the market for all tobacco products except cigars. Both companies had used tough tactics to swallow up competition or to drive it out of business. Not surprisingly, the Supreme Court found both firms guilty of violating Sections 1 and 2 of the Sherman Act and ordered their dissolution.[6]

rule of reason The criterion introduced by the Supreme Court in 1911 to determine whether a particular action was illegal ("unreasonable") or legal ("reasonable") within the terms of the Sherman Act.

The Court made clear, however, that the Sherman Act did not outlaw every action that seemed to restrain trade, only those that were "unreasonable." In enunciating this **rule of reason**, the Court seemed to say that structure alone was not a criterion for unreasonableness. Thus, it was possible for a near-monopoly not to violate the Sherman Act as long as it had won its market using "reasonable" tactics.

Subsequent court cases confirmed that a firm could be convicted of violating the Sherman Act only if it had exhibited *unreasonable conduct*. Between 1911 and 1920, cases were brought against Eastman Kodak, International Harvester, United Shoe Machinery, and United States Steel. The first three companies controlled overwhelming shares of their respective markets, and the fourth controlled 60 percent of the country's capacity to produce steel. Nonetheless, all four cases were dismissed on the grounds that these companies had shown no evidence of "unreasonable conduct."

New technologies have also created challenges for the courts in defining reasonable conduct. Perhaps the largest antitrust case recently has been the case launched by the U.S. Department of Justice against Microsoft. By the 1990s, Microsoft had more that 90 percent of the market in operating systems for PCs. The government argued that Microsoft had achieved this market share through illegal dealing, while Microsoft argued that the government failed to understand the issues associated with competition in a market with network externalities and dynamic competition. In the end, the case was settled with a *consent decree* in July 1994. A consent decree is a formal agreement between a prosecuting government and defendants that must be approved by the courts. Such decrees can be signed before, during, or after a trial and are often used to save litigation costs. In the case of Microsoft, under the consent decree, it agreed to give computer manufacturers more freedom to install software from other software companies. In 1997, Microsoft found itself charged with violating the terms of the consent decree and was back in court. In 2000, the company was found guilty of violating the antitrust laws and a judge ordered it split into two companies. But Microsoft appealed; and the decision to split the company was replaced with a consent decree requiring Microsoft to behave more competitively, including a provision that computer makers would have the ability to sell competitors' software without fear of retaliation. In the fall of 2005, Microsoft finally ended its antitrust troubles in the United States after agreeing to pay RealNetworks $761 million to settle one final lawsuit.

In 2005, Advanced Micro Devices (AMD) brought suit against Intel, which has an 80 percent share of the x-86 processors used in most of the world's PCs. AMD alleged anticompetitive behavior and attempted monopolization. At present in the United States, private antitrust cases, brought by one firm against another, are 20-plus times more common than government-led cases.

Clayton Act Passed by Congress in 1914 to strengthen the Sherman Act and clarify the rule of reason, the act outlawed specific monopolistic behaviors such as tying contracts, price discrimination, and unlimited mergers.

Federal Trade Commission (FTC) A federal regulatory group created by Congress in 1914 to investigate the structure and behavior of firms engaging in interstate commerce, to determine what constitutes unlawful "unfair" behavior, and to issue cease-and-desist orders to those found in violation of antitrust law.

The Clayton Act and the Federal Trade Commission, 1914 Designed to strengthen the Sherman Act and to clarify the rule of reason, the **Clayton Act** of 1914 outlawed a number of specific practices. First, it made *tying contracts* illegal. Such contracts force a customer to buy one product to obtain another. Second, it limited mergers that would "substantially lessen competition or tend to create a monopoly." The *Economics in Practice* on page 279 highlights a recent government challenge to the Whole Foods–Wild Oats merger. Third, it banned *price discrimination*—charging different customers different prices for reasons other than changes in cost or matching competitors' prices.

The **Federal Trade Commission (FTC)**, created by Congress in 1914, was established to investigate "the organization, business conduct, practices, and management" of companies that engage in interstate commerce. At the same time, the act establishing the commission added another vaguely worded prohibition to the books: "Unfair methods of competition in commerce are hereby declared unlawful." The determination of what constituted "unfair" behavior was left up to the commission. The FTC was also given the power to issue "cease-and-desist orders" where it found behavior in violation of the law.

Nonetheless, the legislation of 1914 retained the focus on *conduct*; thus, the rule of reason remained central to all antitrust action in the courts.

[6] *United States v. Standard Oil Co. of New Jersey*, 221 U.S. 1 (1911); *United States v. American Tobacco Co.*, 221 U.S. 106 (1911).

ECONOMICS IN PRACTICE

The Government Takes on Whole Foods

FTC opposing Wild Oats, Whole Foods merger

The Denver Post

The U.S. Federal Trade Commission has filed a lawsuit to block the proposed acquisition of Boulder-based Wild Oats Markets Inc. by rival Whole Foods Market Inc.

Austin, Texas-based Whole Foods announced in February that it planned to buy Wild Oats for roughly $700 million. The two companies are the largest players in the natural-grocer sector.

Whole Foods operates 194 stores. Wild Oats has 110 locations.

"Whole Foods and Wild Oats are each other's closest competitors in premium natural and organic supermarkets, and are engaged in intense head-to-head competition in markets across the country," Jeffrey Schmidt, director of the FTC's Bureau of Competition, said in a press release. "If Whole Foods is allowed to devour Wild Oats, it will mean higher prices, reduced quality, and fewer choices for consumers. That is a deal consumers should not be allowed to swallow."

Wild Oats and Whole Foods said they would "vigorously challenge" the lawsuit.

By Kristi Arellano, Denver Post Staff Writer.

As we see in the remarks of Mr. Schmidt of the FTC, the government is concerned with the likelihood that a merger of Wild Oats Market and Whole Foods Market will result in monopoly power with its attendant higher prices and social welfare losses to consumers. In the United States, the explicit goal of the antitrust laws is to promote consumer welfare.

In responding to the government, Whole Foods has challenged the market definition, arguing that Whole Foods competes not only with other organic food stores but also with conventional food stores that are stocking more natural and organic foods. The key question surrounding this merger is how close the substitutes are for Whole Foods' products.

In the end, the merger was allowed to move forward after a judge ruled against the FTC, arguing that the merger would not harm consumers.

Imperfect Markets: A Review and a Look Ahead

A firm has *market power* when it exercises some control over the price of its output or the prices of the inputs that it uses. The extreme case of a firm with market power is the pure monopolist. In a pure monopoly, a single firm produces a product for which there are no close substitutes in an industry in which all new competitors are barred from entry.

Our focus in this chapter on pure monopoly (which occurs rarely) has served a number of purposes. First, the monopoly model describes a number of industries quite well. Second, the monopoly case illustrates the observation that imperfect competition leads to an inefficient allocation of resources. Finally, the analysis of pure monopoly offers insights into the more commonly encountered market models of monopolistic competition and oligopoly, which we discussed briefly in this chapter and will discuss in detail in the next two chapters.

SUMMARY

1. A number of assumptions underlie the logic of perfect competition. Among them: (1) A large number of firms and households are interacting in each market; (2) firms in a given market produce undifferentiated, or homogeneous, products; and (3) new firms are free to enter industries and compete for profits. The first two imply that firms have no control over input prices or output prices; the third implies that opportunities for positive profit are eliminated in the long run.

IMPERFECT COMPETITION AND MARKET POWER: CORE CONCEPTS *p. 261*

2. A market in which individual firms have some control over price is imperfectly competitive. Such firms exercise *market power*. The three forms of *imperfect competition* are monopoly, oligopoly, and monopolistic competition.
3. A *pure monopoly* is an industry with a single firm that produces a product for which there are no close substitutes and in which there are significant *barriers to entry*.
4. Market power means that firms must make four decisions instead of three: (1) how much to produce, (2) how to produce it, (3) how much to demand in each input market, and (4) *what price to charge for their output*.
5. Market power does not imply that a monopolist can charge any price it wants. Monopolies are constrained by market demand. They can sell only what people will buy and only at a price that people are willing to pay.

PRICE AND OUTPUT DECISIONS IN PURE MONOPOLY MARKETS *p. 263*

6. In perfect competition, many firms supply homogeneous products. With only one firm in a monopoly market, however, there is no distinction between the firm and the industry—the firm *is* the industry. The market demand curve is thus the firm's demand curve, and the total quantity supplied in the market is what the monopoly firm decides to produce.
7. For a monopolist, an increase in output involves not just producing more and selling it but also reducing the price of its output to sell it. Thus, marginal revenue, to a monopolist, is not equal to product price, as it is in competition. Instead, marginal revenue is lower than price because to raise output 1 unit *and to be able to sell* that 1 unit, the firm must lower the price it charges to all buyers.
8. A profit-maximizing monopolist will produce up to the point at which marginal revenue is equal to marginal cost ($MR = MC$).
9. Monopolies have no identifiable supply curves. They simply choose a point on the market demand curve. That is, they choose a price and quantity to produce, which depend on both the marginal cost and the shape of the demand curve.
10. In the short run, monopolists are limited by a fixed factor of production, just as competitive firms are. Monopolies that do not generate enough revenue to cover costs will go out of business in the long run.
11. Compared with a competitively organized industry, a monopolist restricts output, charges higher prices, and earns positive profits. Because *MR* always lies below the demand curve for a monopoly, monopolists always charge a price higher than *MC* (the price that would be set by perfect competition).
12. Barriers to entry prevent new entrants from competing away industry excess profits.
13. Forms of barriers to entry include economies of scale, patents, government rules, ownership of scarce factors, and network effects.
14. When a firm exhibits economies of scale so large that average costs continuously decline with output, it may be efficient to have only one firm in an industry. Such an industry is called a *natural monopoly*.

THE SOCIAL COSTS OF MONOPOLY *p. 273*

15. When firms price above marginal cost, the result is an inefficient mix of output. The decrease in consumer surplus is larger than the monopolist's profit, thus causing a net loss in social welfare.
16. Actions that firms take to preserve positive profits, such as lobbying for restrictions on competition, are called rent seeking. *Rent-seeking behavior* consumes resources and adds to social cost, thus reducing social welfare even further.

PRICE DISCRIMINATION *p. 275*

17. Charging different prices to different buyers is called *price discrimination*. The motivation for price discrimination is fairly obvious: If a firm can identify those who are willing to pay a higher price for a good, it can earn more profit from them by charging a higher price.
18. A firm that charges the maximum amount that buyers are willing to pay for each unit is practicing *perfect price discrimination*.
19. A perfectly price-discriminating monopolist will actually produce the *efficient* quantity of output.
20. Examples of price discrimination are all around us. Airlines routinely charge travelers who stay over Saturday nights a much lower fare than those who do not. Business travelers generally travel during the week, often are unwilling to stay over Saturdays, and generally are willing to pay more for tickets.

REMEDIES FOR MONOPOLY: ANTITRUST POLICY *p. 277*

21. Governments have assumed two roles with respect to imperfectly competitive industries: (1) They *promote* competition and restrict market power, primarily through antitrust laws and other congressional acts; and (2) they *restrict* competition by regulating industries.
22. In 1914, Congress passed the *Clayton Act*, which was designed to strengthen the Sherman Act and to clarify what specific forms of conduct were "unreasonable" restraints of trade. In the same year, the *Federal Trade Commission* was established and given broad power to investigate and regulate unfair methods of competition.

REVIEW TERMS AND CONCEPTS

barrier to entry, *p. 270*
Clayton Act, *p. 278*
Federal Trade Commission (FTC), *p. 278*
government failure, *p. 275*
imperfectly competitive industry, *p. 261*
market power, *p. 261*
natural monopoly, *p. 270*
network externalities, *p. 272*
patent, *p. 271*
perfect price discrimination, *p. 275*
price discrimination, *p. 275*
public choice theory, *p. 275*
pure monopoly, *p. 262*
rent-seeking behavior, *p. 275*
rule of reason, *p. 278*

PROBLEMS

Visit **www.myeconlab.com** to complete the problems marked in orange online. You will receive instant feedback on your answers, tutorial help, and access to additional practice problems.

1. Do you agree or disagree with each of the following statements? Explain your reasoning.
   a. For a monopoly, price is equal to marginal revenue because a monopoly has the power to control price.
   b. Because a monopoly is the only firm in an industry, it can charge virtually any price for its product.
   c. It is always true that when demand elasticity is equal to −1, marginal revenue is equal to 0.
2. Explain why the marginal revenue curve facing a competitive firm differs from the marginal revenue curve facing a monopolist.
3. Assume that the potato chip industry in the Northwest in 2007 was competitively structured and in long-run competitive equilibrium; firms were earning a normal rate of return. In 2008, two smart lawyers quietly bought up all the firms and began operations as a monopoly called "Wonks." To operate efficiently, Wonks hired a management consulting firm, which estimated long-run costs and demand. These results are presented in the following figure.

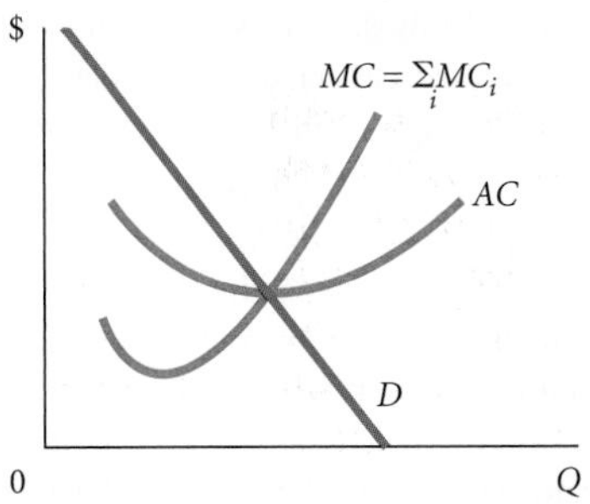

($\Sigma_i MC_i$ = the horizontal sum of the marginal cost curves of the individual branches/firms.)
   a. Indicate 2007 output and price on the diagram.
   b. By assuming that the monopolist is a profit-maximizer, indicate on the graph total revenue, total cost, and total profit after the consolidation.
   c. Compare the perfectly competitive outcome with the monopoly outcome.
   d. In 2008, an old buddy from law school files a complaint with the Antitrust Division of the Justice Department claiming that Wonks has monopolized the potato chip industry. Justice concurs and prepares a civil suit. Suppose you work in the White House and the president asks you to prepare a brief memo (two or three paragraphs) outlining the issues. In your response, be sure to include:
   (1) The economic justification for action.
   (2) A proposal to achieve an efficient market outcome.
4. Willy's Widgets, a monopoly, faces the following demand schedule (sales in widgets per month):

Price	$20	$30	$40	$50	$60	$70	$80	$90	$100
Quantity demanded	40	35	30	25	20	15	10	5	0

Calculate marginal revenue over each interval in the schedule—for example, between $q = 40$ and $q = 35$. Recall that marginal revenue is the added revenue from an additional *unit* of production/sales and assume that *MR* is constant within each interval.

If marginal cost is constant at $20 and fixed cost is $100, what is the profit-maximizing level of output? (Choose one of the specific levels of output from the schedule.) What is the level of profit? Explain your answer using marginal cost and marginal revenue.

Repeat the exercise for $MC = \$40$.
5. The following diagram illustrates the demand curve facing a monopoly in an industry with no economies or diseconomies of scale and no fixed costs. In the short and long run $MC = ATC$. Copy the diagram and indicate the following:

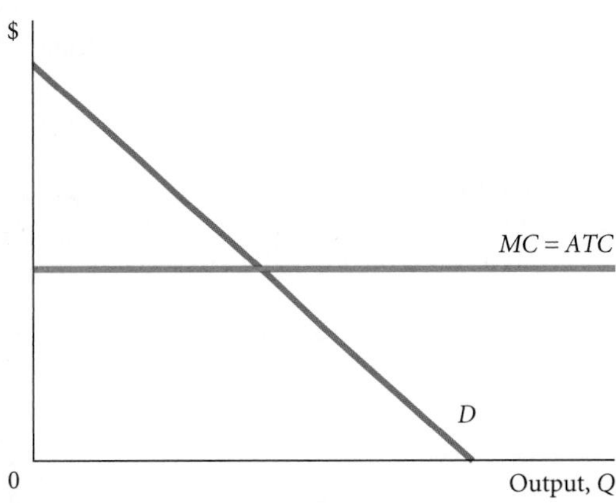

a. Optimal output
b. Optimal price
c. Total revenue
d. Total cost
e. Total monopoly profits
f. Total "excess burden" or "welfare costs" of the monopoly (briefly explain)

6. The following diagram shows the cost structure of a monopoly firm as well as market demand. Identify on the graph and calculate the following:
a. Profit-maximizing output level
b. Profit-maximizing price
c. Total revenue
d. Total cost
e. Total profit or loss

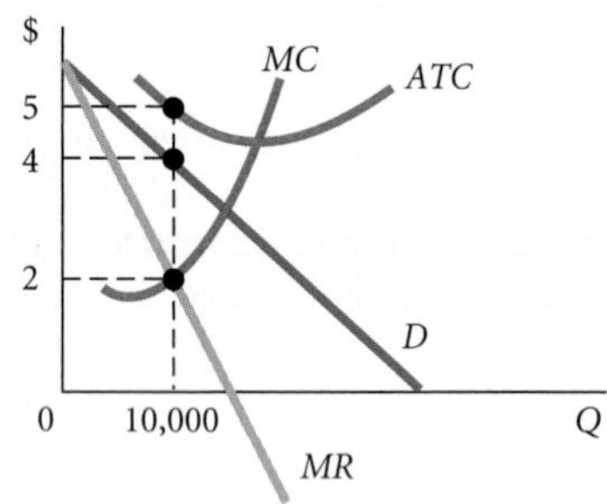

7. Consider the following monopoly that produces paperback books:

fixed costs = $1,000

marginal cost = $1 (and is constant)

a. Draw the average total cost curve and the marginal cost curve on the same graph.
b. Assume that all households have the same demand schedule given by the following relationship:

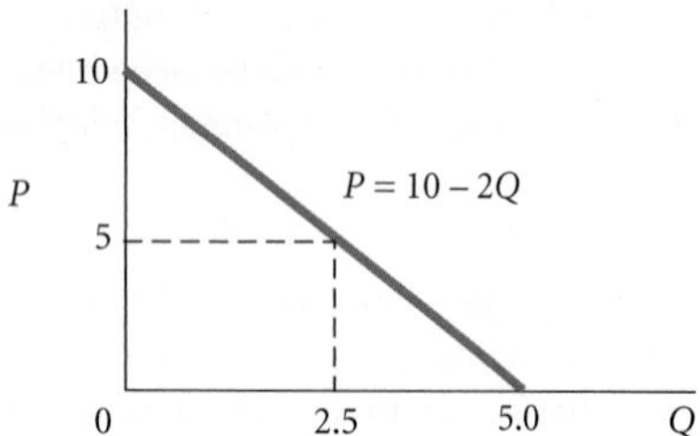

Assuming 400 households are in the economy, draw the market demand curve and the marginal revenue schedule facing the monopolist.
c. What is the monopolist's profit-maximizing output? What is the monopolist's price?
d. What is the "efficient price," assuming no externalities?
e. Suppose the government "imposed" the efficient price by setting a ceiling on price at the efficient level. What is the long-run output of the monopoly?
f. Suggest an alternative approach for achieving an efficient outcome.

*8. In Taiwan, there is only one beer producer, a government-owned monopoly called Taiwan Beer. Suppose that the company were run in a way to maximize profit for the government. That is, assume that it behaved like a private profit-maximizing monopolist. Assuming demand and cost conditions are given on the following diagram, at what level would Taiwan Beer target output and what price would it charge?

Now suppose Taiwan Beer decided to begin competing in the highly competitive American market. Assume further that Taiwan maintains import barriers so that American producers cannot sell in Taiwan but that they are not immediately reciprocated. Assuming Taiwan Beer can sell all that it can produce in the American market at a price $P = P_{US}$ indicate the following:
a. Total output
b. Output sold in Taiwan
c. New price in Taiwan
d. Total sold in the United States
e. Total profits
f. Total profits on U.S. sales
g. Total profits on Taiwan sales

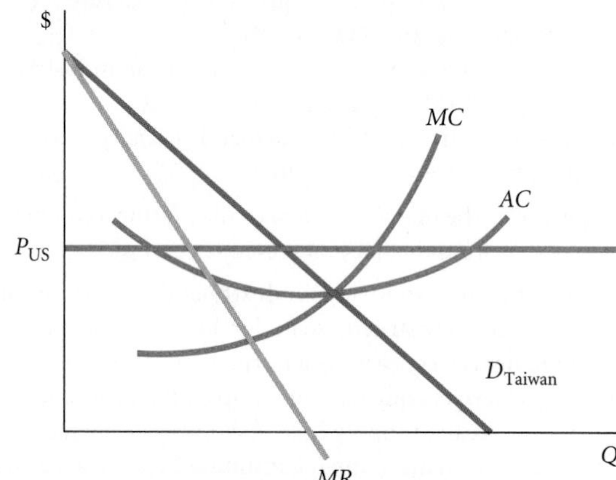

9. One of the big success stories of recent years has been Google. Research the firm and write a memorandum to the head of the Antitrust Division of the Justice Department presenting the case for and against antitrust action against Google. In what ways has Google acted to suppress competition? What private suits have been brought? What are the benefits of a strong, profitable Google?

10. [Related to the *Economics in Practice* on p. 272] When cable television was first introduced, there were few substitutes for it, particularly in areas with poor reception of network TV. In the current environment, a number of companies from outside the industry (for example, AT&T) have begun to develop new ways to compete with cable. What effect should we expect this to have on the cable companies?

11. [Related to the *Economics in Practice* on p. 279] Why might Whole Foods want to merge with Wild Oats?

---

*Note: Problems marked with an asterisk are more challenging.

Oligopoly 14

CHAPTER OUTLINE

We have now examined two "pure" market structures. At one extreme is *perfect competition*, a market structure in which many firms, each small relative to the size of the market, produce undifferentiated products and have no market power at all. Each competitive firm takes price as given and faces a perfectly elastic demand for its product. At the other extreme is *pure monopoly*, a market structure in which only one firm is the industry. The monopoly holds the power to set price and is protected against competition by barriers to entry. Its market power would be complete if it did not face the discipline of the market demand curve. Even a monopoly, however, must produce a product that people want and are willing to pay for.

Most industries in the United States fall somewhere between these two extremes. In the next two chapters, we focus on two types of industries in which firms exercise some market power but at the same time face competition: oligopoly and monopolistic competition. In this chapter, we cover oligopolies, and in Chapter 15, we turn to monopolistic competition.

An **oligopoly** is an industry dominated by a few firms that, by virtue of their individual sizes, are large enough to influence the market price. Oligopolies exist in many forms. Consider the following cases:

oligopoly A form of industry (market) structure characterized by a few dominant firms. Products may be homogenous or differentiated.

In the United States, 90 percent of the music produced and sold comes from one of four studios: Universal, Sony, Warner, or EMI. The competition among these four firms is intense, but most of it involves the search for new talent and the marketing of that talent. Although studios compete less on price, Radiohead's 2007 campaign to have consumers set their own price in buying its new CD may result in a shake-up of the industry.

Stents are small metal devices used to prop open coronary arteries once they have been unblocked by angioplasty surgery. In the United States, the $1 billion stent market is dominated by three firms: Boston Scientific, Johnson & Johnson, and Medtronic. Among the three, there is fierce competition in the area of research and development (R&D) as they try to develop new, improved products. In 2007, Johnson & Johnson tried marketing its stents directly to patients, with an advertisement during the Dallas Cowboys–New York Jets Thanksgiving Day football game. On the other hand, we see very little price competition among these firms.

Airlines are another oligopolistic industry, but price competition can be fierce. When Southwest enters a new market, travelers often benefit from large price drops.

In 2006, Sony and Toshiba each introduced a new technology in the high-definition DVD market. In this case, the two competitors took different strategies in terms of prices versus product quality. Much of the competition took place in the attempts of the two companies to win over studios that would produce movies compatible with one of the firm's new technologies. In the end, Sony's technology won out.

What we see in these examples is the complexity of competition among oligopolists. Oligopolists compete with one another not only in price but also in developing new products, marketing and advertising those products, and developing complements to use with the products.

At times, in some industries, competition in any of these areas can be fierce; in the other industries, there seems to be more of a "live and let live" attitude. The complex interdependence among oligopolists combined with the wide range of strategies that they use to compete makes them difficult to analyze. To find the right strategy, firms need to anticipate the reactions of their customers and their rivals to what the firms do. If I raise my price, will my rivals follow me? If they do not, will my customers leave, or are they attracted enough to what I produce that they will continue to purchase from me? If Universal decides to dramatically cut prices of its music and redo its contracts with artists so that they earn more revenue from concerts, will Sony imitate that strategy? If Sony does, how will that affect Universal? As you can see, these are hard, although interesting, questions. This chapter will introduce you to a range of different models from the fields of game theory and competitive strategy to help you answer these questions.

The four cases just described differ not only in how firms compete but also in some of the fundamental features of their industries. Before we describe the formal models of the way oligopoly firms interact, it is useful to provide a few tools that can be used to analyze the *structure* of the industries to which those firms belong. Knowing more of the structure of an industry can help us figure out which of the models we describe will be most helpful. For this exercise, we will rely on some of the tools developed in the area of competitive strategy used in business schools and in management consulting.

Five Forces model A model developed by Michael Porter that helps us understand the five competitive forces that determine the level of competition and profitability in an industry.

Market Structure in an Oligopoly

One of the standard models used in the competitive strategy area to look at the structure of an oligopoly industry is the **Five Forces model** developed by Michael Porter of Harvard University. Figure 14.1 illustrates the model.

▶ FIGURE 14.1
Forces Driving Industry Competition

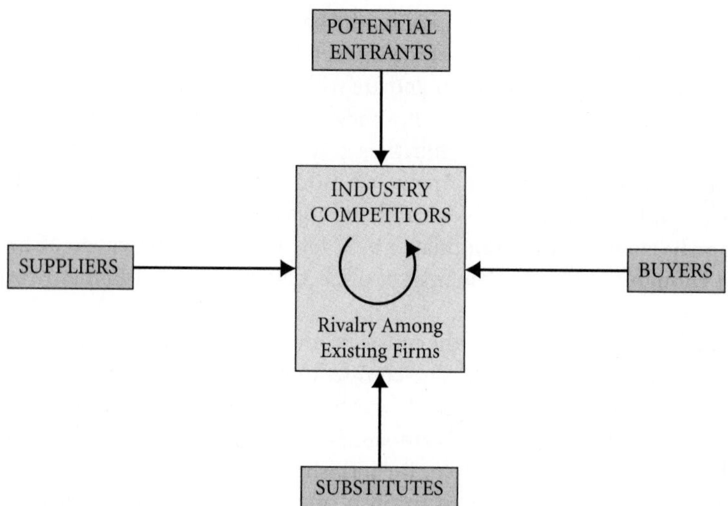

The five forces help us explain the relative profitability of an industry and identify in which area firm rivalry is likely to be most intense.

The center box of the figure focuses on the competition among the existing firms in the industry. In the competitive market, that box is so full of competitors that no individual firm needs to think strategically about any other individual firm. In the case of monopoly, the center box has only one firm. In an oligopoly, there are a small number of firms and each of those firms will spend time thinking about how it can best compete against the other firms.

What characteristics of the existing firms should we look at to see how that competition will unfold? An obvious structural feature of an industry to consider is the number and size distribution of those firms. Do the top two firms have 90 percent of the market or only 20 percent? Is there one very large firm and a few smaller competitors, or are firms similar in size? Table 14.1 shows the distribution of market shares in a range of different U.S. industries, based on census data using value of shipments. Market share can also be constructed using employment data. We can see that even within industries that are highly *concentrated*, there are differences. Ninety percent of U.S. beer is made by the top four firms (Anheuser-Busch itself produces 50 percent of the beer sold in the

United States), but there is a relatively large fringe of much smaller firms. In the copper industry, we find only large firms. As we will see shortly in the models, with fewer firms, all else being equal competition is reduced.

TABLE 14.1 Percentage of Value of Shipments Accounted for by the Largest Firms in High-Concentration Industries, 2002

Industry Designation	Four Largest Firms	Eight Largest Firms	Number of Firms
Primary copper	99	100	10
Cigarettes	95	99	15
Household laundry equipment	93	100	13
Cellulosic man-made fiber	93	100	8
Breweries	90	94	344
Electric lamp bulbs	89	94	57
Household refrigerators and freezers	85	95	18
Small arms ammunition	83	89	109
Cereal breakfast foods	82	93	45
Motor vehicles	81	91	308

Source: U.S. Department of Commerce, Bureau of the Census, 2002 Economic Census, *Concentration Ratios: 2002* ECO2-315R-1, May 2006.

We are also interested in the size distribution of firms among the top firms. Again, looking at the beer industry, while Anheuser-Busch produces half of the U.S. beer consumed, MillerCoors (a recently merged pair) is now up to 30 percent of the market, giving us a two-firm **concentration ratio** of 80 percent. In the market for conventional DVD players, Sony controls 20 percent of the market, but the next three or four firms in the industry have similar shares. When we discuss the price leadership model of oligopoly, we will highlight this question of size distribution. In our discussion of government merger policy, we will discuss measures other than the concentration ratio that can be used to measure firm shares.

concentration ratio The share of industry output in sales or employment accounted for by the top firms.

The final feature of existing firms that we want to look at is the amount of product differentiation we see in the industry. Are the firms all making the same product, or are the products very different from one another? This takes us back to the issue of how close products are as substitutes, a topic introduced in Chapter 13 in the description of monopoly. The more differentiated products produced by oligopolists are, the more their behavior will resemble that of the monopolist.

Now look at the boxes to the north and south of the competitive rivalry box in Figure 14.1. To the north, we see potential entrants. In the last chapter, we described the major sources of entry barriers. When entry barriers are low, new firms can come in to compete away any excess profits that existing firms are earning. In an oligopoly, we find that the threat of entry by new firms can play an important role in how competition in the industry unfolds. In some cases, the threat alone may be enough to make an industry with only a few firms behave like a perfectly competitive firm. Markets in which entry and exit are easy so that the threat of potential entry holds down prices to a competitive level are known as **contestable markets**.

contestable markets Markets in which entry and exit are easy.

Consider, for example, a small airline that can move its capital stock from one market to another with little cost. Cape Air flies between Boston, Martha's Vineyard, Nantucket, and Cape Cod during the summer months. During the winter, the same planes are used in Florida, where they fly up and down that state's west coast between Naples, Fort Meyers, Tampa, and other cities. A similar situation may occur when a new industrial complex is built at a fairly remote site and a number of trucking companies offer their services. Because the trucking companies' capital stock is mobile, they can move their trucks somewhere else at no great cost if business is not profitable. Existing firms in this market are continuously faced with the threat of competition. In contestable markets, even large oligopolistic firms end up behaving like perfectly competitive firms. Prices are pushed to long-run average cost by competition, and positive profits do not persist.

To the south of the competitor box, we see substitutes. For oligopolists—just like the monopolists described in the last chapter—the availability of substitute products outside the industry will limit the ability of firms to earn high profits.

ECONOMICS IN PRACTICE

Why are Record Labels Losing Key Stars like Madonna?

How can we use the Five Forces model to help us understand the competition record labels face? Notice first that the defectors from the labels—Madonna, Radiohead, and Nine Inch Nails—are well-known stars. For the record labels, these stars are suppliers. As these stars gain in popularity, they can drive harder bargains with the record labels. (This is one reason record labels sign artists to multiple record contracts, but no contract lasts forever.) While the supply of unknown singers is likely quite elastic, the supply of branded stars like Madonna is much more inelastic. Some people would argue that venues such as YouTube reduce the power of the record labels, even for young artists, by providing low-cost exposure. Here, YouTube serves as a *substitute* for the record labels from the perspective of the unknown artists. Buyers are also gaining power. With easy access to downloaded music, often pirated, listeners are willing to spend less on music and concerts play a bigger role in generating revenue for artists. Most observers think that the sum of these changes brought by new technology will be negative for record label profits.

Madonna (and the Internet) Disrupts Another Business

Wall Street Journal

Madonna has always had a keen eye for the latest trends and her new megadeal is no exception. But this time it's not due to the latest musical styles she's embracing. It's the fact that the Internet is disrupting traditional business models.

Rather than renewing her contract with her longtime record label Warner Bros., the Material Girl is signing a 10-year, $120-million deal with a concert-promotion company, the *Journal* reports. The promoter, Live Nation, probably won't make that back by selling the three albums worth of music Madonna's agreed to record for them. Instead, it intends to make a profit by selling everything from concert tickets to Madonna-brand perfumes to corporate sponsorships.

It's a textbook example of how the Internet is disrupting an industry. The record labels used to be the key players in the music industry. Getting music to fans meant negotiating a complex supply chain that included printing records and delivering them to stores. Looking at it this way, the record labels are more or less distribution companies. Yes, it's a simplified view, but it also makes it easier to see the broader implications, because most successful companies have had to master two skills: making stuff and distributing stuff.

The Internet is the world's most efficient distribution channel, which makes it a threat to any business whose business model relies on getting product to customers. In the case of the music industry, anyone can now distribute their music over the Internet for little or no cost. This, in turn, changes the value of recorded music. Madonna and bands like Radiohead and Nine Inch Nails realize that the best way to make money is to use their music as a way to promote their overall brands.

The music industry is just the most obvious example of the way the Internet is changing the way an industry distributes, values and indeed defines its product. Newspapers–including the Business Technology Blog's employer–are going through their own version of this disruption right now. And it's just a matter of time before it impacts other industries.

Source: October 10, 2007

Now take a look at the horizontal boxes in Figure 14.1. One of the themes in this book has been the way in which input and output markets are linked. Firms that sell in the product market also buy in the input market. Conditions faced by firms in their input markets are described in the left-hand box, suppliers. The circular flow diagram in Chapter 3 emphasizes this point. We see this same point in the Five Forces horizontal boxes. Airlines, which have some market power in the airline industry, face strong oligopolists when they try to buy or lease airplanes. In the airplane market, Boeing and Airbus control almost the entire market for commercial airplanes. In the market for leasing planes, GE has a dominant position. When a firm with market power faces another firm with market power in the input markets, interesting bargaining dynamics may result in terms of who ends up with the profits.

Finally, on the right side of the Five Forces diagram, we see the buyer or consumer—in some ways the most important part of the schema. Buyer preferences, which we studied as we looked at individual demand and utility functions—help to determine how successful a firm will be when it tries to differentiate its products. Some buyers can also exert bargaining power, even when faced with a relatively powerful seller. When people think of buyers, they usually think of the retail buyer of consumer goods. These buyers typically have little power. But many products in the U.S. economy are sold to other firms, and in many of these markets firms face highly concentrated buyers. Intel sells its processors to the relatively concentrated personal computer market, in which Dell has a large share. Proctor & Gamble (P&G) sells its consumer products to Wal-Mart, which currently controls 25 percent of the retail grocery market. Wal-Mart's power has enormous effects on how P&G can compete in its markets.

We have now identified a number of the key features of an oligopolistic industry. Understanding these features will help us predict the strategies firms will use to compete with their rivals for business. We turn now to some of the models of oligopolistic behavior.

Oligopoly Models

Because many different types of oligopolies exist, a number of different oligopoly models have been developed. The following provides a sample of the alternative approaches to the behavior (or conduct) of oligopolistic firms. As you will see, all kinds of oligopolies have one thing in common: The behavior of any given oligopolistic firm depends on the behavior of the other firms in the industry composing the oligopoly.

The Collusion Model

In Chapter 13, we examined what happens when a perfectly competitive industry falls under the control of a single profit-maximizing firm. We saw that when many competing firms act independently, they produce more, charge a lower price, and earn less profit than if they had acted as a single unit. If these firms get together and agree to cut production and increase price—that is, if firms can agree *not* to price compete—they will have a bigger total-profit pie to carve. When a group of profit-maximizing oligopolists colludes on price and output, the result is the same as it would be if a monopolist controlled the entire industry. That is, the colluding oligopoly will face market demand and produce only up to the point at which marginal revenue and marginal cost are equal ($MR = MC$) and price will be set above marginal cost.

A group of firms that gets together and makes price and output decisions jointly is called a **cartel**. Perhaps the most familiar example of a cartel today is the Organization of Petroleum Exporting Countries (OPEC). The OPEC cartel consists of 13 countries, including Saudi Arabia and Kuwait, that agree on oil production levels. As early as 1970, the OPEC cartel began to cut petroleum production. Its decisions in this matter led to a 400 percent increase in the price of crude oil on world markets during 1973 and 1974.

cartel A group of firms that gets together and makes joint price and output decisions to maximize joint profits.

OPEC is a cartel of governments. Cartels consisting of firms, by contrast, are illegal under U.S. antitrust laws described in Chapter 13. Price fixing has been defined by courts as any agreement among individual competitors concerning prices. All agreements aimed at fixing prices or output levels, regardless of whether the resulting prices are high, are illegal. Moreover, price fixing is a criminal offense, and the penalty for being found guilty can involve jail time as well as fines. In the 1950s, a group of 12 executives from five different companies in the electrical equipment industry were found guilty of a price-fixing scheme to rotate winning bids among the firms. All were fined and sentenced to jail. In 2005, a former executive from Bayer AG, a major German pharmaceutical company, was sentenced to four months in jail and given a $50,000 fine for price fixing. In 2007, the U.S. government launched suits charging price fixing against a number of firms in industries ranging from car rental to board game manufacturers. Despite the clear illegality of price fixing, the lure of profits seems to attract some executives to agree on prices.

For a cartel to work, a number of conditions must be present. First, demand for the cartel's product must be inelastic. If many substitutes are readily available, the cartel's price increases may become self-defeating as buyers switch to substitutes. Here we see the importance of understanding the substitutes box in Figure 14.1. Second, the members of the cartel must play by the rules. If a cartel is holding up prices by restricting output, there is a big incentive for members to cheat by increasing output. Breaking ranks can mean huge profits.

Incentives of the various members of a cartel to "cheat" rather than cooperate on the cartel highlights the role of the size distribution of firms in an industry. Consider an industry with one large firm and a group of small firms that has agreed to charge relatively high prices. For each firm, the price will be above its marginal cost of production. Gaining market share by selling more units is thus very appealing. On the other hand, if every firm drops prices to gain a market share, the cartel will collapse. For small players in an industry, the attraction of the added market share is often hard to resist, while the top firms in the industry have more to lose if the cartel collapses and have less added market share to gain. In most cartels, it is the small firms that begin pricing at below cartel prices.

tacit collusion Collusion occurs when price- and quantity-fixing agreements among producers are explicit. *Tacit collusion* occurs when such agreements are implicit.

Collusion occurs when price- and quantity-fixing agreements are explicit, as in a cartel. **Tacit collusion** occurs when firms end up fixing prices without a specific agreement or when such agreements are implicit. A small number of firms with market power may fall into the practice of setting similar prices or following the lead of one firm without ever meeting or setting down formal agreements. The fewer and more similar the firms, the easier it will be for tacit collusion to occur. As we will see later in this chapter, antitrust laws also play a role in trying to discourage tacit collusion.

The Price-Leadership Model

price leadership A form of oligopoly in which one dominant firm sets prices and all the smaller firms in the industry follow its pricing policy.

In another form of oligopoly, one firm dominates an industry and all the smaller firms follow the leader's pricing policy—hence its name **price leadership**. If the dominant firm knows that the smaller firms will follow its lead, it will derive its own demand curve by subtracting from total market demand the amount of demand that the smaller firms will satisfy at each potential price.

The price-leadership model is best applied when the industry is made up of one large firm and a number of smaller competitive firms. Under these conditions, we can think of the dominant firm as maximizing profit subject to the constraint of market demand *and* subject to the behavior of the smaller competitive firms. Smaller firms then can essentially sell all they want at this market price. The difference between the quantity demanded in the market and the amount supplied by the smaller firms is the amount that the dominant firm will produce.

Under price leadership, the quantity demanded in the market will be produced by a mix of the smaller firms and the dominant firm. Contrast this situation with that of the monopolist. For a monopolist, the only constraint it faces comes from consumers, who at some price will forgo the good the monopolist produces. In an oligopoly, with a dominant firm practicing price leadership, the existence of the smaller firms (and their willingness to produce output) is also a constraint. For this reason, the output expected under price leadership lies between that of the monopolist and the competitive firm, with prices also set between the two price levels.

The fact that the smaller firms constrain the behavior of the dominant firm suggests that that firm might have an incentive to try to push those smaller firms out of the market by buying up or merging with the smaller firms. We have already seen in the monopoly chapter how moving from many firms to one firm can help a firm increase profits, even as it reduces social welfare. Antitrust rules governing mergers, discussed later in this chapter, reflect the potential social costs of such mergers. An alternative way for a dominant firm to reduce the number of smaller firms in its industry is through aggressive price setting. Rather than accommodate the small firms, as is done in the price leadership situation, the dominant firm can try cutting prices aggressively until the smaller firms leave. The practice by which a large, powerful firm tries to drive smaller firms out of the market by temporarily selling at an artificially low price is called *predatory pricing*. Such behavior can be very expensive for the larger firm and is often ineffective. Changing prices below average variable costs to push other firms out of an industry in the expectation of later recouping through price increases is also illegal under antitrust laws.

The Cournot Model

A very simple model that illustrates the idea of interdependence among firms in an oligopoly is the Cournot model, introduced in the 19th century by the mathematician Antoine Augustin Cournot. The model was based on Cournot's observations of competition between two producers of spring water. Despite the age of the model and some if its restrictive assumptions, the intuition that emerges from it has proven to be helpful to economists and policy makers.

The original Cournot model focused on an oligopoly with only two firms. A two-firm oligopoly is known as a **duopoly**. We assume the firms produce identical products. We will also assume that the firms have identical cost structures and that, in contrast to the example we described earlier in this chapter, the firms cannot collude.

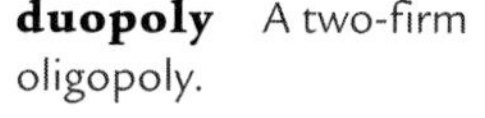

The key feature of an oligopoly, compared to the competitive firm, is that a firm's optimal decisions depend on the actions of the other individual firms in its industry. In a duopoly, as we are modeling here, the right output choice for each of the two firms will depend on what the other firm does. Cournot provides us with one way to model how firms take each other's behavior into account.

Return to the monopoly example that we used in the last chapter in Figure 13.9 on p. 273, reproduced here as Figure 14.2(a). Marginal cost is constant at \$2, and the demand curve facing the monopolist firm is the downward-sloping market demand curve. Recall that the marginal revenue curve lies below the demand curve because in order to increase sales the monopoly firm must lower its per-unit price. In this example, the marginal revenue curve hits zero at an output of 3,000 units. In this market, the monopolist maximizes profits at a quantity of 2,000 units and a price of \$4 as we saw in the last chapter. What happens in this market if, instead of having one monopoly firm, we have a Cournot duopoly? What does the duopoly equilibrium look like?

In choosing the optimal output, the monopolist had only to consider its own costs and the demand curve that it faced. The duopolist has another factor to consider: how much output will its rival produce? The more the rival produces, the less market is left for the other firm in the duopoly. In the Cournot model, each firm looks at the market demand, subtracts what it expects the rival firm to produce, and chooses its output to maximize its profits based on the market that is left.

Let's illustrate the Cournot duopoly solution to this problem with two firms, Firm A and Firm B. Recall the key feature of the duopoly: Firms must take each other's output into account when choosing their own output. Given this feature, it is helpful to look at how each firm's optimal output might vary with its rival's output. In Figure 14.2(b), we have drawn two *reaction functions*, showing each firm's optimal, profit-maximizing output as it depends on its rival's output. The *Y*-axis shows levels of Firm A's output, denoted q_A and the *X*-axis shows Firm B's output denoted as q_B.

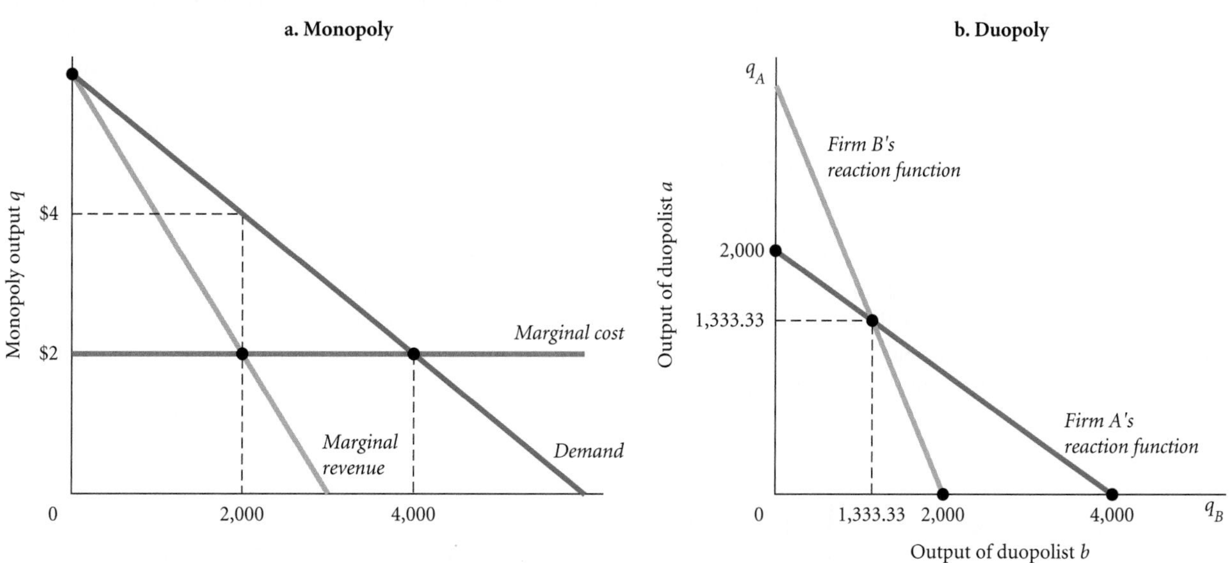

▲ **FIGURE 14.2 Graphical Depiction of the Cournot Model**
The left graph shows a profit-maximizing output of 2,000 units for a monopolist with marginal cost of \$2. The right graph shows output of 1,333.33 units *each* for two duopolists with the same marginal cost of \$2, facing the same demand curve. Total industry output increases as we go from the monopolist to the Cournot duopolists, but it does not rise as high as the competitive output (here 4,000 units).

Several of the points along Firm A's reaction function should look familiar. Consider the point where Firm A's reaction function crosses the vertical axis. At this point, Firm A's task is to choose the optimal output assuming Firm B produces 0. But we know what this point is from solving the monopoly problem. If Firm B produces nothing, then Firm A is a monopolist and it optimally produces 2,000 units. So *if* Firm A expects Firm B to produce 0, it should produce 2,000 to maximize its profits.

Look at the point at which Firm A's reaction function crosses the horizontal axis. At this point Firm B is producing 4,000 units. Look back at Figure 14.2(a). At an output level of 4,000 units the market price is $2, which is the marginal cost of production. If Firm A expects Firm B to produce 4,000 units, there is no profitable market left for Firm A and it will produce 0. If you start there, where the output of Firm B (measured on the horizontal axis) is 4,000 units each period, and you let Firm B's output fall moving to the left, Firm A will find it in its interest to increase output. If you carefully figure out what Firms A's profit-maximizing output is at every possible level of output for Firm B, you will discover that Firm A's reaction function is just a downward-sloping line between 2,000 on the *Y*-axis and 4,000 on the *X*-axis. The downward slope reflects the way in which firm A chooses its output. It looks at the market demand, subtracts its rival's output and then chooses its own optimal output. The more the rival produces, the less market is profitably left for the other firm in the duopoly.

Next, we do the same thing for Firm B. How much will Firm B produce if it maximizes profit and accepts Firm A's output as given? Since the two firms are exactly alike in costs and type of product, Firm B's reaction function looks just like Firm A's: When Firm B thinks it is alone in the market (Firm A's output on the vertical axis is 0) it produces the monopoly output of 2,000; when Firm B thinks Firm A is going to produce 4,000 units, it chooses to produce 0.

As you can see, the two reaction functions cross. Each firm's reaction function shows what it wants to do, conditional on the other firm's output. At the point of intersection, each firm is doing the best it can, given the actual output of the other firm. This point is sometimes called the *best response equilibrium*. As you can see from the graph, the Cournot duopoly equilibrium to this problem occurs when each firm is producing 1,333.33 units for an industry total of 2,666.66. This output is more than the original monopolist produced in this market, but less than the 4,000 units that a competitive industry would produce.

It turns out that the crossing point is the only equilibrium point in Figure 14.2(b). To see why, consider what happens if you start off with a monopoly and then let a second firm compete. Suppose, for example, Firm A expected Firm B to stay out of the market, to produce nothing, leaving Firm A as a monopolist. With that expectation, Firm A would choose to produce 2,000 units. But now look at Firm B's reaction function. If Firm A is now producing 2,000 units, Firm B's profit-maximizing output is not zero, it is 1,000 units. Draw a horizontal line from Firm A's output level of 2,000 to Firm B's reaction function and then go down to the *X*-axis and you will discover that Firm B's optimal output lies at 1,000 units. So an output level for Firm A of 2,000 units is not an equilibrium because it was predicated on a production level for Firm B that was incorrect. Going one step further, with Firm B now producing 1,000 units, Firm A will cut back from 2,000. This will in turn lead to a further increase in Firm B's output and the process will go on until both are producing 1,333.33.

As we have seen, the output level predicted by the Cournot model is between that of the monopoly and that of a perfectly competitive industry. Later extensions of the Cournot model tell us that the more firms we have, behaving as Cournot predicted, the closer output (and thus prices) will be to the competitive levels. This type of intuitive result is one reason the Cournot model has been widely used. A criticism of the model is that it provides an oversimplified view of firm interaction, with each firm taking its rival output as fixed. The field of game theory, to which we now turn, offers a more sophisticated and complete view of firm interactions.

Game Theory

The firms in Cournot's model do not anticipate the moves of the competition. Instead, they try to guess the output levels of their rivals and then choose optimal outputs of their own. But notice, the firms do not try to anticipate or influence what the rival firms will do in response to their own actions. In many situations, it does not seem realistic for firms to just take their rival's output as independent of their own. We might think that Intel, recognizing how important Advanced Micro Devices (AMD) is in the processor market, would try to influence AMD's business decisions. **Game theory** is a subfield of economics that analyzes the choices made by rival firms, people, and even governments when they are trying to maximize their own well-being while anticipating and reacting to the actions of others in their environment.

game theory Analyzes the choices made by rival firms, people, and even governments when they are trying to maximize their own well-being while anticipating and reacting to the actions of others in their environment.

Game theory began in 1944 with the work of mathematician John von Neumann and economist Oskar Morgenstern who published path-breaking work in which they analyzed a set of problems, or *games*, in which two or more people or organizations pursue their own interests and in which neither one of them can dictate the outcome. Game theory has become an increasingly popular field of study and research. The notions of game theory have been applied to analyses of firm behavior, politics, international relations, nuclear war, military strategy, and foreign policy. In 1994, the Nobel Prize in Economic Science was awarded jointly to three early game theorists: John F. Nash of Princeton University, John C. Harsanyi of the University of California at Berkeley, and Reinhard Selten of the University of Bonn. You may have seen the movie *A Beautiful Mind* about John Nash and his contribution to game theory.

Game theory begins by recognizing that in all conflict situations, there are decision makers (or players), rules of the game, and payoffs (or prizes). Players choose strategies without knowing with certainty what strategy the opposition will use. At the same time, though, some information that indicates how their opposition may be "leaning" may be available to the players. Most centrally, understanding that the other players are also trying to do their best will be helpful in predicting their actions.

Figure 14.3 illustrates what is called a payoff matrix for a simple game. Each of two firms, A and B, must decide whether to mount an expensive advertising campaign. If each firm decides not to advertise, it will earn a profit of $50,000. If one firm advertises and the other does not, the firm that does will increase its profit by 50 percent (to $75,000) while driving the competition into the loss column. If both firms decide to advertise, they will each earn profits of $10,000. They may generate a bit more demand by advertising, but not enough to offset the expense of the advertising.

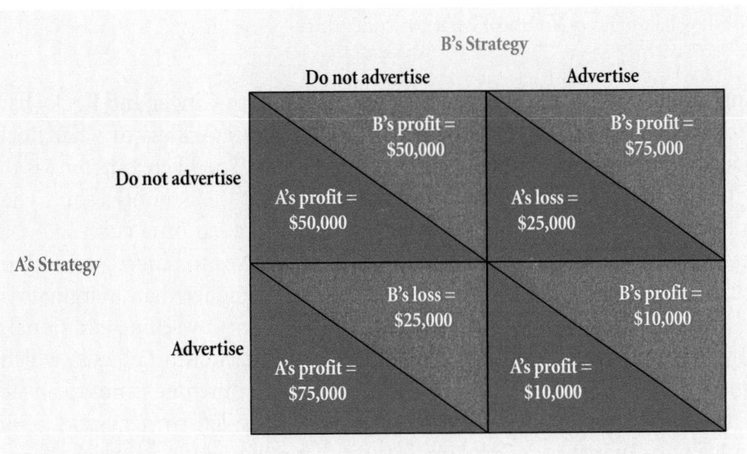

FIGURE 14.3 Payoff Matrix for Advertising Game

Both players have a dominant strategy. If B does not advertise, A will because $75,000 beats $50,000. If B does advertise, A will also advertise because a profit of $10,000 beats a loss of $25,000. A will advertise regardless of what B does. Similarly, B will advertise regardless of what A does. If A does not advertise, B will because $75,000 beats $50,000. If A does advertise, B will too because a $10,000 profit beats a loss of $25,000.

If firms A and B could collude (and we assume that they cannot), their optimal strategy would be to agree not to advertise. That solution maximizes the joint profits to both firms. If both firms do not advertise, joint profits are $100,000. If both firms advertise, joint profits are only $20,000. If only one of the firms advertises, joint profits are $75,000 − $25,000 = $50,000.

We see from Figure 14.3 that each firm's *payoff* depends on what the other firm does. In considering what firms should do, however, it is more important to ask whether a firm's *strategy* depends on what the other firm does. Consider A's choice of strategy. Regardless of what B does, it pays A to advertise. If B does not advertise, A makes $25,000 more by advertising than by not advertising. Thus, A will advertise. If B does advertise, A must advertise to avoid a loss. The same logic holds for B. Regardless of the strategy pursued by A, it pays B to advertise. A **dominant strategy** is one that is best no matter what the opposition does. In this game, both players have a dominant strategy, which is to advertise.

dominant strategy In game theory, a strategy that is best no matter what the opposition does.

prisoners' dilemma A game in which the players are prevented from cooperating and in which each has a dominant strategy that leaves them both worse off than if they could cooperate.

The result of the game in Figure 14.4 is an example of what is called a **prisoners' dilemma.** The term comes from a game in which two prisoners (call them Ginger and Rocky) are accused of robbing the local 7-Eleven together, but the evidence is shaky. If both confess, they each get 5 years in prison for armed robbery. If each one refuses to confess, they are convicted of a lesser charge, shoplifting, and get 1 year in prison each. The problem is that the district attorney has offered each of them a deal independently. If Ginger confesses and Rocky does not, Ginger goes free and Rocky gets 7 years. If Rocky confesses and Ginger does not, Rocky goes free and Ginger gets 7 years. The payoff matrix for the prisoners' dilemma is given in Figure 14.4.

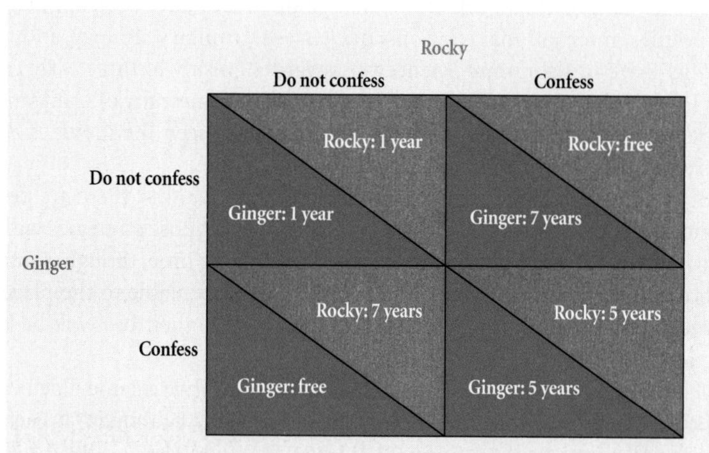

▲ **FIGURE 14.4 The Prisoners' Dilemma**

Both players have a dominant strategy and will confess. If Rocky does *not* confess, Ginger will because going free beats a year in jail. Similarly, if Rocky *does* confess, Ginger will confess because 5 years in the slammer is better than 7. Rocky has the same set of choices. If Ginger does *not* confess, Rocky will because going free beats a year in jail. Similarly, if Ginger *does* confess, Rocky also will confess because 5 years in the slammer is better than 7. Both will confess *regardless* of what the other does.

By looking carefully at the payoffs, you may notice that both Ginger and Rocky have dominant strategies: to confess. That is, Ginger is better off confessing regardless of what Rocky does and Rocky is better off confessing regardless of what Ginger does. The likely outcome is that both will confess even though they would be better off if they both kept their mouths shut. There are many cases in which we see games like this one. In a class that is graded on a curve, all students might consider agreeing to moderate their performance. But incentives to "cheat" by studying would be hard to resist. In an oligopoly, the fact that prices tend to be higher than marginal costs provides incentives for firms to "cheat" on output—restricting agreements by selling additional units.

Is there any way out of this dilemma? There may be, under circumstances in which the game is played over and over. Look back at Figure 14.3. The best joint outcome is not to advertise. But the power of the dominant strategy makes it hard to get to the top-left corner. Suppose firms interact over and over again for many years. Now opportunities for cooperating are richer. Suppose firm A decided not to advertise for one period to see how firm B would respond. If firm B continued to advertise, A would have to resume advertising to survive. Suppose B decided to match A's strategy. In this case, both firms might—with no explicit collusion—end up not advertising after A figures out what B is doing. We return to this in the discussion of repeated games, which follows.

There are many games in which one player does not have a dominant strategy, but in which the outcome is predictable. Consider the game in Figure 14.5(a) in which C does not have a dominant strategy. If D plays the left strategy, C will play the top strategy. If D plays the right strategy, C will play the bottom strategy. What strategy will D choose to play? If C knows the options, it will see that D has a dominant strategy and is likely to play that same strategy. D does better playing the right-hand strategy regardless of what C does. D can guarantee a $100 win by choosing right and is guaranteed to win nothing by playing left. Because D's behavior is predictable (it will play the right-hand strategy), C will play bottom. When all players are playing their best strategy *given* what their competitors are doing, the result is called a **Nash equilibrium**, named after John Nash. We have already seen one example of a Nash equilibrium in the Cournot model.

Nash equilibrium In game theory, the result of all players' playing their best strategy given what their competitors are doing.

Now suppose the game in Figure 14.5(a) were changed. Suppose all the payoffs are the same except that if D chooses left and C chooses bottom, C loses $10,000, as shown in Figure 14.5(b). While D still has a dominant strategy (playing right), C now stands to lose a great deal by choosing bottom on the off chance that D chooses left instead. When uncertainty and risk are introduced, the game changes. C is likely to play top and guarantee itself a $100 profit instead of playing bottom and risk losing $10,000 in the off chance that D plays left. A **maximin strategy** is a strategy chosen by a player to maximize the minimum gain that it can earn. In essence, one who plays a maximin strategy assumes that the opposition will play the strategy that does the most damage.

maximin strategy In game theory, a strategy chosen to maximize the minimum gain that can be earned.

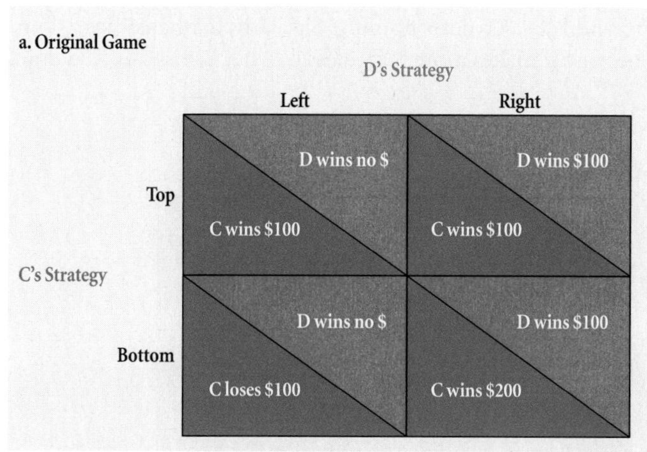

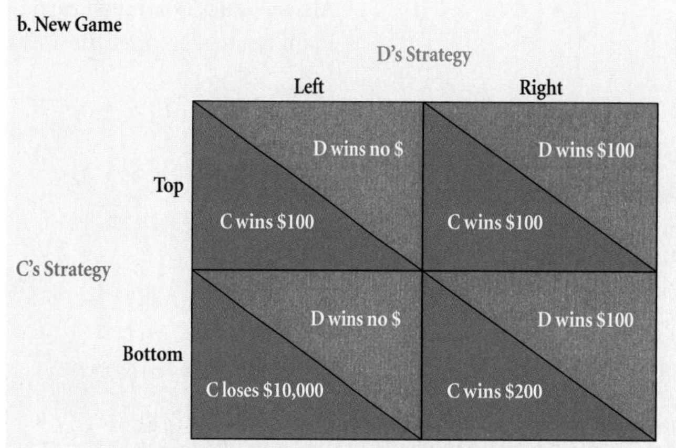

▲ **FIGURE 14.5 Payoff Matrixes for Left/Right–Top/Bottom Strategies**

In the original game (*a*), C does not have a dominant strategy. If D plays left, C plays top; if D plays right, C plays bottom. D, on the other hand, *does* have a dominant strategy: D will play right regardless of what C does. If C believes that D is rational, C will predict that D will play right. If C concludes that D will play right, C will play bottom. The result is a Nash equilibrium because each player is doing the best that it can *given* what the other is doing.

In the new game (b), C had better be very sure that D will play right because if D plays left and C plays bottom, C is in big trouble, losing $10,000. C will probably play top to minimize the potential loss if the probability of D's choosing left is at all significant.

Repeated Games

Clearly, games are not played once. Firms must decide on advertising budgets, investment strategies, and pricing policies continuously. Pepsi and Coca-Cola have competed against each other for 100 years, in countries across the globe. While explicit collusion violates the antitrust statutes, strategic reaction does not. Yet strategic reaction in a repeated game may have the same effect as tacit collusion.

Consider the game in Figure 14.6. Suppose British Airways and Lufthansa were competing for business on the New York to London route during the offseason. To lure travelers, they were offering discount fares. The question is how much to discount. Both airlines were considering a deep discount of $400 round-trip or a moderate discount of $600. Suppose costs are such that each $600 ticket produces profit of $400 and each $400 ticket produces profit of $200.

Clearly, demand is sensitive to price. Assume that studies of demand elasticity have determined that if *both* airlines offer tickets for $600, they will attract 6,000 passengers per week (3,000 for each airline) and each airline will make a profit of $1.2 million per week ($400 dollar profit times 3,000 passengers). However, if both airlines offer the deep discount fares of $400, they will attract 2,000 additional customers per week for a total of 8,000 (4,000 for each airline). While they will have more passengers, each ticket brings in less profit and total profit falls to $800,000 per week ($200 profit times 4,000 passengers). In this example, we can make some inferences about demand elasticity. With a price cut from $600 to $400, revenues fall from $3.6 million (6,000 passengers times $600) to $3.2 million (8,000 passengers times $400). We know from Chapter 5 that if a price cut reduces revenue, we are operating on an *inelastic* portion of the demand curve.

What if the two airlines offer different prices? To keep things simple, we will ignore brand loyalty and assume that whichever airline offers the deep discount gets all of the 8,000 passengers. If British Airways offers the $400 fare, it will sell 8,000 tickets per week and make $200 profit each, for a total of $1.6 million. Since Lufthansa holds out for $600, it sells no tickets and makes no profit. Similarly, if Lufthansa were to offer tickets for $400, it would make $1.6 million per week while British Airways would make zero.

Looking carefully at the payoff matrix in Figure 14.6, do you conclude that either or both of the airlines have a dominant strategy? In fact, both do. If Lufthansa prices at $600, British Airways will price at the deep discount, $400, because $1.6 million per week is more than $1.2 million. On the other hand, if Lufthansa offers the deep discount, British Airways must do so as well. If British Airways does not, it will earn nothing, and $800,000 beats nothing! Similarly, Lufthansa has a dominant strategy to offer the $400 fare because it makes more regardless of what British Airways does.

▶ FIGURE 14.6

Payoff Matrix for Airline Game

In a single play, both British Airways (BA) and Lufthansa Airlines (LA) have dominant strategies. If LA prices at $600, BA will price at $400 because $1.6 million beats $1.2 million. If, on the other hand, LA prices at $400, BA will again choose to price at $400 because $800,000 beats zero. Similarly, LA will choose to price at $400 regardless of which strategy BA chooses.

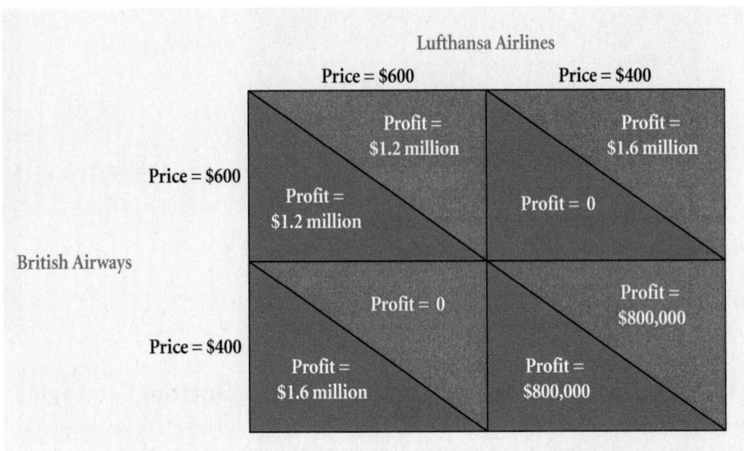

The result is that both airlines will offer the deep discount fare and each will make $800,000 per week. This is a classic prisoners' dilemma. If they were permitted to collude on price, they would both charge $600 per ticket and make $1.2 million per week instead—a 50 percent increase.

It was precisely this logic that led American Airlines President Robert Crandall to suggest to Howard Putnam of Braniff Airways in 1983, "I think this is dumb as hell...to sit here and pound the @#%* out of each other and neither one of us making a @#%* dime." ... "I have a suggestion for you, raise your @#%* fares 20 percent. I'll raise mine the next morning."

Since competing firms are prohibited from even talking about prices, Crandall got into trouble with the Justice Department when Putnam turned over a tape of the call in which these comments were made. But could they have colluded without talking to each other? Suppose prices are announced each week at a given time. It is like playing the game in Figure 14.6 a number of times in succession, a repeated game. After a few weeks of making $800,000, British Airways raises its price to $600. Lufthansa knows that if it sits on its $400 fare, it will double its profit from $800,000 to $1.6 million per week. But what is British Airways up to? It must know that its profit will drop to zero unless Lufthansa raises its fare too. The fare increase could just be a signal that both firms would be better off at the higher price and that if one leads and can count on the other to follow, they will both be better off. The strategy to respond in kind to a competitor is called a **tit-for-tat strategy**.

tit-for-tat strategy A repeated game strategy in which a player responds in kind to an opponent's play.

If Lufthansa figures out that British Airways will play the same strategy that Lufthansa is playing, both will end up charging $600 per ticket and earning $1.2 million instead of charging $400 and earning only $800,000 per week even though there has been no explicit price-fixing.

A Game with Many Players: Collective Action Can Be Blocked by a Prisoner's Dilemma

Some games have many players and can result in the same kinds of prisoners' dilemmas as we have just discussed. The following game illustrates how coordinated collective action in everybody's interest can be blocked under some circumstances.

Suppose I am your professor in an economics class of 100 students. I ask you to bring $10 to class. In front of the room I place two boxes marked Box A and Box B. I tell you that you must put the sum of $10 split any way you would like in the two boxes. You can put all $10 in Box A and nothing in Box B. You can put all $10 in Box B and nothing in Box A. On the other hand, you can put $2.50 in Box A and $7.50 in Box B. Any combination totaling $10 is all right, and I am the only person who will ever know how you split up your money.

At the end of the class, every dollar put into Box A will be returned to the person who put it in. You get back exactly what you put in. But Box B is special. I will add 20 cents to Box B for every dollar put into it. That is, if there is $100 in the box, I will add $20. But here is the wrinkle: The money that ends up in Box B, *including* my 20 percent contribution, will be divided equally among everyone in the class regardless of the amount that an individual student puts in.

You can think of Box A as representing a private market where we get what we pay for. We pay $10, and we get $10 in value back. Think of Box B as representing something we want to do collectively where the benefits go to all members of the class regardless of whether they have contributed. In Chapter 12, we discussed the concept of a *public good.* People cannot be excluded from enjoying the benefits of a public good once it is produced. Examples include clean air, a lower crime rate from law enforcement, and national defense. You can think of Box B as representing a public good.

Now where do you put your money? If you were smart, you would call a class meeting and get everyone to agree to put his or her entire $10 in Box B. Then everybody would walk out with $12. There would be $1,000 in the box, I would add $200, and the total of $1,200 would be split evenly among the 100 students.

But suppose you were not allowed to get together, in the same way that Ginger and Rocky were kept in separate cells in the jailhouse? Further suppose that everyone acts in his or her best interest. Everyone plays a strategy that maximizes the amount that he or she walks out with. If you think carefully, the dominant strategy for each class member is to put all $10 in Box A. *Regardless of what anyone else does,* you get more if you put all your money into Box A than you would get from any other split of the $10. And if you put all your money into A, no one will walk out of the room with more money than you will!

How can this be? It is simple. Suppose everyone else puts the $10 in B but you put your $10 in A. Box B ends up with $990 plus a 20 percent bonus from you of $198, for a grand total of $1,188, just $12 short of the maximum possible of $1,200. What do you get? Your share of Box B—which is $11.88, *plus* your $10 back, for a total of $21.88. Pretty slimy but clearly optimal for you. If you had put all your money into B, you would get back only $12. You can do the same analysis for cases in which the others split up their income in any way, and the optimal strategy is still to put the whole $10 in Box A.

Here is another way to think about it is: What part of what you ultimately get out is linked to or dependent upon what you put in? For every dollar you put in A, you get a dollar back. For every dollar *you yourself* put in B, you get back only 1 cent, one one-hundredth of a dollar, because your dollar gets split up among all 100 members of the class.

Thus, the game is a classic prisoners' dilemma, where collusion if it could be enforced would result in an optimal outcome but where dominant strategies result in a suboptimal outcome.

How do we break this particular dilemma? We call a town meeting (class meeting) and pass a law that requires us to contribute to the production of public goods by paying taxes. Then, of course, we run the risk that government becomes a player. We will return to this theme in Chapters 16 and 18.

To summarize, oligopoly is a market structure that is consistent with a variety of behaviors.The only necessary condition of oligopoly is that firms are large enough to have some control over price. Oligopolies are concentrated industries. At one extreme is the cartel, in which a few firms get together and jointly maximize profits—in essence, acting as a monopolist. At the other extreme, the firms within the oligopoly vigorously compete for small, contestable markets by moving capital quickly in response to observed profits. In between are a number of alternative models, all of which emphasize the interdependence of oligopolistic firms.

ECONOMICS IN PRACTICE

Price Fixing or Price Competition?

The section on game theory describes a two-firm game where each firm sets a high or low price. This kind of game can result in prisoners' dilemma, a destructive price war in which both firm suffer big losses and consumers gain. However, if the game is repeated, both firms might end up charging a high price, taking consumer surplus away from car renters. Also recall that for competition to work efficiently, consumers need to know prices. That means accurate advertising.

The following article describes a 2007 case in which a group of consumers filed suit claiming auto rental firms were colluding to fix prices. Is this an example of true competition, or is it an unfair and potentially illegal form of collusion? What would you do if you were the judge?

Suit Accuses Car Rental Firms of Price-Fixing

Los Angeles Times

In December 2006, the average daily rate for a mid-size rental car booked via the Internet at Los Angeles International Airport was about $60. A month later, the rate had climbed to $79, according to a study by a consumer group.

A class-action lawsuit filed by the group Wednesday alleged that the spike was the result of illegal price-fixing by rental-car companies—enabled by a new state law that allows the companies to change the way they advertise rates at many airports.

The amended law, which was drafted at the urging of rental car companies, was rushed through the Legislature with three minutes of debate in a late-night session only hours before legislators adjourned last year.

Consumer advocates contend in the suit that the companies are using the law as cover for a coordinated price increase, and that car renters have lost tens of millions of dollars as a result.

"They are allowed to charge excessive rates because they changed the law," said Gary Gramkow, 52, a plaintiff in the lawsuit that was filed by a group of five attorneys, including two with the Center for Public Interest Law in San Diego. Gramkow, who travels twice a month for his San Diego footwear business, said he noted the higher prices in January but initially blamed them on inflation.

The law allowed car rental firms to remove an 11% airport concession fee from their widely advertised base rental rate and bill it as a separate cost on each invoice. But rather than rates immediately dropping 11% when the fee was removed, they went up, the lawsuit alleges, and consumers were billed the 11% fee on top of a higher base rate.

That resulted in "a multimillion-dollar illegal windfall to the rental car industry," said University of San Diego Law Professor Robert C. Fellmeth, an author of the lawsuit.

Car rental company representatives, including Hertz's Richard D. Broome, denied Wednesday that they had fixed prices and said the legislation actually helped the consumer by separating out all costs that contributed to the final bill.

Rental car prices

Here is an example of how a new state law has affected car rental rates, in this case the average daily base price quoted by seven companies on the Internet for a medium-sized car rented at LAX:

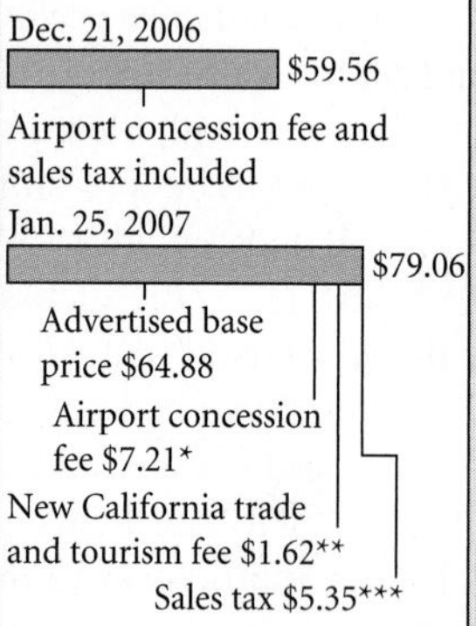

Dec. 21, 2006
$59.56
Airport concession fee and sales tax included

Jan. 25, 2007
$79.06
Advertised base price $64.88
Airport concession fee $7.21*
New California trade and tourism fee $1.62**
Sales tax $5.35***

* Rate = 11.11% ** Rate = 2.5%
*** Rate = 8.25%

Source: Crater for Public Interest Law

By Patrick McGreevy and Jean-Paul Renaud, Los Angeles Times Staff Writers November 15, 2007

Oligopoly and Economic Performance

How well do oligopolies perform? Should they be regulated or changed? Are they efficient, or do they lead to an inefficient use of resources? On balance, are they good or bad?

With the exception of the contestable-markets model, all the models of oligopoly we have examined lead us to conclude that concentration in a market leads to pricing above marginal cost and output below the efficient level. When price is above marginal cost at equilibrium, consumers are paying more for the good than it costs to produce that good in terms of products forgone in other industries. To increase output would be to create value that exceeds the social cost of the good, but profit-maximizing oligopolists have an incentive not to increase output.

Entry barriers in many oligopolistic industries also prevent new capital and other resources from responding to profit signals. Under competitive conditions or in contestable markets, positive profits would attract new firms and thus increase production. This does not happen in most oligopolistic industries. The problem is most severe when entry barriers exist and firms explicitly or tacitly collude. The results of collusion are identical to the results of a monopoly. Firms jointly maximize profits by fixing prices at a high level and splitting up the profits.

On the other hand, it is useful to ask why oligopolies exist in an industry in the first place and what benefits larger firms might bring to a market. When there are economies of scale, larger and fewer firms bring cost efficiencies even as they reduce price competition.

Vigorous product competition among oligopolistic competitors may produce variety and lead to innovation in response to the wide variety of consumer tastes and preferences. The connection between market structure and the rate of innovation is the subject of some debate in research literature.

Industrial Concentration and Technological Change

One of the major sources of economic growth and progress throughout history has been technological advance. Innovation, both in methods of production and in the creation of new and better products, is one of the engines of economic progress. Much innovation starts with R&D efforts undertaken by firms in search of profit.

Several economists, notably Joseph Schumpeter and John Kenneth Galbraith, argued in works now considered classics that industrial concentration, where a relatively small number of firms control the marketplace, actually increases the rate of technological advance. As Schumpeter put it in 1942:

> As soon as we...inquire into the individual items in which progress was most conspicuous, the trail leads not to the doors of those firms that work under conditions of comparatively free competition but precisely to the doors of the large concerns ...and a shocking suspicion dawns upon us that big business may have had more to do with creating that standard of life than keeping it down.[1]

This interpretation caused the economics profession to pause and take stock of its theories. The conventional wisdom had been that concentration and barriers to entry insulate firms from competition and lead to sluggish performance and slow growth.

The evidence concerning where innovation comes from is mixed. Certainly, most small businesses do not engage in R&D and most large firms do. When R&D expenditures are considered as a percentage of sales, firms in industries with high concentration ratios spend more on R&D than firms in industries with low concentration ratios.

Many oligopolistic companies do considerable research. In the opening segment of this chapter, we noted three firms dominated the medical devices market—Johnson & Johnson, Boston Scientific, and Medtronic. Each of these firms spends more than 10 percent of its revenues on R&D. Johnson & Johnson alone spent $8 billion on R&D in 2007. Microsoft spends a similar amount.

---

[1] J. A. Schumpeter, *Capitalism, Socialism, and Democracy* (New York: Harper, 1942); and J. K. Galbraith, *American Capitalism* (Boston: Houghton Mifflin, 1952).

However, the "high-tech revolution" grew out of many tiny start-up operations. Companies such as Sun Microsystems, Cisco Systems, and even Microsoft barely existed only a generation ago. The new biotechnology firms that are just beginning to work miracles with genetic engineering are still tiny operations that started with research done by individual scientists in university laboratories.

Significant ambiguity on this subject remains. Indeed, there may be no right answer. Technological change seems to come in fits and starts, sometimes from small firms and sometimes from large ones.

The Role of Government

As we suggested earlier, one way that oligopolies increase the market concentration is through mergers. Not surprisingly, the government has passed laws to control the growth of market power through mergers.

Regulation of Mergers

Celler-Kefauver Act Extended the government's authority to control mergers.

The Clayton Act of 1914 (as mentioned in Chapter 13) had given government the authority to limit mergers that might "substantially lessen competition in an industry." The **Celler-Kefauver Act** (1950) enabled the Justice Department to monitor and enforce these provisions. In the early years of the Clayton Act, firms that worked to merge did so knowing there was a risk of government opposition. Firms could spend large amounts of money on lawyers and negotiation. Firms could spend resources on negotiations only to have the government take the firms to court.

In 1968, the Justice Department issued its first guidelines designed to reduce uncertainty about the mergers it would find acceptable. The 1968 guidelines were strict. For example, if the largest four firms in an industry controlled 75 percent or more of a market, an acquiring firm with a 15 percent market share would be challenged if it wanted to acquire a firm that controlled as little as an additional 1 percent of the market.

Herfindahl-Hirschman Index (HHI) An index of market concentration found by summing the square of percentage shares of firms in the market.

In 1982, the Antitrust Division—in keeping with President Reagan's hands-off policy toward big business—issued a new set of guidelines. Revised in 1984, they remain in place today. The standards are based on a measure of market structure called the **Herfindahl-Hirschman Index (HHI)**. The HHI is calculated by expressing the market share of each firm in the industry as a percentage, squaring these figures, and summing. For example, in an industry in which two firms each control 50 percent of the market, the index is

$$50^2 + 50^2 = 2{,}500 + 2{,}500 = 5{,}000$$

For an industry in which four firms each control 25 percent of the market, the index is

$$25^2 + 25^2 + 25^2 + 25^2 = 625 + 625 + 625 + 625 = 2{,}500$$

Table 14.2 shows HHI calculations for several hypothetical industries. The Justice Department's courses of action, summarized in Figure 14.7, are as follows: If the Herfindahl-Hirschman Index is less than 1,000, the industry is considered unconcentrated and any proposed merger will go unchallenged by the Justice Department. If the index is between 1,000 and 1,800, the department will challenge any merger that would increase the index by over 100 points. Herfindahl indexes above 1,800 mean that the industry is considered concentrated already; and the Justice Department will challenge any merger that pushes the index up more than 50 points.

TABLE 14.2 Calculation of a Simple Herfindahl-Hirschman Index for Four Hypothetical Industries, Each with No More Than Four Firms

	Percentage Share of:				
	Firm 1	Firm 2	Firm 3	Firm 4	Herfindahl Hirschman Index
Industry A	50	50	–	–	$50^2 + 50^2 = 5{,}000$
Industry B	80	10	10	–	$80^2 + 10^2 + 10^2 = 6{,}600$
Industry C	25	25	25	25	$25^2 + 25^2 + 25^2 + 25^2 = 2{,}500$
Industry D	40	20	20	20	$40^2 + 20^2 + 20^2 + 20^2 = 2{,}800$

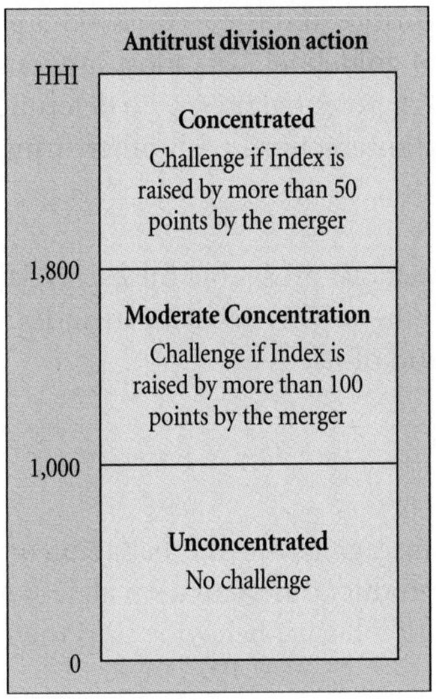

Antitrust division action

HHI	
1,800 –	**Concentrated** Challenge if Index is raised by more than 50 points by the merger
1,000 – 1,800	**Moderate Concentration** Challenge if Index is raised by more than 100 points by the merger
0 – 1,000	**Unconcentrated** No challenge

FIGURE 14.7 Department of Justice Merger Guidelines (revised 1984)

You should be able to see that the HHI combines two features of an industry that we identified as important in our Five Forces discussion: the number of firms in an industry and their relative sizes.

In the previous arithmetic example, we looked at the share of the market controlled by each of several firms. Before we can make these calculations, however, we have to answer another question: How do we define the market? What are we taking a share of? Think back to our discussion of market power in Chapter 13. Coca-Cola has a "monopoly" in the production of Coke but is one of several firms making cola products, one of many more firms making soda in general, and one of hundreds of firms making beverages. Coca-Cola's market power depends on how much substitutability there is among cola products, among sodas in general, and among beverages in general. Before the government can calculate an HHI, it must *define the market*, a task that involves figuring out which products are good substitutes for the products in question.

An interesting example of the difficulty in defining markets and the use of the HHI in merger analysis comes from the 1997 opposition by the FTC to the proposed merger between Staples and Office Depot. At that time, Office Depot and Staples were the number one and number two firms, respectively, in terms of market share in dedicated sales of office supplies. The FTC argued that in sales of office supplies, office superstores such as Office Depot and Staples had a strong advantage in the mind of the consumer. As a result of the one-stop shopping that they offered, it was argued that other stores selling stationery were not good substitutes for the sales of these two stores. So the FTC defined the market over which it intended to calculate the HHI to decide on the merger as the sale of office supplies in office superstores. Practically, this meant that stationery sold in the corner shop or in Wal-Mart was not part of the market, not a substantial constraint on the pricing of Office Depot or Staples. Using this definition, depending on where in the United States one looked, the HHI resulting from the proposed merger was between 5,000 and 10,000, clearly above the threshold. Economists working for Staples, on the other hand, argued that the market should include all sellers of office supplies. By that definition, a merger between Office Depot and Staples would result in a HHI well below the threshold since these two firms together controlled only 5 percent of the total market and the HHI in the overall market was well below 1,000. In the end, the merger was not allowed.

In Table 14.3, we present HHIs for a few different markets. Notice in one case—Las Vegas gaming—that the market has both a product and a geographic component. This definition, which was used by the government in one merger case, assumes that casinos in Las Vegas do not effectively compete with casinos in Atlantic City, for example. Other markets (for example, beer) are national markets. In general, the broader the definition of the market, the lower the HHI.

TABLE 14.3

Industry Definition	Some Sample HHIs
Beer	3,525
Ethanol	326
Las Vegas gaming	1,497
Critical care patient monitors	2,661

In 1997, the Department of Justice and the FTC issued joint Horizontal Merger Guidelines, updating and expanding the 1984 guidelines. The most interesting part of the new provisions is that the government examines each potential merger to determine whether it enhances the firms' power to engage in "coordinated interaction" with other firms in the industry. The guidelines define "coordinated interaction" as

> actions by a group of firms that are profitable for each of them only as the result of the accommodating reactions of others. This behavior includes tacit or express collusion, and may or may not be lawful in and of itself. [2]

A Proper Role?

Certainly, there is much to guard against in the behavior of large, concentrated industries. Barriers to entry, large size, and product differentiation all lead to market power and to potential inefficiency. Barriers to entry and collusive behavior stop the market from working toward an efficient allocation of resources.

For several reasons, however, economists no longer attack industry concentration with the same fervor they once did. First, even firms in highly concentrated industries can be pushed to produce efficiently under certain market circumstances. Second, the benefits of product differentiation and product competition are real. After all, a constant stream of new products and new variations of old products comes to the market almost daily. Third, the effects of concentration on the rate of R&D spending are, at worst, mixed. It is true that large firms do a substantial amount of the total research in the United States. Finally, in some industries, substantial economies of scale simply preclude a completely competitive structure.

In addition to the debate over the desirability of industrial concentration, there is a never-ending debate concerning the role of government in regulating markets. One view is that high levels of concentration lead to inefficiency and that government should act to improve the allocation of resources—to help the market work more efficiently. This logic has been used to justify the laws and other regulations aimed at moderating noncompetitive behavior.

An opposing view holds that the clearest examples of effective barriers to entry are those created by government. This view holds that government regulation in past years has been ultimately anticompetitive and has made the allocation of resources less efficient than it would have been with no government involvement. Recall from Chapter 13 that those who earn positive profits have an incentive to spend resources to protect themselves and their profits from competitors. This *rent-seeking* behavior may include using the power of government.

Complicating the debate further is international competition. Increasingly, firms are faced with competition from foreign firms in domestic markets at the same time they are competing with other multinational firms for a share of foreign markets. We live in a truly global economy today. Thus, firms that dominate a domestic market may be fierce competitors in the international arena. This has implications for the proper role of government. Some contend that instead of breaking up AT&T, the government should have allowed it to be a bigger, stronger international competitor. We will return to this debate in a later chapter.

---

[2] U.S. Department of Justice, Federal Trade Commission, *Horizontal Merger Guidelines*, 2005.

SUMMARY

MARKET STRUCTURE IN AN OLIGOPOLY *p. 284*

1. An *oligopoly* is an industry dominated by a few firms that, by virtue of their individual sizes, are large enough to influence market price. The behavior of a single oligopolistic firm depends on the reactions it expects of all the other firms in the industry. Industrial strategies usually are very complicated and difficult to generalize about.

2. The Five Forces model is a helpful way to organize economic knowledge about the structure of oligopolistic industries. By gathering data on an industry's structure in terms of the existing rivals, new entrants, substitutes, and buyer and supplier characteristics, we can better understand the sources of excess profits in an industry.

OLIGOPOLY MODELS *p. 287*

3. When firms collude, either explicitly or tacitly, they jointly maximize profits by charging an agreed-to price or by setting output limits and splitting profits. The result is the same as it would be if one firm monopolized the industry: The firm will produce up to the point at which $MR = MC$, and price will be set above marginal cost.
4. The *price-leadership* model of oligopoly leads to a result similar but not identical to the collusion model. In this organization, the dominant firm in the industry sets a price and allows competing firms to supply all they want at that price. An oligopoly with a dominant price leader will produce a level of output between what would prevail under competition and what a monopolist would choose in the same industry. An oligopoly will also set a price between the monopoly price and the competitive price.
5. The *Cournot model* of oligopoly is based on three assumptions: (1) that there are few firms in an industry, (2) that each firm takes the output of the other as a given, and (3) that firms maximize profits. The model holds that a series of output-adjustment decisions leads to a final level of output between that which would prevail under perfect competition and that which would be set by a monopoly.

GAME THEORY *p. 290*

6. *Game theory* analyzes the behavior of firms as if their behavior were a series of strategic moves and countermoves. It helps us understand the problem of oligopoly but leaves us with an incomplete and inconclusive set of propositions about the likely behavior of individual oligopolistic firms.

OLIGOPOLY AND ECONOMIC PERFORMANCE *p. 297*

7. Concentration in markets often leads to price above marginal cost and output below the efficient level. Market concentration, however, can also lead to gains from economies of scale and may promote innovation.

THE ROLE OF GOVERNMENT *p. 298*

8. The *Clayton Act* of 1914 (see Chapter 13) gave the government the authority to limit mergers that might "substantially lessen competition in an industry." The *Celler-Kefauver Act* (1950) enabled the Justice Department to move against a proposed merger. Currently, the Justice Department uses the *Herfindahl-Hirschman Index* to determine whether it will challenge a proposed merger.
9. Some argue that the regulation of mergers is no longer a proper role for government.

REVIEW TERMS AND CONCEPTS

cartel, *p. 287*
Celler-Kefauver Act, *p. 298*
concentration ratio, *p. 285*
contestable markets, *p. 285*
dominant strategy, *p. 291*
duopoly, *p. 288*
Five Forces model, *p. 284*
game theory, *p. 291*
Herfindahl-Hirschman Index (HHI), *p. 298*
maximin strategy, *p. 293*
Nash equilibrium, *p. 292*
oligopoly, *p. 283*
price leadership, *p. 290*
prisoners' dilemma, *p. 292*
tacit collusion, *p. 288*
tit-for-tat strategy, *p. 294*

PROBLEMS

Visit **www.myeconlab.com** to complete the problems marked in orange online. You will receive instant feedback on your answers, tutorial help, and access to additional practice problems.

1. Which of the following industries would you classify as an oligopoly? Which would you classify as monopolistically competitive? Explain your answer. If you are not sure, what information do you need to know to decide?
   a. Athletic shoes
   b. Restaurants
   c. Watches
   d. Aircraft
   e. Ice cream
2. **[Related to the *Economics in Practice* on *p. 286*]** In the last decade, many movie theaters have closed and others have seen a fall in yearly revenues. Use the Five Forces apparatus to analyze why this might have occurred.
3. Which of the following markets are likely to be perfectly contestable? Explain your answers.
   a. Shipbuilding
   b. Trucking
   c. Housecleaning services
   d. Wine production
4. Assume that you are in the business of building houses. You have analyzed the market carefully, and you know that at a price of $120,000, you will sell 800 houses per year. In addition, you know that at any price above $120,000, no one will buy your houses because the government provides equal-quality houses to anyone who wants one at $120,000. You also know that for every $20,000 you lower your price, you will be able to sell an additional 200 units. For example, at a price of $100,000, you can sell 1,000 houses; at a price of $80,000, you can sell 1,200 houses; and so on.
   a. Sketch the demand curve that your firm faces.
   b. Sketch the effective marginal revenue curve that your firm faces.
   c. If the marginal cost of building a house is $100,000, how many will you build and what price will you charge? What if $MC = \$85,000$?

5. The matrix in Figure 1 shows payoffs based on the strategies chosen by two firms. If they collude and hold prices at $10, each firm will earn profits of $5 million. If A cheats on the agreement, lowering its price, but B does not, A will get 75 percent of the business and earn profits of $8 million and B will lose $2 million. Similarly, if B cheats and A does not, B will earn $8 million and A will lose $2 million. If both firms cut prices, they will end up with $2 million each in profits.

Which strategy minimizes the maximum potential loss for A and for B? If you were A, which strategy would you choose? Why? If A cheats, what will B do? If B cheats, what will A do? What is the most likely outcome of such a game? Explain.

6. The payoff matrixes in Figure 2 show the payoffs for two games. The payoffs are given in parentheses. The figure on the left refers to the payoff to A; the figure on the right refers to the payoff to B. Hence, (2, 25) means a $2 payoff to A and a $25 payoff to B.
   a. Is there a dominant strategy in each game for each player?
   b. If game 1 were repeated a large number of times and you were A and you could change your strategy, what might you do?
   c. Which strategy would you play in game 2? why?

7. [Related to the *Economics in Practice* on *p. 296*] During 2007 and 2008, dozens of lawsuits were brought against U.S. firms for conspiracy to fix prices of things as diverse as homeowners insurance, gasoline, and rental cars. Choose one of these lawsuits or cases and describe the economic and legal issues. Using Google or another search engine, find the details of the case. What law was allegedly violated? How was the case settled? Was justice done? Explain your answer.

8. Suppose we have an industry with two firms producing the same product. Firm A produces 90 units, while firm B produces 10 units. The price in the market is $100, and both firms have marginal costs of production of $50. What incentives do the two firms have to lower prices as a way of trying to get consumers to switch the firm they buy from? Which firm is more likely to lower its price?

9. For each of the following, state whether you agree or disagree. Explain your reasoning.
   a. Oligopolies are always bad for society.
   b. The beer industry has a few large firms and many small firms. Therefore, we would not call it an oligopoly.

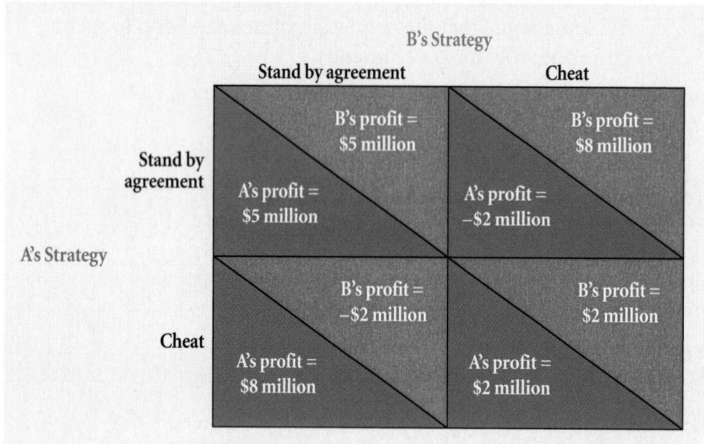

▲ FIGURE 1

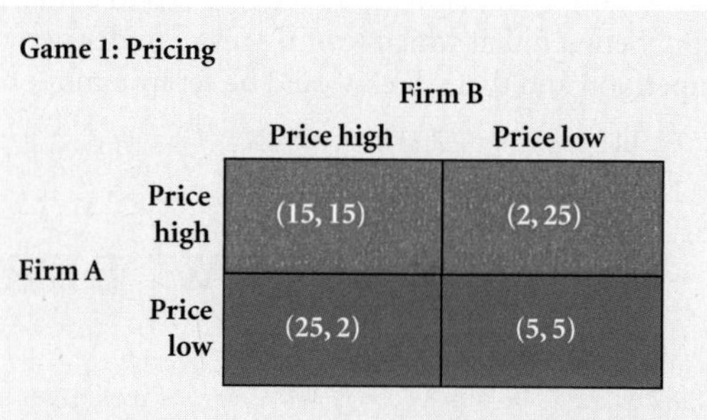

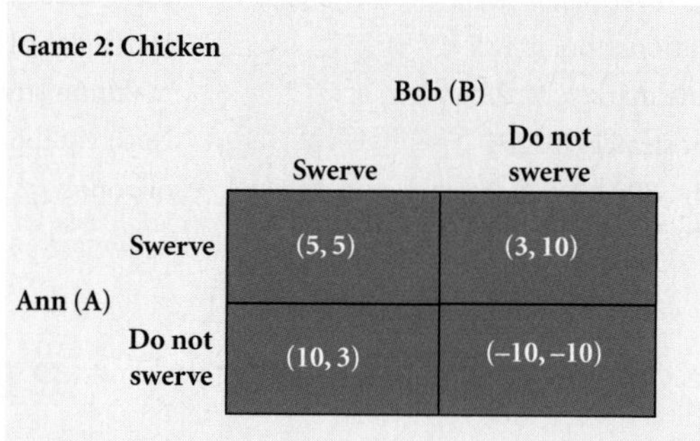

▲ FIGURE 2

Monopolistic Competition

15

We come now to our last broad type of market structure: *monopolistic competition*. Like perfect competition, a monopolistically competitive industry is an industry in which entry is easy and many firms are the norm. In contrast to the perfectly competitive firm, however, firms in this industry type do not produce homogeneous goods. Rather, each firm produces a slightly different version of a product. These product differences give rise to some market power. In the monopolistically competitive industry, a firm can charge a higher price than a competitor and not lose all of its customers. We will spend some time in this chapter looking at pricing in these industries.

But pricing is only one part of the story in these industries. When we look at firms in an industry characterized by monopolistic competition, we naturally focus on how firms make decisions about what kinds of products to sell and how to market and advertise them. Why do we see a dozen different types of shampoo in a store? Is a dozen too many, too few, or just the right amount? Why are beverages and automobiles advertised a great deal but semiconductors and economics textbooks are not? Advertising is expensive: Is it a waste of money, or does it serve some social function? In this chapter, we will also explore briefly some ideas from *behavioral economics*. Can consumers ever be offered too many choices? Why does nutritional cereal sell better in the extra large size while candy sells better by the bar?

By the end of this chapter, we will have covered the four basic types of market structure. Figure 15.1 summarizes the four types: perfect competition, monopoly, oligopoly, and monopolistic competition. The behavior of firms in an industry, the key decisions facing firms, and the key policy issues government faces in dealing with those firms differ depending on the market structure we are in. Although not every industry fits neatly into one of these categories, they do provide a useful and convenient framework for thinking about industry structure and behavior.

CHAPTER OUTLINE

	Number of firms	Products differentiated or homogeneous	Price a decision variable	Easy entry	Distinguished by	Examples
Perfect competition	Many	Homogeneous	No	Yes	Market sets price	Wheat farmer Textile firm
Monopoly	One	One version or many versions of a product	Yes	No	Still constrained by market demand	Public utility Patented drug
Monopolistic competition	Many	Differentiated	Yes, but limited	Yes	Price and quality competition	Restaurants Hand soap
Oligopoly	Few	Either	Yes	Limited	Strategic behavior	Automobiles Aluminum

▲ **FIGURE 15.1 Characteristics of Different Market Organizations**

Industry Characteristics

monopolistic competition A common form of industry (market) structure in the United States, characterized by a large number of firms, no barriers to entry, and product differentiation.

A **monopolistically competitive industry** has the following characteristics:

1. A large number of firms
2. No barriers to entry
3. Product differentiation

While pure monopoly and perfect competition are rare, monopolistic competition is common in the United States, for example, in the restaurant business. In a Yahoo search of San Francisco restaurants, there are 8,083 listed in the area. Each produces a slightly different product and attempts to distinguish itself in consumers' minds. Entry to the market is not blocked. At one location near Union Square in San Francisco, five different restaurants opened and went out of business in 5 years. Although many restaurants fail, small ones can compete and survive because there are few economies of scale in the restaurant business.

The feature that distinguishes monopolistic competition from monopoly and oligopoly is that firms that are monopolistic competitors cannot influence market price by virtue of their size. No one restaurant is big enough to affect the market price of a prime rib dinner even though all restaurants can control their *own* prices. Instead, firms gain control over price in monopolistic competition by *differentiating* their products. You make it in the restaurant business by producing a product that people want that others are not producing or by establishing a reputation for good food and good service. By producing a unique product or establishing a particular reputation, a firm becomes, in a sense, a "monopolist"—that is, no one else can produce the exact same good.

The feature that distinguishes monopolistic competition from pure monopoly is that good substitutes are available in a monopolistically competitive industry. With 8,083 restaurants in the San Francisco area, there are dozens of good Italian, Chinese, and French restaurants. San Francisco's Chinatown, for example, has about 50 small Chinese restaurants, with over a dozen packed on a single street. The menus are nearly identical, and they all charge virtually the same prices. At the other end of the spectrum are restaurants, with established names and prices far above the cost of production, that are always booked. That is the goal of every restaurateur who ever put a stockpot on the range.

Table 15.1 presents some data on nine national manufacturing industries that have the characteristics of monopolistic competition. Each of these industries includes hundreds of individual firms, some larger than others, but all small relative to the industry. The top four firms in book printing, for example, account for 33 percent of total shipments. The top 20 firms account for 68 percent of the market, while the market's remaining 41 percent is split among almost 540 separate firms.

Firms in a monopolistically competitive industry are small relative to the total market. New firms can enter the industry in pursuit of profit, and relatively good substitutes for the firms' products are available. Firms in monopolistically competitive industries try to achieve a degree of market power by differentiating their products—by producing something new, different, or better or by creating a unique identity in the minds of consumers. To discuss the behavior of such firms, we begin with product differentiation and advertising.

TABLE 15.1 Percentage of Value of Shipments Accounted for by the Largest Firms in Selected Industries, 2002

Industry Designation	Four Largest Firms	Eight Largest Firms	Twenty Largest Firms	Number of Firms
Travel trailers and campers	38	45	58	733
Games, toys	39	48	63	732
Wood office furniture	34	43	56	546
Book printing	33	54	68	560
Curtains and draperies	17	25	38	1,778
Fresh or frozen seafood	14	24	48	529
Women's dresses	18	23	48	528
Miscellaneous plastic products	6	10	18	6,775

Source: U.S. Department of Commerce, Bureau of the Census, 2002 Census of Manufacturers, *Concentration Ratios in Manufacturing.* Subject Ec02 315R, May 2006.

Product Differentiation and Advertising

Monopolistically competitive firms achieve whatever degree of market power they command through **product differentiation**. But what determines how much differentiation we see in a market and what form it takes?

product differentiation A strategy that firms use to achieve market power. Accomplished by producing products that have distinct positive identities in consumers' minds.

How Many Varieties?

As you look around your neighborhood, notice the sidewalks that connect individual homes with the common outside walk. In some areas, you will see an occasional brick or cobblestone walk; but in most places in the United States, these sidewalks are made of concrete. In almost every case, that concrete is gray. Now look at the houses that these sidewalks lead up to. Except in developments with tight controls, house colors vary across the palate. Why do we have one variety of concrete sidewalk while we have multiple varieties of house colors?

Whenever we see limited varieties of a product, a first thought might be that all consumers—here homeowners—have similar preferences. Perhaps everyone has a natural affection for gray, at least in concrete. The wide variety in the colors of the houses that these sidewalks lead up to might make you skeptical of this explanation, but it is possible. Another possible explanation for the common gray sidewalks might be a desire for coordination: Maybe everyone wants his or her sidewalk to look like the neighbor's, and the fact that the sidewalk connecting the houses—often provided by the city—is gray serves to make gray a focal point. In fashion, for example, coordination and conformity play an enormous role. There is no inherent reason that oversized jeans should be more or less attractive than narrow-cut, low-rise jeans except that they are made so at certain times by the fact that many people are wearing them. Again, you might wonder why conformity is important in sidewalk color but not in house color, something even more visible to the neighbors.

In explaining the narrow variety of concrete sidewalks, a better explanation may come from a review of the material we covered in Chapter 8 when we looked at cost structures. As you know, concrete is made in large mixer trucks. The average capacity of these trucks is 9 or more cubic yards, well more than you would need for a sidewalk. An obvious way to color this concrete is to mix a coloring agent in the mixer truck along with the cement and other ingredients. When done this way, however, we need to find several neighbors who want the same color cement that we want at the same time—concrete is not storable. Even doing it this way is potentially problematic because the inside of the mixer unit can be affected, leaving a residue of our purple concrete, for example, for the next customer. Alternatively, we could add dye after the concrete comes out of the truck, which is done in some places; but the resulting colors are limited, and the process is expensive. So the lack of variety in concrete and not in houses may reflect the scale economies in homogeneous production of concrete not found in house painting.

The example of the sidewalks versus the houses helps explain the wide variety in some product areas and the narrowness in others. In some cases, consumers may have very *different tastes*. It should be no surprise that immigration brings with it an increase in the variety of restaurant types in an area and in the food offerings at the local grocery store. Immigration typically increases the heterogeneity of consumer tastes. Product variety is narrower when there are gains to coordination. In Chapter 13, we described products in which there are network externalities. Here *coordination needs* can dramatically narrow product choice. For example, it will be more important to most people to use the same word processing program their friends use than to use one that suits them perfectly. Finally, scale economies that make producing different varieties more expensive than a single type can reduce variety. People prefer a relatively inexpensive standardized good over a more expensive custom product that perfectly suits them. The development of the Levitt house in the postwar period in Pennsylvania and New York was a testament to the cost savings in housing that came from standardization, creating uniform tract houses for affordable prices.

In sum, in well-working markets, the level of product variety reflects the underlying heterogeneity of consumers' tastes in that market, the gains if any from coordination, and cost economies from standardization. In industries that are monopolistically competitive, differences in consumer tastes, lack of need for coordination, and modest or no scale economies from standardization give rise to a large number of firms, each of which has a different product. Even within this industry structure, however, these same forces play a role in driving levels of variety.

In recent years, quite a few people have taken up the sport of running. The market has responded in a big way. Now there are numerous running magazines; hundreds of orthotic shoes designed specifically for runners with particular running styles; running suits of every color, cloth, and style; weights for the hands, ankles, and shoelaces; tiny radios to slip into sweatbands; and so on. Even physicians have differentiated their products: Sports medicine clinics have diets for runners, therapies for runners, and doctors specializing in shin splints or Morton's toe.

Why has this increase in variety in the running market taken place? More runners—each with a different body, running style, and sense of aesthetics—increase consumer heterogeneity. The increased market size also tells us that if you produce a specialized running product, it is more likely you will sell enough to cover whatever fixed costs you had in developing the product. So market size allows for more variety. New York has a wider range of ethnic restaurants than does Eden Prairie, Minnesota, not only because of the difference in the heterogeneity of the populations but also because of the sheer size of the two markets.

How Do Firms Differentiate Products?

We have learned that differentiation occurs in response to demands by consumers for products that meet their individual needs and tastes, constrained by the forces of costs of coordination and scale economies. We can go one step further and characterize the kinds of differentiation we see in markets.

Return to the restaurant example we brought up earlier. Of the 8,083 restaurants in San Francisco, some are French, some are Chinese, and some are Italian. Economists would call this form of differentiation across the restaurants **horizontal differentiation**. Horizontal differentiation is a product difference that improves the product for some people but makes it worse for others. If we were to poll San Francisco residents, asking for the best restaurant in town, we would undoubtedly get candidates from a number of different categories. Indeed, many people might not even consider this to be a legitimate question.

horizontal differentiation Products differ in ways that make them better for some people and worse for others.

If you add sea salt and vinegar to potato chips, that makes them more attractive to some people and less attractive to others. Horizontal differentiation creates variety to reflect differences in consumers' tastes in the market.

For some products, people choose a type and continue with it for a long time. For many of us, breakfast cereals have this feature. Day after day we eat Cheerios or corn flakes. Brand preference for mayonnaise has the same stability. For dinner, however, most of us are *variety-seeking*. Even small cities can support some variety in restaurant types because people get tired of eating at the same place every week.

People who visit planned economies often comment on the lack of variety. Before the Berlin Wall came down in 1989 and East and West Germany were reunited in 1990, those who were allowed passed from colorful and exciting West Berlin into dull and gray East Berlin; variety seemed to vanish. As the wall came down, thousands of Germans from the East descended on the department stores of the West. Visitors to China since the economic reforms of the mid-1980s claim that the biggest visible sign of change is the increase in the selection of products available to the population.

Recent work in the area of *behavioral economics* suggests, however, that there may be times in which too much variety is a bad thing.[2] **Behavioral economics** is a branch of economics that uses the insight of psychology and economics to investigate decision making.

behavioral economics A branch of economics that uses the insights of psychology and economics to investigate decision making.

Researchers set up an experiment in an upscale grocery, Draeger's, located in Menlo Park, California. Draeger's is known for its large selection, carrying, for example, 250 varieties of mustard. A tasting booth was set up in the store on two consecutive Saturdays. On one day, consumers were offered one of six exotic jams to taste, while on the other day, 24 varieties were offered. The results of the experiment were striking. While more customers approached the 24-jam booth for a taste than approached the booth with a limited selection, almost none of the tasters at the 24-jam booth bought anything; in contrast, almost 30 percent of tasters at the six-jam booth made a purchase.[3] The researchers conclude that while some choice is highly valued by people, too much choice can reduce purchases.

The jam experiment offers a case in which individuals react to a wide choice range by not making any decision at all. Behavioral economists also note that when the number of choices is large, individuals may avoid the decision-making burden by using a rule of thumb or by reverting to the default option. In the area of retirement savings, for example, some studies have found a tendency for people to allocate savings evenly across a range of investment options without paying much attention to the earnings characteristics of those funds. In other cases, people appear to favor whatever option is the default designated by the government body or by the firm offering the plan. For this reason, some economists have argued that one way to increase consumer savings (if that is desirable) is to make participation rather than no participation the default in pension plans. In this way, individuals would be enrolled in a retirement plan unless they chose not to be. These plans are sometimes called opt-out plans rather than opt-in plans.

Behavioral economics also has something to say about another form of horizontal differentiation—package size and pricing form.[4] Many consumer goods come in small, large, and extra large packages. Many goods (for example, health club visits and magazines) can be bought per visit or issue or via membership or subscription. Many of us think of these differences as matters of convenience. Firms can use these differences to create products targeted at consumer types. Small households buy small boxes of cereals, and large families purchase extra large sizes. Occasional readers buy *Us Weekly* on the newsstand, and fans subscribe to the magazine. Clearly, these kinds of differences play a role. But behavioral economists have also suggested that some of these differences survive in the market because some consumers are interested in trying to control their purchasing behavior. People buy small containers of ice cream but large bottles of vitamins. Why? Because they want to *commit* themselves to taking a vitamin every day but only occasionally eating ice cream. People buy memberships to health clubs as an incentive to work out; they make the marginal cost of a visit zero even though in the end, they may pay more than they would have by paying a per-visit fee. We subscribe to *The Economist* but buy *Us Weekly* on the newsstand at high per-issue prices in the hopes that we will read more of *The Economist* and less of *Us Weekly*. Some students choose classes that reward attendance as a way of ensuring that they go to class. Firms can be creative about using product differentiation to offer consumers commitment devices that help them control their own impulses. A **commitment device** is an action taken by an individual now to try to control his or her behavior in the future.

commitment device Actions that individuals take in one period to try to control their behavior in a future period.

Behavioral economics is an exciting new field that is challenging and deepening our understanding of a number of areas of economics. New ideas from behavioral economics have entered both microeconomics and macroeconomics.

---

[2] The classic paper that describes the study reported here is I. Yengar and L. Epper, "When Choice Is Demotivating: Can One Desire Too Much of a Good Thing?" *Journal of Personality and Social Psychology*, 2000, 995–1006.

[3] The subsample of six brands was carefully selected to be neither the best nor the worst of the flavors; and to actually buy, consumers had to go to a shelf that contained all the varieties of jam.

[4] Papers described in this paragraph include Klaus W. Ertenbroch, "Self-Rationing: Self-Control in Consumer Choice," INSEAD Working Paper, 2001, on the package size topic; Ulrike Malmendier and Stefano Della Vigna, "Paying Not to Go to the Gym," AER, June 2006, 694–719, on health club memberships; and Sharon Oster and Fiona Scott Morton, "Behavioral Biases Meet the Market," *BEPress Journal of Economic Advance and Policy*, 2005, on magazines.

ECONOMICS IN PRACTICE

An Economist Makes Tea

You have probably seen Honest Tea, a slightly sweetened bottled iced tea made from green, black, and herbal blends in your local grocery store. It is probably not the only iced tea on the shelf. In addition to the popular brands Lipton and Snapple, you may also see SoBe, Tazo, and Turkey Hill, depending on where you live. Bottled iced tea is a classic example of a monopolistically competitive market. None of the brands are exactly alike. Honest Tea, for example, prides itself on being made with high-end tea leaves and only a hint of sweetener, while Snapple uses lower-quality leaves and a hefty dose of sweetener. Nor are the teas priced the same. In a typical store, the retail price of Honest Tea and SoBe are likely to be about $1.89, while Snapple would likely cost about $1.39. If you spend time in the beverage aisle of a grocery store, you will notice that despite the higher price of Honest Tea, some consumers choose it over the alternatives.

What you may not know about Honest Tea is that it was started a decade ago by Seth Goldman, an entrepreneur, and Barry Nalebuff, an economist. In figuring out how to differentiate his tea from others in the industry, Nalebuff used some of the economic theory that we covered in Chapter 6 of this book. Look at the following graph, which shows the placement of one of Honest Tea's most popular flavors, Green Dragon. The graph shows how taste varies with sugar for Goldman and Nalebuff's potential customers. Tea taste improves for the first few grams of sugar, but shortly begins to flatten out and then fall. Note that Green Dragon is somewhat to the left of the taste peak. Some economists looking at this graph criticized Nalebuff for choosing too little sugar content for his tea. What were the critics thinking, and why were they wrong?

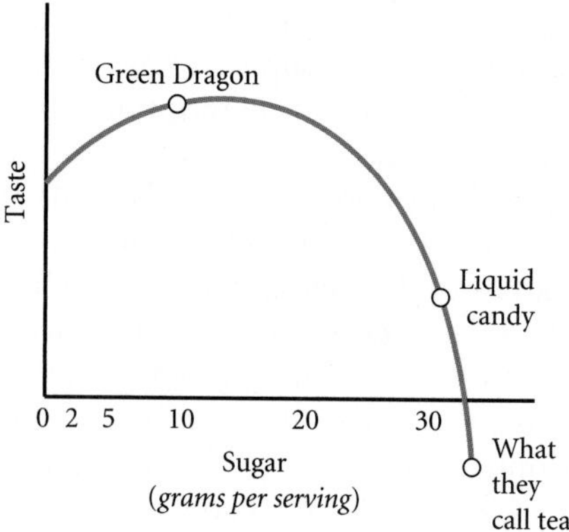

The critics clearly noticed that Green Dragon is not at the peak of the taste curve. That is, a little more sugar would improve the taste of the tea. Why did Nalebuff stop short of that point? This is product differentiation at its best. Goldman and Nalebuff are out to produce a new product that will attract demand. That is, at a reasonable price they must attract consumers away from other products. Goldman and Nalebuff discovered that sugar beyond some point adds little taste, yet comes at a health cost—more calories. Given consumers' new awareness of healthy and natural foods, Honest Tea became an overnight success. Since Nalebuff is an economist, he couldn't resist a graph on the label of the tea bottles

vertical differentiation A product difference that, from everyone's perspective, makes a product better than rival products.

Products can be differentiated not only horizontally but also **vertically**. A new BMW with GPS is better than one without for almost everyone. A hard drive with more capacity is better than one with less. The Hilton is better than a Motel 6 if they are located in the same place. How can a product survive in a competitive marketplace when another better product is available? The answer, of course, is in the price. The better products cost more, and only some people find it worthwhile to pay the higher price to get a better product. So differences among people also give rise to vertical differentiation. Some people value quality in a specific product more than others do and are willing to pay for that quality. If you are on a special date, it might be worthwhile to go to the best restaurant in town. On the other hand, while on a casual dinner with friends, watching your budget might be more important.

We have described the forces that help determine how much differentiation we will see in a market and the major forms that differentiation can take. We turn now to advertising, which plays a special role in the area of monopolistic competition.

Advertising

Advertising fits into the differentiation story in two different ways. One role advertising plays is to inform people about the real differences that exist among products. Advertising can also *create* or contribute to product differentiation, creating a brand image for a product that has little to do with its physical characteristics. We can all think of examples of each type.

Recent Coca-Cola ads trumpeting the "Coke Side of Life" have little to do with Coke's taste, for example. The dancers in iPod's ads create an image of hip and happy people rather than describe the technical features of the device. On the other hand, the advertising circulars in local newspapers carry specific information about what products are on sale that week in the local grocery store.

In 2006, firms spent about $250 billion on advertising, as Table 15.2 shows. Advertising reaches us through every medium of communication. Table 15.3 shows national advertising expenditures by major industrial category. The automobile industry leads the pack with expenditures of nearly $20 billion advertising in 2006. In 2008, 30 seconds of prime commercial advertising time during Super Bowl XLII cost $2.7 million.

TABLE 15.2 Total Advertising Expenditures in 2006

	Billions of Dollars
Newspapers	$49.0
Television	66.8
Direct mail	59.6
Yellow pages	14.4
Internet	15.0
Radio	19.1
Magazines	24.0
Total	247.9

Source: www.plunkettresearch.com

Many observers believe that the Internet is rapidly changing the way advertising works. Traditionally, companies have targeted their advertisements in both print and media. Beer commercials are shown during televised sporting events, toy commercials air during children's programs, and so on. The Internet has dramatically improved the ability of advertising to target a specific market. Consider advertising on Google. Under Google's AdWords system, which is a click-and-pay system, advertisers pay only when a Web surfer clicks to their site. In this way, advertisers are sure that people who see their advertisements are interested in the product. In 2006, Google earned over $6 billion from this form of targeted advertising.

YouTube, another new entrant into the advertising business, offers firms the opportunity to actively interact with customers. In addition to the standard video ads, firms can create online contests and brand channels to learn from customers about their preferences. Advertising as information has become more of a transparent two-way street as a result of the Internet.

The effects of product differentiation in general (and advertising in particular) on the allocation of resources have been hotly debated for years. Advocates claim that these forces give the market system its vitality and power. Critics argue that they cause waste and inefficiency. Before we proceed to the models of monopolistic competition and oligopoly, let us look at this debate.

TABLE 15.3 Domestic Advertising Spending by Category in 2006 in Billions of Dollars

Rank	Category	2006
1	Automotive	$19.8
2	Retail	19.1
3	Telecommunications	11.0
4	Medicine & Remedies	9.2
5	General services	8.7
6	Financial services	8.7
7	Food, beverages, & candy	7.2
8	Personal care	5.7
9	Airlines, hotels, car rental, travel	5.4
10	Movies, recorded video, & music	5.4
11	Restaurants	5.3
12	Media	5.1
13	Government, politics, religion	3.5
14	Insurance	3.5
15	Real estate	3.1
16	Apparel	2.9
17	Computers, software	2.5
18	Home furnishings	2.2
19	Beer, wine, & liquor	2.1
20	Education	1.9

Source: TNS Media Intelligence

The Case for Advertising For product differentiation to be successful, consumers must know about product quality and availability. In perfect competition, where all products are alike, we assume that consumers have perfect information; without it, the market fails to produce an efficient allocation of resources. Complete information is even more important when we allow for product differentiation. Consumers get this information through advertising, at least in part. The basic function of advertising, according to its proponents, is to assist consumers in making informed, rational choices. When we think of advertising, many of us think of the persuasive ads shown on television geared to changing our image of a product. Over the years, Budweiser has developed a reputation for clever ads of this sort, especially those delivered during the Super Bowl. But much advertising is entirely informational. In most parts of the country, one day a week the newspaper grows in size. On this day, stores advertise and promote their food sales. For many newspapers, advertisements are a big source of revenue; and it is all informational, helping consumers figure out where to buy their orange juice and chicken, for example. During the holiday season, toy advertising, both in print and on television, increases dramatically. For toys, which have a high rate of new product introduction, publicizing them is very important.

Supporters of advertising also note that it can promote competition. New products can compete with old, established brands only when promoters can get their messages through to consumers. The standard of living rises when we have product *innovation*, when new and better products come on the market. Think of all the products today that did not exist 20 years ago: iPods, DVD players, and many features of PCs, to name a few. When consumers are informed about a wide variety of potential substitutes, their market choices help discipline older firms that may have lost touch with consumers' tastes.

Even advertising that seems to function mostly to create and reinforce a brand image can have efficiency effects. Creating a brand name such as Coca-Cola or Tide requires a huge investment in marketing and advertising. The stronger the brand name and the more a firm has invested in creating that name, the more the firm will invest in trying to protect that name. In many cases, those investments provide benefits for consumers. In reacting to the 2007 news about lead in children's toys made in China, large toy companies such as Hasbro and Mattel spent millions in new testing of those toys. Restoring parental trust in the face of the lead toy recalls is vital to the future of the firms.

The advocates of spirited competition believe that differentiated products and advertising give the market system its vitality and are the basis of its power. They are the only ways to begin to satisfy the enormous range of tastes and preferences in a modern economy. Product differentiation helps to ensure high quality and variety, and advertising provides consumers with valuable information on product availability, quality, and price that they need to make efficient choices in the marketplace.

The Case Against Product Differentiation and Advertising Product differentiation and advertising waste society's scarce resources, argue critics. They say enormous sums of money are spent to create minute, meaningless differences among products.

Drugs, both prescription and nonprescription, are an example. Companies spend millions of dollars to promote brand-name drugs that contain the same compounds as those available under the generic names. The antibiotics erythromycin and erythrocin have the same ingredients, yet erythrocin is half as expensive as erythromycin. Aspirin is aspirin, yet we pay twice the price for an advertised brand because the manufacturer has convinced us that there is a tangible—or intangible—difference.

Do we really need 50 different kinds of soap, some of whose prices are increased by the cost of advertising? For a firm producing a differentiated product, advertising is part of the everyday cost of doing business. Its price is built into the average cost curve and thus into the price of the product in the short run and the long run. Thus, consumers pay to finance advertising.

Critics also argue that the information content of advertising is minimal at best and deliberately deceptive at worst. Advertising is meant to change our minds, to persuade us, and to create brand images. Try to determine how much real information there is in the next 10 advertisements you see on television. U.S. firms spend about $250 billion a year on advertising. Critics argue that firms waste a substantial portion of this money if the advertising does not clearly convey information to consumers.

Competitive advertising can also easily turn into unproductive warfare. Suppose there are five firms in an industry and one firm begins to advertise heavily. To survive, the others respond in kind. If one firm drops out of the race, it will certainly lose out. Advertising of this sort may not increase demand for the product or improve profitability for the industry. Instead, it is often a "zero sum game"—a game in which the sum of the gains equals the sum of the losses.

Advertising may also reduce competition by creating a barrier to the entry of new firms into an industry. One famous case study taught at the Harvard Business School calculates the cost of entering the brand-name breakfast cereal market. To be successful, a potential entrant would have to start with millions of dollars in an extensive advertising campaign to establish a brand name recognized by consumers. Entry to the breakfast cereal game is not completely blocked, but such financial requirements make entry very difficult.

Finally, some argue that advertising, by its very nature, imposes a cost on society. We are continuously bombarded by bothersome jingles and obtrusive images. When driving home from school or work, we may pass 50 billboards and listen to 15 minutes of news and 20 minutes of advertising on the radio. When we get home, we throw away 10 pieces of unsolicited junk mail, glance at a magazine containing 50 pages of writing and 75 pages of advertisements, and perhaps watch a television show that is interrupted every 5 minutes for a "message."

The bottom line, critics of product differentiation and advertising argue, is waste and inefficiency. Enormous sums are spent to create minute, meaningless, and possibly nonexistent differences among products. Advertising raises the cost of products and frequently contains very little information. Often, it is merely an annoyance. Product differentiation and advertising have turned the system upside down: People exist to satisfy the needs of the economy, not vice versa. Advertising can lead to unproductive warfare and may serve as a barrier to entry, thus reducing real competition.

ECONOMICS IN PRACTICE

Can Information Reduce Obesity?

Policy makers have been working to increase the level of information that consumers have about products. In the early 1990s, the Food and Drug Administration passed rules requiring most processed foods sold in grocery stores to carry nutrition labels. The current hot topic in the labeling area involves restaurant meals. With growing obesity in the United States, many policy makers think that one way to fight the problem is to require calorie and fat labeling in restaurants. The following article from the *Seattle Times* describes efforts along these lines in Seattle, Washington.

New rules: Menus must say what's in your meal

Seattle Times

Despite objections from restaurant owners and food-industry officials, the King County Board of Health on Thursday banned artificial trans fat and required nutritional labeling for menu items in chain restaurants.

With the vote, King County joins a handful of jurisdictions in the county to ban artificial trans fat in restaurant meals and becomes only the second to require nutrition labeling on menus.

While most restaurant owners and their supporters testified against the trans-fat ban—most said they're already getting rid of trans fats but they simply hate mandates—they saved their harshest words for the nutrition-labeling requirement.

Chris Clifford, a Renton resident who said he's owned several restaurants in King County,

said very few customers need labeling to know that a 16-ounce steak rolled in butter is fattening.

"I have a six-letter word to describe them: It's 'stupid!'" Clifford told the board, "You can't help stupid people." Instead of menu labeling, Clifford suggested a "warning label" on the restaurant door: "Eating here is fattening and could kill you."

On a more serious level, restaurant owners said the labeling requirement was unworkable and expensive, would possibly drive customers elsewhere—and pleaded for more time to find a less onerous solution.

But health providers and a number of diabetic and heart patients in the standing-room-only crowd said customers deserve to have enough information to make healthful choices.

Some economists have suggested that instead of information, the price mechanism should be used to reduce obesity. The proposal is to tax high-fat foods.

Source: Carol M. Ostrom, Seattle Times health reporter. Seattle Times July 25, 2007.

Open Questions You will see over and over as you study economics that many questions remain open. There are strong arguments on both sides of the advertising debate, and even the empirical evidence yields to conflicting conclusions. Some studies show that advertising leads to concentration and positive profits; others, that advertising improves the functioning of the market.

Price and Output Determination in Monopolistic Competition

Recall that monopolistically competitive industries are made up of a large number of firms, each small relative to the size of the total market. Thus, no one firm can affect market price by virtue of its size alone. Firms do differentiate their products, however, in ways we have been discussing. By doing so, they gain some control over price.

Product Differentiation and Demand Elasticity

Perfectly competitive firms face a perfectly elastic demand for their product: All firms in a perfectly competitive industry produce exactly the same product. If firm A tried to raise prices, buyers would go elsewhere and firm A would sell nothing. When a firm can distinguish its product from all others in the minds of consumers, as we assume it can under monopolistic competition, it probably can raise price without losing all quantity demanded. Figure 15.2 shows how product differentiation might make demand somewhat less elastic for a hypothetical firm.

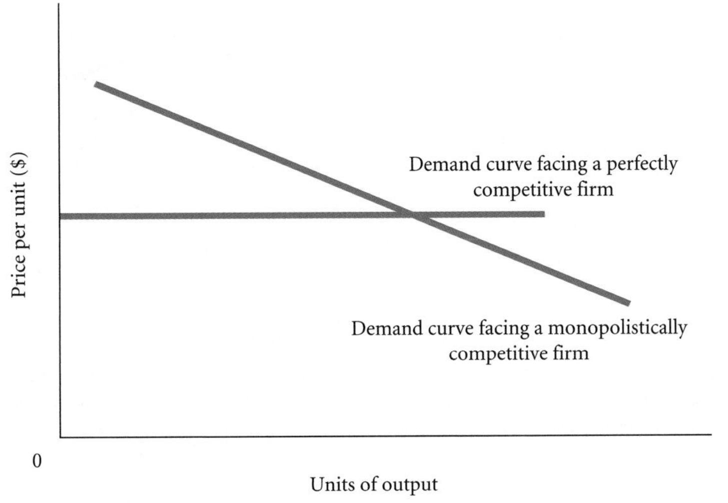

FIGURE 15.2
Product Differentiation Reduces the Elasticity of Demand Facing a Firm
The demand curve that a monopolistic competitor faces is likely to be less elastic than the demand curve that a perfectly competitive firm faces. Demand is more elastic than the demand curve that a monopolist faces because close substitutes for the products of a monopolistic competitor are available.

A monopoly is an industry with a single firm that produces a good for which there are no close substitutes. A monopolistically competitive firm is like a monopoly in that it is the only producer of its unique product. Only one firm can produce Cheerios or Wheat Thins or Johnson's Baby Shampoo or Oreo cookies. However, unlike the product in a monopoly market, the product of a monopolistically competitive firm has many close substitutes competing for the consumer's favor. Although the demand curve that a monopolistic competitor faces is likely to be less elastic than the demand curve that a perfectly competitive firm faces, it is likely to be more elastic than the demand curve that a monopoly faces.

Price/Output Determination in the Short Run

Under conditions of monopolistic competition, a profit-maximizing firm behaves much like a monopolist in the short run. First, marginal revenue is not equal to price because the monopolistically competitive firm has some control over output price. Like a monopolistic firm, a monopolistically competitive firm must lower price to increase output and sell it. The monopolistic competitor's marginal revenue curve thus lies *below* its demand curve, intersecting the quantity axis midway between the origin and the point at which the demand curve intersects it. (If necessary, review Chapter 13 to make sure you understand this idea.) The firm chooses the output/price combination that maximizes profit. To maximize profit, the monopolistically competitive firm will increase production until the marginal revenue from increasing output and selling it no longer exceeds the marginal cost of producing it. This occurs at the point at which marginal revenue equals marginal cost: $MR = MC$.

In Figure 15.3(a), the profit-maximizing output is $q_0 = 2{,}000$, where marginal revenue equals marginal cost. To sell 2,000 units, the firm must charge \$6. Total revenue is $P_0 \times q_0 = \$12{,}000$, or the area of P_0Aq_00. Total cost is equal to average total cost times q_0, which is \$10,000, or CBq_00. Total profit is the difference, \$2,000 (the gray-shaded area P_0ABC).

Nothing guarantees that a firm in a monopolistically competitive industry will earn positive profits in the short run. Figure 15.3(b) shows what happens when a firm with similar cost curves faces a weaker market demand. Even though the firm does have some control over price, market demand is insufficient to make the firm profitable.

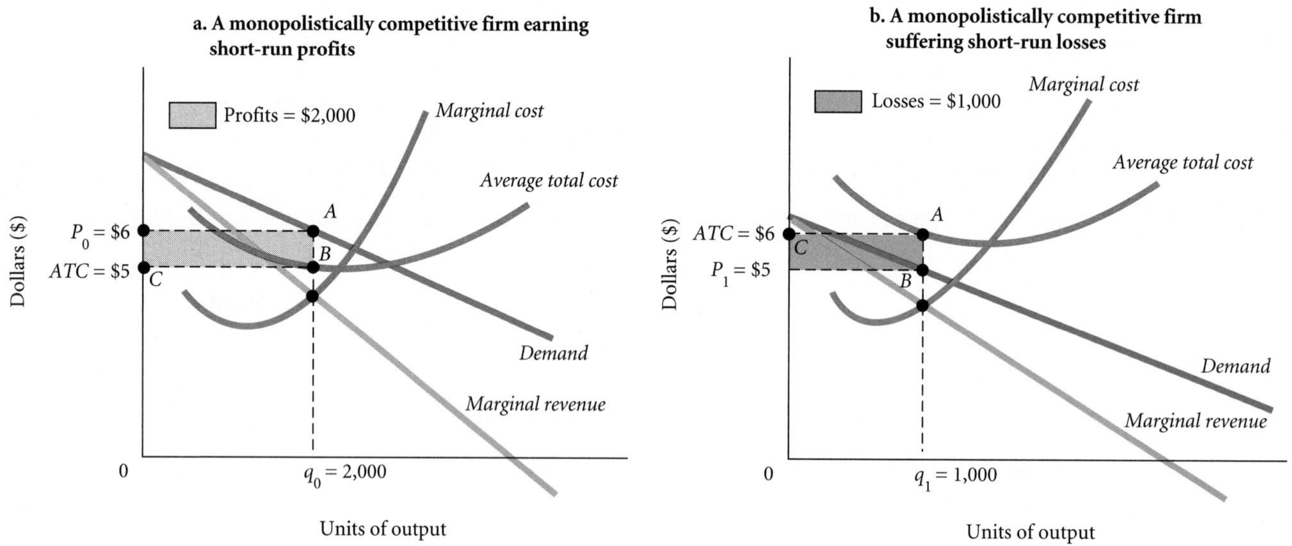

▲ **FIGURE 15.3 Monopolistic Competition in the Short Run**
In the short run, a monopolistically competitive firm will produce up to the point $MR = MC$. At $q_0 = 2{,}000$ in panel a, the firm is earning short-run profits equal to $P_0ABC = \$2{,}000$. In panel b, another monopolistically competitive firm with a similar cost structure is shown facing a weaker demand and suffering short-run losses at $q_1 = 1{,}000$, equal to $CABP_1 = \$1{,}000$.

As in perfect competition, such a firm minimizes its losses by producing up to the point where marginal revenue is equal to marginal cost. Of course, as in perfect competition, the price that the firm charges must be sufficient to cover average variable costs. Otherwise, the firm will shut down and suffer losses equal to total fixed costs instead of increasing losses by producing more. In Figure 15.3(b), the loss-minimizing level of output is $q_1 = 1{,}000$ at a price of \$5. Total revenue is $P_1 \times q_1 = \$5{,}000$, or P_1Bq_10. Total cost is $ATC \times q_1 = \$6{,}000$, or CAq_10. Because total cost is greater than revenue, the firm suffers a loss of \$1,000, equal to the pink-shaded area, $CABP_1$.

Price/Output Determination in the Long Run

In analyzing monopolistic competition, we assume that entry and exit are easy in the long run. Firms can enter an industry when there are profits to be made, and firms suffering losses can go out of business. However, entry into an industry of this sort is somewhat different from entry into perfect competition because products are differentiated in monopolistic competition. A firm that enters a monopolistically competitive industry is producing a close substitute for the good in question, *but not the same good.*

Let us begin with a firm earning positive profits in the short run, as shown on the left-hand side of Figure 15.3. Those profits provide an incentive for new firms to enter the industry. This entry creates new substitutes for the profit-making firm, which, in turn, drives down demand for its product. For example, if several restaurants seem to be doing well in a particular location, others may start up and take business from the existing restaurants.

New firms will continue to enter the market until profits are eliminated. As the new firms enter, the demand curve facing each old firm begins to shift to the left, pushing the marginal revenue curve along with it. (Review Chapter 13 if you are unsure why.) This shift continues until profits are eliminated, which occurs when the demand curve slips down to the average total cost curve. Graphically, this is the point at which the demand curve and the average total cost curve are tangent (the point at which they just touch and have the same slope). Figure 15.4 shows a monopolistically competitive industry in long-run equilibrium. At q^* and P^*, price and average total cost are equal; so there are no profits or losses.

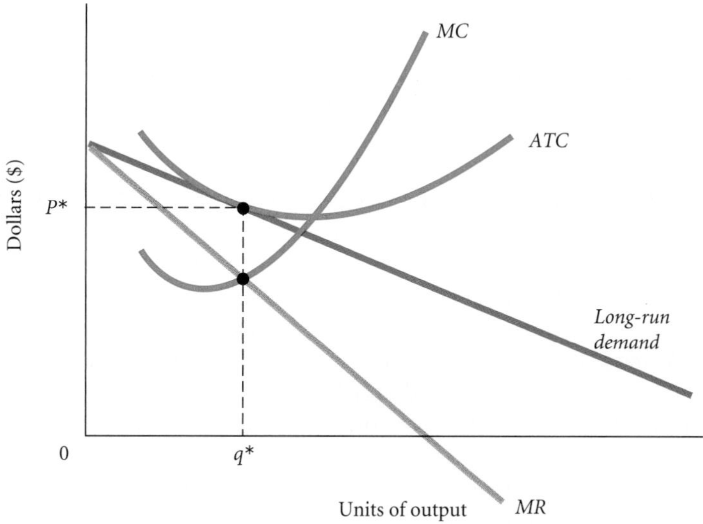

FIGURE 15.4 Monopolistically Competitive Firm at Long-Run Equilibrium

As new firms enter a monopolistically competitive industry in search of profits, the demand curves of profit-making existing firms begin to shift to the left, pushing marginal revenue with them as consumers switch to the new close substitutes. This process continues until profits are eliminated, which occurs for a firm when its demand curve is just tangent to its average total cost curve.

Look carefully at the tangency, which in Figure 15.4, is at output level q^*. The tangency occurs at the profit-maximizing level of output. At this point, marginal cost is equal to marginal revenue. At any level of output other than q^*, *ATC* lies above the demand curve. This means that at any other level of output, *ATC* is greater than the price that the firm can charge. (Recall that the demand curve shows the price that can be charged at every level of output.) Hence, price equals average total cost at q^* and profits equal zero.

This equilibrium must occur at the point at which the demand curve is *just tangent* to the average total cost curve. If the demand curve cuts across the average cost curve, intersecting it at two points, the demand curve would be *above* the average total cost curve at some levels of output. Producing at those levels of output would mean positive profits. Positive profits would attract entrants, shifting the market demand curve to the left and lowering profits. If the demand curve were always *below* the average total cost curve, all levels of output would produce losses for the firm. This would cause firms to exit the industry, shifting the market demand curve to the right and increasing profits (or reducing losses) for those firms still in the industry. The firm's demand curve must end up tangent to its average total cost curve for profits to equal zero. This is the condition for long-run equilibrium in a monopolistically competitive industry.

Even if some monopolistically competitive firms start with losses, the long-run equilibrium will be zero profits for all firms remaining in the industry. (Look back at Figure 15.3(b), which shows a firm suffering losses.) Suppose many restaurants open in a small area, for example. In Columbus, Ohio, near the intersection of I-270 and Fishinger Road, there are a dozen or so "quick dinner" restaurants crowded into a small area. Given so many restaurants, it seems likely that there will be a "shake-out" sometime in the near future—that is, one or more of the restaurants suffering losses will decide to drop out of the market.

When this happens, the firms remaining in the industry will get a larger share of the total business; and their demand curves will shift to the right. Firms will continue to drop out, and the demand curves of the remaining firms will continue to shift until all losses are eliminated. Thus, we end up with the same long-run equilibrium as when we started out, with firms earning positive profits. At equilibrium, demand is tangent to average total cost and there are no profits or losses.

Economic Efficiency and Resource Allocation

We have already noted some of the similarities between monopolistic competition and perfect competition. Because entry is easy and economic profits are eliminated in the long run, we might conclude that the result of monopolistic competition is efficient. There are two problems, however.

First, once a firm achieves any degree of market power by differentiating its product (as is the case in monopolistic competition), its profit-maximizing strategy is to hold down production and charge a price above marginal cost, as you saw in Figure 15.3 and Figure 15.4. Remember from Chapter 12 that price is the value that society places on a good and that marginal cost is the value that society places on the resources needed to produce that good. By holding production down and price above marginal cost, monopolistically competitive firms prevent the efficient use of resources. More product could be produced at a resource cost below the value that consumers place on the product.

Second, as Figure 15.4 shows, the final equilibrium in a monopolistically competitive firm is necessarily to the left of the low point on its average total cost curve. That means a typical firm in a monopolistically competitive industry will not realize all the economies of scale available. (In perfect competition, you will recall, firms are pushed to the bottom of their long-run average cost curves, and the result is an efficient allocation of resources.)

Suppose a number of firms enter an industry and build plants on the basis of initially profitable positions. As more firms compete for those profits, individual firms find themselves with smaller market shares; eventually, they end up with "excess capacity." The firm in Figure 15.4 is not fully using its existing capacity because competition drove its demand curve to the left. In monopolistic competition, we end up with many firms, each producing a slightly different product at a scale that is less than optimal. Would it not be more efficient to have a smaller number of firms, each producing on a slightly larger scale?

The costs of less-than-optimal production, however, need to be balanced against the gains that can accrue from aggressive competition among products. If product differentiation leads to the introduction of new products, improvements in old products, and greater variety, an important gain in economic welfare may counteract (and perhaps outweigh) the loss of efficiency from pricing above marginal cost or not fully realizing all economies of scale.

Most industries that comfortably fit the model of monopolistic competition are very competitive. Price competition coexists with product competition, and firms do not earn incredible profits and do not violate any of the antitrust laws that we discussed in the last chapter. Monopolistically competitive firms have not been a subject of great concern among economic policy makers. Their behavior appears to be sufficiently controlled by competitive forces, and no serious attempt has been made to regulate or control them.

SUMMARY

INDUSTRY CHARACTERISTICS *p. 304*

1. A monopolistically competitive industry has the following structural characteristics: (1) a large number of firms, (2) no barriers to entry, and (3) *product differentiation*. Relatively good substitutes for a monopolistic competitor's products are available. Monopolistic competitors try to achieve a degree of market power by differentiating their products.

PRODUCT DIFFERENTIATION AND ADVERTISING *p. 305*

2. The amount of product differentiation in an industry depends on a number of features of the industry. How different are customers' tastes? Are there gains to customers in buying a product that is identical to one bought by everyone else? Are there large-scale economies associated with making only one variety of a good? Industries with many different products reflect strong heterogeneity of consumers, low gains from coordination, and small cost gains from standardization.

3. Products can be differentiated horizontally or vertically. Horizontal differentiation produces different types of a good with different appeals to different types of people. In vertical differentiation, people agree that one product is better than another; they just may not be willing to pay for the better good.

4. *Behavioral economics* suggests that there may be times when too much variety reduces consumers' purchases.
5. Behavioral economics also suggests that there may be times when consumers prefer one form of a good over another as a way to commit themselves to different actions in the future than they would otherwise take.
6. Advocates of free and open competition believe that differentiated products and advertising give the market system its vitality and are the basis of its power. Critics argue that product differentiation and advertising are wasteful and inefficient.

PRICE AND OUTPUT DETERMINATION IN MONOPOLISTIC COMPETITION *p. 313*

7. By differentiating their products, firms hope to be able to raise prices without losing all demand. The demand curve facing a monopolistic competitor is less elastic than the demand curve faced by a perfectly competitive firm but more elastic than the demand curve faced by a monopoly.
8. To maximize profit in the short run, a monopolistically competitive firm will produce as long as the marginal revenue from increasing output and selling it exceeds the marginal cost of producing it.
9. When firms enter a monopolistically competitive industry, they introduce close substitutes for the goods being produced. This attracts demand away from the firms already in the industry. Demand faced by each firm shifts left, and profits are ultimately eliminated in the long run. This long-run equilibrium occurs at the point where the demand curve is just tangent to the average total cost curve.

ECONOMIC EFFICIENCY AND RESCOURCE ALLOCATION *p. 316*

10. Monopolistically competitive firms end up pricing above marginal cost. This is inefficient, as is the fact that monopolistically competitive firms do not realize all economies of scale available. There may be off-setting gains from increased variety.

REVIEW TERMS AND CONCEPTS

behavioral economics, *p. 307*
commitment device, *p. 307*
horizontal differentiation, *p. 306*
monopolistic competition, *p. 304*
product differentiation, *p. 305*
vertical differentiation, *p. 308*

PROBLEMS

Visit **www.myeconlab.com** to complete the problems marked in orange online. You will receive instant feedback on your answers, tutorial help, and access to additional practice problems.

1. For each of the following, state whether you agree or disagree. Explain your answer.
   a. Monopolistically competitive firms produce their economic profits protected by barriers to entry.
   b. Monopolistically competitive firms are efficient because in the long run, price falls to equal marginal cost.
2. Consider the local music scene in your area. Name some of the local live bands that play in clubs and music halls, both on and off campus. Look in your local newspaper for advertisements of upcoming shows or performances. How would you characterize the market for local musicians? Is there product differentiation? In what specific ways do firms (individual performers or bands) compete? To what degree are they able to exercise market power? Are there barriers to entry? How profitable do you think the musicians are?
3. Write a brief essay explaining this statement: The Beatles were once a monopolistically competitive firm that became a monopolist.
4. In a market in which there is vertical differentiation, we always see price differences among the products. In markets with horizontal differentiation, sometimes the products differ but prices are very much the same. Why does vertical differentiation naturally bring with it price differences?
5. [Related to *Economics in Practice* on *p. 308*] If you look at the prices listed in the *Economics in Practice* on p. 308, you will see that the more well-known brands are being sold for a lower price than the less well-known brands. Is this pattern always true? Explain your answer.
6. [Related to *Economics in Practice* on *p. 312*] The news story tells us that most restaurant owners oppose the labeling requirement. Why? Since restaurants compete with one another, would you not expect some of the healthier restaurants to come out in favor of the rule? Explain.
7. The table shows the relationship for a hypothetical firm between its advertising expenditures and the quantity of its output that it expects it can sell at a fixed price of $5 per unit.

ADVERTISING EXPENDITURES (MILLIONS)	QUANTITY SOLD AT P = $5/IN MILLION UNITS
$1	8
$1.2	9
$1.4	9.4
$1.6	9.6
$1.8	9.7

   a. In economic terms, why might the relationship between advertising and sales look the way it does?

b. Assume that the marginal costs of producing this product (not including the advertising costs) are a constant $4. How much advertising should this firm be doing? What economic principle are you using to make this decision?

8. In the area around a local university, a number of food vendors gather each lunchtime to sell food to university students who are tired of dorm food. The university and the town have no license fees that apply to food vendors, preferring to let the market dictate how many and which vendors show up.

Many different cuisines are represented on the street corner, including a cart sponsored by Madame Defarge selling gumbo and jambalaya. Madame Defarge sells a plate of either gumbo or jambalaya for $5. The food is made in the morning at her nearby restaurant, when the kitchen is otherwise unoccupied. Her crew of three, each of whom earns $15 per hour, takes 2 hours to make the 100 meals required by Madame Defarge. In creating these meals, they use ingredients equal to $100. Madame Defarge hires another worker to load her cart with food and sell it during the lunch hours. That worker costs $10 per hour and typically sells out the entire cart of 100 meals in 2 hours. The cart is rented for $100 per 5-day week. (The carts are not in operation on the weekends, when Madame Defarge is too busy at her restaurant.)

a. What market structure does this business most resemble? What characteristics lead you to this conclusion?

b. What would you expect to see happen in this business? Use the data in the problem to support your conclusions.

c. How would your calculations change if Madame Defarge were to develop a weekday lunch business that used the kitchen's capacity?

Externalities, Public Goods, and Social Choice

16

CHAPTER OUTLINE

In Chapters 6 through 12, we built a complete model of a perfectly competitive economy under a set of assumptions. By Chapter 12, we had demonstrated that the allocation of resources under perfect competition is efficient and we began to relax some of the assumptions on which the perfectly competitive model is based. We introduced the idea of **market failure**, and in Chapters 13, 14, and 15, we talked about three kinds of imperfect markets: monopoly, oligopoly, and monopolistic competition. We also discussed some of the ways government has responded to the inefficiencies of imperfect markets and to the development of market power.

As we continue our examination of market failure, we look first at *externalities* as a source of inefficiency. Often when we engage in transactions or make economic decisions, second or third parties suffer consequences that decision makers have no incentive to consider. For example, for many years, manufacturing firms and power plants had no reason to worry about the impact of smoke from their operations on the quality of the air we breathe. Now we know that air pollution—an externality—harms people.

Next, we consider a second type of market failure that involves products that private firms find unprofitable to produce even if members of society want them. These products are called *public goods* or *social goods*. Public goods yield collective benefits, and in most societies, governments produce them or arrange to provide them. The process of choosing what social goods to produce is very different from the process of private choice.

Finally, while the existence of externalities and public goods are examples of market failure, it is not necessarily true that government involvement always improves matters. Just as markets fail, so too can governments. When we look at the incentives facing government decision makers, we find several reasons behind government failure.

market failure Occurs when resources are misallocated or allocated inefficiently.

Externalities and Environmental Economics

An **externality** exists when the actions or decisions of one person or group impose a cost or bestow a benefit on second or third parties. Externalities are sometimes called *spillovers* or *neighborhood effects*. Inefficient decisions result when decision makers fail to consider social costs and benefits.

The presence of externalities is a significant phenomenon in modern life. Examples are everywhere: Air, water, land, sight, and sound pollution; traffic congestion; automobile accidents; abandoned housing; nuclear accidents; and secondhand cigarette smoke are only a few. The study of externalities is a major concern of *environmental economics.*

externality A cost or benefit imposed or bestowed on an individual or a group that is outside, or external to, the transaction.

The opening of Eastern Europe in 1989 and 1990 revealed that environmental externalities are not limited to free market economies. Part of the logic of a planned economy is that when economic decisions are made socially (by the government, presumably acting on behalf of the people) instead of privately, planners can and will take all costs—private and social—into account. This has not been the case, however. When East and West Germany were reunited and the borders of Europe were opened, we saw the disastrous condition of the environment in virtually all of Eastern Europe.

As societies become more urbanized, externalities become more important: When we live more closely together, our actions are more likely to affect others.

Marginal Social Cost and Marginal-Cost Pricing

Profit-maximizing perfectly competitive firms will produce output up to the point at which price is equal to marginal cost ($P = MC$). Let us take a moment to review why this is essential to the proposition that perfectly competitive markets produce what people want—an efficient mix of output.

When a firm weighs price and marginal cost and no externalities exist, it is weighing the full benefits to society of additional production against the full costs to society of that production. Those who benefit from the production of a product are the people or households who end up consuming it. The price of a product is a good measure of what an additional unit of that product is "worth" because those who value it more highly already buy it. People who value it less than the current price are not buying it. If marginal cost includes all costs—that is, all costs *to society*—of producing a marginal unit of a good, additional production will be efficient, provided P is greater than MC. Up to the point where $P = MC$, each unit of production yields benefits in excess of cost.

Consider a firm in the business of producing laundry detergent. As long as the price per unit that consumers pay for that detergent exceeds the cost of the resources needed to produce one additional unit of it, the firm will continue to produce. Producing up to the point where $P = MC$ is efficient because for every unit of detergent produced, consumers derive benefits that exceed the cost of the resources needed to produce it. Producing at a point where $MC > P$ is inefficient because marginal cost will rise above the unit price of the detergent. For every unit produced beyond the level at which $P = MC$, society uses resources that cost more than the benefits that consumers place on detergent. Figure 16.1 shows a firm and an industry in which no externalities exist.

Suppose, however, that the production of the firm's product imposes external costs on society as well. If the firm does not factor those additional costs into its decisions, it is likely to overproduce. In Figure 16.1(b), a certain measure of external costs is added to the firm's marginal cost curve. We see these external costs in the graph, but the firm is ignoring them. The curve labeled *MSC*, **marginal social cost**, is the sum of the marginal costs of producing the product and the correctly measured damage costs imposed in the process of production.

marginal social cost (*MSC*) The total cost to society of producing an additional unit of a good or service. *MSC* is equal to the sum of the marginal costs of producing the product and the correctly measured damage costs involved in the process of production.

If the firm does not have to pay for these damage costs, it will produce exactly the same level of output (q^*) as before and price (P^*) will continue to reflect only the costs that the firm actually pays to produce its product. The firms in this industry will continue to produce, and consumers will continue to consume their product; but the market price takes into account only part of the full cost of producing the good. At equilibrium (q^*), marginal social costs are considerably greater than *price*. (Recall that *price* is a measure of the full value to consumers of a unit of the product at the margin.)

Suppose our detergent plant freely dumps untreated toxic waste into a river. The waste imposes specific costs on people who live downstream: It kills the fish in the river, it makes the river ugly to look at and rotten to smell, and it destroys the river for recreational use. There may also be health hazards depending on what chemicals the firm is dumping. Obviously, the plant's product provides certain benefits. Its soap is valuable to consumers who are willing and able to pay for it. The firm employs people and capital, and its revenues are sufficient to cover all costs. The issue is how the *net benefits* produced by the plant compare with the damage that it does. You do not need an economic model to know that *someone* should consider the costs of those damages.

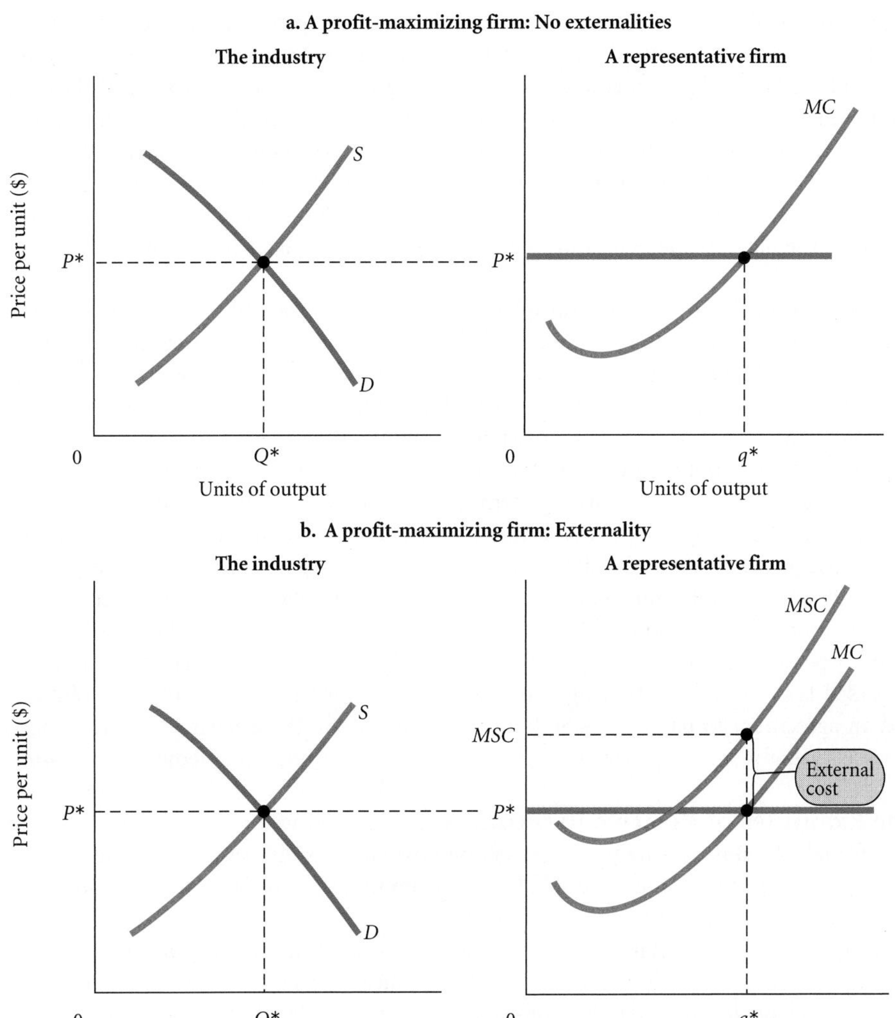

◀ FIGURE 16.1

Profit-Maximizing Perfectly Competitive Firms Will Produce Up to the Point That Price Equals Marginal Cost (*P* = *MC*)

If we assume that the current price reflects what consumers are willing to pay for a product at the margin, firms that create external costs without weighing them in their decisions are likely to produce too much. At q^*, marginal social cost exceeds the price paid by consumers.

Acid Rain and the Clean Air Act Acid rain is an excellent example of an externality and of the issues and conflicts involved in dealing with externalities. Manufacturing firms and power plants in the Midwest burn coal with a high sulfur content. When the smoke from those plants mixes with moisture in the atmosphere, the result is a dilute acid that is windblown north to Canada and east to New York and New England, where it falls to the earth in the rain. The subject of a major conflict between the U.S. and Canadian governments and between industry and environmental groups, this acid rain is imposing enormous costs where it falls. Estimates of damage from fish kills, building deterioration, and deforestation range into the billions of dollars.

Decision makers at the manufacturing firms and public utilities using high-sulfur coal should weigh these costs, of course, but there is another side to this story. Burning cheap coal and not worrying about the acid rain that may be falling on someone else means jobs and cheap power for residents of the Midwest. Forcing coal-burning plants to pay for past damages from acid rain or requiring them to begin weighing the costs that they are presently imposing will undoubtedly raise electricity prices and production costs in the Midwest. Some firms will be driven out of business, and some jobs will be lost. However, if the electricity and other products produced in the Midwest are worth the full costs imposed by acid rain, plants will not shut down, and consumers will pay higher prices. If those goods are not worth the full cost, they should not be produced, at least not in current quantities or through the use of current production methods.

The case of acid rain highlights the fact that efficiency analysis ignores the *distribution* of gains and losses. That is, to establish efficiency, we need only demonstrate that the total value of the gains exceeds the total value of the losses. If midwestern producers and consumers of their products were forced to pay an amount equal to the damages they caused, the gains from reduced damage in the East and in Canada would be at least as great as costs in the Midwest. The beneficiaries of forcing midwestern firms to consider these costs would be the households and firms in the East and in Canada. After many years of debate, Congress passed and President George H. W. Bush signed the Clean Air Act of 1990. Included in the law are strict emissions standards aimed, in part, at controlling the production and distribution of acid rain. An interesting provision of the Clean Air Act is its use of "tradable pollution rights," which we discuss later in this chapter.

Other Externalities Other examples of external effects are all around us. When people drive their cars into the center of the city at rush hour, they contribute to the congestion and impose costs (in the form of lost time and auto emissions) on others. Clearly, the most significant and hotly debated issue of externalities is global warming. The 2007 Nobel Peace Prize was awarded to former Vice President Al Gore and the Intergovernmental Panel on Climate Change, a group of 2,500 researchers from 130 nations that issued a number of reports linking human activity to the recent rise of the average temperature on Earth. Although there is considerable disagreement, many people are convinced that strong measures must be taken to prevent major adverse consequences such as dramatically rising sea levels. We will return to this topic later.

Secondhand cigarette smoke has become a matter of public concern. In December 1994, a judge in Florida ruled that nonsmokers could bring a class-action suit based on the health consequences of passive smoke. Smoking has been banned on domestic air carriers, and many states have passed laws severely restricting smoking in public places. In 1997, the big tobacco firms signed an agreement to pay over $350 billion to compensate those harmed by smoking and to reimburse states for smoking-related medical expenses paid under the Medicaid program.

Some Examples of Positive Externalities Thus far we have described a series of negative externalities. But externalities can also be positive. In some cases, when other people or firms engage in an activity, there are side *benefits* from that activity. From an economics perspective, there are problems with positive externalities as well.

Ian Ayres and Steve Levitt have studied a fascinating example of a product with positive externalities, LoJack. LoJack is a device that allows police to track a car when it is stolen. When a car has a LoJack device installed, the gains to stealing that car are sharply reduced. These devices not only help recover cars but also help catch car thieves. Suppose that 90 percent of the cars in a community had LoJack installed. If all LoJack cars were identified—the way houses are that have burglar alarms—potential thieves could look for the unmarked cars. As it happens, LoJack does not come with any identifying mark. From a thief's perspective, any car has a 90 percent chance of having a LoJack installed. As a result, the benefits from stealing *any* car are reduced. With reduced benefits, fewer thefts occur. Ayres and Levitt have found that the size of these positive externalities are very large; they estimate that the purchaser of a LoJack captures, as an individual, only 10 percent of the value of the device.[1]

We also see positive externalities in the case of vaccinations. The more people who are vaccinated, the less likely a disease will become prevalent. But the less likely the disease, the lower the private benefits to people from getting a vaccination. With communicable diseases, health precautions taken by an individual have positive external benefits to the rest of the community.

The problem with positive externalities should now be clear. For this type of externality, the individuals in charge have too little incentive to engage in the activity. Too few LoJacks are bought; too few people wash their hands often; too few people would vaccinate their children unless forced to do so by school systems.

Private Choices and External Effects

To help us understand externalities, let us use a simple two-person example. Harry lives in a dormitory at a big public college in the Southwest, where he is a first-year student. When he graduated from high school, his family gave him an expensive stereo system. Unfortunately, the walls of

[1] Ian Ayres and Steve Levitt, Measuring Positive Externalities from Unobservable Victim Precautions: An Empirical Analysis of Lojack, *Quarterly Journal of Economics*, Vol. 108, no. 1, 1998.

Harry's dorm are made of quarter-inch drywall over 3-inch aluminum studs. You can hear people sleeping four rooms away. Harry likes bluegrass music of the "twangy" kind. Because of a hearing loss after an accident on the Fourth of July some years ago, he often does not notice the volume of his music.

Jake, who lives next door to Harry, is not much of a music lover; but when he does listen to music, he prefers Brahms and Mozart. So Harry's music bothers Jake.

Let us assume that there are no further external costs or benefits to anyone other than Harry and Jake. Figure 16.2 illustrates the decision process that the two dorm residents face. The downward-sloping curve labeled *MB* represents the value of the marginal benefits that Harry derives from listening to his music. Of course, Harry does not sit down to draw this curve, any more than anyone else (other than an economics student) sits down to draw actual demand curves. Curves like this are simply abstract representations of the way people behave. If you think about it, such a curve must exist. To ask how much an hour of listening to music is worth to you is to ask how much you would be willing to pay to have it. Start at $0.01 and raise the "price" slowly in your mind. Presumably, you must stop at some point. Where you stop depends on your taste for music and your income.

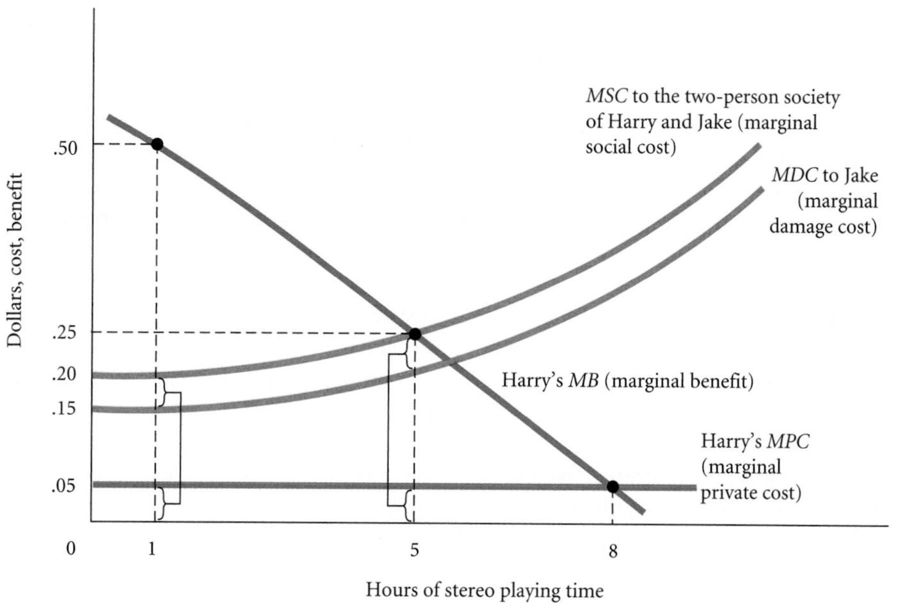

◀ FIGURE 16.2 Externalities in a College Dormitory

The marginal benefits to Harry exceed the marginal costs he must bear to play his stereo system for a period of up to 8 hours. When the stereo is playing, a cost is being imposed on Jake. When we add the costs borne by Harry to the damage costs imposed on Jake, we get the full cost of the stereo to the two-person society made up of Harry and Jake. Playing the stereo more than 5 hours is inefficient because the benefits to Harry are less than the social cost for every hour above 5. If Harry considers only his private costs, he will play the stereo for too long a time from society's point of view.

You can think about the benefits Harry derives from listening to bluegrass as the maximum amount of money that he would be willing to pay to listen to his music for an hour. For the first hour, for instance, the value for *MB* is $0.50. We assume diminishing marginal utility, of course. The more hours Harry listens, the lower the additional benefits from each successive hour. As the graph shows, the *MB* curve falls below $0.05 per hour after 8 hours of listening.

marginal private cost (*MPC*) The amount that a consumer pays to consume an additional unit of a particular good.

We call the cost that Harry must pay for each additional hour of listening to music **marginal private cost**, labeled *MPC* in Figure 16.2. In the present example, this cost is primarily the cost of electricity. This cost is constant at $0.05 per hour.

marginal damage cost (*MDC*) The additional harm done by increasing the level of an externality-producing activity by 1 unit. If producing product *X* pollutes the water in a river, *MDC* is the additional cost imposed by the added pollution that results from increasing output by 1 unit of *X* per period.

Then there is Jake. Although Harry's music does not poison Jake, give him lung cancer, or even cause him to lose money, it damages him nonetheless: He gets a headache, loses sleep, and cannot concentrate on his work. Jake is harmed, and it is possible (at least conceptually) to measure that harm in terms of the maximum amount that he would be willing to pay to avoid it. The damage, or cost, imposed on Jake is represented in Figure 16.2 by the curve labeled *MDC*. Formally, **marginal damage cost (*MDC*)** is the additional harm done by increasing the level of an externality-producing activity by 1 unit. By assuming Jake would be willing to pay some amount of money to avoid the music, it is reasonable to assume the amount increases each successive hour. His headache gets worse with each additional hour he is forced to listen to bluegrass.

In the simple society of Jake and Harry, it is easy to add up social benefits and costs. At every level of output (stereo playing time), total social cost is the sum of the private costs borne by Harry and the damage costs borne by Jake. In Figure 16.2, *MPC* (constant at $0.05 per hour) is added to *MDC* to get *MSC*. The social optimum occurs where the marginal social benefit equals the marginal social cost.

Now consider what would happen if Harry simply ignored Jake.[2] If Harry decides to play the stereo, Jake will be damaged. As long as Harry gains more in personal benefits from an additional hour of listening to music than he incurs in costs, the stereo system will stay on. He will play it for 8 hours (the point where Harry's *MB* = *MPC*). This result is inefficient; for every hour of play beyond 5, the marginal social cost borne by society—in this case, a society made up of Harry and Jake—exceeds the marginal benefits to Harry—that is, *MSC* > Harry's MB. It is generally true that when economic decisions ignore external costs, whether those costs are borne by one person or by society, those decisions are likely to be inefficient. We will return to Harry and Jake to see how they deal with their problem. First, we need to discuss the general problem of correcting for externalities.

Internalizing Externalities

A number of mechanisms are available to provide decision makers with incentives to weigh the external costs and benefits of their decisions, a process called *internalization*. In some cases, externalities are internalized through bargaining and negotiation without government involvement. In other cases, private bargains fail and the only alternative may be government action of some kind.

Five approaches have been taken to solving the problem of externalities: (1) government-imposed taxes and subsidies, (2) private bargaining and negotiation, (3) legal rules and procedures, (4) sale or auctioning of rights to impose externalities, and (5) direct government regulation. While each is best suited for a different set of circumstances, all five provide decision makers with an incentive to weigh the external effects of their decisions.

Taxes and Subsidies Traditionally, economists have advocated marginal taxes and subsidies as a direct way of forcing firms to consider external costs or benefits. When a firm imposes an external social cost, the reasoning goes, a per-unit tax should be imposed equal to the damages of each successive unit of output produced by the firm—the tax should be *exactly equal* to marginal damage costs.[3]

Figure 16.3 repeats Figure 16.1(b), but this time the damage costs are paid by the firm in the form of a per-unit tax—that is, the tax = *MDC*. The firm now faces a marginal cost curve that is the same as the marginal social cost curve (MC_1 = *MSC*). Remember that the industry supply curve is the sum of the marginal cost curves of the individual firms. This means that as a result of the tax, the industry supply curve shifts to the left, driving up price from P_0 to P_1. The efficient level of output is q_1, where $P = MC_1$. (Recall our general equilibrium analysis from Chapter 12.)

Because a profit-maximizing firm equates price with marginal cost, the new price to consumers covers the resource costs of producing the product and the damage costs. The consumer decision process is once again efficient at the margin because marginal social benefit as reflected in market price is equal to the full social marginal cost of the product.

An interesting example of the use of taxes to reduce pollution is the tax that London has placed on cars driving into the central part of the city. New York's Mayor Bloomberg considered a similar policy.

Measuring Damages The biggest problem with using taxes and subsidies is that damages must be estimated in financial terms. For the detergent plant polluting the nearby river to be properly taxed, the government must evaluate the damages done to residents downstream in money terms. This evaluation is difficult but not impossible. When legal remedies are pursued, judges are forced to make such estimates as they decide on compensation to be paid. Surveys of

---

[2] It may be easier for individuals to ignore the social costs imposed by their actions when those costs fall on large numbers of other people whom they do not have to look in the eye or they do not know personally. For the moment, however, we assume that Harry takes no account of Jake.

[3] As we discuss later in this chapter, damage costs are difficult to measure. It is often assumed that they are proportional to the volume of pollutants discharged into the air or water. Instead of taxes, governments often impose *effluent charges*, which make the cost to polluters proportional to the amount of pollution caused. We will use "tax" to refer to both taxes and effluent charges.

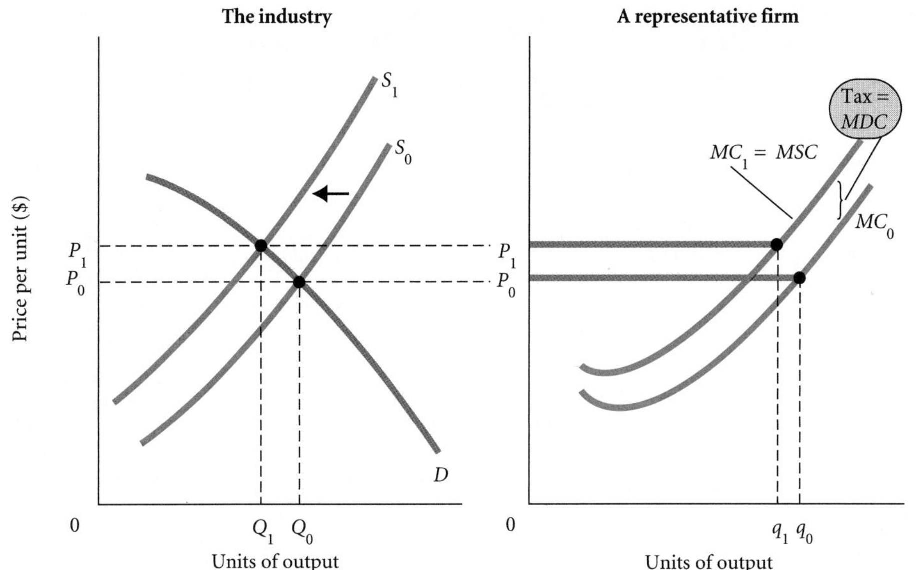

FIGURE 16.3

Tax Imposed on a Firm Equal to Marginal Damage Cost

If a per-unit tax exactly equal to marginal damage costs is imposed on a firm, the firm will weigh the tax, and thus the damage costs, in its decisions. At the new equilibrium price, P_1, consumers will be paying an amount sufficient to cover full resource costs as well as the cost of damage imposed. The efficient level of output for the firm is q_1.

"willingness to pay," studies of property values in affected versus nonaffected areas, and sometimes the market value of recreational activities can provide basic data.

The monetary value of damages to health and loss of life is, naturally, more difficult to estimate, and any measurement of such losses is controversial. Even here, policy makers frequently make judgments that implicitly set values on life and health. Tens of thousands of deaths and millions of serious injuries result from traffic accidents in the United States every year, yet Americans are unwilling to give up driving or to reduce the speed limit to 40 miles per hour—the costs of either course of action would be too high. If most Americans are willing to increase the risk of death in exchange for shorter driving times, the value we place on life has its limits.

Keep in mind that taxing externality-producing activities may not eliminate damages. Taxes on these activities are not designed to eliminate externalities; they are simply meant to force decision makers to consider the full costs of their decisions. Even if we assume that a tax correctly measures all the damage done, the decision maker may find it advantageous to continue causing the damage. The detergent manufacturer may find it most profitable to pay the tax and go on polluting the river. It can continue to pollute because the revenues from selling its product are sufficient to cover the cost of resources used *and to compensate the damaged parties fully*. In such a case, producing the product in spite of the pollution is "worth it" to society. It would be inefficient for the firm to stop polluting. Only if damage costs were very high would it make sense to stop. Thus, you can see the importance of proper measurement of damage costs.

Reducing Damages to an Efficient Level Taxes also provide firms with an incentive to use the most efficient technology for dealing with damage. If a tax reflects true damages and it is reduced when damages are reduced, firms may choose to avoid or reduce the tax by using a different technology that causes less damage. Suppose our soap manufacturer is taxed $10,000 per month for polluting the river. If the soap plant can ship its waste to a disposal site elsewhere at a cost of $7,000 per month and thereby avoid the tax, it will do so. If a plant belching sulfides into the air can install smoke scrubbers that eliminate emissions for an amount less than the tax imposed for polluting the air, it will do so.

The Incentive to Take Care and to Avoid Harm You should understand that all externalities involve at least two parties and that it is not always clear which party is "causing" the damage. Take our friends Harry and Jake. Harry enjoys music; Jake enjoys quiet. If Harry plays his music, he imposes a cost on Jake. If Jake can force Harry to stop listening to music, he imposes a cost on Harry.

Often, the best solution to an externality problem may not involve stopping the externality-generating activity. Suppose Jake and Harry's dormitory has a third resident, Pete. Pete hates silence and loves bluegrass music. The resident adviser on Harry's floor arranges for Pete and Jake to switch rooms. What was once an external cost has been transformed into an external benefit. Everyone is better off. Harry and Pete get to listen to music, and Jake gets his silence.

ECONOMICS IN PRACTICE

Externalities Are All Around Us

Externalities arise from many sources. The most common examples involve smoking factories and the automobile. But externalities are everywhere. Here are two examples of externalities that you may have experienced.

THE CRYING BABY

Peter Scott, once employed as a research assistant on this book and now a writer in Hollywood, wrote the following lines about crying babies on airplanes:

"The best example of this [an externality] is on airplanes. For most of my life, a crying baby on an airplane felt like some kind of torture method used to get spies to reveal national secrets. There was actually a deleted scene in *Goldfinger* where Goldfinger locks James Bond in a room with crying babies. The problem was that Bond then shot himself, thus destroying the franchise. So they rewrote the scene and had Goldfinger try and slice Bond in half with a laser. Bond could easily escape from that because lasers are obviously less terrifying than crying babies."[1]

John Tierney wrote about the same externality in the *New York Times*:[2] "If you think of a screaming child as an environmental disturbance, then giving a child a discount is like offering subsidy to a polluter. A child should at least pay full fare, and the fairest policy would be to impose a surcharge."

CHRISTMAS DECORATIONS

Abominable Snowmen: The War on Lawn Decorations

Wall Street Journal

Jim McDilda's holiday display last year included a 28-foot lighted arch, 50-foot tree, 50,000 lights, and dozens of animated silhouettes. The spectacle—he needed a crane to set it all up—lit up the sky and drew thousands of gawking visitors to his Redding, Calif., house.

But nearby neighbors weren't so thrilled. Cars, limos, and tour buses clogged the cul-de-sac, and trash was strewn across lawns. Christmas music blasting from Mr. McDilda's display kept neighbors awake. They complained to the city, which required that Mr. McDilda get a special-events permit and demanded that he remove the nearby cargo containers he used to store the display most of the year. After months of sniping between Mr. McDilda and the city, he decided to throw in the towel. This year, his house is unadorned.

By Sara Schaefer Muñoz December 20, 2007

1. Peter Scott, *There's a Spouse in the House: A Humorous Journey Through the First Years of Marriage. COPYRIGHT© 2007–2008 PETER SCOTT. ALL RIGHTS RESERVED.* 2. John Tierney, *"The Big City: Urban Menace Stalks Streets in Diapers,"* New York Times, *June 24, 2000.*

Sometimes the most efficient solution to an externality problem is for the damaged party to avoid the damage. However, if full compensation is paid by the damager, damaged parties may have no incentive to do so. Consider a laundry located next to the exhaust fans from the kitchen of a Chinese restaurant. Suppose damages run to $1,000 per month because the laundry must use special air filters in its dryers so that the clothes will not smell of Szechuan spices. The laundry looks around and finds a perfectly good alternative location away from the restaurant that rents for only $500 per month above its current rent. Without any compensation from the Chinese restaurant, the laundry will move and the total damage will be the $500 per month extra rent that it must pay. But if the restaurant compensates the laundry for damages of $1,000 a month, why should the laundry move? Under these conditions, a move is unlikely even though it would be efficient.

Subsidizing External Benefits Sometimes activities or decisions generate external benefits instead of costs, as in the case of Harry and Pete, or in the LoJack example. Real estate investment provides another example. Investors who revitalize a downtown area—an old theater district in a big city, for example—provide benefits to many people, both in the city and in surrounding areas.

Activities that provide such external social benefits may be subsidized at the margin to give decision makers an incentive to consider them. Just as ignoring social costs can lead to inefficient decisions, so too can ignoring social benefits. Government subsidies for housing and other development, either directly through specific expenditure programs or indirectly through tax exemptions, have been justified on such grounds.

Bargaining and Negotiation

In a notable article written in 1960, economist Ronald Coase pointed out that the government does not need to be involved in every case of externality.[4] Coase argued that private bargains and negotiations are likely to lead to an efficient solution in many social damage cases, without any government involvement at all. This argument is referred to as the **Coase theorem**.

Coase theorem Under certain conditions, when externalities are present, private parties can arrive at the efficient solution without government involvement.

For Coase's solution to work, three conditions must be satisfied. First, the basic rights at issue must be clearly understood. Either Harry has the right to play his stereo system or Jake has the right to silence. These rights will probably be spelled out in dorm rules. Second, there must be no impediments to bargaining. Parties must be willing and able to discuss the issues openly and without cost. Third, only a few people can be involved. Serious problems can develop when one of the parties to a bargain is a large group of people, such as all the residents of a large town.

For the sake of our example, let us say that all three of these conditions hold for Harry and Jake and that no room swap with someone like Pete is possible. The dorm rules establish basic rights in this case by specifying that during certain hours of the day, Harry has the right to play his stereo as loudly as he pleases. Returning to Figure 16.2 and our earlier discussion, suppose that under the rules, Harry is free to choose any number of music-playing hours between 0 and 8.

Because Harry is under no legal constraint to pay any attention to Jake's wishes, you might be tempted to think that he will ignore Jake and play his stereo for 8 hours. (Recall that up to 8 hours, the marginal benefits to Harry exceed the marginal costs that he must pay.) However, Jake is willing to pay Harry to play his stereo fewer than 8 hours. For the first hour of play, the marginal damage to Jake is $0.15; so Jake would be willing to pay Harry $0.15 in the first hour to have Harry turn off his stereo. The opportunity cost to Harry of playing the first hour is thus $0.15 plus the (constant) marginal private cost of $0.05, or $0.20. Because the marginal gain to Harry in the first hour is $0.50, Harry would not accept the bribe. Likewise, for hours 2 through 5 the marginal benefit to Harry exceeds the bribe that Jake would be willing to pay plus the marginal private cost.

After 5 hours, however, Jake is willing to pay $0.20 per hour to have Harry turn off his stereo. This means that the opportunity cost to Harry is $0.25. After 5 hours, the marginal benefit to Harry of another hour of listening to his stereo falls below $0.25. Harry will thus accept the bribe not to listen to his music in the sixth hour. Similarly, a bribe of $0.25 per hour is sufficient to have Harry not play the stereo in the seventh and eighth hours, and Jake would be willing to pay such a bribe. Five hours is the efficient amount of playing time. More hours or fewer hours reduce net total benefits to Harry and Jake.

Coase also pointed out that bargaining will bring the contending parties to the right solution regardless of where rights are initially assigned. For example, suppose that the dorm rules state that Jake has the right to silence. This being the case, Jake can go to the dorm administrators and

[4] See Ronald Coase, "The Problem of Social Cost," *Journal of Law and Economics*, 1960.

have them enforce the rule. Now when Harry plays the stereo and Jake asks him to turn it off, Harry must comply.

Now the tables are turned. Accepting the dorm rules (as he must), Harry knocks on Jake's door. Jake's damages from the first hour are only $0.15. This means that if he was compensated by more than $0.15, he would allow the music to be played. Now the stage is set for bargaining. Harry gets $0.45 in net benefit from the first hour of playing the stereo ($0.50 minus private cost of $0.05). Thus, he is willing to pay up to $0.45 for the privilege. If there are no impediments to bargaining, money will change hands. Harry will pay Jake some amount between $0.15 and $0.45; and just as before, the stereo will continue to play. Jake has, in effect, sold his right to have silence to Harry. As before, bargaining between the two parties will lead to 5 hours of stereo playing. At exactly 5 hours, Jake will stop taking compensation and tell Harry to turn the stereo off. (Look again at Figure 16.2 to see that this is true.)

In both cases, the offer of compensation might be made in some form other than cash. Jake may offer Harry goodwill, a favor or two, or the use of his Harley-Davidson for an hour.

Coase's critics are quick to point out that the conditions required for bargaining to produce the efficient result are not always present. The biggest problem with Coase's system is also a common problem. Very often one party to a bargain is a large group of people, and our reasoning may be subject to a fallacy of composition.

Suppose a power company in Pittsburgh is polluting the air. The damaged parties are the 100,000 people who live near the plant. Let us assume the plant has the right to pollute. The Coase theorem predicts that the people who are damaged by the smoke will get together and offer a bribe (as Jake offered a bribe to Harry). If the bribe is sufficient to induce the power plant to stop polluting or reduce the pollutants with air scrubbers, it will accept the bribe and cut down on the pollution. If the bribe is not sufficient, the pollution will continue, but the firm will have weighed all the costs (just as Harry did when he continued to play the stereo) and the result will be efficient.

However, not everyone will contribute to the bribe fund. First, each contribution is so small relative to the whole that no single contribution makes much of a difference. Making a contribution may seem unimportant or unnecessary to some. Second, all people get to breathe the cleaner air whether they contribute to the bribe or not. Many people will not participate simply because they are not compelled to, and the private bargain breaks down—the bribe that the group comes up with will be less than the full damages unless everyone participates. (We discuss these two problems—the *drop-in-the-bucket* and the *free-rider*—later in this chapter.) When the number of damaged parties is large, government taxes or regulation may be the only avenue to a remedy.

Legal Rules and Procedures For bargaining to result in an efficient outcome, the initial assignment of rights must be clear to both parties. When rights are established by law, more often than not some mechanism to protect those rights is also built into the law. In some cases where a nuisance exists, for example, there may be legal remedies. In such cases, the victim can go to court and ask for an **injunction** that forbids the damage-producing behavior from continuing. If the dorm rules specifically give Jake the right to silence, Jake's getting the resident adviser to speak to Harry is something like getting an injunction.

injunction A court order forbidding the continuation of behavior that leads to damages.

Injunctive remedies are irrelevant when the damage has already been done. Consider accidents. If your leg has already been broken as the result of an automobile accident, enjoining the driver of the other car from drinking and driving will not work—it is too late. In these cases, rights must be protected by **liability rules**, rules that require A to compensate B for damages imposed. In theory, such rules are designed to do the same thing that taxing a polluter is designed to do: provide decision makers with an incentive to weigh all the consequences, actual and potential, of their decisions. Just as taxes do not stop all pollution, liability rules do not stop all accidents.

liability rules Laws that require A to compensate B for damages imposed.

However, the threat of liability actions does induce people to take more care than they might otherwise. Product liability is a good example. If a person is damaged in some way because a product is defective, the producing company is, in most cases, held liable for the damages, even if the company took reasonable care in producing the product. Producers have a powerful incentive to be careful. If consumers know they will be generously compensated for any damages, however, they may not have as powerful an incentive to be careful when using the product.

Selling or Auctioning Pollution Rights We have already established that not all externality-generating activities should be banned. Around the world, the private automobile has become the clearest example of an externality-generating activity whose benefits (many believe) outweigh its costs.

Many externalities are imposed when we drive our cars. First, congestion is an externality. Even though the marginal "harm" imposed by any one driver is small, the sum total is a serious cost to all who spend hours in traffic jams. Second, most of the air pollution in the United States comes from automobiles. The problem is most evident in Los Angeles, where smog loaded with harmful emissions (mostly from cars) blankets the city virtually every day. Finally, driving increases the likelihood of accidents, raising insurance costs to all.

While we do not ignore these costs from the standpoint of public policy, we certainly have not banned driving. Athens, Greece, however, has instituted an even-odd system in which inner city driving is restricted to alternative days depending on a person's license plate number. (In a development that some economists predicted, however, this rule has led some people to buy two cars and simply switch off.) In many cases, we have also consciously opted to allow ocean dumping, river pollution, and air pollution within limits.

The right to impose environmental externalities is beneficial to the parties causing the damage. In a sense, the right to dump in a river or to pollute the air or the ocean is a resource. Thinking of the privilege to dump in this way suggests an alternative mechanism for controlling pollution: selling or auctioning the pollution rights to the highest bidder. The Clean Air Act of 1990 takes this cap-and-trade approach to controlling the emissions from our nation's power plants. Emissions from each plant are capped; that is, emissions are limited to a specified level. The lower the level specified, the more air quality will improve. The plant is issued a permit allowing it to emit only at that level. This permit can be used or can be traded to another firm in what has developed into a large auction market. For a firm with low costs of abating pollution, it is often in the firm's best interest to cut back below its permit levels and sell its unused permits to a firm with higher abatement costs. In this way, the given level of emissions chosen by the government will be achieved at the lowest possible costs as a result of market trades. Environmentalists can also buy up permits and leave them unused, resulting in improvements in air quality beyond what the government mandated. These cap-and-trade programs are being used around the world in an attempt to reduce greenhouse gases responsible for global warming.

A simple example will help illustrate the potential gains from a cap-and-trade system. Table 16.1 shows the situation facing two firms, both of which are polluting. Assume that each firm emits 5 units of pollution and the government wants to reduce the total amount of pollution from the current level of 10 to 4. To do this, the government caps each firm's allowed pollution level at 2. Thus, each firm must pay to cut its pollution levels by 3 units. The process of reducing pollution is sometimes called *pollution abatement.* The table shows the marginal cost of abatement for each firm and the total costs. For Firm A, for example, the first unit of pollution reduced or abated costs only $5. As the firm tries to abate more pollution, doing so becomes more difficult; the marginal costs of reducing pollution rise. If Firm A wants to reduce its pollution levels from 5 units to 2, as the government requires, it must spend $21, $5 for the first unit, $7 for the second unit, and $9 for the third unit. Firm B finds reducing pollution to be more difficult. If it tries to reduce pollution by 3 units, it will have costs of $45. A cap-and-trade policy gives each of these firms two permits and allows them to trade permits if they so choose. What will the firms want to do?

TABLE 16.1 Permit Trading

Firm A	Firm A	Firm A	Firm B	Firm B	Firm B
Reduction of pollution by Firm A (in units of pollution)	MC of reducing pollution for Firm A	TC of reducing pollution for Firm A	Reduction of pollution by Firm B (in units of pollution)	MC of reducing pollution for Firm B	TC of reducing pollution for Firm B
1	$ 5	$ 5	1	$ 8	$ 8
2	7	12	2	14	22
3	9	21	3	23	45
4	12	33	4	35	80
5	17	50	5	50	130

Firm A can reduce its emissions from 2 units to 1 unit by spending $12 more on abatement. It would then have a permit to sell to Firm B. How much would Firm B be willing to pay for this permit? At the moment, the firm is abating 3 units, and the marginal cost of that third unit is $23. This tells us that Firm B would be willing to pay up to $23 to buy a permit to allow it to continue polluting up to a level of 3. So there is room for a deal. Indeed, the permit price will be somewhere between the $12 demanded by Firm A and the $23 that Firm B is willing to spend. Because Firm A's marginal costs of abatement are lower than Firm B's, we expect Firm A to do more abatement and sell its extra permit to B. You should be able to see from the numbers that Firm A will not sell its last permit to B. To abate another unit, Firm A would have marginal costs of $17. To avoid abatement, however, Firm B would pay only $14. There is no room for a deal. Once the trade of one permit by A to B has occurred, there are still only 4 units of pollution, but now Firm A is emitting 1 unit and Firm B is emitting 3 units. What are the total costs of this pollution reduction? When both firms were reducing their emission levels equally, the total costs were $21 for Firm A and $45 for Firm B, for a total of $66. Now costs are $33 for A and $22 for B, for a total of $55. (Of course, A will also be receiving a payment for the permit.)

Europe took the problem of global warming seriously by implementing the world's first mandatory trading scheme for carbon dioxide emissions in 2005. Carbon dioxide emissions are a major source of global warming. The first phase of the plan, which was over at the end of 2007, involved around 12,000 factories and other facilities. The participating firms were oil refineries; power generation facilities; and glass, steel, ceramics, lime, paper, and chemical factories. These 12,000 plants represented 45 percent of total European Union (EU) emissions. The EU set an absolute cap on carbon dioxide emissions and then allocated allowances to governments. The nations in turn distributed the allowances to the separate plants. In the second phase from 2008 through 2012, a number of large sectors will be added, including agriculture and petrochemicals.

In both the United States and Europe, the allowances are given out to the selected plants free of charge even though the allowances will trade at a high price once they are distributed. Many are now questioning whether the government should sell them in the market or collect a fee from the firms. As it is, many of the firms that receive the allocations get a huge windfall. During the second phase in Europe, the governments are allowed to auction over 10 percent of the allowances issued.

Another example of selling externality rights comes from Singapore, where the right to buy a car is auctioned each year. Despite very high taxes and the need for permits to drive in downtown areas, the roads in Singapore have become congested. The government decided to limit the number of new cars on the road because the external costs associated with them (congestion and pollution) were becoming very high. With these limits imposed, the decision was made to distribute car ownership rights to those who place the highest value on them. It seems likely that taxi drivers, trucking companies, bus lines, and traveling salespeople will buy the licenses; families who drive for convenience instead of taking public transportation will find the licenses too expensive. Congestion and pollution are not the only externalities that Singapore takes seriously: In 2005 the fine for littering was as high as $1,000; for failing to flush a public toilet, over $100; and for eating on a subway, $300.

Direct Regulation of Externalities Taxes, subsidies, legal rules, and public auctions are all methods of indirect regulation designed to induce firms and households to weigh the social costs of their actions against their benefits. The actual size of the external cost/benefit depends on the reaction of households and firms to the incentives provided by the taxes, subsidies, and rules.

For obvious reasons, many externalities are too important to be regulated indirectly. Dumping cancer-causing chemicals into the ground near a public water supply is simply illegal, and those who do it can be prosecuted and sent to jail.

Direct regulation of externalities takes place at federal, state, and local levels. The Environmental Protection Agency (EPA) is a federal agency established by an act of Congress in 1970. Since the 1960s, Congress has passed a great deal of legislation that sets specific standards for permissible discharges into the air and water. Every state has a division or department charged with regulating activities that are likely to harm the environment. Most airports in the United States have landing patterns and hours that are regulated by local governments to minimize noise.

Many criminal penalties and sanctions for violating environmental regulations are like the taxes imposed on polluters. Not all violations and crimes are stopped, but violators and criminals face "costs." For the outcome to be efficient, the penalties they expect to pay should reflect the damage that their actions impose on society.

ECONOMICS IN PRACTICE

The Debate Over Global Warming

One of the most hotly debated issues involving externalities is the potential cost of global warming. There is currently no incentive for steel producers pumping carbon dioxide into the atmosphere to consider the fact that they may be contributing to widespread damage to the climate in 40 years. While many observers point to the high level of uncertainty in measuring such costs, others stress potentially disastrous results if we do nothing.

In testimony before Congress in July 2005 the president of the National Academy of Sciences addressed the controversial issue of global warming. The following is from that testimony:

> The Earth is warming. Weather station records and ship-based observations indicate that global mean surface air temperature increased about 0.7°F since the early 1970s. Although the magnitude of warming varies locally, the warming trend is widespread and is consistent with an array of other evidence (e.g., melting glaciers and ice caps, sea level rise, extended growing seasons, and changes in the geographical distributions of plant and animal species). The ocean, which represents the largest reservoir of heat in the climate system, has warmed by about 0.12°F.
>
> Laboratory measurements...have shown that for hundreds of thousands of years, changes in temperatures have closely tracked atmospheric carbon dioxide concentrations. Burning fossil fuel for energy, industrial processes, and transportation releases carbon dioxide to the atmosphere. Carbon dioxide in the atmosphere is now at its highest level in 400,000 years and continues to rise. Nearly all climate scientists today believe that much of Earth's current warming has been caused by increases in the amount of greenhouse gases in the atmosphere, mostly from the burning of fossil fuels.
>
> It is important to recognize, however, that while future climate change and its impacts are inherently uncertain, they are far from unknown. The combined effects of ice melting and sea water expansion from ocean warming will likely cause the global average sea level to rise. In colder climates, such warming could bring longer growing seasons and less severe winters. Those in coastal communities, many in developing nations, will experience increased flooding due to sea-level rise and are likely to experience more severe storms and surges. In the Arctic regions, where temperatures have risen more than the global average, the landscape and ecosystems are being altered rapidly.

The Kyoto Protocol is an international treaty on global warming negotiated by the United Nations in the 1990s. It came into force after being ratified by Russia in February 2005. A total of 141 countries have ratified the agreement, which commits them to reduce their emissions of carbon dioxide and five other greenhouse gases or to engage in emissions trading. The United States has not ratified the treaty.

The United Nations turned up the volume considerably in November 2007 when it released with great fanfare a report drawing attention to the serious catastrophes that would result without immediate joint action by the nations of the world. The report argued the following: As early as 2020, 75 million to 250 million people in Africa will suffer water shortages. Asia's large cities will be at great risk from rising ocean waters. According to the report, the world is heading toward warmer temperatures at an accelerating pace, with great human suffering to be the result.

On October 12, 2007, former Vice President Al Gore and the International Panel on Climate Change made up of 2,500 researchers from 130 nations, won the Nobel Peace Prize. Gore had played a major role in bringing the issue of global climate change to the public with a film, *An Inconvenient Truth*, that had won two Academy Awards, one for best documentary.

Despite a greater awareness among the citizenry of the issues that global warming brings to the table, there remains debate about the size of the effect and the optimal policy response. There is no doubt that the issue of global climate change will be on the top of the agenda for a long time.

Source: Ralph J. Cicerone, Ph.D., President, National Academy of Sciences, The National Academies, before the Subcommittee on Global Climate Change and Impacts Committee on Commerce, Science, and Transportation. U.S. Senate, July 20, 2005.

Public (Social) Goods

public goods (social *or* collective goods) Goods that are nonrival in consumption and/or their benefits are nonexcludable.

Another source of market failure lies in **public goods**, often called **social *or* collective goods**. Public goods are defined by two closely related characteristics: They are nonrival in consumption, and/or their benefits are nonexcludable. As we will see, these goods represent a market failure because they have characteristics that make it difficult for the private sector to produce them profitably. In an unregulated market economy with no government to see that they are produced, public goods would at best be produced in insufficient quantity and at worst not produced at all.

The Characteristics of Public Goods

nonrival in consumption A characteristic of public goods: One person's enjoyment of the benefits of a public good does not interfere with another's consumption of it.

A good is **nonrival in consumption** when A's consumption of it does not interfere with B's consumption of it. This means that the benefits of the goods are collective—they accrue to everyone. National defense, for instance, benefits us all. The fact that I am protected in no way detracts from the fact that you are protected; every citizen is protected just as much as every other citizen. If the air is cleaned up, my breathing that air does not interfere with your breathing it, and (under ordinary circumstances) that air is not used up as more people breathe it. Private goods, in contrast, are *rival in consumption*. If I eat a hamburger, you cannot eat it too.

Goods can sometimes generate collective benefits and still be rival in consumption. This happens when crowding occurs. A park or a pool can accommodate many people at the same time, generating collective benefits for everyone. However, when too many people crowd in on a hot day, they begin to interfere with each other's enjoyment.

nonexcludable A characteristic of most public goods: Once a good is produced, no one can be excluded from enjoying its benefits.

Most public goods are also **nonexcludable**. Once the good is produced, people cannot be excluded for any reason from enjoying its benefits. Once a national defense system is established, it protects everyone.

Before we go on, it is very important to note that goods are either public or private by virtue of their characteristics (nonrival and nonexcludable) and *not* by virtue of whether they are produced by the public sector. If the government decided to make it a law that hamburgers were an entitlement (that is, all people could have all the hamburgers they wanted at government expense), that decision would not make hamburgers into public goods. It is an example of the government's providing a private good free of charge to all. The government's decision not to exercise the power to exclude doesn't change the nature of a hamburger.

The real problem with public goods is that private producers may simply not have any incentive to produce them or to produce the right amount. For a private profit-making firm to produce a good and make a profit, it must be able to withhold that good from those who do not pay. McDonald's can make money selling chicken sandwiches only because customers do not get the chicken sandwich unless you pay for it first. If payment were voluntary, McDonald's would not be in business for long.

Consider an entrepreneur who decides to offer better police protection to the city of Metropolis. Careful (and we assume correct) market research reveals that the citizens of Metropolis want high-quality protection and are willing to pay for it. Not everyone is willing to pay the same amount. Some can afford more, others less. People also have different preferences and different feelings about risk. Our entrepreneur hires a sales force and begins to sell his service. Soon he encounters a problem. Because his company is private, payment is voluntary. He cannot force anyone to pay. Payment for a hamburger is voluntary too, but a hamburger can be withheld for nonpayment. The good that our new firm is selling, however, is by nature a public good.

As a potential consumer of a public good, you face a dilemma. You want more police protection, and let us say that you are even willing to pay $50 a month for it. But nothing is contingent on your payment. First, if the good is produced, the crime rate falls and all residents benefit. You get that benefit whether or not you pay for it. You get a free ride. That is why this dilemma is called the **free-rider problem**. Second, your payment is very small relative to the amount that must be collected to provide the service. Thus, the amount of police protection actually produced will not be significantly affected by how much you contribute or whether you contribute at all. This is the **drop-in-the-bucket problem**. Consumers acting in their own self-interest have no incentive to contribute voluntarily to the production of public goods. Some will feel a moral responsibility or social pressure to contribute, and those people indeed may do so. Nevertheless, the economic incentive is missing, and most people do not find room in their budgets for many voluntary payments. The public goods problem can also be thought of as a large-number, prisoners' dilemma game theory problem. (For a full discussion see Chapter 14.)

free-rider problem A problem intrinsic to public goods: Because people can enjoy the benefits of public goods whether or not they pay for them, they are usually unwilling to pay for them.

drop-in-the-bucket problem A problem intrinsic to public goods: The good or service is usually so costly that its provision generally does not depend on whether any single person pays.

Income Distribution as a Public Good?

In Chapter 18, we add the issues of justice and equity to the matters of economic efficiency that we are considering here. There we explain that the government may want to change the distribution of income that results from the operation of the unregulated market on the grounds that the distribution is not fair. Before addressing that topic, we need to note that some economists have argued for redistribution of income on grounds that it generates public benefits.

For example, let us say that many members of U.S. society want to eliminate hunger in the United States. Suppose you are willing to give $200 per year in exchange for the knowledge that people are not going to bed hungry. Many private charities in the United States use the money they raise to feed the poor. If you want to contribute, you can do so privately, through charity. So why do we need government involvement?

To answer this, we must consider the benefits of eliminating hunger. First, it generates collective psychological benefits; simply knowing that people are not starving helps us sleep better. Second, eliminating hunger may reduce disease, and this has many beneficial effects. People who are fit and strong are more likely to stay in school and to get and keep jobs. This reduces welfare claims and contributes positively to the economy. If people are less likely to get sick, insurance premiums for everyone will go down. Robberies may decline because fewer people are desperate for money. This means that all of us are less likely to be victims of crime, now and in the future.

These are goals that members of society may want to achieve. But just as there is no economic incentive to contribute voluntarily to national defense, so there is no economic incentive to contribute to private causes. If hunger is eliminated, you benefit whether you contributed or not—the free-rider problem. At the same time, poverty is a huge problem and your contribution cannot possibly have any influence on the amount of national hunger—the drop-in-the-bucket problem. The goals of income redistribution may be more like national defense than like a chicken sandwich from McDonald's. If we accept the idea that redistributing income generates a public good, private endeavors may fail to do what we want them to do, and government involvement may be called for.

Public Provision of Public Goods

All societies, past and present, have had to face the problem of providing public goods. When members of society get together to form a government, they do so to provide themselves with goods and services that will not be provided if they act separately. Like any other good or service, a body of laws (or system of justice) is produced with labor, capital, and other inputs. Law and the courts yield social benefits, and they must be set up and administered by some sort of collective, cooperative effort.

Notice that we are talking about public *provision*, not public *production*. Once the government decides what service it wants to provide, it often contracts with the private sector to produce the good. Much of the material for national defense is produced by private defense contractors. Highways, government offices, data processing services, and so on, are usually produced by private firms.

One of the immediate problems of public provision is that it frequently leads to public dissatisfaction. It is easy to be angry at government. Part, but certainly not all, of the reason for this dissatisfaction lies in the nature of the goods that government provides. Firms that produce or sell private goods post a price—we can choose to buy any quantity we want, or we can walk away with nothing. It makes no sense to get angry at a shoe store because no one can force you to shop there.

You cannot shop for collectively beneficial public goods. When it comes to national defense, the government must choose one and only one kind and quantity of (collective) output to produce. Because none of us can choose how much should be spent or on what it should be spent, we are all dissatisfied. Even if the government does its job with reasonable efficiency, at any given time, about half of us think that we have too much national defense and about half of us think that we have too little.

Optimal Provision of Public Goods

In the early 1950s, economist Paul Samuelson demonstrated that there exists an *optimal*, or a *most efficient*, level of output for every public good.[5] The discussion of the Samuelson solution that follows leads us straight to the thorny problem of how societies, as opposed to individuals, make choices.

Samuelson's Theory An efficient economy produces what people want. Private producers, whether perfect competitors or monopolists, are constrained by the market demand for their products. If they cannot sell their products for more than it costs to produce them, they will be out of business. Because private goods permit exclusion, firms can withhold their products until households pay. Buying a product at a posted price reveals that it is "worth" at least that amount to you and to everyone who buys it.

Market demand for a private good is the sum of the quantities that each household decides to buy (as measured on the horizontal axis) at each price. The diagrams in Figure 16.4 review the derivation of a market demand curve. Assume that society consists of two people, A and B. At a price of $1, A demands 9 units of the private good and B demands 13. Market demand at a price of $1 is 22 units. If price were to rise to $3, A's quantity demanded would drop to 2 units and B's would drop to 9 units; market demand at a price of $3 is 2 + 9 = 11 units. The point is that the price mechanism forces people to reveal what they want, and it forces firms to produce only what people are willing to pay for, but it works this way only because exclusion is possible.

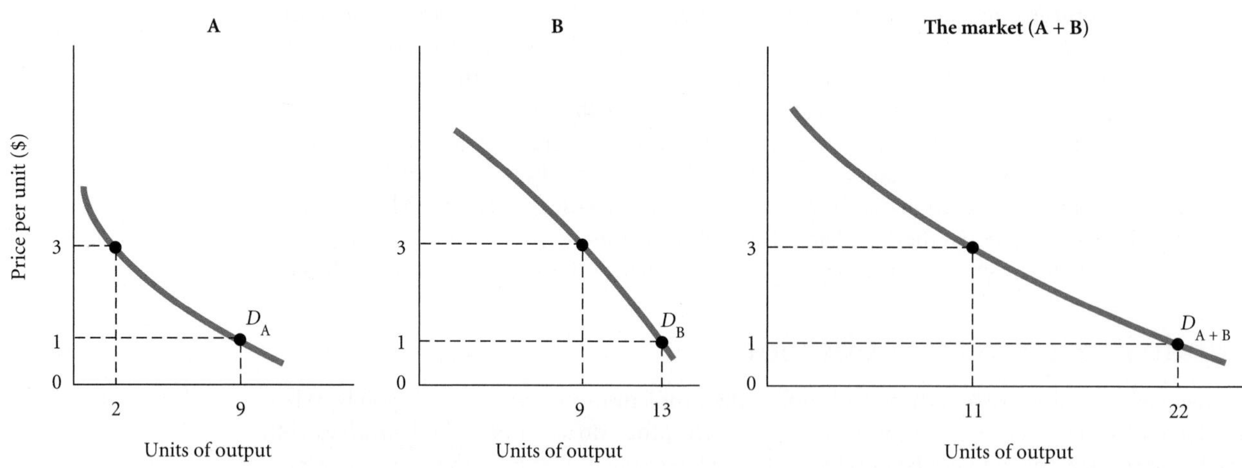

▲ FIGURE 16.4

With Private Goods, Consumers Decide What Quantity to Buy; Market Demand Is the Sum of Those Quantities at Each Price

At a price of $3, A buys 2 units and B buys 9 for a total of 11. At a price of $1, A buys 9 units and B buys 13 for a total of 22. We all buy the quantity of each private good that we want. Market demand is the horizontal sum of all individual demand curves.

[5] Paul A. Samuelson, "Diagrammatic Exposition of a Theory of Public Expenditure," *Review of Economics and Statistics*, 37, 1955, 350–56.

People's preferences and demands for public goods are conceptually no different from their preferences and demands for private goods. You may want fire protection and be willing to pay for it in the same way you want to listen to a CD. To demonstrate that an efficient level of production exists, Samuelson assumes that we know people's preferences. Figure 16.5 shows demand curves for buyers A and B. If the public good were available in the private market at a price of $6, A would buy X_1 units. Put another way, A is willing to pay $6 per unit to obtain X_1 units of the public good. B is willing to pay only $3 per unit to obtain X_1 units of the public good.

Remember, public goods are nonrival and/or nonexcludable—benefits accrue simultaneously to everyone. One and only one quantity can be produced, and that is the amount that everyone gets. When X_1 units are produced, A gets X_1 and B gets X_1. When X_2 units are produced, A gets X_2 and B gets X_2.

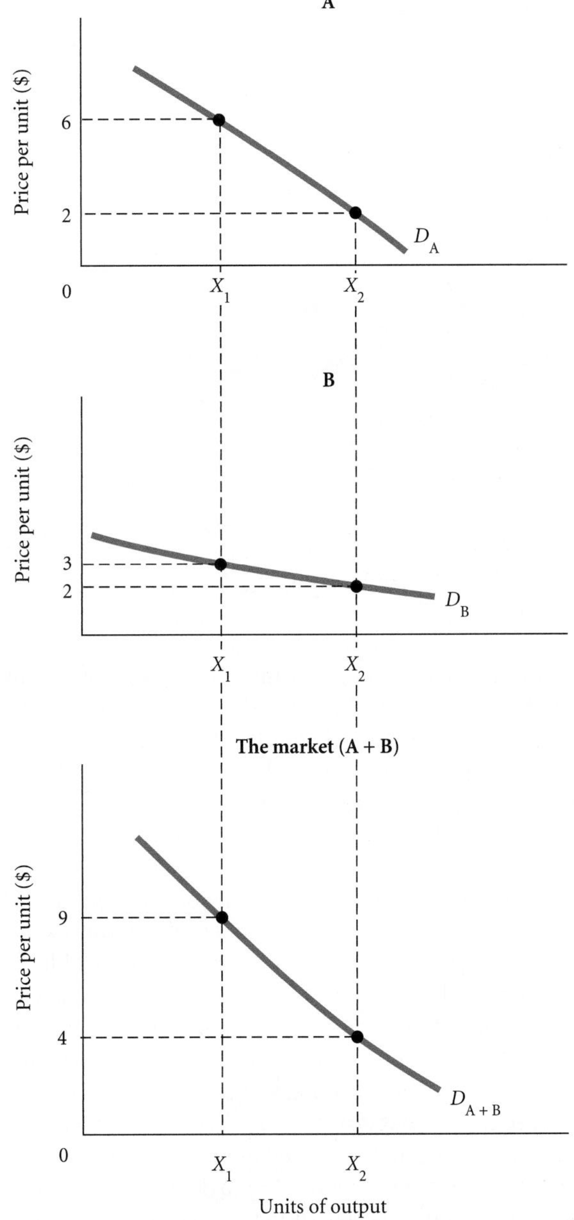

FIGURE 16.5

With Public Goods, There Is Only One Level of Output and Consumers Are Willing to Pay Different Amounts for Each Level

A is willing to pay $6 per unit for X_1 units of the public good. B is willing to pay only $3 for X_1 units. Society—in this case A and B—is willing to pay a total of $9 for X_1 units of the good. Because only one level of output can be chosen for a public good, we must add A's contribution to B's to determine market demand. This means adding demand curves vertically.

To arrive at market demand for public goods, we do not sum quantities. Instead, *we add the amounts that individual households are willing to pay for each potential level of output.* In Figure 16.5, A is willing to pay $6 per unit for X_1 units and B is willing to pay $3 per unit for X_1 units. Thus, if society consists only of A and B, society is willing to pay $9 per unit for X_1 units of public good X. For X_2 units of output, society is willing to pay a total of $4 per unit.

For private goods, market demand is the horizontal sum of individual demand curves—we add the different *quantities* that households consume (as measured on the *horizontal* axis). For public goods, market demand is the vertical sum of individual demand curves—we add the different *amounts* that households are willing to pay to obtain each level of output (as measured on the *vertical* axis).

Samuelson argued that once we know how much society is willing to pay for a public good, we need only compare that amount to the cost of its production. Figure 16.6 reproduces A's and B's demand curves and the total demand curve for the public good. As long as society (in this case, A and B) is willing to pay more than the marginal cost of production, the good should be produced. If A is willing to pay $6 per unit of public good and B is willing to pay $3 per unit, society is willing to pay $9.

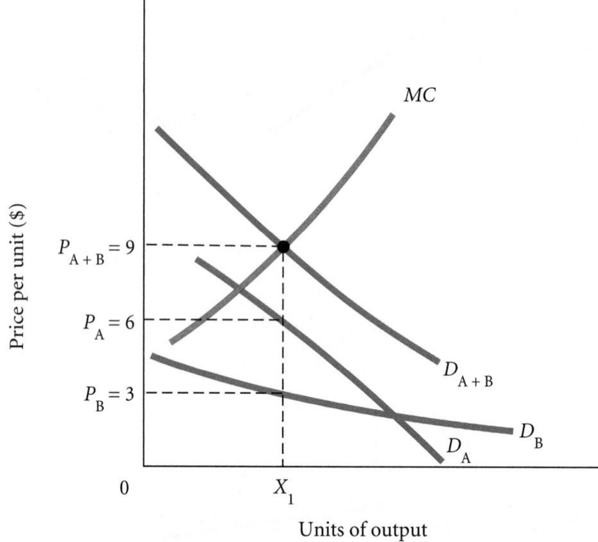

▶ **FIGURE 16.6**

Optimal Production of a Public Good

Optimal production of a public good means producing as long as society's total willingness to pay per unit (D_{A+B}) is greater than the marginal cost of producing the good.

Given the *MC* curve as drawn in Figure 16.6, the efficient level of output is X_1 units. If at that level A is charged a fee of $6 per unit of X produced and B is charged a fee of $3 per unit of X, everyone should be happy. Resources are being drawn from the production of other goods and services only to the extent that people want the public good and are willing to pay for it. We have arrived at the **optimal level of provision for public goods.** At the optimal level, society's total willingness to pay per unit is equal to the marginal cost of producing the good.

optimal level of provision for public goods The level at which society's total willingness to pay per unit is equal to the marginal cost of producing the good.

The Problems of Optimal Provision One major problem exists, however. To produce the optimal amount of each public good, the government must know something that it cannot possibly know—everyone's preferences. Because exclusion is impossible, nothing forces households to reveal their preferences. Furthermore, if we ask households directly about their willingness to pay, we run up against the same problem encountered by our protection-services salesperson mentioned earlier. If your actual payment depends on your answer, you have an incentive to hide your true feelings. Knowing that you cannot be excluded from enjoying the benefits of the good and that your payment is not likely to have an appreciable influence on the level of output finally produced, what incentive do you have to tell the truth—or to contribute?

How does society decide which public goods to provide? We assume that members of society want certain public goods. Private producers in the market cannot make a profit by producing these goods, and the government cannot obtain enough information to measure society's demands accurately. No two societies have dealt with this dilemma in the same way. In some countries, dictators simply decide for the people. In other countries, representative political bodies speak for the people's preferences. In still other countries, people vote directly. None of these solutions works perfectly. We will return to the problem of social choice at the end of the chapter.

Local Provision of Public Goods: Tiebout Hypothesis

In 1956, economist Charles Tiebout made this point: To the extent that local governments are responsible for providing public goods, an efficient market-choice mechanism may exist. Consider a set of towns that are identical except for police protection. Towns that choose to spend a great deal of money on police are likely to have a lower crime rate. A lower crime rate will attract households who are risk-averse and who are willing to pay higher taxes for a lower risk of being a crime victim. Those who are willing to bear greater risk may choose to live in the low-tax/high-crime towns. Also, if some town is efficient at crime prevention, it will attract residents—given that each town has limited space, property values will be bid up in this town. The higher home price in this town is the "price" of the lower crime rate.

According to the **Tiebout hypothesis**, an efficient mix of public goods is produced when local prices (in the form of taxes or higher housing costs) come to reflect consumer preferences just as they do in the market for private goods. What is different in the Tiebout world is that people exercise consumer sovereignty not by "buying" different combinations of goods in a market, but by "voting with their feet" (choosing among bundles of public goods and tax rates produced by different towns and participating in local government).

Tiebout hypothesis An efficient mix of public goods is produced when local land/housing prices and taxes come to reflect consumer preferences just as they do in the market for private goods.

Mixed Goods

Finally, we should mention the case of mixed goods. Most goods are easy to classify as either public or private. A hamburger is a pure private good. It is clearly possible to exclude people from consuming a burger: if I eat it, you cannot. That is, a hamburger is both excludable and rival in consumption. On the other hand, clean air is a pure public good. Once clean air is produced, no one can be excluded from breathing it if he or she did not pay and my breathing it in no way interferes with your breathing it. That is, clean air is *not* excludable and is nonrival in consumption.

Many goods, however, are not easy to classify. Such goods have characteristics that are part public and part private, and we call them **mixed goods**. The classic example of a mixed good is elementary and secondary education.

mixed goods Goods that are part public goods and part private goods. Education is a key example.

First of all, note that education, at least a basic level of primary and secondary education, is a right or an entitlement in every state in the United States. Thus, we have decided that exclusion will not be exercised. But is education "excludable"? The answer is yes. It is possible to exclude a student from attending class at a private school if she or her parents do not pay tuition. Certainly, at both the college level and the high school level, private schools are numerous and the prime benefits of an education belong to the individual student: a higher income in the future, perhaps access to a more desirable profession, or maybe something as simple as learning to appreciate literature, art, or music. Thus, education is essentially a private good.

But many argue that education does produce public benefits that are nonexcludable. The essential argument is that all members of society benefit when citizens are educated. The Nobel laureate Milton Friedman argued that "a stable democratic society is impossible without a minimum degree of literacy and knowledge on the part of most citizens." An educated society is likely to have a lower crime rate, higher productivity, and thus higher wages. Higher wages to others also benefit me because neighborhoods will be more attractive.

Another way of describing the same idea is that education is a private good that creates a positive externality. When mixed goods generate significant positive externalities, we often turn to government involvement to help provide the optimal level of production.

Social Choice

One view of government, or the public sector, holds that it exists to provide things that "society wants." A society is a collection of individuals, and each has a unique set of preferences. Defining what society wants, therefore, becomes a problem of **social choice**—of somehow adding up, or aggregating, individual preferences.

social choice The problem of deciding what society wants. The process of adding up individual preferences to make a choice for society as a whole.

It is also important to understand that government is made up of individuals—politicians and government workers—whose *own* objectives in part determine what government does. To understand government, we must understand the incentives facing politicians and public servants, as well as the difficulties of aggregating the preferences of the members of a society.

The Voting Paradox

Democratic societies use ballot procedures to determine aggregate preferences and to make the social decisions that follow from them. If all votes could be unanimous, efficient decisions would be guaranteed. Unfortunately, unanimity is virtually impossible to achieve when hundreds of millions of people, with their own different preferences, are involved.

impossibility theorem A proposition demonstrated by Kenneth Arrow showing that no system of aggregating individual preferences into social decisions will always yield consistent, nonarbitrary results.

The most common social decision-making mechanism is majority rule—but it is not perfect. In 1951, economist Kenneth Arrow proved the **impossibility theorem**[6]—that it is impossible to devise a voting system that respects individual preferences and gives consistent, nonarbitrary results.

One example of a seemingly irrational result emerging from majority-rule voting is the voting paradox. Suppose that faced with a decision about the future of the institution, the president of a major university opts to let its top three administrators vote on the following options: Should the university (A) increase the number of students and hire more faculty, (B) maintain the current size of the faculty and student body, or (C) cut back on faculty and reduce the student body? Figure 16.7 represents the preferences of the three administrators diagrammatically.

The vice president for finance (VP1) wants growth, preferring A to B and B to C. The vice president for development (VP2), however, does not want to rock the boat, preferring the maintenance of the current size of the institution, option B, to either of the others. If the status quo is out of the question, VP2 would prefer option C. The dean believes in change, wanting to shake the place up and not caring whether that means an increase or a decrease. The dean prefers C to A and A to B.

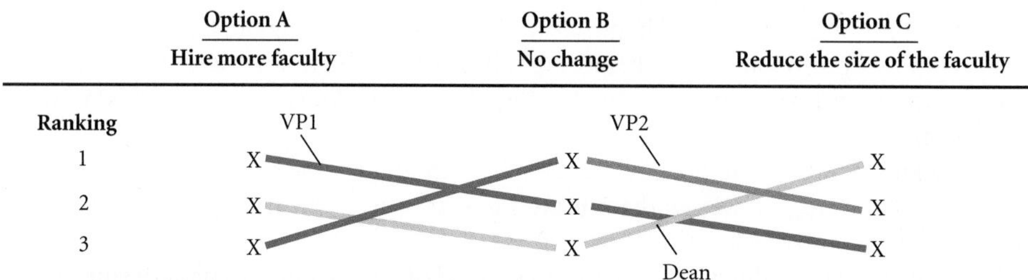

▶ FIGURE 16.7
Preferences of Three Top University Officials
VP1 prefers A to B and B to C. VP2 prefers B to C and C to A. The dean prefers C to A and A to B.

Table 16.2 shows the results of the vote. When the three vote on A versus B, they vote in favor of A—to increase the size of the university instead of keeping it the same size. VP1 and the dean outvote VP2. Voting on B and C produces a victory for option B; two of the three would prefer to hold the line than to decrease the size of the institution. After two votes, we have the result that A (an increase) is preferred to B (no change) and that B (no change) is preferred to C (a decrease).

TABLE 16.2 Results of Voting on University's Plans: The Voting Paradox

	Votes of:			
Vote	VP1	VP2	Dean	Result[a]
A versus B	A	B	A	A wins: A > B
B versus C	B	B	C	B wins: B > C
C versus A	A	C	C	C wins: C > A

[a]A > B is read "A is preferred to B."

[6] Kenneth Arrow, *Social Choice and Individual Values* (New York: John Wiley, 1951).

The problem arises when we have the three vote on A against C. Both VP2 and the dean vote for C, giving it the victory; C is actually preferred to A. Nevertheless, if A beats B and B beats C, how can C beat A? The results are inconsistent.

The **voting paradox** illustrates several points. Most important is that when preferences for public goods differ among individuals, any system for adding up, or aggregating, those preferences can lead to inconsistencies. In addition, it illustrates just how much influence the person who sets the agenda has. If a vote had been taken on A and C first, the first two votes might never have occurred. This is why rules committees in both houses of Congress have enormous power; they establish the rules under which as well as the order in which legislation will be considered.

voting paradox A simple demonstration of how majority-rule voting can lead to seemingly contradictory and inconsistent results. A commonly cited illustration of the kind of inconsistency described in the impossibility theorem.

Another problem with majority-rule voting is that it leads to logrolling. **Logrolling** occurs when representatives trade votes—D helps get a majority in favor of E's program; in exchange, E helps D get a majority on D's program. It is not clear whether any bill could get through any legislature without logrolling. It is also not clear whether logrolling is, on balance, a good thing or a bad thing from the standpoint of efficiency. On the one hand, a program that benefits one region or group of people might generate enormous net social gains, but because the group of beneficiaries is fairly small, it will not command a majority of delegates. If another bill that is likely to generate large benefits to another area is also awaiting a vote, a trade of support between the two sponsors of the bills should result in the passage of two good pieces of efficient legislation. On the other hand, logrolling can also turn out unjustified, inefficient pork barrel legislation.

logrolling Occurs when congressional representatives trade votes, agreeing to help each other get certain pieces of legislation passed.

A number of other problems also follow from voting as a mechanism for public choice. For one, voters do not have much of an incentive to become well informed. When you go out to buy a car or, on a smaller scale, an MP3 player, you are the one who suffers the full consequences of a bad choice. Similarly, you are the beneficiary of the gains from a good choice. This is not so in voting. Although many of us believe that we have a civic responsibility to vote, no one really believes that his or her vote will actually determine the outcome of an election. The time and effort it takes just to get to the polls are enough to deter many people. Becoming informed involves even more costs, and it is not surprising that many people do not do it.

Beyond the fact that a single vote is not likely to be decisive is the fact that the costs and benefits of wise and unwise social choices are widely shared. If the congressperson whom you elect makes a big mistake and wastes a billion dollars, you bear only a small fraction of that cost. Even though the sums involved are large in aggregate, individual voters find little incentive to become informed.

Two additional problems with voting are that choices are almost always limited to *bundles* of publicly provided goods and that we vote infrequently. Many of us vote for Republicans or Democrats. We vote for president only every 4 years. We elect senators for 6-year terms. In private markets, we can look at each item separately and decide how much of each item we want. We also can shop daily. In the public sector, though, we vote for a platform or a party that takes a particular position on a whole range of issues. In the public sector it is very difficult, or impossible, for voters to unbundle issues.

There is, of course, a reason why bundling occurs in the sphere of public choice. It is difficult enough to convince people to go to the polls once a year. If we voted separately on every appropriation bill, we would spend our lives at the polls. This is one reason for representative democracy. We elect officials who we hope will become informed and represent our interests and preferences.

Government Inefficiency: Theory of Public Choice

Recent work in economics has focused not just on the government as an extension of individual preferences but also on government officials as people with their own agendas and objectives. That is, government officials are assumed to maximize their own utility, not the social good. To understand the way government functions, we need to look less at the preferences of individual members of society and more at the incentive structures that exist around public officials.

The officials whom we seem to worry about are the people who run government agencies—the Social Security Administration, the Department of Housing and Urban Development, and state registries of motor vehicles, for example. What incentive do these people have to produce a good product and to be efficient? Might such incentives be lacking?

In the private sector, where firms compete for profits, only efficient firms producing goods that consumers will buy survive. If a firm is inefficient—if it is producing at a higher-than-necessary cost—the market will drive it out of business. This is not necessarily so in the public sector. If a government bureau is producing a necessary service or one that is mandated by law, it does not need to worry about customers. No matter how bad the service is at the registry of motor vehicles, everyone with a car must buy its product.

The efficiency of a government agency's internal structure depends on the way incentives facing workers and agency heads are structured. If the budget allocation of an agency is based on the last period's spending alone, for example, agency heads have a clear incentive to spend more money, however inefficiently. This point is not lost on government officials, who have experimented with many ways of rewarding agency heads and employees for cost-saving suggestions.

However, critics say such efforts to reward productivity and punish inefficiency are rarely successful. It is difficult to punish, let alone dismiss, a government employee. Elected officials are subject to recall, but it usually takes gross negligence to rouse voters into instituting such a measure. Also, elected officials are rarely associated with problems of bureaucratic mismanagement, which they decry daily.

Critics of "the bureaucracy" argue that no set of internal incentives can ever match the discipline of the market. They point to studies of private versus public garbage collection, airline operations, fire protection, mail service, and so on, all of which suggest significantly lower costs in the private sector. One theme of the Reagan and first Bush administrations was "privatization." If the private sector can possibly provide a service, it is likely to do so more efficiently—so the public sector should allow the private sector to take over.

One concern regarding wholesale privatization is the potential effect it may have on distribution. Late in his administration, President Reagan suggested that the federal government sell its entire stock of public housing to the private sector. Would the private sector continue to provide housing to poor people? The worry is that it would not because it may not be profitable to do so.

Like voters, public officials suffer from a lack of incentive to become fully informed and to make tough choices. Consider an elected official. If the real objective of an elected official is to get reelected, then the real incentive must be to provide visible goods for that official's constituency while hiding the costs or spreading them thin. Self-interest may easily lead to poor decisions and public irresponsibility.

Looking at the public sector from the standpoint of the behavior of public officials and the potential for inefficient choices and bureaucratic waste rather than in terms of its potential for improving the allocation of resources has become quite popular. This is the viewpoint of what is called the *public choice* field in economics that builds heavily on the work of Nobel laureate James Buchanan.

Rent-Seeking Revisited

Another problem with public choice is that special-interest groups can and do spend resources to influence the legislative process. As we said before, individual voters have little incentive to become well informed and to participate fully in the legislative process. Favor-seeking special-interest groups have a great deal of incentive to participate in political decision making. We saw in Chapter 13 that a monopolist would be willing to pay to prevent competition from eroding its economic profits. Many—if not all—industries lobby for favorable treatment, softer regulation, or antitrust exemption. This, as you recall, is *rent-seeking*.

Rent-seeking extends far beyond those industries that lobby for government help in preserving monopoly powers. Any group that benefits from a government policy has an incentive to use its resources to lobby for that policy. Farmers lobby for farm subsidies, oil producers lobby for oil import taxes, and the American Association of Retired Persons lobbies against cuts in Social Security.

In the absence of well-informed and active voters, special-interest groups assume an important and perhaps critical role. But there is another side to this story. Some have argued that favorable legislation is, in effect, for sale in the marketplace. Those willing and able to pay the most are more successful in accomplishing their goals than those with fewer resources. Theory may suggest that unregulated markets fail to produce an efficient allocation of resources. This should not lead you to the conclusion that government involvement necessarily leads to efficiency. There are reasons to believe that government attempts to produce the right goods and services in the right quantities efficiently may fail.

Government and the Market

There is no question that government must be involved in both the provision of public goods and the control of externalities. No society has ever existed in which citizens did not get together to protect themselves from the abuses of an unrestrained market and to provide for themselves certain goods and services that the market did not provide. The question is not *whether* we need government involvement. The question is *how much* and *what kind* of government involvement we should have.

Critics of government involvement correctly say that the existence of an "optimal" level of public-goods production does not guarantee that governments will achieve it. It is easy to show that governments will generally fail to achieve the most efficient level. There is no reason to believe that governments are capable of achieving the "correct" amount of control over externalities. Markets may fail to produce an efficient allocation of resources, but governments may make it worse. Measurement of social damages and benefits is difficult and imprecise. For example, estimates of the costs of acid rain range from practically nothing to incalculably high amounts.

Just as critics of government involvement must concede that the market by itself fails to achieve full efficiency, defenders of government involvement must acknowledge government's failures. Many on both sides agree that we get closer to an efficient allocation of resources by trying to control externalities and by doing our best to produce the public goods that people want with the imperfect tools we have than we would by leaving everything to the market.

SUMMARY

EXTERNALITIES AND ENVIRONMENTAL ECONOMICS *p. 319*

1. Often when we engage in transactions or make economic decisions, second or third parties suffer consequences that decision makers have no incentive to consider. These are called *externalities.* A classic example of an external cost is pollution.
2. When external costs are not considered in economic decisions, we may engage in activities or produce products that are not "worth it." When external benefits are not considered, we may fail to do things that are indeed "worth it." The result is an inefficient allocation of resources.
3. A number of alternative mechanisms have been used to control externalities: (1) government-imposed taxes and subsidies, (2) private bargaining and negotiation, (3) legal remedies such as *injunctions* and *liability rules*, (4) sale or auctioning of rights to impose externalities, and (5) direct regulation.

PUBLIC (SOCIAL) GOODS *p. 332*

4. In an unfettered market, certain goods and services that people want will not be produced in adequate amounts. These *public goods* have characteristics that make it difficult or impossible for the private sector to produce them profitably.
5. Public goods are *nonrival in consumption* (their benefits fall collectively on members of society or on groups of members), and/or their benefits are *nonexcludable* (it is generally impossible to exclude people who have not paid from enjoying the benefits of public goods). An example of a public good is national defense.
6. One of the problems of public provision is that it leads to public dissatisfaction. We can choose any quantity of private goods that we want, or we can walk away without buying any. When it comes to public goods such as national defense, the government must choose one and only one kind and quantity of (collective) output to produce.
7. Theoretically, there exists an *optimal level of provision* for each public good. At this level, society's willingness to pay per unit equals the marginal cost of producing the good. To discover such a level, we would need to know the preferences of each individual citizen.
8. According to the *Tiebout hypothesis*, an efficient mix of public goods is produced when local land/housing prices and taxes come to reflect consumer preferences just as they do in the market for private goods.

SOCIAL CHOICE *p. 337*

9. Because we cannot know everyone's preferences about public goods, we are forced to rely on imperfect *social choice* mechanisms such as majority rule.
10. The theory that unfettered markets do not achieve an efficient allocation of resources should not lead us to conclude that government involvement necessarily leads to efficiency. Governments also fail.

GOVERNMENT AND THE MARKET *p. 341*

11. Defenders of government involvement in the economy acknowledge its failures but believe we get closer to an efficient allocation of resources with government than without it. By trying to control externalities and by doing our best to provide the public goods that society wants, we do better than we would if we left everything to the market.

REVIEW TERMS AND CONCEPTS

Coase theorem, *p. 327*
drop-in-the-bucket problem, *p. 333*
externality, *p. 319*
free-rider problem, *p. 333*
impossibility theorem, *p. 338*
injunction, *p. 328*
liability rules, *p. 328*
logrolling, *p. 339*
marginal damage cost (*MDC*), *p. 323*
marginal private cost (*MPC*), *p. 323*
marginal social cost (*MSC*), *p. 320*
market failure, *p. 319*
mixed goods, *p. 337*
nonexcludable, *p. 332*
nonrival in consumption, *p. 332*
optimal level of provision for public goods, *p. 336*
public goods (social *or* collective goods), *p. 332*
social choice, *p. 337*
Tiebout hypothesis, *p. 337*
voting paradox, *p. 339*

PROBLEMS

Visit **www.myeconlab.com** to complete the problems marked in orange online. You will receive instant feedback on your answers, tutorial help, and access to additional practice problems.

1. If government imposes on the firms in a polluting industry penalties (taxes) that exceed the actual value of the damages done by the pollution, the result is an inefficient and unfair imposition of costs on those firms and on the consumers of their products. Discuss that statement. Use a graph to show how consumers are harmed.

2. It has been proposed that toll collection on the Massachusetts Turnpike, a key commuter route into Boston from the west, be discontinued. Proponents argue that tolls have long ago paid for the cost of building the road; now they just provide cash for a fat bureaucracy. A number of economists are opposing the repeal of tolls on the grounds that they serve to internalize externalities. Explain their argument briefly.

3. Many people are concerned with the problem of urban sprawl. As the development of new housing tracts and suburban shopping malls continues over time, metropolitan areas have become more congested and polluted. Open space disappears, and the quality of life changes. Think of your own metropolitan area, city, or town. Using the concept of externalities, consider the issue of land use and development. What are the specific decisions made in the development process that lead to externalities? On whom are the externalities imposed? Do you think that they are measurable? In what specific ways can decision makers be given the incentive to consider them? One of the cities that has paid the most attention to urban sprawl is Portland, Oregon. Search the Web to see what you can find out about Portland's approach.

4. The existence of "public goods" is an example of potential market failure and suggests that a government or public sector can *improve* the outcome of completely free markets. Write a brief summary of the arguments *for* government provision of public goods. (Make sure you consider the discussion of a prisoners' dilemma in the last chapter.) The following three arguments suggest that government may not improve the outcome as much as we might anticipate.

a. *Public goods theory:* Because public goods are collective, the government is constrained to pick a single level of output for all of us. National defense is an example. The government must pick one level of defense expenditure. Some will think it is too much, some will think it is too little, and no one is happy.

b. *Problems of social choice:* It is impossible to choose collectively in a rational way that satisfies voters/consumers of public goods.

c. *Public choice and public officials:* Once elected or appointed, public officials tend to act in accordance with their own preferences and not out of concern for the public.

Which of the three arguments do you find to be most persuasive?

5. It has been argued that the following are examples of "mixed goods." They are essentially private but partly public. For each example, describe the private and public components and discuss briefly why the government should or should not be involved in their provision.

a. Elementary and secondary education
b. Higher education
c. Medical care
d. Air traffic control

6. A paper factory dumps polluting chemicals into the Snake River. Thousands of citizens live along the river, and they bring suit, claiming damages. You are asked by the judge to testify at the trial as an impartial expert. The court is considering four possible solutions, and you are asked to comment on the potential efficiency and equity of each. Your testimony should be brief.

a. Deny the merits of the case and affirm the polluter's right to dump. The parties will achieve the optimal solution without government.

b. Find in favor of the plaintiff. The polluters will be held liable for damages and must fully compensate citizens for all past and future damages imposed.

c. Order an immediate end to the dumping, with no damages awarded.

d. Refer the matter to the Environmental Protection Agency, which will impose a tax on the factory equal to the marginal damage costs. Proceeds will not be paid to the damaged parties.

7. **[Related to the *Economics in Practice* on *p. 326*]** The *Economics in Practice* suggests that children impose negative externalities. What does that imply about discounts for children's meals at restaurants and discount tickets for children at museums? Provide three examples of activities that may, in fact, generate positive externalities.

8. Explain why you agree or disagree with each of the following statements:
   a. The government should be involved in providing housing for the poor because housing is a "public good."
   b. From the standpoint of economic efficiency, an unregulated market economy tends to overproduce public goods.

9. Society is made up of two individuals, A and B, whose demands for public good X are given in Figure 1. Assuming that the public good can be produced at a constant marginal cost of $6, what is the optimal level of output? How much would you charge A and B?

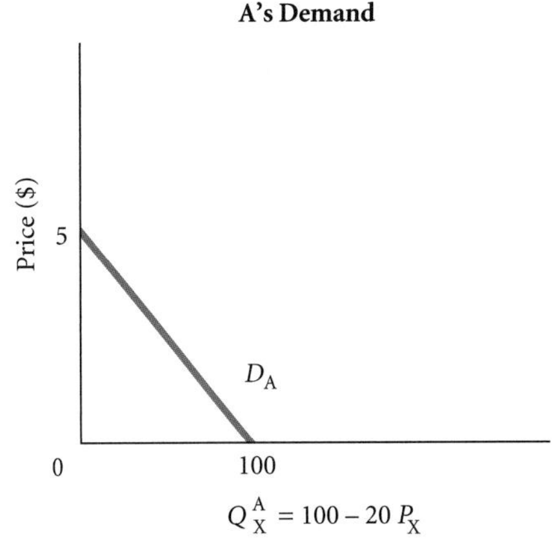

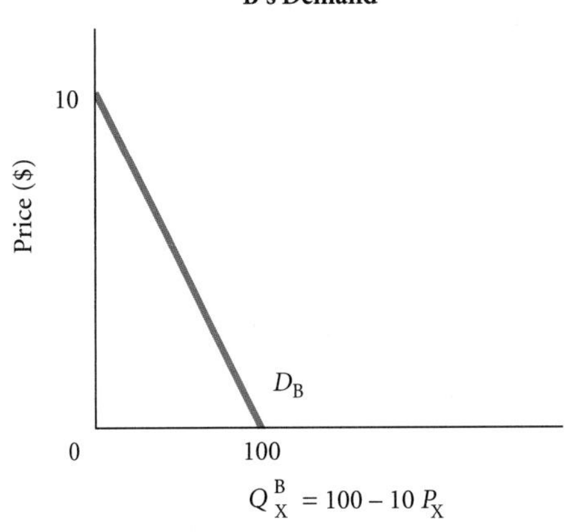

▲ FIGURE 1

10. Government involvement in general scientific research has been justified on the grounds that advances in knowledge are public goods—once produced, information can be shared at virtually no cost. A new production technology in an industry could be made available to all firms, reducing costs of production, driving down price, and benefiting the public. The patent system, however, allows private producers of "new knowledge" to exclude others from enjoying the benefits of that knowledge. Inventors would have little incentive to produce new knowledge if there was no possibility of profiting from their inventions. If one company holds exclusive rights to an advanced production process, it produces at lower cost but can use the exclusion to acquire monopoly power and hold price up.
    a. On balance, is the patent system a good or bad thing? Explain.
    b. Is government involvement in scientific research a good idea? Discuss.

11. The Coase theorem implies that we never need to worry about regulating externalities because the private individuals involved will reach the efficient outcome through negotiations. Is that statement true or false? Justify your answer and use examples.

12. In recent years, events in Eastern Europe have been dramatic. Those events demonstrate that the best economic system is one in which *all* economic decisions are made by individual households and firms without *any* government involvement. Comment briefly.

13. **[Related to the *Economics in Practice* on p. 331]** The discussion between those on both sides of the issue of what to do about climate change is becoming louder. Peter Orszag was director of the Congressional Budget Office in 2008, and he wrote several pieces about global warming as it was perceived in 2007. Search the Internet to find his testimony before the House Budget Committee on November 1, 2007.

    Write a brief essay on the positions of those on both sides of the issue. Summarize the options that Orszag thinks we should consider. Should we take drastic action to stem the tide of global climate change? Why or why not?

Uncertainty and Asymmetric Information

17

CHAPTER OUTLINE

In previous chapters, we assumed that consumers and firms made choices based on perfect information. When consumers choose between two products, we assume that they know the qualities of those products, and as a result their choices reveal their true preferences. Similarly, when firms choose how many workers to hire or how much capital to use, we assume that they know the productivity of those workers or that capital. Of course, in many settings, perfect information seems to be a reasonable assumption to make. Every day you may choose whether to have cereal or eggs for breakfast. Every evening you may decide what to have for dinner and whether to go to the movies or stay home and study. Even for these choices, a little uncertainty can creep in; perhaps a new cereal is on the market or a new movie has been released. But assuming that these choices are made with perfect information does not seem too far a stretch.

In some markets, however, consumers and firms clearly make decisions without perfect information. When you decide to insure your car against theft, you don't know whether the car will be stolen. When you decide to buy a used car, it is not easy to figure out how good that car really is. If you are choosing between a sales job that pays a flat salary and one that pays a commission for every sale you make, you have to predict how good your sales skills will be to determine which is the better offer. In many markets, including some very important markets, consumers as well as firms make decisions while having only some of the information they need. In this chapter, we will explore the economics of these markets.

Decision Making Under Uncertainty: The Tools

In Chapter 6, we laid out the fundamental principles of consumer choice assuming perfect information. To adapt this model to cases in which there is uncertainty, we need to develop a few more tools.

Expected Value

payoff The amount that comes from a possible outcome or result.

expected value The sum of the payoffs associated with each possible outcome of a situation weighted by its probability of occurring.

Suppose I offer you the following deal: You flip a coin 100 times. Every time the coin is a head, you pay me $1. Whenever the coin lands on tails, I pay you a dollar. We call the amount that one player—in this case, me—receives in each of the situations the **payoff**. Here my payoff is +$1 for heads and –$1 for tails. In the case of a coin toss, the probability of heads is ½, as is the probability of tails. This tells us that the financial value of this deal to me, or its expected value, is $0. Half the time I win a dollar, and half the time I lose a dollar. Formally, we define the **expected value** of an uncertain situation or deal as the sum of the payoffs associated with each possible outcome multiplied by the probability that outcome will occur. Again, in the case of a coin toss with the payoffs described, the expected value (EV) is

$$EV = 1/2\ (\$1) + 1/2\ (-\$1) = 0$$

The coin toss is an easy example, in part because there are only two outcomes. But the definition of expected value holds for any deal in which I can describe both the payoffs and the probabilities of all possible outcomes. If I play a game in which I receive $1 every time I roll a die and end up with an even number and I pay $1 every time the die comes up odd, this deal also has an expected value of $0. Half the time (3 of 6 possible outcomes) I recieve $1, and half the time (3 of 6 possible outcomes) I pay $1.

fair game *or* fair bet A game whose expected value is zero.

The two games just described are known as **fair games** or **fair bets**. A fair game has an expected value of $0. The expected financial gains from playing a fair game are equal to the financial costs of that game. In the two fair games we described, the stakes are quite low. Suppose instead of $1 payoffs, we made the payoffs $1,000 for heads and –$1,000 for tails. As you can see, the expected value of that deal is $0 just as it was in the $1 game. But we have learned in watching people's behavior that while some people might be willing to play a fair game with $1 payoffs, very few people will play $1,000-payoff fair games. What is it about people that makes them change their minds about taking a fair bet when the stakes get high? We will explore this question next using some of the tools already covered in Chapter 6.

Expected Utility

Recall from Chapter 6 that consumers make choices to maximize utility. The idea of maximizing utility will also help us understand the way in which those consumers make choices in risky situations.

diminishing marginal utility The more of any one good consumed in a given period, the less incremental satisfaction is generated by consuming a marginal or incremental unit of the same good.

Chapter 6 introduced you to the idea of **diminishing marginal utility**—the more of any one good consumed in a period, the less incremental satisfaction (utility) will be generated by each additional (marginal) unit of that good. Review Figure 6.4 on p. 120 and notice the form the utility curve takes when we have diminishing marginal utility for a good. The curve flattens as we increase units of the good consumed. Now think about what happens to your utility level when we increase not the number of units of a particular good, but your overall income. Figure 17.1 graphs the total utility of a typical consumer, Jacob, as a function of his income. On the *Y*-axis, we have assigned units of total utility, while on the *X*-axis we have annual income. The shape of the utility curve tells us that the consumer has diminishing marginal utility from income. The first $20,000 of income is very important to this consumer, moving him from a total utility level of 0 to 10; this first $20,000 might allow him to buy food and shelter, for example. Moving from $20,000 to $40,000 brings an increase in well-being from 10 to 15. Notice that the second $20,000 adds 5 to the total utility level, while the first $20,000 adds 10. And the pattern continues as we add $20,000 increments to income. Each dollar increases total utility, but at a decreasing rate. The result is a curve as shown in Figure 17.1 that flattens as we move from left to right, with smaller gains in total utility from equal gains in income.

You should see that the assumption of diminishing marginal utility of income reflects the diminishing marginal utility of goods that we talked about in Chapter 6. Income counts for less the more we have because the value of what we can buy with that money on the margin falls as we buy more.

As you think about Figure 17.1, remember that we are describing the relationship between utility and income for a *given individual*. The figure does not tell us that rich people get less utility from an incremental dollar than do poor people. Indeed, it might be argued that one reason some rich people work so hard to make money is that they get a great deal of utility from increases in income relative to the average person. But rich or poor, Figure 17.1 tells us that as your income increases, the marginal utility of another dollar falls.

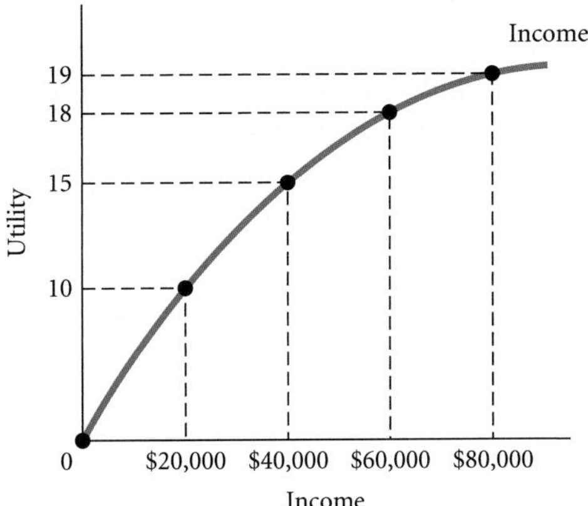

◀ **FIGURE 17.1 The Relationship Between Utility and Income**

The figure shows the way in which utility increases with income for a hypothetical person, Jacob. Notice that utility increases with income but at a decreasing rate: the curve gets flatter as income increases. This curve shows diminishing marginal utility of income.

How does Figure 17.1 help us explain people's unwillingness to play fair games with larger stakes? Suppose Jacob, the individual whose preferences are shown in Figure 17.1, is currently earning $40,000. We see that $40,000 corresponds to a total utility level of 15. Now a firm offers Jacob a different type of salary structure. Rather than earning $40,000 for sure, at the end of the year, a manager will toss a coin. If it is heads, Jacob will earn $60,000; but if the coin turns up tails, his earnings will fall to $20,000. This is a high stakes game of the sort described earlier. Notice that the expected value of the two salaries is the same. With one, Jacob earns $40,000 with certainty. With the second, he earns $20,000 half the time and $60,000 half the time, for an expected value of

$$EV = 1/2(\$20{,}000) + 1/2\,(60{,}000) = \$40{,}000$$

From an expected value perspective, the two salary offers are identical. So if we simply looked at the expected values, we might expect Jacob to be indifferent between the two wage offers. But if you put yourself in Jacob's shoes, probably you would not find the coin-tossing salary to be as attractive as the fixed $40,000 wage. If we think back to the model introduced in Chapter 6, we can see why. Consumers make choices not to maximize income per se but to maximize their utility levels. Figure 17.1 tells us that while utility increases with income, the relationship is not linear. So to decide what Jacob will do, we need to look at his utility under the two contracts.

What can we say about Jacob's utility under the two salary contracts? With a fixed $40,000 salary, total utility is at a level of 15, as we saw earlier. If his income falls to $20,000, that utility level falls from 15 to 10, a substantial drop. With a possible earnings level of $60,000, the total utility level goes up; but notice that it only increases from 15 to only 18. The drop in income causes a bigger loss in utility than comes from a gain in income. Of course, this results from the diminishing marginal utility of income. In fact, we can define **expected utility** as the sum of the utilities coming from all possible outcomes of a deal, weighted by the probability of each occurring. You can see that the expected utility is like the expected value, but the payoffs are in utility terms rather than in dollars. In the coin-toss salary offer, if you look again at Figure 17.1, the expected utility (EU) is

expected utility The sum of the utilities coming from all possible outcomes of a deal, weighted by the probability of each occurring.

$$EU = 1/2\ U(\$20{,}000) + 1/2\ U(60{,}000), \text{ which reduces to}$$

$$EU = 1/2\,(10) + 1/2\,(18) = 14$$

Since Jacob's utility from a fixed salary of $40,000 is 15, he will not take the coin-toss salary alternative.

Of course, in practice, workers are not paid wages based on the toss of a coin. Nevertheless, many wage contracts contain some uncertainty. Many of you have probably had jobs where your wages were uncertain in ways you could not control. Understanding the difference between expected value maximization and expected utility maximization helps us understand these and other similar contracts.

In uncertain situations, consumers make choices to maximize their expected utility. Looking at Figure 17.1, you should now see why people may take small fair bets but will avoid fair games with high stakes. For small games, people are making choices within a very small region of the utility curve. The utility of gaining one more dollar or losing it is almost identical. When we compare outcomes at very different points on the utility curve, the differences in marginal utility become more pronounced. This makes large fair bets quite unattractive.

Attitudes Toward Risk

risk-averse Refers to a person's preference of a certain payoff over an uncertain one with the same expected value.

risk-neutral Refers to a person's willingness to take a bet with an expected value of zero.

risk-loving Refers to a person's preference for an uncertain deal over a certain deal with an equal expected value.

risk premium The maximum price a risk-averse person will pay to avoid taking a risk.

We have now seen that diminishing marginal utility of income means that the typical individual will not play a large stakes fair game. Individuals, like Jacob, who prefer a certain payoff to an uncertain payoff with an equal expected value are called **risk-averse**. Risk aversion thus comes from the assumption of diminishing marginal utility of income and can be seen in the shape of the utility curve. You are unwilling to take a risk because the costs of losing in terms of your well-being or utility exceed the gains of possibly winning. People who are willing to take a fair bet, one that has an expected value of zero, are known as **risk-neutral**. For these individuals, the marginal utility of income is constant so that the relationship between total utility and income in a graph like Figure 17.1, for example, would be a straight, upward-sloping line. Again, we have seen that some people will be risk-neutral when the stakes are low. Finally, some people, in some circumstances, may actually prefer uncertain games to certain outcomes. Individuals who pay to play a game with an expected value of zero or less are known as **risk-loving**. Since most people are risk-averse in most situations, we will concentrate on this case.

The fact that people are, in general, risk-averse is seen in many markets. Most people who own houses buy fire insurance even when not required to do so. In general, a fire insurance policy costs a homeowner more than it is worth in terms of expected value; this is how insurance companies make money. People pay for this insurance because they are risk-averse: The possible loss of their home is very important relative to the value of the premiums they have to pay to protect it. When people invest in a risky business, there has to be some chance that they will "make it big" to induce them to put up their money. The riskier the business in the sense that it may fail, the bigger the upside potential needs to be. This too is an indication of risk aversion.

The presence of risk and uncertainty do not by themselves pose a problem for the workings of the market. The risk that your house might burn down does not prevent you from buying a house; it simply encourages you, if you are risk-averse, to buy insurance. In fact, many markets are designed to allow people to trade risk. Individuals who are risk-averse seek out other individuals (or more commonly firms) who are willing to take on those risks for a price.

The **risk premium** is the maximum price a risk-averse person will pay to avoid taking a risk. Figure 17.2 gives us another look at the same individual, Jacob, we examined in Figure 17.1. Suppose Jacob is currently earning \$40,000 but faces a 50 percent chance of suffering an unpreventable disability that will reduce his income level to \$0. Thus, the expected value of Jacob's income is

$$EV = .5(\$40{,}000) + .5(\$0) = \$20{,}000$$

Suppose further that there are many individuals just like Jacob. On average, in any year, half would become disabled and half would not. If an insurance company offered policies to all of them, offering to replace their \$40,000 salaries should they become disabled, on average, this policy would cost the company \$20,000 per person. In other words, the expected value tells us what, on average, it would cost a firm that pooled large numbers of identical people to offer them insurance against an income loss of this size. If the individuals are willing to pay the insurance company more than this expected value, there is a potential deal to be made. In fact, looking at Figure 17.2 shows us that the deal offered by the insurance company to cover earnings losses in the case of a disability is worth more than \$20,000 to a risk-averse individual like Jacob. Uninsured, Jacob faces a 50 percent chance of earning \$0 and a 50 percent chance of earning \$40,000. Looking at the graph, we see that the expected utility of Jacob in his uninsured state is

$$EU = .5\ U\ (\$0) + .5\ U(\$40{,}000)$$

$$EU = .5(0) + .5(15) = 7.5$$

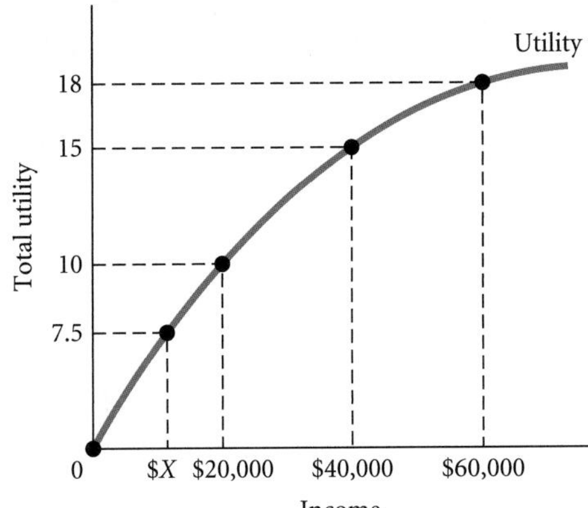

FIGURE 17.2

Risk Aversion and Insurance Markets

With a 50 percent chance of earning $40,000 and a 50 percent chance of becoming disabled and earning $0, Jacob has an EV of income of $20,000. But his expected utility is halfway between the utility of $40,000 (15) and the utility of 0 (0), or 7.5. $X is the amount of certain earnings Jacob would accept to avoid a 50 percent chance of earning $0.

But a utility level of 7.5 corresponds, as we look at Figure 17.2, to a certain income level of *x*, which is below the $20,000 level. In other words, Jacob would be indifferent between a certain income of $x and remaining uninsured. But notice that $x is less than $20,000, which tells us that Jacob is willing to pay more than $20,000 to avoid this disability risk. So there is room for a deal between the insurance company and risk-averse individuals. Because insurance companies can pool risks across many different people, they will be risk-neutral, willing to take on the risks of individuals for a price. In this example, the distance between $20,000, the expected value of the risk, and $x tells us the risk premium.

You may now be wondering how economists explain gambling. Every day people throughout the United States buy lottery tickets even though they know that lotteries are not a fair bet. The Powerball lottery in Connecticut is one example. The winning number is generated by choosing 5 numbers out of a pool of 49, then choosing another number from a pool of 42. The probability of getting all 6 numbers correct and winning the lottery's top prize is 1 in 80 million. The top prize in the lottery varies but is typically in the $10 million to $150 million range. The prize is taxable, and winning the top prize would push a winner into the top tax bracket with a tax rate of almost 40 percent. When the prize level is very high, many people play the lottery and there is a risk of multiple winners, with prize sharing. Thus, in almost all cases, the expected value of the typical lottery is highly negative. Playing the slots at a casino also has a negative expected value, as do all professional games of chance. If this were not true, casinos would go out of business. Nevertheless, individuals buy lottery tickets and gamble in a range of forms. One explanation for this risk-taking behavior may, of course, be that some people find gambling fun and gamble not just in the hopes of winning but for the experience. For other people, gambling may be an addiction. Trying to understand more fully why people gamble while they seem to be risk-averse in most other ways remains an interesting research area in economics.

Asymmetric Information

In the discussion so far, we have described the way people behave in situations in which everyone involved in the deal is equally uncertain. Again, the coin toss is a classic case. When you offer me a coin toss game, neither you nor I know how the coin will fall. It is an unknowable game of chance. Under these situations, we have seen how to use the idea of expected utility to understand choices and we have seen how markets arise to enable risk trading. In other situations, though, the playing field may be less even, with one party to the transaction having more information relevant to the transaction than the other party. Economists refer to these circumstances as ones of **asymmetric information**. Asymmetric information creates possibilities of market failure by making it harder for individuals to make deals that would otherwise be attractive.

asymmetric information One of the parties to a transaction has information relevant to the transaction that the other party does not have.

We are surrounded by situations with asymmetric information. A homeowner has better information than does his or her insurance company about how careful his or her family is, how often family members use candles, and whether anyone smokes. All of these factors are important to an insurance company trying to set an insurance price. When you applied to college, you likely knew more about your work ethic than did the colleges to which you applied.

In this section, we will explore several classic types of asymmetric situations. We will look at the nature of the market failure that arises when we have asymmetric information, and we will consider some of the mechanisms that individuals and markets use to deal with these problems.

Adverse Selection

adverse selection A situation in which asymmetric information results in high-quality goods or high-quality consumers being squeezed out of transactions because they cannot demonstrate their quality.

A common saying in the car market is that once you drive a new car off the lot, it loses a substantial part of its original value. Why might this be true? Physical depreciation is likely small after only a few miles, for example. The answer can be found in the theory of adverse selection, a theory whose development was cited by the Nobel Committee in its award to George Akerlof in 2001. **Adverse selection** is a category of asymmetric information problems. In adverse selection, the quality of what is being offered in a transaction matters and is not easily demonstrated. For example, consumers might be willing to pay for high-quality used cars. But it is hard to tell which cars are good and which cars are not, and sellers will not, in general, have an incentive to be completely truthful. Insurance companies might be willing to offer inexpensive health insurance to people who take good care of themselves. But it is not easy to figure out who those people are, and insurance buyers are not likely to want to tell the company about their bad habits. As we will see, under these conditions, high-quality products and high-quality consumers are often squeezed out of markets, giving rise to the term *adverse selection*. We will explore adverse selection in the used car market, the setting Akerlof first wrote about, and then turn to insurance markets.

Adverse Selection and Lemons Suppose you were in the market for a slightly used car of a particular make, perhaps from 2005. Having read a number of automotive magazines, you learned that half of these cars are lemons (bad cars) and half are peaches (good cars). Given your own tastes, a peach of this model year is worth $12,000 to you while a lemon is worth only $3,000. What would you pay if you were unable to tell a peach from a lemon?

One possible solution to this problem might involve thinking back to the lesson on expected value. The data we described suggest that the expected value of this type of used car is $7,500, which we calculate as ½($12,000) + ½($3,000). From expected utility theory, you might conclude that you would pay somewhat less than this—let's say $7,000.

The problem with this calculation, however, is that you have forgotten that you will be trying to buy this car from a rational, utility-maximizing car seller. Under these circumstances, it will not be equally likely that the car offered will be a peach or a lemon. Let us see how a potential seller of a used car sees the situation.

Suppose you offer current owners of a random 2005 car the $7,000 that we calculated. Which owners will want to sell? Owners of cars likely know whether they have peaches or lemons. After all, they have been driving these cars for a while. The game we are playing here is very different from the coin toss. Owners of the peaches will not, on average, find your offer attractive because their cars are worth $12,000 and you are offering only $7,000. Owners of lemons, on the other hand, will leap at the chance of unloading their cars at that price. In fact, with an offer of only $7,000, only lemon owners will offer their cars for sale. Over time, buyers come to understand that the probability of getting a lemon on the used market is greater than the probability of getting a peach and the price of the used cars will fall. In fact, in this situation, since you know with certainty that only lemons will be offered for sale, the most you will offer for the 2005 car is $3,000, the value to you of a lemon. In the end, Akerlof suggests, only lemons will be left in the market. Indeed, Akerlof called his paper "The Market for Lemons."

The used car example highlights the market failure associated with adverse selection. Because one party to the transaction—the seller here—has better information than the other party and because people behave opportunistically, owners of high-quality cars will have difficulty selling them. Buyers who are interested in peaches will find it hard to buy one because they cannot tell a lemon from a peach and thus are not willing to offer a high enough price to make the transaction. Thus, while there are buyers who value a peachy car more than it is valued by its current seller, no transaction will occur. The market, which is normally so good at moving goods from consumers who place a lower value on a good to consumers with higher values, does not work properly.

You should now see why the simple act of driving a car off the lot reduces its price dramatically: Potential buyers assume you are selling the car because you must have bought a lemon, and it is hard for you to prove otherwise.

Adverse Selection and Insurance Adverse selection is a problem in a number of markets. Consider the very important market for insurance. We have already seen that risk aversion causes people to want to buy health insurance. But individuals often know more about their own health than anyone else, even with required medical exams. For a given premium level, those who know themselves to be most in need of medical care will be most attracted to the insurance. As unhealthy people swell the ranks of the insured, premiums will rise. The higher the rates, the less attractive healthy people will find such insurance. Similar problems are likely in markets for insurance on auto theft and fire. As with used cars, it will be difficult for insurance companies to transact business with lower-risk (high-quality) individuals.

Reducing Adverse Selection Problems In practice, there are a number of ways in which individuals and markets try to respond to adverse selection problems. Mechanics offer would-be used car buyers an inspection service that levels the information playing field a bit. Of course, these inspection services have a price. Buyers can also look for other clues to quality. Some buyers have come to recognize that the best used cars to buy are from individuals who have to relocate to another state. Many students buy used cars from graduating seniors for example. People who need to relocate, like graduating seniors, often want to sell their cars even if they are peaches, and they may be willing to do so at prices that do not quite reflect what they know to be the high quality of the car they are selling. If a car is being sold by a dealer, he or she can offer a warranty that covers repairs for the first few years. The fact that a dealer is willing to offer a warranty tells the potential buyer that the car is not likely to be a lemon. Dealers also develop reputations for selling peaches or lemons. The government also plays a role in trying to reduce adverse selection problems in the used car market. All states have lemon laws that allow buyers to return a used car for a full refund within a few days of purchase on the grounds that some major problems can be detected after modest driving.

Insurance markets also employ strategies to reduce the problem of adverse selection. Companies require medical exams, for example, and often impose restrictions on their willingness to pay for treatment for preexisting conditions. Some companies offer better prices to people based on verifiable health-related behavior such as not smoking.

Understanding the problem of adverse selection is also useful when we think about the policy issue of universal health coverage. In the United States, health coverage is provided by a mix of the private sector (through employers and private purchase) and by the government through Medicare and Medicaid programs. Under the U.S. system currently in use, many people have a choice about what, if any, kind of health insurance they want to purchase given the premiums that insurers offer. By contrast, in some countries, including much of Western Europe, everyone receives health insurance, typically through a government program. A government program in which everyone is covered, at least at some level, is known as *universal health coverage.* While there is considerable debate about the merits of moving to a universal health coverage system, most economists agree that universal coverage reduces problems of adverse selection. When individuals can choose whether to be covered, on average, those who expect to most need medical care will be most attracted to the insurance offer. To the extent that universal coverage reduces choice, it reduces the adverse selection problem.

ECONOMICS IN PRACTICE

Recycled Lemons

All 50 states have lemons laws to try to deal with the problem of adverse selection in the used car market that we described in the text. But as this article points out, some lemons just never go away.

The problem of laundered lemons has stimulated activity not only by government but also in markets. Google *laundered lemons* and you will find advertisements for books to help you avoid these cars and companies that provide services in which you can track lemons via vehicle identification numbers. There may be profitable opportunities in helping people reduce problems of asymmetric information.

Their Titles Laundered, the Cars Are Still Lemons

New York Times

WHEN Stephen and Michelle Steiner won their lemon-law case against Volkswagen of America last fall, the Stratham, N.H., couple were thrilled. At last they were free of the 2003 Passat wagon that they were afraid to drive.

But delight turned to dismay early this year when Mrs. Steiner, curious about what had become of the car, searched the Internet and found it advertised by a used-car dealer near Rochester as a "perfect family car" with a "clean title."

The Passat had been anything but perfect. The car had already had three repairs for fuel-pump problems, and the Steiners had become so worried about its stalling that they stopped driving it last summer. New Hampshire had declared it a lemon, so Mrs. Steiner could not believe there was no warning in the online ad about its troubled past.

"I was flabbergasted," she said. "I thought they would have to let it be known that it was a lemon."

A few states to the west, Julia and Manuel Moreno found themselves on the other end of a transaction involving a used lemon. In 2005 while living in Wooster, Ohio, they bought a used 1998 Kia Sportage. After a series of problems, they discovered that in 2000 Kia Motors America had bought the vehicle back from its original owner as a lemon. The Morenos said the SUV had steering and suspension problems.

The definition of a lemon varies by state, but in general the vehicle has had a serious problem that remains uncorrected despite several attempts to fix it. A car could also be a lemon if it has had a series of different problems that has made it unavailable to the consumer for a long period, often 30 days.

All 50 states have lemon laws, according to the International Association of Lemon Law Administrators. Once a car is determined to be a lemon, usually by an independent arbitration board, the manufacturer is required to buy it back.

But as the Steiners and Morenos have learned, the car can cause problems after that, because of inconsistent state laws on how lemons are handled. Even if one state requires the title to be branded a "lemon" or "buyback," consumer advocates and state officials say there is a good chance the car can be sold in another state with no indication on the title of its troubled past.

By Christopher Jensen, New York Times, August 26, 2007

Market Signaling

We have discussed how asymmetric information between buyers and sellers can lead to adverse selection. However, there are many things that can be done to overcome or at least reduce the information problem. Michael Spence, who shared the Nobel Prize in Economics with George Akerlof and Joseph Stiglitz in 2001, defined the concept of **market signaling** to help explain how buyers and sellers communicate quality in a world of uncertainty.

market signaling
Actions taken by buyers and sellers to communicate quality in a world of uncertainty.

The college admission process is a good example of how signaling works. In the year 2008–2009, the age group applying to college in the United States peaked. This is the result of 4.1 million births in 1990, record immigration, and an economy that provided young people with an incentive to get a good education. Thus, the demand for spaces at the top schools far exceeded the spaces available. Harvard University alone received over 27,000 applications for membership in a class with fewer than 2,000 students. At the same time, many schools are far less selective and some cannot even fill the chairs in their classrooms.

In selective admissions, the student is clearly "selling" in the admissions process and the colleges and universities are buying. Signaling results because the matching between students and colleges involves communicating quality in a world of uncertainty.

The selective colleges and universities have uncertain information about the students that they admit. While schools have concrete information such as test scores and grades, they do not have concrete measures for other qualities that they are seeking. Thus, schools must look for *signals* of those characteristics.

First, selective schools want students who are likely to be successful. They are seeking students who are willing to work hard and who will do well academically. But schools also want students who will contribute to society by becoming good scientists, artists, humanists, dancers, musicians, businesspeople, and leaders. In their admissions forms, brochures, and Web sites, many selective colleges and universities explain that they are "seeking students who will make a difference."

Developing a set of signals for identifying quality in admissions candidates is a difficult task, but there are some generally accepted signals that the colleges and universities look at. Clearly, they look beyond grades and standardized tests. "Quality of the program" is a term used to describe the difficulty of the classes that the applicant took in high school. How many advanced placement courses did the student take? How many years of math, science, and foreign language? Did the student challenge himself or herself?

In addition to courses, extracurricular activities serve as a signal for future success. Here are several examples of the type of student that admissions professionals notice: students who are the president of a group or club rather than only a member, students who have written for the school paper for three years and have become editors by senior year, and students who have done some community service. Admissions professionals also see hours of practicing the violin or piano or soccer as signals of students who dedicate energy to difficult challenges. Admissions professionals make these assumptions about students because they have imperfect information.

Even without knowing about the theory of signals, most high school students recognize that colleges reward extracurricular activities. Not surprisingly, this knowledge increases the incentive of all students to engage in such activities. But how can extracurricular activities be a good signal of interests and productivity if everyone begins to do them? If every high school senior belongs to the French Club, membership ceases to have a signaling effect.

For extracurricular activities to remain useful as a good signal, they must be more easily done by well-rounded and productive students than by other students. If a student who is truly interested in writing and is well-organized about time management finds it easier to write for the school paper, colleges can correctly infer that the newspaper writer is more likely to be interested in writing and is a good manager. It would be too costly in terms of lost time and fun for someone who dislikes writing and is disorganized to join the newspaper staff just to signal colleges. For signals to work, they must be costly and the cost of using them must be less for people who have the trait that is valued. College admissions committees are, for this reason, beginning to think about things like how many hours a given activity takes. Time-intensive activities are more painful if a student does not really like the activity, and they involve more of a trade-off with other academic pursuits.

For a signal to reduce the problem of adverse selection, then, it must be less costly for the high quality-type person to obtain. Extracurricular activities work as a signal when the most committed and brightest students are most able to do the activities and do well at school. Under those conditions, these activities are thought of as a *strong signal*. In the job market, education is a strong signal.

ECONOMICS IN PRACTICE

How to Read Advertisements

Many high-end magazines, including alumni magazines for colleges, have a section at the back with advertisements for rentals of vacation homes. Consider the following ad recently found in one of those magazines.

St. Thomas Rental: "Lovely villa on the Caribbean island of St. Thomas. Sleeps 6. Beautiful garden and pool area. Covered veranda and barbecue. Available by the week or month."

What conclusion should a discerning reader of this ad draw about the property beyond what is written? The obvious conclusion to be drawn from this ad by anyone who has studied economics is that the property is not on or even near the beach.

Why do we conclude this? Ads are designed by people who want to attract customers. So a first step in our deduction is to recognize that the villa owner will mention any attractive and important positive feature that the villa has. On a Caribbean island, beachfront is a key attraction; thus, no mention of the beach tells us that this villa is not on or near the beach. Recognizing that profit-seeking individuals place the ad lets us draw conclusions about the information they do not provide.

This same logic can be used in a corporate setting. In 2002, Congress and the president passed new accounting rules that require firms to inform shareholders of the stock options they give to their executives and the effect of those options on the firms' costs. Information could be embedded in the financial statements or placed in the footnotes. Not surprisingly, those firms—typically the dot-com firms—for whom options costs were large chose the less transparent method of putting the information in the footnotes, while more traditional firms, with fewer options to disclose, were more forthcoming.

Sometimes the lack of information serves as a signal.

Of course, education improves your life in many ways, as a consumer, a citizen, and a worker. Education can directly improve your productivity in most jobs. But it can also signal a potential employer that you are a productive person. Why is education a good signal? Education, like extracurricular activities, is most easily attained by people who are disciplined, bright, and hard-working. All of those qualities are valued in the workplace but are hard to certify—hence, the need for a signal.

Signals are everywhere. Return for a moment to the used car example and the discussion of warranties. We argued that a car for which a dealer offered a warranty was likely to be a peach. Why? A warranty is a promise to pay for repairs for any defects. For a dealer, the warranty is expensive to live up to only if the car is a lemon. Because a lemon will require more repairs than a peach, providing a warranty for it will end up costing the dealer more. So the fact that a seller offers a warranty is a strong signal that the car is a peach.

Under some conditions, a firm's name can signal quality to consumers. Many airports now have nail salons offering manicures to travelers with spare time. On the surface, though, it appears that there might be a problem with adverse selection in the nail salon business. In a community, a nail salon that does a poor job for the money it charges is likely to go out of business. The salon will have few return visitors, and word of mouth of its poor quality is likely to spread. In an airport salon, return business is infrequent; thus, one might think that low-quality nail salons would not be forced out of business. Given that quality is more expensive in terms of labor costs and that consumers do not know whether a salon is good before they have a manicure, one might expect bad salons to crowd out good salons in airports. Savvy consumers would come to realize that only the desperate or those unconcerned with quality should get their nails done in an airport. In fact, there is an offset to this story about the crowding out of good salons. What we see in many airports is a shop that is part of a large chain of salons. The firm that owns the chain recognizes that providing good care in a shop at the Dallas-Fort Worth airport, for example, will have positive reputation effects in the same-named shop at the St. Louis airport. This gives the firm an incentive to provide better quality care at each airport. As a result, airport visitors can view the brand name of the salon as a signal of its quality. One of the economic advantages of a chain is its ability to provide some assurance to customers who are not local of a common level of product quality at different locations. Next time you are traveling along the interstate, look at the hotel and food choices at the rest stops. Most are chains for the reasons we just described.

Moral Hazard

Another information problem that arises in insurance markets is *moral hazard*. Often people enter into contracts in which the result of the contract, at least in part, depends on one of the parties' future behavior. A **moral hazard** problem arises when one party to a contract changes behavior in response to that contract and thus passes the cost of its behavior on to the other party to the contract. For example, accident insurance policies are contracts that agree to pay for repairs to your car if it is damaged in an accident. Whether you have an accident depends in part on whether you drive cautiously. Similarly, apartment leases may specify that the landlord will perform routine maintenance around the apartment. If you punch the wall every time you get angry, your landlord ultimately pays the repair bill.

moral hazard Arises when one party to a contract changes behavior in response to that contract and thus passes on the costs of that behavior change to the other party.

Such contracts can lead to inefficient behavior. The problem is like the externality problem in which firms and households have no incentive to consider the full costs of their behavior. If your car is fully insured against theft, why should you lock it? If health insurance provides new glasses whenever you lose a pair, it is likely that you will be less careful.

Like adverse selection, the moral hazard problem is an information problem. Contracting parties cannot always determine the future behavior of the person with whom they are contracting. If all future behavior could be predicted, contracts could be written to try to eliminate undesirable behavior. Sometimes this is possible. Life insurance companies do not pay off in the case of suicide during the first two years the policy is in force. Fire insurance companies will not write a policy unless you have smoke detectors. If you cause unreasonable damage to an apartment, your landlord can retain your security deposit. It is impossible to know everything about behavior and intentions. If a contract absolves one party of the consequences of his or her action and people act in their own self-interest, the result is inefficient.

Incentives

The discussion of moral hazard provides us with a number of examples in which individuals who buy insurance may have the wrong *incentives* when they make decisions. Incentives play an important role in other areas of life as well. When firms hire, they want to make sure that their workers have the incentive to work hard. Many employers provide bonuses for exemplary performance to create incentives for their employees. In class, teachers try to provide incentives in the form of positive feedback and grades to encourage students to learn the material. In designing policies to deal with unemployment, poverty, and even international relations, governments constantly worry about designing appropriate incentives.

In fact, most of our interest in incentives comes because of uncertainty. Because your teacher or employer cannot always see how hard you are working, he or she wants to design incentives to ensure that you work even when no one is watching. Grades and salary bonuses play this role. Because insurance companies cannot monitor whether you lock your car door, they would like to create incentives to encourage you to lock your doors even though you have theft insurance.

Within economics, the area of **mechanism design** explores how transactions and contracts can be designed so that, even under conditions of asymmetric information, self-interested people have the incentive to behave properly. In 2007, Leonid Hurwicz, Roger Myerson, and Eric Maskin won the Nobel Prize for their work in this area. While the field of mechanism design is a complex

mechanism design A contract or an institution that aligns the interests of two parties in a transaction. A piece rate, for example, creates incentives for a worker to work hard, just as his or her superior wants. A co-pay in the health care industry encourages more careful use of health care, just as the insurance company wants.

one, a simple idea in the field is that different incentive schemes can cause people to reveal the truth about themselves. In the following discussion, we will look at a few examples in the labor market and the health care market to see how incentives can help reduce both adverse selection and moral hazard in this way.

Labor Market Incentives

In the section on expected utility versus expected value, we described an employee trying to choose between a job that offered a wage of $40,000 versus a coin toss that could bring him either $20,000 or $60,000. We suggested that few employees would take such a deal, given risk aversion. And yet many people do have wage contracts that contain some uncertainty. For many CEOs of large U.S. companies, less than half of their compensation is in the form of a fixed salary. Most of their pay comes from bonuses based on the firm's profits or its stock market performance. Many factory jobs pay piece wages that depend on how fast the worker is. Some of you may have had summer jobs selling magazines where wages were uncertain. Why do we see these contracts, given the risk aversion of most people?

These types of contracts occur because variable compensation can help firms get better performance from their workforce. Suppose you are hiring one individual as a salesperson and have two candidates, George and Harry. Both men seem to be affable, good with people, and hardworking. How can you tell who will be a better salesperson? In this case, incentives can play a powerful role. Suppose you offer George and Harry the following deal: The base pay for this job is $25,000, but for every sale made beyond a certain level, a large commission is paid. How valuable is this salary offer? That depends on how good George and Harry are as salespeople. If George knows he is an excellent salesperson, while Harry recognizes that despite his good nature, he is lazy, only George will want to take this salary offer. The way the incentive package is designed has caused the right person, the better salesperson, to *select* into the job. Notice that in contrast to the problem of adverse selection described earlier in this chapter, this incentive scheme creates *beneficial* selection dynamics. One reason that many companies design compensation with a component that varies with performance is that they want to attract the right kind of employees. In this case, the compensation scheme has *screened out* the poor worker. Harry has revealed his own laziness by his job choice, as a result of the design of the incentive.

Performance compensation plays another role as well. Once George has taken the job, the fact that some of his salary depends on his hard work will encourage him to work even harder. Of course, it is important that his compensation depend on things he can, in part, control. This is one reason that in most companies, the CEO's compensation is tied more to firm profitability than is the salary of his or her executive assistant. Because the CEO has more control over profitability, he or she should face the strongest performance incentives.

In recent years, there have been efforts in some states to use more incentive compensation for public school teachers. In some cases, bonuses have been tied to student performance on standardized tests. In a related set of experiments, New York City has a pilot program to reward students who earn good grades with gifts such as cell phones. There has been a lot of debate about the efficacy of both programs. Some people think that public school teachers are already highly motivated and that monetary compensation is not likely to have much effect. Others worry that teachers will "teach to the test," suggesting that the wrong behavior will be stimulated. Some worry that incentive pay will screen out committed teachers, while other people believe it will improve retention of hard-working teachers. In the case of public school students, critics worry that these incentives will turn learning from a matter of love to one of commerce. These issues will likely be debated for some time to come.

Incentives in Health Care

For more than the last decade, growing health care costs in the United States have been a major political issue. In 2007, health care costs were more than 15 percent of the total U.S. gross domestic product (GDP). Some people believe that part of the explanation for the growth in health care costs has been the problem of moral hazard on the part of the insured population.

In the health care industry, one might worry about incentives of consumers and physicians. Health insurance provides some protection for individuals against medical costs. We have already seen that risk aversion leads most people to seek health insurance if they can afford it. But the protection provided by health insurance also creates opportunities for moral hazard. In particular, individuals may do less preventive care in areas such as diet and exercise than they would absent such insurance. In effect, insurance protects them, in part, from the consequences of their own behavior.

In the United States, some health insurance is paid for by private employers. The price paid by firms depends on medical claims made by their workers. This system provides an incentive for those firms to reduce the health care costs of their employees. As a result, a number of larger firms offer wellness programs for employees, trying to reduce out-of-pocket costs of activities (for example, exercise) that improve health and reduce overall insurance premiums that the firms must pay.

There are also issues of overuse of the medical system by patients who, as a result of insurance, do not pay the full costs of a procedure and by physicians who are prescribing medicine for people who are not paying full costs. In many circumstances, insurance companies review health treatments and referrals to try to prevent overtreatment by doctors. Remember in our earlier chapters the important role that price plays in the rationing of goods. Insurance blunts that pricing function on both the patient and doctor side of the market.

A number of programs have been designed to improve other incentives in health care. Most insurance programs have *co-pays* and deductibles. Under a co-pay or a deductible, the cost of a medical visit or procedure is shared by the patient. Co-pays are designed to reduce the problem of moral hazard by giving the patient an incentive to pay attention to medical costs, both in choosing preventive care and avoiding unnecessary visits. Ideally, one might want co-pays to be higher for conditions that are preventable by patients, since those are the areas in which incentives are likely to play the largest role. With all health care reform, however, issues of human rights and values commingle with those of efficiency.

Economists are actively exploring ways in which their new ideas on mechanism design and incentives can help solve some of the issues in managing health care costs in the United States. These issues are among the most exciting topics in economic theory.

SUMMARY

DECISION MAKING UNDER UNCERTAINTY: THE TOOLS p. 345

1. To find the expected value of a deal, you identify all possible outcomes of the deal and find the payoffs associated with those outcomes. *Expected value* is the weighted average of those payoffs where the weights are the probability of each payoff occurring.
2. In general, people do not accept uncertain deals with the same expected value as certain deals.
3. *Risk aversion* exists when people prefer a certain outcome to an uncertain outcome with an equal expected value. *Risk-neutral* people are indifferent between these two deals, and *risk-loving* people prefer the uncertain deal to its certain equivalent.
4. Most people are risk-averse unless the payoffs are very small.
5. Income is subject to *diminishing marginal utility*, and this diminishing marginal utility helps explain risk aversion.

ASYMMETRIC INFORMATION p. 349

6. Choices made in the presence of imperfect information may not be efficient. In the face of incomplete information, consumers and firms may encounter the problem of *adverse selection*. When buyers or sellers enter into market exchanges with other parties who have more information, low-quality goods are exchanged in greater numbers than high-quality goods. *Moral hazard* arises when one party to a contract passes the cost of its behavior on to the other party to the contract. If a contract absolves one party of the consequences of its actions and people act in their own self-interest, the result is inefficient. *Asymmetric information* occurs when one of the parties to a transaction has information relevant to the transaction that the other party does not have.
7. In many cases, the market provides solutions to information problems. Profit-maximizing firms will continue to gather information as long as the marginal benefits from continued search are greater than the marginal costs. Consumers will do the same: More time is afforded to the information search for larger decisions. In other cases, government must be called on to collect and disperse information to the public.
8. Market signaling is a process by which sellers can communicate to buyers their quality. For a signal to be meaningful, it must be less expensive for high-quality types to acquire the signal than for low-quality types.

INCENTIVES p. 355

9. Correct incentive design can improve the selection mechanism along with reducing the moral hazard problem.
10. Performance contracts in the labor market and co-pays in the health insurance market are two examples of incentive contracts.

REVIEW TERMS AND CONCEPTS

adverse selection, *p. 350*
asymmetric information, *p. 349*
diminishing marginal utility, *p. 346*
expected utility, *p. 347*
expected value, *p. 346*
fair game *or* fair bet, *p. 346*
market signaling, *p. 353*
mechanism design, *p. 355*
moral hazard, *p. 355*
payoff, *p. 346*
risk-averse, *p. 348*
risk-loving, *p. 348*
risk-neutral, *p. 348*
risk premium, *p. 348*

PROBLEMS

Visit **www.myeconlab.com** to complete the problems marked in orange online. You will receive instant feedback on your answers, tutorial help, and access to additional practice problems.

1. Explain how imperfect information problems such as adverse selection and moral hazard might affect the following markets or situations:
   a. Workers applying for disability benefits from a company
   b. The market for used computers
   c. The market for customized telephone systems for college offices and dorms
   d. The market for automobile collision insurance
2. Figure 17.1 (p. 347) and Figure 17.2 (p. 349) show a utility curve for a person who is risk-averse. Draw a similar curve for an individual who is risk-neutral and for someone who is risk-loving.
*3. Your current salary is a fixed sum of $50,625 per year. You have an offer for another job. The salary there is a flat $25,000 plus a chance to earn $150,000 if the company does well. Assume that your utility from income can be expressed as $U = \sqrt{\text{Income}}$. So, for example, at an income level of $100, your utility level is 10; your utility level from the current salary of $50,625 is 225. How high does the probability of success for the company have to be to induce you to take this job?
4. Last January I bought life insurance; at the end of the year, I am still alive. Was my purchase a mistake? Explain.
5. Many colleges offer pass/fail classes. Use the ideas of adverse selection and moral hazard to explain why teachers in these classes find that pass/fail students rarely score at the top of the class.
6. Signals are also used in social settings. In a new place, what signals do you look for to find people who share your interests?
7. **[Related to the *Economics in Practice* on *p. 354*]** Find a product advertisement in a magazine for which the missing information tells you something important about the product.
8. **[Related to the *Economics in Practice* on *p. 352*]** Why are cars subject to lemons laws but many other products are not?
9. Leopold Bloom runs a local United Parcel Service branch. At present, he pays his workers an hourly wage. He is considering changing to a piece rate, in which workers would be paid based on how many packages they process during a day. Assume on any given day that there are more packages than the work staff can handle. What effect would you expect this change in compensation to have on Bloom's operations?
10. The fast-food restaurants located on major highways are typically part of national chains. Why might this be the case?
11. Mary's local gym has two pricing options. If you pay by the day, the charge is $10 per day. Alternatively, you can pay an annual membership fee that allows you to exercise as often as you like for $1,000. On average, Mary predicts that she would use the gym once a week and the value of the 50 times per year she would go is not enough to warrant a membership. Instead, Mary decides to pay by the day.
    a. At the end of the year, Mary finds that she went to the gym only 25 times rather than the 50 she had predicted. She is still sure, however, that with a membership, she would go 50 times and insists that economic logic supports her prediction. What principle is she thinking about?
    b. Mary's employer has read a new health study that suggests that people who work out at least once a week perform better at work. The firm decides to give Mary and her coworkers a cash bonus of $40 per week to cover the costs of going to the health club four times a month. Do you think this policy would be effective? If not, suggest an alternative that would achieve the firm's goal.

*Note: Problems with an asterisk are more challenging.

Income Distribution and Poverty

18

What role should government play in the economy? Thus far we have focused only on actions the government might be called on to take to improve market efficiency. Even if we achieved markets that are perfectly efficient, would the result be fair? We now turn to the question of **equity**, or fairness.

Somehow the goods and services produced in every society get distributed among its citizens. Some citizens end up with mansions in Palm Beach, ski trips to Gstaad, and Ferraris; other citizens end up without enough to eat, and they live in shacks. This chapter focuses on distribution. Why do some people get more than others? What are the sources of inequality? Should the government change the distribution generated by the market?

CHAPTER OUTLINE

equity Fairness.

The Utility Possibilities Frontier

Ideally, in discussing distribution, we should talk not about the distribution of goods and services, but about the distribution of well-being. In the nineteenth century, philosophers used the concept of *utility* as a measure of well-being. As they saw it, people make choices among goods and services on the basis of the utility those goods and services yield. People act to maximize utility. If you prefer a night at the symphony to a rock concert, the reason is that you expect to get more utility from the symphony. If we extend this thinking, we might argue that if household A gets more total utility than household B, A is better off than B.

Utility is not directly observable or measurable, but thinking about it as if it were can help us understand some of the ideas that underlie debates about distribution. Suppose society consisted of two people, I and J. Next, suppose that the line *PP′* in Figure 18.1 represents all the combinations of I's utility and J's utility that are possible, given the resources and technology available in their society. (This is an extension of the production possibilities frontier in Chapter 2.)

Any point inside *PP′*, or the **utility possibilities frontier**, is inefficient because both I and J could be better off. *A* is one such point. *B* is one of many possible points along *PP′* that society should prefer to *A* because both members are better off at *B* than they are at *A*.

While point *B* is preferable to point *A* from everyone's point of view, how does point *B* compare with point *C*? Both *B* and *C* are efficient; I cannot be made better off without making J worse off, and vice versa. All the points along *PP′* are efficient, but they may not be equally desirable. If all the assumptions of perfectly competitive market theory held, the market system would lead to one of the points along *PP′*. The actual point reached would depend on I's and J's initial endowments of wealth, skills, and so on.

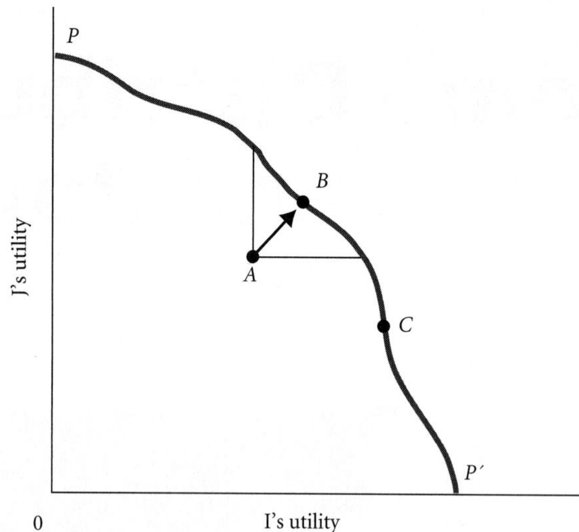

FIGURE 18.1
Utility Possibilities Frontier

If society were made up of two people, I and J, and all the assumptions of perfect competition held, the market system would lead to some point along *PP′*. Every point along *PP′* is efficient; it is impossible to make I better off without making J worse off, and vice versa. Which point is best? Is *B* better than *C*?

utility possibilities frontier A graphic representation of a two-person world that shows all points at which I's utility can be increased only if J's utility is decreased.

In practice, however, the market solution leaves some people out. The rewards of a market system are linked to productivity, and some people in every society are simply not capable of being very productive or have not had the opportunity to become more productive. All societies make some provision for the very poor. Most often, public expenditures on behalf of the poor are financed with taxes collected from the rest of society. Society makes a judgment that those who are better off should give up some of their rewards so that those at the bottom can have more than the market system would allocate to them. In a democratic state, such redistribution is presumably undertaken because a majority of the members of that society think it is fair, or just.

Early economists drew analogies between social choices among alternative outcomes and consumer choices among alternative outcomes. A consumer chooses on the basis of his or her own unique utility function, or measure of his or her own well-being. Society, economists said, chooses on the basis of a social welfare function that embodies the society's ethics.

Such theoretical discussions of fairness and equity focus on the distribution and redistribution of utility. Because utility is neither observable nor measurable, most discussions of social policy center on the *distribution of income* or the *distribution of wealth* as indirect measures of well-being. It is important that you remember throughout this chapter, however, that income and wealth are imperfect measures of well-being. Someone with a profound love of the outdoors may choose to work in a national park for a low wage instead of a consulting firm in a big city for a high wage. The choice reveals that she is better off even though her measured income is lower. As another example, think about five people with $1 each. Now suppose that one of those people has a magnificent voice, and that the other four give up their dollars to hear her sing. The exchange leads to inequality of measured wealth—the singer has $5 and no one else has any—but all are better off than they were before.

Although income and wealth are imperfect measures of utility, they have no observable substitutes and are therefore the measures used throughout this chapter. First, we review the factors that determine the distribution of income in a market setting. Second, we look at the data on income distribution, wealth distribution, and poverty in the United States. Third, we talk briefly about some theories of economic justice. Finally, we describe a number of current redistributional programs, including public assistance (or welfare), food stamps, Medicaid, and public housing.

The Sources of Household Income

Why do some people and some families have more income than others? Before we turn to data on the distribution of income, let us review what we already know about the sources of inequality. Households derive their incomes from three basic sources: (1) from wages or salaries received in exchange for labor; (2) from property—that is, capital, land, and so on; and (3) from government.

Wages and Salaries

More than half of personal income in the United States in 2007 was received in the form of wages and salaries. If you add wage supplements, which include contributions for health insurance and pensions, the figure is 64 percent. Hundreds of different wage rates are paid to employees for their labor in thousands of different labor markets. As you saw in Chapter 10, perfectly competitive market theory predicts that all factors of production (including labor) are paid a return equal to their marginal revenue product—the market value of what they produce at the margin. There are reasons why one type of labor might be more productive than another and why some households have higher incomes than others.

Required Skills, Human Capital, and Working Conditions Some people are born with attributes that translate into valuable skills. Tim Duncan and Shaquille O'Neal are great basketball players, partly because they happen to be 7 feet tall. They did not decide to go out and invest in height; they were born with the right genes. Some people have perfect pitch and beautiful voices; others are tone deaf. Some people have quick mathematical minds; others cannot add 2 and 2.

The rewards of a skill that is in limited supply depend on the demand for that skill. Men's professional basketball is extremely popular, and the top NBA players make millions of dollars per year. There are great women basketball players too, but because women's professional basketball has not become popular in the United States, these women's skills go comparatively unrewarded. In tennis, however, people want to see women play, so women therefore earn prize money similar to the money that men earn.

Some people with rare skills can make enormous salaries in an unfettered market economy. Luciano Pavarotti had a voice that millions of people were willing to pay to hear in person and on CDs. Some baseball players make tens of millions of dollars per year. Before Pablo Picasso died, he could sell small sketches for vast sums of money. Were they worth it? They were worth exactly what the highest bidder was willing to pay.

Not all skills are inborn. Some people have invested in training and schooling to improve their knowledge and skills, and therein lies another source of inequality in wages. When we go to school, we are investing in **human capital** that we expect to yield dividends, partly in the form of higher wages, later on. Human capital, the stock of knowledge and skills that people possess, is also produced through on-the-job training. People learn their jobs and acquire "firm-specific" skills when they are on the job. Thus, in most occupations, there is a reward for experience. Pay scale often reflects numbers of years on the job, and those with more experience earn higher wages than those in similar jobs with less experience.

human capital The stock of knowledge, skills, and talents that people possess; it can be inborn or acquired through education and training.

Some jobs are more desirable than others. Entry-level positions in "glamour" industries such as publishing and television tend to be low-paying. Because talented people are willing to take entry-level jobs in these industries at salaries below what they could earn in other occupations, there must be other, nonwage rewards. It may be that the job itself is more personally rewarding or that a low-paying apprenticeship is the only way to acquire the human capital necessary to advance. In contrast, less desirable jobs often pay wages that include **compensating differentials**. Of two jobs requiring roughly equal levels of experience and skills that compete for the same workers, the job with the poorer working conditions usually has to pay a slightly higher wage to attract workers away from the job with the better working conditions.

compensating differentials Differences in wages that result from differences in working conditions. Risky jobs usually pay higher wages; highly desirable jobs usually pay lower wages.

Compensating differentials are also required when a job is very dangerous. Those who take great risks are usually rewarded with high wages. High-beam workers on skyscrapers and bridges command premium wages. Firefighters in cities that have many old, run-down buildings are usually paid more than firefighters in relatively tranquil rural or suburban areas.

Multiple Household Incomes Another source of wage inequality among households lies in the fact that many households have more than one earner in the labor force. Second, and even third, incomes are becoming more the rule than the exception for U.S. families. In 1960, about 37 percent of women over the age of 16 were in the labor force. By 1978, the figure had increased to over 50 percent, and it continued to climb slowly but steadily to over 60 percent in 2007.

The Minimum Wage Controversy One strategy for reducing wage inequity that has been used for almost 100 years in many countries is the minimum wage. (The minimum wage and price floors were discussed in Chapter 4.) A **minimum wage** is the lowest wage firms are permitted to

minimum wage The lowest wage that firms are permitted to pay workers.

pay workers. The first minimum wage law was adopted in New Zealand in 1894. The United States adopted a national minimum wage with the passage of the Fair Labor Standards Act of 1938, although many individual states had laws on the books much earlier. The minimum wage was raised to $6.55 in the summer of 2008 and is scheduled to be raised to $7.25 in the summer of 2009.

In recent years, the minimum wage has come under increasing attack. Opponents argue that minimum wage legislation interferes with the smooth functioning of the labor market and creates unemployment. Proponents argue that it has been successful in raising the wages of the poorest workers and alleviating poverty without creating much unemployment.

These arguments can best be understood with a simple supply and demand graph. Figure 18.2 shows hypothetical demand and supply curves for unskilled labor. The equilibrium wage rate is $5.40. At that wage, the quantity of unskilled labor supplied and the quantity of unskilled labor demanded are equal. Now suppose that a law is passed setting a minimum wage of $6.55. At that wage rate, the quantity of labor supplied increases from the equilibrium level, L^*, to L_S. At the same time, the higher wage reduces the quantity of labor demanded by firms, from L^* to L_D. As a result, firms lay off $L^* - L_D$ workers.

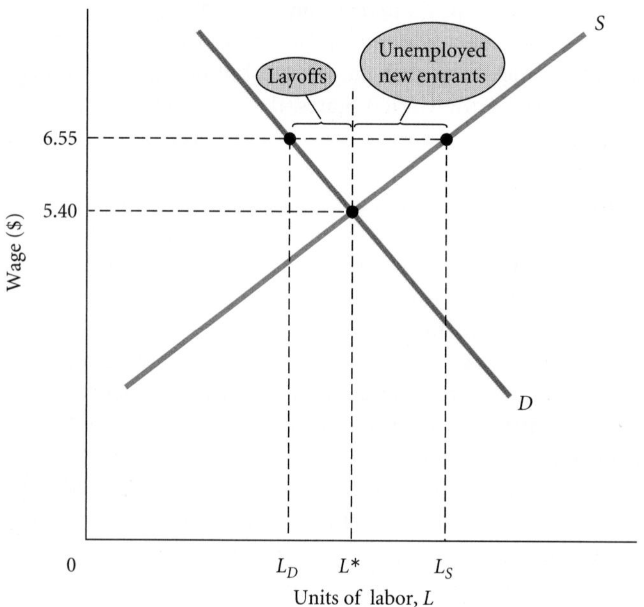

FIGURE 18.2 Effect of Minimum Wage Legislation

If the equilibrium wage in the market for unskilled labor is below the legislated minimum wage, the result is likely to be unemployment. The higher wage will attract new entrants to the labor force (quantity supplied will increase from L^* to L_S), but firms will hire fewer workers (quantity demanded will drop from L^* to L_D).

It is true that those workers who remain on payrolls receive higher wages. With the minimum wage in effect, unskilled workers receive $6.55 per hour instead of $5.40. But is it worth it? Some workers gain while others (including those who had been employed at the equilibrium wage) suffer unemployment.

In fact, the evidence on the extent to which the minimum wage causes jobs to be lost is unclear. Professor Finis Welch at Texas A&M and two colleagues estimated in a recent study that each 10 percent increase in the minimum wage produces job losses of about 1 percent of all minimum wage workers, or about 60,000 workers in total at the time of the study. But other studies find little or no effect on the number of jobs lost when the minimum wage increases. Two earlier studies by David Card of the University of California at Berkeley and one by Lawrence Katz of Harvard and Alan Krueger of Princeton University found that an increase in the minimum wage had virtually no effect on unemployment.

Unemployment Before turning to property income, we need to mention another cause of inequality in the United States that is the subject of much discussion in macroeconomics: *unemployment.*

People earn wages only when they have jobs. In recent years, the United States has been through two severe recessions (economic downturns). In 1975, the unemployment rate hit 9 percent and over 8 million people were unable to find work. In 1982, the unemployment rate was nearly 11 percent and over 12 million were jobless. More recently, the recovery from the milder recession of 1990 to 1991 was slow at first. By 2000, the number of unemployed dropped below 5.5 million (an unemployment rate of 3.9 percent), but by 2007, it was back to 7.2 million, or 4.7 percent.

Unemployment hurts primarily those who are laid off, and thus its costs are narrowly distributed. For some workers, the costs of unemployment are lowered by unemployment compensation benefits paid out of a fund accumulated with receipts from a tax on payrolls.

Income from Property

Another source of income inequality is that some people have **property income**—from the ownership of real property and financial holdings—while many others do not. Some people own a great deal of wealth, and some have no assets at all. Overall, about 22 percent of personal income in the United States in 2007 came from ownership of property. The amount of property income that a household earns depends on (1) how much property it owns and (2) what kinds of assets it owns. Such income generally takes the form of profits, interest, dividends, and rents.

property income Income from the ownership of real property and financial holdings. It takes the form of profits, interest, dividends, and rents.

Households come to own assets through saving and through inheritance. Many of today's large fortunes were inherited from previous generations. The Rockefellers, the Kennedys, and the Fords, to name a few, still have large holdings of property originally accumulated by previous generations. Thousands of families receive smaller inheritances each year from their parents. (Under 2008 tax laws, $2 million can pass from one generation to another free of estate taxes.) Most families receive little through inheritance; most of their wealth or property comes from saving.

Often fortunes accumulate in a single generation when a business becomes successful. The late Sam Walton built a personal fortune estimated at over $70 billion on a chain of retail stores including Wal-Mart. *Forbes* magazine estimates that Bill Gates, founder and chief executive officer of Microsoft, is worth over $56 billion. Karl and Theo Albrecht made $20 billion, beginning with their mother's corner store in Germany and expanding to 4,000 stores in Germany and 10 other countries. In the United States, they own the gourmet food-and-beverage chain Trader Joe's. *Forbes* estimates that there are over 940 billionaires in the world.

Income from the Government: Transfer Payments

About 14 percent of personal income in 2007 came from governments in the form of **transfer payments.** Transfer payments are payments made by government to people who do not supply goods or services in exchange. Some, but not all, transfer payments are made to people with low incomes precisely because they have low incomes. Transfer payments thus reduce the amount of inequality in the distribution of income. Not all transfer income goes to the poor. The biggest single transfer program at the federal level is Social Security. Transfer programs are by and large designed to provide income to those in need. They are part of the government's attempts to offset some of the problems of inequality and poverty.

transfer payments Payments by government to people who do not supply goods or services in exchange.

The Distribution of Income

Despite the many problems with using income as a measure of well-being, it is useful to know something about how income is distributed. Before we examine these data, we should pin down precisely what the data represent.

Economic income is defined as the amount of money a household can spend during a given period without increasing or decreasing its net assets. Economic income includes anything that enhances your ability to spend—wages, salaries, dividends, interest received, proprietors' income, transfer payments, rents, and so on. If you own an asset (such as a share of stock) that increases in value, that gain is part of your income whether or not you sell the asset to "realize" the gain. Normally, we speak of "before-tax" income, with taxes considered a use of income.

economic income The amount of money a household can spend during a given period without increasing or decreasing its net assets. Wages, salaries, dividends, interest income, transfer payments, rents, and so on are sources of economic income.

Income Inequality in the United States

Table 18.1 presents some estimates of the distribution of several income components and of total income for households in 2006. The measure of income used to calculate these figures is very broad; it includes both taxable and nontaxable items, as well as estimates of realized capital gains.

The data are presented by "quintiles"; that is, the total number of households is first ranked by income and then split into five groups of equal size. In 2006, the top quintile earned 46.4 percent of total income while the bottom quintile earned just 3.2 percent. The top 1 percent (which is part of the top quintile) earned more than the bottom 40 percent. Labor income was more evenly distributed than total income.

Income from property is more unevenly distributed than wages and salaries. Property income comes from owning things: Land earns rent, stocks earn dividends and appreciate in value, bonds and deposit accounts earn interest, owners of small businesses earn profits, and so on. The top 20 percent of households earned 65.5 percent of property income, and the top 1 percent earned over 30 percent.

Transfer payments include Social Security benefits, unemployment compensation, and welfare payments, as well as an estimate of nonmonetary transfers from the government to households—food stamps and Medicaid and Medicare program benefits, for example. Transfers flow to low-income households, but not solely to them. Social Security benefits, for example, which account for about half of all transfer payments, flow to everyone who participated in the system for the requisite number of years and who has reached the required age regardless of income. Nonetheless, transfers represent a more important income component at the bottom of the distribution than at the top. Although not shown in Table 18.1, transfers account for more than 80 percent of the income of the bottom 10 percent of households, but only about 3 percent of income among the top 10 percent of households.

TABLE 18.1 Distribution of Total Income and Components in the United States, 2006 (Percentages)

Households	Total Income	Labor Income	Property Income	Transfer Income
Bottom fifth	3.4	1.3	2.2	17.2
Second fifth	9.2	6.7	6.3	24.6
Third fifth	16.3	14.1	11.7	21.2
Fourth fifth	23.6	24.5	14.3	18.3
Top fifth	47.5	53.4	65.5	18.7
Top 1 percent	13.2	10.8	30.6	1.0

Source: Julie-Anne Cronin, U.S. Department of the Treasury, OTA paper 85, p. 19 and author's calculations.

money income The measure of income used by the Census Bureau. Because money income excludes noncash transfer payments and capital gains income, it is less inclusive than economic income.

Changes in the Distribution of Income Table 18.2 presents the distribution of money income among U.S. households[1] at a number of points in time. **Money income**, the measure used by the Census Bureau in its surveys and publications, is slightly less complete than the income measure used in the calculations in Table 18.1. The measure does not include noncash transfer benefits, for example, and does not include capital gains.

Since 1975, there has been a slow but steady drift toward more inequality. During those years, the share of income going to the top 5 percent has increased from 16.4 percent to 22.3 percent while the share going to the bottom 40 percent has fallen from 14.7 percent to 12 percent.

Lorenz curve A widely used graph of the distribution of income, with cumulative percentage of households plotted along the horizontal axis and cumulative percentage of income plotted along the vertical axis.

The Lorenz Curve and the Gini Coefficient The distribution of income can be graphed in several ways. The most widely used graph is the **Lorenz curve**, shown in Figure 18.3. Plotted along the horizontal axis is the percentage of households, and along the vertical axis is the cumulative percentage of income. The curve shown here represents the year 2006, using data from Table 18.2.

During that year, the bottom 20 percent of households earned only 3.4 percent of total money income. The bottom 40 percent earned 12.0 percent (3.4 percent plus 8.6 percent), and so on. If income were distributed equally—that is, if the bottom 20 percent earned 20 percent of the income, the bottom 40 percent earned 40 percent of the income, and so on—the Lorenz curve would be a 45-degree line between 0 and 100 percent. More unequal distributions produce Lorenz curves that are farther from the 45-degree line.

Gini coefficient A commonly used measure of the degree of inequality of income derived from a Lorenz curve. It can range from 0 to a maximum of 1.

The **Gini coefficient** is a measure of the degree of inequality in a distribution. It is the ratio of the shaded area in Figure 18.3 to the total triangular area below and to the right of the diagonal line 0*A*. If income is equally distributed, there is no shaded area (because the Lorenz curve

[1] The term *household* includes unmarried individuals living alone and groups of people living together who are not related by blood, marriage, or adoption. In the United States in 2006, there was a total of 116 million households and 35 million nonfamily households.

and the 45-degree line are the same) and the Gini coefficient is zero. The Lorenz curves for distributions with more inequality are farther down to the right, their shaded areas are larger, and their Gini coefficients are higher. The maximum Gini coefficient is 1. As the Lorenz curve shifts down to the right, the shaded area becomes a larger portion of the total triangular area below 0*A*. If one family earned all the income (with no one else receiving anything), the shaded area and the triangle would be the same and the ratio would equal 1.

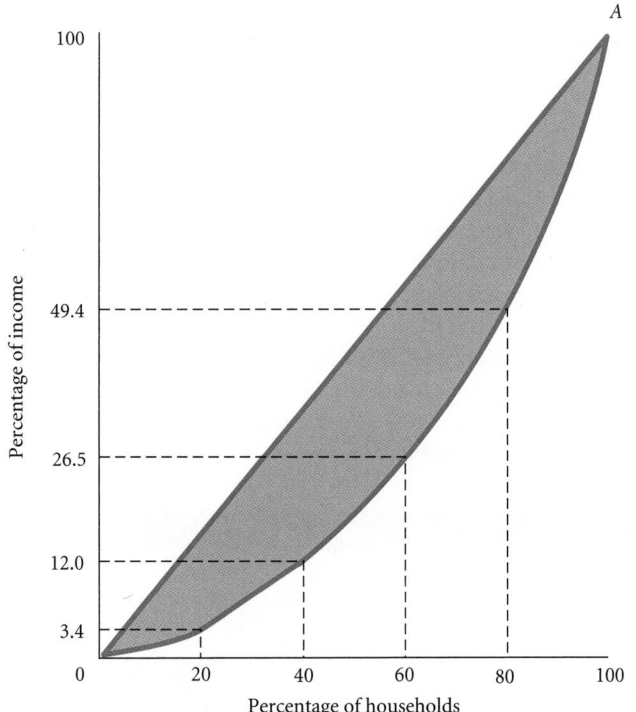

FIGURE 18.3
Lorenz Curve for the United States, 2006

The Lorenz curve is the most common way of presenting income distribution graphically. The larger the shaded area, the more unequal the distribution. If the distribution were equal, the Lorenz curve would be the 45-degree line 0*A*.

TABLE 18.2 Distribution of Money Income of U.S. Households by *Quintiles*, 1967–2006 (Percentages)

	1967	1975	1985	1995	2000	2006
Bottom fifth	4.0	4.3	3.9	3.7	3.6	3.4
Second fifth	10.8	10.4	9.8	9.1	8.9	8.6
Third fifth	17.3	17.0	16.2	15.2	14.8	14.5
Fourth fifth	24.2	24.7	24.4	23.3	23.0	22.9
Top fifth	43.6	43.6	45.6	48.7	49.8	50.5
Top 5%	17.2	16.4	17.6	21.6	22.1	22.3

Source: Bureau of the Census, Current Population Survey, Annual Social and Economic Supplements.

Differences Among African-American Households, White Households, and Single-Person Households Looking just at households without differentiating them in any way hides some needed distinctions. Income distribution differs significantly among African-American, Hispanic, and white households.

Table 18.3 presents data on the distribution of money income for different types of households. The differences among the groupings are dramatic. In 2006, the bottom 20 percent of white households had a mean household income that was twice that of the bottom 20 percent of African-American households. For the middle 20 percent of households, mean income for white households was 62 percent higher than mean income for African-American households. For Hispanics, the figure was 40 percent. The top 5 percent of white households averaged \$315,193 of income. For African-Americans, it was \$200,678; for Hispanics, \$209,819.

TABLE 18.3 Mean Household Income Received by the Top, Middle, and Bottom Fifth of Households in 2006

	White (non-Hispanic)	African-American	Hispanic
Bottom 20%	$ 13,129	$ 6,317	$ 9,671
Middle 20%	52,920	32,575	37,934
Top 20%	178,326	117,346	123,684
Top 5%	315,193	200,678	209,819

Source: U.S. Census Bureau, www.census.gov, Historical Income Tables, Table H3, 2006.

The World Distribution of Income

Data on the distribution of income across rich and poor nations reveal much more inequality, as shown in Table 18.4. The population of the world in 2006 was approximately 6.5 billion. Of that number, 2.4 billion, or 37 percent, live in what the World Bank classifies as low-income countries. The average income per capita in those countries was $650 in 2006. The same year about 1 billion, or 15 percent, lived in high-income countries where per-capita income was $36,487. When you look at total national income, the rich countries with 15 percent of the population earn 77.3 percent of world income while the poor countries with 37 percent of the population get only 3.3 percent of world income. The poorest country in the world in 2006 was Burundi, with 8 million people and a per-capita income of $100 per year. The richest country was Norway, with 5 million people and a per-capita income of $66,000.[2]

TABLE 18.4 Income and Income per Capita Across the World in 2006

	Population		Gross National Income		Per-Capita Income
	Billions	%	Trillions of $	%	(Dollars)
World	6.5	100	48.5	100.0	7,439
Low-Income Countries	2.4	37	1.6	3.3	650
Middle-Income Countries	3.1	48	9.4	19.4	3,051
High-Income Countries	1.0	15	37.5	77.3	36,487

Source: World Bank, *World Development Report 2008*, Key development indicators Table 1.

As we discussed earlier, income inequality has increased within the United States over the last several decades. The evidence also suggests that income inequality is increasing in most other advanced countries as well as in Asia and Latin America. Among the advanced economies, only France has seen decreasing inequality. Inequality has increased everywhere in the developing world except Africa and the Middle East.

Causes of Increased Inequality

The increased income inequality we see in the United States and in many other regions has become the subject of much political debate. Much of the debate concerns what we as a nation and as a member of the world community should do to improve the position of the poorest of our citizens. We will describe these economic issues in the next section of this chapter. But equally debated is the question of what has caused the rise in inequality. Is it the forces of free trade, immigration, and globalization all working together to worsen the position of the middle-income workers who find themselves competing with workers in lower-income countries? Is it the declining power of unions and deregulation that have opened up more labor markets to the forces of competition? Some have argued that a major force in increasing inequality has been technological change that has favored the well-educated worker at the expense of unskilled labor.

These are very difficult questions, questions that are becoming part of the political debate across the world. Consider the role that immigration plays, for example. Most immigrants to the United States come from lower-income countries. Movement of labor from low-income areas to higher-income areas is a natural economic phenomena, a manifestation of the forces of supply

[2] U.S. Bureau of the Census, www.census.gov.

and demand in labor markets. Unchecked, these movements have the capacity to reduce costs of production in the high-wage country, increasing the return to capital, and to reduce world income inequality. Immigration also may play a role in increasing within-country inequality to the extent that it brings a new group of less-skilled workers into a country, potentially competing for jobs with the lower-income population already in the country.

Empirical evidence of the extent to which immigration has in fact reduced wages of lower-income workers is mixed.

The Evidence: The Net Costs of Immigration To determine whether the net benefits of immigration outweigh its net costs, we must ask one important question: To what extent does immigration reduce domestic wages and increase unemployment? A number of recent studies have found that metropolitan areas with greater numbers of immigrants seem to have only slightly lower wages and only slightly higher unemployment rates.

An influential study by economist David Card of the University of California, Berkeley, looks carefully at wages and employment opportunities in the Miami metropolitan area during and after the Mariel boat lift of 1980. Almost overnight about 125,000 Cubans arrived in Florida and increased the labor force in Miami by over 7 percent. Card looked at trends in wages and unemployment among Miami workers between 1980 and 1985 and found virtually no effect. In addition, the data he examined mirrored the experience of workers in Los Angeles, Houston, Atlanta, and similar cities that were not hit by the same shock.[3]

However, a more recent study by Borjas, Freeman, and Katz takes issue with much of the work done to date. They argue that immigrants do not stay in the cities at which they arrive, but rather move within the United States in response to job opportunities and wage differentials. Thus, they argue that the effects of immigration on wages and unemployment must be analyzed at the national level, not the city level. Their study points to the large decline in the wages of high school dropouts relative to workers with more education during the 1980s. Their results suggest that a third of the drop in the relative wages of high school dropouts can be attributed to lower-skilled immigrants.[4]

It is clear that immigration is not an issue simply for the United States. For someone in Guatemala, Mexico offers new opportunities. Per-capita income in Guatemala is $2,640 and is $7,870 in Mexico. Haiti, one of the poorest countries in the world, sends people to the Dominican Republic in search of work. In fact, the World Bank estimates that in 2007, 74 million migrants moved from one developing country to another. Here, too, there are lively debates about the effects of this migration on incomes and inequality.

Technological change also appears to play a role in the increases in inequality. In the last several decades, technological advances have played a strong role in development. In the United States and the developing world, more work is conducted with the aid of computers and less work requires large inputs of unskilled labor. The result has been a wage premium for skilled workers.[5] In fact, work by the International Monetary Fund (IMF) suggests that by looking at the growth in inequality in regions around the world, the central force has been technological change with its increased skill needs. The role of technology in increasing inequality appears to be especially large in Asia. The opening up of economies to free trade has played a modest role relative to technology. In fact, the IMF finds that in the advanced countries, free trade has decreased inequality by replacing low-paid manufacturing jobs with higher-paid jobs in the service sector.

The important role of technology in driving inequality suggests that going forward, education may be key to reducing inequality in the United States and across the world.

Poverty

Most of the government's concern with income distribution and redistribution has focused on poverty. *Poverty* is a very complicated word to define. In simplest terms, it means the condition of people who have very low incomes. The dictionary defines the term simply as "lack of money or material possessions," but how low does your income have to be before you are classified as poor?

---

[3] David Card, "The Impact of the Mariel Boat Lift on the Miami Labor Market," *Industrial and Labor Relations Review*, January 1990, pp. 245–257.

[4] George Borjas, Richard Freeman, and Lawrence Katz, "On the Labor Market Effects of Immigration and Trade," in *Immigration and the Work Force: Economic Consequences for the United States and Source Areas*, eds. George Borjas and Richard Freeman (Chicago: University of Chicago Press, 1992).

[5] Nancy Birdsall, 2007. "Discussion of the Impact of Globalization on the World's Poor," Brookings.

The Problem of Definition Philosophers and social policy makers have long debated the meaning of "poverty." One school of thought argues that poverty should be measured by determining how much it costs to buy the "basic necessities of life." For many years, the Bureau of Labor Statistics published "family budget" data designed to track the cost of specific "bundles" of food, clothing, and shelter that were supposed to represent the minimum standard of living.

Critics argue that defining bundles of necessities is a hopeless task. Although it might be possible to define a minimally adequate diet, what is a "minimum" housing unit? Is a car a necessity? What about medical care? In reality, low-income families end up using what income they have in an enormous variety of ways.

Some say that poverty is culturally defined and is therefore a relative concept, not an absolute one. Poverty in Bangladesh is very different from poverty in the United States. Even within the United States, urban poverty is very different from rural poverty. If poverty is a relative concept, the definition of it might change significantly as a society accumulates wealth and achieves higher living standards.

Although it is difficult to define precisely, the word *poverty* is one that we all understand intuitively to some degree. It conveys images of run-down, overcrowded, rat-infested housing; homeless people; untreated illness; and so on. It is also a word that we have been forced to define formally for purposes of keeping statistics and administering public programs.

The Official Poverty Line In the early 1960s, the U.S. government established an official poverty line. Because poor families tend to spend about one-third of their incomes on food, the official **poverty line** has been set at a figure that is simply three times the cost of the Department of Agriculture's minimum food budget.

poverty line The officially established income level that distinguishes the poor from the nonpoor. It is set at three times the cost of the Department of Agriculture's minimum food budget.

The minimum food budget was only calculated once, in 1963. It has been updated with the Consumer Price Index since that year. Needless to say these figures are somewhat arbitrary, but they are still used to determine the official poverty rate. For 2007, the threshold for a family of four was 21,027.

After years of study and debate, the Department of Health and Human Services began publishing an alternative measure of poverty now called the Poverty Guidelines. The new and somewhat more complex methodology produces income limits that define eligibility for a number of programs including food stamps and Medicaid. The Department set the figure at $21,200 for a family of four in 2008.

Poverty in the United States Since 1960 In 1962, Michael Harrington published *The Other America: Poverty in the United States*, a book that woke the American people to the problem of poverty and stimulated the government to declare a "war on poverty" in 1964. In 1960, official figures had put the number of the poor in the United States at just under 40 million, or 22 percent of the total population. In his book, Harrington argued that the number had reached over 50 million.

By the late 1960s, the number living below the official poverty line had declined to about 25 million, where it stayed for over a decade. Between 1978 and 1983, the number of poor jumped nearly 45 percent, from 24.5 million to 35.3 million, the highest number since 1964. The figure stood at 36.5 million in 2006. As a percentage of the total population, the poor accounted for between 11 percent and 12.6 percent of the population throughout the 1970s. That figure increased sharply to 15.2 percent between 1979 and 1983. From 1983 to 1989, the rate dropped to 12.8 percent, rising back to 14.5 percent in 1995. The rate fell to 12.3 percent in 2006.

While the official 2006 figures put the poverty rate at 12.3 percent of the population, they also show that some groups in society experience more poverty than others. Table 18.5 shows the official poverty count for 1964 and 2006 by demographic group. One of the problems with the official count is that it considers only money income as defined by the census and is therefore somewhat inflated. Many federal programs designed to help people out of poverty include noncash benefits (sometimes called *in-kind benefits*) such as food stamps and public housing. If added to income, these benefits would reduce the number of those officially designated as below the poverty line to about 9 percent of the population.

The poverty rate among African-Americans is more than twice as high as the poverty rate among whites. Nearly one in four African-Americans live in poverty. In addition, a slightly lower proportion of Hispanics than African-Americans had incomes below the poverty line in 2006.

The group with the highest incidence of poverty in 2006 was women living in households with no husband present. In 1964, 45.9 percent of such women lived in poverty. By 2006, the figure was still 28.3 percent. During the 1980s, there was increasing concern about the "feminization of poverty," a concern that continues today.

TABLE 18.5 Percentage of Persons in Poverty by Demographic Group, 1964 and 2006

	Official Measure 1964	Official Measure 2006
All	19.0	12.3
White (Non-Hispanic)	14.9	8.2
African-American	49.6	24.3
Hispanic	NA	20.6
Female householder—no husband present	45.9	28.3
Elderly (65 +)	28.5	9.4
Children under 18	20.7	17.4

Source: U.S. Census Bureau. Income, Poverty and Health Insurance Coverage in the U.S., 2006.

Poverty rates among the elderly have been reduced considerably over the last few decades, dropping from 28.5 percent in 1964 to 9.4 percent in 2006. Certainly, Social Security, supplemental security income, and Medicare have played a role in reducing poverty among the elderly. In 1964, 20.7 percent of all children under 18 lived in poverty; and in 2006, the figure was 17.4 percent.

The Distribution of Wealth

Data on the distribution of wealth are not as readily available as data on the distribution of income. Periodically, however, the government conducts a detailed survey of the holdings that make up wealth. The results show that the top 10 percent of households held just under 70 percent of the total net worth in the United States in 2004 while the bottom 40 percent of households held only 2.6 percent.

The distribution of wealth is more unequal than the distribution of income. Part of the reason is that wealth is passed from generation to generation and accumulates. Large fortunes also accumulate when small businesses become successful large businesses. Some argue that an unequal distribution of wealth is the natural and inevitable consequence of risk taking in a market economy: It provides the incentive necessary to motivate entrepreneurs and investors. Others believe that too much inequality can undermine democracy and lead to social conflict. Many of the arguments for and against income redistribution, discussed in the next section, apply equally well to wealth redistribution.

The Redistribution Debate

Debates about the role of government in correcting for inequity in the distribution of income revolve around philosophical and practical issues. *Philosophical* issues deal with the "ideal." What should the distribution of income be if we could give it any shape we desired? What is "fair"? What is "just"? *Practical* issues deal with what is and what is not possible. Suppose we wanted zero poverty. How much would it cost, and what would we sacrifice? When we take wealth or income away from higher-income people and give it to lower-income people, do we destroy incentives? What are the effects of this kind of redistribution?

Policy makers must deal with both kinds of issues, but it seems logical to confront the philosophical issues first. If you do not know where you want to go, you cannot explain how to get there or how much it costs. You may find that you do not want to go anywhere at all. Many respected economists and philosophers argue quite convincingly that the government should *not* redistribute income.

Arguments Against Redistribution

Those who argue against government redistribution believe that the market, when left to operate on its own, is fair. This argument rests on the proposition that "one is entitled to the fruits of one's efforts."[6] Remember that if market theory is correct, rewards paid in the market are linked to productivity. In other words, labor and capital are paid in accordance with the value of what they produce.

This view also holds that property income—income from land or capital—is no less justified than labor income. All factors of production have marginal products. Capital owners receive profits or interest because the capital they own is productive.

The argument against redistribution also rests on the principles behind "freedom of contract" and the protection of property rights. When you agree to sell your labor or to commit your capital

---

[6] Powerful support for this notion of "entitlement" can be found in the works of the seventeenth-century English philosophers Thomas Hobbes and John Locke.

to use, you do so freely. In return, you contract to receive payment, which becomes your "property." When a government taxes you and gives your income to someone else, that action violates those two basic rights.

The more common arguments against redistribution are not philosophical. Instead, they point to more practical problems. First, it is said that taxation and transfer programs interfere with the basic incentives provided by the market. Taxing higher-income people reduces their incentive to work, save, and invest. Taxing the "winners" of the economic game also discourages risk taking. Furthermore, providing transfers to those at the bottom reduces their incentive to work as well. All of this leads to a reduction in total output that is the "cost" of redistribution.

Another practical argument against redistribution is that it does not work. Some critics see the rise in the poverty rate during the early 1980s, again in the early 1990s, and yet again between 2001 and 2004 as an indication that antipoverty programs simply drain money without really helping the poor out of poverty. Whether these programs actually help people out of poverty, the possibility of bureaucratic inefficiency in administration always exists. Social programs must be administered by people who must be paid. The Department of Health and Human Services employs over 120,000 people to run the Social Security system, process Medicaid claims, and so on. Some degree of waste and inefficiency is inevitable in any sizable bureaucracy.

Arguments in Favor of Redistribution

The argument most often used in favor of redistribution is that a society as wealthy as the United States has a moral obligation to provide all its members with the necessities of life. The Constitution does carry a guarantee of the "right to life." In declaring war on poverty in 1964, President Lyndon Johnson put it this way:

> There will always be some Americans who are better off than others. But it need not follow that the "poor are always with us."...It is high time to redouble and to concentrate our efforts to eliminate poverty....We know what must be done and this nation of abundance can surely afford to do it.[7]

Many people, often through no fault of their own, find themselves left out. Some are born with mental or physical problems that severely limit their ability to "produce." Then there are children. Even if some parents can be held accountable for their low incomes, do we want to punish innocent children for the faults of their parents and thus perpetuate the cycle of poverty? The elderly, without redistribution of income, would have to rely exclusively on savings to survive once they retire, and many conditions can lead to inadequate savings. Should the victims of bad luck be doomed to inevitable poverty? Illness is perhaps the best example. The accumulated savings of very few people can withstand the drain of extraordinary hospital and doctors' bills and the exorbitant cost of nursing home care.

Proponents of redistribution refute "practical" arguments against it by pointing to studies that show little negative effect on the incentives of those who benefit from transfer programs. For many—children, the elderly, the mentally ill—incentives are irrelevant, they say, and providing a basic income to most of the unemployed does not discourage them from working when they have the opportunity to do so. We now turn briefly to several more formal arguments.

utilitarian justice The idea that "a dollar in the hand of a rich person is worth less than a dollar in the hand of a poor person." If the marginal utility of income declines with income, transferring income from the rich to the poor will increase total utility.

Utilitarian Justice First put forth by the English philosophers Jeremy Bentham and John Stuart Mill in the late eighteenth and early nineteenth centuries, the essence of the utilitarian argument in favor of redistribution is that "a dollar in the hand of a rich person is worth less than a dollar in the hand of a poor person." The rich spend their marginal dollars on luxury goods. It is easy to spend over $100 per person for a meal in a good restaurant in New York or Los Angeles. The poor spend their marginal dollars on necessities—food, clothing, and medical care. If the marginal utility of income declines as income rises, the value of a dollar's worth of luxury goods is worth less than a dollar's worth of necessities. Thus, redistributing from the rich to the poor increases total utility. To put this notion of **utilitarian justice** in everyday language: Through income redistribution, the rich sacrifice a little and the poor gain a great deal.

[7] *Economic Report of the President*, 1964.

The utilitarian position is not without problems. People have very different tastes and preferences. Who is to say that you value a dollar more or less than I do? Because utility is unobservable and unmeasurable, comparisons between individuals cannot be easily made. Nonetheless, many people find the basic logic of the utilitarians to be persuasive.

Social Contract Theory—Rawlsian Justice The work of Harvard philosopher John Rawls has generated a great deal of recent discussion, both within the discipline of economics and between economists and philosophers.[8] In the tradition of Hobbes, Locke, and Rousseau, Rawls argues that as members of society, we have a contract with one another. In the theoretical world that Rawls imagines, an original *social contract* is drawn up and all parties agree to it without knowledge of who they are or who they will be in society. This condition is called the "original position" or the "state of nature." With no vested interests to protect, members of society are able to make disinterested choices.

As we approach the contract, everyone has a chance to end up very rich or homeless. On the assumption that we are all "risk-averse," Rawls believes that people will attach great importance to the position of the least fortunate members of society because anyone could end up there. **Rawlsian justice** is argued from the assumption of risk aversion. Rawls concludes that any contract emerging from the original position would call for an income distribution that would "maximize the well-being of the worst-off member of society."

Rawlsian justice A theory of distributional justice that concludes that the social contract emerging from the "original position" would call for an income distribution that would maximize the well-being of the worst-off member of society.

Any society bound by such a contract would allow for inequality, but only if that inequality had the effect of improving the lot of the very poor. If inequality provides an incentive for people to work hard and innovate, for example, those inequalities should be tolerated as long as some of the benefits go to those at the bottom.

The Works of Karl Marx For decades, a rivalry existed between the United States and the Soviet Union. At the heart of this rivalry was a fundamental philosophical difference of opinion about how economic systems work and how they should be managed. At the center of the debate were the writings of Karl Marx.

Marx did not write very much about socialism or communism. His major work, *Das Kapital* (published in the nineteenth century), was a three-volume analysis and critique of the capitalist system that he saw at work in the world around him. We know what Marx thought was wrong with capitalism, but he was not very clear about what should replace it. In one essay late in his life, he wrote, "from each according to his ability, to each according to his needs"[9]; but he was not specific about the applications of this principle.

Marx's view of capital income does have important implications for income distribution. In the preceding chapters, we discussed profit as a return to a productive factor: Capital, like labor, is productive and has a marginal product. However, Marx attributed all value to labor and none to capital. According to Marx's **labor theory of value**, the value of any commodity depends only on the amount of labor needed to produce it. The owners of capital are able to extract profit, or "surplus value," because labor creates more value in a day than it is paid for. Like any other good, labor power is worth only what it takes to "produce" it. In simple words, this means that under capitalism, labor is paid a subsistence wage.

labor theory of value Stated most simply, the theory that the value of a commodity depends only on the amount of labor required to produce it.

Marx saw profit as an illegitimate expropriation by capitalists of the fruits of labor's efforts. It follows that Marxians see the property income component of income distribution as the primary source of inequality in the United States today. Without capital income, the distribution of income would be more equal. (Refer again to Table 18.1 on p. 364.)

Income Distribution as a Public Good Those who argue that the unfettered market produces a just income distribution do not believe private charity should be forbidden. Voluntary redistribution does not involve any violation of property rights by the state.

In Chapter 16, however, you saw that there may be a problem with private charity. Suppose people really do want to end the hunger problem. As they write their checks to charity, they encounter the classic public-goods problem. First, there are free riders. If hunger and starvation are eliminated, the benefits—even the merely psychological benefits—flow to everyone whether they contributed or not. Second, any contribution is a drop in the bucket. One individual contribution is so small that it can have no real effect.

---

[8] See John Rawls, *A Theory of Justice* (Cambridge, MA: Harvard University Press, 1972).
[9] Karl Marx, "Critique of the Gotha Program" (May 1875), in *The Marx-Engels Reader*, ed. Robert Tucker (New York: W. W. Norton), p. 388.

With private charity, as with national defense, nothing depends on whether you pay. Thus, private charity may fail for the same reason that the private sector is likely to fail to produce national defense and other public goods. People will find it in their interest not to contribute. Thus, we turn to government to provide goods and services we want that will not be provided adequately if we act separately—in this case, help for the poor and hungry.

Redistribution Programs and Policies

The role of government in changing the *distribution of income* is hotly debated. The debate involves not only what government programs are appropriate to fight poverty but also the character of the tax system. Unfortunately, the quality of the public debate on the subject is low. Usually, the debate consists of a series of claims and counterclaims about what social programs do to incentives instead of a serious inquiry into what our distributional goal should be.

In this section, we talk about the tools of redistribution policy in the United States. As we do so, you will have a chance to assess for yourself some of the evidence about their effects.

Financing Redistribution Programs: Taxes

Redistribution always involves those who end up with less and those who end up with more. Because redistributional programs are financed by tax dollars, it is important to know who the donors and recipients are—who pays the taxes and who receives the benefits of those taxes. The issue of which households bear the burden of the taxes collected by government is quite complex and requires some analysis. Oftentimes households, firms, and markets react to the presence of taxes in ways that shift burdens off of those on whom they were intended to fall and onto others.

A perfect example is the corporation tax. At both the federal and state levels in most states, a special tax is levied on corporations in proportion to their profit or net income. Although this tax is levied on certain firms, the burden ultimately falls on households in one or more of a number of ways. The tax may result in higher prices for corporate products. The tax may result in lower wages for corporate employees, or the tax may result in lower profits for owners/shareholders of corporations. The ultimate impact of a tax, or set of taxes, on the distribution of income depends on which households end up bearing the burden after shifting has taken place.

The term *incidence* refers to the ultimate burden distribution of a tax. Chapter 19 illustrates the way in which economic analysis can be used to estimate the ultimate incidence of taxes.

The mainstay of the U.S. tax system is the individual income tax, authorized in 1913 by the Sixteenth Amendment to the Constitution. The income tax is *progressive*—those with higher incomes pay a higher percentage of their incomes in taxes. Even though the tax is subject to many exemptions, deductions, and so on, that allow some taxpayers to reduce their tax burdens, all studies of the income tax show that its burden as a percentage of income rises as income rises.

With the passage of the Tax Reform Act of 1986, Congress initiated a major change in income tax rates and regulations. The reforms were to simplify the tax and make it easier for people to comply with and harder to avoid. In addition, the act reduced the number of tax brackets and the overall progressivity of the rates. The largest reduction was in the top rate, cut from 50 percent to 28 percent in 1986. The Act also substantially reduced the tax burdens of those at the very bottom by increasing the amount of income a person can earn before paying any tax at all.

In 1993, President Clinton signed into law a tax bill that increased the top rate to 36 percent for families with taxable incomes over $140,000 and individuals with taxable incomes over $115,000. In addition, families with incomes of over $250,000 paid a surtax (a tax rate on a tax rate) of 10 percent, bringing the marginal rate for those families to 39.6 percent. Families with low incomes received grants and credits under the plan. On May 28, 2003, President Bush signed a tax law that reduced the top rate to 35 percent and changed a number of other provisions of the tax code. (See Chapter 19 for details.)

The individual income tax is only one tax among many. More important to the individual is the *overall* burden of taxation, including all federal, state, and local taxes. Most studies of the effect of taxes on the distribution of income, both before and after the Tax Reform Act, have concluded that the overall burden is roughly proportional. In other words, all people pay about the same percentage of their income in total taxes.

Table 18.6 presents an estimate of effective tax rates paid in 2000 by families that have been ranked by income. Although some progressivity is visible, it is very slight. The bottom 20 percent of the income earners pay 28 percent of their total incomes in tax. The top 1 percent pay 37.0 percent. We can conclude from these data that the tax side of the equation produces very little change in the distribution of income. (For more on taxes, see Chapter 19.)

TABLE 18.6 Effective Rates of Federal, State, and Local Taxes, 2000 (Taxes as a Percentage of Total Income)

	Federal	Total
Bottom 20%	5.9	28.1
Second 20	11.7	26.3
Third 20	17.4	29.2
Fourth 20	20.1	32.6
Top 20	24.6	33.9
Top 10	25.7	34.5
Top 5	26.6	34.9
Top 1	29.1	37.0

Source: Julie-Anne Cronin, U.S. Department of the Treasury, OTA paper 85, and authors' estimate.

Expenditure Programs

Some programs designed to redistribute income or to aid the poor provide cash income to recipients. Others provide benefits in the form of health care, subsidized housing, or food stamps. Still others provide training or help workers find jobs.

Social Security By far the largest income redistribution program in the United States is Social Security. The **Social Security system** is three programs financed through separate trust funds. The *Old Age and Survivors Insurance (OASI) program*, the largest of the three, pays cash benefits to retired workers, their survivors, and their dependents. The *Disability Insurance (DI) program* pays cash benefits to disabled workers and their dependents. The third, *Health Insurance (HI)*, or Medicare, provides medical benefits to workers covered by OASI and DI and the railroad retirement program. The Social Security system has been credited with substantially reducing poverty among the elderly.

Social Security system The federal system of social insurance programs. It includes three separate programs that are financed through separate trust funds: the Old Age and Survivors Insurance (OASI) program, the Disability Insurance (DI) program, and the Health Insurance (HI), or Medicare program.

Most workers in the United States must participate in the Social Security system. For many years, federal employees and employees belonging to certain state and municipal retirement systems were not required to participate, but federal employees are now being brought into the system. Today, well over 90 percent of all workers in the United States contribute to Social Security.

Participants and their employers are required to pay a *payroll tax* to the *Federal Insurance Corporation Association (FICA)* to finance the Social Security system. The tax in 2008 was 7.65 percent paid by employers and 7.65 percent paid by employees on wages up to $102,000. Self-employed people assume the entire FICA burden themselves.

You are entitled to Social Security benefits if you participate in the system for 10 years. Benefits are paid monthly to you after you retire or, if you die, to your survivors. A complicated formula based on your average salary while you were paying into the system determines your benefit level. Those who earned more receive a higher level of benefits, but there are maximum and minimum monthly benefits. By and large, low-salaried workers get more out of the system than they paid into it while they were working. High-salaried workers usually get out of the system considerably less than they put in.

The Social Security system is self-financing, but it is different from funded retirement systems. In a *funded system*, deposits (by the employer, the employee, or both) are made to an account in the employee's name. Those funds are invested and earn interest or dividends that accumulate until the employee's retirement, when they are withdrawn. Funded retirement plans operate very much like a savings plan that you might set up independently, except that you cannot touch the contents until you retire.

In the U.S. Social Security system, the tax receipts from today's workers are used to pay benefits to retired and disabled workers and their dependents today. Currently, the system is collecting more than it is paying out, and the excess is accumulating in the trust funds. This is necessary to keep the system solvent because after the year 2010, there will be a large increase in the number of retirees and a relative decline in the number of workers. These demographic changes are the result of a high birth rate between 1946 and 1964—the so-called baby boom. In 2007, 31.5 million retired workers received Social Security benefits and 7.1 million received disability payments.

public assistance, *or* welfare Government transfer programs that provide cash benefits to: (1) families with dependent children whose incomes and assets fall below a very low level and (2) the very poor regardless of whether they have children.

Public Assistance Next to Social Security, the biggest cash transfer program in the United States is **public assistance**, more commonly called **welfare**. Aimed specifically at the poor, welfare falls into two major categories.

Most welfare is paid in the form of *temporary assistance for needy families*. Benefit levels are set by the states, and they vary widely. In January 2003, the maximum monthly payment to a one-parent family of three was $170 per month in Mississippi, $639 per month in Vermont, and $923 per month in Alaska. The average monthly payment in the United States was $423. To participate, a family must have a very low income and virtually no assets. In 2002, there were 5.1 million recipients of Temporary Assistance for Needy Families in the United States. Those who find jobs and enter the labor force lose benefits quickly as their incomes rise. This loss of benefits acts as a tax on beneficiaries, and some argue that it discourages welfare recipients from seeking jobs.

No topics raise passions more than welfare and welfare reform. The issue has been a focal point of "liberal/conservative" name-calling for more than three decades. In 1996, Congress passed and President Clinton signed a major overhaul of the welfare system in the United States. The name of the program was changed to Temporary Assistance for Needy Families from its former name, Aid to Families with Dependent Children, as of July 1997. The key change mandated that states limit most recipients to no more than five years of benefits over a lifetime. Some argue that the result will be a disaster, with some families left with nothing. Others argue that the previous system led to dependency and that there was no incentive to work.

The new legislation provides funds for added services to parents with young children but leaves a great deal of discretion in states' hands. Only time will tell how it turns out. However, remarkable declines in the Temporary Assistance for Needy Families program (TANF) caseloads occurred between 1994 and 2001. At the end of that year, the average monthly number of TANF recipients was 5.5 million, or 56 percent lower than the Aid to Families with Dependent Children (AFDC) caseload in 1996. From its peak of 14.4 million in March 1994, the number dropped by 64.6 percent to 5.1 million in 2002. Over three-fourths of the reduction in the U.S. average monthly number of recipients since March 1994 occurred following implementation of TANF. These are the largest caseload declines in the history of U.S. public assistance programs.

Supplemental Security Income The *Supplemental Security Income program(SSI)* is a federal program that was set up under the Social Security Administration in 1974. The program is financed out of general revenues. That is, there is no trust fund and there are no earmarked taxes from which SSI benefits are paid out.

SSI is designed to take care of the elderly who end up very poor and have no or very low Social Security entitlement. In 2006, 7.2 million people received SSI payments, about half of whom also received some Social Security benefits. The average SSI payment was $454.75 per month. As with welfare, qualified recipients must have very low incomes and virtually no assets.

unemployment compensation A state government transfer program that pays cash benefits for a certain period of time to laid-off workers who have worked for a specified period of time for a covered employer.

Unemployment Compensation In the first quarter of 2005, governments paid out over $9.5 billion in benefits to 3.3 million recipients. The money to finance this benefit comes from taxes paid by employers into special funds. Companies that hire and fire frequently pay a higher tax rate, while companies with relatively stable employment levels pay a lower tax rate. Tax and benefit levels are determined by the states, within certain federal guidelines.

Workers who qualify for **unemployment compensation** begin to receive benefit checks soon after they are laid off. These checks continue for a period specified by the state. Most unemployment benefits continue for 20 weeks. In times of recession, the benefit period is often extended on a state-by-state basis. Average unemployed workers receive only about 36 percent of their normal wages, and not all workers are covered. To qualify for benefits, an unemployed person must have worked recently for a covered employer for a specified time for a given amount of wages. Recipients must also demonstrate willingness and ability to seek and accept suitable employment.

Unemployment benefits are not aimed at the poor alone, although many of the unemployed are poor. Unemployment benefits are paid regardless of a person's income from other sources and regardless of assets.

Medicaid *and* Medicare In-kind government transfer programs that provide health and hospitalization benefits: Medicare to the aged and their survivors and to certain of the disabled, regardless of income, and Medicaid to people with low incomes.

Medicaid and Medicare The largest in-kind transfer programs in the United States are Medicare and Medicaid. The **Medicaid** program provides health and hospitalization benefits to people with low incomes. Although the program is administered by the states, about 57 percent of the cost is borne by the federal government. In 2007, about 44 million people received benefits with total payments exceeding $290 billion.

Medicare, which is run by the Social Security Administration, is a health insurance program for the aged and certain disabled persons. Most U.S. citizens over age 65 receive Medicare hospital insurance coverage regardless of their income. In addition, they may elect to enroll in a supplementary medical insurance program under Medicare by paying a premium. Medicare pays only a part of total hospital expenses. When their hospital stay is longer than 60 days, for example, patients are responsible for $130 per day.

In 2004, over 41.7 million aged and disabled were covered by Medicare. Benefit payments reached $303 billion in 2004. Medicare has become a political football in Washington in recent years. Projections using conservative assumptions suggest that in 2009, total annual outlays will reach $500 billion and that the Medicare fund will be exhausted by 2020. As the baby boom generation reaches retirement after 2010, the current system is clearly unsustainable. This was an important issue in the most recent presidential election.

Food Stamps The Food Stamp program is an antipoverty program fully funded out of general federal tax revenues, with states bearing 50 percent of the program's administrative costs. **Food stamps** are vouchers that have a face value greater than their cost and that can be used to purchase food at grocery stores. The amount by which the face value of the stamps exceeds their cost depends on income and family size. Only low-income families and single people are eligible to receive food stamps.

food stamps Vouchers that have a face value greater than their cost and that can be used to purchase food at grocery stores.

It is generally acknowledged that a thriving black market in food stamps exists. Families that want or need cash can sell their food stamps to people who will buy them for less than face value but more than the original recipient paid for them.

In 2004, there were 24 million participants in the Food Stamp program. The total cost of the program in 2004 was $27 billion.

Housing Programs Over the years, the federal government and state governments have administered many different housing programs designed to improve the quality of housing for low-income people. The biggest is the Public Housing program, financed by the federal government but administered by local public housing authorities. Public housing tenants pay rents equal to no more than 30 percent of their incomes. In many cases, this means they pay nothing. The largest housing program, called "Section 8," provides housing assistance payments to tenants and slightly above-market rent guarantees to participating landlords.

In 2003, there were 33.5 million rental housing units in the United States, of which 1.9 million were in public housing projects. Another 2.2 million received a government rent subsidy.

The Earned Income Tax Credit An important program that is not well understood by most people is the earned income tax credit (EIC). The program is quite complex but essentially allows lower-income families with children a credit equal to a percentage of all wage and salary income against their income taxes. If the credit exceeds the amount of taxes due, the credit is refundable. To see roughly how the EIC works, consider a family made up of two adults and two children with an income of $11,000 per year, all earned as wages. After the standard deduction and exemptions, such a family would owe no taxes, but it would receive (subject to a number of restrictions) refundable credit of up to $3,800. That means the family would actually get a check for $3,800.

While not well known, the EIC program is very large. In 2006, the EIC was claimed by over 22 million households and totaled more than $43 billion.

How Effective Are Antipoverty Programs?

The number of people officially classified as poor dropped sharply during the 1960s and early 1970s. Between 1978 and 1983, however, the number of poor increased nearly 45 percent. After falling back between 1983 and 1989, the figure hit 39.3 million in 1994, the highest total since 1964. (The figure fell to 36.5 million in 2006.) The changing number of people classified as poor is at the center of a great debate over the effectiveness of antipoverty programs.

Some say economic growth is the best way to cure poverty. Poverty programs are expensive and must be paid for with tax revenues. The high rates of taxation to support these programs, critics say, have eroded the incentive to work, save, and invest, slowing the rate of economic growth. Critics also believe that the rise in poverty is evidence that antipoverty programs do not work.

The opposite view is that poverty would be more widespread without antipoverty programs. Poverty has increased not because of *increasing* programs, but because the "real" level of transfer payments has *fallen* significantly. In other words, transfer payments have not kept up with rising prices.

ECONOMICS IN PRACTICE

Does Price Matter in Charitable Giving?

In the United States, one of the ways in which people try to help the poor is through charity. Almost 90 percent of the population contributes each year to some charitable organization. Recent work in experimental economics has explored the factors that lead people to make these contributions. In experimental economics, experiments are conducted in a laboratory or in the field by using control groups to test economic theories. In some cases, the lessons learned have been put to use by charities as they try to raise funds.

One set of experiments looks at the effect of a matching gift on giving.[1] A matching gift is a commitment by a donor to give funds *conditioned on* another person's donation. A donor might say, for example, "For every dollar you raise up to $20,000, I will match with a dollar of my own." Why might an economist expect a matching gift commitment to increase the likelihood that another person will give to the charity?

There are at least two plausible explanations. In the previous chapter of this book, we described *signals*. In this situation, by offering a matching gift, in a public way, the original donor is telling other potential donors that he or she believes the charity to be worthy. If the donor is a well-known member of the community, this signal can be a powerful incentive to other givers.

Suppose that we think of "giving to charity" the same way we think of buying a good or a service. That is, we do it because we derive "utility" from it. If we do donate to charity, we are giving up the other things that the donation would buy. Now think of the "price of giving" as the amount you need to pay to deliver $10 in aid to a charity. With the matching grant, the price of giving falls to $5. If you give $5, the charity gets $10. If you give $100, the charity gets $200. So matching gifts are like reducing the "price" of a charitable gift.

Under the U.S. Income Tax, many taxpayers can deduct gifts to qualifying charities from their income in calculating their taxes each year. Suppose that a taxpayer were taxed at a marginal rate of 25 percent. Then a gift of $100 results in a tax saving of $25. The deduction reduces income by $100, and that $100 would have been taxed at 25 percent. Thus, just as in the case of the matching grant, the "price of giving" is reduced, in this case the price of giving $100 is reduced to $75. With deductibility, we reduce the price of charity from P to $P(1-t)$ where t is the tax rate that applies to increases or decreases in income. Do you see why?

Whether a reduction in "price" leads people to give more depends on a lot of things. If it is a matching grant, you may give less and deliver more charity due to the match or you may give more to take advantage of the match. In the Karlan and List experiments, matching gift programs increased rates of giving.

1. Dean Karlan and John List, "Does Price Matter in Charitable Giving" *American Economics Review*, 2008.

Despite the anti-big-government rhetoric of recent years, most of what the government did to change the distribution of income 15 years ago it still does today. The volume of redistribution is less, but most major programs have remained largely intact. Many still argue we do too little. The poverty rate was 12.3 percent in 2006, and homelessness was a serious problem in many U.S. cities.

Government or the Market? A Review

In Part II (Chapter 6 to 12), you were introduced to the behavior of households and firms in input and output markets. You learned that if all the assumptions of perfect competition held in the real world, the outcome would be perfectly efficient.

As we began to relax the assumptions of perfect competition in Part III (Chapter 13 to Chapter 19), we began to see a potential role for government in the economy. Some firms acquire market power and tend to underproduce and overprice. Unregulated markets give private decision makers no incentives to weigh the social costs of externalities. Goods that provide collective benefits may not be produced in sufficient quantities without government involvement. As we saw in this chapter, the final distribution of well-being determined by the unfettered market may not be considered equitable by society.

Remember, however, that government is not a cure for all economic woes. There is no guarantee that public-sector involvement will improve matters. Many argue that government involvement may bring about even more inequity and inefficiency because bureaucrats are often driven by self-interest, not public interest.

SUMMARY

THE UTILITY POSSIBILITIES FRONTIER *p. 359*

1. Even if all markets were perfectly efficient, the result might not be fair. Even in relatively unfettered market economies, governments redistribute income and wealth, usually in the name of fairness, or *equity*.
2. Because utility is neither directly observable nor measurable, most policy discussions deal with the distributions of income and wealth as imperfect substitutes for the concept of "the distribution of well-being."

THE SOURCES OF HOUSEHOLD INCOME *p. 360*

3. Households derive their incomes from three basic sources: (1) from wages or salaries received in exchange for labor (about 64 percent), (2) from property such as capital and land (about 22 percent), and (3) from government (about 14 percent).
4. Differences in wage and salary incomes across households result from differences in the characteristics of workers (skills, training, education, experience, and so on) and from differences in jobs (dangerous, exciting, glamorous, difficult, and so on). Household income also varies with the number of household members in the labor force, and it can decline sharply if members become unemployed.
5. The amount of property income that a household earns depends on the amount and kinds of property it owns. Transfer income from governments flows substantially but not exclusively to lower-income households. Except for Social Security, transfer payments are by and large designed to provide income to those in need.

THE DISTRIBUTION OF INCOME *p. 363*

6. The 20 percent of families at the top of the income distribution received 50.5 percent of the money income in the United States in 2006, while the bottom 20 percent earned just 3.4 percent. Income distribution in the United States has remained basically stable over a long period of time.
7. The Lorenz curve is a commonly used graphic device for describing the distribution of income. The Gini coefficient is an index of income inequality that ranges from 0 for perfect equality to 1 for total inequality.
8. Poverty is very difficult to define. Nonetheless, the official poverty line in the United States is fixed at three times the cost of the Department of Agriculture's minimum food budget. In 2006, the poverty line for a family of four was $17,628.
9. Between 1960 and 1970, the number of people officially classified as poor fell from 40 million to 25 million. That number did not change much between 1970 and 1978. Between 1978 and 1983, the number of poor people increased by nearly 45 percent to 35.3 million. In 2006, the figure was 36.5 million.
10. Data on the distribution of wealth are not as readily available as data on the distribution of income. The distribution of wealth in the United States is more unequal than the distribution of income. The wealthiest 10 percent of households own just under 70 percent of all household net worth in 2004.

THE REDISTRIBUTION DEBATE *p. 369*

11. The basic philosophical argument against government redistribution rests on the proposition that one is entitled to the fruits of one's efforts. The argument also rests on the principles of freedom of contract and protection of property rights. More common arguments focus on the negative effects of redistribution on incentives to work, save, and invest.
12. The basic philosophical argument in favor of redistribution is that a society as rich as the United States has a moral obligation to provide all its members with the basic necessities of life. More formal arguments can be found in the works of the utilitarians, Rawls, and Marx.

REDISTRIBUTION PROGRAMS AND POLICIES *p. 372*

13. In the United States, redistribution is accomplished through taxation and through a number of government transfer programs. The largest of these programs are Social Security, public assistance, supplemental security, unemployment compensation, Medicare and Medicaid, food stamps, and various housing subsidy programs (including public housing).
14. The increase in poverty during the 1980s and 1990s is at the center of a great debate over the effectiveness of antipoverty programs. One view holds that the best way to cure poverty is with economic growth. Poverty programs are expensive and must be paid for with tax revenues. The high rates of taxation required to support these programs have eroded the incentive to work, save, and invest, thus slowing the rate of economic growth. In addition, the rise in poverty is cited as evidence that antipoverty programs do not work. The opposite view holds that without antipoverty programs, poverty would be much worse.

REVIEW TERMS AND CONCEPTS

compensating differentials, *p. 361*
economic income, *p. 363*
equity, *p. 359*
food stamps, *p. 375*
Gini coefficient, *p. 364*
human capital, *p. 361*
labor theory of value, *p. 371*
Lorenz curve, *p. 364*
Medicaid *and* Medicare, *p. 374*
minimum wage, *p. 361*
money income, *p. 364*
poverty line, *p. 368*
property income, *p. 363*
public assistance, *or* welfare, *p. 374*
Rawlsian justice, *p. 371*
Social Security system, *p. 373*
transfer payments, *p. 363*
unemployment compensation, *p. 374*
utilitarian justice, *p. 370*
utility possibilities frontier, *p. 360*

PROBLEMS

Visit **www.myeconlab.com** to complete the problems marked in orange online. You will receive instant feedback on your answers, tutorial help, and access to additional practice problems.

1. One of the issues that is debated in virtually every election is whether to raise the minimum wage, which stood at $6.55 per hour in 2008. Assume that you are married with a child, living on the minimum wage. By assuming that you pay taxes of about 10 percent of your total pay, how much do you "take home" each month? How much does it cost to rent a "reasonable" apartment near where you live? How much would you have left after paying rent? How much would it cost for other items such as food? Work out a hypothetical "budget" for this family.

2. By using the data in the following table, create two graphs. The first graph should plot the Lorenz curves for African-American families and white families. The second graph should plot the Lorenz curve for the 1980 "all" data and the Lorenz curve for the 1995 "all" data.

   In each graph, which has the higher Gini coefficient? How do you interpret the result?

	PERCENT OF INCOME			
	AFRICAN-AMERICAN	WHITE	1995 ALL	1980 ALL
Lowest fifth	3.2	4.6	4.2	5.1
Second fifth	8.5	10.3	10.0	11.6
Third fifth	15.1	15.8	15.7	17.5
Fourth fifth	24.7	23.0	23.3	24.3
Highest fifth	48.7	46.3	46.9	41.6

3. Economists call education "an investment in human capital." Define *capital*. In what sense is education capital? Investments are undertaken to earn a rate of return. Describe the return to an investment in a college education. How would you go about measuring it? How would you decide if it is good enough to warrant the investment?

4. Following is a list of establishment categories and average weekly earnings for nonsupervisory employees in a recent year. Using the concepts of "human capital" and "compensating differentials," explain why they might be expected to differ in these areas:

Computer programming	$724.85
Heavy construction firms	535.29
Logging firms	447.02
Gas stations	218.13
Car washes	161.19

5. During the mid-1980s and again between 1995 and 2006, house values and rents rose sharply in California and in the northeastern United States. But starting in 2006, prices began to fall. Homeowners, who have higher incomes on average than renters, benefit from house-price increases and are protected from housing-cost increases. Falling house prices, on the other hand, make housing more affordable but inflict pain on homeowners. Renters experience rising rents and falling standards of living if incomes do not keep up with rents. Using the *Statistical Abstract of the United States*, other data sources, www.census.gov, www.ofheo.gov, or http://macromarkets.com, look up residential rent, home prices, and income levels for your area. What has happened in the last 10 years? Do you think the performance of the housing market in recent years has increased or decreased inequality in your area? Explain.

6. New PhDs in economics entering the job market find that academic jobs (jobs teaching at colleges and universities) pay about 30 percent less than nonacademic jobs such as working at a bank or a consulting firm. Those who take academic jobs are clearly worse off than those who take nonacademic jobs. Do you agree? Explain your answer.

7. Should welfare benefits be higher in California and New York than in Mississippi? Defend your answer.

8. Poverty among the elderly has been sharply reduced in the last quarter-century. How has this reduction been accomplished?

9. "Income inequality is evidence that our economic system is working well, not poorly." Do you agree or disagree? Defend your answer.

10. The official poverty line has been the subject of much debate over the last few decades. On Google or another search engine, look up and read the work of Molly Orshansky. Her work focused on finding a measure of poverty that reflected a bundle of goods that people in different circumstances must be able to purchase. Describe the debate and the resulting system for setting the poverty thresholds. How would you change them?

11. **[Related to the *Economics in Practice* on *p. 376*]** Some economists predict that an increase in the marginal income tax rate would increase the amount of charitable giving that people do even though this increase would require wealthier people to pay more taxes. Why do you think economists are predicting this effect?

Public Finance: The Economics of Taxation

19

The previous chapters in Part III have analyzed the potential role of government in the economy. Together those chapters discuss much of the field of *public economics*. In this chapter, we make the transition to *public finance*. No matter what functions we end up assigning to government, to do anything at all, government must first raise revenues. The primary vehicle that the government uses to finance itself is taxation.

Taxes may be imposed on transactions, institutions, property, meals, and other things, but in the final analysis they are paid by individuals or households.

CHAPTER OUTLINE

The Economics of Taxation

To begin our analysis of the U.S. tax system, we need to clarify some terms. There are many kinds of taxes and tax analysts use a specific language to describe them.

Taxes: Basic Concepts

Every tax has two parts: a *base* and a *rate structure*. The **tax base** is the measure or value upon which the tax is levied. In the United States, taxes are levied on a variety of bases, including income, sales, property, and corporate profits. The **tax rate structure** determines the portion of the tax base that must be paid in taxes. A tax rate of 25 percent on income, for example, means that you pay a tax equal to 25 percent of your income.

tax base The measure or value upon which a tax is levied.

tax rate structure The percentage of a tax base that must be paid in taxes—25 percent of income, for example.

Taxes on Stocks versus Taxes on Flows Tax bases may be either stock measures or flow measures. The local property tax is a tax on the value of residential, commercial, or industrial property. A homeowner, for instance, is taxed on the current assessed value of his or her home. Current value is a *stock variable*—that is, it is measured or estimated at a point in time.

Other taxes are levied on *flows*. Income is a flow. Most people are paid on a monthly basis, and they have taxes taken out every month. Retail sales take place continuously and a retail sales tax takes a portion of that flow. Figure 19.1 diagrams in simple form the important continuous payment flows between households and firms and the points at which the government levies six different taxes.

Table 19.1 shows the evolution of federal tax receipts since 1960. While the individual income tax has remained around 45 percent of federal receipts since 1960, other taxes have changed share. The corporation income tax, levied on incorporated businesses only, has fallen from 23.2 percent of the total in 1960 to only 11.8 percent of receipts in 2008. The payroll tax, almost all of which is earmarked for the Social Security system and Medicare, has grown from just under 16 percent of the total to nearly 35 percent in 2008.

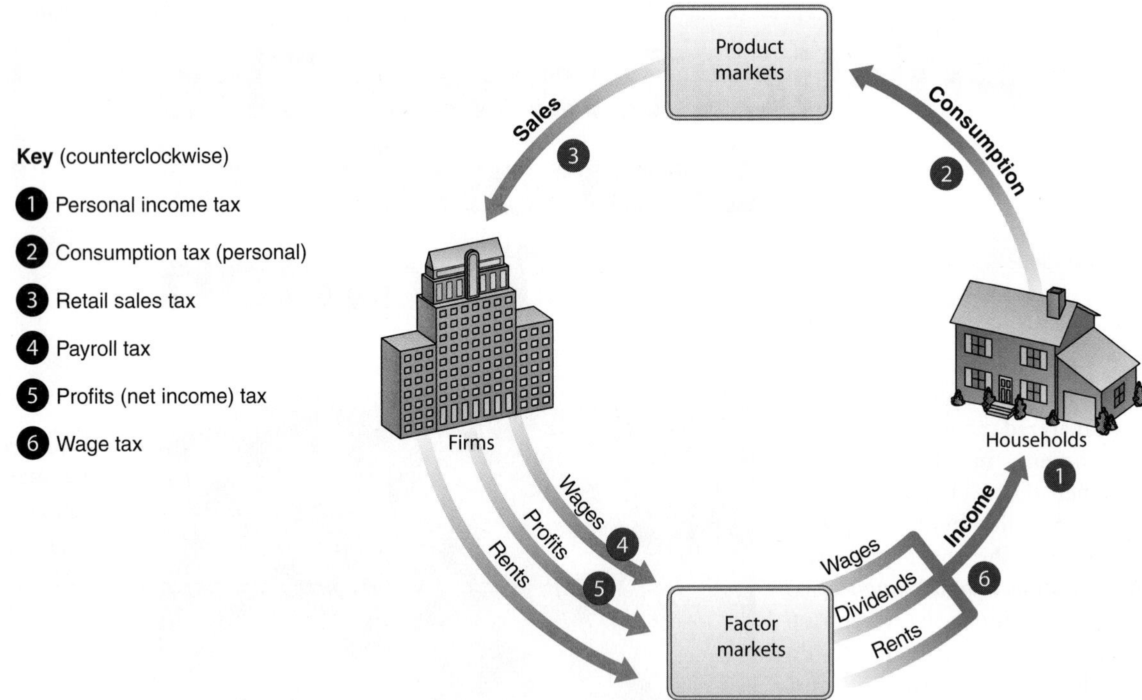

▲ **FIGURE 19.1 Taxes on Economic "Flows"**
Most taxes are levied on measurable economic flows. For example, a profits, or net income, tax is levied on the annual profits earned by corporations.

TABLE 19.1 Federal Government Receipts 1960–2008 (billions of dollars)

	Individual Income Tax	Corporation Income Tax	Social Insurance Payroll Taxes	Excise Taxes	Other Receipts	Total
1960	40.7	21.5	14.7	11.7	3.9	92.5
%	**44.0**	**23.2**	**15.9**	**12.6**	**4.2**	**100**
1970	90.4	32.8	44.4	15.7	9.5	192.8
%	**46.9**	**17.0**	**23.0**	**8.1**	**4.9**	**100**
1980	244.1	64.6	157.8	24.3	26.3	517.1
%	**47.2**	**12.5**	**30.1**	**4.7**	**5.1**	**100**
1990	466.9	93.5	380.0	35.3	56.2	1,032.0
%	**45.2**	**9.1**	**36.8**	**3.4**	**5.4**	**100**
2000	1004.5	207.3	652.9	68.9	92.0	2025.5
%	**49.6**	**10.2**	**32.2**	**3.4**	**4.5**	**100**
2008	1,246.6	314.9	927.2	68.1	105.6	2,662.0
%	**46.8**	**11.8**	**34.8**	**2.6**	**4.0**	**100**

Source: United States, Office of Management and Budget. Percentages may not add to 100 due to rounding.

proportional tax A tax whose burden is the same proportion of income for all households.

progressive tax A tax whose burden, expressed as a percentage of income, increases as income increases.

Proportional, Progressive, and Regressive Taxes All taxes are ultimately paid out of income. A tax whose burden is the same proportion of income for all households is a **proportional tax.** A tax of 20 percent on all forms of income, with no deductions or exclusions, is a proportional tax.

A tax that exacts a higher percentage of income from higher-income households than from lower-income households is a **progressive tax.** Because its rate structure increases with income, the U.S. individual income tax is a progressive tax. Under current law, a family with a taxable income of under $14,000 would pay a tax of 10 percent while a family with an income of $100,000 would pay about 19 percent.

A tax that exacts a lower percentage of income from higher-income families than from lower-income families is a **regressive tax**. *Excise taxes* (taxes on specific commodities such as gasoline and telephone calls) are regressive. The retail sales tax is also a regressive tax. Suppose the retail sales tax in your state is 5 percent. You might assume that it is a proportional tax because everyone pays 5 percent. But all people do not spend the same fraction of their income on taxable goods and services. In fact, higher-income households save a larger fraction of their incomes. Even though they spend more on expensive things and may pay more taxes in *dollars* than lower-income families, they end up paying a smaller *proportion* of their incomes in sales tax.

regressive tax A tax whose burden, expressed as a percentage of income, falls as income increases.

Table 19.2 shows this principle at work in three families. The lowest-income family saves 20 percent of its $10,000 income, leaving $8,000 for consumption. With a hypothetical 5 percent sales tax, the household pays $400, or 4 percent of total income, in tax. The $50,000 family saves 50 percent of its income, or $25,000, leaving $25,000 for consumption. With the 5 percent sales tax, the household pays $1,250, only 2.5 percent of its total income, in tax.

TABLE 19.2 The Burden of a Hypothetical 5% Sales Tax Imposed on Three Households with Different Incomes

Household	Income	Saving Rate, %	Saving	Consumption	5% Tax on Consumption	Tax as a % of Income
A	$10,000	20	$ 2,000	$ 8,000	$ 400	4.0
B	20,000	40	8,000	12,000	600	3.0
C	50,000	50	25,000	25,000	1,250	2.5

Marginal versus Average Tax Rates When discussing a specific tax or taxes in general, we should distinguish between average tax rate and marginal tax rates. Your **average tax rate** is the total amount of tax you pay divided by your total income. If you earned a total income of $15,000 and paid income taxes of $1,500, your average income tax rate would be 10 percent ($1,500 divided by $15,000). If you paid $3,000 in taxes, your average rate would be 20 percent ($3,000 divided by $15,000). Your **marginal tax rate** is the tax rate you pay on any additional income you earn. If you take a part-time job and pay an additional $280 in tax on the extra $1,000 you've earned, your marginal tax rate is 28 percent ($280 divided by $1,000).

average tax rate Total amount of tax paid divided by total income.

marginal tax rate The tax rate paid on any additional income earned.

Marginal and average tax rates are usually different. The U.S. individual income tax shows how and why marginal tax rates can differ. Each year you must file a tax return with the Internal Revenue Service on or before April 15. On that form, you first figure out the total tax you are responsible for paying. Next, you determine how much was withheld from your income and sent to the IRS by your employer. If too much was withheld, you get a refund; if not enough was withheld, you have to write a check to the government for the difference.

In figuring out the total amount of tax you must pay, you first add up all your income. You are then allowed to subtract certain items from it. Among the things that virtually all taxpayers can subtract are the *personal exemption* and the *standard deduction.*[1] After everything is subtracted, you are left with *taxable income*. Taxable income is then subject to a set of marginal rates that rise with income. Table 19.3 presents the marginal individual income tax rates for 2007.

Suppose you are a single taxpayer who earned $100,000 in 2007. It was a very good year! During 2007, you had tax withheld by your employer. By April 15, 2008, you had to file a return to see if your employer withheld too much or too little. Rushing to meet the deadline, you had to do the following calculations, which are summarized in Table 19.4.

[1] Deductions and exemptions have no definition other than they are amounts that you are allowed to subtract from income before figuring your tax. In 2007, a single taxpayer could subtract a *personal exemption* of $3,400. A married couple could subtract twice that amount plus $3,400 for every dependent child in the family. If your parents claim you as a dependent, you cannot claim an exemption for yourself when you file as an individual. Taxpayers in 2007 were also permitted to subtract either a *standard deduction* of $5,350 ($10,700 for a married couple) or itemized deductions if they exceeded $5,350. Expenditures that can be itemized and deducted include extraordinary medical expenses, state and local income and property taxes, mortgage interest paid, and charitable contributions. The standard deduction is larger for those who are over 65 and/or blind.

TABLE 19.3 Individual Income Tax Rates, 2007

Married Couples Filing Jointly Taxable Income	Tax Rate
$0–15,650	10%
$15,651–63,700	15%
$63,701–128,500	25%
$128,501–195,850	28%
$195,851–349,700	33%
More than $349,700	35%

Single Taxpayer Taxable Income	Tax Rate
$0–7,825	10%
$7,826–31,850	15%
$31,851–77,100	25%
$77,101–160,850	28%
$160,851–349,700	33%
More than $349,700	35%

Source: The Internal Revenue Service.

TABLE 19.4 Tax Calculations for a Single Taxpayer Who Earned $100,000 in 2007

Total income	$ 100,000
−Personal exemption	3,400
−Standard deduction	5,350
= Taxable income	$ 91,250
Tax Calculation	
0–$7,825 taxed at 10% = 7,825 × .10 =	$782.50
$7,825–$31,850 taxed at 15% ($31,850 − $7,825) × .15 = $24,025 × .15 =	$ 3,603.75
$31,850–$77,100 taxed at 25% = ($77,100 − $31,850) × .25 = $45,250 × .25 =	$11,312.50
Income over $77,100 taxed at 28% = ($91,250 − $77,100) × .28 = $14,150 × .28 =	$ 3,962
Total tax	$19,660.75
Average tax rate	19.7%
Marginal tax rate	28%

First, take your total income, $100,000, and subtract the personal exemption ($3,400) and the standard deduction ($5,350), leaving "Taxable Income" of $91,250. To figure the tax, in principle, four separate calculations are involved.[2] The first $7,825 is taxed at 10 percent. (See Table 19.3). The tax on this amount is simply .10 × $7,825, or $782.50.

The second "slice" of income, between $7,825 and $31,850, is taxed at 15 percent. The difference between $7,825 and $31,850 is $24,025. The tax on this amount is .15 × $24,025, or $3,603.75. The third "slice" of income, between $31,850 and $77,100, is taxed at 25 percent. The difference between $31,850 and $77,100 is $45,250. The tax on this amount is .25 × $45,250, or $11,312.50. Finally, the last "slice" of income, from $77,100 up to our taxable income of $91,250, is taxed at 28 percent. The tax at this amount is .28 × $14,150, or $3,962. Thus, the total tax due is $782.50 + $3,603.75 + $11,312.50 + $3,962 = $19,660.75. You now check to see if the amount withheld by your employer was too little or too much. If you paid too much, you get a refund; if you did not pay enough, you must send Uncle Sam a check for the shortfall by April 15.

You can now see the difference between average and marginal tax rates. Your average rate in 2007 was $19,660.75 as a percentage of $100,000, or 19.7 percent. But note that any *additional* income that you might have earned up to $160,850 would be taxed at 28 percent because it is more income over $77,101.

[2] Taxpayers do not have to do these calculations. Rather, filers simply look up the tax due for their particular income level in the tax table that accompanies their tax form package. Many use commercial software such as Turbo Tax.

How Much Does a Deduction Save You in Taxes? As you saw in the example, you were allowed to subtract $5,350 from your income as a "standard deduction." However, you may be able to do better (that is, pay less tax) if you can come up with "itemized deductions" in excess of $5,350. Taxpayers may deduct income taxes paid to a state, charitable contributions to qualifying organizations, real estate taxes, and interest paid on a mortgage to finance the purchase of a home, as well as other items.

For many taxpayers, itemized deductions are much higher than the standard deduction. Let's say that you paid $7,700 in interest on your condo loan in 2007. Your local property tax on the condo was $2,300, you paid state income taxes of $3,800, and gave $2,000 to your church. Your total deductions are equal to $15,800, which is $10,450 more than the standard deduction of $5,350.

As a result, your taxable income is reduced by $10,450 from $91,250 (see Table 19.4) to $80,800. Now if you figure the tax on $80,800, it is $16,734.75 instead of $19,660.75. You can work through the calculations in Table 19.4 to verify this. Your taxes have been reduced by $2,926. If you perform the calculations, you will see that the only thing that has changed is the amount of income taxed at the 28 percent rate. By increasing the amount that you deduct by $10,450, you reduce your taxes by exactly 28 percent of that amount. That is, your tax savings is $2,926, which is 28 percent of $10,450.

Note that because *marginal* dollars of income are subject to a 28 percent tax rate, any reduction of your taxable income through an additional deduction saves you a tax of 28 percent of that amount. If you were to give an extra $1,000 to the Red Cross, a qualifying charity, you would save $280 (28 percent) in taxes.

Some people complain that high-income households receive a bigger benefit from deductions. For example, if a single person with very high income—let's say over $400,000—gave the same contribution of $1,000, she would save $350 (35 percent in taxes). The highest rate applied to income in the highest bracket is 35 percent. If another person had a taxable income of only $20,000, the same $1,000 charitable contribution would save her only $150 because she would face a marginal rate of only 15 percent.

This example gives you a taste of the U.S. Individual Income Tax. It is a very complex tax, and most people need help in figuring out how to comply with the law. One of the top priorities of each of the past five presidents of the United States has been to simplify the tax code, and while the Tax Reform Act of 1986 made some progress, the code seems to get more complex with every passing year.

Part of the reason taxes are such a political issue is because people differ in how they define fairness. But people also differ in the effect they think different tax structures will have on behavior of the people and institutions in the economy. Here the distinction we have made between marginal and average tax rates plays a big role. Suppose you have a job with a salary of $100,000 per year and you have the opportunity to work a little harder and earn another $1,000. With no taxes at all, your efforts reward you with the full $1,000. With a marginal tax rate of 28 percent, your increased efforts give you an added $720. In some European countries, marginal tax rates are in excess of 50 percent, meaning that the majority of the gains from the incremental $1,000 go to the government. At least some economists believe that individuals react to high marginal tax rates by working less. Notice that the relevant rate is the marginal tax rate—the rate charged on the incremental earnings—and not the average rate. In the area of charitable giving, some economists have found that increasing the marginal tax rate increases charitable giving by making it "cheaper" to give. Changes in the marginal tax rate facing corporations can also affect their investment levels and even their location decisions.

Tax Equity

One of the criteria for evaluating the economy that we defined in Chapter 1 (and returned to in Chapter 18) was fairness, or *equity*. Everyone agrees that tax burdens should be distributed fairly, that all of us should pay our "fair share" of taxes, but there is endless debate about what constitutes a fair tax system.

One theory of fairness is called the **benefits-received principle**. Dating back to the eighteenth-century economist Adam Smith and earlier writers, the benefits-received principle holds that taxpayers should contribute to government according to the benefits they derive

benefits-received principle A theory of fairness holding that taxpayers should contribute to government (in the form of taxes) in proportion to the benefits they receive from public expenditures.

from public expenditures. This principle ties the tax side of the fiscal equation to the expenditure side. For example, the owners and users of cars pay gasoline and automotive excise taxes, which are paid into the Federal Highway Trust Fund to build and maintain the federal highway system. The beneficiaries of public highways are thus taxed in rough proportion to their use of those highways.

The difficulty with applying the benefits principle is that many public expenditures are for public goods—national defense, for example. The benefits of public goods fall collectively on all members of society, and there is no way to determine what value individual taxpayers receive from them.

ability-to-pay principle A theory of taxation holding that citizens should bear tax burdens in line with their ability to pay taxes.

A different principle, and one that has dominated the formulation of tax policy in the United States for decades, is the **ability-to-pay principle**. This principle holds that taxpayers should bear tax burdens in line with their ability to pay. Here the tax side of the fiscal equation is viewed separately from the expenditure side. Under this system, the problem of attributing the benefits of public expenditures to specific taxpayers or groups of taxpayers is avoided.

Horizontal and Vertical Equity If we accept the idea that ability to pay should be the basis for the distribution of tax burdens, two principles follow. First, the principle of *horizontal equity* holds that those with equal ability to pay should bear equal tax burdens. Second, the principle of *vertical equity* holds that those with greater ability to pay should pay more.

Although these notions seem appealing, we must have answers to two interdependent questions before they can be meaningful. First, how is ability to pay measured? What is the "best" tax base? Second, if A has a greater ability to pay than B, *how much* more should A contribute?

What is the "Best" Tax Base?

The three leading candidates for best tax base are *income*, *consumption*, and *wealth*. Before we consider each as a basis for taxation, let us see what they mean.

Income—to be precise, *economic income*—is anything that enhances your ability to command resources. The technical definition of economic income is the value of what you consume plus any change in the value of what you own:

Economic Income = Consumption + Change in Net Worth

This broad definition is essentially consumption + saving, but it includes many items not counted by the Internal Revenue Service and some items the Census Bureau does not include in its definition of "money income." Economic income includes all money receipts, whether from employment, interest on savings, dividends, profits, or transfers from the government. It also includes the value of benefits not received in money form, such as medical benefits, employer retirement contributions, paid country club memberships, and so on. Increases or decreases in the value of stocks or bonds, whether or not they are "realized" through sale, are part of economic income. For income tax purposes, capital gains (increases in the value of assets, like shares of stock) count as income only when they are realized; but for purposes of defining economic income, all increases in asset values count, whether they are realized or not.

A few other items that we do not usually think of as income are included in a comprehensive definition of income. If you own your house outright and live in it rent free, income flows from your house just as interest flows from a bond or profit from a share of stock. By owning the house, you enjoy valuable housing benefits for which you would otherwise have to pay rent. You are your own landlord, and you are, in essence, earning your own rent. Other components of economic income include any gifts and bequests received and food grown at home. In economic terms, income is income regardless of source and use.

Consumption is the total value of goods and services that a household consumes in a given period.

Wealth, or *net worth*, is the value of all the goods and services you own after your liabilities are subtracted. If today you were to sell everything of value you own—stocks, bonds, houses, cars, and so on—at their current market prices and pay off all your debts—loans, mortgages, and so on—you would end up with your net worth.

Net worth = Assets − Liabilities

Remember, income and consumption are *flow* measures. We speak of income per month or per year. Wealth and net worth are *stock* measures at a point in time.

For years, conventional wisdom among economists held that income was the best measure of ability to pay taxes. Many who believe that consumption is a better measure have recently challenged that assumption. The following arguments are not just arguments about fairness and ability to pay; they are also arguments about the best base for taxation.

Remember as you proceed that the issue is which *base* is the best base, not which *tax* is the best tax or whether taxes ought to be progressive or regressive. Sales taxes are regressive, but it is possible to have a personal consumption tax that is progressive. Under such a system, individuals would report their income as they do now, but all documented saving would be deductible. The difference between income and saving is a measure of personal consumption that could be taxed with progressive rates.

Consumption as the Best Tax Base The view favoring consumption as the best tax base dates back to at least the seventeenth-century English philosopher Thomas Hobbes, who argued that people should pay taxes in accordance with "what they actually take out of the common pot, not what they leave in." The standard of living, the argument goes, depends not on income, but on how much income is spent. If we want to redistribute well-being, therefore, the tax base should be consumption because consumption is the best measure of well-being.

A second argument with a distinguished history dates back to work done by Irving Fisher in the early part of the last century. Fisher and many others have argued that a tax on income discourages saving by taxing savings twice. A story told originally by Fisher illustrates this theory nicely.[3]

Suppose Alex builds a house for Frank. In exchange, Frank pays Alex $10,000 and gives him an orchard containing 100 apple trees. Alex spends the $10,000 today, but he saves the orchard, and presumably he will consume or sell the fruit it bears every year in the future. At year's end, the state levies a 10 percent tax on Alex's total income, which includes the $10,000 and the orchard. First, the government takes 10 percent of the $10,000, which is 10 percent of Alex's consumption. Second, it takes 10 percent of the orchard—10 trees—which is 10 percent of Alex's saving. If this is all the government did, there would be no double taxation of saving. If, however, the income tax is also levied the following year, Alex will be taxed on the income generated by the 90 trees that he still owns. If the income tax is levied in the year after that, Alex will again be taxed on the income generated by his orchard, and so on. The income tax is thus taxing Alex's saving more than once. To tax the orchard fairly, the system should take 10 percent of the trees *or* 10 percent of the fruit going forward—*but not both!* To avoid the double taxation of savings, either the original savings of 100 trees should not be taxed or the income generated from the after-tax number of trees (90) should not be taxed.

The same logic can be applied to cash savings. Suppose the income tax rate is 25 percent and you earn $20,000. Out of the $20,000, you consume $16,000 and save $4,000. At the end of the year, you owe the government 25 percent of your total income, or $5,000. You can think of this as a tax of 25 percent on consumption ($4,000) and 25 percent on savings ($1,000). Why, then, do we say that the income tax is a double tax on savings? To see why, you have to think about the $4,000 that is saved.

If you save $4,000, you will no doubt put it to some use. Saving possibilities include putting it in an interest-bearing account or buying a bond. If you do either, you will earn interest that you can consume in future years. In fact, when we save and earn interest, we are spreading some of our present earnings over future years of consumption. Just as the orchard yields future fruit, the bond yields future interest, which is considered income in the year it is earned and is taxed as such. The only way you can earn that future interest income is by leaving your money tied up in the bond or the account. You can consume the $4,000 today, *or* you can have the future flow of interest; you can't have both. Yet both are taxed!

Taxing consumption is also more efficient than taxing income. As you will see later, a tax that distorts economic choices creates *excess burdens*. By double-taxing savings, an income tax distorts the choice between consumption and saving, which is really the choice between present consumption and future consumption. Double-taxing also tends to reduce the saving rate and the rate of investment—and ultimately the rate of economic growth.

Income as the Best Tax Base Your ability to pay is your ability to command resources, and many argue that your income is the best measure of your capacity to command resources today. According to proponents of income as a tax base, you should be taxed not on what you

[3] Irving Fisher and Herbert Fisher, *Constructive Income Taxation: A Proposal for Reform* (New York: Harper, 1942), Ch. 8, p. 56.

actually draw out of the common pot, but rather on the basis of your *ability* to draw from that pot. In other words, your decision to save or consume is no different from your decision to buy apples, to go out for dinner, or to give money to your mother. It is your *income* that enables you to do all these things, and it is income that should be taxed, regardless of its sources and regardless of how you use it. Saving is just another use of income.

If income is the best measure of ability to pay, the double taxation argument doesn't hold true. An income tax taxes savings twice only if consumption is the measure used to gauge a person's ability to pay. It does not do so if income is the measure used. Acquisition of the orchard enhances your ability to pay today; a bountiful crop of fruit enhances your ability to pay when it is produced. Interest income is no different from any other form of income; it too enhances your ability to pay. Taxing both is thus fair.

Wealth as the Best Tax Base Still others argue that the real power to command resources comes not from any single year's income, but from accumulated wealth. Aggregate net worth in the United States is many times larger than aggregate income.

If two people have identical annual incomes of $10,000 but one of them also has an accumulated net worth of $1 million, is it reasonable to argue that these two people have the same ability to pay or that they should pay equal taxes? Most people would answer no.

Those who promote a wealth-based system also argue that the only real way to redistribute economic power is to tax the very high concentrations of wealth. Of course, it is important to note that if income is already taxed, a wealth tax, in essence, taxes the same dollars again.

No Simple Answer Recall that these arguments are about the definition of "horizontal equity": What is the single best measure of ability to pay? In fact, policy debates about the system of taxes in the United States or in any other country involve much more. Virtually every country in the world has a system of taxation that taxes all three bases. In the United States, for example, there are sales and excise taxes (consumption taxes), the Federal Gift and Estate Tax (a wealth tax), the Individual Income Tax, and the local property tax (another wealth tax).

It is important to point out that for many U.S. taxpayers, the Individual Income Tax is probably closer to being a consumption tax than an income tax since much of household savings can be deducted from income before the tax is figured. The tax code (or law) is full of subsidies and incentives. Among the most significant incentives built into the system are provisions designed to encourage people to save. For example, an important exclusion from income for purposes of defining the income tax base is employers' contributions to employee pension accounts. For many workers, retirement is in part financed by payments from pension funds. As long as a person is working, many employers will make deposits or match employee deposits to retirement or pension accounts. Those contributions are part of a household's economic income and part of household savings, but they are not taxed. Recall that income is essentially consumption plus savings (change in net worth). In addition, deposits to specific kinds of accounts (such as Individual Retirement Accounts, or IRAs) can be excluded from income for tax purposes. A good portion of capital gains income (increases in the value of things that a household owns), such as increases in the value of corporate stocks or houses, is left out of the base or taxed at lower rates.

There is ongoing debate in the United States about whether it would be better to shift toward a more comprehensive consumption tax. In the fall of 2005, President Bush's Advisory Panel on Federal Tax Reform presented its report on reforming and simplifying the nation's tax code. The commission stopped short of full implementation of a consumption tax such as a national sales tax or a version of a national sales tax called a *value-added tax* (VAT) that is popular in Europe. But the panel did recommend moving to a system that rewards saving and discourages consumption more than the current one. An important goal of the commission was to recommend ways of simplifying the code.

The Gift and Estate Tax

estate The property that a person owns at the time of his or her death.

estate tax A tax on the total value of a person's estate.

One of the oldest and most common forms of taxation in the world is the taxation of property held by an individual at the time of his or her death. The property owned at the time of a person's death is called the person's **estate**. An **estate tax** is a tax on the total value of a person's estate regardless of how it is distributed. The United States levies a Gift and Estate Tax on gifts made over a person's lifetime and the value of the person's estate. The Federal Gift and Estate Tax,

ECONOMICS IN PRACTICE

The Gift and Estate Tax: A Call to Restore It in 2007

The Federal Gift and Estate Tax has been in the process of being phased out since 2001. Unable to agree on a final bill, Congress put off a decision until 2010, when the tax will revert back to the 2001 rules. During the next two years, Congress will once again address the question of repealing the tax altogether or reducing it by raising the amount of wealth that can be passed down to others as a gift or at death without a tax.

In the middle of the debate, the second richest person in the world (at least according to *Fortune* magazine), Warren Buffett, added his voice to those who are against an outright repeal.

Buffett Tells Congress to Keep Estate Tax

Wall Street Journal

For years, Warren Buffet has been urging Congress to keep the federal estate tax. Now, he's suggesting how the government should use the money: a $1,000 annual tax credit for the 23 million U.S. households with incomes under $20,000.

The billionaire investing guru told the Senate Finance Committee that many of those families face a marginal payroll tax rate of 15.3%, higher than the current top rate on capital gains, dividends and carried interest for assets held long term. In contrast, repealing the estate tax would help families of the richest Americans who have seen their wealth take off like a "rocket ship" in the last two decades.

Buffett noted that of 2.4 million Americans who died last year, only about 12,000 paid estate tax, assessed on an individual's net worth at death. "You'd have to attend 200 funerals to be at one" where an estate tax was owed, Buffett said.

Source: John Godfrey, November 15, 2007.

which raises less than 2 percent of total tax revenues, is scheduled to be phased out in 2010. The law phasing out the Gift and Estate Tax was passed by Congress in 2001. The law gradually raises what is called the unified credit each year until 2010, when the tax is no longer paid. What is strange is that if Congress and the president do not formally extend the law shutting down the Gift and Estate Tax, it will come back automatically in its pre-2001 form. Most find this outcome to be unlikely. In fact, the House of Representatives voted to repeal the tax in 2005.

Some are strongly opposed to the elimination of the Gift and Estate Tax on the grounds that it is an important progressive element in the tax code. As of 2008, the unified credit effectively exempts estates from the tax that are under $2 million. Critics say that elimination of the tax will significantly reduce federal revenues precisely when the federal government is having fiscal problems. Those who favor elimination point to the fact that the tax reduces the incentive to save—and thus the nation's saving rate. They also argue that taxing accumulated income that has already been taxed is yet again a form of double taxing.

Tax Incidence: Who Pays?

When a government levies a tax, it writes a law assigning responsibility for payment to specific people or specific organizations. To understand a tax, we must look beyond those named in the law as the initial taxpayers.

First, remember the principle of tax analysis: The burden of a tax is ultimately borne by individuals or households; institutions such as business firms and colleges have no real taxpaying capacity. Taxes paid by a firm ultimately fall on customers or owners or workers. Second, the burden of a tax is not always borne by those initially responsible for paying it. Directly or indirectly, tax burdens are often *shifted* to others. When we speak of the **incidence of a tax**, we are referring to the ultimate distribution of its burden.

tax incidence The ultimate distribution of a tax burden.

The simultaneous reactions of many households and/or firms to the presence of a tax may cause relative prices to change, and price changes affect households' well-being. Households may feel the impact of a tax on the sources side or on the uses side of the income equation. (We use the term *income equation* because the amount of income from all *sources* must be equal to the amount of income allocated to all *uses*—including saving—in a given period.) On the **sources side**, a household is hurt when the net wages or profits that it receives fall; on the **uses side**, a household is hurt when the prices of the goods and services that it buys rise. If your wages remain the same but the price of every item that you buy doubles, you are in the same position you would have been in if your wages had been cut by 50 percent and prices hadn't changed. In short, the imposition of a tax or a change in a tax can change behavior. Changes in behavior can affect supply and demand in markets and cause prices to change. When prices change in input or output markets, some households are made better off and some are made worse off. These final changes determine the ultimate burden of the tax.

sources side/uses side The impact of a tax may be felt on one or the other or on both sides of the income equation. A tax may cause net income to fall (damage on the sources side), or it may cause prices of goods and services to rise so that income buys less (damage on the uses side).

Tax shifting takes place when households can alter their behavior and do something to avoid paying a tax. Such shifting is easily accomplished when only certain items are singled out for taxation. Suppose a heavy tax were levied on bananas. Initially, the tax would make the price of bananas much higher, but there are many potential substitutes for bananas. Consumers can avoid the tax by not buying bananas, and that is what many will do. But as demand drops, the market price of bananas falls and banana growers lose money. The tax shifts from consumers to the growers, at least in the short run.

tax shifting Occurs when households can alter their behavior and do something to avoid paying a tax.

A tax such as the retail sales tax, which is levied at the same rate on *all* consumer goods, is harder to avoid. The only thing consumers can do to avoid such a tax is to consume less of everything. If consumers consume less, saving will increase, but otherwise there are few opportunities for tax avoidance and therefore for tax shifting. Broad-based taxes are less likely to be shifted and more likely to "stick" where they are levied than "partial taxes" are.

The Incidence of Payroll Taxes

In 2008, about 35 percent of federal revenues came from social insurance taxes, also called *payroll taxes*. The revenues from payroll taxes go to support Social Security, unemployment compensation, and other health and disability benefits for workers. (These are discussed in Chapter 18.) Some of these taxes are levied on employers as a percentage of payroll, and some are levied on workers as a percentage of wages or salaries earned.

To analyze the payroll tax, let us take a tax levied on employers and sketch the reactions that are likely to follow. When the tax is first levied, firms find that the price of labor increases. Firms may react in two ways. First, they may substitute capital for the now more-expensive labor. Second, higher costs and lower profits may lead to a cut in production. Both reactions mean a lower demand for labor. Lower demand for labor reduces wages, and part of the tax is thus passed on (or *shifted to*) the workers, who end up earning less. The extent to which the tax is shifted to workers depends on how workers can react to the lower wages.

We can develop a more formal analysis of this situation with a picture of the market before the tax is levied. Figure 19.2 shows equilibrium in a hypothetical labor market with no payroll tax. Before we proceed, we should review the factors that determine the shapes of the supply and demand curves.

Labor Supply and Labor Demand Curves in Perfect Competition: A Review Recall that the demand for labor in perfectly competitive markets depends on its productivity. As you saw in Chapter 10, a perfectly competitive, profit-maximizing firm will hire labor up to the point at which the market wage is equal to labor's marginal revenue product. The shape of the demand curve for labor shows how responsive *firms* are to changes in wages.

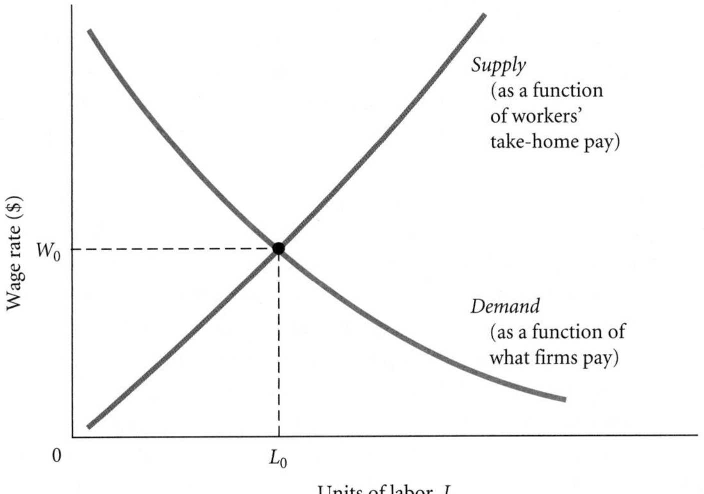

◀ **FIGURE 19.2**

Equilibrium in a Competitive Labor Market—No Taxes

With no taxes on wages, the wage that firms pay is the same as the wage that workers take home. At a wage of W_0, the quantity of labor supplied and the quantity of labor demanded are equal.

Recall from Chapter 6 that household behavior and thus the shape of the labor supply curve depend on the relative strengths of income and substitution effects. The labor supply curve represents the reaction of workers to changes in the wage rate. Household behavior depends on the *after-tax* wage that workers actually take home per hour of work. In contrast, labor demand is a function of the full amount that firms must pay per unit of labor, an amount that may include a tax if it is levied directly on payroll, as it is in our example. Such a tax, when present, drives a "wedge" between the price of labor that firms face and take-home wages.

Imposing a Payroll Tax: Who Pays? In Figure 19.2, there were no taxes and the wage that firms paid was the same as the wage that workers took home. At a wage of W_0, quantity of labor supplied and quantity of labor demanded were equal and the labor market was in equilibrium.[4]

But suppose employers must pay a tax of $\$T$ per unit of labor. Figure 19.3 shows a new curve that is parallel to the supply curve but above it by a distance T. The new curve, S_1, shows labor supply as a function of what firms pay. Note that S_1 is not really a new supply curve. Supply is still determined by what workers take home. S_1 simply adds T to the supply curve. Regardless of how the ultimate burden of the tax is shared, there is a difference between what firms pay and what workers take home.

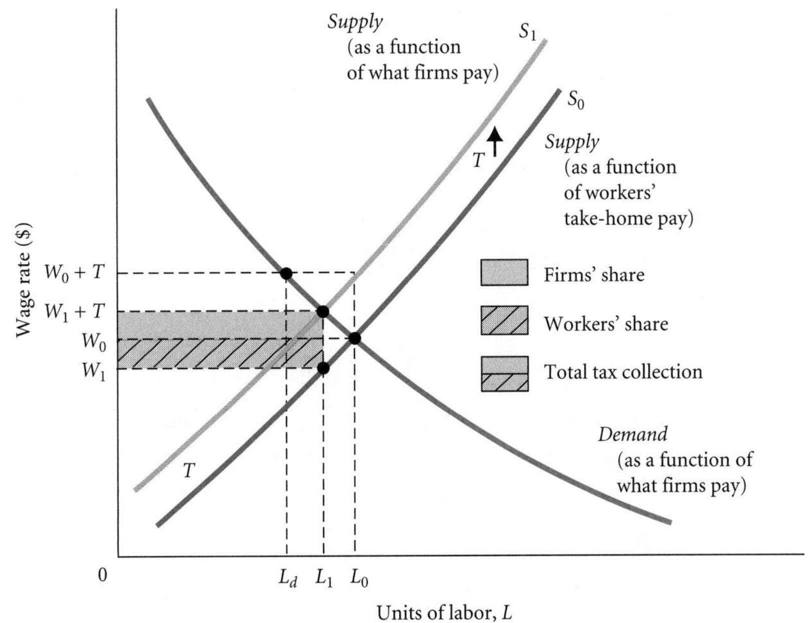

◀ **FIGURE 19.3**

Incidence of a Per-Unit Payroll Tax in a Perfectly Competitive Labor Market

With a tax on firms of $\$T$ per unit of labor hired, the market will adjust, shifting the tax partially to workers. When the tax is levied, firms must first pay $W_0 + T$. This reduces the labor demand to L_d. The result is excess supply, which pushes wages down to W_1 and passes some of the burden of the tax on to workers.

[4] Although the supply curve has a positive slope, that slope implies nothing about the actual shape of the labor supply curve in the United States.

If the initial wage is W_0 per hour, firms will face a price of $W_0 + T$ per unit of labor immediately after the tax is levied. Workers still receive only W_0, however. The higher wage rate—that is, the higher price of labor that firms now face—reduces the quantity of labor demanded from L_0 to L_d, and the firms lay off workers. Workers initially still receive W_0, so that amount of labor supplied does not change, and the result is an excess supply of labor equal to $(L_0 - L_d)$.

The excess supply applies downward pressure to the market wage, and wages fall, shifting some of the tax burden onto workers. The issue is how far wages will fall. Figure 19.3 shows that a new equilibrium is achieved at W_1, with firms paying $W_1 + T$. When workers take home W_1, they supply L_1 units of labor. If firms must pay $W_1 + T$, they will demand L_1 units of labor, and the market clears. Quantity supplied again equals quantity demanded.

In this case, then, employers and employees share the burden of the payroll tax. Initially, firms paid W_0; after the tax, they pay $W_1 + T$. Initially, workers received W_0; after the tax, they end up with the lower wage W_1. Total tax collections by the government are equal to $T \times L_1$. Geometrically, tax collections are equal to the entire shaded area in Figure 19.3. The workers' share of the tax burden is the lower portion, $(W_0 - W_1) \times L_1$. The firms' share is the upper portion, $[(W_1 + T) - W_0] \times L_1$.

The relative sizes of the firms' share and the workers' share of the total tax burden depend on the shapes of the demand and supply curves. Figure 19.4, parts a and b, show that the ultimate burden of a payroll tax depends, at least in part, on the *elasticity of labor supply*. If labor supply is very elastic (that is to say, responsive to price), take-home wages do not fall very much and workers bear only a small portion of the tax. But if labor supply is inelastic, or unresponsive to price, *most* of the burden is borne by workers. Workers bear the bulk of the burden of a payroll tax if labor supply is relatively inelastic, and firms bear the bulk of the burden of a payroll tax if labor supply is relatively elastic.

▶ **FIGURE 19.4**
Payroll Tax with Elastic (a) and Inelastic (b) Labor Supply
The ultimate burden of a payroll tax depends on the elasticities of labor supply and labor demand. For example, if supply is relatively elastic, as in part a, the burden falls largely on employers; if the supply is relatively inelastic, as in part b, the burden falls largely on workers.

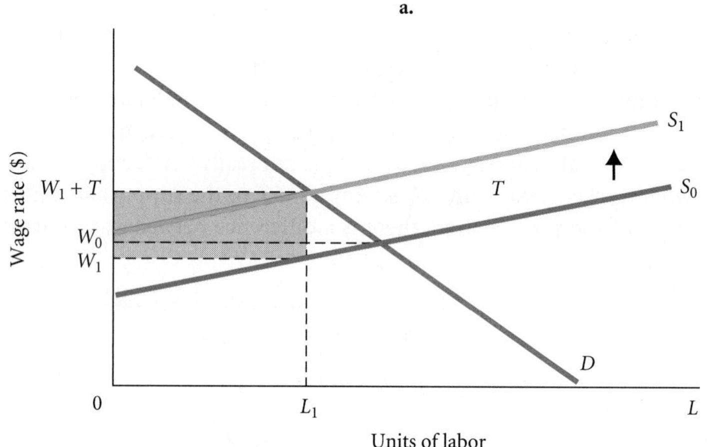

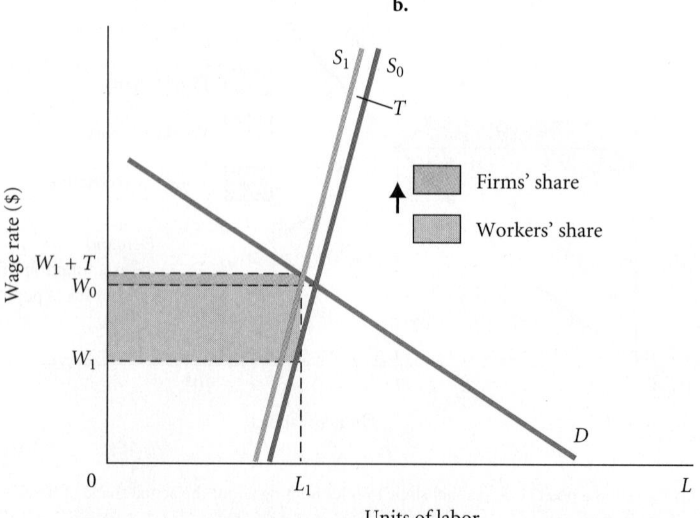

Empirical studies of labor supply behavior in the United States suggest that for most of the workforce, the elasticity of labor supply is close to zero. Therefore; most of the payroll tax in the United States is probably borne by workers. The result would be exactly the same if the tax were initially levied on workers rather than on firms. Go back to the equilibrium in Figure 19.3 on p. 389, with wages at W_0. But now assume that the tax of $\$T$ per hour is levied on workers rather than firms. The burden will end up being shared by firms and workers in the *exact same proportions*. Initially, take-home wages will fall to $W_0 - T$. Workers will supply less labor, creating excess demand and pushing market wages up. That shifts part of the burden back to employers. The "story" is different, but the result is the same.

Table 19.5 presents an estimate of the incidence of payroll taxes (Social Security taxes) in the United States in 2007. This estimate assumes that both the employers' share and employees' share of the payroll taxes are ultimately *borne by employees*.

TABLE 19.5 Estimated Incidence of Payroll Taxes in the United States in 2007

Population Ranked by Income	Tax as a % of Total Income
Bottom 20%	7.5
Second 20%	9.9
Third 20%	10.6
Fourth 20%	11.4
Top 20%	8.0
Top 10%	6.3
Top 5%	5.1
Top 1%	2.5

Source: Authors' estimate.

The payroll tax is regressive at the top income levels for two reasons. First, in 2007, most of the tax (6.2 percent of total wage and salary income levied on both employers and employees) did not apply to wages and salaries above $97,500. The remainder of the total 7.65 percent tax—1.45 percent—applied to all wage and salary income. Second, wages and salaries fell as a percentage of total income as we move up the income scale. Those with higher incomes earn a larger portion of their incomes from profits, dividends, rents, and so on, and these kinds of income are not subject to the payroll tax.

Some economists dispute the conclusion that the payroll tax is borne entirely by wage earners. Even if labor supply is inelastic, some wages are set in the process of collective bargaining between unions and large firms. If the payroll tax results in a higher gross wage in the bargaining process, firms may find themselves faced with higher costs. Higher costs either reduce profits to owners or are passed on to consumers in the form of higher product prices.

The Incidence of Corporate Profits Taxes

Another tax that requires careful analysis is the corporate profits tax that is levied by the federal government as well as by most states. The *corporate profits tax* or *corporation income tax*, is a tax on the profits of firms that are organized as corporations. *Corporations* are firms granted limited liability status by the government. Limited liability means that shareholders/owners can lose only what they have invested. The owners of *partnerships* and *proprietorships* do not enjoy limited liability and do not pay this tax; rather, they report their firms' income directly on their individual income tax returns.

We can think of the corporate tax as a tax on *capital income*, or profits, in one sector of the economy. For simplicity, we assume that there are only two sectors of the economy, corporate and noncorporate, and only two factors of production, labor and capital. Owners of capital receive profits, and workers (labor) are paid a wage.

Like the payroll tax, the corporate tax may affect households on the sources or the uses side of the income equation. The tax may affect profits earned by owners of capital, wages earned by workers, or prices of corporate and noncorporate products. Once again, the key question is how large these changes are likely to be.

When first imposed, the corporate profits tax initially reduces net (after-tax) profits in the corporate sector. Assuming the economy was in long-run equilibrium before the tax was levied, firms in both the corporate and noncorporate sectors were earning a *normal rate of return*; there was no reason to expect higher profits in one sector than in the other. Suddenly, firms in the corporate sector become significantly less profitable as a result of the tax. (In 2007, for example, the tax rate applicable to most corporations was 35 percent.)

In response to these lower profits, capital investment begins to favor the nontaxed sector because after-tax profits are higher there. Firms in the taxed sector contract in size or (in some cases) go out of business, while firms in the nontaxed sector expand and new firms enter its various industries. As this happens, the flow of capital from the taxed to the nontaxed sector reduces the profit rate in the nontaxed sector: More competition springs up, and product prices are driven down. Some of the tax burden shifts to capital income earners in the noncorporate sector, who end up earning lower profits.

As capital flows out of the corporate sector in response to lower after-tax profits, the profit rate in that sector rises somewhat because fewer firms means less supply, which means higher prices, and so on. Presumably, capital will continue to favor the nontaxed sector until the after-tax profit rates in the two sectors are equal. Even though the tax is imposed on just one sector, it eventually depresses after-tax profits in all sectors equally.

Under these circumstances, the products of corporations will probably become more expensive and products of proprietorships and partnerships will probably become less expensive. But because almost everyone buys both corporate and noncorporate products, these *excise effects* (that is, effects on the prices of products) are likely to have a minimal impact on the distribution of the tax burden. In essence, the price increases in the corporate sector and the price decreases in the noncorporate sector cancel each other out.

Finally, what effect does the imposition of a corporate income tax have on labor? Wages could actually rise or fall, but the effect is not likely to be large. Taxed firms will have an incentive to substitute labor for capital because capital income is now taxed. This could benefit labor by driving up wages. In addition, the contracting sector will use less labor *and* capital, but if the taxed sector is the capital-intensive corporate sector, the bulk of the effect will be felt by capital. The price of capital will fall more than the price of labor.

The Burden of the Corporate Tax The ultimate burden of the corporate tax appears to depend on several factors: the relative capital/labor intensity of the two sectors, the ease with which capital and labor can be substituted in the two sectors, and elasticities of demand for the products of each sector. In 1962, economist Arnold Harberger, then of the University of Chicago, analyzed this and concluded that owners of corporations, proprietorships, and partnerships all bear the burden of the corporate tax in rough proportion to profits, even though it is directly levied only on corporations. Harberger also found that wage effects of the corporate tax were small and that excise effects, as we just noted, probably cancel each other out.[5]

Although most economists accept Harberger's view of the corporate tax, there are arguments against it. For example, a profits tax on a monopoly firm earning above-normal profits is *not* shifted to other sectors unless the tax drives profits below the competitive level.

You might be tempted to conclude that because monopolists can control market price, they will simply pass on the profits tax in the form of higher prices to consumers of monopoly products. But theory predicts just the opposite: that the tax burden will remain with the monopolist.

Remember that monopolists are constrained by market demand. That is, they choose the combination of price and output that is consistent with market demand and that maximizes profit. If a proportion of that profit is taxed, the choice of price and quantity will not change. Why not? Quite simply, if you behave so as to maximize profit and then I come and take half of your profit, you maximize your half by maximizing the whole, which is exactly what you would do in the absence of the tax. Thus, your price and output do not change, the tax is shifted, and you end up paying the tax. In the long run, capital will not leave the taxed monopoly sector, as it did in the competitive case. Even with the tax, the monopolist is earning higher profits than are possible elsewhere.

The great debate about whom the corporate tax hurts illustrates the advantage of broad-based direct taxes over narrow-based indirect taxes. Because it is levied on an institution, the corporate tax is indirect, and therefore it is always shifted. Furthermore, it taxes only one factor (capital) in only one part of the economy (the corporate sector). The income tax, in contrast, taxes all forms of income in all sectors of the economy and is virtually impossible to shift. It is difficult to argue that a tax is a good tax if we can't be sure who ultimately ends up paying it.

[5] Arnold Harberger, "The Incidence of the Corporate Income Tax," *Journal of Political Economy*, LXX, June 1962.

Table 19.6 presents an estimate of the actual incidence of the U.S. corporate income tax in 2007. The burden of the corporate income tax is clearly progressive because profits and capital income make up a much bigger part of the incomes of high-income households.

TABLE 19.6 Estimated Burden of the U.S. Corporation Income Tax in 2007

Population Ranked by Income	Corporate Tax Burden as a % of Total Income
Bottom 20%	1.2
Second 20%	1.1
Third 20%	1.5
Fourth 20%	1.6
Top 20%	4.7
Top 10%	5.6
Top 5%	7.3
Top 1%	9.0

Source: Authors' estimate.

The Overall Incidence of Taxes in the United States: Empirical Evidence

Many researchers have done complete analyses under varying assumptions about tax incidence, and in most cases their results are similar. State and local taxes (with sales taxes playing a big role) seem as a group to be mildly regressive. Federal taxes, dominated by the individual income tax but increasingly affected by the regressive payroll tax, are mildly progressive. The overall system is mildly progressive.

Excess Burdens and the Principle of Neutrality

You have seen that when households and firms make decisions in the presence of a tax that differ from decisions they would make in its absence, the burden of the tax can be shifted from those for whom it was originally intended. Now we can take the same logic one step further. When taxes distort economic conditions, they impose burdens on society that, in aggregate, exceed the revenue collected by the government.

The amount by which the burden of a tax exceeds the total revenue collected by the government is called the **excess burden** of the tax. The *total burden* of a tax is the sum of the revenue collected from the tax and the excess burden created by the tax. Because excess burdens are a form of waste, or lost value, tax policy should be written to minimize them. (Excess burdens are also called *deadweight losses.*)

excess burden The amount by which the burden of a tax exceeds the total revenue collected. Also called deadweight loss.

The size of the excess burden imposed by a tax depends on the extent to which economic decisions are distorted. The general principle that emerges from the analysis of excess burdens is the **principle of neutrality**. *Ceteris paribus*, or all else equal,[6] a tax that is neutral with respect to economic decisions is preferred to one that distorts economic decisions.

principle of neutrality All else equal, taxes that are neutral with respect to economic decisions (that is, taxes that do not distort economic decisions) are generally preferable to taxes that distort economic decisions. Taxes that are not neutral impose excess burdens.

In practice, all taxes change behavior and distort economic choices. A product-specific excise tax raises the price of the taxed item, and people can avoid the tax by buying substitutes. An income tax distorts the choice between present and future consumption and between work and leisure. The corporate tax influences investment and production decisions—investment is diverted away from the corporate sector, and firms may be induced to substitute labor for capital.

How Do Excess Burdens Arise?

The idea that a tax can impose an extra cost, or excess burden, by distorting choices can be illustrated by example. Consider a perfectly competitive industry that produces an output, *X*, using the technology shown in Figure 19.5. Using technology A, firms can produce 1 unit of output with 7 units of

[6] The phrase *ceteris paribus* (all else equal) is important. In judging the merits of a tax or a change in tax policy, the degree of neutrality is only one criterion among many, and it often comes into conflict with others. For example, tax A may impose a larger excess burden than tax B, but society may deem A more equitable.

capital (K) and 3 units of labor (L). Using technology B, the production of 1 unit of output requires 4 units of capital and 7 units of labor. A is thus the more capital-intensive technology.

FIGURE 19.5

Firms Choose the Technology That Minimizes the Cost of Production

If the industry is perfectly competitive, long-run equilibrium price will be \$20 per unit of X. If 1,000 units of X are sold, consumers will pay a total of \$20,000 for X.

Technology	Input requirements per unit of output X: K	L	Per-unit cost of X $= K(P_K) + L(P_L)$; $P_K = \$2$, $P_L = \$2$	
A	7	3	\$20	Least cost
B	4	7	\$22	

If we assume labor and capital each cost \$2 per unit, it costs \$20 to produce each unit of output with technology A and \$22 to produce each unit of output with technology B. Firms will choose technology A. Because we assume perfect competition, output price will be driven to cost of production and the price of output will in the long run be driven to \$20 per unit.

Now let us narrow our focus to the distortion of technology choice that is brought about by the imposition of a tax. Assume that demand for the good in question is perfectly inelastic at 1,000 units of output. That is, regardless of price, households will buy 1,000 units of the good. A price of \$20 per unit means consumers pay a total of \$20,000 for 1,000 units of X.

Now suppose the government levies a tax of 50 percent on capital. This has the effect of raising the price of capital, P_K, to \$3. Figure 19.6 shows what would happen to unit cost of production after the tax is imposed. With capital now more expensive, the firm switches to the more labor-intensive technology B. With the tax in place, X can be produced at a cost of \$27 per unit using technology A but for \$26 per unit using technology B.

FIGURE 19.6

Imposition of a Tax on Capital Distorts the Choice of Technology

If the industry is perfectly competitive, price will be \$26 per unit of X when a tax of \$1 per unit of capital is imposed. If technology B is used and if we assume that total sales remain at 1,000 units, total tax collections will be 1,000 × 4 × \$1 = \$4,000. But consumers will pay a total of \$26,000 for the good—\$6,000 more than before the tax. Thus, there is an excess burden of \$2,000.

Technology	Input requirements per unit of output X: K	L	Per-unit cost of X $= K(P_K) + L(P_L)$; $P_K = \$2 + \$1 \text{ tax} = \$3$, $P_L = \$2$	
A	7	3	\$27	
B	4	7	\$26	Least cost

If demand is inelastic, buyers continue to buy 1,000 units of X regardless of its price. (We shall ignore any distortions of consumer choices that might result from the imposition of the tax.) Recall that the tax is 50 percent, or \$1 per unit of capital used. Because it takes 4 units of capital to produce each unit of output, firms—which are now using technology B—will pay a total tax to the government of \$4 per unit of output produced. With 1,000 units of output produced and sold, total tax collections amount to \$4,000.

But if you look carefully, you will see that the burden of the tax exceeds \$4,000. After the tax, consumers will be paying \$26 per unit for the good. Twenty-six dollars is now the unit cost of producing the good using the best available technology in the presence of the capital tax. Consumers will pay \$26,000 for 1,000 units of the good. This represents an increase of \$6,000 over the previous total of \$20,000. The revenue raised from the tax is \$4,000, but its total burden is \$6,000. There is an *excess burden* of \$2,000.

How did this excess burden arise? Look back at Figure 19.5. You can see that technology B is less efficient than technology A. (Unit costs of production are \$2 higher per unit using technology B.) But the tax on capital has caused firms to switch to this less efficient, labor-intensive mode of production. The result is a waste of \$2 per unit of output. The total burden of the tax is equal to the revenue collected plus the loss due to the wasteful choice of technology, and the excess burden is \$2 per unit times 1,000 units, or \$2,000.

The same principle holds for taxes that distort consumption decisions. Suppose that you prefer to consume bundle X to bundle Y when there is no tax, but choose bundle Y when there is a tax in place. Not only do you pay the tax, you also end up with a bundle of goods that is worth less than the bundle you would have chosen had the tax not been levied. Again, we have the burden of an extra cost. The larger the distortion that a tax causes in behavior, the larger the excess burden of the tax. Taxes levied on broad bases tend to distort choices less and impose smaller excess burdens than taxes on more sharply defined bases. This follows from our discussion earlier in this chapter: The more partial the tax, the easier it is to avoid. An important part of the logic behind the recommendation of the president's tax reform commission in 2005 was that broader bases and lower rates reduce the distorting effects of the tax system and minimize excess burdens.

The only tax that has no excess burden is the lump-sum tax, where the tax you pay does not depend on your behavior or your income or your wealth. Everyone pays the same amount; there is no way to avoid the tax. In 1990, the government of Prime Minister Margaret Thatcher of Great Britain replaced the local property tax with a tax that was very similar to a lump-sum tax. Such a tax is highly regressive, and the perceived unfairness of it led her successor, John Major, to call for its repeal in 1991.

The Principle of Second Best

Now that we have established the connection between taxes that distort decisions and excess burdens, we can add more complexity to our earlier discussions. Although it may seem that distorting taxes always creates excess burdens, this is not necessarily the case. A distorting tax is sometimes desirable when other distortions already exist in the economy. This is called the **principle of second best**. At least two kinds of circumstances favor nonneutral (that is, distorting) taxes: the presence of externalities and the presence of other distorting taxes.

principle of second best The fact that a tax distorts an economic decision does not always imply that such a tax imposes an excess burden. If there are previously existing distortions, such a tax may actually improve efficiency.

We already examined externalities at some length in Chapter 16. If some activity by a firm or household imposes costs on society that are not considered by decision makers, firms and households are likely to make economically inefficient choices. Pollution is the classic example of an externality, but there are thousands of others. An efficient allocation of resources can be restored if a tax is imposed on the externality-generating activity that is equal to the value of the damages caused by it. Such a tax forces the decision maker to consider the full economic cost of the decision.

Because taxing for externalities changes decisions that would otherwise be made, it does in a sense "distort" economic decisions. But its purpose is to force decision makers to consider real costs that they would otherwise ignore. In the case of pollution, for example, the distortion caused by a tax is desirable. Instead of causing an excess burden, it results in an efficiency gain. (Review Chapter 16 if this is not clear.)

A distorting tax can also improve economic welfare when other taxes are present that already distort decisions. Suppose there were only three goods, *X*, *Y*, and *Z*, and a 5 percent excise tax on *Y* and *Z*. The taxes on *Y* and *Z* distort consumer decisions away from those goods and toward *X*. Imposing a similar tax on *X* reduces the distortion of the existing system of taxes. When consumers face equal taxes on all goods, they cannot avoid the tax by changing what they buy. The distortion caused by imposing a tax on *X* corrects for a preexisting distortion—the taxes on *Y* and *Z*.

Let's return to the example described earlier in Figures 19.5 and 19.6 on p. 394. Imposing the tax of 50 percent on the use of capital generated revenues of $4,000 but imposed a burden of $6,000 on consumers. A distortion now exists. But what would happen if the government imposed an additional tax of 50 percent, or $1 per unit, on labor? Such a tax would push our firm back toward the more efficient technology A. In fact, the labor tax would generate a total revenue of $6,000, but the burden it imposes on consumers would be only $4,000. (It is a good idea for you to work these figures out yourself.)

Optimal Taxation

The idea that taxes work together to affect behavior has led tax theorists to search for optimal taxation systems. Knowing how people will respond to taxes would allow us to design a system that would minimize the overall excess burden. For example, if we know the elasticity of demand for all traded goods, we can devise an optimal system of excise taxes that are heaviest on those goods with relatively inelastic demand and lightest on those goods with relatively elastic demands.

Of course, it is impossible to collect all the information required to implement the optimal tax systems that have been suggested. This point brings us full circle, and we end up where we started, with the *principle of neutrality*: All else equal, taxes that are neutral with respect to economic decisions are generally preferable to taxes that distort economic decisions. Taxes that are not neutral impose excess burdens.

ECONOMICS IN PRACTICE

Federal Tax Reform

During the campaign for the White House in 2008, the candidates focused broadly on the tax changes that had been put in place during the Bush administration and on the need for a tax cut to stimulate the economy and prevent a recession during 2008. One of the major issues was the ultimate elimination of the Gift and Estate Tax discussed on p. 387. But two other important issues were first presented by an advisory panel appointed by the president in 2005.

Panel Urges Big Cut in Mortgage Deduction

New York Times

President Bush's advisory commission on taxes unanimously recommended a vastly simplified tax system on Tuesday that would limit the deduction of interest payments on large mortgages and erase other tax breaks that many Americans enjoy.

The commission, officially named the President's Advisory Panel on Federal Tax Reform, presented two alternative plans. For individuals, the two plans are similar, but they differ in the way they treat business taxes.

The panel, made up of politicians and tax experts from outside the government, rejected as impractical replacing the income tax with a completely different system like a value-added tax or a national retail sales tax.

In addition to the limits on write-offs for mortgage interest, the main elements of the proposals would abolish the alternative minimum tax, erase deductions for state and local income and property taxes, restrict tax-free employer-paid health insurance, and reduce the deductions that many taxpayers can claim for charitable donations.

Source: David E. Rosenbaum, November 2, 2005.

Two controversial provisions of the proposed law were (1) elimination of the provision that allows federal taxpayers to deduct state and local taxes from taxable income, and (2) a substantial change in and reduction in the deduction for home mortgage interest paid.

Why eliminate the deduction of state and local taxes? After all, if you pay taxes to a state or a local government, that is income that you do not get. Isn't ability to pay based on "after-tax" income? Clearly people who thought of it that way favored keeping the deduction. But there is a counterargument. We pay state and local taxes for services that those governments produce for us. Local government, for example, provides police protection, fire protection, and schools. We decide on those budgets, and in a way it is similar to a firm producing a product for us. In the case of a government, deductibility "reduces the price" to taxpayers of services provided by state and local governments. If you and your fellow citizens decide to vote for added school spending, and if you are in the top income tax bracket (which was 35 percent in 2005), each dollar of additional spending costs you only 65 cents! Why? Because for every dollar you are able to deduct, you save 35 cents in tax. This encourages those governments to overspend.

Those who want to disallow the deduction argue the deductibility of home mortgage interest was the largest and most popular of all the provisions of the tax code, and many thought that a proposal to eliminate it would stall the progress of the proposals as they moved through the legislative process. After all, nearly 70 percent of households are home owners and they would, by and large, be hurt. The proposal replaced the deduction with a 15 percent credit. Suppose that you have paid $10,000 in interest this year. That is roughly what you would pay if you had borrowed $160,000 to buy a home. If you were in the 25 percent marginal income tax bracket, you would gain $2,500 from the deduction. But if you got a 15 percent credit, you would only gain $1,500. Recall that a credit is a reduction in taxes, so a $1 credit results in a tax saving of $1. In addition, the proposal called for limits on the deduction by capping the size of the mortgage that would receive full deductibility.

Those in favor of this reduction pointed to inefficient "overinvestment in housing" resulting from the implicit subsidy to home ownership. Those in favor of retaining deductibility pointed to the "external public good" resulting from home ownership. Home owners, it is argued, are better neighbors and citizens because they have a higher stake in the locality.

Measuring Excess Burdens

It is possible to measure the size of excess burdens if we know something about how people respond to price changes. Look at the demand curve in Figure 19.7. The product originally sold for a price, P_0, equal to marginal cost (which, for simplicity, we assume is constant). Recall that when input prices are determined in competitive markets, marginal cost reflects the real value of the resources used in producing the product.

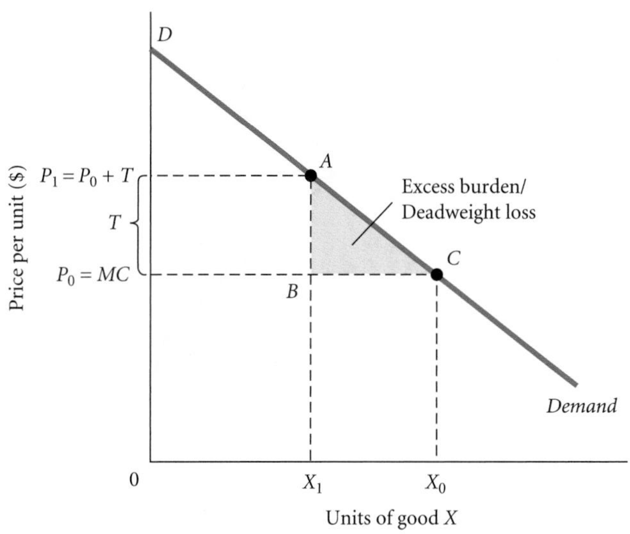

FIGURE 19.7

The Excess Burden of a Distorting Excise Tax

A tax that alters economic decisions imposes a burden that exceeds the amount of taxes collected. An excise tax that raises the price of a good above marginal cost drives some consumers to buy less desirable substitutes, reducing consumer surplus.

To measure the total burden of the tax, we need to recall the notion of consumer surplus from Chapter 4. At any price, some people pay less for a product than it is worth to them. All we reveal when we buy a product is that it is worth *at least* the price being charged. For example, if only 1 unit of product *X* were auctioned, someone would pay a price close to *D* in Figure 19.7. By paying only P_0, that person received a "surplus" equal to $(D - P_0)$. (For a review of consumer surplus and how it is measured, see Chapters 4 and 6.)

Consider what happens when an excise tax raises the price of *X* from P_0 to $P_1 = P_0 + T$, where *T* is the tax per unit of *X*. First, the government collects revenue. The amount of revenue collected is equal to *T* times the number of units of *X* purchased (X_1). You can see that $T \times X_1$ is equal to the area of rectangle P_1ABP_0. Second, because consumers must now pay a price of P_1, the consumer surplus generated in the market is reduced from the area of triangle DCP_0 to the area of the smaller triangle DAP_1. The excess burden is equal to the original (pre-tax) consumer surplus *minus* the after-tax surplus *minus* the total taxes collected by the government.

In other words, the original value of consumer surplus (triangle DCP_0) has been broken up into three parts: the area of triangle DAP_1 that is still consumer surplus, the area of rectangle P_1ABP_0 that is tax revenue collected by the government, and the area of triangle *ACB* that is lost.

Thus, the area *ACB* is an approximate measure of the excess burden of the tax. The total burden of the tax is the sum of the revenue collected and the excess burden: the area of P_1ACP_0.

Excess Burdens and the Degree of Distortion

The size of the excess burden that results from a decision-distorting tax depends on the degree to which decisions change in response to that tax. In the case of an excise tax, consumer behavior is reflected in elasticity of demand. The more elastic the demand curve, the greater the distortion caused by any given tax rate.

Figure 19.8 shows how the size of the consumer response determines the size of the excess burden. At price P_0, the quantity demanded by consumers is X_0. Now suppose that the government imposes a tax of $\$T$ per unit of *X*. The two demand curves (D_1 and D_2) illustrate two possible responses by consumers. The change in quantity demanded along D_1 (from X_0 to X_1) is greater than the change in quantity demanded along D_2 (from X_0 to X_2). In other words, the response of consumers illustrated by D_1 is more elastic than the response of consumers along D_2.

The excess burdens that would result from the tax under the two assumptions about demand elasticity are approximately equal to the areas of the shaded triangles in Figure 19.8. As you can see, where demand is more responsive (more elastic), the excess burden is larger.

FIGURE 19.8

The Size of the Excess Burden of a Distorting Excise Tax Depends on the Elasticity of Demand

The size of the excess burden from a distorting tax depends on the degree to which decisions or behaviors change in response to it.

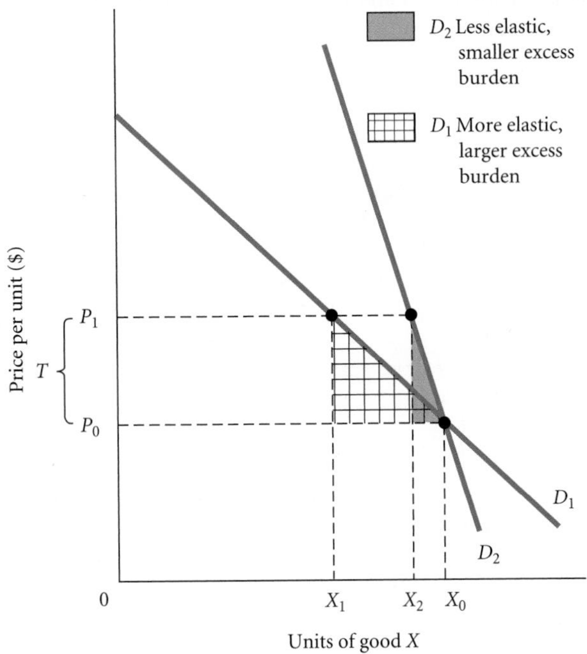

If demand were perfectly inelastic, no distortion would occur and there would be no excess burden. The tax would simply transfer part of the surplus being earned by consumers to the government. That is why some economists favor uniform land taxes over other taxes. Because land is in perfectly inelastic supply, a uniform tax on all land uses distorts economic decisions less than taxes levied on other factors of production that are in variable supply.

SUMMARY

THE ECONOMICS OF TAXATION *p. 379*

1. Public finance is one of the major subfields of applied economics. A major interest within this subfield is the economics of taxation.

2. Taxes are ultimately paid by people. Taxes may be imposed on transactions, institutions, property, and all kinds of other things, but in the final analysis, taxes are paid by individuals or households.

3. The *base* of a tax is the measure or value upon which the tax is levied. The *rate structure* of a tax determines the portion of the base that must be paid in tax.
4. A tax whose burden is a constant proportion of income for all households is a *proportional tax*. A tax that exacts a higher proportion of income from higher-income households is a *progressive tax*. A tax that enacts a lower proportion of income from higher-income households is a *regressive tax*. In the United States, income taxes are progressive and sales and excise taxes are regressive.
5. Your average tax rate is the total amount of tax you pay divided by your total income. Your marginal tax rate is the tax rate that you pay on any additional income that you have earned. Marginal tax rates have the most influence on behavior.
6. There is much disagreement over what constitutes a fair tax system. One theory contends that people should bear tax burdens in proportion to the benefits that they receive from government expenditures. This is the *benefits-received principle*. Another theory contends that people should bear tax burdens in line with their ability to pay. This *ability-to-pay principle* has dominated U.S. tax policy.
7. The three leading candidates for best tax base are income, consumption, and wealth.

TAX INCIDENCE: WHO PAYS? *p. 387*

8. As a result of behavioral changes and market adjustments, tax burdens are often not borne by those initially responsible for paying them. When we speak of the *incidence of a tax*, we are referring to the ultimate distribution of its burden.
9. Taxes change behavior, and changes in behavior can affect supply and demand in markets, causing prices to change. When prices change in input markets or in output markets, some people may be made better off and some worse off. These final changes determine the ultimate burden of a tax.
10. *Tax shifting* occurs when households can alter their behavior and do something to avoid paying a tax. In general, broad-based taxes are less likely to be shifted and more likely to stick where they are levied than partial taxes are.
11. When labor supply is more elastic, firms bear the bulk of a tax imposed on labor. When labor supply is more inelastic, workers bear the bulk of the tax burden. Because the elasticity of labor supply in the United States is close to zero, most economists conclude that most of the payroll tax in the United States is probably borne by workers.
12. The payroll tax is regressive at top incomes for two reasons. First, in 2007, most of the tax (6.2 percent of total income levied on both employers and employees) did not apply to wages and salaries above $97,500. The remainder of the total 7.65 percent—only 1.45 percent—applied to all wage and salary income. Second, wages and salaries fall as a percentage of total income as we move up the income scale. Those with higher incomes earn a larger portion of their incomes from profits, dividends, rents, and so on, and these kinds of income are not subject to the payroll tax.
13. The ultimate burden of the corporate tax appears to depend on several factors. One generally accepted study shows that the owners of corporations, proprietorships, and partnerships all bear the burden of the corporate tax in rough proportion to profits, even though it is directly levied only on corporations, that wage effects are small, and that excise effects are roughly neutral. However, there is still much debate about whom the corporate tax "hurts." The burden of the corporate tax is progressive because profits and capital income make up a much bigger part of the incomes of the high-income households.
14. Under a reasonable set of assumptions about tax shifting, state and local taxes seem as a group to be mildly regressive. Federal taxes, dominated by the individual income tax but increasingly affected by the regressive payroll tax, are mildly progressive. The overall system is mildly progressive.

EXCESS BURDENS AND THE PRINCIPLE OF NEUTRALITY *p. 393*

15. When taxes distort economic decisions, they impose burdens that, in aggregate, exceed the revenue collected by the government. The amount by which the burden of a tax exceeds the revenue collected by the government is called the *excess burden*. The size of excess burdens depends on the degree to which economic decisions are changed by the tax. The *principle of neutrality* holds that the most efficient taxes are broad-based taxes that do not distort economic decisions.
16. The *principle of second best* holds that a tax that distorts economic decisions does not necessarily impose an excess burden. If previously existing distortions or externalities exist, such a tax may actually improve efficiency.

MEASURING EXCESS BURDENS *p. 397*

17. The excess burden imposed by a tax is equal to the pre-tax consumer surplus minus the after-tax consumer surplus minus the total taxes collected by the government. The more elastic the demand curve, the greater the distortion caused by any given tax rate.

REVIEW TERMS AND CONCEPTS

ability-to-pay principle, *p. 384*
average tax rate, *p. 381*
benefits-received principle, *p. 383*
estate, *p. 386*
estate tax, *p. 386*
excess burden, *p. 393*
marginal tax rate, *p. 381*
principle of neutrality, *p. 393*
principle of second best, *p. 395*
progressive tax, *p. 380*
proportional tax, *p. 380*
regressive tax, *p. 381*
sources side/uses side, *p. 388*
tax base, *p. 379*
tax incidence, *p. 388*
tax rate structure, *p. 379*
tax shifting, *p. 388*

PROBLEMS

Visit www.myeconlab.com to complete the problems marked in orange online. You will receive instant feedback on your answers, tutorial help, and access to additional practice problems.

1. Suppose that in 2009, Congress passed and the president signed a new simple income tax with a flat rate of 25 percent on all income over $25,000 (no tax on the first $25,000). Assume that the tax is imposed on every individual separately. For each of the following total income levels, calculate taxes due and compute the average tax rate. Plot the average tax rate on a graph with income along the horizontal axis. Is the tax proportional, progressive, or regressive? Explain why.
   a. $25,000
   b. $35,000
   c. $45,000
   d. $60,000
   e. $80,000
   f. $100,000
2. Using the tax brackets and rates for 2007 in Table 19.3 and footnote 1, compute the total tax for each of the following. In each case, calculate average and marginal tax rates. Assume in each case that the taxpayer chooses the standard deduction.
   a. A single taxpayer earning $35,000
   b. A married couple with two dependent children earning $50,000
   c. A single taxpayer earning $90,000
   d. A married couple with two dependent children earning $110,000
3. A number of specific tax provisions passed the Congress and were enacted into law in 2008. Assume that you were a prospective candidate for Congress in 2008. Write a brief essay describing the changes and explaining why they are good or bad.
4. A citizens' group in the Pacific Northwest has the following statement in its charter:

   "Our goal is to ensure that large, powerful corporations pay their fair share of taxes in this country."

   To implement this goal, the group has recommended and lobbied for an increase in the corporation income tax and a reduction in the individual income tax. Would you support such a petition? Explain your logic.
5. Taxes on necessities that have low demand elasticities impose large excess burdens because consumers can't avoid buying them. Do you agree or disagree with that statement? Explain.
6. For each of the following statements, do you agree or disagree? Why?
   a. Economic theory predicts unequivocally that a payroll tax reduction will increase the supply of labor.
   b. Corporation income taxes levied on a monopolist are likely to be regressive because the monopoly can pass on its burden to consumers.
   c. All nonneutral taxes are undesirable.
7. In calculating total faculty compensation, the administration of Doughnut University includes payroll taxes (Social Security taxes) paid as a *benefit* to faculty. After all, those tax payments are earning future entitlements for the faculty under Social Security. However, the American Association of University Professors has argued that, far from being a benefit, the employer's contribution is simply a tax and that its burden falls on the faculty even though it is paid by the university. Discuss both sides of this debate.
8. Developing countries rarely have a sophisticated income tax structure like that in the United States. The primary means of raising revenues in many developing countries is through commodity taxes. What problems do you see with taxing particular goods in these countries? (*Hint:* Think about elasticities of demand.)
9. Suppose a special tax was introduced that used the value of one's automobile as the tax base. Each person would pay taxes equal to 10 percent of the value of his or her car. Would the tax be proportional, regressive, or progressive? What assumptions do you make in answering this question? What distortions do you think would appear in the economy if such a tax were introduced?
10. You are given the following information on a proposed "restaurant meals tax" in the Republic of Olympus. Olympus collects no other specific excise taxes, and all other government revenues come from a neutral lump-sum tax. (A lump-sum tax is a tax of a fixed sum paid by all people regardless of their circumstances.) Assume further that the burden of the tax is fully borne by consumers.

    Now consider the following data:
    - Meals consumed before the tax: 12 million
    - Meals consumed after the tax: 10 million
    - Average price per meal: $15 (not including the tax)
    - Tax rate: 10 percent

    Estimate the size of the excess burden of the tax. What is the excess burden as a percentage of revenues collected from the tax?
11. **[Related to *Economics in Practice* on *p. 387*]** In an interview, Warren Buffett, worth over $50 billion, stated his opposition to a repeal of the Gift and Estate Tax. Go to the Web and search using the key words Federal Gift and Estate Tax. See what changes were made in the tax in 2008 or 2009. Was the tax repealed? Were the rates changed? What amount of assets can be passed on to one's children tax-free this year?
12. **[Related to *Economics in Practice* on *p. 396*]** The president's tax reform commission in 2005 argued for shifting the country's main revenue system closer to being a tax on consumption by expanding opportunities to save tax-free. Would you favor such a shift? What are the arguments for and against it?
13. **[Related to *Economics in Practice* on *p. 396*]** Beginning in 2006, U.S. house prices began falling and the mortgage market experienced sky-high defaults and millions of foreclosures. Many people blamed low interest rates and the federal tax treatment of owner-occupied housing for pumping up the housing market during the boom years from 1995 through 2005. Review the *Economics in Practice* on p. 396 and explain the opponents' argument. Do you agree that federal tax policy may have made the boom cycle bigger than it would otherwise have been? Explain.

Introduction to Macroeconomics 20

CHAPTER OUTLINE

Macroeconomics is part of our everyday lives. If the macroeconomy is doing well, few people do not have a job who want one, people's incomes are generally rising, and profits of corporations are generally high. In this type of an economy, it is relatively easy for new entrants into the labor force, such as students who have just graduated, to find jobs. On the other hand, if the macroeconomy is in a slump, new jobs are hard to find, incomes are not growing well, and profits are low. Students who entered the job market in the boom of the late 1990s in the United States, on average, had an easier time finding a job than did those who entered in the recession of 2001. Given the large effect that the macroeconomy can have on our lives, it is important that we understand how it works.

We begin by discussing the differences between microeconomics and macroeconomics that we glimpsed in Chapter 1. **Microeconomics** examines the functioning of individual industries and the behavior of individual decision-making units, typically firms and households. With a few assumptions about how these units behave (firms maximize profits; households maximize utility), we can derive useful conclusions about how markets work, how resources are allocated, and so on.

microeconomics Examines the functioning of individual industries and the behavior of individual decision-making units—firms and households.

Macroeconomics, instead of focusing on the factors that influence the production of particular products and the behavior of individual industries, focuses on the determinants of total national output. Macroeconomics studies not household income but *national* income, not individual prices but the *overall* price level. It does not analyze the demand for labor in the automobile industry but instead total employment in the economy.

macroeconomics Deals with the economy as a whole. Macroeconomics focuses on the determinants of total national income, deals with aggregates such as aggregate consumption and investment, and looks at the overall level of prices instead of individual prices.

Both microeconomics and macroeconomics are concerned with the decisions of households and firms. Microeconomics deals with individual decisions; macroeconomics deals with the sum of these individual decisions. *Aggregate* is used in macroeconomics to refer to sums. When we speak of **aggregate behavior**, we mean the behavior of all households and firms together. We also speak of aggregate consumption and aggregate investment, which refer to total consumption and total investment in the economy, respectively.

aggregate behavior The behavior of all households and firms together.

Because microeconomists and macroeconomists look at the economy from different perspectives, you might expect that they would reach somewhat different conclusions about the way the economy behaves. This is true to some extent. Microeconomists generally conclude that markets work well. They see prices as flexible, adjusting to maintain equality between quantity supplied and quantity demanded. Macroeconomists, however, observe that important prices in the economy—for example, the wage rate (or price of labor)—often seem "sticky." **Sticky prices** are prices that do not always adjust rapidly to maintain equality between quantity supplied and quantity demanded. Microeconomists do not expect to see the quantity of apples supplied exceeding the

sticky prices Prices that do not always adjust rapidly to maintain equality between quantity supplied and quantity demanded.

quantity of apples demanded because the price of apples is not sticky. On the other hand, macroeconomists—who analyze aggregate behavior—examine periods of high unemployment, where the quantity of labor supplied appears to exceed the quantity of labor demanded. At such times, it appears that wage rates do not adjust fast enough to equate the quantity of labor supplied and the quantity of labor demanded.

Macroeconomic Concerns

Three of the major concerns of macroeconomics are

- Output growth
- Unemployment
- Inflation and deflation

Government policy makers would like to have high output growth, low unemployment, and low inflation. We will see that these goals may conflict with one another and that an important point in understanding macroeconomics is understanding these conflicts.

Output Growth

business cycle The cycle of short-term ups and downs in the economy.

aggregate output The total quantity of goods and services produced in an economy in a given period.

recession A period during which aggregate output declines. Conventionally, a period in which aggregate output declines for two consecutive quarters.

depression A prolonged and deep recession.

expansion *or* boom The period in the business cycle from a trough up to a peak during which output and employment grow.

contraction, recession, *or* slump The period in the business cycle from a peak down to a trough during which output and employment fall.

Instead of growing at an even rate at all times, economies tend to experience short-term ups and downs in their performance. The technical name for these ups and downs is the **business cycle**. The main measure of how an economy is doing is **aggregate output**, the total quantity of goods and services produced in the economy in a given period. When less is produced (in other words, when aggregate output decreases), there are fewer goods and services to go around and the average standard of living declines. When firms cut back on production, they also lay off workers, increasing the rate of unemployment.

Recessions are periods during which aggregate output declines. It has become conventional to classify an economic downturn as a "recession" when aggregate output declines for two consecutive quarters. A prolonged and deep recession is called a **depression**, although economists do not agree on when a recession becomes a depression. Since the beginning of the twentieth century, the United States has experienced one depression (during the 1930s), three severe recessions (1946, 1974–1975, and 1980–1982), and a number of less severe and shorter recessions (1954, 1958, 1990–1991, and 2001). Other countries also experienced recessions in the twentieth century, some roughly coinciding with U.S. recessions and some not.

A typical business cycle is illustrated in Figure 20.1. Since most economies, on average, grow over time, the business cycle in Figure 20.1 shows a positive trend—the *peak* (the highest point) of a new business cycle is higher than the peak of the previous cycle. The period from a *trough*, or bottom of the cycle, to a peak is called an **expansion** or a **boom**. During an expansion, output and employment grow. The period from a peak to a trough is called a **contraction**, **recession**, or **slump**, when output and employment fall.

In judging whether an economy is expanding or contracting, note the difference between the level of economic activity and its rate of change. If the economy has just left a trough (point *A* in Figure 20.1), it will be growing (rate of change is positive), but its level of output will still be low. If the economy has just started to decline from a peak (point *B*), it will be contracting (rate of change is negative), but its level of output will still be high.

The business cycle in Figure 20.1 is symmetrical, which means that the length of an expansion is the same as the length of a contraction. Most business cycles are not symmetrical, however. It is possible, for example, for the expansion phase to be longer than the contraction phase. When contraction comes, it may be fast and sharp, while expansion may be slow and gradual. Moreover, the economy is not nearly as regular as the business cycle in Figure 20.1 indicates. The ups and downs in the economy tend to be erratic.

Figure 20.2 shows the actual business cycles in the United States between 1900 and 2007. Although many business cycles have occurred in the last 108 years, each has been unique. The economy is not so simple that it has regular cycles.

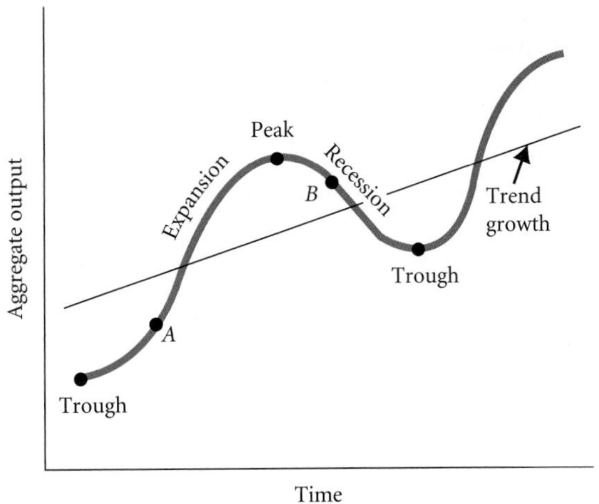

FIGURE 20.1 A Typical Business Cycle

In this business cycle, the economy is expanding as it moves through point *A* from the trough to the peak. When the economy moves from a peak down to a trough, through point *B*, the economy is in recession.

The periods of the Great Depression and World Wars I and II show the largest fluctuations in Figure 20.2, although other large contractions and expansions have taken place. Note the expansion in the 1960s and the recessions at the beginning of the 1980s and 1990s. Some of the cycles have been long; some have been very short. Note also that aggregate output actually increased between 1933 and 1937, even though it was still quite low in 1937. The economy did not come out of the Depression until the defense buildup prior to the start of World War II. Note also that business cycles were more extreme before World War II than they have been since then.

FIGURE 20.2 U.S. Aggregate Output (Real GDP), 1900–2007

The periods of the Great Depression and World Wars I and II show the largest fluctuations in aggregate output.

Unemployment

You cannot listen to the news or read a newspaper without noticing that data on the unemployment rate are released each month. The **unemployment rate**—the percentage of the labor force that is unemployed—is a key indicator of the economy's health. Because the unemployment rate is usually closely related to the economy's aggregate output, announcements of each month's new figure are followed with great interest by economists, politicians, and policy makers.

unemployment rate The percentage of the labor force that is unemployed.

Although macroeconomists are interested in learning why the unemployment rate has risen or fallen in a given period, they also try to answer a more basic question: Why is there any unemployment at all? We do not expect to see zero unemployment. At any time, some firms may go bankrupt due to competition from rivals, bad management, or bad luck. Employees of such firms typically are not able to find new jobs immediately, and while they are looking for work, they will be unemployed. Also, workers entering the labor market for the first time may require a few weeks or months to find a job.

If we base our analysis on supply and demand, we would expect conditions to change in response to the existence of unemployed workers. Specifically, when there is unemployment beyond some minimum amount, there is an excess supply of workers—at the going wage rates, there are people who want to work who cannot find work. In microeconomic theory, the response to excess supply is a decrease in the price of the commodity in question and therefore an increase in the quantity demanded, a reduction in the quantity supplied, and the restoration of equilibrium. With the quantity supplied equal to the quantity demanded, the market clears.

The existence of unemployment seems to imply that the aggregate labor market is not in equilibrium—that something prevents the quantity supplied and the quantity demanded from equating. Why do labor markets not clear when other markets do, or is it that labor markets are clearing and the unemployment data are reflecting something different? This is another main concern of macroeconomists.

Inflation and Deflation

inflation An increase in the overall price level.

hyperinflation A period of very rapid increases in the overall price level.

Inflation is an increase in the overall price level. Keeping inflation low has long been a goal of government policy. Especially problematic are **hyperinflations**, or periods of very rapid increases in the overall price level.

Most Americans are unaware of what life is like under very high inflation. In some countries at some times, people were accustomed to prices rising by the day, by the hour, or even by the minute. During the hyperinflation in Bolivia in 1984 and 1985, the price of one egg rose from 3,000 pesos to 10,000 pesos in 1 week. In 1985, three bottles of aspirin sold for the same price as a luxury car had sold for in 1982. At the same time, the problem of handling money became a burden. Banks stopped counting deposits—a $500 deposit was equivalent to about 32 million pesos, and it just did not make sense to count a huge sack full of bills. Bolivia's currency, printed in West Germany and England, was the country's third biggest import in 1984, surpassed only by wheat and mining equipment.

Skyrocketing prices in Bolivia are a small part of the story. When inflation approaches rates of 2,000 percent per year, the economy and the whole organization of a country begin to break down. Workers may go on strike to demand wage increases in line with the high inflation rate, and firms may find it hard to secure credit.

Hyperinflations are rare. Nonetheless, economists have devoted much effort to identifying the costs and consequences of even moderate inflation. Does anyone gain from inflation? Who loses? What costs does inflation impose on society? How severe are they? What causes inflation? What is the best way to stop it? These are some of the main concerns of macroeconomists.

deflation A decrease in the overall price level.

A decrease in the overall price level is called **deflation**. In some periods in U.S. history and recently in Japan, deflation has occurred over an extended period of time. The goal of policy makers is to avoid prolonged periods of deflation as well as inflation in order to pursue the macroeconomic goal of stability.

The Components of the Macroeconomy

Understanding how the macroeconomy works can be challenging because a great deal is going on at one time. Everything seems to affect everything else. To see the big picture, it is helpful to divide the participants in the economy into four broad groups: (1) *households*, (2) *firms*, (3) the *government*, and (4) the *rest of the world*. Households and firms make up the private sector, the government is the public sector, and the rest of the world is the foreign sector. These four groups interact in the economy in a variety of ways, many involving either receiving or paying income.

The Circular Flow Diagram

A useful way of seeing the economic interactions among the four groups in the economy is a **circular flow** diagram, which shows the income received and payments made by each group. A simple circular flow diagram is pictured in Figure 20.3.

circular flow A diagram showing the income received and payments made by each sector of the economy.

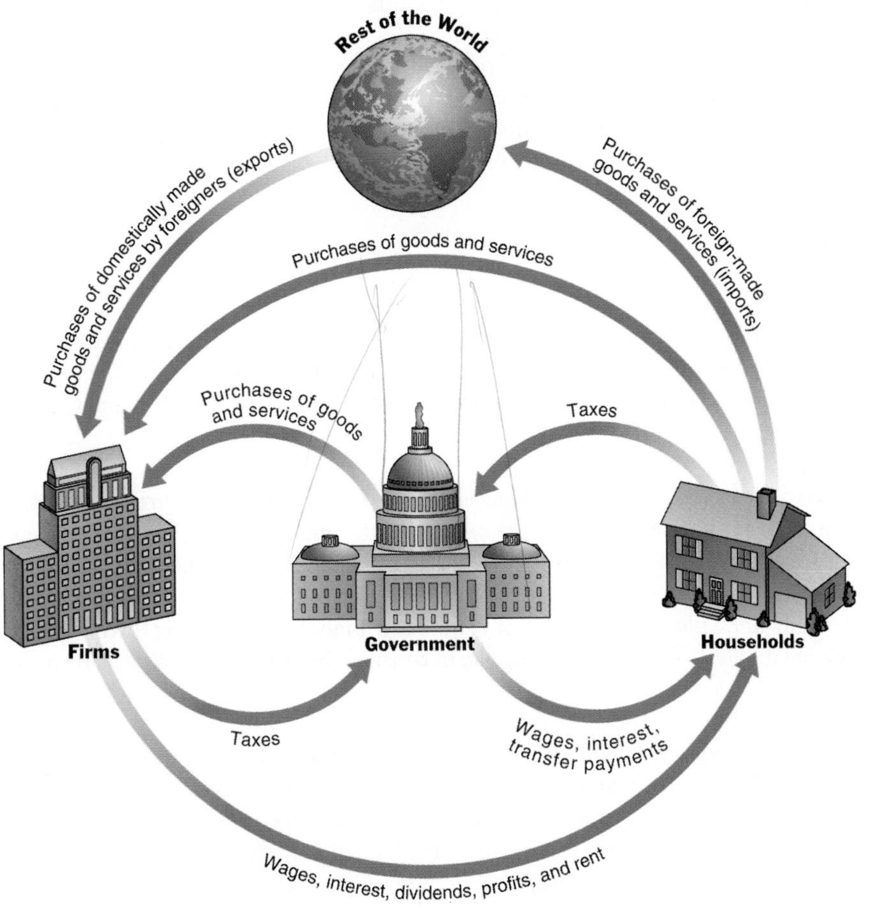

◀ **FIGURE 20.3 The Circular Flow of Payments**

Households receive income from firms and the government, purchase goods and services from firms, and pay taxes to the government. They also purchase foreign-made goods and services (imports). Firms receive payments from households and the government for goods and services; they pay wages, dividends, interest, and rents to households and taxes to the government. The government receives taxes from firms and households, pays firms and households for goods and services—including wages to government workers—and pays interest and transfers to households. Finally, people in other countries purchase goods and services produced domestically (exports).

Note: Although not shown in this diagram, firms and governments also purchase imports.

Let us walk through the circular flow step by step. Households work for firms and the government, and they receive wages for their work. Our diagram shows a flow of wages *into* households as payment for those services. Households also receive interest on corporate and government bonds and dividends from firms. Many households receive other payments from the government, such as Social Security benefits, veterans' benefits, and welfare payments. Economists call these kinds of payments from the government (for which the recipients do not supply goods, services, or labor) **transfer payments**. Together, these receipts make up the total income received by the households.

transfer payments Cash payments made by the government to people who do not supply goods, services, or labor in exchange for these payments. They include Social Security benefits, veterans' benefits, and welfare payments.

Households spend by buying goods and services from firms and by paying taxes to the government. These items make up the total amount paid out by the households. The difference between the total receipts and the total payments of the households is the amount that the households save or dissave. If households receive more than they spend, they *save* during the period. If they receive less than they spend, they *dissave*. A household can dissave by using up some of its previous savings or by borrowing. In the circular flow diagram, household spending is shown as a flow *out* of households. Saving by households is sometimes termed a "leakage" from the circular flow because it withdraws income, or current purchasing power, from the system.

Firms sell goods and services to households and the government. These sales earn revenue, which shows up in the circular flow diagram as a flow *into* the firm sector. Firms pay wages, interest, and dividends to households, and firms pay taxes to the government. These payments are shown flowing *out* of firms.

The government collects taxes from households and firms. The government also makes payments. It buys goods and services from firms, pays wages and interest to households, and makes transfer payments to households. If the government's revenue is less than its payments, the government is dissaving.

Finally, households spend some of their income on *imports*—goods and services produced in the rest of the world. Similarly, people in foreign countries purchase *exports*—goods and services produced by domestic firms and sold to other countries.

One lesson of the circular flow diagram is that everyone's expenditure is someone else's receipt. If you buy a personal computer from Dell, you make a payment to Dell and Dell receives revenue. If Dell pays taxes to the government, it has made a payment and the government has received revenue. Everyone's expenditures go somewhere. It is impossible to sell something without there being a buyer, and it is impossible to make a payment without there being a recipient. Every transaction must have two sides.

The Three Market Arenas

Another way of looking at the ways households, firms, the government, and the rest of the world relate to one another is to consider the markets in which they interact. We divide the markets into three broad arenas: (1) the goods-and-services market, (2) the labor market, and (3) the money (financial) market.

Goods-and-Services Market Households and the government purchase goods and services from firms in the *goods-and-services market.* In this market, firms also purchase goods and services from each other. For example, Levi Strauss buys denim from other firms to make its blue jeans. In addition, firms buy capital goods from other firms. If General Motors needs new robots on its assembly lines, it may buy them from another firm instead of making them. The *Economics in Practice* in Chapter 1 describes how Apple, in constructing its iPod, buys parts from a number of other firms.

Firms *supply* to the goods-and-services market. Households, the government, and firms *demand* from this market. Finally, the rest of the world buys from and sells to the goods-and-services market. The United States imports hundreds of billions of dollars' worth of automobiles, DVDs, oil, and other goods. In the case of Apple's iPod, inputs come from other firms located in countries all over the world. At the same time, the United States exports hundreds of billions of dollars' worth of computers, airplanes, and agricultural goods.

Labor Market Interaction in the *labor market* takes place when firms and the government purchase labor from households. In this market, households *supply* labor and firms and the government *demand* labor. In the U.S. economy, firms are the largest demanders of labor, although the government is also a substantial employer. The total supply of labor in the economy depends on the sum of decisions made by households. Individuals must decide whether to enter the labor force (whether to look for a job at all) and how many hours to work.

Labor is also supplied to and demanded from the rest of the world. In recent years, the labor market has become an international market. For example, vegetable and fruit farmers in California would find it very difficult to bring their product to market if it were not for the labor of migrant farm workers from Mexico. For years, Turkey has provided Germany with "guest workers" who are willing to take low-paying jobs that more prosperous German workers avoid. Call centers run by major U.S. corporations are sometimes staffed by labor in India and other developing countries.

Money Market In the *money market*—sometimes called the *financial market*—households purchase stocks and bonds from firms. Households *supply* funds to this market in the expectation of earning income in the form of dividends on stocks and interest on bonds. Households also *demand* (borrow) funds from this market to finance various purchases. Firms borrow to build new facilities in the hope of earning more in the future. The government borrows by issuing bonds. The rest of the world borrows from and lends to the money market. Every morning there are reports on TV and radio about the Japanese and British stock markets. Much of the borrowing and lending of households, firms, the government, and the rest of the world are coordinated by financial institutions—commercial banks, savings and loan associations, insurance companies, and the like. These institutions take deposits from one group and lend them to others.

When a firm, a household, or the government borrows to finance a purchase, it has an obligation to pay that loan back, usually at some specified time in the future. Most loans also involve payment of interest as a fee for the use of the borrowed funds. When a loan is made, the borrower usually signs a "promise to repay," or *promissory note*, and gives it to the lender. When the federal government borrows, it issues "promises" called **Treasury bonds, notes,** or **bills** in exchange for money. Firms can borrow by issuing **corporate bonds.**

Treasury bonds, notes, *and* bills Promissory notes issued by the federal government when it borrows money.

corporate bonds Promissory notes issued by firms when they borrow money.

Instead of issuing bonds to raise funds, firms can also issue shares of stock. A **share of stock** is a financial instrument that gives the holder a share in the firm's ownership and therefore the right to share in the firm's profits. If the firm does well, the value of the stock increases and the stockholder receives a *capital gain*[1] on the initial purchase. In addition, the stock may pay **dividends**—that is, the firm may return some of its profits directly to its stockholders instead of retaining the profits to buy capital. If the firm does poorly, so does the stockholder. The capital value of the stock may fall, and dividends may not be paid.

shares of stock Financial instruments that give to the holder a share in the firm's ownership and therefore the right to share in the firm's profits.

dividends The portion of a firm's profits that the firm pays out each period to its shareholders.

Stocks and bonds are simply contracts, or agreements, between parties. I agree to loan you a certain amount, and you agree to repay me this amount plus something extra at some future date, or I agree to buy part ownership in your firm, and you agree to give me a share of the firm's future profits.

A critical variable in the money market is the *interest rate*. Although we sometimes talk as if there is only one interest rate, there is never just one interest rate at any time. Instead, the interest rate on a given loan reflects the length of the loan and the perceived risk to the lender. A business that is just getting started must pay a higher rate than General Motors pays. A 30-year mortgage has a different interest rate than a 90-day loan. Nevertheless, interest rates tend to move up and down together, and their movement reflects general conditions in the financial market.

The Role of the Government in the Macroeconomy

The government plays a major role in the macroeconomy, so a useful way of learning how the macroeconomy works is to consider how the government uses policy to affect the economy. The two main policies are (1) fiscal policy and (2) monetary policy. Much of the study of macroeconomics is learning how fiscal and monetary policies work.

Fiscal policy refers to the government's decisions about how much to tax and spend. The federal government collects taxes from households and firms and spends those funds on goods and services ranging from missiles to parks to Social Security payments to interstate highways. Taxes take the form of personal income taxes, Social Security taxes, and corporate profits taxes, among others. An *expansionary* fiscal policy is a policy in which taxes are cut and/or government spending increases. A *contractionary* fiscal policy is the reverse.

fiscal policy Government policies concerning taxes and spending.

Monetary policy in the United States is controlled by the Federal Reserve, the nation's central bank. The Fed, as it is usually called, determines the quantity of money in the economy, which in turn affects interest rates. The Fed's decisions have important effects on the economy. In fact, the task of trying to smooth out business cycles in the United States is primarily left to the Fed (that is, to monetary policy). The chair of the Federal Reserve is sometimes said to be the second most powerful person in the United States after the president.

monetary policy The tools used by the Federal Reserve to control the quantity of money, which in turn affects interest rates.

A Brief History of Macroeconomics

The severe economic contraction and high unemployment of the 1930s, the decade of the **Great Depression**, spurred a great deal of thinking about macroeconomic issues, especially unemployment. Figure 20.2 shows that this period had the largest and longest aggregate output contraction in the twentieth century in the United States. The 1920s had been prosperous years for the U.S. economy. Virtually everyone who wanted a job could get one, incomes rose substantially, and prices were stable. Beginning in late 1929, things took a sudden turn for the worse. In 1929, 1.5 million people were unemployed. By 1933, that had increased to 13 million out of a labor force of 51 million. In 1933, the United States produced about 27 percent fewer goods and services than it had in 1929. In October 1929, when stock prices collapsed on Wall Street, billions of

Great Depression The period of severe economic contraction and high unemployment that began in 1929 and continued throughout the 1930s.

[1] A *capital gain* occurs whenever the value of an asset increases. If you bought a stock for $1,000 and it is now worth $1,500, you have earned a capital gain of $500. A capital gain is "realized" when you sell the asset. Until you sell, the capital gain is *accrued* but not *realized*.

dollars of personal wealth were lost. Unemployment remained above 14 percent of the labor force until 1940. (See the *Economics in Practice*, p. 409, "Macroeconomics in Literature," for Fitzgerald's and Steinbeck's take on the 1920s and 1930s.)

Before the Great Depression, economists applied microeconomic models, sometimes referred to as "classical" or "market clearing" models, to economy-wide problems. For example, classical supply and demand analysis assumed that an excess supply of labor would drive down wages to a new equilibrium level; as a result, unemployment would not persist.

In other words, classical economists believed that recessions were self-correcting. As output falls and the demand for labor shifts to the left, the argument went, the wage rate will decline, thereby raising the quantity of labor demanded by firms that will want to hire more workers at the new lower wage rate. However, during the Great Depression, unemployment levels remained very high for nearly 10 years. In large measure, the failure of simple classical models to explain the prolonged existence of high unemployment provided the impetus for the development of macroeconomics. It is not surprising that what we now call macroeconomics was born in the 1930s.

One of the most important works in the history of economics, *The General Theory of Employment, Interest and Money*, by John Maynard Keynes, was published in 1936. Building on what was already understood about markets and their behavior, Keynes set out to construct a theory that would explain the confusing economic events of his time.

Much of macroeconomics has roots in Keynes's work. According to Keynes, it is not prices and wages that determine the level of employment, as classical models had suggested; instead, it is the level of aggregate demand for goods and services. Keynes believed that governments could intervene in the economy and affect the level of output and employment. The government's role during periods when private demand is low, Keynes argued, is to stimulate aggregate demand and, by so doing, to lift the economy out of recession. (Keynes was a larger-than-life figure, one of the Bloomsbury group in England that included, among others, Virginia Woolf and Clive Bell. See the *Economics in Practice*, p. 411, "John Maynard Keynes.")

After World War II and especially in the 1950s, Keynes's views began to gain increasing influence over both professional economists and government policy makers. Governments came to believe that they could intervene in their economies to attain specific employment and output goals.They began to use their powers to tax and spend as well as their ability to affect interest rates and the money supply for the explicit purpose of controlling the economy's ups and downs. This view of government policy became firmly established in the United States with the passage of the Employment Act of 1946. This act established the President's Council of Economic Advisers, a group of economists who advise the president on economic issues. The act also committed the federal government to intervening in the economy to prevent large declines in output and employment.

The notion that the government could and should act to stabilize the macroeconomy reached the height of its popularity in the 1960s. During these years, Walter Heller, the chairman of the Council of Economic Advisers under both President Kennedy and President Johnson, alluded to **fine-tuning** as the government's role in regulating inflation and unemployment. During the 1960s, many economists believed the government could use the tools available to manipulate unemployment and inflation levels fairly precisely.

fine-tuning The phrase used by Walter Heller to refer to the government's role in regulating inflation and unemployment.

In the 1970s and early 1980s, the U.S. economy had wide fluctuations in employment, output, and inflation. In 1974–1975 and again in 1980–1982, the United States experienced a severe recession. Although not as catastrophic as the Great Depression of the 1930s, these two recessions left millions without jobs and resulted in billions of dollars of lost output and income. In 1974–1975 and again in 1979–1981, the United States also saw very high rates of inflation.

The 1970s was thus a period of stagnation and high inflation, which came to be called stagflation. **Stagflation** is defined as a situation in which there is high inflation at the same time there are slow or negative output growth and high unemployment. Until the 1970s, high inflation had been observed only in periods when the economy was prospering and unemployment was low. The problem of stagflation was vexing both for macroeconomic theorists and policy makers concerned with the health of the economy.

stagflation A situation of both high inflation and high unemployment.

It was clear by 1975 that the macroeconomy was more difficult to control than Heller's words or textbook theory had led economists to believe. The events of the 1970s and early 1980s had an important influence on macroeconomic theory. Much of the faith in the simple Keynesian model and the "conventional wisdom" of the 1960s was lost. Although we are now 30 years past the

ECONOMICS IN PRACTICE

Macroeconomics in Literature

As you know, the language of economics includes a heavy dose of graphs and equations. But the underlying phenomena that economists study are the stuff of novels as well as graphs and equations. The following two passages, from *The Great Gatsby* by F. Scott Fitzgerald and *The Grapes of Wrath* by John Steinbeck, capture in graphic, although not graphical, form the economic growth and spending of the Roaring Twenties and the human side of the unemployment of the Great Depression.

The Great Gatsby, written in 1925, is set in the 1920s, while *The Grapes of Wrath*, written in 1939, is set in the early 1930s. If you look at Figure 20.2 for these two periods, you will see the translation of Fitzgerald and Steinbeck into macroeconomics.

From *The Great Gatsby*

At least once a fortnight a corps of caterers came down with several hundred feet of canvas and enough colored lights to make a Christmas tree of Gatsby's enormous garden. On buffet tables, garnished with glistening hors d'œuvre, spiced baked hams crowded against salads of harlequin designs and pastry pigs and turkeys bewitched to a dark gold. In the main hall a bar with a real brass rail was set up, and stocked with gins and liquors and with cordials so long forgotten that most of his female guests were too young to know one from another.

By seven o'clock the orchestra has arrived—no thin five piece affair but a whole pit full of oboes and trombones and saxophones and viols and cornets and piccolos and low and high drums. The last swimmers have come in from the beach now and are dressing upstairs; the cars from New York are parked five deep in the drive, and already the halls and salons and verandas are gaudy with primary colors and hair shorn in strange new ways and shawls beyond the dreams of Castile.

From *The Grapes of Wrath*

The moving, questing people were migrants now. Those families who had lived on a little piece of land, who had lived and died on forty acres, had eaten or starved on the produce of forty acres, had now the whole West to rove in. And they scampered about, looking for work; and the highways were streams of people, and the ditch banks were lines of people. Behind them more were coming. The great highways streamed with moving people.

And the migrants streamed in on the highways and their hunger was in their eyes, and their need was in their eyes. They had no argument, no system, nothing but their numbers and their needs. When there was work for a man, ten men fought for it—fought with a low wage. If that fella'll work for thirty cents, I'll work for twenty-five.

1970s, the discipline of macroeconomics is still in flux and there is no agreed-upon view of how the macroeconomy works. Many important issues have yet to be resolved. This makes macroeconomics hard to teach but exciting to study.

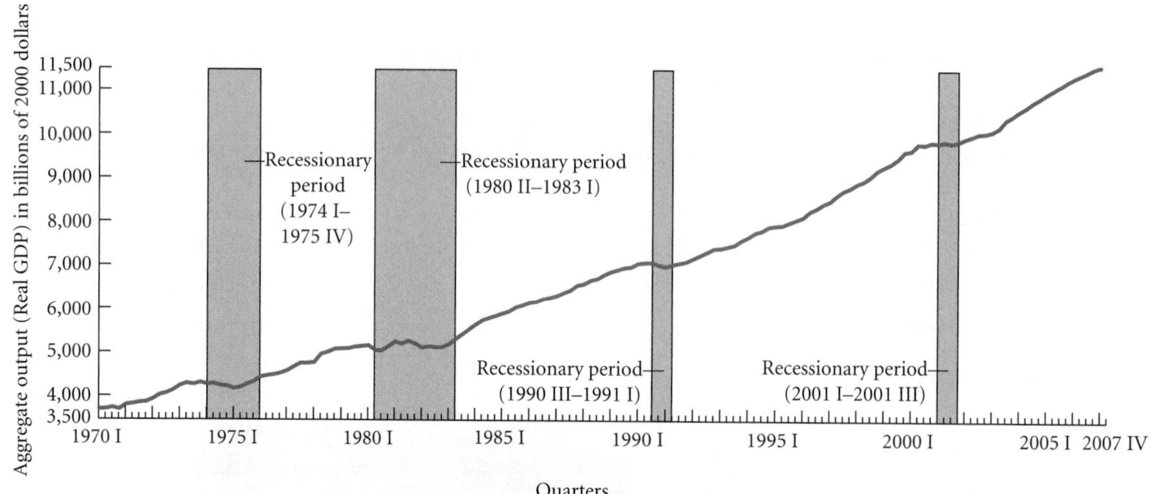

▲ **FIGURE 20.4 Aggregate Output (Real GDP), 1970 I–2007 IV**
Aggregate output in the United States since 1970 has risen overall, but there have been four recessionary periods: 1974 I–1975 IV, 1980 II–1983 I, 1990 III–1991 I, and 2001 I–2001 III.

The U.S Economy Since 1970

In the following chapters, it will be useful to have a picture of how the U.S. economy has performed in recent history. Since 1970, the U.S. economy has experienced four recessions and two periods of high inflation. The period since 1970 is illustrated in Figures 20.4, 20.5, and 20.6. These figures are based on quarterly data (that is, data for each quarter of the year). The first quarter consists of January, February, and March; the second quarter consists of April, May, and June; and so on. The Roman numerals I, II, III, and IV denote the four quarters. For example, 1972 III refers to the third quarter of 1972. The measurement of aggregate output, real GDP, in Figure 20.4 is discussed in the next chapter. In Figure 20.6, the measurement of inflation, the percentage change in the GDP deflator, is also discussed in the next chapter.

Figure 20.4 plots aggregate output for 1970 I–2007 IV. The four recessionary periods are 1974 I–1975 IV, 1980 II–1983 I, 1990 III–1991 I, and 2001 I–2001 III.[2] These four periods are shaded in the figure. Figure 20.5 plots the unemployment rate for the same overall period with the same shading for the recessionary periods. Note that unemployment rose in all four recessions. In the 1974–1975 recession, the unemployment rate reached a maximum of 8.8 percent in the second quarter of 1975. During the 1980–1982 recession, it reached a maximum of 10.7 percent in the fourth quarter of 1982. The unemployment rate continued to rise after the 1990–1991 recession and reached a peak of 7.6 percent in 1992 III. By the end of 1994, the unemployment rate had fallen to 5.6 percent, and by the second quarter of 2000, it had fallen to 4.0 percent. It then rose to 5.8 percent by the second quarter of 2002. It began falling again in the fourth quarter of 2003.

Figure 20.6 plots the inflation rate for 1970 I–2007 IV. The two high inflation periods are 1973 IV–1975 IV and 1979 I–1981 IV, which are shaded. In the first high inflation period, the inflation rate peaked at 11 percent in the first quarter of 1975. In the second high inflation period, inflation peaked at 10.1 percent in the first quarter of 1981. Since 1983, the inflation rate has been quite low by the standards of the 1970s. Since 1994, it has been between about 2 and 3 percent.

[2] As Figure 20.4 shows, output rose in the middle of 1981 before falling again in the last quarter of 1981. Given this fact, one possibility would be to treat the 1980 II–1983 I period as if it included two separate recessionary periods: 1980 II–1981 I and 1981 IV–1983 I. Because expansion in 1981 was so short-lived, however, we have chosen not to separate the period into two parts.

ECONOMICS IN PRACTICE

John Maynard Keynes

Much of the framework of modern macroeconomics comes from the works of John Maynard Keynes, whose *General Theory of Employment, Interest and Money* was published in 1936. The following excerpt by Robert L. Heilbroner provides some insights into Keynes's life and work.

By 1933 the nation was virtually prostrate. On street corners, in homes, in Hoovervilles (communities of makeshift shacks), 14 million unemployed sat, haunting the land....

It was the unemployment that was hardest to bear. The jobless millions were like an embolism in the nation's vital circulation; and while their indisputable existence argued more forcibly than any text that something was wrong with the system, the economists wrung their hands and racked their brains... but could offer neither diagnosis nor remedy. Unemployment—this kind of unemployment—was simply not listed among the possible ills of the system: it was absurd, impossible, unreasonable, and paradoxical. But it was there.

It would seem logical that the man who would seek to solve this impossible paradox of not enough production existing side by side with men fruitlessly seeking work would be a Left-winger, an economist with strong sympathies for the proletariat, an angry man. Nothing could be further from the fact. The man who tackled it was almost a dilettante with nothing like a chip on his shoulder. The simple truth was that his talents inclined in every direction. He had, for example, written a most recondite book on mathematical probability, a book that Bertrand Russell had declared "impossible to praise too highly"; then he had gone on to match his skill in abstruse logic with a flair for making money—he accumulated a fortune of £500,000 by way of the most treacherous of all roads to riches: dealing in international currencies and commodities. More impressive yet, he had written his mathematics treatise on the side, as it were, while engaged in Government service, and he piled up his private wealth by applying himself for only half an hour a day while still abed.

But this is only a sample of his many-sidedness. He was an economist, of course—a Cambridge don with all the dignity and erudition that go with such an appointment.... He managed to be simultaneously the darling of the Bloomsbury set, the cluster of Britain's most avant-garde intellectual brilliants, and also the chairman of a life insurance company, a niche in life rarely noted for its intellectual abandon. He was a pillar of stability in delicate matters of international diplomacy, but his official correctness did not prevent him from acquiring a knowledge of other European politicians that included their... neuroses and financial prejudices.... He ran a theater, and he came to be a Director of the Bank of England. He knew Roosevelt and Churchill and also Bernard Shaw and Pablo Picasso....

His name was John Maynard Keynes, an old British name (pronounced to rhyme with "rains") that could be traced back to one William de Cahagnes and 1066. Keynes was a traditionalist; he liked to think that greatness ran in families, and it is true that his own father was John Neville Keynes, an illustrious enough economist in his own right. But it took more than the ordinary gifts of heritage to account for the son; it was as if the talents that would have sufficed half a dozen men were by happy accident crowded into one person.

By a coincidence he was born in 1883, in the very year that Karl Marx passed away. But the two economists who thus touched each other in time, although each was to exert the profoundest influence on the philosophy of the capitalist system, could hardly have differed from one another more. Marx was bitter, at bay, heavy and disappointed; as we know, he was the draftsman of Capitalism Doomed. Keynes loved life and sailed through it buoyant, at ease, and consummately successful to become the architect of Capitalism Viable.

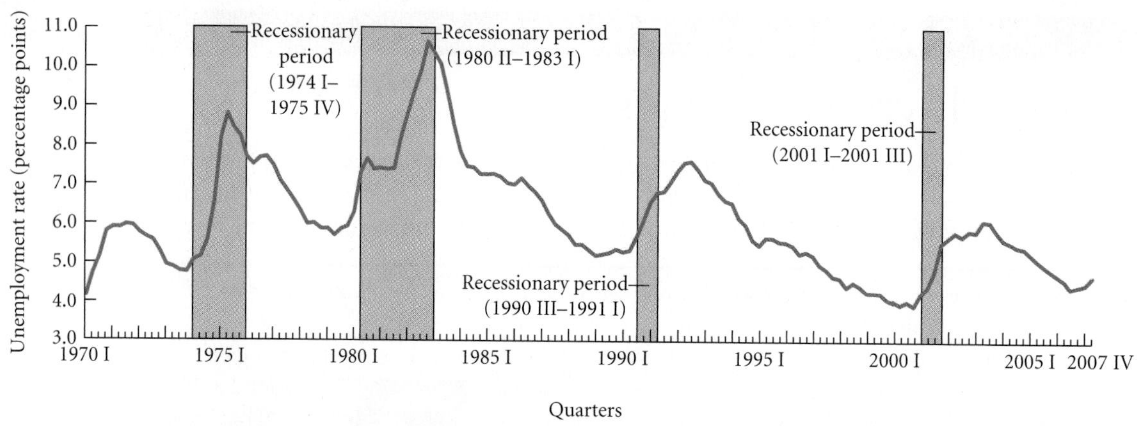

▲ **FIGURE 20.5 Unemployment Rate, 1970 I–2007 IV**

The U.S. unemployment rate since 1970 shows wide variations. The four recessionary reference periods show increases in the unemployment rate.

In the following chapters, we will explain the behavior of and the connections among variables such as output, unemployment, and inflation. When you understand the forces at work in creating the movements shown in Figures 20.4, 20.5, and 20.6, you will have come a long way in understanding how the macroeconomy works.

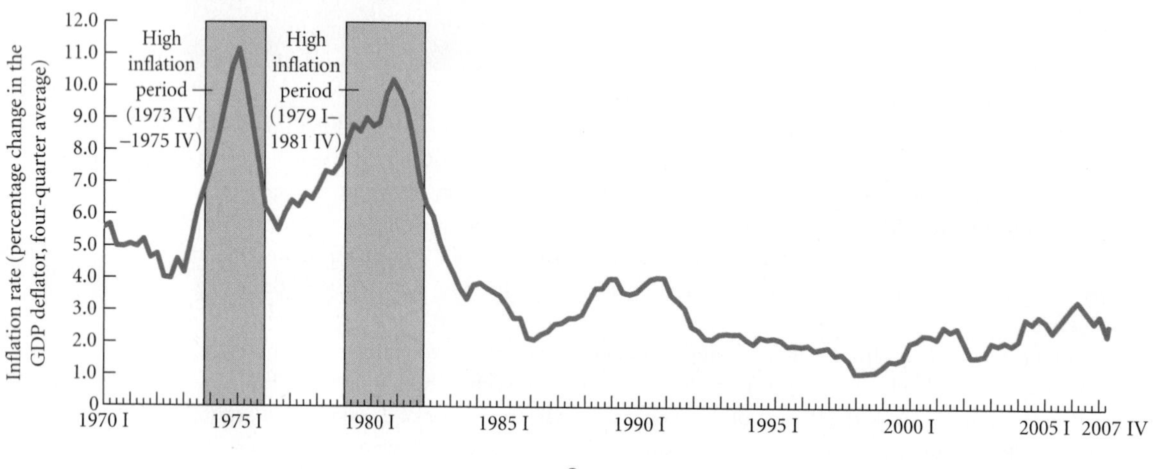

▲ **FIGURE 20.6 Inflation Rate (Percentage Change in the GDP Deflator, Four-Quarter Average), 1970 I–2007 IV**

Since 1970, inflation has been high in two periods: 1973 IV–1975 IV and 1979 I–1981 IV. Inflation between 1983 and 1992 was moderate. Since 1992, it has been fairly low.

ECONOMICS IN PRACTICE

Pearson Prentice Hall is committed to providing the most current content possible. Starting December 15, 2008, all printed Student Editions of **Case/Fair/Oster's** ninth edition will include this newly updated *Economics in Practice* content. You can view this updated content at www.pearsonhighered.com/case on November 20, 2008.

SUMMARY

1. *Microeconomics* examines the functioning of individual industries and the behavior of individual decision-making units. *Macroeconomics* is concerned with the sum, or aggregate, of these individual decisions—the consumption of *all* households in the economy, the amount of labor supplied and demanded by *all* individuals and firms, and the total amount of *all* goods and services produced.

MACROECONOMIC CONCERNS *p. 402*

2. The three topics of primary concern to macroeconomists are the growth rate of aggregate output; the level of unemployment; and increases in the overall price level, or *inflation*.

THE COMPONENTS OF THE MACROECONOMY *p. 404*

3. The *circular flow* diagram shows the flow of income received and payments made by the four groups in the economy—households, firms, the government, and the rest of the world. Everybody's expenditure is someone else's receipt—every transaction must have two sides.

4. Another way of looking at how households, firms, the government, and the rest of the world relate is to consider the markets in which they interact: the goods-and-services market, labor market, and money (financial) market.

5. Among the tools that the government has available for influencing the macroeconomy are *fiscal policy* (decisions on

taxes and government spending) and *monetary policy* (control of the money supply, which affects interest rates).

A BRIEF HISTORY OF MACROECONOMICS *p. 407*

6. Macroeconomics was born out of the effort to explain the *Great Depression* of the 1930s. Since that time, the discipline has evolved, concerning itself with new issues as the problems facing the economy have changed. Through the late 1960s, it was believed that the government could "fine-tune" the economy to keep it running on an even keel at all times. The poor economic performance of the 1970s, however, showed that *fine-tuning* does not always work.

THE U.S. ECONOMY SINCE 1970 *p. 410*

7. Since 1970, the U.S. economy has seen four *recessions* and two periods of high inflation.

REVIEW TERMS AND CONCEPTS

aggregate behavior, *p. 401*
aggregate output, *p. 402*
business cycle, *p. 402*
circular flow, *p. 405*
contraction, recession, *or* slump, *p. 402*
corporate bonds, *p. 407*
deflation, *p. 404*
depression, *p. 402*
dividends, *p. 407*
expansion *or* boom, *p. 402*
fine-tuning, *p. 408*
fiscal policy, *p. 407*
Great Depression, *p. 407*
hyperinflation, *p. 404*
inflation, *p. 404*
macroeconomics, *p. 401*
microeconomics, *p. 401*
monetary policy, *p. 407*
recession, *p. 402*
shares of stock, *p. 407*
stagflation, *p. 408*
sticky prices, *p. 401*
transfer payments, *p. 405*
Treasury bonds, notes, *and* bills, *p. 407*
unemployment rate, *p. 403*

PROBLEMS

Visit **www.myeconlab.com** to complete the problems marked in orange online. You will receive instant feedback on your answers, tutorial help, and access to additional practice problems.

1. Define inflation. Assume that you live in a simple economy in which only three goods are produced and traded: fish, fruit, and meat. Suppose that on January 1, 2007, fish sold for $2.50 per pound, meat was $3.00 per pound, and fruit was $1.50 per pound. At the end of the year, you discover that the catch was low and that fish prices had increased to $5.00 per pound, but fruit prices stayed at $1.50 and meat prices had actually fallen to $2.00. Can you say what happened to the overall "price level"? How might you construct a measure of the "change in the price level"? What additional information might you need to construct your measure?

2. Define *unemployment*. Should everyone who does not hold a job be considered "unemployed"? To help with your answer, draw a supply and demand diagram depicting the labor market. What is measured along the demand curve? What factors determine the quantity of labor demanded during a given period? What is measured along the labor supply curve? What factors determine the quantity of labor supplied by households during a given period? What is the opportunity cost of holding a job?

3. **[Related to the *Economics in Practice* on p. 409]** The *Economics in Practice* describes prosperity and recession as they are depicted in literature. At the beginning of 2008, there was a debate about whether the U.S. economy was in recession. Look at the data on real GDP growth and unemployment and describe the pattern since 2007. You can find raw data on employment and unemployment at www.bls.gov, and you can find raw data on real GDP growth at www.bea.gov. (In both cases, use the data described in "Current Releases.") Summarize what happened during 2008. Did we have a recession? Explain.

4. A recession occurred in the U.S. economy during the first three quarters of 2001. National output of goods and services fell during this period. But during the fourth quarter of 2001, output began to increase and it increased at a slow rate through the first quarter of 2003. At the same time, between March 2001 and April 2003, employment declined almost continuously with a loss of over 2 million jobs. How is it possible that output rises while at the same time employment is falling?

5. Describe the economy of your state. What is the most recently reported unemployment rate? How has the number of payroll jobs changed over the last 3 months and over the last year? How does your state's performance compare to the U.S. economy's performance over the last year? What explanations have been offered in the press? How accurate are they?

6. Explain briefly how macroeconomics is different from microeconomics. How can macroeconomists use microeconomic theory to guide them in their work, and why might they want to do so?

7. During 1993 when the economy was growing very slowly, President Clinton recommended a series of spending cuts and tax increases designed to reduce the deficit. These were passed by Congress in the Omnibus Budget Reconciliation Act of 1993. Some who opposed the bill argue that the United States was pursuing a "contractionary fiscal policy" at precisely the wrong time. Explain their logic.

8. Many of the expansionary periods during the twentieth century occurred during wars. Why do you think this is true?

9. In the 1940s, you could buy a soda for 5 cents, eat dinner at a restaurant for less than $1, and purchase a house for $10,000. From this statement, it follows that consumers today are worse off than consumers in the 1940s. Comment.

10. **[Related to *Economics in Practice* on *p. 411*]** John Maynard Keynes was the first to show that government policy could be used to change aggregate output and prevent recessions by stabilizing the economy. Describe the economy of the world at the time Keynes was writing. Describe the economy of the United States today. What measures were being proposed by the Presidential candidates in the election of 2008 to prevent or end a recession in 2008-2009? Where the actions taken appropriate from the standpoint of John Maynard Keynes? Did they have the desired effect?

Measuring National Output and National Income

21

We saw in the last chapter that three main concerns of macroeconomics are aggregate output, unemployment, and inflation. In this chapter, we discuss the measurement of aggregate output and inflation. In the next chapter, we discuss the measurement of unemployment. Accurate measures of these variables are critical for understanding the economy. Without good measures, economists would have a hard time analyzing how the economy works and policy makers would have little to guide them on which policies are best for the economy.

Much of the macroeconomic data are from the **national income and product accounts**, which are compiled by the Bureau of Economic Analysis (BEA) of the U.S. Department of Commerce. It is hard to overestimate the importance of these accounts. They are, in fact, one of the great inventions of the twentieth century. (See the *Economics in Practice*, p. 425.) They not only convey data about the performance of the economy but also provide a conceptual framework that macroeconomists use to think about how the pieces of the economy fit together. When economists think about the macroeconomy, the categories and vocabulary they use come from the national income and product accounts.

The national income and product accounts can be compared with the mechanical or wiring diagrams for an automobile engine. The diagrams do not explain how an engine works, but they identify the key parts of an engine and show how they are connected. Trying to understand the macroeconomy without understanding national income accounting is like trying to fix an engine without a mechanical diagram and with no names for the engine parts.

There are literally thousands of variables in the national income and product accounts. In this chapter, we discuss only the most important. This chapter is meant to convey the way the national income and product accounts represent or organize the economy and the *sizes* of the various pieces of the economy.

CHAPTER OUTLINE

Gross Domestic Product

The key concept in the national income and product accounts is **gross domestic product (GDP)**.

> GDP is the total market value of a country's output. It is the market value of all final goods and services produced within a given period of time by factors of production located within a country.

U.S. GDP for 2007—the value of all output produced by factors of production in the United States in 2007—was $13,841.3 billion.

national income and product accounts Data collected and published by the government describing the various components of national income and output in the economy.

gross domestic product (GDP) The total market value of all final goods and services produced within a given period by factors of production located within a country.

GDP is a critical concept. Just as an individual firm needs to evaluate the success or failure of its operations each year, so the economy as a whole needs to assess itself. GDP, as a measure of the total production of an economy, provides us with a country's economic report card. Because GDP is so important, we need to take time to explain exactly what its definition means.

Final Goods and Services

final goods and services Goods and services produced for final use.

intermediate goods Goods that are produced by one firm for use in further processing by another firm.

First, note that the definition refers to **final goods and services.** Many goods produced in the economy are not classified as *final* goods, but instead as intermediate goods. **Intermediate goods** are produced by one firm for use in further processing by another firm. For example, tires sold to automobile manufacturers are intermediate goods. The parts that go in Apple's iPod are also intermediate goods. The value of intermediate goods is not counted in GDP.

Why are intermediate goods not counted in GDP? Suppose that in producing a car, General Motors (GM) pays $200 to Goodyear for tires. GM uses these tires (among other components) to assemble a car, which it sells for $24,000. The value of the car (including its tires) is $24,000, not $24,000 + $200. The final price of the car already reflects the value of all its components. To count in GDP both the value of the tires sold to the automobile manufacturers and the value of the automobiles sold to the consumers would result in double counting.

value added The difference between the value of goods as they leave a stage of production and the cost of the goods as they entered that stage.

Double counting can also be avoided by counting only the value added to a product by each firm in its production process. The **value added** during some stage of production is the difference between the value of goods as they leave that stage of production and the cost of the goods as they entered that stage. Value added is illustrated in Table 21.1. The four stages of the production of a gallon of gasoline are: (1) oil drilling, (2) refining, (3) shipping, and (4) retail sale. In the first stage, value added is the value of the crude oil. In the second stage, the refiner purchases the oil from the driller, refines it into gasoline, and sells it to the shipper. The refiner pays the driller $3.00 per gallon and charges the shipper $3.30. The value added by the refiner is thus $0.30 per gallon. The shipper then sells the gasoline to retailers for $3.60. The value added in the third stage of production is $0.30. Finally, the retailer sells the gasoline to consumers for $4.00. The value added at the fourth stage is $0.40; and the total value added in the production process is $4.00, the same as the value of sales at the retail level. Adding the total values of sales at each stage of production ($3.00 + $3.30 + $3.60 + $4.00 = $13.90) would significantly overestimate the value of the gallon of gasoline.

In calculating GDP, we can sum up the value added at each stage of production or we can take the value of final sales. We do not use the value of total sales in an economy to measure how much output has been produced.

TABLE 21.1 Value Added in the Production of a Gallon of Gasoline (Hypothetical Numbers)

Stage of Production	Value of Sales	Value Added
(1) Oil drilling	$3.00	$3.00
(2) Refining	3.30	0.30
(3) Shipping	3.60	0.30
(4) Retail sale	4.00	0.40
Total value added		$4.00

Exclusion of Used Goods and Paper Transactions

GDP is concerned only with new, or current, production. Old output is not counted in current GDP because it was already counted when it was produced. It would be double counting to count sales of used goods in current GDP. If someone sells a used car to you, the transaction is not counted in GDP because no new production has taken place. Similarly, a house is counted in GDP only at the time it is built, not each time it is resold. In short:

GDP does not count transactions in which money or goods changes hands but in which no new goods and services are produced.

Sales of stocks and bonds are not counted in GDP. These exchanges are transfers of ownership of assets, either electronically or through paper exchanges, and do not correspond to current production. However, what if you sell the stock or bond for more than you originally paid for it? Profits from the stock or bond market have nothing to do with current production, so they are not counted in GDP. However, if you pay a fee to a broker for selling a stock of yours to someone else, this fee is counted in GDP because the broker is performing a service for you. This service is part of current production. Be careful to distinguish between exchanges of stocks and bonds for money (or for other stocks and bonds), which do not involve current production, and fees for performing such exchanges, which do.

Exclusion of Output Produced Abroad by Domestically Owned Factors of Production

GDP is the value of output produced by factors of production *located within a country.*

The three basic factors of production are land, labor, and capital. The labor of U.S. citizens counts as a domestically owned factor of production for the United States. The output produced by U.S. citizens abroad—for example, U.S. citizens working for a foreign company—is *not* counted in U.S. GDP because the output is not produced within the United States. Likewise, profits earned abroad by U.S. companies are not counted in U.S. GDP. However, the output produced by foreigners working in the United States is counted in U.S. GDP because the output is produced within the United States. Also, profits earned in the United States by foreign-owned companies are counted in U.S. GDP.

It is sometimes useful to have a measure of the output produced by factors of production owned by a country's citizens regardless of where the output is produced. This measure is called **gross national product (GNP)**. For most countries, including the United States, the difference between GDP and GNP is small. In 2007, GNP for the United States was $13,937.1 billion, which is close to the $13,841.3 billion value for U.S. GDP.

gross national product (GNP) The total market value of all final goods and services produced within a given period by factors of production owned by a country's citizens, regardless of where the output is produced.

The distinction between GDP and GNP can be tricky. Consider the Honda plant in Marysville, Ohio. The plant is owned by the Honda Corporation, a Japanese firm, but most of the workers employed at the plant are U.S. workers. Although all the output of the plant is included in U.S. GDP, only part of it is included in U.S. GNP. The wages paid to U.S. workers are part of U.S. GNP, while the profits from the plant are not. The profits from the plant are counted in Japanese GNP because this is output produced by Japanese-owned factors of production (Japanese capital in this case). The profits, however, are not counted in Japanese GDP because they were not earned in Japan.

Calculating GDP

GDP can be computed two ways. One way is to add up the total amount spent on all final goods and services during a given period. This is the **expenditure approach** to calculating GDP. The other way is to add up the income—wages, rents, interest, and profits—received by all factors of production in producing final goods and services. This is the **income approach** to calculating GDP. These two methods lead to the same value for GDP for the reason we discussed in the previous chapter: *Every payment (expenditure) by a buyer is at the same time a receipt (income) for the seller.* We can measure either income received or expenditures made, and we will end up with the same total output.

expenditure approach A method of computing GDP that measures the total amount spent on all final goods and services during a given period.

income approach A method of computing GDP that measures the income—wages, rents, interest, and profits—received by all factors of production in producing final goods and services.

Suppose the economy is made up of just one firm and the firm's total output this year sells for $1 million. Because the total amount spent on output this year is $1 million, this year's GDP is $1 million. (Remember: The expenditure approach calculates GDP on the basis of the total amount spent on final goods and services in the economy.) However, *every one* of the million dollars of GDP either is paid to someone or remains with the owners of the firm as profit. Using the income approach, we add up the wages paid to employees of the firm, the interest paid to those who lent money to the firm, and the rents paid to those who leased land, buildings, or equipment to the firm. What is left over is profit, which is, of course, income to the owners of the firm. If we add up the incomes of all the factors of production, including profits to the owners, we get a GDP of $1 million.

The Expenditure Approach

Recall from the previous chapter the four main groups in the economy: households, firms, the government, and the rest of the world. There are also four main categories of expenditure:

- Personal consumption expenditures (*C*): household spending on consumer goods
- Gross private domestic investment (*I*): spending by firms and households on new capital, that is, plant, equipment, inventory, and new residential structures
- Government consumption and gross investment (*G*)
- Net exports (*EX* – *IM*): net spending by the rest of the world, or exports (*EX*) minus imports (*IM*)

The expenditure approach calculates GDP by adding together these four components of spending. It is shown here in equation form:

$$GDP = C + I + G + (EX - IM)$$

U.S. GDP was $13,841.3 billion in 2007. The four components of the expenditure approach are shown in Table 21.2, along with their various categories.

TABLE 21.2 Components of U.S. GDP, 2007: The Expenditure Approach

	Billions of Dollars		Percentage of GDP	
Personal consumption expenditures (C)	9,734.2		70.3	
Durable goods		1,078.2		7.8
Nondurable goods		2,833.2		20.5
Services		5,822.8		42.1
Gross private domestic investment (I)	2,125.4		15.4	
Nonresidential		1,481.8		10.7
Residential		640.7		4.6
Change in business inventories		2.9		0.0
Government consumption and gross investment (G)	2,689.8		19.4	
Federal		976.0		7.1
State and local		1,713.8		12.4
Net exports (*EX* – *IM*)	–708.0		–5.1	
Exports (*EX*)		1,643.0		11.9
Imports (*IM*)		2,351.0		17.0
Gross domestic product	13,841.3		100.0	

Note: Numbers may not add exactly because of rounding.

Source: U.S. Department of Commerce, Bureau of Economic Analysis.

personal consumption expenditures (*C*) Expenditures by consumers on goods and services.

durable goods Goods that last a relatively long time, such as cars and household appliances.

nondurable goods Goods that are used up fairly quickly, such as food and clothing.

services The things we buy that do not involve the production of physical things, such as legal and medical services and education.

Personal Consumption Expenditures (*C*) The largest part of GDP consists of **personal consumption expenditures (*C*)**. Table 21.2 shows that in 2007, the amount of personal consumption expenditures accounted for 70.3 percent of GDP. These are expenditures by consumers on goods and services.

There are three main categories of consumer expenditures: durable goods, nondurable goods, and services. **Durable goods**, such as automobiles, furniture, and household appliances, last a relatively long time. **Nondurable goods**, such as food, clothing, gasoline, and cigarettes, are used up fairly quickly. Payments for **services**—those things we buy that do not involve the production of physical items—include expenditures for doctors, lawyers, and educational institutions. As Table 21.2 shows, in 2007, durable goods expenditures accounted for 7.8 percent of GDP, nondurables for 20.5 percent, and services for 42.1 percent.

Gross Private Domestic Investment (*I*) *Investment*, as we use the term in economics, refers to the purchase of new capital—housing, plants, equipment, and inventory. The economic use of the term is in contrast to its everyday use, where *investment* often refers to purchases of stocks, bonds, or mutual funds.

ECONOMICS IN PRACTICE

Where Does eBay Get Counted?

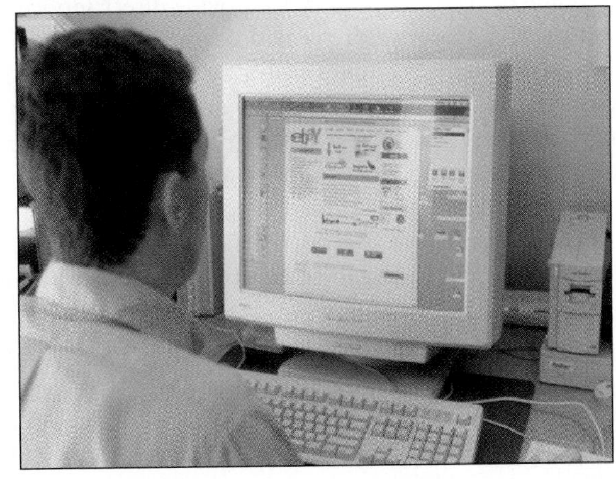

eBay runs an online marketplace with over 220 million registered users who buy and sell 2.4 billion items a year, ranging from children's toys to oil paintings. In December 2007, one eBay user auctioned off a 1933 Chicago World's Fair pennant. The winning bid was just over $20.

eBay is traded on the New York Stock Exchange, employs hundreds of people, and has a market value of about $40 billion. With regard to eBay, what do you think gets counted as part of current GDP?

That 1933 pennant, for example, does not get counted. The production of that pennant was counted back in 1933. The many cartons of K'nex bricks sent from one home to another don't count either. Their value was counted when the bricks were first produced. What about a newly minted Scrabble game? One of the interesting features of eBay is that it has changed from being a market in which individuals market their hand-me-downs to a place that small and even large businesses use as a sales site. The value of the new Scrabble game would be counted as part of this year's GDP if it were produced in the year.

So do any of eBay's services count as part of GDP? eBay's business is to provide a marketplace for exchange. In doing so, it uses labor and capital and creates value. In return for creating this value, eBay charges fees to the sellers that use its site. The value of these fees do enter into GDP. So while the old knickknacks that people sell on eBay do not contribute to current GDP, the cost of finding an interested buyer for those old goods does indeed get counted.

Total investment in capital by the private sector is called **gross private domestic investment** (*I*). Expenditures by firms for machines, tools, plants, and so on make up **nonresidential investment.**[1] Because these are goods that firms buy for their own final use, they are part of "final sales" and counted in GDP. Expenditures for new houses and apartment buildings constitute **residential investment.** The third component of gross private domestic investment, the **change in business inventories,** is the amount by which firms' inventories change during a period. Business inventories can be looked at as the goods that firms produce now but intend to sell later. In 2007, gross private domestic investment accounted for 15.4 percent of GDP. Of that, 10.7 percent was nonresidential investment, 4.6 percent was residential investment, and 0.0 percent (rounded to one decimal point) was change in business inventories.

gross private domestic investment (*I*) Total investment in capital—that is, the purchase of new housing, plants, equipment, and inventory by the private (or nongovernment) sector.

nonresidential investment Expenditures by firms for machines, tools, plants, and so on.

residential investment Expenditures by households and firms on new houses and apartment buildings.

change in business inventories The amount by which firms' inventories change during a period. Inventories are the goods that firms produce now but intend to sell later.

Change in Business Inventories It is sometimes confusing to students that inventories are counted as capital and that changes in inventory are counted as part of gross private domestic investment, but conceptually it makes sense. The inventory a firm owns has a value, and it serves a purpose (or provides a service) to the firm. That inventory has value is obvious. Think of the inventory of a new car dealer or of a clothing store or stocks of newly produced but unsold computers awaiting shipment. All these have value.

[1] The distinction between what is considered investment and what is considered consumption is sometimes fairly arbitrary. A firm's purchase of a car or a truck is counted as investment, but a household's purchase of a car or a truck is counted as consumption of durable goods. In general, expenditures by firms for items that last longer than a year are counted as investment expenditures. Expenditures for items that last less than a year are seen as purchases of intermediate goods.

However, what *service* does inventory provide? Firms keep stocks of inventory for a number of reasons. One is to meet unforeseen demand. Firms are never sure how much they will sell from period to period. Sales go up and down. To maintain the goodwill of their customers, firms need to be able to respond to unforeseen increases in sales. The only way to do that is with inventory.

Some firms use inventory to provide direct services to customers—the main function of a retail store. A grocery store provides a service—convenience. The store itself does not produce any food. It simply assembles a wide variety of items and puts them on display so consumers with varying tastes can come and shop in one place for what they want. The same is true for clothing and hardware stores. To provide their services, such stores need light fixtures, counters, cash registers, buildings, and stocks of inventory. Capital stocks are made up of plant, equipment, and inventory. Inventory accumulation is part of the change in capital stocks, or investment.

Remember that GDP is not the market value of total final *sales* during a period—it is the market value of total *production*. The relationship between total production and total sales is as follows:

GDP = Final sales + Change in business inventories

Total production (GDP) equals final sales of domestic goods plus the change in business inventories. In 2007, production in the United States exceeded sales by $2.9 billion. Inventories at the end of 2007 were $2.9 billion *greater* than they were at the end of 2006.

Gross Investment versus Net Investment During the process of production, capital (especially machinery and equipment) produced in previous periods gradually wears out. GDP does not give us a true picture of the real production of an economy. GDP includes newly produced capital goods but does not take account of capital goods "consumed" in the production process.

depreciation The amount by which an asset's value falls in a given period.

gross investment The total value of all newly produced capital goods (plant, equipment, housing, and inventory) produced in a given period.

net investment Gross investment minus depreciation.

Capital assets decline in value over time. The amount by which an asset's value falls each period is called its **depreciation.**[2] A personal computer purchased by a business today may be expected to have a useful life of 4 years before becoming worn out or obsolete. Over that period, the computer steadily depreciates.

What is the relationship between gross investment (I) and depreciation? **Gross investment** is the total value of all newly produced capital goods (plant, equipment, housing, and inventory) produced in a given period. It takes no account of the fact that some capital wears out and must be replaced. **Net investment** is equal to gross investment minus depreciation. Net investment is a measure of how much the stock of capital *changes* during a period. Positive net investment means that the amount of new capital produced exceeds the amount that wears out, and negative net investment means that the amount of new capital produced is less than the amount that wears out. Therefore, if net investment is positive, the capital stock has increased, and if net investment is negative, the capital stock has decreased. Put another way, the capital stock at the end of a period is equal to the capital stock that existed at the beginning of the period plus net investment:

$$\text{capital}_{\text{end of period}} = \text{capital}_{\text{beginning of period}} + \text{net investment}$$

government consumption and gross investment (G) Expenditures by federal, state, and local governments for final goods and services.

Government Consumption and Gross Investment (G) **Government consumption and gross investment (G)** include expenditures by federal, state, and local governments for final goods (bombs, pencils, school buildings) and services (military salaries, congressional salaries, school teachers' salaries). Some of these expenditures are counted as government consumption, and some are counted as government gross investment. Government transfer payments (Social Security benefits, veterans' disability stipends, and so on) are not included in G because these transfers are not purchases of anything currently produced. The payments are not made in exchange for any goods or services. Because interest payments on the government debt are also counted as transfers, they are excluded from GDP on the grounds that they are not payments for current goods or services.

As Table 21.2 shows, government consumption and gross investment accounted for $2,689.8 billion, or 19.4 percent of U.S. GDP, in 2007. Federal government consumption and gross investment in 2007 accounted for 7.1 percent of GDP, and state and local government consumption and gross investment accounted for 12.4 percent.

[2] This is the formal definition of economic depreciation. Because depreciation is difficult to measure precisely, accounting rules allow firms to use shortcut methods to approximate the amount of depreciation that they incur each period. To complicate matters even more, the U.S. tax laws allow firms to deduct depreciation for tax purposes under a different set of rules.

Net Exports ($EX - IM$) The value of **net exports ($EX - IM$)** is the difference between *exports* (sales to foreigners of U.S.-produced goods and services) and *imports* (U.S. purchases of goods and services from abroad). This figure can be positive or negative. In 2007, the United States exported less than it imported, so the level of net exports was negative (−$708.0 billion). Before 1976, the United States was generally a net exporter—exports exceeded imports, so the net export figure was positive.

The reason for including net exports in the definition of GDP is simple. Consumption, investment, and government spending (C, I, and G, respectively) include expenditures on goods produced at home and abroad. Therefore, $C + I + G$ overstates domestic production because it contains expenditures on foreign-produced goods—that is, imports (IM), which have to be subtracted from GDP to obtain the correct figure. At the same time, $C + I + G$ understates domestic production because some of what a nation produces is sold abroad and therefore is not included in C, I, or G—exports (EX) have to be added in. If a U.S. firm produces computers and sells them in Germany, the computers are part of U.S. production and should be counted as part of U.S. GDP.

net exports ($EX - IM$) The difference between exports (sales to foreigners of U.S.-produced goods and services) and imports (U.S. purchases of goods and services from abroad). The figure can be positive or negative.

The Income Approach

We now turn to calculating GDP using the income approach, which looks at GDP in terms of who receives it as income rather than as who purchases it.

We begin with the concept of **national income**, which is defined in Table 21.3. National income is the sum of eight income items. **Compensation of employees**, the largest of the eight items by far, includes wages and salaries paid to households by firms and by the government, as well as various supplements to wages and salaries such as contributions that employers make to social insurance and private pension funds. **Proprietors' income** is the income of unincorporated businesses. **Rental income**, a minor item, is the income received by property owners in the form of rent. **Corporate profits**, the second-largest item of the eight, is the income of corporations. **Net interest** is the interest paid by business. (Interest paid by households and the government is not counted in GDP because it is not assumed to flow from the production of goods and services.)

national income The total income earned by the factors of production owned by a country's citizens.

compensation of employees Includes wages, salaries, and various supplements—employer contributions to social insurance and pension funds, for example—paid to households by firms and by the government.

proprietors' income The income of unincorporated businesses.

rental income The income received by property owners in the form of rent.

corporate profits The income of corporations.

net interest The interest paid by business.

TABLE 21.3 National Income, 2007

	Billions of Dollars		Percentage of National Income	
National income	12,221.1		100.0	
Compensation of employees		7,874.2		64.4
Proprietors' income		1,042.6		8.5
Rental income		65.4		0.5
Corporate profits		1,598.2		13.1
Net interest		602.6		4.9
Indirect taxes minus subsidies		961.4		7.9
Net business transfer payments		94.2		0.8
Surplus of government enterprises		−14.5		−0.1

Source: See Table 21.2.

The sixth item, **indirect taxes minus subsidies**, includes taxes such as sales taxes, customs duties, and license fees less subsidies that the government pays for which it receives no goods or services in return. (Subsidies are like negative taxes.) The value of indirect taxes minus subsidies is thus net income received by the government. **Net business transfer payments** are net transfer payments by businesses to others and are thus income of others. The final item is the **surplus of government enterprises**, which is the income of government enterprises. Table 21.3 shows that this item was negative in 2007: government enterprises on net ran at a loss.

National income is the total income of the country, but it is not quite GDP. Table 21.4 shows what is involved in going from national income to GDP. Table 21.4 first shows that in moving from gross domestic product (GDP) to gross national product (GNP), we need to add receipts of factor income from the rest of the world and subtract payments of factor income to the rest of the world. National income is income of the country's citizens, not the income of the residents of the country. So we first need to move from GDP to GNP. This, as discussed earlier, is a minor adjustment.

indirect taxes minus subsidies Taxes such as sales taxes, customs duties, and license fees less subsidies that the government pays for which it receives no goods or services in return.

net business transfer payments Net transfer payments by businesses to others.

surplus of government enterprises Income of government enterprises.

TABLE 21.4 GDP, GNP, NNP, and National Income, 2007

	Dollars (Billions)
GDP	13,841.3
Plus: Receipts of factor income from the rest of the world	+817.5
Less: Payments of factor income to the rest of the world	−721.8
Equals: **GNP**	13,937.1
Less: Depreciation	−1,686.6
Equals: **Net national product (NNP)**	12,250.5
Less: Statistical discrepancy	−29.4
Equals: **National income**	12,221.1

Source: See Table 21.2

net national product (NNP) Gross national product minus depreciation; a nation's total product minus what is required to maintain the value of its capital stock.

We then need to subtract depreciation from GNP, which is a large adjustment. GNP less depreciation is called **net national product (NNP)**. Why is depreciation subtracted? To see why, go back to the example earlier in this chapter in which the economy is made up of just one firm and total output (GDP) for the year is $1 million. Assume that after the firm pays wages, interest, and rent, it has $100,000 left. Assume also that its capital stock depreciated by $40,000 during the year. National income includes corporate profits (see Table 21.3); and in calculating corporate profits, the $40,000 depreciation is subtracted from the $100,000, leaving profits of $60,000. When we calculate GDP using the expenditure approach, depreciation is not subtracted. We simply add consumption, investment, government spending, and net exports. In our simple example, this is just $1 million. We thus must subtract depreciation from GDP (actually GNP when there is a rest-of-the-world sector) to get national income.

statistical discrepancy Data measurement error.

Table 21.4 shows that net national product and national income are the same except for a **statistical discrepancy**, a data measurement error. If the government were completely accurate in its data collection, the statistical discrepancy would be zero. The data collection, however, is not perfect, and the statistical discrepancy is the measurement error in each period. Table 21.4 shows that in 2007, this error was −$29.4 billion, which is small compared to national income of $12,221.1 billion.

personal income The total income of households.

We have so far seen from Table 21.3 the various income items that make up total national income, and we have seen from Table 21.4 how GDP and national income are related. A useful way to think about national income is to consider how much of it goes to households. The total income of households is called **personal income**, and it turns out that almost all of national income is personal income. Table 21.5 shows that of the $12,221.1 billion in national income in 2007, $11,659.5 billion was personal income. Although not shown in Table 21.5, one of the differences between national income and personal income is the profits of corporations not paid to households in the form of dividends, called the *retained earnings* of corporations. This is income that goes to corporations rather than to households, and so it is part of national income but not personal income.

TABLE 21.5 National Income, Personal Income, Disposable Personal Income, and Personal Saving, 2007

	Dollars (Billions)
National income	12,221.1
Less: Amount of national income not going to households	−561.6
Equals: **Personal income**	11,659.5
Less: Personal income taxes	−1,482.5
Equals: **Disposable personal income**	10,177.0
Less: Personal consumption expenditures	−9,734.2
Personal interest payments	−262.8
Transfer payments made by households	−137.1
Equals: **Personal saving**	42.9
Personal saving as a percentage of disposable personal income:	0.4%

Source: See Table 21.2

ECONOMICS IN PRACTICE

GDP: One of the Great Inventions of the 20th Century

As the 20th century drew to a close, the U.S. Department of Commerce embarked on a review of its achievements. At the conclusion of this review, the Department named the development of the national income and product accounts as "its achievement of the century."

J. Steven Landefeld *Director, Bureau of Economic Analysis*

While the GDP and the rest of the national income accounts may seem to be arcane concepts, they are truly among the great inventions of the twentieth century.

Paul A. Samuelson and William D. Nordhaus

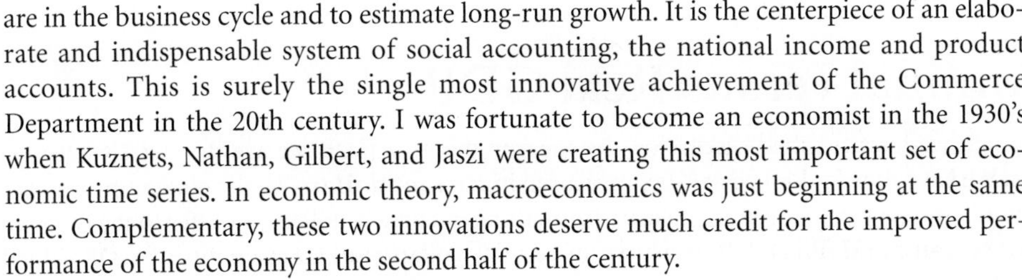

GDP! The right concept of economy-wide output, accurately measured. The U.S. and the world rely on it to tell where we are in the business cycle and to estimate long-run growth. It is the centerpiece of an elaborate and indispensable system of social accounting, the national income and product accounts. This is surely the single most innovative achievement of the Commerce Department in the 20th century. I was fortunate to become an economist in the 1930's when Kuznets, Nathan, Gilbert, and Jaszi were creating this most important set of economic time series. In economic theory, macroeconomics was just beginning at the same time. Complementary, these two innovations deserve much credit for the improved performance of the economy in the second half of the century.

James Tobin

FROM THE *SURVEY OF CURRENT BUSINESS*

Prior to the development of the NIPAs [national income and product accounts], policymakers had to guide the economy using limited and fragmentary information about the state of the economy. The Great Depression underlined the problems of incomplete data and led to the development of the national accounts:

> One reads with dismay of Presidents Hoover and then Roosevelt designing policies to combat the Great Depression of the 1930's on the basis of such sketchy data as stock price indices, freight car loadings, and incomplete indices of industrial production. The fact was that comprehensive measures of national income and output did not exist at the time. The Depression, and with it the growing role of government in the economy, emphasized the need for such measures and led to the development of a comprehensive set of national income accounts.
>
> Richard T. Froyen

In response to this need in the 1930's, the Department of Commerce commissioned Nobel laureate Simon Kuznets of the National Bureau of Economic Research to develop a set of national economic accounts....Professor Kuznets coordinated the work of researchers at the National Bureau of Economic Research in New York and his staff at Commerce. The original set of accounts was presented in a report to Congress in 1937 and in a research report, *National Income, 1929–35*....

The national accounts have become the mainstay of modern macroeconomic analysis, allowing policymakers, economists, and the business community to analyze the impact of different tax and spending plans, the impact of oil and other price shocks, and the impact of monetary policy on the economy as a whole and on specific components of final demand, incomes, industries, and regions....

Source: U.S. Department of Commerce, Bureau of Economics, "GDP: One of the Great Inventions of the 20th Century," Survey of Current Business, *January 2000, pp. 6–9.*

disposable personal income *or* after-tax income Personal income minus personal income taxes. The amount that households have to spend or save.

personal saving The amount of disposable income that is left after total personal spending in a given period.

personal saving rate The percentage of disposable personal income that is saved. If the personal saving rate is low, households are spending a large amount relative to their incomes; if it is high, households are spending cautiously.

Personal income is the income received by households before they pay personal income taxes. The amount of income that households have to spend or save is called **disposable personal income**, or **after-tax income**. It is equal to personal income minus personal income taxes, as shown in Table 21.5.

Because disposable personal income is the amount of income that households can spend or save, it is an important income concept. Table 21.5 on p. 424 shows there are three categories of spending: (1) personal consumption expenditures, (2) personal interest payments, and (3) transfer payments made by households. The amount of disposable personal income left after total personal spending is **personal saving**. If your monthly disposable income is $500 and you spend $450, you have $50 left at the end of the month. Your personal saving is $50 for the month. Your personal saving level can be negative: If you earn $500 and spend $600 during the month, you have *dissaved* $100. To spend $100 more than you earn, you will have to borrow the $100 from someone, take the $100 from your savings account, or sell an asset you own.

The **personal saving rate** is the percentage of disposable personal income saved, an important indicator of household behavior. A low saving rate means households are spending a large amount of their income. A high saving rate means households are cautious in their spending. As Table 21.5 shows, the U.S. personal saving rate in 2007 was 0.4 percent. Saving rates tend to rise during recessionary periods, when consumers become anxious about their future, and fall during boom times, as pent-up spending demand gets released.

Nominal versus Real GDP

current dollars The current prices that we pay for goods and services.

nominal GDP Gross domestic product measured in current dollars.

Although we have finished discussing the measurement of GDP, we are not yet close to being done. We have thus far looked at GDP measured in **current dollars**, or the current prices we pay for goods and services. When we measure something in current dollars, we refer to it as a *nominal* value. **Nominal GDP** is GDP measured in current dollars—all components of GDP valued at their current prices.

In most applications in macroeconomics, however, nominal GDP is not what we are after. It is not a good measure of aggregate output over time. Why? Assume that there is only one good—say, pizza, which is the same quality year after year. In each year 1 and 2, 100 units (slices) of pizza were produced. Production thus remained the same for year 1 and year 2. Suppose the price of pizza increased from $1.00 per slice in year 1 to $1.10 per slice in year 2. Nominal GDP in year 1 is $100 (100 units × $1.00 per unit), and nominal GDP in year 2 is $110 (100 units × $1.10 per unit). Nominal GDP has increased by $10 even though no more slices of pizza were produced. If we use nominal GDP to measure growth, we can be misled into thinking production has grown when all that has really happened is a rise in the price level (inflation).

If there were only one good in the economy—for example, pizza—it would be easy to measure production and compare one year's value to another's. We would add up all the pizza slices produced each year. In the example, production is 100 in both years. If the number of slices had increased to 105 in year 2, we would say production increased by 5 slices between year 1 and year 2, which is a 5 percent increase. Alas, however, there is more than one good in the economy.

The following is a discussion of how the BEA adjusts nominal GDP for price changes. As you read the discussion, keep in mind that this adjustment is not easy. Even in an economy of just apples and oranges, it would not be obvious how to add up apples and oranges to get an overall measure of output. The BEA's task is to add up thousands of goods, each of whose price is changing over time.

weight The importance attached to an item within a group of items.

In the following discussion, we will use the concept of a **weight**, either price weights or quantity weights. What is a weight? It is easiest to define the term by an example. Suppose in your economics course there is a final exam and two other tests. If the final exam counts for one-half of the grade and the other two tests for one-fourth each, the "weights" are one-half, one-fourth, and one-fourth. If instead the final exam counts for 80 percent of the grade and the other two tests for 10 percent each, the weights are .8, .1, and .1. The more important an item is in a group, the larger its weight.

Calculating Real GDP

Nominal GDP adjusted for price changes is called *real GDP*. All the main issues involved in computing real GDP can be discussed using a simple three-good economy and 2 years. Table 21.6 presents all the data that we will need. The table presents price and quantity data for 2 years and three goods. The goods are labeled *A*, *B*, and *C*, and the years are labeled 1 and 2. *P* denotes price, and *Q* denotes quantity. Keep in mind that everything in the following discussion, including the discussion of the GDP deflation, is based on the numbers in Table 21.6. Nothing has been brought in from the outside. The table is the entire economy.

The first thing to note from Table 21.6 is that *nominal output*—in current dollars—in year 1 for good *A* is the price of good *A* in year 1 ($0.50) times the number of units of good *A* produced in year 1 (6), which is $3.00. Similarly, nominal output in year 1 is 7 × $0.30 = $2.10 for good *B* and 10 × $0.70 = $7.00 for good *C*. The sum of these three amounts, $12.10 in column 5, is nominal GDP in year 1 in this simple economy. Nominal GDP in year 2—calculated by using the year 2 quantities and the year 2 prices—is $19.20 (column 8). Nominal GDP has risen from $12.10 in year 1 to $19.20 in year 2, an increase of 58.7 percent.[3]

TABLE 21.6 A Three-Good Economy

	(1)	(2)	(3)	(4)	(5)	(6)	(7)	(8)
	Production		Price per Unit		GDP in Year 1 in Year 1 Prices	GDP in Year 2 in Year 1 Prices	GDP in Year 1 in Year 2 Prices	GDP in Year 2 in Year 2 Prices
	Year 1 Q_1	Year 2 Q_2	Year 1 P_1	Year 2 P_2	$P_1 \times Q_1$	$P_1 \times Q_2$	$P_2 \times Q_1$	$P_2 \times Q_2$
Good *A*	6	11	$0.50	$0.40	$3.00	$5.50	$2.40	$4.40
Good *B*	7	4	0.30	1.00	2.10	1.20	7.00	4.00
Good C	10	12	0.70	0.90	7.00	8.40	9.00	10.80
Total					$12.10	$15.10	$18.40	$19.20
					Nominal GDP in year 1			Nominal GDP in year 2

You can see that the price of each good changed between year 1 and year 2—the price of good *A* fell (from $0.50 to $0.40) and the prices of goods *B* and *C* rose (*B* from $0.30 to $1.00; *C* from $0.70 to $0.90). Some of the change in nominal GDP between years 1 and 2 is due to price changes and not production changes. How much can we attribute to price changes and how much to production changes? Here things get tricky. The procedure that the BEA used prior to 1996 was to pick a **base year** and to use the prices in that base year as weights to calculate real GDP. This is a **fixed-weight procedure** because the weights used, which are the prices, are the same for all years—namely, the prices that prevailed in the base year.

base year The year chosen for the weights in a fixed-weight procedure.

fixed-weight procedure A procedure that uses weights from a given base year.

Let us use the fixed-weight procedure and year 1 as the base year, which means using year 1 prices as the weights. Then in Table 21.6, real GDP in year 1 is $12.10 (column 5) and real GDP in year 2 is $15.10 (column 6). Note that both columns use year 1 prices and that nominal and real GDP are the same in year 1 because year 1 is the base year. Real GDP has increased from $12.10 to $15.10, an increase of 24.8 percent.

Let us now use the fixed-weight procedure and year 2 as the base year, which means using year 2 prices as the weights. In Table 21.6, real GDP in year 1 is $18.40 (column 7) and real GDP in year 2 is $19.20 (column 8). Note that both columns use year 2 prices and that nominal and real GDP are the same in year 2 because year 2 is the base year. Real GDP has increased from $18.40 to $19.20, an increase of 4.3 percent.

This example shows that growth rates can be sensitive to the choice of the base year—24.8 percent using year 1 prices as weights and 4.3 percent using year 2 prices as weights. The old

[3] The percentage change is calculated as [(19.20 − 12.10)/12.10] × 100 = .587 × 100 = 58.7 percent.

BEA procedure simply picked one year as the base year and did all the calculations using the prices in that year as weights. The new procedure makes two important changes. The first (using the current example) is to "split the difference" between 24.8 percent and 4.3 percent. What does "splitting the difference" mean? One way is to take the average of the two numbers, which is 14.55 percent. What the BEA does is to take the *geometric* average, which for the current example is 14.09 percent.[4] These two averages (14.55 percent and 14.09 percent) are quite close, and the use of either would give similar results. The point here is not that the geometric average is used, but that the first change is to split the difference using some average. Note that this new procedure requires two "base" years because 24.8 percent was computed using year 1 prices as weights and 4.3 percent was computed using year 2 prices as weights.

The second BEA change is to use years 1 and 2 as the base years when computing the percentage change between years 1 and 2, then use years 2 and 3 as the base years when computing the percentage change between years 2 and 3, and so on. The two base years change as the calculations move through time. The series of percentage changes computed this way is taken to be the series of growth rates of real GDP. So in this way, nominal GDP is adjusted for price changes. To make sure you understand this, review the calculations in Table 21.6, which provides all the data you need to see what is going on.

Calculating the GDP Deflator

We now switch gears from real GDP, a quantity measure, to the GDP deflator, a price measure. One of economic policy makers' goals is to keep changes in the overall price level small. For this reason, policy makers not only need good measures of how real output is changing but also good measures of how the overall price level is changing. The GDP deflator is one measure of the overall price level. We can use the data in Table 21.6 to show how the BEA computes the GDP deflator.

In Table 21.6, the price of good *A* fell from $0.50 in year 1 to $0.40 in year 2, the price of good *B* rose from $0.30 to $1.00, and the price of good *C* rose from $0.70 to $0.90. If we are interested only in how individual prices change, this is all the information we need. However, if we are interested in how the overall price *level* changes, we need to weight the individual prices in some way. The obvious weights to use are the quantities produced, but which quantities—those of year 1 or year 2? The same issues arise here for the quantity weights as for the price weights in computing real GDP.

Let us first use the fixed-weight procedure and year 1 as the base year, which means using year 1 quantities as the weights. Then in Table 21.6, the "bundle" price in year 1 is $12.10 (column 5) and the bundle price in year 2 is $18.40 (column 7). Both columns use year 1 quantities. The bundle price has increased from $12.10 to $18.40, an increase of 52.1 percent.

Next, use the fixed-weight procedure and year 2 as the base year, which means using year 2 quantities as the weights. Then the bundle price in year 1 is $15.10 (column 6), and the bundle price in year 2 is $19.20 (column 8). Both columns use year 2 quantities. The bundle price has increased from $15.10 to $19.20, an increase of 27.2 percent.

This example shows that overall price increases can be sensitive to the choice of the base year: 52.1 percent using year 1 quantities as weights and 27.2 percent using year 2 quantities as weights. Again, the old BEA procedure simply picked one year as the base year and did all the calculations using the quantities in the base year as weights. First, the new procedure splits the difference between 52.1 percent and 27.2 percent by taking the geometric average, which is 39.1 percent. Second, it uses years 1 and 2 as the base years when computing the percentage change between years 1 and 2, years 2 and 3 as the base years when computing the percentage change between years 2 and 3, and so on. The series of percentage changes computed this way is taken to be the series of percentage changes in the GDP deflator, that is, a series of inflation rates.

The Problems of Fixed Weights

To see why the BEA switched to the new procedure, let us consider a number of problems using fixed-price weights to compute real GDP. First, 1987 price weights, the last price weights the BEA used before it changed procedures, are not likely to be very accurate for, say, the 1950s. Many

[4] The geometric average is computed as the square root of 124.8×104.3, which is 114.09.

structural changes have taken place in the U.S. economy in the last 40 to 50 years, and it seems unlikely that 1987 prices are good weights to use for the 1950s.

Another problem is that the use of fixed-price weights does not account for the responses in the economy to supply shifts. Perhaps bad weather leads to a lower production of oranges in year 2. In a simple supply-and-demand diagram for oranges, this corresponds to a shift of the supply curve to the left, which leads to an increase in the price of oranges and a decrease in the quantity demanded. As consumers move up the demand curve, they are substituting away from oranges. If technical advances in year 2 result in cheaper ways of producing computers, the result is a shift of the computer supply curve to the right, which leads to a decrease in the price of computers and an increase in the quantity demanded. Consumers are substituting toward computers. (You should be able to draw supply-and-demand diagrams for both cases.) Table 21.6 on p. 427 shows this tendency. The quantity of good *A* rose between years 1 and 2 and the price decreased (the computer case), whereas the quantity of good *B* fell and the price increased (the orange case). The computer supply curve has been shifting to the right over time, due primarily to technical advances. The result has been large decreases in the price of computers and large increases in the quantity demanded.

To see why these responses pose a problem for the use of fixed-price weights, consider the data in Table 21.6. Because the price of good *A* was higher in year 1, the increase in production of good *A* is weighted more if we use year 1 as the base year than if we used year 2 as the base year. Also, because the price of good *B* was lower in year 1, the decrease in production of good *B* is weighted less if we use year 1 as the base year. These effects make the overall change in real GDP larger if we use year 1 price weights than if we use year 2 price weights. Using year 1 price weights ignores the kinds of substitution responses discussed in the previous paragraph and leads to what many believe are too-large estimates of real GDP changes. In the past, the BEA tended to move the base year forward about every 5 years, resulting in the past estimates of real GDP growth being revised downward. It is undesirable to have past growth estimates change simply because of the change to a new base year. The new BEA procedure avoids many of these fixed-weight problems.

Similar problems arise when using fixed-quantity weights to compute price indexes. For example, the fixed-weight procedure ignores the substitution away from goods whose prices are increasing and toward goods whose prices are decreasing or increasing less rapidly. The procedure tends to overestimate the increase in the overall price level. As discussed in the next chapter, there are still a number of price indexes that are computed using fixed weights. The GDP deflator differs because it does not use fixed weights. It is also a price index for all the goods and services produced in the economy. Other price indexes cover fewer domestically produced goods and services but also include some imported (foreign-produced) goods and services.

It should finally be stressed that there is no "right" way of computing real GDP. The economy consists of many goods, each with its own price, and there is no exact way of adding together the production of the different goods. We can say that the BEA's new procedure for computing real GDP avoids the problems associated with the use of fixed weights, and it seems to be an improvement over the old procedure. We will see in the next chapter, however, that the consumer price index (CPI)—a widely used price index—is still computed using fixed weights.

Limitations of the GDP Concept

We generally think of increases in GDP as good. Increasing GDP (or preventing its decrease) is usually considered one of the chief goals of the government's macroeconomic policy. Because some serious problems arise when we try to use GDP as a measure of happiness or well-being, we now point out some of the limitations of the GDP concept as a measure of welfare.

GDP and Social Welfare

If crime levels went down, society would be better off, but a decrease in crime is not an increase in output and is not reflected in GDP. Neither is an increase in leisure time. Yet to the extent that households want extra leisure time (instead of having it forced on them by a lack of jobs in the economy), an increase in leisure is also an increase in social welfare. Furthermore, some increases in social welfare are associated with a *decrease* in GDP. An increase in leisure during a time of full employment, for example, leads to a decrease in GDP because less time is spent on producing output.

Most nonmarket and domestic activities, such as housework and child care, are not counted in GDP even though they amount to real production. However, if I decide to send my children to day care or hire someone to clean my house or drive my car for me, GDP increases. The salaries of day care staff, cleaning people, and chauffeurs are counted in GDP; but the time I spend doing the same things is not counted. A mere change of institutional arrangements, even though no more output is being produced, can show up as a change in GDP.

Furthermore, GDP seldom reflects losses or social ills. GDP accounting rules do not adjust for production that pollutes the environment. The more production there is, the larger the GDP, regardless of how much pollution results in the process.

GDP also has nothing to say about the distribution of output among individuals in a society. It does not distinguish, for example, between the case in which most output goes to a few people and the case in which output is evenly divided among all people. We cannot use GDP to measure the effects of redistributive policies (which take income from some people and give income to others). Such policies have no direct impact on GDP. GDP is also neutral about the kinds of goods an economy produces. Symphony performances, handguns, cigarettes, professional football games, Bibles, soda pop, milk, economics textbooks, and comic books all get counted similarly without regard to their differing value to society.

The Underground Economy

Many transactions are missed in the calculation of GDP even though, in principle, they should be counted. Most illegal transactions are missed unless they are "laundered" into legitimate business. Income that is earned but not reported as income for tax purposes is usually missed, although some adjustments are made in the GDP calculations to take misreported income into account. The part of the economy that should be counted in GDP but is not is sometimes called the **underground economy**.

underground economy The part of the economy in which transactions take place and in which income is generated that is unreported and therefore not counted in GDP.

Tax evasion is usually thought to be the major incentive for people to participate in the underground economy. Studies estimate that the size of the U.S. underground economy, ranging from 5 percent to 30 percent of GDP,[5] is comparable to the size of the underground economy in most European countries and probably much smaller than the size of the underground economy in the Eastern European countries. Estimates of Italy's underground economy range from 10 percent to 35 percent of Italian GDP. At the lower end of the scale, estimates for Switzerland range from 3 percent to 5 percent.

Why should we care about the underground economy? To the extent that GDP reflects only a part of economic activity instead of a complete measure of what the economy produces, it is misleading. Unemployment rates, for example, may be lower than officially measured if people work in the underground economy without reporting this fact to the government. Also, if the size of the underground economy varies among countries—as it does—we can be misled when we compare GDP among countries. For example, Italy's GDP would be much higher if we considered its underground sector as part of the economy, while Switzerland's GDP would change very little.

Gross National Income per Capita

gross national income (GNI) GNP converted into dollars using an average of currency exchange rates over several years adjusted for rates of inflation.

Making comparisons across countries is difficult because such comparisons need to be made in a single currency, generally U.S. dollars. Converting GNP numbers for Japan into dollars requires converting from yen into dollars. Since exchange rates can change quite dramatically in short periods of time, such conversions are tricky. Recently, the World Bank adopted a new measuring system for international comparisons. The concept of **gross national income (GNI)** is GNP converted into dollars using an average of currency exchange rates over several years adjusted for

[5] See, for example, Edgar L. Feige, "Defining and Estimating Underground and Informal Economies: The New Industrial Economic Approach," *World Development* 19(7), 1990, and "The Underground Economy in the United States," Occasional Paper No. 2, U.S. Department of Labor, September 1992.

rates of inflation. Figure 21.1 lists the gross national income per capita (GNI divided by population) for various countries in 2006. Norway has the highest per capita GNI followed by Switzerland, Denmark, Ireland, and the United States. Ethiopia was estimated to have per capita GNI of only $180 in 2006.

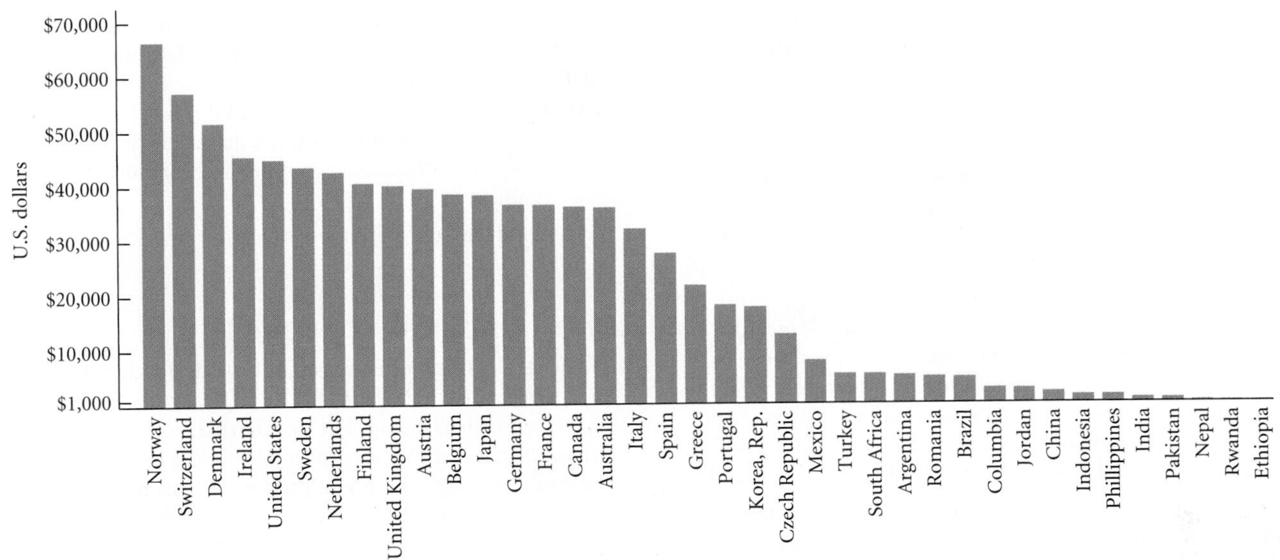

▲ **FIGURE 21.1 Per Capita Gross National Income for Selected Countries, 2006**

Source: World Bank, September 2007.

Looking Ahead

This chapter has introduced many key variables in which macroeconomists are interested, including GDP and its components. There is much more to be learned about the data that macroeconomists use. In the next chapter, we will discuss the data on employment, unemployment, and the labor force. In Chapters 25 and 26, we will discuss the data on money and interest rates. Finally, in Chapter 35, we will discuss in more detail the data on the relationship between the United States and the rest of the world.

SUMMARY

1. One source of data on the key variables in the macroeconomy is the *national income and product accounts*. These accounts provide a conceptual framework that macroeconomists use to think about how the pieces of the economy fit together.

GROSS DOMESTIC PRODUCT *p. 417*

2. *Gross domestic product* (*GDP*) is the key concept in national income accounting. GDP is the total market value of all final goods and services produced within a given period by factors of production located within a country. GDP excludes *intermediate goods*. To include goods when they are purchased as inputs and when they are sold as final products would be double counting and would result in an overstatement of the value of production.

3. GDP excludes all transactions in which money or goods change hands but in which no new goods and services are produced. GDP includes the income of foreigners working in the United States and the profits that foreign companies earn in the United States. GDP excludes the income of U.S. citizens working abroad and profits earned by U.S. companies in foreign countries.

4. *Gross national product* (*GNP*) is the market value of all final goods and services produced during a given period by factors of production owned by a country's citizens.

CALCULATING GDP *p. 419*

5. The *expenditure approach* to GDP adds up the amount spent on all final goods and services during a given period. The four main categories of expenditures are *personal consumption expenditures* (*C*), *gross private domestic investment* (*I*), *government consumption and gross investment* (*G*), and *net exports* (*EX* − *IM*). The sum of these categories equals GDP.
6. The three main components of *personal consumption expenditures* (*C*) are *durable goods, nondurable goods*, and *services.*
7. *Gross private domestic investment* (*I*) is the total investment made by the private sector in a given period. There are three kinds of investment: *nonresidential investment, residential investment*, and *changes in business inventories*. Gross investment does not take *depreciation*—the decrease in the value of assets—into account. *Net investment* is equal to gross investment minus depreciation.
8. *Government consumption and gross investment* (*G*) include expenditures by state, federal, and local governments for final goods and services. The value of *net exports* (*EX* − *IM*) equals the differences between exports (sales to foreigners of U.S.-produced goods and services) and imports (U.S. purchases of goods and services from abroad).
9. Because every payment (expenditure) by a buyer is a receipt (income) for the seller, GDP can be computed in terms of who receives it as income—the *income approach* to calculating gross domestic product.
10. GNP minus depreciation is *net national product* (*NNP*). *National income* is the total amount earned by the factors of production in the economy. It is equal to NNP except for a statistical discrepancy. *Personal income* is the total income of households. *Disposable personal income* is what households have to spend or save after paying their taxes. The *personal saving rate* is the percentage of disposable personal income saved instead of spent.

NOMINAL VERSUS REAL GDP *p. 426*

11. GDP measured in current dollars (the current prices that one pays for goods) is *nominal GDP*. If we use nominal GDP to measure growth, we can be misled into thinking that production has grown when all that has happened is a rise in the price level, or inflation. A better measure of production is *real GDP*, which is nominal GDP adjusted for price changes.
12. The GDP deflator is a measure of the overall price level.

LIMITATIONS OF THE GDP CONCEPT *p. 429*

13. We generally think of increases in GDP as good, but some problems arise when we try to use GDP as a measure of happiness or well-being. The peculiarities of GDP accounting mean that institutional changes can change the value of GDP even if real production has not changed. GDP ignores most social ills, such as pollution. Furthermore, GDP tells us nothing about what kinds of goods are being produced or how income is distributed across the population. GDP also ignores many transactions of the *underground economy*.
14. The concept of *gross national income* (*GNI*) is GNP converted into dollars using an average of currency exchange rates over several years adjusted for rates of inflation.

REVIEW TERMS AND CONCEPTS

base year, *p. 427*
change in business inventories, *p. 421*
compensation of employees, *p. 423*
corporate profits, *p. 423*
current dollars, *p. 426*
depreciation, *p. 422*
disposable personal income, *or* after-tax income, *p. 426*
durable goods, *p. 420*
expenditure approach, *p. 419*
final goods and services, *p. 418*
fixed-weight procedure, *p. 427*
government consumption and gross investment (*G*), *p. 422*
gross domestic product (GDP), *p. 417*
gross investment, *p. 422*
gross national income (GNI), *p. 430*
gross national product (GNP), *p. 419*
gross private domestic investment (*I*), *p. 421*
income approach, *p. 419*
indirect taxes minus subsidies, *p. 423*
intermediate goods, *p. 418*
national income, *p. 423*
national income and product accounts, *p. 417*
net business transfer payments, *p. 423*
net exports (*EX* − *IM*), *p. 423*
net interest, *p. 423*
net investment, *p. 422*
net national product (NNP), *p. 424*
nominal GDP, *p. 426*
nondurable goods, *p. 420*
nonresidential investment, *p. 421*
personal consumption expenditures (*C*), *p. 420*
personal income, *p. 424*
personal saving, *p. 426*
personal saving rate, *p. 426*
proprietors' income, *p. 423*
rental income, *p. 423*
residential investment, *p. 421*
services, *p. 420*
statistical discrepancy, *p. 424*
surplus of government enterprises, *p. 423*
underground economy, *p. 430*
value added, *p. 418*
weight, *p. 426*
Expenditure approach to GDP: $GDP = C + I + G + (EX - IM)$, *p. 420*
GDP = Final sales + Change in business inventories, *p. 422*
Net investment = Capital end of period − Capital beginning of period, *p. 422*

PROBLEMS

Visit www.myeconlab.com to complete the problems marked in orange online. You will receive instant feedback on your answers, tutorial help, and access to additional practice problems.

1. **[Related to the *Economics in Practice* on p. 421]** In a simple economy suppose that all income is either compensation of employees or profits. Suppose also that there are no indirect taxes. Calculate gross domestic product from the following set of numbers. Show that the expenditure approach and the income approach add up to the same figure.

Consumption	$5,000
Investment	1,000
Depreciation	600
Profits	900
Exports	500
Compensation of employees	5,300
Government purchases	1,000
Direct taxes	800
Saving	1,100
Imports	700

2. How do we know that calculating GDP by the expenditure approach yields the same answer as calculating GDP by the income approach?

3. As the following table indicates, GNP and real GNP were almost the same in 1972, but there was a $300 billion difference by mid-1975. Explain why. Describe what the numbers here suggest about conditions in the economy at the time. How do the conditions compare with conditions today?

DATE	GNP (BILLIONS OF DOLLARS)	REAL GNP (BILLIONS OF DOLLARS)	REAL GNP (% CHANGE)	GNP DEFLATOR (% CHANGE)
72:2	1,172	1,179	7.62	2.93
72:3	1,196	1,193	5.11	3.24
72:4	1,233	1,214	7.41	5.30
73:1	1,284	1,247	10.93	5.71
73:2	1,307	1,248	.49	7.20
73:3	1,338	1,256	2.44	6.92
73:4	1,377	1,266	3.31	8.58
74:1	1,388	1,253	−4.00	7.50
74:2	1,424	1,255	.45	10.32
74:3	1,452	1,247	−2.47	10.78
74:4	1,473	1,230	−5.51	12.03
75:1	1,480	1,204	−8.27	10.86
75:2	1,517	1,219	5.00	5.07

4. What are some of the problems in using fixed weights to compute real GDP and the GDP price index? How does the BEA's approach attempt to solve these problems?

5. Explain what double counting is and discuss why GDP is not equal to total sales.

6. The following table gives some figures from a forecast of real GDP (in 2000 dollars) and population done in 2008. According to the forecast, approximately how much real growth will there be between 2009 and 2010? What is per capita GDP projected to be in 2009 and in 2010? Compute the forecast rate of change in real GDP and per capita real GDP between 2009 and 2010.

Real GDP 2009 (billions)	$12,043
Real GDP 2010 (billions)	$12,464
Population 2009 (millions)	306.4
Population 2010 (millions)	308.8

7. Look at a recent edition of *The Economist*. Go to the section on economic indicators. Go down the list of countries and make a list of the ones with the fastest and slowest GDP growth. Look also at the forecast rates of GDP growth. Go back to the table of contents at the beginning of the journal to see if there are articles about any of these countries. Write a paragraph or two describing the events or the economic conditions in one of the countries. Explain why they are growing or not growing rapidly.

8. During 2002, real GDP in Japan rose about 1.3 percent. During the same period, retail sales in Japan fell 1.8 percent in real terms. What are some possible explanations for retail sales to consumers falling when GDP rises? (*Hint:* Think of the composition of GDP using the expenditure approach.)

9. **[Related to the *Economics in Practice* on p. 425]** Which of the following transactions would not be counted in GDP? Explain your answers.
   a. General Motors issues new shares of stock to finance the construction of a plant.
   b. General Motors builds a new plant.
   c. Company A successfully launches a hostile takeover of company B, in which company A purchases all the assets of company B.
   d. Your grandmother wins $10 million in the lottery.
   e. You buy a new copy of this textbook.
   f. You buy a used copy of this textbook.
   g. The government pays out Social Security benefits.
   h. A public utility installs new antipollution equipment in its smokestacks.
   i. Luigi's Pizza buys 30 pounds of mozzarella cheese, holds it in inventory for 1 month, and then uses it to make pizza (which it sells).
   j. You spend the weekend cleaning your apartment.
   k. A drug dealer sells $500 worth of illegal drugs.

10. If you buy a new car, the entire purchase is counted as consumption in the year in which you make the transaction. Explain briefly why this is in one sense an "error" in national income accounting. (*Hint:* How is the purchase of a car different from the purchase of a pizza?) How might you correct this error?

11. Explain why imports are subtracted in the expenditure approach to calculating GDP.

12. GDP calculations do not directly include the economic costs of environmental damage—for example, global warming and acid rain. Do you think these costs should be included in GDP? Why or why not? How could GDP be amended to include environmental damage costs?

13. Beginning in 2005, the housing market, which had been booming for years, turned. Housing construction dropped sharply in 2006. Go to www.bea.gov. Look at the GDP release and at past releases from 2002 onward. In real dollars, how much private residential fixed investment (houses, apartments, condominiums, and cooperatives) took place in each quarter from 2002 through 2008? What portion of GDP did housing construction represent? After 2006, residential fixed investment was declining sharply, yet GDP was growing. What categories of aggregate output kept the economy growing into 2008?

14. At the beginning of 2008, most people were convinced that the U.S. economy was in a recession. Define *recession*. Go to www.bea.gov and look at the growth of GDP during 2008. In addition, go to www.bls.gov and look at payroll employment and the unemployment rate. Was the United States in a recession? What do you see in the data? Can you tell by reading the newspapers or watching CNN whether the country was in a recession? Explain.

Unemployment, Inflation, and Long-Run Growth

22

CHAPTER OUTLINE

Each month the U.S. Bureau of Labor Statistics (BLS) announces the value of the unemployment rate for the previous month. For example, on February 1, 2008, it announced that the unemployment rate for January 2008 was 4.9 percent. The unemployment rate is a key measure of how the economy is doing. This announcement is widely watched, and if the announced unemployment rate is different from what the financial markets expect, there can be large movements in those markets. It is thus important to know how the BLS computes the unemployment rate. The first part of this chapter describes how the unemployment rate is computed and discusses its various components.

Inflation is another key macroeconomic variable. The previous chapter discussed how the GDP deflator, the price deflator for the entire economy, is computed. The percentage change in the GDP deflator is a measure of inflation. There are, however, other measures of inflation, each pertaining to some part of the economy. The most widely followed price index is the consumer price index (CPI), and its measurement is discussed next in this chapter. The CPI is also announced monthly by the BLS, and this announcement is widely followed by the financial markets as well. For example, on February 20, 2008, the BLS announced that the percentage change in the CPI for January was 4.9 percent at an annual rate. After discussing the measurement of the CPI, this chapter discusses various costs of inflation.

The last topic considered in this chapter is long-run growth. Although much of macroeconomics is concerned with explaining business cycles, long-run growth is also a major concern. The average yearly growth rate of U.S. real GDP depicted in Figure 20.2 on p. 403 is 3.4 percent. So while there were many ups and downs during the 108 years depicted in Figure 20.2, on average, the economy was growing at a 3.4 percent rate. In the last part of this chapter, we discuss the sources of this growth.

Keep in mind that this chapter is still descriptive. We begin our analysis of how the economy works in the next chapter.

Unemployment

We begin our discussion of unemployment with its measurement.

Measuring Unemployment

The unemployment data released each month by the BLS are based on a survey of households. Each month the BLS draws a sample of 65,000 households and completes interviews with all but about 2,500 of them. Each interviewed household answers questions concerning the work

employed Any person 16 years old or older (1) who works for pay, either for someone else or in his or her own business for 1 or more hours per week, (2) who works without pay for 15 or more hours per week in a family enterprise, or (3) who has a job but has been temporarily absent with or without pay.

unemployed A person 16 years old or older who is not working, is available for work, and has made specific efforts to find work during the previous 4 weeks.

not in the labor force A person who is not looking for work because he or she does not want a job or has given up looking.

labor force The number of people employed plus the number of unemployed.

unemployment rate The ratio of the number of people unemployed to the total number of people in the labor force.

labor force participation rate The ratio of the labor force to the total population 16 years old or older.

activity of household members 16 years of age or older during the calendar week that contains the twelfth of the month. (The survey is conducted in the week that contains the twelfth of the month.)

If a household member 16 years of age or older worked 1 hour or more as a paid employee, either for someone else or in his or her own business or farm, the person is classified as **employed**. A household member is also considered employed if he or she worked 15 hours or more without pay in a family enterprise. Finally, a household member is counted as employed if the person held a job from which he or she was temporarily absent due to illness, bad weather, vacation, labor-management disputes, or personal reasons, regardless of whether he or she was paid.

Those who are not employed fall into one of two categories: (1) unemployed or (2) not in the labor force. To be considered **unemployed**, a person must be 16 years old or older, available for work, and have made specific efforts to find work during the previous 4 weeks. A person not looking for work because he or she does not want a job or has given up looking is classified as **not in the labor force**. People not in the labor force include full-time students, retirees, individuals in institutions, and those staying home to take care of children or elderly parents.

The total **labor force** in the economy is the number of people employed plus the number of unemployed:

$$\text{labor force} = \text{employed} + \text{unemployed}$$

The total population 16 years of age or older is equal to the number of people in the labor force plus the number not in the labor force:

$$\text{population} = \text{labor force} + \text{not in labor force}$$

With these numbers, several ratios can be calculated. The **unemployment rate** is the ratio of the number of people unemployed to the total number of people in the labor force:

$$\text{unemployment rate} = \frac{\text{unemployed}}{\text{employed} + \text{unemployed}}$$

In January 2008, the labor force contained 153.824 million people, 146.248 million of whom were employed and 7.576 million of whom were unemployed and looking for work. The unemployment rate was 4.9 percent:

$$\frac{7.576}{146.248 + 7.576} = 4.9\%$$

The ratio of the labor force to the population 16 years old or over is called the **labor force participation rate**:

$$\text{labor force participation rate} = \frac{\text{labor force}}{\text{population}}$$

In January 2008, the population of 16 years old or over was 232.616 million. So the labor force participation rate was .66 (= 153.824/232.616).

Table 22.1 shows values of these variables for selected years since 1953. The year 1982 shows the effects of the recession. Although the unemployment rate has gone up and down, the labor force participation rate has grown steadily since 1953. Much of this increase is due to the growth in the participation rate of women between the ages of 25 and 54. Column 3 in Table 22.1 shows how many new workers the U.S. economy has absorbed in recent years. The number of employed workers increased by about 38 million between 1953 and 1982 and by about 47 million between 1982 and 2007.

TABLE 22.1 Employed, Unemployed, and the Labor Force, 1953–2007

	(1) Population 16 Years Old or Over (Millions)	(2) Labor Force (Millions)	(3) Employed (Millions)	(4) Unemployed (Millions)	(5) Labor Force Participation Rate (Percentage Points)	(6) Unemployment Rate (Percentage Points)
1953	107.1	63.0	61.2	1.8	58.9	2.9
1960	117.2	69.6	65.8	3.9	59.4	5.5
1970	137.1	82.8	78.7	4.1	60.4	4.9
1980	167.7	106.9	99.3	7.6	63.8	7.1
1982	172.3	110.2	99.5	10.7	64.0	9.7
1990	189.2	125.8	118.8	7.0	66.5	5.6
2000	212.6	142.6	136.9	5.7	67.1	4.0
2007	231.9	153.1	146.0	7.1	66.0	4.6

Note: Figures are civilian only (military excluded).
Source: Economic Report of the President, 2008, Table B-35.

Components of the Unemployment Rate

The unemployment rate by itself conveys some but not all information about the unemployment picture. To get a better picture, it is useful to look at unemployment rates across groups of people, regions, and industries.

Unemployment Rates for Different Demographic Groups There are large differences in rates of unemployment across demographic groups. Table 22.2 shows the unemployment rate for November 1982—the worst month of the recession in 1982—and for March 2008, broken down by race, sex, and age. In November 1982, when the overall unemployment rate hit 10.8 percent, the rate for whites was 9.6 percent while the rate for African Americans was more than twice that—20.2 percent.

TABLE 22.2 Unemployment Rates by Demographic Group, 1982 and 2008

	Years	Nov. 1982	March 2008
Total		10.8	5.1
White		9.6	4.5
Men	20+	9.0	4.1
Women	20+	8.1	4.1
Both sexes	16–19	21.3	13.2
African American		20.2	9.0
Men	20+	19.3	8.4
Women	20+	16.5	7.5
Both sexes	16–19	49.5	31.3

Source: U.S. Department of Labor, Bureau of Labor Statistics. Data are seasonally adjusted.

During the recession in 1982, men fared worse than women. In November 1982, 9.0 percent of white men 20 years and over but only 8.1 percent of white women 20 years and over were unemployed. For African Americans, 19.3 percent of men 20 years and over and 16.5 percent of women 20 years and over were unemployed. Teenagers between 16 and 19 years of age fared worst. African Americans between 16 and 19 experienced an unemployment rate of 49.5 percent in November 1982. For whites between 16 and 19, the unemployment rate was 21.3 percent. Although the rates were lower for all groups in March 2008, the pattern was similar. The highest unemployment rates were for African-American teenagers—31.3 percent. The main point of Table 22.2 is that an unemployment rate of, say, 5.1 percent does not mean every group in society has a 5.1 percent unemployment rate. There are large differences in unemployment rates across demographic groups.

Unemployment Rates in States and Regions Unemployment rates vary by geographic location. For a variety of reasons, not all states and regions have the same level of unemployment. States and regions have different combinations of industries, which do not all grow and decline at the same time and at the same rate. Also, the labor force is not completely mobile—workers often cannot or do not want to pack up and move to take advantage of job opportunities in other parts of the country.

As Table 22.3 shows, in the last 30 years remarkable changes have occurred in the relative prosperity of regions, particularly in the Northeast and the oil-rich Southwest. During the early 1970s, the Northeast (New England, in particular) was hit by a serious decline in its industrial base. Textile mills, leather goods plants, and furniture factories closed in the face of foreign competition or moved south to states with lower wages. During the recession of 1975, Massachusetts and Michigan had very high unemployment rates (11.2 percent and 12.5 percent, respectively). Riding the crest of rising oil prices, Texas had one of the lowest unemployment rates at that time (5.6 percent).

During the recession of 1982, Texas continued to do well and Massachusetts took a sharp turn for the better. The unemployment rate in Massachusetts went from nearly three points above the national average during the 1975 recession to nearly two points below during the 1982 recession.

By 1987, things had changed. Although not shown in Table 22.3, Massachusetts had one of the lowest unemployment rates in the country in 1987 (an amazing 2.8 percent) and Texas (at 8.5 percent) had one of the highest. In Massachusetts, high-tech firms such as Wang Laboratories and Digital Equipment, two firms that employed a total of over 100,000 people, had grown dramatically. In contrast, the fall in crude oil prices from over $30 per barrel to under $15 per barrel in the early 1980s forced the oil-based economy of Texas into a deep and prolonged recession. Then, in 1991, Massachusetts experienced yet another reversal with an unemployment rate of 9 percent.

TABLE 22.3 Regional Differences in Unemployment, 1975, 1982, 1991, and 2003

	1975	1982	1991	2003
U.S. avg.	8.5	9.7	6.7	6.0
Cal.	9.9	9.9	7.5	6.7
Fla.	10.7	8.2	7.3	5.1
Ill.	7.1	11.3	7.1	6.7
Mass.	11.2	7.9	9.0	5.8
Mich.	12.5	15.5	9.2	7.3
N.J.	10.2	9.0	6.6	5.9
N.Y.	9.5	8.6	7.2	6.3
N.C.	8.6	9.0	5.8	6.5
Ohio	9.1	12.5	6.4	6.1
Tex.	5.6	6.9	6.6	6.8

Source: Statistical Abstract of the United States, various editions.

The economy of Michigan is heavily tied to the fortunes of the automobile industry. During the recession of 1982, Michigan had the highest unemployment rate in the country at 15.5 percent. The automobile industry not only suffered from the decline in the U.S. economy but also faced stiff foreign competition, primarily from Japan. Michigan also suffered in 1991, with an unemployment rate of 9.2 percent.

The recession of 2001 was mild by comparison, and the impact was more uniform around the country. By the second quarter of 2003, the national unemployment rate had risen to 6.1 percent from 3.9 percent in the fourth quarter of 2000. For the states listed in Table 22.3, the unemployment rate in 2003 varied from 5.1 percent for Florida to 7.3 percent for Michigan. Again, the national unemployment rate does not tell the whole story. A low national rate of unemployment does not mean that the entire nation is growing and producing at the same rate.

ECONOMICS IN PRACTICE

A Quiet Revolution: Women Join the Labor Force

Table 22.1 shows that the labor force participation rate in the United States increased from 58.9 percent in 1953 to 66.0 percent in 2007. Much of this increase was due to the increased participation of women in the labor force. In 1955, the labor force participation rate of women was 36 percent. For married women, the rate was even lower at 29 percent. By the 1990s, these numbers shifted considerably. In 1996, the labor force participation rate was 60 percent for all women and 62 percent for married women. The reasons for these changes are complex. Certainly, in the 1960s, there was a change in society's attitude toward women and paid work. In addition, the baby boom became the baby bust as greater availability of birth control led to fewer births.

By comparison, the participation rate for men declined over this period—from 85 percent in 1955 to 75 percent in 1996. Why the labor force participation rate for men fell is less clear than why the women's rate rose. No doubt, some men dropped out to assume more traditional women's roles, such as child care. Whatever the causes, the economy grew in a way that absorbed virtually all the new entrants during the period in question.

As women began joining the labor force in greater numbers in the 1970s and 1980s, their wages relative to men's wages actually fell. Most economists attribute this decline to the fact that less experienced women were entering the labor force, pointing out the importance of correcting for factors such as experience and education when we analyze labor markets.

At least some of the women entering the labor force at this time hired housecleaners and child care workers to perform tasks they had once done themselves. As we learned in Chapter 21, the salaries of daycare staff and cleaning people are counted in GDP, while the value of these tasks when done by a husband or wife in a household is not part of GDP.

If you are interested in learning more about the economic history of American women, read the book *Understanding the Gender Gap: An Economic History of American Women* by Harvard University economist Claudia Goldin.

Discouraged-Worker Effects Remember, people who stop looking for work are classified as having dropped out of the labor force instead of being unemployed. During recessions, people may become discouraged about finding a job and stop looking. This lowers the unemployment rate because those no longer looking for work are no longer counted as unemployed.

To demonstrate how this **discouraged-worker effect** lowers the unemployment rate, suppose there are 10 million unemployed out of a labor force of 100 million. This means an unemployment rate of 10/100 = .10, or 10 percent. If 1 million of these 10 million unemployed people stopped looking for work and dropped out of the labor force, 9 million would be unemployed out of a labor force of 99 million. The unemployment rate would then drop to 9/99 = .091, or 9.1 percent.

discouraged-worker effect The decline in the measured unemployment rate that results when people who want to work but cannot find jobs grow discouraged and stop looking, thus dropping out of the ranks of the unemployed and the labor force.

The BLS survey provides some evidence on the size of the discouraged-worker effect. Respondents who indicate that they have stopped searching for work are asked why they stopped. If the respondent cites inability to find employment as the sole reason for not searching, that person might be classified as a discouraged worker.

The number of discouraged workers seems to hover around 1 percent of the size of the labor force in normal times. During the 1980–1982 recession, the number of discouraged workers increased steadily to a peak of 1.5 percent. By the end of the first quarter of 1991, the recession of

1990–1991 had produced 997,000 discouraged workers. Some economists argue that adding the number of discouraged workers to the number who are now classified as unemployed gives a better picture of the unemployment situation.

The Duration of Unemployment The unemployment rate measures unemployment at a given point in time. It tells us nothing about how long the average unemployed worker is out of work. Table 22.4 shows that during recessionary periods, the average duration of unemployment rises. Between 1979 and 1983, the average duration of unemployment rose from 10.8 weeks to 20.0 weeks. The slow growth following the 1990–1991 recession resulted in an increase in duration of unemployment to 17.7 weeks in 1992 and to 18.8 weeks in 1994. In 2000, average duration was down to 12.6 weeks, which then rose to 19.6 weeks in 2004. In 2006 and 2007, it was 16.8 weeks.

TABLE 22.4 Average Duration of Unemployment, 1979–2007

	Weeks		Weeks
1979	10.8	1993	18.0
1980	11.9	1994	18.8
1981	13.7	1995	16.6
1982	15.6	1996	16.7
1983	20.0	1997	15.8
1984	18.2	1998	14.5
1985	15.6	1999	13.4
1986	15.0	2000	12.6
1987	14.5	2001	13.1
1988	13.5	2002	16.6
1989	11.9	2003	19.2
1990	12.0	2004	19.6
1991	13.7	2005	18.4
1992	17.7	2006	16.8
		2007	16.8

Sources: U.S. Department of Labor, Bureau of Labor Statistics.

The Costs of Unemployment

In the Employment Act of 1946, Congress declared that it was the

> continuing policy and responsibility of the federal government to use all practicable means...to promote maximum employment, production, and purchasing power.

In 1978, Congress passed the Full Employment and Balanced Growth Act, commonly referred to as the *Humphrey-Hawkins Act*, which formally established a specific unemployment target of 4 percent. Why should full employment be a policy objective of the federal government? What costs does unemployment impose on society?

Some Unemployment Is Inevitable Before we discuss the costs of unemployment, we must realize that some unemployment is simply part of the natural workings of the labor market. Remember, to be classified as unemployed, a person must be looking for a job. Every year thousands of people enter the labor force for the first time. Some have dropped out of high school, some are high school or college graduates, and still others are finishing graduate programs. At the same time, new firms are starting up and others are expanding and creating new jobs while other firms are contracting or going out of business.

At any moment, there is a set of job seekers and a set of jobs that must be matched with one another. It is important that the right people end up in the right jobs. The right job for a person will depend on that person's skills, preferences concerning work environment (large firm or small, formal or informal), location of the individual's home, and willingness to commute. At the same time, firms want workers who can meet the requirements of the job and grow with the company.

To make a good match, workers must acquire information on job availability, wage rates, location, and work environment. Firms must acquire information on worker availability and skills. Information gathering consumes time and resources. The search may involve travel, interviews, preparation of a résumé, telephone calls, and hours going through the newspaper. To the extent that these efforts lead to a better match of workers and jobs, they are well spent. As long as the gains to firms and workers exceed the costs of search, the result is efficient.

When we consider the various costs of unemployment, it is useful to categorize unemployment into three types:

- Frictional unemployment
- Structural unemployment
- Cyclical unemployment

Frictional, Structural, and Cyclical Unemployment When the BLS does its survey about work activity for the week containing the twelfth of each month, it interviews many people who are involved in the normal search for work. Some are either entering the labor force or switching jobs. This unemployment is both natural and beneficial for the economy.

The portion of unemployment due to the normal working of the labor market is called **frictional unemployment**. The frictional unemployment rate can never be zero. It may, however, change over time. As jobs become more differentiated and the number of required skills increases, matching skills and jobs becomes more complex and the frictional unemployment rate may rise.

frictional unemployment The portion of unemployment that is due to the normal working of the labor market; used to denote short-run job/skill matching problems.

The concept of frictional unemployment is somewhat abstract because it is hard to know what "the normal working of the labor market" means. The industrial structure of the U.S. economy is continually changing. Manufacturing, for instance, has yielded part of its share of total employment to services and to finance, insurance, and real estate. Within the manufacturing sector, the steel and textile industries have contracted sharply, while high-technology sectors such as electronic components have expanded.

Although the unemployment that arises from such structural shifts could be classified as frictional, it is usually called **structural unemployment**. The term *frictional unemployment* is used to denote short-run job/skill matching problems, problems that last a few weeks. *Structural unemployment* denotes longer-run adjustment problems—those that tend to last for years. Although structural unemployment is expected in a dynamic economy, it is painful to the workers who experience it. In some ways, those who lose their jobs because their skills are obsolete experience the greatest pain. The fact that structural unemployment is natural and inevitable does not mean that it costs society nothing.

structural unemployment The portion of unemployment that is due to changes in the structure of the economy that result in a significant loss of jobs in certain industries.

Economists sometimes use the term **natural rate of unemployment** to refer to unemployment that occurs as a normal part of the functioning of the economy. This concept is also somewhat vague because *natural* is not a precise word. It is probably best to think of the natural rate as the sum of the frictional rate and the structural rate. Estimates of the natural rate range from 4 percent to 6 percent.

natural rate of unemployment The unemployment that occurs as a normal part of the functioning of the economy. Sometimes taken as the sum of frictional unemployment and structural unemployment.

Although some unemployment is natural, there are times when the unemployment rate seems to be above the natural rate. In 1979, the unemployment rate was 5.8 percent, but it did not fall below 6 percent again until 1987, 8 years later. In the meantime, the United States experienced a major recession, during which the unemployment rate rose substantially. The increase in unemployment that occurs during recessions and depressions is called **cyclical unemployment**.

cyclical unemployment The increase in unemployment that occurs during recessions and depressions.

Social Consequences The costs of unemployment are neither evenly distributed across the population nor easily quantified. The social consequences of the Depression of the 1930s are perhaps the hardest to comprehend. Most people alive today did not live through the Great Depression and can only read about it in books or hear stories told by parents and grandparents. Few emerged from this period unscathed. At the bottom were the poor and the fully unemployed, about 25 percent of the labor force. Even those who kept their jobs found themselves working part-time. Many people lost all or part of their savings as the stock market crashed and thousands of banks failed.

Congressional committees heard story after story. In Cincinnati, where the labor force totaled about 200,000, about 48,000 were wholly unemployed, 40,000 more were on short time, and relief payments to the needy averaged $7 to $8 per week:

> Relief is given to a family one week and then they are pushed off for a week in the hope that somehow or other the breadwinner may find some kind of work....We are paying no rent at all. That, of course, is a very difficult problem because we are continually having evictions, and social workers...are hard put to find places for people whose furniture has been put out on the street.[1]

From Birmingham, Alabama, in 1932:

> ...we have about 108,000 wage and salary workers in my district. Of that number, it is my belief that not exceeding 8000 have their normal incomes. At least 25,000 men are altogether without work. Some of them have not had a stroke of work for more than 12 months. Perhaps 60,000 or 70,000 are working from one to five days a week, and practically all have had serious cuts in wages and many of them do not average over $1.50 per day.[2]

Economic hardship accompanied the 1980–1982 recession as well. Between 1979 and 1983, the number of people officially classified as living in poverty in the United States rose from 26.1 million (11.7 percent of the population) to 35.5 million (15.3 percent). In addition to economic hardship, prolonged unemployment may also bring with it social and personal ills: anxiety, depression, deterioration of physical and psychological health, drug abuse (including alcoholism), and suicide.

Inflation

It is important to note that not all price increases constitute inflation. Prices of individual goods and services are determined in many ways. In competitive markets, the interaction of many buyers and many sellers—the operation of supply and demand—determines prices. In imperfectly competitive markets, prices are determined by producers' decisions. (This is the core of microeconomic theory.) In any economy, prices are continuously changing as markets adjust to changing conditions. Lack of rain may dry up corn and wheat fields, reducing supply and pushing up the price of agricultural products. At the same time, high levels of production by oil producers may be driving down the price of oil and petroleum products. Simultaneously, the United Auto Workers may be negotiating a contract with the Ford Motor Company that raises (or lowers) wage rates.

When prices of some goods are rising and others are falling, these are *relative* price changes. Inflation, on the other hand, occurs when there is an increase in the overall price level and deflation occurs when there is a decrease in the overall price level. We measure overall price levels by looking at all or a large number of goods and services in the economy. The GDP deflator, which was discussed in the last chapter, is the price deflator for all goods and services in the economy. The consumer price index, on the other hand, covers a smaller market basket of goods. We turn to this topic now.

The Consumer Price Index

consumer price index (CPI) A price index computed each month by the Bureau of Labor Statistics using a bundle that is meant to represent the "market basket" purchased monthly by the typical urban consumer.

The **consumer price index (CPI)** is the most widely followed price index. Unlike the GDP deflator, it is a fixed-weight index. It was first constructed during World War I as a basis for adjusting shipbuilders' wages, which the government controlled during the war. Currently, the CPI is computed by the BLS each month using a bundle of goods meant to represent the "market basket" purchased monthly by the typical urban consumer. The quantities of each good in the bundle that are used for the weights are based on extensive surveys of consumers. In fact, the BLS

[1] U.S. Senate Hearings before a subcommittee of the Committee of Manufacturers, 72nd Congress, first session (1931), p. 239. Cited in Lester Chandler, *America's Greatest Depression, 1929–1941* (New York: Harper & Row, 1970), p. 43.

[2] Senate Hearings, in Lester Chandler, *America's Greatest Depression, 1929–1941* (New York: Harper & Row, 1970), p. 43.

collects prices each month for about 71,000 goods and services from about 22,000 outlets in 44 geographic areas. For example, the cost of housing is included in the data collection by surveying about 5,000 renters and 1,000 homeowners each month. Figure 22.1 shows the CPI market basket for December 2007.

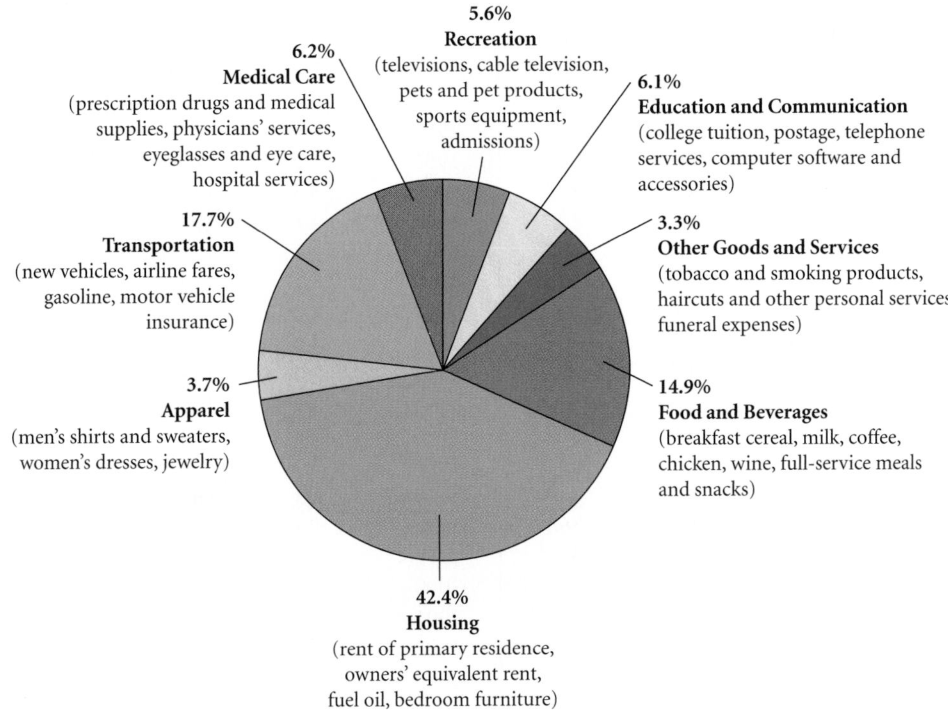

FIGURE 22.1
The CPI Market Basket
The CPI market basket shows how a typical consumer divides his or her money among various goods and services. Most of a consumer's money goes toward housing, transportation, and food and beverages.

Source: The Bureau of Labor Statistics

Table 22.5 shows values of the CPI since 1950. The base period for this index is 1982–1984, which means that the index is constructed to have a value of 100.0 when averaged across these three years. The percentage change for a given year in the table is a measure of inflation in that year. For example, from 1970 to 1971, the CPI increased from 38.8 to 40.5, a percentage change of 4.9 percent. [The percentage change is (40.5 – 38.8)/38.8 times 100.] The table shows the high inflation rates in the 1970s and early 1980s and the fairly low inflation rates since 1992.

Since the CPI is a fixed-weight price index (with the current base period 1982–1984), it suffers from the substitution problem discussed in the last chapter. With fixed weights, it does not account for consumers' substitution away from high-priced goods. The CPI thus has a tendency to overestimate the rate of inflation. This problem has important policy implications because government transfers such as Social Security payments are tied to the CPI. If inflation as measured by percentage changes in the CPI is biased upward, Social Security payments will grow more rapidly than they would with a better measure: The government is spending more than it otherwise would.

In response to the fixed-weight problem, in August 2002, the BLS began publishing a version of the CPI called the Chained Consumer Price Index, which uses changing weights. Although this version is not yet the main version, it may be that within a few years the BLS completely moves away from the fixed-weight version of the CPI. Remember, however, that even if this happens, the CPI will still differ in important ways from the GDP deflator, discussed in the last chapter. The CPI covers only consumer goods and services—those listed in Figure 22.1—whereas the GDP deflator covers all goods and services produced in the economy. Also, the CPI includes prices of imported goods, which the GDP deflator does not.

Other popular price indexes are **producer price indexes (PPIs)**, once called *wholesale price indexes*. These are indexes of prices that producers receive for products at all stages in the production process, not just the final stage. The indexes are calculated separately for various stages in the production process. The three main categories are *finished goods, intermediate materials*, and *crude materials*, although there are subcategories within each of these categories.

producer price indexes (PPIs) Measures of prices that producers receive for products at all stages in the production process.

TABLE 22.5 The CPI, 1950–2007

	Percentage Change in CPI	CPI		Percentage Change in CPI	CPI
1950	1.3	24.1	1979	11.3	72.6
1951	7.9	26.0	1980	13.5	82.4
1952	1.9	26.5	1981	10.3	90.9
1953	0.8	26.7	1982	6.2	96.5
1954	0.7	26.9	1983	3.2	99.6
1955	−0.4	26.8	1984	4.3	103.9
1956	1.5	27.2	1985	3.6	107.6
1957	3.3	28.1	1986	1.9	109.6
1958	2.8	28.9	1987	3.6	113.6
1959	0.7	29.1	1988	4.1	118.3
1960	1.7	29.6	1989	4.8	124.0
1961	1.0	29.9	1990	5.4	130.7
1962	1.0	30.2	1991	4.2	136.2
1963	1.3	30.6	1992	3.0	140.3
1964	1.3	31.0	1993	3.0	144.5
1965	1.6	31.5	1994	2.6	148.2
1966	2.9	32.4	1995	2.8	152.4
1967	3.1	33.4	1996	3.0	156.9
1968	4.2	34.8	1997	2.3	160.5
1969	5.5	36.7	1998	1.6	163.0
1970	5.7	38.8	1999	2.2	166.6
1971	4.4	40.5	2000	3.4	172.2
1972	3.2	41.8	2001	2.8	177.1
1973	6.2	44.4	2002	1.6	179.9
1974	11.0	49.3	2003	2.3	184.0
1975	9.1	53.8	2004	2.7	188.9
1976	5.8	56.9	2005	3.4	195.3
1977	6.5	60.6	2006	3.2	201.6
1978	7.6	65.2	2007	2.8	207.3

Sources: Bureau of Labor Statistics, U.S. Department of Labor.

One advantage of some of the PPIs is that they detect price increases early in the production process. Because their movements sometimes foreshadow future changes in consumer prices, they are considered to be leading indicators of future consumer prices.

The Costs of Inflation

If you asked most people why inflation is bad, they would tell you that it lowers the overall standard of living by making goods and services more expensive. That is, it cuts into people's purchasing power. People are fond of recalling the days when a bottle of Coca-Cola cost a dime and a hamburger cost a quarter. Just think what we could buy today if prices had not changed. What people usually do not think about is what their incomes were in the "good old days." The fact that the cost of a Coke has increased from 10 cents to a dollar does not mean anything in real terms if people who once earned $5,000 now earn $50,000. Why? The reason is simple: People's income from wages and salaries, profits, interest, and rent increases during inflations. The wage rate is the price of labor, rent is the price of land, and so on. During inflations, most prices—including input prices—tend to rise together; and input prices determine both the incomes of workers and the incomes of owners of capital and land.

Inflation May Change the Distribution of Income Whether you gain or lose during a period of inflation depends on whether your income rises faster or slower than the prices of the things you buy. The group most often mentioned when the impact of inflation is discussed is people living on fixed incomes. If your income is fixed and prices rise, your ability to purchase goods and services falls proportionately.

Although the elderly are often thought of as living on fixed incomes, many pension plans pay benefits that are *indexed* to inflation. The benefits these plans provide automatically increase when the general price level rises. If prices rise 10 percent, benefits also rise 10 percent. The biggest source of income for the elderly is Social Security. These benefits are fully indexed; when prices rise—that is, when the CPI rises—by 5 percent, Social Security benefits also increase by 5 percent.

Wages are also sometimes indexed to inflation through cost of living adjustments (COLAs) written into labor contracts. These contracts usually stipulate that future wage increases will be larger the larger is the rate of inflation. If wages are fully indexed, workers do not suffer a fall in real income when inflation rises, although wages are not always fully indexed.

One way of thinking about the effects of inflation on the distribution of income is to distinguish between *anticipated* and *unanticipated* inflation. If inflation is anticipated and contracts are made and agreements written with the anticipated value of inflation in mind, there need not be any effects of inflation on income distribution. Take, for example, debtors versus creditors. It is commonly believed that debtors benefit at the expense of creditors during an inflation because with inflation they pay back less in the future in real terms than they borrowed. But this is not the case if the inflation is anticipated and the loan contract is written with this in mind.

Suppose that you want to borrow $100 from me to be paid back in a year and that we both agree that if there is no inflation the appropriate interest rate is 5 percent. Suppose also that we both anticipate that the inflation rate will be 10 percent. In this case we will agree on a 15 percent interest rate—you will pay me back $115 at the end of the year. By charging you 15 percent I have taken into account the fact that you will be paying me back with dollars worth 10 percent less in real terms than when you borrowed them. I am then not hurt by inflation and you are not helped if the actual inflation rate turns out to equal our anticipated rate. I am earning a 5 percent **real interest rate**—the difference between the interest rate on a loan and the inflation rate.

real interest rate The difference between the interest rate on a loan and the inflation rate.

Unanticipated inflation, on the other hand, is a different story. If the actual inflation rate during the year turns out to be 20 percent, I as a creditor will be hurt. I charged you 15 percent interest, expecting to get a 5 percent real rate of return, when I needed to charge you 25 percent to get the same 5 percent real rate of return. Because inflation was higher than anticipated, I got a negative real return of 5 percent. Inflation that is higher than anticipated benefits debtors; inflation that is lower than anticipated benefits creditors.

To summarize, the effects of anticipated inflation on the distribution of income are likely to be fairly small, since people and institutions will adjust to the anticipated inflation. Unanticipated inflation, on the other hand, may have large effects, depending, among other things, on how much indexing to inflation there is. If many contracts are not indexed and are based on anticipated inflation rates that turn out to be wrong, there can be big winners and losers. In general, there is more uncertainty and risk when inflation is unanticipated. This uncertainty may prevent people from signing long-run contracts that would otherwise be beneficial for both parties.

Administrative Costs and Inefficiencies There may also be costs associated even with anticipated inflation. One is the administrative cost associated with simply keeping up. During the rapid inflation in Israel in the early 1980s, a telephone hotline was set up to give the hourly price index. Store owners had to recalculate and repost prices frequently, and this took time that could have been used more efficiently. In Zimbabwe, where the inflation rate in June 2008 was estimated by some to be over 1 million percent at an annual rate, the government was forced to print ever-increasing denominations of money.

More frequent banking transactions may also be required when anticipated inflation is high. For example, interest rates tend to rise with anticipated inflation. When interest rates are high, the opportunity costs of holding cash outside of banks is high. People therefore hold less cash and need to stop at the bank more often. (We discuss this effect in more detail in the next part of this book.)

Public Enemy Number One? Economists have debated the seriousness of the costs of inflation for decades. Some, among them Alan Blinder, say, "Inflation, like every teenager, is grossly misunderstood, and this gross misunderstanding blows the political importance of inflation out of all proportion to its economic importance."[3] Others such as Phillip Cagan and Robert Lipsey argue, "It was once thought that the economy would in time make all the necessary adjustments [to inflation], but many of them are proving to be very difficult.... For financial institutions and markets, the effects of inflation have been extremely unsettling."[4]

No matter what the real economic cost of inflation, people do not like it. It makes us uneasy and unhappy. In 1974, President Ford verbalized some of this discomfort when he said, "Our inflation, our public enemy number one, will unless whipped destroy our country, our homes, our liberties, our property, and finally our national pride, as surely as any well-armed wartime enemy."[5] In this belief, our elected leaders have vigorously pursued policies designed to stop inflation.

Long-Run Growth

output growth The growth rate of the output of the entire economy.

per-capita output growth The growth rate of output per person in the economy.

productivity growth The growth rate of output per worker.

In discussing long-run growth, it will be useful to begin with a few definitions. **Output growth** is the growth rate of the output of the entire economy. **Per-capita output growth** is the growth rate of output per person in the economy. If the population of a country is growing at the same rate as output, then per-capita output is not growing: Output growth is simply keeping up with population growth. Not everyone in a country works, and so output per worker is not the same as output per person. Output per worker is larger than output per person, and it is called productivity. **Productivity growth** is thus the growth rate of output per worker.

If we take as the measure of economic welfare of a country its per-capita output, a rapid growth rate of output does not necessarily improve individual welfare. If population is growing as rapidly as output, per-capita output is not growing, which means that the economic welfare of the average person is not growing. If the fraction of the population that is working remains the same and productivity increases, per-capita output will increase because more output is being produced per person. Per-capita output will also increase if productivity does not change but the fraction of the population that is working increases. In this case, more output is also being produced per person, although this is so because more people are working.

Output and Productivity Growth

We have pointed out that aggregate output in the United States has grown at an annual rate of 3.4 percent since 1900. Some years are better than this and some years worse, but, on average, the growth rate has been 3.4 percent. An area of economics called *growth theory* is concerned with the question of what determines this rate. Why 3.4 percent and not 2 percent or 4 percent? We take up this question in Chapter 32, but a few points are useful to make now.

Before we begin our discussion of economic growth, it is important to review what is meant by *capital*. Capital is anything that is produced that is then used as an input to produce other goods and services. Capital can be tangible, such as buildings and equipment, or intangible. The knowledge and skills acquired through education and training can be thought of as intangible *human capital*. Capital can be private or public. The roads and bridges that we drive on are a part of the public capital stock. Capital, thus, can take many forms. To simplify the discussion, however, we will sometimes refer to capital as simply "machines."

In a simplified economy, machines (capital) and workers (labor) are needed to produce output. Suppose that an economy consists of six machines and 60 workers, with 10 workers working on each machine, and that the length of the workweek is 40 hours, with this workweek resulting in 50 units of output per month per machine. Total output (GDP) for the month is thus 300 units (6 machines times 50 units per machine) in this simple economy.

How can output increase in this economy? There are a number of ways. One way is to add more workers. If, for example, 12 workers are added, 2 extra per machine, more output can be produced per machine per hour worked because there are more workers helping out on each machine. Another way is to add more machines. For example, if 4 machines are added, the

---

[3] Alan Blinder, *Hard Heads, Soft Hearts: Tough-Minded Economics for a Just Society* (Reading, MA: Addison-Wesley, 1987).

[4] Phillip Cagan and Robert Lipsey, "The Financial Effects of Inflation," National Bureau of Economic Research (Cambridge, MA: General Series No. 103, 1978), pp. 67–68.

[5] U.S. President, Weekly Compilation of Presidential Documents, vol. 10, no. 41, p. 1247. Cited in Blinder, *Hard Heads.*

60 workers have a total of 10 machines to work with instead of 6 and more output can be produced per worker per hour worked. A third way is to increase the length of the workweek (for example, from 40 hours to 45 hours). With workers and machines working more hours, more output can be produced. Output can thus increase if labor or capital increases or if the amount of time that labor and capital are working per week increases.

Another way for output to increase in our economy is for the quality of the workers to increase. If, for example, the education of the workers increases, this may add to their skills and thus increase their ability to work on the machines. Output per machine might then rise from 50 units per month to some larger number per month. Also, if workers become more physically fit by exercising more and eating less fat and more whole grains and fresh fruits and vegetables, their greater fitness may increase their output on the machines. People are sometimes said to be adding to their *human capital* when they increase their mental or physical skills.

The quality of the machines may also increase. In particular, new machines that replace old machines may allow more output to be produced per hour with the same number of workers. In our example, it may be that 55 instead of 50 units of output can be produced per month per new machine with 10 workers per machine and a 40-hour workweek. An obvious example is the replacement of an old computer with a new, faster one that allows more to be done per minute of work on the computer.

To summarize, output can increase when there are more workers, more skills per worker, more machines, better machines, or a longer workweek.

Turning now to the actual economy, an interesting variable to look at is the ratio of total output to the total number of worker hours. Output per worker hour is called *labor productivity* or sometimes just *productivity*. Output per worker hour is plotted in Figure 22.2 for the 1952 I–2007 IV period. Two features are immediately clear from the figure. First, there is an upward trend. Second, there are fairly sizable short-run fluctuations around the trend. We will see in Chapter 31 why there are short-run fluctuations. This has to do with the possibility that the employed workforce is not always fully utilized. For now, however, the main interest is the long-run trend.

To smooth out the short-run fluctuations in Figure 22.2, we have added straight-line segments to the figure, where the segments roughly go through the high values. The slope of each line segment is the growth rate of productivity along the segment. The growth rates are listed in the figure. The different productivity growth rates in the figure tell an interesting story. From the 1950s through the mid-1960s, the growth rate was 3.1 percent. The rate then fell to 2.5 percent in the last half of the 1960s and early 1970s. Between the early 1970s and the early 1990s, the growth rate was much lower at 1.5 percent. Since the early 1990s, it has been 1.9 percent.

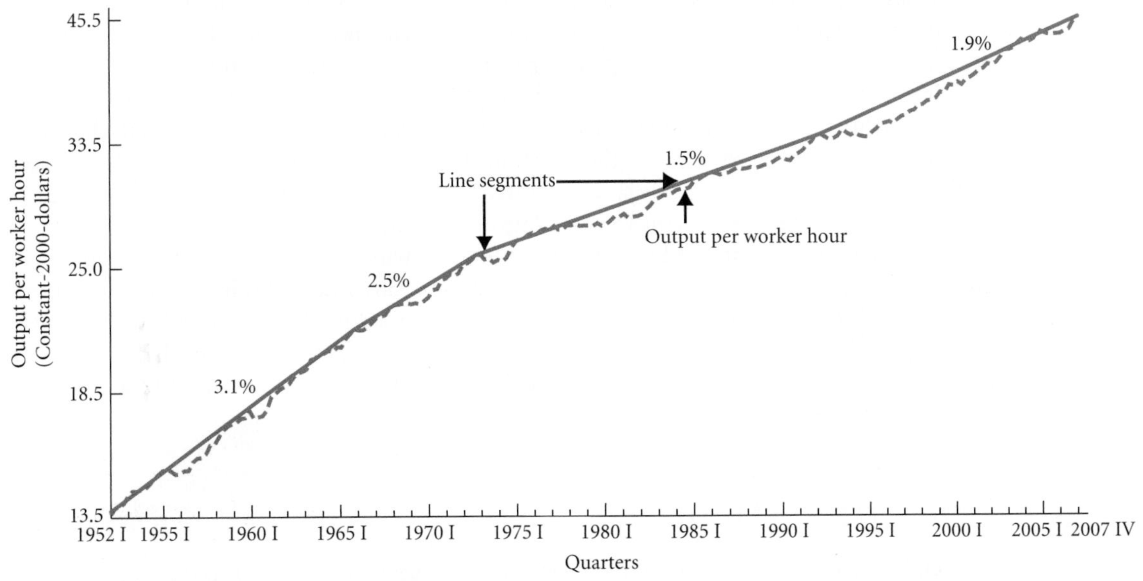

▲ **FIGURE 22.2 Output per Worker Hour (Productivity), 1952 I–2007 IV**

Productivity grew much faster in the 1950s and 1960s than since.

Why are the growth rates positive in Figure 22.2? In other words, why has the amount of output that a worker can produce per hour risen in the last half century? Part of the answer is that the amount of capital per worker has increased. In Figure 22.3 capital per worker is plotted for the same 1952 I–2007 IV period. It is clear from the figure that the amount of capital per worker has generally been rising. Therefore, with more capital per worker, more output can be produced per worker. The other part of the answer is that the quality of labor and capital has been increasing. Both the average skill of workers and the average quality of capital have been increasing. This means that more output can be produced per worker for a given quantity of capital because both workers and capital are getting better.

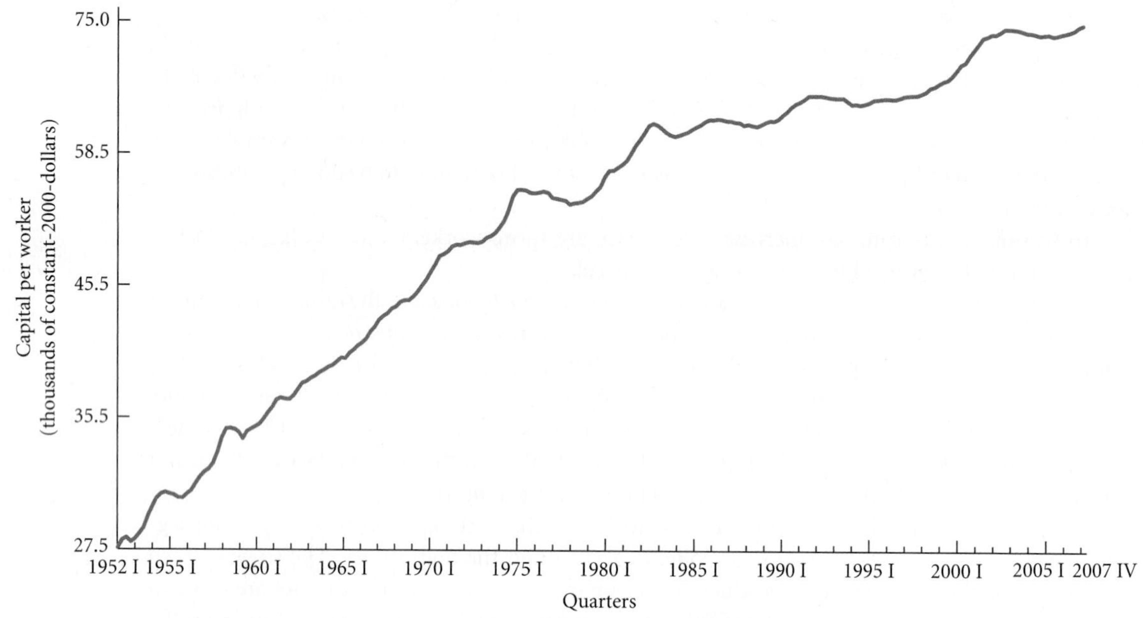

▲ **FIGURE 22.3 Capital per Worker, 1952 I–2007 IV**
Capital per worker grew until about 1980 and then leveled off somewhat.

A harder question to answer concerning Figure 22.2 is why the growth rate of productivity was much higher in the 1950s and 1960s than it has been since the early 1970s. Again, part of the answer is that the amount of capital per worker rose more rapidly in the 1950s and 1960s than it has since then. This can be seen in Figure 22.3. The other part of the answer is, of course, that the quality of labor and capital must have increased more in the 1950s and 1960s than later, although this, to some extent, begs the question. The key question is why the quality of labor and capital has grown more slowly since the early 1970s. We take up this question in Chapter 32, where we will see that there seems to be no one obvious answer. An interesting question for the future is whether the continued growth of the Internet will lead to a much larger productivity growth rate, perhaps as large as the growth rate in the 1950s and 1960s. In the present context, you can think about the growth of the Internet as an increase in physical capital (wires, servers, switchers, and so on) and an increase in the quality of capital (an increase in what can be done per minute using the Internet). Time will tell whether the Internet will lead to a "new age" of productivity growth.

Looking Ahead

This ends our introduction to the basic concepts and problems of macroeconomics. The first chapter of this part introduced the field; the second chapter discussed the measurement of national product and national income; and this chapter discussed unemployment, inflation and long-run growth. We are now ready to begin the analysis of how the macroeconomy works.

SUMMARY

UNEMPLOYMENT *p. 435*

1. The *unemployment rate* is the ratio of the number of *unemployed* people to the number of people in the *labor force*. To be considered unemployed and in the labor force, a person must be looking for work.
2. Big differences in rates of unemployment exist across demographic groups, regions, and industries. African Americans, for example, experience much higher unemployment rates than whites.
3. A person who decides to stop looking for work is considered to have dropped out of the labor force and is no longer classified as unemployed. People who stop looking because they are discouraged about finding a job are sometimes called *discouraged workers*.
4. Some unemployment is inevitable. Because new workers are continually entering the labor force, because industries and firms are continuously expanding and contracting, and because people switch jobs, there is a constant process of job search as workers and firms try to match the best people to the available jobs. This unemployment is both natural and beneficial for the economy.
5. The unemployment that occurs because of short-run job/skill-matching problems is called *frictional unemployment*. The unemployment that occurs because of longer-run structural changes in the economy is called *structural unemployment*. The *natural rate of unemployment* is the sum of the frictional rate and the structural rate. The increase in unemployment that occurs during recessions and depressions is called *cyclical unemployment*.

INFLATION *p. 442*

6. The *consumer price index (CPI)* is a fixed-weight price index. It represents the "market basket" purchased by the typical urban consumer.
7. Whether people gain or lose during a period of inflation depends on whether their income rises faster or slower than the prices of the things they buy. The elderly are more insulated from inflation than most people think because Social Security benefits and many pensions are indexed to inflation.
8. Inflation is likely to have a larger effect on the distribution of income when it is unanticipated than when it is anticipated.

LONG-RUN GROWTH *p. 446*

9. Output growth depends on: (1) the growth rate of the capital stock, (2) the growth rate of output per unit of the capital stock, (3) the growth rate of labor, and (4) the growth rate of output per unit of labor.
10. Output per worker hour (labor productivity) rose faster in the 1950s and 1960s than it rose from the 1970s to 2007. An interesting question is whether labor productivity will rise faster in the future because of the Internet.

REVIW TERMS AND CONCEPTS

consumer price index (CPI), *p. 442*
cyclical unemployment, *p. 441*
discouraged-worker effect, *p. 439*
employed, *p. 436*
frictional unemployment, *p. 441*
labor force, *p. 436*
labor force participation rate, *p. 436*
natural rate of unemployment, *p. 441*
not in the labor force, *p. 436*
output growth, *p. 446*
per-capita output growth, *p. 446*
producer price indexes (PPIs), *p. 443*
productivity growth, *p. 446*
real interest rate, *p. 445*
structural unemployment, *p. 441*
unemployed, *p. 436*
unemployment rate, *p. 436*

1. labor force = employed + unemployed
2. population = labor force + not in labor force
3. $\text{unemployment rate} = \dfrac{\text{unemployed}}{\text{employed} + \text{unemployed}}$
4. $\text{labor force participation rate} = \dfrac{\text{labor force}}{\text{population}}$

PROBLEMS

Visit **www.myeconlab.com** to complete the problems marked in orange online. You will receive instant feedback on your answers, tutorial help, and access to additional practice problems.

1. In early 2008, economists were debating whether the U.S. economy was in a recession even though the unemployment rate was close to full employment at only 5.1 percent. How can they make this assertion?
2. When an inefficient firm or a firm producing a product that people no longer want goes out of business, people are unemployed, but that is part of the normal process of economic growth and development. The unemployment is part of the

natural rate and need not concern policy makers. Discuss that statement and its relevance to the economy today.

3. What is the unemployment rate in your state today? What was it in 1970, 1975, 1982, and 2008? How has your state done relative to the national average? Do you know or can you determine why?

4. Suppose all wages, salaries, welfare benefits, and other sources of income were indexed to inflation. Would inflation still be considered a problem? Why or why not?

5. **[Related to the *Economics in Practice* on *p. 439*]** Go to www.bls.gov and click on the links for state and area employment and unemployment. Look at your home state and describe what changes have taken place in the workforce. Has the labor force participation rate gone up or down? Provide an explanation for the rate change. Are your state's experiences the same as the rest of the country? Provide an explanation of why your state's experiences are the same as or different from the rest of the country.

6. What do the CPI and the PPI measure? Why do we need both of these price indexes? (Think about what purpose you would use each one for.)

7. The consumer price index (CPI) is a fixed-weight index. It compares the price of a fixed bundle of goods in one year with the price of the same bundle of goods in some base year. Calculate the price of a bundle containing 100 units of good *X*, 150 units of good *Y*, and 25 units of good *Z* in 2006, 2007, and 2008. Convert the results into an index by dividing each bundle price figure by the bundle price in 2006. Calculate the percentage change in your index between 2006 and 2007 and again between 2007 and 2008. Was there inflation between 2007 and 2008?

GOOD	QUANTITY CONSUMED	PRICES 2006	PRICES 2007	PRICES 2008
X	100	$1.00	$1.50	$1.75
Y	150	1.50	2.00	2.00
Z	25	3.00	3.25	3.00

8. Consider the following statements:
   a. More people are employed in Tappania now than at any time in the past 50 years.
   b. The unemployment rate in Tappania is higher now than it has been in 50 years.

   Can both of those statements be true at the same time? Explain.

9. Policy makers talk about the "capacity" of the economy to grow. What specifically is meant by the "capacity" of the economy? How might capacity be measured? In what ways is capacity limited by labor constraints and by capital constraints? What are the consequences if demand in the economy exceeds capacity? What signs would you look for?

10. What was the rate of growth in real GDP during the most recent quarter? You can find the answer in publications such as the *Survey of Current Business, The Economist*, and *Business Week*. Has growth been increasing or decreasing? What policies might you suggest for increasing the economy's potential long-run rate of growth?

11. Suppose the stock of capital and the workforce are both increasing at 3 percent annually in the country of Wholand. At the same time, real output is growing at 6 percent. How is that possible in the short run and in the long run?

part V
The Core of Macroeconomic Theory

We now begin our discussion of the theory of how the macroeconomy works. We know how to calculate gross domestic product (GDP), but what factors *determine* it? We know how to define and measure inflation and unemployment, but what circumstances *cause* inflation and unemployment? What, if anything, can government do to reduce unemployment and inflation?

Analyzing the various components of the macroeconomy is a complex undertaking. The level of GDP, the overall price level, and the level of employment—three chief concerns of macroeconomists—are influenced by events in three broadly defined "markets":

- Goods-and-services market
- Financial (money) market
- Labor market

We will explore each market, as well as the links between them, in our discussion of macroeconomic theory. Figure V.1 presents the plan of the next seven chapters, which form the

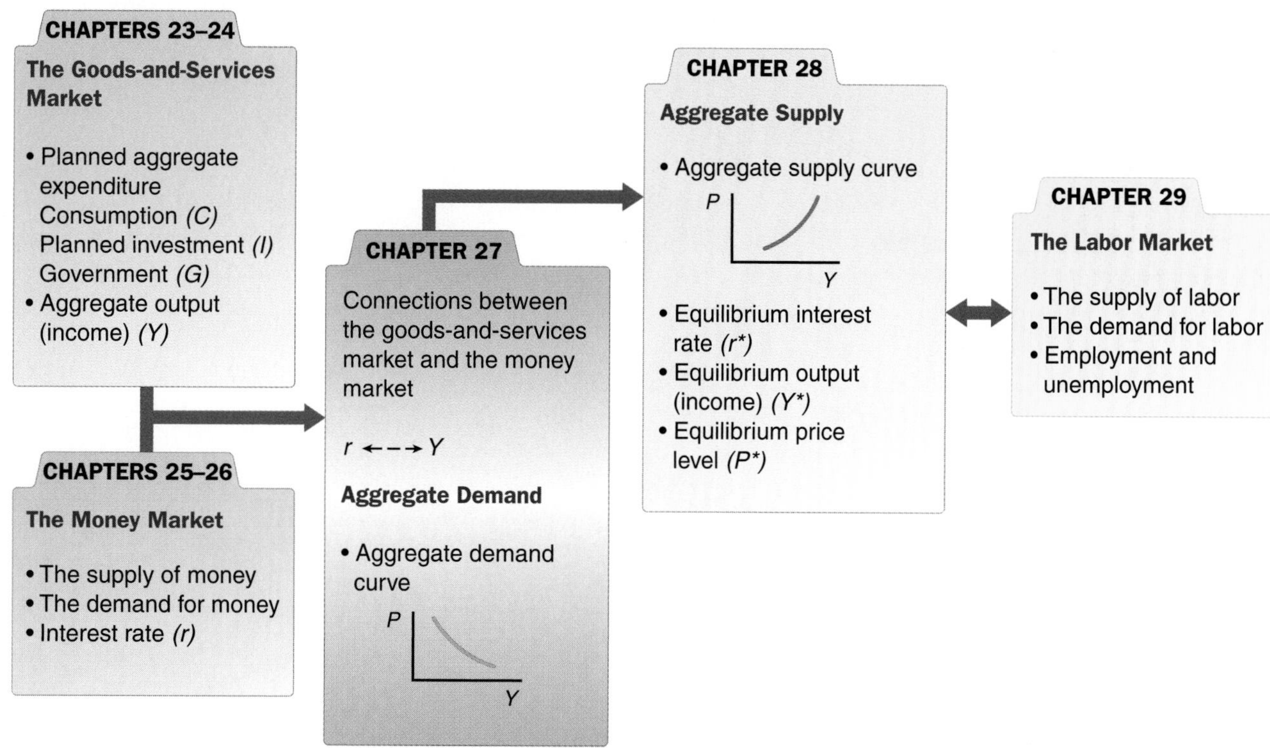

▲ **FIGURE V.1 The Core of Macroeconomic Theory**

We build up the macroeconomy slowly. In Chapters 23 and 24, we examine the market for goods and services. In Chapters 25 and 26, we examine the money market. Then in Chapter 27, we bring the two markets together, in so doing explaining the links between aggregate output (Y) and the interest rate (r), and derive the aggregate demand curve. In Chapter 28, we introduce the aggregate supply curve and determine the price level (P). We then explain in Chapter 29 how the labor market fits into the macroeconomic picture.

core of macroeconomic theory. In Chapters 23 and 24, we describe the market for goods and services, often called the *goods market*. In Chapter 23, we explain several basic concepts and show how the equilibrium level of output is determined in a simple economy with no government and no imports or exports. In Chapter 24, we add the government to the economy.

In Chapters 25 and 26, we focus on the *money market*. Chapter 25 introduces the money market and the banking system and discusses the way the U.S. central bank (the Federal Reserve) controls the money supply. Chapter 26 analyzes the demand for money and the way interest rates are determined. Chapter 27 then examines the relationship between the goods market and the money market and derives the aggregate demand curve. At the end of Chapter 27, the equilibrium values of aggregate output and the interest rate are determined for a given price level. Chapter 28 then uses the analysis from Chapter 27, adds the aggregate supply curve, and determines the price level. Having then determined output, the interest rate, and the price level, we are ready to analyze the effects of fiscal and monetary policies on the economy. This is done in the second half of Chapter 28. Finally, Chapter 29 discusses the supply of and demand for labor and the functioning of the *labor market* in the macroeconomy. This material is essential to understanding employment and unemployment.

Before we begin our discussion of aggregate output and income, we need to stress that production, consumption, and other activities that we will be discussing in the following chapters are ongoing activities. Nonetheless, it is helpful to think about these activities as if they took place in a series of *production periods*. A period might be a month long or 3 months long. During each period, output is produced, income is generated, and spending takes place. At the end of each period, we can examine the results. Was everything that was produced in the economy sold? What percentage of income was spent? What percentage was saved? Is output (income) likely to rise or fall in the next period?

Aggregate Expenditure and Equilibrium Output

23

CHAPTER OUTLINE

In this chapter, we explain how equilibrium output is determined in an economy with no government. We build slowly, and the only theory we use is that consumption depends on income and that the goods market is in equilibrium. Having determined equilibrium output, we then discuss how an economy that is out of equilibrium adjusts back to equilibrium.

In Chapter 21, we introduced real gross domestic product as a measure of the total quantity of output produced in the economy in a given period. Output includes the production of services, consumer goods, and investment goods. We saw that GDP can be calculated in terms of income or expenditures. Because every dollar of expenditure is received by someone as income, we can compute total GDP by adding up the total spent on all final goods and services during a period or by adding up all the income—wages, rents, interest, and profits—received by all factors of production.

We will use the variable Y to refer to both **aggregate output** and **aggregate income** because they are the same seen from two different points of view. When output increases, additional income is generated. More workers may be hired and paid, workers may put in and be paid for more hours, and owners may earn more profits. When output is cut, income falls, workers may be laid off or work fewer hours (and be paid less), and profits may fall.

aggregate output The total quantity of goods and services produced (or supplied) in an economy in a given period.

aggregate income The total income received by all factors of production in a given period.

> In any given period, there is an exact equality between aggregate output (production) and aggregate income. You should be reminded of this fact whenever you encounter the combined term **aggregate output (income) (Y)**.

aggregate output (income) (Y) A combined term used to remind you of the exact equality between aggregate output and aggregate income.

Aggregate output can also be considered the aggregate quantity supplied because it is the amount that firms are supplying (producing) during a period. In the discussions that follow, we use the term *aggregate output (income)* instead of *aggregate quantity supplied*, but keep in mind that the two are equivalent. Also remember that *aggregate output* means "real GDP."

From the outset, you must think in "real terms." For example, when we talk about output (Y), we mean real output, not nominal output. Although we discussed in Chapter 21 that the calculation of real GDP is complicated, you can ignore these complications in the following analysis. To help make things easier to read, we will frequently use dollar values for Y. But do not confuse Y with nominal output. The main point is to think of Y as being in real terms—the quantities of goods and services produced, not the dollars circulating in the economy.

The Keynesian Theory of Consumption

In 2005, the average American family spent about $1,350 on clothing. For high-income families earning more than $148,000, the amount spent on clothing was substantially higher, at $3,700. We all recognize that for consumption as a whole, as well as for consumption of most specific categories of goods and services, consumption rises with income. This relationship between consumption and income is central to Keynes's model of the economy. While Keynes recognized that many factors, including wealth and interest rates, play a role in determining consumption levels in the economy, in his classic *The General Theory of Employment, Interest and Money*, current income played the key role:

> The fundamental psychological law, upon which we are entitled to depend with great confidence both *a priori* from our knowledge of human nature and from the detailed facts of experience, is that men [and women, too] are disposed, as a rule and on average, to increase their consumption as their incomes increase, but not by as much as the increase in their income.[1]

Keynes is telling us two things in this quote. First, if you find your income going up, you will spend more than you did before. But Keynes is also saying something about how much more you will spend: He predicts—based on his looking at the data and his understanding of people—that the rise in consumption will be less than the full rise in income. This simple observation plays a large role in helping us understand the workings of the aggregate economy.

consumption function The relationship between consumption and income.

The relationship between consumption and income is called a **consumption function.** Figure 23.1 shows a hypothetical consumption function for an individual household. The curve is labeled $c(y)$, which is read "c is a function of y," or "consumption is a function of income." Note that we have drawn the line with an upward slope, reflecting that consumption increases with income. To reflect Keynes's view that consumption increases less than one for one with income, we have drawn the consumption function with a slope of less than 1. The consumption function in Figure 23.1 is a straight line, telling us that an increase in income of $1 leads to the same increase in consumption regardless of the initial value of income. In practice, the consumption function may be curved, with the slope decreasing as income increases. This would tell us that the typical consumer spends less of the incremental income received as his or her income rises.

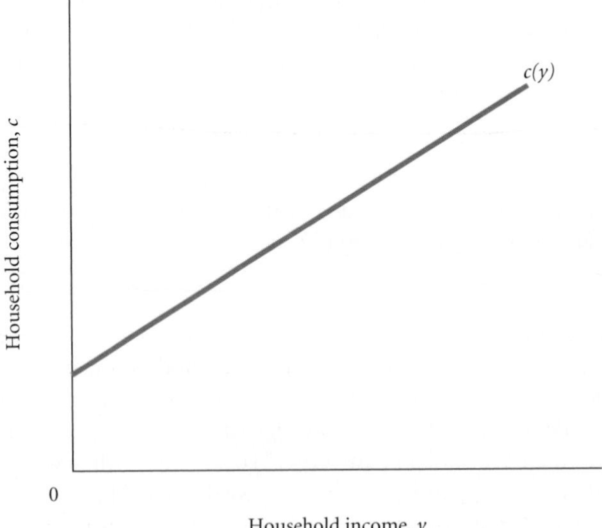

FIGURE 23.1 A Consumption Function for a Household
A consumption function for an individual household shows the level of consumption at each level of household income.

The consumption function in Figure 23.1 represents an individual household. In macroeconomics, however, we are interested in the behavior of the economy as a whole, the aggregate consumption of all households in the economy in relation to aggregate income. Figure 23.2 shows this

[1] John Maynard Keynes, *The General Theory of Employment, Interest, and Money* (1936), First Harbinger Ed. (New York: Harcourt Brace Jovanovich, 1964), p. 96.

aggregate consumption function, again using a straight line, or constant slope, for simplicity. With a straight line consumption curve, we can use the following equation to describe the curve:

$$C = a + bY$$

Y is aggregate output (income), *C* is aggregate consumption, and *a* is the point at which the consumption function intersects the *C*-axis—a constant. The letter *b* is the slope of the line, in this case $\Delta C/\Delta Y$ [because consumption (*C*) is measured on the vertical axis and income (*Y*) is measured on the horizontal axis].[2] Every time income increases (say by ΔY), consumption increases by *b* times ΔY. Thus, $\Delta C = b \times \Delta Y$ and $\Delta C/\Delta Y = b$. Suppose, for example, that the slope of the line in Figure 23.2 is .75 (that is, $b = .75$). An increase in income (ΔY) of \$1,000 would then increase consumption by $b\Delta Y = .75 \times \$1{,}000$, or \$750.

Aggregate consumption, C

$C = a + bY$

ΔC

ΔY

a

Slope = $\dfrac{\Delta C}{\Delta Y} = b$

0

Aggregate income, Y

FIGURE 23.2 An Aggregate Consumption Function

The aggregate consumption function shows the level of aggregate consumption at each level of aggregate income. The upward slope indicates that higher levels of income lead to higher levels of consumption spending.

The **marginal propensity to consume (*MPC*)** is the fraction of a change in income that is consumed. In the consumption function here, *b* is the *MPC*. An *MPC* of .75 means consumption changes by .75 of the change in income. The slope of the consumption function is the *MPC*. An *MPC* less than 1 tells us that individuals spend less than 100 percent of their income increase, just as Keynes suggested.

marginal propensity to consume (*MPC*) That fraction of a change in income that is consumed, or spent.

$$\text{marginal propensity to consume} \equiv \text{slope of consumption function} \equiv \frac{\Delta C}{\Delta Y}$$

Aggregate saving (*S*) in the economy, denoted *S*, is the difference between aggregate income and aggregate consumption:

aggregate saving (*S*) The part of aggregate income that is not consumed.

$$S \equiv Y - C$$

The triple equal sign means that this equation is an **identity**, or something that is always true by definition. This equation simply says that income that is not consumed must be saved. If \$0.75 of a \$1.00 increase in income goes to consumption, \$0.25 must go to saving. If income decreases by \$1.00, consumption will decrease by \$0.75 and saving will decrease by \$0.25. The **marginal propensity to save (*MPS*)** is the fraction of a change in income that is saved: $\Delta S/\Delta Y$, where ΔS is the change in saving. Because everything not consumed is saved, the *MPC* and the *MPS* must add up to 1.

identity Something that is always true.

marginal propensity to save (*MPS*) That fraction of a change in income that is saved.

$$MPC + MPS \equiv 1$$

[2] The Greek letter Δ (delta) means "change in." For example, ΔY (read "delta *Y*") means the "change in income." If income (*Y*) in 2007 is \$100 and income in 2008 is \$110, then ΔY for this period is \$110 − \$100 = \$10. For a review of the concept of slope, see Appendix, Chapter 1.

Because the *MPC* and the *MPS* are important concepts, it may help to review their definitions. The marginal propensity to consume (*MPC*) is the fraction of an increase in income that is consumed (or the fraction of a decrease in income that comes out of consumption). The marginal propensity to save (*MPS*) is the fraction of an increase in income that is saved (or the fraction of a decrease in income that comes out of saving).

The numerical examples used in the rest of this chapter are based on the following consumption function:

$$C = \underbrace{100}_{a} + \underbrace{.75}_{b}Y$$

This equation is simply an extension of the generic $C = a + bY$ consumption function we have been discussing, where a is 100 and b is .75. This function is graphed in Figure 23.3.

▶ FIGURE 23.3 The Aggregate Consumption Function Derived from the Equation $C = 100 + .75Y$

In this simple consumption function, consumption is 100 at an income of zero. As income rises, so does consumption. For every 100 increase in income, consumption rises by 75. The slope of the line is .75.

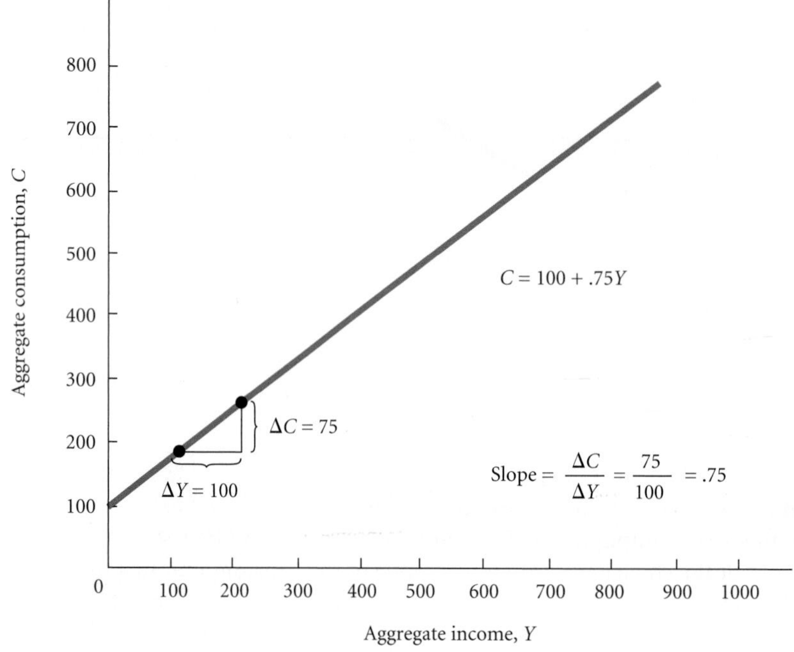

Aggregate Income, Y	Aggregate Consumption, C
0	100
80	160
100	175
200	250
400	400
600	550
800	700
1,000	850

Since saving and consumption by definition add up to income, we can use the consumption curve to tell us about both consumption and saving. We do this in Figure 23.4. In this figure, we have drawn a 45° line from the origin. Everywhere along this line aggregate consumption is equal to aggregate income. Therefore, saving is zero. Where the consumption curve is *above* the 45° line, consumption exceeds income and saving is negative. Where the consumption function *crosses* the 45° line, consumption is equal to income and saving is zero. Where the consumption function is *below* the 45° line, consumption is less than income and saving is positive. Note that the slope of the saving function is $\Delta S/\Delta Y$, which is equal to the marginal propensity to save (*MPS*). The consumption function and the saving function are mirror images of each other. No information appears in one that does not appear in the other. These functions tell us how households in the aggregate will divide income between consumption spending and saving at every possible income level. In other words, they embody aggregate household behavior.

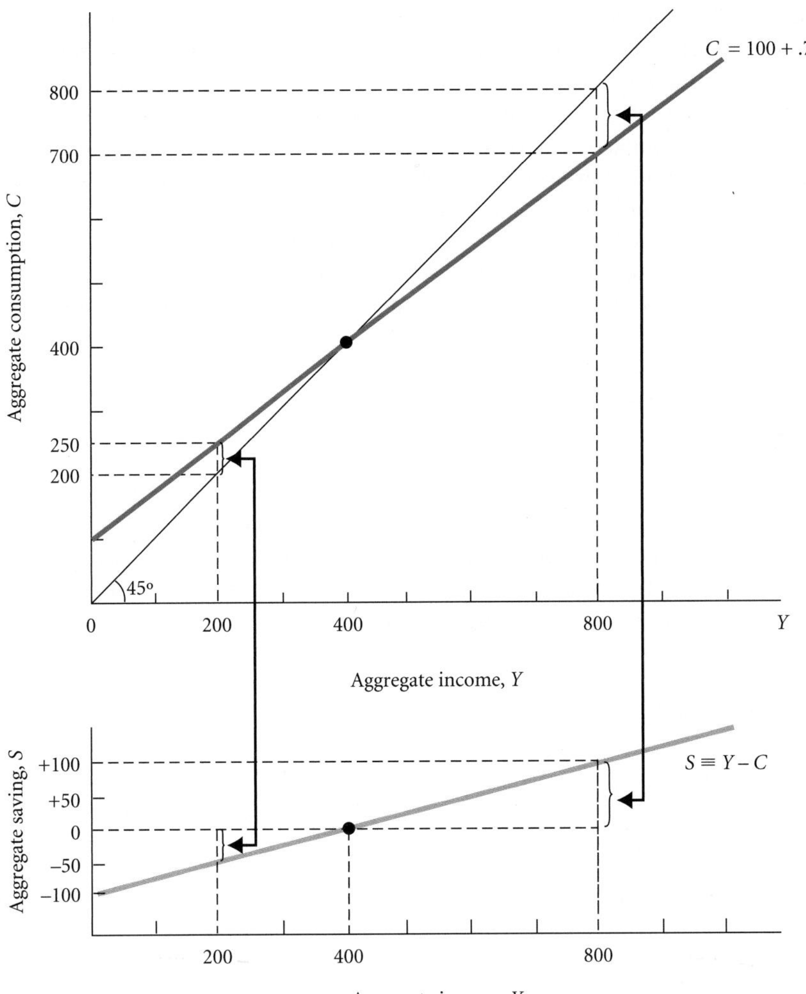

FIGURE 23.4 Deriving the Saving Function from the Consumption Function in Figure 23.3

Because $S \equiv Y - C$, it is easy to derive the saving function from the consumption function. A 45° line drawn from the origin can be used as a convenient tool to compare consumption and income graphically. At $Y = 200$, consumption is 250. The 45° line shows us that consumption is larger than income by 50. Thus, $S \equiv Y - C = -50$. At $Y = 800$, consumption is less than income by 100. Thus, $S = 100$ when $Y = 800$.

Y	–	C	=	S
Aggregate Income		Aggregate Consumption		Aggregate Saving
0		100		–100
80		160		–80
100		175		–75
200		250		–50
400		400		0
600		550		50
800		700		100
1,000		850		150

Other Determinants of Consumption

The assumption that consumption depends only on income is obviously a simplification. In practice, the decisions of households on how much to consume in a given period are also affected by their wealth, by the interest rate, and by their expectations of the future. Households with higher wealth are likely to spend more, other things being equal, than households with less wealth.

In 2007, Steve Schwarzman, CEO of Blackstone, a private equity firm, spent $3 million on a lavish 60th birthday party for himself, considerably more than most people would spend. While Schwarzman's spending is likely influenced by his income ($750 million in 2006/2007 combined), it also reflects his enormous wealth.

For many households, interest rates also figure in to consumption and saving decisions. Lower interest rates reduce the cost of borrowing, so lower interest rates are likely to stimulate spending. (Conversely, higher interest rates increase the cost of borrowing and are likely to decrease spending.)

Finally, as households think about what fraction of incremental income to consume versus save, their expectations about the future may also play a role. If households are optimistic and expect to do better in the future, they may spend more at present than if they think the future will be bleak.

Household expectations are also important regarding households' responses to changes in their income. If, for example, the government announces a tax cut, which increases after-tax income, households' responses to the tax cut will likely depend on whether the tax cut is expected to be temporary or permanent. If households expect that the tax cut will be in effect for only two years, their responses are likely to be smaller than if they expect the tax cut to be permanent.

We examine these issues in Chapter 31, where we take a closer look at household behavior regarding both consumption and labor supply. But for now, we will focus only on income as affecting consumption.

Planned Investment (I)

In Chapter 27, we present a theory as to why the investment decisions of firms are likely to be affected by the interest rate, where low interest rates stimulate investment and high interest rates discourage investment. Then in Chapter 31, we look more carefully at firms' decisions, including their investment decisions. For now, however, we are treating firms' investment decisions in a very simple way. We assume that the investment that firms plan to make, denoted I, is fixed. In particular, it does not depend on income. This assumption is depicted in Figure 23.5. In this figure, planned investment is 25 for all values of income.

FIGURE 23.5 The Planned Investment Function

For the time being, we will assume that planned investment is fixed. It does not change when income changes, so its graph is a horizontal line.

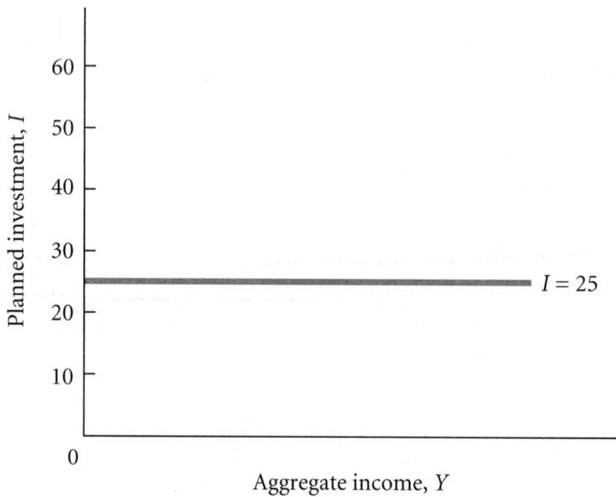

We know from Chapter 21 that investment includes both plant and equipment investment as well as the change in inventories. If a firm buys a machine, its stock of capital increases since machines are part of the capital stock. Part of the capital stock, however, also includes the stock of inventories. If an automobile firm has 10,000 cars in inventory, these cars are considered part of the firm's capital stock. If in the current period the firm produces 20,000 cars and sells 18,000, its change in inventories is the value of 2,000 cars and its capital stock has increased by the value of 2,000 cars.

The difference between planned investment and actual investment plays a major role in this chapter in the discussion of equilibrium. We will use I to refer to planned investment only. **Planned investment (I)** is the investment that firms plan to make. Remember that investment includes investment in plant and equipment as well as the change in inventories. **Actual investment** is the actual amount of investment that takes place. How can planned and actual investment differ? Consider the automobile firm again. Assume that it plans to buy $5 million in machines and to have no change in inventories. Assume that it buys the $5 million in machines, produces 20,000 cars expecting to sell all of them, and sells only 18,000. The firm's actual investment is the $5 million plus the value of 2,000 cars. So its actual investment was larger than its planned investment. Actual investment can differ from planned investment if a firm misestimates how much it will sell in the period. Any misestimation means that the change in its inventories, which is part of its actual investment, will be different from what it planned the change to be. We will see that the economy is in equilibrium only when planned investment is equal to actual investment. Otherwise, the actual change in inventories is different from planned: Firms have misestimated their sales.

planned investment (I) Those additions to capital stock and inventory that are planned by firms.

actual investment The actual amount of investment that takes place; it includes items such as unplanned changes in inventories.

ECONOMICS IN PRACTICE

Behavioral Biases in Saving Behavior

This chapter has described how saving is related to income. Economists have generally assumed that people make their saving decisions rationally, just as they make other decisions about choices in consumption and the labor market. Saving decisions involve thinking about trade-offs between present and future consumption. Recent work in behavioral economics has highlighted the role of psychological biases in saving behavior and has demonstrated that seemingly small changes in the way saving programs are designed can result in big behavioral changes.

Many retirement plans are designed with an opt-in feature. That is, you need to take some action to enroll. Typically, when you begin a job, you need to check yes on the retirement plan enrollment form. Recent work in economics by James Choi of Yale University and Bridget Madrian and Dennis Shea of the University of Chicago suggests that simply changing the enrollment process from the opt-in structure just described to an opt-out system in which people are automatically enrolled unless they check the no box dramatically increases enrollment in retirement pension plans. In one study, the change from an opt-in to an opt-out system increased pension plan enrollment after 3 months of work from 65 percent to 98 percent of workers.

Behavioral economists have administered a number of surveys suggesting that people, on average, think they save too little of their income for retirement. Shlomo Benartzi, from the University of California, Los Angeles, and Richard Thaler, from the University of Chicago, devised a retirement program to try to increase saving rates. Under this plan, called Save More Tomorrow, employees are offered a program that allows them to precommit to save more whenever they get a pay raise. Behavioral economists argue that people find this option attractive because it is easier for them to commit to making sacrifices tomorrow than it is for them to make those sacrifices today. (This is why many people resolve to diet some time in the future but continue to overeat today.) The Save More Tomorrow retirement plans have been put in place in a number of companies, including Vanguard, T. Rowe Price, and TIAA-CREF. Early results suggest dramatic increases in the saving rates of those enrolled, with saving rates quadrupling after 4 years and 4 pay raises.

The Determination of Equilibrium Output (Income)

Thus far, we have described the behavior of firms and households. We now discuss the nature of equilibrium and explain how the economy achieves equilibrium.

A number of definitions of **equilibrium** are used in economics. They all refer to the idea that at equilibrium, there is no tendency for change. In microeconomics, equilibrium is said to exist in a particular market (for example, the market for bananas) at the price for which the quantity demanded is equal to the quantity supplied. At this point, both suppliers and demanders are satisfied. The equilibrium price of a good is the price at which suppliers want to furnish the amount that demanders want to buy.

equilibrium Occurs when there is no tendency for change. In the macroeconomic goods market, equilibrium occurs when planned aggregate expenditure is equal to aggregate output.

planned aggregate expenditure (AE) The total amount the economy plans to spend in a given period. Equal to consumption plus planned investment: $AE \equiv C + I$.

To define equilibrium, we start with a new variable, **planned aggregate expenditure (AE)**. Planned aggregate expenditure is, by definition, consumption plus planned investment:

$$AE \equiv C + I$$

Note that I is planned investment spending only. It does not include any unplanned increases or decreases in inventory. Note also that this is a definition. Aggregate expenditure is always equal to $C + I$, and we write it with the triple equal sign.

The economy is defined to be in equilibrium when aggregate output (Y) is equal to planned aggregate expenditure (AE).

$$\text{Equilibrium: } Y = AE$$

Because AE is, by definition, $C + I$, equilibrium can also be written:

$$\text{Equilibrium: } Y = C + I$$

It will help in understanding the equilibrium concept to consider what happens if the economy is out of equilibrium. First, suppose aggregate output is greater than planned aggregate expenditure:

$$Y > C + I$$

$$\text{aggregate output} > \text{planned aggregate expenditure}$$

When output is greater than planned spending, there is unplanned inventory investment. Firms planned to sell more of their goods than they sold, and the difference shows up as an unplanned increase in inventories.

Next, suppose planned aggregate expenditure is greater than aggregate output:

$$C + I > Y$$

$$\text{planned aggregate expenditure} > \text{aggregate output}$$

When planned spending exceeds output, firms have sold more than they planned to. Inventory investment is smaller than planned. Planned and actual investment are not equal. Only when output is exactly matched by planned spending will there be no unplanned inventory investment. If there is unplanned inventory investment, this will be a state of disequilibrium. The mechanism by which the economy returns to equilibrium will be discussed later. Equilibrium in the goods market is achieved only when aggregate output (Y) and planned aggregate expenditure ($C + I$) are equal, or when actual and planned investment are equal.

Table 23.1 derives a planned aggregate expenditure schedule and shows the point of equilibrium for our numerical example. (Remember, all our calculations are based on $C = 100 + .75Y$). To determine planned aggregate expenditure, we add consumption spending (C) to planned investment spending (I) at every level of income. Glancing down columns 1 and 4, we see one and only one level at which aggregate output and planned aggregate expenditure are equal: $Y = 500$.

TABLE 23.1 Deriving the Planned Aggregate Expenditure Schedule and Finding Equilibrium. The Figures in Column 2 are Based on the Equation $C = 100 + .75Y$.

(1) Aggregate Output (Income) (Y)	(2) Aggregate Consumption (C)	(3) Planned Investment (I)	(4) Planned Aggregate Expenditure (AE) $C + I$	(5) Unplanned Inventory Change $Y - (C + I)$	(6) Equilibrium? ($Y = AE$?)
100	175	25	200	−100	No
200	250	25	275	−75	No
400	400	25	425	−25	No
500	475	25	500	0	Yes
600	550	25	575	+25	No
800	700	25	725	+75	No
1,000	850	25	875	+125	No

Figure 23.6 illustrates the same equilibrium graphically. Figure 23.6a adds planned investment, constant at 25, to consumption at every level of income. Because planned investment is a constant, the planned aggregate expenditure function is simply the consumption function displaced vertically by that constant amount. Figure 23.6b shows the planned aggregate expenditure function with the 45° line. The 45° line represents all points on the graph where the variables on the horizontal and vertical axes are equal. Any point on the 45° line is a potential equilibrium point. The planned aggregate expenditure function crosses the 45° line at a single point, where $Y = 500$. (The point at which the two lines cross is sometimes called the *Keynesian cross.*) At that point, $Y = C + I$.

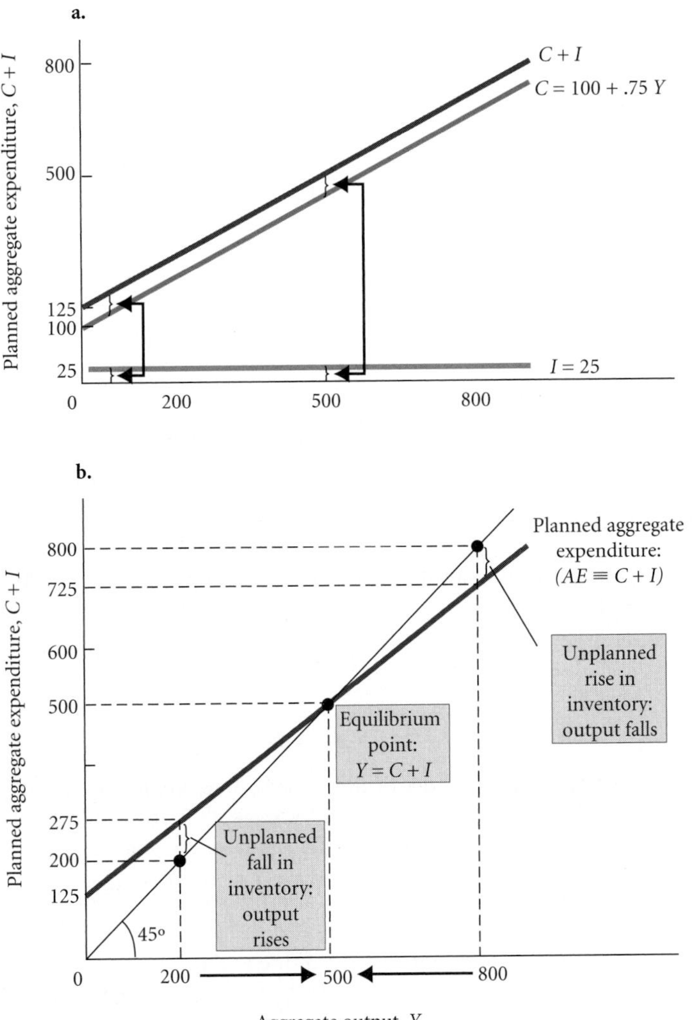

FIGURE 23.6 Equilibrium Aggregate Output

Equilibrium occurs when planned aggregate expenditure and aggregate output are equal. Planned aggregate expenditure is the sum of consumption spending and planned investment spending.

Now let us look at some other levels of aggregate output (income). First, consider $Y = 800$. Is this an equilibrium output? Clearly, it is not. At $Y = 800$, planned aggregate expenditure is 725 (see Table 23.1). This amount is less than aggregate output, which is 800. Because output is greater than planned spending, the difference ends up in inventory as unplanned inventory investment. In this case, unplanned inventory investment is 75. In the aggregate, firms have more inventory than desired. As a result, firms have an incentive to change their production plans going forward. In this sense, the economy will not be in equilibrium.

Next, consider $Y = 200$. Is this an equilibrium output? No. At $Y = 200$, planned aggregate expenditure is 275. Planned spending (AE) is greater than output (Y), and there is unplanned inventory disinvestment of 75. Again, firms in the aggregate will experience a different result from what they expected.

At $Y = 200$ and $Y = 800$, planned investment and actual investment are unequal. There is unplanned investment, and the system is out of balance. Only at $Y = 500$, where planned aggregate expenditure and aggregate output are equal, will planned investment equal actual investment.

Finally, let us find the equilibrium level of output (income) algebraically. Recall that we know the following:

$$(1)\ Y = C + I \qquad \text{(equilbrium)}$$

$$(2)\ C = 100 + .75Y \qquad \text{(consumption function)}$$

$$(3)\ I = 25 \qquad \text{(planned investment)}$$

By substituting (2) and (3) into (1), we get:

$$Y = \underbrace{100 + .75Y}_{C} + \underbrace{25.}_{I}$$

There is only one value of Y for which this statement is true, and we can find it by rearranging terms:

$$Y - .75Y = 100 + 25$$

$$Y - .75Y = 125$$

$$.25Y = 125$$

$$Y = \frac{125}{.25} = 500$$

The equilibrium level of output is 500, as shown in Table 23.1 and Figure 23.6.

The Saving/Investment Approach to Equilibrium

Because aggregate income must be saved or spent, by definition, $Y \equiv C + S$, which is an identity. The equilibrium condition is $Y = C + I$, but this is not an identity because it does not hold when we are out of equilibrium.[3] By substituting $C + S$ for Y in the equilibrium condition, we can write:

$$C + S = C + I$$

Because we can subtract C from both sides of this equation, we are left with:

$$S = I$$

Thus, only when planned investment equals saving will there be equilibrium.

Figure 23.7 reproduces the saving schedule derived in Figure 23.4 and the horizontal investment function from Figure 23.5. Notice that $S = I$ at one and only one level of aggregate output, $Y = 500$. At $Y = 500$, $C = 475$ and $I = 25$. In other words, $Y = C + I$; therefore, equilibrium exists.

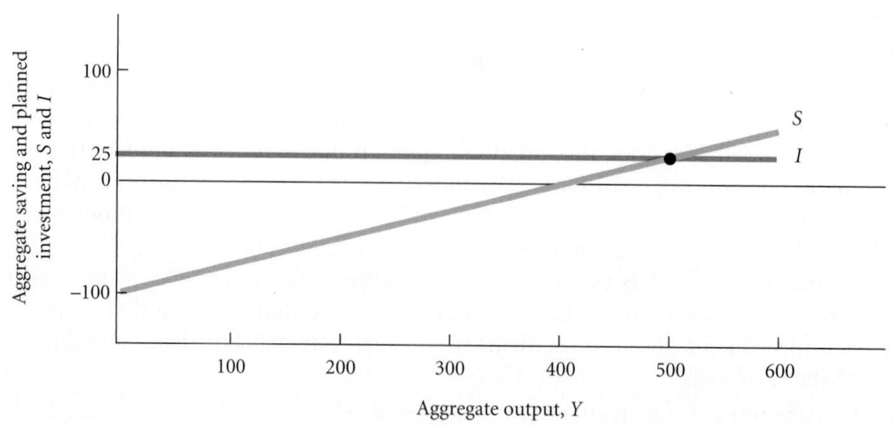

FIGURE 23.7 The $S = I$ Approach to Equilibrium

Aggregate output is equal to planned aggregate expenditure only when saving equals planned investment ($S = I$). Saving and planned investment are equal at $Y = 500$.

[3] It would be an identity if I included unplanned inventory accumulations—in other words, if I were actual investment instead of planned investment.

Adjustment to Equilibrium

We have defined equilibrium and learned how to find it, but we have said nothing about how firms might react to *disequilibrium*. Let us consider the actions firms might take when planned aggregate expenditure exceeds aggregate output (income).

We already know the only way firms can sell more than they produce is by selling some inventory. This means that when planned aggregate expenditure exceeds aggregate output, unplanned inventory reductions have occurred. It seems reasonable to assume that firms will respond to unplanned inventory reductions by increasing output. If firms increase output, income must also increase. (Output and income are two ways of measuring the same thing.) As GM builds more cars, it hires more workers (or pays its existing workforce for working more hours), buys more steel, uses more electricity, and so on. These purchases by GM represent income for the producers of labor, steel, electricity, and so on. When firms try to keep their inventories intact by increasing production, this will generate more income in the economy as a whole. This will lead to more consumption. Remember, when income rises, so does consumption. The adjustment process will continue as long as output (income) is below planned aggregate expenditure. If firms react to unplanned inventory reductions by increasing output, an economy with planned spending greater than output will adjust to equilibrium, with Y higher than before. If planned spending is less than output, there will be unplanned increases in inventories. In this case, firms will respond by reducing output. As output falls, income falls, consumption falls, and so on, until equilibrium is restored, with Y lower than before.

As Figure 23.6 shows, at any level of output above $Y = 500$, such as $Y = 800$, output will fall until it reaches equilibrium at $Y = 500$, and at any level of output below $Y = 500$, such as $Y = 200$, output will rise until it reaches equilibrium at $Y = 500$.[4]

The Multiplier

Now that we know how the equilibrium value of income is determined, we ask: How does the equilibrium level of output change when planned investment changes? If there is a sudden change in planned investment, how will output respond, if it responds at all? Suppose firms in aggregate decide that instead of a desired or planned investment of 25 as in the example we have been using, planned investment rises to 50. What will this do to the level of aggregate output in the economy? We also will see that, the change in equilibrium output is *greater* than the initial change in planned investment. Output changes by a *multiple* of the change in planned investment.

The **multiplier** is defined as the ratio of the change in the equilibrium level of output to a change in some exogenous variable. An **exogenous variable** is a variable that is assumed not to depend on the state of the economy—that is, a variable is exogenous if it does not change in response to changes in the economy. In this chapter, we consider planned investment to be exogenous. This simplifies our analysis and provides a foundation for later discussions.

multiplier The ratio of the change in the equilibrium level of output to a change in some exogenous variable.

exogenous variable A variable that is assumed not to depend on the state of the economy—that is, it does not change when the economy changes.

With planned investment exogenous, we can ask how much the equilibrium level of output changes when planned investment changes. Remember that we are not trying to explain *why* planned investment changes; we are simply asking how much the equilibrium level of output changes when (for whatever reason) planned investment changes. (Beginning in Chapter 27, we will no longer take planned investment as given and will explain how planned investment is determined.)

Consider a sustained increase in planned investment of 25—that is, suppose I increases from 25 to 50 and stays at 50. If equilibrium existed at $I = 25$, an increase in planned investment of 25 will cause a disequilibrium, with planned aggregate expenditure greater than aggregate output by 25. Firms immediately see unplanned reductions in their inventories. As a result, firms begin to increase output.

[4] In discussing simple supply and demand equilibrium in Chapters 3 and 4, we saw that when quantity supplied exceeds quantity demanded, the price falls and the quantity supplied declines. Similarly, when quantity demanded exceeds quantity supplied, the price rises and the quantity supplied increases. In the analysis here, we are ignoring potential changes in prices or in the price level and focusing on changes in the level of real output (income). Later, after we have introduced money and the price level into the analysis, prices will be very important. At this stage, however, only aggregate output (income) (Y) adjusts when aggregate expenditure exceeds aggregate output (with inventory falling) or when aggregate output exceeds aggregate expenditure (with inventory rising).

Let us say the increase in planned investment comes from an anticipated increase in travel that leads airlines to purchase more airplanes, car rental companies to increase purchases of automobiles, and bus companies to purchase more buses (all capital goods). The firms experiencing unplanned inventory declines will be automobile manufacturers, bus producers, and aircraft producers—GM, Ford, Boeing, and so on. In response to declining inventories of planes, buses, and cars, these firms will increase output.

Now suppose these firms raise output by the full 25 increase in planned investment. Does this restore equilibrium? No, it does not because when output goes up, people earn more income and a part of that income will be spent. This increases planned aggregate expenditure even further. In other words, an increase in I also leads indirectly to an increase in C. To produce more airplanes, Boeing has to hire more workers or ask its existing employees to work more hours. It also must buy more engines from General Electric, more tires from Goodyear, and so on. Owners of these firms will earn more profits, produce more, hire more workers, and pay out more in wages and salaries. This added income does not vanish into thin air. It is paid to households that spend some of it and save the rest. The added production leads to added income, which leads to added consumption spending.

If planned investment (I) goes up by 25 initially *and is sustained at this higher level*, an increase of output of 25 will *not* restore equilibrium because it generates even more consumption spending (C). People buy more consumer goods. There are unplanned reductions of inventories of basic consumption items—washing machines, food, clothing, and so on—and this prompts other firms to increase output. The cycle starts all over again.

Output and income can rise significantly more than the initial increase in planned investment, but how much and how large is the multiplier? This is answered graphically in Figure 23.8. Assume that the economy is in equilibrium at point A, where equilibrium output is 500. The increase in I of 25 shifts the $AE \equiv C + I$ curve up by 25 because I is higher by 25 at every level of income. The new equilibrium occurs at point B, where the equilibrium level of output is 600. Like point A, point B is on the 45° line and is an equilibrium value. Output (Y) has increased by 100 (600 − 500), or four times the initial increase in planned investment of 25, between point A and point B. The multiplier in this example is 4. At point B, aggregate spending is also higher by 100. If 25 of this additional 100 is investment (I), as we know it is, the remaining 75 is added consumption (C). From point A to point B then, $\Delta Y = 100$, $\Delta I = 25$, and $\Delta C = 75$.

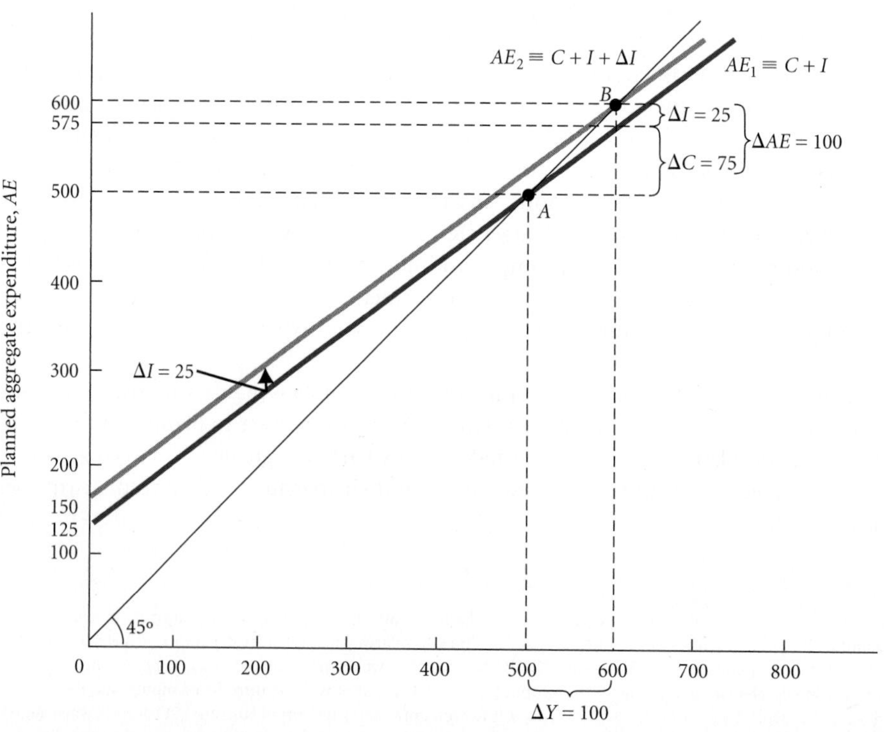

FIGURE 23.8

The Multiplier as Seen in the Planned Aggregate Expenditure Diagram

At point A, the economy is in equilibrium at $Y = 500$. When I increases by 25, planned aggregate expenditure is initially greater than aggregate output. As output rises in response, additional consumption is generated, pushing equilibrium output up by a multiple of the initial increase in I. The new equilibrium is found at point B, where $Y = 600$. Equilibrium output has increased by 100 (600 − 500), or *four times* the amount of the increase in planned investment.

Why doesn't the multiplier process go on forever? The answer is that only a fraction of the increase in income is consumed in each round. Successive increases in income become smaller and smaller in each round of the multiplier process, due to leakage as saving, until equilibrium is restored.

The size of the multiplier depends on the slope of the planned aggregate expenditure line. The steeper the slope of this line, the greater the change in output for a given change in investment. When planned investment is fixed, as in our example, the slope of the $AE \equiv C + I$ line is just the marginal propensity to consume ($\Delta C/\Delta Y$). The greater the *MPC*, the greater the multiplier. This should not be surprising. A large *MPC* means that consumption increases a great deal when income increases. The more consumption changes, the more output has to change to achieve equilibrium.

The Multiplier Equation

Is there a way to determine the size of the multiplier without using graphic analysis? Yes, there is.

Assume that the market is in equilibrium at an income level of $Y = 500$. Now suppose planned investment (I)—thus, planned aggregate expenditure (AE)—increases and remains higher by 25. Planned aggregate expenditure is greater than output, there is an unplanned inventory reduction, and firms respond by increasing output (income) (Y). This leads to a second round of increases, and so on.

What will restore equilibrium? Look at Figure 23.7 and recall: Planned aggregate expenditure ($AE \equiv C + I$) is not equal to aggregate output (Y) unless $S = I$; the leakage of saving must exactly match the injection of planned investment spending for the economy to be in equilibrium. Recall also that we assumed that planned investment jumps to a new, higher level and stays there; it is a *sustained* increase of 25 in planned investment spending. As income rises, consumption rises and so does saving. Our $S = I$ approach to equilibrium leads us to conclude that equilibrium will be restored only when saving has increased by exactly the amount of the initial increase in I. Otherwise, I will continue to be greater than S and $C + I$ will continue to be greater than Y. (The $S = I$ approach to equilibrium leads to an interesting paradox in the macroeconomy. See the following Economics in Practice, "The Paradox of Thrift.")

It is possible to figure how much Y must increase in response to the additional planned investment before equilibrium will be restored. Y will rise, pulling S up with it until the change in saving is exactly equal to the change in planned investment—that is, until S is again equal to I at its new higher level. Because added saving is a *fraction* of added income (the *MPS*), the increase in *income* required to restore equilibrium must be a *multiple* of the increase in planned investment.

Recall that the marginal propensity to save (*MPS*) is the fraction of a change in income that is saved. It is defined as the change in S (ΔS) over the change in income (ΔY):

$$MPS = \frac{\Delta S}{\Delta Y}$$

Because ΔS must be equal to ΔI for equilibrium to be restored, we can substitute ΔI for ΔS and solve:

$$MPS = \frac{\Delta I}{\Delta Y}$$

Therefore,

$$\Delta Y = \Delta I \times \frac{1}{MPS}$$

As you can see, the change in equilibrium income (ΔY) is equal to the initial change in planned investment (ΔI) times $1/MPS$. The multiplier is $1/MPS$:

$$\text{multiplier} \equiv \frac{1}{MPS}$$

Because $MPS + MPC \equiv 1$, $MPS \equiv 1 - MPC$. It follows that the multiplier is equal to

$$\text{multiplier} \equiv \frac{1}{1 - MPC}$$

ECONOMICS IN PRACTICE

The Paradox of Thrift

An interesting paradox can arise when households attempt to increase their saving. What happens if households become concerned about the future and want to save more today to be prepared for hard times tomorrow? If households increase their planned saving, the saving schedule in the graph below shifts upward from S_0 to S_1. The plan to save more is a plan to consume less, and the resulting drop in spending leads to a drop in income. Income drops by a multiple of the initial shift in the saving schedule. Before the increase in saving, equilibrium exists at point *A*, where $S_0 = I$ and $Y = 500$. Increased saving shifts the equilibrium to point *B*, the point at which $S_1 = I$. New equilibrium output is 300—a 200 decrease (ΔY) from the initial equilibrium.

By consuming less, households have actually *caused* the hard times about which they were apprehensive. Worse, the new equilibrium finds saving at the same level as it was before consumption dropped (25). In their attempt to save more, households have caused a contraction in output, and thus in income. They end up consuming less, but they have not saved any more.

It should be clear why saving at the new equilibrium is equal to saving at the old equilibrium. Equilibrium requires that saving equals planned investment, and because planned investment is unchanged, saving must remain unchanged for equilibrium to exist. This paradox shows that the interactions among sectors in the economy can be of crucial importance.

The paradox of thrift is "paradoxical" because it contradicts the widely held belief that "a penny saved is a penny earned." This may be true for an individual, but when society as a whole saves more, the result is a drop in income but no increased saving.

Does the paradox of thrift always hold? Recall our assumption that planned investment is fixed. Let us drop this assumption for a moment. If the extra saving that households want to do to ward off hard times is channeled into additional investment through financial markets, there is a shift up in the *I* schedule. The paradox could then be averted. If investment increases, a new equilibrium can be achieved at a higher level of saving and income. This result, however, depends critically on the existence of a channel through which additional household saving finances additional investment.

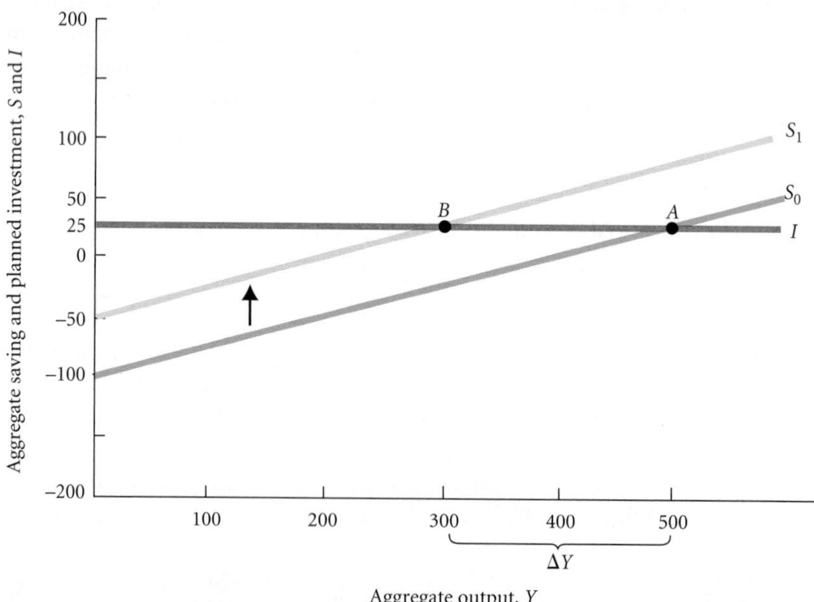

The Paradox of Thrift

An increase in planned saving from S_0 to S_1 causes equilibrium output to decrease from 500 to 300. The decreased consumption that accompanies increased saving leads to a contraction of the economy and to a reduction of income. But at the new equilibrium, saving is the same as it was at the initial equilibrium. Increased efforts to save have caused a drop in income but no overall change in saving.

In our example, the *MPC* is .75; so the *MPS* must equal 1 − .75, or .25. Thus, the multiplier is 1 divided by .25, or 4. The change in the equilibrium level of *Y* is 4 × 25, or 100.[5] Also note that the same analysis holds when planned investment falls. If planned investment falls by a certain amount and is sustained at this lower level, output will fall by a multiple of the reduction in *I*. As the initial shock is felt and firms cut output, they lay people off. The result: Income, and subsequently consumption, falls.

The Size of the Multiplier in the Real World

In considering the size of the multiplier, it is important to realize that the multiplier we derived in this chapter is based on a *very* simplified picture of the economy. First, we have assumed that planned investment is exogenous and does not respond to changes in the economy. Second, we have thus far ignored the role of government, financial markets, and the rest of the world in the macroeconomy. For these reasons, it would be a mistake to move on from this chapter thinking that national income can be increased by $100 billion simply by increasing planned investment spending by $25 billion.

As we relax these assumptions in the following chapters, you will see that most of what we add to make our analysis more realistic has the effect of *reducing* the size of the multiplier. For example:

1. The Appendix to Chapter 24 shows that when tax payments depend on income (as they do in the real world), the size of the multiplier is reduced. As the economy expands, tax payments increase and act as a drag on the economy. The multiplier effect is smaller.
2. We will see in Chapter 27 that planned investment (*I*) is not exogenous; instead, it depends on the interest rate in the economy. This too has the effect of reducing the size of the multiplier.
3. Thus far we have not discussed how the overall price level is determined in the economy. When we do (in Chapter 28), we will see that part of an expansion of the economy is likely to take the form of an increase in the price level instead of an increase in output. When this happens, the size of the multiplier is reduced.
4. The multiplier is also reduced when imports are introduced (in Chapter 35), because some domestic spending leaks into foreign markets.

These juicy tidbits give you something to look forward to as you proceed through the rest of this book. For now, however, it is enough to point out that in reality the size of the multiplier is about 1.4. That is, a sustained increase in exogenous spending of $10 billion into the U.S. economy can be expected to raise real GDP over time by about $14 billion. This is a far cry from the value of 4.0 that we used in this chapter.

Looking Ahead

In this chapter, we took the first step toward understanding how the economy works. We assumed that consumption depends on income, that planned investment is fixed, and that there is equilibrium. We discussed how the economy might adjust back to equilibrium when it is out of equilibrium. We also discussed the effects on equilibrium output from a change in planned investment and derived the multiplier. In the next chapter, we retain these assumptions and add the government to the economy.

---

[5] The multiplier can also be derived algebraically, as the Appendix to this chapter demonstrates.

SUMMARY

THE KEYNESIAN THEORY OF CONSUMPTION *p. 454*

1. Aggregate consumption is assumed to be a function of aggregate income.

2. The *marginal propensity to consume* (*MPC*) is the fraction of a change in income that is consumed, or spent. The *marginal propensity to save* (*MPS*) is the fraction of a change in income that is saved. Because all income must be saved or spent, $MPS + MPC \equiv 1$.

PLANNED INVESTMENT *p. 458*

3. Planned investment is assumed to be fixed. Planned investment may differ from actual investment because of unanticipated changes in inventories.

THE DETERMINATION OF EQUILIBRIUM OUTPUT (INCOME) *p. 459*

4. *Planned aggregate expenditure* (*AE*) equals consumption plus planned investment: $AE \equiv C + I$. *Equilibrium* in the goods market is achieved when planned aggregate expenditure equals aggregate output: $C + I = Y$. This holds if and only if planned investment and actual investment are equal.

5. Because aggregate income must be saved or spent, the equilibrium condition $Y = C + I$ can be rewritten as $C + S = C + I$, or $S = I$. Only when planned investment equals saving will there be equilibrium. This approach to equilibrium is the *saving/ investment approach* to equilibrium.

6. When planned aggregate expenditure exceeds aggregate output (*income*), there is an unplanned fall in inventories. Firms will increase output. This increased output leads to increased income and even more consumption. This process will continue as long as output (income) is below planned aggregate expenditure. If firms react to unplanned inventory reductions by increasing output, an economy with planned spending greater than output will adjust to a new equilibrium, with *Y* higher than before.

THE MULTIPLIER *p. 463*

7. Equilibrium output changes by a multiple of the change in planned investment or any other *exogenous variable*. The *multiplier* is $1/MPS$.

8. When households increase their planned saving, income decreases and saving does not change. Saving does not increase because in equilibrium, saving must equal planned investment and planned investment is fixed. If planned investment also increased, this *paradox of thrift* could be averted and a new equilibrium could be achieved at a higher level of saving and income. This result depends on the existence of a channel through which additional household saving finances additional investment.

REVIEW TERMS AND CONCEPTS

actual investment, *p. 458*
aggregate income, *p. 453*
aggregate output, *p. 453*
aggregate output (income) (*Y*), *p. 453*
aggregate saving (*S*), *p. 455*
consumption function, *p. 454*
equilibrium, *p. 459*
exogenous variable, *p. 463*
identity, *p. 455*
marginal propensity to consume (*MPC*), *p. 455*
marginal propensity to save (*MPS*), *p. 455*
multiplier, *p. 463*
planned aggregate expenditure (*AE*), *p. 460*
planned investment (*I*), *p. 458*

1. $S \equiv Y - C$
2. $MPC \equiv$ slope of consumption function $\equiv \dfrac{\Delta C}{\Delta Y}$
3. $MPC + MPS \equiv 1$
4 $AE \equiv C + I$
5. Equilibrium condition: $Y = AE$ or $Y = C + I$
6. Saving/investment approach to equilibrium: $S = I$
7. Multiplier $\equiv \dfrac{1}{MPS} \equiv \dfrac{1}{1 - MPC}$

PROBLEMS

Visit www.myeconlab.com to complete the problems marked in orange online. You will receive instant feedback on your answers, tutorial help, and access to additional practice problems.

1. Briefly define the following terms and explain the relationship between them:

MPC . . . . Multiplier
Actual investment . . . . Planned investment
Aggregate expenditure . . . . Real GDP
Aggregate output . . . . Aggregate income

The Government and Fiscal Policy

24

CHAPTER OUTLINE

Nothing in macroeconomics or microeconomics arouses as much controversy as the role of government in the economy.

In microeconomics, the active presence of government in regulating competition, providing roads and education, and redistributing income is applauded by those who believe a free market simply does not work well when left to its own devices. Opponents of government intervention say it is the government, not the market, that performs badly. They say bureaucracy and inefficiency could be eliminated or reduced if the government played a smaller role in the economy.

In macroeconomics, the debate over what the government can and should do has a similar flavor, although the issues are somewhat different. At one end of the spectrum are the Keynesians and their intellectual descendants who believe that the macroeconomy is likely to fluctuate too much if left on its own and that the government should smooth out fluctuations in the business cycle. These ideas can be traced to Keynes's analysis in *The General Theory*, which suggests that governments can use their taxing and spending powers to increase aggregate expenditure (and thereby stimulate aggregate output) in recessions or depressions. At the other end of the spectrum are those who claim that government spending is incapable of stabilizing the economy, or worse, is destabilizing and harmful.

Perhaps the one thing most people can agree on is that, like it or not, governments are important actors in the economies of virtually all countries. For this reason alone, it is worth our while to analyze the way government influences the functioning of the macroeconomy.

The government has a variety of powers—including regulating firms' entry into and exit from an industry, setting standards for product quality, setting minimum wage levels, and regulating the disclosure of information—but in macroeconomics, we study a government with general but limited powers. Specifically, government can affect the macroeconomy through two policy channels: fiscal policy and monetary policy. **Fiscal policy**, the focus of this chapter, refers to the government's spending and taxing behavior—in other words, its budget policy. (The word *fiscal* comes from the root *fisc*, which refers to the "treasury" of a government.) Fiscal policy is generally divided into three categories: (1) policies concerning government purchases of goods and services, (2) policies concerning taxes, and (3) policies concerning transfer payments (such as unemployment compensation, Social Security benefits, welfare payments, and veterans' benefits) to households. **Monetary policy**, which we consider in the next two chapters, refers to the behavior of the nation's central bank, the Federal Reserve, concerning the nation's money supply.

fiscal policy The government's spending and taxing policies.

monetary policy The behavior of the Federal Reserve concerning the nation's money supply.

Government in the Economy

Given the scope and power of local, state, and federal governments, there are some matters over which they exert great control and some matters beyond their control. We need to distinguish between variables that a government controls directly and variables that are a consequence of government decisions *combined with the state of the economy.*

For example, tax rates are controlled by the government. By law, Congress has the authority to decide who and what should be taxed and at what rate. Tax *revenue*, on the other hand, is not subject to complete control by the government. Revenue from the personal income tax system depends on personal tax rates (which Congress sets) *and* on the income of the household sector (which depends on many factors not under direct government control, such as how much households decide to work). Revenue from the corporate profits tax depends on both corporate profits tax rates and the size of corporate profits. The government controls corporate tax rates but not the size of corporate profits.

Some government spending also depends on government decisions and on the state of the economy. For example, in the United States, the unemployment insurance program pays benefits to unemployed people. When the economy goes into a recession, the number of unemployed workers increases and so does the level of government unemployment insurance payments.

Because taxes and spending often go up or down in response to changes in the economy instead of as the result of deliberate decisions by policy makers, we will occasionally use **discretionary fiscal policy** to refer to changes in taxes or spending that are the result of deliberate changes in government policy.

discretionary fiscal policy Changes in taxes or spending that are the result of deliberate changes in government policy.

Government Purchases (G), Net Taxes (T), and Disposable Income (Y_d)

We now add the government to the simple economy in Chapter 23. To keep things simple, we will combine two government activities—the collection of taxes and the payment of transfer payments—into a category we call **net taxes (T)**. Specifically, net taxes are equal to the tax payments made to the government by firms and households minus transfer payments made to households by the government. The other variable we will consider is government purchases of goods and services (G).

net taxes (T) Taxes paid by firms and households to the government minus transfer payments made to households by the government.

Our earlier discussions of household consumption did not take taxes into account. We assumed that all the income generated in the economy was spent or saved by households. When we take into account the role of government, as Figure 24.1 does, we see that as income (Y) flows toward households, the government takes income from households in the form of net taxes (T). The income that ultimately gets to households is called **disposable**, or **after-tax, income (Y_d)**:

disposable, *or* after-tax, income (Y_d) Total income minus net taxes: $Y - T$.

$$\text{disposable income} \equiv \text{total income} - \text{net taxes}$$
$$Y_d \equiv Y - T$$

Y_d excludes taxes paid by households and includes transfer payments made to households by the government. For now, we are assuming that T does not depend on Y—that is, net taxes do not depend on income. This assumption is relaxed in Appendix B to this chapter. Taxes that do not depend on income are sometimes called *lump-sum taxes.*

As Figure 24.1 shows, the disposable income (Y_d) of households must end up as either consumption (C) or saving (S). Thus,

$$Y_d \equiv C + S$$

This equation is an identity—something that is always true.

Because disposable income is aggregate income (Y) minus net taxes (T), we can write another identity:

$$Y - T \equiv C + S$$

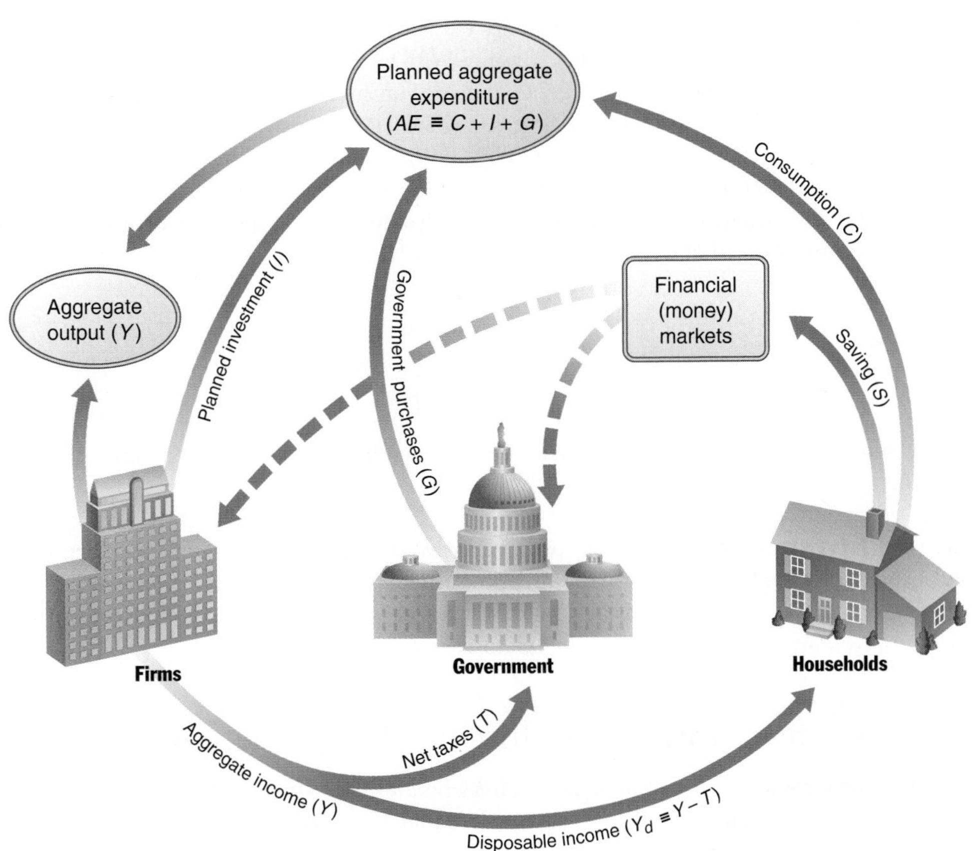

◀ **FIGURE 24.1**
Adding Net Taxes (T) and Government Purchases (G) to the Circular Flow of Income

By adding T to both sides:

$$Y \equiv C + S + T$$

This identity says that aggregate income gets cut into three pieces. Government takes a slice (net taxes, T), and then households divide the rest between consumption (C) and saving (S).

Because governments spend money on goods and services, we need to expand our definition of planned aggregate expenditure. Planned aggregate expenditure (AE) is the sum of consumption spending by households (C), planned investment by business firms (I), *and* government purchases of goods and services (G).

$$AE \equiv C + I + G$$

A government's **budget deficit** is the difference between what it spends (G) and what it collects in taxes (T) in a given period:

budget deficit The difference between what a government spends and what it collects in taxes in a given period: $G - T$.

$$\text{budget deficit} \equiv G - T$$

If G exceeds T, the government must borrow from the public to finance the deficit. It does so by selling Treasury bonds and bills (more on this later). In this case, a part of household saving (S) goes to the government. The dashed lines in Figure 24.1 mean that some S goes to firms to finance investment projects and some goes to the government to finance its deficit. If G is less than T, which means that the government is spending less than it is collecting in taxes, the government is running a *surplus*. A budget surplus is simply a negative budget deficit.

Adding Taxes to the Consumption Function In Chapter 23, we assumed that aggregate consumption (C) depends on aggregate income (Y), and for the sake of illustration, we used a specific linear consumption function:

$$C = a + bY$$

where b is the marginal propensity to consume. We need to modify this consumption function because we have added government to the economy. With taxes a part of the picture, it makes sense to assume that disposable income (Y_d), instead of before-tax income (Y), determines consumption behavior. If you earn a million dollars but have to pay $950,000 in taxes, you have no more disposable income than someone who earns only $50,000 but pays no taxes. What you have available for spending on current consumption is your disposable income, not your before-tax income.

To modify our aggregate consumption function to incorporate disposable income instead of before-tax income, instead of $C = a + bY$, we write

$$C = a + bY_d$$

or

$$C = a + b(Y - T)$$

Our consumption function now has consumption depending on disposable income instead of before-tax income.

Planned Investment What about planned investment? The government can affect investment behavior through its tax treatment of depreciation and other tax policies. Investment may also vary with economic conditions and interest rates, as we will see later. For our present purposes, however, we continue to assume that planned investment (I) is fixed.

The Determination of Equilibrium Output (Income)

We know from Chapter 23 that equilibrium occurs where $Y = AE$—that is, where aggregate output equals planned aggregate expenditure. Remember that planned aggregate expenditure in an economy with a government is $AE \equiv C + I + G$, so equilibrium is

$$Y = C + I + G$$

The equilibrium analysis in Chapter 23 applies here also. If output (Y) exceeds planned aggregate expenditure ($C + I + G$), there will be an unplanned increase in inventories—actual investment will exceed planned investment. Conversely, if $C + I + G$ exceeds Y, there will be an unplanned decrease in inventories.

An example will illustrate the government's effect on the macroeconomy and the equilibrium condition. First, our consumption function, $C = 100 + .75Y$ before we introduced the government sector, now becomes

$$C = 100 + .75Y_d$$

or

$$C = 100 + .75(Y - T)$$

Second, we assume that G is 100 and T is 100.[1] In other words, the government is running a balanced budget, financing all of its spending with taxes. Third, we assume that planned investment (I) is 100.

Table 24.1 calculates planned aggregate expenditure at several levels of disposable income. For example, at $Y = 500$, disposable income is $Y - T$, or 400. Therefore, $C = 100 + .75(400) = 400$. Assuming that I is fixed at 100 and assuming that G is fixed at 100, planned aggregate expenditure is 600 ($C + I + G = 400 + 100 + 100$). Because output ($Y$) is only 500, planned spending is greater than output by 100. As a result, there is an unplanned inventory decrease of 100, giving firms an incentive to raise output. Thus, output of 500 is below equilibrium.

[1] As we pointed out earlier, the government does not have complete control over tax revenues and transfer payments. We ignore this problem here, however, and set T, tax revenues minus transfers, at a fixed amount. Things will become more realistic later in this chapter and in Appendix B.

TABLE 24.1 Finding Equilibrium for I = 100, G = 100, and T = 100

(1) Output (Income) Y	(2) Net Taxes T	(3) Disposable Income $Y_d \equiv Y - T$	(4) Consumption Spending $C = 100 + .75\ Y_d$	(5) Saving S $Y_d - C$	(6) Planned Investment Spending I	(7) Government Purchases G	(8) Planned Aggregate Expenditure $C + I + G$	(9) Unplanned Inventory Change $Y - (C + I + G)$	(10) Adjustment to Disequilibrium
300	100	200	250	−50	100	100	450	−150	Output ↑
500	100	400	400	0	100	100	600	−100	Output ↑
700	100	600	550	50	100	100	750	−50	Output ↑
900	100	800	700	100	100	100	900	0	Equilibrium
1,100	100	1,000	850	150	100	100	1,050	+50	Output ↓
1,300	100	1,200	1,000	200	100	100	1,200	+100	Output ↓
1,500	100	1,400	1,150	250	100	100	1,350	+150	Output ↓

If $Y = 1{,}300$, then $Y_d = 1{,}200$, $C = 1{,}000$, and planned aggregate expenditure is 1,200. Here planned spending is *less* than output, there will be an unplanned inventory increase of 100, and firms have an incentive to cut back output. Thus, output of 1,300 is above equilibrium. Only when output is 900 are output and planned aggregate expenditure equal, and only at $Y = 900$ does equilibrium exist.

In Figure 24.2, we derive the same equilibrium level of output graphically. First, the consumption function is drawn, taking into account net taxes of 100. The old function was $C = 100 + .75Y$. The new function is $C = 100 + .75(Y - T)$ or $C = 100 + .75(Y - 100)$, rewritten as $C = 100 + .75Y - 75$, or $C = 25 + .75Y$. For example, consumption at an income of zero is 25 ($C = 25 + .75Y = 25 + .75(0) = 25$). The marginal propensity to consume has not changed—we assume that it remains .75. Note that the consumption function in Figure 24.2 plots the points in columns 1 and 4 of Table 24.1.

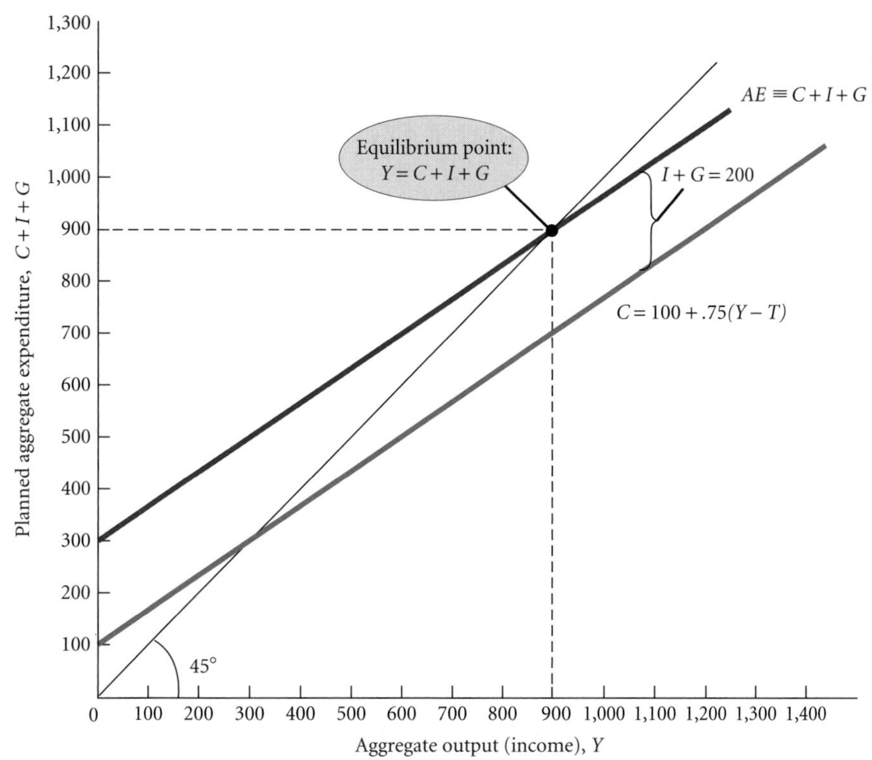

FIGURE 24.2 Finding Equilibrium Output/Income Graphically

Because G and I are both fixed at 100, the aggregate expenditure function is the new consumption function displaced upward by $I + G = 200$. Equilibrium occurs at $Y = C + I + G = 900$.

Planned aggregate expenditure, recall, adds planned investment to consumption. Now in addition to 100 in investment, we have government purchases of 100. Because I and G are constant at 100 each at all levels of income, we add $I + G = 200$ to consumption at every level of income. The result is the new *AE* curve. This curve is just a plot of the points in columns 1 and 8 of Table 24.1. The 45° line helps us find the equilibrium level of real output, which, we already know, is 900. If you examine any level of output above or below 900, you will find disequilibrium. Look, for example, at $Y = 500$ on the graph. At this level, planned aggregate expenditure is 600, but output is only 500. Inventories will fall below what was planned, and firms will have an incentive to increase output.

The Saving/Investment Approach to Equilibrium As in the last chapter, we can also examine equilibrium using the saving/investment approach. Look at the circular flow of income in Figure 24.1. The government takes out net taxes (T) from the flow of income—a leakage—and households save (S) some of their income—also a leakage from the flow of income. The planned spending injections are government purchases (G) and planned investment (I). If leakages ($S + T$) equal planned injections ($I + G$), there is equilibrium:

saving/investment approach to equilibrium: $S + T = I + G$

To derive this, we know that in equilibrium, aggregate output (income) (Y) equals planned aggregate expenditure (AE). By definition, AE equals $C + I + G$; and by definition, Y equals $C + S + T$. Therefore, at equilibrium

$$C + S + T = C + I + G$$

Subtracting C from both sides leaves:

$$S + T = I + G$$

Note that equilibrium does *not* require that $G = T$ (a balanced government budget) or that $S = I$. It is only necessary that the sum of S and T equals the sum of I and G.

Column 5 of Table 24.1 calculates aggregate saving by subtracting consumption from disposal income at every level of disposable income ($S \equiv Y_d - C$). Because I and G are fixed, $I + G$ equals 200 at every level of income. Using the table to add saving and taxes ($S + T$), we see that $S + T$ equals 200 only at $Y = 900$. Thus, the equilibrium level of output (income) is 900, the same answer we arrived at through numerical and graphic analysis.

Fiscal Policy at Work: Multiplier Effects

You can see from Figure 24.2 that if the government were able to change the levels of either G or T, it would be able to change the equilibrium level of output (income). At this point, we are assuming that the government controls G and T. In this section, we will review three multipliers:

- Government spending multiplier
- Tax multiplier
- Balanced-budget multiplier

The Government Spending Multiplier

Suppose you are the chief economic adviser to the president and the economy is sitting at the equilibrium output pictured in Figure 24.2. Output and income are 900, and the government is currently buying 100 worth of goods and services each year and is financing them with 100 in taxes. The budget is balanced. In addition, firms are investing (producing capital goods) 100. The president calls you into the Oval Office and says, "Unemployment is too high. We need to lower unemployment by increasing output and income." After some research, you determine that an acceptable unemployment rate can be achieved only if aggregate output increases to 1,100.

You now need to determine how the government can use taxing and spending policy—fiscal policy—to increase the equilibrium level of national output. Suppose the president has let it be known that taxes must remain at present levels—Congress just passed a major tax reform package—so adjusting T is out of the question for several years. That leaves you with G. Your only option is to increase government spending while holding taxes constant.

To increase spending without raising taxes (which provides the government with revenue to spend), the government must borrow. When G is bigger than T, the government runs a deficit and the difference between G and T must be borrowed. For the moment, we will ignore the possible effect of the deficit and focus only on the effect of a higher G with T constant.

Meanwhile, the president is awaiting your answer. How much of an increase in spending would be required to generate an increase of 200 in the equilibrium level of output, pushing it from 900 to 1,100 and reducing unemployment to the president's acceptable level? You might be tempted to say that because we need to increase income by 200 (1,100 − 900), we should increase government spending by the same amount—but what will happen? The increased government spending will throw the economy out of equilibrium. Because G is a component of aggregate spending, planned aggregate expenditure will increase by 200. Planned spending will be greater than output, inventories will be lower than planned, and firms will have an incentive to increase output. Suppose output rises by the desired 200. You might think, "We increased spending by 200 and output by 200, so equilibrium is restored."

There is more to the story than this. The moment output rises, the economy is generating more income. This was the desired effect: the creation of more employment. The newly employed workers are also consumers, and some of their income gets spent. With higher consumption spending, planned spending will be greater than output, inventories will be lower than planned, and firms will raise output (and thus raise income) again. This time firms are responding to the new consumption spending. Already, total income is over 1,100.

This story should sound familiar. It is the multiplier in action. Although this time it is government spending (G) that is changed rather than planned investment (I), the effect is the same as the multiplier effect we described in Chapter 23. An increase in government spending has the same impact on the equilibrium level of output and income as an increase in planned investment. A dollar of extra spending from either G or I is identical with respect to its impact on equilibrium output. The equation for the government spending multiplier is the same as the equation for the multiplier for a change in planned investment.

$$\text{government spending multiplier} \equiv \frac{1}{MPS}$$

We derive the government spending multiplier algebraically in Appendix A to this chapter.

Formally, the **government spending multiplier** is defined as the ratio of the change in the equilibrium level of output to a change in government spending. This is the same definition we used in the previous chapter, but now the autonomous variable is government spending instead of planned investment.

government spending multiplier The ratio of the change in the equilibrium level of output to a change in government spending.

Remember that we were thinking of increasing government spending (G) by 200. We can use the multiplier analysis to see what the new equilibrium level of Y would be for an increase in G of 200. The multiplier in our example is 4. (Because b—the MPC—is .75, the MPS must be $1 - .75 = .25$; and $1/.25 = 4$.) Thus, Y will increase by 800 (4×200). Because the initial level of Y was 900, the new equilibrium level of Y is $900 + 800 = 1{,}700$ when G is increased by 200.

The level of 1,700 is much larger than the level of 1,100 that we calculated as being necessary to lower unemployment to the desired level. Let us back up then. If we want Y to increase by 200 and if the multiplier is 4, we need G to increase by only $200/4 = 50$. If G changes by 50, the equilibrium level of Y will change by 200 and the new value of Y will be 1,100 (900 + 200), as desired.

Looking at Table 24.2, we can check our answer to make sure it is an equilibrium. Look first at the old equilibrium of 900. When government purchases (G) were 100, aggregate output (income) was equal to planned aggregate expenditure ($AE \equiv C + I + G$) at $Y = 900$. Now G has increased to 150. At $Y = 900$, $(C + I + G)$ is greater than Y, there is an unplanned fall in inventories, and output will rise but by how much? The multiplier told us that equilibrium income would rise by four times the 50 change in G. Y should rise by $4 \times 50 = 200$, from 900 to 1,100, before equilibrium is restored. Let us check. If $Y = 1{,}100$, consumption is $C = 100 + .75Y_d = 100 + .75(1{,}000) = 850$. Because I equals 100 and G now equals 100 (the original level of G) + 50 (the additional G brought about by the fiscal policy change) = 150, $C + I + G = 850 + 100 + 150 = 1{,}100$. $Y = AE$, and the economy is in equilibrium.

TABLE 24.2 Finding Equilibrium After a Government Spending Increase of 50 (G Has Increased from 100 in Table 24.1 to 150 Here)

(1) Output (Income) Y	(2) Net Taxes T	(3) Disposable Income $Y_d \equiv Y - T$	(4) Consumption Spending $C = 100 + .75\,Y_d$	(5) Saving S $Y_d - C$	(6) Planned Investment Spending I	(7) Government Purchases G	(8) Planned Aggregate Expenditure $C + I + G$	(9) Unplanned Inventory Change $Y - (C + I + G)$	(10) Adjustment to Disequilibrium
300	100	200	250	−50	100	150	500	−200	Output ↑
500	100	400	400	0	100	150	650	−150	Output ↑
700	100	600	550	50	100	150	800	−100	Output ↑
900	100	800	700	100	100	150	950	−50	Output ↑
1,100	100	1,000	850	150	100	150	1,100	0	Equilibrium
1,300	100	1,200	1,000	200	100	150	1,250	+50	Output ↓

The graphic solution to the president's problem is presented in Figure 24.3. An increase of 50 in G shifts the planned aggregate expenditure function up by 50. The new equilibrium income occurs where the new AE line (AE_2) crosses the 45° line, at $Y = 1{,}100$.

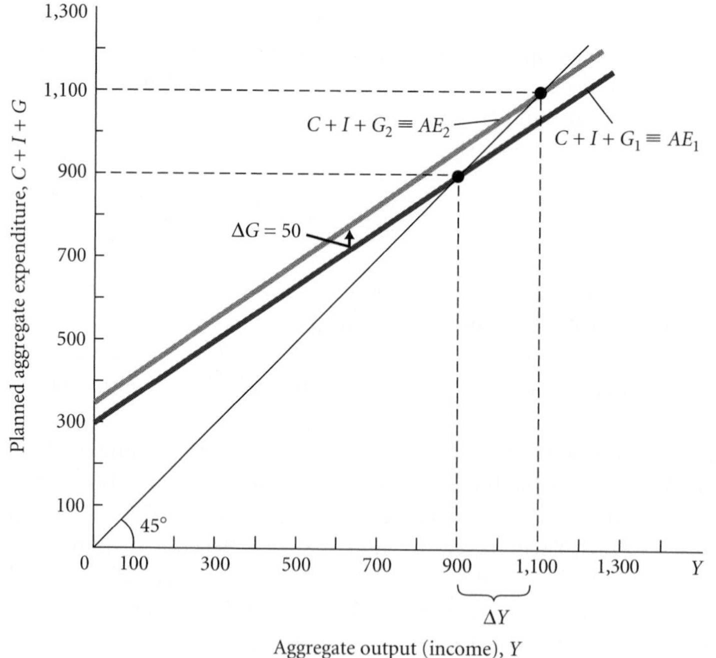

▸ FIGURE 24.3
The Government Spending Multiplier
Increasing government spending by 50 shifts the AE function up by 50. As Y rises in response, additional consumption is generated. Overall, the equilibrium level of Y increases by 200, from 900 to 1,100.

The Tax Multiplier

Remember that fiscal policy comprises policies concerning government spending *and* policies concerning taxation. To see what effect a change in tax policy has on the economy, imagine the following. You are still chief economic adviser to the president, but now you are instructed to devise a plan to reduce unemployment to an acceptable level *without* increasing the level of government spending. In your plan, instead of increasing government spending (G), you decide to cut taxes and maintain the current level of spending. A tax cut increases disposable income, which is likely to lead to added consumption spending. (Remember our general rule that increased income leads to increased consumption.) Would the decrease in taxes affect aggregate output (income) the same as an increase in *G*?

A decrease in taxes would increase income. The government spends no less than it did before the tax cut, and households find that they have a larger after-tax (or disposable) income than they had before. This leads to an increase in consumption. Planned aggregate expenditure will increase, which will lead to inventories being lower than planned, which will lead to a rise in output. When output rises, more workers will be employed and more income will be generated, causing a second-round increase in consumption, and so on. Thus, income will increase by a multiple of the decrease in taxes, but there is a "wrinkle." The multiplier for a change in taxes is *not the same* as the multiplier for a change in government spending. Why does the **tax multiplier**—the ratio of change in the equilibrium level of output to a change in taxes—differ from the spending multiplier? To answer that question, we need to compare the ways in which a tax cut and a spending increase work their way through the economy.

tax multiplier The ratio of change in the equilibrium level of output to a change in taxes.

Look at Figure 24.1 on p. 473. When the government increases spending, there is an immediate and direct impact on the economy's *total* spending. Because *G* is a component of planned aggregate expenditure, an increase in *G* leads to a dollar-for-dollar increase in planned aggregate expenditure. When taxes are cut, there is no direct impact on spending. Taxes enter the picture only because they have an effect on the household's disposable income, which influences household's consumption (which is part of total spending). As Figure 24.1 shows, the tax cut flows through households before affecting aggregate expenditure.

Let us assume that the government decides to cut taxes by $1. By how much would spending increase? We already know the answer. The marginal propensity to consume (*MPC*) tells us how much consumption spending changes when disposable income changes. In the example running through this chapter, the marginal propensity to consume out of disposable income is .75. This means that if households' after-tax incomes rise by $1.00, they will increase their consumption not by the full $1.00, but by only $0.75.[2]

In summary, when government spending increases by $1, planned aggregate expenditure increases initially by the full amount of the rise in *G*, or $1. When taxes are cut, however, the initial increase in planned aggregate expenditure is only the *MPC* times the change in taxes. Because the initial increase in planned aggregate expenditure is smaller for a tax cut than for a government spending increase, the final effect on the equilibrium level of income will be smaller.

We figure the size of the tax multiplier in the same way we derived the multiplier for an increase in investment and an increase in government purchases. The final change in the equilibrium level of output (income) (*Y*) is

$$\Delta Y = (\text{initial increase in aggregate expenditure}) \times \left(\frac{1}{MPS}\right)$$

Because the initial change in aggregate expenditure caused by a tax change of ΔT is $(-\Delta T \times MPC)$, we can solve for the tax multiplier by substitution:

$$\Delta Y = (-\Delta T \times MPC) \times \left(\frac{1}{MPS}\right) = -\Delta T \times \left(\frac{MPC}{MPS}\right)$$

Because a tax cut will cause an *increase* in consumption expenditures and output and a tax increase will cause a *reduction* in consumption expenditures and output, the tax multiplier is a negative multiplier:

$$\text{tax multiplier} \equiv -\left(\frac{MPC}{MPS}\right)$$

We derive the tax multiplier algebraically in Appendix A to this chapter.

[2] What happens to the other $0.25? Remember that whatever households do not consume is, by definition, saved. The other $0.25 thus gets allocated to saving.

If the *MPC* is .75, as in our example, the multiplier is $-.75/.25 = -3$. A tax cut of 100 will increase the equilibrium level of output by $-100 \times -3 = 300$. This is very different from the effect of our government spending multiplier of 4. Under those same conditions, a 100 increase in *G* will increase the equilibrium level of output by 400 (100×4).

The Balanced-Budget Multiplier

We have now discussed (1) changing government spending with no change in taxes and (2) changing taxes with no change in government spending. What if government spending and taxes are increased by the same amount? That is, what if the government decides to pay for its extra spending by increasing taxes by the same amount? The government's budget deficit would not change because the increase in expenditures would be matched by an increase in tax income.

You might think in this case that equal increases in government spending and taxes have no effect on equilibrium income. After all, the extra government spending equals the extra amount of tax revenues collected by the government. This is not so. Take, for example, a government spending increase of $40 billion. We know from the preceding analysis that an increase in *G* of 40, with taxes (*T*) held constant, should increase the equilibrium level of income by $40 \times$ the government spending multiplier. The multiplier is $1/MPS$ or $1/.25 = 4$. The equilibrium level of income should rise by 160 (40×4).

Now suppose that instead of keeping tax revenues constant, we finance the 40 increase in government spending with an equal increase in taxes so as to maintain a balanced budget. What happens to aggregate spending as a result of the rise in *G* and the rise in *T*? There are two initial effects. First, government spending rises by 40. This effect is direct, immediate, and positive. Now the government also collects 40 more in taxes. The tax increase has a *negative* impact on overall spending in the economy, but it does not fully offset the increase in government spending.

The final impact of a tax increase on aggregate expenditure depends on how households respond to it. The only thing we know about household behavior so far is that households spend 75 percent of their added income and save 25 percent. We know that when disposable income falls, both consumption and saving are reduced. A tax *increase* of 40 reduces disposable income by 40, and that means consumption falls by $40 \times MPC$. Because $MPC = .75$, consumption falls by 30 $(40 \times .75)$. The net result in the beginning is that government spending rises by 40 and consumption spending falls by 30. Aggregate expenditure increases by 10 right after the simultaneous balanced-budget increases in *G* and *T*.

So a balanced-budget increase in *G* and *T* will raise output, but by how much? How large is this **balanced-budget multiplier**? The answer may surprise you:

balanced-budget multiplier The ratio of change in the equilibrium level of output to a change in government spending where the change in government spending is balanced by a change in taxes so as not to create any deficit. The balanced-budget multiplier is equal to 1: The change in *Y* resulting from the change in *G* and the equal change in *T* are exactly the same size as the initial change in *G* or *T*.

$$\text{balanced-budget multiplier} \equiv 1$$

Let us combine what we know about the tax multiplier and the government spending multiplier to explain this. To find the final effect of a simultaneous increase in government spending and increase in net taxes, we need to add the multiplier effects of the two. The government spending multiplier is $1/MPS$. The tax multiplier is $-MPC/MPS$. Their sum is $(1/MPS) + (-MPC/MPS) \equiv (1 - MPC)/MPS$. Because $MPC + MPS \equiv 1$, $1 - MPC \equiv MPS$. This means that $(1 - MPC)/MPS \equiv MPS/MPS \equiv 1$. (We also derive the balanced-budget multiplier in Appendix A to this chapter.)

Returning to our example, recall that by using the government spending multiplier, a 40 increase in *G* would *raise* output at equilibrium by 160 $(40 \times$ the government spending multiplier of 4). By using the tax multiplier, we know that a tax hike of 40 will *reduce* the equilibrium level of output by 120 $(40 \times$ the tax multiplier, $-3)$. The net effect is 160 minus 120, or 40. It should be clear then that the effect on equilibrium *Y* is equal to the balanced increase in *G* and *T*. In other words, the net increase in the equilibrium level of *Y* resulting from the change in *G* and the change in *T* are exactly the size of the initial change in *G* or *T*.

If the president wanted to raise *Y* by 200 without increasing the deficit, a simultaneous increase in *G* and *T* of 200 would do it. To see why, look at the numbers in Table 24.3. In Table 24.1, we saw an equilibrium level of output at 900. With both *G* and *T* up by 200, the new equilibrium is 1,100—higher by 200. At no other level of *Y* do we find $(C + I + G) = Y$. An increase in government spending has a direct initial effect on planned aggregate expenditure; a tax increase does not. The initial effect of the tax increase is that households cut consumption by the *MPC* times the change in taxes. This change in consumption is less than the change in taxes because the *MPC* is less than 1. The positive stimulus from the government spending increase is thus greater than the negative stimulus from the tax increase. The net effect is that the balanced-budget multiplier is 1.

TABLE 24.3 Finding Equilibrium After a Balanced-Budget Increase in *G* and *T* of 200 Each (Both *G* and *T* Have Increased from 100 in Table 24.1 to 300 Here)

(1) Output (Income) Y	(2) Net Taxes T	(3) Disposable Income $Y_d \equiv Y - T$	(4) Consumption Spending $C = 100 + .75\,Y_d$	(5) Planned Investment Spending I	(6) Government Purchases G	(7) Planned Aggregate Expenditure $C + I + G$	(8) Unplanned Inventory Change $Y - (C + I + G)$	(9) Adjustment to Disequilibrium
500	300	200	250	100	300	650	−150	Output ↑
700	300	400	400	100	300	800	−100	Output ↑
900	300	600	550	100	300	950	−50	Output ↑
1,100	300	800	700	100	300	1,100	0	Equilibrium
1,300	300	1,000	850	100	300	1,250	+50	Output ↓
1,500	300	1,200	1,000	100	300	1,400	+100	Output ↓

Table 24.4 summarizes everything we have said about fiscal policy multipliers.

TABLE 24.4 Summary of Fiscal Policy Multipliers

	Policy Stimulus	Multiplier	Final Impact on Equilibrium *Y*
Government spending multiplier	Increase or decrease in the level of government purchases: ΔG	$\frac{1}{MPS}$	$\Delta G \times \frac{1}{MPS}$
Tax multiplier	Increase or decrease in the level of net taxes: ΔT	$\frac{-MPC}{MPS}$	$\Delta T \times \frac{-MPC}{MPS}$
Balanced-budget multiplier	Simultaneous balanced-budget increase or decrease in the level of government purchases and net taxes: $\Delta G = \Delta T$	1	ΔG

A Warning Although we have added government, the story told about the multiplier is still incomplete and oversimplified. For example, we have been treating net taxes (T) as a lump-sum, fixed amount, whereas in practice, taxes depend on income. Appendix B to this chapter shows that the size of the multiplier is reduced when we make the more realistic assumption that taxes depend on income. We continue to add more realism and difficulty to our analysis in the chapters that follow.

The Federal Budget

Because fiscal policy is the manipulation of items in the federal budget, we need to consider those aspects of the budget relevant to our study of macroeconomics. The **federal budget** is an enormously complicated document, up to thousands of pages each year. It lists in detail all the things the government plans to spend money on and all the sources of government revenues for the coming year. It is the product of a complex interplay of social, political, and economic forces.

federal budget The budget of the federal government.

The "budget" is really three different budgets. First, it is a *political document* that dispenses favors to certain groups or regions (the elderly benefit from Social Security, farmers from agricultural price supports, students from federal loan programs, and so on) and places burdens (taxes) on others. Second, it is a *reflection of goals* the government wants to achieve. For example, in addition to assisting farmers, agricultural price supports are meant to preserve the "family farm." Tax breaks for corporations engaging in research and development of new products are meant to encourage research. Finally, the budget may be an *embodiment of some beliefs about how (if at all) the government should manage the macroeconomy.* The macroeconomic aspects of the budget are only a part of a more complicated story, a story that may be of more concern to political scientists than to economists.

The Budget in 2007

A highly condensed version of the federal budget is shown in Table 24.5. In 2007, the government had total receipts of $2,671.4 billion, largely from personal income taxes ($1,162.1 billion) and contributions for social insurance ($953.0 billion). (Contributions for social insurance are employer and employee Social Security taxes.) Receipts from corporate income taxes accounted for $380.8 billion, or only 14.3 percent of total receipts. Not everyone is aware of the fact that corporate income taxes as a percentage of government receipts are quite small relative to personal income taxes and Social Security taxes.

TABLE 24.5 Federal Government Receipts and Expenditures, 2007 (Billions of Dollars)

	Amount	Percentage of Total
Current receipts		
Personal income taxes	1,162.1	43.5
Excise taxes and customs duties	99.9	3.7
Corporate income taxes	380.8	14.3
Taxes from the rest of the world	13.4	0.5
Contributions for social insurance	953.0	35.7
Interest receipts and rents and royalties	25.1	0.9
Current transfer receipts from business and persons	39.4	1.5
Current surplus of government enterprises	-2.3	-0.0
Total	2,671.4	100.0
Current expenditures		
Consumption expenditures	856.0	29.6
Transfer payments to persons	1,270.7	43.9
Transfer payments to the rest of the world	38.6	1.3
Grants-in-aid to state and local governments	377.5	13.1
Interest payments	302.4	10.5
Subsidies	46.7	1.6
Total	2,892.0	100.0
Net federal government saving—surplus (+) or deficit (−)		
(Total current receipts − Total current expenditures)	−220.6	

Source: U.S. Department of Commerce, Bureau of Economic Analysis.

The federal government also spent $2,892.0 billion in expenditures in 2007. Of this, $1,270.7 billion represented transfer payments to persons (Social Security benefits, military retirement benefits, and unemployment compensation).[3] Consumption ($856.0 billion) was the next-largest component, followed by grants-in-aid to state and local governments ($377.5 billion), which are grants given to the state and local governments by the federal government, and interest payments on the federal debt ($302.4 billion).

federal surplus (+) *or* **deficit (−)** Federal government receipts minus expenditures.

The difference between the federal government's receipts and its expenditures is the **federal surplus (+)** or **deficit (−)**, which is federal government saving. Table 24.5 shows that the federal government spent more than it took in during 2007, resulting in a deficit of $220.6 billion.

[3] Remember that there is an important difference between transfer payments and government purchases of goods and services (consumption expenditures). Much of the government budget goes for things that an economist would classify as transfers (payments that are grants or gifts) instead of purchases of goods and services. Only the latter are included in our variable *G*. Transfers are counted as part of net taxes.

Fiscal Policy Since 1993: The Clinton and Bush Administrations

Since 1993, there have been large fluctuations in many fiscal policy variables. These fluctuations reflect the different behavior of the two Clinton administrations (1993–2000) and the two Bush administrations (2001–2007). Figure 24.4 plots total federal personal income taxes as a percentage of total taxable income for the 1993 I–2007 IV period. This is a graph of the average personal income tax rate. As the figure shows, the average tax rate increased substantially during the Clinton administrations. Much of this increase was due to a tax bill that was passed in 1993 during the first Clinton administration. The figure then shows the dramatic effects of the tax cuts during the first Bush administration. The large fall in the average tax rate in 2001 III was due to a tax rebate passed after the 9/11 terrorist attacks. Although the average tax rate went back up in 2001 IV, it then fell substantially as the Bush tax cuts began to be felt. The overall tax policy of the federal government since 1993 is thus clear from Figure 24.4. The average tax rate rose sharply under President Clinton and fell sharply under President Bush.

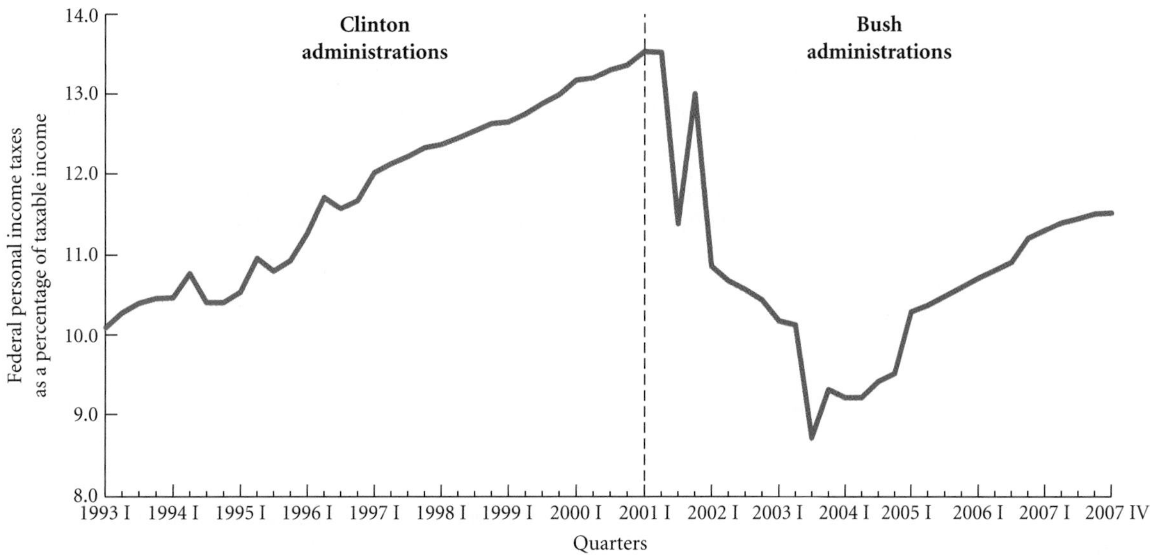

▲ **FIGURE 24.4 Federal Personal Income Taxes as a Percentage of Taxable Income, 1993 I–2007 IV**

Table 24.5 shows that the three most important spending variables of the federal government are consumption expenditures, transfer payments to persons, and grants-in-aid to state and local governments. Consumption expenditures, which are government expenditures on goods and services, are part of GDP. Transfer payments and grants-in-aid are not spending on current output (GDP), but just transfers from the federal government to people and state and local governments. Figure 24.5 plots two spending ratios. One is federal government consumption expenditures as a percentage of GDP, and the other is transfer payments to persons plus grants-in-aid to state and local governments as a percentage of GDP. The figure shows that consumption expenditures as a percentage of GDP generally fell during the Clinton administrations and generally rose during the Bush administrations. The increase during the Bush administrations reflects primarily the spending on the Iraq war. The figure also shows that transfer payments as a percentage of GDP generally rose during the Bush administrations. The figure was flat or slightly falling during the Clinton administrations. Some of the fall between 1996 and 2000 was due to President Clinton's welfare reform legislation. Some of the rise from 2001 on is due to increased Medicare payments.

Figure 24.6 plots the federal government surplus (+) or deficit (–1) as a percentage of GDP for the 1993 I–2007 IV period. The figure shows that during the Clinton administrations the federal budget moved from substantial deficit to noticeable surplus. This, of course, should not be surprising since the average tax rate generally rose during this period and spending as a percentage of GDP generally fell. Figure 24.6 then shows that the surplus turned into a substantial deficit during the first Bush administration. This also should not be surprising since the average tax rate generally fell during this period and spending as a percentage of GDP generally rose.

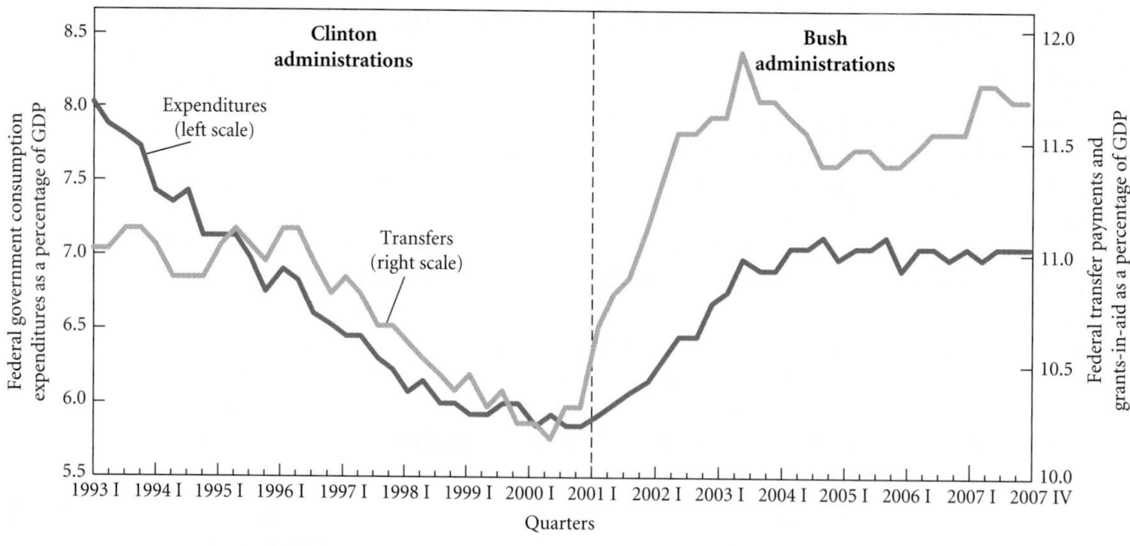

▲ **FIGURE 24.5 Federal Government Consumption Expenditures as a Percentage of GDP and Federal Transfer Payments and Grants-in-Aid as a Percentage of GDP, 1993 I–2007 IV**

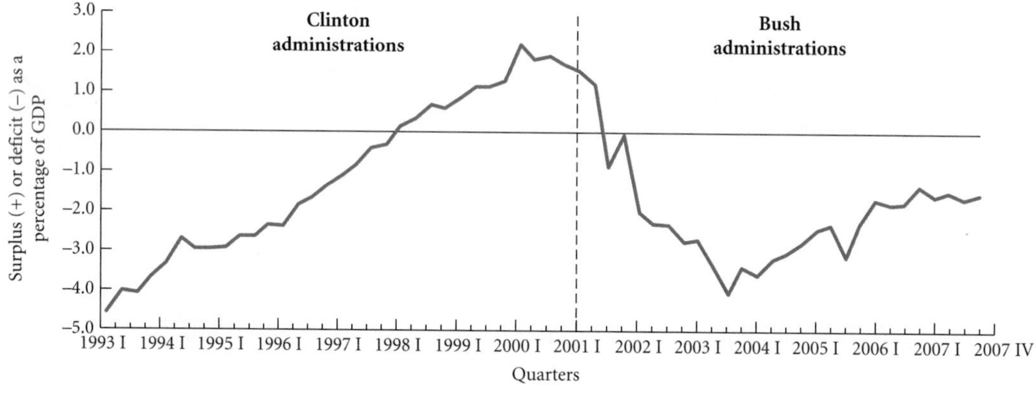

▲ **FIGURE 24.6**

The Federal Government Surplus (+) or Deficit (–) as a Percentage of GDP, 1993 I–2007 IV

To summarize, Figures 24.4, 24.5, and 24.6 show clearly the large differences in the fiscal policies of the Clinton and Bush administrations. Tax rates generally rose and spending as a percentage of GDP generally fell during the Clinton administrations, and the opposite generally happened during the Bush administrations.

As you look at these differences, you should remember that the decisions that governments make about levels of spending and taxes reflect not only macroeconomic concerns but also microeconomic issues and political philosophy. President Clinton's welfare reform program resulted in a decrease in government transfer payments but was motivated in part by interest in improving market incentives. President Bush's early tax cuts were based less on macroeconomic concerns than on political philosophy, while the increased spending came from international relations. Even when tax and spending policies are not motivated by macroeconomic concerns, however, they have macroeconomic consequences.

The Federal Government Debt

federal debt The total amount owed by the federal government.

When the government runs a deficit, it must borrow to finance it. To borrow, the federal government sells government securities to the public. It issues pieces of paper promising to pay a certain amount, with interest, in the future. In return, it receives funds from the buyers of the paper and uses these funds to pay its bills. This borrowing increases the **federal debt**, the total amount owed by the federal government. The federal debt is the total of all accumulated deficits minus surpluses over time. Conversely, if the government runs a surplus, the federal debt falls.

Some of the securities that the government issues end up being held by the federal government at the Federal Reserve or in government trust funds, the largest of which is Social Security. The term **privately held federal debt** refers only to the *privately held* debt of the U.S. government. At the beginning of December 2007, the federal debt was $9.2 trillion, of which $5.2 trillion was privately held.

privately held federal debt The privately held (non-government-owned) debt of the U.S. government.

The federal government debt (privately held) as a percentage of GDP is plotted in Figure 24.7 for the 1993 I–2007 IV period. The percentage fell during the second Clinton administration, when the budget was in surplus, and it mostly rose during the Bush administrations, when the budget was in deficit. In 2007 IV, the percentage was 36.5 percent.

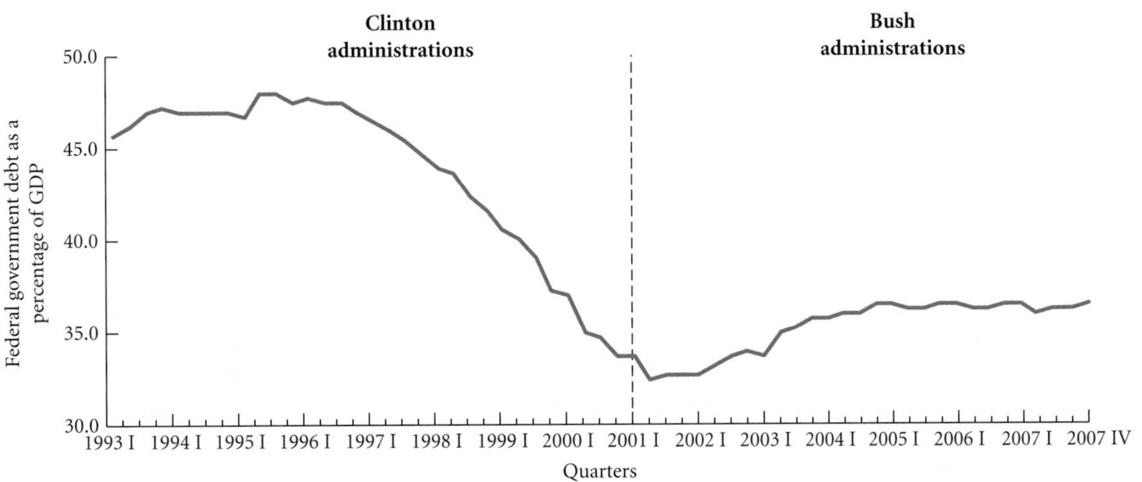

▲ FIGURE 24.7
The Federal Government Debt as a Percentage of GDP, 1993 I–2007 IV

The Economy's Influence on the Government Budget

Some parts of the government's budget depend on the state of the economy, over which the government has no direct control. Following are some of the ways in which the economy affects the budget.

Tax Revenues Depend on the State of the Economy

Consider the revenue side of the budget. The government passes laws that set tax rates and tax brackets, variables the government does control. Tax revenue, on the other hand, depends on taxable income, and income depends on the state of the economy, which the government does *not* completely control. The government can set a personal income tax rate of 20 percent, but the revenue that the tax brings in will depend on the average income that households earn. The government will collect more revenue when average income is $60,000 than when average income is $40,000.

Some Government Expenditures Depend on the State of the Economy

Some items on the expenditure side of the government budget also depend on the state of the economy. As the economy expands, unemployment falls. The result is a decrease in unemployment benefits. Welfare payments and food stamp allotments also decrease somewhat. Some of the people who receive these benefits during bad times are able to find jobs when the state of the economy improves, and they begin earning enough income that they no longer qualify. Transfer payments

ECONOMICS IN PRACTICE

Fiscal Policy In 2008

At the beginning of 2008, many worried that the economy was slipping into a recession. The Bureau of Labor Statistics reported that the number of payroll jobs was falling and GDP growth stalled from over 4 percent annually in the third quarter of 2007 to under 1 percent in the fourth quarter. A decline in house prices and a huge drop in new construction was leading the way. Against this backdrop, Congress and the president agreed on expansionary fiscal policy. Specifically, they passed a rapid-fire tax cut that is described in the following article.

Congress Approves Economic-Stimulus Bill

Wall Street Journal

WASHINGTON—Congress approved a $168 billion bill to boost the economy, paving the way for more than 130 million households to start receiving rebate checks this spring.

The measure passed the Senate, 81-16, after Democrats dropped demands for billions in extra spending and tax breaks, which were opposed by most Republicans. The House quickly adopted the Senate's changes last night, in a 380-34 vote.

The speedy action on the legislation marked a rare bipartisan effort in an election year, as lawmakers more accustomed to fighting decided to work together on the economy, a top concern for many voters. The last hurdle for the bill was cleared earlier yesterday, as Senate leaders agreed to a compromise that closely mirrored a bipartisan House agreement worked out with the Bush administration last month.

In a statement, President Bush made clear he intends to sign the legislation, calling it "an example of bipartisan cooperation at a time when the American people most expect it."

The new Senate bill disappointed many Democrats in that chamber, who had tried unsuccessfully to pick up enough Republican votes for a more-expansive package that would have extended unemployment-insurance benefits, boosted funding for home-heating subsidies for the poor, and supplied $500 checks to millions of Social Security recipients.

Under the final bill, most taxpayers would receive checks of up to $600 for individuals, or $1,200 for married couples, amounts that would begin to phase out at incomes above $75,000 for individuals and $150,000 for married couples. Millions of people who don't pay income taxes but have incomes of at least $3,000 would receive smaller rebates of $300, or $600 for married couples. This group would include Social Security recipients and military veterans receiving disability payments, as well as their surviving spouses—a provision generated by the Senate. People receiving rebates would receive $300 credits for each child.

Source: Sarah Lueck, February 8, 2008.

tend to go down automatically during an expansion. (During a slump, transfer payments tend to increase because there are more people without jobs and more poor people generally.)

Another reason that government spending is not completely controllable is that inflation often picks up when the economy is expanding. This can lead the government to spend more than it had planned to spend. Suppose the government has ordered 20 planes at $2 million each and inflation causes the actual price to be higher than expected. If the government decides to go ahead and buy the planes anyway, it will be forced to increase its spending. Finally, any change in the interest rate changes government interest payments. An increase in interest rates means that the government spends more in interest payments.

Automatic Stabilizers

As the economy expands, the government's tax receipts increase. Also, transfer payments fall as the economy expands, which leads to a decrease in government expenditures. The revenue and expenditure items that change in response to changes in economic activity in such a way as to moderate changes in GDP are known as **automatic stabilizers**. As the economy expands or contracts, "automatic" changes in government revenues and expenditures take place that tend to reduce the change in, or to stabilize, GDP.

automatic stabilizers Revenue and expenditure items in the federal budget that automatically change with the state of the economy in such a way as to stabilize GDP.

The fact that some revenues *automatically* tend to rise and some expenditures *automatically* tend to fall in an expansion means that the government surplus is larger (or the deficit is smaller) in an expansion than it otherwise would be. Suppose we wanted to assess whether a government is practicing a policy designed to increase spending and income. If we looked only at the size of the government budget deficit, we might be fooled into thinking that the government is trying to stimulate the economy when, in fact, the real source of the deficit is a slump in the economy that caused revenues to fall and transfer payments to increase.

Fiscal Drag

If the economy is doing well, income will be high and so will tax revenue. Tax revenue rises with increases in income for two reasons. First, there is more income to be taxed when people are earning more. Second, as people earn more income, they move into higher tax brackets and the average tax rate that they pay increases. This type of increase in tax rates is a **fiscal drag** because the increase in average tax rates that results when people move into higher brackets acts as a "drag" on the economy. As the economy expands and income increases, the automatic tax increase mechanism built into the system goes to work. Tax rates go up, reducing the after-tax wage, which slows down the expansion.

fiscal drag The negative effect on the economy that occurs when average tax rates increase because taxpayers have moved into higher income brackets during an expansion.

Before 1982, people found themselves pushed into higher tax brackets by inflation alone. Suppose my income rose 10 percent in 1981 but the price level also rose by 10 percent that year. My income did not increase at all in real terms; but because the tax brackets were not legislated in real terms, I ended up paying more taxes. Since 1982, however, tax brackets have been indexed—that is, adjusted for inflation—and this change has substantially reduced the automatic fiscal drag built into the system.

Full-Employment Budget

Because the condition of the economy affects the budget deficit so strongly, we cannot accurately judge either the intent or the success of fiscal policies just by looking at the surplus or deficit. Instead of looking simply at the size of the surplus or deficit, economists have developed an alternative way to measure how effective fiscal policy actually is. By examining what the budget would be like if the economy were producing at the full-employment level of output—the so-called **full-employment budget**—we can establish a benchmark for evaluating fiscal policy.

full-employment budget What the federal budget would be if the economy were producing at the full-employment level of output.

The distinction between the actual and full-employment budget is important. Suppose the economy is in a slump and the deficit is \$250 billion. Also suppose that if there were full employment, the deficit would fall to \$75 billion. The \$75 billion deficit that would remain even with full employment would be due to the structure of tax and spending programs instead of the state of the economy. This deficit—the deficit that remains at full employment—is sometimes called the **structural deficit**. The \$175 billion (\$250 billion − \$75 billion) part of the deficit caused by the fact the economy is in a slump is known as the **cyclical deficit**. The existence of the cyclical deficit depends on where the economy is in the business cycle, and it ceases to exist when full employment is reached. By definition, the cyclical deficit of the full-employment budget is zero.

structural deficit The deficit that remains at full employment.

cyclical deficit The deficit that occurs because of a downturn in the business cycle.

Looking Ahead

We have now seen how households, firms, and the government interact in the goods market, how equilibrium output (income) is determined, and how the government uses fiscal policy to influence the economy. In the following two chapters, we analyze the money market and monetary policy—the government's other major tool for influencing the economy.

SUMMARY

1. The government can affect the macroeconomy through two specific policy channels. *Fiscal policy* refers to the government's taxing and spending behavior. *Discretionary fiscal policy* refers to changes in taxes or spending that are the result of deliberate changes in government policy. *Monetary policy* refers to the behavior of the Federal Reserve concerning the nation's money supply.

GOVERNMENT IN THE ECONOMY *p. 472*

2. The government does not have complete control over tax revenues and certain expenditures, which are partially dictated by the state of the economy.
3. As a participant in the economy, the government makes purchases of goods and services (G), collects taxes, and makes transfer payments to households. *Net taxes* (T) is equal to the tax payments made to the government by firms and households minus transfer payments made to households by the government.
4. *Disposable*, or *after-tax, income* (Y_d) is equal to the amount of income received by households after taxes: $Y_d \equiv Y - T$. After-tax income determines households' consumption behavior.
5. The *budget deficit* is equal to the difference between what the government spends and what it collects in taxes: $G - T$. When G exceeds T, the government must borrow from the public to finance its deficit.
6. In an economy in which government is a participant, planned aggregate expenditure equals consumption spending by households (C) plus planned investment spending by firms (I) plus government spending on goods and services (G): $AE \equiv C + I + G$. Because the condition $Y = AE$ is necessary for the economy to be in equilibrium, it follows that $Y = C + I + G$ is the macroeconomic equilibrium condition. The economy is also in equilibrium when leakages out of the system equal injections into the system. This occurs when saving and net taxes (the leakages) equal planned investment and government purchases (the injections): $S + T = I + G$.

FISCAL POLICY AT WORK: MULTIPLIER EFFECTS *p. 476*

7. Fiscal policy has a multiplier effect on the economy. A change in government spending gives rise to a multiplier equal to $1/MPS$. A change in taxation brings about a multiplier equal to $-MPC/MPS$. A simultaneous equal increase or decrease in government spending and taxes has a multiplier effect of 1.

THE FEDERAL BUDGET *p. 481*

8. During the two Clinton administrations, the federal budget went from being in deficit to being in surplus. This was reversed during the two Bush administrations, driven by tax rate decreases and government spending increases.

THE ECONOMY'S INFLUENCE ON THE GOVERNMENT BUDGET *p. 485*

9. *Automatic stabilizers* are revenue and expenditure items in the federal budget that automatically change with the state of the economy and tend to stabilize GDP. For example, during expansions, the government automatically takes in more revenue because people are making more money that is taxed. Higher income and tax brackets also mean fewer transfer payments.
10. *Fiscal drag* is the negative effect on the economy that occurs when average tax rates increase because taxpayers have moved into higher income brackets during an expansion. These higher taxes reduce disposable income and slow down the expansion. Since 1982, tax brackets have been indexed to inflation. This change has reduced the fiscal drag built into the tax system.
11. The *full-employment budget* is an economist's construction of what the federal budget would be if the economy were producing at a full-employment level of output. The *structural deficit* is the federal deficit that remains even at full employment. A *cyclical deficit* occurs when there is a downturn in the business cycle.

REVIEW TERMS AND CONCEPTS

automatic stabilizers, *p. 487*
balanced-budget multiplier, *p. 480*
budget deficit, *p. 473*
cyclical deficit, *p. 487*
discretionary fiscal policy, *p. 472*
disposable, *or* after-tax, income (Y_d), *p. 472*
federal budget, *p. 481*
federal debt, *p. 484*
federal surplus (+) *or* deficit (−), *p. 482*
fiscal drag, *p. 487*
fiscal policy, *p. 472*
full-employment budget, *p. 487*
government spending multiplier, *p. 477*
monetary policy, *p. 472*
net taxes (T), *p. 472*
privately held federal debt, *p. 485*
structural deficit, *p. 487*
tax multiplier, *p. 479*

1. Disposable income $Y_d \equiv Y - T$
2. $AE \equiv C + I + G$
3. Government budget deficit $\equiv G - T$
4. Equilibrium in an economy with a government: $Y = C + I + G$
5. Saving/investment approach to equilibrium in an economy with a government: $S + T = I + G$
6. Government spending multiplier $\equiv \frac{1}{MPS}$
7. Tax multiplier $\equiv -\left(\frac{MPC}{MPS}\right)$
8. Balanced-budget multiplier $\equiv 1$

PROBLEMS

Visit **www.myeconlab.com** to complete the problems marked in orange online. You will receive instant feedback on your answers, tutorial help, and access to additional practice problems.

1. You are appointed secretary of the treasury of a recently independent country called Rugaria. The currency of Rugaria is the lav. The new nation began fiscal operations this year, and the budget situation is that the government will spend 10 million lavs and taxes will be 9 million lavs. The 1-million-lav difference will be borrowed from the public by selling 10-year government bonds paying 5 percent interest. The interest on the outstanding bonds must be added to spending each year, and we assume that additional taxes are raised to cover that interest. Assuming that the budget stays the same except for the interest on the debt for 10 years, what will be the accumulated debt? What will the size of the budget be after 10 years?

2. Suppose that the government of Lumpland is enjoying a fat budget surplus with fixed government expenditures of $G = 150$ and fixed taxes of $T = 200$. Assume that consumers of Lumpland behave as described in the following consumption function:

$$C = 150 + 0.75(Y - T)$$

Suppose further that investment spending is fixed at 100. Calculate the equilibrium level of GDP in Lumpland. Solve for equilibrium levels of Y, C, and S. Next, assume that the Republican Congress in Lumpland succeeds in reducing taxes by 20 to a new fixed level of 180. Recalculate the equilibrium level of GDP using the tax multiplier. Solve for equilibrium levels of Y, C, and S after the tax cut and check to ensure that the multiplier worked. What arguments are likely to be used in support of such a tax cut? What arguments might be used to oppose such a tax cut?

3. For each of the following statements, decide whether you agree or disagree and explain your answer:
   a. During periods of budget surplus (when $G < T$), the government debt grows.
   b. A tax cut will increase the equilibrium level of GDP if the budget is in deficit but will decrease the equilibrium level of GDP if the budget is in surplus.
   c. If the $MPS = .90$, the tax multiplier is actually larger than the expenditure multiplier.

4. Define *saving* and *investment*. Data for the simple economy of Newt show that in 2005, saving exceeded investment and the government is running a balanced budget. What is likely to happen? What would happen if the government were running a deficit and saving were equal to investment?

5. Expert economists in the economy of Yuk estimate the following:

	BILLION YUKS
Real output/income	1,000
Government purchases	200
Total net taxes	200
Investment spending (planned)	100

Assume that Yukkers consume 75 percent of their disposable incomes and save 25 percent.
   a. You are asked by the business editor of the *Yuk Gazette* to predict the events of the next few months. By using the data given, make a forecast. (Assume that investment is constant.)
   b. If no changes were made, at what level of GDP (Y) would the economy of Yuk settle?
   c. Some local conservatives blame Yuk's problems on the size of the government sector. They suggest cutting government purchases by 25 billion Yuks. What effect would such cuts have on the economy? (Be specific.)

6. A $1 increase in government spending will raise equilibrium income more than a $1 tax cut will, yet both have the same impact on the budget deficit. So if we care about the budget deficit, the best way to stimulate the economy is through increases in spending, not cuts in taxes. Comment.

7. Assume that in 2008, the following prevails in the Republic of Nurd:

Y = \$200	G = \$0
C = \$160	T = \$0
S = \$40	
I (planned) = \$30	

Assume that households consume 80 percent of their income, they save 20 percent of their income, $MPC = .8$, and $MPS = .2$. That is, $C = .8Y_d$ and $S = .2Y_d$.
   a. Is the economy of Nurd in equilibrium? What is Nurd's equilibrium level of income? What is likely to happen in the coming months if the government takes no action?
   b. If $200 is the "full-employment" level of Y, what fiscal policy might the government follow if its goal is full employment?
   c. If the full-employment level of Y is $250, what fiscal policy might the government follow?
   d. Suppose $Y = \$200$, $C = \$160$, $S = \$40$, and $I = \$40$. Is Nurd's economy in equilibrium?
   e. Starting with the situation in part d, suppose the government starts spending $30 each year with no taxation and continues to spend $30 every period. If I remains constant, what will happen to the equilibrium level of Nurd's domestic product (Y)? What will the new levels of C and S be?
   f. Starting with the situation in part d, suppose the government starts taxing the population $30 each year without spending anything and continues to tax at that rate every period. If I remains constant, what will happen to the equilibrium level of Nurd's domestic product (Y)? What will be the new levels of C and S? How does your answer to part f differ from your answer to part e? Why?

8. Some economists claim World War II ended the Great Depression of the 1930s. The war effort was financed by borrowing massive sums of money from the public. Explain how a war could end a recession. Look at recent and back issues of the *Economic Report of the President* or the *Statistical Abstract of the United States*. How large was the federal government's debt as a percentage of GDP in 1946? How large is it today?

9. Suppose all tax collections are fixed (instead of dependent on income) and all spending and transfer programs are fixed (in the sense that they do not depend on the state of the economy, as, for example, unemployment benefits now do). In this case, would there be any automatic stabilizers in the government budget? Would there be any distinction between the full-employment deficit and the actual budget deficit? Explain.

10. Answer the following:
   a. $MPS = .4$. What is the government spending multiplier?
   b. $MPC = .9$. What is the government spending multiplier?
   c. $MPS = .5$. What is the government spending multiplier?
   d. $MPC = .75$. What is the tax multiplier?
   e. $MPS = .1$. What is the tax multiplier?
   f. If the government spending multiplier is 6, what is the tax multiplier?
   g. If the tax multiplier is -2, what is the government spending multiplier?
   h. If government purchases and taxes are increased by $100 billion simultaneously, what will the effect be on equilibrium output (income)?

11. **[Related to the *Economics in Practice* on *p. 486*]** While many thought that the 2008 fiscal stimulus plan described in the feature on p. 486 was a good idea, some did not. Some even thought that Congress didn't go far enough. In retrospect, who was right? Did the economy experience a recession in 2008 or 2009? What happened to employment during the rest of 2008? What are some of the alternatives to a tax cut that might have been used?

APPENDIX A

DERIVING THE FISCAL POLICY MULTIPLIERS

THE GOVERNMENT SPENDING AND TAX MULTIPLIERS

In the chapter, we noted that the government spending multiplier is $1/MPS$. (This is the same as the investment multiplier.) We can also derive the multiplier algebraically using our hypothetical consumption function:

$$C = a + b(Y - T)$$

where b is the marginal propensity to consume. As you know, the equilibrium condition is

$$Y = C + I + G$$

By substituting for C, we get

$$Y = a + b(Y - T) + I + G$$
$$Y = a + bY - bT + I + G$$

This equation can be rearranged to yield

$$Y - bY = a + I + G - bT$$
$$Y(1 - b) = a + I + G - bT$$

Now solve for Y by dividing through by $(1 - b)$:

$$Y = \frac{1}{(1 - b)}(a + I + G - bT)$$

We see from this last equation that if G increases by 1 with the other determinants of Y (a, I, and T) remaining constant, Y increases by $1/(1 - b)$. The multiplier is, as before, simply $1/(1 - b)$, where b is the marginal propensity to consume. Of course, $1 - b$ equals the marginal propensity to save, so the government spending multiplier is $1/MPS$.

We can also derive the tax multiplier. The last equation says that when T increases by $1, holding a, I, and G constant, income decreases by $b/(1 - b)$ dollars. The tax multiplier is $-b/(1 - b)$, or $-MPC/(1 - MPC) = -MPC/MPS$. (Remember, the negative sign in the resulting tax multiplier shows that it is a *negative* multiplier.)

THE BALANCED-BUDGET MULTIPLIER

It is easy to show formally that the balanced-budget multiplier = 1. When taxes and government spending are simultaneously increased by the same amount, there are two effects on planned aggregate expenditure: one positive and one negative. The initial impact of a balanced-budget increase in government spending and taxes on aggregate expenditure would be the *increase* in government purchases (ΔG) minus the *decrease* in consumption (ΔC) caused by the tax increase. The decrease in consumption brought about by the tax increase is equal to $\Delta C = \Delta T\,(MPC)$.

increase in spending:	ΔG
− decrease in spending:	$\Delta C = \Delta T(MPC)$
= net increase in spending	$\Delta G - \Delta T(MPC)$

In a balanced-budget increase, $\Delta G = \Delta T$; so we can substitute:

net initial increase in spending:

$$\Delta G - \Delta G(MPC) = \Delta G\,(1 - MPC)$$

Because $MPS = (1 - MPC)$, the net initial increase in spending is:

$$\Delta G(MPS)$$

We can now apply the expenditure multiplier $\left(\frac{1}{MPS}\right)$ to this net initial increase in spending:

$$\Delta Y = \Delta G(MPS)\left(\frac{1}{MPS}\right) = \Delta G$$

Thus, the final total increase in the equilibrium level of Y is just equal to the initial balanced increase in G and T. That means the balanced-budget multiplier = 1, so the final increase in real output is of the same magnitude as the initial change in spending.

APPENDIX B

THE CASE IN WHICH TAX REVENUES DEPEND ON INCOME

In this chapter, we used the simplifying assumption that the government collects taxes in a lump sum. This made our discussion of the multiplier effects somewhat easier to follow. Now suppose that the government collects taxes not solely as a lump sum that is paid regardless of income but also partly in the form of a proportional levy against income. This is a more realistic assumption. Typically, tax collections either are based on income (as with the personal income tax) or follow the ups and downs in the economy (as with sales taxes). Instead of setting taxes equal to some fixed amount, let us say that tax revenues depend on income. If we call the amount of net taxes collected *T*, we can write $T = T_0 + tY$.

This equation contains two parts. First, we note that net taxes (*T*) will be equal to an amount T_0 if income (*Y*) is zero. Second, the tax rate (*t*) indicates how much net taxes change as income changes. Suppose T_0 is equal to −200 and *t* is 1/3. The resulting tax function is $T = -200 + 1/3Y$, which is graphed in Figure 24B.1. Note that when income is zero, the government collects "negative net taxes," which simply means that it makes transfer payments of 200. As income rises, tax collections increase because every extra dollar of income generates \$0.33 in extra revenues for the government.

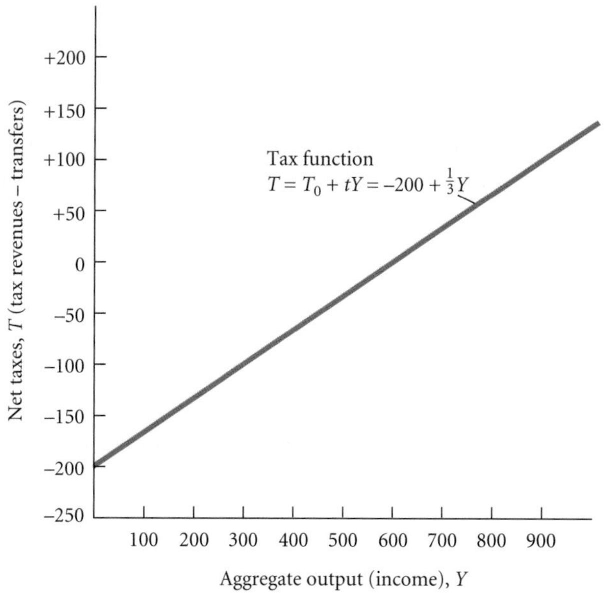

▲ **FIGURE 24B.1 The Tax Function**
This graph shows net taxes (taxes minus transfer payments) as a function of aggregate income.

How do we incorporate this new tax function into our discussion? All we do is replace the old value of *T* (in the example in the chapter, *T* was set equal to 100) with the new value, −200 + 1/3*Y*. Look first at the consumption equation. Consumption (*C*) still depends on disposable income, as it did before. Also, disposable income is still $Y - T$, or income minus taxes. Instead of disposable income equaling $Y - 100$, however, the new equation for disposable income is

$$Y_d \equiv Y - T$$
$$Y_d \equiv Y - (-200 + 1/3Y)$$
$$Y_d \equiv Y + 200 - 1/3Y$$

Because consumption still depends on after-tax income, exactly as it did before, we have

$$C = 100 + .75Y_d$$
$$C = 100 + .75(Y + 200 - 1/3Y)$$

Nothing else needs to be changed. We solve for equilibrium income exactly as before, by setting planned aggregate expenditure equal to aggregate output. Recall that planned aggregate expenditure is $C + I + G$ and aggregate output is *Y*. If we assume, as before, that $I = 100$ and $G = 100$, the equilibrium is

$$Y = C + I + G$$
$$Y = \underbrace{100 + .75(Y + 200 - 1/3Y)}_{C} + \underbrace{100}_{I} + \underbrace{100}_{G}$$

This equation may look difficult to solve, but it is not. It simplifies to

$$Y = 100 + .75Y + 150 - .25Y + 100 + 100$$
$$Y = 450 + .5Y$$
$$.5Y = 450$$

This means that $Y = 450/.5 = 900$, the new equilibrium level of income.

Consider the graphic analysis of this equation as shown in Figure 24B.2, where you should note that when we make taxes a function of income (instead of a lump-sum amount), the *AE* function becomes *flatter* than it was before. Why? When tax collections do not depend on income, an increase in income of \$1 means disposable income also increases by a dollar. Because taxes are a constant amount, adding more income does not raise the amount of taxes paid. Disposable income therefore changes dollar for dollar with any change in income.

When taxes depend on income, a \$1 increase in income does not increase disposable income by a full dollar because some of the additional dollar goes to pay extra taxes. Under the modified tax function of Figure 24B.2, an extra dollar of income will increase disposable income by only \$0.67 because \$0.33 of the extra dollar goes to the government in the form of taxes.

No matter how taxes are calculated, the marginal propensity to consume out of disposable (or after-tax) income is the same—each extra dollar of disposable income will increase consumption spending by \$0.75. However, a \$1 change in before-tax income does not have the same effect on disposable income in each case. Suppose we were to increase income by \$1. With the lump-sum tax function, disposable income would rise by \$1.00, and consumption would increase by the *MPC* times the change

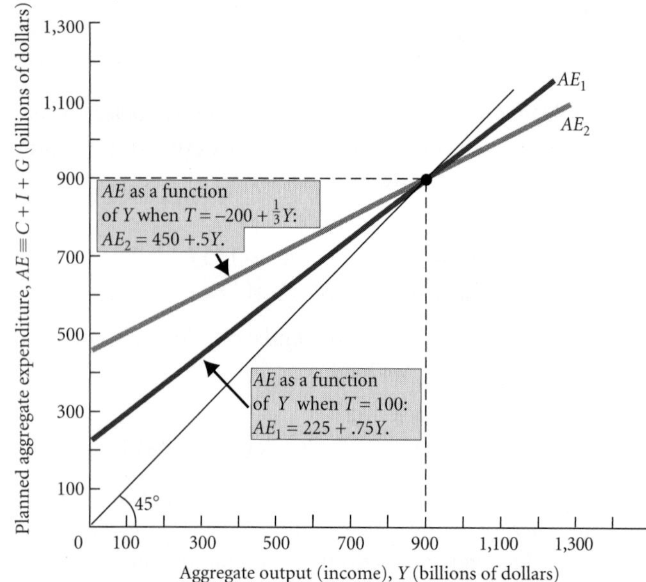

▲ **FIGURE 24B.2**

Different Tax Systems

When taxes are strictly lump-sum ($T = 100$) and do not depend on income, the aggregate expenditure function is steeper than when taxes depend on income.

in Y_d, or \$0.75. When taxes depend on income, disposable income would rise by only \$0.67 from the \$1.00 increase in income and consumption would rise by only the *MPC* times the change in disposable income, or $\$0.75 \times .67 = \$0.50$.

If a \$1.00 increase in income raises expenditure by \$0.75 in one case and by only \$0.50 in the other, the second aggregate expenditure function must be flatter than the first.

THE GOVERNMENT SPENDING AND TAX MULTIPLIERS ALGEBRAICALLY

All this means that if taxes are a function of income, the three multipliers (investment, government spending, and tax) are less than they would be if taxes were a lump-sum amount. By using the same linear consumption function we used in Chapters 22 and 23, we can derive the multiplier:

$$C = a + b(Y - T)$$
$$C = a + b(Y - T_0 - tY)$$
$$C = a + bY - bT_0 - btY$$

We know that $Y = C + I + G$. Through substitution we get

$$Y = \underbrace{a + bY - bT_0 - btY}_{C} + I + G$$

Solving for Y:

$$Y = \frac{1}{1 - b + bt}(a + I + G - bT_0)$$

This means that a \$1 increase in G or I (holding a and T_0 constant) will increase the equilibrium level of Y by

$$\frac{1}{1 - b + bt}$$

If $b = MPC = .75$ and $t = .20$, the spending multiplier is 2.5. (Compare this to 4, which would be the value of the spending multiplier if taxes were a lump sum, that is, if $t = 0$.)

Holding a, I, and G constant, a fixed or lump-sum tax cut (a cut in T_0) will increase the equilibrium level of income by

$$\frac{b}{1 - b + bt}$$

Thus, if $b = MPC = .75$ and $t = .20$, the tax multiplier is -1.875. (Compare this to -3, which would be the value of the tax multiplier if taxes were a lump sum.)

SUMMARY

1. When taxes depend on income, a \$1 increase in income does not increase disposable income by a full dollar because some of the additional dollar must go to pay extra taxes. This means that if taxes are a function of income, the three multipliers (investment, government spending, and tax) are less than they would be if taxes were a lump-sum amount.

PROBLEMS

1. Assume the following for the economy of a country:
   a. Consumption function: $C = 85 + 0.5Y_d$
   b. Investment function: $I = 85$
   c. Government spending: $G = 60$
   d. Net taxes: $T = -40 + 0.25Y$
   e. Disposable income: $Y_d \equiv Y - T$
   f. Equilibrium: $Y = C + I + G$

   Solve for equilibrium income. (*Hint*: Be very careful in doing the calculations. They are not difficult, but it is easy to make careless mistakes that produce wrong results.) How much does the government collect in net taxes when the economy is in equilibrium? What is the government's budget deficit or surplus?

The Money Supply and the Federal Reserve System

25

CHAPTER OUTLINE

In the last two chapters, we explored how consumers, firms, and the government interact in the goods market. In this chapter and the next, we show how money markets work in the macroeconomy. We begin with what money is and what role it plays in the U.S. economy. We then discuss the forces that determine the supply of money and show how banks create money. Finally, we discuss the workings of the nation's central bank, the Federal Reserve (the Fed), and the tools at its disposal to control the money supply.

Microeconomics has little to say about money. Microeconomic theories and models are concerned primarily with *real* quantities (apples, oranges, hours of labor) and *relative* prices (the price of apples relative to the price of oranges or the price of labor relative to the prices of other goods). Most of the key ideas in microeconomics do not require that we know anything about money. As we shall see, this is not the case in macroeconomics.

An Overview of Money

You often hear people say things like, "He makes a lot of money" (in other words, "He has a high income") or "She's worth a lot of money" (meaning "She is very wealthy"). It is true that your employer uses money to pay you your income, and your wealth may be accumulated in the form of money. However, *money is not income, and money is not wealth.*

To see that money and income are not the same, think of a $20 bill. That bill may pass through a thousand hands in a year, yet never be used to pay anyone a salary. Suppose you get a $20 bill from an automatic teller machine, and you spend it on dinner. The restaurant puts that $20 bill in a bank in the next day's deposit. The bank gives it to a woman cashing a check the following day; she spends it at a baseball game that night. The bill has been through many hands but not as part of anyone's income.

What Is Money?

Most people take the ability to obtain and use money for granted. When the whole monetary system works well, as it generally does in the United States, the basic mechanics of the system are virtually invisible. People take for granted that they can walk into any store, restaurant, boutique, or gas station and buy whatever they want as long as they have enough green pieces of paper.

The idea that you can buy things with money is so natural and obvious that it seems absurd to mention it, but stop and ask yourself: "How is it that a store owner is willing to part with a steak and a loaf of bread that I can eat in exchange for some pieces of paper that are intrinsically worthless?" Why, on the other hand, are there times and places where it takes a shopping cart full of money to purchase a dozen eggs? The answers to these questions lie in what money is—a means of payment, a store of value, and a unit of account.

A Means of Payment, or Medium of Exchange Money is vital to the working of a market economy. Imagine what life would be like without it. The alternative to a monetary economy is **barter**, people exchanging goods and services for other goods and services directly instead of exchanging via the medium of money.

barter The direct exchange of goods and services for other goods and services.

How does a barter system work? Suppose you want bacon, eggs, and orange juice for breakfast. Instead of going to the store and buying these things with money, you would have to find someone who has the items and is willing to trade them. You would also have to have something the bacon seller, the orange juice purveyor, and the egg vendor want. Having pencils to trade will do you no good if the bacon, orange juice, and egg sellers do not want pencils.

A barter system requires a *double coincidence of wants* for trade to take place. That is, to effect a trade, you have to find someone who has what you want and that person must also want what you have. Where the range of goods traded is small, as it is in relatively unsophisticated economies, it is not difficult to find someone to trade with and barter is often used. In a complex society with many goods, barter exchanges involve an intolerable amount of effort. Imagine trying to find people who offer for sale all the things you buy in a typical trip to the supermarket and who are willing to accept goods that you have to offer in exchange for their goods.

medium of exchange, *or* means of payment What sellers generally accept and buyers generally use to pay for goods and services.

Some agreed-to **medium of exchange** (or **means of payment**) neatly eliminates the double-coincidence-of-wants problem. Under a monetary system, money is exchanged for goods or services when people buy things; goods or services are exchanged for money when people sell things. No one ever has to trade goods for other goods directly. Money is a lubricant in the functioning of a market economy.

A Store of Value Economists have identified other roles for money aside from its primary function as a medium of exchange. Money also serves as a **store of value**—an asset that can be used to transport purchasing power from one time period to another. If you raise chickens and at the end of the month sell them for more than you want to spend and consume immediately, you may keep some of your earnings in the form of money until the time you want to spend it.

store of value An asset that can be used to transport purchasing power from one time period to another.

There are many other stores of value besides money. You could have decided to hold your "surplus" earnings by buying such things as antique paintings, baseball cards, or diamonds, which you could sell later when you want to spend your earnings. Money has several advantages over these other stores of value. First, it comes in convenient denominations and is easily portable. You do not have to worry about making change for a Renoir painting to buy a gallon of gasoline. Second, because money is also a means of payment, it is easily exchanged for goods at all times. (A Renoir is not easily exchanged for other goods.) These two factors compose the **liquidity property of money**. Money is easily spent, flowing out of your hands like liquid. Renoirs and ancient Aztec statues are neither convenient nor portable and are not readily accepted as a means of payment.

liquidity property of money The property of money that makes it a good medium of exchange as well as a store of value: It is portable and readily accepted and thus easily exchanged for goods.

The main disadvantage of money as a store of value is that the value of money falls when the prices of goods and services rise. If the price of potato chips rises from $1 per bag to $2 per bag, the value of a dollar bill in terms of potato chips falls from one bag to half a bag. When this happens, it may be better to use potato chips (or antiques or real estate) as a store of value.

A Unit of Account Money also serves as a **unit of account**—a consistent way of quoting prices. All prices are quoted in monetary units. A textbook is quoted as costing $90, not 150 bananas or 5 DVDs, and a banana is quoted as costing 60 cents, not 1.4 apples or 6 pages of a textbook. Obviously, a standard unit of account is extremely useful when quoting prices. This function of money may have escaped your notice—what else would people quote prices in except money?

unit of account A standard unit that provides a consistent way of quoting prices.

Commodity and Fiat Monies

Introductory economics textbooks are full of stories about the various items that have been used as money by various cultures—candy bars, cigarettes (in World War II prisoner-of-war camps), huge wheels of carved stone (on the island of Yap in the South Pacific), cowrie shells (in West Africa), beads (among North American Indians), cattle (in southern Africa), and small green scraps of paper (in contemporary North America). The list goes on. These various kinds of money are generally divided into two groups, commodity monies and fiat money.

ECONOMICS IN PRACTICE

Dolphin Teeth as Currency

In most countries commodity monies are not used anymore, but the world is a big place and there are exceptions. The following article discusses the use of dolphin teeth as currency in the Solomon Islands. Dolphin teeth are being used as a means of payment and a store of value. Note that even with a currency like dolphin teeth there is a concern about counterfeit currency, namely fruit-bat teeth. Tooth decay is also a problem.

Shrinking Dollar Meets Its Match In Dolphin Teeth

Wall Street Journal

HONIARA, Solomon Islands—Forget the euro and the yen. In this South Pacific archipelago, people are pouring their savings into another appreciating currency: dolphin teeth.

Shaped like miniature ivory jalapeños, the teeth of spinner dolphins have facilitated commerce in parts of the Solomon Islands for centuries. This traditional currency is gaining in prominence now after years of ethnic strife that have undermined the country's economy and rekindled attachment to ancient customs.

Over the past year, one spinner tooth has soared in price to about two Solomon Islands dollars (26 U.S. cents), from as little as 50 Solomon Islands cents. The official currency, pegged to a global currency basket dominated by the U.S. dollar, has remained relatively stable in the period.

Even Rick Houenipwela, the governor of the Central Bank of the Solomon Islands, says he is an investor in teeth, having purchased a "huge amount" a few years ago. "Dolphin teeth are like gold," Mr. Houenipwela says. "You keep them as a store of wealth—just as if you'd put money in the bank."

Few Solomon Islanders share Western humane sensibilities about the dolphins. Hundreds of animals are killed at a time in regular hunts, usually off the large island of Malaita. Dolphin flesh provides protein for the villagers. The teeth are used like cash to buy local produce. Fifty teeth will purchase a pig; a handful are enough for some yams and cassava.

The tradition has deep roots. Dolphin teeth and other animal products were used as currency in the Solomon Islands and other parts of Melanesia long before European colonizers arrived here in the late nineteenth century.

An exhibit of traditional money in the central bank's lobby displays the now-worthless garlands of dog teeth. Curled pig tusks have played a similar role in the neighboring nation of Vanuatu and parts of Papua New Guinea. Whale, rather than dolphin, teeth were collected in Fiji. While the use of these traditional currencies is dying off elsewhere in the region, there is no sign of the boom in dolphin teeth abating here. Mr. Houenipwela, the central bank governor, says that some entrepreneurs have recently asked him for permission to establish a bank that would take deposits in teeth.

A dolphin-tooth bank with clean, insect-free vaults would solve the problem of tooth decay under inappropriate storage conditions, and would also deter counterfeiters who pass off fruit-bat teeth, which resemble dolphin teeth, for the genuine article. Mr. Houenipwela, however, says he had to turn down the request because only institutions accepting conventional currencies can call themselves banks under Solomon Islands law.

Source: Yaroslav Trofimov, April 30, 2008.

commodity monies Items used as money that also have intrinsic value in some other use.

Commodity monies are those items used as money that also have an intrinsic value in some other use. For example, prisoners of war made purchases with cigarettes, quoted prices in terms of cigarettes, and held their wealth in the form of accumulated cigarettes. Of course, cigarettes could also be smoked—they had an alternative use apart from serving as money. Gold represents another form of commodity money. For hundreds of years gold could be used directly to buy things, but it also had other uses, ranging from jewelry to dental fillings.

fiat, *or* token, money Items designated as money that are intrinsically worthless.

By contrast, money in the United States today is mostly fiat money. **Fiat money**, sometimes called **token money**, is money that is intrinsically worthless. The actual value of a 1-, 10-, or 50-dollar bill is basically zero; what other uses are there for a small piece of paper with some green ink on it?

Why would anyone accept worthless scraps of paper as money instead of something that has some value, such as gold, cigarettes, or cattle? If your answer is "because the paper money is backed by gold or silver," you are wrong. There was a time when dollar bills were convertible directly into gold. The government backed each dollar bill in circulation by holding a certain amount of gold in its vaults. If the price of gold were $35 per ounce, for example, the government agreed to sell 1 ounce of gold for 35 dollar bills. However, dollar bills are no longer backed by any commodity—gold, silver, or anything else. They are exchangeable only for dimes, nickels, pennies, other dollars, and so on.

legal tender Money that a government has required to be accepted in settlement of debts.

The public accepts paper money as a means of payment and a store of value because the government has taken steps to ensure that its money is accepted. The government declares its paper money to be **legal tender**. That is, the government declares that its money must be accepted in settlement of debts. It does this by fiat (hence *fiat money*). It passes laws defining certain pieces of paper printed in certain inks on certain plates to be legal tender, and that is that. Printed on every Federal Reserve note in the United States is "This note is legal tender for all debts, public and private." Often the government can get a start on gaining acceptance for its paper money by requiring that it be used to pay taxes. (Note that you cannot use chickens, baseball cards, or Renoir paintings to pay your taxes.)

currency debasement The decrease in the value of money that occurs when its supply is increased rapidly.

Aside from declaring its currency legal tender, the government usually does one other thing to ensure that paper money will be accepted: It promises the public that it will not print paper money so fast that it loses its value. Expanding the supply of currency so rapidly that it loses much of its value has been a problem throughout history and is known as **currency debasement**. Debasement of the currency has been a special problem of governments that lack the strength to take the politically unpopular step of raising taxes. Printing money to be used on government expenditures of goods and services can serve as a substitute for tax increases, and weak governments have often relied on the printing press to finance their expenditures. A recent example is Zimbabwe. In 2007, faced with a need to improve the public water system, Zimbabwe's president, Robert Mugabe, said "Where money for projects cannot be found, we will print it" (reported in the *Washington Post*, July 29, 2007). In later chapters we will see the way in which this strategy for funding public projects can lead to serious inflation.

Measuring the Supply of Money in the United States

We now turn to the various kinds of money in the United States. Recall that money is used to buy things (a means of payment), to hold wealth (a store of value), and to quote prices (a unit of account). Unfortunately, these characteristics apply to a broad range of assets in the U.S. economy. As we will see, it is not at all clear where we should draw the line and say, "Up to this is money, beyond this is something else."

To solve the problem of multiple monies, economists have given different names to different measures of money. The two most common measures of money are transactions money, also called M1, and broad money, also called M2.

M1: Transactions Money What should be counted as money? Coins and dollar bills, as well as higher denominations of currency, must be counted as money—they fit all the requirements. What about checking accounts? Checks, too, can be used to buy things and can serve as a store of value. Debit cards provide even easier access to funds in checking accounts. In fact, bankers call checking accounts *demand deposits* because depositors have the right to go to the bank and cash in (demand) their entire checking account balance at any time. That makes your checking account balance virtually equivalent to bills in your wallet, and it should be included as part of the amount of money you hold.

If we take the value of all currency (including coins) held outside of bank vaults and add to it the value of all demand deposits, traveler's checks, and other checkable deposits, we have defined **M1**, or **transactions money**. As its name suggests, this is the money that can be directly used for transactions—to buy things.

M1, *or* transactions money Money that can be directly used for transactions.

M1 ≡ currency held outside banks + demand deposits + traveler's checks + other checkable deposits

M1 at the end of February 2008 was $1,372.5 billion. M1 is a stock measure—it is measured at a point in time. It is the total amount of coins and currency outside of banks and the total dollar amount in checking accounts *on a specific day*. Until now, we have considered supply as a flow—a variable with a time dimension: the quantity of wheat supplied *per year*, the quantity of automobiles supplied to the market *per year*, and so on. However, M1 is a stock variable.

M2: Broad Money Although M1 is the most widely used measure of the money supply, there are others. Should savings accounts be considered money? Many of these accounts cannot be used for transactions directly, but it is easy to convert them into cash or to transfer funds from a savings account into a checking account. What about money market accounts (which allow only a few checks per month but pay market-determined interest rates) and money market mutual funds (which sell shares and use the proceeds to purchase short-term securities)? These can be used to write checks and make purchases, although only over a certain amount.

If we add **near monies**, close substitutes for transactions money, to M1, we get **M2**, called **broad money** because it includes not-quite-money monies such as savings accounts, money market accounts, and other near monies.

near monies Close substitutes for transactions money, such as savings accounts and money market accounts.

M2, *or* broad money M1 plus savings accounts, money market accounts, and other near monies.

M2 ≡ M1 + Savings accounts + Money market accounts + Other near monies

M2 at the end of February 2008 was $7,586.0 billion, considerably larger than the total M1 of $1,372.5 billion. The main advantage of looking at M2 instead of M1 is that M2 is sometimes more stable. For instance, when banks introduced new forms of interest-bearing checking accounts in the early 1980s, M1 shot up as people switched their funds from savings accounts to checking accounts. However, M2 remained fairly constant because the fall in savings account deposits and the rise in checking account balances were both part of M2, canceling each other out.

Beyond M2 Because a wide variety of financial instruments bear some resemblance to money, some economists have advocated including almost all of them as part of the money supply. In recent years, for example, credit cards have come to be used extensively in exchange. Everyone who has a credit card has a credit limit—you can charge only a certain amount on your card before you have to pay it off. Usually we pay our credit card bills with a check. One of the very broad definitions of money includes the amount of available credit on credit cards (your charge limit minus what you have charged but not paid) as part of the money supply.

There are no rules for deciding what is and is not money. This poses problems for economists and those in charge of economic policy. However, *for our purposes, "money" will always refer to transactions money, or M1*. For simplicity, we will say that M1 is the sum of two *general* categories: currency in circulation and deposits. Keep in mind, however, that M1 has *four* specific components: currency held outside banks, demand deposits, traveler's checks, and other checkable deposits.

The Private Banking System

Most of the money in the United States today is "bank money" of one sort or another. M1 is made up largely of checking account balances instead of currency, and currency makes up an even smaller part of M2 and other broader definitions of money. Any understanding of money requires some knowledge of the structure of the private banking system.

Banks and banklike institutions borrow from individuals or firms with excess funds and lend to those who need funds. For example, commercial banks receive funds in various forms, including deposits in checking and savings accounts. They take these funds and loan them out in the form of car loans, mortgages, commercial loans, and so on. Banks and banklike institutions are called **financial intermediaries** because they "mediate," or act as a link between people who have funds to lend and those who need to borrow.

financial intermediaries Banks and other institutions that act as a link between those who have money to lend and those who want to borrow money.

The main types of financial intermediaries are commercial banks, followed by savings and loan associations, life insurance companies, and pension funds. Since about 1970, the legal distinctions among the different types of financial intermediaries have narrowed considerably. It used to be, for example, that checking accounts could be held only in commercial banks and that commercial banks could not pay interest on checking accounts. Savings and loan associations were prohibited from offering certain kinds of deposits and were restricted primarily to making loans for mortgages.

The Depository Institutions Deregulation and Monetary Control Act, enacted by Congress in 1980, eliminated many of the previous restrictions on the behavior of financial institutions. Many types of institutions now offer checking accounts, and interest is paid on many types of checking accounts. Savings and loan associations now make loans for many things besides home mortgages.

How Banks Create Money

So far we have described the general way that money works and the way the supply of money is measured in the United States, but how much money is available at a given time? Who supplies it, and how does it get supplied? We are now ready to analyze these questions in detail. In particular, we want to explore a process that many find mysterious: the way banks *create money*.

A Historical Perspective: Goldsmiths

To begin to see how banks create money, consider the origins of the modern banking system. In the fifteenth and sixteenth centuries, citizens of many lands used gold as money, particularly for large transactions. Because gold is both inconvenient to carry around and susceptible to theft, people began to place their gold with goldsmiths for safekeeping. On receiving the gold, a goldsmith would issue a receipt to the depositor, charging him a small fee for looking after his gold. After a time, these receipts themselves, rather than the gold that they represented, began to be traded for goods. The receipts became a form of paper money, making it unnecessary to go to the goldsmith to withdraw gold for a transaction. The receipts of the de Medici's, who were both art patrons and goldsmith-bankers in Italy in the Renaissance period, were reputedly accepted in wide areas of Europe as currency.

At this point, all the receipts issued by goldsmiths were backed 100 percent by gold. If a goldsmith had 100 ounces of gold in his safe, he would issue receipts for 100 ounces of gold, and no more. Goldsmiths functioned as warehouses where people stored gold for safekeeping. The goldsmiths found, however, that people did not come often to withdraw gold. Why should they, when paper receipts that could easily be converted to gold were "as good as gold"? (In fact, receipts were better than gold—more portable, safer from theft, and so on.) As a result, goldsmiths had a large stock of gold continuously on hand.

Because they had what amounted to "extra" gold sitting around, goldsmiths gradually realized that they could lend out some of this gold without any fear of running out of gold. Why would they do this? Because instead of just keeping their gold idly in their vaults, they could earn interest on loans. Something subtle, but dramatic, happened at this point. The goldsmiths changed from mere depositories for gold into banklike institutions that had the power to create money. This transformation occurred as soon as goldsmiths began making loans. Without adding any more real gold to the system, the goldsmiths increased the amount of money in circulation by creating additional claims to gold—that is, receipts that entitled the bearer to receive a certain number of ounces of gold on demand.[1] Thus, there were more claims than there were ounces of gold.

---

[1] Remember, these receipts circulated as money, and people used them to make transactions without feeling the need to cash them in—that is, to exchange them for gold itself.

A detailed example may help to clarify this. Suppose you go to a goldsmith who is functioning only as a depository, or warehouse, and ask for a loan to buy a plot of land that costs 20 ounces of gold. Also suppose that the goldsmith has 100 ounces of gold on deposit in his safe and receipts for exactly 100 ounces of gold out to the various people who deposited the gold. If the goldsmith decides he is tired of being a mere goldsmith and wants to become a real bank, he will loan you some gold. You don't want the gold itself, of course; rather, you want a slip of paper that represents 20 ounces of gold. The goldsmith in essence "creates" money for you by giving you a receipt for 20 ounces of gold (even though his entire supply of gold already belongs to various other people).[2] When he does, there will be receipts for 120 ounces of gold in circulation instead of the 100 ounces worth of receipts before your loan and the supply of money will have increased.

People think the creation of money is mysterious. Far from it! The creation of money is simply an accounting procedure, among the most mundane of human endeavors. You may suspect the whole process is fundamentally unsound or somehow dubious. After all, the banking system began when someone issued claims for gold that already belonged to someone else. Here you may be on slightly firmer ground.

Goldsmiths-turned-bankers did face certain problems. Once they started making loans, their receipts outstanding (claims on gold) were greater than the amount of gold they had in their vaults at any given moment. If the owners of the 120 ounces worth of gold receipts all presented their receipts and demanded their gold at the same time, the goldsmith would be in trouble. With only 100 ounces of gold on hand, people could not get their gold at once.

In normal times, people would be happy to hold receipts instead of real gold, and this problem would never arise. If, however, people began to worry about the goldsmith's financial safety, they might begin to have doubts about whether their receipts really were as good as gold. Knowing there were more receipts outstanding than there were ounces of gold in the goldsmith's vault, they might start to demand gold for receipts.

This situation leads to a paradox. It makes perfect sense for people to hold paper receipts (instead of gold) if they know they can always get gold for their paper. In normal times, goldsmiths could feel perfectly safe in loaning out more gold than they actually had in their possession. But once people start to doubt the safety of the goldsmith, they are foolish not to demand their gold back from the vault.

A run on a goldsmith (or in our day, a **run on a bank**) occurs when many people present their claims at the same time. These runs tend to feed on themselves. If I see you going to the goldsmith to withdraw your gold, I may become nervous and decide to withdraw my gold as well. It is the *fear* of a run that usually causes the run. Runs on a bank can be triggered by a variety of causes: rumors that an institution may have made loans to borrowers who cannot repay, wars, failures of other institutions that have borrowed money from the bank, and so on. As you will see later in this chapter, today's bankers differ from goldsmiths—today's banks are subject to a "required reserve ratio." Goldsmiths had no legal reserve requirements, although the amount they loaned out was subject to the restriction imposed on them by their fear of running out of gold.

run on a bank Occurs when many of those who have claims on a bank (deposits) present them at the same time.

The Modern Banking System

To understand how the modern banking system works, you need to be familiar with some basic principles of accounting. Once you are comfortable with the way banks keep their books, the whole process of money creation will seem logical.

A Brief Review of Accounting Central to accounting practices is the statement that "the books always balance." In practice, this means that if we take a snapshot of a firm—any firm, including a bank—at a particular moment in time, then by definition:

$$\text{Assets} - \text{Liabilities} \equiv \text{Net Worth}$$

or

$$\text{Assets} \equiv \text{Liabilities} + \text{Net Worth}$$

[2] In return for lending you the receipt for 20 ounces of gold, the goldsmith expects to get an IOU promising to repay the amount (in gold itself or with a receipt from another goldsmith) with interest after a certain period of time.

Assets are things a firm owns that are worth something. For a bank, these assets include the bank building, its furniture, its holdings of government securities, cash in its vaults, bonds, stocks, and so on. Most important among a bank's assets, for our purposes at least, are the loans it has made. A borrower gives the bank an *IOU*, a promise to repay a certain sum of money on or by a certain date. This promise is an asset of the bank because it is worth something. The bank could (and sometimes does) sell the IOU to another bank for cash.

Federal Reserve Bank (the Fed) The central bank of the United States.

Other bank assets include cash on hand (sometimes called *vault cash*) and deposits with the U.S. central bank—the **Federal Reserve Bank (the Fed)**. As we will see later in this chapter, federal banking regulations require that banks keep a certain portion of their deposits on hand as vault cash or on deposit with the Fed.

A firm's *liabilities* are its debts—what it owes. A bank's liabilities are the promises to pay, or IOUs, that it has issued. A bank's most important liabilities are its deposits. *Deposits* are debts owed to the depositors because when you deposit money in your account, you are in essence making a loan to the bank.

The basic rule of accounting says that if we add up a firm's assets and then subtract the total amount it owes to all those who have lent it funds, the difference is the firm's net worth. *Net worth* represents the value of the firm to its stockholders or owners. How much would you pay for a firm that owns $200,000 worth of diamonds and had borrowed $150,000 from a bank to pay for them? The firm is worth $50,000—the difference between what it owns and what it owes. If the price of diamonds were to fall, bringing their value down to only $150,000, the firm would be worth nothing.

We can keep track of a bank's financial position using a simplified balance sheet called a T-account. By convention, the bank's assets are listed on the left side of the T-account and its liabilities and net worth are on the right side. By definition, the balance sheet always balances, so that the sum of the items on the left side of the T-account is equal to the sum of the items on the right side.

reserves The deposits that a bank has at the Federal Reserve bank plus its cash on hand.

The T-account in Figure 25.1 shows a bank having $110 million in *assets*, of which $20 million are **reserves**, the deposits the bank has made at the Fed, and its cash on hand (coins and currency). Reserves are an asset to the bank because it can go to the Fed and get cash for them, the same way you can go to the bank and get cash for the amount in your savings account. Our bank's other asset is its loans, worth $90 million.

▶ **FIGURE 25.1**

T-Account for a Typical Bank (millions of dollars)

The balance sheet of a bank must always balance, so that the sum of assets (reserves and loans) equals the sum of liabilities (deposits and net worth).

	Assets	Liabilities	
Reserves	20	100	Deposits
Loans	90	10	Net worth
Total	110	110	Total

Why do banks hold reserves/deposits at the Fed? There are many reasons, but perhaps the most important is the legal requirement that they hold a certain percentage of their deposit liabilities as reserves. The percentage of its deposits that a bank must keep as reserves is known as the **required reserve ratio**. If the reserve ratio is 20 percent, a bank with deposits of $100 million must hold $20 million as reserves, either as cash or as deposits at the Fed. To simplify, we will assume that banks hold all of their reserves in the form of deposits at the Fed.

required reserve ratio The percentage of its total deposits that a bank must keep as reserves at the Federal Reserve.

On the liabilities side of the T-account, the bank has taken deposits of $100 million, so it owes this amount to its depositors. This means that the bank has a net worth of $10 million to its owners ($110 million in assets – $250 million in liabilities = $10 million net worth). The net worth of the bank is what "balances" the balance sheet. Remember that when some item on a bank's balance sheet changes, there must be at least one other change somewhere else to maintain balance. If a bank's reserves increase by $1, one of the following must also be true: (1) Its other assets (for example, loans) decrease by $1, (2) its liabilities (deposits) increase by $1, or (3) its net worth increases by $1. Various fractional combinations of these are also possible.

The Creation of Money

Like the goldsmiths, today's bankers seek to earn income by lending money out at a higher interest rate than they pay depositors for use of their money.

In modern times, the chances of a run on a bank are fairly small; and even if there is a run, the central bank protects the private banks in various ways. Therefore, banks usually make loans up to the point where they can no longer do so because of the reserve requirement restriction. A bank's required amount of reserves is equal to the required reserve ratio times the total deposits in the bank. If a bank has deposits of $100 and the required ratio is 20 percent, the required amount of reserves is $20. The difference between a bank's actual reserves and its required reserves is its **excess reserves**:

excess reserves The difference between a bank's actual reserves and its required reserves.

$$\text{excess reserves} \equiv \text{actual reserves} - \text{required reserves}$$

If banks make loans up to the point where they can no longer do so because of the reserve requirement restriction, this means that banks make loans up to the point where their excess reserves are zero.

To see why, note that when a bank has excess reserves, it has credit available and it can make loans. Actually, a bank can make loans *only* if it has excess reserves. When a bank makes a loan, it creates a demand deposit for the borrower. This creation of a demand deposit causes the bank's excess reserves to fall because the extra deposits created by the loan use up some of the excess reserves the bank has on hand. An example will help demonstrate this.

Assume that there is only one private bank in the country, the required reserve ratio is 20 percent, and the bank starts off with nothing, as shown in panel 1 of Figure 25.2. Now suppose dollar bills are in circulation and someone deposits 100 of them in the bank. The bank deposits the $100 with the central bank, so it now has $100 in reserves, as shown in panel 2. The bank now has assets (reserves) of $100 and liabilities (deposits) of $100. If the required reserve ratio is 20 percent, the bank has excess reserves of $80.

Panel 1		Panel 2		Panel 3	
Assets	Liabilities	Assets	Liabilities	Assets	Liabilities
Reserves 0	0 Deposits	Reserves 100	100 Deposits	Reserves 100 Loans 400	500 Deposits

▲ **FIGURE 25.2 Balance Sheets of a Bank in a Single-Bank Economy**
In panel 2, there is an initial deposit of $100. In panel 3, the bank has made loans of $400.

How much can the bank lend and still meet the reserve requirement? For the moment, let us assume that anyone who gets a loan keeps the entire proceeds in the bank or pays them to someone else who does. Nothing is withdrawn as cash. In this case, the bank can lend $400 and still meet the reserve requirement. Panel 3 shows the balance sheet of the bank after completing the maximum amount of loans it is allowed with a 20 percent reserve ratio. With $80 of excess reserves, the bank can have up to $400 of additional deposits. The $100 in reserves plus $400 in loans (which are made as deposits) equals $500 in deposits. With $500 in deposits and a required reserve ratio of 20 percent, the bank must have reserves of $100 (20 percent of $500)—and it does. The bank can lend no more than $400 because its reserve requirement must not exceed $100. When a bank has no excess reserves and thus can make no more loans, it is said to be *loaned up*.

Remember, the money supply (M1) equals cash in circulation plus deposits. Before the initial deposit, the money supply was $100 ($100 cash and no deposits). After the deposit and the loans, the money supply is $500 (no cash outside bank vaults and $500 in deposits). It is clear then that when loans are converted into deposits, the supply of money can change.

The bank whose T-accounts are presented in Figure 25.2 is allowed to make loans of $400 based on the assumption that loans that are made *stay in the bank* in the form of deposits. Now suppose you borrow from the bank to buy a personal computer and you write a check to the computer store. If the store also deposits its money in the bank, your check merely results in a reduction in your account balance and an increase to the store's account balance within the bank. No cash has left the bank. As long as the system is closed in this way—remember that so far we have assumed that there is only one bank—the bank knows that it will never be called on to release any of its $100 in reserves. It can expand its loans up to the point where its total deposits are $500.

Of course, there are many banks in the country, a situation that is depicted in Figure 25.3. As long as the banking system as a whole is closed, it is still possible for an initial deposit of $100 to result in an expansion of the money supply to $500, but more steps are involved when there is more than one bank.

	Panel 1		Panel 2		Panel 3	
	Assets	Liabilities	Assets	Liabilities	Assets	Liabilities
Bank 1	Reserves 100	100 Deposits	Reserves 100 Loans 80	180 Deposits	Reserves 20 Loans 80	100 Deposits
Bank 2	Reserves 80	80 Deposits	Reserves 80 Loans 64	144 Deposits	Reserves 16 Loans 64	80 Deposits
Bank 3	Reserves 64	64 Deposits	Reserves 64 Loans 51.20	115.20 Deposits	Reserves 12.80 Loans 51.20	64 Deposits

Summary:	Loans	Deposits
Bank 1	80	100
Bank 2	64	80
Bank 3	51.20	64
Bank 4	40.96	51.20
⋮	⋮	⋮
Total	400.00	500.00

▲ **FIGURE 25.3 The Creation of Money When There Are Many Banks**

In panel 1, there is an initial deposit of $100 in bank 1. In panel 2, bank 1 makes a loan of $80 by creating a deposit of $80. A check for $80 by the borrower is then written on bank 1 (panel 3) and deposited in bank 2 (panel 1). The process continues with bank 2 making loans and so on. In the end, loans of $400 have been made and the total level of deposits is $500.

To see why, assume that Mary makes an initial deposit of $100 in bank 1 and the bank deposits the entire $100 with the Fed (panel 1 of Figure 25.3). All loans that a bank makes are withdrawn from the bank as the individual borrowers write checks to pay for merchandise. After Mary's deposit, bank 1 can make a loan of up to $80 to Bill because it needs to keep only $20 of its $100 deposit as reserves. (We are assuming a 20 percent required reserve ratio.) In other words, bank 1 has $80 in excess reserves.

Bank 1's balance sheet at the moment of the loan to Bill appears in panel 2 of Figure 25.3. Bank 1 now has loans of $80. It has credited Bill's account with the $80, so its total deposits are $180 ($80 in loans plus $100 in reserves). Bill then writes a check for $80 for a set of shock absorbers for his car. Bill wrote his check to Sam's Car Shop, and Sam deposits Bill's check in bank 2. When the check clears, bank 1 transfers $80 in reserves to bank 2. Bank 1's balance sheet now looks like the top of panel 3. Its assets include reserves of $20 and loans of $80; its liabilities are $100 in deposits. Both sides of the T-account balance: The bank's reserves are 20 percent of its deposits, as required by law, and it is fully loaned up.

Now look at bank 2. Because bank 1 has transferred $80 in reserves to bank 2, bank 2 now has $80 in deposits and $80 in reserves (panel 1, bank 2). Its reserve requirement is also 20 percent, so it has excess reserves of $64 on which it can make loans.

Now assume that bank 2 loans the $64 to Kate to pay for a textbook and Kate writes a check for $64 payable to the Manhattan College Bookstore. The final position of bank 2, after it honors

Kate's $64 check by transferring $64 in reserves to the bookstore's bank, is reserves of $16, loans of $64, and deposits of $80 (panel 3, bank 2).

The Manhattan College Bookstore deposits Kate's check in its account with bank 3. Bank 3 now has excess reserves because it has added $64 to its reserves. With a reserve ratio of 20 percent, bank 3 can loan out $51.20 (80 percent of $64, leaving 20 percent in required reserves to back the $64 deposit).

As the process is repeated over and over, the total amount of deposits created is $500, the sum of the deposits in each of the banks. Because the banking system can be looked on as one big bank, the outcome here for many banks is the same as the outcome in Figure 25.2 for one bank.[3]

The Money Multiplier

In practice, the banking system is not completely closed—there is some leakage out of the system. Still, the point here is that an increase in bank reserves leads to a greater than one-for-one increase in the money supply. Economists call the relationship between the final change in deposits and the change in reserves that caused this change the money multiplier. Stated somewhat differently, the **money multiplier** is the multiple by which deposits can increase for every dollar increase in reserves. Do not confuse the money multiplier with the spending multipliers we discussed in the last two chapters. They are not the same thing.

money multiplier The multiple by which deposits can increase for every dollar increase in reserves; equal to 1 divided by the required reserve ratio.

In the example we just examined, reserves increased by $100 when the $100 in cash was deposited in a bank and the amount of deposits increased by $500 ($100 from the initial deposit, $400 from the loans made by the various banks from their excess reserves). The money multiplier in this case is $500/$100 = 5. Mathematically, the money multiplier can be defined as follows:

$$\text{money multiplier} \equiv \frac{1}{\text{required reserve ratio}}$$

In the United States, the required reserve ratio varies depending on the size of the bank and the type of deposit. For large banks and for checking deposits, the ratio is currently 10 percent, which makes the potential money multiplier 1/.10 = 10. This means that an increase in reserves of $1 could cause an increase in deposits of $10 if there were no leakage out of the system.

The Federal Reserve System

We have seen how the private banking system creates money by making loans. However, private banks are not free to create money at will. Their ability to create money is controlled by the volume of reserves in the system, which is controlled by the Fed. The Fed therefore has the ultimate control over the money supply. We will now examine the structure and function of the Fed.

Founded in 1913 by an act of Congress (to which major reforms were added in the 1930s), the Fed is the central bank of the United States. The Fed is a complicated institution with many responsibilities, including the regulation and supervision of over 7,500 commercial banks. The organization of the Federal Reserve System is presented in Figure 25.4.

The *Board of Governors* is the most important group within the Federal Reserve System. The board consists of seven members, each appointed for 14 years by the president of the United States. The *chair* of the Fed, who is appointed by the president and whose term runs for 4 years, usually dominates the entire Federal Reserve System and is sometimes said to be the second most powerful person in the United States. The Fed is an independent agency in that it does not take orders from the president or from Congress.

The United States is divided into 12 Federal Reserve districts, each with its own Federal Reserve bank. These districts are indicated on the map in Figure 25.4. The district banks are like branch offices of the Fed in that they carry out the rules, regulations, and functions of the central system in their districts and report to the Board of Governors on local economic conditions.

---

[3] If banks create money when they make loans, does repaying a loan "destroy" money? The answer is yes.

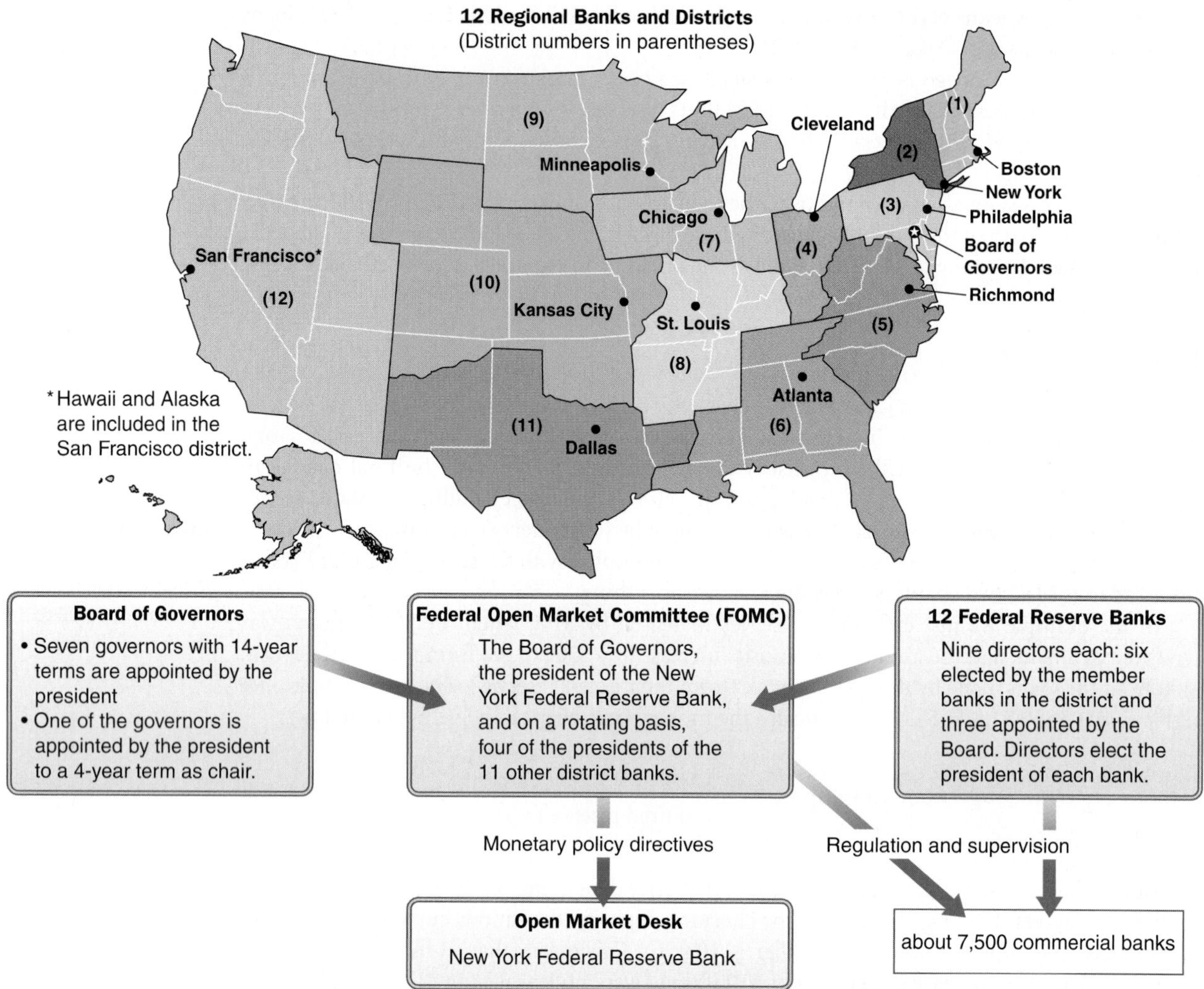

▲ FIGURE 25.4 **The Structure of the Federal Reserve System**

Federal Open Market Committee (FOMC) A group composed of the seven members of the Fed's Board of Governors, the president of the New York Federal Reserve Bank, and four of the other 11 district bank presidents on a rotating basis; it sets goals concerning the money supply and interest rates and directs the operation of the Open Market Desk in New York.

Open Market Desk The office in the New York Federal Reserve Bank from which government securities are bought and sold by the Fed.

U.S. monetary policy—the behavior of the Fed concerning the money supply—is formally set by the **Federal Open Market Committee (FOMC)**. The FOMC consists of the seven members of the Fed's Board of Governors, the president of the New York Federal Reserve Bank and on a rotating basis, four of the presidents of the 11 other district banks. The FOMC sets goals concerning the money supply and interest rates, and it directs the **Open Market Desk** in the New York Federal Reserve Bank to buy and/or sell government securities. (We discuss the specifics of open market operations later in this chapter.)

Functions of the Federal Reserve

The Fed is the central bank of the United States. Central banks are sometimes known as "bankers' banks" because only banks (and occasionally foreign governments) can have accounts in them. As a private citizen, you cannot go to the nearest branch of the Fed and open a checking account or apply to borrow money.

Although from a macroeconomic point of view the Fed's crucial role is to control the money supply, the Fed also performs several important functions for banks. These functions include clearing interbank payments, regulating the banking system, and assisting banks in a difficult financial position. The Fed is also responsible for managing exchange rates and the nation's foreign exchange reserves.[4] In addition, it is often involved in intercountry negotiations on international economic issues.

---

[4] *Foreign exchange reserves* are holdings of the currencies of other countries—for example, Japanese yen—by the U.S. government. We discuss exchange rates and foreign exchange markets at length in Chapter 35.

Clearing Interbank Payments Suppose you write a $100 check drawn on your bank, the First Bank of Fresno (FBF), to pay for tulip bulbs from Crockett Importers of Miami, Florida. Because Crockett Importers does not bank at FBF, but at Banco de Miami, how does your money get from your bank to the bank in Florida?

The answer: The Fed does it. Both FBF and Banco de Miami have accounts at the Fed. When Crockett Importers receives your check and deposits it at Banco de Miami, the bank submits the check to the Fed, asking it to collect the funds from FBF. The Fed presents the check to FBF and is instructed to debit FBF's account for the $100 and to credit the account of Banco de Miami. Accounts at the Fed count as reserves, so FBF loses $100 in reserves, and Banco de Miami gains $100 in reserves. The two banks effectively have traded ownerships of their deposits at the Fed. The *total* volume of reserves has not changed, nor has the money supply.

This function of clearing interbank payments allows banks to shift money around virtually instantaneously. All they need to do is wire the Fed and request a transfer, and the funds move at the speed of electricity from one computer account to another.

Other Duties of the Fed Besides facilitating the transfer of funds between banks, the Fed performs several other important duties. It is responsible for many of the regulations governing banking practices and standards. For example, the Fed has the authority to control mergers between banks, and it is responsible for examining banks to ensure that they are financially sound and that they conform to a host of government accounting regulations. As we saw earlier, the Fed also sets reserve requirements for all financial institutions.

One of the most important responsibilities of the Fed is to act as the **lender of last resort** for the banking system. As our discussion of goldsmiths suggested, banks are subject to the possibility of runs on their deposits. In the United States, most deposits of less than $100,000 are insured by the Federal Deposit Insurance Corporation (FDIC), a U.S. government agency that was established in 1933 during the Great Depression. Deposit insurance makes panics less likely. Because depositors know they can always get their money, even if the bank fails, they are less likely to withdraw their deposits. Not all deposits are insured, so the possibility of bank panics remains. However, the Fed stands ready to provide funds to a troubled bank that cannot find any other sources of funds.

lender of last resort One of the functions of the Fed: It provides funds to troubled banks that cannot find any other sources of funds.

The Fed is the ideal lender of last resort for two reasons. First, providing funds to a bank that is in dire straits is risky and not likely to be very profitable, and it is hard to find private banks or other private institutions willing to do this. The Fed is a nonprofit institution whose function is to serve the overall welfare of the public. Thus, the Fed would certainly be interested in preventing catastrophic banking panics such as those that occurred in the late 1920s and the 1930s.

Second, the Fed has an essentially unlimited supply of funds with which to bail out banks facing the possibility of runs. The reason, as we shall see, is that the Fed can create reserves at will. A promise by the Fed that it will support a bank is very convincing. Unlike any other lender, the Fed can never run out of money. Therefore, the explicit or implicit support of the Fed should be enough to assure depositors that they are in no danger of losing their funds.

In March 2008, the Fed, in a major change in policy, began loaning money to financial institutions other than commercial banks. The change was in response to financial problems in the United States that resulted from falling housing prices and mortgage foreclosures. In an even larger change, the Fed guaranteed $30 billion of Bear Stearns' liabilities to JPMorgan in a deal that had JPMorgan buying Bear Stearns. It is hard to know how these changes in policy will play out, but it does suggest that the Fed may take a more active role in the private financial sector than merely as a lender of last resort.

The Federal Reserve Balance Sheet

Although it is a special bank, the Fed is in some ways similar to an ordinary commercial bank. Like an ordinary bank, the Fed has a balance sheet that records its asset and liability position at any moment in time. The balance sheet for the Fed is presented in Table 25.1.

As the asset side of the balance sheet shows, the Fed owns about $11 billion of gold. *Do not think that this gold has anything to do with the supply of money.* Most of the gold was acquired during the 1930s, when it was purchased from the U.S. Treasury Department. Since 1934, the dollar has not been backed by (is not convertible into) gold. You cannot take a dollar bill to the Fed to

TABLE 25.1 Assets and Liabilities of the Federal Reserve System, October 24, 2007 (Millions of Dollars)

Assets			Liabilities
Gold	$ 11,037	$776,701	Federal Reserve notes (outstanding)
Loans to banks	502		Deposits:
U.S. Treasury securities	779,574	21,107	Bank Reserves (from depository institutions)
All other assets	93,860	4,737	U.S. Treasury
Total	$884,973	82,428	All other liabilities and net worth
		$884,973	Total

Source: Board of Governors of the Federal Reserve System.

receive gold for it; all you can get for your old dollar bill is a new dollar bill.[5] Although it is unrelated to the money supply, the Fed's gold counts as an asset on its balance sheet because it is something of value the Fed owns.

The balance sheet mentions an asset called "loans to banks." These loans are an asset of the Fed in the same way a private commercial bank's loans are among its assets. The Fed sometimes makes loans to commercial banks that are short of reserves.[6] The $502 million in Table 25.1 represents these kinds of loans.

The largest of the Fed's assets by far consists of government (U.S. Treasury) securities: $779,574 million worth on October 24, 2007. Government securities such as Treasury bills and bonds are obligations of the federal government that the Fed has purchased over the years. The way in which these bonds are acquired has important implications for the Fed's control of the money supply. (We return to this topic after our survey of the Fed's balance sheet.)

The bulk of the Fed's liabilities are Federal Reserve notes. The dollar bill you use to buy a pack of gum is clearly an asset from your point of view—it is something you own that has value. Because every financial asset is by definition a liability of some other agent in the economy, whose liability is that dollar bill? That dollar bill, and bills of all other denominations in the economy, are a liability—an IOU—of the Fed. They are rather strange IOUs because all they can be redeemed for are other IOUs of exactly the same type. They are, nonetheless, classified as liabilities of the Fed.

The balance sheet shows that, like an ordinary commercial bank, the Fed has accepted deposits. These deposits are liabilities. The bulk of the Fed's deposits come from commercial banks. Remember, commercial banks are required to keep a certain share of their own deposits as deposits at the Fed. A bank's deposits at the Fed (its reserves) are an asset from the bank's point of view, and those same reserves must be a liability from the Fed's point of view.

Table 25.1 shows that the Fed has accepted a small volume of deposits from the U.S. Treasury. In effect, the Fed acts as the bank for the U.S. government. When the government needs to pay for something such as a new aircraft carrier, it may write a check to the supplier of the ship drawn on its "checking account" at the Fed. Similarly, when the government receives revenues from tax collections, fines, or sales of government assets, it may deposit these funds in its account at the Fed.

How the Federal Reserve Controls the Money Supply

To see how the Fed controls the supply of money in the U.S. economy, we need to understand the role of reserves. As we have said, the required reserve ratio establishes a link between the reserves of the commercial banks and the deposits (money) that commercial banks are allowed to create. The reserve requirement effectively determines how much a bank has available to lend. If the required reserve

---

[5] The fact that the Fed is not obliged to provide gold for currency means it can never go bankrupt. When the currency was backed by gold, it would have been possible for the Fed to run out of gold if too many of its depositors came to it at the same time and asked to exchange their deposits for gold. If depositors come to the Fed to withdraw their deposits today, all they can get is dollar bills. The dollar was convertible into gold internationally until August 15, 1971.

[6] Recall that commercial banks are required to keep a set percentage of their deposit liabilities on deposit at the Fed. If a bank suddenly finds itself short of reserves, one of its alternatives is to borrow the reserves it needs from the Fed.

ratio is 20 percent, each $1 of reserves can support $5 in deposits. A bank that has reserves of $100,000 cannot have more than $500,000 in deposits. If it did, it would fail to meet the required reserve ratio.

If you recall that the *money supply* is equal to the sum of deposits inside banks and the currency in circulation outside banks, you can see that reserves provide the leverage that the Fed needs to control the money supply. If the Fed wants to increase the supply of money, it creates more reserves, thereby freeing banks to create additional deposits by making more loans. If it wants to decrease the money supply, it reduces reserves.

Three tools are available to the Fed for changing the money supply: (1) changing the required reserve ratio, (2) changing the discount rate, and (3) engaging in open market operations. Although (3) is almost exclusively used to change the money supply, an understanding of how (1) and (2) work is useful in understanding how (3) works. We thus begin our discussion with the first two tools.

The Required Reserve Ratio

One way for the Fed to alter the supply of money is to change the required reserve ratio. This process is shown in Table 25.2. Let us assume the initial required reserve ratio is 20 percent.

In panel 1, a simplified version of the Fed's balance sheet (in billions of dollars) shows that reserves are $100 billion and currency outstanding is $100 billion. The total value of the Fed's assets is $200 billion, which we assume to be all in government securities. Assuming there are no excess reserves—banks stay fully loaned up—the $100 billion in reserves supports $500 billion in deposits at the commercial banks. ((Remember, the money multiplier equals 1/required reserve ratio = 1/.20 = 5. Thus, $100 billion in reserves can support $500 billion ($100 billion × 5) in deposits when the required reserve ratio is 20 percent.)) The supply of money (M1, or transactions money) is therefore $600 billion: $100 billion in currency and $500 billion in (checking account) deposits at the commercial banks.

TABLE 25.2 A Decrease in the Required Reserve Ratio from 20 Percent to 12.5 Percent Increases the Supply of Money (All Figures in Billions of Dollars)

Panel 1: Required Reserve Ratio = 20%

Federal Reserve				Commercial Banks			
Assets		Liabilities		Assets		Liabilities	
Government securities	$200	$100	Reserves	Reserves	$100	$500	Deposits
		$100	Currency	Loans	$400		

Note: Money supply (M1) = currency + deposits = $600.

Panel 2: Required Reserve Ratio = 12.5%

Federal Reserve				Commercial Banks			
Assets		Liabilities		Assets		Liabilities	
Government securities	$200	$100	Reserves	Reserves	$100	$800 (+$300)	Deposits
		$100	Currency	Loans (+$300)	$700		

Note: Money supply (M1) = currency + deposits = $900.

Now suppose the Fed wants to increase the supply of money to $900 billion. If it lowers the required reserve ratio from 20 percent to 12.5 percent (as in panel 2 of Table 25.2), the same $100 billion of reserves could support $800 billion in deposits instead of only $500 billion. In this case, the money multiplier is 1/.125, or 8. At a required reserve ratio of 12.5 percent, $100 billion in reserves can support $800 billion in deposits. The total money supply would be $800 billion in deposits plus the $100 billion in currency, for a total of $900 billion.[7]

[7] To find the maximum volume of deposits (D) that can be supported by an amount of reserves (R), divide R by the required reserve ratio. If the required reserve ratio is g, because $R = gD$, then $D = R/g$.

Put another way, with the new lower reserve ratio, banks have excess reserves of $37.5 billion. At a required reserve ratio of 20 percent, they needed $100 billion in reserves to back their $500 billion in deposits. At the lower required reserve ratio of 12.5 percent, they need only $62.5 billion of reserves to back their $500 billion of deposits; so the remaining $37.5 billion of the existing $100 billion in reserves is "extra." With that $37.5 billion of excess reserves, banks can lend out more money. If we assume the system loans money and creates deposits to the *maximum* extent possible, the $37.5 billion of reserves will support an additional $300 billion of deposits ($37.5 billion × the money multiplier of 8 = $300 billion). The change in the required reserve ratio has injected an additional $300 billion into the banking system, at which point the banks will be fully loaned up and unable to increase their deposits further. Decreases in the required reserve ratio allow banks to have more deposits with the existing volume of reserves. As banks create more deposits by making loans, the supply of money (currency + deposits) increases. The reverse is also true: If the Fed wants to restrict the supply of money, it can raise the required reserve ratio, in which case banks will find that they have insufficient reserves and must therefore reduce their deposits by "calling in" some of their loans.[8] The result is a decrease in the money supply.

For many reasons, the Fed has tended not to use changes in the reserve requirement to control the money supply. In part, this reluctance stems from the era when only some banks were members of the Fed and therefore subject to reserve requirements. The Fed reasoned that if it raised the reserve requirement to contract the money supply, banks might choose to stop being members. (Because reserves pay no interest, the higher the reserve requirement, the more the penalty imposed on those banks holding reserves.) This argument no longer applies. Since the passage of the Depository Institutions Deregulation and Monetary Control Act in 1980, all depository institutions are subject to Fed requirements.

It is also true that changing the reserve requirement ratio is a crude tool. Because of lags in banks' reporting to the Fed on their reserve and deposit positions, a change in the requirement today does not affect banks for about 2 weeks. (However, the fact that changing the reserve requirement expands or reduces credit in every bank in the country makes it a very powerful tool when the Fed does use it.)

The Discount Rate

discount rate The interest rate that banks pay to the Fed to borrow from it.

Banks may borrow from the Fed. The interest rate they pay the Fed is the **discount rate**. When banks increase their borrowing, the money supply increases. To see why this is true, assume that there is only one bank in the country and that the required reserve ratio is 20 percent. The initial position of the bank and the Fed appear in panel 1 of Table 25.3, where the money supply (currency + deposits) is $480 billion. In panel 2, the bank has borrowed $20 billion from the Fed. By using this $20 billion as a reserve, the bank can increase its loans by $100 billion, from $320 billion to $420 billion. (Remember, a required reserve ratio of 20 percent gives a money multiplier of 5; having excess reserves of $20 billion allows the bank to create an additional $20 billion × 5, or $100 billion, in deposits.) The money supply has thus increased from $480 billion to $580 billion. Bank borrowing from the Fed thus leads to an increase in the money supply.

The Fed can influence bank borrowing, and thus the money supply, through the discount rate. The higher the discount rate, the higher the cost of borrowing and the less borrowing banks will want to do. If the Fed wants to curtail the growth of the money supply, for example, it will raise the discount rate and discourages banks from borrowing from it, restricting the growth of reserves (and ultimately deposits).

Historically, the Fed has not used the discount rate to control the money supply. Prior to 2003 it usually set the discount rate lower than the rate that banks had to pay to borrow money in the private market. Although this provided an incentive for banks to borrow from the Fed, the Fed discouraged borrowing by putting pressure in various ways on the banks not to borrow. This

---

[8] To reduce the money supply, banks never really have to "call in" loans before they are due. First, the Fed is almost always expanding the money supply slowly because the real economy grows steadily and, as we shall see, growth brings with it the need for more circulating money. So when we speak of "contractionary monetary policy," we mean the Fed is slowing down the rate of money growth, not reducing the money supply. Second, even if the Fed were to cut reserves (instead of curb their expansion), banks would no doubt be able to comply by reducing the volume of new loans they make while old ones are coming due.

TABLE 25.3 The Effect on the Money Supply of Commercial Bank Borrowing from the Fed (All Figures in Billions of Dollars)

Panel 1: No Commercial Bank Borrowing from the Fed

Federal Reserve				Commercial Banks			
Assets		Liabilities		Assets		Liabilities	
Securities	$160	$80	Reserves	Reserves	$80	$400	Deposits
		$80	Currency	Loans	$320		

Note: Money supply (M1) = currency + deposits = $480.

Panel 2: Commercial Bank Borrowing $20 from the Fed

Federal Reserve				Commercial Banks			
Assets		Liabilities		Assets		Liabilities	
Securities	$160	$100	Reserves (+$20)	Reserves (+$20)	$100	$500	Deposits (+$300)
Loans	$20	$80	Currency	Loans (+$100)	$420	$20	Amount owed to Fed (+$20)

Note: Money supply (M1) = currency + deposits = $580.

pressure was sometimes called **moral suasion.** On January 9, 2003, the Fed announced a new procedure. Henceforth, the discount rate would be set above the rate that banks pay to borrow money in the private market and moral suasion would no longer be used. Although banks can now borrow from the Fed if they want to, they are unlikely to do so except in unusual circumstances because borrowing is cheaper in the private market. It is thus clear that the Fed is not using the discount rate as a tool to try to change the money supply on a regular basis.

moral suasion The pressure that in the past the Fed exerted on member banks to discourage them from borrowing heavily from the Fed.

Open Market Operations

By far the most significant of the Fed's tools for controlling the supply of money is **open market operations.** Congress has authorized the Fed to buy and sell U.S. government securities in the open market. When the Fed purchases a security, it pays for it by writing a check that, when cleared, *expands* the quantity of reserves in the system, increasing the money supply. When the Fed sells a bond, private citizens or institutions pay for it with a check that, when cleared, *reduces* the quantity of reserves in the system.

open market operations The purchase and sale by the Fed of government securities in the open market; a tool used to expand or contract the amount of reserves in the system and thus the money supply.

To see how open market operations and reserve controls work, we need to review several key ideas.

Two Branches of Government Deal in Government Securities The fact that the Fed is able to buy and sell government securities—bills and bonds—may be confusing. In fact, *two* branches of government deal in financial markets for different reasons; and you must keep the two separate in your mind.

First, keep in mind that the Treasury Department is responsible for collecting taxes and paying the federal government's bills. Salary checks paid to government workers, payments to General Dynamics for a new Navy ship, Social Security checks to retirees, and so on, are all written on accounts maintained by the Treasury. Tax receipts collected by the Internal Revenue Service, a Treasury branch, are deposited to these accounts.

If total government spending exceeds tax receipts, the law requires the Treasury to borrow the difference. Recall that the government deficit is $(G - T)$, or government purchases minus net taxes. $(G - T)$ is the amount the Treasury must borrow each year to finance the deficit. This means that the Treasury *cannot* print money to finance the deficit. The Treasury borrows by issuing bills, bonds, and notes that pay interest. These government securities, or IOUs, are sold to individuals and institutions. Often foreign countries as well as U.S. citizens buy them. As discussed in Chapter 24, the total amount of privately held government securities is the *privately held federal debt.*

The Fed is not the Treasury. Instead, it is a quasi-independent agency authorized by Congress to buy and sell *outstanding* (preexisting) U.S. government securities on the open market. The bonds and bills initially sold by the Treasury to finance the deficit are continuously resold and traded among ordinary citizens, firms, banks, pension funds, and so on. The Fed's participation in that trading affects the quantity of reserves in the system, as we will see.

Because the Fed owns some government securities, some of what the government owes it owes to itself. Recall that the Federal Reserve System's largest single asset is government securities. These securities are nothing more than bills and bonds initially issued by the Treasury to finance the deficit. They were acquired by the Fed over time through direct open market purchases that the Fed made to expand the money supply as the economy expanded.

The Mechanics of Open Market Operations How do open market operations affect the money supply? Look again at Table 25.1 on p. 506. As you can see, most of the Fed's assets consist of the government securities we have been talking about.

Suppose the Fed wants to decrease the supply of money. If it can reduce the volume of bank reserves on the liabilities side of its balance sheet, it will force banks, in turn, to reduce their own deposits (to meet the required reserve ratio). Since these deposits are part of the supply of money, the supply of money will contract.

What will happen if the Fed sells some of its holdings of government securities to the general public? The Fed's holdings of government securities must decrease because the securities it sold will now be owned by someone else. How do the purchasers of securities pay for what they have bought? They pay by writing checks drawn on their banks and payable to the Fed.

Let us look more carefully at how this works, with the help of Table 25.4. In panel 1, the Fed initially has $100 billion of government securities. Its liabilities consist of $20 billion of deposits (which are the reserves of commercial banks) and $80 billion of currency. With the required reserve ratio at 20 percent, the $20 billion of reserves can support $100 billion of deposits in the commercial banks. The commercial banking system is fully loaned up. Panel 1 also shows the financial position of a private citizen, Jane Q. Public. Jane has assets of $5 billion (a large checking account deposit in the bank) and no debts, so her net worth is $5 billion.

TABLE 25.4 Open Market Operations (The Numbers in Parentheses in Panels 2 and 3 Show the Differences Between Those Panels and Panel 1. All Figures in Billions of Dollars)

Panel 1

Federal Reserve				Commercial Banks				Jane Q. Public			
Assets		Liabilities		Assets		Liabilities		Assets		Liabilities	
Securities	$100	$20	Reserves	Reserves	$20	$100	Deposits	Deposits	$5	$0	Debts
		$80	Currency	Loans	$80					$5	Net Worth

Note: Money supply (M1) = currency + deposits = $180.

Panel 2

Federal Reserve				Commercial Banks				Jane Q. Public			
Assets		Liabilities		Assets		Liabilities		Assets		Liabilities	
Securities (−$5)	$95	$15	Reserves (−$5)	Reserves (−$5)	$15	$95	Deposits (−$5)	Deposits (−$5)	$0	$0	Debts
		$80	Currency	Loans	$80			Securities (+$5)	$5	$5	Net Worth

Note: Money supply (M1) = currency + deposits = $175.

Panel 3

Federal Reserve				Commercial Banks				Jane Q. Public			
Assets		Liabilities		Assets		Liabilities		Assets		Liabilities	
Securities (−$5)	$95	$15	Reserves (−$5)	Reserves (−$5)	$15	$75	Deposits (−$25)	Deposits (−$5)	$0	$0	Debts
		$80	Currency	Loans (−$20)	$60			Securities (+$5)	$5	$5	Net Worth

Note: Money supply (M1) = currency + deposits = $155.

Now imagine that the Fed sells $5 billion in government securities to Jane. Jane pays for the securities by writing a check to the Fed, drawn on her bank. The Fed then reduces the reserve account of her bank by $5 billion. The balance sheets of all the participants after this transaction are shown in panel 2. Note that the supply of money (currency plus deposits) has fallen from $180 billion to $175 billion.

This is not the end of the story. As a result of the Fed's sale of securities, the amount of reserves has fallen from $20 billion to $15 billion, while deposits have fallen from $100 billion to $95 billion. With a required reserve ratio of 20 percent, banks must have .20 × $95 billion, or $19 billion, in reserves. Banks are under their required reserve ratio by $4 billion [$19 billion (the amount they should have) minus $15 billion (the amount they do have)]. To comply with the federal regulations, banks must decrease their loans and their deposits.[9]

The final equilibrium position is shown in panel 3, where commercial banks have reduced their loans by $20 billion. Notice that the change in deposits from panel 1 to panel 3 is $25 billion, which is five times the size of the change in reserves that the Fed brought about through its $5 billion open market sale of securities. This corresponds exactly to our earlier analysis of the money multiplier. The change in money (−$25 billion) is equal to the money multiplier (5) times the change in reserves (−$5 billion).

Now consider what happens when the Fed *purchases* a government security. Suppose you hold $100 in Treasury bills, which the Fed buys from you. The Fed writes you a check for $100, and you turn in your Treasury bills. You then take the $100 check and deposit it in your local bank. This increases the reserves of your bank by $100 and begins a new episode in the money expansion story. With a reserve requirement of 20 percent, your bank can now lend out $80. If that $80 is spent and ends up back in a bank, that bank can lend $64, and so on. (Review Figure 25.3.) The Fed can expand the money supply by buying government securities from people who own them, just the way it reduces the money supply by selling these securities.

Each business day the Open Market Desk in the New York Federal Reserve Bank buys or sells millions of dollars' worth of securities, usually to large security dealers who act as intermediaries between the Fed and the private markets. We can sum up the effect of these open market operations this way:

- An open market *purchase* of securities by the Fed results in an *increase* in reserves and an *increase* in the supply of money by an amount equal to the money multiplier times the change in reserves.
- An open market *sale* of securities by the Fed results in a *decrease* in reserves and a *decrease* in the supply of money by an amount equal to the money multiplier times the change in reserves.

Open market operations are the Fed's preferred means of controlling the money supply for several reasons. First, open market operations can be used with some precision. If the Fed needs to change the money supply by just a small amount, it can buy or sell a small volume of government securities. If it wants a larger change in the money supply, it can buy or sell a larger amount. Second, open market operations are extremely flexible. If the Fed decides to reverse course, it can easily switch from buying securities to selling them. Finally, open market operations have a fairly predictable effect on the supply of money. Because banks are obliged to meet their reserve requirements, an open market sale of $100 in government securities will reduce reserves by $100, which will reduce the supply of money by $100 times the money multiplier.

Where does the Fed get the money to buy government securities when it wants to expand the money supply? The Fed simply creates it! In effect, it tells the bank from which it has bought a $100 security that its reserve account (deposit) at the Fed now contains $100 more than it did previously. This is where the power of the Fed, or any central bank, lies. The Fed has the ability to create money at will. In the United States, the Fed exercises this power when it creates money to buy government securities.

---

[9] Once again, banks never really have to call in loans. Loans and deposits would probably be reduced by slowing the rate of new lending as old loans come due and are paid off.

The Supply Curve for Money

Thus far we know how the Fed can control the money supply by controlling the amount of reserves in the economy. If the Fed wants the quantity of money to be $1,350 billion on a given date, it can aim for this target by changing the discount rate by changing the required reserve ratio, or by engaging in open market operations. (As discussed earlier, the Fed almost always uses open market operations as its tool.) Because the Fed can choose whatever value of the money supply that it wants, it is useful to begin with the case in which the Fed picks a value independent of anything in the economy. In other words, we will assume for now that the Fed's choice of the value of the money supply does not depend on things like the interest rate, inflation, unemployment, and aggregate output. This assumption is relaxed in Chapter 28. We will see in Chapter 28 that in practice, the Fed chooses a value of the money supply to hit a particular value of the interest rate, where the Fed's choice for the target interest rate depends on things like inflation and unemployment. But this is jumping ahead of the story.

If the Fed's choice of the value for the money supply does not depend on the interest rate, then in Figure 25.5 we can draw the money supply curve as a vertical line. Therefore, until we get to Chapter 28, we will assume that the money supply curve is vertical.

▶ **FIGURE 25.5**
The Supply of Money
If the Fed's money supply behavior is not influenced by the interest rate, the money supply curve is a vertical line. Through open market operations, the Fed can have the money supply be whatever value it wants.

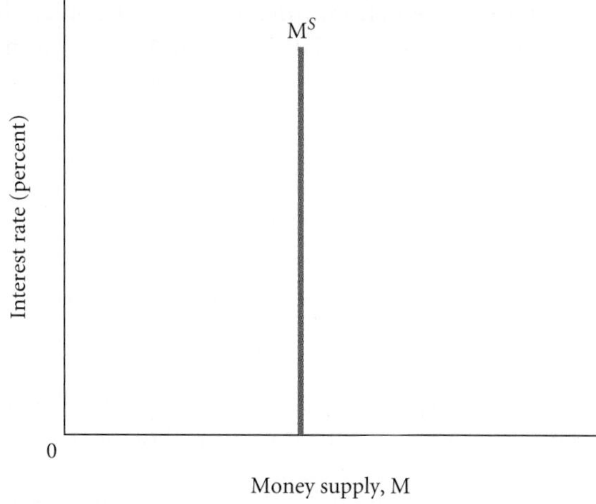

Looking Ahead

This chapter has discussed only the supply side of the money market. We have seen what money is, how banks create money by making loans, and how the Fed controls the money supply. In the next chapter, we turn to the demand side of the money market. We will examine the demand for money and see how the supply of and demand for money determine the equilibrium interest rate.

SUMMARY

AN OVERVIEW OF MONEY *p. 493*

1. Money has three distinguishing characteristics: (1) a *means of payment*, or *medium of exchange*; (2) *a store of value*; and (3) *a unit of account*. The alternative to using money is *barter*, in which goods are exchanged directly for other goods. Barter is costly and inefficient in an economy with many different kinds of goods.

2. *Commodity monies* are items that are used as money and that have an intrinsic value in some other use—for example, gold and cigarettes. *Fiat monies* are intrinsically worthless apart from their use as money. To ensure the acceptance of fiat monies, governments use their power to declare money *legal tender* and promise the public they will not debase the currency by expanding its supply rapidly.

3. There are various definitions of money. Currency plus demand deposits plus traveler's checks plus other checkable deposits compose M1, or *transactions money*—money that can be used directly to buy things. The addition of savings accounts and money market accounts (*near monies*) to M1 gives M2, or *broad money*.

HOW BANKS CREATE MONEY *p. 498*

4. The *required reserve ratio* is the percentage of a bank's deposits that must be kept as *reserves* at the nation's central bank, the *Federal Reserve*.
5. Banks create money by making loans. When a bank makes a loan to a customer, it creates a deposit in that customer's account. This deposit becomes part of the money supply. Banks can create money only when they have *excess reserves*—reserves in excess of the amount set by the required reserve ratio.
6. The *money multiplier* is the multiple by which the total supply of money can increase for every dollar increase in reserves. The money multiplier is equal to 1/required reserve ratio.

THE FEDERAL RESERVE SYSTEM *p. 503*

7. The Fed's most important function is controlling the nation's money supply. The Fed also performs several other functions: It clears interbank payments, is responsible for many of the regulations governing banking practices and standards, and acts as a *lender of last resort* for troubled banks that cannot find any other sources of funds. The Fed also acts as the bank for the U.S. government.

HOW THE FEDERAL RESERVE CONTROLS THE MONEY SUPPLY *p. 506*

8. The key to understanding how the Fed controls the money supply is the role of reserves. If the Fed wants to increase the supply of money, it creates more reserves, freeing banks to create additional deposits. If it wants to decrease the money supply, it reduces reserves.
9. The Fed has three tools to control the money supply: (1) changing the required reserve ratio, (2) changing the *discount rate* (the interest rate member banks pay when they borrow from the Fed), and (3) engaging in *open market operations* (the buying and selling of already-existing government securities). To increase the money supply, the Fed can create additional reserves by lowering the discount rate or by buying government securities or the Fed can increase the number of deposits that can be created from a given quantity of reserves by lowering the required reserve ratio. To decrease the money supply, the Fed can reduce reserves by raising the discount rate or by selling government securities or it can raise the required reserve ratio.
10. If the Fed's money supply behavior is not influenced by the interest rate, the supply curve for money is a vertical line.

REVIEW TERMS AND CONCEPTS

barter, *p. 494*
commodity monies, *p. 496*
currency debasement, *p. 496*
discount rate, *p. 508*
excess reserves, *p. 501*
Federal Open Market Committee (FOMC), *p. 504*
Federal Reserve Bank (the Fed), *p. 500*
fiat, *or* token, money, *p. 496*
financial intermediaries, *p. 498*
legal tender, *p. 496*
lender of last resort, *p. 505*
liquidity property of money, *p. 494*
M1, *or* transactions money, *p. 497*
M2, *or* broad money, *p. 497*
medium of exchange, *or* means of payment, *p. 494*
money multiplier, *p. 503*
moral suasion, *p. 509*
near monies, *p. 497*
Open Market Desk, *p. 504*
open market operations, *p. 509*
required reserve ratio, *p. 500*
reserves, *p. 500*
run on a bank, *p. 499*
store of value, *p. 494*
unit of account, *p. 494*

1. M1 ≡ currency held outside banks + demand deposits + traveler's checks + other checkable deposits
2. M2 ≡ M1 + savings accounts + money market accounts + other near monies
3. Assets ≡ Liabilities + Net Worth
4. Excess reserves ≡ actual reserves – required reserves
5. $\text{Money multiplier} \equiv \dfrac{1}{\text{required reserve ratio}}$

PROBLEMS

Visit **www.myeconlab.com** to complete the problems marked in orange online. You will receive instant feedback on your answers, tutorial help, and access to additional practice problems.

1. In the Republic of Ragu, the currency is the rag. During 2009, the Treasury of Ragu sold bonds to finance the Ragu budget deficit. In all, the Treasury sold 50,000 10-year bonds with a face value of 100 rags each. The total deficit was 5 million rags. Further, assume that the Ragu Central Bank reserve requirement was 20 percent and that in the same year, the bank bought 500,000 rags' worth of outstanding bonds on the open market. Finally, assume that all of the Ragu debt is held by either the private sector (the public) or the central bank.
   a. What is the combined effect of the Treasury sale and the central bank purchase on the total Ragu debt outstanding? on the debt held by the private sector?
   b. What is the effect of the Treasury sale on the money supply in Ragu?
   c. Assuming no leakage of reserves out of the banking system, what is the effect of the central bank purchase of bonds on the money supply?

2. In 2000, the federal debt was being paid down because the federal budget was in surplus. Recall that surplus means that tax collections (T) exceed government spending (G). The surplus ($T - G$) was used to buy back government bonds from the public, reducing the federal debt. As we discussed in this chapter, the main method by which the Fed increases the money supply is to buy government bonds by using open market operations. What is the impact on the money supply of using the fiscal surplus to buy back bonds? In terms of their impacts on the money supply, what is the difference between Fed open market purchases of bonds and Treasury purchases of bonds using tax revenues?

3. For each of the following, determine whether it is an asset or a liability on the accounting books of a bank. Explain why in each case.

   Cash in the vault
   Demand deposits
   Savings deposits
   Reserves
   Loans
   Deposits at the Federal Reserve

4. **[Related to the *Economics in Practice* on p. 495]** It is well known that cigarettes served as money for prisoners of war in World War II. Do a Google search using the keyword *cigarettes* and write a description of how this came to be and how it worked.

5. If the head of the Central Bank of Japan wanted to expand the supply of money in Japan in 2009, which of the following would do it? Explain your answer.

   Increase the required reserve ratio
   Decrease the required reserve ratio
   Increase the discount rate
   Decrease the discount rate
   Buy government securities in the open market
   Sell government securities in the open market

6. Suppose in the Republic of Madison that the regulation of banking rested with the Madison Congress, including the determination of the reserve ratio. The Central Bank of Madison is charged with regulating the money supply by using open market operations. In April 2006, the money supply was estimated to be 52 million hurls. At the same time, bank reserves were 6.24 million hurls and the reserve requirement was 12 percent. The banking industry, being "loaned up," lobbied the Congress to cut the reserve ratio. The Congress yielded and cut required reserves to 10 percent. What is the potential impact on the money supply? Suppose the central bank decided that the money supply should not be increased. What countermeasures could it take to prevent the Congress from expanding the money supply?

7. The U.S. money supply (M1) at the beginning of 2000 was $1,148 billion broken down as follows: $523 billion in currency, $8 billion in traveler's checks, and $616 billion in checking deposits. Suppose the Fed decided to reduce the money supply by increasing the reserve requirement from 10 percent to 11 percent. Assuming all banks were initially loaned up (had no excess reserves) and currency held outside of banks did not change, how large a change in the money supply would have resulted from the change in the reserve requirement?

8. As king of Medivalia, you are constantly strapped for funds to pay your army. Your chief economic wizard suggests the following plan: "When you collect your tax payments from your subjects, insist on being paid in gold coins. Take those gold coins, melt them down, and remint them with an extra 10 percent of brass thrown in. You will then have 10 percent more money than you started with." What do you think of the plan? Will it work?

9. Why is M2 sometimes a more stable measure of money than M1? Explain in your own words using the definitions of M1 and M2.

10. Do you agree or disagree with each of the following statements? Explain your answers.
    a. When the Treasury of the United States issues bonds and sells them to the public to finance the deficit, the money supply remains unchanged because every dollar of money taken in by the Treasury goes right back into circulation through government spending. This is not true when the Fed sells bonds to the public.
    b. The money multiplier depends on the marginal propensity to save.

*11. When the Fed adds new reserves to the system, some of these new reserves find their way out of the country into foreign banks or foreign investment funds. In addition, some portion of the new reserves ends up in people's pockets and mattresses instead of bank vaults. These "leakages" reduce the money multiplier and sometimes make it very difficult for the Fed to control the money supply precisely. Explain why this is true.

12. You are given this account for a bank:

ASSETS		LIABILITIES	
Reserves	$ 500	$3,500	Deposits
Loans	3,000		

The required reserve ratio is 10 percent.
   a. How much is the bank required to hold as reserves given its deposits of $3,500?
   b. How much are its excess reserves?
   c. By how much can the bank increase its loans?
   d. Suppose a depositor comes to the bank and withdraws $200 in cash. Show the bank's new balance sheet, assuming the bank obtains the cash by drawing down its reserves. Does the bank now hold excess reserves? Is it meeting the required reserve ratio? If not, what can it do?

* Note: Problems marked with an asterisk are more challenging.

Money Demand and the Equilibrium Interest Rate

26

Having discussed the supply of money in the last chapter, we now turn to the *demand* for money. One goal of this and the previous chapter is to provide a theory of how the interest rate is determined in the macroeconomy. Once we have seen how the interest rate is determined, we can turn to how the Federal Reserve (Fed) affects the interest rate through its ability to change the money supply.

CHAPTER OUTLINE

Interest Rates and Bond Prices

Interest is the fee that borrowers pay to lenders for the use of their funds. Firms and governments borrow funds by issuing bonds, and they pay interest to the lenders that purchase the bonds. Households also borrow, either directly from banks and finance companies or by taking out mortgages.

interest The fee that borrowers pay to lenders for the use of their funds.

Some loans are very simple. You might borrow $1,000 from a bank to be paid back a year from the date you borrowed the funds. If the bank charged you, say, $100 for doing this, the interest rate on the loan would be 10 percent. You would receive $1,000 now and pay back $1,100 at the end of the year—the original $1,000 plus the interest of $100. In this simple case the interest rate is just the interest payment divided by the amount of the loan, namely 10 percent.

Bonds are more complicated loans. Bonds have several properties. First, they are issued with a face value, typically in denominations of $1,000. Second, they come with a maturity date, which is the date the borrower agrees to pay the lender the face value of the bond. Third, there is a fixed payment of a specified amount that is paid to the bondholder each year. This payment is known as a coupon.

Say that company XYZ on January 2, 2008, issued a 15-year bond that had a face value of $1,000 and paid a coupon of $100 per year. On this date the company sold the bond in the bond market. The price at which the bond sold would be whatever price the market determined it to be. Say that the market-determined price was in fact $1,000. (Firms when issuing bonds try to choose the coupon to be such that the price that the bond initially sells for is roughly equal to its face value.) The lender would give XYZ a check for $1,000 and every January for the next 14 years XYZ would send the lender a check for $100. Then on January 2, 2023, XYZ would send the lender a check for the face value of the bond—$1,000—plus the last coupon payment—$100—and that would square all accounts. In this example the interest rate that the lender receives each year on his or her $1,000 investment is 10 percent. If, on the other hand, the market-determined price of the XYZ bond at the time of issue were only $900, then the interest rate that the lender receives would be larger than 10 percent. The lender pays $900 and receives $100 each year. This is an interest rate of roughly 11.1 percent.

A key relationship that we will use in this chapter is that market-determined prices of existing bonds and interest rates are inversely related. The fact that the coupon on a bond is unchanged over

ECONOMICS IN PRACTICE

Professor Serebryakov Makes an Economic Error

In Chekhov's play *Uncle Vanya*, Alexander Vladimirovitch Serebryakov, a retired professor, but apparently not of economics, calls his household together to make an announcement. He has retired to his country estate, but he does not like living there. Unfortunately, the estate does not derive enough income to allow him to live in town. To his gathered household, he thus proposes the following:

> Omitting details, I will put it before you in rough outline. Our estate yields on an average not more than two per cent, on its capital value. I propose to sell it. If we invest the money in suitable securities, we should get from four to five per cent, and I think we might even have a few thousand roubles to spare for buying a small villa in Finland.

This idea was not well received by the household, especially by Uncle Vanya, who lost it for a while and tried to kill Professor Serebryakov, but no one pointed out that this was bad economics. As the beginning of this chapter discusses, if you buy a bond and interest rates rise, the price of your bond falls. What Professor Serebryakov does not realize is that what he is calling the capital value of the estate, on which he is earning 2 percent, is not the value for which he could sell the estate if the interest rate on "suitable" securities is 5 percent. If an investor in Russia can earn 5 percent on these securities, why would he or she buy an estate earning only 2 percent? The price of the estate would have to fall until the return to the investor was 5 percent. To make matters worse, it may have been that the estate was a riskier investment than the securities, and if this were so, a return higher than 5 percent would have been required on the estate purchase to compensate the investor for the extra risk. This would, of course, lower the price of the estate even more. In short, this is not a scheme by which the professor could earn more money than what the estate is currently yielding. Perhaps had Uncle Vanya taken an introductory economics course and known this, he would have been less agitated.

time does not mean that a bond's price is insulated from interest rate movements. Say that after XYZ issued its bond, interest rates went up so that a company similar to XYZ when issuing a 15-year bond had to choose a coupon of $200 to have its bond initially sell for $1,000. At $1,000 this bond is clearly a better deal than the XYZ bond at $1,000 because the coupon is larger. If the owner of the XYZ bond wanted to sell it, what price could he or she get? It should be obvious that he or she could not get $1,000 since people could buy the other bond for $1,000 and earn more. The price of the XYZ bond would have to fall to have investors be indifferent between buying it and buying the other bond. In other words, when interest rates rise, the prices of existing bonds fall.

It is important to realize that the bond market directly determines prices of bonds, not interest rates. Given a bond's market-determined price, its face value, its maturity, and its coupon, the interest rate, or yield, on that bond can be calculated. Interest rates are thus *indirectly* determined by the bond market. Although each bond generally has at least a slightly different interest rate, we will assume for simplicity in this and the following chapters that there is only one interest rate. (Appendix A to this chapter provides some detail on various types of interest rates.) In fact, we will assume in the following analysis that there is only one type of bond. The (one) interest rate is the market-determined interest rate on this bond.

The Demand for Money

What factors and what forces determine the demand for money are central issues in macroeconomics. As we shall see, the interest rate and the level of national income (*Y*) influence how much money households and firms choose to hold.

Before we proceed, we must stress one point that may be troublesome. When we speak of the demand for money, we are not asking these questions: How much cash would you like to have? How much income would you like to earn? How much wealth would you like? (The answer to these questions is presumably "as much as possible.") Instead, we are concerned with how much of your financial assets you want to hold *in the form of money*, which does not earn interest, versus how much you want to hold in interest-bearing securities such as bonds. We take as given the *total* amount of financial assets. Our concern here is with how these assets are divided between money and interest-bearing securities.

The Transaction Motive

How much money to hold involves a trade-off between the liquidity of money and the interest income offered by other kinds of assets. The main reason for holding money instead of interest-bearing assets is that money is useful for buying things. Economists call this the **transaction motive**. This rationale for holding money is at the heart of the discussion that follows.[1]

transaction motive The main reason that people hold money—to buy things.

To keep our analysis of the demand for money clear, we need a few simplifying assumptions. First, we assume that there are only two kinds of assets available to households: bonds and money. By "bonds" we mean interest-bearing securities of all kinds. As noted above, we are assuming that there is only one type of bond and only one market-determined interest rate. By "money" we mean currency in circulation and deposits in checking accounts that do not pay interest.[2]

Second, we assume that income for the typical household is "bunched up." It arrives once a month at the beginning of the month. Spending, by contrast, is spread out over time; we assume that spending occurs at a completely uniform rate throughout the month—that is, that the same amount is spent each day (Figure 26.1). The mismatch between the timing of money inflow and the timing of money outflow is sometimes called the **nonsynchronization of income and spending**.

nonsynchronization of income and spending The mismatch between the timing of money inflow to the household and the timing of money outflow for household expenses.

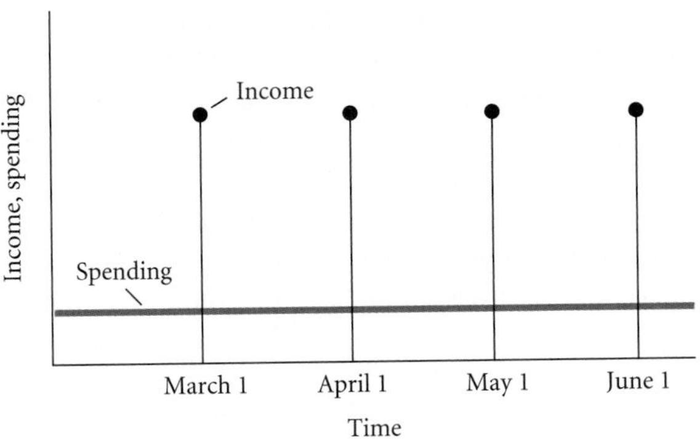

◀ FIGURE 26.1
The Nonsynchronization of Income and Spending
Income arrives only once a month, but spending takes place continuously.

Finally, we assume that spending for the month is equal to income for the month. Because we are focusing on the transactions demand for money and not on its use as a store of value, this assumption is perfectly reasonable.

---

[1] The model that we discuss here is known in the economics profession as the Baumol/Tobin model, after the two economists who independently derived it, William Baumol and James Tobin.

[2] Although we are assuming that checking accounts do not pay interest, many do. Fortunately, all that we really need to assume here is that the interest rate on checking accounts is less than the interest rate on "bonds." Suppose bonds pay 10 percent interest and checking accounts pay 5 percent. (Checking accounts must pay less than bonds. Otherwise, everyone would hold all their wealth in checking accounts and none in bonds because checking accounts are more convenient.) When it comes to choosing whether to hold bonds or money, the difference in the interest rates on the two matters. People are concerned about how much extra interest they will earn from holding bonds instead of money. For simplicity, we are assuming in the following discussion that the interest rate on checking accounts is zero.

Given these assumptions, how would a rational person (household) decide how much of monthly income to hold as money and how much to hold as interest-bearing bonds? Suppose Jim decides to deposit his entire paycheck in his checking account. Let us say that Jim earns $1,200 per month. The pattern of Jim's bank account balance is illustrated in Figure 26.2. At the beginning of the month, Jim's balance is $1,200. As the month rolls by, Jim draws down his balance, writing checks or withdrawing cash to pay for the things he buys. At the end of the month, Jim's bank account balance is down to zero. Just in time, he receives his next month's paycheck, deposits it, and the process begins again.

▸ **FIGURE 26.2**

Jim's Monthly Checking Account Balances: Strategy 1

Jim could decide to deposit his entire paycheck ($1,200) into his checking account at the start of the month and run his balance down to zero by the end of the month. In this case, his average balance would be $600.

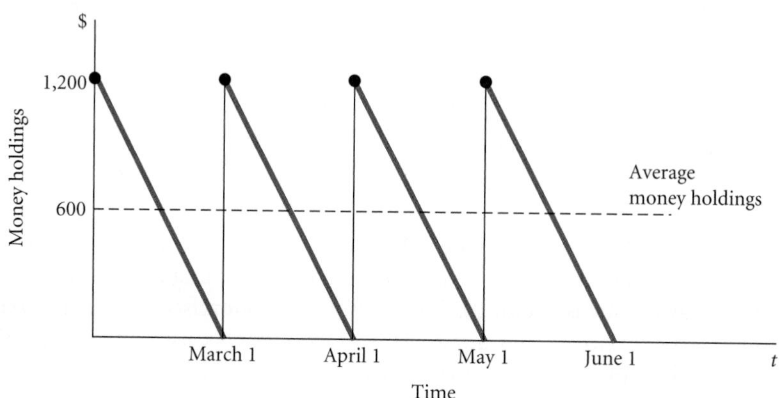

One useful statistic we need to calculate is the *average balance* in Jim's account. Jim spends his money at a constant $40 per day ($40 per day times 30 days per month = $1,200). His average balance is just his starting balance ($1,200) plus his ending balance (0) divided by 2, or ($1,200 + 0)/2 = $600. For the first half of the month, Jim has more than his average of $600 on deposit, and for the second half of the month, he has less than his average.

Is anything wrong with Jim's strategy? Yes. If he follows the plan described, Jim is giving up interest on his funds, interest he could be earning if he held some of his funds in interest-bearing bonds instead of in his checking account. How could he manage his funds to give himself more interest?

Instead of depositing his entire paycheck in his checking account at the beginning of the month, Jim could put half his paycheck into his checking account and buy a bond with the other half. By doing this, he would run out of money in his checking account halfway through the month. At a spending rate of $40 per day, his initial deposit of $600 would last only 15 days. Jim would have to sell his bond halfway through the month and deposit the $600 from the sale of the bond in his checking account to pay his bills during the second half of the month.

Jim's money holdings (checking account balances) if he follows this strategy are shown in Figure 26.3. When he follows the buy-a-$600-bond strategy, Jim reduces the average amount of money in his checking account. Comparing the dashed green lines (old strategy) with the solid green lines (buy-$600-bond strategy), his average bank balance is exactly half of what it was with the first strategy.[3]

The buy-a-$600-bond strategy seems sensible. The object of this strategy was to keep some funds in bonds, where they could earn interest, instead of being "idle" money. Why should he stop there? Another possibility would be for Jim to put only $400 into his checking account on the first of the month and buy two $400 bonds. The $400 in his account will last only 10 days if he spends $40 per day, so after 10 days he must sell one of the bonds and deposit the $400 from the sale in his checking account. This will last through the 20th of the month, at which point he must sell the second bond and deposit the other $400. This strategy lowers Jim's average money holding (checking account balance) even further, reducing his money holdings to an average of only $200 per month, with correspondingly higher average holdings of interest-earning bonds.

[3] Jim's average balance for the first half of the month is (starting balance + ending balance)/2, or ($600 + 0)/2 = $300. His average for the second half of the month is also $300. His average for the month as a whole is $300.

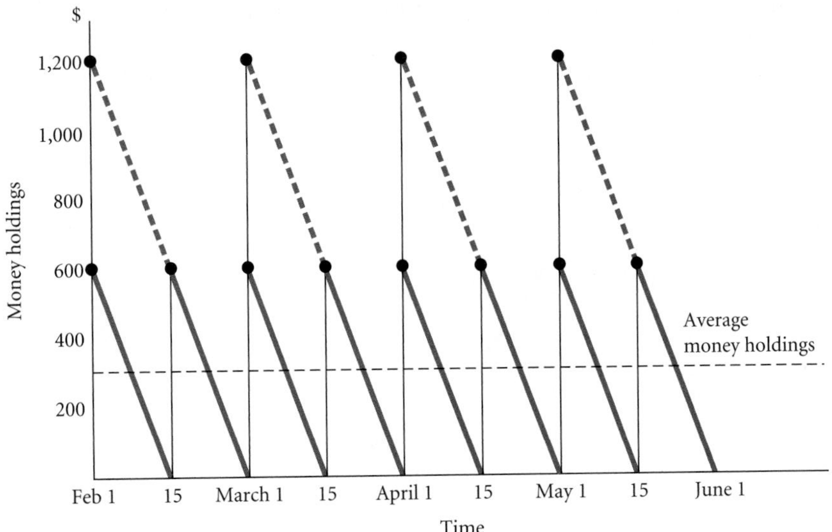

FIGURE 26.3

Jim's Monthly Checking Account Balances: Strategy 2

Jim could also choose to put half of his paycheck into his checking account and buy a bond with the other half of his income. At mid-month, Jim would sell the bond and deposit the $600 into his checking account to pay the second half of the month's bills. Following this strategy, Jim's average money holdings would be $300.

You can imagine Jim going even further. Why not hold all wealth in the form of bonds (where it earns interest) and make transfers from bonds to money every time he makes a purchase? If selling bonds, transferring funds to checking accounts, and making trips to the bank were without cost, Jim would never hold money for more than an instant. Each time he needed to pay cash for something or to write a check, he would go to the bank or call the bank, transfer the exact amount of the transaction to his checking account, and withdraw the cash or write the check to complete the transaction. If he did this constantly, he would squeeze the most interest possible out of his funds because he would never hold assets that did not earn interest.

In practice, money management of this kind is costly. There are brokerage fees and other costs to buy or sell bonds, and time must be spent waiting in line at the bank or at an ATM. At the same time, it is costly to hold assets in non-interest-bearing form because they lose potential interest revenue.

We have a trade-off problem of the type that pervades economics. Switching more often from bonds to money raises the interest revenue Jim earns (because the more times he switches, the less, on average, he has to hold in his checking account and the more he can keep in bonds), but this increases his money management costs. Less switching means more interest revenue lost (because average money holdings are higher) but lower money management costs (fewer purchases and sales of bonds, less time spent waiting in bank lines, fewer trips to the bank, and so on). Given this trade-off, there is a level of average money balances that earns Jim the most profit, taking into account both the interest earned on bonds and the costs paid for switching from bonds to money. This level is his *optimal balance*.

How does the interest rate affect the number of switches that Jim makes and thus the average money balance he chooses to hold? It is easy to see why an increase in the interest rate lowers the optimal money balance. If the interest rate were only 2 percent, it would not be worthwhile to give up much liquidity by holding bonds instead of cash or checking balances. However, if the interest rate were 30 percent, the opportunity cost of holding money instead of bonds would be quite high and we would expect people to keep most of their funds in bonds and to spend considerable time managing their money balances. The interest rate represents the opportunity cost of holding money (and therefore not holding bonds, which pay interest). The higher the interest rate, the higher the opportunity cost of holding money and the less money people will want to hold. When interest rates are high, people want to take advantage of the high return on bonds, so they choose to hold very little money. Appendix B to this chapter provides a detailed example of this principle.

A demand curve for money, with the interest rate representing the "price" of money, would look like the curve labeled M^d in Figure 26.4. At higher interest rates, bonds are more attractive than money, so people hold less money because they must make a larger sacrifice in interest for each dollar of money they hold. The curve in Figure 26.4 slopes downward, just like an ordinary demand curve for oranges or shoes. There is an inverse relationship between the interest rate and the quantity of money demanded.[4]

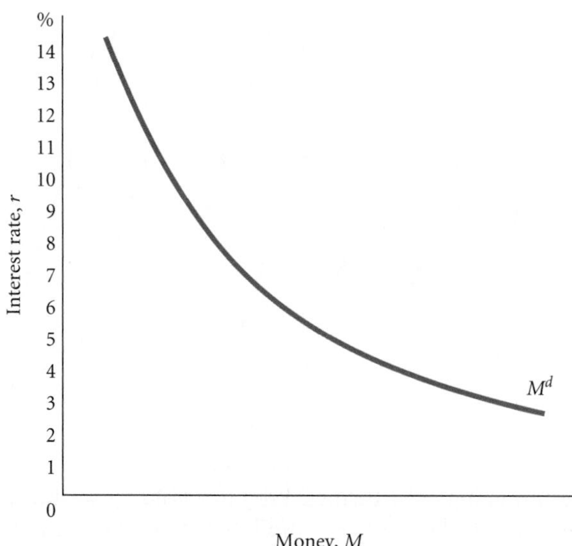

FIGURE 26.4
The Demand Curve for Money Balances
The quantity of money demanded (the amount of money households and firms want to hold) is a function of the interest rate. Because the interest rate is the opportunity cost of holding money balances, increases in the interest rate reduce the quantity of money that firms and households want to hold and decreases in the interest rate increase the quantity of money that firms and households want to hold.

The Speculation Motive

A number of theories have been offered to explain why the quantity of money households want to hold may rise when interest rates fall and fall when interest rates rise. One theory involves household expectations and the fact, as discussed at the beginning of this chapter, that interest rates and bond prices are inversely related.

Consider your desire to hold money balances instead of bonds. If market interest rates are higher than normal, you may expect them to come down in the future. If and when interest rates fall, the bonds that you bought when interest rates were high will increase in price. When interest rates are high, the opportunity cost of holding cash balances is high and there is a **speculation motive** for holding bonds in lieu of cash. You are "speculating" that interest rates will fall in the future and thus that bond prices will rise.

speculation motive One reason for holding bonds instead of money: Because the market price of interest-bearing bonds is inversely related to the interest rate, investors may want to hold bonds when interest rates are high with the hope of selling them when interest rates fall.

Similarly, when market interest rates are lower than normal, you may expect them to rise in the future. Rising interest rates will bring about a decline in the price of existing bonds. Thus, when interest rates are low, it is a good time to be holding money and not bonds. When interest rates are low, not only is the opportunity cost of holding cash balances low, but also there is a speculative motive for holding a larger amount of money. Why should you put money into bonds now when you expect interest rates to rise in the future and thus bond prices to fall?

The Total Demand for Money

So far we have talked only about household demand for checking account balances. However, the total quantity of money demanded in the economy is the sum of the demand for checking account balances *and cash* by both households *and firms*.

The trade-off for firms is the same as it was for Jim. Like households, firms must manage their money. They have payrolls to meet and purchases to make, they receive cash and checks from sales, and many firms that deal with the public must make change—they need cash in the cash register. Thus, just like Jim, firms need money to engage in ordinary transactions.

---

[4] The theory of money demand presented here assumes that people know the exact timing of their income and spending. In practice, both have some uncertainty attached to them. For example, some income payments may be unexpectedly delayed a few days or weeks, and some expenditures may arise unexpectedly (such as the cost of repairing a plumbing problem). Because people know that this uncertainty exists, as a precaution against unanticipated delays in income receipts or unanticipated expenses, they may choose to hold more money than the strict transactions motive would suggest. This reason for holding money is sometimes called the *precautionary motive*.

ECONOMICS IN PRACTICE

ATMs and the Demand for Money

Twenty years ago the typical college student spent many a Friday afternoon visiting a bank to make sure he or she had enough cash for weekend activities. Today the typical student, whether in the United States or abroad, doesn't need to plan ahead. As a result of automated teller machines (ATMs), access to your bank account is available 24-7. What difference has the spread of ATMs made on the demand for money?

Italy makes a great case study of the effects of the spread of ATMs on the demand for money. In Italy, virtually all checking accounts pay interest. What doesn't pay interest is cash. So from the point of view of the model in this chapter, we can think of Italian checking accounts as (interest-earning) "bonds" and cash as (non-interest-earning) "money." In other words, in Italy there is an interest cost to carrying cash instead of depositing the cash in a checking account. A recent paper by three economists—Orazio Attansio from University College London, Luigi Guiso from the University of Sassari, Italy, and Tullio Jappelli from the University of Salerno, Italy—took advantage of this institutional fact to see how the availability of ATMs influence the demand for cash (non-interest-earning money).[1]

Why do we think there might be an effect? Think back to the college student of 20 years ago. On Friday, he or she might have withdrawn cash in excess of expected weekly needs just in case. With ATMs everywhere, cash can be withdrawn as needed. This means that the amount of cash needed to support a given level of consumption should fall as ATMs proliferate. This is exactly what Attansio, Guiso, and Jappelli found in Italy in the first six years of ATM adoption. In 1989, ATM adoption in Italy was relatively low, about 15 percent of the population. By 1995, ATM use had risen to about 40 percent. What happened to cash holdings in this period? The amount of cash divided by total consumption fell from 3.8 percent to 2.8 percent. The study also found, as we would expect from our discussion in the text, that the demand for cash responds to changes in the interest rate paid on checking accounts. The higher the interest rate, the less cash held. In other words, when the interest rate on checking accounts rises, people go to ATM machines more often and take out less in cash each time, thereby keeping, on average, more in checking accounts earning the higher interest rate.

[1] *Orazio Attansio, Luigi Guiso, and Tullio Jappelli, "The Demand for Money, Financial Innovation and the Welfare Costs of Inflation: An Analysis with Household Data," Journal of Political Economy, April 2002.*

However, firms as well as households can hold their assets in interest-earning form. Firms manage their assets the same way households do, keeping some in cash, some in their checking accounts, and some in bonds. A higher interest rate raises the opportunity cost of money for firms as well as for households and thus reduces the demand for money.

The same trade-off holds for cash. We all walk around with some money in our pockets, but not thousands of dollars, for routine transactions. We carry, on average, about what we think we will need, not more, because there are costs—risks of being robbed and forgone interest. At any given moment, there is a demand for money—for cash and checking account balances. Although households and firms need to hold balances for everyday transactions, their demand has a limit. For both households and firms, the quantity of money demanded at any moment depends on the opportunity cost of holding money, a cost determined by the interest rate.

The Effects of Income and the Price Level on the Demand for Money

The money demand curve in Figure 26.4 is a function of the interest rate. There are, however, other factors besides the interest rate that influence total desired money holdings. One is the dollar value of transactions made during a given period of time. Suppose Jim's income were to increase. Instead of making $1,200 in purchases each month, he will now spend more. He thus needs to hold more money. The reason is simple: To buy more things, he needs more money.

What is true for Jim is true for the economy as a whole. The total demand for money in the economy depends on the total dollar volume of transactions made. The total dollar volume of transactions in the economy, in turn, depends on two things: the total *number* of transactions and the average transaction *amount*. Although there are no data on the actual number of transactions in the economy, a reasonable indicator is likely to be aggregate output (income) (Y). A rise in aggregate output—real gross domestic product (GDP)—means that there is more economic activity. Firms are producing and selling more output, more people are on payrolls, and household incomes are higher. In short, there are more transactions and firms, and households together will hold more money when they are engaging in more transactions. Thus, an increase in aggregate output (income) will increase the demand for money. Figure 26.5 shows a shift of the money demand curve resulting from an increase in Y. For a given interest rate, a higher level of output means an increase in the *number* of transactions and more demand for money. The money demand curve shifts to the right when Y rises. Similarly, a decrease in Y means a decrease in the number of transactions and a lower demand for money. The money demand curve shifts to the left when Y falls.

FIGURE 26.5

An Increase in Aggregate Output (Income) (Y) Will Shift the Money Demand Curve to the Right

An increase in Y means that there is more economic activity. Firms are producing and selling more, and households are earning more income and buying more. There are more transactions, for which money is needed. As a result, both firms and households are likely to increase their holdings of money balances at a given interest rate.

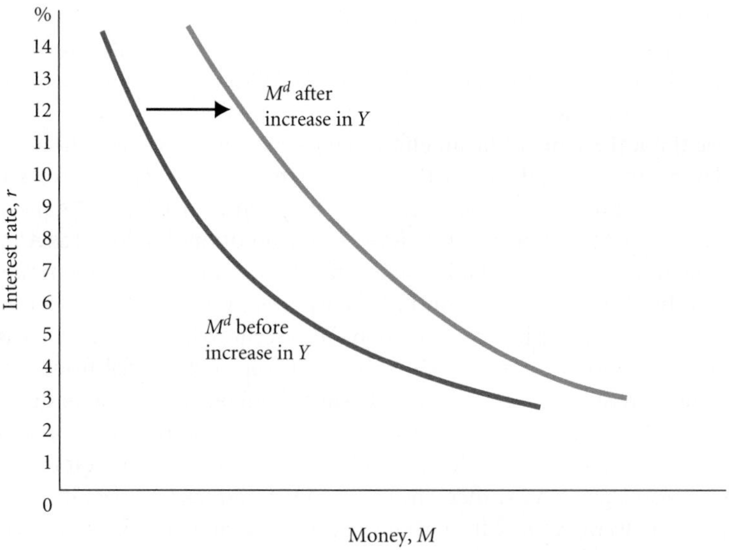

The amount of money that firms and households need to facilitate their day-to-day transactions also depends on the average *dollar amount* of each transaction. In turn, the average amount of each transaction depends on prices, or instead, on the *price level*. If all prices, including the price of labor (the wage rate) were to double, firms and households would need more money balances to carry out their day-to-day transactions—each transaction would require twice as much money. If the price of your lunch increases from $3.50 to $7.00, you will begin carrying more cash. If your end-of-the-month bills are twice as high as they used to be, you will keep more money in your checking account. Increases in the price level shift the money demand curve to the right, and decreases in the price level shift the money demand curve to the left. Even though the number of transactions may not have changed, the quantity of money needed to engage in them has.

Table 26.1 summarizes everything we have said about the demand for money. First, because the interest rate (r) is the opportunity cost of holding money balances for both firms and households, increases in the interest rate are likely to decrease the quantity of money demanded; decreases in the interest rate will increase the quantity of money demanded. Thus, the quantity of money demanded is a negative function of the interest rate.

The demand for money also depends on the dollar volume of transactions in a given period. The dollar volume of transactions depends on both aggregate output (income), Y, and the price level, P. The relationship of money demand to Y and the relationship of money demand to P are both positive. Increases in Y or in P will shift the money demand curve to the right; decreases in Y or P will shift the money demand curve to the left.

TABLE 26.1 Determinants of Money Demand

1. The interest rate: r (The quantity of money demanded is a negative function of the interest rate.)
2. The dollar volume of transactions
   a. Aggregate output (income): Y (An increase in Y shifts the money demand curve to the right.)
   b. The price level: P (An increase in P shifts the money demand curve to the right.)

The Equilibrium Interest Rate

We are now in a position to consider one of the key questions in macroeconomics: How is the interest rate determined in the economy?

Financial markets (what we call the money market) work very well in the United States. Almost all financial markets clear—that is, almost all reach an equilibrium where quantity demanded equals quantity supplied. In the money market, the point at which the quantity of money demanded equals the quantity of money supplied determines the equilibrium interest rate in the economy. This explanation sounds simple, but it requires elaboration.

Supply and Demand in the Money Market

We saw in Chapter 25 that the Fed controls the money supply through its manipulation of the amount of reserves in the economy. Because we are assuming that the Fed's money supply behavior does not depend on the interest rate, the money supply curve is a vertical line. (Review Figure 25.5 on p. 512.) In other words, we are assuming that the Fed uses its three tools (the required reserve ratio, the discount rate, and open market operations) to achieve its fixed target for the money supply.

Figure 26.6 superimposes the vertical money supply curve from Figure 25.5 on the downward-sloping money demand curve. Only at interest rate r^* is the quantity of money in circulation (the money supply) equal to the quantity of money demanded. To understand why r^* is an equilibrium, we need to ask what forces drive the interest rate to r^*. Keep in mind in the

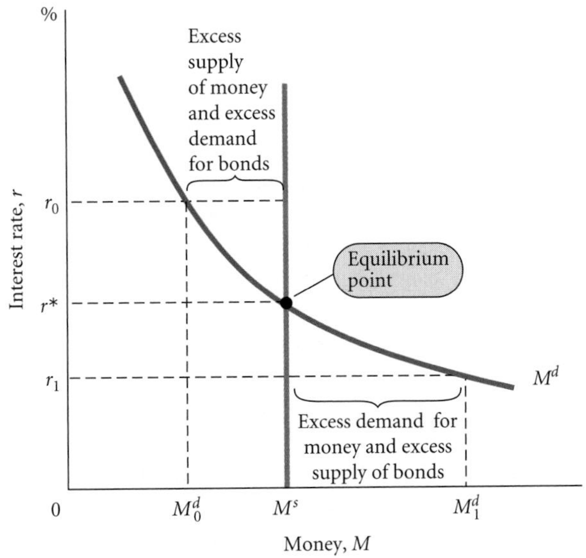

FIGURE 26.6 Adjustments in the Money Market

Equilibrium exists in the money market when the supply of money is equal to the demand for money and thus when the supply of bonds is equal to the demand for bonds. At r_0 the price of bonds would be bid up (and thus the interest rate down), and at r_1 the price of bonds would be bid down (and thus the interest rate up).

following discussion that when the Fed fixes the money supply it also fixes the supply of bonds. The decision of households and firms is to decide what fraction of their funds to hold in non-interest-bearing money versus interest-bearing bonds. At the equilibrium interest rate r^* in Figure 26.6 the demand for bonds by households and firms is equal to the supply.

Consider r_0 in Figure 26.6, an interest rate higher than the equilibrium rate. At this interest rate households and firms would want to hold more bonds than the Fed is supplying (and less money than the Fed is supplying). They would bid the price of bonds up and thus the interest rate down. The bond market would clear when the price of bonds fell enough to correspond to an interest rate of r^*. At interest rate r_1 in Figure 26.6, which is lower than the equilibrium rate, households and firms would want to hold fewer bonds than the fed is supplying (and more money than the Fed is supplying). They would bid the price of bonds down and thus the interest rate up. The bond market would clear when the price of bonds rose enough to correspond to an interest rate of r^*.

Changing the Money Supply to Affect the Interest Rate

With an understanding of equilibrium in the money market, we now see how the Fed can affect the interest rate. Suppose the current interest rate is 7 percent and the Fed wants to reduce the interest rate. To do so, it would expand the money supply. Figure 26.7 shows how such an expansion would work. To expand M^s, the Fed can reduce the reserve requirement, cut the discount rate, or buy U.S. government securities on the open market. All these practices expand the quantity of reserves in the system. Banks can make more loans, and the money supply expands even more. (Review Chapter 25 if you are unsure why.) In Figure 26.7, the initial money supply curve, M_0^s, shifts to the right, to M_1^s. At M_1^s the supply of bonds is smaller than it was at M_0^s.

As the money supply expands from M_0^s to M_1^s, the supply of bonds is decreasing, which drives up the price of bonds. At M_1^s the equilibrium price of bonds corresponds to an interest rate of 4 percent. So the new equilibrium interest rate is 4 percent.

If the Fed wanted to increase the interest rate, it would contract the money supply. It could do so by increasing the reserve requirement, by raising the discount rate, or by selling U.S. government securities in the open market. Whichever tool the Fed chooses, the result would be lower reserves and a lower supply of money. The supply of money curve in Figure 26.7 would shift to the left, and the equilibrium interest rate would rise. (As an exercise, draw a graph of this situation and explain why the interest rate would rise.)

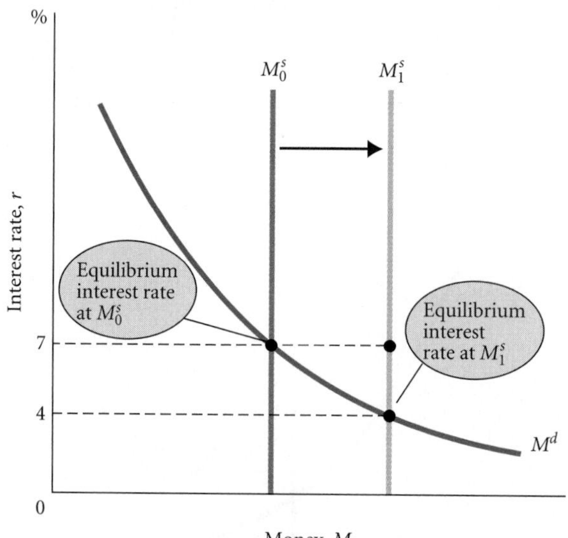

FIGURE 26.7

The Effect of an Increase in the Supply of Money on the Interest Rate

An increase in the supply of money from M_0^s to M_1^s lowers the rate of interest from 7 percent to 4 percent.

Increases in *Y* and Shifts in the Money Demand Curve

Changes in the supply of money are not the only factors that influence the equilibrium interest rate. Shifts in money demand can do the same thing.

Recall that the demand for money depends on both the interest rate and the volume of transactions. As a rough measure of the volume of transactions, we use *Y*, the level of aggregate output (income). Remember that the relationship between money demand and *Y* is positive—increases in *Y* mean a higher level of real economic activity. More is being produced, income is higher, and there are more transactions in the economy. Consequently, the demand for money on the part of firms and households in aggregate is higher. An increase in *Y* shifts the money demand curve to the right.

Figure 26.8 illustrates such a shift. *Y* increases, causing money demand to shift from M_0^d to M_1^d. The result is an increase in the equilibrium level of the interest rate from 4 percent to 7 percent. A decrease in *Y* would shift M^d to the left, and the equilibrium interest rate would fall.

The money demand curve also shifts when the price level changes. If the price level rises, the money demand curve shifts to the right because people want more money to engage in their day-to-day transactions. In this case the equilibrium interest rate also rises. An increase in the price level is like an increase in *Y* in that both events increase the demand for money. The result is an increase in the equilibrium interest rate.

If the price level *falls*, the money demand curve shifts to the left because people want less money for their transactions. However, with the quantity of money supplied unchanged, the equilibrium interest rate falls. A decrease in the price level thus leads to a decrease in the equilibrium interest rate. We explore this relationship in more detail in Chapter 28.

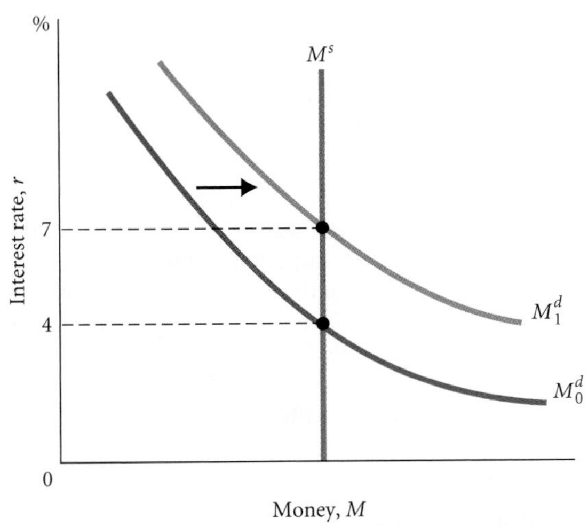

FIGURE 26.8

The Effect of an Increase in Income on the Interest Rate

An increase in aggregate output (income) shifts the money demand curve from M_0^d to M_1^d, which raises the equilibrium interest rate from 4 percent to 7 percent.

Looking Ahead: The Federal Reserve and Monetary Policy

We now know that the Fed can change the interest rate by changing the quantity of money supplied. If the Fed increases the quantity of money, the interest rate falls. If the Fed decreases the quantity of money, the interest rate rises.

Nonetheless, we have not yet said *why* the Fed might want to change the interest rate or what happens to the economy when the interest rate changes. We have hinted at why: A low interest rate stimulates spending, particularly investment; a high interest rate reduces spending. By changing the interest rate, the Fed can change aggregate output (income). In the next chapter, we will combine our discussions of the goods and money markets and discuss how the interest rate affects the equilibrium level of aggregate output (income) (*Y*) in the goods market.

The Fed's use of its power to influence events in the goods market as well as in the money market is the center of the government's monetary policy. When the Fed moves to contract the money supply and thus raise interest rates in an effort to restrain the economy, economists call it a **tight monetary policy**. Conversely, when the Fed stimulates the economy by expanding the money supply and thus lower interest rates, it has an **easy monetary policy**. We will discuss the way in which the economy affects the Fed's behavior in Chapter 28.

tight monetary policy Fed policies that contract the money supply and thus raise interest rates in an effort to restrain the economy.

easy monetary policy Fed policies that expand the money supply and thus lower interest rates in an effort to stimulate the economy.

SUMMARY

INTEREST RATES AND BOND PRICES *p. 515*

1. *Interest* is the fee that borrowers pay to lenders for the use of their funds. Interest rates and bond prices are inversely related. Although there are many different interest rates in the United States, we assume for simplicity that there is only one interest rate in the economy.

THE DEMAND FOR MONEY *p. 517*

2. The demand for money depends negatively on the interest rate. The higher the interest rate, the higher the opportunity cost (more interest forgone) from holding money and the less money people will want to hold. An increase in the interest rate reduces the quantity demanded for money, and the money demand curve slopes downward.
3. The volume of transactions in the economy affects money demand. The total dollar volume of transactions depends on both the total number of transactions and the average transaction amount.
4. A reasonable measure of the number of transactions in the economy is aggregate output (income) (Y). When Y rises, there is more economic activity, more is being produced and sold, and more people are on payrolls—there are more transactions in the economy. An increase in Y causes the money demand curve to shift to the right. This effect follows because households and firms need more money when they are engaging in more transactions. A decrease in Y causes the money demand curve to shift to the left.
5. Changes in the price level affect the average dollar amount of each transaction. *Increases* in the price level increase the demand for money (shift the money demand curve to the right) because households and firms need more money for their expenditures. *Decreases* in the price level decrease the demand for money (shift the money demand curve to the left).

THE EQUILIBRIUM INTEREST RATE *p. 523*

6. The point at which the quantity of money supplied equals the quantity of money demanded determines the equilibrium interest rate in the economy. An excess supply of money will cause households and firms to buy more bonds, driving the interest rate down. An excess demand for money will cause households and firms to move out of bonds, driving the interest rate up.
7. The Fed can affect the equilibrium interest rate by changing the supply of money using one of its three tools—the required reserve ratio, the discount rate, or open market operations.
8. An increase in the price level is like an increase in Y in that both events cause an increase in money demand. The result is an increase in the equilibrium interest rate. A decrease in the price level leads to reduced money demand and a decrease in the equilibrium interest rate.
9. *Tight monetary policy* refers to Fed policies that contract the money supply and thus raise interest rates in an effort to restrain the economy. *Easy monetary policy* refers to Fed policies that expand the money supply and thus lower interest rates in an effort to stimulate the economy. The Fed chooses between these two types of policies for different reasons at different times.

REVIEW TERMS AND CONCEPTS

easy monetary policy, *p. 525*
interest, *p. 515*
nonsynchronization of income and spending, *p. 517*
speculation motive, *p. 520*
tight monetary policy, *p. 525*
transaction motive, *p. 517*

PROBLEMS

Visit **www.myeconlab.com** to complete the problems marked in orange online. You will receive instant feedback on your answers, tutorial help, and access to additional practice problems.

1. State whether you agree or disagree with the following statements and explain why.
   a. When the real economy expands (Y rises), the demand for money expands. As a result, households hold more cash and the supply of money expands.
   b. Inflation, a rise in the price level, causes the demand for money to decline. Because inflation causes money to be worth less, households want to hold less of it.
   c. If the Fed buys bonds in the open market and at the same time we experience a recession, interest rates will no doubt rise.

2. During 2003, we began to stop worrying that inflation was a problem. Instead, we began to worry about deflation, a decline in the price level. Assume that the Fed decided to hold the money supply constant. What impact would deflation have on interest rates?

3. **[Related to *Economics in Practice* on p. 521]** How many times a week do you use an ATM? If ATMs were not available, would you carry more cash? Would you keep more money in your checking account? How many times a day do you use cash?

4. What if, at a low level of interest rates, the money demand curve became nearly horizontal, as in the following graph. That is, with interest rates so low, the public would not find it attractive to hold bonds; thus, money demand would be very high. Many argue that this was the position of the U.S. economy in 2003. If the Fed decided to expand the money supply in the graph, what would be the impact on interest rates?

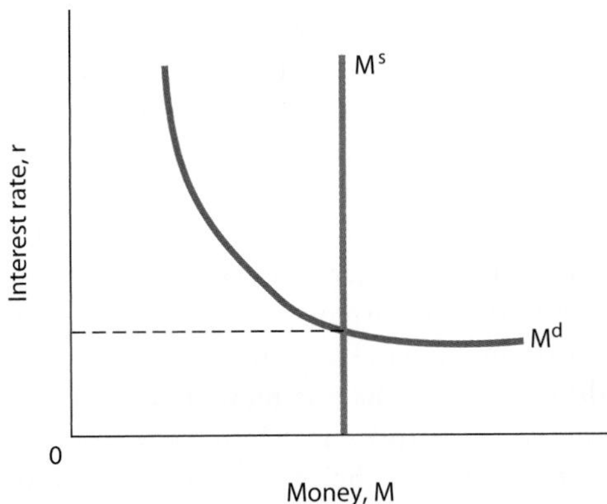

5. During the fourth quarter of 1993, real GDP in the United States grew at an annual rate of over 7 percent. During 1994, the economy continued to expand with modest inflation. (Y rose at a rate of 4 percent and P increased about 3 percent.) At the beginning of 1994, the prime interest rate (the interest rate that banks offer their best, least risky customers) stood at 6 percent, where it remained for over a year. By the beginning of 1995, the prime rate had increased to over 8.5 percent.
   a. By using money supply and money demand curves, show the effects of the increase in Y and P on interest rates, assuming *no change* in the money supply.
   b. On a separate graph, show that the interest rate can rise even if the Federal Reserve expands the money supply as long as it does so more slowly than money demand is increasing.

6. Illustrate the following situations using supply and demand curves for money:
   a. The Fed buys bonds in the open market during a recession.
   b. During a period of rapid inflation, the Fed increases the reserve requirement.
   c. The Fed acts to hold interest rates constant during a period of high inflation.
   d. During a period of no growth in GDP and zero inflation, the Fed lowers the discount rate.
   e. During a period of rapid real growth of GDP, the Fed acts to increase the reserve requirement.

7. During a recession, interest rates may fall even if the Fed takes no action to expand the money supply. Why? Use a graph to explain.

8. During the summer of 1997, Congress and the president agreed on a budget package to balance the federal budget. The "deal," signed into law by President Clinton in August as the Taxpayer Relief Act of 1997, contained substantial tax cuts and expenditure reductions. The tax reductions were scheduled to take effect immediately, however, while the expenditure cuts would come mostly in 1999 to 2002. Thus, in 1998, the package was seen by economists to be mildly expansionary. If the result is an increase in the growth of real output/income, what would you expect to happen to interest rates if the Fed holds the money supply (or the rate of growth of the money supply) constant? What would the Fed do if it wanted to raise interest rates? What if it wanted to lower interest rates? Illustrate with graphs.

9. The demand for money in a country is given by

$$M^d = 10{,}000 - 10{,}000r + Y$$

where M^d is money demand in dollars, r is the interest rate (a 10 percent interest rate means $r = 0.1$), and Y is national income. Assume that Y is initially 5,000.
   a. Graph the amount of money demanded (on the horizontal axis) against the interest rate (on the vertical axis).
   b. Suppose the money supply (M^s) is set by the central bank at \$10,000. On the same graph you drew for part a., add the money supply curve. What is the equilibrium rate of interest? Explain how you arrived at your answer.
   c. Suppose income rises from $Y = 5{,}000$ to $Y = 7{,}500$. What happens to the money demand curve you drew in part a.? Draw the new curve if there is one. What happens to the equilibrium interest rate if the central bank does not change the supply of money?
   d. If the central bank wants to keep the equilibrium interest rate at the same value as it was in part b., by how much should it increase or decrease the supply of money given the new level of national income?
   e. Suppose the shift in part c. has occurred and the money supply remains at \$10,000 but there is no observed change in the interest rate. What might have happened that could explain this?

10. **[Related to *Economics in Practice* on p. 516]** Between the end of 2007 and mid-2008, the Fed moved to cut interest rates to stimulate aggregate spending in the economy and to try and prevent a recession. Lower interest rates reduce the cost of borrowing and encourage firms to borrow and invest. They also have an effect on the value of the bonds (private and government) outstanding in the economy. Explain briefly but clearly why the value of bonds changes when interest rates change. Go to federalreserve.gov, click on "Economic Research & Data" and click on "Flow of Funds." Look at the most recent release and find balance sheet table B.100. How big is the value of Credit Market Instruments held by households?

APPENDIX A

THE VARIOUS INTEREST RATES IN THE U.S. ECONOMY

Although there are many different interest rates in the economy, they tend to move up or down with one another. Here we discuss some of their differences. We first look at the relationship between interest rates on securities with different *maturities*, or terms. We then briefly discuss some of the main interest rates in the U.S. economy.

THE TERM STRUCTURE OF INTEREST RATES

The *term structure of interest rates* is the relationship among the interest rates offered on securities of different maturities. The key here is understanding issues such as these: How are these different rates related? Does a 2-year security (an IOU that promises to repay principal, plus interest, after 2 years) pay a lower annual rate than a 1-year security (an IOU to be repaid, with interest, after 1 year)? What happens to the rate of interest offered on 1-year securities if the rate of interest on 2-year securities increases?

Assume that you want to invest some money for 2 years and at the end of the 2 years you want it back. Assume that you want to buy government securities. For this analysis, we restrict your choices to two: (1) You can buy a 2-year security today and hold it for 2 years, at which time you cash it in (we will assume that the interest rate on the 2-year security is 9 percent per year), or (2) you can buy a 1-year security today. At the end of 1 year, you must cash this security in; you can then buy another 1-year security. At the end of the second year, you will cash in the second security. Assume that the interest rate on the first 1-year security is 8 percent.

Which would you prefer? Currently, you do not have enough data to answer this question. To consider choice (2) sensibly, you need to know the interest rate on the 1-year security that you intend to buy in the second year. This rate will not be known until the second year. All you know now is the rate on the 2-year security and the rate on the current 1-year security. To decide what to do, you must form an *expectation* of the rate on the 1-year security a year from now. If you expect the 1-year rate (8 percent) to remain the same in the second year, you should buy the 2-year security. You would earn 9 percent per year on the 2-year security but only 8 percent per year on the two 1-year securities. If you expect the 1-year rate to rise to 12 percent a year from now, you should make the second choice. You would earn 8 percent in the first year, and you expect to earn 12 percent in the second year. The expected rate of return over the 2 years is about 10 percent, which is better than the 9 percent you can get on the 2-year security. If you expect the 1-year rate a year from now to be 10 percent, it does not matter very much which of the two choices you make. The rate of return over the 2-year period will be roughly 9 percent for both choices.

We now alter the focus of our discussion to get to the topic we are really interested in—how the 2-year rate is determined. Assume that the 1-year rate has been set by the Fed and it is 8 percent. Also assume that people expect the 1-year rate a year from now to be 10 percent. What is the 2-year rate? According to a theory called the *expectations theory of the term structure of interest rates*, the 2-year rate is equal to the average of the current 1-year rate and the 1-year rate expected a year from now. In this example, the 2-year rate would be 9 percent (the average of 8 percent and 10 percent).

If the 2-year rate were lower than the average of the two 1-year rates, people would not be indifferent as to which security they held. They would want to hold only the short-term 1-year securities. To find a buyer for a 2-year security, the seller would be forced to increase the interest rate it offers on the 2-year security until it is equal to the average of the current 1-year rate and the expected 1-year rate for next year. The interest rate on the 2-year security will continue to rise until people are once again indifferent between one 2-year security and two 1-year securities.[1]

Let us now return to Fed behavior. We know that the Fed can affect the short-term interest rate by changing the money supply, but does it also affect long-term interest rates? The answer is "somewhat." Because the 2-year rate is an average of the current 1-year rate and the expected 1-year rate a year from now, the Fed influences the 2-year rate to the extent that it influences the current 1-year rate. The same holds for 3-year rates and beyond. The current short-term rate is a means by which the Fed can influence longer-term rates.

In addition, Fed behavior may directly affect people's expectations of the future short-term rates, which will then affect long-term rates. If the chair of the Fed testifies before Congress that raising short-term interest rates is under consideration, people's expectations of higher future short-term interest rates are likely to increase. These expectations will then be reflected in current long-term interest rates.

TYPES OF INTEREST RATES

The following are some widely followed interest rates in the United States.

THREE-MONTH TREASURY BILL RATE

Government securities that mature in less than a year are called *Treasury bills*, or sometimes *T-bills*. The interest rate on 3-month Treasury bills is probably the most widely followed short-term interest rate.

GOVERNMENT BOND RATE

Government securities with terms of 1 year or more are called *government bonds*. There are 1-year bonds, 2-year bonds, and so on, up to 30-year bonds. Bonds of different terms have different interest rates. The relationship among the interest rates on the various maturities is the term structure of interest rates that we discussed in the first part of this Appendix.

FEDERAL FUNDS RATE

Banks borrow not only from the Fed but also from each other. If one bank has excess reserves, it can lend some of those reserves to other banks through the federal funds market. The

[1] For longer terms, additional future rates must be averaged in. For a 3-year security, for example, the expected 1-year rate a year from now and the expected 1-year rate 2 years from now are added to the current 1-year rate and averaged.

interest rate in this market is called the *federal funds rate*—the rate banks are charged to borrow reserves from other banks.

The federal funds market is really a desk in New York City. From all over the country, banks with excess reserves to lend and banks in need of reserves call the desk and negotiate a rate of interest. Account balances with the Fed are changed for the period of the loan without any physical movement of money.

This borrowing and lending, which takes place near the close of each working day, is generally for 1 day ("overnight"), so the federal funds rate is a 1-day rate. It is the rate on which the Fed has the most effect through its open market operations.

COMMERCIAL PAPER RATE

Firms have several alternatives for raising funds. They can sell stocks, issue bonds, or borrow from a bank. Large firms can also borrow directly from the public by issuing "commercial paper," which is essentially short-term corporate IOUs that offer a designated rate of interest. The interest rate offered on commercial paper depends on the financial condition of the firm and the maturity date of the IOU.

PRIME RATE

Banks charge different interest rates to different customers depending on how risky the banks perceive the customers to be. You would expect to pay a higher interest rate for a car loan than General Motors would pay for a $1 million loan to finance investment. Also, you would pay more interest for an unsecured loan, a "personal" loan, than for one that was secured by some asset, such as a house or car, to be used as collateral.

The *prime rate* is a benchmark that banks often use in quoting interest rates to their customers. A very low-risk corporation might be able to borrow at (or even below) the prime rate. A less well-known firm might be quoted a rate of "prime plus three-fourths," which means that if the prime rate is, say, 10 percent, the firm would have to pay interest of 10.75 percent. The prime rate depends on the cost of funds to the bank; it moves up and down with changes in the economy.

AAA CORPORATE BOND RATE

Corporations finance much of their investment by selling bonds to the public. Corporate bonds are classified by various bond dealers according to their risk. Bonds issued by General Motors are in less risk of default than bonds issued by a new risky biotech research firm. Bonds differ from commercial paper in one important way: Bonds have a longer maturity.

Bonds are graded in much the same way students are. The highest grade is AAA, the next highest AA, and so on. The interest rate on bonds rated AAA is the *triple A corporate bond rate*, the rate that the least risky firms pay on the bonds that they issue.

PROBLEMS

1. The following table gives three key U.S. interest rates in 1980 and again in 1993:

	1980 (%)	1993 (%)
Three-month U.S. government bills	11.39	3.00
Long-term U.S. government bonds	11.27	6.59
Prime rate	15.26	6.00

Provide an explanation for the extreme differences that you see. Specifically, comment on (1) the fact that rates in 1980 were much higher than in 1993 and (2) the fact that the long-term rate was higher than the short-term rate in 1993 but lower in 1980.

APPENDIX B

THE DEMAND FOR MONEY: A NUMERICAL EXAMPLE

This Appendix presents a numerical example showing how optimal money management behavior can be derived.

We have seen that the interest rate represents the opportunity cost of holding funds in non-interest-bearing checking accounts (as opposed to bonds, which yield interest). We have also seen that costs are involved in switching from bonds to money. Given these costs, our objective is to determine the optimum amount of money for an individual to hold. The optimal average level of money holdings is the amount that maximizes the profits from money management. Interest is earned on average bond holdings, but the cost per switch multiplied by the number of switches must be subtracted from interest revenue to obtain the net profit from money management.

Suppose the interest rate is .05 (5 percent), it costs $2 each time a bond is sold,[1] and the proceeds from the sale are deposited in one's checking account. Suppose also that the individual's income is $1,200 and that this income is spent evenly throughout the period. This situation is depicted in the top half of Table 26B.1. The optimum value for average money holdings is the value that achieves the largest possible profit in column 6 of the table. When the interest rate is 5 percent, the

[1] In this example, we will assume that the $2 cost does not apply to the original purchase of bonds.

TABLE 26B.1 Optimum Money Holdings

1 Number Of Switches[a]	2 Average Money Holdings[b]	3 Average Bond Holdings[c]	4 Interest Earned[d]	5 Cost Of Switching[e]	6 Net Profit[f]
			r = 5 percent		
0	$600.00	$ 0.00	$ 0.00	$0.00	$ 0.00
1	300.00	300.00	15.00	2.00	13.00
2	200.00	400.00	20.00	4.00	16.00
3	150.00*	450.00	22.50	6.00	16.50
4	120.00	480.00	24.00	8.00	16.00
Assumptions: Interest rate $r = 0.05$. Cost of switching from bonds to money equals $2 per transaction.					
			r = 3 percent		
0	$600.00	$ 0.00	$ 0.00	$0.00	$0.00
1	300.00	300.00	9.00	2.00	7.00
2	200.00*	400.00	12.00	4.00	8.00
3	150.00	450.00	13.50	6.00	7.50
4	120.00	480.00	14.40	8.00	6.40
Assumptions: Interest rate $r = 0.03$. Cost of switching from bonds to money equals $2 per transaction.					

*Optimum money holdings. [a]That is, the number of times you sell a bond. [b]Calculated as 600/(col. 1 + 1). [c]Calculated as 600 - col. 2. [d]Calculated as $r \times$ col. 3, where r is the interest rate. [e]Calculated as $t \times$ col. 1, where t is the cost per switch ($2). [f]Calculated as col. 4 − col. 5

optimum average money holdings are $150 (which means that the individual makes three switches from bonds to money).

In the bottom half of Table 26B.1, the same calculations are performed for an interest rate of 3 percent instead of 5 percent. In this case, the optimum average money holdings is $200 (which means the person/household makes two instead of three switches from bonds to money). The lower interest rate has led to an increase in the optimum average money holdings. Under the assumption that people behave optimally, the demand for money is a negative function of the interest rate: The lower the rate, the more money on average is held, and the higher the rate, the less money on average is held.

PROBLEMS

1. Sherman Peabody earns a monthly salary of $1,500, which he receives at the beginning of each month. He spends the entire amount each month at the rate of $50 per day. (Assume 30 days in a month.) The interest rate paid on bonds is 10 percent per month. It costs $4 every time Peabody sells a bond.
   a. Describe briefly how Mr. Peabody should decide how much money to hold.
   b. Calculate Peabody's optimal money holdings. (*Hint:* It may help to formulate a table such as Table 26B.1 in this Appendix. You can round to the nearest $0.50, and you need to consider only average money holdings of more than $100.)
   c. Suppose the interest rate rises to 15 percent. Find Peabody's optimal money holdings at this new interest rate. What will happen if the interest rate increases to 20 percent?
   d. Graph your answers to b. and c. with the interest rate on the vertical axis and the amount of money demanded on the horizontal axis. Explain why your graph slopes downward.

Aggregate Demand in the Goods and Money Markets

27

CHAPTER OUTLINE

In Chapters 23 and 24, we discussed the market for goods and services—the **goods market**—without mentioning money, the money market, or the interest rate. We described how the equilibrium level of aggregate output (income) (Y) is determined in the goods market. At given levels of planned investment spending (I), government spending (G), and net taxes (T), we were able to determine the equilibrium level of output in the economy.

In Chapters 25 and 26, we discussed the financial market, or **money market**, barely referring to the goods market, as we explained how the equilibrium level of the interest rate is determined in the money market.

The goods market and the money market do not operate independently, however. When the Fed increases the money supply and reduces the interest rate, this likely affects the demand for housing, autos, and a range of other goods. Similarly, when the rate of household formation increases the demand for housing, the equilibrium in the money market is likely changed. Events in the money market affect what goes on in the goods market, and events in the goods market affect what goes on in the money market. Only by analyzing the two markets together can we determine the values of aggregate output (income) (Y) and the interest rate (r) that are consistent with the existence of equilibrium in *both* markets.

Looking at both markets simultaneously also reveals how fiscal policy affects the money market and how monetary policy affects the goods market. This is what we will do in this chapter. By establishing how the two markets affect each other, we will show how open market purchases of government securities (which expand the money supply) affect the equilibrium level of aggregate output. Similarly, we will show how fiscal policy measures affect the interest rate.

The relationship between aggregate output and the price level that exists when the goods and money markets are combined can be summarized in a curve called the aggregate demand (AD) curve. Every point on the AD curve reflects equilibrium in both the goods and money markets for the given price level. In the last part of this chapter, we derive the AD curve from the relationships in the goods and money markets. The AD curve is then used in the next chapter in determining the price level.

Planned Investment and the Interest Rate

We have so far assumed for simplicity that planned investment is fixed, and we now must relax this assumption. In practice planned investment depends on many factors, but we focus here on just one: the interest rate. In the theory of household behavior in Chapter 23 we postulated that consumption depends only on income, and in the theory of firm behavior in this chapter we postulate that investment depends only on the interest rate. We will see that investment falls as the interest rate rises.

goods market The market in which goods and services are exchanged and in which the equilibrium level of aggregate output is determined.

money market The market in which financial instruments are exchanged and in which the equilibrium level of the interest rate is determined.

Recall that investment refers to a firm's purchase of new capital—new machines and plants. Whether a firm decides to invest in a project depends on whether the expected profits from the project justify its costs. And one cost of an investment project is the interest cost. Consider a firm opening a new plant, or a new ice cream store. When a manufacturing firm builds a new plant, the contractor must be paid at the time the plant is built. When an entrepreneur decides to open a new ice cream parlor, freezers, tables, chairs, light fixtures, and signs are needed. These too must be paid for when they are installed. The money needed to carry out such projects is generally borrowed and paid back over an extended period. The real cost of an investment project thus depends in part on the interest rate—the cost of borrowing. When the interest rate rises, it becomes more expensive to borrow and fewer projects are likely to be undertaken; increasing the interest rate, *ceteris paribus*, is likely to reduce the level of planned investment spending. When the interest rate falls, it becomes less costly to borrow and more investment projects are likely to be undertaken; reducing the interest rate, *ceteris paribus*, is likely to increase the level of planned investment spending.

The relationship between the interest rate and planned investment is illustrated by the downward-sloping demand curve in Figure 27.1. The higher the interest rate, the lower the level of planned investment. At an interest rate of 3 percent, planned investment is I_0. When the interest rate rises from 3 to 6 percent, planned investment falls from I_0 to I_1. As the interest rate falls, however, more projects become profitable, so more investment is undertaken. The curve in Figure 27.1 is sometimes called the "marginal efficiency of investment" curve.

FIGURE 27.1
Planned Investment Schedule

Planned investment spending is a negative function of the interest rate. An increase in the interest rate from 3 percent to 6 percent reduces planned investment from I_0 to I_1.

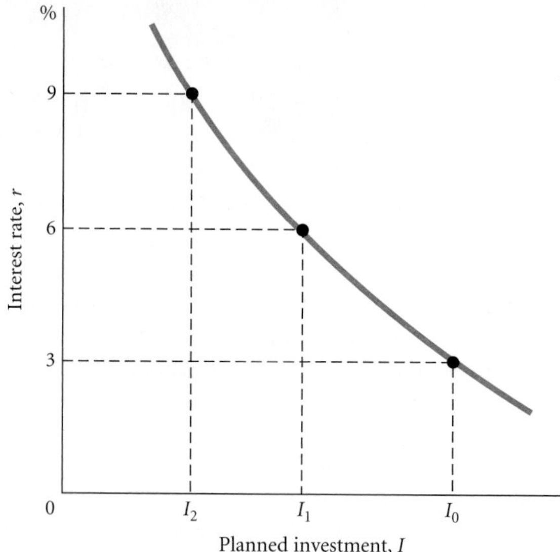

Other Determinants of Planned Investment

The assumption that planned investment depends only on the interest rate is obviously a simplification, just as is the assumption that consumption depends only on income. In practice, the decision of a firm on how much to invest depends on, among other things, its expectation of future sales. If a firm expects that its sales will increase in the future, it may begin to build up its capital stock—that is, to invest—now so that it will be able to produce more in the future to meet the increased level of sales. The optimism or pessimism of entrepreneurs about the future course of the economy can have an important effect on current planned investment. Keynes used the phrase *animal spirits* to describe the feelings of entrepreneurs, and he argued that these feelings affect investment decisions.

We come back to this issue in Chapter 31, where we take a closer look at firm behavior (and household behavior), but for now we will assume that planned investment simply depends on the interest rate.

Planned Aggregate Expenditure and the Interest Rate

We can use the fact that planned investment depends on the interest rate to consider how planned aggregate expenditure (*AE*) depends on the interest rate. Recall that planned aggregate expenditure is the sum of consumption, planned investment, and government purchases. That is,

ECONOMICS IN PRACTICE

Interest Rates and Investment Spending

The text discusses the idea that there is a negative relationship between the interest rate (r) and the investment spending of firms (I). A higher rate means a higher cost for firms that borrow to finance their capital expenditures and hence a higher cost of capital. Similarly, a lower interest rate is likely to stimulate additional investment spending.

A recent study by Simon Gilchrist, Fabio Natalucci, and Egon Zakrajsek finds that interest rates have a powerful effect on the behavior of firms.

> "The notion that business spending on fixed capital falls when interest rates rise is a theoretically unambiguous relationship that lies at the heart of the monetary transmission mechanism. Nonetheless, the presence of a robust negative relationship between investment expenditures has been difficult to document in actual data. In this paper we revisit this long-standing empirical anomaly. We do so by constructing a new data set . . . for more than 900 large U.S. non-financial corporations. Our results indicate that investment expenditures are highly sensitive—both economically and statistically—to changes in interest rates."[1]

According to their estimates, a one-percentage-point increase in the interest rate appropriate for a firm's borrowing leads to a drop in investment spending of more than one percentage point.

In 2007, interest rates were falling and many believed that the decline in interest rates would prevent a recession in 2008. The chairman of the President's Council for Economic Advisors, Ed Lazear, wrote in the annual Economics Report of the President:

> "During the four quarters of 2007, real business investment on equipment and software grew at 3.7%. Its fastest growing components during 2007 included computer software and communication equipment. . . . Business investment growth is projected to remain solid during 2008. . . ."

[1] *Simon Gilchrist, Fabio Natalucci, and Egon Zakrajsek, "Interest Rate and Investment Redux," Federal Reserve Board of Governors, March 2007; Economic Report of the President, February 2008.*

$$AE \equiv C + I + G$$

We now know that there are many possible levels of I, each corresponding to a different interest rate. When the interest rate changes, planned investment changes. Therefore, a change in the interest rate (r) will lead to a change in total planned spending ($C + I + G$) as well.[1]

Figure 27.2 shows what happens to planned aggregate expenditure and output when the interest rate rises from 3 percent to 6 percent. At the higher interest rate, planned investment is lower; planned aggregate expenditure thus shifts *downward*. Recall from Chapters 23 and 24 that a fall in any component of aggregate spending has an even larger (or "multiplier") effect on equilibrium income (Y). When the interest rate rises, planned investment (and planned aggregate expenditure) falls and equilibrium output (income) falls by even more than the fall in planned investment. In Figure 27.2, equilibrium Y falls from Y_0 to Y_1 when the interest rate rises from 3 percent to 6 percent.

[1] When we look in detail in Chapter 31 at the behavior of households in the macroeconomy, we will see that consumption spending (C) is also stimulated by lower interest rates and discouraged by higher interest rates.

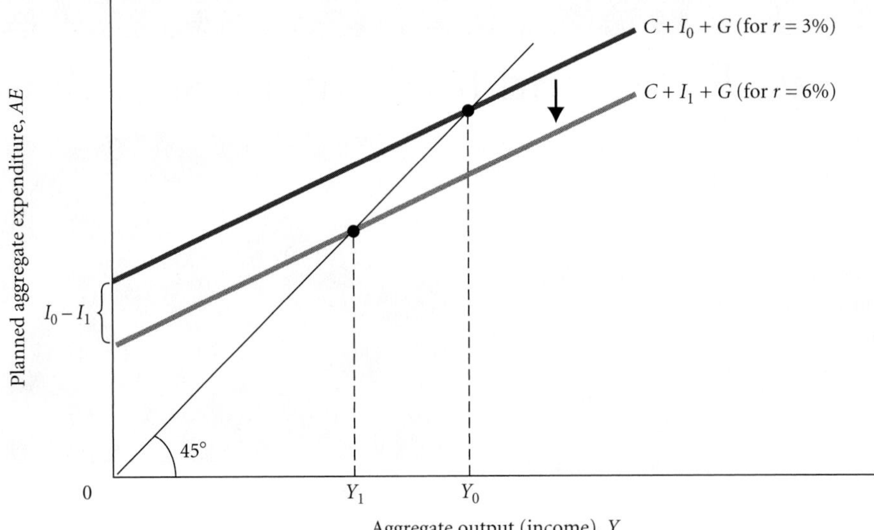

FIGURE 27.2
The Effect of an Interest Rate Increase on Planned Aggregate Expenditure
An increase in the interest rate from 3 percent to 6 percent lowers planned aggregate expenditure and thus reduces equilibrium income from Y_0 to Y_1.

We can summarize the effects of a change in the interest rate on the equilibrium level of output. The effects of a change in the interest rate include:

- A high interest rate (r) discourages planned investment (I).
- Planned investment is a part of planned aggregate expenditure (AE).
- Thus, when the interest rate rises, planned aggregate expenditure (AE) at every level of income falls.
- Finally, a decrease in planned aggregate expenditure lowers equilibrium output (income) (Y) by a multiple of the initial decrease in planned investment.

Using a convenient shorthand:

$$r \uparrow \rightarrow I \downarrow \rightarrow AE \downarrow \rightarrow Y \downarrow$$
$$r \downarrow \rightarrow I \uparrow \rightarrow AE \uparrow \rightarrow Y \uparrow$$

Equilibrium in Both the Goods and Money Markets

It is now straightforward to see how the goods and money markets are linked. We have just seen that an increase in the interest rate (r) decreases output (Y) in the goods market because an increase in r lowers planned investment. This is the first link.

The second link can be seen from Figure 26.8 on p. 525. When income (Y) increase, this shifts the money demand curve to the right, which increases the interest rate (r) with a fixed money supply. We can thus write:

$$Y \uparrow \rightarrow M^d \uparrow \rightarrow r \uparrow$$
$$Y \downarrow \rightarrow M^d \downarrow \rightarrow r \downarrow$$

In other words, an increase in Y increases r in the money market and a decrease in Y decreases r.

Figure 27.3 summarize the links between the two markets. Given this figure, we are essentially done with the analysis. Given the interest rate, the equilibrium level of output can be determined from the goods market. Given output, the equilibrium interest rate can be determined from the money market. Putting both markets together allows the one pair of equilibrium values of Y and r to be determined. The equilibrium value of Y is the value that is consistent with the equilibrium value of r. There is equilibrium in both markets for the particular pair of values. This overall equilibrium is derived formally in the Appendix to this chapter.

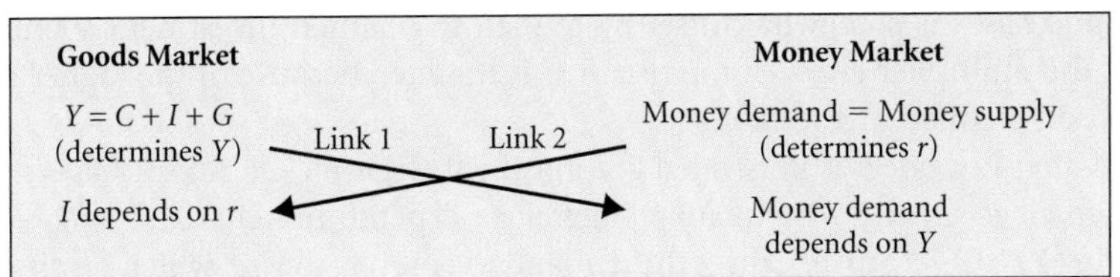

FIGURE 27.3
Links Between the Goods Market and the Money Market
Planned investment depends on the interest rate, and money demand depends on aggregate output.

Policy Effects in the Goods and Money Markets

A useful way to examine the links between the goods and money markets is to consider the effects of changes in fiscal and monetary policy actions on the economy. We want to examine what happens to the equilibrium levels of output (Y) and interest rate (r) when policy changes. The three policy variables are government spending (G), net taxes (T), and the money supply (M^S).

Expansionary Policy Effects

Any government policy aimed at stimulating aggregate output (income) (Y) is said to be expansionary. An **expansionary fiscal policy** is an increase in government spending (G) or a reduction in net taxes (T) aimed at increasing aggregate output (income) (Y). An **expansionary monetary policy** is an increase in the money supply aimed at increasing aggregate output (income) (Y).

expansionary fiscal policy An increase in government spending or a reduction in net taxes aimed at increasing aggregate output (income) (Y).

expansionary monetary policy An increase in the money supply aimed at increasing aggregate output (income) (Y).

Expansionary Fiscal Policy: An Increase in Government Purchases (G) or a Decrease in Net Taxes (T) As you know from Chapter 24, government purchases (G) and net taxes (T) are the two tools of government fiscal policy. The government can stimulate the economy—that is, it can increase aggregate output (income) (Y)—either by *increasing* government purchases or by *reducing* net taxes. Although the impact of a tax cut is somewhat smaller than the impact of an increase in G, both have a multiplier effect on the equilibrium level of Y.

Consider an increase in government purchases (G) of $10 billion. This increase in expenditure causes firms' inventories to be smaller than planned. Unplanned inventory reductions stimulate production, and firms increase output (Y). However, because added output means added income, some of which is subsequently spent, consumption spending (C) also increases. Again, inventories will be smaller than planned and output will rise even further. The final equilibrium level of output is higher by a multiple of the initial increase in government purchases.

This multiplier story is incomplete, however. Until this chapter, we have assumed that planned investment (I) is fixed at a certain level, but we now know that planned investment depends on the interest rate. We can now discuss what happens to the multiplier when investment varies because we have an understanding of the money market, in which the interest rate is determined.

Return to our multiplier story at the point that firms first begin to raise output in response to an increase in government purchases. As aggregate output (income) (Y) increases, an impact is felt in the money market—the increase in income (Y) increases the demand for money (M^d). (For the moment, assume that the Fed holds the quantity of money supplied [M^s] constant.) The resulting disequilibrium, with the quantity of money demanded greater than the quantity of money supplied, causes the interest rate to rise. The increase in G increases both Y and r.

The increase in r has a side effect—a higher interest rate causes planned investment spending (I) to decline. Because planned investment spending is a component of planned aggregate expenditure ($C + I + G$), the decrease in I works against the increase in G. An increase in government spending (G) increases planned aggregate expenditure and increases aggregate output, but a decrease in planned investment reduces planned aggregate expenditure and *decreases* aggregate output.

This tendency for increases in government spending to cause reductions in private investment spending is called the **crowding-out effect**. Without any expansion in the money supply to accommodate the rise in income and increased money demand, planned investment spending is partially crowded out by the higher interest rate. The extra spending created by the rise in

crowding-out effect The tendency for increases in government spending to cause reductions in private investment spending.

government purchases is somewhat offset by the fall in planned investment spending. Income still rises, but the multiplier effect of the rise in *G* is lessened because of the higher interest rate's negative effect on planned investment.

This crowding-out effect is illustrated graphically in Figure 27.4. An increase in government purchases from G_0 to G_1 shifts the planned aggregate expenditure curve $(C + I_0 + G_0)$ upward. The increase in (*Y*) from Y_0 to Y_1 causes the demand for money to rise, which results in a disequilibrium in the money market. The excess demand for money raises the interest rate, causing *I* to decrease from I_0 to I_1. The fall in *I* pulls the planned aggregate expenditure curve back down, which lowers the equilibrium level of income to Y^*. (Remember that equilibrium is achieved when $Y = AE$.) The possibility of some crowding out of firm investment by increased government spending is a subject of political debate as well as economic analysis. To the extent that there is some crowding out, an increase in government spending as a way to increase aggregate output leads to a reduced share of private-sector (that is, firm) investment in GDP. There is considerable disagreement among voters and politicians in the United States about what constitutes the right mix of private investment and public spending in a healthy economy.

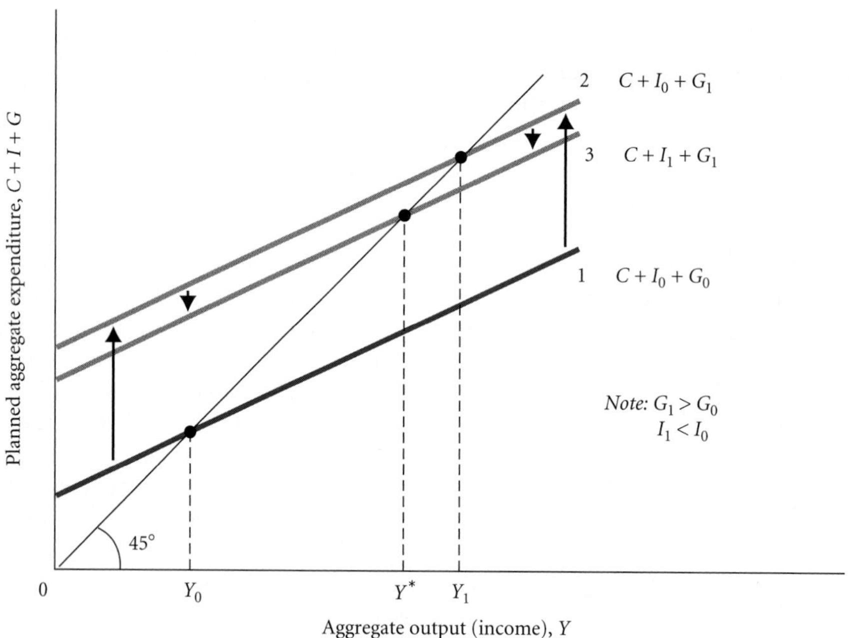

FIGURE 27.4
The Crowding-Out Effect
An increase in government spending *G* from G_0 to G_1 shifts the planned aggregate expenditure schedule from 1 to 2. The crowding-out effect of the decrease in planned investment (brought about by the increased interest rate) then shifts the planned aggregate expenditure schedule from 2 to 3.

Note that the size of the crowding-out effect and the ultimate size of the government spending multiplier depend on several things. First, we assumed that the Fed did not change the quantity of money supplied. If we were to assume instead that the Fed expanded the quantity of money to accommodate the increase in G, the multiplier would be larger. In this case, the higher demand for money would be satisfied with a higher quantity of money supplied and the interest rate would not rise. Without a higher interest rate, there would be no crowding out.

Second, the crowding-out effect depends on the **sensitivity** or **insensitivity of planned investment** spending to changes in the interest rate. Crowding out occurs because a higher interest rate reduces planned investment spending. Investment depends on factors other than the interest rate, however, and investment may at times be quite insensitive to changes in the interest rate. If planned investment does not fall when the interest rate rises, there is no crowding-out effect. These effects are summarized next.

interest sensitivity *or* **insensitivity of planned investment** The responsiveness of planned investment spending to changes in the interest rate. *Interest sensitivity* means that planned investment spending changes a great deal in response to changes in the interest rate; *interest insensitivity* means little or no change in planned investment as a result of changes in the interest rate.

Effects of an expansionary fiscal policy:

$$G\uparrow \rightarrow Y\uparrow \rightarrow M^d\uparrow \rightarrow r\uparrow \rightarrow I\downarrow$$

→ *Y* increases less than if *r* did not increase

Exactly the same reasoning holds for changes in net taxes. The ultimate effect of a tax cut on the equilibrium level of output depends on how the money market reacts. The expansion of Y that a tax cut brings about will lead to an increase in the interest rate and thus a decrease in planned investment spending. The ultimate increase in Y will therefore be less than it would be if the interest rate did not rise.

Expansionary Monetary Policy: An Increase in the Money Supply

Now let us consider what will happen when the Fed decides to increase the supply of money through open market operations. At first, open market operations inject new reserves into the system and expand the quantity of money supplied (the money supply curve shifts to the right). Because the quantity of money supplied is now greater than the amount households want to hold, the equilibrium rate of interest falls. Planned investment spending (which is a component of planned aggregate expenditure) increases when the interest rate falls.

Increased planned investment spending means planned aggregate expenditure is now greater than aggregate output. Firms experience unplanned decreases in inventories, and they raise output (Y). An increase in the money supply decreases the interest rate and increases Y. However, the higher level of Y increases the demand for money (the demand for money curve shifts to the right), which keeps the interest rate from falling as far as it otherwise would.

If you review the sequence of events that follows the monetary expansion, you can see the links between the injection of reserves by the Fed into the economy and the increase in output. First, the increase in the quantity of money supplied pushes down the interest rate. Second, the lower interest rate causes planned investment spending to rise. Third, the increased planned investment spending means higher planned aggregate expenditure, which means increased output as firms react to unplanned decreases in inventories. Fourth, the increase in output (income) leads to an increase in the demand for money (the demand for money curve shifts to the right), which means the interest rate decreases less than it would have if the demand for money had not increased.

Effects of an expansionary monetary policy:

$$M^s\uparrow \rightarrow r\downarrow \rightarrow I\uparrow \rightarrow Y\uparrow \rightarrow M^d\uparrow$$

→ r decreases less than if M^d did not increase

The power of monetary policy to affect the goods market depends on how much of a reaction occurs at each link in this chain. Perhaps the most critical link is the link between r and I. Monetary policy can be effective *only* if I reacts to changes in r.[2] If firms sharply increase the number of investment projects undertaken when the interest rate falls, expansionary monetary policy works well at stimulating the economy. If, however, firms are reluctant to invest even at a low interest rate, expansionary monetary policy will have limited success. In other words, the effectiveness of monetary policy depends on the slope of the investment function. If it is nearly vertical, indicating very little responsiveness of investment to the interest rate, the middle link in this chain will be weak, rendering monetary policy ineffective.

Contractionary Policy Effects

Any government policy that is aimed at reducing aggregate output (income) (Y) is said to be *contractionary*. Where expansionary policy is used to boost the economy, contractionary policy is used to slow the economy.

Contractionary Fiscal Policy: A Decrease in Government Spending (G) or an Increase in Net Taxes (T)

A **contractionary fiscal policy** is a decrease in government spending (G) or an increase in net taxes (T) aimed at decreasing aggregate output (income) (Y). The effects of this policy are the opposite of the effects of an expansionary fiscal policy.

contractionary fiscal policy A decrease in government spending or an increase in net taxes aimed at decreasing aggregate output (income) (Y).

A decrease in government purchases or an increase in net taxes leads to a decrease in aggregate output (income) (Y), a decrease in the demand for money (M^d), and a decrease in

[2] As we discuss in Chapter 31, consumption (C) may also depend on r, which further increases the effectiveness of monetary policy.

the interest rate (r). The decrease in Y that accompanies a contractionary fiscal policy is less than it would be if we did not take the money market into account because the decrease in r also causes planned investment (I) to *increase*. This increase in I offsets some of the decrease in planned aggregate expenditure brought about by the decrease in G. (This also means the multiplier effect is smaller than it would be if we did not take the money market into account.) The effects of a decrease in G, or an increase in T, can be represented as shown.

Effects of a contractionary fiscal policy:

$$G\downarrow \text{ or } T\uparrow \rightarrow Y\downarrow \rightarrow M^d\downarrow \rightarrow r\downarrow \rightarrow I\uparrow$$

→ Y decreases less than if r did not decrease

contractionary monetary policy A decrease in the money supply aimed at decreasing aggregate output (income) (Y).

Contractionary Monetary Policy: A Decrease in the Money Supply A **contractionary monetary policy** is a decrease in the money supply aimed at decreasing aggregate output (income) (Y). As you recall, the level of planned investment spending is a negative function of the interest rate: The higher the interest rate, the less planned investment there will be. The less planned investment there is, the lower planned aggregate expenditure will be and the lower the equilibrium level of output (income) (Y) will be. The lower equilibrium income results in a decrease in the demand for money, which means that the increase in the interest rate will be less than it would be if we did not take the goods market into account.

Effects of a contractionary monetary policy:

$$M^s\downarrow \rightarrow r\uparrow \rightarrow I\downarrow \rightarrow Y\downarrow \rightarrow M^d\downarrow$$

→ r increases less than if M^d did not decrease

The Macroeconomic Policy Mix

Although we have been treating fiscal and monetary policy separately, it should be clear that fiscal and monetary policy can be used simultaneously. For example, both government purchases (G) and the money supply (M^s) can be increased at the same time. We have seen that an increase in G by itself raises both Y and r, while an increase in M^s by itself raises Y but lowers r. Therefore, if the government wanted to increase Y without changing r, it could do so by increasing both G and M^s by the appropriate amounts.

policy mix The combination of monetary and fiscal policies in use at a given time.

Policy mix refers to the combination of monetary and fiscal policies in use at a given time. A policy mix that consists of a decrease in government spending and an increase in the money supply favors private investment spending over government spending. The reason is that both the increased money supply and the fall in government purchases cause the interest rate to fall, which leads to an increase in planned investment. The opposite is true for a mix that consists of an expansionary fiscal policy and a contractionary monetary policy. This mix favors government spending over investment spending. Such a policy has the effect of increasing government spending and reducing the money supply. Tight money and expanded government spending drives the interest rate up and planned investment down.

There is no rule about what constitutes the "best" policy mix or the "best" composition of output. On this issue, as on many other issues, economists (and others) disagree. In part, someone's preference for a certain composition of output—say, one weighted heavily toward private spending with relatively little government spending—depends on how that person stands on such issues as the proper role of government in the economy.

Table 27.1 summarizes the effects of various combinations of policies on several important macroeconomic variables. If you can explain the reasoning underlying each of the effects shown in the table, you can be satisfied that you have a good understanding of the links between the goods market and the money market.

TABLE 27.1 The Effects of the Macroeconomic Policy Mix

		Fiscal Policy	
		Expansionary ($\uparrow$ G or $\downarrow$ T)	Contractionary ($\downarrow$ G or $\uparrow$ T)
Monetary Policy	Expansionary ($\uparrow$ M^s)	$Y\uparrow$, $r?$, $I?$, $C\uparrow$	$Y?$, $r\downarrow$, $I\uparrow$, $C?$
	Contractionary ($\downarrow$ M^s)	$Y?$, $r\uparrow$, $I\downarrow$, $C?$	$Y\downarrow$, $r?$, $I?$, $C\downarrow$

Key:
$\uparrow$: Variable increases.
$\downarrow$: Variable decreases.
?: Forces push the variable in different directions. Without additional information, we cannot specify which way the variable moves.

The Aggregate Demand (*AD*) Curve

Having determined equilibrium in the goods and money markets, we can now derive the aggregate demand (*AD*) curve. **Aggregate demand** is the total demand for goods and services in the economy. The *AD* curve shows the equilibrium levels of aggregate output associated with different price levels in the economy. The *AD* curve plays a key role in the next chapter in determining the price level (*P*). The aggregate demand curve is derived by assuming that the fiscal policy variables—government expenditures (*G*) and net taxes (*T*)—and the monetary policy variable (M^S) remain unchanged. In other words, the assumption is that the government does not take any action to affect the economy in response to changes in the price level.

aggregate demand The total demand for goods and services in the economy.

To derive the aggregate demand curve, we examine what happens to aggregate output (*Y*) when the price level (*P*) changes, taking into account both the money and the goods markets. Begin with an exogenous increase in the price level. For now, you need not worry about where the price increase comes from. What happens as a result of this price increase? From the last chapter, we know that a price increase, all else equal, shifts the demand for money curve to the right. We have shown this in Figure 27.5(a). The supply of money curve is shown as a fixed vertical line since we have assumed that the Fed's money supply choice is independent of the interest rate. In the figure, we see that the price increase increases the interest rate from 6 percent to 9 percent as a result of the shift of the money demand curve. This new higher interest rate leads other things to change. Figure 27.5(b) shows the effect of the interest rate increase on planned investment. With higher borrowing costs, planned investment falls, from I_0 to I_1. But planned investment is one of the components of aggregate expenditure (*AE*), and so the fall in planned investment shifts the AE curve down, as we see in Figure 27.5(c). Lower *AE* means inventories are greater than planned, firms cut back on output, and *Y* falls from Y_0 to Y_1. An increase in the price level thus leads the level of aggregate output (income) to fall.

The situation is reversed when the price level declines. A lower price level shifts the money demand curve to the left, which leads to a lower interest rate. A lower interest rate stimulates planned investment spending, increasing planned aggregate expenditure, which leads to an increase in *Y*. A decrease in the price level thus leads the level of aggregate output (income) to rise.

This negative relationship between aggregate output (income) and the price level is called the **aggregate demand (*AD*) curve**, shown in Figure 27.6. Each point on the aggregate demand curve represents equilibrium in both the goods market *and* the money market. We have derived the *AD* curve using the analysis of the links between the goods market and the money market. Each value of *Y* on the aggregate demand curve corresponds to a value at which both the goods market and the money market are in equilibrium for the given value of the price level.

aggregate demand (*AD*) curve A curve that shows the negative relationship between aggregate output (income) and the price level. Each point on the *AD* curve is a point at which both the goods market and the money market are in equilibrium.

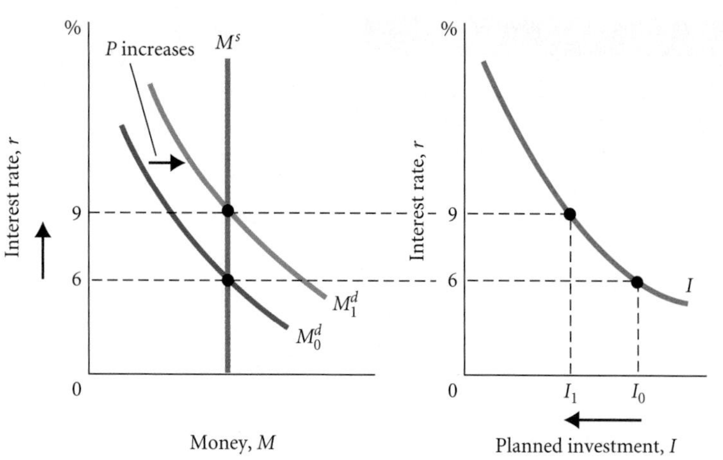

a. An increase in the price level (P) increases the demand for money from M_0^d to M_1^d. With the supply of money unchanged, the interest rate increases from 6 percent to 9 percent.

b. The higher interest rate decreases planned investment from I_0 to I_1.

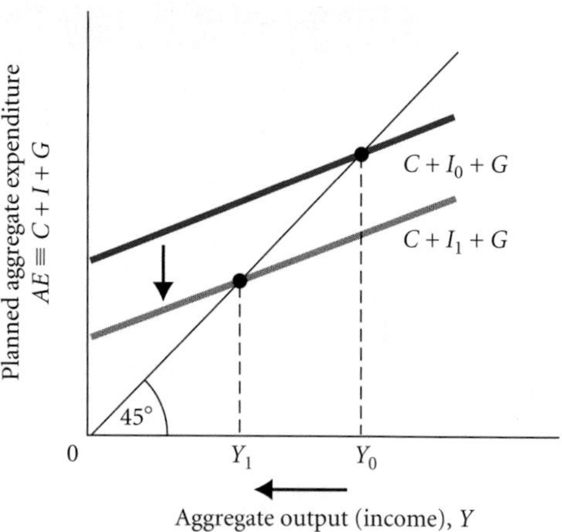

c. Decreased planned investment reduces planned aggregate expenditure and causes equilibrium output (income) to fall from Y_0 to Y_1.

▲ **FIGURE 27.5 The Impact of an Increase in the Price Level on the Economy—Assuming No Changes in *G*, *T*, and M^s**

This figure shows that when P increases, Y decreases.

▶ **FIGURE 27.6**

The Aggregate Demand (*AD*) Curve

At all points along the *AD* curve, both the goods market and the money market are in equilibrium. The policy variables G, T, and M^s are fixed.

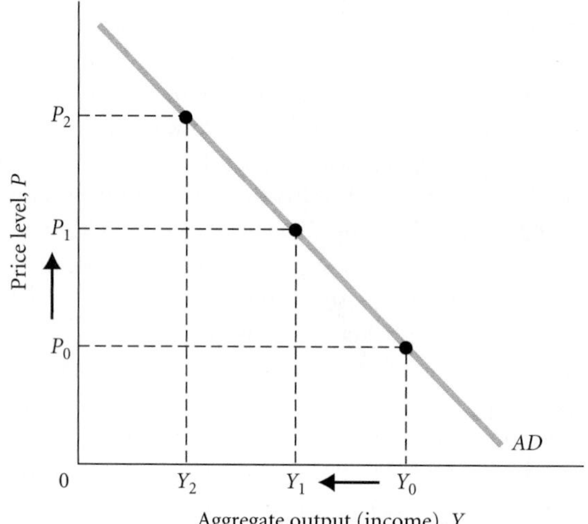

The Aggregate Demand Curve: A Warning

It is important that you realize what the aggregate demand curve represents. The aggregate demand curve is more complex than a simple individual or market demand curve. The *AD* curve is *not* a market demand curve, and it is *not* the sum of all market demand curves in the economy. To understand why, recall the logic behind a simple downward-sloping household demand curve. A demand curve shows the quantity of output demanded (by an individual household or in a single market) at every possible price, *ceteris paribus*. In drawing a simple demand curve, we are assuming that *other prices* and *income* are fixed. From these assumptions, it follows that one reason the quantity demanded of a particular good falls when its price rises is that other prices do *not* rise. The good in question therefore becomes more expensive relative to other goods, and households respond by substituting other goods for the good whose price increased. In addition, if income does not rise when the price of a good does, real income falls. This may also lead to a lower quantity demanded of the good whose price has risen.

Things are different when the *overall price level* rises. When the overall price level rises many prices—including many wage rates (many people's income)—rise together. For this reason, we cannot use the *ceteris paribus* assumption to draw the *AD* curve. The logic that explains why a simple demand curve slopes downward fails to explain why the *AD* curve also has a negative slope. Aggregate demand falls when the price level increases because the higher price level causes the demand for money (M^d) to rise. With the money supply constant, the interest rate will rise to reestablish equilibrium in the money market. *It is the higher interest rate that causes aggregate output to fall.* The *AD* curve traces the relationship between the overall price level and aggregate demand, taking into account the behavior of firms and households in the goods and money markets at the same time.

You do not need to understand anything about the money market to understand a simple individual or market demand curve. However, to understand what the *aggregate* demand curve represents, you must understand the interaction between the goods market and the money markets. The *AD* curve in Figure 27.6 embodies everything we have learned about the goods market and the money market up to now.

Other Reasons for a Downward-Sloping Aggregate Demand Curve

In addition to the effects of money supply and money demand on the interest rate, two other factors lie behind the downward slope of the *AD* curve. These are the consumption link and the real wealth effect.

The Consumption Link We noted in Chapter 22 (and will discuss in detail in Chapter 31) that consumption (*C*) depends on the interest rate. Other things being equal, consumption expenditures tend to rise when the interest rate falls and to fall when the interest rate rises—just as planned investment does. This tendency is another link between the goods market and the money market. If something happens to change the interest rate in the money market, both consumption and planned investment are affected in the goods market.

The *consumption* link provides another reason for the *AD* curve's downward slope. An increase in the price level increases the demand for money, which leads to an increase in the interest rate, which leads to a decrease in consumption (as well as planned investment), which leads to a decrease in aggregate output (income). The initial decrease in consumption (brought about by the increase in the interest rate) contributes to the overall decrease in output. Planned investment does not bear all the burden of providing the link from a higher interest rate to a lower level of aggregate output. Decreased consumption brought about by a higher interest rate also contributes to this effect.

The Real Wealth Effect We also noted in Chapter 23 (and will discuss in detail in Chapter 31 that consumption depends on wealth. Other things being equal, the more wealth households have, the more they consume. Wealth includes holdings of money, shares of stock, bonds, and housing, among other things. If household wealth decreases, the result will be less consumption now and in the future.

The price level has an effect on some kinds of wealth. Suppose you are holding $1,000 in a checking account or in a money market fund and the price level rises by 10 percent. Your holding is now worth 10 percent less because the prices of the goods that you could buy with your $1,000 have all increased by 10 percent. The purchasing power (or "real value") of your holding has decreased by 10 percent.

An increase in the price level may also lower the real value of stocks and housing, although whether it does depends on what happens to stock prices and housing prices when the overall price level rises. If stock prices and housing prices rise by the same percentage as the overall price level, the real value of stocks and housing will remain unchanged. If an increase in the price level does lower the real value of wealth, this is another reason for the downward slope of the *AD* curve. If real wealth falls, this leads to a decrease in consumption, which leads to a decrease in aggregate output (income). So if real wealth falls when there is an increase in the price level, there is a negative relationship between the price level and output through this **real wealth effect** or **real balance effect**.

real wealth, *or* **real balance, effect** The change in consumption brought about by a change in real wealth that results from a change in the price level.

Aggregate Expenditure and Aggregate Demand

Throughout our discussion of macroeconomics so far, we have referred to the total planned spending by households (C), firms (I), and the government (G) as planned aggregate expenditure. At equilibrium, planned aggregate expenditure ($AE \equiv C + I + G$) and aggregate output (Y) are equal:

$$\text{equilibrium condition: } C + I + G = Y$$

How does planned aggregate expenditure relate to aggregate demand? At every point along the aggregate demand curve, the aggregate quantity demanded is exactly equal to planned aggregate expenditure, $C + I + G$. You can see this in Figures 27.5 and 27.6 on p. 540. When the price level rises, it is planned aggregate expenditure that decreases, moving us up the aggregate demand curve.

However, the aggregate demand curve represents more than just planned aggregate expenditure. Each point on the *AD* curve represents the *particular* level of planned aggregate expenditure that is consistent with equilibrium in the goods market and the money market at the given price level. Notice that the variable on the horizontal axis of the aggregate demand curve in Figure 27.6 is Y. At every point along the *AD* curve, $Y = C + I + G$.

Shifts of the Aggregate Demand Curve

The aggregate demand curve in Figure 27.6 is based on the assumption that the government policy variables G, T, and M^s are fixed. If any of these variables change, the aggregate demand curve will shift.

Consider an increase in the quantity of money supplied. If the quantity of money is expanded at any given price level, the interest rate will fall, causing planned investment spending (and planned aggregate expenditure) to rise. The result is an increase in output at the given price level. As Figure 27.7 shows, an increase in the quantity of money supplied at a given price level shifts the aggregate demand curve to the right.

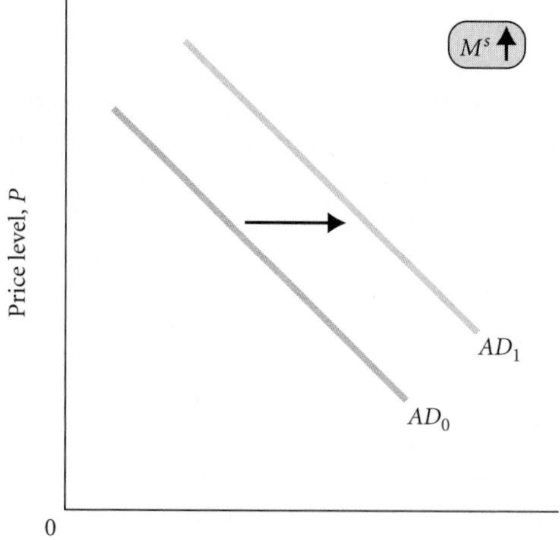

FIGURE 27.7

The Effect of an Increase in Money Supply on the *AD* Curve

An increase in the money supply (M^s) causes the aggregate demand curve to shift to the right, from AD_0 to AD_1. This shift occurs because the increase in M^s lowers the interest rate, which increases planned investment (and thus planned aggregate expenditure). The final result is an increase in output at each possible price level.

An increase in government purchases or a decrease in net taxes also increases aggregate output (income) at each possible price level even though some of the increase will be crowded out if the money supply is held constant. An increase in government purchases directly increases planned aggregate expenditure, which leads to an increase in output. A decrease in net taxes results in a rise in consumption, which increases planned aggregate expenditure, which also leads to an increase in output. As Figure 27.8 shows, an increase in government purchases or a decrease in net taxes shifts the aggregate demand curve to the right.

The same kind of reasoning applies to decreases in the quantity of money supplied, decreases in government purchases, and increases in net taxes. All of these shift the aggregate demand curve to the left.

Figure 27.9 summarizes the ways the aggregate demand curve shifts in response to changes in M^s, G, and T. To test your understanding of the *AD* curve, go through the figure piece by piece and explain the necessary steps for each of its components to create the shift in aggregate demand.

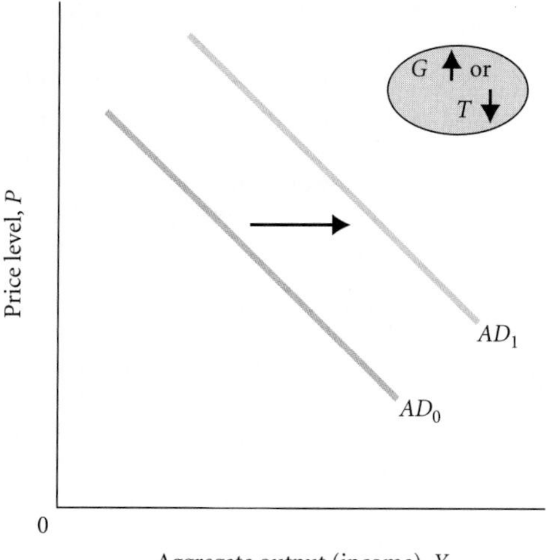

▲ FIGURE 27.8 **The Effect of an Increase in Government Purchases or a Decrease in Net Taxes on the *AD* Curve**

An increase in government purchases (*G*) or a decrease in net taxes (*T*) causes the aggregate demand curve to shift to the right, from AD_0 to AD_1. The increase in *G* increases planned aggregate expenditure, which leads to an increase in output at each possible price level. A decrease in *T* causes consumption to rise. The higher consumption then increases planned aggregate expenditure, which leads to an increase in output at each possible price level.

Expansionary monetary policy	Contractionary monetary policy
$M^s \uparrow \rightarrow$ *AD* curve shifts to the right	$M^s \downarrow \rightarrow$ *AD* curve shifts to the left
Expansionary fiscal policy	**Contractionary fiscal policy**
$G \uparrow \rightarrow$ *AD* curve shifts to the right	$G \downarrow \rightarrow$ *AD* curve shifts to the left
$T \downarrow \rightarrow$ *AD* curve shifts to the right	$T \uparrow \rightarrow$ *AD* curve shifts to the left

◀ FIGURE 27.9 **Factors That Shift the Aggregate Demand Curve**

Looking Ahead: Determining the Price Level

Our discussion of aggregate output (income) and the interest rate in the goods and money markets is now complete. You should have a good understanding of how the two markets work together. The *AD* curve is a useful summary of this analysis in that every point on the curve corresponds to equilibrium in both the goods and money markets for the given value of the price level. We have not yet, however, determined the price level. This is the task of the next chapter.

SUMMARY

1. The *goods market* and the *money market* do not operate independently. Events in the money market have effects on the goods market, and events in the goods market have effects on the money market.

PLANNED INVESTMENT AND THE INTEREST RATE *p. 531*

2. There is a negative relationship between planned investment and the interest rate because the interest rate affects the cost of investment projects. When the interest rate rises, planned investment decreases, and when the interest rate falls, planned investment increases.

3. For every value of the interest rate, there is a different level of planned investment spending and a different equilibrium level of output.

EQUILIBRIUM IN BOTH THE GOODS AND MONEY MARKETS *p. 534*

4. In the goods market, there is a negative relationship between the interest rate and output because there is a negative relationship between the interest rate and planned investment. In the money market, there is a positive relationship between the interest rate and output for a fixed money supply

because if output increases, the interest rate must increase to achieve equilibrium in the money market.

5. Combining the goods and money markets determines the equilibrium values of both the interest rate and output.

POLICY EFFECTS IN THE GOODS AND MONEY MARKETS p. 535

6. An *expansionary fiscal policy* is an increase in government spending (*G*) or a reduction in net taxes (*T*) aimed at increasing aggregate output (income) (*Y*). An expansionary fiscal policy based on increases in government spending tends to lead to a *crowding-out effect*: Because increased government expenditures mean more transactions in the economy and thus an increased demand for money, the interest rate will rise. The decrease in planned investment spending that accompanies the higher interest rate will then partially offset the increase in aggregate expenditures brought about by the increase in G.

7. The size of the crowding-out effect, affecting the size of the government spending multiplier, depends on two things: the assumption that the Fed does not change the quantity of money supplied and the *sensitivity or insensitivity of planned investment* to changes in the interest rate.

8. An *expansionary monetary policy* is an increase in the money supply aimed at increasing aggregate output (income) (*Y*). An increase in the money supply leads to a lower interest rate, increased planned investment, increased planned aggregate expenditure, and ultimately a higher equilibrium level of aggregate output (income) (*Y*). Expansionary policies have been used to lift the economy out of recessions.

9. A *contractionary fiscal policy* is a decrease in government spending or an increase in net taxes aimed at decreasing aggregate output (income) (*Y*). A decrease in government spending or an increase in net taxes leads to a decrease in aggregate output (income) (*Y*), a decrease in the demand for money, and a decrease in the interest rate. However, the decrease in *Y* is somewhat offset by the additional planned investment resulting from the lower interest rate.

10. A *contractionary monetary policy* is a decrease in the money supply aimed at decreasing aggregate output (income) (*Y*). The higher interest rate brought about by the reduced money supply causes a decrease in planned investment spending and a lower level of equilibrium output. However, the lower equilibrium level of output brings about a decrease in the demand for money, which means the increase in the interest rate will be less than it would be if we did not take the goods market into account. Contractionary policies have been used to fight inflation.

11. The *policy mix* is the combination of monetary and fiscal policies in use at a given time. There is no rule about what constitutes the best policy mix or the best composition of output. In part, one's preference for a certain composition of output depends on one's stance concerning such issues as the proper role of government in the economy.

THE AGGREGATE DEMAND (*AD*) CURVE p. 539

12. *Aggregate demand* is the total demand for goods and services in the economy. The *aggregate demand (AD) curve* illustrates the negative relationship between aggregate output (income) and the price level. Each point on the *AD* curve is a point at which both the goods market and the money market are in equilibrium for a given value of the price level. The *AD* curve is *not* the sum of all the market demand curves in the economy.

13. At every point along the aggregate demand curve, the aggregate quantity demanded in the economy is exactly equal to planned aggregate expenditure for the given value of the price level.

14. An increase in the quantity of money supplied, an increase in government purchases, or a decrease in net taxes at a given price level shifts the aggregate demand curve to the right. A decrease in the quantity of money supplied, a decrease in government purchases, or an increase in net taxes shifts the aggregate demand curve to the left.

REVIEW TERMS AND CONCEPTS

aggregate demand, *p. 539*
aggregate demand (*AD*) curve, *p. 539*
contractionary fiscal policy, *p. 537*
contractionary monetary policy, *p. 538*
crowding-out effect, *p. 535*
expansionary fiscal policy, *p. 535*
expansionary monetary policy, *p. 535*
goods market, *p. 531*
interest sensitivity *or* insensitivity of planned investment, *p. 536*
money market, *p. 532*
policy mix, *p. 538*
real wealth, *or* real balance, effect, *p. 541*

PROBLEMS

Visit www.myeconlab.com to complete the problems marked in orange online. You will receive instant feedback on your answers, tutorial help, and access to additional practice problems.

1. On June 5, 2003, the European Central Bank acted to decrease the short-term interest rate in Europe by half a percentage point, to 2 percent. The bank's president at the time, Willem Duisenberg, suggested that, in the future, the bank could reduce rates further. The rate cut was made because European countries were growing very slowly or were in recession. What effect did the bank hope the action would have on the economy? Be specific. What was the hoped-for result on *C*, *I*, and *Y*?

2. [Related to the *Economics in Practice* on p. 533] In 2007, the Federal Reserve began a series of cuts in interest rates designed to stimulate investment spending by firms. At the same time, housing construction, a component of investment, was dropping sharply. Go to www.census.gov and click on "Housing and New Construction" to see what happened between 2007 and 2009. Also go to www.bea.gov and look at the current GDP release to see what happened to both residential and nonresidential fixed investment spending between 2007 and 2009. Besides the drop in interest rates, what other factors might have influenced the level of investment spending during those years? Do you think the Federal Reserve achieved its goal? Explain.

3. During the third quarter of 1997, Japanese GDP was falling at an annual rate of over 11 percent. Many blamed the big increase in Japan's taxes in the spring of 1997, which was designed to balance the budget. Explain how an increase in taxes with the economy growing slowly could precipitate a recession. Do not skip steps in your answer. If you were head of the Japanese central bank, how would you respond? What impact would your policy have on the level of investment?

4. Some economists argue that the "animal spirits" of investors are so important in determining the level of investment in the economy that interest rates do not matter at all. Suppose that this were true—that investment in no way depends on interest rates.
   a. How would Figure 27.1 be different?
   b. What would happen to the level of planned aggregate expenditures if the interest rate changed?
   c. What would be different about the relative effectiveness of monetary and fiscal policy?

5. For each of the following scenarios, tell a story and predict the effects on the equilibrium levels of aggregate output (Y) and the interest rate (r):
   a. During 2005, the Federal Reserve was tightening monetary policy in an attempt to slow the economy. Congress passed a substantial cut in the individual income tax at the same time.
   b. During the summer of 2003, Congress passed and President George W. Bush signed the third tax cut in 3 years. Many of the tax cuts took effect in 2005. Assume that the Fed holds M^s fixed.
   c. In 1993, the government raised taxes. At the same time, the Fed was pursuing an expansionary monetary policy.
   d. In 2005, conditions in Iraq led to a sharp drop in consumer confidence and a drop in consumption. Assume that the Fed holds the money supply constant.
   e. The Fed attempts to increase the money supply to stimulate the economy, but plants are operating at 65 percent of their capacities and businesses are pessimistic about the future.

6. Occasionally, the Federal Open Market Committee (FOMC) sets a policy designed to "track" the interest rate. This means that the FOMC is pursuing policies designed to keep the interest rate constant. If, in fact, the Fed were acting to counter any increases or decreases in the interest rate to keep it constant, what specific actions would you expect to see the Fed take if the following were to occur? (In answering, indicate the effects of each set of events on Y, C, S, I, M^s, M^d, and r.)
   a. An unexpected increase in investor confidence leads to a sharp increase in orders for new plants and equipment.
   b. A major New York bank fails, causing a number of worried people (not trusting even the FDIC) to withdraw a substantial amount of cash from other banks and put it in their cookie jars.

7. Paranoia, the largest country in central Antarctica, receives word of an imminent penguin attack. The news causes expectations about the future to be shaken. As a consequence, there is a sharp decline in investment spending plans.
   a. Explain in detail the effects of such an event on the economy of Paranoia assuming no response on the part of the central bank or the Treasury. (M^s, T, and G all remain constant.) Make sure you discuss the adjustments in the goods market and the money market.
   b. To counter the fall in investment, the king of Paranoia calls for a proposal to increase government spending. To finance the program, the chancellor of the exchequer has proposed three alternative options:
      (1) Finance the expenditures with an equal increase in taxes
      (2) Keep tax revenues constant and borrow the money from the public by issuing new government bonds
      (3) Keep taxes constant and finance the expenditures by printing new money

   Consider the three financing options and rank them from most expansionary to least expansionary. Explain your ranking.

8. Why might investment not respond positively to low interest rates during a recession? Why might investment not respond negatively to high interest rates during a boom?

9. The aggregate demand curve slopes downward because when the price level is lower, people can afford to buy more and aggregate demand rises. When prices rise, people can afford to buy less and aggregate demand falls. Is this a good explanation of the shape of the *AD* curve? Why or why not?

APPENDIX

The *IS-LM* Diagram

There is a useful way of depicting graphically the determination of aggregate output (income) and the interest rate in the goods and money markets. Two curves are involved in this diagram, the *IS* curve and the *LM* curve. In this Appendix, we will derive these two curves and use them to see how changes in government purchases (G) and the money supply (M^s) affect the equilibrium values of aggregate output (income) and the interest rate. The effects we describe here are the same as the effects we described in the main text; here we illustrate the effects graphically.

THE *IS* CURVE

We know that in the goods market there is an equilibrium level of aggregate output (income) (Y) for each value of the interest rate (r). For a given value of r, we can determine the equilibrium value of Y. The equilibrium value of Y falls when r rises and rises when r falls. There is thus a *negative* relationship between the equilibrium value of Y and r. The reason for this negative relationship is the negative relationship between planned investment and the interest rate. When the interest rate rises, planned investment (I) falls, and this decrease in I leads to a decrease in the equilibrium value of Y. The negative relationship between the equilibrium value of Y and r is shown in Figure 27A.1. This curve is called the **IS curve.**[1] Each point on the *IS* curve represents the equilibrium point in the goods market for the given interest rate.

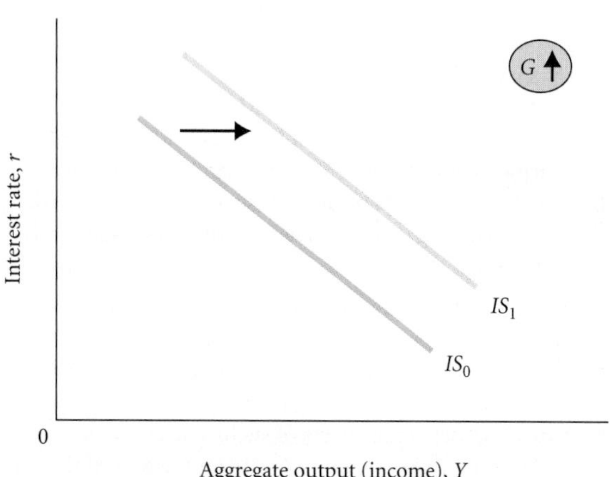

▲ **FIGURE 27A.1 The *IS* Curve**
Each point on the *IS* curve corresponds to the equilibrium point in the goods market for the given interest rate. When government spending (G) increases, the *IS* curve shifts to the right, from IS_0 to IS_1.

We also know from our earlier analysis of the goods market that when government purchases (G) increase with a constant interest rate, the equilibrium value of Y increases. This means the *IS* curve shifts to the right when G increases. With the same value of r and a higher value of G, the equilibrium value of Y is larger; when G decreases, the *IS* curve shifts to the left.

THE *LM* CURVE

In the money market, there is an equilibrium value of the interest rate (r) for every value of aggregate output (income) (Y). The equilibrium value of r is determined at the point at which the quantity of money demanded equals the quantity of money supplied. For a given value of Y, we can determine the equilibrium value of r in the money market. We also know from Figure 27.5 that the equilibrium value of r rises when Y rises and falls when Y falls—a *positive* relationship between the equilibrium value of r and Y. The reason for this positive relationship is the positive relationship between the demand for money and Y. When Y increases, the demand for money increases because more money is demanded for the increased volume of transactions in the economy. An increase in the demand for money increases the equilibrium value of r—thus the positive relationship between the equilibrium value of r and Y.

The positive relationship between the equilibrium value of r and Y is shown in Figure 27A.2. This curve is called the ***LM* curve.**[2] Each point on the *LM* curve represents equilibrium in the money market for the given value of aggregate output (income).

We also know from our analysis of the money market that when the money supply (M^s) increases with a constant level of Y, the equilibrium value of r decreases. As Figure 27A.2 shows, this means that the *LM* curve shifts to the right when M^s increases. With the same value of Y and a higher value of M^s, the equilibrium value of r is lower. When M^s decreases, the *LM* curve shifts to the left.

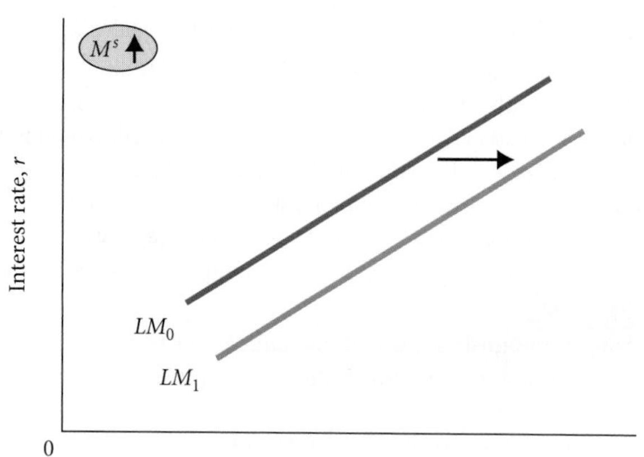

▲ **FIGURE 27A.2 The *LM* Curve**
Each point on the *LM* curve corresponds to the equilibrium point in the money market for the given value of aggregate output (income). Money supply (M^s) increases shift the *LM* curve to the right, from LM_0 to LM_1.

THE *IS-LM* DIAGRAM

Figure 27A.3 shows the *IS* and *LM* curves together on one graph. The point at which the two curves intersect is the point at which equilibrium exists in *both* the goods market and the money market. There is equilibrium in the goods market because the point is on the *IS* curve, and there is equilibrium in the money market because the point is on the *LM* curve.

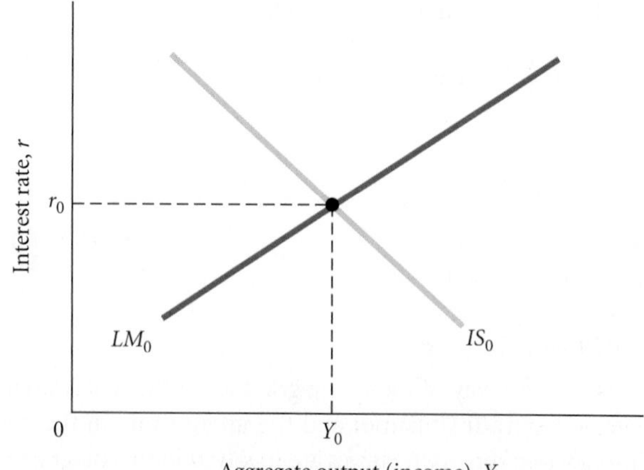

▲ **FIGURE 27A.3 The *IS-LM* Diagram**
The point at which the *IS* and *LM* curves intersect corresponds to the point at which both the goods market and the money market are in equilibrium. The equilibrium values of aggregate output and the interest rate are Y_0 and r_0.

---

[1] The letter I stands for investment, and the letter S stands for saving. *IS* refers to the fact that in equilibrium in the goods market, planned investment equals saving.
[2] The letter L stands for liquidity, a characteristic of money. The letter M stands for money.

We now have only two tasks left. The first is to see how the equilibrium values of Y and r are affected by changes in G—fiscal policy. This is easy. We have just seen that an increase in G shifts the *IS* curve to the right. Thus, an increase in G leads to higher equilibrium values of Y and r. This situation is illustrated in Figure 27A.4. Conversely, a decrease in G leads to lower equilibrium values of Y and r because the lower level of G causes the *IS* curve to shift to the left. (The effects are similar for changes in net taxes, T.)

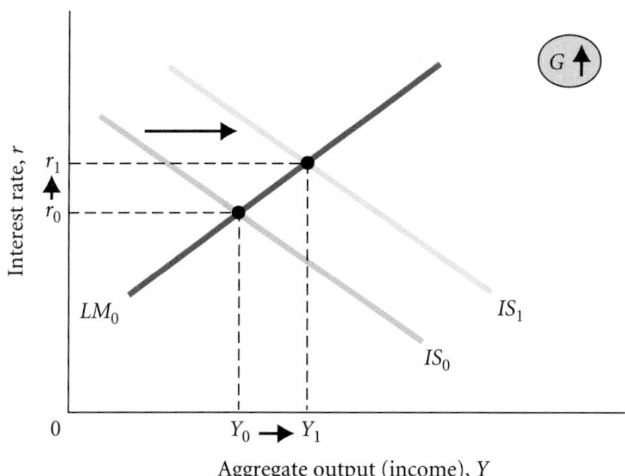

▲ **FIGURE 27A.4 An Increase in Government Purchases (G)**

When G increases, the *IS* curve shifts to the right. This increases the equilibrium value of both Y and r.

Our second task is to see how the equilibrium values of Y and r are affected by changes in M^s—monetary policy. This is also easy. We have just seen that an increase in M^s shifts the *LM* curve to the right. Thus, an increase in M^s leads to a higher equilibrium value of Y and a lower equilibrium value of r. This is illustrated in Figure 27A.5. Conversely, a decrease in M^s leads to a lower equilibrium value of Y and a higher equilibrium value of r because a decreased money supply causes the *LM* curve to shift to the left.

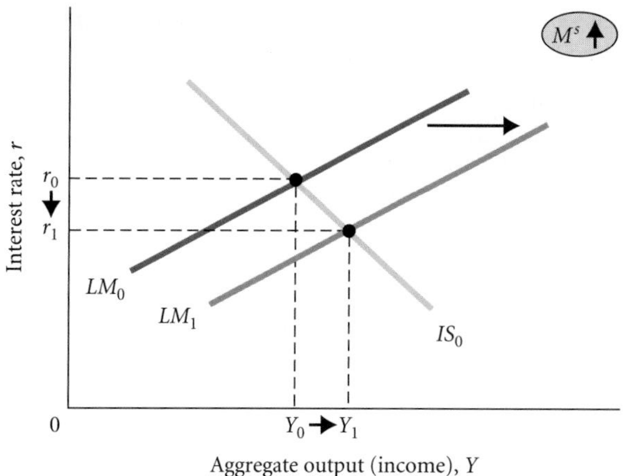

▲ **FIGURE 27A.5 An Increase in the Money Supply (M^s)**

When M^s increases, the *LM* curve shifts to the right. This increases the equilibrium value of Y and decreases the equilibrium value of r.

The *IS-LM* diagram is a useful way of seeing the effects of changes in monetary and fiscal policies on equilibrium aggregate output (income) and the interest rate through shifts in the two curves. Always keep in mind the economic theory that lies *behind* the two curves. Do not memorize what curve shifts when; be able to understand and explain *why* the curves shift. This means going back to the behavior of households and firms in the goods and money markets.

It is easy to use the *IS-LM* diagram to see how there can be a monetary and fiscal policy mix that leads to, say, an increase in aggregate output (income) but no increase in the interest rate. If both G and M^s increase, both curves shift to the right and the shifts can be controlled in such a way as to bring about no change in the equilibrium value of the interest rate.

SUMMARY

An *IS curve* illustrates the negative relationship between the equilibrium value of aggregate output (income) (Y) and the interest rate in the goods market. An *LM curve* illustrates the positive relationship between the equilibrium value of the interest rate and aggregate output (income) (Y) in the money market. The point at which the *IS* and *LM* curves intersect is the point at which equilibrium exists in both the goods market and the money market.

REVIEW TERMS AND CONCEPTS

***IS* curve** A curve illustrating the negative relationship between the equilibrium value of aggregate output (income) (Y) and the interest rate in the goods market. *p. 546*

***LM* curve** A curve illustrating the positive relationship between the equilibrium value of the interest rate and aggregate output (income) (Y) in the money market. *p. 546*

PROBLEMS

1. Illustrate each of the following situations with *IS-LM* curves:
   a. An increase in G with the money supply held constant by the Fed
   b. An increase in G with the Fed changing M^s by enough to keep interest rates constant
   c. A decrease in G and an increase in T while the Fed expands M^s
   d. An increase in G and T while the Fed holds M^s constant during a period of inflation

Aggregate Supply and the Equilibrium Price Level

28

In the summer of 2008 both the United States and Europe were facing increases in their price levels. The president of the European Central Bank (ECB), Jean-Claude Trichet, made a number of announcements during that summer suggesting that the ECB was likely to take action to try to control inflation. Ben Bernanke, the head of the Federal Reserve Bank, who had been less hawkish on inflation, also indicated some concern with rising price levels. What causes price levels to rise and why might rising price levels be a problem for an economy? What tools do Trichet and Bernanke have to try to control inflation? These are the subjects of this chapter.

The determination of the overall price level in an economy is one of the central issues in macroeconomics. As the examples of Trichet and Bernanke in the summer of 2008 suggest, inflation—an increase in the overall price level—is one of the key concerns of macroeconomists and government policy makers. In Chapter 22, we discussed how inflation is measured and the costs of inflation, but made no mention of the *causes* of inflation. For simplicity, our analysis in Chapters 23 through 27 took the price level as fixed. This allowed us to discuss the links between the goods market and the money market without the complication of a changing price level. Having considered how the two markets work, we are ready to take up flexible prices.

We derived the aggregate demand curve in Chapter 27. The first step in this chapter is to introduce the aggregate supply curve. Given the aggregate demand and aggregate supply curves, the equilibrium price level is just the intersection of the two curves. Once the equilibrium price level is determined, we can examine how fiscal and monetary policies affect the price level.

The Aggregate Supply Curve

Aggregate supply is the total supply of goods and services in an economy. Although there is little disagreement among economists about how the aggregate demand curve is derived, there is a great deal of disagreement about how the aggregate supply curve is derived. Differences among economists regarding the shape of the aggregate supply curve is one important factor giving rise to differences in policies they suggest to deal with macroeconomic problems such as inflation and unemployment.

The Aggregate Supply Curve: A Warning

The **aggregate supply (*AS*) curve** shows the relationship between the aggregate quantity of output supplied by all the firms in an economy and the overall price level. To understand the aggregate supply curve, we need to understand something about the behavior of the individual firms that make up the economy.

aggregate supply The total supply of all goods and services in an economy.

aggregate supply (*AS*) curve A graph that shows the relationship between the aggregate quantity of output supplied by all firms in an economy and the overall price level.

It may seem logical to derive the aggregate supply curve by adding together the supply curves of all the individual firms in the economy. However, the logic behind the relationship between the overall price level in the economy and the level of aggregate output (income)—that is, the *AS* curve—is very different from the logic behind an individual firm's supply curve. The aggregate supply curve is *not* a market supply curve, and it is *not* the simple sum of all the individual supply curves in the economy. (Recall a similar warning for the aggregate demand curve in the last chapter.) The reason is that many firms (some would argue most firms) do not simply respond to prices determined in the market. Instead, they actually *set prices*. Only in perfectly competitive markets do firms simply react to prices determined by market forces. Firms in other kinds of industries (imperfectly competitive industries) make both output and price decisions based on their perceptions of demand and costs. Price-setting firms do not have individual supply curves because these firms are choosing both output and price at the same time. To derive an individual supply curve, we need to imagine calling out a price to a firm and having the firm tell us how much output it will supply at that price. We cannot do this if firms are also setting prices. If supply curves do not exist for imperfectly competitive firms, we certainly cannot add them together to get an aggregate supply curve!

What can we say about the relationship between aggregate output and the overall price level? Because many firms in the economy set prices as well as output, it is clear that an "aggregate supply curve" in the traditional sense of the word *supply* does not exist. What does exist is what we might call a "price/output response" curve—a curve that traces out the price decisions and output decisions of all firms in the economy under a given set of circumstances.

What might such a curve look like?

Aggregate Supply in the Short Run

Many argue that the aggregate supply curve (or the price/output response curve) has a positive slope, at least in the short run. (We will discuss the short-run/long-run distinction in more detail later in this chapter.) In addition, many argue that at very low levels of aggregate output—for example, when the economy is in a recession—the aggregate supply curve is fairly flat and that at high levels of output—for example, when the economy is experiencing a boom—it is vertical or nearly vertical. Such a curve is shown in Figure 28.1.

▶ **FIGURE 28.1**

The Short-Run Aggregate Supply Curve

In the short run, the aggregate supply curve (the price/output response curve) has a positive slope. At low levels of aggregate output, the curve is fairly flat. As the economy approaches capacity, the curve becomes nearly vertical. At capacity, the curve is vertical.

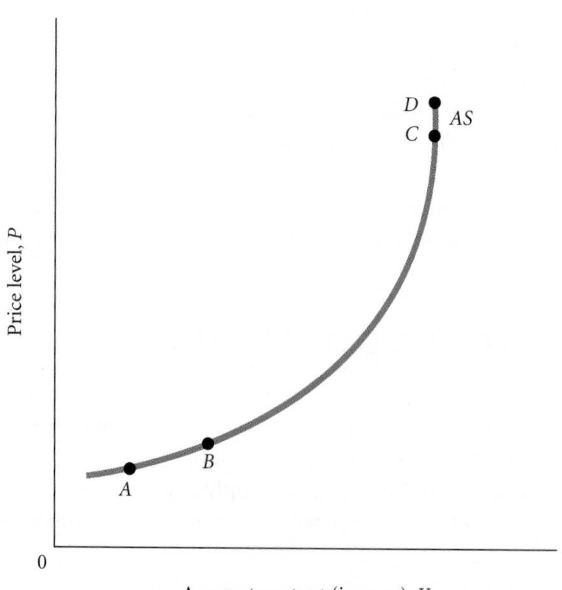

Why might the *AS* curve have a positive slope in the short run? One reason is that wages may lag prices in responding to a change in demand. Consider the case in which there is an increase in aggregate demand, and assume that firms in the economy are imperfectly competitive. The increase in aggregate demand shifts the demand curves facing individual firms out. If the firms' marginal cost curves do not also shift, then firms can increase their profits by raising prices and increasing output.[1] In other words, the response of the overall economy to the aggregate demand increase will be an increase in output and the price level—a positive slope of the short-run *AS* curve.

A key assumption in this story is that firms' marginal cost curves do not also shift. This is where wages come into the picture. A key input into the production processes of firms is labor, and labor costs are a large fraction of total costs. If wages do not respond quickly to price increases, there may be some period of time in which firms raise prices without seeing wage rates rise. In practice wages do tend to lag prices. We discuss in the next chapter various reasons that have been advanced for why wages might be "sticky" in the short run. The main point of this chapter is that if wages are sticky in the short run in the sense that wages lag prices, this is a reason for an upward-sloping short-run *AS* curve. Firms' demand curves will shift without a corresponding shift in their marginal cost curves.

We should add a word of caution at this point. It may be that some of a firm's input costs are rising even in the short run after the aggregate demand increase has taken place because some of a firm's inputs may be purchased from other firms who are raising prices. For example, one input to a Dell computer is a chip produced by Intel or AMD. The fact that some of a firm's input costs rise along with a shift in the demand for its product complicates the picture because it means that at the same time that there is an outward shift in a firm's demand curve there is a upward shift in its marginal cost curve. In deriving an upward-sloping *AS* curve, we are in effect assuming that these kinds of input costs are small relative to wage costs. So the story is that wages are a large fraction of total costs and that wage changes lag price changes. This gives us an upward-sloping short-run *AS* curve.

So far we have explained why the short-run *AS* curve might be upward sloping, but we have not explained why it may have the shape in Figure 28.1 with a flat part and then a steeper part. To do this, we need to turn to the concept of capacity utilization. Capacity utilization is a measure of how much of a firm's existing capital and labor the firm is using. When firms are at low levels of capacity utilization, increasing output can be accomplished without large cost increases. On the other hand, when firms are approaching full capacity utilization, further expansions are harder to do. It is this difference in the levels of firms' capacity utilization that gives rise to the flat and then steep parts of the short-run *AS* curve.

Let us first consider the flat segment of the short-run *AS* curve, pictured in Figure 28.1 between points *A* and *B*. Here the economy is operating at a low level of output, and thus firms are likely to have excess capacity. At this point, firms may be holding more capital and labor than they need for their current production levels. In Chapter 31, we will discuss further some of the reasons firms might hold excess capital and excess labor. It may be hard in the short run for firms to sell off their capital equipment. If there are costs of getting rid of capital once it is in place, a firm may choose to hold on to some of this capital even if the economy is in a downturn and the firm has decreased its output. In this case, the firm will not be fully utilizing its capital stock. Firms may be especially likely to behave this way if they expect that the downturn will be short and that they will need the capital in the future to produce a higher level of output. Firms may have similar reasons for holding excess labor. It may be costly, both in worker morale and administrative costs, to lay off a large number of workers. With excess labor and capital, the costs of producing an additional unit of output in response to demand increases will not rise much. The response of a firm in this position will be primarily to increase output rather than to increase its price. In moving from *A* to *B* in Figure 28.1, there is a large increase in output and only a small increase in the price level. The short-run *AS* (price/output response) curve is fairly flat at levels of output in which there is excess capacity.

If demand continues to expand, things will change. As firms move closer to capacity, their responses to demand increases change from mainly increasing output to mainly increasing prices. As demand increases firms move toward holding no excess capital and excess labor. Now firms begin to come up against the constraints imposed by their inability to quickly expand their

---

[1] This is a standard result in microeconomics. An outward demand shift for an imperfectively competitive firm with an unchanged marginal cost curve leads the firm to raise its price and its quantity produced. In the perfectly competitive case the industry output price is determined in the market, and firms take this price as given in deciding how much output to produce. If aggregate demand increases and results in a larger industry output price and if there is no increase in firms' costs, they will respond by increasing output. There will thus be an increase in both industry output prices and output, resulting in a positive sloping short-run *AS* curve.

capacity. In any short-run period, firms' output decisions are constrained by some fixed factor of production. Manufacturing firms will find it difficult to expand the physical size of their plant in the short run. Farmers are constrained in the short run by the number of acres of land on their farms. Because firms cannot easily expand their capital stock, increasing output typically involves rising marginal costs, perhaps by running a plant on double or triple shifts. At this point, increases in demand will be met by the firms mostly increasing prices rather than output. At some level of aggregate demand, it is virtually impossible for firms to expand any further, and firms will respond to any further increases in demand only by raising prices. This case is pictured in Figure 28.1 at points *C* and *D*. Moving from *C* to *D* results in no increase in aggregate output but a large increase in the price level.

Shifts of the Short-Run Aggregate Supply Curve

Given the above discussion, it is straightforward to consider what shifts the short-run *AS* curve: Anything that shifts a firm's marginal cost curve shifts the short-run *AS* curve. If wage rates change, this will shift the short-run *AS* curve. In fact, in deriving the long-run *AS* curve below, we use the fact that as wage rates increase in response to price increases this shifts the short-run *AS* curve back (to the left). A leftward shift of a firm's marginal cost curve with no change in demand leads the firm to raise its price and lower its output.

Another important input aside from labor in firms' production processes is energy. Many energy prices, like the price of oil, are determined in world markets. We can think of the short-run *AS* curve as being derived under the assumption of fixed energy prices (as well as fixed wage rates). In other words, we can treat energy like labor in deriving the short-run *AS* curve. If we do this, then, as with wage rates, when the price of, say, oil changes, this shifts the short-run *AS* curve. An increase in the price of oil shifts firms' marginal costs curves to the left and thus the short-run *AS* curve to the left.

Not only is oil a large component of U.S. energy use, its price undergoes large fluctuations. During the summer of 2005, the price of oil doubled from about $35 to $70 a barrel. Once it became clear that the severe hurricanes of that year would not cause a large disruption of oil supplies, the price fell back below $60. In contrast, in 1973–1974 and again in 1979, the price of oil increased substantially and remained at a higher level. In the summer of 2008, the price of oil rose to over $140 a barrel. Given that oil price changes shift the short-run *AS* curve, this is a lot of shifting.

Figure 28.2(a) shows a leftward shift of the short-run *AS* curve. This can be caused by an increase in wages rates or energy prices. Figure 28.2(b) shows a rightward shift of the short-run *AS* curve. This can be caused by a decrease in wage rates or energy prices. Shifts like these that are brought about by a change in costs are referred to as **cost shocks** or **supply shocks**. One of the sources of the concerns in 2008 raised by both the Federal Reserve chair and the president of the European Central Bank, described in the opening of this chapter, was the large increase in the price of oil in the first half of 2008. This was a fairly large cost shock.

cost shock, *or* **supply shock** A change in costs that shifts the short-run aggregate supply (*AS*) curve.

Natural disasters, such as a drought or a flood, shift the *AS* curve to the left. For a given set of prices firms produce less because their production processes have been damaged. The resource base of the economy has been reduced.

One can also think of the *AS* curve shifting to the right over time due to technical progress and labor force growth. Recall that the vertical part of the short run *AS* curve represents the economy's maximum (capacity) output. This maximum output is determined by the economy's existing resources, like the size of its labor force and the current state of technology. The labor force grows naturally with an increase in the working-age population, but it can also increase for other reasons. Since the 1960s, for example, the percentage of women in the labor force has grown sharply. This increase in the supply of women workers has shifted the *AS* curve to the right. Immigration can also shift the *AS* curve. During the 1970s, Germany, faced with a serious labor shortage, opened its borders to large numbers of "guest workers," largely from Turkey. The United States has experienced significant immigration, legal and illegal, from Mexico, from Central and South American countries, and from Asia. (We discuss economic growth in more detail in Chapter 32.)

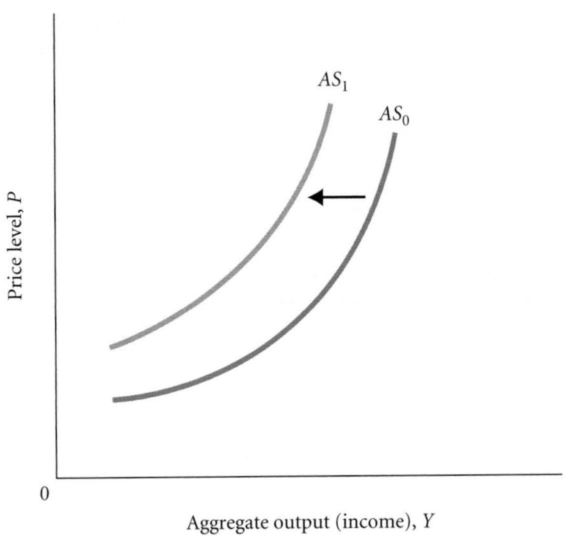

a. A decrease in aggregate supply

A leftward shift of the *AS* curve from AS_0 to AS_1 could be caused by an increase in costs—for example, an increase in wage rates or energy prices.

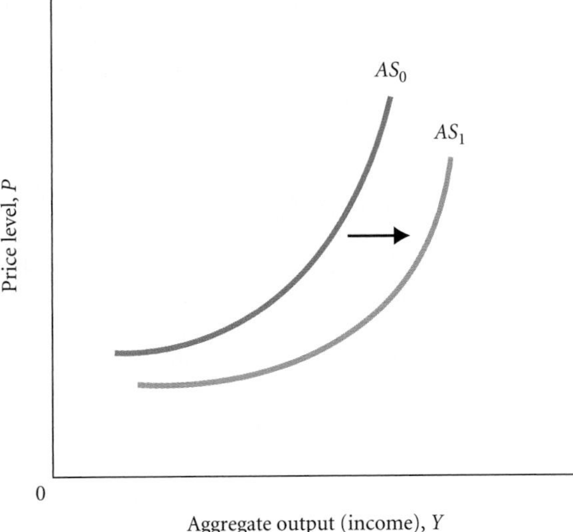

b. An increase in aggregate supply

A rightward shift of the *AS* curve from AS_0 to AS_1 could be caused by a decrease in costs—for example, a decrease in wage rates or energy prices.

▲ FIGURE 28.2 **Shifts of the Short-Run Aggregate Supply Curve**

The Equilibrium Price Level

The **equilibrium price level** in the economy occurs at the point at which the *AD* curve and the *AS* curve intersect, shown in Figure 28.3, where the equilibrium price level is P_0 and the equilibrium level of aggregate output (income) is Y_0.

equilibrium price level The price level at which the aggregate demand and aggregate supply curves intersect.

Figure 28.3 looks simple, but it is a powerful device for analyzing a number of macroeconomic questions. Consider first what is true at the intersection of the *AS* and *AD* curves. Each point on the *AD* curve corresponds to equilibrium in both the goods market and the money market. Each point on the *AS* curve represents the price/output responses of all the firms in the economy. That means that the point at which the *AS* and *AD* curves intersect corresponds to equilibrium in the goods and money markets and to a set of price/output decisions on the part of all the firms in the economy.

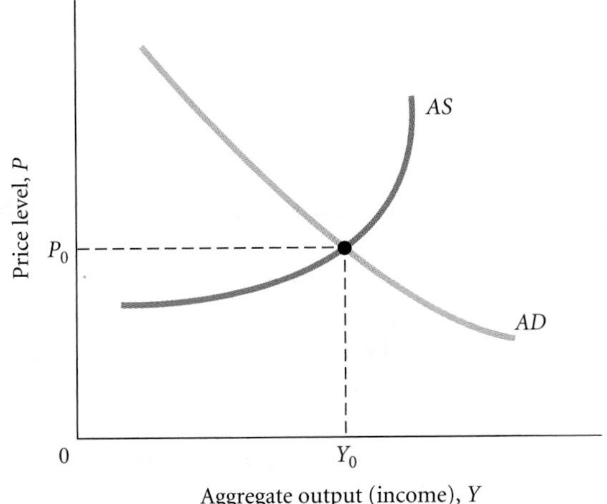

◀ FIGURE 28.3
The Equilibrium Price Level

At each point along the *AD* curve, both the money market and the goods market are in equilibrium. Each point on the *AS* curve represents the price/output decisions of all the firms in the economy. P_0 and Y_0 correspond to equilibrium in the goods market and the money market and to a set of price/output decisions on the part of all the firms in the economy.

We will use this *AS/AD* framework to analyze the effects of monetary and fiscal policy on the economy and to analyze the causes of inflation. For example, what can Trichet and Bernanke do if they are worried about inflation? To answer these kinds of questions, we need to return to the *AS* curve and discuss its shape in the long run.

The Long-Run Aggregate Supply Curve

We derived the short-run *AS* curve under the assumption that wage changes lag price changes. This does not mean, however, that, say, wages never increase after prices increases. Over time, wages adjust to higher prices. When workers negotiate with firms over their wages, they take into account what prices have been doing in the recent past. If wages fully adjust to prices in the long run, then the long-run *AS* curve will be vertical. We can see why in Figure 28.4. Initially, the economy is in equilibrium at a price level of P_0 and aggregate output of Y_0 (the point *A* at which AD_0 and AS_0 intersect). Now imagine a shift of the *AD* curve from AD_0 to AD_1. In response to this shift, both the price level and aggregate output rise in the short run, to P_1 and Y_1, respectively (the point *B* at which AD_1 and AS_0 intersect). The movement along the upward-sloping AS_0 curve as *Y* increases from Y_0 to Y_1 assumes that wages lag prices.

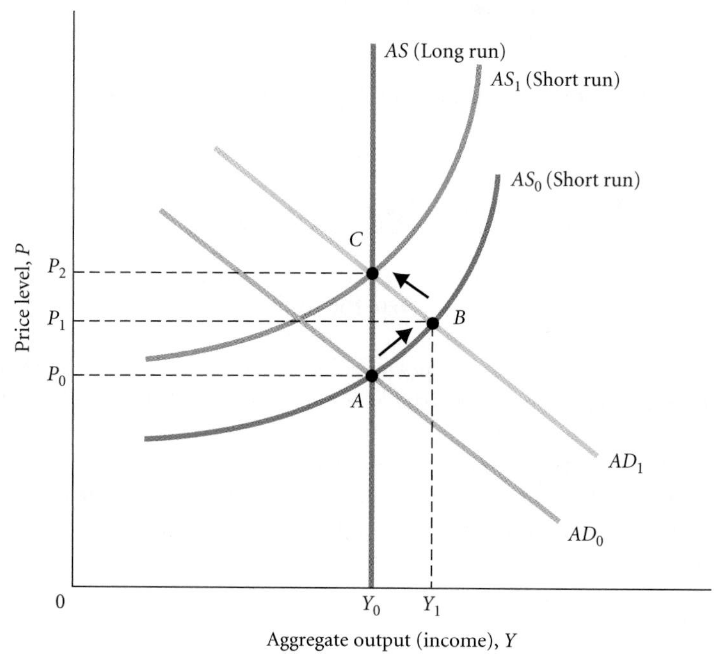

FIGURE 28.4
The Long-Run Aggregate Supply Curve
When the *AD* curve shifts from AD_0 to AD_1, the equilibrium price level initially rises from P_0 to P_1 and output rises from Y_0 to Y_1. Wages respond in the longer run, shifting the *AS* curve from AS_0 to AS_1. If wages fully adjust, output will be back at Y_0. Y_0 is sometimes called *potential GDP*.

Now, as wages increase the short-run *AS* curve shifts to the left. If wages fully adjust, the *AS* curve will over time have shifted from AS_0 to AS_1 in Figure 28.4, and output will be back to Y_0 (the point C at which AD_1 and AS_1 intersect). So when wages fully adjust to prices, the long-run *AS* curve is vertical.

By looking at Figure 28.4, you can begin to see why arguments about the shape of the *AS* curve are so important in policy debates. If the long-run *AS* curve is vertical as we have drawn it, factors that shift the *AD* curve to the right—including policy actions such as increasing government spending—simply end up increasing the price level. If the short-run *AS* curve also is quite steep, even in the short run, most of the effect of any shift in the *AD* curve will be felt in an increase in the price level rather than an increase in aggregate output. If the *AS* curve, on the other hand, is flat, *AD* shifts can have a large effect on aggregate output, at least in the short run. We discuss these effects of policy in more detail later in this chapter.

ECONOMICS IN PRACTICE

The Simple "Keynesian" Aggregate Supply Curve

There is a great deal of disagreement concerning the shape of the *AS* curve. One view of the aggregate supply curve, the simple "Keynesian" view, holds that at any given moment, the economy has a clearly defined capacity, or maximum, output. This maximum output, denoted by Y_F, is defined by the existing labor force, the current capital stock, and the existing state of technology. If planned aggregate expenditure increases when the economy is producing *below* this maximum capacity, this view holds, inventories will be lower than planned, and firms will increase output, but the price level will not change. Firms are operating with underutilized plants (excess capacity), and there is cyclical unemployment. Expansion does not exert any upward pressure on prices. However, if planned aggregate expenditure increases when the economy is producing near or at its maximum (Y_F), inventories will be lower than planned, but firms cannot increase their output. The result will be an increase in the price level, or inflation.

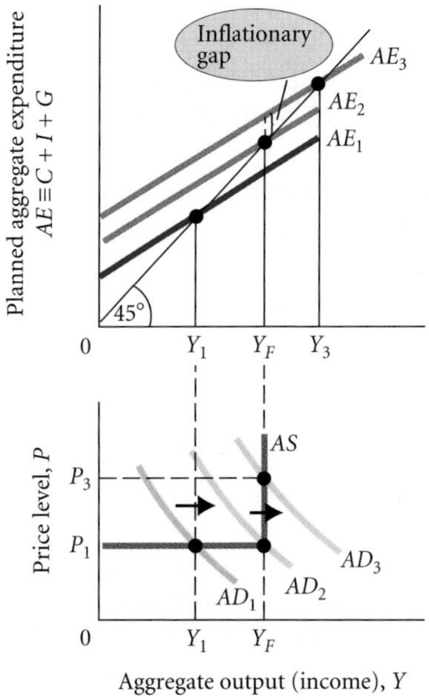

With planned aggregate expenditure of AE_1 and aggregate demand of AD_1, equilibrium output is Y_1. A shift of planned aggregate expenditure to AE_2, corresponding to a shift of the *AD* curve to AD_2, causes output to rise but the price level to remain at P_1. If planned aggregate expenditure and aggregate demand exceed Y_F, however, there is an inflationary gap and the price level rises to P_3.

This view is illustrated in the figure. In the top half of the diagram, aggregate output (income) (Y) and planned aggregate expenditure ($C + I + G \equiv AE$) are initially in equilibrium at AE_1, Y_1, and price level P_1. Now suppose a tax cut or an increase in government spending increases planned aggregate expenditure. If such an increase shifts the *AE* curve from AE_1 to AE_2 and the corresponding aggregate demand curve from AD_1 to AD_2, the equilibrium level of output will rise from Y_1 to Y_F. (Remember, an expansionary policy shifts the *AD* curve to the right.) Because we were initially producing below capacity output (Y_1 is lower than Y_F), the price level will be unaffected, remaining at P_1.

Now consider what would happen if *AE* increased even further. Suppose planned aggregate expenditure shifted from AE_2 to AE_3, with a corresponding shift of AD_2 to AD_3. If the economy were producing below capacity output, the equilibrium level of output would rise to Y_3. However, the output of the economy cannot exceed the maximum output of Y_F. As inventories fall below what was planned, firms encounter a fully employed labor market and fully utilized plants. Therefore, they cannot increase their output. The result is that the aggregate supply curve becomes vertical at Y_F, and the price level is driven up to P_3.

The difference between planned aggregate expenditure and aggregate output at full capacity is sometimes referred to as an *inflationary gap*. You can see the inflationary gap in the top half of the figure. At Y_F (capacity output), planned aggregate expenditure (shown by AE_3) is greater than Y_F. The price level rises to P_3 until the aggregate quantity supplied and the aggregate quantity demanded are equal.

Despite the fact that the kinked aggregate supply curve provides some insights, most economists find it unrealistic. It does not seem likely that the whole economy suddenly runs into a capacity "wall" at a specific level of output. As output expands, some firms and industries will hit capacity before others.

Potential GDP

Recall that even the short-run *AS* curve becomes vertical at some particular level of output. The vertical portion of the short-run *AS* curve exists because there are physical limits to the amount that an economy can produce in any given time period. At the physical limit, all plants are operating around the clock, many workers are on overtime, and there is no cyclical unemployment.

Note that the vertical portions of the short-run *AS* curves in Figure 28.4 on p. 554 are to the right of Y_0. If the vertical portions of the short-run *AS* curves represent "capacity," what is the nature of Y_0, the level of output corresponding to the long-run *AS* curve? Y_0 represents the level of aggregate output that can be *sustained* in the long run without inflation. It is sometimes called **potential output** or **potential GDP**. Output can be pushed above Y_0 under a variety of circumstances, but when it is, there is upward pressure on wages. As the economy approaches short-run capacity, wage rates tend to rise as firms try to attract more people into the labor force and to induce more workers to work overtime. Rising wages shift the short-run *AS* curve to the left (in Figure 28.4 from AS_0 to AS_1) and drive output back to Y_0.

potential output, *or* **potential GDP** The level of aggregate output that can be sustained in the long run without inflation.

Short-Run Equilibrium Below Potential Output Thus far we have argued that if the short-run aggregate supply and aggregate demand curves intersect to the right of Y_0 in Figure 28.4, wages will rise, causing the short-run *AS* curve to shift to the left and pushing aggregate output back down to Y_0. Although different economists have different opinions on how to determine whether an economy is operating at or above potential output, there is general agreement that there is a maximum level of output (below the vertical portion of the short-run aggregate supply curve) that can be sustained without inflation.

What about short-run equilibria that occur to the *left* of Y_0? If the short-run aggregate supply and aggregate demand curves intersect at a level of output below potential output, what will happen? Here again economists disagree. Those who believe the aggregate supply curve is vertical in the long run believe that when short-run equilibria exist below Y_0, output will tend to rise—just as output tends to fall when short-run equilibria exist above Y_0. The argument is that when the economy is operating below full employment with excess capacity and high unemployment, wages are likely to *fall*. A decline in wages shifts the aggregate supply curve to the *right*, causing the price level to fall and the level of aggregate output to rise back to Y_0. This automatic adjustment works only if wages fall when excess capacity and unemployment exist. We will discuss wage adjustment during periods of unemployment in detail in Chapter 29.

Monetary and Fiscal Policy Effects

We are now ready to use the *AS/AD* framework to consider the effects of monetary and fiscal policy. We will first consider the short-run effects.

Recall that the two fiscal policy variables are government purchases (G) and net taxes (T). The monetary policy variable is the quantity of money supplied (M^s). An *expansionary* policy aims at stimulating the economy through an increase in G or M^s or a decrease in T. A *contractionary* policy aims at slowing down the economy through a decrease in G or M^s or an increase in T. We saw earlier in this chapter that an expansionary policy shifts the *AD* curve to the right and that a contractionary policy shifts the *AD* curve to the left. How do these policies affect the equilibrium values of the price level (P) and the level of aggregate output (income)?

When considering the effects of a policy change, we must be careful to note where along the (short-run) *AS* curve the economy is at the time of the change. If the economy is initially on the flat portion of the *AS* curve, as shown by point *A* in Figure 28.5, an expansionary policy, which shifts the *AD* curve to the right, will result in a small price increase relative to the output increase: The increase in equilibrium Y (from Y_0 to Y_1) is much greater than the increase in equilibrium P (from P_0 to P_1). This is the case in which an expansionary policy works well. There is an increase in output with little increase in the price level.

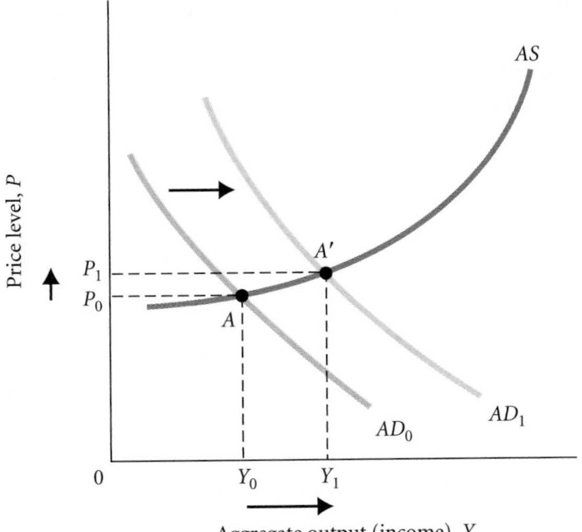

FIGURE 28.5

A Shift of the Aggregate Demand Curve When the Economy Is on the Nearly Flat Part of the *AS* Curve

Aggregate demand can shift to the right for a number of reasons, including an increase in the money supply, a tax cut, or an increase in government spending. If the shift occurs when the economy is on the nearly flat portion of the *AS* curve, the result will be an increase in output with little increase in the price level from point *A* to point *A'*.

If the economy is initially on the steep portion of the *AS* curve, as shown by point *B* in Figure 28.6, an expansionary policy will result in a small increase in equilibrium output (from Y_0 to Y_1) and a large increase in the equilibrium price level (from P_0 to P_1). In this case, an expansionary policy does not work well. It results in a much higher price level with little increase in output. The multiplier is therefore close to zero: Output is initially close to capacity, and attempts to increase it further lead mostly to a higher price level.

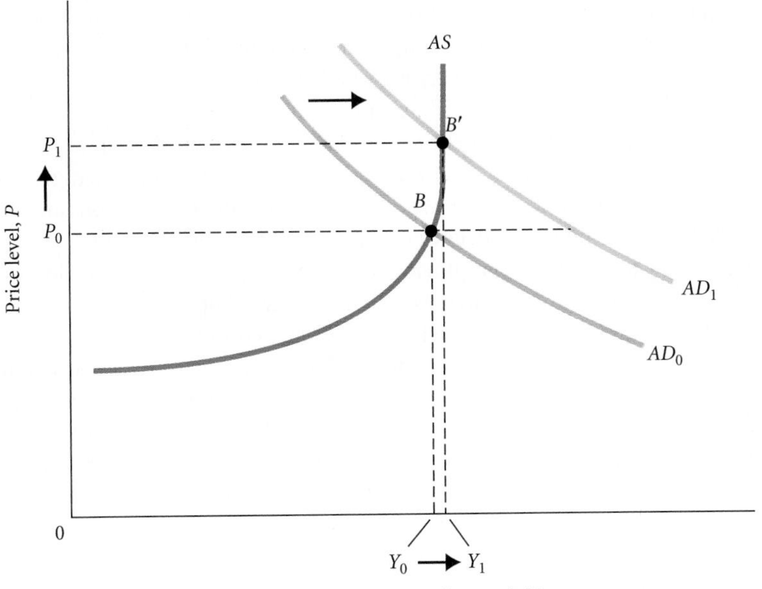

FIGURE 28.6

A Shift of the Aggregate Demand Curve When the Economy Is Operating at or Near Maximum Capacity

If a shift of aggregate demand occurs while the economy is operating near full capacity, the result will be an increase in the price level with little increase in output from point *B* to point *B'*.

Figures 28.5 and 28.6 show that it is important to know where the economy is *before* a policy change is put into effect. The economy is producing on the nearly flat part of the *AS* curve when most firms are producing well below capacity. When this is the case, firms will respond to an increase in demand by increasing output much more than they increase prices. When the economy is producing on the steep part of the *AS* curve, firms are close to capacity and will respond to an increase in demand by increasing prices much more than they increase output.

To see what happens when the economy is on the steep part of the *AS* curve, consider the effects of an increase in *G* with no change in the money supply. What will happen is that when *G* is increased, there will be virtually no increase in *Y*. In other words, the expansionary fiscal policy will fail to stimulate the economy. To consider this, we need to go back to Chapter 27 and review what is behind the *AD* curve.

The first thing that happens when G increases is an unanticipated decline in firms' inventories. Because firms are very close to capacity output when the economy is on the steep part of the *AS* curve, they cannot increase their output very much. The result, as Figure 28.6 shows, is a substantial increase in the price level. The increase in the price level increases the demand for money, which (with a fixed money supply) leads to an increase in the interest rate, decreasing planned investment. *There is nearly complete crowding out of investment.* If firms are producing at capacity, prices and interest rates will continue to rise until the increase in G is completely matched by a decrease in planned investment and there is complete crowding out.

Long-Run Aggregate Supply and Policy Effects

We have so far been considering monetary and fiscal policy effects in the short run. It is important to realize that if the *AS* curve is vertical in the long run, neither monetary policy nor fiscal policy has any effect on aggregate output in the long run. Look back at Figure 28.4 on p. 554. Monetary and fiscal policy shift the *AD* curve. If the long-run *AS* curve is vertical, output always comes back to Y_0. In this case, policy affects *only* the price level in the long run and the multiplier effect of a change in government spending on aggregate output in the long run is zero. Under the same circumstances, the tax multiplier is also zero.

The conclusion that policy has no effect on aggregate output in the long run is perhaps startling. Do most economists agree that the aggregate supply curve is vertical in the long run? Most economists agree that wages tend to lag behind output prices in the short run, giving the *AS* curve some positive slope. Most also agree the *AS* curve is likely to be steeper in the long run, but how long is the long run? The longer the lag time, the greater the potential impact of monetary and fiscal policy on aggregate output. If wages follow output prices within, say, 3 to 6 months, policy has little chance to affect output. If the long run is 3 or 4 years, policy can have significant effects. A good deal of research in macroeconomics focuses on the length of time lags between wages and output prices. In a sense, the length of the long run is one of the most important open questions in macroeconomics.

Another source of disagreement centers on whether equilibria below potential output, Y_0 in Figure 28.4, are self-correcting (that is, without government intervention). Recall that those who believe in a vertical long-run *AS* curve believe that slack in the economy will put downward pressure on wages, causing the short-run *AS* curve to shift to the right and pushing aggregate ouput back toward Y_0. However, some argue that wages do *not* fall during slack periods and that the economy can get "stuck" at an equilibrium below potential output. In this case, monetary and fiscal policy would be necessary to restore full employment. We will return to this debate in Chapter 29.

The "new classical" economics, which we will discuss in Chapter 33, assumes that prices and wages are fully flexible and adjust very quickly to changing conditions. New classical economists believe, for example, that wage rate changes do not lag behind price changes. The new classical view is consistent with the existence of a vertical *AS* curve, even in the short run. At the other end of the spectrum is what is sometimes called the simple "Keynesian" view of aggregate supply. Those who hold this view believe there is a kink in the *AS* curve at capacity output, as we discussed in *Economics in Practice*, "The Simple 'Keynesian' Aggregate Supply Curve."

Causes of Inflation

We now turn to inflation and use the *AS/AD* framework to consider the causes of inflation.

Demand-Pull Inflation

demand-pull inflation Inflation that is initiated by an increase in aggregate demand.

Inflation initiated by an increase in aggregate demand is called **demand-pull inflation**. You can see how demand-pull inflation works by looking at Figures 28.5 and 28.6. In both, the inflation begins with a shift of the aggregate demand schedule from AD_0 to AD_1, which causes the price level to increase from P_0 to P_1. (Output also increases, from Y_0 to Y_1.) If the economy is operating on the steep portion of the *AS* curve at the time of the increase in aggregate demand, as in Figure 28.6, most of the effect will be an increase in the price level instead of an increase in output. If the economy is operating on the flat portion of the *AS* curve, as in Figure 28.5, most of the effect will be an increase in output instead of an increase in the price level.

Remember, in the long run the initial increase in the price level will cause the *AS* curve to shift to the left as wages respond to the increase in output prices. If the long-run *AS* curve is vertical, as depicted in Figure 28.4, the increase in wages will shift the short-run *AS* curve (AS_0) to the left to AS_1, pushing the price level even higher, to P_2. If the long-run *AS* curve is vertical, a shift in aggregate demand from AD_0 to AD_1 will result, in the long run, in *no* increase in output and a price-level increase from P_0 to P_2.

Cost-Push, or Supply-Side, Inflation

Inflation can also be caused by an increase in costs, referred to as **cost-push**, or **supply-side, inflation**. Several times in the last three decades oil prices in world markets increased sharply. Because oil is used in virtually every line of business, costs increased.

cost-push, *or* supply-side, inflation Inflation caused by an increase in costs.

An increase in costs (a cost shock) shifts the *AS* curve to the left, as Figure 28.7 shows. If we assume the government does not react to this shift in *AS* by changing fiscal or monetary policy, the *AD* curve will not shift. The supply shift will cause the equilibrium price level to rise (from P_0 to P_1) and the level of aggregate output to decline (from Y_0 to Y_1). Recall from Chapter 20 that **stagflation** occurs when output is falling at the same time prices are rising—in other words, when the economy is experiencing both a contraction and inflation simultaneously. Figure 28.7 shows that one possible cause of stagflation is an increase in costs.

stagflation Occurs when output is falling at the same time that prices are rising.

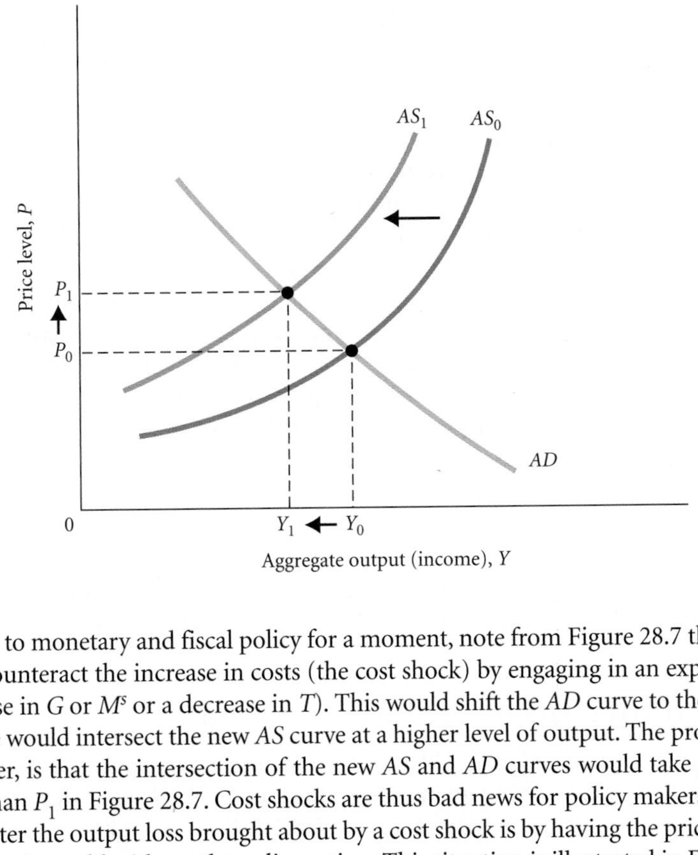

Price level, *P*
P_1
P_0
0
AS_1
AS_0
AD
Y_1 ← Y_0
Aggregate output (income), *Y*

◀ **FIGURE 28.7**
Cost-Push, or Supply-Side, Inflation
An increase in costs shifts the *AS* curve to the left. By assuming the government does not react to this shift, the *AD* curve does not shift, the price level rises, and output falls.

To return to monetary and fiscal policy for a moment, note from Figure 28.7 that the government could counteract the increase in costs (the cost shock) by engaging in an expansionary policy (an increase in *G* or M^s or a decrease in *T*). This would shift the *AD* curve to the right, and the new *AD* curve would intersect the new *AS* curve at a higher level of output. The problem with this policy, however, is that the intersection of the new *AS* and *AD* curves would take place at a price even higher than P_1 in Figure 28.7. Cost shocks are thus bad news for policy makers. The only way they can counter the output loss brought about by a cost shock is by having the price level increase even more than it would without the policy action. This situation is illustrated in Figure 28.8.

Expectations and Inflation

When firms are making their price/output decisions, their *expectations* of future prices may affect their current decisions. If a firm expects that its competitors will raise their prices, in anticipation, it may raise its own price.

Consider a firm that manufactures toasters in an imperfectly competitive market. The toaster maker must decide what price to charge retail stores for its toaster. If it overestimates price and charges much more than other toaster manufacturers are charging, it will lose many customers. If

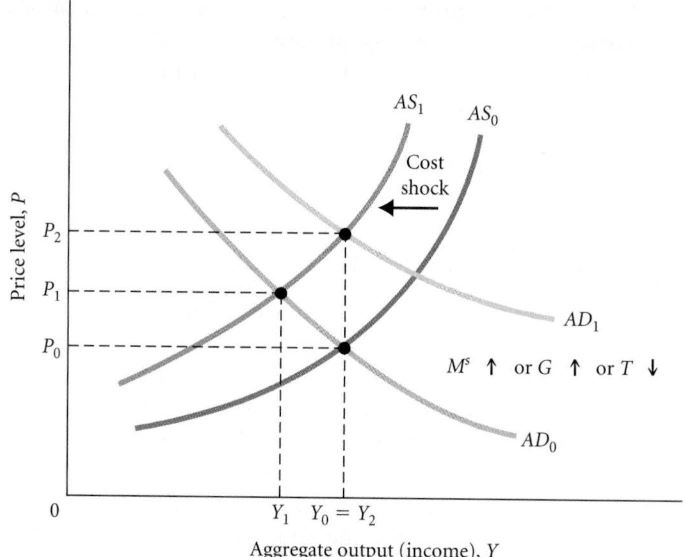

FIGURE 28.8

Cost Shocks Are Bad News for Policy Makers

A cost shock with no change in monetary or fiscal policy would shift the aggregate supply curve from AS_0 to AS_1, lower output from Y_0 to Y_1, and raise the price level from P_0 to P_1. Monetary or fiscal policy could be changed enough to have the *AD* curve shift from AD_0 to AD_1. This policy would raise aggregate output *Y* again, but it would raise the price level further, to P_2.

it underestimates price and charges much less than other toaster makers are charging, it will gain customers but at a considerable loss in revenue per sale. The firm's *optimum price*—the price that maximizes the firm's profits—is presumably not too far from the average of its competitors' prices. If it does not know its competitors' projected prices before it sets its own price, as is often the case, it must base its price on what it expects its competitors' prices to be.

Suppose inflation has been running at about 10 percent per year. Our firm probably expects its competitors will raise their prices about 10 percent this year, so it is likely to raise the price of its own toaster by about 10 percent. This response is how expectations can get "built into the system." If every firm expects every other firm to raise prices by 10 percent, every firm will raise prices by about 10 percent. Every firm ends up with the price increase it expected.

The fact that expectations can affect the price level is vexing. Expectations can lead to an inertia that makes it difficult to stop an inflationary spiral. If prices have been rising and if people's expectations are *adaptive*—that is, if they form their expectations on the basis of past pricing behavior—firms may continue raising prices even if demand is slowing or contracting. In terms of the *AS/AD* diagram, an increase in inflationary expectations that causes firms to increase their prices shifts the *AS* curve to the left. Remember that the *AS* curve represents the price/output responses of firms. If firms increase their prices because of a change in inflationary expectations, the result is a leftward shift of the *AS* curve.

Given the importance of expectations in inflation, the central banks of many countries survey consumers about their expectations. In Great Britain, for example, a survey of consumers by the Bank of England found a rise in expectations of inflation from 3.9 percent in February 2008 to 4.9 percent in May 2008. One of the aims of central banks is to try to keep these expectations low.

Money and Inflation

It is easy to see that an increase in the money supply can lead to an increase in the aggregate price level. As Figures 28.5 and 28.6 show, an increase in the money supply (M^s) shifts the *AD* curve to the right and results in a higher price level. This is simply a demand-pull inflation.

However, the supply of money may also play a role in creating inflation that persists over a long period of time, which we will call a "sustained" inflation. Consider an initial increase in government spending (*G*) with the money supply (M^s) unchanged. Because the money supply is unchanged, this is an increase in *G* that is not "accommodated" by the Fed. The increase in *G* shifts the *AD* curve to the right and results in a higher price level. This is shown in Figure 28.9 as a shift from AD_0 to AD_1. (In Figure 28.9, the economy is assumed to be operating on the vertical portion of the *AS* curve.)

Remember what happens when the price level increases. The higher price level causes the demand for money to increase. With an unchanged money supply and an increase in the quantity of money demanded, the interest rate will rise and the result will be a decrease in planned investment (*I*) spending. The new equilibrium corresponds to higher *G*, lower *I*, a higher interest rate, and a higher price level.

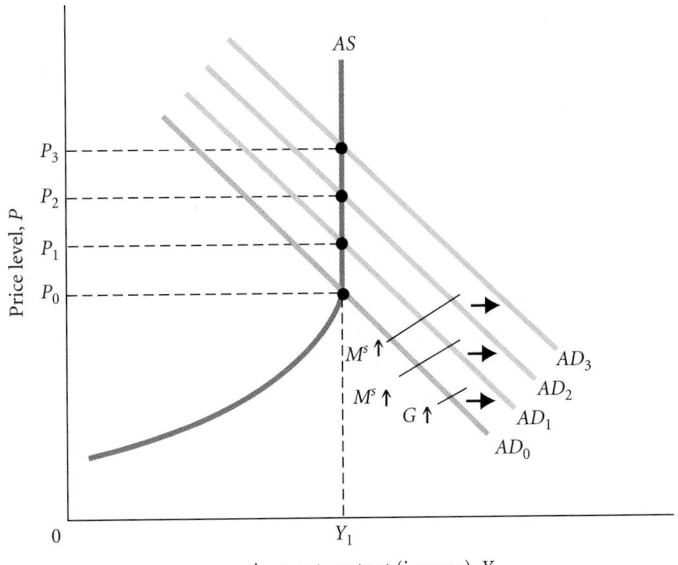

◀ **FIGURE 28.9**

Sustained Inflation from an Initial Increase in G and Fed Accommodation

An increase in G with the money supply constant shifts the AD curve from AD_0 to AD_1. Although not shown in the figure, this leads to an increase in the interest rate and crowding out of planned investment. If the Fed tries to keep the interest rate unchanged by increasing the money supply, the AD curve will shift farther and farther to the right. The result is a sustained inflation, perhaps even hyperinflation.

Now let us take our example one step further. Suppose that the Fed is sympathetic to the expansionary fiscal policy (the increase in G we just discussed) and decides to expand the supply of money to keep the interest rate constant. As the higher price level pushes up the demand for money, the Fed expands the supply of money with the goal of keeping the interest rate unchanged, eliminating the crowding-out effect of a higher interest rate.

When the supply of money is expanded, the AD curve shifts to the right again, from AD_1 to AD_2. This shift of the AD curve, brought about by the increased money supply, pushes prices up even further. Higher prices, in turn, increase the demand for money further, which requires a further increase in the money supply and so on.

What would happen if the Fed tried to keep the interest rate constant when the economy was operating on the steep part of the AS curve? The situation could lead to a hyperinflation, a period of very rapid increases in the price level. If no more output can be coaxed out of the economy and if planned investment is not allowed to fall (because the interest rate is kept unchanged), it is not possible to increase G. As the Fed keeps pumping more and more money into the economy to keep the interest rate unchanged, the price level will keep rising.

Sustained Inflation as a Purely Monetary Phenomenon

Virtually all economists agree that an increase in the price level can be caused by anything that causes the AD curve to shift to the right or the AS curve to shift to the left. These include expansionary fiscal policy actions, monetary expansion, cost shocks, changes in expectations, and so on. It is also generally agreed that for a *sustained* inflation to occur, the Fed must accommodate it. In this sense, a sustained inflation can be thought of as a purely monetary phenomenon.

This argument, first put forth by monetarists (coming in Chapter 33), has gained wide acceptance. It is easy to show, as we just did, how expanding the money supply can continuously shift the AD curve. It is not as easy to come up with other reasons for continued shifts of the AD curve if the money supply is constant. One possibility is for the government to increase spending continuously without increasing taxes, but this process cannot continue forever. To finance spending without taxes, the government must borrow. Without any expansion of the money supply, the interest rate will rise dramatically because of the increase in the supply of government bonds. The public must be willing to buy the government bonds that are being issued to finance the spending increases. At some point, the public may be unwilling to buy any more bonds even though the interest rate is very high.[2] At this point, the government is no longer able to increase non-tax-financed spending without the Fed's cooperation. If this is true, a sustained inflation cannot exist without the Fed's cooperation.

[2] This means that the public's demand for money no longer depends on the interest rate. Even though the interest rate is very high, the public cannot be induced to have its real money balances fall any farther. There is a limit concerning how much the public can be induced to have its real money balances fall.

The Behavior of the Fed

We have so far in this book talked about monetary policy as consisting of changes in the money supply (M^S), which affects the interest rate (r). We saw in Chapter 25 that the Fed can change the money supply by (1) changing the required reserve ratio, (2) changing the discount rate, and (3) engaging in open market operations (buying and selling government securities). We also pointed out that the main way in which the Fed changes the money supply is by engaging in open market operations. Through these operations the Fed can achieve whatever value of the money supply it wants.

We must add two key points to the monetary policy story to make the story realistic, as we do in this section. The first point is that *in practice, the Fed controls the interest rate rather than the money supply*. The second point is that *the interest rate value that the Fed chooses depends on the state of the economy*. We will first explain these two points and then turn to a discussion of actual Fed policy from 1970 on. Figure 28.10 outlines how the Fed behaves in practice. It will be useful to keep this figure in mind in the following discussion.

▶ **FIGURE 28.10**
Fed Behavior

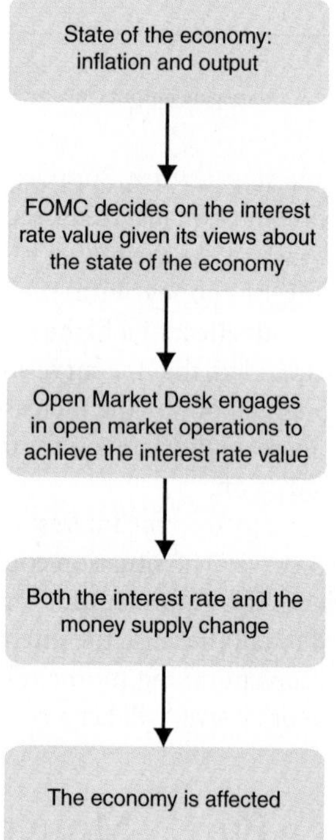

Controlling the Interest Rate

Figure 26.7 on page 524 in Chapter 26 shows that when the Fed increases the money supply, the interest rate falls. As the money supply curve shifts to the right, there is a movement of the equilibrium interest rate down the money demand curve. The buying and selling of government securities by the Fed thus has two effects at the same time: It changes the money supply, and it changes the interest rate. If the Fed buys securities, this purchase increases the money supply and lowers the interest rate, and if the Fed sells securities, this sale decreases the money supply and raises the interest rate. How much the interest rate changes depends on the shape of the money demand curve. The steeper the money demand curve, the larger the change in the interest rate for a given size change in government securities.

What this means is that if the Fed wants to achieve a particular value of the money supply, it must accept whatever interest rate value is implied by this choice. (Again, the interest rate value depends on the shape of the money demand curve.) Conversely, if the Fed wants to achieve a particular value of the interest rate, it must accept whatever money supply value is implied by this. If, for example, the Fed wants to lower the interest rate by one percentage point, it must keep buying government securities until the interest rate value is reached. As the Fed is buying government securities, the money supply is increasing. In short, the Fed can pick a money supply value and accept the interest rate consequences, or it can pick an interest rate value and accept the money supply consequences. The first key point is that in practice, the Fed chooses the interest rate value and accepts the money supply consequences, rather than vice versa.

Why might the Fed want to control the interest rate rather than the money supply? In practice, it is the interest rate that directly affects economic activity, for example, by affecting firms' decisions about investing. Controlling the interest rate thus gives the Fed more control over the key variable that matters to the economy. Focusing on the money supply leaves the Fed one step removed from the key processes.

The Federal Open Market Committee (FOMC) meets every 6 weeks and sets the value of the interest rate. It then instructs the Open Market Desk at the New York Federal Reserve Bank to keep buying or selling government securities until the desired interest rate value is achieved.

The FOMC announces the interest rate value at 2:15 P.M. eastern time on the day it meets. This is a key time for financial markets around the world. At 2:14 P.M., thousands of people are staring at their computer screens waiting for the word from on high. If the announcement is a surprise, it can have very large and immediate effects on bond and stock markets.

For most of the rest of this text, we will talk about monetary policy as being a change in the interest rate. Keep in mind, of course, that monetary policy also changes the money supply. We can talk about an expansionary monetary policy as one in which the money supply is increased or one in which the interest rate is lowered. We will talk about the interest rate being lowered because the interest rate is what the Fed targets in practice. However we talk about it, an expansionary monetary policy is achieved by the Fed's buying government securities.

The Fed's Response to the State of the Economy

When the FOMC meets every 6 weeks to set the value of the interest rate, it does not set the value in a vacuum. An important question in macroeconomics is what influences the interest rate decision. To answer this, we must consider the main goals of the Fed. What ultimately is the Fed trying to achieve?

The Fed's main goals are high levels of output and employment and a low rate of inflation. From the Fed's point of view, the best situation is a fully employed economy with an inflation rate near zero. The worst situation is *stagflation*—high unemployment and high inflation.

If the economy is in a low output/low inflation situation, it will be producing on the relatively flat portion of the aggregate supply (*AS*) curve (Figure 28.11). In this case, the Fed can increase output by lowering the interest rate (and thus increasing the money supply) with little effect on the price level. The expansionary monetary policy will shift the aggregate demand (*AD*) curve to the right, leading to an increase in output with little change in the price level. The Fed is likely to lower the interest rate (and thus increase the money supply) during times of low output and low inflation.

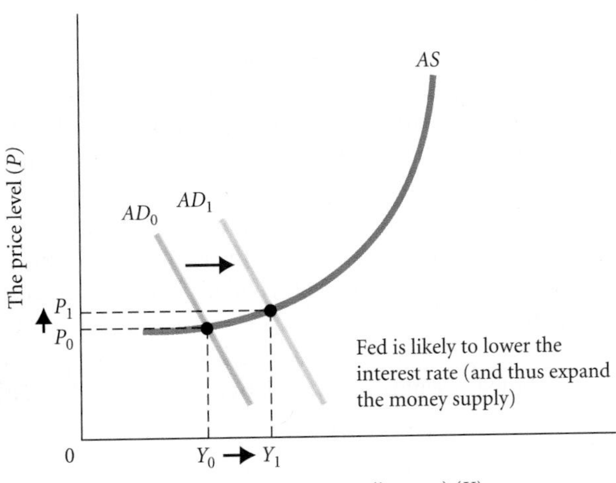

FIGURE 28.11

The Fed's Response to Low Output/Low Inflation

During periods of low output/low inflation, the economy is on the relatively flat portion of the *AS* curve. In this case, the Fed is likely to lower the interest rate (and thus expand the money supply). This will shift the *AD* curve to the right, from AD_0 to AD_1, and lead to an increase in output with very little increase in the price level.

ECONOMICS IN PRACTICE

Pearson Prentice Hall is committed to providing the most current content possible. Starting December 15, 2008, all printed Student Editions of **Case/Fair/Oster's** ninth edition will include this newly updated *Economics in Practice* content. You can view this updated content at www.pearsonhighered.com/case on November 20, 2008.

The opposite is true in times of high output and high inflation. In this situation, the economy is producing on the relatively steep portion of the *AS* curve (Figure 28.12), and the Fed can increase the interest rate (and thus decrease the money supply) with little effect on output. The contractionary monetary policy will shift the *AD* curve to the left, which will lead to a fall in the price level and little effect on output.[3] The Fed is likely to increase the interest rate (and thus decrease the money supply) during times of high output and high inflation. In this discussion, we see again the role of the shape of *AS* curve in determining the likely effect of government policy.

Stagflation is a more difficult problem to solve. If the Fed lowers the interest rate, output will rise, but so will the inflation rate (which is already too high). If the Fed increases the interest rate, the inflation rate will fall, but so will output (which is already too low). (You should be able to draw *AS/AD* diagrams to see why this is true.) The Fed is faced with a trade-off. In this case, the Fed's decisions depend on how it weights output relative to inflation. If it dislikes high inflation

[3] In practice, the price level rarely falls. What the Fed actually achieves in this case is a decrease in the *rate of inflation*—that is, in the percentage change in the price level—not a decrease in the price level itself. The discussion here is sliding over the distinction between the price level and the rate of inflation. This distinction is discussed further in the next chapter.

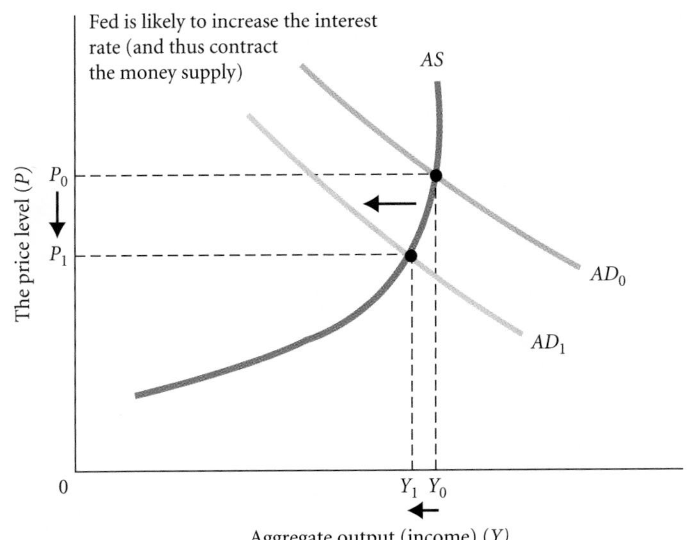

FIGURE 28.12

The Fed's Response to High Output/High Inflation

During periods of high output/high inflation, the economy is on the relatively steep portion of the *AS* curve. In this case, the Fed is likely to increase the interest rate (and thus contract the money supply). This will shift the *AD* curve to the left, from AD_0 to AD_1, and lead to a decrease in the price level with very little decrease in output.

more than low output, it will increase the interest rate; if it dislikes low output more than high inflation, it will lower the interest rate. In practice, the Fed probably dislikes high inflation more than low output, but how the Fed behaves depends in part on the beliefs of the chair of the Fed.

The Fed is sometimes said to "lean against the wind," meaning that as the economy expands, the Fed uses open market operations to raise the interest rate gradually to try to prevent the economy from expanding too quickly. Conversely, as the economy contracts, the Fed lowers the interest rate gradually to lessen (and eventually stop) the contraction.

Fed Behavior Since 1970

Figure 28.13 plots three variables that can be used to describe Fed behavior since 1970. The interest rate is the 3-month Treasury bill rate, which moves closely with the interest rate that the Fed actually controls, which is the federal funds rate. For simplicity, we will take the 3-month Treasury bill rate to be the rate that the Fed controls and we will just call it "the interest rate." Inflation is the percentage change in the GDP deflator over the previous 4 quarters. This variable is also plotted in Figure 20.6 on p. 412. Output is the percentage deviation of real GDP from its trend. (Real GDP itself is plotted in Figure 20.4 on p. 410.) It is easier to see fluctuations in real GDP by looking at percentage deviations from its trend.

Recall from Chapter 20 that we have called four periods since 1970 "recessionary periods" and two periods "high inflation periods." These periods are highlighted in Figure 28.13. The recessionary and high inflation periods have considerable overlap in the last half of the 1970s and early 1980s. After 1981, there are no more high inflation periods and two more fairly short recessionary periods. There is thus some stagflation in the early part of the period since 1970 but not in the later part.

We know from earlier in this chapter that stagflation is bad news for policy makers. Should the Fed raise the interest rate to lessen inflation at a cost of making the output situation worse, or should it lower the interest rate to help output growth at a cost of making inflation worse? What did the Fed actually do? You can see from Figure 28.13 that the Fed generally raised the interest rate when inflation was high—even when output was low. In particular, the interest rate was very high in the 1979–1983 period even though output was low. Had the Fed not had such high interest rates in this period, the recession would likely have been less severe, but inflation would have been even worse.

After inflation got back down to about 4 percent in 1983, the Fed began lowering the interest rate, which helped output. The Fed increased the interest rate in 1988 as inflation began to pick up a little and output was strong. The Fed acted aggressively in lowering the interest rate during the 1990–1991 recession and again in the 2001 recession. The Treasury bill rate got below 1 percent in 2003. The Fed then reversed course, and the interest rate rose to nearly 5 percent in 2006.

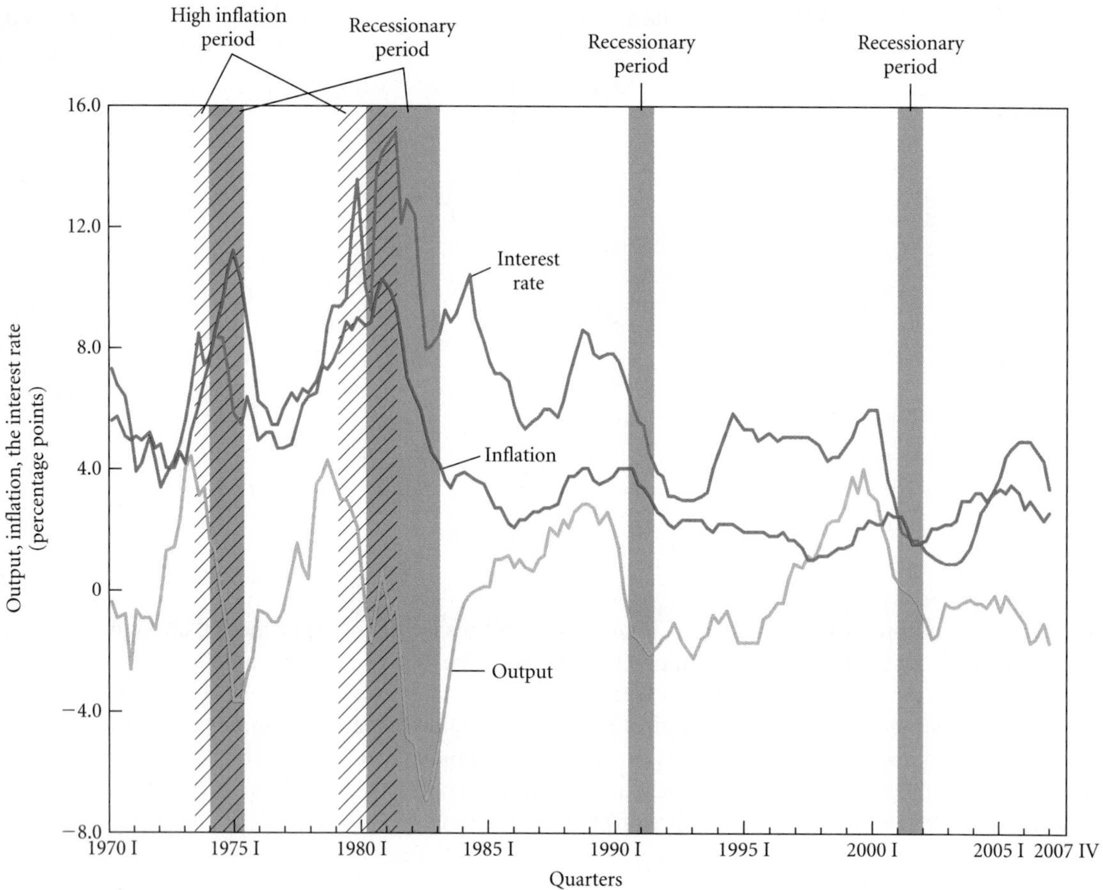

▲ **FIGURE 28.13 Output, Inflation, and the Interest Rate 1970 I–2007 IV**

The Fed generally had high interest rates in the two inflationary periods and low interest rates from the mid 1980s on. It aggressively lowered interest rates in the 1990 IV–1991 I and 2001 I–2001 III recessions. Output is the percentage deviation of real GDP from its trend. Inflation is the 4-quarter average of the percentage change in the GDP deflator. The interest rate is the 3-month Treasury bill rate.

The Fed then reversed course again near the end of 2007 and began lowering the interest rate in an effort to fight a recession that it expected was coming.

Fed behavior in the period since 1970 is thus fairly easy to summarize. The Fed generally had high interest rates in the 1970s and early 1980s as it fought inflation. Since 1983, inflation has been low by historical standards, and the Fed focused in this period on trying to smooth fluctuations in output.

Inflation Targeting

inflation targeting When a monetary authority chooses its interest rate values with the aim of keeping the inflation rate within some specified band over some specified horizon.

Some monetary authorities in the world engage in what is called **inflation targeting**. If a monetary authority behaves this way, it announces a *target* value of the inflation rate, usually for a horizon of a year or more, and then it chooses its interest rate values with the aim of keeping the actual inflation rate within some specified band around the target value. For example, the target value might be 2 percent with a band of 1 to 3 percent. Then the monetary authority would try to keep the actual inflation rate between 1 and 3 percent. With a horizon of a year or more, the monetary authority would not expect to keep the inflation rate between 1 and 3 percent each month because there are a number of temporary factors that move the inflation rate around each month (such as weather) over which the monetary authority has no control. But over a year or more, the expectation would be that the inflation rate would be between 1 and 3 percent. For example, in Hungary in 2008 the central bank set a medium term inflation target of 3 percent. In the United Kingdom the chancellor of the Exchequer sets the inflation target.

ECONOMICS IN PRACTICE

Rising Food Prices Worry Central Banks Around the World

Some central banks in the world (for example, the European Central Bank (ECB)) are primarily inflation targeters, whereas others (for example, the Fed) are not. All central banks, however, even the Fed, worry about inflation. The following article shows the concern of the ECB and the Bank of China, among others, regarding possible inflationary pressures on 2008 from rising food prices. It is clear from the third paragraph that Jean-Claude Trichet, the president of the ECB, will do his best to keep inflation from getting out of hand.

Food Prices Worry Central Bankers

Wall Street Journal

BASEL, Switzerland—Central bankers from around the globe voiced concern about the risks that rising food and commodity prices present for the worldwide inflation outlook.

"On a global level, inflationary risks are significant," European Central Bank President Jean-Claude Trichet told reporters Monday, in his capacity as chairman of the global economy meeting at the Bank for International Settlements. Global policy makers gather at the BIS—often called the central bankers' central bank—every other month.

"There is no time for complacency for central banks in any respect," Mr. Trichet said, "The present level of inflation must be transitory."

The ECB is expected to keep interest rates steady at 4% when it meets on Thursday, as policy makers struggle to balance the risks of slowing growth and high inflation.

"Food prices are an issue everywhere for two reasons: First, the impact on inflation, and second, the impact on the situation of many poor people around the world," said ECB Governing Council member Erkki Liikanen of Finland.

Some policy makers said there may be little that monetary policy can do to slow runaway food prices. "It's a global problem.... But we cannot use monetary policy to manage this problem," said Slawomir Skrzypek, president of the Polish central bank.

People's Bank of China governor Zhou Xiaochuan said interest rates were one way to control price gains, but they weren't the Chinese central bank's only option: "We always say there is [the] possibility to use interest rates to go further to control the inflation in China. But whether we chose this instrument or that instrument, we still have some options."

Source: Nina Koeppen, May 6, 2008

In the discussion at the beginning of this section about the Fed's response to the state of the economy, we assumed that the Fed was concerned about both inflation and output. When output is low, other things being equal, it was argued that the Fed is likely to lower the interest rate to stimulate the economy. If at the same time inflation is high (stagflation), the Fed is faced with a trade-off, and whether it raises or lowers the interest rate depends on how it weights output relative to inflation. In the case of inflation targeting, all the weight is on inflation. So inflation targeting is a special case of Fed behavior just discussed—namely, the case in which all of the Fed's focus is on setting the interest rate to keep the inflation rate within some band over some horizon.

There has been much debate about whether inflation targeting is a good idea. The Fed under Alan Greenspan and previous chairs never engaged in inflation targeting, but the issue arose in the United States with the appointment of Ben Bernanke in 2006 as the new Fed chair. Bernanke had argued in the past in favor of inflation targeting, and people wondered whether the Fed would move in this direction under Bernanke. You can see in Figure 28.13 that the Fed began lowering the interest rate in 2007 in anticipation of a recession, which doesn't look like inflation targeting.

Looking Ahead

In Chapters 23 and 24, we discussed the concept of an equilibrium level of aggregate output and income, the idea of the multiplier, and the basics of fiscal policy. Those two chapters centered on the workings of the goods market alone.

In Chapters 25 and 26, we analyzed the money market by discussing the supply of money, the demand for money, the equilibrium interest rate, and the basics of monetary policy. In Chapter 27, we brought our analysis of the goods market together with our analysis of the money market and we derived the aggregate demand curve.

In this chapter, we introduced the aggregate supply curve. By using the aggregate supply and aggregate demand curves, we can determine the equilibrium price level in the economy and understand some causes of inflation.

We have still said little about employment, unemployment, and the functioning of the labor market in the macroeconomy. The next chapter will link everything we have done so far to this third major market arena—the labor market—and to the problem of unemployment.

SUMMARY

THE AGGREGATE SUPPLY CURVE *p. 549*

1. *Aggregate supply* is the total supply of goods and services in an economy. The *aggregate supply (AS) curve* shows the relationship between the aggregate quantity of output supplied by all the firms in an economy and the overall price level. The *AS* curve is *not* a market supply curve, and it is *not* the simple sum of all the individual supply curves in the economy. For this reason, it is helpful to think of the *AS* curve as a "price/output response" curve—that is, a curve that traces out the price decisions and output decisions of all the markets and firms in the economy under a given set of circumstances.
2. The shape of the short-run *AS* curve is a source of much controversy in macroeconomics. Many economists believe that at very low levels of aggregate output, the *AS* curve is fairly flat and that at high levels of aggregate output, the *AS* curve is vertical or nearly vertical. Thus, the *AS* curve slopes upward and becomes vertical when the economy reaches its capacity, or maximum, output.
3. Anything that affects an individual firm's marginal cost curve can shift the *AS* curve. The two main factors are wage rates and energy prices.

THE EQUILIBRIUM PRICE LEVEL *p. 553*

4. The *equilibrium price level* in the economy occurs at the point at which the *AS* and *AD* curves intersect. The intersection of the *AS* and *AD* curves corresponds to equilibrium in the goods and money markets *and* to a set of price/output decisions on the part of all the firms in the economy.

THE LONG-RUN AGGREGATE SUPPLY CURVE *p. 554*

5. If wages fully adjust to prices in the long run, then the long-run *AS* curve will be vertical.
6. The level of aggregate output that can be sustained in the long run without inflation is called *potential output* or *potential GDP*.

MONETARY AND FISCAL POLICY EFFECTS *p. 556*

7. If the economy is initially producing on the flat portion of the *AS* curve, an expansionary policy—which shifts the *AD* curve to the right—will result in a small increase in the equilibrium price level relative to the increase in equilibrium output. If the economy is initially producing on the steep portion of the *AS* curve, an expansionary policy results in a small increase in equilibrium output and a large increase in the equilibrium price level.

8. If the *AS* curve is vertical in the long run, neither monetary nor fiscal policy has any effect on aggregate output in the long run. For this reason, the exact length of the long run is one of the most pressing questions in macroeconomics.

CAUSES OF INFLATION *p. 558*

9. *Demand-pull inflation* is inflation initiated by an increase in aggregate demand. *Cost-push*, or *supply-side, inflation* is inflation initiated by an increase in costs like energy prices. An increase in costs may also lead to *stagflation*—the situation in which the economy is experiencing a contraction and inflation simultaneously.

10. Inflation can become "built into the system" as a result of expectations. If prices have been rising and people form their expectations on the basis of past pricing behavior, firms may continue raising prices even if demand is slowing or contracting.

11. When the price level increases, so too does the demand for money. If the economy is operating on the steep part of the *AS* curve and the Fed tries to keep the interest rate constant by increasing the supply of money, the result could be a *hyperinflation*—a period of very rapid increases in the price level.

THE BEHAVIOR OF THE FED *p. 562*

12. In practice, the Fed controls the interest rate rather than the money supply. The interest rate value that the Fed chooses depends on the state of the economy. The Fed wants high output and low inflation. The Fed is likely to decrease the interest rate during times of low output and low inflation, and is likely to increase the interest rate during times of high output and high inflation.

13. The Fed generally had high interest rates in the 1970s and early 1980s as it fought inflation. Since 1983, inflation has been low by historical standards and the Fed focused in this period on trying to smooth fluctuations in output.

14. Inflation targeting is the case where the monetary authority weights only inflation. It chooses its interest rate values with the aim of keeping the inflation rate within some specified band over some specified horizon.

REVIEW TERMS AND CONCEPTS

aggregate supply, *p. 550*
aggregate supply (*AS*) curve, *p. 550*
cost-push, *or* supply-side, inflation, *p. 559*
cost shock, *or* supply shock, *p. 552*
demand-pull inflation, *p. 558*
equilibrium price level, *p. 553*
inflation targeting, *p. 566*
potential output, *or* potential GDP, *p. 556*
stagflation, *p. 559*

PROBLEMS

Visit www.myeconlab.com to complete the problems marked in orange online. You will receive instant feedback on your answers, tutorial help, and access to additional practice problems.

1. In Japan during the first half of 2000, the Bank of Japan kept interest rates at a near zero level in an attempt to stimulate demand. In addition, the government passed a substantial increase in government expenditure and cut taxes. Slowly, Japanese GDP began to grow with absolutely no sign of an increase in the price level. Illustrate the position of the Japanese economy with aggregate supply and demand curves. Where on the short-run *AS* curve was Japan in 2000?

2. In 2008, the price of oil rose sharply on world markets. What impact would you expect there to be on the aggregate price level and on real GDP? Illustrate your answer with aggregate demand and supply curves. What would you expect to be the effect on interest rates if the Fed held the money supply constant? Tell a complete story.

3. By using aggregate supply and demand curves to illustrate your points, discuss the impacts of the following events on the price level and on equilibrium GDP (*Y*) in the *short run*:
   a. A tax cut holding government purchases constant with the economy operating at near full capacity
   b. An increase in the money supply during a period of high unemployment and excess industrial capacity
   c. An increase in the price of oil caused by a war in the Middle East, assuming that the Fed attempts to keep interest rates constant by accommodating inflation
   d. An increase in taxes and a cut in government spending supported by a cooperative Fed acting to keep output from falling

4. During 1999 and 2000, a debate raged over whether the United States was at or above potential GDP. Some economists feared the economy was operating at a level of output above potential GDP and inflationary pressures were building. They urged the Fed to tighten monetary policy and increase interest rates to slow the economy. Others argued that a worldwide glut of cheap products was causing input prices to be lower, keeping prices from rising.

   By using aggregate supply and demand curves and other useful graphs, illustrate the following:
   a. Those pushing the Fed to act were right, and prices start to rise more rapidly in 2000. The Fed acts belatedly to slow money growth (contract the money supply), driving up interest rates and pushing the economy back to potential GDP.
   b. The worldwide glut gets worse, and the result is a *falling* price level (deflation) in the United States despite expanding aggregate demand.

5. **[Related to the *Economics in Practice* on p. 555]** The *Economics in Practice* describes the simple Keynesian aggregate supply curve as one in which there is a maximum level of output given the constraints of a fixed capital stock and a fixed supply of labor. The presumption is that increases in demand when firms are operating below capacity will result in output increases and no input price or output price changes but that at levels of output above full capacity, firms have no choice but to raise prices of demand increases. In reality, however, the short-run aggregate supply curve isn't flat and then vertical. Rather, it becomes steeper as we move from left to right on the diagram. Explain why. What circumstances might lead to an equilibrium at a very flat portion of the *AS* curve? at a very steep portion?

6. Using aggregate supply and aggregate demand curves to illustrate, describe the effects of the following events on the price level and on equilibrium GDP in the *long run* assuming that input prices fully adjust to output prices after some lag:
   a. An increase occurs in the money supply above potential GDP
   b. A decrease in government spending and in the money supply with GDP above potential GDP occurs
   c. Starting with the economy at potential GDP, a war in the Middle East pushes up energy prices temporarily. The Fed expands the money supply to accommodate the inflation.

7. Two separate capacity constraints are discussed in this chapter: (1) the actual physical capacity of existing plants and equipment, shown as the vertical portion of the short-run *AS* curve, and (2) potential GDP, leading to a vertical long-run *AS* curve. Explain the difference between the two. Which is greater, full-capacity GDP or potential GDP? Why?

8. In country A, all wage contracts are indexed to inflation. That is, each month wages are adjusted to reflect increases in the cost of living as reflected in changes in the price level. In country B, there are no cost-of-living adjustments to wages, but the workforce is completely unionized. Unions negotiate 3-year contracts. In which country is an expansionary monetary policy likely to have a larger effect on aggregate output? Explain your answer using aggregate supply and aggregate demand curves.

9. During 2001, the U.S. economy slipped into a recession. For the next several years, the Fed and Congress used monetary and fiscal policies in an attempt to stimulate the economy. Obtain data on interest rates (such as the prime rate or the federal funds rate). Do you see evidence of the Fed's action? When did the Fed begin its expansionary policy? Obtain data on total federal expenditures, tax receipts, and the deficit. (Try www.commerce.gov). When did fiscal policy become "expansionary"? Which policy seems to have suffered more from policy lags?

10. Describe the Fed's tendency to "lean against the wind." Do the Fed's policies tend to stabilize or destabilize the economy?

11. **[Related to the *Economics in Practice* on p. 567]** The *Economics in Practice* describes the increase in food prices around the world in 2008. Since food, in large measure, affects the real income of households, increasing prices will eventually push up wages and have an impact on the aggregate supply curve. Central banks were very worried about the prospects for inflation becoming generalized. To stop the inflation, what would the Fed be likely to do? What are the consequences for the economy? Illustrate graphically how the *AD* curve is likely to respond? Specifically, what would be the effects on employment and unemployment? How would you, as a board member, decide whether to increase or decrease the money supply?

The Labor Market In the Macroeconomy

29

CHAPTER OUTLINE

In previous chapters, we stressed the three broadly defined markets in which households, firms, the government, and the rest of the world interact: (1) the *goods market*, discussed in Chapters 23 and 24; (2) the *money market*, discussed in Chapters 25 and 26; and (3) the *labor market*. In Chapter 22, we described some features of the U.S. labor market and explained how the unemployment rate is measured. Then in Chapter 28, we considered the labor market briefly in our discussion of the aggregate supply curve. Because labor is an input, what goes on in the labor market affects the shape of the aggregate supply (*AS*) curve. If wages lag prices the *AS* curve will be upward-sloping; if wages are completely flexible and rise every time prices rise by the same percentage, the *AS* curve will be vertical.

In this chapter, we look further at the labor market's role in the macroeconomy. First, we consider the classical view, which holds that wages always adjust to clear the labor market, that is, to equate the supply of and demand for labor. We then consider why the labor market may not always clear and why unemployment may exist. Finally, we discuss the relationship between inflation and unemployment. As we go through the analysis, it is important to recall why unemployment is one of the three primary concerns of macroeconomics. Go back and reread "The Cost of Unemployment" in Chapter 22 (pp. 440–442). It is clear that unemployment imposes heavy costs on the unemployed and on society. In 2008, more than 7 million people in the United States were looking for work and did not have even a part-time job.

The Labor Market: Basic Concepts

Let us briefly review what the unemployment rate measures, which we discussed in Chapter 22. On the first Friday of every month, the Labor Department releases the results of a household survey that provides an estimate of the number of people with a job, the employed (E), as well as the number of people who are looking for work but cannot find a job, the unemployed (U). The labor force (LF) is the number of employed plus unemployed:

$$LF = E + U$$

The **unemployment rate** is the number of people unemployed as a percentage of the labor force:

$$\text{unemployment rate} = \frac{U}{LF}$$

To repeat, to be unemployed, a person must be out of a job and actively looking for work. When a person stops looking for work, he or she is considered *out of the labor force* and is no longer counted as unemployed.

unemployment rate The number of people unemployed as a percentage of the labor force.

frictional unemployment The portion of unemployment that is due to the normal working of the labor market; used to denote short-run job/skill matching problems.

structural unemployment The portion of unemployment that is due to changes in the structure of the economy that result in a significant loss of jobs in certain industries.

cyclical unemployment The increase in unemployment that occurs during recessions and depressions.

It is important to realize that even if the economy is running at or near full capacity, the unemployment rate will never be zero. The economy is dynamic. Students graduate from schools and training programs; some businesses make profits and grow, while others suffer losses and go out of business; people move in and out of the labor force and change careers. It takes time for people to find the right job and for employers to match the right worker with the jobs they have. This **frictional** and **structural unemployment** is inevitable and in many ways desirable. (Review Chapter 22 if these terms are hazy to you.)

In this chapter, we are concerned with **cyclical unemployment**, the increase in unemployment that occurs during recessions and depressions. When the economy contracts, the number of people unemployed and the unemployment rate rise. The United States has experienced several periods of high unemployment. During the Great Depression, the unemployment rate remained high for nearly a decade. In December 1982, more than 12 million people were unemployed, putting the unemployment rate at 10.8 percent.

In one sense, the reason employment falls when the economy experiences a downturn is obvious. When firms cut back on production, they need fewer workers, so people get laid off. Employment tends to fall when aggregate output falls and to rise when aggregate output rises. *Nevertheless, a decline in the demand for labor does not necessarily mean that unemployment will rise.* If markets work as we described in Chapters 3 and 4, a decline in the demand for labor will initially create an excess supply of labor. As a result, the wage rate will fall until the quantity of labor supplied again equals the quantity of labor demanded, restoring equilibrium in the labor market. At the new lower wage rate, everyone who wants a job will have one.

If the quantity of labor demanded and the quantity of labor supplied are brought into equilibrium by rising and falling wage rates, there should be no persistent unemployment above the frictional and structural amount. This was the view held by the classical economists who preceded Keynes, and it is still the view of a number of economists today. Other economists believe that wage rates adjust only slowly to decreases in the demand for labor and, as a result, economies can suffer bouts of involuntary unemployment.

The Classical View of the Labor Market

labor demand curve A graph that illustrates the amount of labor that firms want to employ at each given wage rate.

labor supply curve A graph that illustrates the amount of labor that households want to supply at each given wage rate.

The classical view of the labor market is illustrated in Figure 29.1. Classical economists assumed that the wage rate adjusts to equate the quantity demanded with the quantity supplied, thereby implying that unemployment does not exist. To see how this adjustment might take place, we can use the supply and demand curves in Figure 29.1. Curve D_0 is the **labor demand curve**. Each point on D_0 represents the amount of labor firms want to employ at each given wage rate. Each firm's decision about how much labor to demand is part of its overall profit-maximizing decision. A firm makes a profit by selling output to households. It will hire workers if the value of its output is sufficient to justify the wage that is being paid. Thus, the amount of labor that a firm hires depends on the value of output that workers produce.

Figure 29.1 also shows a **labor supply curve**, labeled *S*. Each point on the labor supply curve represents the amount of labor households want to supply at each given wage rate. Each household's decision concerning how much labor to supply is part of the overall consumer choice problem of a household. Each household member looks at the market wage rate, the prices of outputs, and the value of leisure time (including the value of staying at home and working in the yard or raising children) and chooses the amount of labor to supply (if any). A household member not in the labor force has decided that his or her time is more valuable in nonmarket activities.

Those individuals who stay out of the labor force place a higher value on the use of their time than do potential employers, whose demand reflects the value that those individuals can produce in the formal job market. Consider households in less developed countries. In many such households, the alternative to working for a wage is subsistence farming. If the wage rate in the labor market is very low, many people will choose to farm for themselves. In this case, the value of what these people produce in farming must be greater than the value that society currently places on what they would produce if they worked for a wage. If this were not true, wages would rise and more people would join the labor force.

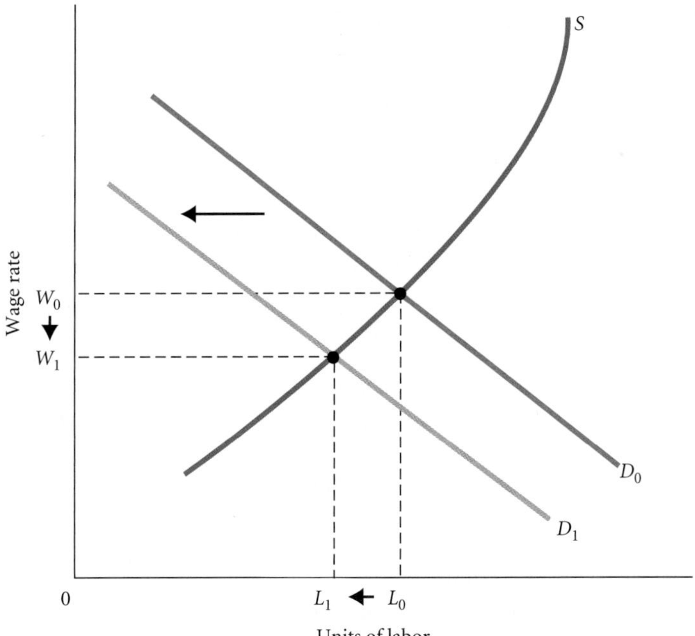

FIGURE 29.1
The Classical Labor Market
Classical economists believe that the labor market always clears. If the demand for labor shifts from D_0 to D_1, the equilibrium wage will fall from W_0 to W_1. Anyone who wants a job at W_1 will have one.

In Figure 29.1 the labor market is initially in equilibrium at W_0 and L_0. Now consider what classical economists think would happen if there is a decrease in the demand for labor. The demand for labor curve shifts in from D_0 to D_1. The new demand curve intersects the labor supply curve at L_1 and W_1. There is a new equilibrium at a lower wage rate, in which fewer people are employed. Note that the fall in the demand for labor has not caused any unemployment. There are fewer people working, but all people interested in working at the wage W_1 are in fact employed.

The classical economists saw the workings of the labor market—the behavior of labor supply and labor demand—as optimal from the standpoint of both individual households and firms and from the standpoint of society. If households want more output than is currently being produced, output demand will increase, output prices will rise, the demand for labor will increase, the wage rate will rise, and more workers will be drawn into the labor force. (Some of those who preferred not to be a part of the labor force at the lower wage rate will be lured into the labor force at the higher wage rate.) At equilibrium, prices and wages reflect a trade-off between the value households place on outputs and the value of time spent in leisure and nonmarket work. At equilibrium, the people who are not working have *chosen* not to work at that market wage. There is always *full employment* in this sense. The classical economists believed that the market would achieve the optimal result if left to its own devices, and there is nothing the government can do to make things better.

The Classical Labor Market and the Aggregate Supply Curve

How does the classical view of the labor market relate to the theory of the vertical *AS* curve we covered in Chapter 28? The classical idea that wages adjust to clear the labor market is consistent with the view that wages respond quickly to price changes. Recall that the argument that the *AS* curve is vertical in the long run involves wage adjustments. If the short-run *AS* and aggregate demand (*AD*) curves intersected above potential output (Y_0 in Figure 28.4), wages would rise, shifting the *AS* curve to the left and pushing *Y* back down to Y_0. Similarly, if the short-run *AS* and *AD* curves intersected to the left of Y_0, unemployment and excess capacity would cause wages to fall, shifting the *AS* curve to the right and pushing *Y* back up to Y_0. Also remember that if the *AS* curve is vertical, monetary and fiscal policy cannot affect the level of output and employment in the economy. It therefore follows that those who believe that the wage rate adjusts quickly to clear the labor market are likely to believe that the *AS* curve is vertical (or almost vertical) and that monetary and fiscal policy have little or no effect on output and employment.

The Unemployment Rate and the Classical View

If, as the classical economists assumed, the labor market works well, how can we account for the fact that the unemployment rate at times seems high? There seem to be times when millions of people who want jobs at prevailing wage rates cannot find them. How can we reconcile this situation with the classical assumption about the labor market?

Some economists answer by arguing that the unemployment rate is not a good measure of whether the labor market is working well. We know the economy is dynamic and at any given time some industries are expanding and some are contracting. Consider, for example, a carpenter who is laid off because of a contraction in the construction industry. He had probably developed specific skills related to the construction industry—skills not necessarily useful for jobs in other industries. If he were earning $40,000 per year as a carpenter, he may be able to earn only $30,000 per year in another industry. He may eventually work his way back up to a salary of $40,000 in the new industry as he develops new skills, but this process will take time. Will this carpenter take a job at $30,000? There are at least two reasons he may not. First, he may believe that the slump in the construction industry is temporary and that he will soon get his job back. Second, he may mistakenly believe that he can earn more than $30,000 in another industry and will continue to look for a better job.

If our carpenter decides to continue looking for a job paying more than $30,000 per year, he will be considered unemployed because he is actively looking for work. This does not necessarily mean that the labor market is not working properly. The carpenter has *chosen* not to work for a wage of $30,000 per year, but if his value to any firm outside the construction industry is no more than $30,000 per year, we would not expect him to find a job paying more than $30,000. In this case, a positive unemployment rate as measured by the government does not necessarily indicate that the labor market is working poorly.

If the degree to which industries are changing in the economy fluctuates over time, there will be more people like our carpenter at some times than at others. This variation will cause the measured unemployment rate to fluctuate. Some economists argue that the measured unemployment rate may sometimes *seem* high even though the labor market is working well. The quantity of labor supplied at the current wage is equal to the quantity demanded at the current wage. The fact that there are people willing to work at a wage higher than the current wage does not mean that the labor market is not working. Whenever there is an upward-sloping supply curve in a market (as is usually the case in the labor market), the quantity supplied at a price higher than the equilibrium price is always greater than the quantity supplied at the equilibrium price.

Economists who view unemployment this way do not see it as a major problem. Yet the haunting images of the bread lines in the 1930s are still with us, and many find it difficult to believe everything was optimal when over 12 million people were looking for work at the end of 1982. There are other views of unemployment, as we will now see.

Explaining the Existence of Unemployment

If unemployment is a major macroeconomic problem—and many economists believe that it is—then we need to explore some of the reasons that have been suggested for its existence. Among these are sticky wages, efficiency wages, imperfect information, and minimum wage laws.

Each of these explanations for unemployment focuses on a particular reason that wage rates do not completely adjust when the demand for labor falls. Because wage rates do not fall as far as needed, there will be more people who wish to work at the current wage rates than there are jobs for those people. This is what one means by unemployment.

Sticky Wages

sticky wages The downward rigidity of wages as an explanation for the existence of unemployment.

One explanation for unemployment (above and beyond normal frictional and structural unemployment) is that wages are **sticky** on the downward side. That is, the equilibrium wage gets stuck at a particular level and does not fall when the demand for labor falls. This situation is illustrated in Figure 29.2, where the equilibrium wage gets stuck at W_0 (the original wage) and does not fall to W^* when demand decreases from D_0 to D_1. The result is unemployment of the amount

$L_0 - L_1$, where L_0 is the quantity of labor that households want to supply at wage rate W_0 and L_1 is the amount of labor that firms want to hire at wage rate W_0. $L_0 - L_1$ is the number of workers who would like to work at W_0 but cannot find jobs.

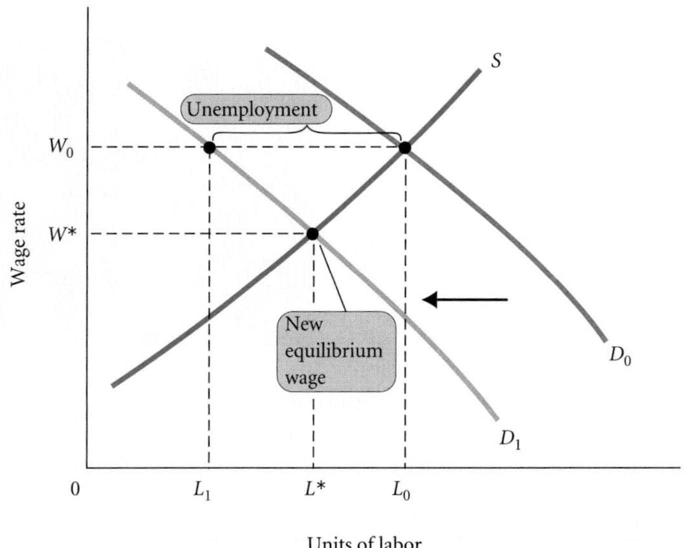

FIGURE 29.2
Sticky Wages
If wages "stick" at W_0 instead of falling to the new equilibrium wage of W^* following a shift of demand from D_0 to D_1, the result will be unemployment equal to $L_0 - L_1$.

The sticky wage explanation of unemployment, however, begs the question. *Why* are wages sticky, if they are, and *why* do wages not fall to clear the labor market during periods of high unemployment? Many answers have been proposed, but as yet no one answer has been agreed on. This lack of consensus is one reason macroeconomics has been in a state of flux for so long. The existence of unemployment continues to be a puzzle. Although we will discuss the major theories that economists have proposed to explain why wages may not clear the labor market, we can offer no conclusions. The question is still open.

Social, or Implicit, Contracts One explanation for downwardly sticky wages is that firms enter into **social**, or **implicit**, **contracts** with workers not to cut wages. It seems that extreme events—deep recession, deregulation, or threat of bankruptcy—are necessary for firms to cut wages. Wage cuts did occur in the Great Depression, in the airline industry following deregulation of the industry in the 1980s, and recently when some U.S. manufacturing firms found themselves in danger of bankruptcy from stiff foreign competition. These are exceptions to the general rule. For reasons that may be more sociological than economic, cutting wages seems close to being a taboo. In a recent study, Truman Bewley of Yale University surveyed hundreds of managers about why they did not reduce wage rates in downturns. The most common response was that wage cuts hurt worker morale and thus negatively affect worker productivity. Breaking the taboo and cutting wages may be costly in this sense.

social, *or* implicit, contracts Unspoken agreements between workers and firms that firms will not cut wages.

A related argument, the **relative-wage explanation of unemployment**, holds that workers are concerned about their wages *relative* to the wages of other workers in other firms and industries and may be unwilling to accept wage cuts unless they know that other workers are receiving similar cuts. Because it is difficult to reassure any one group of workers that all other workers are in the same situation, workers may resist any cut in their wages. There may be an implicit understanding between firms and workers that firms will not do anything that would make their workers worse off relative to workers in other firms.

relative-wage explanation of unemployment An explanation for sticky wages (and therefore unemployment): If workers are concerned about their wages relative to other workers in other firms and industries, they may be unwilling to accept a wage cut unless they know that all other workers are receiving similar cuts.

Explicit Contracts Many workers—in particular unionized workers—sign 1- to 3-year employment contracts with firms. These contracts stipulate the workers' wages for each year of the contract. Wages set in this way do not fluctuate with economic conditions, either upward or downward. If the economy slows down and firms demand fewer workers, the wage will not fall. Instead, some workers will be laid off.

ECONOMICS IN PRACTICE

Graduate School Applications in Recessions

In early 2008, there were a number of indications that the U.S. economy was slowing down. For many soon-to-graduate college students, forecasting the economy became a very personal enterprise. If the economy moved into a recession, as some economists were predicting because of the subprime housing problem, the graduates' job prospects would be poor. As the following article suggests, many students found a way to partially protect themselves from the possibility of a recession: apply to graduate school. Some observers of the economy argue that applications to take the GRE—standardized test required for graduate school admissions—increase when recessions loom. Young people may thus time when they go to graduate school based on their forecasts of the economy.

Graduate School Offers Relief During Economic Recession

***Oklahoma Daily* (U. Oklahoma)**

(U-WIRE) NORMAN, Okla. - A shaky economy may make it difficult for students to find jobs and pay off loans after graduation, but one option for graduates is more promising: Graduate school.

Bette Scott, OU Career Services director, said during her time at Career Services, she has seen economic recession cause graduating students to become more interested in continuing their education rather than entering an uncertain job market.

"Generally, what will happen when the job market slows down is that more students will look at going on to grad school," Scott said. "During good job markets like we've been in, grad school applications are down."

A recession is a decrease in gross domestic product for two straight quarters. Though that isn't the current situation, early indicators, such as a .4 percent rise in national unemployment to 5 percent and a failing stock market, tell economists a recession could occur.

During the last recession between 2001 and 2003, graduate school applications across the nation were up, according to University of Washington researchers.

Students beginning graduate school in the natural sciences and engineering fields increased by 31 percent from before the recession in 1998.

"The high-tech economy siphoned people away from graduate school, and when the bubble burst, that temporarily turned things around," William Zumeta, a University of Washington professor who did the research, said in his published findings from 2004.

Another indicator the researchers found was the number of people who took the Graduate Record Exam increased 9 percent, suggesting more people were preparing for varied programs.

If graduate school is not an option for students, Scott said students should be prepared to look outside their comfort zone when searching for a job.

"Students will be more willing to look at jobs they haven't looked at previously," he said. "In that kind of job market, you take whatever is available."

Scott said she is not seeing employment numbers wavering despite recent reports of a looming recession flood the media.

"We are not yet seeing that in our office in terms of hiring new college graduates," he said. "As a matter of fact, we are looking at a record number of employers wanting to come to the career fair."

Still, Oklahoma's unemployment rose from 4 percent in 2006 to 4.5 percent in December 2007.

Scott said Oklahoma's geographical location helps when economic trouble hits.

"In the past, it's always been worst on the east and west coast[s] before it hits here."

The office can adjust when the signs of recession are prominent on the coasts.

Scott said, though her office may not see an unemployment crunch now, the situation could be different tomorrow.

"We've seen it before change overnight," Scott said.

Kevin Bruns, American Student Loan Providers executive director, said the trend also is in the student loan market.

"The traditional pattern is going back to school during a recession," he said.

Source: Jerry Wofford, February 8, 2008

Although **explicit contracts** can explain why some wages are sticky, a deeper question must also be considered. Workers and firms surely know at the time a contract is signed that unforeseen events may cause the wages set by the contract to be too high or too low. Why do firms and workers bind themselves in this way? One explanation is that negotiating wages is costly. Negotiations between unions and firms can take a considerable amount of time—time that could be spent producing output—and it would be very costly to negotiate wages weekly or monthly. Contracts are a way of bearing these costs at no more than 1-, 2-, or 3-year intervals. There is a trade-off between the costs of locking workers and firms into contracts for long periods of time and the costs of wage negotiations. The length of contracts that minimizes negotiation costs seems to be (from what we observe in practice) between 1 and 3 years.

explicit contracts Employment contracts that stipulate workers' wages, usually for a period of 1 to 3 years.

Some multiyear contracts adjust for unforeseen events by **cost-of-living adjustments (COLAs)** written into the contract. COLAs tie wages to changes in the cost of living: The greater the rate of inflation, the more wages are raised. COLAs thus protect workers from unexpected inflation, although many COLAs adjust wages by a smaller percentage than the percentage increase in prices.

cost-of-living adjustments (COLAs) Contract provisions that tie wages to changes in the cost of living. The greater the inflation rate, the more wages are raised.

Efficiency Wage Theory

Another explanation for unemployment centers on the **efficiency wage theory**, which holds that the productivity of workers increases with the wage rate. If this is true, firms may have an incentive to pay wages *above* the wage at which the quantity of labor supplied is equal to the quantity of labor demanded.

efficiency wage theory An explanation for unemployment that holds that the productivity of workers increases with the wage rate. If this is so, firms may have an incentive to pay wages above the market-clearing rate.

The key argument of the efficiency wage theory is that by offering workers a wage in excess of the market wage, the productivity of those workers is increased. Some economists have likened the payment of this higher wage as a gift-exchange: firms pay a wage in excess of the market wage and in return workers work harder or more productively than they otherwise would. Under these circumstances, there will be people who want to work at the wage paid by firms and cannot find employment. Indeed, for the efficiency wage theory to operate, it must be the case that the wage offered by firms is above the market wage. It is the gap between the two that motivates workers who do have jobs to outdo themselves.

Empirical studies of labor markets have identified several potential benefits that firms receive from paying workers more than the market-clearing wage. Among them are lower turnover, improved morale, and reduced "shirking" of work. Even though the efficiency wage theory predicts some unemployment, the behavior it is describing is unlikely to account for much of the observed large cyclical fluctuations in unemployment over time.

Imperfect Information

Thus far we have been assuming that firms know exactly what wage rates they need to set to clear the labor market. They may not choose to set their wages at this level, but at least they know what the market-clearing wage is. In practice, however, firms may not have enough information at their disposal to know what the market-clearing wage is. In this case, firms are said to have *imperfect information*. If firms have imperfect or incomplete information, they may simply set wages wrong—wages that do not clear the labor market.

If a firm sets its wages too high, more workers will want to work for that firm than the firm wants to employ, resulting in some potential workers being turned away. The result is, of course, unemployment. One objection to this explanation is that it accounts for the existence of unemployment only in the very short run. As soon as a firm sees that it has made a mistake, why would it not immediately correct its mistake and adjust its wages to the correct market-clearing level? Why would unemployment *persist*?

If the economy were simple, it should take no more than a few months for firms to correct their mistakes, but the economy is complex. Although firms may be aware of their past mistakes and may try to correct them, new events are happening all the time. Because constant change—including a constantly changing equilibrium wage level—is characteristic of the economy, firms may find it hard to adjust wages to the market-clearing level. The labor market is not like the stock market or the market for wheat, where prices are determined in organized exchanges every day. Instead, thousands of firms are setting wages and millions of workers are responding to these wages. It may take considerable time for the market-clearing wages to be determined after they have been disturbed from an equilibrium position.

Minimum Wage Laws

minimum wage laws Laws that set a floor for wage rates—that is, a minimum hourly rate for any kind of labor.

Minimum wage laws explain at least a small fraction of unemployment. These laws set a floor for wage rates—a minimum hourly rate for any kind of labor. In 2008, the federal minimum wage was $6.55 per hour. If the market-clearing wage for some groups of workers is below this amount, this group will be unemployed. In Figure 29.2, if the minimum wage is W_0 and the market-clearing wage is W^*, the number of unemployed will be $L_0 - L_1$.

Teenagers, who have relatively little job experience, are most likely to be hurt by minimum wage laws. If some teenagers can produce only $5.90 worth of output per hour, no firm would be willing to hire them at a wage of $6.55. To do so would incur a loss of $0.65 per hour. In an unregulated market, these teenagers would be able to find work at the market-clearing wage of $5.90 per hour. If the minimum wage laws prevent the wage from falling below $6.55, these workers will not be able to find jobs and they will be unemployed. Others who may be hurt include people with very low skills and some recent immigrants.

In response to this argument against the minimum wage, Congress in 1996 established a subminimum wage for teenagers. The law allowed employers to hire teenagers at an "opportunity wage" of $4.25 for up to 90 days.

An Open Question

As we have seen, there are many explanations for why the labor market may not clear. The theories we have just set forth are not necessarily mutually exclusive, and there may be elements of truth in all of them. The aggregate labor market is very complicated, and there are no simple answers to why there is unemployment. Much current work in macroeconomics is concerned directly or indirectly with this question, and it is an exciting area of study. Which argument or arguments will win out in the end is an open question.

The Short-Run Relationship Between the Unemployment Rate and Inflation

At the Boston Fed in June 2008, Ben Bernanke, the Fed chair, gave a speech in which he referred to both the "upside risk to inflation," and the "unwelcome rise in the unemployment rate." Unemployment and inflation are the two central concerns of macroeconomics and of policy makers like Bernanke. But what is the relationship between the two? When Bernanke chooses to fight inflation, is he inevitably increasing unemployment and visa versa? We are now in a position to tackle this question.

We begin by looking at the relation between aggregate output (income) (Y) and the unemployment rate (U). For an economy to increase aggregate output, firms must hire more labor to produce that output. Thus, more output implies greater employment. An increase in employment means more people working (fewer people unemployed) and a lower unemployment rate. An increase in Y corresponds to a *decrease* in U. Thus, U and Y are *negatively* related: when Y rises, the unemployment rate falls, and when Y falls, the unemployment rate rises.

What about the relationship between aggregate output and the overall price level? The *AS* curve, reproduced in Figure 29.3, shows the relationship between Y and the overall price level (P). The relationship is a positive one: When P increases, Y increases, and when P decreases, Y decreases.

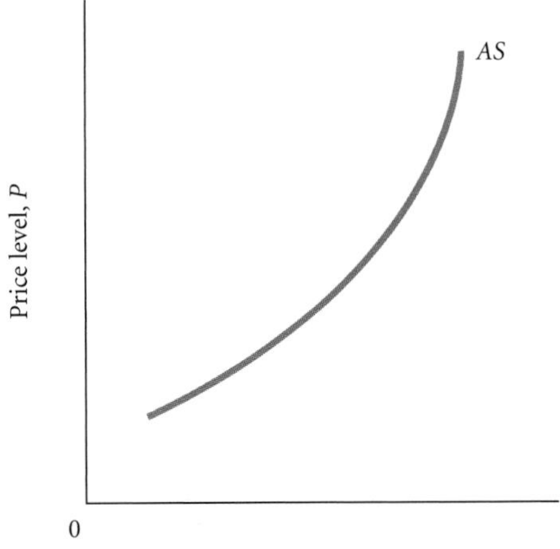

FIGURE 29.3
The Aggregate Supply Curve
The *AS* curve shows a positive relationship between the price level (P) and aggregate output (income) (Y).

As you will recall from the last chapter, the shape of the *AS* curve is determined by the behavior of the firms and how they react to an increase in demand. If aggregate demand shifts to the right and the economy is operating on the nearly flat part of the *AS* curve—far from capacity—output will increase, but the price level will not change much. However, if the economy is operating on the steep part of the *AS* curve—close to capacity—an increase in demand will drive up the price level, but output will be constrained by capacity and will not increase much.

Now let us put the two pieces together and think about what will happen following an event that leads to an increase in aggregate demand. First, firms experience an unanticipated decline in inventories. They respond by increasing output (Y) and hiring workers—the unemployment rate falls. If the economy is not close to capacity, there will be little increase in the price level. If, however, aggregate demand continues to grow, the ability of the economy to increase output will eventually reach its limit. As aggregate demand shifts farther and farther to the right along the *AS* curve, the price level increases more and more and output begins to reach its limit. At the point at which the *AS* curve becomes vertical, output cannot rise any farther. If output cannot grow, the unemployment rate cannot be pushed any lower. There is a negative relationship between the unemployment rate and the price level. As the unemployment rate declines in response to the economy's moving closer and closer to capacity output, the overall price level rises more and more, as shown in Figure 29.4.

FIGURE 29.4
The Relationship Between the Price Level and the Unemployment Rate
This curve shows a negative relationship between the price level (P) and the unemployment rate (U). As the unemployment rate declines in response to the economy's moving closer and closer to capacity output, the price level rises more and more.

inflation rate The percentage change in the price level.

Phillips Curve A curve showing the relationship between the inflation rate and the unemployment rate.

The *AS* curve shows the relationship between the price level and aggregate output and thus implicitly between the price level and the unemployment rate. In policy formulation and discussions, however, economists have focused less on the *AS* curve than on the relationship between the **inflation rate**—the percentage change in the price level—and the unemployment rate. Note that the price level and the percentage change in the price level are not the same. The curve describing the relationship between the inflation rate and the unemployment rate, which is shown in Figure 29.5, is called the **Phillips Curve**, after British economist A. W. Phillips, who first examined it using data for the United Kingdom. Fortunately, the analysis we have just done with the *AS* curve on the price level and aggregate output will enable us to see both why the Phillips Curve initially looked so appealing as an explanation of the relationship between inflation and unemployment and how more recent history has changed our views of the interpretation of the Phillips Curve.

FIGURE 29.5
The Phillips Curve
The Phillips Curve shows the relationship between the inflation rate and the unemployment rate.

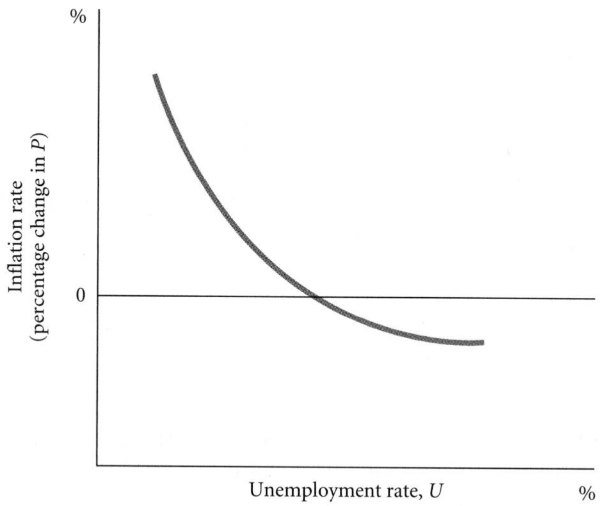

The Phillips Curve: A Historical Perspective

In the 1950s and 1960s, there was a remarkably smooth relationship between the unemployment rate and the rate of inflation, as Figure 29.6 shows for the 1960s. As you can see, the data points fit fairly closely around a downward-sloping curve; in general, the higher the unemployment rate is, the lower the rate of inflation. The Phillips Curve in Figure 29.6 shows a trade-off between inflation and unemployment. To lower the inflation rate, we must accept a higher unemployment rate, and to lower the unemployment rate, we must accept a higher rate of inflation.

FIGURE 29.6
Unemployment and Inflation, 1960–1969
During the 1960s, there seemed to be an obvious trade-off between inflation and unemployment. Policy debates during the period revolved around this apparent trade-off.
Source: see Table 22.5

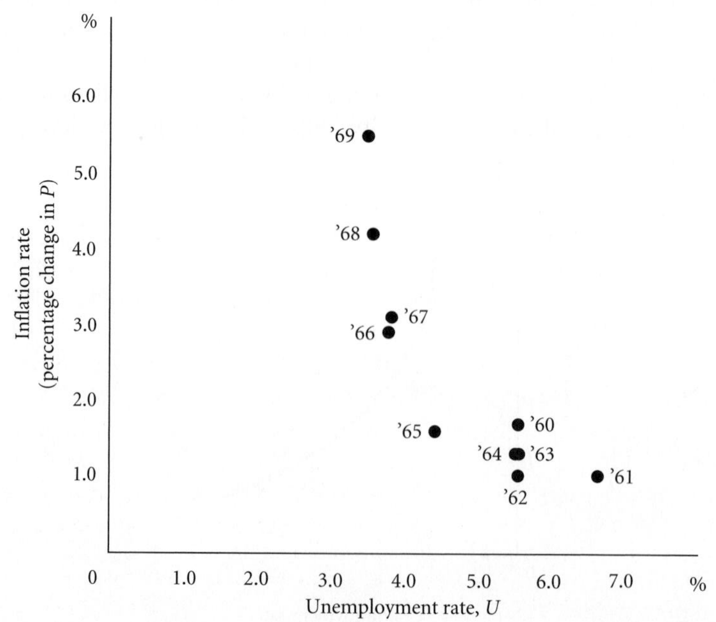

Textbooks written in the 1960s and early 1970s relied on the Phillips Curve as the main explanation of inflation. Things seemed simple—inflation appeared to respond in a fairly predictable way to changes in the unemployment rate. For this reason, policy discussions in the 1960s revolved around the Phillips Curve. The role of the policy maker, it was thought, was to choose a point on the curve. Conservatives usually argued for choosing a point with a low rate of inflation and were willing to accept a higher unemployment rate in exchange for this. Liberals usually argued for accepting more inflation to keep unemployment at a low level.

Life did not turn out to be quite so simple. The Phillips Curve broke down in the 1970s and 1980s. This change can be seen in Figure 29.7, which graphs the unemployment rate and inflation rate for the period from 1970 to 2007. The points in Figure 29.7 show no particular relationship between inflation and unemployment.

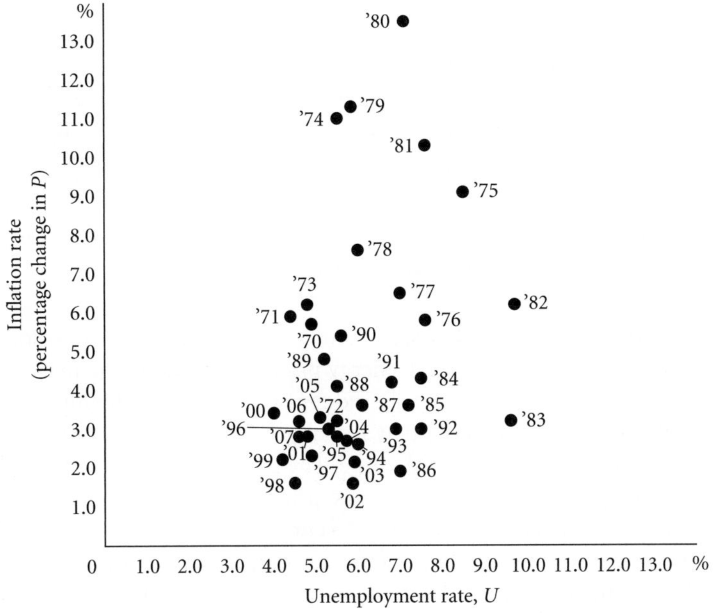

FIGURE 29.7
Unemployment and Inflation, 1970–2007
From the 1970s on, it became clear that the relationship between unemployment and inflation was anything but simple.
Source: See Table 22.5.

Aggregate Supply and Aggregate Demand Analysis and the Phillips Curve

How can we explain the stability of the Phillips Curve in the 1950s and 1960s and the lack of stability after that? To answer, we need to return to *AS/AD* analysis.

If the *AD* curve shifts from year to year but the *AS* curve does not, the values of *P* and *Y* each year will lie along the *AS* curve [Figure 29.8(a)]. The plot of the relationship between *P* and *Y* will be upward-sloping. Correspondingly, the plot of the relationship between the unemployment rate (which decreases with increased output) and the rate of inflation will be a curve that slopes downward. In other words, we would expect to see a negative relationship between the unemployment rate and the inflation rate.

However, the relationship between the unemployment rate and the inflation rate will look different if the *AS* curve shifts from year to year but the *AD* curve does not. A leftward shift of the *AS* curve will cause an *increase* in the price level (*P*) and a *decrease* in aggregate output (*Y*) [Figure 29.8(b)]. When the *AS* curve shifts to the left, the economy experiences both inflation *and* an increase in the unemployment rate (because decreased output means increased unemployment). In other words, if the *AS* curve is shifting from year to year, we would expect to see a positive relationship between the unemployment rate and the inflation rate.

If both the *AS* and the *AD* curves are shifting simultaneously, however, there is no systematic relationship between *P* and *Y* [Figure 29.8(c)] and thus no systematic relationship between the unemployment rate and the inflation rate. One explanation for the change in the Phillips Curve between the 1960s and later periods is that both the *AS* and the *AD* curves appear to be shifting in the later periods. Why might this be?

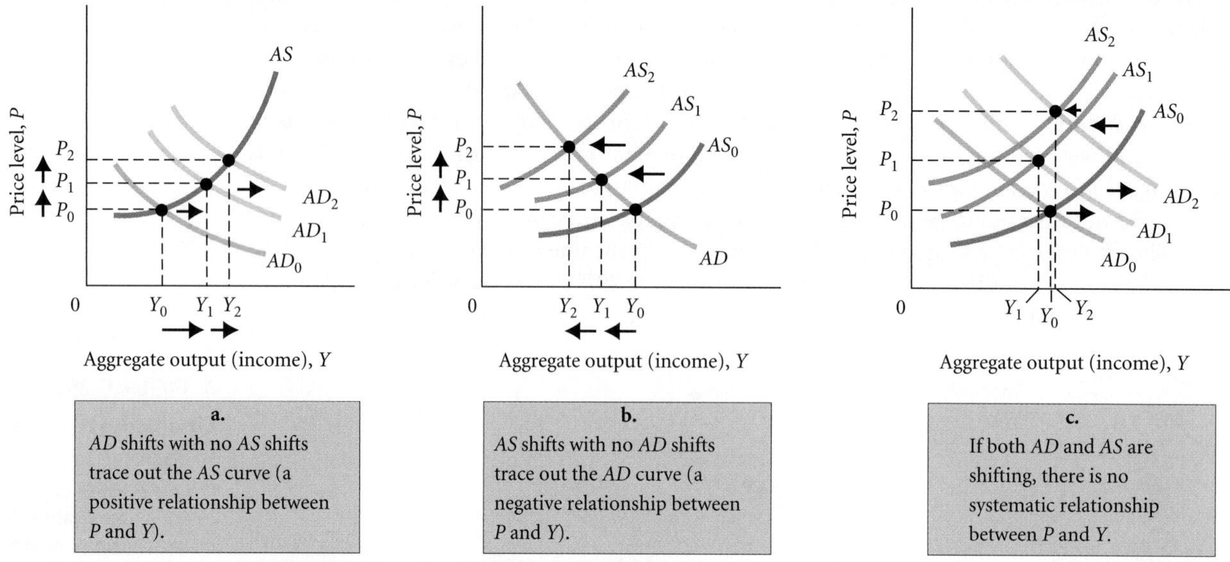

▲ **FIGURE 29.8 Changes in the Price Level and Aggregate Output Depend on Shifts in Both Aggregate Demand and Aggregate Supply**

The Role of Import Prices We discussed in the previous chapter that some of the main factors that causes the *AS* curve to shift are energy prices, particularly the price of oil. Since the United States imports much of its oil, the price index of U.S. imports is highly correlated with the (world) price of oil. We can thus consider that a change in the U.S. import price index, which we will call "the price of imports," shifts the *AS* curve. The price of imports is plotted in Figure 29.9 for the 1960 I–2007 IV period. As you can see, the price of imports changed very little between 1960 and 1970. There were no large shifts in the *AS* curve in the 1960s due to changes in the price of imports. There were also no other large changes in input prices in the 1960s, so overall the *AS* curve shifted very little during the decade. The main variation in the 1960s was in aggregate demand, so the shifting *AD* curve traced out points along the *AS* curve.

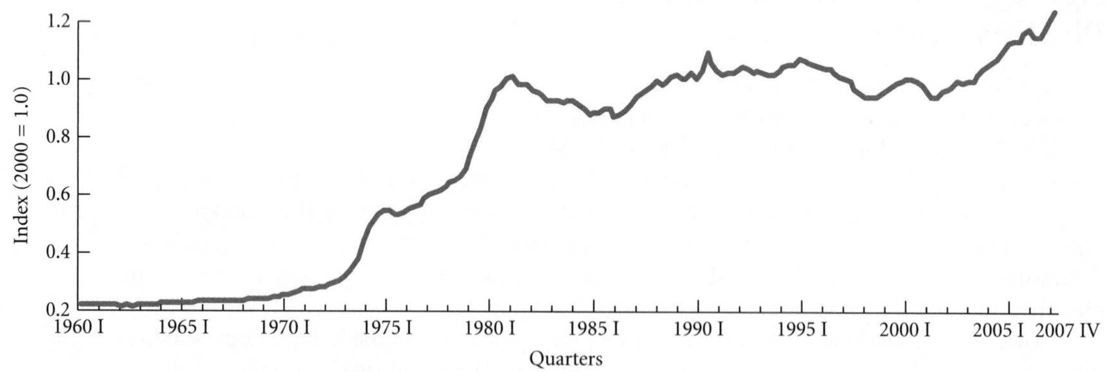

▲ **FIGURE 29.9 The Price of Imports, 1960 I–2007 IV**

The price of imports changed very little in the 1960s and early 1970s. It increased substantially in 1974 and again in 1979–1980. Between 1981 and 2002, the price of imports changed very little. Since 2002, it has been rising.

Figure 29.9 also shows that the price of imports increased considerably in the 1970s. This rise led to large shifts in the *AS* curve during the decade, but the *AD* curve was also shifting throughout the 1970s. With both curves shifting, the data points for *P* and *Y* were scattered all over the graph and the observed relationship between *P* and *Y* was not at all systematic.

This story about import prices and the *AS* and *AD* curves in the 1960s and 1970s carries over to the Phillips Curve. The Phillips Curve was stable in the 1960s because the primary source of variation in the economy was demand, not costs. In the 1970s, both demand *and* costs were varying so no obvious relationship between the unemployment rate and the inflation rate was apparent. To some extent, what is remarkable about the Phillips Curve is not that it was not smooth after the 1960s, but that it ever was smooth.

Expectations and the Phillips Curve

Another reason the Phillips Curve is not stable concerns expectations. We saw in Chapter 28 that if a firm expects other firms to raise their prices, the firm may raise the price of its own product. If all firms are behaving this way, prices will rise because they are expected to rise. In this sense, expectations are self-fulfilling. Similarly, if inflation is expected to be high in the future, negotiated wages are likely to be higher than if inflation is expected to be low. Wage inflation is thus affected by expectations of future price inflation. Because wages are input costs, prices rise as firms respond to the higher wage costs. Price expectations that affect wage contracts eventually affect prices themselves.

If the rate of inflation depends on expectations, the Phillips Curve will shift as expectations change. For example, if inflationary expectations increase, the result will be an increase in the rate of inflation even though the unemployment rate may not have changed. In this case, the Phillips Curve will shift to the right. If inflationary expectations decrease, the Phillips Curve will shift to the left—there will be less inflation at any given level of the unemployment rate.

It so happened that inflationary expectations were quite stable in the 1950s and 1960s. The inflation rate was moderate during most of this period, and people expected it to remain moderate. With inflationary expectations not changing very much, there were no major shifts of the Phillips Curve, a situation that helps explain its stability during the period.

Near the end of the 1960s, inflationary expectations began to increase, primarily in response to the actual increase in inflation that was occurring because of the tight economy caused by the Vietnam War. Inflationary expectations increased even further in the 1970s as a result of large oil price increases. These changing expectations led to shifts of the Phillips Curve and are another reason the curve was not stable during the 1970s.

Is There a Short-Run Trade-Off between Inflation and Unemployment?

Does the fact that the Phillips Curve broke down during the 1970s mean that there is no trade-off between inflation and unemployment in the short run? Not at all: It simply means that other things affect inflation aside from unemployment. Just as the relationship between price and quantity demanded along a standard demand curve shifts when income or other factors change, so does the relationship between unemployment and inflation change when other factors change.

In 1975, for example, inflation and unemployment were both high. As we explained earlier, this stagflation was caused partly by an increase in oil costs that shifted the aggregate supply curve to the left and partly by expectations of continued inflation that kept prices rising despite high levels of unemployment. In the summer of 2008, many observers, including Fed chair Ben Bernanke, were becoming concerned about both rising unemployment and rising inflation. In response to the 1975 situation, the Federal Reserve (Fed) pursued a contractionary monetary policy, which shifted the *AD* curve to the left and led to even higher unemployment. By 1977, the rate of inflation had dropped from over 11 percent to about 6 percent. So the rise in the unemployment rate did lead to a decrease in inflation, an outcome that reflects the trade-off. There *is* a short-run trade-off between inflation and unemployment, but other factors besides unemployment affect inflation. Policy involves more than simply choosing a point along a nice smooth curve.

The Long-Run Aggregate Supply Curve, Potential Output, and the Natural Rate of Unemployment

Recall from Chapter 28 that many economists believe the *AS* curve is vertical in the long run. This situation is illustrated in Figure 29.10. Assume that the initial equilibrium is at the intersection of AD_0 and the long-run aggregate supply curve. Now consider a shift of the aggregate demand curve from AD_0 to AD_1. If wages lag prices, aggregate output will rise from Y_0 to Y_1. (This is a movement along the short-run *AS* curve AS_0.) In the longer run, wages may catch up. For example, next year's labor contracts may make up for the fact that wage increases did not keep up with the cost of living this year. If wages catch up in the longer run, the *AS* curve will shift from AS_0 to AS_1 and drive aggregate output back to Y_0. If wages ultimately rise by exactly the same percentage as output prices, firms will produce the same level of output as they did before the increase in aggregate demand.

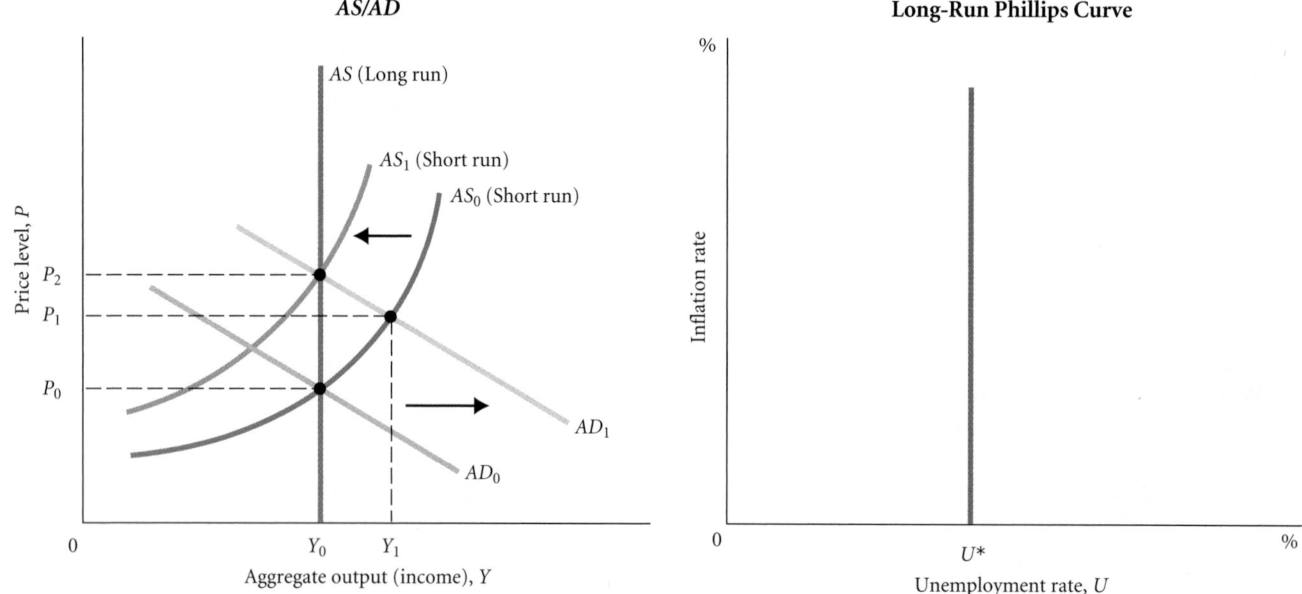

▲ **FIGURE 29.10 The Long-Run Phillips Curve: The Natural Rate of Unemployment**

If the *AS* curve is vertical in the long run, so is the Phillips Curve. In the long run, the Phillips Curve corresponds to the natural rate of unemployment—that is, the unemployment rate that is consistent with the notion of a fixed long-run output at potential output. U^* is the natural rate of unemployment.

In Chapter 28, we said that Y_0 is sometimes called *potential output.* Aggregate output can be pushed above Y_0 in the short run. When aggregate output exceeds Y_0, however, there is upward pressure on input prices and costs. The unemployment rate is already quite low, firms are beginning to encounter the limits of their plant capacities, and so on. At levels of aggregate output above Y_0, costs will rise, the *AS* curve will shift to the left, and the price level will rise. Thus, potential output is the level of aggregate output that can be sustained in the long run without inflation.

This story is directly related to the Phillips Curve. Those who believe that the *AS* curve is vertical in the long run at potential output also believe that the Phillips Curve is vertical in the long run at some natural rate of unemployment. Recall from Chapter 22 that the **natural rate of unemployment** refers to unemployment that occurs as a normal part of the functioning of the economy. It is sometimes taken as the sum of frictional unemployment and structural unemployment. The logic behind the vertical Phillips Curve is that whenever the unemployment rate is pushed below the natural rate, wages begin to rise, thus pushing up costs. This leads to a *lower* level of output, which pushes the unemployment rate back up to the natural rate. At the natural rate, the economy can be considered to be at full employment.

natural rate of unemployment The unemployment that occurs as a normal part of the functioning of the economy. Sometimes taken as the sum of frictional unemployment and structural unemployment.

The Nonaccelerating Inflation Rate of Unemployment (NAIRU)

In Figure 29.10, the long-run vertical Phillips Curve is a graph with the inflation rate on the vertical axis and the unemployment rate on the horizontal axis. The natural rate of unemployment is U^*. In the long run, according to advocates of the long-run vertical Phillips Curve, the actual unemployment rate moves to U^* because of the natural workings of the economy.

Another graph of interest is Figure 29.11, which plots the *change in* the inflation rate on the vertical axis and the unemployment rate on the horizontal axis. Many economists believe that the relationship between the change in the inflation rate and the unemployment rate is as depicted by the *PP* curve in the figure. The value of the unemployment rate where the *PP* curve crosses zero is called the *nonaccelerating inflation rate of unemployment* (**NAIRU**). If the actual unemployment rate is to the left of the NAIRU, the change in the inflation rate will be positive. As depicted in the figure, at U_1, the change in the inflation rate is 1. Conversely, if the actual unemployment rate is to the right of the NAIRU, the change in the inflation rate is negative: At U_2, the change is -1.

NAIRU The nonaccelerating inflation rate of unemployment.

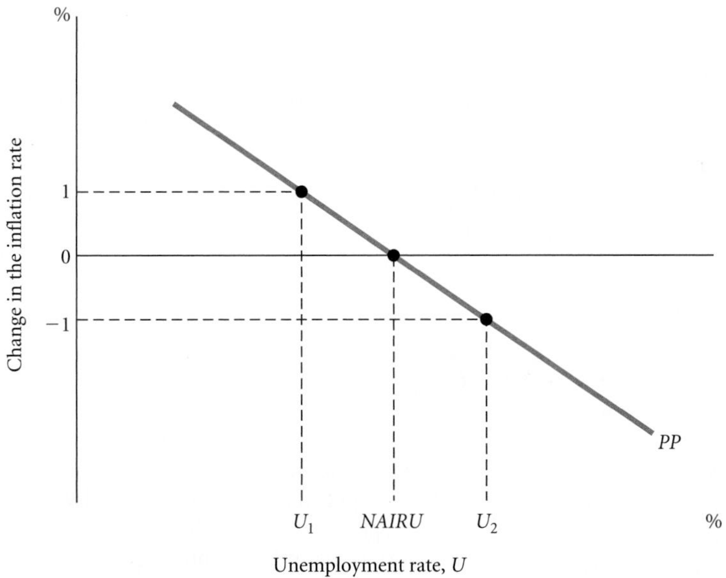

FIGURE 29.11
The NAIRU Diagram
To the left of the NAIRU, the price level is accelerating (positive changes in the inflation rate); to the right of the NAIRU, the price level is decelerating (negative changes in the inflation rate). Only when the unemployment rate is equal to the NAIRU is the price level changing at a constant rate (no change in the inflation rate).

Consider what happens if the unemployment rate decreases from the NAIRU to U_1 and stays at U_1 for many periods. Assume also that the inflation rate at the NAIRU was 2 percent. Then in the first period the inflation rate will increase from 2 percent to 3 percent. The inflation rate does not, however, just stay at the higher 3 percent value. In the next period, the inflation rate will increase from 3 percent to 4 percent and so on. The price level will be accelerating—that is, the change in the inflation rate will be positive—when the actual unemployment rate is below the NAIRU. Conversely, the price level will be decelerating—that is, the change in the inflation rate will be negative—when the actual unemployment rate is above the NAIRU.[1]

The *PP* curve in Figure 29.11 is like the *AS* curve in Figure 29.3—the same factors that shift the *AS* curve, such as cost shocks, can also shift the *PP* curve. Figure 28.8 on p. 560 summarizes the various factors that can cause the *AS* curve to shift, and these are also relevant for the *PP* curve. A favorable shift for the *PP* curve is to the left because the *PP* curve crosses zero at a lower unemployment rate, indicating that the NAIRU is lower. Some have argued that one possible recent source of favorable shifts is increased foreign competition, which may have kept wage costs and other input costs down.

Before about 1995, proponents of the NAIRU theory argued that the value of the NAIRU in the United States was around 6 percent. By the end of 1995, the unemployment rate declined to 5.6 percent, and by 2000, the unemployment rate was down to 3.8 percent. If the NAIRU had been 6 percent, one should have seen a continuing increase in the inflation rate beginning about 1995. In fact, the 1995 to 2000 period saw slightly declining inflation. Not only did inflation not continually increase, it did not even increase once to a new, higher value and then stay there. As the unemployment rate declined during this period, proponents of the NAIRU lowered their estimates of it, more or less in line with the actual fall in the unemployment rate. This recalibration can be justified by arguing that there have been continuing favorable shifts of the *PP* curve, such

[1] The NAIRU is actually misnamed. It is the *price level* that is accelerating or decelerating, not the inflation rate, when the actual unemployment rate differs from the NAIRU. The inflation rate is not accelerating or decelerating, but simply changing by the same amount each period. The namers of the NAIRU forgot their physics.

as possible increased foreign competition. Critics, however, have argued that this procedure is close to making the NAIRU theory vacuous. Can the theory really be tested if the estimate of the NAIRU is changed whenever it is not consistent with the data? How trustworthy is the appeal to favorable shifts?

Macroeconomists are currently debating whether equations estimated under the NAIRU theory are good approximations. More time is needed before any definitive answers can be given.

Looking Ahead

This chapter concludes our basic analysis of how the macroeconomy works. In the preceding seven chapters, we have examined how households and firms behave in the three market arenas—the goods market, the money market, and the labor market. We have seen how aggregate output (income), the interest rate, and the price level are determined in the economy, and we have examined the relationship between two of the most important macroeconomic variables, the inflation rate and the unemployment rate. In Chapter 30, we use everything we have learned up to this point to examine a number of important policy issues.

SUMMARY

THE LABOR MARKET: BASIC CONCEPTS *p. 571*

1. Because the economy is dynamic, *frictional* and *structural unemployment* are inevitable and in some ways desirable. Times of *cyclical unemployment* are of concern to macroeconomic policy makers.
2. In general, employment tends to fall when aggregate output falls and rise when aggregate output rises.

THE CLASSICAL VIEW OF THE LABOR MARKET *p. 572*

3. Classical economists believe that the interaction of supply and demand in the labor market brings about equilibrium and that unemployment (beyond the frictional and structural amounts) does not exist.
4. The classical view of the labor market is consistent with the theory of a vertical aggregate supply curve.

EXPLAINING THE EXISTENCE OF UNEMPLOYMENT *p. 574*

5. Some economists argue that the unemployment rate is not an accurate indicator of whether the labor market is working properly. Unemployed people who are considered part of the labor force may be offered jobs but may be unwilling to take those jobs at the offered salaries. Some of the unemployed may have chosen not to work, but this result does not mean that the labor market has malfunctioned.
6. Those who do not subscribe to the classical view of the labor market suggest several reasons why unemployment exists. Downwardly *sticky wages* may be brought about by *social (implicit)* or *explicit contracts* not to cut wages. If the equilibrium wage rate falls but wages are prevented from falling also, the result will be unemployment.
7. *Efficiency wage theory* holds that the productivity of workers increases with the wage rate. If this is true, firms may have an incentive to pay wages above the wage at which the quantity of labor supplied is equal to the quantity of labor demanded. At all wages above the equilibrium, there will be an excess supply of labor and therefore unemployment.
8. If firms are operating with incomplete or imperfect information, they may not know what the market-clearing wage is. As a result, they may set their wages incorrectly and bring about unemployment. Because the economy is so complex, it may take considerable time for firms to correct these mistakes.
9. *Minimum wage laws*, which set a floor for wage rates, are one factor contributing to unemployment of teenagers and very low-skilled workers. If the market-clearing wage for some groups of workers is below the minimum wage, some members of this group will be unemployed.

THE SHORT-RUN RELATIONSHIP BETWEEN THE UNEMPLOYMENT RATE AND INFLATION *p. 578*

10. There is a negative relationship between the unemployment rate (U) and aggregate output (income) (Y): When Y rises, U falls. When Y falls, U rises.
11. The relationship between the unemployment rate and the price level is negative: As the unemployment rate declines and the economy moves closer to capacity, the price level rises more and more.
12. The *Phillips Curve* represents the relationship between the *inflation rate* and the *unemployment rate*. During the 1950s and 1960s, this relationship was stable and there seemed to be a predictable trade-off between inflation and unemployment. As a result of import price increases (which led to shifts in aggregate supply), the relationship between the inflation rate and the unemployment rate was erratic in the 1970s. There *is* a short-term trade-off between inflation and unemployment, but other things besides unemployment affect inflation.

THE LONG-RUN AGGREGATE SUPPLY CURVE, POTENTIAL OUTPUT, AND THE NATURAL RATE OF UNEMPLOYMENT p. 583

13. Those who believe that the *AS* curve is vertical in the long run also believe that the Phillips Curve is vertical in the long run at the *natural rate of unemployment*. The natural rate is generally the sum of the frictional and structural rates. If the Phillips Curve is vertical in the long run, then there is a limit to how low government policy can push the unemployment rate without setting off inflation.

14. The *NAIRU* theory says that the price level will accelerate when the unemployment rate is below the NAIRU and decelerate when the unemployment rate is above the NAIRU.

REVIEW TERMS AND CONCEPTS

cost-of-living adjustments (COLAs), *p. 577*
cyclical unemployment, *p. 572*
efficiency wage theory, *p. 577*
explicit contracts, *p. 577*
frictional unemployment, *p. 572*
inflation rate, *p. 580*
labor demand curve, *p. 572*
labor supply curve, *p. 572*
minimum wage laws, *p. 578*
NAIRU, *p. 585*
natural rate of unemployment, *p. 584*
Phillips Curve, *p. 580*
relative-wage explanation of unemployment, *p. 575*
social, *or* implicit, contracts, *p. 575*
sticky wages, *p. 574*
structural unemployment, *p. 572*
unemployment rate, *p. 572*

PROBLEMS

Visit **www.myeconlab.com** to complete the problems marked in orange online. You will receive instant feedback on your answers, tutorial help, and access to additional practice problems.

1. In April 2000, the U.S. unemployment rate dropped below 4 percent for the first time in 30 years. At the same time, inflation remained at a very low level by historical standards. Can you offer an explanation for what seems to be an improved trade-off between inflation and unemployment? What factors might improve the trade-off? What factors might make it worse?

2. **[Related to the *Economics in Practice* on *p. 576*]** The *Economics in Practice* describes the potential effects of a decline in employment on graduate school enrollment in the United States. Take time to review how the Bureau of Labor Statistics measures the unemployment rate. (See Chapter 22, pp. 435–437) As of July 2008, the total labor force was 155 million. Of that number, 146 million were classified as employed. That left about 8.8 million unemployed and an unemployment rate of 5.7 percent. Suppose next year that 60,000 students stayed in school without working rather than looking for a job but there were no other changes in the labor force or the number employed. Estimate the size of the change on unemployment and the unemployment rate.

3. Obtain monthly data on the unemployment rate and the inflation rate for the last 2 years. (This data can be found at www.bls.gov or in a recent issue of the *Survey of Current Business* or in the *Monthly Labor Review* or *Employment and Earnings*, all published by the government and available in many college libraries.)
   a. What trends do you observe? Can you explain what you see using aggregate supply and aggregate demand curves?
   b. Plot the 24 monthly rates on a graph with the unemployment rate measured on the x-axis and the inflation rate on the y-axis. Is there evidence of a trade-off between these two variables? Provide an explanation.

4. In 2008, the country of Ruba was suffering from a period of high unemployment. The new president, Clang, appointed Laurel Tiedye as his chief economist. Ms. Tiedye and her staff estimated these supply and demand curves for labor from data obtained from the secretary of labor, Robert Small:

$$Q_D = 100 - 5W$$
$$Q_S = 10W - 20$$

where Q is the quantity of labor supplied/demanded in millions of workers and W is the wage rate in slugs, the currency of Ruba.
   a. Currently, the law in Ruba says that no worker shall be paid less than 9 slugs per hour. Estimate the quantity of labor supplied, the number of unemployed, and the unemployment rate.
   b. President Clang, over the objection of Secretary Small, has recommended to the congress that the law be changed to allow the wage rate to be determined in the market. If such a law was passed and the market adjusted quickly, what would happen to total employment, the size of the labor force, and the unemployment rate? Show the results graphically.
   c. Will the Rubanese labor market adjust quickly to such a change in the law? Why or why not?

5. The following policies have at times been advocated for coping with unemployment. Briefly explain how each might work and explain which type or types of unemployment (frictional, structural, or cyclical) each policy is designed to alter.
   a. A computer list of job openings and a service that matches employees with job vacancies (sometimes called an "economic dating service")
   b. Lower minimum wage for teenagers
   c. Retraining programs for workers who need to learn new skills to find employment
   d. Public employment for people without jobs
   e. Improved information about available jobs and current wage rates
   f. The president's going on nationwide TV and attempting to convince firms and workers that the inflation rate next year will be low

6. Your boss offers you a wage increase of 10 percent. Is it possible that you are worse off with the wage increase than you were before? Explain your answer.

7. How will the following affect labor force participation rates, labor supply, and unemployment?
   a. Because the retired elderly are a larger and larger fraction of the U.S. population, Congress and the president decide to raise the Social Security tax on individuals to continue paying benefits to the elderly.
   b. A national child care program is enacted, requiring employers to provide free child care services.
   c. The U.S. government reduces restrictions on immigration into the United States.
   d. The welfare system is eliminated.
   e. The government subsidizes the purchase of new capital by firms (an investment tax credit).

8. Draw a graph to illustrate the following:
   a. A Phillips Curve based on the assumption of a vertical long-run aggregate supply curve
   b. The effect of a change in inflationary expectations on a recently stable Phillips Curve
   c. Unemployment caused by a recently enacted minimum wage law

9. Obtain data on "average hourly earnings of production workers" and the unemployment rate for your state or area over a recent 2-year period. Has unemployment increased or decreased? What has happened to wages? Does the pattern of unemployment help explain the movement of wages? Provide an explanation.

10. Suppose the inflation–unemployment relationship depicted by the Phillips Curve was stable. Do you think the U.S. trade-off and the Japanese trade-off would be identical? If not, what kinds of factors might make the trade-offs dissimilar?

Policy Timing, Deficit Targeting, and Stock Market Effects

30

CHAPTER OUTLINE

The year 2008 was a national election year in the United States and by the late summer and early fall of the year most polls suggested that the state of the economy would be the central political issue in the presidential election. On almost any day of the year, the front page of most newspapers has at least one article on some macroeconomic issue. Most of the financial investment decisions made both by financial institutions and household investors are affected by the state of the macroeconomy.

In this chapter, we use the tools we have already learned to examine three key issues in macroeconomics. First, how is the use of fiscal and monetary policy influenced by the time lags we see in the economy? It is not easy to get the timing right when we try to stabilize the economy, particularly when using fiscal policy instruments. How do timing lags affect our choice of policy instruments? Second, in recent years, the United States has run large budget deficits. What happens when we try to implement policy initiatives based on targeting the size of those deficits? How does deficit targeting affect stabilization policy more broadly? Third, we look at the connection between financial markets and the macroeconomy. Next time Ben Bernanke, the Chair of the Federal Reserve, is scheduled to make a major announcement about monetary policy, log on to one of the online financial sites. Often you will see that the major stock indices react to Bernanke's announcements. Why might this be true and when exactly do we most expect to see a reaction? These are the questions we treat in this chapter.

Time Lags Regarding Monetary and Fiscal Policy

One of the objectives of monetary and fiscal policy is stabilization of the economy. Consider the two possible time paths for aggregate output (income) (Y) shown in Figure 30.1. In path B (the light blue line), the fluctuations in GDP are smaller than those in path A (the dark blue line). One aim of **stabilization policy** is to smooth out fluctuations in output to try to move the economy along a path like B instead of A. Stabilization policy is also concerned with the stability of prices. Here the goal is not to prevent the overall price level from rising at all, but instead to achieve an inflation rate that is as close as possible to a target rate of about 2 percent given the government's other goals of high and stable levels of output and employment.

stabilization policy Describes both monetary and fiscal policy, the goals of which are to smooth out fluctuations in output and employment and to keep prices as stable as possible.

Stabilization goals are not easy to achieve. The existence of various kinds of **time lags**, or delays in the response of the economy to stabilization policies, can make the economy difficult to control. Economists generally recognize three kinds of time lags: recognition lags, implementation lags, and response lags.

time lags Delays in the economy's response to stabilization policies.

GURE 30.1
Two Possible Time Paths for GDP

Path *A* is less stable—it varies more over time—than path *B*. Other things being equal, society prefers path *B* to path *A*.

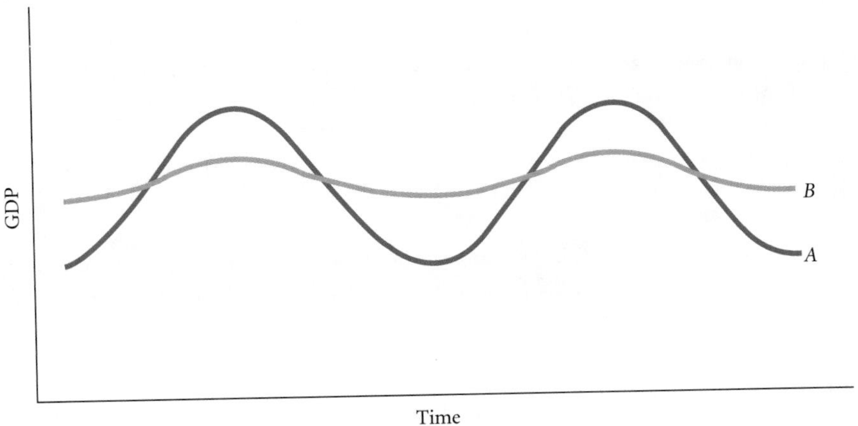

Stabilization

Figure 30.2 shows timing problems a government may face when trying to stabilize the economy. Suppose the economy reaches a peak and begins to slide into recession at point *A* (at time t_0). Policy makers do not observe the decline in GDP until it has sunk to point *B* (at time t_1). By the time they have begun to stimulate the economy (point *C*, time t_2), the recession is well advanced and the economy has almost bottomed out. When the policies finally begin to take effect (point *D*, time t_3), the economy is already on its road to recovery. The policies push the economy to point *E'*—a much greater fluctuation than point *E*, which is where the economy would have been without the stabilization policy. Sometime after point *D*, policy makers may begin to realize that the economy is expanding too quickly. By the time they have implemented contractionary policies and the policies have made their effects felt, the economy is starting to weaken. The contractionary policies therefore end up pushing GDP to point *F'* instead of point *F*.

Because of the various time lags, the expansionary policies that should have been instituted at time t_0 do not begin to have an effect until time t_3, when they are no longer needed. The light blue line in Figure 30.2 shows how the economy behaves as a result of the "stabilization" policies. The dark blue line shows the time path of GDP if the economy had been allowed to run its course and no stabilization policies had been attempted. In this case, stabilization policy makes income more erratic, not less—the policy results in a peak income of *E'* as opposed to *E* and a trough income of *F'* instead of *F*.

Critics of stabilization policy argue that the situation in Figure 30.2 is typical of the interaction between the government and the rest of the economy. This claim is not necessarily true. We need to know more about the nature of the various kinds of lags before deciding whether stabilization policy is good or bad.

FIGURE 30.2
Possible Stabilization Timing Problems

Attempts to stabilize the economy can prove destabilizing because of time lags. An expansionary policy that should have begun to take effect at point *A* does not actually begin to have an impact until point *D*, when the economy is already on an upswing. Hence, the policy pushes the economy to points *E'* and *F'* (instead of points *E* and *F*). Income varies more widely than it would have if no policy had been implemented.

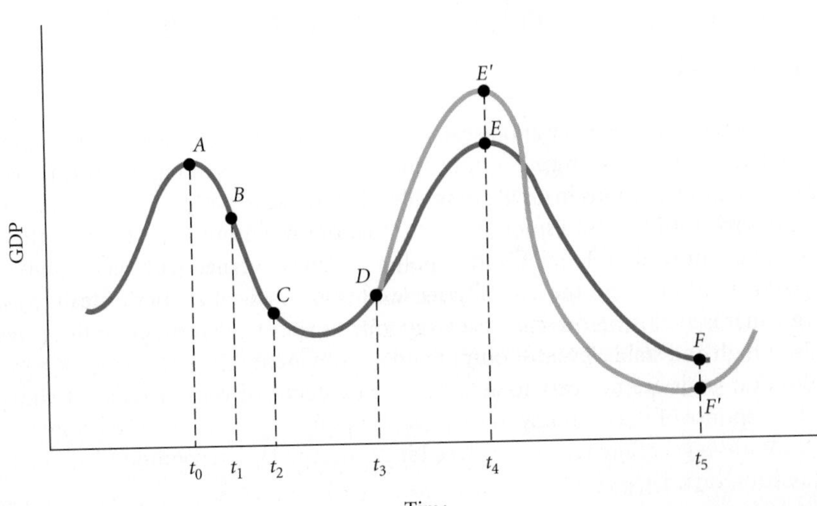

Recognition Lags

It takes time for policy makers to recognize a boom or a slump. Many important data—those from the national income and product accounts, for example—are available only quarterly. It usually takes several weeks to compile and prepare even the preliminary estimates for these figures. If the economy goes into a slump on January 1, the recession may not be detected until the data for the first quarter are available at the end of April.

Moreover, the early national income and product accounts data are only preliminary, based on an incomplete compilation of the various data sources. These estimates can, and often do, change as better data become available. This situation makes the interpretation of the initial estimates difficult, and **recognition lags** result.

recognition lag The time it takes for policy makers to recognize the existence of a boom or a slump.

Implementation Lags

The problems that lags pose for stabilization policy do not end once economists and policy makers recognize that the economy is in a boom or a slump. Even if everyone knows that the economy needs to be stimulated or reined in, it takes time to put the desired policy into effect, especially for actions that involve fiscal policy. **Implementation lags** result.

implementation lag The time it takes to put the desired policy into effect once economists and policy makers recognize that the economy is in a boom or a slump.

Each year Congress decides on the federal government's budget for the coming year. The tax laws and spending programs embodied in this budget are hard to change once they are in place. If it becomes clear that the economy is entering a recession and is in need of a fiscal stimulus during the middle of the year, there is a limited amount that can be done. Until Congress authorizes more spending or a cut in taxes, changes in fiscal policy are not possible.[1]

Monetary policy is less subject to the kinds of restrictions that slow down changes in fiscal policy. As we saw in Chapter 25, the Fed's main tool for controlling the supply of money or the interest rate is open market operations—buying and selling government securities. Transactions in these securities take place in a highly developed market, and if the Fed chooses, it can buy or sell a large volume of securities in a very short period of time. The implementation lag for monetary policy is generally much shorter than for fiscal policy. When the Fed wants to increase the supply of money, it goes into the open market and purchases government securities. This action instantly increases the stock of money (bank reserves held at the Fed), and an expansion of the money supply begins.

Response Lags

Even after a macroeconomic problem has been recognized and the appropriate policies to correct it have been implemented, there are **response lags**—lags that occur because of the operation of the economy itself. Even after the government has formulated a policy and put it into place, the economy takes time to adjust to the new conditions. Although monetary policy can be adjusted and implemented more quickly than fiscal policy, it takes longer to make its effect felt on the economy because of response lags. What is most important is the total lag between the time a problem first occurs and the time the corrective policies are felt.

response lag The time that it takes for the economy to adjust to the new conditions after a new policy is implemented; the lag that occurs because of the operation of the economy itself.

Response Lags for Fiscal Policy One way to think about the response lag in fiscal policy is through the government spending multiplier. This multiplier measures the change in GDP caused by a given change in government spending or net taxes. It takes time for the multiplier to reach its full value. The result is a lag between the time a fiscal policy action is initiated and the time the full change in GDP is realized.

The reason for the response lag in fiscal policy—the delay in the multiplier process—is simple. During the first few months after an increase in government spending or a tax cut, there is not enough time for the firms or individuals who benefit directly from the extra government spending or the tax cut to increase their own spending. Neither individuals nor firms revise their spending plans instantaneously. Until they can make those revisions, extra government spending does not stimulate extra private spending.

[1] Do not forget, however, about the existence of automatic stabilizers (Chapter 24). Many programs contain built-in counter-cyclical features that expand spending or cut tax collections automatically (without the need for congressional or executive action) during a recession.

ECONOMICS IN PRACTICE

Pearson Prentice Hall is committed to providing the most current content possible. Starting December 15, 2008, all printed Student Editions of **Case/Fair/Oster's** ninth edition will include this newly updated *Economics in Practice* content. You can view this updated content at www.pearsonhighered.com/case on November 20, 2008.

Changes in government purchases are a component of aggregate expenditure. When *G* rises, aggregate expenditure increases directly; when *G* falls, aggregate expenditure decreases directly. When personal taxes are changed, however, an additional step intervenes, giving rise to another lag. Suppose a tax cut has lowered personal income taxes across the board. Each household must decide what portion of its tax cut to spend and what portion to save. This decision is the extra step. Before the tax cut gets translated into extra spending, households must take the step of increasing their spending, which usually takes some time.

With a business tax cut, there is a further complication. Firms must decide what to do with their added after-tax profits. If they pay out their added profits to households as dividends, the result is the same as with a personal tax cut. Households must decide whether to spend or to save the extra funds. Firms may also retain their added profits and use them for investment, but investment is a component of aggregate expenditure that requires planning and time.

In practice, it takes about a year for a change in taxes or in government spending to have its full effect on the economy. This response lag means that if we increase spending to counteract a recession today, the full effects will not be felt for 12 months. By that time, the state of the economy might be very different.

Response Lags for Monetary Policy Monetary policy works by changing interest rates, which then change planned investment. Interest rates can also affect consumption spending, as we discuss further in Chapter 31. For now, it is enough to know that lower interest rates usually stimulate consumption spending and that higher interest rates decrease consumption spending.

The response of consumption and investment to interest rate changes takes time. Even if interest rates were to drop by 5 percent overnight, firms would not immediately increase their investment purchases. Firms generally make their investment plans several years in advance. If General Motors (GM) wants to respond to a decrease in interest rates by investing more, it will take time—perhaps up to a year—for the firm to come up with plans for a new factory or assembly line. While drawing up such plans, GM may spend little on new investments. The effect of the decrease in interest rates may not make itself felt for quite some time.

The response lags for monetary policy are even longer than response lags for fiscal policy. When government spending changes, there is a direct change in the sales of firms, which sell more as a result of the increased government purchases. When interest rates change, however, the sales of firms do not change until households change their consumption spending and/or firms change their investment spending. It takes time for households and firms to respond to interest rate changes. In this sense, interest rate changes are like tax-rate changes. The resulting change in firms' sales must wait for households and firms to change their purchases of goods.

Summary Stabilization is not easily achieved. It takes time for policy makers to recognize the existence of a problem, more time for them to implement a solution, and yet more time for firms and households to respond to the stabilization policies taken. Monetary policy can be adjusted more quickly and easily than taxes or government spending, making it a useful instrument in stabilizing the economy. However, because the economy's response to monetary changes is probably slower than its response to changes in fiscal policy, tax and spending changes may also play a useful role in macroeconomic management.

To end on a positive note, the Congress and the president responded quickly to the possibility of a recession in 2008, recognized in late 2007, by passing a stimulus package in February 2008 that began to go into effect in April 2008. The main part of the package was a tax rebate of about a $120 billion, with rebate checks starting in April. This was a very rapid fiscal policy response to an expected recession.

Fiscal Policy: Deficit Targeting

Every year from 2002 through 2008, the U.S. government ran a budget deficit. Despite the overall prosperity of the U.S. economy during most of this period, these persistent deficits worried a number of observers. In fact, during this recent period, as well as early periods of deficits, some policy makers suggested that the government focus on reducing the deficit as a central policy goal. What might the effects be on the overall economy of deficit targeting?

The deficit first emerged as a policy concern in the early 1980s, as you can see from Figure 24.6 on p. 484. In the 1980s the government was simply spending much more than it was receiving in taxes. When the deficit reached 4.7 percent of GDP in 1986, the U.S. Congress passed and President Reagan signed the **Gramm-Rudman-Hollings Act** (named for its three congressional sponsors), referred to as GRH.

Gramm-Rudman-Hollings Act Passed by the U.S. Congress and signed by President Reagan in 1986, this law set out to reduce the federal deficit by $36 billion per year, with a deficit of zero slated for 1991.

GRH set a target for reducing the federal deficit by a set amount each year. As Figure 30.3 shows, the deficit was to decline by $36 billion per year between 1987 and 1991, with a deficit of zero slated for fiscal year 1991. What was interesting about the GRH legislation was that the targets were not merely guidelines. If Congress, through its decisions about taxes and spending programs, produced a budget with a deficit larger than the targeted amount, GRH called for automatic spending cuts. The cuts were divided proportionately among most federal spending programs so that a program that made up 5 percent of total spending was to endure a cut equal to 5 percent of the total spending cut.[2]

[2] Programs such as Social Security were exempt from cuts or were treated differently. Interest payments on the federal debt were also immune from cuts.

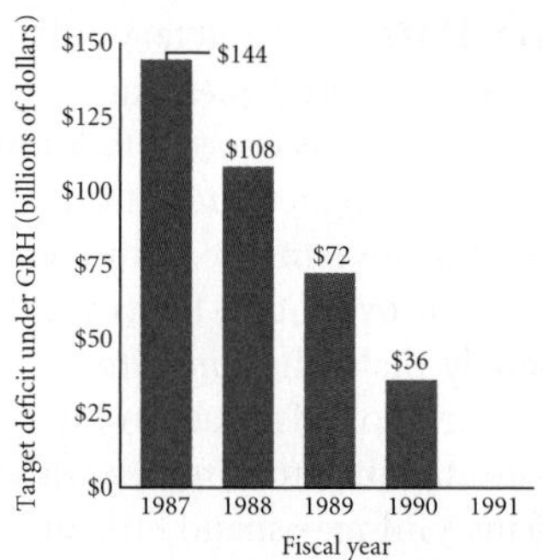

▶ **FIGURE 30.3**
Deficit Reduction Targets under Gramm-Rudman-Hollings
The GRH legislation, passed in 1986, set out to lower the federal deficit by $36 billion per year. If the plan had worked, a zero deficit would have been achieved by 1991.

In 1986, the U.S. Supreme Court declared part of the GRH bill unconstitutional. In effect, the Court said that Congress would have to approve the "automatic" spending cuts before they could take place. The law was changed in 1986 to meet the Supreme Court ruling and again in 1987, when new targets were established. The new targets had the deficit reaching zero in 1993 instead of 1991. The targets were revised again in 1991, when the year to achieve a zero deficit was changed from 1993 to 1996.

In practice, these targets never came close to being achieved. As time wore on, even the revised targets became completely unrealistic, and by the end of the 1980s, the GRH legislation was not taken seriously.

As Figure 24.6 on p. 484 shows, the deficit problem continued in the 1990s, and one of President Clinton's goals when he took office in 1993 was to reduce the deficit. The first step was the Omnibus Budget Reconciliation Act of 1993. The act, which barely made it through Congress, was projected to reduce the deficit in the 5 fiscal years 1994 to 1998 by $504.8 billion—$254.7 billion would come from cuts in federal spending, and $250.1 billion would come from tax increases. Most of the tax increases were levied on high-income taxpayers.

There was also some sentiment in the mid-1990s for the passage of a *balanced-budget amendment*, intended to prevent Congress from doing what it did in the 1980s. The balanced-budget amendment passed the House in early 1995, but it failed by one vote in the Senate. It turned out that the passage of the Omnibus Budget Reconciliation Act of 1993 and a robust economy were enough to lead to a balanced budget by 1998. You can see from Figure 24.6 that by 2000, there was a large budget surplus. Between 1998 and 2001, the federal government was in the process of paying off its debt and there was talk that the debt would be completely paid off. The surplus turned to deficit in 2002, however; and the federal government began again to worry about deficits. As we think about current deficits, it is thus useful to review the approach that the government considered in the late 1980s and early 1990s to cope with the deficit problem, namely the GRH legislation and the balanced-budget amendment. In addition to its policy relevance, this material is a great learning tool. If you understand the macroeconomic consequences of the GRH legislation and the balanced-budget amendment, you have come a long way toward being a macroeconomist.

The Effects of Spending Cuts on the Deficit

Suppose the terms of the balanced-budget amendment or some other deficit-reduction measure dictate that the deficit must be cut by $20 billion. By how much must government spending be cut to achieve this goal? You might be tempted to think the spending cuts should add up to the amount the deficit is to be cut—$20 billion. (This is what GRH dictated: If the deficit needed to be cut by a certain amount, automatic spending cuts were to be equal to that amount.) This approach seems reasonable. If you decrease your personal spending by $100 over a year, your personal deficit will fall by the full $100 of your spending cut.

However, the government is not an individual household. A cut in government spending shifts the *AD* curve to the left and results in a decrease in aggregate output (income) (*Y*) and a contraction in the economy. When the economy contracts, both the taxable income of households and the profits of firms fall. This effect means in turn that revenue from the personal income tax and the corporate profits tax will fall.

How do these events affect the size of the deficit? To estimate the response of the deficit to changes in government spending, we need to go through two steps. First, we must decide how much a $1 change in government spending will change GDP. That means we need to know the size of the government spending multiplier. ((Recall that the government spending multiplier measures the increase (or decrease) in GDP (Y) brought about by a $1 increase (or decrease) in government spending.)) Based on empirical evidence, a reasonable value for the government spending multiplier seems to be around 1.4 after 1 year, and this is the value we will use. A $1 billion decrease in government spending lowers GDP by about $1.4 billion after 1 year.

Next, we must see what happens to the deficit when GDP changes. We have just noted that when GDP falls—the economy contracts—taxable income and corporate profits fall, so tax revenues fall. In addition, some categories of government expenditures tend to rise when the economy contracts. For example, unemployment insurance benefits (a transfer payment) rise as the economy contracts because more people become unemployed and eligible for benefits. Both the decrease in tax revenues and the rise in government expenditures cause the deficit to increase. The deficit tends to rise when GDP falls and tends to fall when GDP rises.

The **deficit response index (DRI)** is the amount by which the deficit changes with a $1 change in GDP. Assume that the DRI is −.22. That is, for every $1 billion decrease in GDP, the deficit rises by $.22 billion. This number seems close to what is true in practice. We can now use the multiplier and the DRI to answer the question that began this section. Suppose government spending is reduced by $20 billion, the exact amount of the necessary deficit reduction. This will lower GDP by 1.4 × $20 billion, or $28 billion, if the value of the multiplier is 1.4. A $28 billion fall in GDP will increase the deficit by .22 × $28 billion, or $6.2 billion, if the value of the DRI is −.22. Because we initially cut government spending (and therefore lowered the deficit from this source) by $20 billion, the net effect of the spending cut is to lower the deficit by $20 billion − $6.2 billion = $13.8 billion.

deficit response index (DRI) The amount by which the deficit changes with a $1 change in GDP.

A $20 billion government spending cut does not lower the deficit by $20 billion. To lower the deficit by $20 billion, we need to cut government spending by about $30 billion. By using 1.4 as the value of the government spending multiplier and −.22 as the value of the DRI, we see that a spending cut of $30 billion lowers GDP by 1.4 × $30 billion, or $42 billion. This raises the deficit by .22 × $42 billion, or $9.2 billion. The net effect on the deficit is −$30 billion (from the government spending cut) + $9.2 billion, which is −$20.8 billion (slightly larger than the necessary $20 billion reduction). This means that the spending cut must be nearly 50 percent larger than the deficit reduction we want to achieve. Congress would have had trouble achieving the deficit targets under the GRH legislation even if it had allowed GRH's automatic spending cuts to take place.

Monetary Policy to the Rescue? Was Congress so poorly informed about macroeconomics that it would pass legislation that could not possibly work? In other words, are there any conditions under which it would be reasonable to assume that a spending cut needs to be only as large as the desired reduction in the deficit? If the government spending multiplier is zero, government spending cuts will not contract the economy and the cut in the deficit will be equal to the cut in government spending.

Could the government spending multiplier ever be zero? Before the GRH bill was passed, some argued that it could. The argument went as follows: If households and firms are worried about the large government deficits and hold back on consumption and investment because of these worries, the passage of GRH might make them more optimistic and induce them to consume and invest more. This increased consumption and investment would offset the effects of the decreased government spending, and the net result would be a multiplier effect of zero.

Another argument in favor of the GRH bill centered on the Fed and monetary policy. We know that an expansionary monetary policy shifts the AD curve to the right. Because a cut in government spending shifts the AD curve to the left, the Fed could respond to the spending cut enough to shift the AD curve back (to the right) to its original position, preventing any change in aggregate output (income). Some argued the Fed would behave this way after the passage of the GRH bill because it would see that Congress finally "got its house in order."

How large would the interest rate cuts have to be to offset the decrease in G completely, thus resulting in a multiplier of zero? Studies at the time of the original GRH bill showed that the decrease in the interest rate that would be necessary for a multiplier of zero—that is, for a government spending cut to have no effect on aggregate output (income)—is quite large. The Fed would have had to engage in extreme behavior with respect to interest rate changes for the multiplier to be zero. A zero multiplier can come about through renewed optimism on the part of households and firms or through very aggressive behavior on the part of the Fed, but because neither of these situations is very plausible, the multiplier is likely to be greater than zero. Thus, it is likely that to lower the deficit by a certain amount, the cut in government spending must be larger than that amount.

Economic Stability and Deficit Reduction

So lowering the deficit by a given amount is likely to require a government spending decrease larger than this amount. However, this is not the only point to learn from our analysis of deficit targeting. We will now show how deficit targeting can adversely affect the way the economy responds to a variety of stimuli.

In a world with no GRH, no balanced-budget amendment, and no similar deficit-targeting measure, the Congress and the president make decisions each year about how much to spend and how much to tax. The federal government deficit is a result of these decisions and the state of the economy. However, with GRH or the balanced-budget amendment, the size of the deficit is set in advance. Taxes and government spending must be adjusted to produce the required deficit. In this situation, the deficit is no longer a consequence of the tax and spending decisions. Instead, taxes and spending become a consequence of the deficit decision.

What difference does it make whether Congress chooses a target deficit and adjusts government spending and taxes to achieve that target or decides how much to spend and tax and lets the deficit adjust itself? The difference may be substantial. Consider a leftward shift of the *AD* curve caused by some negative demand shock. A **negative demand shock** is something that causes a negative shift in consumption or investment schedules or that leads to a decrease in U.S. exports.

negative demand shock Something that causes a negative shift in consumption or investment schedules or that leads to a decrease in U.S. exports.

We know that a leftward shift of the *AD* curve lowers aggregate output (income), which causes the government deficit to increase. In a world without deficit targeting, the increase in the deficit during contractions provides an **automatic stabilizer** for the economy. (Review Chapter 24 if this point is hazy.) The contraction-induced decrease in tax revenues and increase in transfer payments tend to reduce the fall in after-tax income and consumer spending due to the negative demand shock. Thus, the decrease in aggregate output (income) caused by the negative demand shock is lessened somewhat by the growth of the deficit [Figure 30.4(a)].

automatic stabilizers Revenue and expenditure items in the federal budget that automatically change with the economy in such a way as to stabilize GDP.

In a world with deficit targeting, the deficit is not allowed to rise. Some combination of tax increases and government spending cuts would be needed to offset what would have otherwise been an increase in the deficit. We know that increases in taxes or cuts in spending are contractionary in themselves. The contraction in the economy will therefore be larger than it would have been without deficit targeting because the initial effect of the negative demand shock is worsened by the rise in taxes or the cut in government spending required to keep the deficit from rising. As Figure 30.4(b) shows, deficit targeting acts as an **automatic destabilizer**. It requires taxes to be raised and government spending to be cut during a contraction. This reinforces, rather than counteracts, the shock that started the contraction.

automatic destabilizers Revenue and expenditure items in the federal budget that automatically change with the economy in such a way as to destabilize GDP.

FIGURE 30.4
Deficit Targeting as an Automatic Destabilizer
Deficit targeting changes the way the economy responds to negative demand shocks because it does not allow the deficit to increase. The result is a smaller deficit but a larger decline in income than would have otherwise occurred.

a. Without Deficit Targeting

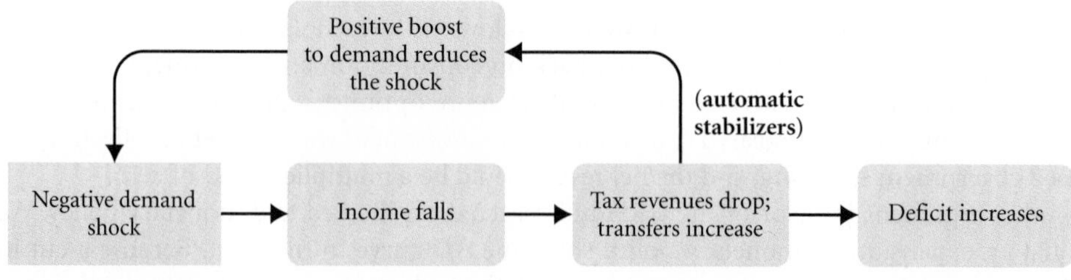

b. With Deficit Targeting

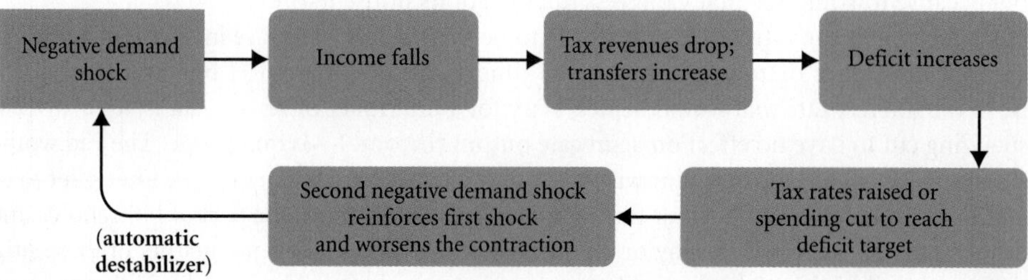

Summary

It is clear that the GRH legislation, the balanced-budget amendment, and similar deficit targeting measures have some undesirable macroeconomic consequences. Deficit targeting requires cuts in spending or increases in taxes at times when the economy is already experiencing problems. This drawback does not mean that Congress should ignore deficits when they arise. Instead, it means that locking the economy into spending cuts during periods of negative demand shocks, as deficit-targeting measures do, is not a good way to manage the economy.

The Stock Market and the Economy

Introductory macroeconomic texts written a decade ago could more or less ignore the stock market. The effects of the stock market on the macroeconomy were small enough to be put aside in introductory discussions. This changed in the 1990s. We will see that the stock market boom that began in 1995 had a large impact on the economy. The economy grew well in the last half of the 1990s, and many came to believe in the existence of a new economy or a "new age." How much of the growth in the last half of the 1990s was due to the stock market boom? Did the economy in fact enter a new age? We try to answer those questions in this section.

Stocks and Bonds

It will be useful to begin by briefly discussing the three main ways in which firms borrow or raise money to finance their investments. How do firms use financial markets in practice?

When a firm wants to make a large purchase to build a new factory or buy machines, it often cannot pay for the purchase out of its own funds. In this case, it must "finance" the investment. One way to do this is to borrow from a bank. The bank loans the money to the firm, the firms uses the money to buy the factory or machine, and the firm pays back the loan (with interest) to the bank over time.

Another possible way for a firm to borrow money is for the firm to issue a bond. If you buy a bond from a firm, you are making a loan to the firm. Bonds were discussed at the beginning of Chapter 26.

A third way for a firm to finance an investment is for it to issue additional shares of **stock**. When a firm issues new shares of stock, it does not add to its debt. Instead, it brings in additional owners of the firm, owners who agree to supply it with funds. Such owners are treated differently than bondholders, who are owed the amount they have loaned.

stock A certificate that certifies ownership of a certain portion of a firm.

A share of common stock is a certificate that represents the ownership of a share of a business, almost always a corporation. For example, Lincoln Electric is a Cleveland-based company that makes welding and cutting equipment. The company has 41 million shares of common stock that are owned by tens of thousands of shareholders, some of whom are simply private individuals, some of whom are institutions such as Carleton College, and some of whom may be employees of the firm. Shareholders are entitled to a share of the company's profit. When profits are paid directly to shareholders, the payment is called a *dividend*. In a recent year, Lincoln Electric made a profit of $54 million, which was $1.31 per share, of which $0.43 was paid out to shareholders as dividends and the rest was retained for investment.

Stockholders who own stocks that increase in value earn what are called **capital gains**. **Realized capital gains** (or losses) are increases (or decreases) in the value of assets, including stocks, that households receive when they actually sell those assets. The government considers realized capital gains net of losses to be income, although their treatment under the tax code has been very complex and subject to change every few years. The total return that an owner of a share of stock receives is the sum of the dividends received and the capital gain or loss.

capital gain An increase in the value of an asset.

realized capital gain The gain that occurs when the owner of an asset actually sells it for more than he or she paid for it.

Determining the Price of a Stock

What determines the price of a stock? If a share of stock is selling for $25, why is someone willing to pay that much for it? As we have noted, when you buy a share of stock, you own part of the firm. If a firm is making profits, it may be paying dividends to its shareholders. If it is not paying dividends but is making profits, people may expect that it will pay dividends in the future. Dividends are important in thinking about stocks because dividends are the form in which shareholders receive income from the firm. So one thing that is likely to affect the price of a stock is what people expect its future dividends will be. The larger the expected future dividends, the larger the current stock price, other things being equal.

Another important consideration in thinking about the price of a stock is the time the dividends are expected to be paid. A $2 per share dividend that is expected to be paid 4 years from now is worth less than a $2 per share dividend that is expected to be paid next year. In other words, the farther into the future the dividend is expected to be paid, the more it will be "discounted." The amount by which expected future dividends are discounted depends on the interest rate. The larger the interest rate, the more expected future dividends will be discounted. If the interest rate is 10 percent, I can invest $100 today and receive $110 a year from now. I am thus willing to pay $100 today to someone who will pay me $110 in a year. If instead, the interest rate were only 5 percent, I would be willing to pay $104.76 today to receive $110 a year from now because the alternative of $104.76 today at a 5 percent interest rate also yields $110.00 at the end of the year. I am thus willing to pay more for the promise of $110 a year from now when the interest rate is lower. In other words, I "discount" the $110 less when the interest rate is lower.

Another discount factor aside from the interest rate must be taken into account; it is the discount for risk. People prefer certain outcomes to uncertain ones for the same expected values. For example, I prefer a certain $50 over a bet in which there is a 50 percent chance I will get $100 and a 50 percent chance I will get nothing. The expected value of the bet is $50, but I prefer the certain $50 over the bet, where there is a 50 percent chance that I will end up with nothing. The same reasoning holds for future dividends. If, say, I expect dividends for both firms A and B to be $2 per share next year but firm B has a much wider range of possibilities (is riskier), I will prefer firm A. Put another way, I will "discount" firm B's expected future dividends more than firm A's because the outcome for firm B is more uncertain.

We can thus say that the price of a stock should equal the discounted value of its expected future dividends, where the discount factors depend on the interest rate and risk. If for some reason (say, a positive surprise news announcement from the firm) expected future dividends increase, this development should lead to an increase in the price of the stock. If the interest rate falls, this decrease should also lead to a stock price increase. Finally, if the perceived risk of a firm falls, this perception should increase the firm's stock price.

Some stock analysts talk about the possibility of stock market "bubbles." Given the preceding discussion, what might a bubble be? Assume that given your expectations about the future dividends of a firm and given the discount rate, you value the firm's stock at $20 per share. Is there any case in which you would pay more than $20 for a share? You can, of course, buy the stock and sell it later; you don't need to hold the stock forever. If the stock is currently selling for $25, which is above your value of $20, but you think that the stock will rise to $30 in the next few months, you might buy it now in anticipation of selling it later for a higher price. If others have similar views, the price of the stock may be driven up.

In this case, what counts is not the discounted value of expected future dividends, but rather your view of what others will pay for the stock in the future. If everyone expects that everyone else expects that the price will be driven up, the price may be driven up. One might call this outcome a bubble because the stock price depends on what people expect that other people expect and so on.

When a firm's stock price has risen rapidly, it is difficult to know whether the reason is that people have increased their expectations of the firm's future dividends or that there is a bubble. Because people's expectations of future dividends are not directly observed, it is hard to test alternative theories.

Dow Jones Industrial Average An index based on the stock prices of 30 actively traded large companies. The oldest and most widely followed index of stock market performance.

NASDAQ Composite An index based on the stock prices of over 5,000 companies traded on the NASDAQ Stock Market. The NASDAQ market takes its name from the National Association of Securities Dealers Automated Quotation System.

Standard and Poor's 500 (S&P 500) An index based on the stock prices of 500 of the largest firms by market value.

The Stock Market Since 1948

If you follow the stock market at all, you know that much attention is paid to two stock price indices: the **Dow Jones Industrial Average** and the **NASDAQ Composite**. From a macroeconomic perspective, however, these two indices cover too small a sample of firms. One would like an index that includes firms whose total market value is close to the market value of all firms in the economy. For this purpose a much better measure is the **Standard and Poor's 500** stock price index, called the **S&P 500**. This index includes most of the companies in the economy by market value.

The S&P 500 index is plotted in Figure 30.5 for 1948 I–2007 IV. What perhaps stands out most in this plot is the huge increase in the index between 1995 and 2000. Between December 31, 1994, and March 31, 2000, the S&P 500 index rose 226 percent, an annual rate of increase of 25 percent.

This is by far the largest stock market boom in U.S. history, completely dominating the boom of the 1920s. This boom added roughly $14 trillion to household wealth, about $2.5 trillion per year.

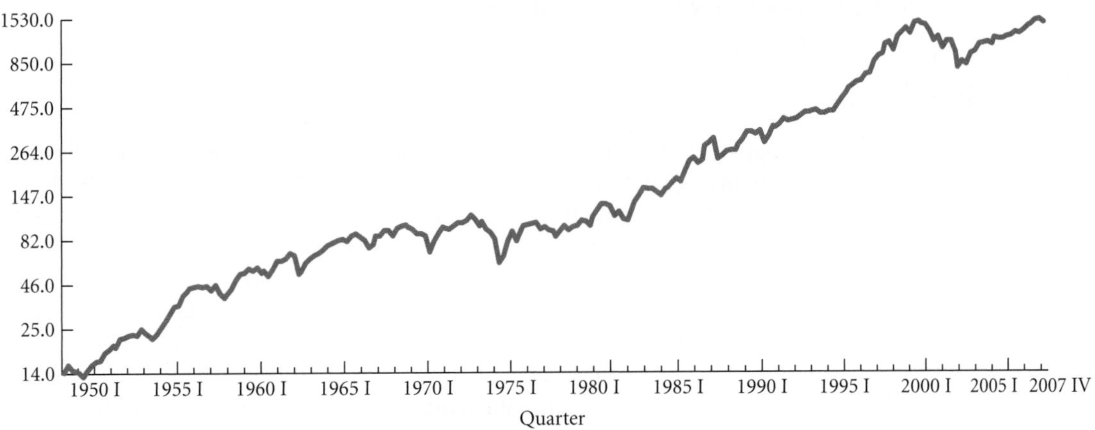

▲ **FIGURE 30.5 The S&P 500 Stock Price Index, 1948 I–2007 IV**

What caused this boom? You can see from Figure 28.13 on p. 566 that interest rates did not change much in the last half of the 1990s, so the boom cannot be explained by any large fall in interest rates. Perhaps profits rose substantially during this period, and this growth led to a large increase in expected future dividends? We know from the preceding discussion that if expected future dividends increase, stock prices should increase. Figure 30.6 plots for 1948 I–2007 IV the ratio of after-tax profits to GDP. It is clear from the figure that nothing unusual happened in the last half of the 1990s. The share of after-tax profits in GDP rose from the middle of 1995 to the middle of 1997, but then generally fell after that through 2000. Thus, there does not appear to be any surge of profits that would have led people to expect much higher future dividends.

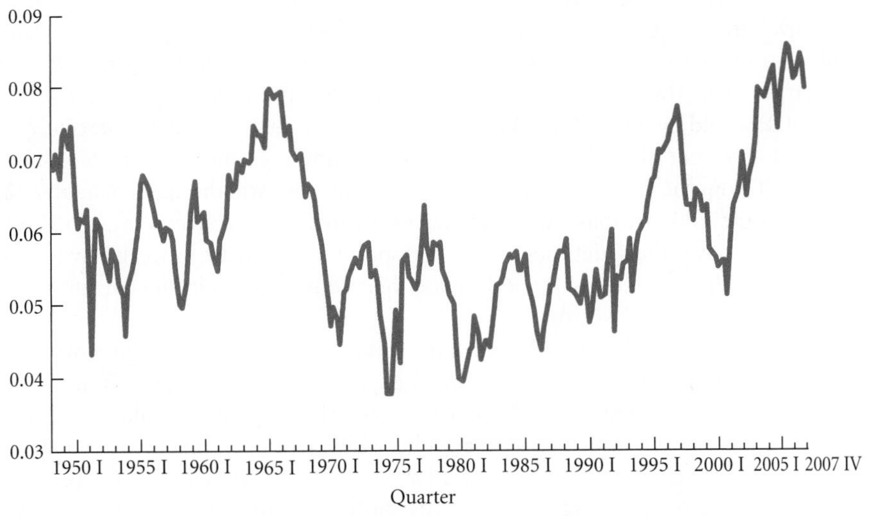

◀ **FIGURE 30.6 Ratio of After-Tax Profits to GDP, 1948 I–2007 IV**

It could be that the perceived riskiness of stocks fell in the last half of the 1990s. This change would have led to smaller discount rates for stocks and thus, other things being equal, to higher stock prices. Although this possibility cannot be completely ruled out, there is no strong independent evidence that perceived riskiness fell.

The stock market boom is thus a puzzle, and many people speculate that it was simply a bubble. For some reason, stock prices started rising rapidly in 1995 and people expected that other people expected that prices would continue to rise. This led stock prices to rise further, thus fulfilling the expectations, which led to expectations of further increases, and so on. Bubble believers note that once stock prices started falling in 2000, they fell a great deal. It is not the case that stock prices just leveled out in 2000; they fell rapidly. People of the bubble view argue that this is simply the bubble bursting.

Remember that we are talking about the S&P 500 index, which includes most of the firms in the U.S. economy by market value. We are not just talking about a few dot-com companies. The entire stock market went up by 25 percent per year for 5 years! We will see in the next section the effects of this increase in wealth on the economy.

Stock Market Effects on the Economy

We mentioned in Chapter 23 that one of the factors that affects consumption expenditures is wealth. Other things being equal, the more wealth a family has, the more it spends. We discuss this in detail in the next chapter, but all we need for now is to note that an increase in wealth increases consumer spending. An increase in stock prices may also affect investment. If a firm is considering an investment project, one way in which it can finance the project is to issue additional shares of stock. The higher the price of the firm's stock, the more money it can get per additional share. A firm is thus likely to undertake more investment projects the higher its stock price. The cost of an investment project in terms of shares of stock is smaller the higher the price of the stock. This is the way in which a stock market boom may increase investment.

The effect of the stock market on the economy is thus fairly straightforward. If stock prices increase, the wealth of households increases, as in turn does consumer spending. Investment also increases because firms can raise more money per share to finance investment projects. As a rough rule of thumb, a $1.00 change in the value of stocks leads to about a $0.03 to $0.04 change in consumer and investor spending per year. We will use the $0.04 number in the following discussion.

The Crash of October 1987 Before considering the boom of the late 1990s, it is useful to review a crash—namely, the crash of October 1987. The value of stocks in the United States fell by about a trillion dollars between August 1987 and the end of October 1987. In one day—October 19, 1987—the value of stocks fell nearly $700 billion. If we assume that a $1.00 decrease in stock prices results in a $0.04 decrease in consumer and investor spending per year, we can see that the $1 trillion decrease in wealth in 1987 implies a $40 billion lower level of spending in 1988. The level of gross domestic product (GDP) was around $4 trillion in 1987, so a $40 billion decrease in spending is around 1.0 percent of GDP. A multiplier effect would also be at work here. A decrease in spending leads to a decrease in aggregate output (income), which leads to a further decrease in spending and so on. The total decrease in GDP would be somewhat larger than the initial decrease of $40 billion. If the multiplier is 1.4, the total decrease in GDP would be about 1.4 × $40 billion = $56 billion, or about 1.4 percent of GDP.

Although 1.4 percent of GDP is a large amount, it is not large enough to imply that a recession would result from the crash. The life-cycle theory, which we will discuss in Chapter 32, helps explain why. If households are making lifetime decisions and want to have as smooth a consumption path as possible over their lifetimes, they will respond to a decrease in wealth by cutting consumption a little each year. They will *not* decrease their consumption in the current year by the full amount of the decrease in wealth.

Why were people predicting that the economy would go into a recession, or worse, a depression, after the crash? The reasons all pertain to expectations. If households and firms had expected the economy to contract sharply after the crash, they probably would have cut back on consumption and investment much more than otherwise. (This reaction would be Keynes's animal spirits at work.) These expectations would have become self-fulfilling in the sense that the economy would have gone into a recession because of the cuts in consumption and investment brought about by lowered expectations.

However, the economy did not go into a recession in 1988. Expectations were not changed drastically following the crash. The Fed helped out by easing monetary policy right after the crash to counteract any large negative reaction. The 3-month Treasury bill rate fell from 6.4 percent to 5.8 percent between October and November 1987. In addition, the value of stocks gradually increased over time to their earlier levels. Because the initial decrease in wealth turned out to be temporary, the negative wealth effect was not nearly as large as it otherwise would have been.

The Boom of 1995–2000 We pointed out earlier that between 1995 and 2000, the value of stocks increased about $2.5 trillion per year. If we assume that a $1.00 increase in stock prices results in a $0.04 increase in consumption and investment per year and if we use a multiplier of 1.4, the added increase in spending is .04 × $2.5 trillion × 1.4, which is $140 billion per year. In 1998, GDP was around $9 trillion, and so an increase of $140 billion is 1.5 percent of GDP.

The annual growth rate of GDP from the end of 1995 to the middle of 2000 was 4.5 percent. The preceding numbers thus suggest that about 1.5 of the 4.5 percent was due to the stock market boom. In other words, had there been no boom, the growth rate would likely have been around 3.0 percent instead of 4.5 percent. Households simply spent much more than they would have had there been no huge increase in their wealth, and firms invested much more than they would have had stock prices not risen so much.

A more detailed analysis of the effects of the stock market boom on the economy is presented in Figure 30.7–30.13. This analysis uses a model of the economy[3] to see what the economy would have been like had there been no stock market boom. In each figure, the "actual" line represents the actual values of the variable over the 1995 I–2002 III period. These values reflect the stock market boom (because the boom actually took place!). The "no boom" line represents the values that the model estimates would have taken place had overall stock prices simply grown at a normal rate. In the no boom case, there was neither the huge increase in stock prices between 1995 and 2000 nor the large fall in prices from 2000 on.

The plots in the seven figures are interesting. They show that had there been no stock market boom, the U.S. economy would not have looked unusual in the last half of the 1990s. There would have been no talk of a "new economy" or a "new age." It would have been more or less business as usual. We will now discuss the figures one by one. Given what you have learned so far about macroeconomics, you should be able to understand the reasons for the various results.

Figure 30.7 shows that the personal saving rate is considerably higher in the no boom case. No longer are the values below the range of historical experience. This is the wealth effect on consumption at work. With no huge increase in wealth, households consume less.

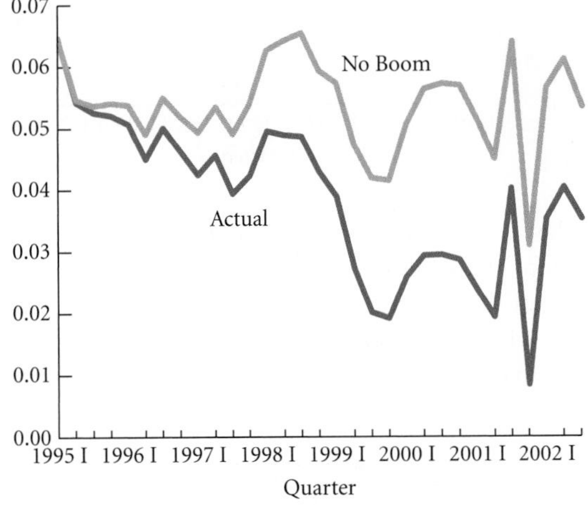

FIGURE 30.7 Personal Saving Rate, 1995 I–2002 III

Figure 30.8 shows that investment also is less in the no boom case. Firms invest less in plant and equipment because the cost to them in terms of extra shares issued is higher (the price per share is lower). Many people believe that investment was excessively high in the late 1990s, a phenomenon that led to the large falls in 2000 and 2001. Figure 30.8 shows that much of this would not have happened had there been no stock market boom.

[3] Ray C. Fair, *Estimating How the Macroeconomy Works* (Cambridge, MA: Harvard University Press, 2004).

▶ **FIGURE 30.8**
Investment-Output Ratio, 1995 I–2002 III

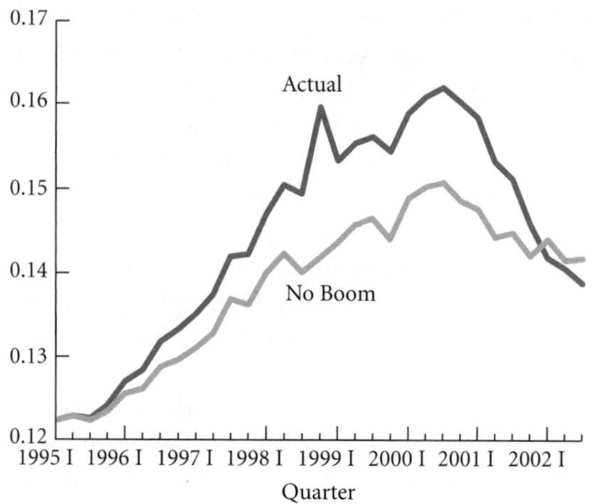

Figure 30.9 shows that the federal government surplus would not have been as high in the late 1990s and in 2000 were it not for the stock market boom. It should be clear why this is the case. In the no boom case, taxable income and profits are less, and so there is less tax revenue. Also, spending on unemployment benefits is greater because (as we will see) unemployment is higher.

▶ **FIGURE 30.9**
Ratio of Federal Government Budget Surplus to GDP, 1995 I–2002 III

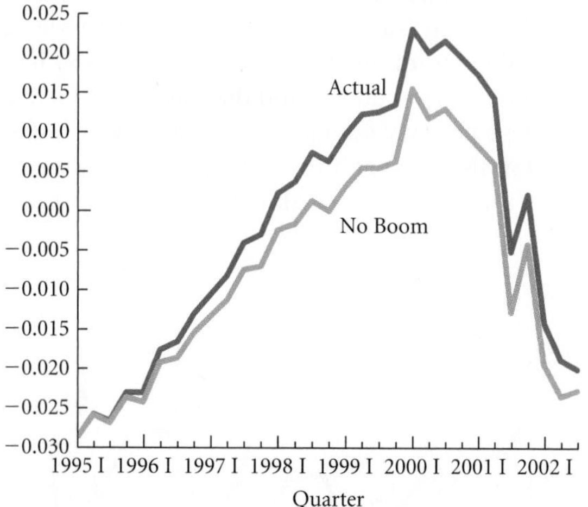

Figure 30.10 shows that real growth was higher in the last half of the 1990s than would have been the case with no boom. This figure gives a more accurate impression of the growth rate effects than the simple use of the 4 percent wealth spending response and the 1.4 multiplier on p. 600. Note from Figure 30.10 that the growth rate is higher in the no boom case in 2001 and 2002 because in the no boom case, there is no large stock market correction in these two years.

▶ **FIGURE 30.10**
Growth Rate of Real GDP, 1995 I–2002 III

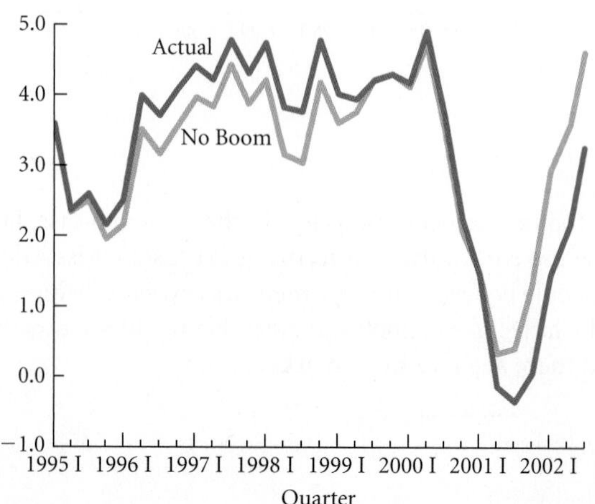

Figure 30.11 shows that the fall in the unemployment rate in the last half of the 1990s to 4 percent from 5.5 percent was due to the stock market boom. Had there been no boom, the unemployment rate would have remained at about 5.5 percent.

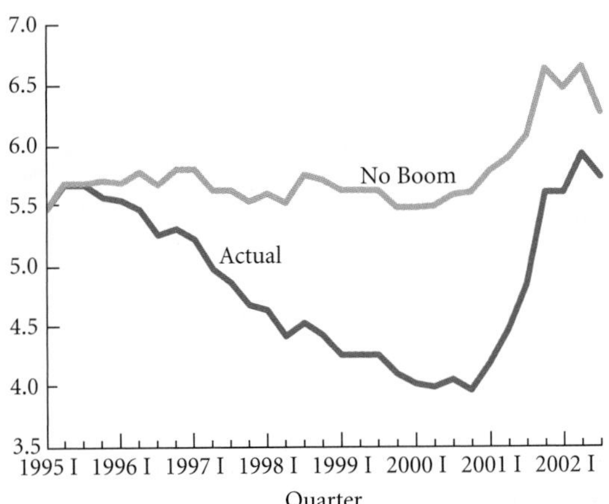

FIGURE 30.11
The Unemployment Rate, 1995 I–2002 III

Figure 30.12 shows that inflation would have been lower in the no boom case. The simple reason is that output would have been lower and thus demand pressure would have been less. In either case, however, the inflation rate is not high by historical standards.

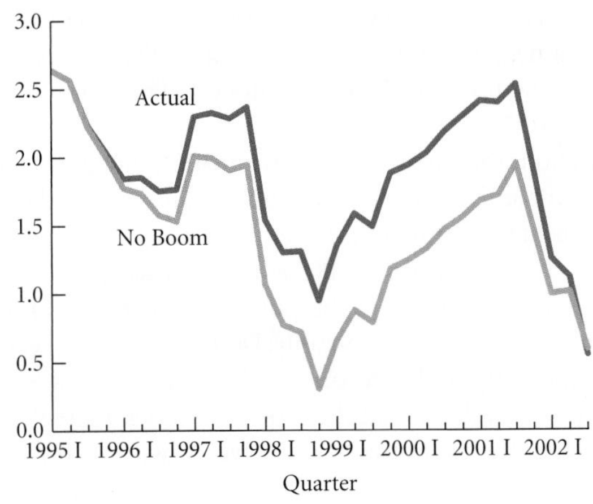

FIGURE 30.12
Inflation Rate, 1995 I–2002 III

Finally, Figure 30.13 plots the 3-month Treasury bill rate. Remember from the last chapter that this rate reflects the behavior of the Fed. The Fed essentially decides each 6 weeks what it wants the rate to be and uses open market operations to achieve this value. The figure shows that the interest rate would have been lower in the last half of the 1990s had there been no boom. This should make sense from the last chapter. Without the boom, real growth would have been lower and the unemployment rate higher and the Fed would have responded with lower interest rates.

Fed Policy and the Stock Market Figure 30.13 is useful for thinking about how Fed policy is related to the stock market. Policy questions arise from time to time as to whether the Fed should be influenced by the stock market. Should the Fed try to influence stock prices by changing interest rates? Figure 30.13 says that the Fed is in fact influenced by the stock market. The Fed kept the interest rate higher than it would have had there been no stock market boom. It should be clear why this is the case. If ultimately the Fed cares about output, unemployment, and inflation and if the stock market affects these variables, the Fed will be indirectly affected by the stock market. In other words, the Fed cares about the stock market to the extent that the stock market affects the things that it ultimately cares about—namely, output, unemployment, and inflation.

▶ FIGURE 30.13
3-Month Treasury Bill Rate, 1995 I–2002 III

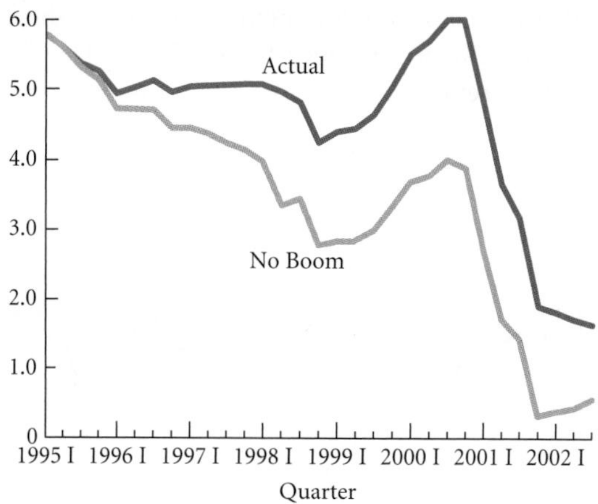

The Post-Boom Economy Figure 30.5 shows that there was a fairly large fall in stock prices between the fourth quarter of 2000 and the third quarter of 2002. In this period, the fall in household wealth from the stock market was about $7 trillion. We mentioned earlier that the stock market boom in the last half of the 1990s added about $14 trillion to household wealth, and so about half of this increase was reversed in the 2000 IV–2002 III period.

Given that the stock market boom in the last half of the 1990s led to a more expansionary economy than would otherwise have been the case, it seems likely that the stock market correction in 2000–2002 led to a less expansionary economy. This is in fact the case: The $7 trillion fall in household wealth had a negative effect on the economy. There were two quarters of negative growth in 2001, and the growth rate in 2002 was modest. The economy did not begin growing well again until the middle of 2003.

What is remarkable about the sluggish economy in 2001 and 2002 is that it came at a time of very expansionary monetary and fiscal policy. Figure 28.13 on p. 566 shows that the Fed lowered the bill rate by over 4 percentage points in this period, perhaps the most expansionary policy in its history. Figures 24.4 and 24.5 on pp. 483–484 show that fiscal policy was also very expansionary. Tax rates were lowered substantially in the Bush administration and government spending and transfer payments were increased considerably. Despite these huge expansionary policies, the economy did not do particularly well, and one of the main reasons was the fall in household wealth from the stock market decline. Had there been no stock market correction but the same monetary and fiscal policies, the economy would have grown much more rapidly in 2001 and 2002 than it in fact did.

The importance of the stock market in the economy should now be clear. It played a big role in the economic boom of the last half of the 1990s and in the economic slack of 2000–2002. This is why introductory macroeconomic texts can no longer ignore the stock market.

A final point that is interesting about the post-boom U.S. economy is the role that housing values played from 2003 through 2005. The stock market began to recover in this period, as can be seen from Figure 30.5 on p. 599, but perhaps more important, the housing market boomed. Many homeowners saw the value of their homes soar. Many responded to this rise by taking out "home equity" loans, which were available at low interest rates, and increasing their spending on consumer goods and services. Consumption was thus stimulated by this increase in housing wealth, which helped fuel the recovery. So both stock market wealth and housing wealth have important effects on the economy.

Some believed by 2005 that a housing bubble was just waiting to be burst. Would housing prices continue to increase or at least not fall? Or was the economy in for a large and rapid fall in prices, as had occurred in the stock market a few years earlier? In fact, in 2006 there began to be a large correction in housing prices, with prices falling in many parts of the country. This had serious repercussions on the mortgage market and by the end of 2007 on real output growth. So this is another example where housing wealth (in this case, the fall in housing wealth from the fall in house prices) has important effects on the economy.

ECONOMICS IN PRACTICE

Bubbles or Rational Investors?

We discussed in the text that the huge increase in U.S. stock prices in the last half of the 1990s is a puzzle. So also is the huge increase in U.S. housing prices between 2002 and 2006. Recently, many other countries also have seen large increases in asset prices. An interesting question is whether these rapid run-ups in prices are bubbles, generated by irrational consumers and investors, or are instead the result of actions of rational investors that simply turned out with hindsight to be wrong. This question is of interest to both academics and policy makers. A key policy question is whether the Fed should ignore asset prices or try to use interest rates to control them. The following article discusses some research that is currently being done on bubbles and its implications for Fed behavior.

Bernanke's Bubble Laboratory: Princeton Protégés of Fed Chief Study the Economics of Manias

Wall Street Journal

PRINCETON, N.J.—First came that tech-stock bubble. Then there were bubbles in housing and credit. Chinese stocks took off like a rocket. Now, as prices soar on every material from oil to corn, some suggest there's a bubble in commodities.

But how and why do bubbles form? Economists traditionally haven't offered much insight. From World War II till the mid-1990s, there weren't many U.S. investing manias for them to look at. The study of bubbles was left to economic historians sifting through musty records of 17th-century Dutch tulip-bulb prices and the like.

The dot-com boom began to change that. "You were seeing live, in action, the unfolding of lots of examples of valuations disconnecting from fundamentals," says Princeton economist Harrison Hong. Now, the study of financial bubbles is hot.

Its hub is Princeton, 40 miles south of Wall Street, home to a band of young scholars hired by former professor Ben Bernanke, now the nation's chief bubble watcher as Federal Reserve chairman. The group includes Mr. Hong, a Vietnam native raised in Silicon Valley; a Chinese wunderkind who started as a physicist [Wei Xiong]; and a German who'd been groomed to take over the family carpentry business [Markus Brunnermeier]. Among their conclusions:

Bubbles emerge at times when investors profoundly disagree about the significance of a big economic development, such as the birth of the Internet. Because it's so much harder to bet on prices going down than up, the bullish investors dominate.

Once they get going, financial bubbles are marked by huge increases in trading, making them easier to identify.

Manias can persist even though many smart people suspect a bubble, because no one of them has the firepower to successfully attack it. Only when skeptical investors act simultaneously—a moment impossible to predict—does the bubble pop.

As a result of all that and more, the Princeton squad argues that the Fed can and should try to restrain bubbles, rather than following former Chairman Alan Greenspan's approach: watchful waiting while prices rise and then cleaning up the mess after a bubble bursts.

If the tech-stock collapse didn't make that clear, the damage done by the housing and credit bubbles should, argues José Scheinkman, 60 years old, a theorist Mr. Bernanke recruited in 1999 from the University of Chicago. "Advanced economies are very dependent on the health of the financial system. What this bubble did was destroy the capacity of the financial system to finance the U.S. economy," Mr. Scheinkman says.

The Fed is giving the activist approach some thought. In a speech scheduled for delivery Thursday night, Fed Governor Frederic Mishkin suggested that while it was inappropriate to use the blunt instrument of interest-rate increases to prick bubbles, if too-easy credit appeared to be fueling a mania, policy makers might craft a regulatory response that could "help reduce the magnitude of the bubble."

Yet the very concept of bubbles is at odds with the view of some that market prices reflect the collective knowledge of multitudes. There are economists who dispute the existence of bubbles—arguing, for instance, that what happened to prices in the dot-com boom was a rational response to the possibility that nascent Internet firms might turn into Microsofts. But these economists' numbers are thinning.

Source: Justin Lahart, May 16, 2008

SUMMARY

TIME LAGS REGARDING MONETARY AND FISCAL POLICY *p. 589*

1. *Stabilization policy* describes both fiscal and monetary policy, the goals of which are to smooth out fluctuations in output and employment and to keep prices as stable as possible. Stabilization goals are not necessarily easy to achieve because of the existence of certain *time lags*, or delays in the response of the economy to macroeconomic policies.
2. A *recognition lag* is the time it takes for policy makers to recognize the existence of a boom or a slump. An *implementation lag* is the time it takes to put the desired policy into effect once economists and policy makers recognize that the economy is in a boom or a slump. A *response lag* is the time it takes for the economy to adjust to the new conditions after a new policy is implemented—in other words, a lag that occurs because of the operation of the economy itself. In general, monetary policy can be implemented more rapidly than fiscal policy but fiscal policy generally has a shorter response lag than monetary policy.

FISCAL POLICY: DEFICIT TARGETING *p. 593*

3. In fiscal year 1986, Congress passed and President Reagan signed the *Gramm-Rudman-Hollings Act* (*GRH*), which set out to reduce the federal deficit by $36 billion per year, with a zero deficit slated for fiscal year 1991. If Congress passed a budget with a deficit larger than the targeted amount, the law called for automatic spending cuts. A Supreme Court ruling later overturned this provision, and the actual figures for each year never came close to the targets. Thanks to the Omnibus Budget Reconciliation Act of 1993 and a robust economy, the federal deficit had been eliminated by 1998.
4. The deficit tends to rise when GDP falls and to fall when GDP rises. The *deficit response index (DRI)* is the amount by which the deficit changes with a $1 change in GDP.
5. For spending cuts of a certain amount to reduce the deficit by the same amount, the government spending multiplier must be zero. Before GRH was passed, some argued that a government spending multiplier of zero can be achieved through renewed optimism on the part of households or through very aggressive behavior by the Fed to decrease the interest rate. Empirical evidence has shown that both situations are not very plausible. So to lower the deficit by a certain amount, government spending cuts must be larger than that amount to lower the deficit.
6. Deficit-targeting measures that call for automatic spending cuts to eliminate or reduce the deficit may have the effect of destabilizing the economy because they prevent automatic stabilizers from working.

THE STOCK MARKET AND THE ECONOMY *p. 597*

7. A firm can finance an investment project by borrowing from banks, by issuing *bonds*, or by issuing new shares of its *stock*. People who own shares of stock own a fraction of the firm.
8. The price of a stock should equal the discounted value of its expected future dividends, where the discount factors depend on the interest rate and risk.
9. A bubble exists when the price of a stock exceeds the discounted value of its expected future dividends. In this case, what matters is what people expect that other people expect about how much the stock can be sold for in the future.
10. The largest stock market boom in U.S. history occurred between 1995 and 2000, when the S&P 500 index rose by 25 percent per year. The boom added $14 trillion to household wealth.
11. Why there was a stock market boom in 1995–2000 appears to be a puzzle. There was nothing unusual about earnings that would predict such a boom. Many people believe that the boom was merely a bubble.

12. The boom of 1995–2000 and the large fall in stock prices after that had significant effects on millions of people's lives. Many people overspent during the boom years and were seriously affected when the boom didn't last.

13. When stock prices increase, household wealth increases, which leads to increased consumer spending. Investment also rises because firms can raise more money per share to finance investment projects. As a rough rule of thumb, a \$1.00 change in the value of stocks leads to about a \$0.03 to \$0.04 change in consumer and investor spending per year.

14. The boom in the economy between 1995 and 2000 was fueled by the stock market boom. Estimates show that had there been no stock market boom, the economy would not have looked historically unusual in the last half of the 1990s.

15. The economy in 2001–2002 was more sluggish than it would have been had there been no stock market "correction" following the boom.

16. The boom in housing prices in 2003–2005 helped sustain the recovery, and the fall in housing prices in 2006–2007 had a serious negative impact on the economy.

REVIEW TERMS AND CONCEPTS

automatic destabilizers, *p. 596*
automatic stabilizers, *p. 596*
capital gain, *p. 597*
deficit response index (DRI), *p. 595*
Dow Jones Industrial Average, *p. 598*
Gramm-Rudman-Hollings Act, *p. 593*
implementation lag, *p. 591*
NASDAQ Composite, *p. 598*
negative demand shock, *p. 596*
realized capital gain, *p. 597*
recognition lag, *p. 591*
response lag, *p. 591*
stabilization policy, *p. 589*
Standard and Poor's 500 (S&P 500), *p. 598*
stock, *p. 597*
time lags, *p. 589*

PROBLEMS

Visit **www.myeconlab.com** to complete the problems marked in orange online. You will receive instant feedback on your answers, tutorial help, and access to additional practice problems.

1. In July 2003, the S&P 500 index was at 1,000.
   a. What is the S&P 500 index?
   b. Where is the S&P today?
   c. If you had invested \$10,000 in July 2003 and your investments had increased in value by the same percentage as the S&P 500 index had increased, how much would you have today?
   d. Assume that the total stock market holdings of the household sector were about \$12 trillion and that the entire stock market went up/down by the same percentage as the S&P. Evidence suggests that the "wealth effect" of stock market holdings on consumer spending is about 4 percent of wealth annually. How much additional or reduced spending would you expect to see as a result of the stock market moves since July 2003? Assuming a multiplier of 2 and a GDP of \$10,000 billion, how much additional/less GDP would you predict for next year if all of this was true?

2. During 1997, stock markets in Asia collapsed. Hong Kong's was down nearly 30 percent, Thailand's was down 62 percent, and Malaysia's was down 60 percent. Japan and Korea experienced big drops as well. What impacts would these events have on the economies of the countries themselves? Explain your answer. In what ways would you have expected these events to influence the U.S. economy? How might the spending of Asians on American goods be affected? What about Americans who have invested in these countries?

3. Explain why the government deficit rises as the economy contracts.

4. You are given the following information about the economy in 2001 (all in billions of dollars):

Consumption function:	$C = 100 + (.8 \times Y_d)$
Taxes:	$T = -150 + (.25 \times Y)$
Investment function:	$I = 60$
Disposable income:	$Y_d = Y - T$
Government spending:	$G = 80$
Equilibrium:	$Y = C + I + G$

Hint: Deficit is $D = G - T = G - [-150 + (.25 \times Y)]$.

   a. Find equilibrium income. Show that the government budget deficit (the difference between government spending and tax revenues) is \$5 billion.
   b. Congress passes the Foghorn-Leghorn (F-L) amendment, which requires that the deficit be zero this year. If the budget adopted by Congress has a deficit that is larger than zero, the deficit target must be met by cutting spending. Suppose spending is cut by \$5 billion (to \$75 billion). What is the new value for equilibrium GDP? What is the new deficit? Explain carefully why the deficit is not zero.
   c. What is the deficit response index, and how is it defined? Explain why the DRI must equal .25 in this example. By using this information, by how much must we cut spending to achieve a deficit of zero?
   d. Suppose the F-L amendment was not in effect and planned investment falls to $I = 55$. What is the new value of GDP? What is the new government budget deficit? What happens to GDP if the F-L amendment is in effect and spending is cut to reach the deficit target? (*Hint:* Spending must be cut by \$21.666 billion to balance the budget.)

5. Some states are required to balance their budgets. Is this measure stabilizing or destabilizing? Suppose all states were committed to a balanced-budget philosophy and the economy moved into a recession. What effects would this philosophy have on the size of the federal deficit?

6. Explain why stabilization policy may be difficult to carry out. How is it possible that stabilization policies can actually be destabilizing?

7. **[Related to the *Economics in Practice* on *p. 605*]** The housing boom of 2000–2005 created wealth of over $10 trillion. Many claim that the spending of this new wealth prevented a serious recession in the early 2000s. If people spent 4% of that new housing wealth annually by taking out home equity loans or simply saving less, what would be the increase in annual consumption expenditures? (Be careful in counting decimal places.) What would happen to GDP growth as a result?

Household and Firm Behavior in the Macroeconomy: A Further Look*

31

CHAPTER OUTLINE

In Chapters 23 through 29, we considered the interactions of households, firms, and the government in the goods, money, and labor markets. The macroeconomy is complicated, and there is much to learn about these interactions. To keep our discussions as uncomplicated as possible, so far we have assumed simple behavior of households and firms—the two basic decision-making units in the economy. We assumed that household consumption (C) depends only on income and that firms' planned investment (I) depends only on the interest rate. We did not consider that households make consumption and labor supply decisions simultaneously and that firms make investment and employment decisions simultaneously.

Now that we understand the basic interactions in the economy, we must relax these assumptions. In the first part of this chapter, we present a more realistic picture of the influences on households' consumption and labor supply decisions. In the second part, we present a more detailed and realistic picture of the influences on firms' investment and employment decisions. We then use what we have learned to analyze more macroeconomic issues.

Households: Consumption and Labor Supply Decisions

For most of our analysis so far, we have been assuming that consumption depends simply on income. While this is a useful starting point, it is far from a complete description of the consumption decision of households. We need to consider other theories of consumption to build a more realistic case.

The Life-Cycle Theory of Consumption

The main idea of the **life-cycle theory of consumption** is that people make lifetime consumption plans. By realizing that they are likely to earn more in their prime working years than they earn earlier or later, people make consumption decisions based on their expectations of lifetime income. People tend to consume less than they earn during their main working years—they *save* during those years—and people tend to consume more than they earn during their early and

* This chapter is somewhat more advanced, but it contains a lot of interesting information!

life-cycle theory of consumption A theory of household consumption: Households make lifetime consumption decisions based on their expectations of lifetime income.

later years—they *dissave*, or use up savings, during those years. Students in medical school generally have very low current incomes, but few live in the poverty that those incomes might predict. Instead, they borrow now and plan to pay back later when their incomes improve.

The lifetime income and consumption pattern of a representative individual is shown in Figure 31.1. As you can see, this person has a low income during the first part of her life, high income in the middle, and low income again in retirement. Her income in retirement is not zero because she has income from sources other than her own labor—Social Security payments, interest and dividends, and so on.

FIGURE 31.1

Life-Cycle Theory of Consumption

In their early working years, people consume more than they earn. This is also true in the retirement years. In between, people save (consume less than they earn) to pay off debts from borrowing and to accumulate savings for retirement.

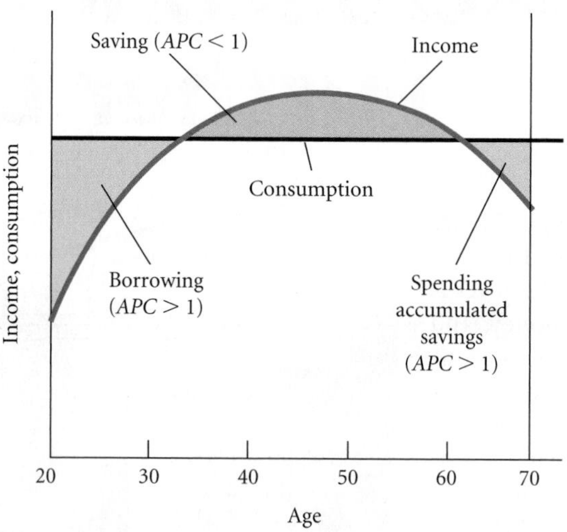

The consumption path as drawn in Figure 31.1 is constant over the person's life. This is an extreme assumption, but it illustrates the point that the path of consumption over a lifetime is likely to be more stable than the path of income. We consume an amount greater than our incomes during our early working careers. We do so by borrowing against future income by taking out a car loan, a mortgage to buy a house, or a loan to pay for college. This debt is repaid when our incomes have risen and we can afford to use some of our income to pay off past borrowing without substantially lowering our consumption. The reverse is true for our retirement years. Here, too, our incomes are low. Because we consume less than we earn during our prime working years, we can save up a "nest egg" that allows us to maintain an acceptable standard of living during retirement.

Fluctuations in wealth are also an important component of the life-cycle story. Many young households borrow in anticipation of higher income in the future. Some households actually have *negative wealth*—the value of their assets is less than the debts they owe. A household in its prime working years saves to pay off debts and to build up assets for its later years, when income typically goes down. Households whose assets are greater than the debts they owe have *positive wealth*. With its wage earners retired, a household consumes its accumulated wealth. Generally speaking, wealth starts out negative, turns positive, and then approaches zero near the end of life. Wealth, therefore, is intimately linked to the cumulative saving and dissaving behavior of households.

The key difference between the Keynesian theory of consumption and the life-cycle theory is that the life-cycle theory suggests that consumption and saving decisions are likely to be based not only on current income but also on expectations of future income. The consumption behavior of households immediately following World War II clearly supports the life-cycle story. Just after the war ended, income fell as wage earners moved out of war-related work. However, consumption spending did not fall commensurately, as Keynesian theory would predict. People expected to find jobs in other sectors eventually, and they did not adjust their consumption spending to the temporarily lower incomes they were earning in the meantime.

permanent income The average level of a person's expected future income stream.

The term **permanent income** is sometimes used to refer to the average level of a person's expected future income stream. If you expect your income will be high in the future (even though it may not be high now), your permanent income is said to be high. With this concept, we can sum up the life-cycle theory by saying that current consumption decisions are likely to be based on permanent income instead of current income.[1] This means that policy changes such as tax-rate changes are likely to have more of an effect on household behavior if they are expected to be permanent instead of temporary.

One-time tax rebates such as we saw in the United States in 2001 and 2008 provide an interesting test of the permanent income hypothesis. In both cases, the tax rebate was a one-time stimulus. In 2008, for example, the tax rebate was $300 to $600 for individual tax payers eligible for the rebate. How much would we expect this rebate to influence consumption? The simple Keynesian model that we introduced earlier in this text would just apply the marginal propensity to consume to the $600. If the marginal propensity to consume is .8, we would expect the $600 to generate $480 in incremental spending per rebate. The permanent income hypothesis instead looks at the $600 in the context of an individual's permanent income. As a fraction of one's lifetime income, $600 is a modest number, and we would thus expect individuals to increase their spending only modestly in response to the rebate. Research on the 2001 tax rebate by Matthew Shapiro and Joel Slemrod, based on surveys of consumers, suggested that most people planned to use their rebates to lower debt, rather than increase spending.

Although the life-cycle model enriches our understanding of the consumption behavior of households, the analysis is still missing something. What is missing is the other main decision of households: the labor supply decision.

The Labor Supply Decision

The size of the labor force in an economy is of obvious importance. A growing labor force is one of the ways in which national income/output can be expanded, and the larger the percentage of people who work, the higher the potential output per capita.

So far we have said little about what determines the size of the labor force. Of course, demographics are a key; the number of children born in 2008 will go a long way toward determining the potential number of 20-year-old workers in 2028. In addition, immigration, both legal and illegal, plays a role.

Behavior also plays a role. Households make decisions about whether to work and how much to work. These decisions are closely tied to consumption decisions because for most households, the bulk of their spending is financed out of wages and salaries. Households make consumption and labor supply decisions simultaneously. Consumption cannot be considered separately from labor supply because it is precisely by selling your labor that you earn income to pay for your consumption.

As we discussed in Chapter 3, the alternative to supplying your labor in exchange for a wage or a salary is leisure or other nonmarket activities. Nonmarket activities include raising a child, going to school, keeping a house, or—in a developing economy—working as a subsistence farmer. What determines the quantity of labor supplied by a household? Among the list of factors are the wage rate, prices, wealth, and nonlabor income.

The Wage Rate A changing wage rate can affect labor supply, but whether the effect is positive or negative is ambiguous. An increase in the wage rate affects a household in two ways. First, work becomes more attractive relative to leisure and other nonmarket activities. Because every hour spent in leisure now requires giving up a higher wage, the opportunity cost of leisure is higher. As a result, you would expect that a higher wage would lead to a larger quantity of labor supplied—a larger workforce. This is called the *substitution effect of a wage rate increase.*

On the other hand, household members who work are clearly better off after a wage rate increase. By working the same number of hours as they did before, they will earn more income. If we assume that leisure is a normal good, people with higher income will spend some of it on leisure by working less. This is the *income effect of a wage rate increase.*

[1] The pioneering work on this topic was done by Milton Friedman, *A Theory of the Consumption Function* (Princeton, NJ: Princeton University Press, 1957). In the mid-1960s, Franco Modigliani did closely related work that included the formulation of the life-cycle theory.

When wage rates rise, the substitution effect suggests that people will work more, while the income effect suggests that they will work less. The ultimate effect depends on which separate effect is more powerful. The data suggest that the substitution effect seems to win in most cases. That is, higher wage rates usually lead to a larger labor supply and lower wage rates usually lead to a lower labor supply.

Prices Prices also play a major role in the consumption/labor supply decision. In our discussions of the possible effects of an increase in the wage rate, we have been assuming that the prices of goods and services do not rise at the same time. If the wage rate and all other prices rise simultaneously, the story is different. To make things clear, we need to distinguish between the nominal wage rate and the real wage rate.

nominal wage rate The wage rate in current dollars.

real wage rate The amount the nominal wage rate can buy in terms of goods and services.

The **nominal wage rate** is the wage rate in current dollars. When we adjust the nominal wage rate for changes in the price level, we obtain the **real wage rate**. The real wage rate measures the amount that wages can buy in terms of goods and services. Workers do not care about their nominal wage—they care about the purchasing power of this wage—the real wage.

Suppose skilled workers in Indianapolis were paid a wage rate of $20 per hour in 2008. Now suppose their wage rate rose to $22 in 2009, a 10 percent increase. If the prices of goods and services were the same in 2009 as they were in 2008, the real wage rate would have increased by 10 percent. An hour of work in 2009 ($22) buys 10 percent more than an hour of work in 2008 ($20). What if the prices of all goods and services also increased by 10 percent between 2008 and 2009? The purchasing power of an hour's wages has not changed. The real wage rate has not increased at all. In 2009, $22 bought the same quantity of goods and services that $20 bought in 2008.

To measure the real wage rate, we adjust the nominal wage rate with a price index. As we saw in Chapter 22, there are several such indexes that we might use, including the consumer price index and the GDP price index.[2]

We can now apply what we have learned from the life-cycle theory to our wage/price story. Recall that the life-cycle theory says that people look ahead in making their decisions. Translated to real wage rates, this idea says that households look at expected future real wage rates as well as the current real wage rate in making their current consumption and labor supply decisions. Consider, for example, medical students who expect that their real wage rate will be higher in the future. This expectation obviously has an effect on current decisions about things like how much to buy and whether to take a part-time job.

Wealth and Nonlabor Income Life-cycle theory says that wealth fluctuates over the life cycle. Households accumulate wealth during their working years to pay off debts accumulated when they were young and to support themselves in retirement. This role of wealth is clear, but the existence of wealth poses another question. Consider two households that are at the same stage in their life cycle and have similar expectations about future wage rates, prices, and so on. They expect to live the same length of time, and both plan to leave the same amount to their children. They differ only in their wealth. Because of a past inheritance, household 1 has more wealth than household 2. Which household is likely to have a higher consumption path for the rest of its life? Household 1 is because it has more wealth to spread out over the rest of its life. Holding everything else constant (including the stage in the life cycle), the more wealth a household has, the more it will consume both now and in the future.

Now consider a household that has a sudden unexpected increase in wealth, perhaps an inheritance from a distant relative. How will the household's consumption pattern be affected? The household will increase its consumption both now and in the future as it spends the inheritance over the course of the rest of its life.

nonlabor, *or* nonwage, income Any income received from sources other than working—inheritances, interest, dividends, transfer payments, and so on.

An increase in wealth can also be looked on as an increase in nonlabor income. **Nonlabor,** or **nonwage, income** is income received from sources other than working—inheritances, interest, dividends, and transfer payments such as welfare payments and Social Security payments. As

[2] To calculate the real wage rate, we divide the nominal wage rate by the price index. Suppose the wage rate rose from $10 per hour in 1994 to $18 per hour in 2006 and the price level rose 50 percent during the same period. Using 1994 as the base year, the price index would be 1.00 in 1994 and 1.50 in 2006. The real wage rate is W/P, where W is the nominal wage rate and P is the price level. Using 1994 as the base year, the real wage rate is $10 in 1994 ($10.00/1.00) and $12 in 2006 ($18.00/1.50).

with wealth, an unexpected increase in nonlabor income will have a positive effect on a household's consumption.

What about the effect of an increase in wealth or nonlabor income on labor supply? We already know that an increase in income results in an increase in the consumption of normal goods, including leisure. Therefore, an unexpected increase in wealth or nonlabor income results in an increase in consumption and an increase in leisure. With leisure increasing, labor supply must fall. So an unexpected increase in wealth or nonlabor income leads to a *decrease* in labor supply. This point should be obvious. If you suddenly win a million dollars in the state lottery or make a killing in the stock market, you will probably work less in the future than you otherwise would have.

Interest Rate Effects on Consumption

Recall from the last few chapters that the interest rate affects a firm's investment decision. A higher interest rate leads to a lower level of planned investment and vice versa. This was a key link between the money market and the goods market, and it was the channel through which monetary policy had an impact on planned aggregate expenditure.

We can now expand on this link: The interest rate also affects household behavior. Consider the effect of a fall in the interest rate on consumption. A fall in the interest rate lowers the reward to saving. If the interest rate falls from 10 percent to 5 percent, you earn 5¢ instead of 10¢ per year on every dollar saved. This means that the opportunity cost of spending a dollar today (instead of saving it and consuming it plus the interest income a year from now) has fallen. You will substitute toward current consumption and away from future consumption when the interest rate falls: You consume more today and save less. A rise in the interest rate leads you to consume less today and save more. This effect is called the *substitution effect*.

There is also an *income effect* of an interest rate change on consumption. If a household has positive wealth and is earning interest on that wealth, a fall in the interest rate leads to a fall in interest income. This is a decrease in its nonlabor income, which, as we just saw, has a negative effect on consumption. For households with positive wealth, the income effect works in the opposite direction from the substitution effect. On the other hand, if a household is a debtor and is paying interest on its debt, a fall in the interest rate will lead to a fall in interest payments. The household is better off in this case and will consume more. In this case, the income and substitution effects work in the same direction. The total household sector in the United States has positive wealth, and so in the aggregate, the income and substitution effects work in the opposite direction.

On balance, the data suggest that the substitution effect dominates the income effect so that the interest rate has a negative net effect on consumption: Interest rate increases cause consumption to fall. There is also some evidence, however, that the income effect is getting larger over time. U.S. households own most of the U.S. government debt, and the size of this debt has increased dramatically in the last 25 years. This means that the change in government interest payments (and so the change in household interest income) is now larger for a given change in interest rates than before, which leads to a larger income effect than before for a given change in interest rates. On net, this tells us that interest rate increases will cause consumption to fall less as the income effect grows.

Government Effects on Consumption and Labor Supply: Taxes and Transfers

The government influences household behavior mainly through income tax rates and transfer payments. When the government raises income tax rates, after-tax real wages decrease, lowering consumption. When the government lowers income tax rates, after-tax real wages increase, raising consumption. A change in income tax rates also affects labor supply. If the substitution effect dominates, as we are generally assuming, an increase in income tax rates, which lowers after-tax wages, will lower labor supply. A decrease in income tax rates will increase labor supply.

Transfer payments are payments such as Social Security benefits, veterans' benefits, and welfare benefits. An increase in transfer payments is an increase in nonlabor income, which we have seen has a positive effect on consumption and a negative effect on labor supply. Increases in transfer payments thus increase consumption and decrease labor supply, while decreases in transfer payments decrease consumption and increase labor supply. Table 31.1 summarizes these results.

TABLE 31.1 The Effects of Government on Household Consumption and Labor Supply

	Income Tax Rates		Transfer Payments	
	Increase	Decrease	Increase	Decrease
Effect on consumption	Negative	Positive	Positive	Negative
Effect on labor supply	Negative*	Positive*	Negative	Positive

*If the substitution effect dominates.
Note: The effects are larger if they are expected to be permanent instead of temporary.

A Possible Employment Constraint on Households

Our discussion of the labor supply decision has so far proceeded as if households were free to choose how much to work each period. If a member of a household decides to work an additional 5 hours a week at the current wage rate, we have assumed that the person *can* work 5 hours more—that work is available. If someone who has not been working decides to work at the current wage rate, we have assumed that the person *can find a job*.

There are times when these assumptions do not hold. The Great Depression, when unemployment rates reached 25 percent of the labor force, led to the birth of macroeconomics in the 1930s. Since the mid-1970s, the United States has experienced four recessions, with millions of unemployed workers unable to find work.

When there is unemployment, some households feel an additional constraint on their behavior. Some people may want to work 40 hours per week at the current wage rates but may find only part-time work. Others may not find any work at all.

How does a household respond when it is constrained from working as much as it would like? It consumes less. If your current wage rate is $10 per hour and you normally work 40 hours a week, your normal income from wages is $400 per week. If your average tax rate is 20 percent, your after-tax wage income is $320 per week. You are likely to spend much of this income during the week. If you are prevented from working, this income will not be available to you and you will have less to spend. You will spend something, of course. You may receive some form of nonlabor income, and you may have assets such as savings deposits or stocks and bonds that can be withdrawn or sold. You also may be able to borrow during your period of unemployment. Even though you will spend something during the week, you almost certainly will spend less than you would have if you had your usual income of $320 in after-tax wages.

A household constrained from working as much as it would like at the current wage rate faces a different decision from the decision facing a household that can work as much as it wants. The work decision of the former household is, in effect, forced on it. The household works as much as it can—a certain number of hours per week or perhaps none at all—but this amount is less than the household would choose to work at the current wage rate if it could find more work. The amount that a household would like to work at the current wage rate if it could find the work is called its **unconstrained supply of labor**. The amount that the household actually works in a given period at current wage rates is called its **constrained supply of labor**.

unconstrained supply of labor The amount a household would like to work within a given period at the current wage rate if it could find the work.

constrained supply of labor The amount a household actually works in a given period at the current wage rate.

A household's constrained supply of labor is not a variable over which it has any control. The amount of labor the household supplies is imposed on it from the outside by the workings of the economy. However, the household's consumption *is* under its control. We have just seen that the less a household works—that is, the smaller the household's constrained supply of labor is—the lower its consumption. Constraints on the supply of labor are an important determinant of consumption when there is unemployment.

Keynesian Theory Revisited Recall the Keynesian theory that current income determines current consumption. We now know the consumption decision is made jointly with the labor supply decision and the two depend on the real wage rate. It is incorrect to think that consumption depends only on income, at least when there is full employment. However, if there is unemployment, Keynes is closer to being correct because income is not determined by households. When there is unemployment, the level of income (at least workers' income) depends exclusively on the employment decisions made by firms. There are unemployed workers who are willing to work at the current wage rate, and their income is in effect determined by firms' hiring decisions. This income affects current consumption, which is consistent with Keynes's theory. This is one of the reasons Keynesian theory is considered to pertain to periods of unemployment. It was, of course, precisely during such a period that the theory was developed.

A Summary of Household Behavior

This completes our discussion of household behavior in the macroeconomy. Household consumption depends on more than current income. Households determine consumption and labor supply simultaneously, and they look ahead in making their decisions.

The following factors affect household consumption and labor supply decisions:

- Current and expected future real wage rates
- Initial value of wealth
- Current and expected future nonlabor income
- Interest rates
- Current and expected future tax rates and transfer payments

If households are constrained in their labor supply decisions, income is directly determined by firms' hiring decisions. In this case, we can say (in the traditional, Keynesian way) that "income" affects consumption.

The Household Sector Since 1970

To better understand household behavior, let us examine how some of the aggregate household variables have changed over time. We will discuss the period 1970 I–2007 IV. (Remember, Roman numerals refer to quarters, that is, 1970 I means the first quarter of 1970.) Within this span, there have been four recessionary periods: 1974 I–1975 IV, 1980 II–1983 I, 1990 III–1991 I, and 2001 I–2001 III. How did the household variables behave during each period?

Consumption Data on the total consumption of the household sector are in the national income accounts. As we saw in Table 21.2 on p. 420, personal consumption expenditures accounted for 70.3 percent of GDP in 2007. The three basic categories of consumption expenditures are services, nondurable goods, and durable goods.

Figure 31.2 plots the data for consumption expenditures on services and nondurable goods combined and for consumption expenditures on durable goods. The variables are in real terms. You can see that expenditures on services and nondurable goods are "smoother" over time than expenditures on durable goods. For example, the decrease in expenditures on services and nondurable goods was much smaller during the four recessionary periods than the decrease in expenditures on durable goods.

Why do expenditures on durables fluctuate more than expenditures on services and nondurables? When times are bad, people can postpone the purchase of durable goods, which they do. It follows that expenditures on these goods change the most. When times are tough, you do not *have* to have a new car or a new washer-dryer; you can make do with your old Chevy or Maytag until things get better. When your income falls, it is not as easy to postpone the service costs of day care or health care. Nondurables fall into an intermediate category, with some items (such as new clothes) easier to postpone than others (such as food).

▶ **FIGURE 31.2**
Consumption Expenditures, 1970 I–2007 IV
Over time, expenditures on services and nondurable goods are "smoother" than expenditures on durable goods.

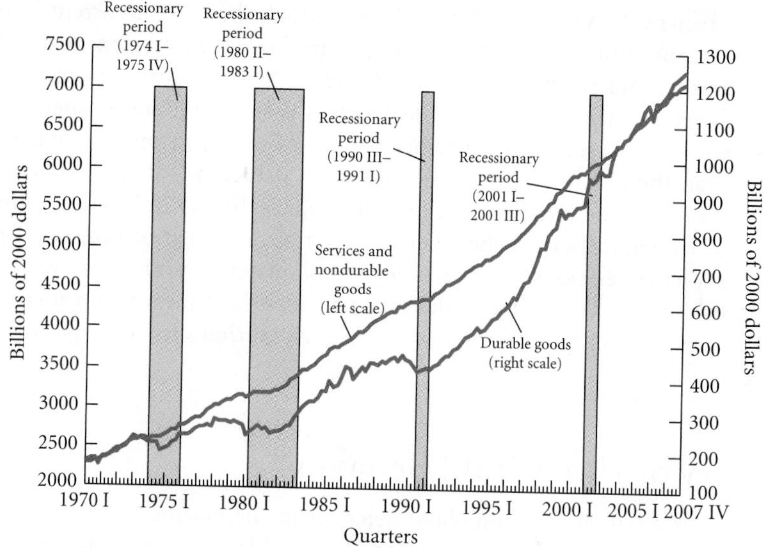

Housing Investment Another important expenditure of the household sector is housing investment (purchases of new housing), plotted in Figure 31.3. This variable fluctuates greatly, for at least two reasons. Housing investment is the most easily postponable of all household expenditures. Also, housing investment is sensitive to the general level of interest rates, and interest rates fluctuate considerably over time. When interest rates are low, housing investment is high and vice versa.

▶ **FIGURE 31.3**
Housing Investment of the Household Sector, 1970 I–2007 IV
Housing investment fell during the four recessionary periods since 1970. Like expenditures for durable goods, expenditures for housing investment are postponable.

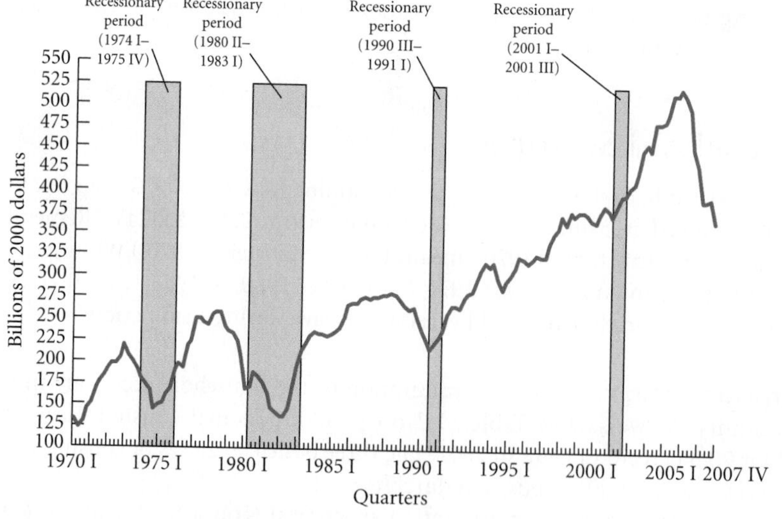

Labor Supply As we noted in Chapters 22 and 29, a person is considered a part of the labor force when he or she is working or has been actively looking for work in the past few weeks. The ratio of the labor force to the total working-age population—those 16 and over—is the *labor force participation rate.*

It is informative to divide the labor force into three categories: males 25 to 54, females 25 to 54, and all others 16 and over. Ages 25 to 54 are sometimes called "prime" ages, presuming that a person is in the prime of working life during these ages. The participation rates for these three groups are plotted in Figure 31.4.

As the figure shows, most men of prime age are in the labor force, although the participation rate has fallen slightly since 1970—from .961 in 1970 I to .909 in 2007 IV. (A rate of .909 means that

ECONOMICS IN PRACTICE

Housing Problems Spread to the Rest of the Economy

Housing prices fell across much of the United States in 2007 and 2008. For many households, housing constitutes a large portion of their wealth. So a fall in housing prices translates into a large fall in wealth for households. The lessons of this chapter suggest—as the following article confirms—that the consequence of a housing-related wealth decrease is a cutback in other household consumption. The article describes the recent housing slowdown and its consequences for the U.S. economy, along with the attempts by the Federal Reserve (Fed) to counteract these effects with an interest rate cut.

Decline in Home Prices Accelerates: Fed's Efforts Have Only Muted Effect On Mortgage Rates

Wall Street Journal

The decline in U.S. home prices accelerated in the fourth quarter, according to two leading barometers, compounding two of the biggest threats facing the nation's economy: faltering consumer spending and tight credit markets.

The S&P/Case-Shiller national home-price index for the fourth quarter fell 8.9% from a year earlier, the largest drop in its 20 years of data. And the Office of Federal Housing Enterprise Oversight's index—which tracks only homes purchased with mortgages guaranteed by home-loan giants Fannie Mae or Freddie Mac—was down 0.3%, the first year-to-year decline in the measure's 16 years.

Lower home prices threaten the economy's growth by making consumers feel less wealthy and thus less willing to spend. They also curtail homeowners' ability to borrow against the value of their homes to finance other purchases. In addition, lower housing prices erode the value of banks' collateral, prompting them to tighten their lending standards, which further damps the economic growth.

A top Federal Reserve official indicated the housing slump and its broadening impact on the economy probably would keep the central bank biased in favor of more interest-rate cuts. "It appears that the correction in the housing market has further to go," Fed Vice Chairman Donald Kohn said yesterday in a speech in North Carolina. Mr. Kohn said that the downturn, after being "contained" for nearly two years, "appears to have spread to other sectors of the economy." He added that if the housing market deteriorates more than expected, "lenders might further reduce credit availability."

The housing-market slump also is taking its toll on consumer sentiment, which could lead to further pullbacks in spending, depressing the economy. The Conference Board, a New York-based business-research group, said yesterday that its index of consumer confidence fell sharply to 75.0 in February from 87.3 in January. The index is closely watched because consumer spending drives much of the U.S. economy.

"Consumer spending is going to take a hit," said Patrick Newport, an economist at Global Insight in Waltham, Mass. "The hit will be bigger the more home prices drop."

Source: Kelly Evans, Serena Ng and Ruth Simon, February 27, 2008

90.9 percent of prime-age men were in the labor force.) The participation rate for prime-age women, on the other hand, rose dramatically between 1970 and 1990—from .501 in 1970 I to .741 in 1990 I. Although economic factors account for some of this increase, a change in social attitudes and preferences probably explains much of the increase. Since 1990, the participation rate for prime-age women has changed very little. In 2007 IV, it was .755, still considerably below the .909 rate for prime-age men.

Figure 31.4 also shows the participation rate for all individuals 16 and over except prime-age men and women. This rate has some cyclical features—it tends to fall in recessions and to rise or fall less during expansions. These features reveal the operation of the *discouraged-worker effect*, discussed in Chapter 22. During recessions, some people get discouraged about ever finding a job. They stop looking and are then not considered a part of the labor force. During expansions, people become encouraged again. Once they begin looking for jobs, they are again considered a part of the labor force. Because prime-age women and men are likely to be fairly attached to the labor force, the discouraged-worker effect for them is quite small.

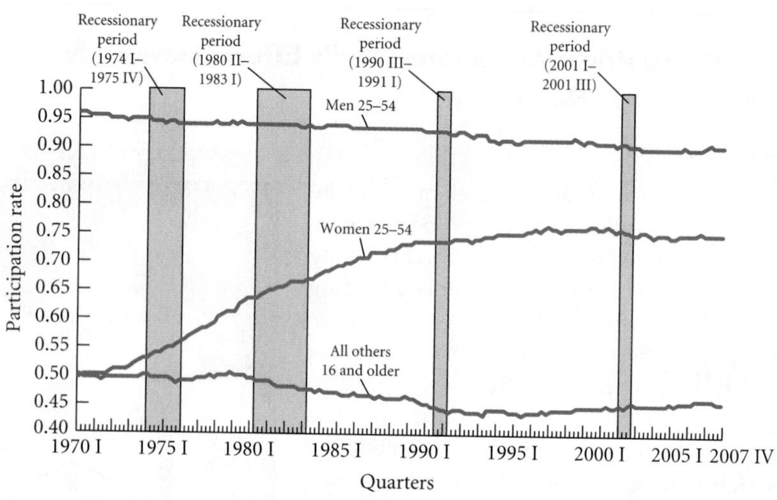

FIGURE 31.4 Labor Force Participation Rates for Men 25 to 54, Women 25 to 54, and All Others 16 and Over, 1970 I–2007 IV

Since 1970, the labor force participation rate for prime-age men has been decreasing slightly. The rate for prime-age women has been increasing dramatically. The rate for all others 16 and over has been declining since 1979 and shows a tendency to fall during recessions (the discouraged-worker effect).

Firms: Investment and Employment Decisions

Having taken a closer look at the behavior of households in the macroeconomy, we now look more closely at the behavior of firms—the other major decision-making unit in the economy. In discussing firm behavior earlier, we assumed that planned investment depends only on the interest rate. However, there are several other determinants of planned investment. We now discuss them and the factors that affect firms' employment decisions. Once again, microeconomic theory can help us gain some insight into the working of the macroeconomy.

In a market economy, firms determine which goods and services are available to consumers today and which will be available in the future, how many workers are needed for what kinds of jobs, and how much investment will be undertaken. Stated in macroeconomic terms, the decisions of firms, taken together, determine output, labor demand, and investment.

Expectations and Animal Spirits

Time is a key factor in investment decisions. Capital has a life that typically extends over many years. A developer who decides to build an office tower is making an investment that will be around (barring earthquakes, floods, or tornadoes) for several decades. In deciding where to build a plant, a manufacturing firm is committing a large amount of resources to purchase capital that will presumably yield services over a long time. Furthermore, the decision to build a plant or to purchase large equipment must often be made years before the actual project is completed. Whereas the acquisition of a small business computer may take only a few days, the planning process for downtown developments in large U.S. cities has been known to take decades.

For these reasons, investment decisions require looking into the future and forming expectations about it. In forming their expectations, firms consider numerous factors. At a minimum, they gather information about the demand for their specific products, about what their competitors are planning, and about the macroeconomy's overall health. A firm is not likely to increase its production capacity if it does not expect to sell more of its product in the future. Hilton will not put up a new hotel if it does not expect to fill the rooms at a profitable rate. Ford will not build a new plant if it expects the economy to enter a long recession.

Forecasting the future is fraught with dangers. Many events cannot be foreseen. Investments are therefore always made with imperfect knowledge. Keynes pointed this out in 1936:

> The outstanding fact is the extreme precariousness of the basis of knowledge on which our estimates of prospective yield have to be made. Our knowledge of the factors which will govern the yield of an investment some years hence is usually very slight and often negligible. If we speak frankly, we have to admit that our basis of knowledge for estimating the yield ten years hence of a railway, a copper mine, a textile factory, the goodwill of a patent medicine, an Atlantic liner, a building in the City of London amounts to little and sometimes nothing.

Keynes concludes from this line of thought that much investment activity depends on psychology and on what he calls the **animal spirits of entrepreneurs**:

animal spirits of entrepreneurs A term coined by Keynes to describe investors' feelings.

> Our decisions . . . can only be taken as a result of animal spirits. In estimating the prospects of investment, we must have regard, therefore, to nerves and hysteria and even the digestions and reactions to the weather of those upon whose spontaneous activity it largely depends.[3]

Because expectations about the future are, as Keynes points out, subject to great uncertainty, they may change often. Thus, animal spirits help to make investment a volatile component of GDP.

The Accelerator Effect Expectations, at least in part, determine the level of planned investment spending. At any interest rate, the level of investment is likely to be higher if businesses are optimistic. If businesses are pessimistic, the level of planned investment will be lower, but what determines expectations?

One possibility, is that expectations are optimistic when aggregate output (Y) is rising and pessimistic when aggregate output is falling. At any given level of the interest rate, expectations may be more optimistic and planned investment higher when output is growing rapidly than when it is growing slowly or falling. It is easy to see why this might be so. When firms expect future prospects to be good, they may plan now to add productive capacity, and one indicator of future prospects is the current growth rate.

If this is the case in reality, the ultimate result will be an **accelerator effect**. If aggregate output (income) (Y) is rising, investment will increase even though the level of Y may be low. Higher investment spending leads to an added increase in output, further "accelerating" the growth of aggregate output. If Y is falling, expectations are dampened and investment spending will be cut even though the level of Y may be high, accelerating the decline.

accelerator effect The tendency for investment to increase when aggregate output increases and to decrease when aggregate output decreases, accelerating the growth or decline of output.

Profit Maximization

When firms decide to increase output, perhaps because of new animal spirits, they will typically need to increase their inputs. By **inputs**, we mean the goods and services that firms purchase and turn into output. Two important inputs that firms use are capital and labor. (Other inputs are energy, raw materials, and semifinished goods.) Each period firms must decide how much capital and labor to use in producing output.

inputs The goods and services that firms purchase and turn into output.

At any point in time, a firm has a certain stock of capital on hand. *Stock of capital* means the factories and buildings (sometimes called "plants") that firms own, the equipment they need to do business, and their inventories of partly or wholly finished goods. Firms add to their capital stock by buying machinery and building new factories. This kind of addition to the capital stock is **plant-and-equipment investment**.

plant-and-equipment investment Purchases by firms of additional machines, factories, or buildings within a given period.

[3] John Maynard Keynes, *The General Theory of Employment, Interest, and Money (1936)*, First Harbinger Ed. (New York: Harcourt Brace Jovanovich, 1964), pp. 149, 152.

In addition to decisions about capital investments, firms also make employment decisions. At the beginning of each period, a firm has a certain number of workers on its payroll. On the basis of its current situation and its upcoming plans, the firm must decide whether to hire additional workers, keep the same number, or reduce its workforce by laying off some employees.

To start our analysis, we assume that firms make choices about capital investment and employment levels to maximize their profits. One of the most important profit-maximizing decisions that a firm must make is how to produce its output. In most cases, a firm must choose among alternative methods of production, or technologies. Different technologies generally require different combinations of capital and labor.

Consider a factory that manufactures shirts. Shirts can be made entirely by hand, with workers cutting the pieces of fabric and sewing them together. However, shirts like those can be made on complex machines that cut and sew and produce shirts with very little human supervision. Between these two extremes are dozens of alternative technologies. Shirts can be partly hand-sewn, with the stitching done on electric sewing machines.

Firms' decisions concerning the amount of capital and labor they will use in production are closely related. If firms maximize profits, they will choose the technology that minimizes the cost of production. That is, it is logical to assume that firms will choose the technology that is most efficient.

The most efficient technology depends on the relative prices of capital and labor. A shirt factory in the Philippines that decides to increase its production faces a large supply of relatively inexpensive labor. Wage rates in the Philippines are quite low. Capital equipment must be imported and is very expensive. A shirt factory in the Philippines is likely to choose a **labor-intensive technology**—a large amount of labor relative to capital. When labor-intensive technologies are used, expansion is likely to increase the demand for labor substantially while increasing the demand for capital only modestly.

labor-intensive technology A production technique that uses a large amount of labor relative to capital.

A shirt factory in Germany that decides to expand production is likely to buy a large amount of capital equipment and to hire relatively few new workers. It will probably choose a **capital-intensive technology**—a large amount of capital relative to labor. German wage rates are quite high, higher in many occupations than in the United States. Capital, however, is plentiful. Firms' decisions about labor demand and investment are likely to depend on the relative costs of labor and capital. The relative impact of an expansion of output on employment and investment demand depends on the wage rate and the cost of capital.

capital-intensive technology A production technique that uses a large amount of capital relative to labor.

Excess Labor and Excess Capital Effects

In practice, firms appear at times to hold what we will call **excess labor** and/or **excess capital**. A firm holds excess labor (or capital) if it can reduce the amount of labor it employs (or capital it holds) and still produce the same amount of output. Why would a firm want to employ more workers or have more capital on hand than it needs? Both labor and capital are costly—a firm has to pay wages to its workers, and it forgoes interest on funds tied up in machinery or buildings. Why would a firm want to incur costs that do not yield revenue?

excess labor, excess capital Labor and capital that are not needed to produce the firm's current level of output.

To see why, suppose a firm suffers a sudden and large decrease in sales, but it expects the lower sales level to last only a few months, after which it believes sales will pick up again. In this case, the firm is likely to lower production in response to the sales change to avoid too large an increase in its stock of inventories. This decrease in production means that the firm could get rid of some workers and some machines because it needs less labor and less capital to produce the now-lower level of output.

However, things are not that simple. Decreasing its workforce and capital stock quickly can be costly for a firm. Abrupt cuts in the workforce hurt worker morale and may increase personnel administration costs, and abrupt reductions in capital stock may be disadvantageous because of the difficulty of selling used machines. These types of costs are sometimes called **adjustment costs** because they are the costs of adjusting to the new level of output. There are also adjustment costs to increasing output. For example, it is usually costly to recruit and train new workers.

adjustment costs The costs that a firm incurs when it changes its production level—for example, the administration costs of laying off employees or the training costs of hiring new workers.

Adjustment costs may be large enough that a firm chooses not to decrease its workforce and capital stock when production falls. The firm may at times choose to have more labor and capital on hand than it needs to produce its current amount of output simply because getting rid of them is more costly than keeping them. In practice, excess labor takes the form of workers not working at their normal level of activity (more coffee breaks and more idle time, for instance). Some of this excess labor may receive new training so that productivity will be higher when production picks up again.

The existence of excess labor and capital at any given moment is likely to affect future employment and investment decisions. Suppose a firm already has excess labor and capital due to a fall in its sales and production. When production picks up again, the firm will not need to hire as many new workers or acquire as much new capital as it would otherwise. The more excess capital a firm already has, the less likely it is to invest in new capital in the future. The more excess labor it has, the less likely it is to hire new workers in the future.

Inventory Investment

We now turn to a brief discussion of the inventory investment decision. **Inventory investment** is the change in the stock of inventories. Although inventory investment is another way in which a firm adds to its capital stock, the inventory investment decision is quite different from the plant-and-equipment investment decision.

inventory investment The change in the stock of inventories.

The Role of Inventories Recall the distinction between a firm's sales and its output. If a firm can hold goods in inventory, which is usually the case unless the good is perishable or unless the firm produces services, then within a given period, it can sell a quantity of goods that differs from the quantity of goods it produces during that period. When a firm sells more than it produces, its stock of inventories decreases; when it sells less than it produces, its stock of inventories increases.

Stock of inventories (end of period) = Stock of inventories (beginning of period)
+ Production − Sales

If a firm starts a period with 100 umbrellas in inventory, produces 15 umbrellas during the period, and sells 10 umbrellas in this same interval, it will have 105 umbrellas (100 + 15 − 10) in inventory at the end of the period. A change in the stock of inventories is actually investment because inventories are counted as part of a firm's capital stock. In our example, inventory investment during the period is a positive number, 5 umbrellas (105 − 100). When the number of goods produced is less than the number of goods sold, such as 5 produced and 10 sold, inventory investment is negative.

The Optimal Inventory Policy We can now consider firms' inventory decisions. Firms are concerned with what they are going to sell and produce in the future as well as what they are selling and producing currently. At each point in time, a firm has some idea of how much it is going to sell in the current period and in future periods. Given these expectations and its knowledge of how much of its good it already has in stock, a firm must decide how much to produce in the current period.

Inventories are costly to a firm because they take up space and they tie up funds that could be earning interest. However, if a firm's stock of inventories gets too low, the firm may have difficulty meeting the demand for its product, especially if demand increases unexpectedly. The firm may lose sales. The point between too low and too high a stock of inventory is called the **desired**, or **optimal, level of inventories**. This is the level at which the extra cost (in lost sales) from decreasing inventories by a small amount is just equal to the extra gain (in interest revenue and decreased storage costs).

desired, *or* **optimal, level of inventories** The level of inventory at which the extra cost (in lost sales) from lowering inventories by a small amount is just equal to the extra gain (in interest revenue and decreased storage costs).

A firm that had no costs other than inventory costs would always aim to produce in a period exactly the volume of goods necessary to make its stock of inventories at the end of the period equal to the desired stock. If the stock of inventory fell lower than desired, the firm would produce more than it expected to sell to bring the stock up. If the stock of inventory grew above the desired level, the firm would produce less than it expected to sell to reduce the stock.

There are other costs to running a firm besides inventory costs. In particular, large and abrupt changes in production can be very costly because it is often disruptive to change a production process geared to a certain rate of output. If production is to be increased, there may be adjustment costs for hiring more labor and increasing the capital stock. If production is to be decreased, there may be adjustment costs in laying off workers and decreasing the capital stock.

Because holding inventories and changing production levels are both costly, firms face a trade-off between them. Because of adjustment costs, a firm is likely to smooth its production path relative to its sales path. This means that a firm is likely to have its production fluctuate less than its sales, with changes in inventories to absorb the difference each period. However, because there are incentives not to stray too far from the optimal level of inventories, fluctuations in production are not eliminated completely. Production is still likely to fluctuate, just not as much as sales fluctuate.

Two other points need to be made here. First, if a firm's stock of inventories is unusually or unexpectedly high, the firm is likely to produce less in the future than it otherwise would have in order to decrease its high stock of inventories. In other words, although the stock of inventories fluctuates over time because production is smoothed relative to sales, at any point in time, inventories may be unexpectedly high or low because sales have been unexpectedly low or high. An unexpectedly high stock will have a negative effect on production in the future, and an unexpectedly low stock will have a positive effect on production in the future. An unexpected increase in inventories has a negative effect on future production, and an unexpected decrease in inventories has a positive effect on future production.

Second, firms do not know their future sales exactly. They have expectations of future sales, and these expectations may not turn out to be exactly right. This has important consequences. If sales turn out to be less than expected, inventories will be higher than expected and there will be less production in the future. Furthermore, *future* sales expectations are likely to have an important effect on *current* production. If a firm expects its sales to be high in the future, it will adjust its planned production path accordingly. Even though a firm smooths production relative to sales, over a long time, it must produce as much as it sells. If it does not, it will eventually run out of inventories. The level of a firm's planned production path depends on the level of its expected future sales path. If a firm's expectations of the level of its future sales path decrease, the firm is likely to decrease the level of its planned production path, including its actual production in the current period. Current production depends on expected future sales.

Because production is likely to depend on expectations of the future, animal spirits may play a role. If firms become more optimistic about the future, they are likely to produce more now. Keynes's view that animal spirits affect investment is also likely to pertain to output.

A Summary of Firm Behavior

The following factors affect firms' investment and employment decisions:

- Firms' expectations of future output
- Wage rate and cost of capital (the interest rate is an important component of the cost of capital)
- Amount of excess labor and excess capital on hand

The most important points to remember about the relationship among production, sales, and inventory investment are

- Inventory investment—that is, the change in the stock of inventories—equals production minus sales.
- An unexpected increase in the stock of inventories has a negative effect on future production.
- Current production depends on expected future sales.

The Firm Sector Since 1970

To close our discussion of firm behavior, we now examine some aggregate investment and employment variables for the period 1970 I–2007 IV.

Plant-and-Equipment Investment Plant-and-equipment investment by the firm sector is plotted in Figure 31.5. Investment fared poorly in the four recessionary periods after 1970. This observation is consistent with the observation that investment depends in part on output. An examination of the plot of real GDP in Figure 20.4 in on p. 410 and the plot of investment in Figure 31.5 shows that investment generally does poorly when GDP does poorly and that investment generally does well when GDP does well.

Figure 31.5 also shows that investment fluctuates greatly. This is not surprising. The animal spirits of entrepreneurs are likely to be volatile, and if animal spirits affect investment, it follows that investment too will be volatile.

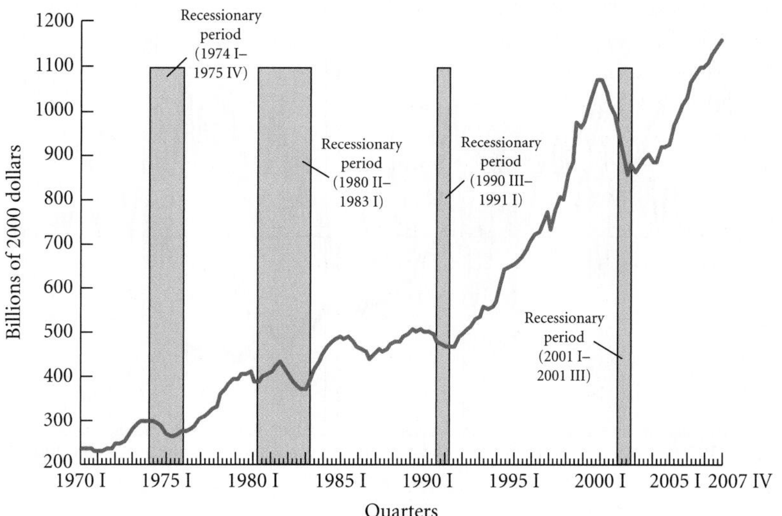

FIGURE 31.5
Plant-and-Equipment Investment of the Firm Sector, 1970 I–2007 IV
Overall, plant-and-equipment investment declined in the four recessionary periods since 1970.

Despite the volatility of plant-and-equipment investment, however, it is still true that housing investment fluctuates more than plant-and-equipment investment (as you can see by comparing Figures 31.3 and 31.5). Plant-and-equipment investment is not the most volatile component of GDP.

Employment Employment in the firm sector is plotted in Figure 31.6, which shows that employment fell in all four recessionary periods. This is consistent with the theory that employment depends in part on output. Otherwise, employment has grown over time in response to the growing economy. Employment in the firm sector rose from 72.7 million in 1970 I to 132.8 million in 2007 IV.

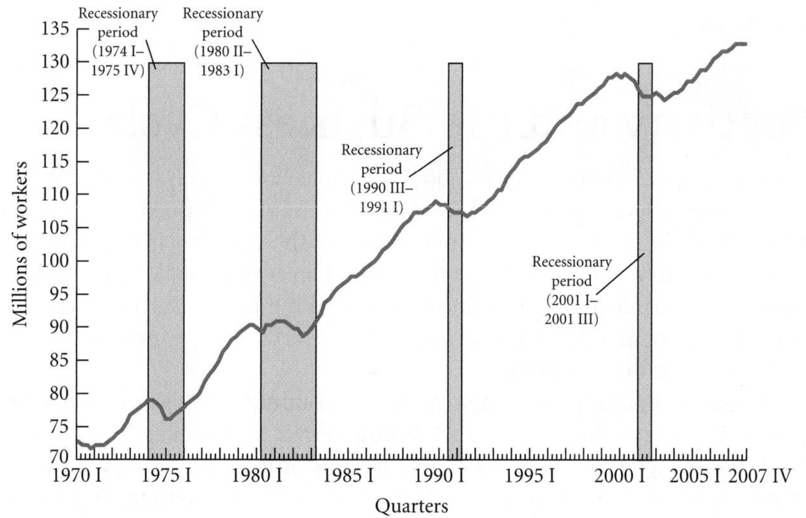

FIGURE 31.6
Employment in the Firm Sector, 1970 I–2007 IV
Growth in employment was generally negative in the four recessions the U.S. economy has experienced since 1970.

Inventory Investment Recall that *inventory investment* is the difference between the level of output and the level of sales. Recall also that some inventory investment is usually unplanned. This occurs when the actual level of sales is different from the expected level of sales.

Inventory investment of the firm sector is plotted in Figure 31.7. Also plotted in this figure is the ratio of the stock of inventories to the level of sales—the *inventory/sales ratio*. The figure shows that inventory investment is very volatile—more volatile than housing investment and plant-and-equipment investment. Some of this volatility is undoubtedly due to the unplanned component of inventory investment, which is likely to fluctuate greatly from one period to the next.

▶ FIGURE 31.7

Inventory Investment of the Firm Sector and the Inventory/Sales Ratio, 1970 I–2007 IV

The inventory/sales ratio is the ratio of the firm sector's stock of inventories to the level of sales. Inventory investment is very volatile.

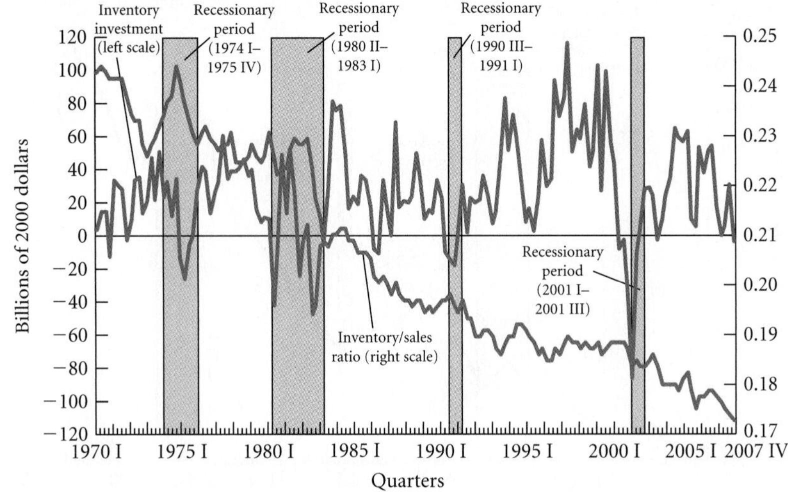

When the inventory/sales ratio is high, the actual stock of inventories is likely to be larger than the desired stock. In such a case, firms have overestimated demand and produced too much relative to sales and they are likely to want to produce less in the future to draw down their stock. You can find several examples of this trend in Figure 31.7—the clearest occurred during the 1974–1975 period. At the end of 1974, the stock of inventories was very high relative to sales, an indication that firms probably had undesired inventories at the end of 1974. In 1975, firms worked off these undesired inventories by producing less than they sold. Thus, inventory investment was very low in 1975. The year 1975 is clearly a year in which output would have been higher had the stock of inventories at the beginning of the year not been so high. There was a huge fall in inventory investment in 2001.

On average, the inventory/sales ratio has been declining over time, evidence that firms are becoming more efficient in their management of inventory stocks. Firms are becoming more efficient in the sense of being able (other things equal) to hold smaller and smaller stocks of inventories relative to sales.

Productivity and the Business Cycle

productivity, *or* labor productivity Output per worker hour; the amount of output produced by an average worker in 1 hour.

We can now use what we have just learned about firm behavior to analyze movements in productivity. **Productivity**, sometimes called **labor productivity**, is defined as output per worker hour. If output is Y and the number of hours worked in the economy is H, productivity is Y/H. Simply stated, productivity measures how much output an average worker produces in 1 hour.

Productivity fluctuates over the business cycle, tending to rise during expansions and fall during contractions. The fact that firms at times hold excess labor explains why productivity fluctuates in the same direction as output.

Figure 31.8 shows the pattern of employment and output over time for a hypothetical economy. Employment does not fluctuate as much as output over the business cycle. It is precisely this pattern that leads to higher productivity during periods of high output and lower productivity during periods of low output. During expansions in the economy, output rises by a larger percentage than employment and the ratio of output to workers rises. During downswings, output falls faster than employment and the ratio of output to workers falls.

The existence of excess labor when the economy is in a slump means that productivity as measured by the ratio Y/H tends to fall at such times. Does this trend mean that labor is in some sense "less productive" during recessions than before? Not really: It means only that firms choose to employ more labor than they need. For this reason, some workers are in effect idle some of the time even though they are considered employed. They are not less productive in the sense of having less potential to produce output; they are merely not working part of the time that they are *counted* as working.

Productivity in the Long Run Theories of long-run economic behavior, which attempt to explain how and why economies grow over time, focus on productivity, usually measured in this case as *output per worker* or its closely related measure, *GDP per capita*. Productivity defined

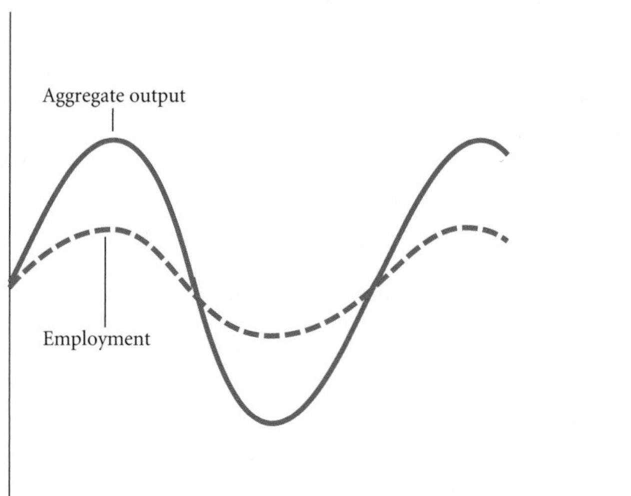

◀ FIGURE 31.8
Employment and Output over the Business Cycle
In general, employment does not fluctuate as much as output over the business cycle. As a result, measured productivity (the output-to-labor ratio) tends to rise during expansionary periods and decline during contractionary periods.

this way is a key index of an economy's performance over the long run. Productivity figures can, however, be misleading when used to diagnose the health of the economy over the short run because business cycles can distort the meaning of productivity measurements. Output per worker falls in recessions because firms hold excess labor during slumps. Output per worker rises in expansions because firms put the excess labor back to work. Neither of these conditions has anything to do with the economy's long-run potential to produce output. We discuss long-run growth in the next chapter.

The Short-Run Relationship Between Output and Unemployment

We can also use what we have learned about household and firm behavior to analyze the relationship between output and unemployment. When we discussed the connections between the *AS/AD* diagram and the Phillips Curve in Chapter 29, we mentioned that output (*Y*) and the unemployment rate (*U*) are inversely related. When output rises, the unemployment rate falls, and when output falls, the unemployment rate rises. At one time, it was believed that the short-run relationship between the two variables was fairly stable. **Okun's Law** (after U.S. economist Arthur Okun, who first studied the relationship) stated that in the short run the unemployment rate decreased about 1 percentage point for every 3 percent increase in real GDP. As with the Phillips Curve, Okun's Law has not turned out to be a "law." The economy is far too complex for there to be such a simple and stable relationship between two macroeconomic variables.

Okun's Law The theory, put forth by Arthur Okun, that in the short run the unemployment rate decreases about 1 percentage point for every 3 percent increase in real GDP. Later research and data have shown that the relationship between output and unemployment is not as stable as Okun's "Law" predicts.

Although the short-run relationship between output and the unemployment rate is not the simple relationship Okun believed, it is true that a 1 percent increase in output tends to correspond to a less than 1 percentage point decrease in the unemployment rate in the short run. In other words, there are a number of "slippages" between changes in output and changes in the unemployment rate.

The first slippage is between the change in output and the change in the number of jobs in the economy. When output increases by 1 percent, the number of jobs does not tend to rise by 1 percent in the short run. There are two reasons for this. First, a firm is likely to meet some of the increase in output by increasing the number of hours worked per job. Instead of having the labor force work 40 hours per week, the firm may pay overtime and have the labor force work 42 hours per week. Second, if a firm is holding excess labor at the time of the output increase, at least part of the increase in output can come from putting the excess labor back to work. For both reasons, the number of jobs is likely to rise by a smaller percentage than the increase in output.

The second slippage is between the change in the number of *jobs* and the change in the *number of people employed*. If you have two jobs, you are counted twice in the job data but only once in the persons-employed data. Because some people have two jobs, there are more jobs than there are people employed. When the number of jobs increases, some of the new jobs are filled by people who already have one job (instead of by people who are unemployed). This means that the increase in the number of people employed is less than the increase in the number of jobs. This is a slippage between output and the unemployment rate because the unemployment rate is calculated from data on the number of people employed, not the number of jobs.

The third slippage concerns the response of the labor force to an increase in output. Let E denote the number of people employed, let L denote the number of people in the labor force, and let u denote the unemployment rate. In these terms, the unemployment rate is

$$u = 1 - E/L$$

The unemployment rate is 1 minus the employment rate, E/L.

discouraged-worker effect The decline in the measured unemployment rate that results when people who want to work but cannot find work grow discouraged and stop looking, dropping out of the ranks of the unemployed and the labor force.

When we discussed how the unemployment rate is measured in Chapter 22, we introduced the **discouraged-worker effect**. A discouraged worker is one who would like a job but has stopped looking because the prospects seem so bleak. When output increases, job prospects begin to look better and some people who had stopped looking for work begin looking again. When they do, they are once again counted as part of the labor force. The labor force increases when output increases because discouraged workers are moving back into the labor force. This is another reason the unemployment rate does not fall as much as might be expected when output increases.

These three slippages show that the link from changes in output to changes in the unemployment rate is complicated. All three combine to make the change in the unemployment rate less than the percentage change in output in the short run. They also show that the relationship between changes in output and changes in the unemployment rate is not likely to be stable. The size of the first slippage, for example, depends on how much excess labor is being held at the time of the output increase, and the size of the third slippage depends on what else is affecting the labor force (such as changes in real wage rates) at the time of the output increase. The relationship between output and unemployment depends on the state of the economy at the time of the output change.

The Size of the Multiplier

We can finally bring together the material in this chapter and in previous chapters to consider the size of the multiplier. We mentioned in Chapter 23 that much of the analysis we would do after deriving the simple multiplier would have the effect of decreasing the size of the multiplier. We can now summarize why.

1. There are *automatic stabilizers*. We saw in the Appendix to Chapter 24 that if taxes are not a fixed amount but instead depend on income (which is surely the case in practice), the size of the multiplier is decreased. When the economy expands and income increases, the amount of taxes collected increases. The rise in taxes acts to offset some of the expansion (thus, a smaller multiplier). When the economy contracts and income decreases, the amount of taxes collected decreases. This decrease in taxes helps to lessen the contraction. Some transfer payments also respond to the state of the economy and act as automatic stabilizers, lowering the value of the multiplier. Unemployment benefits are the best example of transfer payments that increase during contractions and decrease during expansions.
2. There is the *interest rate*. We saw in Chapter 27 that if government spending increases and the money supply remains unchanged, the interest rate increases, which decreases planned investment and aggregate output (income). This *crowding out* of planned investment decreases the value of the multiplier. As we saw earlier in this chapter, increases in the interest rate also have a negative effect on consumption. Consumption is also crowded out in the same way that planned investment is, and this effect lowers the value of the multiplier even further.
3. There is the response of the *price level*. We also saw in Chapter 27 that some of the effect of an expansionary policy is to increase the price level. The multiplier is smaller because of this price response. The multiplier is particularly small when the economy is on the steep part of the *AS* curve, where most of the effect of an expansionary policy is to increase prices.

4. There are *excess capital* and *excess labor*. When firms are holding excess labor and capital, part of any output increase can come from putting the excess labor and capital back to work instead of increasing employment and investment. This lowers the value of the multiplier because (1) investment increases less than it would have if there were no excess capital and (2) consumption increases less than it would have if employment (and thus household income) had increased more.
5. There are *inventories*. Part of any initial increase in sales can come from drawing down inventories instead of increasing output. To the extent that firms draw down their inventories in the short run, the value of the multiplier is lower because output does not respond as quickly to demand changes.
6. There are people's *expectations* about the future. People look ahead, and they respond less to temporary changes than to permanent changes. The multiplier effects for policy changes perceived to be temporary are smaller than those for policy changes perceived to be permanent.

The Size of the Multiplier in Practice In practice, the multiplier probably has a value of around 1.4. Its size also depends on how long ago the spending increase began. For example, in the first quarter of an increase in government spending, the multiplier is only about 1.1. If government spending rises by $1 billion, GDP will increase by about $1.1 billion during the first quarter. In the second quarter, the multiplier will rise to about 1.3. The multiplier then will rise to its peak of about 1.4 in the third or fourth quarter.

One of the main points to remember here is that if the government is contemplating a monetary or fiscal policy change, the response of the economy to the change is not likely to be large and quick. It takes time for the full effects to be felt, and in the final analysis, the effects are much smaller than the simple multiplier we discussed in Chapter 23 would lead one to believe.

A good way to review much of the material since Chapter 23 is to make sure you clearly understand how the value of the multiplier is affected by each of the additions to the simple model in Chapter 23. We have come a long way since then, and this review may help you to put all the pieces together.

SUMMARY

HOUSEHOLDS: CONSUMPTION AND LABOR SUPPLY DECISIONS *p. 609*

1. The *life-cycle theory of consumption* says that households make lifetime consumption decisions based on their expectations of lifetime income. Generally, households consume an amount less than their incomes during their prime working years and an amount greater than their incomes during their early working years and after they have retired.
2. Households make consumption and labor supply decisions simultaneously. Consumption cannot be considered separately from labor supply because it is precisely by selling your labor that you earn the income that makes consumption possible.
3. There is a trade-off between the goods and services that wage income will buy and leisure or other nonmarket activities. The wage rate is the key variable that determines how a household responds to this trade-off.
4. Changes in the wage rate have both an income effect and a substitution effect. The evidence suggests that the substitution effect seems to dominate for most people, which means that the aggregate labor supply responds positively to an increase in the wage rate.
5. Consumption increases when the wage rate increases.
6. The *nominal wage rate* is the wage rate in current dollars. The *real wage rate* is the amount the nominal wage can buy in terms of goods and services. Households look at expected future real wage rates as well as the current real wage rate in making their consumption and labor supply decisions.
7. Holding all else constant (including the stage in the life cycle), the more wealth a household has, the more it will consume both now and in the future.
8. An unexpected increase in *nonlabor income* (any income received from sources other than working, such as inheritances,

interest, and dividends) will have a positive effect on a household's consumption and will lead to a decrease in labor supply.

9. The interest rate also affects consumption, although the direction of the total effect depends on the relative sizes of the income and substitution effects. There is some evidence that the income effect is larger now than it used to be, making monetary policy less effective than it used to be.

10. The government influences household behavior mainly through income tax rates and transfer payments. If the substitution effect dominates, an increase in tax rates lowers after-tax income, decreases consumption, and decreases the labor supply; a decrease in tax rates raises after-tax income, increases consumption, and increases labor supply. Increases in transfer payments increase consumption and decrease labor supply; decreases in transfer payments decrease consumption and increase labor supply.

11. During times of unemployment, households' labor supply may be constrained. Households may want to work a certain number of hours at current wage rates but may not be allowed to do so by firms. In this case, the level of income (at least workers' income) depends exclusively on the employment decisions made by firms. Households consume less if they are constrained from working.

FIRMS: INVESTMENT AND EMPLOYMENT DECISIONS p.618

12. Expectations affect investment and employment decisions. Keynes used the term *animal spirits of entrepreneurs* to refer to investors' feelings.

13. At any level of the interest rate, expectations are likely to be more optimistic and planned investment is likely to be higher when output is growing rapidly than when it is growing slowly or falling. The result is an *accelerator effect* that can cause the economy to expand more rapidly during an expansion and contract more quickly during a recession.

14. Firms purchase *inputs* and turn them into outputs. Each period firms must decide how much capital and labor (two major inputs) to use in producing output. Firms can invest in plants and equipment or in inventory.

15. Because output can be produced using many different technologies, firms must make capital and labor decisions simultaneously. A *labor-intensive technique* uses a large amount of labor relative to capital. A *capital-intensive technique* uses a large amount of capital relative to labor. Which technology to use depends on the wage rate and the cost of capital.

16. *Excess labor and capital* are labor and capital not needed to produce a firm's current level of output. Holding excess labor and capital may be more efficient than laying off workers or selling used equipment. The more excess capital a firm has, the less likely it is to invest in new capital in the future. The more excess labor it has, the less likely it is to hire new workers in the future.

17. Holding inventories is costly to a firm because they take up space and they tie up funds that could be earning interest. Not holding inventories can cause a firm to lose sales if demand increases. The *desired*, or *optimal, level of inventories* is the level at which the extra cost (in lost sales) from lowering inventories by a small amount is equal to the extra gain (in interest revenue and decreased storage costs).

18. An unexpected increase in inventories has a negative effect on future production, and an unexpected decrease in inventories has a positive effect on future production.

19. The level of a firm's planned production path depends on the level of its expected future sales path. If a firm's expectations of its future sales path decrease, the firm is likely to decrease the level of its planned production path, including its actual production in the current period.

PRODUCTIVITY AND THE BUSINESS CYCLE p. 624

20. *Productivity*, or *labor productivity*, is output per worker hour—the amount of output produced by an average worker in 1 hour. Productivity fluctuates over the business cycle, tending to rise during expansions and fall during contractions. That workers are less productive during contractions does not mean that they have less potential to produce output; it means that excess labor exists and that workers are not working at their capacity.

THE SHORT-RUN RELATIONSHIP BETWEEN OUTPUT AND UNEMPLOYMENT p. 625

21. There is a negative relationship between output and unemployment: When output (Y) rises, the unemployment rate (U) falls, and when output falls, the unemployment rate rises. *Okun's Law* stated that in the short run the unemployment rate decreases about 1 percentage point for every 3 percent increase in GDP. Okun's Law is not a "law"—the economy is too complex for there to be a stable relationship between two macroeconomic variables. In general, the relationship between output and unemployment depends on the state of the economy at the time of the output change.

THE SIZE OF THE MULTIPLIER p. 626

22. There are several reasons why the actual value of the multiplier is smaller than the size that would be expected from the simple multiplier model: (1) Automatic stabilizers help to offset contractions or limit expansions. (2) When government spending increases, the increased interest rate crowds out planned investment and consumption spending. (3) Expansionary policies increase the price level. (4) Firms sometimes hold excess capital and excess labor. (5) Firms may meet increased demand by drawing down inventories instead of increasing output. (6) Households and firms change their behavior less when they expect changes to be temporary instead of permanent.

23. In practice, the size of the multiplier at its peak is about 1.4.

REVIEW TERMS AND CONCEPTS

accelerator effect, *p. 619*
adjustment costs, *p. 620*
animal spirits of entrepreneurs, *p. 619*
capital-intensive technology, *p. 620*
constrained supply of labor, *p. 614*
desired, *or* optimal, level of inventories, *p. 621*
discouraged-worker effect, *p. 626*
excess capital, *p. 620*
excess labor, *p. 620*
inputs, *p. 619*
inventory investment, *p. 621*
labor-intensive technology, *p. 620*
life-cycle theory of consumption, *p. 610*
nominal wage rate, *p. 612*
nonlabor, *or* nonwage, income, *p. 612*
Okun's Law, *p. 625*
permanent income, *p. 610*
plant-and-equipment investment, *p. 619*
productivity, *or* labor productivity, *p. 624*
real wage rate, *p. 612*
unconstrained supply of labor, *p. 614*

PROBLEMS

Visit **www.myeconlab.com** to complete the problems marked in orange online. You will receive instant feedback on your answers, tutorial help, and access to additional practice problems.

1. Between October 2004 and October 2005, real GDP in the United States increased by 3.6 percent, while nonfarm payroll jobs increased by only 1.4 percent. How is it possible for output to increase without a proportional increase in the number of workers?

2. **[Related to the *Economics in Practice* on *p. 617*]** Starting in 2006, home prices in the United States fell substantially. By the middle of 2008, house prices were down approximately 15 percent nationwide. Many worried that the decline in housing wealth would reduce consumption spending and slow the economy. In 2007, household holding of real estate (essentially single-family homes and condominiums) stood at about \$20 trillion. In 2000, it was about \$11 trillion. Go to www.federalreserve.gov and click on "Economic Research & Data," then on "Flow of Funds." Look at the most recent release and find balance sheet table B.100. What has happened to the value of household real estate holdings since 2008? Have they gone up or down? by how much? If consumption spending rises by 3 percent of any increase in real estate holdings, how much additional annual consumption would result from a \$5 trillion increase in home values? What about a 15 percent decline from their level in 2007? Some argue that the effect of housing on spending is asymmetric. That is, when home values rise, spending increases; but when home values fall, spending does not fall. Provide an explanation for such an asymmetry.

3. During 2005, the Federal Reserve Bank raised interest rates in an effort to prevent an increase in the rate of inflation.

a. What direct effects do higher interest rates have on household and firm behavior?

b. One of the consequences of higher interest rates was that the value of existing bonds (both corporate bonds and government bonds) fell substantially. Explain why higher interest rates would decrease the value of existing fixed-rate bonds held by the public.

c. Some economists argue that the wealth effect of higher interest rates on consumption is as important as the direct effect of higher interest rates on investment. Explain what economists mean by "wealth effects on consumption" and illustrate with *AS/AD* curves.

4. In 2005, President Bush's tax reform commission proposed and Congress enacted a decrease in taxes. One of the cuts was in the income tax rate for higher-income wage earners. Republicans claimed that raising the rewards for working (the net after-tax wage rate) would lead to more work effort and a higher labor supply. Critics of the tax cuts replied that this criticism was baseless because it "ignored the income effect of the tax cut (net wage increase)." Explain what these critics meant.

5. Graph the following two consumption functions:

$$(1) C = 300 + .5Y$$
$$(2) C = .5Y$$

a. For each function, calculate and graph the average propensity to consume (*APC*) when income is \$100, \$400, and \$800.

b. For each function, what happens to the *APC* as income rises?

c. For each function, what is the relationship between the *APC* and the marginal propensity to consume?

d. Under the first consumption function, a family with income of \$50,000 consumes a smaller proportion of its income than a family with income of \$20,000; yet if we take a dollar of income away from the rich family and give it to the poor family, total consumption by the two families does not change. Explain how this is possible.

6. Throughout the late 1990s, the price of houses increased steadily around the country.

a. What impact would you expect increases and decreases in home value to have on the consumption behavior of home owners? Explain.

b. In what ways might events in the housing market have influenced the rest of the economy through their effects on consumption spending? Be specific.

*7. Adam Smith is 45 years old. He has assets (wealth) of $20,000 and has no debts or liabilities. He knows that he will work for 20 more years and will live 5 years after that, when he will earn nothing. His salary each year for the rest of his working career is $14,000. (There are no taxes.) He wants to distribute his consumption over the rest of his life in such a way that he consumes the same amount each year. He cannot consume in total more than his current wealth plus the sum of his income for the next 20 years. Assume that the rate of interest is zero and that Smith decides not to leave any inheritance to his children.
   a. How much will Adam consume this year and next year? How did you arrive at your answer?
   b. Plot on a graph Adam's income, consumption, and wealth from the time he is 45 until he is 70 years old. What is the relationship between the annual increase in his wealth and his annual saving (income minus consumption)? In what year does Adam's wealth start to decline? Why? How much wealth does he have when he dies?
   c. Suppose Adam receives a tax rebate of $100 per year, so his income is $14,100 per year for the rest of his working career. By how much does his consumption increase this year and next year?
   d. Now suppose Adam receives a 1-year-only tax refund of $100—his income this year is $14,100; but in all succeeding years, his income is $14,000. What happens to his consumption this year? in succeeding years?

8. Explain why a household's consumption and labor supply decisions are interdependent. What impact does this interdependence have on the way in which consumption and income are related?

9. Why do expectations play such an important role in investment demand? How, if at all, does this explain why investment is so volatile?

10. How can a firm maintain a smooth production schedule even when sales are fluctuating? What the benefits of a smooth production schedule? What are the costs?

* Note: Problems marked with an asterisk are more challenging.

Long-Run Growth

32

In 1975, the per capita GDP of the sub-Saharan African nations was $1,928. By 2005, that number had fallen to $1,768. In the same period, nations in East Asia and the Pacific increased GDP per capita from $905 to $4,595. On almost any measure that one could use, the economies of most of the sub-Saharan countries have been languishing, while much of Asia has seen rapid growth. How do we explain these differences? Will China continue to grow, becoming as some have predicted, the next economic superpower? Is the very recent economic progress we observe in parts of sub-Saharan Africa likely to continue? Even the United States has seen substantial differences in growth over time. In the mid-nineteenth century, U.S. growth was over 5 percent. The 1930s, as you may recall from Chapter 20, experienced growth rates of less than 2 percent. As China and other Asian countries grow rapidly, many observers wonder whether the United States can keep up. These questions form the heart of the study of economic growth.

Recall from Chapter 1 that **economic growth** occurs when an economy experiences an increase in total output. The increase in real output that began in the Western world with the Industrial Revolution and continues today has been so sustained and so rapid that economists refer to this as the period of **modern economic growth**.

It is through economic growth that living standards improve, but growth brings change. New things are produced while others become obsolete. Some believe that growth is the fundamental objective of a society because it lifts people out of poverty and enhances the quality of their lives. Others say that economic growth erodes traditional values and leads to exploitation, environmental destruction, and corruption.

The first part of this chapter describes economic growth in some detail and identifies sources of economic growth across the world. We then turn to look more narrowly at the U.S. growth picture. After a review of the U.S. economy's growth record since the nineteenth century, we examine the role of public policy in the growth process. We conclude with a discussion of growth and the environment, returning to the world perspective.

CHAPTER OUTLINE

economic growth An increase in the total output of an economy.

modern economic growth The period of rapid and sustained increase in output that began in the Western world with the Industrial Revolution.

The Growth Process: From Agriculture to Industry

The easiest way to understand the growth process and to identify its causes is to think about a simple economy. Recall from Chapter 2, Colleen and Bill washed up on a deserted island. At first, they had only a few simple tools and whatever human capital they brought with them to the island. They gathered nuts and berries and built a small cabin. Their "GDP" consisted of basic food and shelter.

Over time, things improved. The first year they cleared some land and began to cultivate a few vegetables they found growing on the island. They made some tools and dug a small reservoir to store rainwater. As their agricultural efforts became more efficient, they shifted their resources—their time—into building a larger, more comfortable home.

Colleen and Bill were accumulating capital in two forms. First, they built *physical capital*, material things used in the production of goods and services—a better house, tools, a water system, perhaps a boat to let them fish farther off shore. Second, they acquired more *human capital*—knowledge, skills, and talents. Through trial and error, they learned about the island and its soil and its climate and learned what did and did not work. Both kinds of capital made them more efficient and increased their productivity. Because it took less time to produce the food they needed to survive, they could devote more energy to producing other things or to leisure.

At any given time, Colleen and Bill faced limits on what they could produce. These limits were imposed by the existing state of their technical knowledge and the resources at their disposal. Over time, they expanded their possibilities, developed new technologies, accumulated capital, and made their labor more productive. In Chapter 2, we defined a society's *production possibility frontier (ppf)*, which shows all possible combinations of output that can be produced given present technology and whether all available resources are fully and efficiently employed. Economic growth expands those limits and shifts society's production possibilities frontier out to the right, as Figure 32.1 shows.

FIGURE 32.1

Economic Growth Shifts Society's Production Possibility Frontier Up and to the Right

The production possibility frontier shows all the combinations of output that can be produced if all society's scarce resources are fully and efficiently employed. Economic growth expands society's production possibilities, shifting the ppf up and to the right.

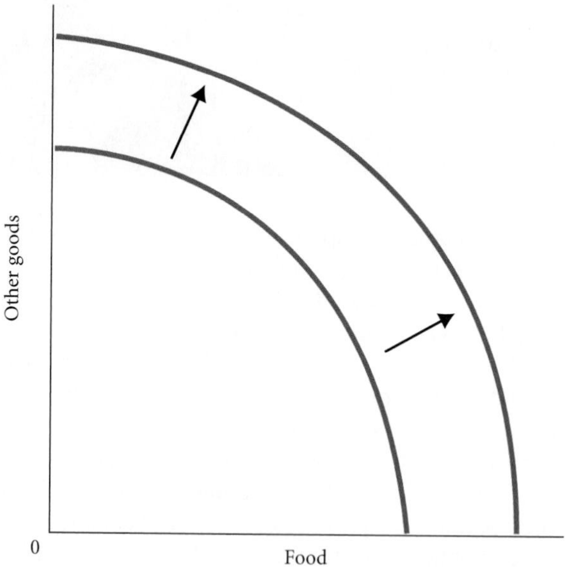

From Agriculture to Industry: The Industrial Revolution Before the Industrial Revolution in Great Britain, every society in the world was agrarian. Towns and cities existed here and there, but almost everyone lived in rural areas. People spent most of their time producing food and other basic subsistence goods. Then beginning in England around 1750, technical change and capital accumulation increased productivity significantly in two important industries: agriculture and textiles. New and more efficient methods of farming were developed. New inventions and new machinery in spinning and weaving meant that more could be produced with fewer resources. Just as new technology, capital equipment, and resulting higher productivity made it possible for Colleen and Bill to spend time working on other projects and new "products," the British turned from agricultural production to industrial production. In both cases, growth meant new products, more output, and wider choice.

Those changes meant that peasants and workers in eighteenth-century England who in the past would have continued in subsistence farming could make a better living as urban workers. A rural agrarian society was very quickly transformed into an urban industrial society.

The transition from agriculture to industry has been more recent in developing countries in Asia. One of the hallmarks of current growth in China and Vietnam, for example, has been the focus on manufacturing exports as a growth strategy. A visitor to Vietnam cannot help but be struck by the pace of industrialization.

Growth in Modern Society Economic growth continues today in the developed world. And while the underlying process is still the same, the face is different. Just as Colleen and Bill devoted time to building a boat and designing tools, the developed economies are still creating capital to increase productivity. Just as a shovel makes it possible to dig a bigger hole, new microwave towers bring cell phone service to places that had been out of range. Scientists work on finding a cure for Alzheimer's disease using tools they couldn't have dreamed of a decade ago. Tools available on the Web make it possible for a single law clerk in a busy law office to check hundreds of documents for the opinions of potential expert witnesses in a court case in an hour, a task that took a dozen law clerks weeks to perform just a few years ago. In each case, we have become more proficient at producing what we want and need and we have freed up resources to produce new things that we want and need. For Colleen and Bill, it was a better diet; with a boat they could catch more fish in less time. Today it may be better cell phone service; a fast, inexpensive color printer; or a better medical procedure.

The basic building blocks are the same. Growth comes from a bigger workforce and more productive workers. Higher productivity comes from tools (capital), a better-educated and more highly skilled workforce (human capital), and increasingly from innovation and technical change (new techniques of production) and newly developed products and services.

Growth Patterns and the Possibility of Catch-Up Table 32.1 provides estimates of the growth of GDP for a number of developed and developing countries. One fact that should strike you as you look at these numbers is the high rates of growth of China and India relative to those of the developed countries. Some economists argue that when poorer, less developed countries begin to develop, they typically have higher growth rates as they **catch-up** with the more developed countries. This idea is called *convergence theory* since it suggests that gaps in national incomes tend to close over time. Indeed, more than 50 years ago, the economic historian Alexander Gerschenkron coined the term *the advantages of backwardness* as a description of the phenomenon by which less developed countries could leap ahead by borrowing technology from more developed countries. This idea seems to fit the current experiences of China and India as shown in the table. On the other hand, growth rates in Africa are more modest. For a country such as Zimbabwe, growth in real GDP has been poor, resulting in a growing disadvantage relative to much of the rest of the world. Understanding why some countries appear to be converging and others are falling further behind is the subject of considerable political, economic, and social interest. We turn now to look at the sources of economic growth.

catch-up The theory stating that the growth rates of less developed countries will exceed the growth rates of developed countries, allowing the less developed countries to catch up.

TABLE 32.1 Growth of Real GDP: 1999–2007

Country	Average Growth Rates per Year, 1999–2007
United States	2.7
Japan	1.5
Germany	1.5
France	2.1
United Kingdom	2.7
China	9.6
India	7.0
Africa (continent)	4.5
Republic of South Africa (2002–2007)	3.9
Cameroon (2002–2007)	4.0
Zimbabwe (2002–2007)	1.0

Source: Economic Report of the President, 2008.

The Sources of Economic Growth

Economic growth occurs when (1) society acquires more resources or (2) society discovers ways of using available resources more efficiently. For economic growth to increase living standards, the rate of growth must exceed the rate of population increase. Economic growth is generally defined as *an increase in real GDP per capita.*

aggregate production function The mathematical representation of the relationship between inputs and national output, or gross domestic product.

As we discuss the factors that contribute to economic growth, it will be helpful to think of an **aggregate production function.** An individual firm's production function is a mathematical representation of the relationship between the firm's inputs and its output. Output for an aggregate production function is national output, or GDP. Stated simply, GDP (output) (Y) depends on the amount of labor (L) and the amount of capital (K) available in the economy (assuming the amount of land is fixed).[1] If you think of GDP as a function of both labor and capital, you can see the following:

An increase in GDP can come about through

1. An increase in the labor supply.
2. An increase in physical or human capital.
3. An increase in productivity (the amount of product produced by each unit of capital or labor).

An Increase in Labor Supply

Consider what would happen if another person joined Colleen and Bill on the island. That individual would join in the work and produce, so GDP would rise. Suppose that a person who had not been a part of the labor force were to begin to work and use time and energy to produce pottery. Real output would rise in this case also. An increase in labor supply can generate more output.

Whether output *per capita* rises when the labor supply increases is another matter. If the capital stock remains fixed while labor increases, the new labor will likely be less productive than the old labor. This effect is called *diminishing returns,* and it worried Thomas Malthus, David Ricardo, and other early economists.

Malthus and Ricardo, who lived in England during the nineteenth century, were concerned that the fixed supply of land would lead to diminishing returns. With land in strictly limited supply, the ppf could be pushed out only so far as population increased. To increase agricultural output, people would be forced to farm less productive land or to farm land more intensively. In either case, the returns to successive increases in population would diminish. Both Malthus and Ricardo predicted a gloomy future as population outstripped the land's capacity to produce. What both economists left out of their calculations was technological change and capital accumulation. New and better farming techniques have raised agricultural productivity so much that less than 3 percent of the U.S. population now provides enough food for the country's entire population.

Diminishing returns can also occur if a nation's capital stock grows more slowly than its workforce. Capital enhances workers' productivity. A person with a shovel digs a bigger hole than a person without one, and a person with a steam shovel outdoes them both. If a society's stock of plant and equipment does not grow and the technology of production does not change, additional workers will not be as productive because they do not have machines with which to work.

labor productivity Output per worker hour; the amount of output produced by an average worker in 1 hour.

Table 32.2 illustrates how growth in the labor force, without a corresponding increase in the capital stock or technological change, might lead to growth of output but declining productivity and a lower standard of living. As labor increases, output rises from 300 units in period 1 to 320 in period 2, to 339 in period 3, and so forth, but **labor productivity** (output per worker hour) falls. Output per worker hour, Y/L, is a measure of labor's productivity.

The fear that new workers entering the labor force will displace existing workers and generate unemployment has been with us for a long time. New workers can come from many places. They might be immigrants, young people looking for their first jobs, or older people entering the labor force for the first time. Between 1947 and 2007, the number of women in the labor force quadrupled, jumping from 17 million to 71 million. Table 32.3 shows that in the United States since World War II, the civilian noninstitutional population (those not in jails or mental institutions) over 16 years of age increased by 127.8 percent, while the labor force grew by 157.7 percent.

[1] All the numbers in the tables to follow were derived from the simple production function $Y = 3 \times K^{1/3} L^{2/3}$.

TABLE 32.2 Economic Growth from an Increase in Labor—More Output but Diminishing Returns and Lower Labor Productivity

Period	Quantity of Labor L (Hours)	Quantity of Capital K (Units)	Total Output Y (Units)	Measured Labor Productivity Y/L
1	100	100	300	3.0
2	110	100	320	2.9
3	120	100	339	2.8
4	130	100	357	2.7

The U.S. economy, however, has shown a remarkable ability to expand right along with the labor force. The number of people employed jumped by 89.0 million—156.1 percent—during the same period. As long as the economy and the capital stock are expanding rapidly enough, new entrants into the labor force do not displace other workers.

TABLE 32.3 Employment, Labor Force, and Population Growth, 1947–2007

	Civilian Noninstitutional Population Over 16 Years Old (Millions)	Civilian Labor Force		Employment (Millions)
		Number (Millions)	Percentage of Population	
1947	101.8	59.4	58.3	57.0
1960	117.3	69.6	59.3	65.8
1970	137.1	82.8	60.4	78.7
1980	167.7	106.9	63.7	99.3
1990	189.2	125.8	66.5	118.8
2000	212.6	142.6	67.1	136.9
2007	231.9	153.1	66.0	146.0
Percentage change, 1947–2007	+127.8%	+157.7%		+156.1%
Annual rate	+1.4%	+1.6%		+1.6%

Source: Economic Report of the President, 2008, Table B-35.

Increases in Physical Capital

An increase in the stock of capital can also increase output even if it is not accompanied by an increase in the labor force. Physical capital both enhances the productivity of labor and provides valuable services directly.

It is easy to see how capital provides services directly. Consider what happened on Bill and Colleen's island. In the first few years, they built a house, putting many hours of work into it that could have gone into producing other things for immediate consumption. With the house for shelter, Colleen and Bill can spend time on other things. In the same way, capital equipment produced in 1 year can add to the value of a product over many years. For example, we still derive use and value from bridges and tunnels built decades ago.

It is also easy to see how capital used in production enhances the productivity of labor. Computers enable us to do almost instantly tasks that once were impossible or might have taken years to complete. An airplane with a small crew can transport hundreds of people thousands of miles in a few hours. A bridge over a river at a critical location may save thousands of labor hours that would be spent transporting materials and people the long way around. New technology is opening up communications impossible to imagine a decade ago. The strongest growth area today for cell phones is in Africa. Technology has allowed phone services to reach geographically remote areas, increasing the productivity of villages. It is precisely this yield in the form of future valuable services that provides private and public investors with the incentive to devote resources to capital production.

Table 32.4 shows how an increase in capital without a corresponding increase in labor might increase output. Observe several things about these numbers. First, additional capital increases measured productivity; output per worker hour (Y/L) increases from 3.0 to 3.1, to 3.2, and finally to 3.3 as the quantity of capital (K) increases. Second, there are diminishing returns to capital. Increasing capital by 10 units first increases output by 10 units—from 300 in period 1 to 310 in period 2. However, the second increase of 10 units yields only 9 units of output, and the third increase yields only 8 units.

TABLE 32.4 Economic Growth from an Increase in Capital—More Output, Diminishing Returns to Added Capital, Higher Measured Labor Productivity

Period	Quantity of Labor L (Hours)	Quantity of Capital K (Units)	Total Output Y (Units)	Measured Labor Productivity Y/L
1	100	100	300	3.0
2	100	110	310	3.1
3	100	120	319	3.2
4	100	130	327	3.3

Table 32.5 shows the values of the private nonresidential capital stock in the United States since 1960. The increase in capital stock is the difference between gross investment and depreciation. (Remember, some capital becomes obsolete and some wears out every year.) Between 1960 and 2006, the stock of equipment increased at a rate of 4.4 percent per year and the stock of structures increased at a rate of 2.4 percent per year.

TABLE 32.5 Fixed Private Nonresidential Net Capital Stock, 1960–2006 (Billions of 2000 Dollars)

	Equipment	Structures
1960	645.7	2,273.3
1970	1,108.5	3,094.8
1980	1,910.0	4,047.7
1990	2,613.3	5,304.5
2000	4,090.5	6,301.6
2006	4,841.8	6,776.9
Percentage change, 1960–2006	+649.9%	+198.1%
Annual rate	+4.4%	+2.4%

Source: Survey of Current Business, September 2007, Table 15, p. 32 and authors' estimates.

By comparing Table 32.3 and Table 32.5, you can see that in the United States, capital has been increasing faster than labor since 1960. In all economies experiencing modern economic growth, capital expands at a more rapid rate than labor. That is, the ratio of capital to labor (K/L) increases, and this too is a source of increasing productivity.

Role of Institutions in Attracting Capital The importance of capital in a country's economic growth naturally leads one to ask the question of what determines a country's stock of capital. In the modern open economy, new capital can come from the saving of a country's residents and/or from the investments of foreigners. **Foreign direct investment** is any investment in enterprises made in a country by residents outside that country. Foreign direct investment has been quite influential in providing needed capital for growth in much of Southeast Asia. In Vietnam, for example, rapid growth has been led by foreign direct investment. Very recently, we have seen signs of Chinese foreign direct investment in parts of Africa and in other parts of Asia.

foreign direct investment (FDI) Investment in enterprises made in a country by residents outside that country.

Recent work in economics has focused on the role that institutions play in creating a capital-friendly environment that encourages home savings and foreign investment. In a series of papers, LaPorta, Lopez de Silanes, Shleifer, and Vishny argue that countries with English common law origins (as opposed to French) provide the strongest protection for shareholders, less corrupt governments, and better court systems. In turn, these financial and legal institutions promote growth by encouraging capital investment. Countries with poor institutions, corruption, and inadequate protection for lenders and investors struggle to attract capital. The World Bank calls countries with weak institutions *fragile countries.*

Many of the World Bank's fragile countries are in sub-Saharan Africa. Many observers believe that the relative stagnation of some of the sub-Saharan African nations comes in part from their relatively weak institutions. High costs of doing business, including corruption and investment risks associated with conflict, have made countries such as Zimbabwe less attractive to domestic and foreign capital. Ethnic and linguistic fractionalization have also played a role.

China's growth in the last several decades, however, suggests that weak institutions may not completely block growth. Beginning in 1978, the Chinese government embarked on a series of reforms that introduced private profit-making business to the economy. Growth since that period has been quite rapid, averaging 9 percent in the years since reform. This growth period was accomplished despite a relatively weak set of property rights protections and financial institutions. Stock exchanges were introduced only in 1990, and the two Chinese exchanges, the Shanghai Exchange and the ShenZhen Exchange, remain small given the size of the economy. Most of the lending is controlled by four state-owned banks. In the early 1980s, corruption continued to be a problem. While many observers now believe that better institutions will be necessary to sustain the Chinese growth miracle (and the government is clearly moving in that direction), it is clear that China's early growth spurt was accomplished despite a relatively weak set of institutions.

Increases in Human Capital

Investment in human capital is another source of economic growth. People in good health are more productive than people in poor health; people with skills are more productive than people without skills.

Consider again the sub-Saharan African nations. The World Bank estimated in 2007 that there were 72 million primary-aged school children in the world who were not in school. Of those children, 37 percent were in the fragile states of Africa. Another key problem facing this area in terms of human capital is health. Rates of HIV/AIDS infections remain very high, particularly in southern Africa. Moreover, HIV/AIDS, unlike many other diseases, affects prime-age workers. Parts of southern Africa have seen reductions in life expectancy in the last 20 years. Interesting work trying to measure the size of the effects of health issues on growth in Africa is being done by a number of economists, including Simon Johnson of the IMF and Daron Acemoglu of MIT.

Human capital can be produced in many ways. Individuals can invest in themselves by going to college or by completing vocational training programs. Firms can invest in human capital through on-the-job training. The government invests in human capital with programs to improve health and to provide schooling and job training.

Table 32.6 shows that the level of educational attainment in the United States has risen significantly since 1940. The percentage of the population with at least 4 years of college rose from under 5 percent in 1940 to 28.0 percent in 2006. In 1940, fewer than 1 person in 4 had completed high school; in 2006, 85.5 percent had.

TABLE 32.6 Years of School Completed by People Over 25 Years Old, 1940–2006

	Percentage with Less than 5 Years of School	Percentage with 4 Years of High School or More	Percentage with 4 Years of College or More
1940	13.7	24.5	4.6
1950	11.1	34.3	6.2
1960	8.3	41.1	7.7
1970	5.5	52.3	10.7
1980	3.6	66.5	16.2
1990	NA	77.6	21.3
2000	NA	84.1	25.6
2006	NA	85.5	28.0

NA = not available.

Source: Statistical Abstract of the United States, 1990, Table 215; and 2008, Table 217.

Increases in Productivity

Growth that cannot be explained by increases in the *quantity* of inputs can be explained only by an increase in the *productivity* of those inputs—each unit of input must be producing more output. The **productivity of an input** can be affected by factors including technological change, other advances in knowledge, and economies of scale.

productivity of an input The amount of output produced per unit of an input.

Technological Change The Industrial Revolution was in part sparked by new technological developments. New techniques of spinning and weaving—the invention of the machines known as the mule and the spinning jenny, for example—were critical. The high-tech boom that swept the United States in the early 1980s was driven by the rapid development and dissemination of semiconductor technology. In India, new high-yielding seeds in the 1960s helped to create a "green revolution" in agriculture.

Technological change affects productivity in two stages. First, there is an advance in knowledge, or an **invention**. However, knowledge by itself does nothing unless it is used. When new knowledge is used to produce a new product or to produce an existing product more efficiently, there is **innovation**.

invention An advance in knowledge.

innovation The use of new knowledge to produce a new product or to produce an existing product more efficiently.

Technological change cannot be measured directly. Some studies have presented data on "indicators" of the rate of technical change—the number of new patents, for example—but none are satisfactory. Still, we know that technological changes that have improved productivity are all around us. Wireless technology has revolutionized the office, hybrid seeds have increased the productivity of land, and more efficient and powerful aircraft have made air travel routine and inexpensive.

Over and above invention and innovation in new products and technology, advances in other kinds of knowledge can also improve productivity. One is what we might call managerial knowledge. For example, because of the very high cost of capital during the early 1980s, firms learned to manage their inventories much better. Many were able to keep production lines and distribution lines flowing with a much lower stock of inventories. Inventories are part of a firm's capital stock, and trimming them reduces costs and raises productivity. This is an example of a *capital-saving* innovation. Many of the advances that we are used to thinking about, such as the introduction of robotics, are *labor-saving*.

In addition to managerial knowledge, improved personnel management techniques, accounting procedures, data management, and the like can also make production more efficient, reduce costs, and increase measured productivity.

Economies of Scale *External economies of scale* are cost savings that result from increases in the size of industries. The economies that accompany growth in size may arise from a variety of causes. For example, as firms in a growing industry build plants at new locations, they may lower transport costs. There may also be some economies of scale associated with research and development (R&D) spending and job-training programs.

Other Influences on Productivity In addition to technological change, other advances in knowledge, and economies of scale, other forces may affect productivity. During the 1970s and 1980s, the U.S. government required many firms to reduce the air and water pollution they were producing. These requirements diverted capital and labor from the production of measured output, therefore *reducing* measured productivity. Similarly, in recent years, requirements imposed by the Occupational Safety and Health Act (OSHA) have required firms to protect workers better from accidental injuries and potential health problems. These laws also divert resources from measured output.

Negative effects such as these are more a problem of *measurement* than of declining productivity. The Environmental Protection Agency (EPA) regulates air and water quality because clean air and water presumably have a value to society. The resources diverted to produce that value are not wasted. A perfect measure of output produced that is of value to society includes environmental quality and good health.

Recent experiences in the Chinese economy point to another set of influences on productivity. Working with the IMF, Zuliu Hu and Mohsin Khan have pointed to the large role of productivity gains in the 20 years following the market reforms in China. In the period after the reforms, productivity growth rates tripled, averaging almost 4 percent a year. Hu and Khan argue that the productivity gains came principally from the unleashing of profit incentives that came with the opening of business to the private sector.

Climate and geography also play a role in productivity. Daron Acemoglu of MIT, Simon Johnson of the IMF, and James Robinson of Harvard have argued that the geography and climate of Africa, by creating high mortality rates among early colonial settlers, gave rise to a colonial strategy of expropriation rather than development. In turn, the weak institutions that emerged from this colonial strategy have hampered further economic development in the area. The role of geography in growth and development remains a fascinating area in economic research.

Growth and Productivity in the United States

Modern economic growth in the United States began in the middle of the nineteenth century. After the Civil War, railroads spread across the country and the economy took off. Table 32.7 shows the growth rate of real output in the United States for selected subperiods since 1871. Between 1871 and 1909, the growth rate was very strong—5.5 percent in the 1871–1889 period and 4.0 percent in the 1889–1909 period. The growth rate slowed to 2.8 percent in the 1909–1929 period and even further to 1.6 percent in the period that includes the Great Depression, 1929–1940. The growth rate was a strong 5.6 percent in the period that includes World War II, 1940–1950. It was then 3.5 percent in the 1950s, 4.2 percent in the 1960s, and roughly 3.2 percent since then.

TABLE 32.7 Growth of Real GDP in the United States, 1871-2000

Period	Average Growth Rate per Year	Period	Average Growth Rate per Year
1871-1889	5.5	1950-1960	3.5
1889-1909	4.0	1960-1970	4.2
1909-1929	2.8	1970-1980	3.2
1929-1940	1.6	1980-1990	3.2
1940-1950	5.6	1990-2000	3.2

Sources: Historical Statistics of the United States: Colonial Times to 1970, Tables F47-70, F98-124; U.S. Department of Commerce, Bureau of Economic Analysis.

Sources of Growth in the U.S. Economy

For many years, Edward Denison of the Brookings Institution in Washington studied the growth process in the United States and sorted out the relative importance of the various causal factors. Table 32.8 presents some of his results. Denison estimates that about half of U.S. growth in output over the entire period from 1929 to 1982 came from increases in factors of production and the other half from increases in productivity. Growth in the labor force accounted for about 20 percent of overall growth, while growth in capital stock (both human and physical) accounted for 33 percent. Of the capital stock growth figure, human capital (education and training) accounted for 19 percent of the total and physical capital accounted for 14 percent. Growth of knowledge was the most important factor contributing to increases in the productivity of inputs.

TABLE 32.8 Sources of Growth in the United States, 1929-1982

	Percent of Growth Attributable to Each Source			
	1929-1982	1929-1948	1948-1973	1973-1979
Increases in inputs	**53**	**49**	**45**	**94**
Labor	20	26	14	47
Capital	14	3	16	29
Education (human capital)	19	20	15	18
Increases in productivity	**47**	**51**	**55**	**6**
Advances in knowledge	31	30	39	8
Other factors[a]	16	21	16	−2
Annual growth rate in real national income	2.8	2.4	3.6	2.6

[a]Economies of scale, weather, pollution abatement, worker safety and health, crime, labor disputes, and so on.

Source: Edward Denison, *Trends in American Economic Growth, 1929–1982* (Washington: Brookings Institution, 1985). Reprinted with permission of The Brookings Institution.

The relative importance of these causes of growth varied considerably over the years. Between 1929 and 1948, for example, physical capital played a much smaller role than it did in other periods. Each period included times that were atypical for one reason or another. The period between 1929 and 1948 included the dislocations and uncertainties of the Great Depression and World War II. From 1948 to 1973, the economy enjoyed a period of unusual stability and expansion.

In looking at the sources of U.S. growth since the 1970s, Professor Dale Jorgenson of Harvard University and a number of colleagues have done a similar accounting that breaks out the contributions of a specific kind of capital: information technology (IT) capital, including computers, software, and communications equipment. The results are presented in Table 32.9. The precise meaning of these numbers is quite complex, but they clearly indicate a number of trends. You can see that the portion of overall growth contributed by productivity is rising and that information technology has played a big role in recent years.

TABLE 32.9 Sources of U.S. Growth, 1995–2004

	Percent Contribution 1995–2004	
Increases in inputs		71.6
Labor	20.6	
Capital	50.7	
IT capital	22.8	
Non-IT capital	27.9	
Increases in productivity		28.4

Source: Information Technology and the American Growth Resurgence. Dale W. Jorgenson, Mun S. Ho and Kevin J. Stiroh (Cambridge, MA: MIT Press, 2005). Data update provided by the authors.

Labor Productivity: 1952 I–2007 IV

In Figure 22.2 on p. 447, we presented a plot of labor productivity for the 1952 I–2007 IV period. It is now time to return to this figure, and it is repeated as Figure 32.2. Productivity in the figure is output per worker hour. Remember that the line segments are drawn to smooth out the short-run fluctuations in productivity. We saw in the last chapter that productivity as it is measured moves with the business cycle because firms tend to hold excess labor in recessions. We are not interested in business cycles in this chapter, and the line segments are a way of ignoring business cycle effects.

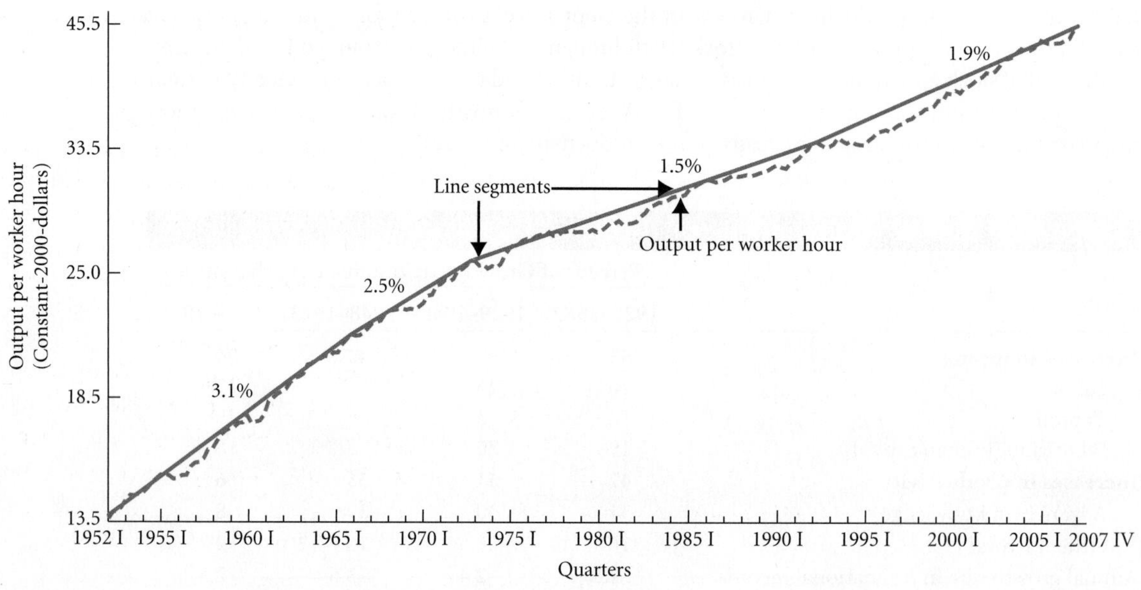

▲ **FIGURE 32.2 Output per Worker Hour (Productivity), 1952 I–2007 IV**

ECONOMICS IN PRACTICE

Improving Productivity in Health Care

In the United States, health care spending has become an increasingly large share of the GDP. For a number of people, part of their health care costs are borne by their employers. These firms thus have strong incentives to find ways to increase the productivity of health care. But productivity growth in health care has been hard to measure. In manufacturing, we often look to capital expenditures to reduce production costs. In health care, most capital investments result in an increase in the quality of care, not a reduction of its costs. New medical devices to stabilize heart rhythm, for example, have the potential to reduce mortality, but they come at a high price. Fewer investments are made that allow doctors to produce a fixed quality of care at a lower cost, a form of productivity growth familiar in the manufacturing world. As the following article suggests, firms have looked elsewhere to lower costs of health care: increasing the availability of preventive services and wellness programs such as smoking cessation and exercise. In other words, firms have looked at trying to change the production technology to lower costs.

Firms' Health Clinics Cut Costs

Wall Street Journal

In the latest attempt to motivate workers to adopt more-healthful lifestyles, American employers are offering wellness coaching to employees at on-site clinics.

While American employers may like the idea of getting out of the business of providing health care, a growing number of corporations are discovering they can save money and boost employee productivity by getting more closely involved at an earlier stage.

"On-site clinics have undergone a huge transformation," said Marne Bell, a senior consultant at Watson Wyatt. "There's much more emphasis on prevention."

Gone are the days when on-site clinics were the sole preserve of manufacturing companies that founded facilities to treat employees' work-related injuries. Some three in 10 large employers–from financial firms to hair-care companies–have on-site clinics, offering everything from primary care to travel medicine, pregnancy support and nutrition counseling. Walt Disney Co. just broke ground on a $6 million, 15,000-square-foot health-and-wellness center for employees at Walt Disney World.

Preventive services, such as health screenings and immunizations, are the most common type at the latest wave of clinics, according to a recent survey by Watson Wyatt and the National Business Group on Health. Four in 10 clinics offer pharmacy services, making it easier for those taking medications to fill their prescriptions.

Faced with escalating health-care costs, Harrah's Entertainment Inc. three years ago opened its first health-and-wellness center in Atlantic City, N.J. Since then, the casino-entertainment company has opened four more facilities, most recently in Las Vegas, where in January 2007 it opened a 7,000-square-foot clinic offering acute and primary-care services, nutritional counseling and physiotherapy. Downstairs there is a 12,000 square-foot gym.

"We recognized that there was going to come a point where we couldn't pass on the additional cost of providing health care to employees," said Jeff Shovlin, vice president of benefits at Harrah's. "We concluded that the only way to control costs was by helping employees to get and stay healthy."

Source: Victoria E. Knight, April 9, 2008

There was much talk in the late 1970s and early 1980s about the "productivity problem." Some economics textbooks published in the early 1980s had entire chapters discussing the decline in productivity that seemed to be taking place during the late 1970s. In January 1981, the Congressional Budget Office published a report, *The Productivity Problem: Alternatives for Action.*

It is clear from Figure 32.2 that there was a slowdown in productivity growth in the 1970s. The growth rate went from 3.1 percent in the 1950s and first half of the 1960s to 2.5 percent in the last half of the 1960s and early 1970s and then to 1.5 percent from the early 1970s to the 1990s. Many explanations were offered at the time for the productivity slowdown of the late 1970s and early 1980s. Some economists pointed to the low rate of saving in the United States compared with other parts of the world. Others blamed increased environmental and government regulation of U.S. business. Still others argued that the country was not spending as much on R&D as it should be. Finally, some suggested that high energy costs in the 1970s led to investment designed to save energy instead of to enhance productivity. (Later in this chapter we discuss how each of these factors influences growth.)

Many of these factors turned around in the 1980s and 1990s and yet, as you can see from Figure 32.2 on p. 640, productivity growth rose to only 1.9 percent in the 1990s and through 2007. This early discussion is now quite dated. The interesting question as we move into the second decade of the twenty-first century is whether the continued growth of the Internet and wireless devices will return productivity growth to the values observed in the 1950s and 1960s or whether the period of the 1950s and 1960s was simply an unusually good period for productivity growth.

Economic Growth and Public Policy in the United States

The decline in productivity in the 1970s that caused so much concern led to a protracted national discussion about the role of government in stimulating economic growth. This debate was spurred in part by increasing concern on the part of many Americans that the United States was not doing as well as the Asian countries.

Suggested Public Policies

Several strategies for increasing the rate of growth in the United States have been suggested, and some have been enacted into law. These strategies include policies aimed toward improving the quality of education, increasing the saving rate, stimulating investment, increasing R&D, reducing regulation, and pursuing an industrial policy.

Policies to Improve the Quality of Education The Denison study shows that the contribution of education and training (human capital production) to growth in the United States has remained relatively constant at about 20 percent since 1929.

The quality of public education has been a concern since the 1970s. Increasingly, attention has been focused on the uneven quality of public education across the country and in particular on the large gap in educational achievement for poor children. Partly in response to perceived educational disparities, in 2001, the Bush administration passed the No Child Left Behind Act. This legislation, which increases state accountability for student performance via a system of increased testing and a wider set of federally imposed "carrots and sticks" for states and local governments, has been very controversial. There is considerable dispute about how to measure educational progress and how to create incentives to produce good outcomes. Nevertheless, there was widespread bipartisan agreement in the United States about the importance of improving education for future prosperity and growth. In the last few years, battles have also been waged in Congress over the amount of federal dollars set aside for scholarships and loans to college students. Whatever the policies of the moment, however, all federal, state, and local expenditures on education acknowledge the need to build the nation's stock of human capital.

The Taxpayer Relief Act of 1997 contained provisions that focused on education. First, the HOPE Scholarship credit allows taxpayers to claim a credit up to $1,500 for postsecondary education expenses on behalf of any family member. Other provisions included an Education Individual Retirement Account that allows savings to earn tax-free returns as long as the balance is used to pay educational expenses.

Policies to Increase the Saving Rate The amount of capital accumulation in an economy is ultimately constrained by its rate of saving. The more saving in an economy, the more funds available for investment. Many people have argued that the tax system and the Social Security system in the United States are biased against saving. Some public finance economists favor shifting to a system of consumption taxation instead of income taxation to reduce the tax burden on saving.

Others claim the Social Security system, by providing guaranteed retirement incomes, reduces the incentive for people to save. Private pension plans make deposits to workers' accounts, the balances of which are invested in the stock market and bond market and are made available to firms for capital investment. In contrast, Social Security benefits are mostly paid out of current tax receipts. Thus, the argument goes, if Social Security substitutes for private saving, the national saving rate is reduced. Evidence on the extent to which taxes and Social Security reduce the saving rate has not been clear to date.

A provision of the 1997 Taxpayer Relief Act allowed for new "backloaded" retirement accounts [the so-called Roth Individual Retirement Accounts (IRAs)] to stimulate saving. Individuals can deposit up to $2,000 annually to specified retirement accounts that accumulate earnings without paying income tax. Withdrawals made after age 59 1/2 or for the purchase of a first home can be made tax free.

Policies to Stimulate Investment For the growth rate to increase, saving must be used to finance new investment. In an effort to revive a slow-growing economy in 1961, President Kennedy proposed and Congress passed the *investment tax credit* (ITC). The ITC provided a tax reduction for firms that invest in new capital equipment. For most investments, the reduction took the form of a direct credit equal to 10 percent of the investment. A firm investing in a new computer system costing $100,000 would have its tax liability reduced by $10,000. The ITC was changed periodically over the years, and it was on the books until it was repealed in 1986. Many states have adopted ITCs against their state corporation taxes.

In 1982, the federal Economic Recovery Tax Act contained a number of provisions designed to encourage investment. Among them was the *Accelerated Cost Recovery System* (*ACRS*), which gave firms the opportunity to reduce their taxes by using artificially rapid rates of depreciation for purposes of calculating taxable profits. Although these rules were complicated, their effect was similar to the effect of the ITC. The government effectively reduced the cost of capital to firms that undertook investment in plant or equipment.

The Bush tax plan, which became law as the Jobs and Growth Tax Relief Reconciliation Act of 2003, was an attempt to stimulate both labor supply and investment. The centerpiece of the plan was a sharp reduction in the taxation of dividends and capital gains. While long-term capital gains have long been afforded special tax treatment, dividends have essentially always been treated as ordinary income. Under the 2003 act, both are taxed at a reduced rate of 15 percent. In addition, the act generally lowered tax rates for most taxpayers. The top rate was reduced to 35 percent, effective in 2003.

In 2005, the president received the report of a federal advisory panel on tax reform. The panel report was entitled *Simple, Fair and Pro-Growth: Proposals to Fix America's Tax System*. The report contained a set of recommendations aimed directly at growth, including allowing businesses to expense all capital purchases immediately rather than depreciating them over time, reducing tax rates on interest, repealing the corporate alternative minimum tax, and reducing tax rates in general. Only time will tell which of those provisions will become law.

Policies to Increase Research and Development In the United States, expenditures on R&D in 2006 were $340 billion. The two largest funders of research and development were industry, with a 67 percent share, and government, with a 28 percent share. High private returns on investment are clearly the stimulus for industry investments. Early work suggests that the private return on investment is quite high, on the order of 30 percent.[2] The large investment by government reflects its view about the role that research plays in long-run economic growth. As Table 32.8 shows, increases in knowledge accounted for 31 percent of total growth in the United States between 1929 and 1982. Although not shown in the table, during the years of high R&D expenditures, 1953 to 1973, the figure reached 40 percent.

---

[2] See M. Nadiri, "Contributions and Determinants of Research and Development Expenditures in the U.S. Manufacturing Industries," in *Capital Efficiency and Growth*, George M. von Furstenberg, ed. (Cambridge, MA: Ballinger Press, 1980).

ECONOMICS IN PRACTICE

Can We Really Measure Productivity Changes?

When the government publishes numbers on changes in productivity, most people consider them to be "true." Even though we don't really know much about how they are constructed, we assume they are the best measurements we can get.

Yet such data are often the source of controversy. Some have argued that the mix of products produced in the United States and the increased pace of technological change in recent years have made it increasingly difficult to measure productivity changes accurately. The observed productivity growth decline in recent decades may be measurement error.

These arguments make a certain amount of sense at an intuitive level. Even in agriculture, where it is relatively easy to measure productivity growth, the possibility of mismeasurement exists. The output of a soybean farm can be measured in bushels; and labor, capital, and land inputs present no serious measurement problems. So over time, as farming techniques improved and farmers acquired new and better machinery, output per acre and output per worker rose and have continued to rise. But today we have biotechnology. Genetic engineering now makes it possible to make soybeans higher in protein and more disease-resistant. Technology has improved and "output" has increased, but these increases do not show up in the data because of crude measures of output.

A similar problem exists with computers. If you simply counted the number of personal computers produced and measured the cost of the inputs used in their production, you would no doubt see some productivity advances. But computers being produced for under $1,000 in 2008 contained processors capable of performing tasks literally thousands of times faster than computers produced a decade earlier. If we were to measure computer outputs not in terms of units produced but in terms of the actual "services" they provided to users, we would find massive productivity advances. The problem is that many of the products we now use are qualitatively different from the comparable products we used only a few years ago, and the standard measures of productivity miss much of these quality changes.

The problems are greater in the service sector, where output is extremely difficult to measure. It is easy to understand the problem if you think of what information technology has done for legal services. As recently as 15 years ago, a lawyer doing research to support a legal case might spend hundreds of hours looking through old cases and public documents. Today's lawyers can log on to a computer and in seconds do a keyword search on a massive legal database. Such time- and labor-saving productivity advances are not counted in the official data.

One of the leading experts on technology and productivity estimates that we have reasonably good measures of output and productivity in only about 31 percent of the U.S. economy. Does this mean that slow productivity growth is not a problem? On this topic economists have agreed to disagree.[a]

[a]This argument was described most clearly by Professor Zvi Grilliches of Harvard in his presidential address to the American Economic Association in January 1994. The full text, entitled "Productivity, R&D, and the Data Constraint," is published in the *American Economic Review*, March 1994. The counterargument is best advanced by Professor Dale Jorgenson in *Productivity* (Harvard University Press, 1995).

Given the centrality of innovation to growth, it is interesting to look at what has been happening to research in the United States over time. A commonly used measure of inputs into research is the fraction of GDP spent. In 2007, the United States spent 2.6 percent of it GDP on R&D, down from a high of 2.9 percent in the early 1960s. Moreover, over time, the balance of research funding has shifted away from government toward industry. Since industry research tends to be more applied, some observers are concerned that the United States will lose some of its edge in technology unless more funding is provided. In 2007, the National Academies of Science argued as follows:

> Although many people assume that the United States will always be a world leader in science and technology, this may not continue to be the case inasmuch as great minds and ideas exist throughout the world. We fear the abruptness with which a lead in science and technology can be lost—and the difficulty of recovering a lead once lost, if indeed it can be recovered at all.[3]

As we suggested earlier, the theory of convergence suggests that newly developing countries can leap forward by exploiting the technology of the developed countries. Indeed, all countries benefit when a better way of doing things is discovered. Innovation and the diffusion of that innovation push the production possibility frontier outward. But there is at least some evidence that a country that leads in a discovery retains some advantage in exploiting it, at least for some time.

What evidence do we have that the United States might be losing its edge? As a share of GDP, the United States ranked seventh among OECD countries in 2006. If we look at patenting data, the evidence is more encouraging: For patents simultaneously sought in the United States, Japan, and the European Union, known as triadic patents, U.S. inventors are the leading source, having taken the lead from the EU in 1989. On the output side, then, the United States appears still to be quite strong.

Industrial Policy In the 1980s, a number of policy makers began to call for increased government involvement in the allocation of capital across manufacturing sectors, a practice known as industrial policy. Those who favored industrial policy, including Robert Reich, the Secretary of Labor under President Clinton, argued that because governments of other nations were "targeting" industries for special subsidies and rapid investment, the United States should do likewise to avoid losing out to global competition.

There is no question that in developing countries, some targeted investment by governments is common. In 2004, for example, Taiwan, which had traditionally been a large exporter of sugar, faced declining world demand and prices. In response, the government made a conscious decision, backed by a strategic investment, to develop a world-class orchid industry for the export market. Low-interest credit was supplied to farmers to help them make the conversion, and a range of industry-specific infrastructure was created. Today Taiwan is a major player in the orchid industry.

Despite the orchids and other stories of government intervention in markets elsewhere, most economists now believe that targeted industrial policy is useful mainly in less developed countries. Dani Rodrik, an economist at Harvard's Kennedy School of Government, has argued that industrial policy is most helpful in less developed economies in which investments in strategic areas can have cascading effects across a range of economic activity. In the case of sectors of activities that are new to an economy—like orchids in Taiwan—the risks to the individual entrepreneur are very high and some government program may be useful. At the same time, many observers are sensitive to charges that many government policy programs in less developed countries are subject to strong political influences that may undermine decision making. Certainly, in the United States, most economists and policy makers at this time favor investments in education and research as ways to increase growth.

---

[3] National Academies, "Rising Above the Gathering Storm: Energizing the Employing America for a Brighter Future," National Academies Press, 2007.

Growth and the Environment and Issues of Sustainability

In 2000, the United Nations unanimously adopted the Millennium Development Goals, a set of quantifiable, time-based targets for developing countries to meet. Included in these targets, as you might expect, were measures of education, mortality, and income growth. But the UN resolution also included a set of environmental criteria. Specific criteria have been developed around clean air, clean water, and conservation management. Table 32.10 provides the 2005 ranking of a series of developing countries on the UN index.

TABLE 32.10 Environmental Scores in the World Bank Country Policy and Institutional Assessment 2005 Scores (min = 1, max = 6)

Country	Score
Albania	3
Angola	2.5
Bhutan	4.5
Cambodia	2.5
Cameroon	4
Gambia	3
Haiti	2.5
Madagascar	4
Mozambique	3
Papua New Guinea	1.5
Sierra Leone	2.5
Sudan	2.5
Tajikistan	2.5
Uganda	4
Vietnam	3.5
Zimbabwe	2.5

Source: World Bank, "Policies and Institutions for Environmental Sustainability."

The inclusion of environmental considerations in the development goals speaks to the importance of environmental infrastructure in the long-run growth prospects of a country. Environmental considerations also address some concerns that in the process of growth, environmental degradation will occur. Evidence on global warming has increased some of the international concerns about growth and the environment. The connections between the environment and growth are complex and remain debated among economists.

The classic work on growth and the environment was done in the mid-1990s by Gene Grossman and Alan Krueger.[4] It is well known that as countries develop, they typically generate air and water pollutants. China's recent rapid growth provides a strong example of this trend. Grossman and Krueger found, however, that as growth progresses and countries become richer, pollution tends to fall. The relationship between growth, as measured in per-capita income, and pollution is an inverted *U*. Figure 32.3 shows Grossman and Krueger's evidence on one measure of air pollution.

How do we explain the inverted *U*? Clean water and clean air are what economists call *normal goods*. That is, as people get richer, they want to consume more of these goods. You have already seen in the Keynesian model that aggregate consumption increases with income. As it happens, microeconomics finds that this relationship is true for most individual types of goods as well. Demand for clean water and clean air turns out to increase with income levels. As countries develop, their populace increasingly demands improvements on these fronts. So while increased industrialization with growth initially degrades the environment, in the long run environmental quality improves.

Grossman and Krueger found this inverted *U* in a number of countries. Economic historians remind us that in the heyday of industrialization, northern England suffered from very serious air pollution. Some of you may recall the description of air pollution in nineteenth-century English novels such as Elizabeth Gaskell's *North and South*.

[4] Gene Grossman and Alan Krueger, "Economic Growth and the Environment," *Quarterly Journal of Economics*, May 1995.

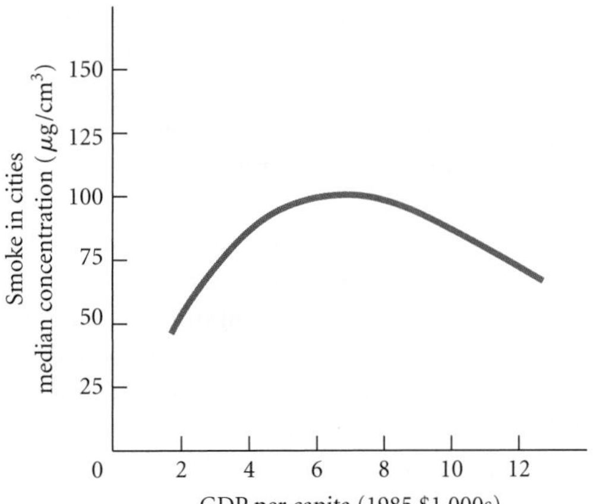

◀ FIGURE 32.3

The Relationship Between Per-Capita GDP and Urban Air Pollution

One measure of air pollution is smoke in cities. The relationship between smoke concentration and per-capita GDP is an inverted *U*: As countries grow wealthier, smoke increases and then declines.

Source: Gene Grossman and Alan Krueger, *QJE*, May 1995.

If environmental pollution eventually declines as growth brings rising per-capita incomes, why should we be worried? First, as Grossman and Krueger point out, the inverted *U* represents historical experience, but it is not inevitable. In particular, if public opinion moves governments and the economy at large toward technologies that reduce pollution, this requires an empowered populace and a responsive government. Here too we see the importance of institutions in growth. A second issue arises in cases in which high levels of current emissions produce irreversible outcomes. Some would argue that by the time nations such as China and Vietnam develop enough to reduce their emissions, it will be too late. Many believe that global warming is such an example.

Another important problem that has made itself known recently comes from pollution sources that move across country boundaries. Carbon emissions associated with global warming are one such by-product of increased industrialization. Other air pollution problems move across national borders as well. In the heyday of industrialization by the Soviet Union, prevailing winds blew much of the Soviet-produced pollution to Finland. Choices that countries make about levels of growth and levels of environmental control affect the well-being of other countries' populations. Nor is it easy for countries at very different levels of GDP per capita to agree on common standards of environmental control. As we suggested earlier, demand for clean air increases with income, when needs for food and shelter are better met. It should surprise no one who has studied economics that there are debates between developing countries and developed countries about optimal levels of environmental control. These debates are further complicated when we recognize the gains that consumers in developed economies reap from economic activity in the developing world. Much of the increased carbon emitted by Chinese businesses, for example, is associated with goods that are transported and traded to Europe and the United States. These consumers thus share the benefits of this air pollution through the cheaper goods they consume.

Sustainability of Resource Extraction Growth Strategies Much of Southeast Asia has fueled its growth through export-led manufacturing. For countries that have based their growth on resource extraction, there is another set of potential sustainability issues. Many of the African nations are in this category. Nigeria relies heavily on oil; South Africa and the Congo are large producers of diamonds and other gems. Extraction methods, of course, may carry environmental problems. Many people also question whether growth based on extraction is economically sustainable: What happens when the oil or minerals run out? The answer is quite complicated and depends in some measure on how the profits from the extraction process are used. Because extraction can be accomplished without a well-educated labor force, while other forms of development are more dependent on a skilled-labor base, public investment in infrastructure is especially important. To the extent that countries use the revenues from extraction to invest in infrastructure such as roads and schools and to increase the education and health of their populace, the basis for growth can be shifted over time. With weak institutions, these proceeds may be expropriated by corrupt governments or invested outside the country, and long-run sustainable growth will not result.

The question of whether the natural resource base imposes strong natural limits on growth has been debated since the time of Malthus. Earlier in this chapter we described the concerns of Thomas Malthus that population growth in England would outstrip the ability of the land to provide. In that case, technology stepped in.

In 1972, the Club of Rome, a group of "concerned citizens," contracted with a group at MIT to do a study entitled *The Limits to Growth*.[5] The book-length final report presented the results of computer simulations that assumed present growth rates of population, food, industrial output, and resource exhaustion. According to these data, sometime after the year 2000 the limits will be reached and the entire world economy will come crashing down:

> Collapse occurs because of nonrenewable resource depletion. The industrial capital stock grows to a level that requires an enormous input of resources. In the very process of that growth, it depletes a large fraction of the resource reserves available. As resource prices rise and mines are depleted, more and more capital must be used for obtaining resources, leaving less to be invested for future growth. Finally, investment cannot keep up with depreciation and the industrial base collapses, taking with it the service and agricultural systems, which have become dependent on industrial inputs (such as fertilizers, pesticides, hospital laboratories, computers, and especially energy for mechanization)....Population finally decreases when the death rate is driven upward by the lack of food and health services.[6]

This argument is similar to one offered almost 200 years ago by Thomas Malthus, mentioned earlier in this chapter.

In the early 1970s, many thought that the Club of Rome's predictions had come true. It seemed the world was starting to run up against the limits of world energy supplies. In the years since, new reserves have been found and new sources of energy have been discovered and developed. At present, issues of global warming and biodiversity are causing many people to question the process of growth. How should one trade off the obvious gains from growth in terms of the lives of those in the poorer nations against environmental goals? Recognizing the existence of these trade-offs and trying to design policies to deal with them is one of the key tasks of policy makers.

---

[5] Donella H. Meadows et al., *The Limits to Growth* (Washington, DC: Potomac Associates, 1972).

[6] Meadows et al., pp. 131–132.

SUMMARY

1. *Modern economic growth* is the period of rapid and sustained increase in real output per capita that began in the Western world with the Industrial Revolution.

THE GROWTH PROCESS: FROM AGRICULTURE TO INDUSTRY *p. 632*

2. All societies face limits imposed by the resources and technologies available to them. Economic growth expands these limits and shifts society's production possibilities frontier up and to the right.
3. There is considerable variation across the globe in growth rates. Some countries—particularly in Southeast Asia—appear to be catching up.
4. The process by which some less developed, poorer countries experience high growth and begin to catch up to more developed areas is known as convergence.

THE SOURCES OF ECONOMIC GROWTH *p. 634*

5. If growth in output outpaces growth in population and if the economic system is producing what people want, growth will increase the standard of living. Growth occurs when (1) society acquires more resources or (2) society discovers ways of using available resources more efficiently.
6. An *aggregate production function* embodies the relationship between inputs—the labor force and the stock of capital—and total national output.
7. A number of factors contribute to *economic growth*: (1) an increase in the labor supply; (2) an increase in physical capital—plant and equipment—and/or human capital—education, training, and health; (3) an increase in productivity brought about by technological change and advances in knowledge (for example, managerial skills); and/or economies of scale.

8. Changes in institutions, including property rights and legal institutions as well as the introduction of incentives, can also contribute to economic growth by attracting capital and improving productivity.

GROWTH AND PRODUCTIVITY IN THE UNITED STATES *p. 639*

9. Modern economic growth in the United States dates to the middle of the nineteenth century. For the last 100 years, the nation's growth in real output has averaged about 3 percent per year. Between 1929 and 1982, about half of U.S. growth in output came from increases in factors of production and half from increases in productivity.

10. There has been much concern that the rate of growth of productivity in the United States is slowing. The growth rate of *labor productivity* decreased from about 3.3 percent in the 1950s and 1960s to about 1.9 percent in the 1990s.

ECONOMIC GROWTH AND PUBLIC POLICY IN THE UNITED STATES *p. 642*

11. A number of public policies have been pursued with the aim of improving the growth of real output. These policies include efforts to improve the quality of education, to encourage saving, to stimulate investment, and to increase research and development. Some economists also argue for increased government involvement in the allocation of capital across manufacturing sectors, a practice known as *industrial policy*.

GROWTH AND THE ENVIRONMENT AND ISSUES OF SUSTAINABILITY *p. 646*

12. As countries begin to develop and industrialize, environmental problems are common. As development progresses further, however, most countries experience improvements in their environmental quality.

13. The limits placed on a country's growth by its natural resources have been debated for several hundred years. Growth strategies based on extraction of resources may pose special challenges to a country's growth.

REVIEW TERMS AND CONCEPTS

aggregate production function, *p. 634*
catch-up, *p. 633*
economic growth, *p. 631*
foreign direct investment (FDI), *p. 636*
innovation, *p. 638*
invention, *p. 638*
labor productivity, *p. 634*
modern economic growth, *p. 631*
productivity of an input, *p. 638*

PROBLEMS

Visit **www.myeconlab.com** to complete the problems marked in orange online. You will receive instant feedback on your answers, tutorial help, and access to additional practice problems.

1. One way that less developed countries catch up with the growth of the more developed countries is by adopting the technology of the developed countries. On average, however, developed countries are capital-rich and labor-short relative to the developing nations. Think of the kinds of technology that a typical developing country with a short supply of capital and a large marginally employed labor force would find when "shopping" for technology in a more developed country. As a hint, the Japanese have developed the field of robotics such as assembly line machines. Such machines are designed to replace expensive workers with capital (robots) in order to lower the overall cost of production. In what ways does it help a developing country to transfer and use a new technology in its country? What are the costs?

2. Tables 1, 2, and 3 present some data on three hypothetical economies. Complete the tables by figuring the measured productivity of labor and the rate of output growth. What do the data tell you about the causes of economic growth? (*Hint*: How fast are *L* and *K* growing?)

TABLE 1

PERIOD	*L*	*K*	*Y*	*Y/L*	GROWTH RATE OF OUTPUT
1	1,052	3,065	4,506		
2	1,105	3,095	4,674		
3	1,160	3,126	4,842		
4	1,218	3,157	5,019		

TABLE 2

PERIOD	*L*	*K*	*Y*	*Y/L*	GROWTH RATE OF OUTPUT
1	1,052	3,065	4,506		
2	1,062	3,371	4,683		
3	1,073	3,709	4,866		
4	1,084	4,079	5,055		

TABLE 3

PERIOD	*L*	*K*	*Y*	*Y/L*	GROWTH RATE OF OUTPUT
1	1,052	3,065	4,506		
2	1,062	3,095	4,731		
3	1,073	3,126	4,967		
4	1,084	3,157	5,216		

3. Go to a recent issue of *The Economist* magazine. In the back of each issue is a section called "economic indicators." That section lists the most recent growth data for a substantial number of countries. Which countries around the world are growing most rapidly according to the most recent data? Which countries around the world are growing more slowly? Flip through the stories in *The Economist* to see if there is any explanation for the pattern that you observe. Write a brief essay on current general economic conditions around the world.

4. In the fall of 2005, the president's tax reform commission issued a final report. The commission called for a general cut in marginal tax rates; lower tax rates on dividends, capital gains, and interest income; and, more importantly, the expensing of investment in capital equipment. These provisions were argued to be "pro-growth." In what ways would you expect each of these proposals to be favorable to economic growth?

5. In earlier chapters, you learned that aggregate expenditure ($C + I + G$) must equal aggregate output for the economy to be in equilibrium. You also saw that when consumption spending rises, $C + I + G$ increases, inventories fall, and aggregate output rises. Thus, policies that simultaneously increase consumer spending and reduce saving lead to a higher level of GDP. In this chapter, we have argued that a higher saving rate, even with lower consumption spending, is the key to long-run GDP growth. How can both arguments be correct?

6. Suppose you have just been elected to Congress and you find yourself on the Ways and Means Committee—the committee in the House that decides on tax matters. The committee is debating a bill that would make major changes in tax policy. First, the corporate tax would be lowered substantially in an effort to stimulate investment. The bill contains a 15 percent investment tax credit—firms would be able to reduce their taxes by 15 percent of the value of investment projects that they undertake. To keep revenues constant, the bill would impose a national sales tax that would raise the price of consumer goods and reduce consumption. What trade-offs do you see implied in this bill? What are the pros and cons? How would you vote?

7. **[Related to the *Economics in Practice* on *p. 641*]** Education, like health care, is another area in which it has been hard to create productivity gains that reduce costs. Collect data on the tuition rates of your own college in the last twenty years and compare that increase to the overall rate of inflation using the CPI. What do you observe? Can you suggest some productivity-enhancing measures?

8. Economists generally agree that high budget deficits today will reduce the growth rate of the economy in the future. Why? Do the reasons for the high budget deficit matter? In other words, does it matter whether the deficit is caused by lower taxes, increased defense spending, more job-training programs, and so on?

9. Why can growth lead to a more unequal distribution of income? By assuming this is true, how is it possible for the poor to benefit from economic growth?

10. **[Related to the *Economics in Practice* on *p. 644*]** For each of the following items how would you measure output? If you used a simple measure of productivity such as output per worker or output per hour of labor, what things might raise productivity in each sector?
    a. Automobiles
    b. Corn
    c. Music players
    d. Insurance
    e. Health care

Debates in Macroeconomics: Monetarism, New Classical Theory, and Supply-Side Economics

33

CHAPTER OUTLINE

Throughout this book, we have noted that there are many disagreements and questions in macroeconomics. For example, economists disagree on whether the aggregate supply curve is vertical, either in the short run or in the long run. Some economists even doubt that the aggregate supply curve is a useful macroeconomic concept. There are different views on whether cyclical employment exists and, if it does, what causes it. Economists disagree about whether monetary and fiscal policies are effective at stabilizing the economy, and they support different views on the primary determinants of consumption and investment spending.

We discussed some of these disagreements in previous chapters, but only briefly. In this chapter, we discuss in more detail a number of alternative views of how the macroeconomy works.

Keynesian Economics

John Maynard Keynes's *General Theory of Employment, Interest, and Money*, published in 1936, remains one of the most important works in economics. While a great deal of the material in the previous 10 chapters is drawn from modern research that postdates Keynes, much of the material is built around a framework constructed by Keynes.

What exactly is *Keynesian economics*? In one sense, it is the foundation of all of macroeconomics. Keynes was the first to stress aggregate demand and links between the money market and the goods market. Keynes also stressed the possible problem of sticky wages. Virtually all the debates in this chapter can be understood in terms of the aggregate output/aggregate expenditure framework suggested by Keynes.

In recent years, the term *Keynesian* has been used narrowly. Keynes believed in an activist federal government. He believed that the government had a role to play in fighting inflation and unemployment, and he believed that monetary and fiscal policy should be used to manage the macroeconomy. This is why *Keynesian* is sometimes used to refer to economists who advocate active government intervention in the macroeconomy.

During the 1970s and 1980s, it became clear that managing the macroeconomy was more easily accomplished on paper than in practice. The inflation problems of the 1970s and early 1980s and the seriousness of the recessions of 1974 to 1975 and 1980 to 1982 led many economists to challenge the idea of active government intervention in the economy. Some of the challenges were simple attacks on the bureaucracy's ability to act in a timely manner. Others were theoretical assaults that claimed to show that monetary and fiscal policy could have *no effect whatsoever* on the economy, even if it were efficiently managed.

Two major schools decidedly against government intervention developed: monetarism and new classical economics.

Monetarism

The debate between "monetarist" and "Keynesian" economics is complicated because they mean different things to different people. If we consider the main monetarist message to be that "money matters," then almost all economists would agree. In the aggregate supply/aggregate demand (*AS/AD*) story, for example, an increase in the money supply shifts the *AD* curve to the right, which leads to an increase in both aggregate output (Y) and the price level (P). Monetary policy thus has an effect on output and the price level. *Monetarism*, however, is usually considered to go beyond the notion that money matters.

The Velocity of Money

velocity of money The number of times a dollar bill changes hands, on average, during a year; the ratio of nominal *GDP* to the stock of money.

To understand monetarist reasoning, you must understand the **velocity of money**. Think of velocity as the number of times a dollar bill changes hands, on average, during a year.

Suppose on January 1 you buy a new ballpoint pen with a $5 bill. The owner of the stationery store does not spend your $5 right away. She may hold it until, say, May 1, when she uses it to buy a dozen doughnuts. The doughnut store owner does not spend the $5 he receives until July 1, when he uses it (along with other cash) to buy 100 gallons of oil. The oil distributor uses the bill to buy an engagement ring for his fiancée on September 1, but the $5 bill is not used again in the remaining 3 months of the year. Because this $5 bill has changed hands four times during the year, its velocity of circulation is 4. A velocity of 4 means that the $5 bill stays with each owner for an average of 3 months, or one quarter of a year.

In practice, we use gross domestic product (GDP), instead of the total value of all transactions in the economy, to measure velocity[1] because GDP data are more readily available. The income velocity of money (V) is the ratio of nominal GDP to the stock of money (M):

$$V \equiv \frac{GDP}{M}$$

If $6 trillion worth of final goods and services is produced in a year and if the money stock is $1 trillion, then the velocity of money is $6 trillion ÷ $1 trillion, or 6.0.

We can expand this definition slightly by noting that nominal income (GDP) is equal to real output (income) (Y) times the overall price level (P):

$$GDP \equiv P \times Y$$

Through substitution:

$$V \equiv \frac{P \times Y}{M}$$

or

$$M \times V \equiv P \times Y$$

At this point, it is worth pausing to ask whether our definition has provided us with any insights into the workings of the economy. The answer is no. Because we defined V as the ratio of GDP to the money supply, the statement $M \times V \equiv P \times Y$ is an identity—it is true by definition. It

[1] Recall that GDP does not include transactions in intermediate goods (for example, flour sold to a baker to be made into bread) or in existing assets (for example, the sale of a used car). If these transactions are made using money, however, they do influence the number of times money changes hands during the course of a year. GDP is an imperfect measure of transactions to use in calculating the velocity of money.

contains no more useful information than the statement "A bachelor is an unmarried man." The definition does not, for example, say anything about what will happen to $P \times Y$ when M changes. The final value of $P \times Y$ depends on what happens to V. If V falls when M increases, the product $M \times V$ could stay the same, in which case the change in M would have had no effect on nominal income. To give monetarism some economic content, a simple version of monetarism known as the **quantity theory of money** is used.

quantity theory of money The theory based on the identity $M \times V \equiv P \times Y$ and the assumption that the velocity of money (V) is constant (or virtually constant).

The Quantity Theory of Money

The key assumption of the quantity theory of money is that the velocity of money is constant (or virtually constant) over time. If we let $\overline{V}$ denote the constant value of V, the equation for the quantity theory can be written as follows:

$$M \times \overline{V} = P \times Y$$

Note that the double equal sign has replaced the triple equal sign because the equation is no longer an identity. The equation is true if velocity is constant (and equal to $\overline{V}$) but not otherwise. If the equation is true, it provides an easy way to explain nominal GDP. Given M, which can be considered a policy variable set by the Federal Reserve (Fed), nominal GDP is just $M \times \overline{V}$. In this case, the effects of monetary policy are clear. Changes in M cause equal percentage changes in nominal GDP. For example, if the money supply doubles, nominal GDP also doubles. If the money supply remains unchanged, nominal GDP remains unchanged.

The key is whether the velocity of money is really constant. Early economists believed that the velocity of money was determined largely by institutional considerations, such as how often people are paid and how the banking system clears transactions between banks. Because these factors change gradually, early economists believed velocity was essentially constant.

When there is equilibrium in the money market, then the quantity of money supplied is equal to the quantity of money demanded. That could mean that M in the quantity-theory equation equals both the quantity of money supplied and the quantity of money demanded. If the quantity-theory equation is looked on as a demand-for-money equation, it says that the demand for money depends on nominal income (GDP, or $P \times Y$), but *not* on the interest rate.[2] If the interest rate changes and nominal income does not, the equation says that the quantity of money demanded will not change. This is contrary to the theory of the demand for money in Chapter 26, which had the demand for money depending on both income and the interest rate.

Testing the Quantity Theory of Money One way to test the validity of the quantity theory of money is to look at the demand for money using recent data on the U.S. economy. The key is this: Does money demand depend on the interest rate? Most empirical work says yes. When demand-for-money equations are estimated (or "fit to the data"), the interest rate usually turns out to be a factor. The demand for money does not appear to depend only on nominal income.

Another way of testing the quantity theory is to plot velocity over time and see how it behaves. Figure 33.1 plots the velocity of money for the 1960 I–2007 IV period. The data show that velocity is far from constant. There is a long-term trend—on average, velocity has been rising during these years—but fluctuations around this trend have also occurred and some have been quite large. Velocity rose from 6.1 in 1980 III to 6.7 in 1981 III, fell to 6.3 in 1983 I, rose to 6.7 in 1984 III, and fell to 5.7 in 1986 IV. Changes of a few tenths of a point may seem small, but they are actually large. For example, the money supply in 1986 IV was \$799 billion. If velocity changes by 0.3 with a money supply of this amount and if the money supply is unchanged, we have a change in nominal GDP ($P \times Y$) of \$240 billion (0.3 × \$799 billion), which is about 5 percent of the level of GDP in 1986.

The debate over monetarist theories is more subtle than our discussion so far indicates. First, there are many definitions of the money supply. M1 is the money supply variable used for the graph in Figure 33.1, but there may be some other measure of the money supply that would lead to a smoother plot. For example, many people shifted their funds from checking account deposits to money market accounts when the latter became available in the late 1970s. Because GDP did not change as a result of this shift while M1 decreased, velocity—the ratio of GDP to M1—must have gone up. Suppose instead we measured the supply of money by M2 (which includes both checking accounts and money market accounts). In this case, the decrease in checking deposits would be exactly offset by the rise in money market account deposits and M2 would not change.

[2] In terms of the Appendix to Chapter 27, this means that the *LM* curve is vertical.

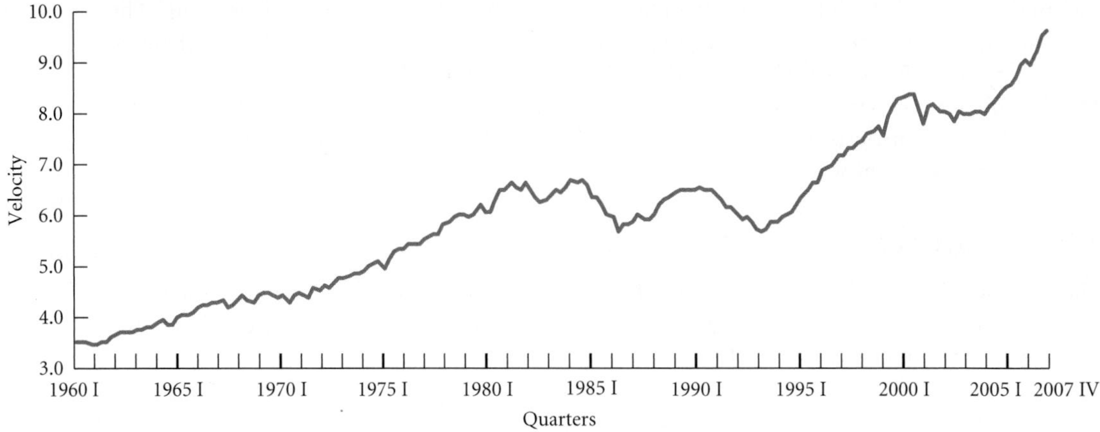

▲ **FIGURE 33.1 The Velocity of Money, 1960 I–2007 IV**
Velocity has not been constant over the period from 1960 to 2007. There is a long-term trend—velocity has been rising. There are also fluctuations, some of them quite large.

With no change in GDP and no change in M2, the velocity of money would not change. Whether or not velocity is constant may depend partly on how we measure the money supply.

Second, there may be a time lag between a change in the money supply and its effects on nominal GDP. Suppose we experience a 10 percent increase in the money supply today, but it takes 1 year for nominal GDP to increase by 10 percent. If we measured the ratio of today's money supply to today's GDP, it would seem that velocity had fallen by 10 percent. However, if we measured today's money supply against GDP 1 year from now, when the increase in the supply of money had its full effect on income, velocity would have been constant.

The debate over the quantity theory of money is primarily empirical. It is a debate that can be resolved by looking at facts about the real world and seeing whether they are in accord with the predictions of theory. Is there a measure of the money supply and a choice of the time lag between a change in the money supply and its effects on nominal GDP such that V is in effect constant? If so, the monetarist theory is a useful approach to understanding how the macroeconomy works and how changes in the money supply will cause a proportionate increase in nominal GDP. If not, some other theory is likely to be more appropriate. (We discuss the testing of alternative theories at the end of this chapter.)

Inflation as a Purely Monetary Phenomenon

So far we have talked only about nominal output ($P \times Y$). We have said nothing about how a monetarist would break down a change in nominal output (due to a money-supply change) into a change in P and a change in Y. Here again it is not possible to make a general statement about what all monetarists believe. Some may believe that all of the change occurs in P, and others may believe that at least sometimes some of the change occurs in Y. If all the change occurs in P, then there is a proportional relationship between changes in the money supply and changes in the price level. For example, a 10 percent change in M will lead to a 10 percent change in P if Y remains unchanged. In this case, inflation (an increase in P) is always a purely monetary phenomenon. The price level will not change if the money supply does not change. We call this view, that changes in M affect only P and not Y, the "strict monetarist" view.

There is considerable disagreement as to whether the strict monetarist view is a good approximation of reality. For example, the strict view is not compatible with a nonvertical *AS* curve in the *AS/AD* model in Chapter 28. In the case of a nonvertical *AS* curve, an increase in M, which shifts the *AD* curve to the right, increases both P and Y. (You may want to review why.)

Almost all economists agree, however, that *sustained* inflation—inflation that continues over many periods—is a purely monetary phenomenon. In the context of the *AS/AD* framework, inflation cannot continue indefinitely unless the Fed "accommodates" it by increasing the money supply. Let us review this.

Consider a continuously increasing level of government spending (G) without any corresponding increase in taxes. The increases in G keep shifting the *AD* curve to the right, which leads to an increasing price level (P). (You may find it useful to draw a graph now.) With a fixed money supply, the increases in P lead to a higher and higher interest rate; but there is a limit to how far this can go. Because taxes are unchanged, the government must finance the increases in G by issuing bonds; and there is a limit to how many bonds the public is willing to hold regardless of how high the interest rate goes. At the point at which the public cannot be induced to hold any more bonds, the government will be unable to borrow any more to finance its expenditures. Only if the Fed is willing to increase the money supply (buy some of the government bonds) can the government spending (with its inflationary consequences) continue. Inflation cannot continue indefinitely without increases in the money supply.

The Keynesian/Monetarist Debate

The debate between Keynesians and monetarists was perhaps the central controversy in macroeconomics in the 1960s. As we will see next, this changed in the 1970s with the rise of new classical macroeconomics. From a historical perspective, however, it is useful to review this debate.

The leading spokesman for monetarism was Milton Friedman from the University of Chicago. Most monetarists, including Friedman, blamed much of the instability in the economy on the Federal Reserve, arguing that the high inflation that the United States encountered from time to time could have been avoided if only the Fed had not expanded the money supply so rapidly. Monetarists were skeptical of the Fed's ability to "manage" the economy—to expand the money supply during bad times and contract it during good times. A common argument against such management is the one discussed in Chapter 30: Time lags may make attempts to stimulate and contract the economy counterproductive.

Friedman advocated instead a policy of steady and slow money growth—specifically, that the money supply should grow at a rate equal to the average growth of real output (income) (Y). That is, the Fed should pursue a constant policy that accommodates real growth but not inflation.

Many Keynesians, on the other hand, advocated the application of coordinated monetary and fiscal policy tools to reduce instability in the economy—to fight inflation and unemployment. However, not all Keynesians advocated an activist federal government. Some rejected the strict monetarist position that changes in money affect only the price level in favor of the view that both monetary and fiscal policies make a difference. *At the same time*, though, they believed that the best possible policy for the government to pursue was basically noninterventionist.

Most economists now agree, after the experience of the 1970s, that monetary and fiscal tools are not finely calibrated. The notion that monetary and fiscal expansions and contractions can "fine-tune" the economy is gone forever. Still, many believe that the experiences of the 1970s also show that stabilization policies can help prevent even bigger economic disasters. Had the government not cut taxes and expanded the money supply in 1975 and in 1982, they argue, the recessions of those years might have been significantly worse. The same people would also argue that had the government not resisted the inflations of 1974 to 1975 and 1979 to 1981 with tight monetary policies, the inflations probably would have become much worse.

As noted previously, the debate between Keynesians and monetarists subsided with the advent of new classical macroeconomics, to which we now turn.

New Classical Macroeconomics

The challenge to Keynesian and related theories has come from a school sometimes referred to as the new classical macroeconomics.[3] Like monetarism and Keynesianism, this term is vague. No two new classical macroeconomists think exactly alike, and no single model completely represents this school. The following discussion, however, conveys the flavor of the new classical views.

The Development of New Classical Macroeconomics

New classical macroeconomics has developed from two different although related sources. These sources are the theoretical and the empirical critiques of existing, or traditional, macroeconomics.

On the theoretical level, there has been growing dissatisfaction with the way traditional models treat expectations. Keynes himself recognized that expectations (in the form of "animal spirits")

[3] The term *new classical* is used because many of the assumptions and conclusions of this group of economists resemble those of the classical economists—that is, those who wrote before Keynes.

play a big part in economic behavior. The problem is that traditional models have assumed that expectations are formed in naive ways. A common assumption, for example, is that people form their expectations of future inflation by assuming present inflation will continue. If they turn out to be wrong, they adjust their expectations by some fraction of the difference between their original forecast and the actual inflation rate. Suppose you expect 10 percent inflation next year. When next year comes, the inflation rate turns out to be only 5 percent, so you have made an error of 5 percentage points. You might then predict an inflation rate for the following year of 7.5 percent, halfway between your earlier expectation (10 percent) and actual inflation last year (5 percent).

The problem with this treatment of expectations is that it is not consistent with the assumptions of microeconomics. It implies that people systematically overlook information that would allow them to make better forecasts, even though there are costs to being wrong. If, as microeconomic theory assumes, people are out to maximize their satisfaction and firms are out to maximize their profits, they should form their expectations in a smarter way. Instead of naively assuming the future will be like the past or the present, they should actively seek to forecast the future. Any other behavior is not in keeping with the microeconomic view of the forward-looking, rational people who compose households and firms.

On the empirical level, there was stagflation in the U.S. economy during the 1970s. Remember, stagflation is simultaneous high unemployment and rising prices. The Phillips Curve theory of the 1960s predicted that demand pressure pushes up prices so that when demand is weak—in times of high unemployment, for example—prices should be stable (or perhaps even falling). The new classical theories were an attempt to explain the apparent breakdown in the 1970s of the simple inflation–unemployment trade-off predicted by the Phillips Curve. Just as the Great Depression of the 1930s motivated the development of Keynesian economics, so the stagflation of the 1970s helped motivate the formulation of new classical economics.

Rational Expectations

In previous chapters, we stressed households' and firms' expectations about the future. A firm's decision to build a new plant depends on its expectations of future sales. The amount of saving a household undertakes today depends on its expectations about future interest rates, wages, and prices.

How are expectations formed? Do people assume that things will continue as they are at present (such as predicting rain tomorrow because it is raining today)? What information do people use to make their guesses about the future? Questions such as these have become central to current macroeconomic thinking and research. One theory, the **rational-expectations hypothesis**, offers a powerful way of thinking about expectations.

rational-expectations hypothesis The hypothesis that people know the "true model" of the economy and that they use this model to form their expectations of the future.

Suppose we want to forecast inflation. What does it mean to say that my expectations of inflation are "rational"? The rational-expectations hypothesis assumes that people know the "true model" that generates inflation—they know how inflation is determined in the economy—and they use this model to forecast future inflation rates. If there were no random, unpredictable events in the economy and if people knew the true model generating inflation, their forecasts of future inflation rates would be perfect. Because it is true, the model would not permit mistakes and thus the people using it would not make mistakes.

However, many events that affect the inflation rate are not predictable—they are random. By "true" model, we mean a model that is, *on average*, correct in forecasting inflation. Sometimes the random events have a positive effect on inflation, which means that the model underestimates the inflation rate, and sometimes they have a negative effect, which means that the model overestimates the inflation rate. On average, the model is correct. Therefore, rational expectations are correct on average even though their predictions are not exactly right all the time.

To see why, suppose you have to forecast how many times a fair coin will come up heads out of 100 tosses. The true model in this case is that the coin has a 50/50 chance of coming up heads on any one toss. Because the outcome of the 100 tosses is random, you cannot be sure of guessing correctly. If you know the true model—that the coin is fair—your rational expectation of the outcome of 100 tosses is 50 heads. You are not likely to be exactly right—the actual number of heads is likely to be slightly higher or slightly lower than 50—but *on average*, you will be correct.

Sometimes people are said to have rational expectations if they use "all available information" in forming their expectations. This definition is vague because it is not always clear what "all available information" means. The definition is precise if by "all available information" we mean that people know and use the true model. We cannot have more or better information than the true model!

If information can be obtained at no cost, people are not behaving rationally when they fail to use all available information. Because there are usually costs to making a wrong forecast, it is not rational to overlook information that could help improve the accuracy of a forecast as long as the costs of acquiring that information do not outweigh the benefits of improving its accuracy.

Rational Expectations and Market Clearing If firms have rational expectations and if they set prices and wages on this basis, on average, prices and wages will be set at levels that ensure equilibrium in the goods and labor markets. When a firm has rational expectations, it knows the demand curve for its output and the supply curve of labor that it faces, except when random shocks disrupt those curves. Therefore, on average, the firm will set the market-clearing prices and wages. The firm knows the true model, and it will not set wages different from those it expects will attract the number of workers it wants. If all firms behave this way, wages will be set in such a way that the total amount of labor supplied will, on average, be equal to the total amount of labor that firms demand. In other words, on average, there will be full employment.

In Chapter 29, we argued that there might be disequilibrium in the labor market (in the form of either unemployment or excess demand for workers) because firms may make mistakes in their wage-setting behavior due to expectation errors. If, on average, firms do not make errors, on average, there will be equilibrium. When expectations are rational, disequilibrium exists only temporarily as a result of random, unpredictable shocks—obviously an important conclusion. If true, it means that disequilibrium in any market is only temporary because firms, on average, set market-clearing wages and prices.

The assumption that expectations are rational radically changes the way we can view the economy. We go from a world in which unemployment can exist for substantial periods and the multiplier can operate to a world in which (on average) all markets clear and there is full employment. In this world, there is no need for government stabilization policies. Unemployment is not a problem that governments need to worry about; if it exists at all, it is because of unpredictable shocks that, on average, amount to zero. There is no more reason for the government to try to change the outcome in the labor market than there is for it to change the outcome in the banana market. On average, prices and wages are set at market-clearing levels.

The Lucas Supply Function The **Lucas supply function**, named after Robert E. Lucas of the University of Chicago, is an important part of a number of new classical macroeconomic theories. It yields, as we shall see, a surprising policy conclusion. The function is deceptively simple. It says that real output (Y) depends on (is a function of) the difference between the actual price level (P) and the expected price level (P^e):

$$Y = f(P - P^e)$$

The actual price level minus the expected price level ($P - P^e$) is the **price surprise**. Before considering the policy implications of this function, we should look at the theory behind it.

Lucas supply function The supply function embodies the idea that output (Y) depends on the difference between the actual price level and the expected price level.

price surprise Actual price level minus expected price level.

Lucas begins by assuming that people and firms are specialists in production but generalists in consumption. If someone you know is a manual laborer, the chances are that she sells only one thing—labor. If she is a lawyer, she sells only legal services. In contrast, people buy a large bundle of goods—ranging from gasoline to ice cream and pretzels—on a regular basis. The same is true for firms. Most companies tend to concentrate on producing a small range of products, but they typically buy a larger range of inputs—raw materials, labor, energy, and capital. According to Lucas, this divergence between buying and selling creates an asymmetry. People know more about the prices of the things they sell than they do about the prices of the things they buy.[4]

At the beginning of each period, a firm has some expectation of the average price level for that period. If the actual price level turns out to be different, there is a price surprise. Suppose the average price level is higher than expected. Because the firm learns about the actual price level slowly, some time goes by before it realizes that all prices have gone up. The firm *does* learn *quickly* that the price of its *output* has gone up. The firm perceives—incorrectly, it turns out—that its price has risen relative to other prices, and this perception leads it to produce more output.

[4] It is not entirely obvious why this should be true, and some critics of the new classical school have argued that this is unrealistic. Some have also criticized the Lucas supply function as being too simple, arguing that other things besides price surprises affect aggregate output.

ECONOMICS IN PRACTICE

How Are Expectations Formed?

A current debate among macroeconomists and policy makers is how people form expectations about the future state of the economy. Of particular interest is the formation of inflationary expectations. One possible way that inflation can be transmitted in an economy is if individuals expect there to be inflation and then, because of these expectations, demand higher wages, leading in turn to increases in inflation. In 2008, a number of central bankers began to worry about the possibility that inflationary expectations were heating up. For example, Thomas Hoenig, the president of the Federal Reserve Bank of Kansas City, said on May 6, 2008: "The bigger concern is that these price increases are beginning to generate an inflation psychology to the extent that I have not seen since the 1970s and early 1980s."

How are expectations in fact formed? Are expectations rational, as some macroeconomists believe, reflecting an accurate understanding of how the economy works? Or are they formed in simpler, more mechanical ways? A recent research paper by Ronnie Driver and Richard Windram from the Bank of England sheds some light on this issue. Since 1999, the Bank of England has done a survey four times a year of 2,000 British consumers about their views of future inflation and future interest rates. The surveys suggest that consumers tend to expect future inflation to be what they perceive past inflation to have been. Also, there are some differences between what consumers perceive past inflation to have been and the actual estimates of past inflation made by the government. In other words, consumers are more influenced by their own experience than by actual government numbers and their expectations of the future are based on their past experiences. Consumers mostly expect the future to look the way they perceive the past to have looked. Two factors that appear to be important in influencing consumer perceptions of inflation are gas prices and the attention the media pays to price increases. All this suggests that, at least for the British consumers surveyed, the formation of inflationary expectations is a less sophisticated process than some economic theorists suggest. This research also suggests that to the extent that gas prices increase and media attention to inflation increases, both of which were occurring in 2008, are important in influencing consumers' expectations, there may be an increase in inflationary expectations in 2008. Thomas Hoenig may have reason to worry.

A similar argument holds for workers. When there is a positive price surprise, workers at first believe that their "price"—their wage rate—has increased relative to other prices. Workers believe that their real wage rate has risen. We know from theory that an increase in the real wage is likely to encourage workers to work more hours.[5] The real wage has not actually risen, but it takes workers a while to figure this out. In the meantime, they supply more hours of work than they would have. This increase means that the economy produces more output when prices are unexpectedly higher than when prices are at their expected level.

This is the rationale for the Lucas supply function. Unexpected increases in the price level can fool workers and firms into thinking that relative prices have changed, causing them to alter the amount of labor or goods they choose to supply.

Policy Implications of the Lucas Supply Function The Lucas supply function in combination with the assumption that expectations are rational implies that anticipated policy changes have no effect on real output. Consider a change in monetary policy. In general, the change will have some effect on the average price level. If the policy change is announced to the public, people will know the effect on the price level because they have rational expectations (and know the way changes in monetary policy affect the price level). This means that the change in

[5] This is true if we assume that the substitution effect dominates the income effect (see Chapter 32).

monetary policy affects the actual price level and the expected price level in the same way. The new price level minus the new expected price level is zero—no price surprise. In such a case, there will be no change in real output because the Lucas supply function states that real output can change from its fixed level only if there is a price surprise.

The general conclusion is that *any* announced policy change—in fiscal policy or any other policy—has no effect on real output because the policy change affects both actual and expected price levels in the same way. If people have rational expectations, known policy changes can produce no price surprises—and no increases in real output. The only way any change in government policy can affect real output is if it is kept in the dark so it is not generally known. Government policy can affect real output only if it surprises people; otherwise, it cannot. Rational-expectations theory combined with the Lucas supply function proposes a very small role for government policy in the economy.

Evaluating Rational-Expectations Theory

What are we to make of all this? It should be clear that the key question concerning the new classical macroeconomics is how realistic is the assumption of rational expectations. If it approximates the way expectations are actually formed, then it calls into question any theory that relies at least in part on expectation errors for the existence of disequilibrium. The arguments in favor of the rational-expectations assumption sound persuasive from the perspective of microeconomic theory. When expectations are not rational, there are likely to be unexploited profit opportunities—most economists believe such opportunities are rare and short-lived.

The argument *against* rational expectations is that it requires households and firms to know too much. This argument says that it is unrealistic to think that these basic decision-making units know as much as they need to know to form rational expectations. People must know the true model (or at least a good approximation of the true model) to form rational expectations, and this knowledge is a lot to expect. Even if firms and households are capable of learning the true model, it may be costly to take the time and gather the relevant information to learn it. The gain from learning the true model (or a good approximation of it) may not be worth the cost. In this sense, there may not be unexploited profit opportunities around. Gathering information and learning economic models may be too costly to bother with, given the expected gain from improving forecasts.

Although the assumption that expectations are rational seems consistent with the satisfaction-maximizing and profit-maximizing postulates of microeconomics, the rational-expectations assumption is more extreme and demanding because it requires more information on the part of households and firms. Consider a firm engaged in maximizing profits. In some way or other, it forms expectations of the relevant future variables; and given these expectations, it figures out the best thing to do from the point of view of maximizing profits. Given a set of expectations, the problem of maximizing profits may not be too hard. What may be hard is forming accurate expectations in the first place. This requires firms to know much more about the overall economy than they are likely to, so the assumption that their expectations are rational is not necessarily realistic. Firms, like the rest of us—so the argument goes—grope around in a world that is difficult to understand, trying to do their best but not always understanding enough to avoid mistakes.

In the final analysis, the issue is empirical. Does the assumption of rational expectations stand up well against empirical tests? This question is difficult to answer. Much work is currently being done to answer it. There are no conclusive results yet, but it is one of the questions that makes macroeconomics an exciting area of research.

Real Business Cycle Theory

Recent work in new classical macroeconomics has been concerned with whether the existence of business cycles can be explained under the assumptions of complete price and wage flexibility (market clearing) and rational expectations. This work is called **real business cycle theory**. As we discussed in Chapter 28, if prices and wages are completely flexible, then the *AS* curve is vertical, even in the short run. If the *AS* curve is vertical, then events or phenomena that shift the *AD* curve (such as changes in the money supply, changes in government spending, and shocks to consumer and investor behavior) have no effect on real output. Real output does fluctuate over time, so the puzzle is how the fluctuations can be explained if they are not due to policy changes or other shocks that shift the *AD* curve. Solving this puzzle is one of the main missions of real business cycle theory.

real business cycle theory An attempt to explain business cycle fluctuations under the assumptions of complete price and wage flexibility and rational expectations. It emphasizes shocks to technology and other shocks.

It is clear that if shifts of the *AD* curve cannot account for real output fluctuations (because the *AS* curve is vertical), then shifts of the *AS* curve must be responsible. However, the task is to come up with convincing explanations as to what causes these shifts and why they persist over a number of periods. The problem is particularly difficult when it comes to the labor market. If prices and wages are completely flexible, then there is never any unemployment aside from frictional unemployment. For example, because the measured U.S. unemployment rate was 9.7 percent in 1982 and 4.2 percent in 1999, the puzzle is to explain why so many more people chose not to work in 1982 than in 1999.

Early real business cycle theorists emphasized shocks to the production technology. Suppose there is a negative shock in a given year that causes the marginal product of labor to decline. This leads to a fall in the real wage, which leads to a decrease in the quantity of labor supplied. People work less because the negative technology shock has led to a lower return from working. The opposite happens when there is a positive shock: The marginal product of labor rises, the real wage rises, and people choose to work more. This early research was not as successful as some had hoped because it required what seemed to be unrealistically large shocks to explain the observed movements in labor supply over time.

Since this initial work, economists have explored other sources of shocks to labor or capital productivity, and work is actively continuing in this area. To date, fluctuations of some variables, but not all, have been explained fairly well. Some argue that this work is doomed to failure because it is based on the unrealistic assumption of complete price and wage flexibility, whereas others hold more hope. Real business cycle theory is another example of the current state of flux in macroeconomics.

Supply-Side Economics

From our discussion of equilibrium in the goods market, beginning with the simple multiplier in Chapter 23 and continuing through Chapter 28, we have focused primarily on *demand*. Supply increases and decreases in response to changes in aggregate expenditure (which is closely linked to aggregate demand). Fiscal policy works by influencing aggregate expenditure through tax policy and government spending. Monetary policy works by influencing investment and consumption spending through increases and decreases in the interest rate. The theories we have been discussing are "demand-oriented."

The 1970s were difficult times for the U.S. economy. The United States found itself in 1974 to 1975 with stagflation—high unemployment and inflation. In the late 1970s, inflation returned to the high levels of 1974 to 1975. It seemed as if policy makers were incapable of controlling the business cycle.

As a result of these seeming failures, orthodox economics came under fire. One assault was from a group of economists who expounded *supply-side economics*. The argument of the supply-siders was simple. Basically, they said, all the attention to demand in orthodox macroeconomic theory distracted our attention from the real problem with the U.S. economy. The real problem, said supply-siders, was that high rates of taxation and heavy regulation had reduced the incentive to work, to save, and to invest. What was needed was not a demand stimulus, but better incentives to stimulate *supply*.

If we cut taxes so people take home more of their paychecks, the argument continued, they will work harder and save more. If businesses get to keep more of their profits and can get away from government regulations, they will invest more. This added labor supply and investment, or capital supply, will lead to an expansion of the supply of goods and services, which will reduce inflation and unemployment at the same time. The ultimate solution to the economy's woes, the supply-siders concluded, was on the *supply side* of the economy.

At their most extreme, supply-siders argued that the incentive effects of supply-side policies were likely to be so great that a major cut in tax rates would actually *increase* tax revenues. Even though *tax rates* would be lower, more people would be working and earning income and firms would earn more profits, so that the increases in the *tax bases* (profits, sales, and income) would then outweigh the decreases in rates, resulting in increased government revenues.

The Laffer Curve Figure 33.2 presents a key diagram of supply-side economics. The tax rate is measured on the vertical axis, and tax revenue is measured on the horizontal axis. The assumption behind this curve is that there is some tax rate beyond which the supply response is large enough to lead to a decrease in tax revenue for further increases in the tax rate. There is obviously some tax rate between zero and 100 percent at which tax revenue is at a maximum. At a tax rate of zero, work effort is high but there is no tax revenue. At a tax rate of 100, the labor supply is presumably zero because people are not allowed to keep any of their income. Somewhere between zero and 100 is the maximum-revenue rate.

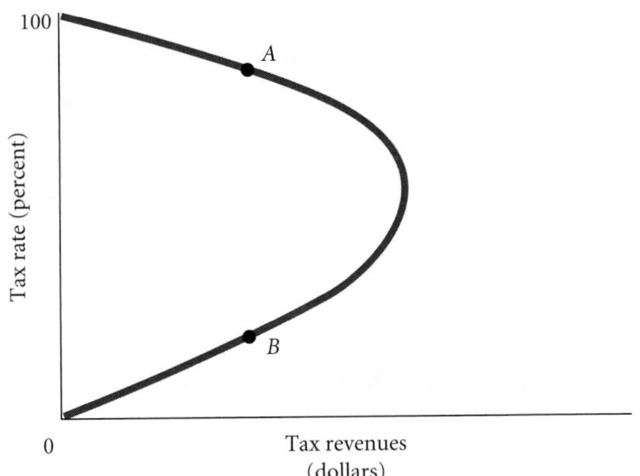

FIGURE 33.2
The Laffer Curve
The Laffer curve shows that the amount of revenue the government collects is a function of the tax rate. It shows that when tax rates are very high, an increase in the tax rate could cause tax revenues to fall. Similarly, under the same circumstances, a cut in the tax rate could generate enough additional economic activity to cause revenues to rise.

The big debate in the 1980s was whether tax rates in the United States put the country on the upper or lower part of the curve in Figure 33.2. The supply-side school claimed that the United States was around *A* and that taxes should be cut. Others argued that the United States was nearer *B* and that tax cuts would lead to lower tax revenue.

The diagram in Figure 33.2 is the **Laffer curve**, named after economist Arthur Laffer, who, legend has it, first drew it on the back of a napkin at a cocktail party. The Laffer curve had some influence on the passage of the Economic Recovery Tax Act of 1981, the tax package put forward by the Reagan administration that brought with it substantial cuts in both personal and business taxes. Individual income tax rates were cut by as much as 25 percent over 3 years. Corporate taxes were cut sharply in a way designed to stimulate capital investment. The new law allowed firms to depreciate their capital at a rapid rate for tax purposes, and the bigger deductions led to taxes that were significantly lower than before.

Laffer curve With the tax rate measured on the vertical axis and tax revenue measured on the horizontal axis, the Laffer curve shows that there is some tax rate beyond which the supply response is large enough to lead to a decrease in tax revenue for further increases in the tax rate.

Evaluating Supply-Side Economics

Supporters of supply-side economics claim that Reagan's tax policies were successful in stimulating the economy. They point to the fact that almost immediately after the tax cuts of 1981 were put into place, the economy expanded and the recession of 1980 to 1982 came to an end. In addition, inflation rates fell sharply from the high rates of 1980 and 1981. Except for 1 year, federal receipts continued to rise throughout the 1980s despite the cut in tax rates.

Critics of supply-side policies do not dispute these facts, but offer an alternative explanation of how the economy recovered. The Reagan tax cuts were enacted just as the U.S. economy was in the middle of its deepest recession since the Great Depression. The unemployment rate stood at 10.8 percent in the fourth quarter of 1982. It was the recession, critics argue, that was responsible for the reduction in inflation—not the supply-side policies. Also among the criticisms of supply-side economics is that it is unlikely a tax cut would substantially increase the supply of labor. In addition, in theory, a tax cut could even lead to a *reduction* in labor supply. Recall our discussion of income and substitution effects in Chapter 31. Although it is true that a higher after-tax wage rate provides a higher reward for each hour of work and thus more incentive to work, a tax cut also means that households receive a higher income for a given number of hours of work. Because they can earn the same amount of money working fewer hours, households might choose to work *less*. They might spend some of their added income on leisure. Research done during the 1980s suggests that tax cuts seem to increase the supply of labor somewhat but that the increases are very modest.

What about the recovery from the recession? Why did real output begin to grow rapidly in late 1982, precisely when the supply-side tax cuts were taking effect? Two reasons have been suggested. First, the supply-side tax cuts had large *demand*-side effects that stimulated the economy. Second, the Fed pumped up the money supply and drove interest rates down at the same time the tax cuts were being put into effect. The money supply expanded about 20 percent between 1981 and 1983, and interest rates succumbed. In 1981, the average 3-month U.S. Treasury bill paid 14 percent interest. In 1983, the figure had dropped to 8.6 percent.

Certainly, traditional theory suggests that a huge tax cut will lead to an increase in disposable income and, in turn, an increase in consumption spending (a component of aggregate expenditure). In addition, although an increase in planned investment (brought about by a lower interest rate) leads to added productive capacity and added supply in the long run, it also increases expenditures on capital goods (new plant and equipment investment) in the short run.

Whether the recovery from the 1981–1982 recession was the result of supply-side expansion or supply-side policies that had demand-side effects, one thing is clear: The extreme promises of the supply-siders did not materialize. President Reagan argued that because of the effect depicted in the Laffer curve, the government could maintain expenditures (and even increase defense expenditures sharply), cut tax rates, *and* balance the budget. This was not the case. Government revenues fell sharply from levels that would have been realized without the tax cuts. After 1982, the federal government ran huge deficits, with nearly $2 trillion added to the national debt between 1983 and 1992.

Testing Alternative Macroeconomic Models

You may wonder why there is so much disagreement in macroeconomics. Why can't macroeconomists test their models against one another and see which performs best?

One problem is that macroeconomic models differ in ways that are hard to standardize. If one model takes the price level to be given, or not explained within the model, and another one does not, the model with the given price level may do better in, for instance, predicting output—not because it is a better model but simply because the errors in predicting prices have not been allowed to affect the predictions of output. The model that takes prices as given has a head start, so to speak.

Another problem arises in the testing of the rational-expectations assumption. Remember, if people have rational expectations, they are using the true model to form their expectations. Therefore, to test this assumption, we need the true model. There is no way to be sure that whatever model is taken to be the true model is in fact the true one. Any test of the rational-expectations hypothesis is therefore a *joint* test (1) that expectations are formed rationally and (2) that the model being used is the true one. If the test rejects the hypothesis, it may be that the model is wrong rather than that the expectations are not rational.

Another problem for macroeconomists is the small amount of data available. Most empirical work uses data beginning about 1950, which in 2008 was about 59 years' (236 quarters) worth of data. Although this may seem like a lot of data, it is not. Macroeconomic data are fairly "smooth," which means that a typical variable does not vary much from quarter to quarter or from year to year. For example, the number of business cycles within this 59-year period is small, about eight. Testing various macroeconomic hypotheses on the basis of eight business cycle observations is not easy, and any conclusions must be interpreted with caution.

To give an example of the problem of a small number of observations, consider trying to test the hypothesis that import prices affect domestic prices. Import prices changed very little in the 1950s and 1960s. Therefore, it would have been very difficult at the end of the 1960s to estimate the effect of import prices on domestic prices. The variation in import prices was not great enough to show any effects. We cannot demonstrate that changes in import prices help explain changes in domestic prices if import prices do not change. The situation was different by the end of the 1970s because by then, import prices had varied considerably. By the end of the 1970s, there were good estimates of the import price effect, but not before. This kind of problem is encountered again and again in empirical macroeconomics. In many cases, there are not enough observations for much to be said and hence there is considerable room for disagreement.

We said in Chapter 1 that it is difficult in economics to perform controlled experiments. Economists, are for the most part, at the mercy of the historical data. If we were able to perform experiments, we could probably learn more about the economy in a shorter time. Alas, we must wait. In time, the current range of disagreements in macroeconomics should be considerably narrowed.

SUMMARY

KEYNESIAN ECONOMICS *p. 651*

1. In a broad sense, Keynesian economics is the foundation of modern macroeconomics. In a narrower sense, *Keynesian* refers to economists who advocate active government intervention in the economy.

MONETARISM *p. 652*

2. The monetarist analysis of the economy places a great deal of emphasis on the *velocity of money*, which is defined as the number of times a dollar bill changes hands, on average, during the course of a year. The velocity of money is the ratio of nominal GDP to the stock of money, or $V \equiv GDP/M \equiv (P \times Y)/M$. Alternately, $M \times V \equiv P \times Y$.

3. The *quantity theory of money* assumes that velocity is constant (or virtually constant). This implies that changes in the supply of money will lead to equal percentage changes in nominal GDP. The quantity theory of money equation is $M \times \overline{V} = P \times Y$. The equation says that demand for money does not depend on the interest rate.
4. Most economists believe that sustained inflation is a purely monetary phenomenon. Inflation cannot continue indefinitely unless the Fed "accommodates" it by expanding the money supply.
5. Most monetarists blame most of the instability in the economy on the federal government and are skeptical of the government's ability to manage the macroeconomy. They argue that the money supply should grow at a rate equal to the average growth of real output (income) (Y)—the Fed should expand the money supply to accommodate real growth but not inflation.

NEW CLASSICAL MACROECONOMICS *p. 655*

6. The *new classical macroeconomics* has developed from two different but related sources: the theoretical and the empirical critiques of traditional macroeconomics. On the theoretical level, there has been growing dissatisfaction with the way traditional models treat expectations. On the empirical level, the stagflation in the U.S. economy during the 1970s caused many people to look for alternative theories to explain the breakdown of the Phillips Curve.
7. The *rational-expectations hypothesis* assumes that people know the "true model" that generates economic variables. For example, rational expectations assumes that people know how inflation is determined in the economy and use this model to forecast future inflation rates.
8. The *Lucas supply function* assumes that real output (Y) depends on the actual price level minus the expected price level, or the *price surprise*. This function combined with the assumption that expectations are rational implies that anticipated policy changes have no effect on real output.
9. *Real business cycle theory* is an attempt to explain business cycle fluctuations under the assumptions of complete price and wage flexibility and rational expectations. It emphasizes shocks to technology and other shocks.

SUPPLY-SIDE ECONOMICS *p. 660*

10. *Supply-side economics* focuses on incentives to stimulate supply. Supply-side economists believe that if we lower taxes, workers will work harder and save more and firms will invest more and produce more. At their most extreme, supply-siders argue that incentive effects are likely to be so great that a major cut in taxes will actually increase tax revenues.
11. The *Laffer curve* shows the relationship between tax rates and tax revenues. Supply-side economists use it to argue that it is possible to generate higher revenues by cutting tax rates. This does not appear to have been the case during the Reagan administration, however, where lower tax rates decreased tax revenues significantly and contributed to the large increase in the federal debt during the 1980s.

TESTING ALTERNATIVE MACROECONOMIC MODELS *p. 662*

12. Economists disagree about which macroeconomic model is best for several reasons: (1) Macroeconomic models differ in ways that are hard to standardize; (2) when testing the rational-expectations assumption, we are never sure that whatever model is taken to be the true model is the true one; and (3) the amount of data available is fairly small.

REVIEW TERMS AND CONCEPTS

Laffer curve, *p. 661*
Lucas supply function, *p. 657*
price surprise, *p. 657*
quantity theory of money, *p. 653*
rational-expectations hypothesis, *p. 656*
real business cycle theory, *p. 659*
velocity of money, *p. 652*

$$V \equiv \frac{GDP}{M}$$
$$M \times V \equiv P \times Y$$
$$M \times \overline{V} = P \times Y$$

PROBLEMS

Visit **www.myeconlab.com** to complete the problems marked in orange online. You will receive instant feedback on your answers, tutorial help, and access to additional practice problems.

1. The table gives estimates of the rate of money supply growth and the rate of real GDP growth for five countries in 2000:
   a. If you were a monetarist, what would you predict about the rate of inflation across the five countries?
   b. If you were a Keynesian and assuming activist central banks, how might you interpret the same data?

	RATE OF GROWTH IN MONEY SUPPLY (M1)	RATE OF GROWTH OF REAL GDP
Australia	+ 9.3	+4.4
Britain	+ 7.6	+4.4
Canada	+18.7	+4.9
Japan	+ 9.0	+0.7
United States	+ 0.2	+5.1

2. The three diagrams in Figure 1 represent in a simplified way the predictions of the three theories presented in this chapter about the likely effects of a major tax cut.
   a. Match each of the following theories with a graph: (1) Keynesian economics, (2) supply-side economics, (3) rational expectations/monetarism. Explain the logic behind the three graphs.
   b. Which theory do you find most convincing? Explain.

3. **[Related to the *Economics in Practice* on p. 658]** Suppose you are thinking about where to live after you finish your degree. You discover that an apartment building near your new job has identical units—one ifor rent and the other for sale as a condominium. Given your salary, both are affordable and you like them. Would you buy or rent? How would you go about deciding? Would your expectations play a role? Be specific. Where do you think those expectations come from? In what ways could expectations change things in the housing market as a whole?

4. In 2000, a well-known economist was heard to say, "The problem with supply-side economics is that when you cut taxes, they have both supply and demand side effects and you cannot separate the effects." Explain this comment. Be specific and use the 1997 tax cuts or the Reagan tax cuts of 1981 as an example.

5. A cornerstone of new classical economics is the notion that expectations are "rational." What do you think will happen to the prices of single-family homes in your community over the next several years? On what do you base your expectations? Is your thinking consistent with the notion of rational expectations? Explain.

6. You are a monetarist given the following information: The money supply is $1,000. The velocity of money is 5. What is nominal income? real income? What happens to nominal income if the money supply is doubled? What happens to real income?

7. When Bill Clinton took office in January 1993, he faced two major economic problems: a large federal budget deficit and high unemployment resulting from a very slow recovery from the recession of 1990 to 1991. In his first State of the Union message, the president called for spending cuts and substantial tax increases to reduce the deficit. Most of these proposed spending cuts were in the defense budget. The following day Alan Greenspan, chair of the Federal Reserve Board of Governors, signaled his support for the president's plan. Many elements of the president's original plan were later incorporated into the deficit reduction bill passed in 1993.
   a. Some said at the time that without the Fed's support, the Clinton plan would be a disaster. Explain this argument.
   b. Supply-side economists and monetarists were very worried about the plan and the support it received from the Fed. What specific problems might a monetarist and a supply-side economist worry about?
   c. Suppose you were hired by the Federal Reserve Bank of St. Louis to report on the events of 1995 and 1996. What specific evidence would you look for to see whether the Clinton plan was effective or whether the critics were right to be skeptical?

8. In an economy with reasonably flexible prices and wages, full employment is almost always maintained. Explain why that statement is true.

9. During the 1980 presidential campaign, Ronald Reagan promised to cut taxes, increase expenditures on national defense, and balance the budget. During the New Hampshire primary of 1980, George Bush called this policy "voodoo economics." The two men were arguing about the relative merits of supply-side economics. Explain their disagreement.

*10. In a hypothetical economy, there is a simple proportional tax on wages imposed at a rate *t*. There are plenty of jobs around; so if people enter the labor force, they can find work. We define total government receipts from the tax as

$$T = t \times W \times L$$

where t = the tax rate, W = the gross wage rate, and L = the total supply of labor. The net wage rate is

$$W_n = (1 - t)\, W$$

The elasticity of labor supply is defined as

$$\frac{\text{Percentage of change in } L}{\text{Percentage of change in } W_n} = \frac{\Delta L/\Delta L}{\Delta W_n/W_n}$$

Suppose t was cut from .25 to .20. For such a cut to *increase* total government receipts from the tax, how elastic must the supply of labor be? (Assume a constant gross wage.) What does your answer imply about the supply-side assertion that a cut in taxes can increase tax revenues?

*Note: Problems marked with an asterisk are more challenging.

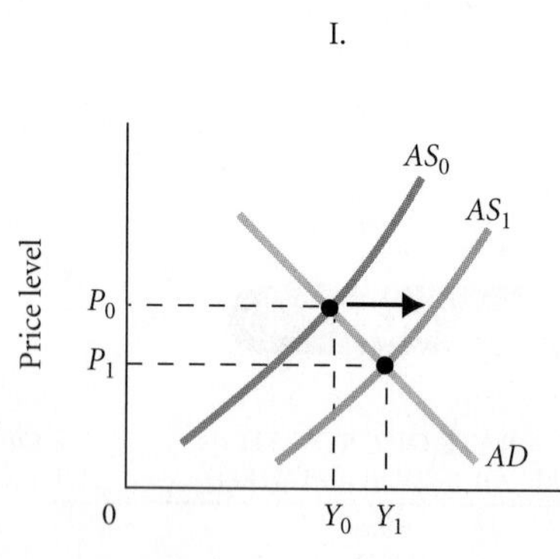

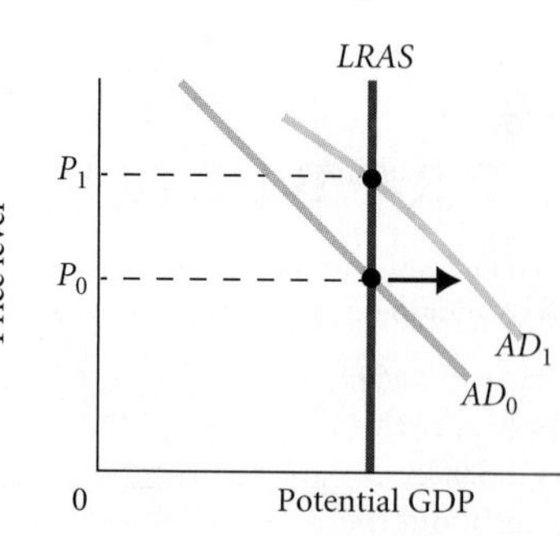

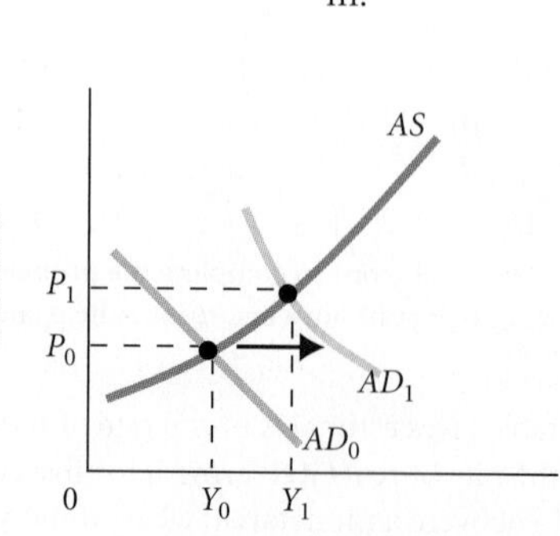

▲ FIGURE 1

International Trade, Comparative Advantage, and Protectionism

34

CHAPTER OUTLINE

Over the last 40 years, international transactions have become increasingly important to the U.S. economy. In 1970, imports represented only about 7 percent of U.S. gross domestic product (GDP). The share is now around 17 percent. In 2007, the United States imported on average more than $195 billion worth of goods and services each month. The increased trade we observe in the United States is mirrored throughout the world. From 1980 to 2005, world trade in real terms grew more than 5 times. This trend has been especially rapid in the newly industrialized Asian economies, but many developing countries such as Malaysia and Vietnam have been increasing their openness to trade.

The "internationalization" or "globalization" of the U.S. economy has occurred in the private and public sectors, in input and output markets, and in firms and households. Once uncommon, foreign products are now everywhere, from the utensils we eat with to the cars we drive. Chinese textiles and Indian software are commonplace. It might surprise you to learn that many of the cut flowers sold in the United States are grown in Africa and South America. In fact, most products today are made in a number of countries. Back in Chapter 1, we presented an *Economics in Practice* that described the production of Apple's iPod. An iPod contains 451 parts made in countries scattered around the world including Korea, Japan, China, and the United States. The bottom of the iPod has the following information: "Assembled in China; Designed in California." Suzuki makes cars in Hungary and employs workers from Romania and Slovakia. Honda started producing Japanese motorcycles in Ohio in 1977 with 64 employees in Marysville. The company now employs over 12,000 workers who assemble Honda automobiles. Bose is based in the United States but has its electronic components assembled in Mexico.

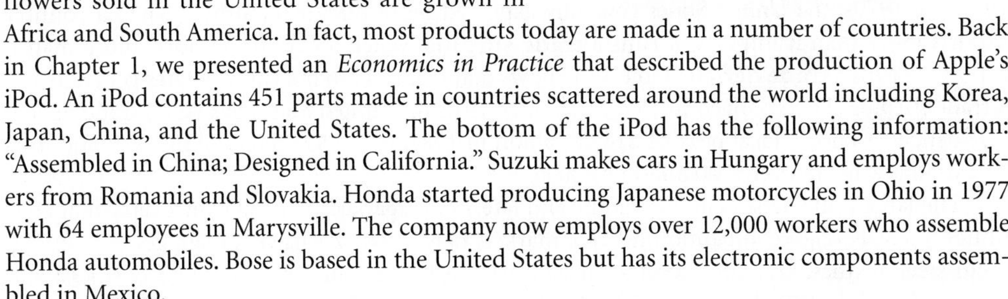

At the same time, the United States exports billions of dollars' worth of agricultural goods, aircraft, and industrial machinery. Korea imports substantial amounts of U.S. beef. In addition,

TABLE 34.1
U.S. Balance of Trade (Exports Minus Imports), 1929–2007 (Billions of Dollars)

	Exports Minus Imports
1929	+0.4
1933	+0.1
1945	−0.8
1955	+0.5
1960	+4.2
1965	+5.6
1970	+4.0
1975	+16.0
1976	−1.6
1977	−23.1
1978	−25.4
1979	−22.5
1980	−13.1
1981	−12.5
1982	−20.0
1983	−51.7
1984	−102.7
1985	−115.2
1986	−132.7
1987	−145.2
1988	−110.4
1989	−88.2
1990	−78.0
1991	−27.5
1992	−33.2
1993	−65.0
1994	−93.6
1995	−91.4
1996	−96.2
1997	−101.6
1998	−159.9
1999	−260.5
2000	−379.5
2001	−367.0
2002	−424.4
2003	−499.4
2004	−615.4
2005	−714.6
2006	−762.0
2007	−708.0

Source: U.S. Department of Commerce, Bureau of Economic Analysis.

the United States exports and imports large quantities of services. When a Pakistani student enrolls in an American college or university, or a sick woman from Chile seeks medical attention in a U.S. hospital, or a Kenyan hires a lawyer in Miami to help him with a real estate deal, or a tourist from Indonesia eats at a restaurant in New York City, the United States is exporting a service. Similarly, when a student from the United States takes her junior year abroad in Scotland, or a tourist stays in a hotel in Singapore or gets a massage at a spa in Jamaica, the United States is importing a service.

Nor are the patterns of trade that we observe in one period set in stone. Consider the case of textiles and apparel. As recently as 2000, Mexico was the major supplier to the United States of textiles and apparel with almost 15 percent of total U.S. imports in this category. By 2006, China had overtaken Mexico's lead with 29 percent of the share of U.S. textile and apparel imports. The Dominican Republic and Honduras, which had been the fourth and fifth largest sources of U.S. imports, respectively, had been replaced by Bangladesh and Indonesia. In 2004, for the first time, India became one of the top five exporters to the United States in this category.

In addition to the fact that goods and services (outputs) flow easily across borders, so too do inputs: capital and labor. Certainly, it is very easy to buy financial assets abroad. Millions of Americans own shares in foreign stocks or have invested in bonds issued by foreign countries. At the same time, millions of foreigners have put money into the U.S. stock and bond markets.

A new phenomenon, outsourcing, is also changing the nature of the global labor market. It is now simple and very common for a customer service call to a software company from a user of its product in Bend, Oregon, to be routed to Bangalore, India, where a young, ambitious Indian man or woman provides assistance to a customer over the Internet. The Internet has in essence made it possible for labor to flow smoothly across international borders.

The inextricable connection of the U.S. economy to the economies of the rest of the world has had a profound impact on the discipline of economics and is the basis of one of its most important insights: All economies, regardless of their size, depend to some extent on other economies and are affected by events outside their borders.

To get you more acquainted with the international economy, this chapter discusses the economics of international trade. First, we describe the recent tendency of the United States to import more than it exports. Next, we explore the basic logic of trade. Why should the United States or any other country engage in international trade? Finally, we address the controversial issue of protectionism. Should a country provide certain industries with protection in the form of import quotas or tariffs, which are taxes imposed on imports? Should a country help a domestic industry compete in international markets by providing subsidies?

Trade Surpluses and Deficits

Until the 1970s, the United States generally exported more than it imported. When a country exports more than it imports, it runs a **trade surplus**. When a country imports more than it exports, it runs a **trade deficit**. Table 34.1 shows that before 1976 the United States generally ran a trade surplus. This changed in 1976, and since 1976 the United States has run a trade deficit. The deficit reached a local peak of $145.2 billion in 1987, fell to $27.5 billion in 1991, and then rose dramatically to over $700 billion by 2005.

trade surplus The situation when a country exports more than it imports.

trade deficit The situation when a country imports more than it exports.

The large trade deficits in the middle and late 1980s sparked political controversy that continues today. Foreign competition hit U.S. markets hard. Less expensive foreign goods—among them steel, textiles, and automobiles—began driving U.S. manufacturers out of business; and thousands of jobs were lost in important industries. Cities such as Pittsburgh, Youngstown, and Detroit had major unemployment problems. In more recent times, the outsourcing of software development to India has caused complaints from white-collar workers.

The natural reaction to trade-related job dislocation is to call for protection of U.S. industries. Many people want the president and Congress to impose taxes and import restrictions that would make foreign goods less available and more expensive, protecting U.S. jobs. This argument is not new. For hundreds of years, industries have petitioned governments for protection and societies have debated the pros and cons of free and open trade. For the last century and a half, the principal argument against protection has been the theory of comparative advantage, first discussed in Chapter 2.

The Economic Basis for Trade: Comparative Advantage

Perhaps the best-known debate on the issue of free trade took place in the British Parliament during the early years of the nineteenth century. At that time, the landed gentry—the landowners—controlled Parliament. For a number of years, imports and exports of grain had been subject to a set of tariffs, subsidies, and restrictions collectively called the **Corn Laws**. Designed to discourage imports of grain and to encourage exports, the Corn Laws' purpose was to keep the price of food high. The landlords' incomes, of course, depended on the prices they got for what their land produced. The Corn Laws clearly worked to the advantage of those in power.

Corn Laws The tariffs, subsidies, and restrictions enacted by the British Parliament in the early nineteenth century to discourage imports and encourage exports of grain.

With the Industrial Revolution, a class of wealthy industrial capitalists emerged. The industrial sector had to pay workers at least enough to live on, and a living wage depended greatly on the price of food. Tariffs on grain imports and export subsidies that kept grain and food prices high increased the wages that capitalists had to pay, cutting into their profits. The political battle raged for years. However, as time went by, the power of the landowners in the House of Lords was significantly reduced. When the conflict ended in 1848, the Corn Laws were repealed.

On the side of repeal was David Ricardo, a businessman, economist, member of Parliament, and one of the fathers of modern economics. Ricardo's principal work, *Principles of Political Economy and Taxation*, was published in 1817, two years before he entered Parliament. Ricardo's **theory of comparative advantage**, which he used to argue against the Corn Laws, claimed that trade enables countries to specialize in producing the products they produce best. According to the theory specialization and free trade will benefit all trading partners (real wages will rise), even those that may be absolutely less efficient producers. This basic argument remains at the heart of free-trade debates even today, as policy makers argue about the effects of tariffs on agricultural development in sub-Saharan Africa and the gains and losses from outsourcing software development to India.

theory of comparative advantage Ricardo's theory that specialization and free trade will benefit all trading partners (real wages will rise), even those that may be absolutely less efficient producers.

The easiest way to understand the theory of comparative advantage is to examine a simple two-person society. Suppose Bill and Colleen, stranded on a deserted island in Chapter 2, have only two tasks to accomplish each week: gathering food to eat and cutting logs to construct a house. If Colleen could cut more logs than Bill in a day and Bill could gather more berries and fruits, specialization would clearly benefit both of them.

But suppose Bill is slow and clumsy and Colleen is better at cutting logs *and* gathering food. Ricardo's point is that it still pays for them to specialize. They can produce more in total by specializing than they can by sharing the work equally. We now turn to look at the application of the powerful idea of comparative advantage to international trade.

Absolute Advantage versus Comparative Advantage

A country enjoys an **absolute advantage** over another country in the production of a good if it uses fewer resources to produce that good than the other country does. Suppose country A and country B produce wheat, but A's climate is more suited to wheat and its labor is more productive. Country A will produce more wheat per acre than country B and use less labor in growing it and bringing it to market. Country A enjoys an absolute advantage over country B in the production of wheat.

absolute advantage The advantage in the production of a good enjoyed by one country over another when it uses fewer resources to produce that good than the other country does.

A country enjoys a **comparative advantage** in the production of a good if that good can be produced at lower cost *in terms of other goods*. Suppose countries C and D both produce wheat and corn and C enjoys an absolute advantage in the production of both—that is, C's climate is better than D's and fewer of C's resources are needed to produce a given quantity of both wheat and corn. Now C and D must each choose between planting land with either wheat or corn. To produce more wheat, either country must transfer land from corn production; to produce more corn, either country must transfer land from wheat production. The cost of wheat in each country can be measured in bushels of corn, and the cost of corn can be measured in bushels of wheat.

comparative advantage The advantage in the production of a good enjoyed by one country over another when that good can be produced at lower cost in terms of other goods than it could be in the other country.

Suppose that in country C, a bushel of wheat has an opportunity cost of 2 bushels of corn. That is, to produce an additional bushel of wheat, C must give up 2 bushels of corn. At the same time, producing a bushel of wheat in country D requires the sacrifice of only 1 bushel of corn. Even though C has an *absolute* advantage in the production of both products, D enjoys a *comparative* advantage in the production of wheat because the *opportunity cost* of producing wheat is lower in D. Under these circumstances, Ricardo claims, D can benefit from trade if it specializes in the production of wheat.

Gains from Mutual Absolute Advantage To illustrate Ricardo's logic in more detail, suppose Australia and New Zealand each have a fixed amount of land and do not trade with the rest of the world. There are only two goods—wheat to produce bread and cotton to produce clothing. This kind of two-country/two-good world does not exist, but its operations can be generalized to many countries and many goods.

To proceed, we have to make some assumptions about the preferences of the people living in New Zealand and the people living in Australia. If the citizens of both countries walk around naked, there is no need to produce cotton, so all the land can be used to produce wheat. However, assume that people in both countries have similar preferences with respect to food and clothing: The populations of both countries use both cotton and wheat, and preferences for food and clothing are such that both countries consume equal amounts of wheat and cotton.

Finally, we assume that each country has only 100 acres of land for planting and that land yields are as given in Table 34.2. New Zealand can produce 3 times the wheat that Australia can on 1 acre of land, and Australia can produce 3 times the cotton that New Zealand can in the same space. New Zealand has an absolute advantage in the production of wheat, and Australia has an absolute advantage in the production of cotton. In cases like this, we say the two countries have *mutual absolute advantage.*

TABLE 34.2 Yield per Acre of Wheat and Cotton

	New Zealand	Australia
Wheat	6 bushels	2 bushels
Cotton	2 bales	6 bales

If there is no trade and each country divides its land to obtain equal units of cotton and wheat production, each country produces 150 bushels of wheat and 150 bales of cotton. New Zealand puts 75 acres into cotton but only 25 acres into wheat, while Australia does the reverse (Table 34.3).

TABLE 34.3 Total Production of Wheat and Cotton Assuming No Trade, Mutual Absolute Advantage, and 100 Available Acres

	New Zealand	Australia
Wheat	25 acres × 6 bushels/acre 150 bushels	75 acres × 2 bushels/acre 150 bushels
Cotton	75 acres × 2 bales/acre 150 bales	25 acres × 6 bales/acre 150 bales

We can organize the same information in graphic form as production possibility frontiers for each country. In Figure 34.1, which presents the positions of the two countries before trade, each country is constrained by its own resources and productivity. If Australia put all its land into cotton, it would produce 600 bales of cotton (100 acres × 6 bales/acre) and no wheat; if it put all its land into wheat, it would produce 200 bushels of wheat (100 acres × 2 bushels/acre) and no cotton. The opposite is true for New Zealand. Recall from Chapter 2 that a country's production possibility frontier represents all combinations of goods that can be produced, given the country's resources and state of technology. Each country must pick a point along its own production possibility curve.

When both countries have an absolute advantage in the production of one product, it is easy to see that specialization and trade will benefit both. Australia should produce cotton, and New Zealand should produce wheat. Transferring all land to wheat production in New Zealand yields 600 bushels, while transferring all land to cotton production in Australia yields 600 bales. An agreement to trade 300 bushels of wheat for 300 bales of cotton would double both wheat and cotton consumption in both countries. (Remember, before trade, both countries produced 150 bushels of wheat and 150 bales of cotton. After trade, each country will have 300 bushels of wheat and 300 bales of cotton to consume. Final production and trade figures are provided in Table 34.4 and Figure 34.2.) Trade enables both countries to move beyond their previous resource and productivity constraints.

The advantages of specialization and trade seem obvious when one country is technologically superior at producing one product and another country is technologically superior at producing another product. However, let us turn to the case in which one country has an absolute advantage in the production of *both* goods.

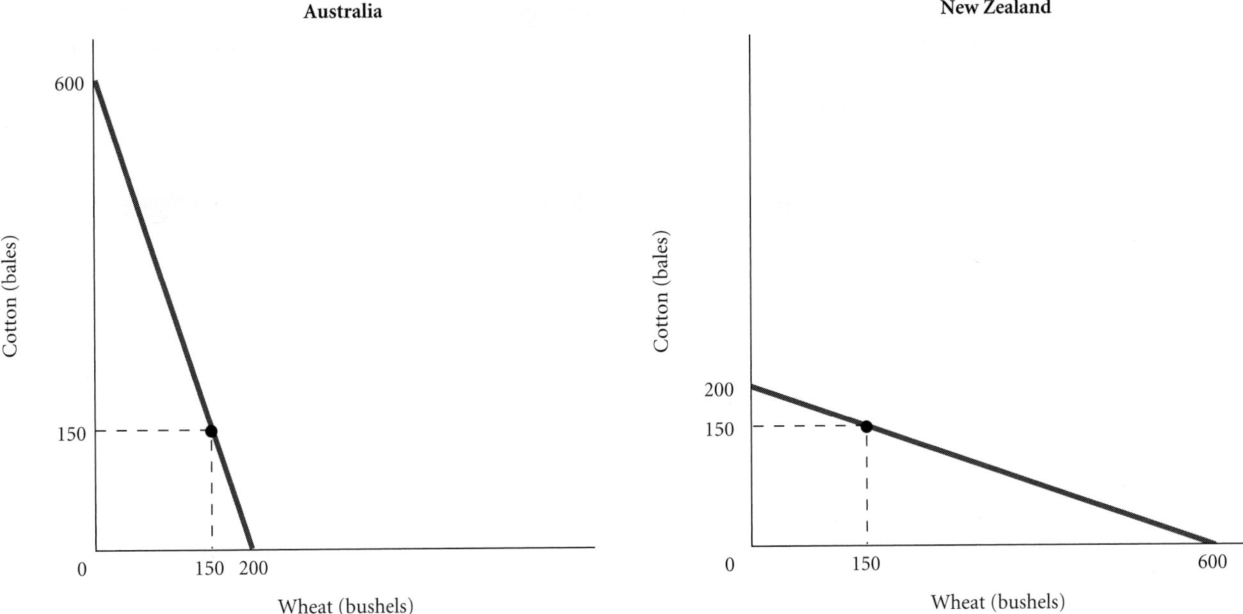

▲ **FIGURE 34.1 Production Possibility Frontiers for Australia and New Zealand Before Trade**

Without trade, countries are constrained by their own resources and productivity.

TABLE 34.4 Production and Consumption of Wheat and Cotton After Specialization

	Production			Consumption	
	New Zealand	Australia		New Zealand	Australia
Wheat	100 acres × 6 bushels/acre 600 bushels	0 acres 0	Wheat	300 bushels	300 bushels
Cotton	0 acres 0	100 acres × 6 bales/acre 600 bales	Cotton	300 bales	300 bales

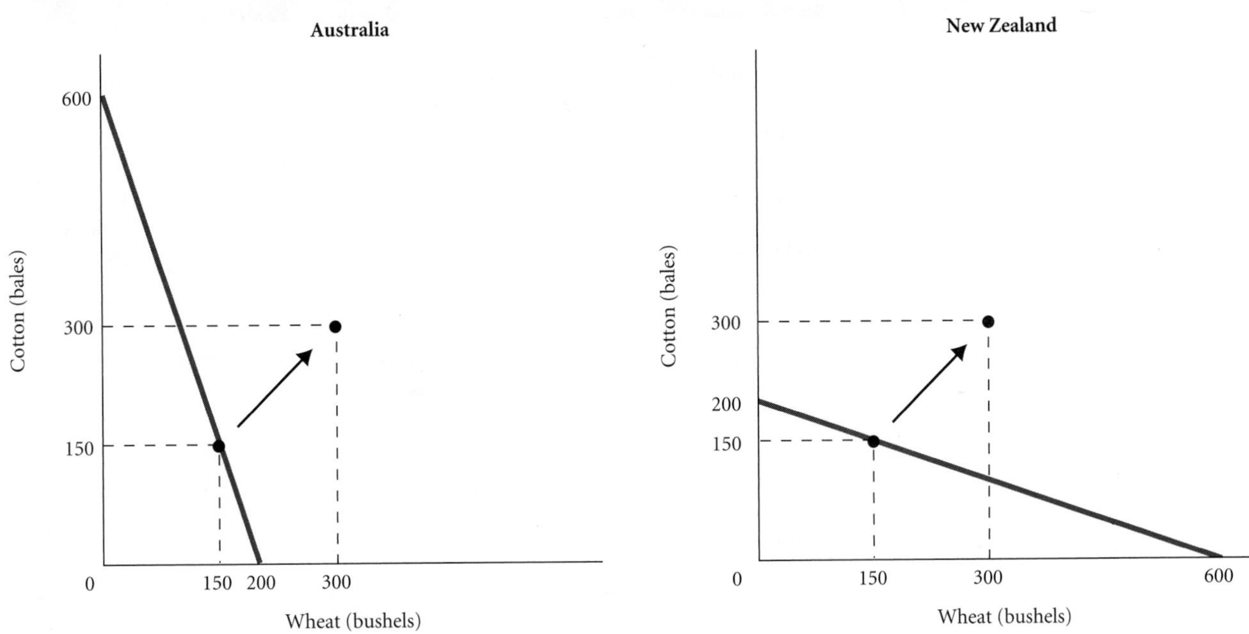

▲ **FIGURE 34.2 Expanded Possibilities After Trade**

Trade enables both countries to move beyond their own resource constraints—beyond their individual production possibility frontiers.

Gains from Comparative Advantage Table 34.5 contains different land yield figures for New Zealand and Australia. Now New Zealand has a considerable absolute advantage in the production of both cotton and wheat, with 1 acre of land yielding 6 times as much wheat and twice as much cotton as 1 acre in Australia. Ricardo would argue that *specialization and trade are still mutually beneficial.*

TABLE 34.5 Yield per Acre of Wheat and Cotton

	New Zealand	Australia
Wheat	6 bushels	1 bushel
Cotton	6 bales	3 bales

Again, preferences imply consumption of equal units of cotton and wheat in both countries. With no trade, New Zealand would divide its 100 available acres evenly, or 50/50, between the two crops. The result would be 300 bales of cotton and 300 bushels of wheat. Australia would divide its land 75/25. Table 34.6 shows that final production in Australia would be 75 bales of cotton and 75 bushels of wheat. (Remember, we are assuming that in each country, people consume equal amounts of cotton and wheat.) Again, before any trade takes place, each country is constrained by its own domestic production possibility curve.

TABLE 34.6 Total Production of Wheat and Cotton Assuming No Trade and 100 Available Acres

	New Zealand	Australia
Wheat	50 acres × 6 bushels/acre 300 bushels	75 acres × 1 bushel/acre 75 bushels
Cotton	50 acres × 6 bales/acre 300 bales	25 acres × 3 bales/acre 75 bales

Imagine we are at a meeting of trade representatives of both countries. As a special adviser, David Ricardo is asked to demonstrate that trade can benefit both countries. He divides his demonstration into three stages, which you can follow in Table 34.7.

TABLE 34.7 Realizing a Gain from Trade When One Country Has a Double Absolute Advantage

STAGE 1

	New Zealand	Australia
Wheat	50 acres × 6 bushels/acre 300 bushels	0 acres 0
Cotton	50 acres × 6 bales/acre 300 bales	100 acres × 3 bales/acre 300 bales

STAGE 2

	New Zealand	Australia
Wheat	75 acres × 6 bushels/acre 450 bushels	0 acres 0
Cotton	25 acres × 6 bales/acre 150 bales	100 acres × 3 bales/acre 300 bales

STAGE 3

	New Zealand	Australia
Wheat	100 bushels (trade) → 350 bushels	 100 bushels
	(after trade)	
Cotton	200 bales (trade) ← 350 bales	 100 bales
	(after trade)	

In stage 1, Australia transfers all its land into cotton production. It will have no wheat and 300 bales of cotton. New Zealand cannot completely specialize in wheat because it needs 300 bales of cotton and will not be able to get enough cotton from Australia. The reason is that we are assuming that each country wants to consume equal amounts of cotton and wheat.

In stage 2, New Zealand transfers 25 acres out of cotton and into wheat. Now New Zealand has 25 acres in cotton that produce 150 bales and 75 acres in wheat that produce 450 bushels.

Finally, the two countries trade. We assume that New Zealand ships 100 bushels of wheat to Australia in exchange for 200 bales of cotton. After the trade, New Zealand has 350 bales of cotton and 350 bushels of wheat; Australia has 100 bales of cotton and 100 bushels of wheat. Both countries are better off than they were before the trade (Table 34.6), and both have moved beyond their own production possibility frontiers.

Why Does Ricardo's Plan Work? To understand why Ricardo's scheme works, let us return to the definition of comparative advantage.

The real cost of producing cotton is the wheat that must be sacrificed to produce it. *When we think of cost this way, it is less costly to produce cotton in Australia than to produce it in New Zealand, even though an acre of land produces more cotton in New Zealand.* Consider the "cost" of 3 bales of cotton in the two countries. In terms of opportunity cost, 3 bales of cotton in New Zealand cost 3 bushels of wheat; in Australia, 3 bales of cotton cost only 1 bushel of wheat. Because 3 bales are produced by 1 acre of Australian land, to get 3 bales, an Australian must transfer 1 acre of land from wheat to cotton production. Because an acre of land produces a bushel of wheat, losing 1 acre to cotton implies the loss of 1 bushel of wheat. *Australia has a comparative advantage in cotton production* because its opportunity cost, in terms of wheat, is lower than New Zealand's. This is illustrated in Figure 34.3.

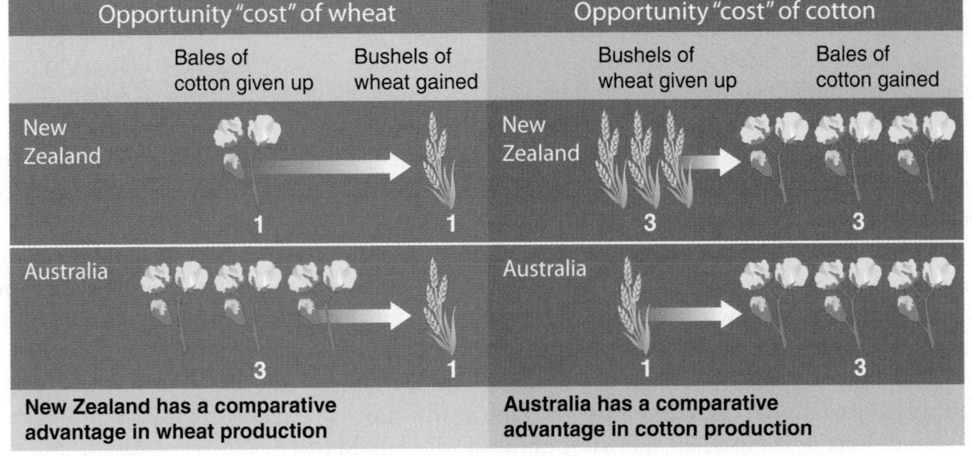

FIGURE 34.3 Comparative Advantage Means Lower Opportunity Cost
The real cost of cotton is the wheat sacrificed to obtain it. The cost of 3 bales of cotton in New Zealand is 3 bushels of wheat (a half acre of land must be transferred from wheat to cotton—refer to Table 34.5). However, the cost of 3 bales of cotton in Australia is only 1 bushel of wheat. Australia has a comparative advantage over New Zealand in cotton production, and New Zealand has a comparative advantage over Australia in wheat production.

Conversely, New Zealand has a comparative advantage in wheat production. A unit of wheat in New Zealand costs 1 unit of cotton, while a unit of wheat in Australia costs 3 units of cotton. When countries specialize in producing goods in which they have a comparative advantage, they maximize their combined output and allocate their resources more efficiently.

Terms of Trade

Ricardo might suggest a number of options for exchanging wheat and cotton to the trading partners. The one we just examined benefited both partners; in percentage terms, Australia made out slightly better. Other deals might have been more advantageous to New Zealand.

The ratio at which a country can trade domestic products for imported products is the **terms of trade**. The terms of trade determine how the gains from trade are distributed among trading partners. In the case just considered, the agreed-to terms of trade were 1 bushel of wheat for 2 bales of cotton. Such terms of trade benefit New Zealand, which can get 2 bales of cotton for each bushel of wheat. If it were to transfer its own land from wheat to cotton, it would get only 1 bale of cotton. The same terms of trade benefit Australia, which can get 1 bushel of wheat for 2 bales of cotton. A direct transfer of its own land would force it to give up 3 bales of cotton for 1 bushel of wheat.

terms of trade The ratio at which a country can trade domestic products for imported products.

If the terms of trade changed to 3 bales of cotton for every bushel of wheat, only New Zealand would benefit. At those terms of trade, *all* the gains from trade would flow to New Zealand. Such terms do not benefit Australia at all because the opportunity cost of producing wheat domestically is *exactly the same* as the trade cost: A bushel of wheat costs 3 bales of cotton. If the terms of trade went the other way—1 bale of cotton for each bushel of wheat—only Australia would benefit. New Zealand gains nothing because it can already substitute cotton for wheat at that ratio. To get a bushel of wheat domestically, however, Australia must give up 3 bales of cotton, and one-for-one terms of trade would make wheat much less costly for Australia.

Both parties must have something to gain for trade to take place. In this case, you can see that both Australia and New Zealand will gain when the terms of trade are set between 1:1 and 3:1, cotton to wheat.

Exchange Rates

The examples used thus far have shown that trade can result in gains to both parties. When trade is free—unimpeded by government-instituted barriers—patterns of trade and trade flows result from the independent decisions of thousands of importers and exporters and millions of private households and firms.

Private households decide whether to buy Toyotas or Chevrolets, and private firms decide whether to buy machine tools made in the United States or machine tools made in Taiwan, raw steel produced in Germany or raw steel produced in Pittsburgh.

But how does this trade actually come about? Before a citizen of one country can buy a product made in another country or sold by someone in another country, a currency swap must take place. Consider Shane, who buys a Toyota from a dealer in Boston. He pays in dollars, but the Japanese workers who made the car receive their salaries in yen. Somewhere between the buyer of the car and the producer, a currency exchange must be made. The regional distributor probably takes payment in dollars and converts them into yen before remitting the proceeds to Japan.

To buy a foreign-produced good, a consumer, in effect, has to buy foreign currency. The price of Shane's Toyota in dollars depends on the price of the car stated in yen and the dollar price of yen. You probably know the ins and outs of currency exchange very well if you have ever traveled in another country.

In May 2008, the British pound was worth $1.97. Now suppose you are in London having dinner. On the menu is a nice bottle of wine for 15 pounds. How can you figure out whether you want to buy it? You know what dollars will buy in the United States, so you have to convert the price into dollars. Each pound will cost you $1.97, so 15 pounds will cost you $1.97 × 15 = $29.55.

exchange rate The ratio at which two currencies are traded. The price of one currency in terms of another.

The attractiveness of foreign goods to U.S. buyers and of U.S. goods to foreign buyers depends in part on the **exchange rate**, the ratio at which two currencies are traded. If the price of pounds were to fall to $1.20, that same bottle of wine would cost $18.

To understand the patterns of trade that result from the actions of hundreds of thousands of independent buyers and sellers—households and firms—we must know something about the factors that determine exchange rates. Exchange rate determination is very complicated. Here, however, we can demonstrate two things. First, for any pair of countries, there is a range of exchange rates that can lead automatically to both countries' realizing the gains from specialization and comparative advantage. Second, within that range, the exchange rate will determine which country gains the most from trade. In short, exchange rates determine the terms of trade.

Trade and Exchange Rates in a Two-Country/Two-Good World Consider first a simple two-country/two-good model. Suppose both the United States and Brazil produce only two goods—raw timber and rolled steel. Table 34.8 gives the current prices of both goods as domestic buyers see them. In Brazil, timber is priced at 3 reals (R) per foot and steel is priced at 4 R per meter. In the United States, timber costs $1 per foot and steel costs $2 per meter.

TABLE 34.8 Domestic Prices of Timber (per Foot) and Rolled Steel (per Meter) in the United States and Brazil

	United States	Brazil
Timber	$1	3 Reals
Rolled steel	$2	4 Reals

Suppose U.S. and Brazilian buyers have the option of buying at home or importing to meet their needs. The options they choose will depend on the exchange rate. For the time being, we will ignore transportation costs between countries and assume that Brazilian and U.S. products are of equal quality.

Let us start with the assumption that the exchange rate is \$1 = 1 R. From the standpoint of U.S. buyers, neither Brazilian steel nor Brazilian timber is competitive at this exchange rate. A dollar buys a foot of timber in the United States, but if converted into a real, it will buy only one-third of a foot. The price of Brazilian timber to an American is \$3 because it will take \$3 to buy the necessary 3 R. Similarly, \$2 buys a meter of rolled steel in the United States, but the same \$2 buys only half a meter of Brazilian steel. The price of Brazilian steel to an American is \$4, twice the price of domestically produced steel.

At this exchange rate, however, Brazilians find that U.S.-produced steel and timber are less expensive than steel and timber produced in Brazil. Timber at home—Brazil—costs 3 R, but 3 R buys \$3, which buys 3 times as much timber in the United States. Similarly, steel costs 4 R at home, but 4 R buys \$4, which buys twice as much U.S.-made steel. At an exchange rate of \$1 = 1 R, Brazil will import steel and timber and the United States will import nothing.

However, now suppose the exchange rate is 1 R = \$0.25. This means that 1 dollar buys 4 R. At this exchange rate, the Brazilians buy timber and steel at home and the Americans import both goods. At this exchange rate, Americans must pay a dollar for a foot of U.S. timber, but the same amount of timber can be had in Brazil for the equivalent of \$0.75. (Because 1 R costs \$0.25, 3 R can be purchased for \$0.75.) Similarly, steel that costs \$2 per meter in the United States costs an American half as much in Brazil because \$2 buys 8 R, which buys 2 meters of Brazilian steel. At the same time, Brazilians are not interested in importing because both goods are cheaper when purchased from a Brazilian producer. In this case, the United States imports both goods and Brazil imports nothing.

So far we can see that at exchange rates of \$1 = 1 R and \$1 = 4 R, we get trade flowing in only one direction. Let us now try an exchange rate of \$1 = 2 R, or 1 R = \$0.50. First, Brazilians will buy timber in the United States. Brazilian timber costs 3 R per foot, but 3 R buys \$1.50, which is enough to buy 1.5 feet of U.S. timber. Buyers in the United States will find Brazilian timber too expensive, but Brazil will import timber from the United States. At this same exchange rate, however, both Brazilian and U.S. buyers will be indifferent between Brazilian and U.S. steel. To U.S. buyers, domestically produced steel costs \$2. Because \$2 buys 4 R, a meter of imported Brazilian steel also costs \$2. Brazilian buyers also find that steel costs 4 R, whether domestically produced or imported. Thus, there is likely to be no trade in steel.

What happens if the exchange rate changes so that \$1 buys 2.1 R? While U.S. timber is still cheaper to both Brazilians and Americans, Brazilian steel begins to look good to U.S. buyers. Steel produced in the United States costs \$2 per meter, but \$2 buys 4.2 R, which buys more than a meter of steel in Brazil. When \$1 buys more than 2 R, trade begins to flow in both directions: Brazil will import timber, and the United States will import steel.

If you examine Table 34.9 carefully, you will see that trade flows in both directions as long as the exchange rate settles between \$1 = 2 R and \$1 = 3 R. Stated the other way around, trade will flow in both directions if the price of a real is between \$0.33 and \$0.50.

TABLE 34.9 Trade Flows Determined by Exchange Rates

Exchange Rate	Price of Real	Result
\$1 = 1 R	\$ 1.00	Brazil imports timber and steel.
\$1 = 2 R	.50	Brazil imports timber.
\$1 = 2.1 R	.48	Brazil imports timber; United States imports steel.
\$1 = 2.9 R	.34	Brazil imports timber; United States imports steel.
\$1 = 3 R	.33	United States imports steel.
\$1 = 4 R	.25	United States imports timber and steel.

Exchange Rates and Comparative Advantage If the foreign exchange market drives the exchange rate to anywhere between 2 and 3 R per dollar, the countries will automatically adjust and comparative advantage will be realized. At these exchange rates, U.S. buyers begin buying all their steel in Brazil. The U.S. steel industry finds itself in trouble. Plants close, and U.S. workers begin to lobby for tariff protection against Brazilian steel. At the same time, the U.S. timber industry does well, fueled by strong export demand from Brazil. The timber-producing sector expands. Resources, including capital and labor, are attracted into timber production.

The opposite occurs in Brazil. The Brazilian timber industry suffers losses as export demand dries up and Brazilians turn to cheaper U.S. imports. In Brazil, lumber companies turn to the government and ask for protection from cheap U.S. timber. However, steel producers in Brazil are happy. They are not only supplying 100 percent of the domestically demanded steel but also selling to U.S. buyers. The steel industry expands, and the timber industry contracts. Resources, including labor, flow into steel.

With this expansion-and-contraction scenario in mind, let us look again at our original definition of comparative advantage. If we assume that prices reflect resource use and resources can be transferred from sector to sector, we can calculate the opportunity cost of steel/timber in both countries. In the United States, the production of a meter of rolled steel consumes twice the resources that the production of a foot of timber consumes. Assuming that resources can be transferred, the opportunity cost of a meter of steel is 2 feet of timber (Table 34.8). In Brazil, a meter of steel uses resources costing 4 R, while a unit of timber costs 3 R. To produce a meter of steel means the sacrifice of only four-thirds (or one and one-third) feet of timber. Because the opportunity cost of a meter of steel (in terms of timber) is lower in Brazil, we say that Brazil has a comparative advantage in steel production.

Conversely, consider the opportunity cost of timber in the two countries. Increasing timber production in the United States requires the sacrifice of half a meter of steel for every foot of timber—producing a meter of steel uses $2 worth of resources, while producing a foot of timber requires only $1 worth of resources. Nevertheless, each foot of timber production in Brazil requires the sacrifice of three-fourths of a meter of steel. Because the opportunity cost of timber is lower in the United States, the United States has a comparative advantage in the production of timber. If exchange rates end up in the right ranges, the free market will drive each country to shift resources into those sectors in which it enjoys a comparative advantage. Only those products in which a country has a comparative advantage will be competitive in world markets.

The Sources of Comparative Advantage

Specialization and trade can benefit all trading partners, even those that may be inefficient producers in an absolute sense. If markets are competitive and if foreign exchange markets are linked to goods-and-services exchange, countries will specialize in producing products in which they have a comparative advantage.

So far, we have said nothing about the sources of comparative advantage. What determines whether a country has a comparative advantage in heavy manufacturing or in agriculture? What explains the actual trade flows observed around the world? Various theories and empirical work on international trade have provided some answers. Most economists look to **factor endowments**—the quantity and quality of labor, land, and natural resources of a country—as the principal sources of comparative advantage. Factor endowments seem to explain a significant portion of actual world trade patterns.

factor endowments The quantity and quality of labor, land, and natural resources of a country.

Heckscher-Ohlin theorem A theory that explains the existence of a country's comparative advantage by its factor endowments: A country has a comparative advantage in the production of a product if that country is relatively well endowed with inputs used intensively in the production of that product.

The Heckscher-Ohlin Theorem

Eli Heckscher and Bertil Ohlin, two Swedish economists who wrote in the first half of the twentieth century, expanded and elaborated on Ricardo's theory of comparative advantage. The **Heckscher-Ohlin theorem** ties the theory of comparative advantage to factor endowments. It assumes that products can be produced using differing proportions of inputs and that inputs are mobile between sectors in each economy but that factors are not mobile *between* economies. According to this theorem, a country has a comparative advantage in the production of a product if that country is relatively well endowed with inputs used intensively in the production of that product.

This idea is simple. A country with a great deal of good fertile land is likely to have a comparative advantage in agriculture. A country with a large amount of accumulated capital is likely to have a comparative advantage in heavy manufacturing. A country well-endowed with human capital is likely to have a comparative advantage in highly technical goods.

Other Explanations for Observed Trade Flows

Comparative advantage is not the only reason countries trade. It does not explain why many countries import and export the same kinds of goods. The United States, for example, exports and imports automobiles.

Just as industries within a country differentiate their products to capture a domestic market, they also differentiate their products to please the wide variety of tastes that exists worldwide. The Japanese automobile industry, for example, began producing small, fuel-efficient cars long before U.S. automobile makers did. In doing so, the Japanese auto industry developed expertise in creating products that attracted a devoted following and considerable brand loyalty. BMWs, made mostly in Germany, and Volvos, made mostly in Sweden, also have their champions in many countries. Just as product differentiation is a natural response to diverse preferences within an economy, it is also a natural response to diverse preferences across economies.

This idea is not inconsistent with the theory of comparative advantage. If the Japanese developed skills and knowledge that gave them an edge in the production of fuel-efficient cars, that knowledge can be thought of as a very specific kind of capital that is not currently available to other producers. The Volvo company invested in a form of intangible capital called *goodwill*. That goodwill, which may come from establishing a reputation for safety and quality over the years, is one source of the comparative advantage that keeps Volvos selling on the international market. Some economists distinguish between gains from *acquired comparative advantages* and gains from *natural comparative advantages*.

Another explanation for international trade is that some economies of scale may be available when firms are producing for a world market that would not be available when they are producing for a more limited domestic market. But because the evidence suggests that economies of scale are exhausted at a relatively small size in most industries, it seems unlikely that they constitute a compelling explanation of world trade patterns.

Trade Barriers: Tariffs, Export Subsidies, and Quotas

Trade barriers—also called *obstacles to trade*—take many forms. The three most common are tariffs, export subsidies, and quotas. All are forms of **protection** shielding some sector of the economy from foreign competition.

protection The practice of shielding a sector of the economy from foreign competition.

A **tariff** is a tax on imports. The average tariff on imports into the United States is less than 5 percent. Certain protected items have much higher tariffs. For example, in 2008, tariffs were 61 percent on rubber footware and 35 percent for canned tuna.

tariff A tax on imports.

Export subsidies—government payments made to domestic firms to encourage exports—can also act as a barrier to trade. One of the provisions of the Corn Laws that stimulated Ricardo's musings was an export subsidy automatically paid to farmers by the British government when the price of grain fell below a specified level. The subsidy served to keep domestic prices high, but it flooded the world market with cheap subsidized grain. Foreign farmers who were not subsidized were driven out of the international marketplace by the artificially low prices.

export subsidies Government payments made to domestic firms to encourage exports.

Farm subsidies remain a part of the international trade landscape today. Many countries continue to appease their farmers by heavily subsidizing exports of agricultural products. The political power of the farm lobby in many countries has had an important effect on recent international trade negotiations aimed at reducing trade barriers. The prevalence of farm subsidies in the developed world has become a major rallying point for less developed countries as they strive to compete in the global marketplace. Many African nations, in particular, have a comparative advantage in agricultural land. In producing agricultural goods for export to the world marketplace, however, they must compete with food produced on heavily subsidized farms in

Europe and the United States. Countries such as France have particularly high farm subsidies, which, it argues, helps preserve the rural heritage of France. One side effect of these subsidies, however, is to make it more difficult for some of the poorer nations in the world to compete. Some have argued that if developed nations eliminated their farm subsidies, this would have a much larger effect on the economies of some African nations than is currently achieved by charitable aid programs.

dumping A firm's or an industry's sale of products on the world market at prices below its own cost of production.

Closely related to subsidies is **dumping**. Dumping occurs when a firm or industry sells its products on the world market at prices lower than its cost of production. Charges of dumping are often brought by a domestic producer that believes itself to be subject to unfair competition. In the United States, claims of dumping are brought before the International Trade Commission. In 2007, for example, a small manufacturer of thermal paper charged China and Germany with dumping. In 2006, the European Union brought a dumping charge against Chinese shoes. Determining whether dumping has actually occurred can be difficult. Domestic producers argue that foreign firms will dump their product in the United States, drive out American competitors, and then raise prices, thus harming consumers. Foreign exporters, on the other hand, claim that their prices are low simply because their costs are low and that no dumping has occurred. Figuring out the costs for German thermal paper or Chinese shoes is not easy. In the case of the Chinese shoe claim, for example, the Chinese government pointed out that shoes are a very labor-intensive product and that given China's low wages, it should not be a surprise that it is able to produce shoes very cheaply. In other words, the Chinese claim that shoes are an example of the theory of comparative advantage at work rather than predatory dumping.

quota A limit on the quantity of imports.

A **quota** is a limit on the quantity of imports. Quotas can be mandatory or voluntary, and they may be legislated or negotiated with foreign governments. The best-known voluntary quota, or "voluntary restraint," was negotiated with the Japanese government in 1981. Japan agreed to reduce its automobile exports to the United States by 7.7 percent, from the 1980 level of 1.82 million units to 1.68 million units. Many quotas limit trade around the world today. Perhaps the best-known recent case is the textile quota imposed in August 2005 by the European Union on imports of textiles from China. Because China had exceeded quotas that had been agreed to earlier in the year, the EU blocked the entry of Chinese-produced textiles into Europe; as a result, more than 100 million garments piled up in European ports.

Smoot-Hawley tariff The U.S. tariff law of the 1930s, which set the highest tariffs in U.S. history (60 percent). It set off an international trade war and caused the decline in trade that is often considered one of the causes of the worldwide depression of the 1930s.

U.S. Trade Policies, GATT, and the WTO

The United States has been a high-tariff nation, with average tariffs of over 50 percent, for much of its history. The highest were in effect during the Great Depression following the **Smoot-Hawley tariff**, which pushed the average tariff rate to 60 percent in 1930. The Smoot-Hawley tariff set off an international trade war when U.S. trading partners retaliated with tariffs of their own. Many economists say the decline in trade that followed was one of the causes of the worldwide depression of the 1930s.[1]

General Agreement on Tariffs and Trade (GATT) An international agreement signed by the United States and 22 other countries in 1947 to promote the liberalization of foreign trade.

In 1947, the United States, with 22 other nations, agreed to reduce barriers to trade. It also established an organization to promote liberalization of foreign trade. This **General Agreement on Tariffs and Trade (GATT)**, at first considered to be an interim arrangement, continues today and has been quite effective. The most recent round of world trade talks sponsored by GATT, the Uruguay Round, began in Uruguay in 1986. It was initialed by 116 countries on December 15, 1993, and was formally approved by the U.S. Congress after much debate following the election in 1994. The Final Act of the Uruguay Round of negotiations is the most comprehensive and complex multilateral trade agreement in history.

World Trade Organization (WTO) A negotiating forum dealing with rules of trade across nations.

In 1995, as part of GATT, the **World Trade Organization (WTO)** was established. The WTO is a negotiating forum designed to deal with rules of trade across nations. It helps facilitate freer trade across countries, negotiate trade disputes that arise, and broker trade agreements.

Doha Development Agenda An initiative of the World Trade Organization focused on issues of trade and development.

While the WTO was founded to promote free trade, its member countries clearly have different incentives as they confront trade cases. In recent years, differences between developed and developing countries have come to the fore. In 2001, at a WTO meeting in Doha, Qatar, the WTO launched a new initiative, the **Doha Development Agenda**, to deal with some of the issues that intersect the areas of trade and development. In 2007, the Doha Development Agenda continued to struggle over

---

[1] See especially Charles Kindleberger, *The World in Depression 1929–1939* (London: Allen Lane, 1973).

the issue of agriculture and farm subsidies that were described earlier in this chapter. The less developed countries, with sub-Saharan Africa taking the lead, seek to eliminate all farm subsidies currently paid by the United States and the European Union (EU). The EU has, for its part, tried to push the less developed countries toward better environmental policies as part of a broader free trade package.

The movement in the United States has been away from tariffs and quotas and toward freer trade. The Reciprocal Trade Agreements Act of 1934 authorized the president to negotiate trade agreements on behalf of the United States. As part of trade negotiations, the president can confer *most-favored-nation status* on individual trading partners. Imports from countries with most-favored-nation status are taxed at the lowest negotiated tariff rates. In addition, in recent years, several successful rounds of tariff-reduction negotiations have reduced trade barriers to their lowest levels ever.

Despite this general trend toward freer trade, most American presidents in the last 50 years have made exceptions to protect one economic sector or another. Eisenhower and Kennedy restricted imports of Japanese textiles; Johnson restricted meat imports to protect Texas beef producers; Nixon restricted steel imports; Reagan restricted automobiles from Japan. In early 2002, President George W. Bush imposed a 30 percent tariff on steel imported from the EU. In 2003, the WTO ruled that these tariffs were unfair and allowed the EU to slap retaliatory tariffs on U.S. products. Shortly thereafter, the steel tariffs were rolled back, at least on EU steel. At present, the United States has high tariffs on sugar-based ethanol, an energy source competitive with corn-based ethanol.

Economic Integration **Economic integration** occurs when two or more nations join to form a free-trade zone. In 1991, the European Community (EC, or the Common Market) began forming the largest free-trade zone in the world. The economic integration process began that December, when the 12 original members (the United Kingdom, Belgium, France, Germany, Italy, the Netherlands, Luxembourg, Denmark, Greece, Ireland, Spain, and Portugal) signed the Maastricht Treaty. The treaty called for the end of border controls, a common currency, an end to all tariffs, and the coordination of monetary and political affairs. The **European Union (EU)**, as the EC is now called, has 27 members and 3 applicants (for a list, see the Summary, p. 685). On January 1, 1993, all tariffs and trade barriers were dropped among the member countries. Border checkpoints were closed in early 1995. Citizens can now travel among member countries without passports.

economic integration Occurs when two or more nations join to form a free-trade zone.

European Union (EU) The European trading bloc composed of 27 countries.

The United States is not a part of the EU. However, in 1988, the United States (under President Reagan) and Canada (under Prime Minister Mulroney) signed the **U.S.-Canadian Free Trade Agreement**, which removed all barriers to trade, including tariffs and quotas, between the two countries in 1998.

During the last days of the George H. W. Bush administration in 1992, the United States, Mexico, and Canada signed the **North American Free Trade Agreement (NAFTA)**, with the three countries agreeing to establish all of North America as a free-trade zone. The agreement eliminated all tariffs over a 10- to 15-year period and removed restrictions on most investments. During the presidential campaign of 1992, NAFTA was hotly debated. Both Bill Clinton and George Bush supported the agreement. Industrial labor unions that might be affected by increased imports from Mexico (such as those in the automobile industry) opposed the agreement, while industries whose exports to Mexico might increase as a result of the agreement—for example, the machine tool industry—supported it. Another concern was that Mexican companies were not subject to the same environmental regulations as U.S. firms, so U.S. firms might move to Mexico for this reason.

U.S.-Canadian Free Trade Agreement An agreement in which the United States and Canada agreed to eliminate all barriers to trade between the two countries by 1998.

North American Free Trade Agreement (NAFTA) An agreement signed by the United States, Mexico, and Canada in which the three countries agreed to establish all North America as a free-trade zone.

NAFTA was ratified by the U.S. Congress in late 1993 and went into effect on the first day of 1994. The U.S. Department of Commerce estimated that as a result of NAFTA, trade between the United States and Mexico increased by nearly $16 billion in 1994. In addition, exports from the United States to Mexico outpaced imports from Mexico during 1994. In 1995, however, the agreement fell under the shadow of a dramatic collapse of the value of the peso. U.S. exports to Mexico dropped sharply, and the United States shifted from a trade surplus to a large trade deficit with Mexico. Aside from a handful of tariffs, however, all of NAFTA's commitments were fully implemented by 2003, and an 8-year report signed by all three countries declared the pact a success. The report concludes, "Eight years of expanded trade, increased employment and investment, and enhanced opportunity for the citizens of all three countries have demonstrated that NAFTA works and will continue to work." In 2007, trade among the NAFTA nations reached $930 billion.

ECONOMICS IN PRACTICE

Trade Barriers Take a Hit in 2008

Sometimes trade barriers rise and fall as a consequence of changes in the international economy. In 2008, the combination of a diminished supply and a rising demand pushed agricultural prices up dramatically worldwide. The arguments posed by the agricultural lobby to maintain trade barriers was offset by the need for an affordable food supply, and tariff barriers fell. The following article describes what happened.

High Food Prices Stir Movement on Tarriffs

The Wall Street Journal

BRUSSELS—The world's scramble for affordable food is tearing at the patchwork of agricultural tariffs that governments have long used to control trade—and offering a glimmer of hope to those trying to kick-start a stalled global trade deal.

Some countries are slashing import duties to attract staples like wheat, rice and cooking oil. Europe, traditionally the world's most outspoken advocate of protected food markets, recently removed cereal-import duties for the first time. Others—notable China—are raising export duties to keep domestic markets well stocked.

So far, the situation hasn't forced a rethinking of subsidies that farmers in the developed world receive. But some say that is an inevitable consequence of higher global food prices. "The market situation now means there's less pressure on farmers," says Peter Mandelson, the European Union's trade commissioner.

Manipulating tariffs to meet market demands isn't new. In the early 1970s, the Soviet Union suffered from shortages of soybeans, wheat and other crops. Western powers set stiff export tariffs or quotas to stop Moscow from buying up too much production. After World War II, weakened European powers protected their battered farm sector with import tariffs and subsidies.

If food prices fall sharply, the global shift on tariffs could reverse. The U.N. and other agencies forecast that prices will remain high, although this year better weather is expected to boost production in Europe and Australia.

"Trade and trade policy are adjusting to a simple fact," says Michael Mann, the EU's agricultural spokesman. "We used to have too much food, and now we have too little."

Source: John W. Miller, February 12, 2008. —Lauren Etter in Chicago contributed to this article.

Free Trade or Protection?

One of the great economic debates of all time revolves around the free-trade-versus-protection controversy. We briefly summarize the arguments in favor of each.

The Case for Free Trade

In one sense, the theory of comparative advantage *is* the case for free trade. Trade has potential benefits for all nations. A good is not imported unless its net price to buyers is below the net price of the domestically produced alternative. When the Brazilians in our earlier example found U.S. timber less expensive than their own, they bought it, yet they continued to pay the same price for homemade steel. Americans bought less expensive Brazilian steel, but they continued to buy domestic timber at the same lower price. Under these conditions, *both Americans and Brazilians ended up paying less and consuming more.*

At the same time, resources (including labor) move out of steel production and into timber production in the United States. In Brazil, resources (including labor) move out of timber production and into steel production. The resources in both countries are used more efficiently. Tariffs, export subsidies, and quotas, which interfere with the free movement of goods and services around the world, reduce or eliminate the gains of comparative advantage.

We can use supply and demand curves to illustrate this. Suppose Figure 34.4 shows domestic supply and demand for textiles. In the absence of trade, the market clears at a price of $4.20. At equilibrium, 450 million yards of textiles are produced and consumed.

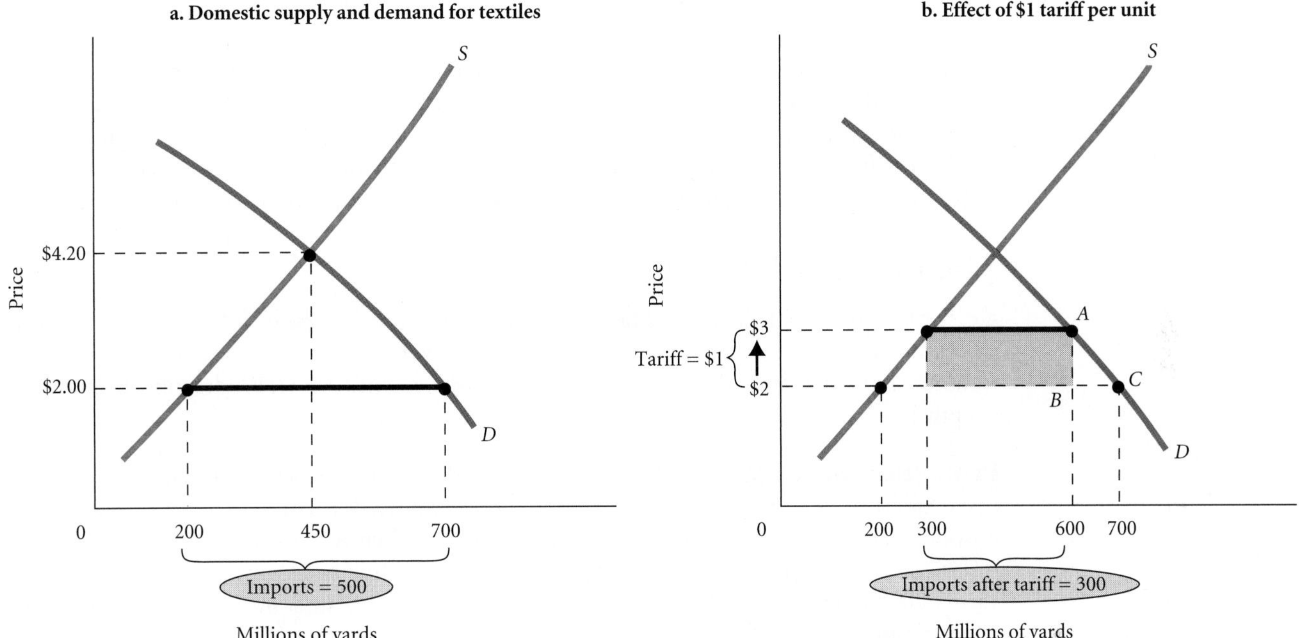

▲ **FIGURE 34.4 The Gains from Trade and Losses from the Imposition of a Tariff**

A tariff of $1 increases the market price facing consumers from $2 per yard to $3 per yard. The government collects revenues equal to the gray shaded area in **b**. The loss of efficiency has two components. First, consumers must pay a higher price for goods that could be produced at lower cost. Second, marginal producers are drawn into textiles and away from other goods, resulting in inefficient domestic production. The triangle labeled ABC in **b** is the dead weight loss or excess burden resulting from the tariff.

Assume now that textiles are available at a world price of $2. This is the price in dollars that Americans must pay for textiles from foreign sources. If we assume that an unlimited quantity of textiles is available at $2 and there is no difference in quality between domestic and foreign textiles, no domestic producer will be able to charge more than $2. In the absence of trade barriers, the world price sets the price in the United States. As the price in the United States falls from $4.20 to $2.00, the quantity demanded by consumers increases from 450 million yards to 700 million yards, but the quantity supplied by domestic producers drops from 450 million yards to 200 million yards. The difference, 500 million yards, is the quantity of textiles imported.

The argument for free trade is that each country should specialize in producing the goods and services in which it enjoys a comparative advantage. If foreign producers can produce textiles at a much lower price than domestic producers, they have a comparative advantage. As the world price of textiles falls to $2, domestic (U.S.) quantity supplied drops and resources are transferred to other sectors. These other sectors, which may be export industries or domestic industries, are not shown in Figure 34.4a. It is clear that the allocation of resources is more efficient at a price of $2. Why should the United States use domestic resources to produce what foreign producers can produce at a lower cost? U.S. resources should move into the production of the things it produces best.

Now consider what happens to the domestic price of textiles when a trade barrier is imposed. Figure 34.4b shows the effect of a set tariff of $1 per yard imposed on imported textiles. The tariff raises the domestic price of textiles to $2 + $1 = $3. The result is that some of the gains from trade are lost. First, consumers are forced to pay a higher price for the same good. The quantity of textiles demanded drops from 700 million yards under free trade to 600 million yards because some consumers are not willing to pay the higher price. Notice in Figure 34.4b the triangle labeled ABC. This is the deadweight loss or excess burden resulting from the tariff. Absent the tariff, these 100 added units of textiles would have generated benefits in excess of the $2 that each one cost.

At the same time, the higher price of textiles draws some marginal domestic producers who could not make a profit at $2 into textile production. (Recall that domestic producers do not pay a tariff.) As the price rises to $3, the quantity supplied by producers rises from 200 million yards to 300 million yards. The result is a decrease in imports from 500 million yards to 300 million yards.

Finally, the imposition of the tariff means that the government collects revenue equal to the shaded area in Figure 34.4b. This shaded area is equal to the tariff rate per unit ($1) times the number of units imported after the tariff is in place (300 million yards). Thus, receipts from the tariff are $300 million.

What is the final result of the tariff? Domestic producers receiving revenues of only $2 per unit before the tariff was imposed now receive a higher price and earn higher profits. However, these higher profits are achieved at a loss of efficiency. Trade barriers prevent a nation from reaping the benefits of specialization, push it to adopt relatively inefficient production techniques, and force consumers to pay higher prices for protected products than they would otherwise pay.

The Case for Protection

A case can also be made in favor of tariffs and quotas. Over the course of U.S. history, protectionist arguments have been made so many times by so many industries before so many congressional committees that it seems all pleas for protection share the same themes. We describe the most frequently heard pleas next.

Protection Saves Jobs The main argument for protection is that foreign competition costs Americans their jobs. When Americans buy imported Toyotas, U.S. produced cars go unsold. Layoffs in the domestic auto industry follow. When Americans buy Chinese textiles, American workers may lose their jobs. When Americans buy shoes or textiles from Korea or Taiwan, the millworkers in Maine and Massachusetts, as well as in South Carolina and Georgia, lose their jobs.

It is true that when we buy goods from foreign producers, domestic producers suffer. However, there is no reason to believe that the workers laid off in the contracting sectors will not ultimately be reemployed in expanding sectors. Foreign competition in textiles, for example, has meant the loss of U.S. jobs in that industry. Thousands of textile workers in New England lost their jobs as the textile mills closed over the last 40 years. Nevertheless, with the expansion of high-tech industries, the unemployment rate in Massachusetts fell to one of the lowest in the country in the mid-1980s, and New Hampshire, Vermont, and Maine also boomed. By the 1990s, New England had suffered another severe downturn, due partly to high-technology hardware manufacturing that had moved abroad. But by the late 1990s, its economy was booming again, this time on the back of what was called a "New Industrial Revolution": the rise of Internet-based business.

The adjustment is far from costless. The knowledge that some other industry, perhaps in some other part of the country, may be expanding is of little comfort to the person whose skills become obsolete or whose pension benefits are lost when his or her company abruptly closes a plant or goes bankrupt. The social and personal problems brought about by industry-specific unemployment, obsolete skills, and bankruptcy as a result of foreign competition are significant.

These problems can be addressed in two ways. We can ban imports and give up the gains from free trade, acknowledging that we are willing to pay premium prices to save domestic jobs in industries that can produce more efficiently abroad; or we can aid the victims of free trade in a constructive way, helping to retrain them for jobs with a future. In some instances, programs to relocate people in expanding regions may be in order. Some programs deal directly with the transition without forgoing the gains from trade.

ECONOMICS IN PRACTICE

A Petition

While most economists argue in favor of free trade, it is important to recognize that some groups are likely to lose from freer trade. Arguments by the losing groups against trade have been around for hundreds of years. In the following article, you will find an essay by a French satirist of the nineteenth century, Frederic Bastiat, complaining about the unfair competition that the sun provides to candle makers. You see that the author proposes a quota, as opposed to a tariff, on the sun.

From the Manufacturers of Candles, Tapers, Lanterns, Sticks, Street Lamps, Snuffers, and Extinguishers, and from Producers of Tallow, Oil, Resin, Alcohol, and Generally of Everything Connected with Lighting.

To the Honourable Members of the Chamber of Deputies.

Gentlemen:

You are on the right track. You reject abstract theories and [have] little regard for abundance and low prices. You concern yourselves mainly with the fate of the producer. You wish to free him from foreign competition, that is, to reserve the *domestic market* for *domestic industry*.

We come to offer you a wonderful opportunity for your—what shall we call it? Your theory? No, nothing is more deceptive than theory. Your doctrine? Your system? Your principle? But you dislike doctrines, you have a horror of systems, as for principles, you deny that there are any in political economy; therefore we shall call it your practice—your practice without theory and without principle.

Screening out the sun would increase the demand for candles. Should candlemakers be protected from unfair competition?

We are suffering from the ruinous competition of a rival who apparently works under conditions so far superior to our own for the production of light that he is *flooding* the *domestic market* with it at an incredibly low price; for the moment he appears, our sales cease, all the consumers turn to him, and a branch of French industry whose ramifications are innumerable is all at once reduced to complete stagnation. This rival, which is none other than the sun, is waging war on us so mercilessly we suspect he is being stirred up against us by perfidious Albion (excellent diplomacy nowadays!), particularly because he has for that haughty island a respect that he does not show for us. [A reference to Britain's reputation as a foggy island.]

We ask you to be so good as to pass a law requiring the closing of all windows, dormers, skylights, inside and outside shutters, curtains, casements, bull's-eyes, deadlights, and blinds—in short, all openings, holes, chinks, and fissures through which the light of the sun is wont to enter houses, to the detriment of the fair industries with which, we are proud to say, we have endowed the country, a country that cannot, without betraying ingratitude, abandon us today to so unequal a combat.

Source: Frederic Bastiat (1801 to 1850), New Australian. Reprinted by permission.

Some Countries Engage in Unfair Trade Practices Attempts by U.S. firms to monopolize an industry are illegal under the Sherman and Clayton acts. If a strong company decides to drive the competition out of the market by setting prices below cost, it would be aggressively prosecuted by the Antitrust Division of the Justice Department. However, the argument goes, if we will not allow a U.S. firm to engage in predatory pricing or monopolize an industry or a market, can we stand by and let a German firm or a Japanese firm do so in the name of free trade? This is a legitimate argument and one that has gained significant favor in recent years. How should we respond when a large international company or a country behaves strategically against a domestic firm or industry? Free trade may be the best solution when everybody plays by the rules, but sometimes we have to fight back. The WTO is the vehicle currently used to negotiate disputes of this sort.

Cheap Foreign Labor Makes Competition Unfair Let us say that a particular country gained its "comparative advantage" in textiles by paying its workers low wages. How can U.S. textile companies compete with companies that pay wages that are less than a quarter of what U.S. companies pay? Questions like this are often asked by those concerned with competition from China and India.

First, remember that wages in a competitive economy reflect productivity: a high ratio of output to units of labor. Workers in the United States earn higher wages because they are more productive. The United States has more capital per worker; that is, the average worker works with better machinery and equipment and its workers are better trained. Second, trade flows not according to *absolute* advantage, but according to *comparative* advantage: All countries benefit, even if one country is more efficient at producing everything.

Protection Safeguards National Security Beyond saving jobs, certain sectors of the economy may appeal for protection for other reasons. The steel industry has argued for years with some success that it is vital to national defense. In the event of a war, the United States would not want to depend on foreign countries for a product as vital as steel. Even if we acknowledge another country's comparative advantage, we may want to protect our own resources.

Virtually no industry has ever asked for protection without invoking the national defense argument. Testimony that was once given on behalf of the scissors and shears industry argued that "in the event of a national emergency and imports cutoff, the United States would be without a source of scissors and shears, basic tools for many industries and trades essential to our national defense." The question lies not in the merit of the argument, but in just how seriously it can be taken if *every* industry uses it.

Protection Discourages Dependency Closely related to the national defense argument is the claim that countries, particularly small or developing countries, may come to rely too heavily on one or more trading partners for many items. If a small country comes to rely on a major power for food or energy or some important raw material in which the large nation has a comparative advantage, it may be difficult for the smaller nation to remain politically neutral. Some critics of free trade argue that larger countries, such as the United States, Russia, and China have consciously engaged in trade with smaller countries to create these kinds of dependencies.

Therefore, should small, independent countries consciously avoid trading relationships that might lead to political dependence? This objective may involve developing domestic industries in areas where a country has a comparative disadvantage. To do so would mean protecting that industry from international competition.

Environmental Concerns In recent years, concern about the environment has led some people to question advantages of free trade. Some environmental groups, for example, argue that the WTO's free trade policies may harm the environment. The central argument is that poor countries will become havens for polluting industries that will operate their steel and auto factories with few environmental controls.

These issues are quite complex, and there is much dispute among economists about the interaction between free trade and the environment. One relatively recent study of sulphur dioxide, for example, found that in the long run, free trade reduces pollution, largely by increasing the income of countries; richer countries typically choose policies to improve the environment.[2] Thus, while free trade and increased development initially may cause pollution levels to rise, in the long run, prosperity is a benefit to the environment. Many also argue that there are complex trade-offs to be made between pollution control and problems such as malnutrition and health for poor countries. The United States and Europe both traded off faster economic growth and income against cleaner air and water at earlier times in their development. Some argue that it is unfair for the developed countries to impose their preferences on other countries facing more difficult trade-offs.

Nevertheless, the concern with global climate change has stimulated new thinking in this area. A recent study by the Tyndall Centre for Climate Change Research in Britain found that in 2004, 23 percent of the greenhouse gas emissions produced by China were created in the production of exports. In other words, these emissions come not as a result of goods that China's population is enjoying as its income rises, but as a consequence of the consumption of the United States and Europe, where most of these goods are going. In a world in which the effects of carbon emissions are global and all countries are not willing to sign binding global agreements to control emissions, trade with China may be a way for developed nations to avoid their commitments to pollution reduction. Some have argued that penalties could be imposed on high-polluting products produced in countries that have not signed international climate control treaties as a way to ensure that the prices of goods imported this way reflect the harm that those products cause the Earth.[3] Implementing these policies is, however, likely to be very complex, and some have argued that it is a mistake to bundle trade and environmental issues. As with other areas covered in this book, there is still disagreement among economists as to the right answer.

Protection Safeguards Infant Industries Young industries in a given country may have a difficult time competing with established industries in other countries. In a dynamic world, a protected **infant industry** might mature into a strong industry worldwide because of an acquired, but real, comparative advantage. If such an industry is undercut and driven out of world markets at the beginning of its life, that comparative advantage might never develop.

infant industry A young industry that may need temporary protection from competition from the established industries of other countries to develop an acquired comparative advantage.

Yet efforts to protect infant industries can backfire. In July 1991, the U.S. government imposed a 62.67 percent tariff on imports of active-matrix liquid crystal display screens (also referred to as "flat-panel displays" used primarily for laptop computers) from Japan. The Commerce Department and the International Trade Commission agreed that Japanese producers were selling their screens in the U.S. market at a price below cost and that this dumping threatened the survival of domestic laptop screen producers. The tariff was meant to protect the infant U.S. industry until it could compete head-on with the Japanese.

Unfortunately for U.S. producers of laptop computers and for consumers who purchase them, the tariff had an unintended (although predictable) effect on the industry. Because U.S. laptop screens were generally recognized to be of lower quality than their Japanese counterparts, imposition of the tariff left U.S. computer manufacturers with three options: (1) They could use the screens available from U.S. producers and watch sales of their final product decline in the face of *higher-quality* competition from abroad, (2) they could pay the tariff for the higher-quality screens and watch sales of their final product decline in the face of *lower-priced* competition from abroad, or (3) they could do what was most profitable for them to do—move their production facilities abroad to avoid the tariff completely. The last option is what Apple and IBM did. In the end, not only were the laptop industry and its consumers hurt by the imposition of the tariff (due to higher costs of production and to higher laptop computer prices), but the U.S. screen industry was hurt as well (due to its loss of buyers for its product) by a policy specifically designed to help it.

---

[2] Werner Antweiler, Brian Copeland, and M. Scott Taylor, "Is Free Trade Good for the Environment?" *AER*, September, 2001.

[3] Judith Chevalier, "A Carbon Cap That Starts in Washington," *New York Times*, December 16, 2007.

The case for free trade has been made across the world as increasing numbers of countries have joined the world marketplace. Figure 34.5 traces the path of tariffs across the world from 1980–2005. The lines show an index of trade openness, calculated as 100 minus the tariff rate. (So higher numbers mean lower tariffs.) We see rapid reductions in the last 25 years across the world, most notably in countries in the emerging and developing markets.

▶ FIGURE 34.5 Trade Openness Across the World (Index is 100 minus the average effective tariff rate in the region.)

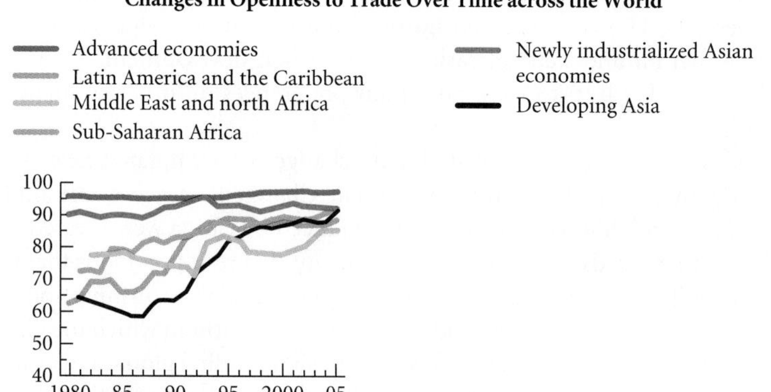

Source: International Monetary Fund, 2007 *World Economic Outlook.*
Trade openness is measured as 100 minus the average effective tariff rate in the region.

Source: International Monetary Fund, 2007 *World Economic Outlook.*
Trade openness is measured as 100 minus the average effective tariff rate in the region.

An Economic Consensus

You now know something about how international trade fits into the structure of the economy.

Critical to our study of international economics is the debate between free traders and protectionists. On one side is the theory of comparative advantage, formalized by David Ricardo in the early part of the nineteenth century. According to this view, all countries benefit from specialization and trade. The gains from trade are real, and they can be large; free international trade raises real incomes and improves the standard of living.

On the other side are the protectionists, who point to the loss of jobs and argue for the protection of workers from foreign competition. Although foreign competition can cause job loss in specific sectors, it is unlikely to cause net job loss in an economy and workers will, over time, be absorbed into expanding sectors. Foreign trade and full employment can be pursued simultaneously. Although economists disagree about many things, the vast majority of them favor free trade.

SUMMARY

1. All economies, regardless of their size, depend to some extent on other economies and are affected by events outside their borders.

TRADE SURPLUSES AND DEFICITS *p. 666*

2. Until the 1970s, the United States generally exported more than it imported—it ran a *trade surplus.* In the mid-1970s, the United States began to import more merchandise than it exported—a *trade deficit.*

THE ECONOMIC BASIS FOR TRADE: COMPARATIVE ADVANTAGE *p. 667*

3. The *theory of comparative advantage,* dating to David Ricardo in the nineteenth century, holds that specialization and free trade will benefit all trading partners, even those that may be absolutely less efficient producers.

4. A country enjoys an *absolute advantage* over another country in the production of a product if it uses fewer resources to produce that product than the other country does. A country has a *comparative advantage* in the production of a product if that product can be produced at a lower cost in terms of other goods.

5. Trade enables countries to move beyond their previous resource and productivity constraints. When countries specialize in producing those goods in which they have a comparative advantage, they maximize their combined output and allocate their resources more efficiently.

6. When trade is free, patterns of trade and trade flows result from the independent decisions of thousands of importers and exporters and millions of private households and firms.

7. The relative attractiveness of foreign goods to U.S. buyers and of U.S. goods to foreign buyers depends in part on *exchange rates*, the ratios at which two currencies are traded for each other.

8. For any pair of countries, there is a range of exchange rates that will lead automatically to both countries realizing the gains from specialization and comparative advantage. Within that range, the exchange rate will determine which country gains the most from trade. This leads us to conclude that exchange rates determine the terms of trade.

9. If exchange rates end up in the right range (that is, in a range that facilitates the flow of goods between nations), the free market will drive each country to shift resources into those sectors in which it enjoys a comparative advantage. Only those products in which a country has a comparative advantage will be competitive in world markets.

THE SOURCES OF COMPARATIVE ADVANTAGE *p. 674*

10. The *Heckscher-Ohlin theorem* looks to relative *factor endowments* to explain comparative advantage and trade flows. According to the theorem, a country has a comparative advantage in the production of a product if that country is relatively well endowed with the inputs that are used intensively in the production of that product.

11. A relatively short list of inputs—natural resources, knowledge capital, physical capital, land, and skilled and unskilled labor—explains a surprisingly large portion of world trade patterns. However, the simple version of the theory of comparative advantage cannot explain why many countries import and export the same goods.

12. Some theories argue that comparative advantage can be acquired. Just as industries within a country differentiate their products to capture a domestic market, they also differentiate their products to please the wide variety of tastes that exists worldwide. This theory is consistent with the theory of comparative advantage.

TRADE BARRIERS: TARIFFS, EXPORT SUBSIDIES, AND QUOTAS *p. 675*

13. Trade barriers take many forms. The three most common are *tariffs, export subsidies*, and *quotas*. All are forms of *protection* through which some sector of the economy is shielded from foreign competition.

14. Although the United States has historically been a high-tariff nation, the general movement is now away from tariffs and quotas. The *General Agreement on Tariffs and Trade (GATT)*, signed by the United States and 22 other countries in 1947, continues in effect today; its purpose is to reduce barriers to world trade and keep them down. Also important are the *U.S.-Canadian Free Trade Agreement*, signed in 1988, and the *North American Free Trade Agreement*, signed by the United States, Mexico, and Canada in the last days of the George H. W. Bush administration in 1992, taking effect in 1994.

15. The World Trade Organization (WTO) was set up by GATT to act as a negotiating forum for trade disputes across countries.

16. The *European Union (EU)* is a free-trade bloc composed of 27 nations: Austria, Belgium, Bulgaria, Cyprus, the Czech Republic, Denmark, Estonia, Finland, France, Germany, Greece, Hungary, Ireland, Italy, Latvia, Lithuania, Luxembourg, Malta, the Netherlands, Poland, Portugal, Romania, Slovakia, Slovenia, Spain, Sweden, and the United Kingdom. Three others have applied for membership: Croatia, the Republic of Macedonia, and Turkey. Many economists believe that the advantages of free trade within the bloc, a reunited Germany, and the ability to work well as a bloc will make the EU the most powerful player in the international marketplace in the coming decades.

FREE TRADE OR PROTECTION? *p. 678*

17. In one sense, the theory of comparative advantage is the case for free trade. Trade barriers prevent a nation from reaping the benefits of specialization, push it to adopt relatively inefficient production techniques, and force consumers to pay higher prices for protected products than they would otherwise pay.

18. The case for protection rests on a number of propositions, one of which is that foreign competition results in a loss of domestic jobs, but there is no reason to believe that the workers laid off in the contracting sectors will not be ultimately reemployed in other expanding sectors. This adjustment process is far from costless, however.

19. Other arguments for protection hold that cheap foreign labor makes competition unfair; that some countries engage in unfair trade practices; that free trade might harm the environment; and that protection safeguards the national security, discourages dependency, and shields *infant industries*. Despite these arguments, most economists favor free trade.

REVIEW TERMS AND CONCEPTS

absolute advantage, *p. 667*
comparative advantage, *p. 667*
Corn Laws, *p. 667*
Doha Development Agenda, *p. 676*
dumping, *p. 676*
economic integration, *p. 677*
European Union (EU), *p. 677*
exchange rate, *p. 672*
export subsidies, *p. 675*
factor endowments, *p. 674*
General Agreement on Tariffs and Trade (GATT), *p. 676*
Heckscher-Ohlin theorem, *p. 674*
infant industry, *p. 683*
North American Free Trade Agreement (NAFTA), *p. 677*
protection, *p. 675*
quota, *p. 676*
Smoot-Hawley tariff, *p. 676*
tariff, *p. 675*
terms of trade, *p. 671*
theory of comparative advantage, *p. 667*
trade deficit, *p. 666*
trade surplus, *p. 666*
U.S.-Canadian Free Trade Agreement, *p. 677*
World Trade Organization (WTO), *p. 676*

PROBLEMS

Visit www.myeconlab.com to complete the problems marked in orange online. You will receive instant feedback on your answers, tutorial help, and access to additional practice problems.

1. Suppose Germany and France each produce only two goods, guns and butter. Both are produced using labor alone. Assuming both countries are at full employment, you are given the following information:

Germany: 10 units of labor required to produce 1 gun
5 units of labor required to produce 1 pound of butter
Total labor force: 1,000,000 units

France: 15 units of labor required to produce 1 gun
10 units of labor required to produce 1 pound of butter
Total labor force: 750,000 units

   a. Draw the production possibility frontiers for each country in the absence of trade.
   b. If transportation costs are ignored and trade is allowed, will France and Germany engage in trade? Explain.
   c. If a trade agreement was negotiated, at what rate (number of guns per unit of butter) would they agree to exchange?

2. The United States and Russia each produce only bearskin caps and wheat. Domestic prices are given in the following table:

	RUSSIA	UNITED STATES	
Bearskin caps	10 Ru	$ 7	Per hat
Wheat	15 Ru	$10	Per bushel

On April 1, the Zurich exchange listed an exchange rate of $1 = 1 Ru.

   a. Which country has an absolute advantage in the production of bearskin caps? wheat?
   b. Which country has a comparative advantage in the production of bearskin caps? wheat?
   c. If the United States and Russia were the only two countries engaging in trade, what adjustments would you predict assuming exchange rates are freely determined by the laws of supply and demand?

3. The following table shows imports and exports of goods during the first half of 2005 for the United States:

	JAN.-JUNE 2005 (BILLIONS OF DOLLARS)	
	EXPORTS	IMPORTS
Total	439.0	795.1
Airplanes	15.5	6.1
Clothing	2.1	35.8
Crude oil	.3	81.6
Vehicles	35.4	95.1
Agricultural goods	30.6	29.8

What, if anything, can you conclude about the comparative advantage that the United States has relative to its trading partners in the production of goods? What stories can you tell about the wide disparities in clothing and airplanes?

4. The following table gives recent figures for yield per acre in Illinois and Kansas:

	WHEAT	SOYBEANS
Illinois	48	39
Kansas	40	24

Source: U.S. Dept. of Agriculture, *Crop Production*.

   a. If we assume that farmers in Illinois and Kansas use the same amount of labor, capital, and fertilizer, which state has an absolute advantage in wheat production? soybean production?
   b. If we transfer land out of wheat into soybeans, how many bushels of wheat do we give up in Illinois per additional bushel of soybeans produced? in Kansas?
   c. Which state has a comparative advantage in wheat production? in soybean production?
   d. The following table gives the distribution of land planted for each state in millions of acres in the same year.

	TOTAL ACRES UNDER TILL	WHEAT	SOYBEANS
Illinois	22.9	1.9 (8.3%)	9.1 (39.7%)
Kansas	20.7	11.8 (57.0%)	1.9 (9.2%)

Are these data consistent with your answer to part c? Explain.

5. You can think of the United States as a set of 50 separate economies with no trade barriers. In such an open environment, each state specializes in the products that it produces best.
   a. What product or products does your state specialize in?
   b. Can you identify the source of the comparative advantage that lies behind the production of one or more of these products (for example, a natural resource, plentiful cheap labor, or a skilled labor force)?
   c. Do you think that the theory of comparative advantage and the Heckscher-Ohlin theorem help to explain why your state specializes the way that it does? Explain your answer.

6. Australia and the United States produce white and red wines. Current domestic prices for each wine are given in the following table:

	AUSTRALIA	UNITED STATES
White wine	5 AU$	10 US$
Red wine	10 AU$	15 US$

Suppose the exchange rate is 1 AU$ = 1 US$.
   a. If the price ratios within each country reflect resource use, which country has a comparative advantage in the production of red wine? white wine?

b. Assume that there are no other trading partners and that the only motive for holding foreign currency is to buy foreign goods. Will the current exchange rate lead to trade flows in both directions between the two countries? Explain.

c. What adjustments might you expect in the exchange rate? Be specific.

d. What would you predict about trade flows between Australia and the United States after the exchange rate has adjusted?

7. Some empirical trade economists have noted that for many products, countries are both importers and exporters. For example, the United States both imports and exports shirts. How do you explain this?

8. **[Related to the *Economics in Practice* on *p. 678*]** Review the *Economics in Practice* on p. 678. Given the fact that food prices rose in world markets during 2008, many countries reduced tariffs and other trade barriers to food. Why did this happen? Who benefits when food prices rise, and who is hurt? Who is likely to be in favor of cutting tariffs on food, and who might be in favor of maintaining those tariffs? Go to newspaper archives such as nytimes.com and online.wsj.com to see if there is evidence to support your answer.

9. **[Related to the *Economics in Practice* on *p. 681*]** When a president presents a trade agreement for ratification to Congress, many domestic industries fight the ratification. In 2005, the United States was negotiating the Central America-Dominican Republic Free Trade Agreement (CAFTA-DR). Write a brief essay on the U.S. political opposition to CAFTA-DR in 2004 and 2005. What industries in the United States opposed the trade agreement? Is it fair to compare the arguments of these industries to the arguments posed by the candle makers?

Open-Economy Macroeconomics: The Balance of Payments and Exchange Rates

35

CHAPTER OUTLINE

The economies of the world have become increasingly interdependent over the last four decades. No economy operates in a vacuum, and economic events in one country can have significant repercussions on the economies of other countries.

International trade is a major part of today's world economy. U.S. imports now account for about 15 percent of U.S. gross domestic product (GDP), and billions of dollars flow through the international capital market each day. In Chapter 34, we explored the main reasons why there is international exchange. Countries trade with one another to obtain goods and services they cannot produce themselves or to take advantage of the fact that other countries can produce goods and services at a lower cost than they can. You can see the various connections between the domestic economy and the rest of the world in the circular flow diagram in Figure 20.3 on p. 405. Foreign countries supply goods and services to the United States, and the United States supplies goods and services to the rest of the world.

From a macroeconomic point of view, the main difference between an international transaction and a domestic transaction concerns currency exchange. When people in countries with different currencies buy from and sell to each other, an exchange of currencies must also take place. Brazilian coffee exporters cannot spend U.S. dollars in Brazil—they need Brazilian reals. A U.S. wheat exporter cannot use Brazilian reals to buy a tractor from a U.S. company or to pay the rent on warehouse facilities. Somehow international exchange must be managed in a way that allows both partners in the transaction to wind up with their own currency.

As you know from Chapter 34, the direction of trade between two countries depends on **exchange rates**—the price of one country's currency in terms of the other country's currency. If the Japanese yen were very expensive (making the dollar cheap), both Japanese and Americans would buy from U.S. producers. If the yen were very cheap (making the U.S. dollar expensive), both Japanese and Americans would buy from Japanese producers. Within a certain range of exchange rates, trade flows in both directions, each country specializes in producing the goods in which it enjoys a comparative advantage, and trade is mutually beneficial.

exchange rate The price of one country's currency in terms of another country's currency; the ratio at which two currencies are traded for each other.

Because exchange rates are a factor in determining the flow of international trade, the way they are determined is very important. Since 1900, the world monetary system has been changed several times by international agreements and events. In the early part of the twentieth century, nearly all currencies were backed by gold. Their values were fixed in terms of a specific number of ounces of gold, which determined their values in international trading—exchange rates.

In 1944, with the international monetary system in chaos as the end of World War II drew near, a large group of experts unofficially representing 44 countries met in Bretton Woods, New Hampshire, and drew up a number of agreements. One of those agreements established a system of essentially fixed exchange rates under which each country agreed to intervene by buying and selling currencies in the foreign exchange market when necessary to maintain the agreed-to value of its currency.

In 1971, most countries, including the United States, gave up trying to fix exchange rates formally and began allowing them to be determined essentially by supply and demand. For example, without government intervention in the marketplace, the price of British pounds in dollars is determined by the interaction of those who want to exchange dollars for pounds (those who "demand" pounds) and those who want to exchange pounds for dollars (those who "supply" pounds). If the quantity of pounds demanded exceeds the quantity of pounds supplied, the price of pounds will rise, just as the price of peanuts or paper clips would rise under similar circumstances. A more detailed discussion of the various monetary systems that have been in place since 1900 is provided in the Appendix to this chapter.

In this chapter, we explore in more detail what has come to be called *open-economy macroeconomics*. First, we discuss the *balance of payments*—the record of a nation's transactions with the rest of the world. We then go on to consider how the analysis changes when we allow for the international exchange of goods, services, and capital.

The Balance of Payments

foreign exchange All currencies other than the domestic currency of a given country.

We sometimes lump all foreign currencies—euros, Swiss francs, Japanese yen, Brazilian reals, and so forth—together as "foreign exchange." **Foreign exchange** is simply all currencies other than the domestic currency of a given country (in the case of the United States, the U.S. dollar). U.S. demand for foreign exchange arises because its citizens want to buy things whose prices are quoted in other currencies, such as Australian jewelry, vacations in Mexico, and bonds or stocks issued by Sony Corporation of Japan. Whenever U.S. citizens make these purchases, they first buy the foreign currencies and then make the purchases.

Where does the *supply* of foreign exchange come from? The answer is simple: The United States (actually U.S. citizens or firms) earns foreign exchange when it sells products, services, or assets to another country. Just as Mexico earns foreign exchange when U.S. tourists visit Cancún, the United States earns foreign exchange (in this case, Mexican pesos) when Mexican tourists come to the United States to visit Disney World. Similarly, Saudi Arabian purchases of stock in General Motors and Colombian purchases of real estate in Miami increase the U.S. supply of foreign exchange.

balance of payments The record of a country's transactions in goods, services, and assets with the rest of the world; also the record of a country's sources (supply) and uses (demand) of foreign exchange.

The record of a country's transactions in goods, services, and assets with the rest of the world is its **balance of payments**. The balance of payments is also the record of a country's sources (supply) and uses (demand) of foreign exchange.[1]

The Current Account

The balance of payments is divided into two major accounts, the *current account* and the *capital account*. These are shown in Table 35.1, which provides data on the U.S. balance of payments for 2007. We begin with the current account.

The first item in the current account is U.S. trade in goods. This category includes exports of computer chips, potato chips, and CDs of U.S. musicians and imports of Scotch whiskey, Chinese toys, and Mexican oil. U.S. exports *earn* foreign exchange for the United States and are a credit (+) item on the current account. U.S. imports *use up* foreign exchange and are a debit (−) item. In 2007, the United States imported $815.4 billion more in goods than it exported.

Next in the current account is services. Like most other countries, the United States buys services from and sells services to other countries. For example, a U.S. firm shipping wheat to

[1] Bear in mind the distinction between the balance of payments and a balance sheet. A *balance sheet* for a firm or a country measures that entity's stock of assets and liabilities at a moment in time. The *balance of payments*, by contrast, measures *flows*, usually over a period of a month, a quarter, or a year. Despite its name, the balance of payments is *not* a balance sheet.

England might purchase insurance from a British insurance company. A Dutch flower grower may fly flowers to the United States aboard an American airliner. In the first case, the United States is importing services and therefore using up foreign exchange; in the second case, it is selling services to foreigners and earning foreign exchange. In 2007, the United States exported $106.9 billion more in services than it imported.

TABLE 35.1 United States Balance of Payments, 2007

All transactions that bring foreign exchange into the United States are credited (+) to the current account; all transactions that cause the United States to lose foreign exchange are debited (–) to the current account

Current Account	Billions of dollars
Goods exports	1,149.2
Goods imports	-1,964.6
(1) Net export of goods	-815.4
Exports of services	479.2
Imports of services	-372.3
(2) Net export of services	106.9
Income received on investments	782.2
Income payments on investments	-707.9
(3) Net investment income	74.3
(4) Net transfer payments	-104.4
(5) Balance on current account (1 + 2 + 3 + 4)	-738.6
Capital Account	
(6) Change in private U.S. assets abroad (increase is -)	-1,183.3
(7) Change in foreign private assets in the United States	1,451.0
(8) Change in U.S. government assets abroad (increase is -)	-23.0
(9) Change in foreign government assets in the United States	412.7
(10) Balance on capital account (6 + 7 + 8 + 9)	657.4
(11) Net capital account transactions	-2.2
(12) Statistical discrepancy	83.6
(13) Balance of payments (5 + 10 + 11 + 12)	0

Source: U.S. Department of Commerce, Survey of Current Business, April 2008.

The difference between a country's exports of goods and services and its imports of goods and services is its **balance of trade**. When exports of goods and services are less than imports of goods and services, a country has a **trade deficit**. The U.S. trade deficit in 2007 was huge: $708.5 billion (that is, $815.4 billion less $106.9 billion).

balance of trade A country's exports of goods and services minus its imports of goods and services.

trade deficit Occurs when a country's exports of goods and services are less than its imports of goods and services.

The third item in the current account concerns investment income. U.S. citizens hold foreign assets (stocks, bonds, and real assets such as buildings and factories). Dividends, interest, rent, and profits paid to U.S. asset holders are a source of foreign exchange. Conversely, when foreigners earn dividends, interest, and profits on assets held in the United States, foreign exchange is used up. In 2007, investment income received from foreigners exceeded investment income paid to foreigners by $74.3 billion.

The fourth item in Table 35.1 is net transfer payments. Transfer payments from the United States to foreigners are another use of foreign exchange. Some of these transfer payments are from private U.S. citizens, and some are from the U.S. government. You may send a check to a relief agency in Africa. Many immigrants in the United States send remittances to their countries of origin to help support extended families. Conversely, some foreigners make transfer payments to the United States. *Net* refers to the difference between payments from the United States to foreigners and payments from foreigners to the United States.

balance on current account Net exports of goods plus net exports of services plus net investment income plus net transfer payments.

If we add net exports of goods, net export of services, net investment income, and net transfer payments, we get the **balance on current account**. The balance on current account shows how much a nation has spent on foreign goods, services, investment income payments, and transfers relative to how much it has earned from other countries. When the balance is negative, which it was for the United States in 2007, a nation has spent more on foreign goods and services (plus investment income and transfers paid) than it has earned through the sales of its goods and services to the rest of the world (plus investment income and transfers received). If a nation has spent more on foreign goods, services, investment income payments, and transfers than it has earned, its net wealth position vis-à-vis the rest of the world must decrease. By *net*, we mean a nation's assets abroad minus its liabilities to the rest of the world. The capital account of the balance of payments records the changes in these assets and liabilities. We now turn to the capital account.

The Capital Account

For each transaction recorded in the current account, there is an offsetting transaction recorded in the capital account. Consider the purchase of a Japanese car by a U.S. citizen. Say that the yen/dollar exchange rate is 100 yen to a dollar and that the yen price of the car is 2.0 million yen, which is $20,000. The U.S. citizen (probably an automobile dealer) takes $20,000, buys 2.0 million yen, and then buys the car. In this case, U.S. imports are increased by $20,000 in the current account and foreign assets in the United States (in this case, Japanese holdings of dollars) are increased by $20,000 in the capital account. The net wealth position of the United States vis-à-vis the rest of the world has decreased by $20,000. The key point to realize is that an increase in U.S. imports results in an increase in foreign assets in the United States. The United States must "pay" for the imports, and whatever it pays with (in this example, U.S. dollars) is an increase in foreign assets in the United States. Conversely, an increase in U.S. exports results in an increase in U.S. assets abroad because foreigners must pay for the U.S. exports.

Table 35.1 shows that U.S. assets abroad are divided into private holdings (line 6) and U.S. government holdings (line 8). Similarly, foreign assets in the United States are divided into foreign private (line 7) and foreign government (line 9). The sum of lines 6, 7, 8, and 9 is the **balance on capital account** (line 10). The next item is called net capital account transactions (line 11). It is quite small in value and includes things such as U.S. government debt forgiveness. These kinds of transactions affect the capital account but not the current account. Ignoring this item, if there were no errors of measurement in the data collection, the balance on capital account would equal the negative of the balance on current account because, as mentioned previously, for each transaction in the current account, there is an offsetting transaction in the capital account. Another way of looking at the balance on capital account is that it is the change in the net wealth position of the country vis-à-vis the rest of the world. When the balance on capital account is positive, this means that the change in foreign assets in the country is greater than the change in the country's assets abroad, which is a decrease in the net wealth position of the country.

balance on capital account In the United States, the sum of the following (measured in a given period): the change in private U.S. assets abroad, the change in foreign private assets in the United States, the change in U.S. government assets abroad, and the change in foreign government assets in the United States.

Table 35.1 shows that in 2007, the U.S. balance on current account was −$738.6 billion, which means that the United States spent considerably more than it made vis-à-vis the rest of the world. If the balance on current account is measured correctly, the net wealth position of the United States vis-à-vis the rest of the world should have decreased by $738.6 billion in 2007 plus the $2.2 billion in line 11 of $740.8 billion. The balance on capital account (line 10) is in fact $657.4 billion; so the error of measurement, called the statistical discrepancy, is $83.6 billion (line 12) in 2007. The balance of payments (line 13) is the sum of the balance on current account, the balance on capital account, net capital account transactions, and the statistical discrepancy. By construction, it is always zero.

It is important to note from Table 35.1 that even though the net wealth position of the United States decreased in 2007, the change in U.S. assets abroad increased considerably ($1,183.3 billion private plus $23.0 billion government). How can this be? Because there was an even larger increase in foreign assets in the United States ($1,451.0 billion private plus $412.7 billion government). It is the *net* change (that is, the change in foreign assets in the United States minus the change in U.S. assets abroad) that is equal to the negative of the balance on current account (aside from the statistical discrepancy), not the change in just U.S. assets abroad. Much of the increase of $412.7 billion in foreign government assets was the accumulation of dollars by Japan and China.

Many transactions get recorded in the capital account that do not pertain to the current account. Consider a purchase of a U.K. security by a U.S. resident. This is done by the U.S.

resident's selling dollars for pounds and using the pounds to buy the U.K. security. After this transaction, U.S. assets abroad have increased (the United States now holds more U.K. securities) and foreign assets in the United States have increased (foreigners now hold more dollars). The purchase of the U.K. security is recorded as a minus item in line 6 in Table 35.1, and the increase in foreign holdings of dollars is recorded as a plus item in line 7. These two balance out. This happens whenever there is a switch of one kind of asset for another vis-à-vis the rest of the world. In recent years, a number of business people from the oil-rich Middle East purchased apartments in U.S. cities like New York and San Francisco. These real estate investments increased foreign assets in the United States (real estate) and increased U.S. assets abroad (foreign currency from the Middle East).

The United States as a Debtor Nation

If a country has a positive net wealth position vis-à-vis the rest of the world, it can be said to be a creditor nation. Conversely, if it has a negative net wealth position, it can be said to be a debtor nation. Remember that a country's net wealth position increases if it has a positive current account balance and decreases if it has a negative current account balance. It is important to realize that the *only* way a country's net wealth position can change is if its current account balance is nonzero. Simply switching one form of asset for another, such as trading real estate for foreign currency, is not a change in a country's net wealth position. Another way of putting this is that a country's net wealth position is the sum of all its past current account balances.

Prior to the mid-1970s, the United States had generally run current account surpluses, and thus its net wealth position was positive. It was a creditor nation. This began to turn around in the mid-1970s, and by the mid-1980s, the United States was running large current account deficits. Sometime during this period, the United States changed from having a positive net wealth position vis-à-vis the rest of the world to having a negative position. In other words, the United States changed from a creditor nation to a debtor nation. The current account deficits persisted into the 1990s, and the United States is now the largest debtor nation in the world. In 2006, foreign assets in the United States totaled $16.3 trillion and U.S. assets abroad totaled $13.8 trillion.[2] The U.S. net wealth position was thus −$2.5 trillion. This large negative position reflects the fact that the United States spent much more in the 1980s, 1990s, and 2000s on foreign goods and services (plus investment income and transfers paid) than it earned through the sales of its goods and services to the rest of the world (plus investment income and transfers received).

Equilibrium Output (Income) in an Open Economy

Everything we have said so far has been descriptive. Now we turn to analysis. How are all these trade and capital flows determined? What impacts do they have on the economies of the countries involved? To simplify our discussion, we will assume that exchange rates are fixed. We will relax this assumption later.

The International Sector and Planned Aggregate Expenditure

Our earlier descriptions of the multiplier took into account the consumption behavior of households (C), the planned investment behavior of firms (I), and the spending of the government (G). We defined the sum of those three components as planned aggregate expenditure (AE).

To analyze the international sector, we must include the goods and services a country exports to the rest of the world as well as what it imports. If we call our exports of goods and services EX, it should be clear that EX is a component of total output and income. A U.S. razor sold to a buyer

[2] U.S. Department of Commerce, *Survey of Current Business*, April 2008, Table F.1.

in Mexico is as much a part of U.S. production as a similar razor sold in Pittsburgh. Exports simply represent demand for domestic products not by domestic households and firms and the government, but by the rest of the world.

What about imports (IM)? Remember, imports are *not a part of domestic output* (Y). By definition, imports are not produced by the country that is importing them. Remember also, when we look at households' total consumption spending, firms' total investment spending, and total government spending, imports are included. Therefore, to calculate domestic output correctly, we must subtract the parts of consumption, investment, and government spending that constitute imports. The definition of planned aggregate expenditure becomes:

Planned aggregate expenditure in an open economy:

$$AE \equiv C + I + G + EX - IM$$

net exports of goods and services ($EX - IM$) The difference between a country's total exports and total imports.

The last two terms ($EX - IM$) together are the country's **net exports of goods and services.**

Determining the Level of Imports What determines the level of imports and exports in a country? For now, we assume that the level of imports is a function of income (Y). The rationale is simple: When U.S. income increases, U.S. citizens buy more of everything, including U.S. cars and peanut butter, Japanese TV sets, and Korean steel and DVD players. When income rises, imports tend to go up. Algebraically,

$$IM = mY$$

marginal propensity to import (MPM) The change in imports caused by a $1 change in income.

where Y is income and m is some positive number. (m is assumed to be less than 1; otherwise, a $1 increase in income generates an increase in imports of more than $1, which is unrealistic.) Recall from Chapter 23 that the marginal propensity to consume (MPC) measures the change in consumption that results from a $1 change in income. Similarly, the **marginal propensity to import**, abbreviated as MPM or m, is the change in imports caused by a $1 change in income. If $m = .2$, or 20 percent, and income is $1,000, then imports, IM, are equal to $.2 \times \$1,000 = \$200$. If income rises by $100 to $1,100, the change in imports will equal $m \times$ (the change in income) $= .2 \times \$100 = \$20$.

For now we will assume that exports (EX) are given (that is, they are not affected, even indirectly, by the state of the economy.) This assumption is relaxed later in this chapter.

Solving for Equilibrium Given the assumption about how imports are determined, we can solve for equilibrium income. This procedure is illustrated in Figure 35.1. Starting from the consumption function (blue line) in Figure 35.1(a), we gradually build up the components of planned aggregate expenditure (red line). Assuming for simplicity that planned investment, government purchases, and exports are all constant and do not depend on income, we move easily from the blue line to the red line by adding the fixed amounts of I, G, and EX to consumption at every level of income. In this example, we take $I + G + EX$ to equal 80.

$C + I + G + EX$, however, includes spending on imports, which are not part of domestic production. To get spending on domestically produced goods, we must subtract the amount that is imported at each level of income. In Figure 35.1(b), we assume $m = .25$, which is the assumption that 25 percent of total income is spent on goods and services produced in foreign countries. Imports under this assumption are a constant fraction of total income; therefore, at higher levels of income, a larger amount is spent on foreign goods and services. For example, at $Y = 200$, $IM = .25\ Y$, or 50. Similarly, at $Y = 400$, $IM = .25\ Y$, or 100. Figure 35.1(b) shows the planned *domestic* aggregate expenditure curve.

Equilibrium is reached when planned domestic aggregate expenditure equals domestic aggregate output (income). This is true at only one level of aggregate output, $Y^* = 200$, in Figure 35.1(b). If Y were below Y^*, planned expenditure would exceed output, inventories would be lower than planned, and output would rise. At levels above Y^*, output would exceed planned expenditure, inventories would be larger than planned, and output would fall.

The Open-Economy Multiplier All of this has implications for the size of the multiplier. Recall the multiplier, introduced in Chapter 23, and consider a sustained rise in government purchases (G). Initially, the increase in G will cause planned aggregate expenditure to be greater

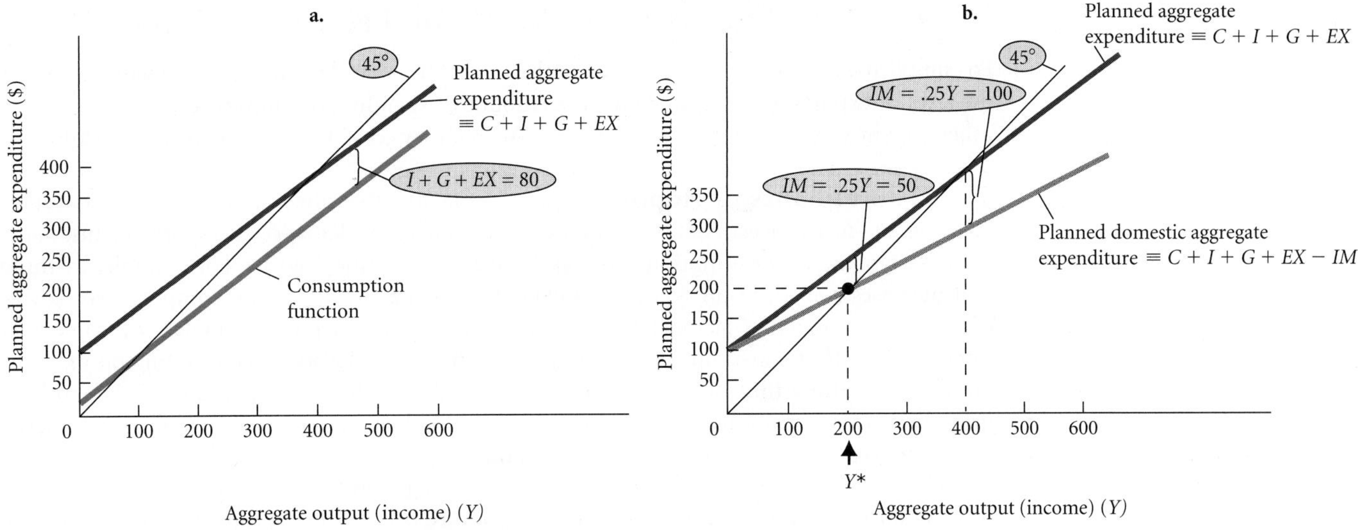

▲ **FIGURE 35.1 Determining Equilibrium Output in an Open Economy**
In **a.**, planned investment spending (*I*), government spending (*G*), and total exports (*EX*) are added to consumption (*C*) to arrive at planned aggregate expenditure. However, *C* + *I* + *G* + *EX* includes spending on imports. In **b.**, the amount imported at every level of income is subtracted from planned aggregate expenditure. Equilibrium output occurs at *Y** = 200, the point at which planned domestic aggregate expenditure crosses the 45-degree line.

than aggregate output. Domestic firms will find their inventories to be lower than planned and thus will increase their output, but added output means more income. More workers are hired, and profits are higher. Some of the added income is saved, and some is spent. The added consumption spending leads to a second round of inventories being lower than planned and raising output. Equilibrium output rises by a multiple of the initial increase in government purchases. This is the multiplier.

In Chapters 23 and 24, we showed that the simple multiplier equals $1/(1 - MPC)$, or $(1/MPS)$. That is, a sustained increase in government purchases equal to ΔG will lead to an increase in aggregate output (income) of $\Delta G\ [1/(1 - MPC)]$. If the *MPC* were .75 and government purchases rose by \$10 billion, equilibrium income would rise by 4 × \$10 billion, or \$40 billion. The multiplier is $[1/(1 - .75)] = [1/.25] = 4.0$.

In an open economy, some of the increase in income brought about by the increase in *G* is spent on imports instead of domestically produced goods and services. The part of income spent on imports does not increase domestic income (*Y*) because imports are produced by foreigners. To compute the multiplier, we need to know how much of the increased income is used to increase domestic consumption. (We are assuming all imports are consumption goods. In practice, some imports are investment goods and some are goods purchased by the government.) In other words, we need to know the marginal propensity to consume *domestic* goods. Domestic consumption is $C - IM$. So the marginal propensity to consume domestic goods is the marginal propensity to consume all goods (the *MPC*) minus the marginal propensity to import (the *MPM*). The marginal propensity to consume domestic goods is $(MPC - MPM)$. Consequently,

$$\text{open-economy multipler} = \frac{1}{1 - (MPC - MPM)}$$

If the *MPC* is .75 and the *MPM* is .25, then the multiplier is 1/.5, or 2.0. This multiplier is smaller than the multiplier in which imports are not taken into account, which is 1/.25, or 4.0. The effect of a sustained increase in government spending (or investment) on income—that is, the multiplier—is smaller in an open economy than in a closed economy. The reason: When government spending (or investment) increases and income and consumption rise, some of the extra consumption spending that results is on foreign products and not on domestically produced goods and services.

Imports and Exports and the Trade Feedback Effect

For simplicity, we have so far assumed that the level of imports depends only on income and that the level of exports is fixed. In reality, the amount of spending on imports depends on factors other than income and exports are not fixed. We will now consider the more realistic picture.

The Determinants of Imports The same factors that affect households' consumption behavior and firms' investment behavior are likely to affect the demand for imports because some imported goods are consumption goods and some are investment goods. For example, anything that increases consumption spending is likely to increase the demand for imports. We saw in Chapters 23 and 26 that factors such as the after-tax real wage, after-tax nonlabor income, and interest rates affect consumption spending; thus, they should also affect spending on imports. Similarly, anything that increases investment spending is likely to increase the demand for imports. A decrease in interest rates, for example, should encourage spending on both domestically produced goods and foreign-produced goods.

There is one additional consideration in determining spending on imports: the *relative prices* of domestically produced and foreign-produced goods. If the prices of foreign goods fall relative to the prices of domestic goods, people will consume more foreign goods relative to domestic goods. When Japanese cars are inexpensive relative to U.S. cars, consumption of Japanese cars should be high and vice versa.

The Determinants of Exports We now relax our assumption that exports are fixed. The demand for U.S. exports by other countries is identical to their demand for imports from the United States. Germany imports goods, some of which are U.S.-produced. France, Spain, and so on do the same. Total expenditure on imports in Germany is a function of the factors we just discussed except that the variables are German variables instead of U.S. variables. This is true for all other countries as well. The demand for U.S. exports depends on economic activity in the rest of the world—rest-of-the-world real wages, wealth, nonlabor income, interest rates, and so forth—as well as on the prices of U.S. goods relative to the price of rest-of-the-world goods. When foreign output increases, U.S. exports tend to increase. U.S. exports also tend to increase when U.S. prices fall relative to those in the rest of the world.

trade feedback effect The tendency for an increase in the economic activity of one country to lead to a worldwide increase in economic activity, which then feeds back to that country.

The Trade Feedback Effect We can now combine what we know about the demand for imports and the demand for exports to discuss the **trade feedback effect**. Suppose the United States finds its exports increasing, perhaps because the world suddenly decides it prefers U.S. computers to other computers. Rising exports will lead to an increase in U.S. output (income), which leads to an increase in U.S. imports. Here is where the trade feedback begins. Because U.S. imports are somebody else's exports, the extra import demand from the United States raises the exports of the rest of the world. When other countries' exports to the United States go up, their output and incomes also rise, in turn leading to an increase in the demand for imports from the rest of the world. Some of the extra imports demanded by the rest of the world come from the United States, so U.S. exports increase. The increase in U.S. exports stimulates U.S. economic activity even more, triggering a further increase in the U.S. demand for imports and so on. An increase in U.S. imports increases other countries' exports, which stimulates those countries' economies and increases their imports, which increases U.S. exports, which stimulates the U.S. economy and increases its imports, and so on. This is the trade feedback effect. In other words, an increase in U.S. economic activity leads to a worldwide increase in economic activity, which then "feeds back" to the United States.

Import and Export Prices and the Price Feedback Effect

We have talked about the price of imports, but we have not yet discussed the factors that influence import prices. The consideration of import prices is complicated because more than one currency is involved. When we talk about "the price of imports," do we mean the price in dollars, in yen, in U.K. pounds, in Mexican pesos, and so on? Because the exports of one country are the imports of another, the same question holds for the price of exports. When Mexico exports auto parts to the United States, Mexican manufacturers are interested in the price of auto parts in terms of pesos because pesos are what they use for transactions in Mexico. U.S. consumers are interested in the price of auto parts in dollars because dollars are what they use for transactions in the United States. The link between the two prices is the dollar/peso exchange rate.

Suppose Mexico is experiencing inflation and the price of radiators in pesos rises from 1,000 pesos to 1,200 pesos per radiator. If the dollar/peso exchange rate remains unchanged at, say, $0.10 per peso, Mexico's export price for radiators in terms of dollars will also rise, from $100 to $120 per radiator. Because Mexico's exports to the United States are, by definition, U.S. imports from Mexico, an increase in the dollar prices of Mexican exports to the United States means an increase in the prices of U.S. imports from Mexico. Therefore, when Mexico's export prices rise with no change in the dollar/peso exchange rate, U.S. import prices rise. Export prices of other countries affect U.S. import prices.

A country's export prices tend to move fairly closely with the general price level in that country. If Mexico is experiencing a general increase in prices, this change likely will be reflected in price increases of all domestically produced goods, both exportable and nonexportable. The general rate of inflation abroad is likely to affect U.S. import prices. If the inflation rate abroad is high, U.S. import prices are likely to rise.

The Price Feedback Effect We have just seen that when a country experiences an increase in domestic prices, the prices of its exports will increase. It is also true that when the prices of a country's *imports* increase, the prices of domestic goods may increase in response. There are at least two ways this effect can occur.

First, an increase in the prices of imported inputs will shift a country's aggregate supply curve to the left. In Chapter 28, we discussed the macroeconomy's response to a cost shock. Recall that a leftward shift in the aggregate supply curve due to a cost increase causes aggregate output to fall and prices to rise (stagflation).

Second, if import prices rise relative to domestic prices, households will tend to substitute domestically produced goods and services for imports. This is equivalent to a rightward shift of the aggregate demand curve. If the domestic economy is operating on the upward-sloping part of the aggregate supply curve, the overall domestic price level will rise in response to an increase in aggregate demand. Perfectly competitive firms will see market-determined prices rise, and imperfectly competitive firms will experience an increase in the demand for their products. Studies have shown, for example, that the price of automobiles produced in the United States moves closely with the price of imported cars.

Still, this is not the end of the story. Suppose a country—say, Mexico—experiences an increase in its domestic price level. This will increase the price of its exports to Canada (and to all other countries). The increase in the price of Canadian imports from Mexico will lead to an increase in domestic prices in Canada. Canada also exports to Mexico. The increase in Canadian prices causes an increase in the price of Canadian exports to Mexico, which then further increases the Mexican price level.

This is called the **price feedback effect**, in the sense that inflation is "exportable." An increase in the price level in one country can drive up prices in other countries, which in turn further increases the price level in the first country. Through export and import prices, a domestic price increase can "feed back" on itself.

price feedback effect The process by which a domestic price increase in one country can "feed back" on itself through export and import prices. An increase in the price level in one country can drive up prices in other countries. This in turn further increases the price level in the first country.

It is important to realize that the discussion so far has been based on the assumption of fixed exchange rates. Life is more complicated under flexible exchange rates, to which we now turn.

The Open Economy with Flexible Exchange Rates

To a large extent, the fixed exchange rates set by the Bretton Woods agreements served as international monetary arrangements until 1971. Then in 1971, the United States and most other countries decided to abandon the fixed exchange rate system in favor of **floating**, or **market-determined, exchange rates**. Although governments still intervene to ensure that exchange rate movements are "orderly," exchange rates today are largely determined by the unregulated forces of supply and demand.

floating, *or* market-determined, exchange rates Exchange rates that are determined by the unregulated forces of supply and demand.

Understanding how an economy interacts with the rest of the world when exchange rates are not fixed is not as simple as when we assume fixed exchange rates. Exchange rates determine the price of imported goods relative to domestic goods and can have significant effects on the level of imports and exports. Consider a 20 percent drop in the value of the dollar against the British pound. Dollars buy fewer pounds, and pounds buy more dollars. Both British residents, who now get more dollars for pounds, and U.S. residents, who get fewer pounds for dollars, find that U.S. goods and services are more attractive. Exchange rate movements have important impacts on imports, exports, and the movement of capital between countries.

The Market for Foreign Exchange

What determines exchange rates under a floating rate system? To explore this question, we assume that there are just two countries, the United States and Great Britain. It is easier to understand a world with only two countries, and most of the points we will make can be generalized to a world with many trading partners.

The Supply of and Demand for Pounds Governments, private citizens, banks, and corporations exchange pounds for dollars and dollars for pounds every day. In our two-country case, those who *demand* pounds are holders of dollars seeking to exchange them for pounds. Those who *supply* pounds are holders of pounds seeking to exchange them for dollars. It is important not to confuse the supply of dollars (or pounds) on the foreign exchange market with the U.S. (or British) money supply. The latter is the sum of all the money currently in circulation. The supply of dollars on the foreign exchange market is the number of dollars that holders seek to exchange for pounds in a given time period. The demand for and supply of dollars on foreign exchange markets determine *exchange* rates; the demand for money balances, and the total domestic money supply determine the *interest* rate.

The common reason for exchanging dollars for pounds is to buy something produced in Great Britain. U.S. importers who purchase Jaguar automobiles or Scotch whiskey must pay with pounds. U.S. citizens traveling in Great Britain who want to ride the train, stay in a hotel, or eat at a restaurant must acquire pounds for dollars to do so. If a U.S. corporation builds a plant in Great Britain, it must pay for that plant in pounds.

At the same time, some people may want to buy British stocks or bonds. Implicitly, when U.S. citizens buy a bond issued by the British government or by a British corporation, they are making a loan, but the transaction requires a currency exchange. The British bond seller must ultimately be paid in pounds.

On the supply side of the market, the situation is reversed. Here we find people—usually British citizens—holding pounds they want to use to buy dollars. Again, the common reason is to buy things produced in the United States. If a British importer decides to import golf carts made in Georgia, the producer must be paid in dollars. British tourists visiting New York may ride in cabs, eat in restaurants, and tour Ellis Island. Doing those things requires dollars. When a British firm builds an office complex in Los Angeles, it must pay the contractor in dollars.

In addition to buyers and sellers who exchange money to engage in transactions, some people and institutions hold currency balances for speculative reasons. If you think that the U.S. dollar is going to decline in value relative to the pound, you may want to hold some of your wealth in the form of pounds. Table 35.2 summarizes some of the major categories of private foreign exchange demanders and suppliers in the two-country case of the United States and Great Britain.

Figure 35.2 shows the demand curve for pounds in the foreign exchange market. When the price of pounds (the exchange rate) is lower, it takes fewer dollars to buy British goods and services, to build a plant in Liverpool, to travel to London, and so on. Lower net prices (in dollars) should increase the demand for British-made products and encourage investment and travel in Great Britain. If prices (in pounds) in Britain do not change, an increase in the quantity of British goods and services demanded by foreigners will increase the quantity of pounds demanded. The demand-for-pounds curve in the foreign exchange market has a negative slope.

Figure 35.3 shows a supply curve for pounds in the foreign exchange market. At a higher exchange rate, each pound buys more dollars, making the price of U.S.-produced goods and services lower to the British. The British are more apt to buy U.S.-made goods when the price of

TABLE 35.2 Some Buyers and Sellers in International Exchange Markets: United States and Great Britain

The Demand for Pounds (Supply of Dollars)

1. Firms, households, or governments that import British goods into the United States or want to buy British-made goods and services
2. U.S. citizens traveling in Great Britain
3. Holders of dollars who want to buy British stocks, bonds, or other financial instruments
4. U.S. companies that want to invest in Great Britain
5. Speculators who anticipate a decline in the value of the dollar relative to the pound

The Supply of Pounds (Demand for Dollars)

1. Firms, households, or governments that import U.S. goods into Great Britain or want to buy U.S.-made goods and services
2. British citizens traveling in the United States
3. Holders of pounds who want to buy stocks, bonds, or other financial instruments in the United States
4. British companies that want to invest in the United States
5. Speculators who anticipate a rise in the value of the dollar relative to the pound

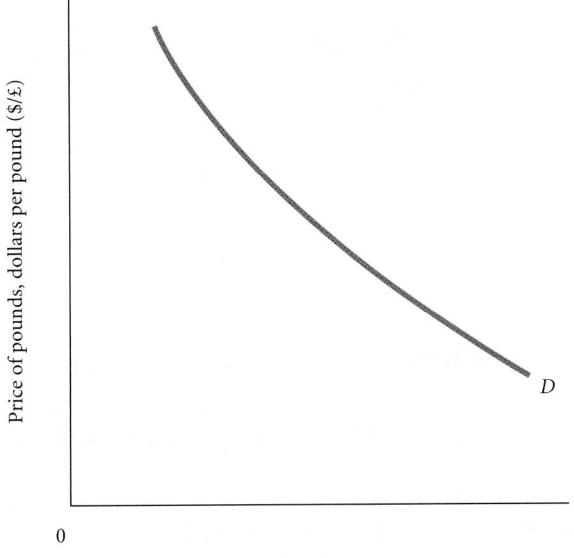

◀ FIGURE 35.2 The Demand for Pounds in the Foreign Exchange Market

When the price of pounds falls, British-made goods and services appear less expensive to U.S. buyers. If British prices are constant, U.S. buyers will buy more British goods and services and the quantity of pounds demanded will rise.

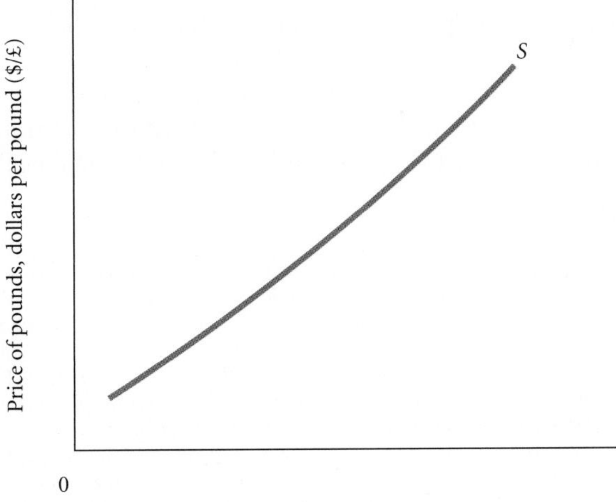

◀ FIGURE 35.3 The Supply of Pounds in the Foreign Exchange Market

When the price of pounds rises, the British can obtain more dollars for each pound. This means that U.S.-made goods and services appear less expensive to British buyers. Thus, the quantity of pounds supplied is likely to rise with the exchange rate.

pounds is high (the value of the dollar is low). An increase in British demand for U.S. goods and services is likely to increase the quantity of pounds supplied. The curve representing the supply of pounds in the foreign exchange market has a positive slope.

appreciation of a currency The rise in value of one currency relative to another.

depreciation of a currency The fall in value of one currency relative to another.

The Equilibrium Exchange Rate When exchange rates are allowed to float, they are determined the same way other prices are determined: The equilibrium exchange rate occurs at the point at which the quantity demanded of a foreign currency equals the quantity of that currency supplied. This is illustrated in Figure 35.4. An excess demand for pounds (quantity demanded in excess of quantity supplied) will cause the price of pounds to rise—the pound will **appreciate** relative to the dollar. An excess supply of pounds will cause the price of pounds to fall—the pound will **depreciate** relative to the dollar.[3]

▶ FIGURE 35.4
The Equilibrium Exchange Rate
When exchange rates are allowed to float, they are determined by the forces of supply and demand. An excess demand for pounds will cause the pound to appreciate against the dollar. An excess supply of pounds will lead to a depreciating pound.

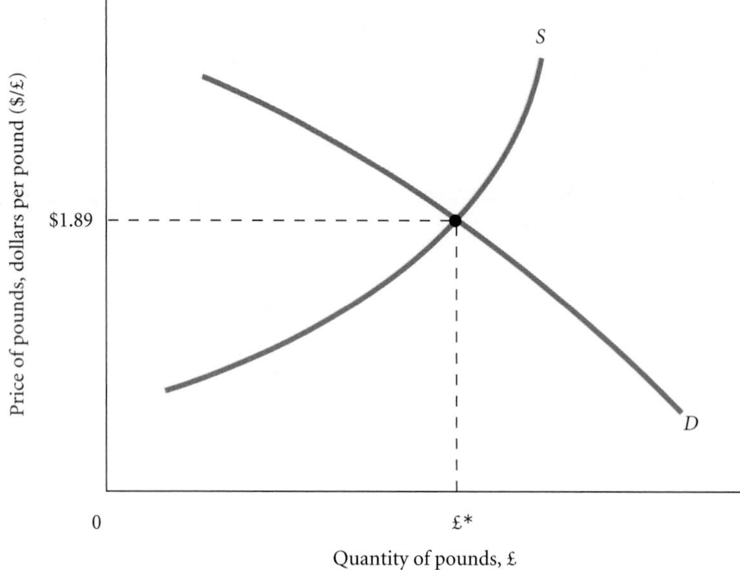

Factors that Affect Exchange Rates

We now know enough to discuss the factors likely to influence exchange rates. Anything that changes the behavior of the people in Table 35.2 can cause demand and supply curves to shift and the exchange rate to adjust accordingly.

Purchasing Power Parity: The Law of One Price If the costs of transporting goods between two countries are small, we would expect the price of the same good in both countries to be roughly the same. The price of basketballs should be roughly the same in Canada and the United States, for example.

It is not hard to see why. If the price of basketballs is cheaper in Canada, it will pay for someone to buy balls in Canada at a low price and sell them in the United States at a higher price. This decreases the supply and pushes up the price in Canada and increases the supply and pushes down the price in the United States. This process should continue as long as the price differential, and therefore the profit opportunity, persists. For a good with trivial transportation costs, we would expect this **law of one price** to hold. The price of a good should be the same regardless of where we buy it.

law of one price If the costs of transportation are small, the price of the same good in different countries should be roughly the same.

---

[3] Although Figure 35.3 shows the supply-of-pounds curve in the foreign exchange market with a positive slope, under certain circumstances the curve may bend back. Suppose the price of a pound rises from $1.50 to $2.00. Consider a British importer who buys 10 Chevrolets each month at $15,000 each, including transportation costs. When a pound exchanges for $1.50, he will supply 100,000 pounds per month to the foreign exchange market—100,000 pounds brings $150,000, enough to buy 10 cars. Now suppose the cheaper dollar causes him to buy 12 cars. Twelve cars will cost a total of $180,000; but at $2 = 1 pound, he will spend only 90,000 pounds per month. The supply of pounds on the market falls when the price of pounds rises. The reason for this seeming paradox is simple. The number of pounds a British importer needs to buy U.S. goods depends on both the quantity of goods he buys and the price of those goods in pounds. If demand for imports is inelastic so that the percentage decrease in price resulting from the depreciated currency is greater than the percentage increase in the quantity of imports demanded, importers will spend fewer pounds and the quantity of pounds supplied in the foreign exchange market will fall. The supply of pounds will slope upward as long as the demand for U.S. imports is elastic.

If the law of one price held for all goods and if each country consumed the same market basket of goods, the exchange rate between the two currencies would be determined simply by the relative price levels in the two countries. If the price of a basketball were $10 in the United States and $12 in Canada, the U.S.–Canada exchange rate would have to be $1 U.S. per $1.20 Canadian. If the rate were instead one-to-one, it would pay people to buy the balls in the United States and sell them in Canada. This would increase the demand for U.S. dollars in Canada, thereby driving up their price in terms of Canadian dollars to $1 U.S. per $1.2 Canadian, at which point no one could make a profit shipping basketballs across international lines and the process would cease.[4]

The theory that exchange rates will adjust so that the price of similar goods in different countries is the same is known as the **purchasing-power-parity theory**. According to this theory, if it takes 10 times as many Mexican pesos to buy a pound of salt in Mexico as it takes U.S. dollars to buy a pound of salt in the United States, the equilibrium exchange rate should be 10 pesos per dollar.

purchasing-power-parity theory A theory of international exchange holding that exchange rates are set so that the price of similar goods in different countries is the same.

In practice, transportation costs for many goods are quite large and the law of one price does not hold for these goods. (Haircuts are often cited as a good example. The transportation costs for a U.S. resident to get a British haircut are indeed large unless that person is an airline pilot.) Also, many products that are potential substitutes for each other are not precisely identical. For instance, a Rolls Royce and a Honda are both cars, but there is no reason to expect the exchange rate between the British pound and the yen to be set so that the prices of the two are equalized. In addition, countries consume different market baskets of goods, so we would not expect the aggregate price levels to follow the law of one price. Nevertheless, a high rate of inflation in one country relative to another puts pressure on the exchange rate between the two countries, and there is a general tendency for the currencies of relatively high-inflation countries to depreciate.

Figure 35.5 shows the adjustment likely to occur following an increase in the U.S. price level relative to the price level in Great Britain. This change in relative prices will affect citizens of both countries. Higher prices in the United States make imports relatively less expensive. U.S. citizens are likely to increase their spending on imports from Britain, shifting the demand for pounds to the right, from D_0 to D_1. At the same time, the British see U.S. goods getting more expensive and reduce their demand for exports from the United States. Consequently, the supply of pounds shifts to the left, from S_0 to S_1. The result is an increase in the price of pounds. Before the change in relative prices, 1 pound sold for $1.89; after the change, 1 pound costs $2.25. The pound appreciates, and the dollar depreciates.

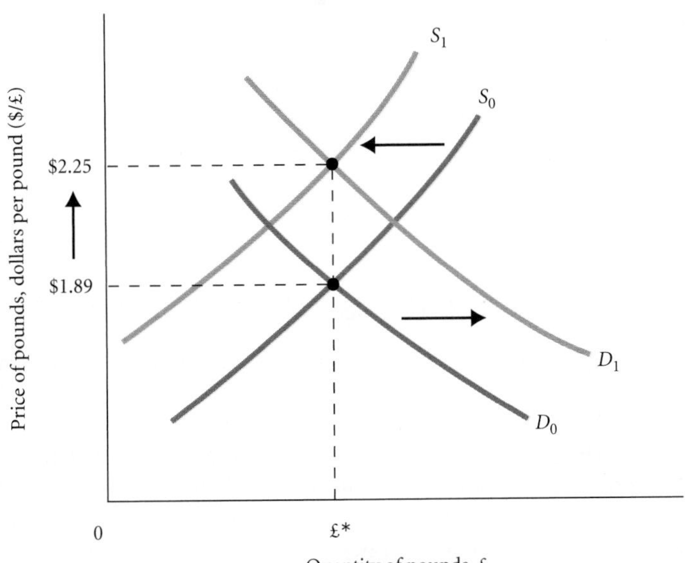

FIGURE 35.5 Exchange Rates Respond to Changes in Relative Prices

The higher price level in the United States makes imports relatively less expensive. U.S. citizens are likely to increase their spending on imports from Britain, shifting the demand for pounds to the right, from D_0 to D_1. At the same time, the British see U.S. goods getting more expensive and reduce their demand for exports from the United States. The supply of pounds shifts to the left, from S_0 to S_1. The result is an increase in the price of pounds. The pound appreciates, and the dollar is worth less.

[4] Of course, if the rate were $1 U.S. to $2 Canadian, it would pay people to buy basketballs in Canada (at $12 Canadian, which is $6 U.S.) and sell them in the United States. This would weaken demand for the U.S. dollar, and its price would fall from $2 Canadian until it reached $1.20 Canadian.

Relative Interest Rates Another factor that influences a country's exchange rate is the level of its interest rate relative to other countries' interest rates. If the interest rate is 6 percent in the United States and 8 percent in Great Britain, people with money to lend have an incentive to buy British securities instead of U.S. securities. Although it is sometimes difficult for individuals in one country to buy securities in another country, it is easy for international banks and investment companies to do so. If the interest rate is lower in the United States than in Britain, there will be a movement of funds out of U.S. securities into British securities as banks and firms move their funds to the higher-yielding securities.

How does a U.S. bank buy British securities? It takes its dollars, buys British pounds, and uses the pounds to buy the British securities. The bank's purchase of pounds drives up the price of pounds in the foreign exchange market. The increased demand for pounds increases the price of the pound (and decreases the price of the dollar). A high interest rate in Britain relative to the interest rate in the United States tends to depreciate the dollar.

Figure 35.6 shows the effect of rising interest rates in the United States on the dollar–pound exchange rate. Higher interest rates in the United States attract British investors. To buy U.S. securities, the British need dollars. The supply of pounds (the demand for dollars) shifts to the right, from S_0 to S_1. The same relative interest rates affect the portfolio choices of U.S. banks, firms, and households. With higher interest rates at home, there is less incentive for U.S. residents to buy British securities. The demand for pounds drops at the same time the supply increases and the demand curve shifts to the left, from D_0 to D_1. The net result is a depreciating pound and an appreciating dollar. The price of pounds falls from $1.89 to $1.25.

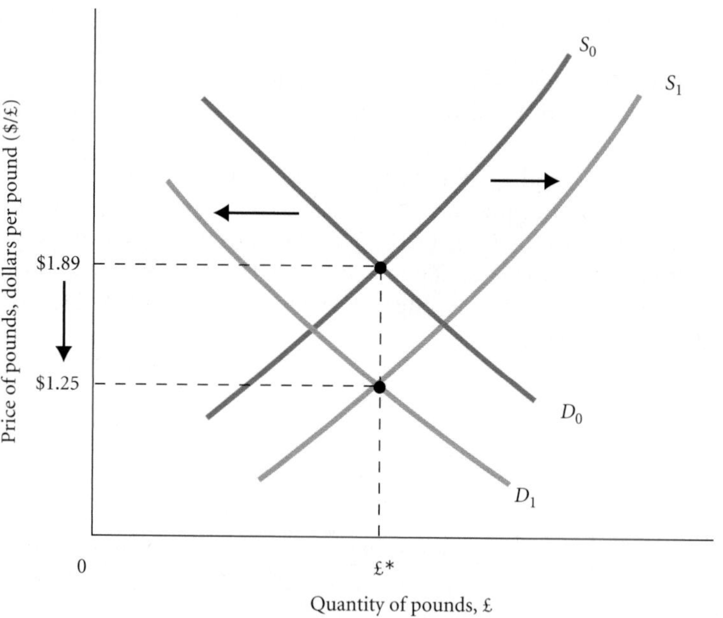

▶ FIGURE 35.6

Exchange Rates Respond to Changes in Relative Interest Rates

If U.S. interest rates rise relative to British interest rates, British citizens holding pounds may be attracted into the U.S. securities market. To buy bonds in the United States, British buyers must exchange pounds for dollars. The supply of pounds shifts to the right, from S_0 to S_1. However, U.S. citizens are less likely to be interested in British securities because interest rates are higher at home. The demand for pounds shifts to the left, from D_0 to D_1. The result is a depreciated pound and a stronger dollar.

The Effects of Exchange Rates on the Economy

We are now ready to discuss some of the implications of floating exchange rates. Recall, when exchange rates are fixed, households spend some of their incomes on imports and the multiplier is smaller than it would be otherwise. Imports are a "leakage" from the circular flow, much like taxes and saving. Exports, in contrast, are an "injection" into the circular flow; they represent spending on U.S.-produced goods and services from abroad and can stimulate output.

The world is far more complicated when exchange rates are allowed to float. First, the level of imports and exports depends on exchange rates as well as on income and other factors. When events cause exchange rates to adjust, the levels of imports and exports will change. Changes in exports and imports can, in turn, affect the level of real GDP and the price level. Further, exchange rates themselves also adjust to changes in the economy. Suppose the government decides to stimulate the economy with an expansionary monetary policy. This will affect interest rates, which may affect exchange rates.

Exchange Rate Effects on Imports, Exports, and Real GDP As we already know, when a country's currency depreciates (falls in value), its import prices rise and its export prices (in foreign currencies) fall. When the U.S. dollar is cheap, U.S. products are more competitive with products produced in the rest of the world and foreign-made goods look expensive to U.S. citizens.

A depreciation of a country's currency can serve as a stimulus to the economy. Suppose the U.S. dollar falls in value, as it did sharply between 1985 and 1988. If foreign buyers increase their spending on U.S. goods, and domestic buyers substitute U.S.-made goods for imports, aggregate expenditure on domestic output will rise, inventories will fall, and real GDP (Y) will increase. A depreciation of a country's currency is likely to increase its GDP.[5]

Exchange Rates and the Balance of Trade: The J Curve Because a depreciating currency tends to increase exports and decrease imports, you might think that it also will reduce a country's trade deficit. In fact, the effect of a depreciation on the balance of trade is ambiguous.

Many economists believe that when a currency starts to depreciate, the balance of trade is likely to worsen for the first few quarters (perhaps three to six). After that, the balance of trade may improve. This effect is graphed in Figure 35.7. The curve in this figure resembles the letter *J*, and the movement in the balance of trade that it describes is sometimes called the **J-curve effect.** The point of the *J* shape is that the balance of trade gets worse before it gets better following a currency depreciation.

J-curve effect Following a currency depreciation, a country's balance of trade may get worse before it gets better. The graph showing this effect is shaped like the letter *J*, hence the name J-curve effect.

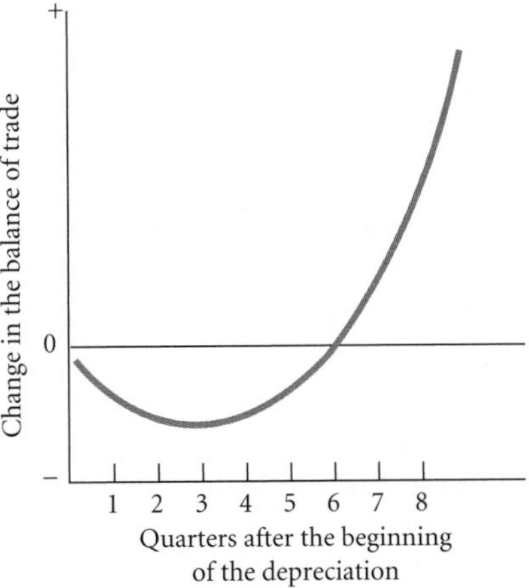

FIGURE 35.7 The Effect of a Depreciation on the Balance of Trade (the J Curve)

Initially, a depreciation of a country's currency may worsen its balance of trade. The negative effect on the price of imports may initially dominate the positive effects of an increase in exports and a decrease in imports.

How does the J curve come about? Recall that the balance of trade is equal to export revenue minus import costs, including exports and imports of services:

$$\begin{aligned}\text{balance of trade} = {} & \text{dollar price of exports} \times \text{quantity of exports} \\ & - \text{dollar price of imports} \times \text{quantity of imports}\end{aligned}$$

A currency depreciation affects the items on the right side of this equation as follows: First, the quantity of exports increases and the quantity of imports decreases; both have a *positive* effect on the balance of trade (lowering the trade deficit or raising the trade surplus). Second, the dollar price of exports is not likely to change very much, at least not initially. The dollar price of exports changes when the U.S. price level changes, but the initial effect of a depreciation on the domestic price level is not likely to be large. Third, the dollar price of imports increases. Imports into the United States are more expensive because $1 U.S. buys fewer yen, euros, and so on, than before. An increase in the dollar price of imports has a *negative* effect on the balance of trade.

[5] For this reason, some countries are tempted at times to intervene in foreign exchange markets, depreciate their currencies, and stimulate their economies. If all countries attempted to lower the value of their currencies simultaneously, there would be no gain in income for any of them. Although the exchange rate system at the time was different, such a situation actually occurred during the early years of the Great Depression. Many countries practiced so-called *beggar-thy-neighbor* policies of competitive devaluations in a desperate attempt to maintain export sales and employment.

An example to clarify this last point follows: The dollar price of a Japanese car that costs 1,200,000 yen rises from $10,000 to $12,000 when the exchange rate moves from 120 yen per dollar to 100 yen per dollar. After the currency depreciation, the United States ends up spending more (in dollars) for the Japanese car than it did before. Of course, the United States will end up buying fewer Japanese cars than it did before. Does the number of cars drop enough so that the quantity effect is bigger than the price effect or vice versa? Does the value of imports increase or decrease?

The net effect of a depreciation on the balance of trade could go either way. The depreciation stimulates exports and cuts back imports, but it also increases the dollar price of imports. It seems that the negative effect dominates initially. The impact of a depreciation on the price of imports is generally felt quickly, while it takes time for export and import quantities to respond to price changes. In the short run, the value of imports increases more than the value of exports, so the balance of trade worsens. The initial effect is likely to be negative; but after exports and imports have had time to respond, the net effect turns positive. The more elastic the demand for exports and imports, the larger the eventual improvement in the balance of trade.

Exchange Rates and Prices The depreciation of a country's currency tends to increase its price level. There are two reasons for this effect. First, when a country's currency is less expensive, its products are more competitive on world markets, so exports rise. In addition, domestic buyers tend to substitute domestic products for the now-more-expensive imports. This means that planned aggregate expenditure on domestically produced goods and services rises and that the aggregate demand curve shifts to the right. The result is a higher price level, a higher output, or both. (You may want to draw an *AS/AD* diagram to verify this outcome.) If the economy is close to capacity, the result is likely to be higher prices. Second, a depreciation makes imported inputs more expensive. If costs increase, the aggregate supply curve shifts to the left. If aggregate demand remains unchanged, the result is an increase in the price level.

Monetary Policy with Flexible Exchange Rates Let us now put everything in this chapter together and consider what happens when monetary policy is used first to stimulate the economy and then to contract the economy.

Suppose the economy is below full employment and the Federal Reserve (Fed) decides to expand the money supply. The volume of reserves in the system is expanded, perhaps through open market purchases of U.S. government securities by the Fed. The result is a decrease in the interest rate. The lower interest rate stimulates planned investment spending and consumption spending.

This added spending causes inventories to be lower than planned and aggregate output (income) (*Y*) to rise, but there are two additional effects: (1) The lower interest rate has an impact in the foreign exchange market. A lower interest rate means a lower demand for U.S. securities by foreigners, so the demand for dollars drops. (2) U.S. investment managers will be more likely to buy foreign securities (which are now paying relatively higher interest rates), so the supply of dollars rises. Both events push down the value of the dollar.

A cheaper dollar is a good thing if the goal of the monetary expansion is to stimulate the domestic economy because a cheaper dollar means more U.S. exports and fewer imports. If consumers substitute U.S.-made goods for imports, both the added exports and the decrease in imports mean more spending on domestic products, so the multiplier actually increases.

Now suppose inflation is a problem and the Fed wants to slow it down with tight money. Here again, floating exchange rates help. Tight monetary policy works through a higher interest rate. A higher interest rate lowers investment and consumption spending, reducing aggregate expenditure, reducing output, and lowering the price level. The higher interest rate also attracts foreign buyers into U.S. financial markets, driving up the value of the dollar, which reduces the price of imports. The reduction in the price of imports causes a shift of the aggregate supply curve to the right, which helps fight inflation.

Fiscal Policy with Flexible Exchange Rates The openness of the economy and flexible exchange rates do not always work to the advantage of policy makers. Consider a policy of cutting taxes to stimulate the economy. Suppose Congress enacts a major tax cut designed to raise output. Spending by households rises, but not all this added spending is on domestic products—some leaks out of the U.S. economy, reducing the multiplier.

ECONOMICS IN PRACTICE

Pearson Prentice Hall is committed to providing the most current content possible. Starting December 15, 2008, all printed Student Editions of **Case/Fair/Oster's** ninth edition will include this newly updated *Economics in Practice* content. You can view this updated content at www.pearsonhighered.com/case on November 20, 2008.

As income rises, so does the demand for money (M^d)—not the demand for dollars in the foreign exchange market, but the amount of money people want to hold for transactions. Unless the Fed is fully accommodating, the interest rate will rise. A higher interest rate tends to attract foreign demand for U.S. securities. This rise in demand tends to drive the price of the dollar up, which further blunts the effectiveness of the tax cut. If the value of the dollar rises, U.S. exports are less competitive in world markets and the quantity of exports will decline. Similarly, a strong dollar makes imported goods look cheaper and U.S. citizens spend more on foreign goods and less on U.S. goods, an effect that again reduces the multiplier.

There is another caveat to the multiplier story of Chapters 23 and 24. Without a fully accommodating Fed, three factors work to reduce the multiplier: (1) A higher interest rate from the increase in money demand may crowd out private investment and consumption; (2) some of the increase in income from the expansion will be spent on imports; and (3) a higher interest rate may cause the dollar to appreciate, discouraging exports and further encouraging imports.

Monetary Policy with Fixed Exchange Rates Although most major countries in the world today have a flexible exchange rate (counting for this purpose the euro zone countries as one country), it is interesting to ask what role monetary policy can play when a country has a fixed exchange rate. The answer is, no role. In order for a country to keep its exchange rate fixed to, say, the U.S. dollar, its interest rate cannot change relative to the U.S. interest rate. If the monetary authority of the country lowered the interest rate because it wanted to stimulate the economy, the country's currency would depreciate (assuming the U.S. interest rate did not change). People would want to sell the country's currency and buy dollars and invest in U.S. securities because the country's interest rate would have fallen relative to the U.S. interest rate. In other words, the monetary authority cannot change its interest rate relative to the U.S. interest rate without having its exchange rate change. The monetary authority is at the mercy of the United States, and it has no independent way of changing its interest rate if it wants to keep its exchange rate fixed to the dollar.

This restriction means that when the various European countries moved in 1999 to a common currency, the euro, each of the countries gave up its monetary policy. There is now only one monetary policy for all the euro zone countries, and it is decided by the European Central Bank (ECB).

The one case in which a country can change its interest rate and keep its exchange rate fixed is if it imposes capital controls. Imposing capital controls means that the country limits or prevents people from buying or selling its currency in the foreign exchange markets. A citizen of the country may be prevented, for example, from using the country's currency to buy dollars. The problem with capital controls is that they are hard to enforce, especially for large countries and for long periods of time.

An Interdependent World Economy

The increasing interdependence of countries in the world economy has made the problems facing policy makers more difficult. We used to be able to think of the United States as a relatively self-sufficient region. Forty years ago economic events outside U.S. borders had relatively little effect on its economy. This situation is no longer true. The events of the past four decades have taught us that the performance of the U.S. economy is heavily dependent on events outside U.S. borders.

This chapter and the previous chapter have provided only the bare bones of open-economy macroeconomics. If you continue your study of economics, more will be added to the basic story we have presented. The next chapter concludes with a discussion of the problems of developing countries.

SUMMARY

1. The main difference between an international transaction and a domestic transaction concerns currency exchange: When people in different countries buy from and sell to each other, an exchange of currencies must also take place.

2. The *exchange rate* is the price of one country's currency in terms of another country's currency.

THE BALANCE OF PAYMENTS *p. 690*

3. *Foreign exchange* is all currencies other than the domestic currency of a given country. The record of a nation's transactions in goods, services, and assets with the rest of the world is its *balance of payments*. The balance of payments is also the record of a country's sources (supply) and uses (demand) of foreign exchange.

EQUILIBRIUM OUTPUT (INCOME) IN AN OPEN ECONOMY *p. 693*

4. In an open economy, some income is spent on foreign produced goods instead of domestically produced goods. To measure planned domestic aggregate expenditure in an open economy, we add total exports but subtract total imports: $C + I + G + EX - IM$. The open economy is in equilibrium when domestic aggregate output (income) (Y) equals planned domestic aggregate expenditure.

5. In an open economy, the multiplier equals $1/[1 - (MPC - MPM)]$, where MPC is the marginal propensity to consume and MPM is the marginal propensity to import. The *marginal propensity to import* is the change in imports caused by a $1 change in income.

6. In addition to income, other factors that affect the level of imports are the after-tax real wage rate, after-tax nonlabor income, interest rates, and relative prices of domestically-produced and foreign-produced goods. The demand for exports is determined by economic activity in the rest of the world and by relative prices.

7. An increase in U.S. economic activity leads to a worldwide increase in economic activity, which then "feeds back" to the United States. An increase in U.S. imports increases other countries' exports, which stimulates economies and increases their imports, which increases U.S. exports, which stimulates the U.S. economy and increases its imports, and so on. This is the *trade feedback effect*.

8. Export prices of other countries affect U.S. import prices. The general rate of inflation abroad is likely to affect U.S. import prices. If the inflation rate abroad is high, U.S. import prices are likely to rise.

9. Because one country's exports are another country's imports, an increase in export prices increases other countries' import prices. An increase in other countries' import prices leads to an increase in their domestic prices—and their export prices. In short, export prices affect import prices and vice versa. This *price feedback effect* shows that inflation is "exportable"; an increase in the price level in one country can drive up prices in other countries, making inflation in the first country worse.

THE OPEN ECONOMY WITH FLEXIBLE EXCHANGE RATES *p. 697*

10. The equilibrium exchange rate occurs when the quantity demanded of a foreign currency in the foreign exchange market equals the quantity of that currency supplied in the foreign exchange market.

11. *Depreciation of a currency occurs* when a nation's currency falls in value relative to another country's currency. *Appreciation of a currency* occurs when a nation's currency rises in value relative to another country's currency.

12. According to the *law of one price*, if the costs of transportation are small, the price of the same good in different countries should be roughly the same. The theory that exchange rates are set so that the price of similar goods in different countries is the same is known as the *purchasing-power-parity* theory. In practice, transportation costs are significant for many goods, and the law of one price does not hold for these goods.

13. A high rate of inflation in one country relative to another country puts pressure on the exchange rate between the two countries. There is a general tendency for the currencies of relatively high-inflation countries to depreciate.

14. A depreciation of the dollar tends to increase U.S. GDP by making U.S. exports cheaper (hence, more competitive abroad) and by making U.S. imports more expensive (encouraging consumers to switch to domestically produced goods and services).

15. The effect of a depreciation of a nation's currency on its balance of trade is unclear. In the short run, a currency depreciation may increase the balance-of-trade deficit because it raises the price of imports. Although this price increase causes a decrease in the quantity of imports demanded, the impact of a depreciation on the price of imports is generally felt quickly, but it takes time for export and import quantities to respond to price changes. The initial effect is likely to be negative; but after exports and imports have had time to respond, the net effect turns positive. The tendency for the balance-of-trade deficit to widen and then to decrease as the result of a currency depreciation is known as the *J-curve effect*.

16. The depreciation of a country's currency tends to raise its price level for two reasons. First, a currency depreciation increases planned aggregate expenditure, an effect that shifts the aggregate demand curve to the right. If the economy is close to capacity, the result is likely to be higher prices. Second, a depreciation makes imported inputs more expensive. If costs increase, the aggregate supply curve shifts to the left. If aggregate demand remains unchanged, the result is an increase in the price level.

17. When exchange rates are flexible, a U.S. expansionary monetary policy decreases the interest rate and stimulates planned investment and consumption spending. The lower interest rate leads to a lower demand for U.S. securities by foreigners and a higher demand for foreign securities by U.S. investment-fund managers. As a result, the dollar depreciates. A U.S. contractionary monetary policy appreciates the dollar.

18. Flexible exchange rates do not always work to the advantage of policy makers. An expansionary fiscal policy can appreciate the dollar and work to reduce the multiplier.

REVIEW TERMS AND CONCEPTS

appreciation of a currency, *p. 700*
balance of payments, *p. 690*
balance of trade, *p. 691*
balance on capital account, *p. 692*
balance on current account, *p. 691*
depreciation of a currency, *p. 700*
exchange rate, *p. 689*
floating, *or* market-determined, exchange rates, *p. 697*
foreign exchange, *p. 690*
J-curve effect, *p. 703*
law of one price, *p. 700*
marginal propensity to import (*MPM*), *p. 694*
net exports of goods and services ($EX - IM$), *p. 694*
price feedback effect, *p. 697*
purchasing-power-parity theory, *p. 701*
trade deficit, *p. 691*
trade feedback effect, *p. 696*
Planned aggregate expenditure in an open economy:
$AE \equiv C + I + G + EX - IM$
Open-economy multiplier =

$$\frac{1}{1 - (MPC - MPM)}$$

PROBLEMS

Visit **www.myeconlab.com** to complete the problems marked in orange online. You will receive instant feedback on your answers, tutorial help, and access to additional practice problems.

1. In June 2008, the euro was trading at \$1.50. Check the Web or any daily newspaper to see what the "price" of a euro is today. What explanations can you give for the change? Make sure you check what has happened to interest rates and economic growth.

2. Suppose the following graph shows what prevailed on the foreign exchange market in 2008 with floating exchange rates.
   a. Name three phenomena that might shift the demand curve to the right.
   b. Which, if any, of these three phenomena might cause a simultaneous shift of the supply curve to the left?
   c. What effects might each of the three phenomena have on the balance of trade if the exchange rate floats?

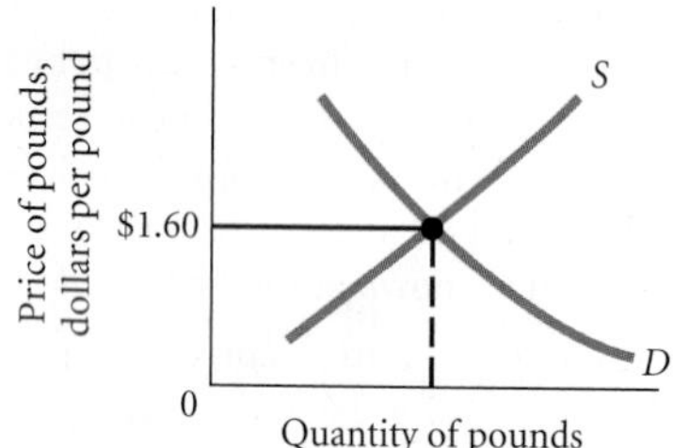

3 Obtain a recent issue of *The Economist*. Turn to the section entitled "Financial Indicators." Look at the table entitled "Trade, exchange rates and budgets." Which country had the largest trade deficit over the last year and during the last month? Which country had the largest trade surplus over the last year and during the last month? How does the current account deficit/surplus compare to the overall trade balance? How can you explain the difference?

4. The exchange rate between the U.S. dollar and the Japanese yen is floating freely—both governments do not intervene in the market for each currency. Suppose a large trade deficit with Japan prompts the United States to impose quotas on certain Japanese products imported into the United States and, as a result, the quantity of these imports falls.
   a. The decrease in spending on Japanese products increases spending on U.S.-made goods. Why? What effect will this have on U.S. output and employment and on Japanese output and employment?
   b. What happens to U.S. imports from Japan when U.S. output (or income) rises? If the quotas initially reduce imports from Japan by \$25 billion, why is the final reduction in imports likely to be less than \$25 billion?
   c. Suppose the quotas do succeed in reducing imports from Japan by \$15 billion. What will happen to the demand for yen? Why?
   d. What will happen to the dollar–yen exchange rate? Why? (*Hint:* There is an excess supply of yen, or an excess demand for dollars.) What effects will the change in the value of each currency have on employment and output in the United States? What about the balance of trade? (Ignore complications such as the J curve.)
   e. Considering the macroeconomic effects of a quota on Japanese imports, could a quota reduce employment and output in the United States? have no effect at all? Explain.

5. What effect will each of the following events have on the current account balance and the exchange rate if the exchange rate is fixed? if the exchange rate is floating?
   a. The U.S. government cuts taxes and income rises.
   b. The U.S. inflation rate increases, and prices in the United States rise faster than those in countries with which the United States trades.
   c. The United States adopts an expansionary monetary policy. Interest rates fall (and are now lower than those in other countries) and income rises.
   d. The textile companies' "Buy American" campaign is successful, and U.S. consumers switch from purchasing imported products to buying products made in the United States.

6. You are given the following model that describes the economy of Hypothetica.
   (1) Consumption function: $C = 100 + .8Y_d$
   (2) Planned investment: $I = 38$
   (3) Government spending: $G = 75$
   (4) Exports: $EX = 25$
   (5) Imports: $IM = .05\, Y_d$
   (6) Disposable income: $Y_d \equiv Y - T$
   (7) Taxes: $T = 40$
   (8) Planned aggregate expenditure:
   $$AE \equiv C + I + G + EX - IM$$
   (9) Definition of equilibrium income: $Y = AE$
   a. What is equilibrium income in Hypothetica? What is the government deficit? What is the current account balance?
   b. If government spending is increased to $G = 80$, what happens to equilibrium income? Explain using the government spending multiplier. What happens to imports?
   c. Now suppose the amount of imports is limited to $IM = 40$ by a quota on imports. If government spending is again increased from 75 to 80, what happens to equilibrium income? Explain why the same increase in G has a bigger effect on income in the second case. What is it about the presence of imports that changes the value of the multiplier?
   d. If exports are fixed at $EX = 25$, what must income be to ensure a current account balance of zero? (*Hint:* Imports depend on income, so what must income be for imports to be equal to exports?) By how much must we cut government spending to balance the current account? (*Hint:* Use your answer to the first part of this question to determine how much of a decrease in income is needed. Then use the multiplier to calculate the decrease in G needed to reduce income by that amount.)

APPENDIX

WORLD MONETARY SYSTEMS SINCE 1900

Since the beginning of the twentieth century, the world has operated under a number of different monetary systems. This Appendix provides a brief history of each and a description of how they worked.

THE GOLD STANDARD

The gold standard was the major system of exchange rate determination before 1914. All currencies were priced in terms of gold—an ounce of gold was worth so much in each currency. When all currencies exchanged at fixed ratios to gold, exchange rates could be determined easily. For instance, 1 ounce of gold was worth $20 U.S.; that same ounce of gold exchanged for £4 (British pounds). Because $20 and £4 were each worth 1 ounce of gold, the exchange rate between dollars and pounds was $20/£4, or $5 to £1.

For the gold standard to be effective, it had to be backed up by the country's willingness to buy and sell gold at the determined price. As long as countries maintain their currencies at a fixed value in terms of gold *and* as long as each country is willing to buy and sell gold, exchange rates are fixed. If at the given exchange rate the number of U.S. citizens who want to buy things produced in Great Britain is equal to the number of British citizens who want to buy things produced in the United States, the currencies of the two countries will simply be exchanged. What if U.S. citizens suddenly decide they want to drink imported Scotch instead of domestic bourbon? If the British do not have an increased desire for U.S. goods, they will still accept U.S. dollars because those dollars can be redeemed in gold. This gold can then be immediately turned into pounds.

As long as a country's overall balance of payments remained in balance, no gold would enter or leave the country and the economy would be in equilibrium. If U.S. citizens bought more from the British than the British bought from the United States, however, the U.S. balance of payments would be in deficit and the U.S. stock of gold would begin to fall. Conversely, Britain would start to accumulate gold because it would be exporting more than it spent on imports.

Under the gold standard, gold was a big determinant of the money supply.[1] An inflow of gold into a country caused that country's money supply to expand, and an outflow of gold caused that country's money supply to contract. If gold were flowing from the United States to Great Britain, the British money supply would expand and the U.S. money supply would contract.

Now recall from earlier chapters the impacts of a change in the money supply. An expanded money supply in Britain will lower British interest rates and stimulate aggregate demand. As a result, aggregate output (income) and the price level in Britain will increase. Higher British prices will discourage U.S. citizens from buying British goods. At the same time, British citizens will have more income and will face relatively lower import prices, causing them to import more from the States.

On the other side of the Atlantic, U.S. citizens will face a contracting domestic money supply. This will cause higher interest rates, declining aggregate demand, lower prices, and falling output (income). The effect will be lower demand in the United States for British goods. Thus, changes in relative prices and incomes that resulted from the inflow and outflow of gold would automatically bring trade back into balance.

PROBLEMS WITH THE GOLD STANDARD

Two major problems were associated with the gold standard. First, the gold standard implied that a country had little control over its money supply. The reason, as we have just seen, is that the money stock increased when the overall balance of payments was in surplus (gold inflow) and decreased when the overall balance was in deficit (gold outflow). A country that was experiencing a balance-of-payments deficit could correct the problem only by the painful process of allowing its money supply to contract. This contraction brought on a slump in economic activity, a slump that would eventually restore balance-of-payments equilibrium, but only after reductions in income and employment. Countries could (and often did) act to protect their gold reserves, and this precautionary step prevented the adjustment mechanism from correcting the deficit.

Making the money supply depend on the amount of gold available had another disadvantage. When major new gold fields were discovered (as in California in 1849 and South Africa in 1886), the world's supply of gold (and therefore of money) increased. The price level rose and income increased. When no new gold was discovered, the supply of money remained unchanged and prices and income tended to fall.

When President Reagan took office in 1981, he established a commission to consider returning the nation to the gold standard. The final commission report recommended against such a move. An important part of the reasoning behind this recommendation was that the gold standard puts enormous economic power in the hands of gold-producing nations.

FIXED EXCHANGE RATES AND THE BRETTON WOODS SYSTEM

As World War II drew to a close, a group of economists from the United States and Europe met to formulate a new set of rules for exchange rate determination that they hoped would avoid the difficulties of the gold standard. The rules they designed became known as the *Bretton Woods system*, after the town in New Hampshire where the delegates met. The Bretton Woods system was based on two (not necessarily compatible) premises. First, countries were to maintain fixed exchange rates

[1] In the days when currencies were tied to gold, changes in the amount of gold influenced the supply of money in two ways. A change in the quantity of gold coins in circulation had a direct effect on the supply of money; indirectly, gold served as a backing for paper currency. A decrease in the central bank's gold holdings meant a decline in the amount of paper money that could be supported.

with one another. Instead of pegging their currencies directly to gold, however, currencies were fixed in terms of the U.S. dollar, which was fixed in value at $35 per ounce of gold. The British pound, for instance, was fixed at roughly $2.40, so that an ounce of gold was worth approximately £14.6. As we shall see, the pure system of fixed exchange rates would work in a manner very similar to the pre-1914 gold standard.

The second aspect of the Bretton Woods system added a new wrinkle to the operation of the international economy. Countries experiencing a "fundamental disequilibrium" in their balance of payments were allowed to change their exchange rates. (The term *fundamental disequilibrium* was necessarily vague, but it came to be interpreted as a large and persistent current account deficit.) Exchange rates were not really fixed under the Bretton Woods system; they were, as someone remarked, only "fixed until further notice."

The point of allowing countries with serious current account problems to alter the value of their currency was to avoid the harsh recessions that the operation of the gold standard would have produced under these circumstances. However, the experience of the European economies in the years between World War I and World War II suggested that it might not be a good idea to give countries complete freedom to change their exchange rates whenever they wanted.

During the Great Depression, many countries undertook so-called competitive devaluations to protect domestic output and employment. That is, countries would try to encourage exports—a source of output growth and employment—by attempting to set as low an exchange rate as possible, thereby making their exports competitive with foreign-produced goods. Unfortunately, such policies had a built-in flaw. A devaluation of the pound against the French franc might help encourage British exports to France; but if those additional British exports cut into French output and employment, France would likely respond by devaluing the franc against the pound, a move that, of course, would undo the effects of the pound's initial devaluation.

To solve this exchange rate rivalry, the Bretton Woods agreement created the International Monetary Fund (IMF). Its job was to assist countries experiencing temporary current account problems.[2] It was also supposed to certify that a "fundamental disequilibrium" existed before a country was allowed to change its exchange rate. The IMF was like an international economic traffic cop whose job was to ensure that all countries were playing the game according to the agreed-to rules and to provide emergency assistance where needed.

"Pure" Fixed Exchange Rates

Under a pure fixed exchange rate system, governments set a particular *fixed* rate at which their currencies will exchange for one another and then commit themselves to maintaining that rate. A true fixed exchange rate system is like the gold standard in that exchange rates are supposed to stay the same forever. Because currencies are no longer backed by gold, they have no fixed, or standard, value relative to one another. There is, therefore, no automatic mechanism to keep exchange rates aligned with each other, as with the gold standard.

The result is that under a pure fixed exchange rate system, governments must at times intervene in the foreign exchange market to keep currencies aligned at their established values. Economists define government intervention in the foreign exchange market as the buying or selling of foreign exchange for the purpose of manipulating the exchange rate. What kind of intervention is likely to occur under a fixed exchange rate system, and how does it work?

We can see how intervention works by looking at Figure 35A.1. Initially, the market for Australian dollars is in equilibrium. At the fixed exchange rate of 0.96, the supply of dollars is exactly equal to the demand for dollars. No government intervention is necessary to maintain the exchange rate at this level. Now suppose Australian wines are found to be contaminated with antifreeze and U.S. citizens switch to California wines. This substitution away from the Australian product shifts the U.S. demand curve for Australian dollars to the left: The United States demands fewer Australian dollars at every exchange rate (cost of an Australian dollar) because it is purchasing less from Australia than it did before.

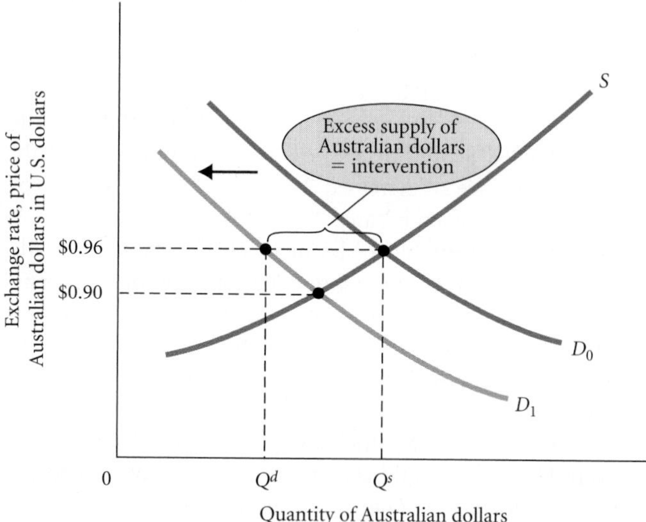

▲ **FIGURE 35A.1 Government Intervention in the Foreign Exchange Market**

If the price of Australian dollars were set in a completely unfettered market, one Australian dollar would cost 0.96 U.S. dollars when demand is D_0 and 0.90 when demand is D_1. If the government has committed to keeping the value at 0.96, it must buy up the excess supply of Australian dollars ($Q^s - Q^d$).

If the price of Australian dollars were set in a completely unfettered market, the shift in the demand curve would lead to a fall in the price of Australian dollars, just the way the price of wheat would fall if there was an excess supply of wheat. Remember, the Australian and U.S. governments have committed themselves to maintaining the rate at 0.96. To do so, either the U.S. government or the Australian government (or both)

[2] The idea was that the IMF would make short-term loans to a country with a current account deficit. The loans would enable the country to correct the current account problem gradually, without bringing on a deep recession, running out of foreign exchange reserves, or devaluing the currency.

must buy up the excess supply of Australian dollars to keep its price from falling. In essence, the fixed exchange rate policy commits governments to making up any difference between the supply of a currency and the demand so as to keep the price of the currency (exchange rate) at the desired level. The government promises to act as the supplier (or demander) of last resort, who will ensure that the amount of foreign exchange demanded by the private sector will equal the supply at the fixed price.

PROBLEMS WITH THE BRETTON WOODS SYSTEM

As it developed after the end of World War II, the system of more-or-less fixed exchange rates had some flaws that led to its abandonment in 1971.

First, there was a basic asymmetry built into the rules of international finance. Countries experiencing large and persistent current account deficits—what the Bretton Woods agreements termed "fundamental disequilibria"—were obliged to devalue their currencies and/or take measures to cut their deficits by contracting their economies. Both of these alternatives were unpleasant because devaluation meant rising prices and contraction meant rising unemployment. However, a country with a current account deficit had no choice because it was losing stock of foreign exchange reserves. When its stock of foreign currencies became exhausted, it had to change its exchange rate because further intervention (selling off some of its foreign exchange reserves) became impossible.

Countries experiencing current account surpluses were in a different position because they were gaining foreign exchange reserves. Although these countries were supposed to stimulate their economies and/or revalue their currencies to restore balance to their current account, they were not obliged to do so. They could easily maintain their fixed exchange rate by buying up any excess supply of foreign exchange with their own currency, of which they had plentiful supply.

In practice, this meant that some countries—especially Germany and Japan—tended to run large and chronic current account surpluses and were under no compulsion to take steps to correct the problem. The U.S. economy, stimulated by expenditures on the Vietnam War, experienced a large and prolonged current account deficit (capital outflow) in the 1960s, which was the counterpart of these surpluses. The United States was, however, in a unique position under the Bretton Woods system. The value of gold was fixed in terms of the U.S. dollar at $35 per ounce of gold. Other countries fixed their exchange rates in terms of U.S. dollars (and therefore only indirectly in terms of gold). Consequently, the United States could never accomplish anything by devaluing its currency in terms of gold. If the dollar was devalued from $35 to $40 per ounce of gold, the yen, pegged at 200 yen per dollar, would move in parallel with the dollar (from 7,000 yen per ounce of gold to 8,000 yen per ounce), with the dollar–yen exchange rate unaffected. To correct its current account deficits vis-à-vis Japan and Germany, it would be necessary for those two countries to adjust their currencies' exchange rates with the dollar. These countries were reluctant to do so for a variety of reasons. As a result, the U.S. current account was chronically in deficit throughout the late 1960s.

A second flaw in the Bretton Woods system was that it permitted devaluations only when a country had a "chronic" current account deficit and was in danger of running out of foreign exchange reserves. This meant that devaluations could often be predicted quite far in advance, and they usually had to be rather large if they were to correct any serious current account problem. The situation made it tempting for speculators to "attack" the currencies of countries with current account deficits.

Problems such as these eventually led the United States to abandon the Bretton Woods rules in 1971. The U.S. government refused to continue pegging the value of the dollar in terms of gold. Thus, the prices of all currencies were free to find their own levels.

The alternative to fixed exchange rates is a system that allows exchange rates to move freely or flexibly in response to market forces. Two types of flexible exchange rate systems are usually distinguished. In a *freely floating system*, governments do not intervene at all in the foreign exchange market.[3] They do not buy or sell currencies with the aim of manipulating the rates. In a *managed floating system*, governments intervene if markets are becoming "disorderly"—fluctuating more than a government believes is desirable. Governments may also intervene if they think a currency is increasing or decreasing too much in value even though the day-to-day fluctuations may be small.

Since the demise of the Bretton Woods system in 1971, the world's exchange rate system can be described as "managed floating." One of the important features of this system has been times of large fluctuations in exchange rates. For example, the yen–dollar rate went from 347 in 1971 to 210 in 1978, to 125 in 1988, and to 80 in 1995. Those are very large changes, changes that have important effects on the international economy, some of which we have covered in this text.

[3] However, governments may from time to time buy or sell foreign exchange for their own needs (instead of influencing the exchange rate). For example, the U.S. government might need British pounds to buy land for a U.S. embassy building in London. For our purposes, we ignore this behavior because it is not "intervention" in the strict sense of the word.

SUMMARY

1. The gold standard was the major system of exchange rate determination before 1914. All currencies were priced in terms of gold. Difficulties with the gold standard led to the Bretton Woods agreement following World War II. Under this system, countries maintained fixed exchange rates with one another and fixed the value of their currencies in terms of the U.S. dollar. Countries experiencing a "fundamental disequilibrium" in their current accounts were permitted to change their exchange rates.
2. The Bretton Woods system was abandoned in 1971. Since then, the world's exchange rate system has been one of managed floating rates. Under this system, governments intervene if foreign exchange markets are fluctuating more than the government thinks desirable.

PROBLEMS

1. The currency of Atlantis is the wimp. In 2008, Atlantis developed a balance-of-payments deficit with the United States as a result of an unanticipated decrease in exports; U.S. citizens cut back on the purchase of Atlantean goods. Assume Atlantis is operating under a system of fixed exchange rates.
   a. How does the drop in exports affect the market for wimps? Identify the deficit graphically.
   b. How must the government of Atlantis act (in the short run) to maintain the value of the wimp?
   c. If originally Atlantis had been operating at full employment (potential GDP), what impact would those events have had on its economy? Explain your answer.
   d. The chief economist of Atlantis suggests an expansionary monetary policy to restore full employment; the secretary of commerce suggests a tax cut (expansionary fiscal policy). Given the fixed exchange rate system, describe the effects of these two policy options on Atlantis's current account.
   e. How would your answers to **a**, **b**, and **c** change if the two countries operated under a floating rate system?

Economic Growth in Developing and Transitional Economies

36

CHAPTER OUTLINE

Our primary focus in this text has been on countries with modern industrialized economies that rely heavily on markets to allocate resources, but what about the economic problems facing countries such as Somalia and Haiti? Can we apply the same economic principles that we have been studying to these less developed nations?

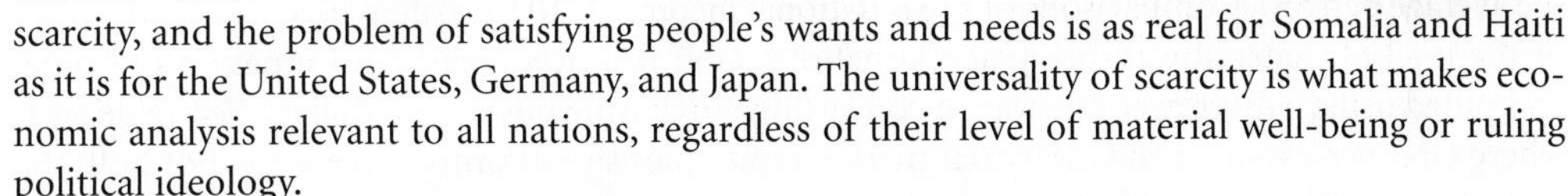

Yes. All economic analysis deals with the problem of making choices under conditions of scarcity, and the problem of satisfying people's wants and needs is as real for Somalia and Haiti as it is for the United States, Germany, and Japan. The universality of scarcity is what makes economic analysis relevant to all nations, regardless of their level of material well-being or ruling political ideology.

The basic tools of supply and demand, theories about consumers and firms, and theories about the structure of markets all contribute to an understanding of the economic problems confronting the world's developing nations. However, these nations often face economic problems quite different from those that richer, more developed countries face. In developing nations, an economist may have to worry about chronic food shortages, explosive population growth, and hyperinflations that reach triple, and even quadruple, digits. The United States and other industrialized economies rarely encounter such difficulties.

The instruments of economic management also vary from nation to nation. The United States has well-developed financial market institutions and a strong central bank (the Federal Reserve) through which the government can control the macroeconomy to some extent. Even limited intervention is impossible in some of the developing countries. In the United States, tax laws can be changed to stimulate saving, to encourage particular kinds of investments, or to redistribute income. In most developing countries, there are neither meaningful personal income taxes nor effective tax policies.

Even though economic problems and the policy instruments available to tackle them vary across nations, economic thinking about these problems can be transferred easily from one setting to another. In this chapter, we discuss several of the economic problems specific to developing nations in an attempt to capture some of the insights that economic analysis can offer.

Life in the Developing Nations: Population and Poverty

In 2008, the population of the world reached over 6.6 billion people. Most of the world's more than 200 nations belong to the developing world, in which about three-fourths of the world's population lives.

In the early 1960s, the nations of the world could be assigned rather easily to categories: The *developed countries* included most of Europe, North America, Japan, Australia, and New Zealand; the *developing countries* included the rest of the world. The developing nations were often referred to as the *Third World* to distinguish them from the Western industrialized nations (the *First World*) and the former Socialist bloc of Eastern European nations (the *Second World*).

In 2008, the world did not divide easily into three neat parts. Rapid economic progress brought some developing nations closer to developed economies. Countries such as Argentina and Chile, still considered to be "developing," are often referred to as middle-income or newly industrialized countries. Other countries, such as those in much of sub-Saharan Africa and some in South Asia, have stagnated and fallen so far behind the economic advances of the rest of the world that the term *Fourth World* has been used to describe them. China and India, while usually labeled developing countries, are fast becoming economic superpowers. It is not clear yet where some of the republics of the former Soviet Union and other formerly Communist countries of Eastern Europe will end up. Production fell sharply in many of them in the early transition stage to a market economy. For example, between 1990 and 1997, real gross domestic product (GDP) fell about 40 percent in the transition economies and over 50 percent in Russia and Central Asia. Post-2000, however, the Russian economy began growing more rapidly, in part fueled by rising energy prices, and by 2008, parts of the Russian economy were thriving.

Although the countries of the developing world exhibit considerable diversity in both their standards of living and their particular experiences of growth, marked differences continue to separate them from the developed nations. The developed countries have a higher average level of material well-being (the amount of food, clothing, shelter, and other commodities consumed by the average person). Comparisons of gross national income (GNI) are often used as a crude index of the level of material well-being across nations. GNI is a new measure of a nation's income, computed using a more accurate way of converting purchasing power into dollars. See Table 36.1, where GNI per-capita in the industrial market economies significantly exceeds GNI of both the low- and middle-income developing economies.

Other characteristics of economic development include improvements in basic health and education. The degree of political and economic freedom enjoyed by individual citizens might also be part of what it means to be a developed nation. Some of these criteria are easy to quantify. Table 36.1 presents data for different types of economies according to some of the more easily measured indexes of development. As you can see, the industrial market economies enjoy higher standards of living according to whatever indicator of development is chosen.

TABLE 36.1 Indicators of Economic Development

Country Group	Population, 2006	Gross National Income per Capita, 2006 (dollars)	Literacy Rate (percent over 15 years of age)	Infant Mortality, 2006 (deaths before age 5 per 1,000 births)	Internet Users per 1,000 people, 2005
Low-income	2.4 billion	650	60.8	114	44
Lower middle-income	2.3 billion	1,778	88.9	39.8	86
Upper middle-income	810 million	5,913	93.1	29.9	194
High-income	1.0 billion	36, 487	98.7	6.9	523

Source: World Bank, www.worldbank.org.

Behind these statistics lies the reality of the very difficult life facing the people of the developing world. For most people, meager incomes provide only the basic necessities. Most meals are the same, consisting of the region's food staple—rice, wheat, or corn. Shelter is primitive. Many people share a small room, usually with an earthen floor and no sanitary facilities. The great majority of the population lives in rural areas where agricultural work is hard and extremely time-consuming. Productivity (output produced per worker) is low because household plots are small and only the crudest of farm implements are available. Low productivity means farm output per person is barely sufficient to feed a farmer's own family, with nothing left to sell to others. School-age children may receive some formal education, but illiteracy remains chronic for young and old. Infant mortality runs 20 times higher than in the United States. Although parasitic infections are common and debilitating, there is only one physician per 5,000 people. In addition, many developing nations are engaged in civil and external warfare.

Life in the developing nations is a continual struggle against the circumstances of poverty, and prospects for dramatic improvements in living standards for most people are dim. As with all generalizations, there are exceptions. Some nations are better off than others, and in any given nation an elite group always lives in considerable luxury. India is on the World Bank's list of low-income countries, yet Mumbai, a state capital, is one of the top 10 centers of commerce in the world, home to Bollywood, the world's largest film industry.

Poverty—not affluence—dominates the developing world. Recent studies suggest that 40 percent of the population of the developing nations has an annual income insufficient to provide for adequate nutrition. While the developed nations account for only about one-quarter of the world's population, they are estimated to consume three-quarters of the world's output. This leaves the developing countries with about three-fourths of the world's people but only one-fourth of the world's income. The simple result is that most of our planet's population is poor.

In the United States in 2005, the poorest one-fifth (bottom 20 percent) of the families received 3.4 percent of total income; the richest one-fifth received 50 percent. Inequality in the world distribution of income is much greater. When we look at the world population, the poorest one-fifth of the families earns about .5 percent and the richest one-fifth earns 79 percent of total world income.

Economic Development: Sources and Strategies

Economists have been trying to understand economic growth and development since Adam Smith and David Ricardo in the eighteenth and nineteenth centuries, but the study of development economics as it applies to the developing nations has a much shorter history. The geopolitical struggles that followed World War II brought increased attention to the developing nations and their economic problems. During this period, the new field of development economics asked simply: Why are some nations poor and others rich? If economists could understand the barriers to economic growth that prevent nations from developing and the prerequisites that would help them to develop, economists could prescribe strategies for achieving economic advancement.

The Sources of Economic Development

Although a general theory of economic development applicable to all nations has not emerged and probably never will, some basic factors that limit a poor nation's economic growth have been suggested. These include insufficient capital formation, a shortage of human resources and entrepreneurial ability, a lack of social overhead capital, and constraints imposed by dependency on the already developed nations.

Capital Formation One explanation for low levels of output in developing nations is insufficient quantities of necessary inputs. Developing nations have diverse resource endowments—Congo, for instance, is abundant in natural resources, while Bangladesh is resource-poor. Almost all developing nations have a scarcity of physical capital relative to other resources, especially labor. The small stock of physical capital (factories, machinery, farm equipment, and other productive capital) constrains labor's productivity and holds back national output.

Nevertheless, citing capital shortages as the cause of low productivity does not explain much. We need to know why capital is in such short supply in developing countries. There are many explanations. One, the **vicious-circle-of-poverty hypothesis**, suggests that a poor nation must consume most of its income just to maintain its already low standard of living. Consuming most of national income implies limited saving, and this implies low levels of investment. Without investment, the capital stock does not grow, the income remains low, and the vicious circle is complete. Poverty becomes self-perpetuating.

vicious-circle-of-poverty hypothesis Suggests that poverty is self-perpetuating because poor nations are unable to save and invest enough to accumulate the capital stock that would help them grow.

The difficulty with the vicious-circle argument is that if it were true, no nation would ever develop. For example, Japanese GDP per capita in 1900 was well below that of many of today's developing nations. The vicious-circle argument fails to recognize that every nation has some surplus above consumption needs that is available for investment. Often this surplus is most visible in the conspicuous consumption habits of the nation's richest families. Poverty alone cannot explain capital shortages, and poverty is not necessarily self-perpetuating.

In a developing economy, scarcity of capital may have more to do with a lack of incentives for citizens to save and invest productively than with any absolute scarcity of income available for capital accumulation. Many of the rich in developing countries invest their savings in Europe or in the United States instead of in their own country, which may have a riskier political climate. Savings transferred to the United States do not lead to physical capital growth in the developing countries. The term **capital flight** refers to the fact that both human capital and financial capital (domestic savings) leave developing countries in search of higher expected rates of return elsewhere or returns with less risk. In addition, government policies in the developing nations—including price ceilings, import controls, and even outright appropriation of private property—tend to discourage investment. There has been increased attention to the role that financial institutions, including accounting systems and property right rules, play in encouraging domestic capital formation.

capital flight The tendency for both human capital and financial capital to leave developing countries in search of higher expected rates of return elsewhere with less risk.

Whatever the causes of capital shortages, it is clear that the absence of productive capital prevents income from rising in any economy. The availability of capital is a necessary, but not a *sufficient*, condition for economic growth. The landscape of the developing countries is littered with idle factories and abandoned machinery. Other ingredients are required to achieve economic progress.

Human Resources and Entrepreneurial Ability Capital is not the only factor of production required to produce output. Labor is equally important. First of all, to be productive, the workforce must be healthy. Disease today is the leading threat to development in much of the world. The most devastating health problem in the world today is the HIV/AIDS pandemic. In 2005 alone, 3.1 million people died of AIDS and 4.9 million were newly infected with HIV. At the end of 2005, more than 40 million people were infected with the virus. In total, more than 25 million have died. AIDS is the leading cause of death in sub-Saharan Africa, where the disease threatens to reverse the developmental achievements of the last 50 years. Beyond AIDS, health and nutrition are essential to workforce development. Programs in nutrition and health can be seen as investments in human capital that lead to increased productivity and higher incomes.

But health is not the only issue. Look back at Table 36.1 You will notice that low-income countries lag behind high-income countries not only in infant health but also in literacy rates. To be productive, the workforce must be educated and trained. The more familiar forms of human capital investment, including formal education and on-the-job training, are essential. Basic literacy as well as specialized training in farm management, for example, can yield high returns to both the individual worker and the economy. Education has grown to become the largest category of government expenditure in many developing nations, in part because of the belief that human resources are the ultimate determinant of economic advance.

Nevertheless, in many developing countries, many children, especially girls, receive only a few years of formal education.

Just as financial capital seeks the highest and safest return, so does human capital. Thousands of students from developing countries, many of whom were supported by their governments, graduate every year from U.S. colleges and universities as engineers, doctors, scientists, economists, and other professionals. After graduation, these people face a difficult choice: to remain in the United States and earn a high salary or to return home and accept a job at a much lower salary. Many remain in the United States. This **brain drain** siphons off many of the most talented minds from developing countries. Recently, economists have begun studying *remittances*, compensation sent back from recent immigrants to their families in less developed countries. While measurement is difficult, estimates of these remittances are approximately $100 billion per year. Remittances fund housing and education for families left behind, but they also can provide investment capital for small businesses. In 2007, it appeared that remittances from illegal immigrants in the United States to Mexico, which had been growing by 20 percent per year, were beginning to fall with tightening of enforcement of immigration rules.

brain drain The tendency for talented people from developing countries to become educated in a developed country and remain there after graduation.

Innovative entrepreneurs who are willing to take risks are an essential human resource in any economy. In a developing nation, new techniques of production rarely need to be invented because they usually can be adapted from the technology already developed by the technologically advanced nations. However, entrepreneurs who are willing and able to organize and carry out economic activity appear to be in short supply. Family and political ties often seem to be more important than ability when it comes to securing positions of authority. Whatever the explanation, development cannot proceed without human resources capable of initiating and managing economic activity

Social Overhead Capital Anyone who has spent time in a developing nation knows how difficult it can be to send a letter, make a local phone call, or travel within the country. Add to this problems with water supplies, frequent electrical power outages—in the few areas where electricity is available—and often ineffective mosquito and pest control, and you soon realize how deficient even the simplest, most basic government-provided goods and services can be.

In any economy, developing or otherwise, the government has considerable opportunity and responsibility for involvement where conditions encourage natural monopoly (as in the utilities industries) and where public goods (such as roads and pest control) must be provided. In a developing economy, the government must put emphasis on creating a basic infrastructure—roads, power generation, and irrigation systems. There are often good reasons why such projects, referred to as **social overhead capital**, cannot successfully be undertaken by the private sector. First, many of these projects operate with economies of scale, which means they can be efficient only if they are very large. In that case, they may be too large for any private company or group of companies to carry out.

social overhead capital Basic infrastructure projects such as roads, power generation, and irrigation systems.

Second, many socially useful projects cannot be undertaken by the private sector because there is no way for private agents to capture enough of the returns to make such projects profitable. This so-called *free-rider problem* is common in the economics of the developed world. Consider national defense: All people in a country benefit from national defense, whether they have paid for it or not. Anyone who attempted to go into the private business of providing national defense would go broke. Why should I buy any national defense if your purchase of defense will also protect me? Why should you buy any if my purchase will also protect you? The governments of developing countries can do important and useful things to encourage development, but many of their efforts must be concentrated in areas that the private sector would never touch. If government action in these realms is not forthcoming, economic development may be curtailed by a lack of social overhead capital. Considerable economic work has been done recently on the role that inefficient government bureaucracies play in retarding economic development. Many less developed countries in sub-Saharan Africa, Asia, and Latin America have only a small fraction of GDP raised in tax revenues and invested by the government. Levels of corruption also matter and vary a great deal by country, as the *Economics in Practice* on p. 718 suggests.

ECONOMICS IN PRACTICE

Corruption

Many people have argued that one barrier to economic development in a number of countries is the level of corruption and inefficiency in the government. Measuring levels of corruption and inefficiency can be difficult. Some researchers have tried surveys and experiments. Ray Fisman[1] had a more unusual way to measure the way in which political connections interfere with the workings of the market in Indonesia.

From 1967 to 1998, Indonesia was ruled by President Suharto. While Suharto ruled, his children and longtime allies were affiliated with a number of Indonesian companies. Fisman had the clever idea of looking at what happened to the stock market prices of those firms connected to the Suharto clan relative to unaffiliated firms when Suharto unexpectedly fell ill. Fisman found a large and significant reduction in the value of those affiliated firms on rumors of illness. What does this tell us? A firm's stock price reflects investors' views of what earnings the firm can expect to have. In the case of firms connected to Suharto, the decline in their stock prices tells us that a large part of the reason investors think that those firms are doing well is because of the family connection rather than the firm's inherent efficiency. One reason corruption is bad for an economy is that it often leads to the wrong firms, the less efficient firms, producing the goods and services in the society.

The following chart shows the World Bank's rating of corruption levels in a number of countries around the world. The countries are ranked from those with the strongest controls on corruption—Germany and France—to those with the lowest controls—Pakistan and Nigeria. Indonesia, as you can see, is near the bottom of the list.

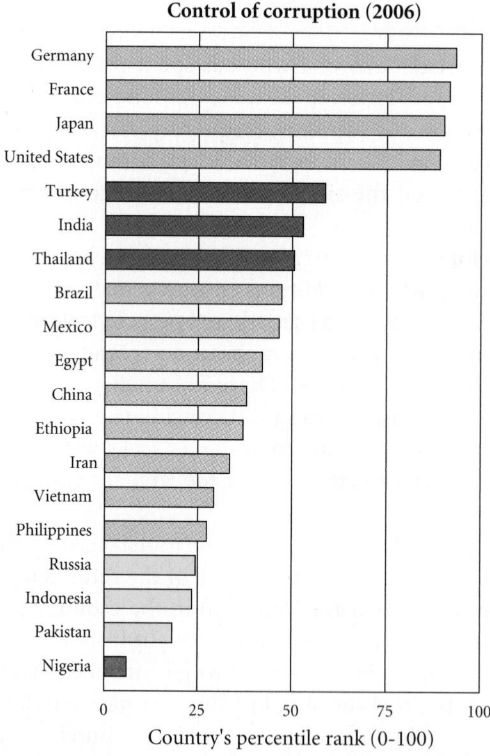

Source: D. Kaufmann, A. Kraay, and M. Mastruzzi, 2007: Governance Matters VI: Governance Indicators for 1996–2006.

Note: The governance indicators presented here aggregate the views on the quality of governance provided by a large number of enterprise, citizen, and expert survey respondents in industrial and developing countries. These data are gathered from a number of survey institutes, think tanks, nongovernmental organizations, and international organizations. The aggregate indicators do not reflect the official views of the World Bank, its executive directors, or the countries they represent.

[1] Raymond Fisman, "Estimating the Value of Political Connections," *The American Economic Review*, September 2001.

Strategies for Economic Development

Just as no single theory appears to explain lack of economic advancement, no one development strategy will likely succeed in all nations. Many alternative development strategies have been proposed over the past years. Although these strategies have been very different, they all recognize that a developing economy faces basic trade-offs. An insufficient amount of both human and physical resources dictates that choices must be made, including those between agriculture and industry, exports and import substitution, and central planning and free markets.

Agriculture or Industry? Most Third World countries began to gain political independence just after World War II. The tradition of promoting industrialization as the solution to the problems of the developing world dates from this time. The early 5-year development plans of India called for promoting manufacturing; the current government in Ethiopia (an extremely poor country) has similar intentions.

Industry has several apparent attractions over agriculture. First, if it is true that capital shortages constrain economic growth, the building of factories will be an obvious step toward increasing a nation's stock of capital. Second, and perhaps most important, one of the primary characteristics of more developed economies is their structural transition away from agriculture toward manufacturing and modern services. As Table 36.2 shows, agriculture's share in GDP declines substantially as per-capita incomes increase. The share of services increases correspondingly, especially in the early phases of economic development.

TABLE 36.2 The Structure of Production in Selected Developed and Developing Economies, 2003

Country	Per-Capita Gross National Income (GNI)	Percentage of Gross Domestic Product		
		Agriculture	Industry	Services
Tanzania	$ 375	45	17	37
Bangladesh	480	20	28	52
China	2,010	12	47	41
Colombia	2,740	12	34	54
Thailand	2,990	10	46	44
Brazil	4,730	5	31	64
Korea (Rep.)	17,690	2	23	75
Japan	38,410	2	30	68
United States	44,970	2	23	75

Source: World Bank, World Development Indicators, 2008; Sectoral numbers for U.S. and Japan are for 2003.

Many economies have pursued industry at the expense of agriculture. In many countries, however, industrialization has been unsuccessful or disappointing—that is, it has not brought the benefits that were expected. Experience suggests that simply trying to replicate the structure of developed economies does not in itself guarantee, or even promote, successful development.

Since the early 1970s, the agricultural sector has received considerably more attention. Agricultural development strategies have had numerous benefits. Although some agricultural projects (such as the building of major dams and irrigation networks) are very capital-intensive, many others (such as services to help teach better farming techniques and small-scale fertilizer programs) have low capital and import requirements. Programs such as these can affect large numbers of households, and because the benefits of these programs are directed at rural areas, they are most likely to help a country's poorest families.

Experience over the last three decades suggests that some balance between these approaches leads to the best outcome—that is, it is important and effective to pay attention to both industry and agriculture. The Chinese have referred to this dual approach to development as "walking on two legs."

Exports or Import Substitution? As developing nations expand their industrial activities, they must decide what type of trade strategy to pursue, usually one of two alternatives: import substitution or export promotion.

import substitution An industrial trade strategy that favors developing local industries that can manufacture goods to replace imports.

Import substitution is an industrial trade strategy to develop local industries that can manufacture goods to replace imports. For example, if fertilizer is imported, import substitution calls for a domestic fertilizer industry to produce replacements for fertilizer imports. This strategy gained prominence throughout South America in the 1950s. At that time, most developing nations exported agricultural and mineral products, goods that faced uncertain and often unstable international markets. Under these conditions, the call for import substitution policies was understandable. Special government actions, including tariff and quota protection and subsidized imports of machinery, were set up to encourage new domestic industries. Multinational corporations were also invited into many countries to begin domestic operations.

Most economists believe that import substitution strategies have failed almost everywhere they have been tried. With domestic industries sheltered from international competition by high tariffs (often as high as 200 percent), major economic inefficiencies were created. For example, Peru has a population of approximately 29 million, only a tiny fraction of whom can afford to buy an automobile. Yet at one time, the country had five or six different automobile manufacturers, each of which produced only a few thousand cars per year. Because there are substantial economies of scale in automobile production, the cost per car was much higher than it needed to be, and valuable resources that could have been devoted to another, more productive, activity were squandered producing cars.

Furthermore, policies designed to promote import substitution often encouraged capital-intensive production methods, which limited the creation of jobs and hurt export activities. A country such as Peru could not export automobiles because it could produce them only at a cost far greater than their price on the world market. Worse still, import substitution policies encouraged the use of expensive domestic products, such as tractors and fertilizer, instead of lower-cost imports. These policies taxed the sectors that might have successfully competed in world markets. To the extent that the Peruvian sugar industry had to rely on domestically produced, high-cost fertilizer, for example, its ability to compete in international markets was reduced because its production costs were artificially raised.

export promotion A trade policy designed to encourage exports.

As an alternative to import substitution, some nations have pursued strategies of export promotion. **Export promotion** is the policy of encouraging exports. As an industrial market economy, Japan was a striking example to the developing world of the economic success that exports can provide. Japan had an average annual per-capita real GDP growth rate of roughly 6 percent per year from 1960–1990. This achievement was, in part, based on industrial production oriented toward foreign consumers.

Several countries in the developing world have attempted to emulate Japan's success. Starting around 1970, Hong Kong, Singapore, Korea, and Taiwan (the "four little dragons" between the two "big dragons," China and Japan) began to pursue export promotion of manufactured goods. Today their growth rates have surpassed Japan's. Other nations, including Brazil, Colombia, and Turkey, have also had some success at pursuing an outward-looking trade policy.

Government support of export promotion has often taken the form of maintaining an exchange rate favorable enough to permit exports to compete with products manufactured in developed economies. For example, many people believe Japan kept the value of the yen artificially low during the 1970s. Because "cheap" yen means inexpensive Japanese goods, in the United States, sales of Japanese goods (especially automobiles) increased dramatically. Governments also have provided subsidies to export industries.

A big issue for countries growing or trying to grow by selling exports on world markets is free trade. In 2003, the United States and Europe were accused of protecting their own agricultural producers with large subsidies that allowed domestic farmers a big advantage selling on world markets. African nations in particular have pushed for reductions in tariffs imposed on their agricultural goods by Europe and the United States, arguing that these tariffs substantially reduce Africa's ability to compete in the world marketplace.

Central Planning or the Market? As part of its strategy for achieving economic development, a nation must decide how its economy will be directed. Its basic choices lie between a market-oriented economic system and a centrally planned one.

In the 1950s and into the 1960s, development strategies that called for national planning commanded wide support. The rapid economic growth of the Soviet Union, a centrally planned economy, provided an example of how fast a less developed agrarian nation could be transformed into a modern industrial power. (The often appalling costs of this strategy—severe discipline, gross violation of human rights, and environmental damage—were less widely known.) In addition, the underdevelopment of many commodity and asset markets in the developing world led many experts to believe that market forces could not direct an economy reliably and that major government intervention was therefore necessary. Even the United States, with its commitment to free enterprise in the marketplace, supported early central planning efforts in many developing nations.

Today, planning takes many forms in the developing nations. In some countries, central planning has replaced market-based outcomes with direct, administratively determined controls over economic variables such as prices, output, and employment. In other countries, national planning amounts to little more than the formulation of general 5- or 10-year goals as rough blueprints for a nation's economic future.

The economic appeal of planning lies theoretically in its ability to channel savings into productive investment and to coordinate economic activities that private actors in the economy might not otherwise undertake. The reality of central planning, however, is that it is a technically difficult, highly politicized nightmare to administer. Given the scarcity of human resources and the unstable political environment in many developing nations, planning itself—let alone the execution of the plan—becomes a formidable task.

The failure of many central planning efforts has brought increasing calls for less government intervention and more market orientation in developing economies. The elimination of price controls, privatization of state-run enterprises, and reductions in import restraints are examples of market-oriented reforms recommended by such international agencies as the **International Monetary Fund (IMF)**, whose primary goals are to stabilize international exchange rates and to lend money to countries that have problems financing their international transactions, and the **World Bank**, which lends money to a country for projects that promote economic development.

International Monetary Fund (IMF) An international agency whose primary goals are to stabilize international exchange rates and to lend money to countries that have problems financing their international transactions.

World Bank An international agency that lends money to individual countries for projects that promote economic development.

Members' contributions to both organizations are determined by the size of their economies. Only 20 percent of the World Bank's funding comes from contributions; 80 percent comes from retained earnings and investments in capital markets. Increasingly, the developing world is recognizing the value of market forces in determining the allocation of scarce resources. Nonetheless, government still has a major role to play. In the decades ahead, the governments of developing nations will need to determine those situations where planning is superior to the market and those where the market is superior to planning.

Microfinance: A New Idea In the mid 1970s, Muhammad Yunus, a young Bangladeshi economist created the Grameen Bank in Bangladesh. Yunus, who trained at Vanderbilt University and was a former professor at Middle Tennessee State University, used this bank as a vehicle to introduce microfinance to the developing world. In 2006, Yunus received a Nobel Peace Prize for his work. Microfinance is the practice of lending very small amounts of money, with no collateral, and accepting very small savings deposits.[2] It is aimed at introducing entrepreneurs in the poorest parts of the developing world to the capital market. By 2002, more than 2,500 institutions were making these small loans, serving over 60 million people. Two-thirds of borrowers were living below the poverty line in their own countries, the poorest of the poor.

Yunus, while teaching economics in Bangladesh, began lending his own money to poor households with entrepreneurial ambitions. He found that with even very small amounts of money, villagers could start simple businesses: bamboo weaving or hair dressing. Traditional banks found these borrowers unprofitable: The amounts were too small, and it was too expensive

[2] An excellent discussion of microfinance is contained in Beatriz Armendariz de Aghion and Jonathan Morduch, *The Economics of Microfinance,* (MIT Press, 2005.)

to figure out which of the potential borrowers was a good risk. With a borrower having no collateral, information about his or her character was key but was hard for a big bank to discover. Local villagers, however, typically knew a great deal about one another's characters. This insight formed the basis for Yunus's microfinance enterprise. Within a village, people who are interested in borrowing money to start businesses are asked to join lending groups of five people. Loans are then made to two of the potential borrowers, later to a second two, and finally to the last. As long as everyone is repaying their loans, the next group receives theirs. But if the first borrowers fail to pay, all members of the group are denied subsequent loans. What does this do? It makes community pressure a substitute for collateral. Moreover, once the peer lending mechanism is understood, villagers have incentives to join only with other reliable borrowers. The mechanism of peer lending is a way to avoid the problems of imperfect information described in an earlier chapter.

The Grameen model grew rapidly. By 2002, Grameen was lending to two million members. Thirty countries and thirty U.S. states have microfinance lending copied from the Grameen model. Relative to traditional bank loans, microfinance loans are much smaller, repayment begins very quickly, and the vast majority of the loans are made to women (who, in many cases, have been underserved by mainstream banks). A growing set of evidence shows that providing opportunities for poor women has stronger spillovers in terms of improving the welfare of children than does comparable opportunities for men. While the field of microfinance has changed considerably since Yunus's introduction and some people question how big a role it will ultimately play in spurring major development and economic growth, it has changed many people's views about the possibilities of entrepreneurship for the poor of the world.

Growth versus Development: The Policy Cycle

Until now, we have used *growth* and *development* as if they meant the same thing, but this may not always be the case. You can easily imagine instances in which a country has achieved higher levels of income (growth) with little or no benefit accruing to most of its citizens (development). Thus, the question is whether economic growth necessarily brings about economic development.

In the past, most development strategies were aimed at increasing the growth rate of income per capita. Many still are, based on the theory that benefits of economic growth will "trickle down" to all members of society. If this theory is correct, growth should promote development.

By the early 1970s, the relationship between growth and development was being questioned more and more. A study by the World Bank in 1974 concluded the following:

> It is now clear that more than a decade of rapid growth in underdeveloped countries has been of little or no benefit to perhaps a third of their population.... Paradoxically, while growth policies have succeeded beyond the expectations of the first development decade, the very idea of aggregate growth as a social objective has increasingly been called into question.

The World Bank study indicated that increases in GDP per capita did not guarantee significant improvements in development indicators such as nutrition, health, and education. Although GDP per capita did rise, its benefits trickled down to a small minority of the population. This very limited success prompted new development strategies that would directly address the problems of poverty. Such new strategies favored agriculture over industry, called for domestic redistribution of income and wealth (especially land), and encouraged programs to satisfy such basic needs as food and shelter.

structural adjustment A series of programs in developing nations designed to: (1) reduce the size of their public sectors through privatization and/or expenditure reductions, (2) decrease their budget deficits, (3) control inflation, and (4) encourage private saving and investment through tax reform.

In the late 1970s and early 1980s, the international macroeconomic crises of high oil prices, worldwide recession, and Third World debt forced attention away from programs designed to eliminate poverty directly. Then, during the 1980s and 1990s, the policy focus turned 180 degrees. The World Bank and the United States began demanding "structural adjustment" in the developing countries as a prerequisite for sending aid to them. **Structural adjustment** programs entail reducing the size of the public sector through privatization and/or expenditure reductions, substantially cutting budget deficits, reining in inflation, and encouraging private saving and investment with tax reforms. These pro-market demands were an attempt to stimulate growth; distributional consequences took a back seat.

ECONOMICS IN PRACTICE

Cell Phones Increase Profits for Fishermen in India

Kerala is a poor state in a region of India. The fishing industry is a major part of the local economy, employing more than one million people and serving as the main source of protein for the population. Every day fishing boats go out; and when they return, the captain of the ship needs to decide where to take the fish to sell. There is much uncertainty in this decision: How much fish will they catch; what other boats will come to a particular location; how many buyers will there be at a location? Moreover, fuel costs are high and timing is difficult, so that once a boat comes ashore, it does not pay for the fishermen to search for a better marketplace. In a recent study of this area, Robert Jensen[1] found on a Tuesday morning in November 1997, 11 fishermen in Badagara were dumping their load of fish because they faced no buyers at the dock. However, unbeknownst to them, 15 kilometers away, 27 buyers were leaving their marketplace empty-handed, with unsatisfied demand for fish.

Beginning in 1997 and continuing for the next several years, mobile phone service was introduced to this region of India. By 2001, the majority of the fishing fleet had mobile phones, which they use to call various vendors ashore to confirm where the buyers are. What was the result? Once the phones were introduced, waste, which had averaged 5 to 8 percent of the total catch, was virtually eliminated. Moreover, just as we would have predicted from the simple laws of supply and demand, the prices of fish across the various villages along the fishing market route were closer to each other than they were before. Jensen found that with less waste fishermen's profits rose on average by 8 percent, while the average price of fish fell by 4 percent.

In fact, cell phones are improving the way markets in less developed countries work by providing price and quantity information so that both producers and consumers can make better economic decisions.

[1] Robert Jensen, "The Digital Provide: Information Technology, Market Performance, and Welfare in the South Indian Fisheries Sector," *The Quarterly Journal of Economics,* August 2007.

Two Examples of Development: China and India

China and India provide two interesting examples of rapidly developing economies. While low per-capita incomes still mean that both countries are typically labeled developing as opposed to developed countries, many expect that to change in the near future. In the 25-year period from 1978 to 2003, China grew, on average, 8 percent per year, a rate faster than any other country in the world. While India's surge has been more recent, in the last 5 years, it too has seen annual growth rates in the 8 to 9 percent range. Many commentators expect India and China to dominate the world economy in the twenty-first century.

How did these two rather different countries engineer their development? Consider institutions: India is a democratic country, has a history of the rule of law, and has an English-speaking heritage—all factors typically thought to provide a development advantage. China is still an authoritarian country politically, and property rights are still not well established—both characteristics that were once thought to hinder growth. Both China and India have embraced free market economics, with China taking the lead as India has worked to remove some of its historical regulatory apparatus.

What about social capital? Both India and China remain densely populated. While China is the most populous country in the world, India, with a smaller land mass, is the world's most densely populated country. Nevertheless, as is true in most developing nations, birth rates in both countries have fallen. Literacy rates and life expectancy in China are quite high, in part a legacy from an earlier period. India, on the other hand, has a literacy rate that is less than that of

China's and a lower life expectancy. In terms of human capital, China appears to have the edge, at least for now.

What about the growth strategies used by the two countries? China has adopted a pragmatic, gradual approach to development, sharply in contrast to that adopted some years ago in Poland. China's approach has been called *moshi guohe*, or "Crossing the river by feeling for stepping stones." In terms of sector, most of China's growth has been fueled by manufacturing. The focus on manufacturing is one reason that China's energy consumption and environmental issues have increased so rapidly in the last decade. In India, services have led growth, particularly in the software industry. In sum, it is clear that there is no single recipe for development.

Issues in Economic Development

Every developing nation has a cultural, political, and economic history all its own and therefore confronts a unique set of problems. Still, it is possible to discuss common economic issues that each nation must face in its own particular way. These issues include rapid population growth and how to manage it.

Population Growth

The populations of the developing nations are estimated to be growing at about 1.7 percent per year. (Compare this with a population growth rate of only .5 percent per year in the industrial market economies.) If the Third World's population growth rate remains at 1.7 percent, within 41 years its population will double from the 1990 level of 4.1 billion to over 8 billion by the year 2031. On the other hand, it will take the industrialized nations 139 years to double their populations. What is so immediately alarming about these numbers is that given the developing nations' current economic problems, it is hard to imagine how they can possibly absorb so many more people in such a relatively short period.

Concern over world population growth is not new. The Reverend Thomas Malthus (who became England's first professor of political economy) expressed his fears about the population increases he observed 200 years ago. Malthus believed that populations grow geometrically at a constant growth rate—thus the absolute size of the increase each year gets larger and larger—but that food supplies grow more slowly because of the diminishing marginal productivity of land.[3] These two phenomena led Malthus to predict the increasing impoverishment of the world's people unless population growth could be slowed.

Malthus's fears for Europe and America proved unfounded. He did not anticipate the technological changes that revolutionized agricultural productivity and the eventual decrease in population growth rates in Europe and North America. Nevertheless, Malthus's prediction may have been right, only premature. Do the circumstances in the developing world now fit his predictions? Although some contemporary observers believe that the Malthusian view is correct and the earth's population will eventually grow to a level that the world's resources cannot support, others say technological change and demographic transitions (to slower population growth rates) will permit further increases in global welfare.

The Consequences of Rapid Population Growth We know far less about the economic consequences of rapid population growth than you might expect. Conventional wisdom warns of dire economic consequences from the developing nations' "population explosion," but these predictions are difficult to substantiate with the available evidence. The rapid economic growth of the United States, for example, was accompanied by relatively rapid population growth by historical standards. Any slowing of population growth has not been necessary for the economic progress achieved by many of the newly industrialized countries. Nonetheless, population expansion in many of today's poorest nations is of a magnitude unprecedented in world history,

[3] The law of diminishing marginal productivity says that with a fixed amount of a resource (land), additions of more and more of a variable resource (labor) will produce smaller and smaller gains in output.

as Figure 36.1 clearly shows. From the year 1 A.D. until the mid-1600s, populations grew slowly, at rates of only about .04 percent per year. Since then, and especially since 1950, rates have skyrocketed. Today populations are growing at rates of 1.5 percent to 4.0 percent per year throughout the developing world.

Because growth rates like these never occurred before the twentieth century, no one knows what impact they will have on future economic development. However, a basic economic concern is that such rapid population growth may limit investment and restrain increases in labor productivity and income. Rapid population growth changes the age composition of a population, generating many dependent children relative to the number of productive working adults. Such a situation may diminish saving rates, and hence investment, as the immediate consumption needs of the young take priority over saving for the future.

Even if low saving rates are not a necessary consequence of rapid population growth, as some authorities contend, other economic problems remain. The ability to improve human capital through a broad range of programs, from infant nutrition to formal secondary education, may be severely limited if the population explosion continues. Such programs are most often the responsibility of the state, and governments that are already weak cannot be expected to improve their

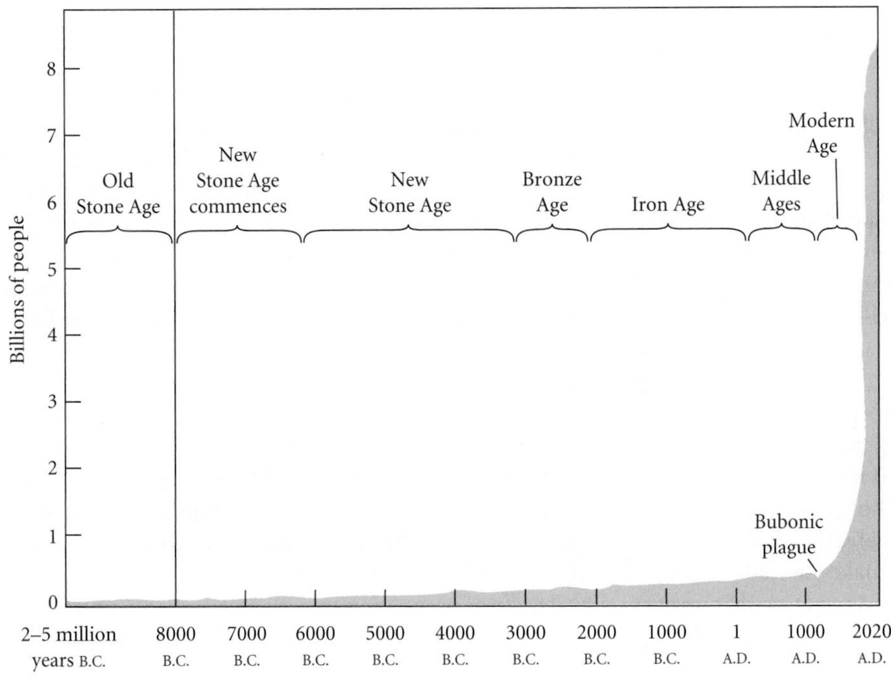

◀ **FIGURE 36.1**
The Growth of World Population, Projected to A.D. 2020
For thousands of years, population grew slowly. From A.D. 1 until the mid-1600s, population grew at about .04 percent per year. Since the Industrial Revolution, population growth has occurred at an unprecedented rate.

services under the burden of population pressures that rapidly increase demands for all kinds of public goods and services.

For example, Uganda's 2008 population growth rate—3.6 percent—is one of the highest in the world. Its 2003 population of 25.8 million had grown by 5 million people by 2007. This is a daunting prospect, and it is hard to imagine how in so little time, Uganda, with per-capita GNP of $300, will be able to provide its population with the physical and human capital needed to maintain, let alone improve, already low standards of living.

Causes of Rapid Population Growth Population growth is determined by the relationship between births and deaths—that is, between **fertility rates** and **mortality rates.** The **natural rate of population increase** is defined as the difference between the birth rate and the death rate. If the birth rate is 4 percent, for example, and the death rate is 3 percent, the population is growing at a rate of 1 percent per year.

Historically, low rates of population growth were maintained because of high mortality rates despite high levels of fertility. That is, families had many children, but average life expectancies were low and many children (and adults) died young. In Europe and North America, improvements in nutrition, in public health programs (especially those concerned with drinking water

fertility rate The birth rate. Equal to (the number of births per year divided by the population) × 100.

mortality rate The death rate. Equal to (the number of deaths per year divided by the population) × 100.

natural rate of population increase The difference between the birth rate and the death rate.

and sanitation services), and in medical practices have led to a drop in the mortality rate and hence to more rapid population growth. Eventually, fertility rates also fell, returning population growth to a low and stable rate.

Public health programs and improved nutrition over the past 30 years also have brought about precipitous declines in mortality rates in the developing nations. However, fertility rates have not declined as quickly, and the result has been high natural rates of population growth. Reduced population growth depends to some extent on decreased birth rates, but attempts to lower fertility rates must take into account how different cultures feel and behave with regard to fertility.

Family planning and modern forms of birth control are important mechanisms for decreasing fertility, but by themselves have had rather limited success in most countries where they have been tried. If family-planning strategies are to be successful, they must make sense to the people who are supposed to benefit from them. The planners of such strategies must understand why families in developing nations have so many children.

To a great extent, in developing countries, people want large families because they believe they need them. Economists have attempted to understand fertility patterns in the developing countries by focusing on the determinants of the demand for children. In agrarian societies, children are sources of farm labor and they may make significant contributions to household income. In societies without public old-age-support or social security programs, children may also provide a source of income for parents who are too old to support themselves. With the high value of children enhanced by high rates of infant mortality, it is no wonder that families try to have many children to ensure that a sufficient number will survive into adulthood.

Cultural and religious values also affect the number of children families want to have, but the economic incentives to have large families are extremely powerful. Only when the relationship between the costs and benefits of having children changes will fertility rates decline. The expansion of employment opportunities for women in an economy increases the opportunity costs of childrearing (by giving women a more highly valued alternative to raising children) and often leads to lower birth rates. Government incentives for smaller families, such as subsidized education for families with fewer than three children, can have a similar effect. In general, rising incomes appear to decrease fertility rates, indicating that economic development itself reduces population growth rates.

Economic theories of population growth suggest that fertility decisions made by poor families should not be viewed as uninformed and uncontrolled. An individual family may find that having many children is a rational strategy for economic survival given the conditions in which it finds itself. This does not mean, however, that having many children is a net benefit to society as a whole. When a family decides to have a large number of children, it imposes costs on the rest of society; the children must be educated, their health provided for, and so on. In other words, what makes sense for an individual household may create negative effects for the nation as a whole. Any nation that wants to slow its rate of population growth will probably find it necessary to have in place economic incentives for fewer children as well as family-planning programs.

The Transition to a Market Economy

In the last several decades, a number of countries have made the transition from a planned economy to a market economy. Russia and the formerly Communist countries of Eastern Europe led the way in this transition beginning in the late-1980s. For a number of these countries, the early transition period was difficult, and there has been considerable debate about the optimal speed of transitions and ways to manage the social upheaval that often comes with economic reform.

For example, between 1992 and 2002, while per-capita income grew by 51 percent in Poland, it shrank by 63 percent in the Ukraine. Countries of the former USSR seem to have had a particularly difficult transition to market economies. Economists have attributed differences in ease of transition to reform strategies (slow versus fast), resource endowments of the country, and differences in institutions.

In more recent years, China and Vietnam have joined the collection of transition economies, coming to rely less on central planning for economic decisions and more on the market. India too is sometimes thought to be a transition economy, as it has in the last decade dismantled much of its government ownership and elaborate rules governing market transactions.

Six Basic Requirements for Successful Transition

Economists generally agree on six basic requirements for a successful transition to a market-based system: (1) macroeconomic stabilization, (2) deregulation of prices and liberalization of trade, (3) privatization of state-owned enterprises and development of new private industry, (4) establishment of market-supporting institutions such as property and contract laws and accounting systems, (5) a social safety net to deal with unemployment and poverty, and (6) external assistance. We now discuss each component.

Macroeconomic Stabilization Many countries in transition have had a problem with inflation, but nowhere has it been worse than in Russia. As economic conditions worsened, the government found itself with serious budget problems. As revenue flows slowed and expenditure commitments increased, large budget deficits resulted. At the same time, each of the new republics established its own central bank. Each central bank began issuing "ruble credits" to keep important enterprises afloat and to pay the government's bills. The issuance of these credits, which were generally accepted as a means of payment throughout the country, led to a dramatic expansion of the money supply.

Almost from the beginning, the expanded money supply meant too much money was chasing too few goods. This was made worse by government-controlled prices set substantially below market-clearing levels. The combination of monetary expansion and price control was deadly. Government-run shops that sold goods at controlled prices were empty. People waited in line for days and often became violent when their efforts to buy goods at low official prices were thwarted. At the same time, suppliers found that they could charge much higher prices for their products on the black market—which grew bigger by the day, further exacerbating the shortage of goods at government shops. Over time, the ruble became worth less and less as black market prices continued to rise more rapidly. Russia found itself with near hyperinflation in 1992. To achieve a properly functioning market system, prices must be stabilized. To do so, the government must find a way to move toward a balanced budget and to bring the supply of money under control. China and India, in contrast to Russia and Eastern European states, initially suffered only modest inflation as they decontrolled their prices, though more recently inflation appears to be increasing in China.

Deregulation of Prices and Liberalization of Trade To move successfully from central planning to a market system, individual prices must be deregulated. A system of freely moving prices forms the backbone of a market system. When people want more of a good than is currently being produced, its price will rise. This higher price increases producers' profits and provides an incentive for existing firms to expand production and for new firms to enter the industry. Conversely, if an industry is producing a good for which there is no market or a good that people no longer want in the same quantity, the result will be excess supply and the price of that good will fall. This outcome reduces profits or creates losses, providing an incentive for some existing firms to cut back on production and for others to go out of business. In short, an unregulated price mechanism ensures an efficient allocation of resources across industries. Until prices are deregulated, this mechanism cannot function. In practice, transition economies have moved at varying speeds in decontrolling prices. Vietnam, for example, decontrolled prices very quickly in moving to a market economy, as did Poland. China, on the other hand, took a slower path in freeing prices from state control.

Trade barriers must also be removed. Reform-minded countries must be able to import capital, technology, and ideas. In addition, it makes no sense to continue to subsidize industries that cannot be competitive on world markets. If it is cheaper to buy steel from an efficient West German steel mill than to produce it in a subsidized antiquated Russian mill, the Russian mill should be modernized or shut down. Ultimately, as the theory of comparative advantage suggests, liberalized trade will push each country to produce the products it produces best.

Deregulating prices and eliminating subsidies can bring serious political problems. Many products in Russia and the rest of the socialist world were priced below market-clearing levels for equity reasons. Housing, food, and clothing were considered by many to be entitlements. Making them more expensive, at least relative to their prices in previous times, is not likely to be popular. In 2008, rising rice prices in Southeast Asia caused considerable unrest in Vietnam, Thailand, and

Cambodia. In addition, forcing inefficient firms to operate without subsidies will lead many of them to go out of business, and jobs will be lost. So while price deregulation and trade liberalization are necessary, they are very difficult politically.

Privatization One problem with a system of central ownership is a lack of accountability. Under a system of private ownership, owners reap the rewards of their successes and suffer the consequences of their failures. Private ownership provides a strong incentive for efficient operation, innovation, and hard work that is lacking when ownership is centralized and profits are distributed to the people.

tragedy of commons The idea that collective ownership may not provide the proper private incentives for efficiency because individuals do not bear the full costs of their own decisions but do enjoy the full benefits.

The classic story to illustrate this point is called the **tragedy of commons**, which is the idea that collective ownership may not provide the proper private incentives for efficiency because individuals do not bear the full costs of their own decisions but do enjoy the full benefits. Suppose an agricultural community has 10,000 acres of grazing land. If the land was held in common so that all farmers had unlimited rights to graze their animals, each farmer would have an incentive to overgraze. He or she would reap the full benefits from grazing additional calves while the costs of grazing the calves would be borne collectively. The system provides no incentive to manage the land efficiently. Similarly, if the efficiency and benefits of your hard work and managerial skills accrue to others or to the state, what incentive do you have to work hard or to be efficient?

One solution to the tragedy of commons attempted in eighteenth-century Britain was to divide up the land into private holdings. Today, many economists argue, the solution to the incentive problem encountered in state-owned enterprises is to privatize them and let the owners compete.

In addition to increasing accountability, privatization means creating a climate in which new enterprises can flourish. If there is market demand for a product not currently being produced, individual entrepreneurs should be free to set up a business and make a profit. During the last months of the Soviet Union's existence, private enterprises such as taxi services, car repair services, restaurants, and even hotels began to spring up all over the country.

Like deregulation of prices, privatization is difficult politically. Privatization means that many protected enterprises will go out of business because they cannot compete at world prices, resulting in a loss of jobs, at least temporarily.

Market-Supporting Institutions Between 1991 and 1997, U.S. firms raced to Eastern Europe in search of markets and investment opportunities and immediately became aware of a major obstacle. The institutions that make the market function relatively smoothly in the United States did not exist in Eastern Europe. For example, the capital market, which channels private saving into productive capital investment in developed capitalist economies, is made up of hundreds of different institutions. The banking system, venture capital funds, the stock market, the bond market, commodity exchanges, brokerage houses, investment banks, and so on, have developed in the United States over hundreds of years, and they could not be replicated overnight in the formerly Communist world.

Similar problems exist in the Chinese economy. While the Chinese equity market has grown rapidly in the last decade, that growth has been accompanied by problems with weak governance and lack of transparency. These issues discourage investments by western firms.

Many market-supporting institutions are so basic that Americans take them for granted. The institution of private property, for example, is a set of rights that must be protected by laws that the government must be willing to enforce. Suppose the French hotel chain Novotel decides to build a new hotel in Moscow or Beijing. Novotel must first acquire land. Then it will construct a building based on the expectation of renting rooms to customers. These investments are made with the expectation that the owner has a right to use them and a right to the profits that they produce. For such investments to be undertaken, these rights must be guaranteed by a set of property laws. This is equally true for large business firms and for local entrepreneurs who want to start their own enterprises. China's ambiguous property rights laws may also be problematic. While farmers can own their own homes, for example, all rural land is collectively owned by villages. Farmers have the right to manage farmland, but not own it. As a result, transfer of land is difficult.

Similarly, the law must provide for the enforcement of contracts. In the United States, a huge body of law determines what happens if you break a formal promise made in good faith. Businesses exist on promises to produce and promises to pay. Without recourse to the law when a contract is breached, contracts will not be entered into, goods will not be manufactured, and services will not be provided.

Protection of intellectual property rights is also an important feature of developed market economies. When an artist puts out a record, the artist and his or her studio are entitled to reap revenues from it. When Apple developed the iPod, it too earned the right to collect revenue for its patent ownership. Many less developed countries lack laws and enforcement mechanisms to protect intellectual property of foreign investments and their own current and future investors. The lack of protection discourages trade and home-grown invention. For example, in late 2007, China, in recognition of some of these issues, began drafting a new set of laws for intellectual property protection.

Another seemingly simple matter that turns out to be quite complex is the establishment of a set of accounting principles. In the United States, the rules of the accounting game are embodied in a set of generally accepted accounting principles (GAAP) that carry the force of law. Companies are required to keep track of their receipts, expenditures, and liabilities so that their performance can be observed and evaluated by shareholders, taxing authorities, and others who have an interest in the company. If you have taken a course in accounting, you know how detailed these rules have become. Imagine trying to do business in a country operating under hundreds of different sets of rules. That is what happened in Russia during its transition.

Another institution is insurance. Whenever a venture undertakes a high-risk activity, it buys insurance to protect itself. Several years ago Amnesty International (a nonprofit organization that works to protect civil liberties around the world) sponsored a worldwide concert tour with a number of well-known rock bands and performers. The most difficult part of organizing the tour was obtaining insurance for the artists and their equipment when they played in the then-Communist countries of Eastern Europe.

Social Safety Net In a centrally planned socialist economy, the labor market does not function freely. Everyone who wants a job is guaranteed one somewhere. The number of jobs is determined by a central plan to match the number of workers. There is essentially no unemployment. This, it has been argued, is one of the great advantages of a planned system. In addition, a central planning system provides basic housing, food, and clothing at very affordable levels for all. With no unemployment and necessities available at very low prices, there is no need for unemployment insurance, welfare, or other social programs.

Transition to a free labor market and liberalization of prices means that some workers will end up unemployed and that everyone will pay higher prices for necessities. Indeed, during the early phases of the transition process, unemployment will be high. Inefficient state-owned enterprises will go out of business; some sectors will contract while others expand. As more and more people experience unemployment, popular support for reform is likely to drop unless some sort of social safety net is erected to ease the transition. This social safety net might include unemployment insurance, aid for the poor, and food and housing assistance. The experiences of the developed world have shown that such programs are expensive.

External Assistance Very few believe that the transition to a market system can be achieved without outside support and some outside financing. Knowledge of and experience with capitalist institutions that exist in the United States, Western Europe, and Japan are of vital interest to the Eastern European nations. The basic skills of accounting, management, and enterprise development can be taught to developing nations; many say it is in everyone's best interest to do so.

There is little agreement about the extent of *financial* support that should be given, however. In the case of Russia, the United States pushed for a worldwide effort to provide billions of dollars in aid, to stabilize its macroeconomy, and to buy desperately needed goods from abroad. For China, no such aid was thought to be necessary.

shock therapy The approach to transition from socialism to market capitalism that advocates rapid deregulation of prices, liberalization of trade, and privatization.

Shock Therapy or Gradualism? Although economists generally agreed on what the former socialist economies needed to do, they debated the sequence and timing of specific reforms.

The popular press described the debate as one between those who believe in "shock therapy" (sometimes called the Big Bang approach) and those who prefer a more gradual approach. Advocates of **shock therapy** believe that the economies in transition should proceed immediately on all fronts. They should stop printing money, deregulate prices and liberalize trade, privatize, develop market institutions, build a social safety net, and acquire external aid—all as quickly as possible. The pain will be severe, the argument goes, but in the end, it will be forgotten as the transition raises living standards. Advocates of a *gradualist* approach believe the best course is to build up market institutions first, gradually decontrol prices, and privatize only the most efficient government enterprises first.

Those who favor moving quickly point to the apparent success of Poland, which moved rapidly through the first phases of reform. Russia's experience during the first years of its transition demonstrated that, at least in that country, change must, to some extent, be gradual. In theory, stabilization and price liberalization can be achieved instantaneously. To enjoy the benefits of liberalization, a good deal of privatization must have taken place—and that takes time. One analyst has said that privatization means "selling assets with no value to people with no money." Some estimates suggest that half of Russian state-owned enterprises were incapable of making a profit at world prices. Simply cutting them loose would create chaos. In a sense, Russia had no choice but to move slowly.

SUMMARY

1. The economic problems facing the developing countries are often quite different from those confronting industrialized nations. The policy options available to governments may also differ. Nonetheless, the tools of economic analysis are as useful in understanding the economies of less developed countries as in understanding the U.S. economy.

LIFE IN THE DEVELOPING NATIONS: POPULATION AND POVERTY *p. 714*

2. The central reality of life in the developing countries is poverty. Although there is considerable diversity across the developing nations, most of the people in most developing countries are extremely poor by U.S. standards.

ECONOMIC DEVELOPMENT: SOURCES AND STRATEGIES *p. 715*

3. Almost all developing nations have a scarcity of physical capital relative to other resources, especially labor. The *vicious-circle-of-poverty hypothesis* says that poor countries cannot escape from poverty because they cannot afford to postpone consumption—that is, to save—to make investments. In its crude form, the hypothesis is wrong inasmuch as some prosperous countries were at one time poorer than many developing countries are today. However, it is often difficult to mobilize saving efficiently in many developing nations.

4. Human capital—the stock of education and skills embodied in the workforce—plays a vital role in economic development.

5. Developing countries are often burdened by inadequate *social overhead capital*, ranging from poor public health and sanitation facilities to inadequate roads, telephones, and court systems. Such social overhead capital is often expensive to provide, and many governments are not in a position to undertake many useful projects because they are too costly.

6. Inefficient and corrupt bureaucracies also play a role in retarding economic development in places.

7. Because developed economies are characterized by a large share of output and employment in the industrial sector, many developing countries seem to believe that development and industrialization are synonymous. In many cases, developing countries have pursued industry at the expense of agriculture, with mixed results. Recent evidence suggests that some balance between industry and agriculture leads to the best outcome.

8. *Import-substitution* policies, a trade strategy that favors developing local industries that can manufacture goods to replace imports, were once very common in developing nations. In general, such policies have not succeeded as well as those promoting open, export-oriented economies.

9. The failure of many central planning efforts has brought increasing calls for less government intervention and more market orientation in developing economies.

10. Microfinance—lending small amounts to poor borrowers using peer lending groups—has become an important new tool in encouraging entrepreneurship in developing countries.

11. China and India have followed quite different paths in recent development.

ISSUES IN ECONOMIC DEVELOPMENT p. 724

12. Rapid population growth is characteristic of many developing countries. Large families can be economically rational because parents need support in their old age or because children offer an important source of labor. However, having many children does not mean a net benefit to society as a whole. Rapid population growth can put a strain on already overburdened public services such as education and health.

THE TRANSITION TO A MARKET ECONOMY p. 726

13. Economists generally agree on six requirements for a successful transition from socialism to a market-based system: (1) macroeconomic stabilization, (2) deregulation of prices and liberalization of trade, (3) privatization, (4) establishment of market-supporting institutions, (5) a social safety net, and (6) external assistance.

14. Much debate exists about the sequence and timing of specific reforms. The idea of *shock therapy* is to proceed immediately on all six fronts, including rapid deregulation of prices and privatization. The *gradualist* approach is to build up market institutions first, gradually decontrol prices, and privatize only the most efficient government enterprises first.

REVIEW TERMS AND CONCEPTS

PROBLEMS

Visit **www.myeconlab.com** to complete the problems marked in orange online. You will receive instant feedback on your answers, tutorial help, and access to additional practice problems.

1. The biggest problem facing developing countries across the globe in 2006 was disease. The HIV/AIDS pandemic had infected more than 40 million worldwide and up to 40 percent of the adult populations of some African countries, such as Botswana. Describe the effects of HIV/AIDS on the economies of these countries. Make sure you discuss the sources of economic growth and the use of scarce resources.
2. For a developing country to grow, it needs capital. The major source of capital in most countries is domestic saving, but the goal of stimulating domestic saving usually is in conflict with government policies aimed at reducing inequality in the distribution of income. Comment on this trade-off between equity and growth. How would you go about resolving the issue if you were the president of a small, poor country?
3. The GDP of any country can be divided into two kinds of goods: capital goods and consumption goods. The proportion of national output devoted to capital goods determines, to some extent, the nation's growth rate.
   a. Explain how capital accumulation leads to economic growth.
   b. Briefly describe how a market economy determines how much investment will be undertaken each period.
   c. Consumption versus investment is a more painful conflict to resolve for developing countries. Comment on that statement.
   d. If you were the benevolent dictator of a developing country, what plans would you implement to increase per capita GDP?
4. The World Bank and the International Monetary Fund were scheduled to formally cancel the debts of 18 very poor countries in 2006, and the African Development Bank was committed to taking the same action during its 2006 annual meeting. Go online and find out whether these debts were indeed canceled. How much debt was forgiven during that year in each of the countries involved? What are the expected benefits to those countries?
5. Poor countries are trapped in a vicious circle of poverty. For output to grow, they must accumulate capital. To accumulate capital, they must save (consume less than they produce). Because they are poor, they have little or no extra output available for savings—it must all go to feed and clothe the present generation. Thus they are doomed to stay poor forever. Comment on each step in that argument.
6. Famines are acts of God resulting from bad weather or other natural disasters. There is nothing we can do about them except to send food relief after they occur. Explain why that position is inaccurate. Concentrate on agricultural pricing policies and distributional issues.
7. In China, rural property is owned collectively by the village while being managed under long-term contracts by individual farmers. Why might this be a problem in terms of optimal land managment, use, and allocation?

8. How does peer lending used in microfinance help to solve the problem of adverse selection?

9. [Related to the *Economics in Practice* on *p. 723*] Find another example of the use of cell phones as a way to improve market functioning in a developing economy.

10. [Related to the *Economics in Practice* on *p. 718*] Corruption in a government is often accompanied by inefficiency in the economy. Why should this be true?

11. The distribution of income in a capitalist economy is likely to be more unequal than it is in a socialist economy. Why is this so? Is there a tension between the goal of limiting inequality and the goal of motivating risk taking and hard work? Explain your answer in detail.

Glossary

ability-to-pay principle A theory of taxation holding that citizens should bear tax burdens in line with their ability to pay taxes. *p. 384*

absolute advantage A producer has an absolute advantage over another in the production of a good or service if he or she can produce that product using fewer resources. *p. 29 p. 667*

accelerator effect The tendency for investment to increase when aggregate output increases and to decrease when aggregate output decreases, accelerating the growth or decline of output. *p. 619*

actual investment The actual amount of investment that takes place; it includes items such as unplanned changes in inventories. *p. 458*

adjustment costs The costs that a firm incurs when it changes its production level—for example, the administration costs of laying off employees or the training costs of hiring new workers. *p. 620*

adverse selection A situation in which asymmetric information results in high-quality goods or high-quality consumers being squeezed out of transactions because they cannot demonstrate their quality. *p. 350*

aggregate behavior The behavior of all households and firms together. *p. 401*

aggregate demand The total demand for goods and services in the economy. *p. 539*

aggregate demand (*AD*) curve A curve that shows the negative relationship between aggregate output (income) and the price level. Each point on the AD curve is a point at which both the goods market and the money market are in equilibrium. *p. 539*

aggregate income The total income received by all factors of production in a given period. *p. 453*

aggregate output The total quantity of goods and services produced in an economy in a given period. *p. 402 p. 453*

aggregate output (income) (*Y*) A combined term used to remind you of the exact equality between aggregate output and aggregate income. *p. 453*

aggregate production function The mathematical representation of the relationship between inputs and national output, or gross domestic product. *p. 634*

aggregate saving (*S*) The part of aggregate income that is not consumed. *p. 455*

aggregate supply The total supply of all goods and services in an economy. *p. 550*

aggregate supply (*AS*) curve A graph that shows the relationship between the aggregate quantity of output supplied by all firms in an economy and the overall price level. *p. 550*

animal spirits of entrepreneurs A term coined by Keynes to describe investors' feelings. *p. 619*

appreciation of a currency The rise in value of one currency relative to another. *p. 412*

asymmetric information One of the parties to a transaction has information relevant to the transaction that the other party does not have. *p. 349*

automatic destabilizers Revenue and expenditure items in the federal budget that automatically change with the economy in such a way as to destabilize GDP. *p. 596*

automatic stabilizers Revenue and expenditure items in the federal budget that automatically change with the state of the economy in such a way as to stabilize GDP. *p. 487 p. 596*

average fixed cost (*AFC*) Total fixed cost divided by the number of units of output; a per-unit measure of fixed costs. *p. 157*

average product The average amount produced by each unit of a variable factor of production. *p. 142*

average tax rate Total amount of tax paid divided by total income. *p. 381*

average total cost (*ATC*) Total cost divided by the number of units of output. *p. 163*

average variable cost (*AVC*) Total variable cost divided by the number of units of output. *p. 162*

balance of payments The record of a country's transactions in goods, services, and assets with the rest of the world; also the record of a country's sources (supply) and uses (demand) of foreign exchange. *p. 402*

balance of trade A country's exports of goods and services minus its imports of goods and services. *p. 403*

balance on capital account In the United States, the sum of the following (measured in a given period): the change in private U.S. assets abroad, the change in foreign private assets in the United States, the change in U.S. government assets abroad, and the change in foreign government assets in the United States. *p. 404*

balance on current account Net exports of goods plus net exports of services plus net investment income plus net transfer payments. *p. 403*

balanced-budget multiplier The ratio of change in the equilibrium level of output to a change in government spending where the change in government spending is balanced by a change in taxes so as not to create any deficit. The balanced-budget multiplier is equal to 1: The change in Y resulting from the change in G and the equal change in T are exactly the same size as the initial change in G or T. *p. 480*

barriers to entry Factors that prevent new firms from entering and competing in imperfectly competitive industries. *p. 270*

barter The direct exchange of goods and services for other goods and services. *p. 494*

base year The year chosen for the weights in a fixed-weight procedure. *p. 427*

behavioral economics A branch of economics that uses the insights of psychology and economics to investigate decision making. *p. 307*

benefits-received principle A theory of fairness holding that taxpayers should contribute to govern-ment (in the form of taxes) in proportion to the benefits they receive from public expenditures. *p. 383*

black market A market in which illegal trading takes place at market-determined prices. *p. 77*

bond A contract between a borrower and a lender, in which the borrower agrees to pay the loan at some time in the future, along with interest payments along the way. *p. 225*

brain drain The tendency for talented people from developing countries to become educated in a developed country and remain there after graduation. *p. 717*

breaking even The situation in which a firm is earning exactly a normal rate of return. *p. 178*

budget constraint The limits imposed on household choices by income, wealth, and product prices. *p. 112*

budget deficit The difference between what a government spends and what it collects in taxes in a given period: *G–T*. *p. 473*

business cycle The cycle of short-term ups and downs in the economy. *p. 402*

capital Things that are produced and then used in the production of other goods and services. *p. 25 p. 221*

capital flight The tendency for both human capital and financial capital to leave developing countries in search of higher expected rates of return elsewhere with less risk. *p. 716*

capital gain An increase in the value of an asset. *p. 597*

capital income Income earned on savings that have been put to use through financial capital markets. *p. 225*

capital market The input/factor market in which households supply their savings, for interest or for claims to future profits, to firms that demand funds to buy capital goods. *p. 47 p. 224*

capital stock For a single firm, the current market value of the firm's plant, equipment, inventories, and intangible assets. *p. 223*

capital-intensive technology Technology that relies heavily on capital instead of human labor. *p. 140 p. 620*

cartel A group of firms that gets together and makes joint price and output decisions to maximize joint profits. *p. 287*

Cartesian coordinate system A common method of graphing two variables that makes use of two perpendicular lines against which the variables are plotted. *p. 19 p. 22*

catch-up The theory stating that the growth rates of less developed countries will exceed the growth rates of developed countries, allowing the less developed countries to catch up. *p. 633*

Celler-Kefauver Act Extended the government's authority to control mergers. *p. 298*

***ceteris paribus, or* all else equal** A device used to analyze the relationship between two variables while the values of other variables are held unchanged. *p. 12*

change in business inventories The amount by which firms' inventories change during a period. Inventories are the goods that firms produce now but intend to sell later. *p. 421*

choice set *or* opportunity set The set of options that is defined and limited by a budget constraint. *p. 113*

circular flow A diagram showing the income received and payments made by each sector of the economy. *p. 405*

Clayton Act Passed by Congress in 1914 to strengthen the Sherman Act and clarify the rule of reason, the act outlawed specific monopolistic behaviors such as tying contracts, price discrimination, and unlimited mergers. *p. 278*

Coase theorem Under certain conditions, when externalities are present, private parties can arrive at the efficient solution without government involvement. *p. 327*

command economy An economy in which a central government either directly or indirectly sets output targets, incomes, and prices. *p. 39*

commitment device Actions that individuals take in one period to try to control their behavior in a future period. *p. 307*

commodity monies Items used as money that also have intrinsic value in some other use. *p. 496*

comparative advantage A producer has a comparative advantage over another in the production of a good or service if he or she can produce that product at a lower *opportunity cost*. *p. 29 p. 403 p. 667*

compensating differentials Differences in wages that result from differences in working conditions. Risky jobs usually pay higher wages; highly desirable jobs usually pay lower wages. *p. 361*

compensation of employees Includes wages, salaries, and various supplements—employer contributions to social insurance and pension funds, for example—paid to households by firms and by the government. *p. 423*

complements, complementary goods Goods that "go together"; a decrease in the price of one results in an increase in demand for the other and vice versa. *p. 52*

concentration ratio The share of industry output in sales or employment accounted for by the top firms. *p. 285*

constant returns to scale An increase in a firm's scale of production has no effect on costs per unit produced. *p. 185*

constant-cost industry An industry that shows no economies or diseconomies of scale as the industry grows. Such industries have flat, or horizontal, long-run supply curves. *p. 200 p. 201*

constrained supply of labor The amount a household actually works in a given period at the current wage rate. *p. 614*

consumer goods Goods produced for present consumption. *p. 32*

consumer price index (CPI) A price index computed each month by the Bureau of Labor Statistics using a bundle that is meant to represent the "market basket" purchased monthly by the typical urban consumer. *p. 442*

consumer sovereignty The idea that consumers ultimately dictate what will be produced (or not produced) by choosing what to purchase (and what not to purchase). *p. 39*

consumer surplus The difference between the maximum amount a person is willing to pay for a good and its current market price. *p. 82*

consumption function The relationship between consumption and income. *p. 454*

contestable markets Markets in which entry and exit are easy. *p. 285*

contraction, recession, *or* slump The period in the business cycle from a peak down to a trough during which output and employment fall. *p. 402*

contractionary fiscal policy A decrease in government spending or an increase in net taxes aimed at decreasing aggregate output (income) (Y). *p. 537*

contractionary monetary policy A decrease in the money supply aimed at decreasing aggregate output (income) (Y). *p. 538*

Corn Laws The tariffs, subsidies, and restrictions enacted by the British Parliament in the early nineteenth century to discourage imports and encourage exports of grain. *p. 667*

corporate bonds Promissory notes issued by firms when they borrow money. *p. 407*

corporate profits The income of corporations. *p. 423*

cost shock, *or* supply shock A change in costs that shifts the short-run aggregate supply (*AS*) curve. *p. 552*

cost-of-living adjustments (COLAs) Contract provisions that tie wages to changes in the cost of living. The greater the inflation rate, the more wages are raised. *p. 577*

cost-push, *or* supply-side, inflation Inflation caused by an increase in costs. *p. 559*

cross-price elasticity of demand A measure of the response of the quantity of one good demanded to a change in the price of another good. *p. 102*

crowding-out effect The tendency for increases in government spending to cause reductions in private investment spending. *p. 535*

currency debasement The decrease in the value of money that occurs when its supply is increased rapidly. *p. 496*

current dollars The current prices that we pay for goods and services. *p. 426*

cyclical deficit The deficit that occurs because of a downturn in the business cycle. *p. 487*

cyclical unemployment The increase in unemployment that occurs during recessions and depressions. *p. 441 p. 572*

deadweight loss The total loss of producer and consumer surplus from underproduction or overproduction. *p. 84*

decreasing returns to scale, *or* diseconomies of scale An increase in a firm's scale of production leads to higher costs per unit produced. *p. 185*

decreasing-cost industry An industry that realizes external economies—that is, average costs decrease as the industry grows. The long-run supply curve for such an industry has a negative slope. *p. 200 p. 201*

deficit response index (DRI) The amount by which the deficit changes with a $1 change in GDP. *p. 595*

deflation A decrease in the overall price level. *p. 404*

demand curve A graph illustrating how much of a given product a household would be willing to buy at different prices. *p. 49*

demand schedule A table showing how much of a given product a household would be willing to buy at different prices. *p. 49*

demand-determined price The price of a good that is in fixed supply; it is determined exclusively by what households and firms are willing to pay for the good. *p. 212*

demand-pull inflation Inflation that is initiated by an increase in aggregate demand. *p. 558*

depreciation The amount by which an asset's value falls in a given period. *p. 224 p. 422*

depreciation of a currency The fall in value of one currency relative to another. *p. 224, p. 412*

depression A prolonged and deep recession. *p. 402*

derived demand The demand for resources (inputs) that is dependent on the demand for the outputs those resources can be used to produce. *p. 204*

descriptive economics The compilation of data that describe phenomena and facts. *p. 10*

desired, *or* optimal, level of inventories The level of inventory at which the extra cost (in lost sales) from lowering inventories by a small amount is just equal to the extra gain (in interest revenue and decreased storage costs). *p. 621*

diamond/water paradox A paradox stating that (1) the things with the greatest value in use frequently have little or no value in exchange and (2) the things with the greatest value in exchange frequently have little or no value in use. *p. 119*

diminishing marginal utility The more of any one good consumed in a given period, the less incremental satisfaction is generated by consuming a marginal or incremental unit of the same good. *p. 346*

discount rate The interest rate that banks pay to the Fed to borrow from it. *p. 508*

discouraged-worker effect The decline in the measured unemployment rate that results when people who want to work but cannot find jobs grow discouraged and stop looking, thus dropping out of the ranks of the unemployed and the labor force. *p. 436 p. 626*

discretionary fiscal policy Changes in taxes or spending that are the result of deliberate changes in government policy. *p. 472*

disposable personal income *or* after-tax income Personal income minus personal income taxes. The amount that households have to spend or save. *p. 426*

disposable, *or* after-tax, income (Y_d) Total income minus net taxes: $Y - T$. *p. 472*

dividends The portion of a firm's profits that the firm pays out each period to its shareholders. *p. 407*

Doha Development Agenda An initiative of the World Trade Organization focused on issues of trade and development. *p. 676*

dominant strategy In game theory, a strategy that is best no matter what the opposition does. *p. 291*

Dow Jones Industrial Average An index based on the stock prices of 30 actively traded large companies. The oldest and most widely followed index of stock market performance. *p. 598*

drop-in-the-bucket problem A problem intrinsic to public goods: The good or service is usually so costly that its provision generally does not depend on whether any single person pays. *p. 333*

dumping A firm's or an industry's sale of products on the world market at prices below its own cost of production. *p. 676*

durable goods Goods that last a relatively long time, such as cars and household appliances. *p. 420*

duopoly A two-firm oligopoly. *p. 289*

easy monetary policy Fed policies that expand the money supply and thus lower interest rates in an effort to stimulate the economy. *p. 525*

economic growth An increase in the total output of an economy. It occurs when a society acquires new resources or when it learns to produce more using existing resources. *p. 15 p. 36 p. 631*

economic income The amount of money a household can spend during a given period without increasing or decreasing its net assets. Wages, salaries, dividends, interest income, transfer payments, rents, and so on are sources of economic income. *p. 363*

economic integration Occurs when two or more nations join to form a free-trade zone. *p. 677*

economic theory A statement or set of related statements about cause and effect, action and reaction. *p. 10*

economics The study of how individuals and societies choose to use the scarce resources that nature and previous generations have provided. *p. 2*

efficiency In economics, allocative efficiency. An efficient economy is one that produces what people want at the least possible cost. *p. 14 p. 242*

efficiency wage theory An explanation for unemployment that holds that the productivity of workers increases with the wage rate. If this is so, firms may have an incentive to pay wages above the market-clearing rate. *p. 577*

efficient market A market in which profit opportunities are eliminated almost instantaneously. *p. 3*

elastic demand A demand relationship in which the percentage change in quantity demanded is larger than the percentage change in price in absolute value (a demand elasticity with an absolute value greater than 1). *p. 92*

elasticity A general concept used to quantify the response in one variable when another variable changes. *p. 89*

elasticity of labor supply A measure of the response of labor supplied to a change in the price of labor. *p. 103*

elasticity of supply A measure of the response of quantity of a good supplied to a change in price of that good. Likely to be positive in output markets. *p. 103*

empirical economics The collection and use of data to test economic theories. *p. 13*

employed Any person 16 years old or older (1) who works for pay, either for someone else or in his or her own business for 1 or more hours per week, (2) who works without pay for 15 or more hours per week in a family enterprise, or (3) who has a job but has been temporarily absent with or without pay. *p. 436*

entrepreneur A person who organizes, manages, and assumes the risks of a firm, taking a new idea or a new product and turning it into a successful business. *p. 46*

equilibrium The condition that exists when quantity supplied and quantity demanded are equal. At equilibrium, there is no tendency for price to change. In the macroeconomic goods market, equilibrium occurs when planned aggregate expenditure is equal to aggregate output. *p. 62 p. 459*

equilibrium price level The price level at which the aggregate demand and aggregate supply curves intersect. *p. 553*

equity Fairness. *p. 14 p. 359*

estate The property that a person owns at the time of his or her death. *p. 386*

estate tax A tax on the total value of a person's estate. *p. 386*

European Union (EU) The European trading bloc composed of 27 countries. *p. 677*

excess burden The amount by which the burden of a tax exceeds the total revenue collected. Also called deadweight loss. *p. 393*

excess demand *or* shortage The condition that exists when quantity demanded exceeds quantity supplied at the current price. *p. 62*

excess labor, excess capital Labor and capital that are not needed to produce the firm's current level of output. *p. 620*

excess supply *or* surplus The condition that exists when quantity supplied exceeds quantity demanded at the current price. *p. 63*

excess reserves The difference between a bank's actual reserves and its required reserves. *p. 501*

exchange rate The ratio at which two currencies are traded. The price of one country's currency in terms of another country's currency. *p. 672 p. 401*

exogenous variable A variable that is assumed not to depend on the state of the economy—that is, it does not change when the economy changes. *p. 463*

expansion *or* boom The period in the business cycle from a trough up to a peak during which output and employment grow. *p. 402*

expansionary fiscal policy An increase in government spending or a reduction in net taxes aimed at increasing aggregate output (income) (Y). *p. 535*

expansionary monetary policy An increase in the money supply aimed at increasing aggregate output (income) (Y). *p. 535*

expected rate of return The annual rate of return that a firm expects to obtain through a capital investment. *p. 231*

expected utility The sum of the utilities coming from all possible outcomes of a deal, weighted by the probability of each occurring. *p. 347*

expected value The sum of the payoffs associated with each possible outcome of a situation weighted by its probability of occurring. *p. 346*

expenditure approach A method of computing GDP that measures the total amount spent on all final goods and services during a given period. *p. 419*

explicit contracts Employment contracts that stipulate workers' wages, usually for a period of 1 to 3 years. *p. 577*

export promotion A trade policy designed to encourage exports. *p. 720*

export subsidies Government payments made to domestic firms to encourage exports. *p. 675*

external economies and diseconomies When industry growth results in a decrease of long-run average costs, there are *external economies*; when industry growth results in an increase of long-run average costs, there are *external diseconomies*. *p. 198 p. 201*

externality A cost or benefit imposed or bestowed on an individual or a group that is outside, or external to, the transaction. *p. 256 p. 319*

factor endowments The quantity and quality of labor, land, and natural resources of a country. *p. 674*

factor substitution effect The tendency of firms to substitute away from a factor whose price has risen and toward a factor whose price has fallen. *p. 210*

factors of production (*or* factors) The inputs into the process of production. Another term for resources. Land, labor, and capital are the three key factors of production. *p. 25 p. 47*

fair game *or* fair bet A game whose expected value is zero. *p. 346*

fallacy of composition The erroneous belief that what is true for a part is necessarily true for the whole. *p. 13*

favored customers Those who receive special treatment from dealers during situations of excess demand. *p. 76*

federal budget The budget of the federal government. *p. 481*

federal debt The total amount owed by the federal government. *p. 484*

Federal Open Market Committee (FOMC) A group composed of the seven members of the Fed's Board of Governors, the president of the New York Federal Reserve Bank, and four of the other 11 district bank presidents on a rotating basis; it sets goals concerning the money supply and interest rates and directs the operation of the Open Market Desk in New York. *p. 504*

Federal Reserve Bank (the Fed) The central bank of the United States. *p. 500*

federal surplus (+) *or* deficit (–) Federal government receipts minus expenditures. *p. 482*

Federal Trade Commission (FTC) A federal regulatory group created by Congress in 1914 to investigate the structure and behavior of firms engaging in interstate commerce, to determine what constitutes unlawful "unfair" behavior, and to issue cease-and-desist orders to those found in violation of antitrust law. *p. 278*

fertility rate The birth rate. Equal to (the number of births per year divided by the population) $\times$ 100. *p. 725*

fiat, *or* token, money Items designated as money that are intrinsically worthless. *p. 496*

final goods and services Goods and services produced for final use. *p. 418*

financial capital market The complex set of institutions in which suppliers of capital (households that save) and the demand for capital (firms wanting to invest) interact. *p. 127 p. 225*

financial intermediaries Banks and other institutions that act as a link between those who have money to lend and those who want to borrow money. *p. 498*

fine-tuning The phrase used by Walter Heller to refer to the government's role in regulating inflation and unemployment. *p. 408*

firm An organization that comes into being when a person or a group of people decides to produce a good or service to meet a perceived demand. A firm transforms resources (inputs) into products (outputs). Firms are the primary producing units in a market economy. *p. 46 p. 136*

fiscal drag The negative effect on the economy that occurs when average tax rates increase because taxpayers have moved into higher income brackets during an expansion. *p. 487*

fiscal policy Government policies concerning taxes and spending. *p. 407 p. 482*

Five Forces model A model developed by Michael Porter that helps us understand the five competitive forces that determine the level of competition and profitability in an industry. *p. 284*

fixed cost Any cost that does not depend on the firms' level of output. These costs are incurred even if the firm is producing nothing. There are no fixed costs in the long run. *p. 156*

fixed-weight procedure A procedure that uses weights from a given base year. *p. 427*

floating, *or* market-determined, exchange rates Exchange rates that are determined by the unregulated forces of supply and demand. *p. 409*

food stamps Vouchers that have a face value greater than their cost and that can be used to purchase food at grocery stores. *p. 375*

foreign direct investment (FDI) Investment in enterprises made in a country by residents outside that country. *p. 636*

foreign exchange All currencies other than the domestic currency of a given country. *p. 409*

free enterprise The freedom of individuals to start and operate private businesses in search of profits. *p. 40*

free-rider problem A problem intrinsic to public goods: Because people can enjoy the benefits of public goods whether or not they pay for them, they are usually unwilling to pay for them. *p. 333*

frictional unemployment The portion of unemployment that is due to the normal working of the labor market; used to denote short-run job/skill matching problems. *p. 441 p. 572*

full-employment budget What the federal budget would be if the economy were producing at the full-employment level of output. *p. 487*

game theory Analyzes the choices made by rival firms, people, and even governments when they are trying to maximize their own well-being while anticipating and reacting to the actions of others in their environment. *p. 291*

General Agreement on Tariffs and Trade (GATT) An international agreement signed by the United States and 22 other countries in 1947 to promote the liberalization of foreign trade. *p. 676*

general equilibrium The condition that exists when all markets in an economy are in simultaneous equilibrium. *p. 242*

Gini coefficient A commonly used measure of the degree of inequality of income derived from a Lorenz curve. It can range from 0 to a maximum of 1. *p. 364*

goods market The market in which goods and services are exchanged and in which the equilibrium level of aggregate output is determined. *p. 531*

government consumption and gross investment (G) Expenditures by federal, state, and local governments for final goods and services. *p. 422*

government failure Occurs when the government becomes the tool of the rent seeker and the allocation of resources is made even less efficient by the intervention of government. *p. 275*

government spending multiplier The ratio of the change in the equilibrium level of output to a change in government spending. *p. 477*

graph A two-dimensional representation of a set of numbers, or data. *p. 18 p. 22*

Gramm-Rudman-Hollings Act Passed by the U.S. Congress and signed by President Reagan in 1986, this law set out to reduce the federal deficit by $36 billion per year, with a deficit of zero slated for 1991. *p. 593*

Great Depression The period of severe economic contraction and high unemployment that began in 1929 and continued throughout the 1930s. *p. 407*

gross domestic product (GDP) The total market value of all final goods and services produced within a given period by factors of production located within a country. *p. 417*

gross investment The total value of all newly produced capital goods (plant, equipment, housing, and inventory) produced in a given period. *p. 422*

gross national income (GNI) GNP converted into dollars using an average of currency exchange rates over several years adjusted for rates of inflation. *p. 430*

gross national product (GNP) The total market value of all final goods and services produced within a given period by factors of production owned by a country's citizens, regardless of where the output is produced. *p. 419*

gross private domestic investment (*I*) Total investment in capital—that is, the purchase of new housing, plants, equipment, and inventory by the private (or nongovernment) sector. *p. 421*

Heckscher-Ohlin theorem A theory that explains the existence of a country's comparative advantage by its factor endowments: A country has a comparative advantage in the production of a product if that country is relatively well endowed with inputs used intensively in the production of that product. *p. 674*

Herfindahl-Hirschman Index (HHI) An index of market concentration found by summing the square of percentage shares of firms in the market. *p. 298*

homogenous products Undifferentiated products; products that are identical to, or indistinguishable from, one another. *p. 109 p. 167*

horizontal differentiation Products differ in ways that make them better for some people and worse for others. *p. 306*

households The consuming units in an economy. *p. 46*

human capital A form of intangible capital that includes the skills and other knowledge that workers have or acquire through education and training and that yields valuable services to a firm over time. *p. 222 p. 361*

hyperinflation A period of very rapid increases in the overall price level. *p. 404*

identity Something that is always true. *p. 455*

imperfect competition An industry in which single firms have some control over price and competition. Imperfectly competitive industries give rise to an inefficient allocation of resources. *p. 254*

imperfect information The absence of full knowledge concerning product characteristics, available prices, and so on. *p. 256*

imperfectly competitive industry An industry in which individual firms have some control over the price of their output. *p. 261*

implementation lag The time it takes to put the desired policy into effect once economists and policy makers recognize that the economy is in a boom or a slump. *p. 591*

import substitution An industrial trade strategy that favors developing local industries that can manufacture goods to replace imports. *p. 720*

impossibility theorem A proposition demonstrated by Kenneth Arrow showing that no system of aggregating individual preferences into social decisions will always yield consistent, nonarbitrary results. *p. 338*

income The sum of all a household's wages, salaries, profits, interest payments, rents, and other forms of earnings in a given period of time. It is a flow measure. *p. 51*

income approach A method of computing GDP that measures the income—wages, rents, interest, and profits—received by all factors of production in producing final goods and services. *p. 419*

income elasticity of demand A measure of the responsiveness of demand to changes in income. *p. 102*

increasing returns to scale, *or* economies of scale An increase in a firm's scale of production leads to lower costs per unit produced. *p. 185*

increasing-cost industry An industry that encounters external diseconomies—that is, average costs increase as the industry grows. The long-run supply curve for such an industry has a positive slope. *p. 200 p. 201*

Indifference curve A set of points, each point representing a combination of goods X and Y, all of which yield the same total utility. *p. 130 p. 134*

indirect taxes minus subsidies Taxes such as sales taxes, customs duties, and license fees less subsidies that the government pays for which it receives no goods or services in return. *p. 423*

Industrial Revolution The period in England during the late eighteenth and early nineteenth centuries in which new manufacturing technologies and improved transportation gave rise to the modern factory system and a massive movement of the population from the countryside to the cities. *p. 4*

inelastic demand Demand that responds somewhat, but not a great deal, to changes in price. Inelastic demand always has a numerical value between zero and –1. *p. 92*

infant industry A young industry that may need temporary protection from competition from the established industries of other countries to develop an acquired comparative advantage. *p. 683*

inferior goods Goods for which demand tends to fall when income rises. *p. 52*

inflation An increase in the overall price level. *p. 404*

inflation rate The percentage change in the price level. *p. 580*

inflation targeting When a monetary authority chooses its interest rate values with the aim of keeping the inflation rate within some specified band over some specified horizon. *p. 566*

injunction A court order forbidding the continuation of behavior that leads to damages. *p. 328*

innovation The use of new knowledge to produce a new product or to produce an existing product more efficiently. *p. 638*

input *or* factor markets The markets in which the resources used to produce goods and services are exchanged. *p. 46*

inputs The goods and services that firms purchase and turn into output. *p. 619*

inputs *or* resources Anything provided by nature or previous generations that can be used directly or indirectly to satisfy human wants. *p. 26*

intangible capital Nonmaterial things that contribute to the output of future goods and services. *p. 222*

interest The payments made for the use of money; The fee that borrowers pay to lenders for the use of their funds. *p. 225 p. 515*

interest rate Interest payments expressed as a percentage of the loan. *p. 225*

interest sensitivity *or* insensitivity of planned investment The responsiveness of planned investment spending to changes in the interest rate. *Interest sensitivity* means that planned investment spending changes a great deal in response to changes in the interest rate; *interest insensitivity* means little or no change in planned investment as a result of changes in the interest rate. *p. 536*

intermediate goods Goods that are produced by one firm for use in further processing by another firm. *p. 418*

International Monetary Fund (IMF) An international agency whose primary goals are to stabilize international exchange rates and to lend money to countries that have problems financing their international transactions. *p. 721*

invention An advance in knowledge. *p. 638*

inventory investment The change in the stock of inventories. *p. 621*

investment The process of using resources to produce new capital; New capital additions to a firm's capital stock. Although capital is measured at a given point in time (a stock), investment is measured over a period of time (a flow). The flow of investment increases the capital stock. *p. 32 p. 223*

***IS* curve** A curve illustrating the negative relationship between the equilibrium value of aggregate output (income) (*Y*) and the interest rate in the goods market. *p. 546 p. 547*

isocost line A graph that shows all the combinations of capital and labor available for a given total cost. *p. 151 p. 153*

isoquant A graph that shows all the combinations of capital and labor that can be used to produce a given amount of output. *p. 150 p. 153*

J-curve effect Following a currency depreciation, a country's balance of trade may get worse before it gets better. The graph showing this effect is shaped like the letter *J*, hence the name J-curve effect. *p. 415*

labor demand curve A graph that illustrates the amount of labor that firms want to employ at each given wage rate. *p. 572*

labor force The number of people employed plus the number of unemployed. *p. 436*

labor force participation rate The ratio of the labor force to the total population 16 years old or older. *p. 436*

labor market The input/factor market in which households supply work for wages to firms that demand labor. *p. 47*

labor productivity Output per worker hour; the amount of output produced by an average worker in 1 hour. *p. 634*

labor supply curve A curve that shows the quantity of labor supplied at different wage rates. Its shape depends on how households react to changes in the wage rate. *p. 124 p. 572*

labor theory of value Stated most simply, the theory that the value of a commodity depends only on the amount of labor required to produce it. *p. 371*

labor-intensive technology Technology that relies heavily on human labor instead of capital. *p. 140 p. 620*

Laffer curve With the tax rate measured on the vertical axis and tax revenue measured on the horizontal axis, the Laffer curve shows that there is some tax rate beyond which the supply response is large enough to lead to a decrease in tax revenue for further increases in the tax rate. *p. 661*

laissez-faire economy Literally from the French: "allow [them] to do." An economy in which individual people and firms pursue their own self-interest without any central direction or regulation. *p. 39*

land market The input/factor market in which households supply land or other real property in exchange for rent. *p. 47*

law of demand The negative relationship between price and quantity demanded: As price rises, quantity demanded decreases; as price falls, quantity demanded increases. *p. 49*

law of diminishing marginal utility The more of any one good consumed in a given period, the less satisfaction (utility) generated by consuming each additional (marginal) unit of the same good. *p. 116*

law of diminishing returns When additional units of a variable input are added to fixed inputs after a certain point, the marginal product of the variable input declines. *p. 141*

law of one price If the costs of transportation are small, the price of the same good in different countries should be roughly the same. *p. 412*

law of supply The positive relationship between price and quantity of a good supplied: An increase in market price will lead to an increase in quantity supplied, and a decrease in market price will lead to a decrease in quantity supplied. *p. 57*

legal tender Money that a government has required to be accepted in settlement of debts. *p. 496*

lender of last resort One of the functions of the Fed: It provides funds to troubled banks that cannot find any other sources of funds. *p. 505*

liability rules Laws that require A to compensate B for damages imposed. *p. 328*

life-cycle theory of consumption A theory of household consumption: Households make lifetime consumption decisions based on their expectations of lifetime income. *p. 610*

liquidity property of money The property of money that makes it a good medium of exchange as well as a store of value: It is portable and readily accepted and thus easily exchanged for goods. *p. 494*

***LM* curve** A curve illustrating the positive relationship between the equilibrium value of the interest rate and aggregate output (income) (Y) in the money market. *p. 546 p. 547*

logrolling Occurs when congressional representatives trade votes, agreeing to help each other get certain pieces of legislation passed. *p. 339*

long run That period of time for which there are no fixed factors of production: Firms can increase or decrease the scale of operation, and new firms can enter and existing firms can exit the industry. *p. 139*

long-run average cost curve (*LRAC*) The "envelope" of a series of short-run cost curves. *p. 186*

long-run competitive equilibrium When $P = SRMC = SRAC = LRAC$ and profits are zero. *p. 195*

long-run industry supply curve (*LRIS*) A graph that traces out price and total output over time as an industry expands. *p. 200 p. 201*

Lorenz curve A widely used graph of the distribution of income, with cumulative percentage of households plotted along the horizontal axis and cumulative percentage of income plotted along the vertical axis. *p. 364*

Lucas supply function The supply function embodies the idea that output (Y) depends on the difference between the actual price level and the expected price level. *p. 657*

M1, *or* transactions money Money that can be directly used for transactions. *p. 497*

M2, *or* broad money M1 plus savings accounts, money market accounts, and other near monies. *p. 497*

macroeconomics The branch of economics that examines the economic behavior of aggregates—income, employment, output, and so on—on a national scale. *p. 8 p. 401*

marginal cost (*MC*) The increase in total cost that results from producing 1 more unit of output. Marginal costs reflect changes in variable costs. *p. 159*

marginal damage cost (*MDC*) The additional harm done by increasing the level of an externality-producing activity by 1 unit. If producing product X pollutes the water in a river, *MDC* is the additional cost imposed by the added pollution that results from increasing output by 1 unit of X per period. *p. 323*

marginal private cost (*MPC*) The amount that a consumer pays to consume an additional unit of a particular good. *p. 323*

marginal product The additional output that can be produced by adding one more unit of a specific input, *ceteris paribus*. *p. 141*

marginal product of labor (MP_L) The additional output produced by 1 additional unit of labor. *p. 204*

marginal productivity theory of income distribution At equilibrium, all factors of production end up receiving rewards determined by their productivity as measured by marginal revenue product. *p. 217*

marginal propensity to consume (*MPC*) That fraction of a change in income that is consumed, or spent. *p. 455*

marginal propensity to import (*MPM*) The change in imports caused by a $1 change in income. *p. 406*

marginal propensity to save (*MPS*) That fraction of a change in income that is saved. *p. 455*

Marginal rate of substitution MU_X/MU_Y; the ratio at which a household is willing to substitute good *Y* for good *X*. *p. 130 p. 134*

marginal rate of technical substitution The rate at which a firm can substitute capital for labor and hold output constant. *p. 150 p. 153*

marginal rate of transformation (*MRT*) The slope of the production possibility frontier (ppf). *p. 35*

marginal revenue (*MR*) The additional revenue that a firm takes in when it increases output by one additional unit. In perfect competition, $P = MR$. *p. 168*

marginal revenue product (*MRP*) The additional revenue a firm earns by employing 1 additional unit of input, *ceteris paribus*. *p. 205*

marginal social cost (*MSC*) The total cost to society of producing an additional unit of a good or service. *MSC* is equal to the sum of the marginal costs of producing the product and the correctly measured damage costs involved in the process of production. *p. 320*

marginal tax rate The tax rate paid on any additional income earned. *p. 381*

marginal utility (*MU*) The additional satisfaction gained by the consumption or use of one more unit of a good or service. *p. 116*

marginalism The process of analyzing the additional or incremental costs or benefits arising from a choice or decision. *p. 2*

market The institution through which buyers and sellers interact and engage in exchange. *p. 39*

market demand The sum of all the quantities of a good or service demanded per period by all the households buying in the market for that good or service. *p. 55*

market failure Occurs when resources are misallocated, or allocated inefficiently. The result is waste or lost value. *p. 254 p. 319*

market power An imperfectly competitive firm's ability to raise price without losing all of the quantity demanded for its product. *p. 261*

market signaling Actions taken by buyers and sellers to communicate quality in a world of uncertainty. *p. 353*

market supply The sum of all that is supplied each period by all producers of a single product. *p. 61*

maximin strategy In game theory, a strategy chosen to maximize the minimum gain that can be earned. *p. 293*

mechanism design A contract or an institution that aligns the interests of two parties in a transaction. A piece rate, for example, creates incentives for a worker to work hard, just as his or her superior wants. A co-pay in the health care industry encourages more careful use of health care, just as the insurance company wants. *p. 355*

Medicaid *and* Medicare In-kind government transfer programs that provide health and hospitalization benefits: Medicare to the aged and their survivors and to certain of the disabled, regardless of income, and Medicaid to people with low incomes. *p. 374*

medium of exchange, *or* means of payment What sellers generally accept and buyers generally use to pay for goods and services. *p. 494*

microeconomics The branch of economics that examines the functioning of individual industries and the behavior of individual decision-making units—that is, firms and households. *p. 8 p. 401*

midpoint formula A more precise way of calculating percentages using the value halfway between P_1 and P_2 for the base in calculating the percentage change in price and the value halfway between Q_1 and Q_2 as the base for calculating the percentage change in quantity demanded. *p. 94*

minimum efficient scale (MES) The smallest size at which the long-run average cost curve is at its minimum. *p. 186*

minimum wage A price floor set for the price of labor; the lowest wage that firms are permitted to pay workers. *p. 79 p. 361*

minimum wage laws Laws that set a floor for wage rates—that is, a minimum hourly rate for any kind of labor. *p. 572*

mixed goods Goods that are part public goods and part private goods. Education is a key example. *p. 337*

model A formal statement of a theory, usually a mathematical statement of a presumed relationship between two or more variables. *p. 11*

modern economic growth The period of rapid and sustained increase in real output per capita that began in the Western World with the Industrial Revolution. *p. 631*

monetary policy The tools used by the Federal Reserve to control the quantity of money, which in turn affects interest rates. *p. 407 p. 472*

money income The measure of income used by the Census Bureau. Because money income excludes noncash transfer payments and capital gains income, it is less inclusive than economic income. *p. 364*

money market The market in which financial instruments are exchanged and in which the equilibrium level of the interest rate is determined. *p. 532*

money multiplier The multiple by which deposits can increase for every dollar increase in reserves; equal to 1 divided by the required reserve ratio. *p. 503*

monopolistic competition A common form of industry (market) structure in the United States, characterized by a large number of firms, no barriers to entry, and product differentiation. *p. 304*

monopoly An industry composed of only one firm that produces a product for which there are no close substitutes and in which significant barriers exist to prevent new firms from entering the industry. *p. 254*

moral hazard Arises when one party to a contract changes behavior in response to that contract and thus passes on the costs of that behavior change to the other party. *p. 355*

moral suasion The pressure that in the past the Fed exerted on member banks to discourage them from borrowing heavily from the Fed. *p. 509*

mortality rate The death rate. Equal to (the number of deaths per year divided by the population) × 100. *p. 725*

movement along a demand curve The change in quantity demanded brought about by a change in price. *p. 54*

movement along a supply curve The change in quantity supplied brought about by a change in price. *p. 59*

multiplier The ratio of the change in the equilibrium level of output to a change in some exogenous variable. *p. 463*

NAIRU The nonaccelerating inflation rate of unemployment. *p. 585*

NASDAQ Composite An index based on the stock prices of over 5,000 companies traded on the NASDAQ Stock Market. The NASDAQ market takes its name from the National Association of Securities Dealers Automated Quotation System. *p. 598*

Nash equilibrium In game theory, the result of all players' playing their best strategy given what their competitors are doing. *p. 292*

national income The total income earned by the factors of production owned by a country's citizens. *p. 423*

national income and product accounts Data collected and published by the government describing the various components of national income and output in the economy. *p. 417*

natural monopoly An industry that realizes such large economies of scale in producing its product that single-firm production of that good or service is most efficient. *p. 270*

natural rate of population increase The difference between the birth rate and the death rate. *p. 725*

natural rate of unemployment The unemployment that occurs as a normal part of the functioning of the economy. Sometimes taken as the sum of frictional unemployment and structural unemployment. *p. 441* *p. 584*

near monies Close substitutes for transactions money, such as savings accounts and money market accounts. *p. 497*

negative demand shock Something that causes a negative shift in consumption or investment schedules or that leads to a decrease in U.S. exports. *p. 596*

negative relationship A relationship between two variables, *X* and *Y*, in which a decrease in *X* is associated with an increase in *Y* and an increase in *X* is associated with a decrease in *Y*. *p. 19* *p. 22*

net business transfer payments Net transfer payments by businesses to others. *p. 423*

net exports (*EX* – *IM*) The difference between exports (sales to foreigners of U.S.-produced goods and services) and imports (U.S. purchases of goods and services from abroad). The figure can be positive or negative. *p. 423*

net exports of goods and services (*EX* – *IM*) The difference between a country's total exports and total imports. *p. 406*

net interest The interest paid by business. *p. 423*

net investment Gross investment minus depreciation. *p. 422*

net national product (NNP) Gross national product minus depreciation; a nation's total product minus what is required to maintain the value of its capital stock. *p. 424*

net taxes (*T*) Taxes paid by firms and households to the government minus transfer payments made to households by the government. *p. 472*

network externalities The value of a product to a consumer increases with the number of that product being sold or used in the market. *p. 272*

nominal GDP Gross domestic product measured in current dollars. *p. 426*

nominal wage rate The wage rate in current dollars. *p. 612*

nondurable goods Goods that are used up fairly quickly, such as food and clothing. *p. 420*

nonexcludable A characteristic of most public goods: Once a good is produced, no one can be excluded from enjoying its benefits. *p. 332*

nonlabor, *or* nonwage, income Any income received from sources other than working—inheritances, interest, dividends, transfer payments, and so on. *p. 612*

nonresidential investment Expenditures by firms for machines, tools, plants, and so on. *p. 421*

nonrival in consumption A characteristic of public goods: One person's enjoyment of the benefits of a public good does not interfere with another's consumption of it. *p. 332*

nonsynchronization of income and spending The mismatch between the timing of money inflow to the household and the timing of money outflow for household expenses. *p. 517*

normal goods Goods for which demand goes up when income is higher and for which demand goes down when income is lower. *p. 51*

normal rate of return A rate of return on capital that is just sufficient to keep owners and investors satisfied. For relatively risk-free firms, it should be nearly the same as the interest rate on risk-free government bonds. *p. 137*

normative economics An approach to economics that analyzes outcomes of economic behavior, evaluates them as good or bad, and may prescribe courses of action. Also called *policy economics*. *p. 10*

North American Free Trade Agreement (NAFTA) An agreement signed by the United States, Mexico, and Canada in which the three countries agreed to establish all North America as a free-trade zone. *p. 677*

not in the labor force A person who is not looking for work because he or she does not want a job or has given up looking. *p. 436*

Ockham's razor The principle that irrelevant detail should be cut away. *p. 11*

Okun's Law The theory, put forth by Arthur Okun, that in the short run the unemployment rate decreases about 1 percentage point for every 3 percent increase in real GDP. Later research and data have shown that the relationship between output and unemployment is not as stable as Okun's "Law" predicts. *p. 625*

oligopoly A form of industry (market) structure characterized by a few dominant firms. Products may be homogenous or differentiated. *p. 283*

Open Market Desk The office in the New York Federal Reserve Bank from which government securities are bought and sold by the Fed. *p. 504*

open market operations The purchase and sale by the Fed of government securities in the open market; a tool used to expand or contract the amount of reserves in the system and thus the money supply. *p. 509*

opportunity cost The best alternative that we forgo, or give up, when we make a choice or a decision. *p. 2* *p. 27*

optimal level of provision for public goods The level at which society's total willingness to pay per unit is equal to the marginal cost of producing the good. *p. 336*

optimal method of production The production method that minimizes cost. *p. 139*

optimal scale of plant The scale of plant that minimizes average cost. *p. 189*

origin On a Cartesian coordinate system, the point at which the horizontal and vertical axes intersect. *p. 19* *p. 22*

output effect of a factor price increase (decrease) When a firm decreases (increases) its output in response to a factor price increase (decrease), this decreases (increases) its demand for all factors. *p. 212*

output growth The growth rate of the output of the entire economy. *p. 446*

outputs Goods and services of value to households. *p. 26*

Pareto efficiency *or* Pareto optimality A condition in which no change is possible that will make some members of society better off without making some other members of society worse off. *p. 248*

partial equilibrium analysis The process of examining the equilibrium conditions in individual markets and for households and firms separately. *p. 242*

patent A barrier to entry that grants exclusive use of the patented product or process to the inventor. *p. 271*

payoff The amount that comes from a possible outcome or result. *p. 346*

per-capita output growth The growth rate of output per person in the economy. *p. 446*

perfect competition An industry structure in which there are many firms, each being small relative to the industry and producing virtually identical products, and in which no firm is large enough to have any control over prices. In perfectly competitive industries, new competitors can freely enter and exit the market. *p. 109* *p. 167*

perfect knowledge The assumption that households possess a knowledge of the qualities and prices of everything available in the market and that firms have all available information concerning wage rates, capital costs, and output prices. *p. 109*

perfect price discrimination Occurs when a firm charges the maximum amount that buyers are willing to pay for each unit. *p. 275*

perfect substitutes Identical products. *p. 52*

perfectly elastic demand Demand in which quantity drops to zero at the slightest increase in price. *p. 92*

perfectly inelastic demand Demand in which quantity demanded does not respond at all to a change in price. *p. 91*

permanent income The average level of a person's expected future income stream. *p. 610*

personal consumption expenditures (C) Expenditures by consumers on goods and services. *p. 420*

personal income The total income of households. *p. 424*

personal saving The amount of disposable income that is left after total personal spending in a given period. *p. 426*

personal saving rate The percentage of disposable personal income that is saved. If the personal saving rate is low, households are spending a large amount relative to their incomes; if it is high, households are spending cautiously. *p. 426*

Phillips Curve A curve showing the relationship between the inflation rate and the unemployment rate. *p. 580*

physical, *or* tangible, capital Material things used as inputs in the production of future goods and services. The major categories of physical capital are nonresidential structures, durable equipment, residential structures, and inventories. *p. 222*

planned aggregate expenditure (*AE*) The total amount the economy plans to spend in a given period. Equal to consumption plus planned investment: $AE \equiv C + I$. *p. 460*

planned investment (*I*) Those additions to capital stock and inventory that are planned by firms. *p. 458*

plant-and-equipment investment Purchases by firms of additional machines, factories, or buildings within a given period. *p. 619*

policy mix The combination of monetary and fiscal policies in use at a given time. *p. 538*

positive economics An approach to economics that seeks to understand behavior and the operation of systems without making judgments. It describes what exists and how it works. *p. 10*

positive relationship A relationship between two variables, *X* and *Y*, in which a decrease in *X* is associated with a decrease in *Y*, and an increase in *X* is associated with an increase in *Y*. *p.* 19 *p. 22*

post hoc, ergo propter hoc Literally, "after this (in time), therefore because of this." A common error made in thinking about causation: If Event A happens before Event B, it is not necessarily true that A caused B. *p. 12*

potential output, *or* potential GDP The level of aggregate output that can be sustained in the long run without inflation. *p. 556*

poverty line The officially established income level that distinguishes the poor from the nonpoor. It is set at three times the cost of the Department of Agriculture's minimum food budget. *p. 368*

Preference map A consumer's set of indifference curves. *p. 131 p. 134*

present discounted value (PDV) *or* present value (PV) The present discounted value of R dollars to be paid *t* years in the future is the amount you need to pay today, at current interest rates, to ensure that you end up with *R* dollars *t* years from now. It is the current market value of receiving *R* dollars in *t* years. *p. 237 p. 240*

price ceiling A maximum price that sellers may charge for a good, usually set by government. *p. 75*

price discrimination Charging different prices to different buyers. *p. 275*

price elasticity of demand The ratio of the percentage of change in quantity demanded to the percentage of change in price; measures the responsiveness of quantity demanded to changes in price. *p. 91*

price feedback effect The process by which a domestic price increase in one country can "feed back" on itself through export and import prices. An increase in the price level in one country can drive up prices in other countries. This in turn further increases the price level in the first country. *p. 409*

price floor A minimum price below which exchange is not permitted. *p. 79*

price leadership A form of oligopoly in which one dominant firm sets prices and all the smaller firms in the industry follow its pricing policy. *p. 288*

price rationing The process by which the market system allocates goods and services to consumers when quantity demanded exceeds quantity supplied. *p. 73*

price surprise Actual price level minus expected price level. *p. 657*

principle of neutrality All else equal, taxes that are neutral with respect to economic decisions (that is, taxes that do not distort economic decisions) are generally preferable to taxes that distort economic decisions. Taxes that are not neutral impose excess burdens. *p. 393*

principle of second best The fact that a tax distorts an economic decision does not always imply that such a tax imposes an excess burden. If there are previously existing distortions, such a tax may actually improve efficiency. *p. 395*

prisoners' dilemma A game in which the players are prevented from cooperating and in which each has a dominant strategy that leaves them both worse off than if they could cooperate. *p. 292*

private goods Goods and services produced by firms for sale to individual households. *p. 255*

privately held federal debt The privately held (non-government-owned) debt of the U.S. government. *p. 485*

producer price indexes (PPIs) Measures of prices that producers receive for products at all stages in the production process. *p. 446*

producer surplus The difference between the current market price and the full cost of production for the firm. *p. 83*

product differentiation A strategy that firms use to achieve market power. Accomplished by producing products that have distinct positive identities in consumers' minds. *p. 305*

product *or* output markets The markets in which goods and services are exchanged. *p. 46*

production The process that transforms scarce resources into useful goods and services. *p. 25 p. 135*

production function *or* total product function A numerical or mathematical expression of a relationship between inputs and outputs. It shows units of total product as a function of units of inputs. *p. 140*

production possibility frontier (ppf) A graph that shows all the combinations of goods and services that can be produced if all of society's resources are used efficiently. *p. 32*

production technology The quantitative relationship between inputs and outputs. *p. 140*

productivity growth The growth rate of output per worker. *p. 446*

productivity of an input The amount of output produced per unit of that input. *p. 204 p. 638*

productivity, *or* labor productivity Output per worker hour; the amount of output produced by an average worker in 1 hour. *p. 624*

profit The difference between revenues and costs. *p. 57 p. 136*

progressive tax A tax whose burden, expressed as a percentage of income, increases as income increases. *p. 380*

property income Income from the ownership of real property and financial holdings. It takes the form of profits, interest, dividends, and rents. *p. 363*

proportional tax A tax whose burden is the same proportion of income for all households. *p. 380*

proprietors' income The income of unincorporated businesses. *p. 423*

protection The practice of shielding a sector of the economy from foreign competition. *p. 411 p. 675*

public assistance, *or* welfare Government transfer programs that provide cash benefits to: (1) families with dependent children whose incomes and assets fall below a very low level, and (2) the very poor regardless of whether they have children. *p. 374*

public choice theory An economic theory that the public officials who set economic policies and regulate the players act in their own self-interest, just as firms do. *p. 275*

public goods, (*or* social *or* collective goods) Goods and services that bestow collective benefits on members of society. Generally, no one can be excluded from enjoying their benefits. The classic example is national defense. *p. 255 p. 332*

purchasing-power-parity theory A theory of international exchange holding that exchange rates are set so that the price of similar goods in different countries is the same. *p. 413*

pure monopoly An industry with a single firm that produces a product for which there are no close substitutes and in which significant barriers to entry prevent other firms from entering the industry to compete for profits. *p. 262*

pure rent The return to any factor of production that is in fixed supply. *p. 212*

quantity demanded The amount (number of units) of a product that a household would buy in a given period if it could buy all it wanted at the current market price. *p. 48*

quantity supplied The amount of a particular product that a firm would be willing and able to offer for sale at a particular price during a given time period. *p. 57*

quantity theory of money The theory based on the identity $M \times V \equiv P \times Y$ and the assumption that the velocity of money (V) is constant (or virtually constant). *p. 653*

queuing Waiting in line as a means of distributing goods and services: a nonprice rationing mechanism. *p. 76*

quota A limit on the quantity of imports. *p. 412 p. 676*

ration coupons Tickets or coupons that entitle individuals to purchase a certain amount of a given product per month. *p. 76*

rational-expectations hypothesis The hypothesis that people know the "true model" of the economy and that they use this model to form their expectations of the future. *p. 656*

Rawlsian justice A theory of distributional justice that concludes that the social contract emerging from the "original position" would call for an income distribution that would maximize the well-being of the worst-off member of society. *p. 371*

real business cycle theory An attempt to explain business cycle fluctuations under the assumptions of complete price and wage flexibility and rational expectations. It emphasizes shocks to technology and other shocks. *p. 659*

real income The set of opportunities to purchase real goods and services available to a household as determined by prices and money income. *p. 114*

real interest rate The difference between the interest rate on a loan and the inflation rate. *p. 445*

real wage rate The amount the nominal wage rate can buy in terms of goods and services. *p. 612*

real wealth, *or* real balance, effect The change in consumption brought about by a change in real wealth that results from a change in the price level. *p. 541*

realized capital gain The gain that occurs when the owner of an asset actually sells it for more than he or she paid for it. *p. 597*

recession A period during which aggregate output declines. Conventionally, a period in which aggregate output declines for two consecutive quarters. *p. 402*

recognition lag The time it takes for policy makers to recognize the existence of a boom or a slump. *p. 591*

regressive tax A tax whose burden, expressed as a percentage of income, falls as income increases. *p. 381*

relative-wage explanation of unemployment An explanation for sticky wages (and therefore unemployment): If workers are concerned about their wages relative to other workers in other firms and industries, they may be unwilling to accept a wage cut unless they know that all other workers are receiving similar cuts. *p. 575*

rent-seeking behavior Actions taken by households or firms to preserve positive profits. *p. 275*

rental income The income received by property owners in the form of rent. *p. 423*

required reserve ratio The percentage of its total deposits that a bank must keep as reserves at the Federal Reserve. *p. 500*

reserves The deposits that a bank has at the Federal Reserve bank plus its cash on hand. *p. 500*

residential investment Expenditures by households and firms on new houses and apartment buildings. *p. 421*

response lag The time that it takes for the economy to adjust to the new conditions after a new policy is implemented; the lag that occurs because of the operation of the economy itself. *p. 591*

risk premium The maximum price a risk-averse person will pay to avoid taking a risk. *p. 348*

risk-averse Refers to a person's preference of a certain payoff over an uncertain one with the same expected value. *p. 348*

risk-loving Refers to a person's preference for an uncertain deal over a certain deal with an equal expected value. *p. 348*

risk-neutral Refers to a person's willingness to take a bet with an expected value of zero. *p. 348*

rule of reason The criterion introduced by the Supreme Court in 1911 to determine whether a particular action was illegal ("unreasonable") or legal ("reasonable") within the terms of the Sherman Act. *p. 278*

run on a bank Occurs when many of those who have claims on a bank (deposits) present them at the same time. *p. 499*

scarce Limited. *p. 2*

services The things we buy that do not involve the production of physical things, such as legal and medical services and education. *p. 420*

shares of stock Financial instruments that give to the holder a share in the firm's ownership and therefore the right to share in the firm's profits. *p. 407*

shift of a demand curve The change that takes place in a demand curve corresponding to a new relationship between quantity demanded of a good and price of that good. The shift is brought about by a change in the original conditions. *p. 53*

shift of a supply curve The change that takes place in a supply curve corresponding to a new relationship between quantity supplied of a good and the price of that good. The shift is brought about by a change in the original conditions. *p. 59*

shock therapy The approach to transition from socialism to market capitalism that advocates rapid deregulation of prices, liberalization of trade, and privatization. *p. 730*

short run The period of time for which two conditions hold: The firm is operating under a fixed scale (fixed factor) of production, and firms can neither enter nor exit an industry. *p. 139*

short-run industry supply curve The sum of the marginal cost curves (above *AVC*) of all the firms in an industry. *p. 183*

shut-down point The lowest point on the average variable cost curve. When price falls below the minimum point on *AVC*, total revenue is insufficient to cover variable costs and the firm will shut down and bear losses equal to fixed costs. *p. 182*

slope A measurement that indicates whether the relationship between variables is positive or negative and how much of a response there is in *Y* (the variable on the vertical axis) when *X* (the variable on the horizontal axis) changes. *p. 20 p. 22*

Smoot-Hawley tariff The U.S. tariff law of the 1930s, which set the highest tariffs in U.S. history (60 percent). It set off an international trade war and caused the decline in trade that is often considered one of the causes of the worldwide depression of the 1930s. *p. 676*

social capital, *or* infrastructure Capital that provides services to the public. Most social capital takes the form of public works (roads and bridges) and public services (police and fire protection). *p. 222*

social choice The problem of deciding what society wants. The process of adding up individual preferences to make a choice for society as a whole. *p. 337*

social overhead capital Basic infrastructure projects such as roads, power generation, and irrigation systems. *p. 717*

social, *or* implicit, contracts Unspoken agreements between workers and firms that firms will not cut wages. *p. 575*

Social Security system The federal system of social insurance programs. It includes three separate programs that are financed through separate trust funds: the Old Age and Survivors Insurance (OASI) program, the Disability Insurance (DI) program, and the Health Insurance (HI), or Medicare program. *p. 373*

sources side/uses side The impact of a tax may be felt on one or the other or on both sides of the income equation. A tax may cause net income to fall (damage on the sources side), or it may cause prices of goods and services to rise so that income buys less (damage on the uses side). *p. 388*

speculation motive One reason for holding bonds instead of money: Because the market price of interest-bearing bonds is inversely related to the interest rate, investors may want to hold bonds when interest rates are high with the hope of selling them when interest rates fall. *p. 520*

spreading overhead The process of dividing total fixed costs by more units of output. Average fixed cost declines as quantity rises. *p. 157*

stability A condition in which national output is growing steadily, with low inflation and full employment of resources. *p. 15*

stabilization policy Describes both monetary and fiscal policy, the goals of which are to smooth out fluctuations in output and employment and to keep prices as stable as possible. *p. 589*

stagflation A situation of both high inflation and high unemployment. Occurs when output is falling at the same time that prices are rising. *p. 408 p. 559*

Standard and Poor's 500 (S&P 500) An index based on the stock prices of 500 of the largest firms by market value. *p. 598*

statistical discrepancy Data measurement error. *p. 424*

sticky prices Prices that do not always adjust rapidly to maintain equality between quantity supplied and quantity demanded. *p. 401*

sticky wages The downward rigidity of wages as an explanation for the existence of unemployment. *p. 574*

stock A share of stock is an ownership claim on a firm, entitling its owner to a profit share. *p. 226 p. 597*

store of value An asset that can be used to transport purchasing power from one time period to another. *p. 494*

structural adjustment A series of programs in developing nations designed to: (1) reduce the size of their public sectors through privatization and/or expenditure reductions, (2) decrease their budget deficits, (3) control inflation, and (4) encourage private saving and investment through tax reform. *p. 722*

structural deficit The deficit that remains at full employment. *p. 487*

structural unemployment The portion of unemployment that is due to changes in the structure of the economy that result in a significant loss of jobs in certain industries. *p. 441 p. 572*

substitutes Goods that can serve as replacements for one another; when the price of one increases, demand for the other increases. *p. 52*

sunk costs Costs that cannot be avoided because they have already been incurred. *p. 3*

supply curve A graph illustrating how much of a product a firm will sell at different prices. *p. 57*

supply schedule A table showing how much of a product firms will sell at alternative prices. *p. 57*

surplus of government enterprises Income of government enterprises. *p. 423*

tacit collusion Collusion occurs when price- and quantity-fixing agreements among producers are explicit. *Tacit collusion* occurs when such agreements are implicit. *p. 288*

tariff A tax on imports. *p. 675*

tax base The measure or value upon which a tax is levied. *p. 379*

tax incidence The ultimate distribution of a tax burden. *p. 388*

tax multiplier The ratio of change in the equilibrium level of output to a change in taxes. *p. 479*

tax rate structure The percentage of a tax base that must be paid in taxes—25 percent of income, for example. *p. 379*

tax shifting Occurs when households can alter their behavior and do something to avoid paying a tax. *p. 388*

technological change The introduction of new methods of production or new products intended to increase the productivity of existing inputs or to raise marginal products. *p. 217*

terms of trade The ratio at which a country can trade domestic products for imported products. *p. 671*

theory of comparative advantage Ricardo's theory that specialization and free trade will benefit all trading parties, even those that may be "absolutely" more efficient producers. *p. 27 p. 667*

Tiebout hypothesis An efficient mix of public goods is produced when local land/ housing prices and taxes come to reflect consumer preferences just as they do in the market for private goods. *p. 337*

tight monetary policy Fed policies that contract the money supply and thus raise interest rates in an effort to restrain the economy. *p. 525*

time lags Delays in the economy's response to stabilization policies. *p. 589*

time series graph A graph illustrating how a variable changes over time. *p. 18 p. 22*

tit-for-tat strategy A repeated game strategy in which a player responds in kind to an opponent's play. *p. 294*

total cost (*TC*) Total fixed costs plus total variable costs. *p. 156*

total cost (total economic cost) The total of (1) out-of-pocket costs and (2) opportunity cost of all factors of production. *p. 136*

total fixed costs (*TFC*) *or* overhead The total of all costs that do not change with output even if output is zero. *p. 156*

total revenue (*TR*) The amount received from the sale of the product; The price per unit times the quantity of output the firm decides to produce ($P \times q$). *p. 136 p. 168*

total utility The total amount of satisfaction obtained from consumption of a good or service. *p. 116*

total variable cost (*TVC*) The total of all costs that vary with output in the short run. *p. 157*

total variable cost curve A graph that shows the relationship between total variable cost and the level of a firm's output. *p. 158*

trade deficit Occurs when a country's exports of goods and services are less than its imports of goods and services in a given period. *p. 666 p. 403*

trade feedback effect The tendency for an increase in the economic activity of one country to lead to a worldwide increase in economic activity, which then feeds back to that country. *p. 408*

trade surplus The situation when a country exports more than it imports. *p. 666*

tragedy of commons The idea that collective ownership may not provide the proper private incentives for efficiency because individuals do not bear the full costs of their own decisions but do enjoy the full benefits. *p. 728*

transaction motive The main reason that people hold money—to buy things. *p. 517*

transfer payments Cash payments made by the government to people who do not supply goods, services, or labor in exchange for these payments. They include Social Security benefits, veterans' benefits, and welfare payments. *p. 363 p. 405*

Treasury bonds, notes, *and* bills Promissory notes issued by the federal government when it borrows money. *p. 407*

U.S.-Canadian Free Trade Agreement An agreement in which the United States and Canada agreed to eliminate all barriers to trade between the two countries by 1998. *p. 677*

unconstrained supply of labor The amount a household would like to work within a given period at the current wage rate if it could find the work. *p. 614*

underground economy The part of the economy in which transactions take place and in which income is generated that is unreported and therefore not counted in GDP. *p. 430*

unemployed A person 16 years old or older who is not working, is available for work, and has made specific efforts to find work during the previous 4 weeks. *p. 436*

unemployment compensation A state government transfer program that pays cash benefits for a certain period of time to laid-off workers who have worked for a specified period of time for a covered employer. *p. 374*

unemployment rate The percentage of the labor force that is unemployed. That is, the ratio of the number of people unemployed to the total number of people in the labor force. *p. 403 p. 436 p. 572*

unit of account A standard unit that provides a consistent way of quoting prices. *p. 494*

unitary elasticity A demand relationship in which the percentage change in quantity of a product demanded is the same as the percentage change in price in absolute value (a demand elasticity of –1). *p. 92*

utilitarian justice The idea that "a dollar in the hand of a rich person is worth less than a dollar in the hand of a poor person." If the marginal utility of income declines with income, transferring income from the rich to the poor will increase total utility. *p. 370*

utility The satisfaction a product yields. *p. 116*

utility possibilities frontier A graphic representation of a two-person world that shows all points at which I's utility can be increased only if J's utility is decreased. *p. 360*

utility-maximizing rule Equating the ratio of the marginal utility of a good to its price for all goods. *p. 119*

value added The difference between the value of goods as they leave a stage of production and the cost of the goods as they entered that stage. *p. 418*

variable A measure that can change from time to time or from observation to observation. *p. 11*

variable cost A cost that depends on the level of production chosen. *p. 156*

velocity of money The number of times a dollar bill changes hands, on average, during a year; the ratio of nominal GDP to the stock of money. *p. 652*

vertical differentiation A product difference that, from everyone's perspective, makes a product better than rival products. *p. 308*

vicious-circle-of-poverty hypothesis Suggests that poverty is self-perpetuating because poor nations are unable to save and invest enough to accumulate the capital stock that would help them grow. *p. 716*

voting paradox A simple demonstration of how majority-rule voting can lead to seemingly contradictory and inconsistent results. A commonly cited illustration of the kind of inconsistency described in the impossibility theorem. *p. 339*

wealth *or* net worth The total value of what a household owns minus what it owes. It is a stock measure. *p. 51*

weight The importance attached to an item within a group of items. *p. 426*

World Bank An international agency that lends money to individual countries for projects that promote economic development. *p. 721*

World Trade Organization (WTO) A negotiating forum dealing with rules of trade across nations. *p. 676*

X-axis On a Cartesian coordinate system, the horizontal line against which a variable is plotted. *p. 19 p. 22*

X-intercept The point at which a graph intersects the X-axis. *p. 19 p. 22*

Y-axis On a Cartesian coordinate system, the vertical line against which a variable is plotted. *p. 19 p. 22*

Y-intercept The point at which a graph intersects the Y-axis. *p. 19 p. 22*

Index

Notes: Key terms and the page on which they are defined appear in **boldface**. Page numbers followed by *n* refer to information in footnotes.

C

D

G

J

K

L

Q

R

S

T

Photo Credits

Chapter 1: page 1, Corbis – Moodboard; page 6, Alamy.com.

Chapter 2: page 25, Niedorf Photography, Steve/Getty Images Inc. - Image Bank; page 28, Tony Freeman/PhotoEdit Inc.

Chapter 3: page 45, Sunny Photography.com/Alamy Images.

Chapter 4: page 73, ©Judy Griesedieck/CORBIS All Rights Reserved/CORBIS-NY; page 79, Arvind Garg/Alamy Images.

Chapter 5: page 89, ©Monica M. Davey/EPA/CORBIS All Rights Reserved/CORBIS-NY; page 100, Paul Sakuma/AP Wide World Photos.

Chapter 6: page 111, Marija Kasao/vario images GmbH & Co. KG/Alamy Images; page 123, Tanya Constantine/Corbis Royalty Free; page 126, Eros Hoagland/Redux Pictures.

Chapter 7: page 135, ©Harry Melchert/dba/CORBIS All Rights Reserved/CORBIS-NY; page 144, Charles Rex Arbogast/AP Wide World Photos; page 146, Kitt Cooper-Smith/Alamy Images.

Chapter 8: page 155, Tetra Images/Alamy Images Royalty Free; page 170, Jeff Greenberg/age fotostock/Art Life Images.

Chapter 9: page 177, Photo Shelter/Levine Roberts Photography; page 187, John Stuart/Creative Eye/MIRA.com; page 194, Courtesy of Ray Fair and Sharon Oster.

Chapter 10: page 203, Jon Mitchell/Lightroom/Digital Railroad Marketplace; page 211, Keith Bedford/Corbis/Reuters America LLC; page 214, Peter/Georgina Bowater/Creative Eye/MIRA.com.

Chapter 11: page 221, ©Gabe Palmer/Alamy Images; page 231, Ashley Cooper/Alamy Images.

Chapter 12: page 241, top, Wesley R. Hitt/Creative Eye/MIRA.com, bottom, Novastock/Stock Connection; page 252, Steve Lipofsky/Photolibrary.com.

Chapter 13: page 261, Jeff Scheid/Getty Images, Inc. - Liaison; page 272, J. Emilio Flores/The New York Times/Redux Pictures; page 279, Justin Sullivan/Getty Images, Inc. AFP.

Chapter 14: page 283, Peter Widmann/Alamy Images; page 286, Anthony Harvey/AP Wide World Photos.

Chapter 15: page 303, Kim Karpeles/Alamy Images; page 312, Robert Sullivan/Agence France Presse/Getty Images.

Chapter 16: page 319, Swerve/ Alamy Images; page 326, Photolibrary.com; page 331, Peter Arnold, Inc.

Chapter 17: page 345, Dennis MacDonald/PhotoEdit.Inc.; page 352, Thinkstock.com/Jupiter Images; page 354, Chris A. Crumley/Alamy Images.

Chapter 18: page 359, ©Tony Aruza/CORBIS All Rights Reserved/CORBIS-NY; page 376, Jupiter Images/Brand X/Alamy Images.

Chapter 19: page 379, David Kohl/AP Wide World Photos; page 387, Alex Wong/Getty Images, Inc.-GINS/Entertainment News & Sports; page 396, © Ron Sachs/CORBIS All Rights Reserved/CORBIS-NY.

Chapter 20: page 401, Kayte M. Deioma/PhotoEdit, Inc.; page 409, top, ©Edward Steichen/Conde Nast Archive/CORBIS All Rights Reserved, bottom, Courtesy of the Library of Congress; page 411, National Archives and Records Administration.

Chapter 21: page 417, Kiichiro Sato/AP Wide World Photos; page 421, David Young-Wolff/PhotoEdit; page 425, Corbis Royalty Free.

Chapter 22: page 435, Sara D. Davis/AP Wide World Photos; page 439, Photos.com.

Chapter 23: page 453, Jeff Greenberg/PhotoEdit, Inc.; page 459, vario images GmbH & Co. KG/Alamy Images.

Chapter 24: page 471, George Bridges/MCT/Newscom; page 486, Scott J. Ferrell/Congressional Quarterly/Newscom.

Chapter 25: page 493, John Neubauer/PhotoEdit, Inc.; page 495, Biosphoto/Klein J.L. & Hubert M.L./Peter Arnold, Inc.

Chapter 26: page 515, Michael Newman/PhotoEdit, Inc.; page 516, Picture Desk, Inc./Kobal Collection; page 521, Stock Italia/Alamy Images.

Chapter 27: page 531, Alex Segre/Alamy Images; page 533, Jeff Greenberg/PhotoEdit, Inc.

Chapter 28: page 549, Corbis - Moodboard; page 567, Chitose Suzuki/AP Wide World Photos.

Chapter 29: page 571, Jeff Greenberg/PhotoEdit, Inc.; page 575, Hannamariah/Shutterstock.

Chapter 30: page 589, Courtesy of Ray Fair and Sharon Oster; page 605, Shutterstock.

Chapter 31: page 609, Getty Images - Stockbyte; page 617, Photographers Choice/Superstock Royalty Free.

Chapter 32: page 631, PCL/Alamy Images.; page 641, Wesley R. Hitt/Creative Eye/MIRA.com; page 644, Mark Richards/PhotoEdit, Inc.

Chapter 33: page 651, Gary Conner/PhotoEdit, Inc.; page 658, Janine Wiedel Photolibrary/Alamy Images.

Chapter 34: page 665, Gautam Singh/AP Wide World Photos; page 678, Luis Liwanag/Agence France Presse/Getty Images; page 681, Austrian Archives/Corbis/Bettmann.

Chapter 35: page 401, Jason Lee/Corbis/Reuters America LLC.

Chapter 36: page 713, Ron Giling/Peter Arnold, Inc.; page 723, Deshakalyan Chowdhury/Agence France Presse/Getty Images.

Monetary: 25, 26

Financial: 11, 30: 597-605

inflation: unemployment: 23, 24, 28, 29, 30,
↳ 589-96

Trade, Global Economy: 33, 34, 35

MICROECONOMIC STRUCTURE

The organization of the microeconomics chapters continues to reflect the authors' belief that the best way to understand how market economies operate—and the best way to understand basic economic theory—is to work through a simple model of a perfectly competitive market system first, including discussions of output markets (goods and services) and input markets (land, labor, and capital), and the connections between them. Only then do the authors turn to noncompetitive market structures such as monopoly and oligopoly. When students have worked through a simple model of a perfectly competitive market system, they begin to understand how the pieces of the economy "fit together." Learning perfect competition first also enables students to see the power of the market system. It is impossible to discuss the efficiency of markets as well as the problems that arise from markets until students have seen how a simple perfectly competitive market produces and distributes goods and services. The accompanying visual gives you an overview of the structure.

CHAPTERS 6-8 provide an overview of firm and household decision making in simple perfectly competitive markets.

CHAPTERS 9–11 show how firms and households interact in output markets (goods and services) and input markets (labor, land, and capital) to determine prices, wages, and profits.

CHAPTER 12 is a pivotal chapter that links simple perfectly competitive markets with a discussion of market imperfections and the role of government.

CHAPTERS 13–19 cover the three noncompetitive market structures (monopoly, oligopoly, and monopolistic competition), externalities, public goods, uncertainty and asymmetric information, and income distribution as well as taxation and government finance.

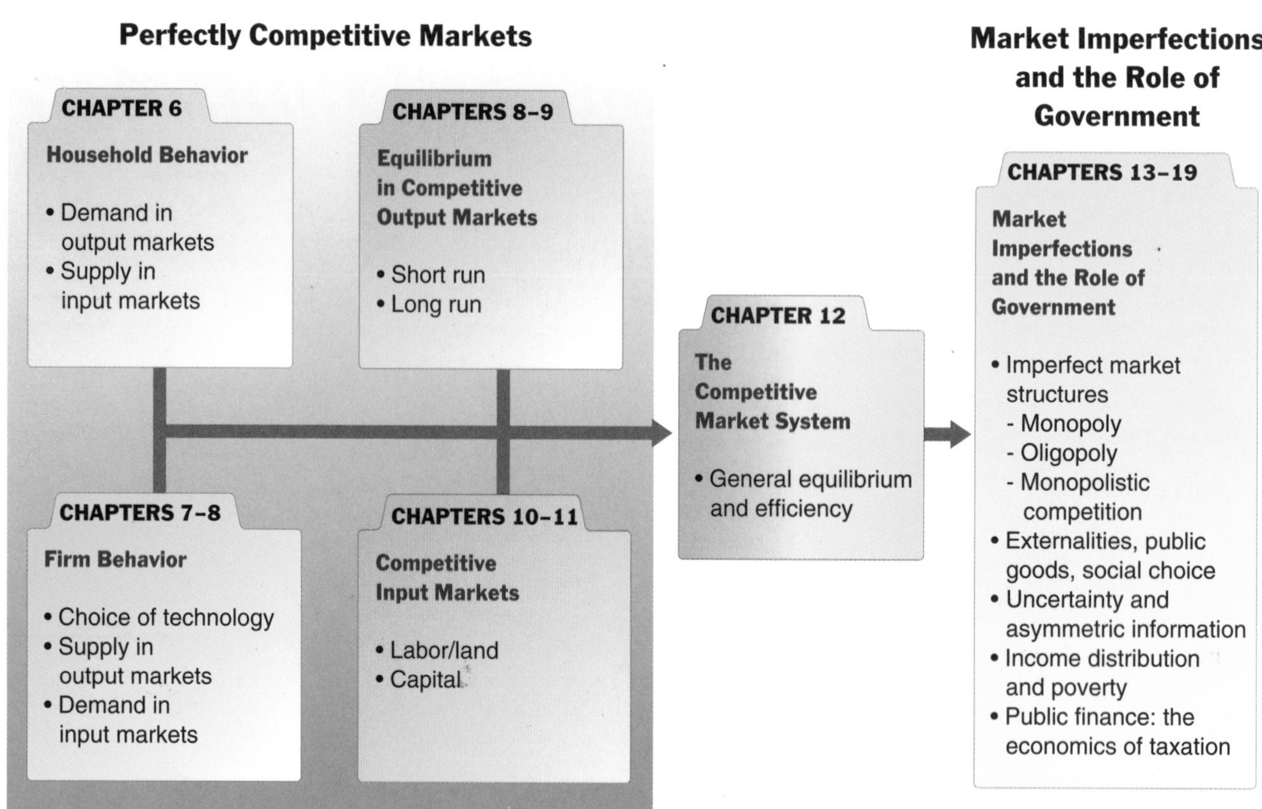

▲ Understanding the Microeconomy and the Role of Government